Metis Families

Volume 11

Sutherland - Zace

Gail Morin

Third Edition

Copyright 2016

TABLE OF CONTENTS

AUTHOR'S NOTE

Métis research is exciting, frustrating, and easy. Records are abundant and often given birth, marriage, death dates, and parents, spouse and children's names. There are some difficulties. The scrip information sometimes conflict with church records. There is a twenty-five-year gap in the St. Boniface Church records, because of the Cathedral fire. Many of the Manitoba church records are not available on interlibrary loan. The St. Norbert, Ste. Agathe, St.Vital and St. Boniface records are available as marriage repertoires and occasionally as extractions in the scrip.

The original intent was to find everyone related to the Morin family. It didn't take long to realize most of the early families living in the Red River were included. Eventually a data base was started and every record available was entered. Sometimes the family relationships were obvious.

This project was possible because of the following people:

Mary McClammy found a copy of the St. Francois Xavier Roman Catholic Church records and the St. Boniface Catholic Church records (that survived the fire) at the Portland Genealogical Forum. She went to the National Archives, Washington, D.C. and located records for the Lake Superior Chippewa and for the Turtle Mountain Chippewa.

David Courchane shared his Métis Families, registers from Duck Lake, Saskatchewan; Pembina, North Dakota; and St. Laurent, Saskatchewan; as well as the 1870 Manitoba Census. He also patiently taught the skills needed for family research.

Geoff Burtonshaw shared his 1834 to 1900 St. Francois Xavier, Manitoba Index written by Clarence Kipling and access to the most important individually owned Métis research library in Alberta.

Al Yerbury shared his Red River Families and Registers of Assumption, Pembina, North Dakota; St. Boniface, Manitoba; Lebret, Saskatchewan; Willow Bunch, Saskatchewan; Yamaska, Quebec Province; St.Joseph, Leroy, North Dakota; Olga, North Dakota; and the early Red River Census records.

Many thanks go to the assistance of Mary McClammy, Al Yerbury, David Courchane, and Denis Garand for translating the (pre-fire) St. Boniface Catholic Church records.

Rod MacQuarrie, an excellent researcher from Saskatchewan, provided extensive reports, problem solving assistance, and translations of the French records.

Rosemary Morrissette Rozyk extracted the St. Boniface (post fire) records in addition to two other important works: St. Norbert, Manitoba (1857-1900) and the Anglican Church index records for the Manitoba area.

Heather Hallett provided much valuable information on the Anglican Church families related to Henry Hallett and also assisted with the Saskatchewan birth, marriage and death records.

Marie Beaupre provided the Lac la Biche, Fort Resolution and Fort Providence records.

Brenda Snider for her assistance with the Little Shell families.

The Ancestor reports would not have been possible without the assistance of Normand Chaunt, Linda Turcotte, Jean Marie Hebert, and Therese Perron. Also important contributors in the ancestor research were Pat Turrene and the Société historique de Saint-Boniface, Manitoba.

The Glenbow Museum and Archives lent the eighteen microfilm of the Charles D. Denney Papers. Mr. Denney's research helped in the identification of the Selkirk settlers and fur trade families and their descendants. Often the Denney research included correspondence and additional information from Clarence Kipling.

The Glenbow also provided microfilm records of the Manitoba Scrip, the North West Half-Breed Scrip (1885); and the 1900 Scrip. Many of the Métis families settled in Saskatchewan and some of them eventually settled in North Dakota and Montana.

Others who contributed: Research: Joyce Gunn Anaka, Carleen Desautel Anderson, Eleanor C. Anderson, Mo Aschenbrenner, Melvin Beaudry, Brenda Page Bercier, Andre Bergeron, Joyce Black, Edsel Bourque, Wendell Brave, Frank Camp, Lauri Cambell, James Carten, Denis Charest, Cindy Charlebois, Dorthy J. Chartrand, James W. Chesebro PhD, John A. Coldwell, Lionel V. DeRagon, Dan Diserlais, Kathy McGregor Donahue, Leah Dorion, Jane Dubois, Len Dubois, Bruce Dumont, Mavis Dumont, Dr. Charles Durham, Debbie Eden, Jan Evans, Art Fisher, Cathy Foley, Lee Fraychineaud, Louella Frederickson, Lorraine Freeman, Peter Gagne, Alain Gariepy, Denis Garand, Andrea Garnier, Wilfred Gayleard, June Morin Haybittle, Jan Hintz, Stan Hulme, Jay Hunter, Donald John Inkster, Debbie Morin Ivers, Alice Belgarde Jackson, John C. Jackson, Ed Jerome, George Johnstone, Nancy Jones, Jackie Gladue Jordon, Lisa Kisch, Leanne Laberge, Alfred Stanislaus Lafleur, Agathe Lafrance, Linda Lamagdeleine, Ernie Lampi, Millie Lansing, Ginger Landrie, John

Laroche, Terry Larocque, Richard Larson, Charmaine Cecile Letourneau, Roger W. Lawrence, Richard Lindsay, Bonnie Lingle-Harrington, Berneice Lomond, Melanie MacFarlane, Kenneth J. Madson, Len Mariner, Patricia McCarthy, Terrance McDougall, Harriet McKay, Justina McKay, T. R. "Pat" McCloy, Debby Merriweather, Valencia T. R. Miller, Robin Miotke, Faye Morin, Francis Morin, Gilbert Morin, Raymond Morin, Robin Mowry, Jeffery Murray, Nellie Nault, Pat Neibergall, Tannis Nielson, Margaret Nunn, Cheryl Osborne, Ethel Otterson, Tammy Hannibal Paci, Wayne Paquin, Garnet Parenteau, Henrietta Parenteau, Howard Piepenbrink, Mathew Pulscher, Larry Quinto, Toby Racette, May Grandbois Racine, Rarihokwats, James Riel, Bonnie Robillard, Lynn Roden, George and Joanne Ross, Clara Royer, Gloria Overbey Ruben, Chane Salois, Faye Sampson Seagraves, Ron Schell, Wanda Brien Sinclair, Thelma Soden, Carrie Stave, Anita Steele, Suzanne Marie Steele, Anne Marie St. Jean, Trevor R. Teed, Ann Vasconi, Kevin Veenstra Eugene E. Venne, Louis Verhagen, Franceene Watson, Cheryl Whited, Elaine Wiseman, Shirley Wishart, and Peggy Fidler Zoraska. (Omissions are not intentional.)

Technology: Richard Avey, Larry Hall, Monte Joseph, Ruth Lampi, Bill Moore, Bernie Morin, Ron Pachosa, Tim Payne, Kathy Proctor, Sharol Seal.

Libraries: Coulee Dam, Washington Family History Center; Calgary, Alberta, Glenbow Archives, Grand Coulee, Washington Public Library, Hudsons Bay Company Archives, Lake Roosevelt, Coulee Dam, Washington High School Library, Manitoba Omak, Washington Public Library, Spokane, Washington Public Library, Wenatchee, Washington Public Library.

Moral Support: My husband Bernie Morin and sons Mike and Bob.

The errors and omissions are inevitable and the sole responsibility of the author. Corrections may be sent to:

Gail Morin
P. O. Box 275
Elmer City, WA 99124-0275

INTRODUCTION

The word *métis* was originally used to identify children of French Canadian and Indian parents. It is now widely used to describe any of the descendants of Indian and non-Indian parents. For a more technical review of the word, see *The Canadian Encyclopedia*, Volume II, pages 1124-1127. V. Harvard, M.D., the Assistant Surgeon, U.S.A, in his report on The French Half-Breeds of the Northwest, which appeared in the *1879 Annual Report Board of Regents of the Smithsonian Institution*, reported the mixed-blood offspring could be traced back to the middle of the 17th century. The half-breed *coureurs de bois* visited the natives at Sault Ste. Marie as early as 1654. Before Lord Selkirk began his settlement on Red River in 1811, there were large villages of mixed bloods at Pembina, and Fort Rouge, later called Fort Garry. By 1879, the Métis population in Canada and the northern United States was estimated to be about 40,000.

The Genealogy of the First Métis Nation, complied by D. N. Sprague and R. P. Frye, maintained that the marriages and the geographical distribution of the people of the Red River Settlement, between 1820 and 1870, were well documented. Taking them at their word, we have searched for our Métis ancestors.

When I looked at the first draft of this book in June 1995, it was impressive. If your ancestors appear in this book, there is a record out there. If they aren't here, do not give up hope. There are other church registers, censuses and scrip records that remain to be discovered and included.

How does a book like this get researched and written? For us, this one began simply enough.

Three sons of Andrew Morin, Sr., and Adelaide Grandboise married three daughters of Moise LaFrance and Marie Cloutier. About 1908, the three sons, with wives and families, moved from Belcourt, N.D. to the northeast corner of Montana to their Turtle Mountain allotments. Later the parents and some of the other brothers and sisters came to the area also. By the time the next generation (ours) was born, some family members had started to move to other areas in northeast Montana, and some went back to North Dakota. During World War II many uncles and cousins entered the services. Some of our parents and grandparents went to the west coast to work in the shipyards. Some never left those areas. Our generation went even further away from home and most of our children and grandchildren have never lived or even seen where we grew up.

In 1988, it was decided the family no longer got together except for funerals, and we were losing contact with one another. We were losing our parents, aunts and uncles. The younger people had no idea who their relatives were, even first cousins. A few people hosted the first family reunion in Superior, Montana, gathered some family information and addresses, and sent it to me to add to what I already had. I was blessed with an aunt, Isabelle Morin Mickelson, who raised my brother and me when our mother died. She helped me for some time gather information on our family. She kept everything, wedding and birth announcements, funeral cards, letters, and newspaper clippings. She also lent me her old family photographs to have copies made, and wrote on the back the names of those in the pictures. When I sent out the first request for additional family information, Gail Overbey Morin was one of the people who responded with both her family and the Morin family details.

During this time I was living in Washington, D.C., with access to the National Archives and the many other sources of information in that area. As time passed, the family information I entered into my computer program became a two-pound bundle of paper when it was mailed to interested relatives. Our yearly family reunions, hosted by relatives in different states, continued. Gail had been working on her family, but our side was growing more interesting. She finally got a computer and proceeded to enter all the information we had into her program. She started typing in a friend's group sheets, binder after binder full.

As we got more information, Gail decided that all of the Turtle Mountain roll of 1892 should be entered, as we probably were related to all of them anyway! In 1992, I went to the Turtle Mountain Agency in Belcourt, North Dakota, and left with a great deal more information on our ancestors. In 1993, I was in Portland, Oregon, on business. At the Genealogical Forum, they had copies of the St. Francis-Xavier Church register in French, and extracted in English, and a copy of the records that survived the fire at St. Boniface, Manitoba. These records took our family back an additional two generations.

This work has been aided and abetted by the generosity of people, in Canada and state side, who were willing to share their information, read film, make copies, and who kept a look out for additional sources. The 1870 Manitoba census, the Hudson Bay Red River census, scrip records, Charles Denny Papers, and other church registers were located, sent to us, and all duly entered by Gail into the database. Many of the records were read directly from microfilm or microfiche. The handwriting on many records requires a magnifying glass.

In doing research on this group of ancestors, there were no birth certificates, applications for marriage, or death certificates available at county offices. Names posed a continuous challenge. The French spelling of Beauchemin, became Bushman in English. Morin could be Moran, Morand or Morain. Records could be in French, Latin, or English, many of them not very readable. Old French church registers may not indicate the person was an Indian or mixed-blood.

It is not unusual to find a different birth date or age on every record you find. In this book, where possible, the earliest record is used. Baptism records often gave a birth date. If the Métis were close to a parish, the child was often baptized the same day it was born. During the buffalo hunts, they may have been born on the plains and baptized by the priest traveling with them. At other times, the wife and children may have all been baptized at the same time, and the parents married. Marriage records for many couples will never be found. They may have been lost in the St. Boniface fire, or they may never have been married. Some were married by tribal custom "in the manner of the country." At most Hudson Bay posts there were "country wives."

Locating the wife's Indian name and tribe is probably not possible for many women. The baptism and marriage records for Indians kept by some of the priests give only a Christian first name, and usually not the name of the parents. There are a few church registers where you will find every effort has been made to record the Indian names. The Hudson Bay records very often state the tribe and name of Indians with whom they had dealings.

Early Hudson Bay census records only gave the head of household's name, and numbers for the family members. The 1870 Manitoba census, done by parish, gives the father's name, if known, for each person. This was a marvelous idea! Given the lifestyle of the Métis, deaths were not uncommon. If a child died, the next child born of that same sex may be given the same name. If a husband or wife died, it was common for them to marry the brother or sister of the former spouse. Usually this took place rather soon after the death of the former spouse. This can cause real confusion, especially since every family seemed to name all their children after their parents, grandparents, and brothers and sisters. In a second or third marriage, the children may be named the same as their half-brothers and half-sisters. Using the various church records, and scrip applications helped sorting.

One of the most impressive items, to me, is the Canadian scrip record. In addition to the application, they often include marriage and baptism records obtained from the parish priests. This is also a source of finding records for deceased children who may not appear elsewhere. So often we hear that the Métis were not educated, illiterate. But in those records we often find where those ancestors signed their name instead of making the "x" mark. This is a thrill I hope will happen to many who are researching their family ancestral lines. Do not take it for granted that they could not read or write. Some of the early Hudson Bay employees sent their children away to be educated. After the missionaries arrived, schooling was given to many of the children. The Turtle Mountain Indian treaty has all full-blood Indians and the half-breeds making an "x" mark. My grandfather, who died in 1915, was one of the "x" marks, but we have documents showing he had beautiful handwriting.

If you are beginning your research, consider getting a book such as Angus Baxter's *In search of your Canadian roots. Tracing your family tree in Canada*. Such a book will help you locate where records are deposited, and where to write for them. Do not overlook the Charles Denny Papers at the Glenbow Archives in Calgary, Alberta. They contain newspaper stories and obituaries in addition to family groups, names and dates.

The Métis were a mobile people, and did not consider the boundary between Canada and United States as applying to them. Parts of our family have appeared in U.S. treaty, scrip, census, and church records in Michigan, Minnesota, North Dakota, Montana, Idaho, Washington, and Oregon, and in Canadian records of the Hudson Bay Company, census records, scrip applications, and church records from Quebec, Ontario, Manitoba, Saskatchewan, and Alberta.

Hopefully this book will help you to find the sources necessary to trace your family lines back far enough to allow you to use such helpful publications as the *Dictionnaire généalogique des familles canadiennes* by l'Abbé Cyprien Tanguay, the *Complément au dictionnaire généalogique Tanguay* by J. Arthur LeBoeuf, and *Dictionnaire généalogique des familles du Québec* by René Jetté to take some of those lines back even further.

Happy hunting!
Mary Mae McClammy
Superior, Montana

Descendants of James Sutherland (b. c1770)

Generation One

1. James Sutherland was born circa 1770 Burra, Orkneys, Scotland (Rod MacQuarrie Research, 18 Oct 2010.). He married **Nancy Cook**, daughter of **William Hemmings Cook** and **Kashnapawamakan (Cree Indian),** before 1803 (Denney Papers, Charles D. Denney, Glenbow Archives, Calgary, Alberta, widow of James Sutherland.). He died on 21 Dec 1806 York Factory (HBCA-B Hudson's Bay Company Archives - biographical sketches, Hudson's Bay Company Archives; Winnipeg, Manitoba.). He was buried on 23 Dec 1806 York Factory (Ibid.).

Nancy Cook was born circa 1787 North West (MBS Scrip Applications, Original White Settlers & Halfbreeds residing in Manitoba on 15 July 1870, RG15-19, C-14928.) (HBCA-B.). She was baptized on 27 May 1821 (Fort Douglas), St.Johns, (Manitoba) (HBCR Hudson Bay Company Register of Anglican Church Baptisms, Marriages, and Burials for the Red River Settlement, 1821-1841; Hudson's Bay Company Archives, Winnipeg, Manitoba, E.4/1a, folio 33d. Hereinafter cited as HBCR.). She married according to the custom of the country **William Garrioch** before 1811. She married **William Garrioch** on 27 May 1821 (Fort Douglas), St.Johns, (Manitoba) (Ibid., M-22.). She was buried on 15 Nov 1875 St.Mary's Anglican Church, Portage la Prairie, Manitoba (SMACPLP St.Marys Anglican Church, Portage La Prairie, Manitoba, Baptisms, Marriages, Burials, 1855-1883, transcribed by Clarence Kipling , page 15, S-114.).

Children of **James Sutherland** and **Nancy Cook** were as follows:

2   i. James Sutherland, b. circa 1803 Ruperts Land; m. Elizabeth "Betsy" Calder; d. 13 Aug 1844 St.Andrews, (Manitoba).

ii. William Sutherland was born before 1806 (HBCA-B.). He was baptized on 27 May 1821 St.Johns, Red River Colony, (Manitoba) (HBCR, E.4/1a, folio 33d.). He married Josephte Trottier, daughter of Andre Trottier and Marguerite Paquette, on 26 Dec 1834 St.Johns, Red River Settlement, (Manitoba) (Ibid., No. 289.).

Josephte Trottier was born in Jul 1812 North West (MBS, C-14928.). She married **Alexis Gonneville**, son of **Antoine Gonneville** and **Marguerite Labine dit Lacouture,** on 10 Jan 1837 St.Francois Xavier, (Manitoba) (SFXI: 1834-1852 St.Francois Xavier 1834-1852 Register Index, M-26. Hereinafter cited as SFXI: 1835-1852.).

Generation Two

2. James Sutherland was born circa 1803 Ruperts Land (1843C RRS HBCA E5/11 1843 Census of the Red River Settlement, HBCA E5/11, Hudson's Bay Company Archives, Provincial Archives, 200 Vaughan Street, Winnipeg, MB R3C 1T5, Canada., page 22.). He was baptized on 8 Jun 1823 St.Johns, Red River Settlement, (Manitoba) (HBCR, E.4/1a, folio 44.). He married **Elizabeth "Betsy" Calder**, daughter of **James Calder** and **Nancy Lindsay**, on 12 May 1829 St.Johns, Red River Settlement, (Manitoba) (Ibid., M-178.). He died on 13 Aug 1844 St.Andrews, (Manitoba) (Denney.).

Elizabeth "Betsy" Calder was born on 15 Dec 1813 North West (MBS, C-14926.). She was baptized on 28 Oct 1825 St.Johns, (Manitoba) (Denney.). She married **Cuthbert Cummings**, son of **Cuthbert Cummings** and **Susette McKee or Mackie,** before 1870 St.Andrews, (Manitoba) (Ibid.). She died on 29 Jul 1907 at age 93 (Ibid.).

Children of **James Sutherland** and **Elizabeth "Betsy" Calder** were as follows:

3   i. Anne Sutherland, b. 14 Jul 1832 St.Johns, Red River Settlement, (Manitoba); m. Murdoch McLennan; d. 13 Apr 1864.

4   ii. William Richard Sutherland, b. 8 Dec 1833 St.Andrews, (Manitoba); m. Margaret Inkster; d. 15 Nov 1906 St.Andrews, Manitoba.

iii. John Sutherland was baptized on 24 Nov 1835 (St.Andrews), Rapids of Red River, (Manitoba) (HBCR, E.4/1a, folio 124d.).

iv. Henry Sutherland was born in 1838 (Denney.).

Generation Three

3. Anne Sutherland was baptized on 14 Jul 1832 St.Johns, Red River Settlement, (Manitoba) (HBCR, E.4/1a, folio 91.). She married **Murdoch McLennan** circa 1856. She died on 13 Apr 1864 at age 31 (Denney.).

Murdoch McLennan was born in 1826 Stornoway, Isle of Lewis, Outer Hebrides, Scotland (Ibid.). He married **Ann Bird**, daughter of **James Bird** and **Isabella Gibson**, before 1868. He died circa 1916 (Ibid.).

4. William Richard Sutherland was born on 8 Dec 1833 St.Andrews, (Manitoba) (MBS, C-14933.). He was baptized on 23 Dec 1833 St.Johns, Red River Settlement, (Manitoba) (HBCR, E.4/1a, folio 106.). He married **Margaret Inkster**, daughter of **John Inkster** and **Mary Sinclair**, on 21 Oct 1861 St.Mary's Anglican Church, Portage la Prairie, (Manitoba) (SMACPLP, page 9, M-18.). He died on 15 Nov 1906 St.Andrews, Manitoba, at age 72 (Denney.).

Margaret Inkster was born on 24 Apr 1827 Kildonan, (Manitoba) (MBS, C-14933.). She was baptized on 1 Jul 1827 St.Johns, (Manitoba) (HBCR, #637.). She died on 14 Dec 1904 St.Andrews, Manitoba, at age 77 (MB Vital Statistics, Death Reg. #1905,004304.).

Children of **William Richard Sutherland** and **Margaret Inkster** were as follows:

5   i. George Thomas Sutherland, b. 18 Feb 1862 St.Andrews, (Manitoba); m. Ann Leask.

ii. William Robert Sutherland was born in Jan 1864 St.Paul, (Manitoba) (Denney.). He died on 14 Mar 1865 St.Paul, (Manitoba), at age 1 (Ibid.).

6 iii. Mary Inkster Sutherland, b. 24 Jan 1864 St.Andrews, (Manitoba); m. William Graham Watt Leask; d. 25 May 1934.

7   iv. John Richard Sutherland, b. 21 Jul 1865 St.Andrews, (Manitoba); m. Margaret Brown; d. 29 Sep 1929 St.Andrews, Manitoba.

8   v. Isabella Ann Sutherland, b. 30 Aug 1868 St.Andrews, (Manitoba); m. Alexander 'Big Alex' Setter; d. 5 Jul 1934 Winnipeg, Manitoba.

9   vi.   William Colin Sutherland, b. 12 Feb 1871 St.Andrews, (Manitoba); m. Catherine 'Kate' Taylor; m. May Matilda Corrigal; m. Rosabel McDonald; d. 16 Mar 1931 St.Andrews, Manitoba.

     vii.   Robert James Sutherland was born in 1873 St.Andrews, Manitoba (Ibid.). He died on 19 Nov 1873 St.Andrews, Manitoba (Ibid.).

    viii.   Elizabeth Victoria Jane Sutherland was born circa 1877 (Ibid.). She died on 2 Mar 1899 Baie St.Paul, Manitoba (Ibid.).

Generation Four

5. George Thomas Sutherland was baptized on 18 Feb 1862 St.Andrews, (Manitoba) (Ibid.). He married **Ann Leask**, daughter of **John Leask** and **Mary Ann Moar**, on 4 Dec 1884 St.Andrews, Manitoba (MB Vital Statistics, Marriage Reg. #1884,001418.).

  Ann Leask was born on 16 Sep 1864 (Denney.) (HBCA-B.) (1901 Canada, District 11-l-6, page 6, family 52, line 34-42.). She died on 5 Dec 1949 Wakefield at age 85 (Denney.).

Children of **George Thomas Sutherland** and **Ann Leask** were as follows:

      i.   Walter Colin Sutherland was born on 2 Jan 1886 R.M. of St.Andrews, Manitoba (MB Vital Statistics, Birth Reg. #1886,003805.). He married Elizabeth McBain, daughter of Alexander McBain and (--?--) Clifford, on 22 Feb 1911 RM St.Andrews, Manitoba (Ibid., Marriage Reg. #1911,001930.). He died on 21 Feb 1949 at age 63 (Denney.).
            Elizabeth McBain was born on 3 Nov 1885 (Ibid.).

     ii.   Guilford Dudley Booth Sutherland was born on 31 Mar 1888 R.M. of St.Andrews, Manitoba (MB Vital Statistics, Birth Reg. #1888,004694.). He married Edna Brown, daughter of Arthur Brown and Alice Naylor, on 9 Jan 1918 (Denney.). He died on 14 Oct 1972 at age 84 (Ibid.).
            Edna Brown was born on 12 May 1900 Ontario (Ibid.).

    iii.   Thomas Herbert Sutherland was born on 16 Oct 1889 R.M. of St.Andrews, Manitoba (MB Vital Statistics, Birth Reg. #1889,002713.). He married Ellen Elizabeth Madigan on 21 Jun 1916 (Denney.). He died on 13 Apr 1982 at age 92 (Ibid.).
            Ellen Elizabeth Madigan was born on 4 Apr 1893 Reynolds, North Dakota (Ibid.). She died on 24 Sep 1965 Assiniboia at age 72 (Ibid.).

     iv.   William Reginald Sutherland was born on 28 Jan 1892 St.Andrews, Manitoba (1901 Canada, District 11-l-6, page 6, family 52, line 34-42.). He married Elsie Isabella McDonald, daughter of George McDonald and Elizabeth Jane McKay, on 16 Jul 1927 St.Andrews, Manitoba (MB Vital Statistics, Marriage Reg. #1927,033523.). He died on 25 Apr 1967 Winnipeg, Manitoba, at age 75 (Denney.).
            Elsie Isabella McDonald was born on 19 Dec 1898 R. M. of St.Andrews, Manitoba (MB Vital Statistics, Birth Reg. #1898,001426.). She died on 2 Mar 1978 at age 79 (Denney.).

      v.   Mary Margaret Sutherland was born on 12 Apr 1894 R.M. of St.Andrews, Manitoba (MB Vital Statistics, Birth Reg. #1894,001843.). She married Geoffrey Arthur McNab, son of Jacob McNab and Henrietta White, on 23 Dec 1914 St.Andrews, Manitoba (Ibid., Marriage Reg. #1914,145264.). She died on 12 Sep 1955 at age 61 (Denney.).
            Geoffrey Arthur McNab was born on 21 Jul 1886 R.M. of St.Andrews, Manitoba (1901 Canada, #11, l-6, page 4, family 36, line 43-48.) (MB Vital Statistics, Birth Reg. #1886,001612.). He died on 6 Mar 1970 at age 83 (Denney.).

     vi.   John Leask Sutherland was born on 25 Jul 1896 R.M. of St.Andrews, Manitoba (MB Vital Statistics, Birth Reg. #1896,002851.). He died on 7 Jul 1942 Winnipeg, Manitoba, at age 45 (Ibid., Death Reg. #1942,028128.).

    vii.   Victor James Sutherland was born on 12 Feb 1899 R.M. of St.Andrews, Manitoba (Ibid., Birth Reg. #1899,006866.). He married Amy Leone McPherson, daughter of Hugh Andrew McPherson and Laura Bristow, on 15 Oct 1924 St.Andrews, Manitoba (Ibid., Marriage Reg. #1924,039305.). He married Freda Brown on 27 May 1967 (Denney.).
            Amy Leone McPherson was born on 29 Oct 1899 R.M. of Rockwood, Manitoba (MB Vital Statistics, Birth Reg. #1899,003079.). She died on 30 Sep 1964 at age 64 (Denney.).
            Freda Brown was born on 20 Aug 1906 (Ibid.).

   viii.   Rosa Ethel Sutherland was born on 8 Jan 1902 R.M. of St.Andrews, Manitoba (MB Vital Statistics, Birth Reg. #1902,004231.). She married William McRae, son of William McRae and Mary McKay, on 19 Nov 1924 Selkirk, Manitoba (Denney.). She died on 28 Jul 1927 Selkirk, Manitoba, at age 25 (MB Vital Statistics, Death Reg. #1927,035029.).
            William McRae was born on 24 Jun 1897 R.M. of St.Andrews, Manitoba (1901 Canada, #11, 1-6, page 1, family 1, line 1-7.) (MB Vital Statistics, Birth Reg. #1897,004003.).

     ix.   Hurbert Sutherland was born on 19 Oct 1905 R.M. of St.Andrews, Manitoba (Ibid., Birth Reg. #1905,002142.).

      x.   Arthur Hamlyn Sutherland was born on 18 Feb 1906 R.M. of St.Andrews, Manitoba (Ibid., Birth Reg. #1906,005104.). He married Myrtle Root on 4 Oct 1930 Emerson, Manitoba (Ibid., Marriage Reg. #1930,048352.).
            Myrtle Root was born on 8 May 1900 (Denney.).

6. Mary Inkster Sutherland was baptized on 24 Jan 1864 St.Andrews, (Manitoba) (Ibid.). She married **William Graham Watt Leask**, son of **John Leask** and **Mary Ann Moar**, on 18 Mar 1883 St.Johns, Manitoba (Ibid.). She died on 25 May 1934 at age 70 (Ibid.).
William Graham Watt Leask was born on 24 Mar 1858 (Ibid.) (HBCA-B.). He died on 8 Jun 1929 at age 71 (Denney.).

7. John Richard Sutherland was born on 21 Jul 1865 St.Andrews, (Manitoba) (1901 Canada, #11, 1-6, page 3, family 27, line 44-50.). He was baptized on 13 Aug 1865 St.Andrews, (Manitoba) (Denney.). He married **Margaret Brown**, daughter of **Thomas Henry Brown** and **Jane Scott**, on 15 Jun 1889 St.Andrews, Manitoba (MB Vital Statistics, Marriage Reg. #1889,002116.). He died on 29 Sep 1929 St.Andrews, Manitoba, at age 64 (Ibid., Death Reg. #1929,060240.).

Margaret Brown was born on 13 Oct 1867 St.Andrews, (Manitoba) (MBS, C-14925.). She was baptized on 26 Nov 1867 St.Andrews, (Manitoba) (Ibid.).

Children of **John Richard Sutherland** and **Margaret Brown** were as follows:

    i.   John Dougall Sutherland was born on 20 Sep 1889 R.M. of St.Andrews, Manitoba (MB Vital Statistics, Birth Reg. #1889,002710.).

    ii.   Harriet Maud Mary Sutherland was born on 21 Oct 1890 R.M. of St.Andrews, Manitoba (Ibid., Birth Reg. #1890,003560.).

    iii.   John Inkster Sutherland was born on 24 Jan 1893 R.M. of St.Andrews, Manitoba (Ibid., Birth Reg. #1893,005111.).

    iv.   Victoria Evelyn Sutherland was born on 22 Jan 1895 R.M. of St.Andrews, Manitoba (Ibid., Birth Reg. #1895,003895.). She died in 1964 (Denney.).

    v.   Isabella Jane Sutherland was born on 12 Feb 1897 R.M. of St.Andrews, Manitoba (MB Vital Statistics, Birth Reg. #1897,001190.). She died in Jan 1936 Moose Jaw, Saskatchewan, at age 38 (Denney.).

    vi.   William Colin Sutherland was born on 20 May 1898 R.M. of St.Andrews, Manitoba (MB Vital Statistics, Birth Reg. #1899,006863.). He married Elizabeth Jane McDonald, daughter of George McDonald and Elizabeth Jane McKay, on 1 Jun 1927 St.Andrews, Manitoba (Ibid., Marriage Reg. #1927,028341.). He died on 30 Nov 1972 at age 74 (Denney.).

        Elizabeth Jane McDonald was born on 26 Jun 1901 R. M. of St.Andrews, Manitoba (MB Vital Statistics, Birth Reg. #1901,002597.). She died on 30 Nov 1950 at age 49 (Denney.).

    vii.   Jessie Gertrude Sutherland was born on 19 Jul 1901 R.M. of St.Andrews, Manitoba (MB Vital Statistics, Birth Reg. #1901,002604.).

    viii.   Florence Margaret Sutherland was born on 31 Jul 1902 R.M. of St.Andrews, Manitoba (Ibid., Birth Reg. #1902,007941.).

    ix.   Esther Marie Sutherland was born on 26 Sep 1904 R.M. of St.Andrews, Manitoba (Ibid., Birth Reg. #1905,004115.).

    x.   Hubert Sutherland was born on 19 Oct 1905 R.M. of St.Andrews, Manitoba (Ibid., Birth Reg. #1905,002142.).

    xi.   Rose Anne Sutherland was born on 15 Sep 1910 R.M. of St.Andrews, Manitoba (Ibid., Birth Reg. #1910,004925.).

    xii.   Vera Sutherland was born in 1911 (Denney.). She died in 1928 Winnipeg, Manitoba (Ibid.).

8. Isabella Ann Sutherland was baptized on 30 Aug 1868 St.Andrews, (Manitoba) (Ibid.). She married **Alexander 'Big Alex' Setter**, son of **James Setter** and **Jane Morwick,** on 15 Dec 1887 St.Andrews, Manitoba (MB Vital Statistics, Marriage Reg. #1887,001912.). She died on 5 Jul 1934 Winnipeg, Manitoba, at age 65 (Ibid., Death Reg. #1934,028087.).

Alexander 'Big Alex' Setter was born on 1 Jan 1857 St.Andrews, (Manitoba) (Denney.). He was baptized on 12 Jan 1857 St.Andrews, (Manitoba) (Ibid.). He died on 19 Dec 1924 St.Andrews, Manitoba, at age 67 (MB Vital Statistics, Death Reg. #1924,048450.).

9. William Colin Sutherland was baptized on 12 Feb 1871 St.Andrews, (Manitoba) (Denney.). He married **Catherine 'Kate' Taylor**, daughter of **William McKay Taylor** and **Mary Birston,** on 5 Jan 1898 St.Andrews, Manitoba (MB Vital Statistics, Marriage Reg. #1898,002414.). He married **May Matilda Corrigal**, daughter of **John Henry Corrigal** and **Maria Halcrow,** on 12 Jul 1905 St.Andrews, Manitoba (Ibid., Marriage Reg. #1905,001642.). He married **Rosabel McDonald**, daughter of **Robert McDonald** and **Charlotte Harcus,** on 30 Oct 1912 St.Andrews, Manitoba (Ibid., Marriage Reg. #1912,004721.). He died on 16 Mar 1931 St.Andrews, Manitoba, at age 60 (Denney.) (MB Vital Statistics, Death Reg. #1931,015247.).

Catherine 'Kate' Taylor was born on 20 Jan 1875 (Denney.). She died on 25 Jun 1904 R.M. of St.Andrews, Manitoba, at age 29 (MB Vital Statistics, Death Reg. #1904,003559.).

Children of **William Colin Sutherland** and **Catherine 'Kate' Taylor** all born R.M. of St.Andrews, Manitoba, were as follows:

    i.   Mildred Mary Sutherland was born on 11 Nov 1898 (Ibid., Birth Reg. #1898,001455.).

    ii.   John Hector Sutherland was born on 2 Apr 1900 (Ibid., Birth Reg. #1900,002101.). He died on 12 Dec 1961 Selkirk, Manitoba, at age 61 (Denney.). He was buried St.Andrews, Manitoba (Ibid.).

    iii.   Agnes Margaret Sutherland was born on 12 Sep 1902 (MB Vital Statistics, Birth Reg. #1902,007941.).

May Matilda Corrigal was born on 26 May 1880 St.Andrews, Manitoba (1901 Canada, St.Andrews, page 3, family 25, line 10-16.).

Children of **William Colin Sutherland** and **May Matilda Corrigal** were:

    i.   Colin Howard Sutherland was born on 27 Jun 1906 R.M. of St.Andrews, Manitoba (MB Vital Statistics, Birth Reg. #1906,005106.). He died on 10 Aug 1906 St.Andrews, Manitoba (Ibid., Death Reg. #1906,003487.).

Rosabel McDonald was born on 28 Oct 1887 R.M. of St.Clements, Manitoba (1901 Canada, #11, m-2, page 3, family 28, line 32-38.) (MB Vital Statistics, Birth Reg. #1887,001852.).

Children of **William Colin Sutherland** and **Rosabel McDonald** are as follows:

    i.   Walter Lorne Sutherland.

    ii.   Maude Sarah Sutherland.

    iii.   Dorothy Sutherland.

    iv.   Lillian Victoria Sutherland was born circa 1914 (1921 Census of Canada from the National Archives of Canada (Transcription by ancestry.com), Ottawa, Canada, page 10.).

    v.   Gertrude Sutherland was born circa 1916 (Ibid.).

    vi.   Irene Sutherland was born circa 1918 (Ibid.).

    vii.   Robert George Sutherland was born circa 1920 (Ibid.).

Descendants of James Sutherland (b. c1777)

Generation One

1. James Sutherland was born circa 1777 (1828C RRS HBCA E5/2 1828 Census of the Red River Settlement, HBCA E5/2, Hudson's Bay Company Archives, Provincial Archives, 200 Vaughan Street, Winnipeg, MB R3C 1T5, Canada., page 8.). He married according to the custom of the country **Jane Flett (Indian)** before 1800. He married **Jane Flett (Indian)** on 20 May 1828 St.Johns, (Manitoba) (HBCR Hudson Bay Company Register of Anglican Church Baptisms, Marriages, and Burials for the Red River Settlement, 1821-1841; Hudson's Bay Company Archives, Winnipeg, Manitoba, M-151. Hereinafter cited as HBCR.). He died on 30 Sep 1844 (Manitoba) (Denney Papers, Charles D. Denney, Glenbow Archives, Calgary, Alberta.) (HBCA-B Hudson's Bay Company Archives - biographical sketches, Hudson's Bay Company Archives; Winnipeg, Manitoba.).

Jane Flett (Indian) was born circa 1785. She died on 7 Jul 1835 (Manitoba) (Ibid.).

Children of **James Sutherland** and **Jane Flett (Indian)** were as follows:

    2   i.   Sarah "Sally" Sutherland, b. circa 1800; m. Roderick McKenzie Jr; d. 1829 Quebec.
    3   ii.   William Sutherland, b. 23 Apr 1806 North West; m. Elizabeth Logan; d. 31 Jan 1879 St.Paul, Middlechurch, Manitoba.
    4   iii. Nancy Sutherland, b. circa 1810; m. Robert Clouston.
    5   iv.   Elizabeth Sutherland, b. 1 Dec 1810 Cumberland House, (Saskatchewan); m. James Inkster; d. 9 Aug 1899 Prince Albert, (Saskatchewan).
    6   v.   Letitia Sutherland, b. 1815 North West; m. James Inkster; d. 20 Nov 1883 Woodlands, Manitoba.
    7   vi.   James Sutherland, b. 3 Jan 1817 North West; m. Maria Bird.
    8   vii. John Sutherland, b. 8 Jan 1819 St.Johns, (Manitoba); m. Catherine Cunningham.
    9   viii. Roderic Sutherland, b. 12 Aug 1821 St.Johns, Norway House; m. Marie Emily Lowman.
         ix.   Donald Sutherland was baptized on 16 Sep 1830 St.Johns, (Manitoba) (Denney.).

Generation Two

2. Sarah "Sally" Sutherland was born circa 1800 (Ibid.). She was baptized on 12 May 1821 St.Johns, (Manitoba) (Ibid.). She was baptized on 12 Aug 1821 St.Johns, Norway House (HBCR, E.4/1a, folio 34d.). She married **Roderick McKenzie Jr.**, son of **Hon. Roderick McKenzie**, on 20 Mar 1823 Fort Alexander (Ibid., M-56.). She died in 1829 Quebec.

Roderick McKenzie Jr was born circa 1791 Gaerloch, Ross-shire, Scotland (Denney.). He died on 10 Jan 1830 Portneuf (Ibid.).

3. William Sutherland was born on 23 Apr 1806 North West (MBS, C-14934.). He married **Elizabeth Logan**, daughter of **Robert Logan** and **Mary Sauteaux Indian Woman**, on 31 Dec 1831 St.Johns, (Manitoba) (HBCR, M-227.). He died on 31 Jan 1879 St.Paul, Middlechurch, Manitoba, at age 72 (Denney.).

Elizabeth Logan was born on 1 Dec 1810 Sault Ste.Marie, (Ontario) (MBS, C-14934.). She was baptized on 13 Jan 1821 St.Johns, Red River Colony, (Manitoba) (HBCR, E.4/1a, folio 29.). She died on 18 Nov 1889 at age 78 (Denney.). She was buried in Nov 1889 St.Johns, Manitoba (Ibid.).

Children of **William Sutherland** and **Elizabeth Logan** were as follows:

    10   i.   James Robert Sutherland, b. 19 Dec 1832 St.Johns, Red River Settlement, (Manitoba); m. Mary Ann Settee.
         ii.   Margaret Sutherland was baptized on 4 Dec 1834 St.Johns, Red River Settlement, (Manitoba) (HBCR, E.4/1a, folio 116d.). She died on 10 Apr 1845 St.Johns, (Manitoba), at age 10 (Denney.).
    11   iii. Mary Sutherland, b. 21 Aug 1836 St.Johns, Red River Settlement, (Manitoba); m. Frederick Watts; d. Aug 1871.
         iv.   William Thomas Sutherland was born on 20 Jun 1838 (Ibid.). He was baptized on 2 Sep 1838 St.Johns, Red River Settlement, (Manitoba) (HBCR, E.4/1a, folio 155d.). He died on 12 Sep 1904 St.Clements, Manitoba, at age 66 (Denney.).
         v.   John Sutherland was born on 10 May 1840 (Ibid.). He was baptized on 14 Jun 1840 St.Johns, Red River Settlement, (Manitoba) (HBCR, E.4/1a, folio 166d.). He died on 13 Jul 1901 Richland at age 61 (Denney.). He was buried Milbrook (Ibid.).
    12   vi.   Roderick Kenneth Sutherland, b. 10 Jun 1842; m. Isabelle Flora Flett; d. 16 Feb 1909 Selkirk, Manitoba.
         vii. Jane Sarah Ann Sutherland was baptized on 6 Oct 1844 St.Johns, (Manitoba) (Ibid.). She died on 8 Nov 1845 St.Johns, (Manitoba), at age 1 (Ibid.).
    13   viii. Ann Sutherland, b. 10 Jul 1846; m. John Norris.
    14   ix.   Alexander Sutherland, b. 3 Nov 1848; m. Lydia Ann Settee; d. 21 May 1902 Selkirk, Manitoba.
         x.   Nathaniel Logan Sutherland was baptized on 24 Apr 1850 St.Paul, (Manitoba) (Ibid.).
         xi.   Elizabeth Sutherland was baptized on 27 Dec 1851 St.Paul, (Manitoba) (Ibid.). She died in Jul 1852 (Ibid.). She was buried St.Johns, (Manitoba) (Ibid.).

4. Nancy Sutherland was born circa 1810. She was baptized on 12 Aug 1821 St.Johns, Norway House (HBCR, E.4/1a, folio 34d.). She married **Robert Clouston** on 2 Apr 1828 St.Johns, (Manitoba) (Denney.).

Robert Clouston was born circa 1794 Orphir, Orkney, Scotland (Ibid.). He died on 14 Jul 1850 (Ibid.). Question: *Marriage No. 154-177 in 1828-1829 are not found in the HBCA records.*

5. Elizabeth Sutherland was born on 1 Dec 1810 Cumberland House, (Saskatchewan) (Denney.). She was baptized on 12 Aug 1821 St.Johns, Norway House (HBCR, E.4/1a, folio 34d.). She married **James Inkster**, son of **John Inkster** and **Margaret Gunn**, on 16 Dec 1830 St.Johns, Red River Settlement, (Manitoba) (Ibid., M-210.). She died on 9 Aug 1899 Prince Albert, (Saskatchewan), at age 88 (Denney.).

James Inkster was born on 5 Aug 1804 Norquay, Orphir County, Orkney, Scotland (Lee Fraychineaud, *The Inkster Family of Lee Fraychineaud*, January 1999), page 4, source: Film #101956, Orphir, (23), Orkney Scotland Births and Marriages, 1708-1854.) (HBCA-B.). He died on 17 May 1865 St.Johns, (Manitoba), at age 60 (Ibid.).

6. Letitia Sutherland was born in 1815 North West (MBS, C-14929.). She was baptized on 12 Aug 1821 St.Johns, Norway House (HBCR, E.4/1a, folio 34d.). She married **James Inkster**, son of **James Inkster** and **Mary Cree**, on 16 Dec 1830 St.Johns, Red River Settlement, (Manitoba) (Ibid., M-211.). She died on 20 Nov 1883 Woodlands, Manitoba (MB Vital Statistics, Death Reg. #1883,001822.).

James Inkster was born on 6 Apr 1809 Brandon House, North West (MBS, C-14929.). He was baptized on 23 Jan 1821 (Brandon House), St.Johns, (Manitoba) (HBCA-B.) (HBCR, E.4/1a, folio 30.). He died on 5 Jun 1888 St.Andrews, Manitoba, at age 79 (MB Vital Statistics, Death Reg. #1888,001754.).

7. **James Sutherland** was born on 3 Jan 1817 North West (MBS, C-14934.). He was baptized on 12 Aug 1821 St.Johns, Norway House, (Manitoba) (HBCR, E.4/1a, folio 34d.). He married **Maria Bird**, daughter of **Joseph Bird** and **Elisabeth Thomas**, on 6 Nov 1838 Middle Church, Red River Settlement, (Manitoba) (Ibid., No. 400.).

Maria Bird was born in 1822 St.Paul, (Manitoba) (MBS, Supplementary Returns, C-14934.). She was baptized on 24 Mar 1822 St.Johns, Red River Colony, (Manitoba) (AI-Rozyk   Anglican Index of Baptisms, Marriages and Burials Extractions, Hudson Bay Company Archives, Winnipeg, Manitoba, Canada, Selected and Compiled by Rosemary Rozyk. Hereinafter cited as AI-Rozyk.) (HBCR, E.4/1a, folio 36d.). She died on 22 Nov 1891 Halcro, (Saskatchewan) (Denney.).

Children of **James Sutherland** and **Maria Bird** were as follows:

15   i.   Elizabeth Sutherland, b. circa 1839 St.Paul, (Manitoba); m. James Brown.

    ii.   George James Sutherland was baptized on 4 Apr 1841 St.Johns, Red River Settlement, (Manitoba) (HBCR, E.4/1a, folio 140d.). He died on 6 Sep 1842 St.Johns, (Manitoba), at age 1 (Denney.).

    iii.   Jemima Sutherland was baptized on 7 Jul 1843 St.Johns, (Manitoba) (Ibid.). She died in 1844 St.Johns, (Manitoba) (Ibid.).

    iv.   Joseph William Sutherland was baptized on 15 Feb 1845 St.Johns, (Manitoba) (Ibid.).

16   v.   Mary Jane Sutherland, b. 1 Nov 1848 St.Paul, (Manitoba); m. William George Bird.

    vi.   Thomas Sutherland was born on 23 Jan 1849 St.Paul, (Manitoba) (MBS, C-14934.). He died on 16 Mar 1882 High Bluff, Manitoba, at age 33 (Denney.).

17   vii.   Jessie Ann Sutherland, b. 23 Feb 1851 St.Paul, (Manitoba); m. Malcolm McLeod.

    viii.   Edwin J. Sutherland was born on 31 May 1853 St.Paul, (Manitoba) (MBS, C-14933.). He died on 14 Sep 1892 Halcro, (Saskatchewan), at age 39 (Denney.).

18   ix.   Catherine Marie Sutherland, b. 18 Oct 1855 St.Paul, (Manitoba); m. Duncan Richard Setter.

    x.   Sarah Sutherland was born on 15 Feb 1862 (HBC-PN , Poplar Point and High Bluff, #290.). She was baptized on 18 Mar 1862 St.Paul, (Manitoba) (Denney.).

19   xi.   Charles John Sutherland, b. 16 Apr 1866; m. Jemima Monkman; d. 18 Jul 1921 Halcro, Saskatchewan.

8. **John Sutherland** was born on 8 Jan 1819 St.Johns, (Manitoba) (MBS, C-14934.) (1901 Canada, #11, R-1, page 4, family 1110-111, line 7-13.). He was baptized on 12 Aug 1821 St.Johns, Norway House (HBCR, E.4/1a, folio 34d.). He married **Catherine Cunningham**, daughter of **Patrick Cunningham** and **Nancy Bruce**, on 20 Dec 1849 St.Johns, (Manitoba) (Denney.).

Catherine Cunningham was born on 10 Mar 1832 (1901 Canada, #11, R-1, page 4, family 1110-111, line 7-13.). She was born in Nov 1832 North West (MBS, C-14934.). She was baptized on 14 Aug 1833 St.Johns, (Manitoba) (HBCA-B.) (HBCR, E.4/1a, folio 104.).

Children of **John Sutherland** and **Catherine Cunningham** were as follows:

    i.   Sarah Sutherland was baptized on 10 Jan 1851 St.Paul, (Manitoba) (Denney.). She died on 10 Nov 1860 St.Paul, (Manitoba), at age 9 (Ibid.).

    ii.   Maria Sutherland was baptized on 7 Aug 1852 St.Paul, (Manitoba) (Ibid.). She died on 8 Apr 1866 St.Paul, (Manitoba), at age 13 (Ibid.).

20   iii.   John George Sutherland, b. 24 Jul 1853 St.Paul, (Manitoba); m. Emma McLennan; d. 22 Nov 1889 St.Paul, Manitoba.

    iv.   Roderick James Sutherland was baptized on 2 Mar 1856 St.Paul, (Manitoba) (Ibid.). He died on 7 Sep 1856 St.Paul, (Manitoba) (Ibid.).

    v.   Jane Sutherland was born in 1857 St.Paul, (Manitoba) (Ibid.). She died on 24 Nov 1860 St.Paul, (Manitoba) (Ibid.).

    vi.   Patrick James Sutherland was baptized in Aug 1857 St.Paul, (Manitoba) (Ibid.). He died on 13 Nov 1863 St.Paul, (Manitoba), at age 6 (Ibid.).

    vii.   Jemima Mary Sutherland was born on 17 Nov 1861 St.Paul, (Manitoba) (Ibid.). She died on 14 Jan 1869 St.Paul, (Manitoba), at age 7 (Ibid.).

    viii.   Alice Sutherland was baptized on 25 Oct 1863 St.Paul, (Manitoba) (Ibid.). She died on 5 Jan 1864 St.Paul, (Manitoba) (Ibid.).

    ix.   John Sutherland was born in 1864.

21   x.   Alfred William Sutherland, b. 18 Oct 1864 St.Paul, (Manitoba); m. Mary M. (--?--).

    xi.   Albert Edward Sutherland was baptized in Mar 1867 St.Paul, (Manitoba) (Ibid.).

22   xii.   Letitia Elizabeth Sutherland, b. 27 Apr 1869 St.Paul, (Manitoba).

    xiii.   Catherine Ann Sutherland was baptized on 25 Mar 1871 St.Paul, (Manitoba) (Ibid.). She died on 8 May 1871 St.Paul, Manitoba (Ibid.).

    xiv.   Robert James Sutherland was baptized on 7 Apr 1872 St.Paul, Manitoba (Ibid.).

9. **Roderic Sutherland** was baptized on 12 Aug 1821 St.Johns, Norway House (HBCR, E.4/1a, folio 34d.). He married **Marie Emily Lowman** on 18 Jan 1849 White Cottage, Red River Settlement, (Manitoba) (Ibid., No. 420.).

Children of **Roderic Sutherland** and **Marie Emily Lowman** were as follows:

    i.   Alice Mary Sutherland was baptized on 24 Jan 1850 St.Johns, (Manitoba) (Denney.).

    ii.   Edith Jane Sutherland was baptized on 15 May 1853 St.Paul, (Manitoba) (Ibid.).

Generation Three

10. **James Robert Sutherland** was baptized on 19 Dec 1832 St.Johns, Red River Settlement, (Manitoba) (HBCR, E.4/1a, folio 94.). He married **Mary Ann Settee**, daughter of **James Settee (Cree)** and **Sarah "Sally" Cook**, before 1861 (1870C-MB, page 212, #237.).

Mary Ann Settee was baptized on 28 Jan 1842 St.Johns, (Manitoba) (Denney.) (HBCA-B, E4/2 fo. 5d.). She married **Henry McKlin** on 8 Feb 1883 St.Andrews, Manitoba (MB Vital Statistics, Marriage Reg. #1883,001451.).

Children of **James Robert Sutherland** and **Mary Ann Settee** were as follows:

23   i.   Alexander Sutherland, b. Dec 1859.

24   ii.   Christie Alice Sutherland, b. 23 Mar 1866 Fort Pelly, (Saskatchewan); m. Alexander Pruden; m. John James Louis or Lewis; d. 1 Apr 1947; bur. 3 Apr 1947.

iii.   Roderick Sutherland was born circa 1868 (Manitoba) (1870C-MB, page 212, #240.).

iv.   Margaret Sutherland was born circa 1868 (Manitoba) (Ibid., page 212, #241.).

11. Mary Sutherland was baptized on 21 Aug 1836 St.Johns, Red River Settlement, (Manitoba) (HBCR, E.4/1a, folio 130.). She married **Frederick Watts**, son of **Thimothy Watts**, before 1860. She died in Aug 1871 (Denney.).

Frederick Watts was born circa 1828 England (1870C-MB, page 158, #55.).

12. Roderick Kenneth Sutherland was born on 10 Jun 1842 (Denney.) (1901 Canada, District 11-j-2, page 5-6, family 44, line 41-50, 1-4.). He was baptized on 16 Aug 1842 St.Johns, (Manitoba) (Denney.). He married **Isabelle Flora Flett**, daughter of **Peter Flett** and **Euphemia Halcrow,** on 24 Dec 1874 St.Paul, Manitoba (Ibid.). He died on 16 Feb 1909 Selkirk, Manitoba, at age 66 (MB Vital Statistics, Death Reg. #1909,004203.).

Isabelle Flora Flett was born on 6 Apr 1856 (1901 Canada, District 11-j-2, page 5-6, family 44, line 41-50, 1-4.). She was baptized on 11 May 1856 St.Paul, (Manitoba) (Denney.). She died on 28 Feb 1932 Winnipeg, Manitoba, at age 75 (MB Vital Statistics, Death Reg. #1932,012098.).

Children of **Roderick Kenneth Sutherland** and **Isabelle Flora Flett** were as follows:

i.   William T. Sutherland was born on 16 Nov 1875 (1901 Canada, District 11-j-2, page 5-6, family 44, line 41-50, 1-4.).

25   ii.   Peter Henry Sutherland, b. 30 Mar 1877; m. Daisy Mary Elizabeth Stevens.

iii.   Norman Alexander Frederick Sutherland was baptized on 13 Dec 1878 Kildonan, Manitoba (Denney.). He died on 8 Apr 1887 Selkirk, Manitoba, at age 8 (MB Vital Statistics, Death Reg. #1887,001241.).

iv.   Effie E. Sutherland was born on 14 Aug 1880 (1901 Canada, District #11-j-2, page 5-6, family 44, line 41-50, 1-4.).

v.   Mary Margaret Sutherland was born on 7 Aug 1882 (Ibid.). She married James Augustin Smith on 12 Apr 1905 Selkirk, Manitoba (MB Vital Statistics, Marriage Reg. #1905,002072.). She died on 23 Jan 1930 St.Boniface, Manitoba, at age 47 (Denney.).

vi.   Isabel Ann Sutherland was baptized on 12 Dec 1884 (1901 Canada, District #11-j-2, page 5-6, family 44, line 41-50, 1-4.). She married Richard Havelock Hogg on 29 Dec 1908 Selkirk, Manitoba (MB Vital Statistics, Marriage Reg. #1908,001122.).

vii.   John Dudley Sutherland was born on 26 Feb 1887 Little Britain, Manitoba (Ibid., Birth Reg. #1887,002728.). He died on 11 May 1888 Selkirk, Manitoba, at age 1 (Ibid., Death Reg. #1888,001287.).

viii.   Sarah Adelaide Sutherland was born on 8 Jul 1889 Selkirk, Manitoba (Ibid., Birth Reg. #1889,001323.).

ix.   Alice Maude Sutherland was born on 7 Oct 1891 Selkirk, Manitoba (Ibid., Birth Reg. #1891,003032.).

x.   Flossie May Sutherland was born on 6 May 1894 Selkirk, Manitoba (Ibid., Birth Reg. #1894,006005.). She died on 30 Jul 1915 Selkirk, Manitoba, at age 21 (Ibid., Death Reg. #1915,187049.).

xi.   William Thomas Sutherland was baptized on 24 Dec 1895 St.Paul, Manitoba (Denney.). He died on 27 Feb 1945 at age 49 (Ibid.).

xii.   Lottie Viola Sutherland was born on 24 Jun 1896 Selkirk, Manitoba (MB Vital Statistics, Birth Reg. #1896,001069.).

xiii.   Roderick Kenneth Sutherland was born on 13 Jan 1899 Selkirk, Manitoba (Ibid., Birth Reg. #1899,004894.). He died on 17 Aug 1909 Mapleton, Manitoba, at age 10 (Denney.).

xiv.   James Aldwin Sutherland was born on 10 Jan 1901 Selkirk, Manitoba (MB Vital Statistics, Birth Reg. #1901,004072.). He died on 23 Jan 1921 Winnipeg, Manitoba, at age 20 (Ibid., Death Reg. #1921,003188.).

13. Ann Sutherland was born on 10 Jul 1846 (Denney.). She was baptized on 27 Sep 1846 St.Johns, (Manitoba) (Ibid.). She married **John Norris**, son of **John Norris** and **Marie Kayattowue,** in Apr 1876 St.Paul, (Manitoba) (NWHBS, C-14940.).

John Norris was born circa Jun 1858 Fort Pitt, (Saskatchewan) (LLBR1 Notre Dame des Tidoren, St.Paul Diocese, Lac La Biche, Registre des Baptemes, Mariages & Seplutures, Volume 1, 1853-1898., page 30, B-163. Hereinafter cited as LLBR1.) (NWHBS, C-14940.). He was baptized on 3 Sep 1858 Lac la Biche, (Alberta) (LLBR1, page 30, B-163.).

14. Alexander Sutherland was born on 3 Nov 1848 (Denney.). He was baptized on 23 Nov 1848 St.Johns, (Manitoba) (Ibid.). He married **Lydia Ann Settee**, daughter of **James Settee (Cree)** and **Sarah "Sally" Cook,** circa 1880 (Rod Mac Quarrie, 20 Sep 2009.). He died on 21 May 1902 Selkirk, Manitoba, at age 53 (MB Vital Statistics, Death Reg. #1902,001723.).

Lydia Ann Settee was born circa 1856 (Denney.) (1870C-MB, page 213, #277.). She died on 11 Jan 1935 Selkirk, Manitoba (MB Vital Statistics, Death Reg. #1935,004287.).

Children of **Alexander Sutherland** and **Lydia Ann Settee** were as follows:

i.   Elizabeth S. Sutherland was born in Jan 1881 St.Paul, Manitoba (1881 Church of Latter Day Saints Census Transcription Project of Census Images from the National Archives of Canada, Ottawa, Canada, http://www.familysearch.org, NA Film #C-13283, District 185, Sub-district A, page 8, house 27.).

ii.   George Sutherland was born circa 1884 Manitoba (1891 Census of Canada from the National Archives of Canada, Ottawa, Canada.).

iii.   Thomas Sutherland was born circa 1887 Manitoba (Ibid.).

iv.   Walter Philip Sutherland was born on 13 Nov 1889 Selkirk, Manitoba (MB Vital Statistics, Birth Reg. #1889,001330.).

     v.   Lydia Christie Sutherland was born on 28 Mar 1892 Selkirk, Manitoba (Ibid., Birth Reg. #1892,004640.). She died on 24 Jan 1893 Selkirk, Manitoba (Ibid., Death Reg. #1893,001949.).

     vi.   Donald Sutherland was born on 19 Feb 1894 Selkirk, Manitoba (Ibid., Birth Reg. #1894,005992.).

     vii.   Harriet Louisa Sutherland was born on 15 Mar 1896 Selkirk, Manitoba (Ibid., Birth Reg. #1896,004031.).

     viii.   Alexander Sutherland was born on 24 Jul 1900 Selkirk, Manitoba (Ibid., Birth Reg. #1900,003509.).

15. Elizabeth Sutherland was born circa 1839 St.Paul, (Manitoba) (MBS, C-14934.) (HBCR, E.4/1a, folio 163d.). She was baptized on 27 Oct 1839 St.Johns, Red River Settlement, (Manitoba) (Ibid.). She married **James Brown**, son of **Henry Brown** and **Isabella Slater**, on 9 Dec 1858 St.Paul, (Manitoba) (Denney.).

James Brown was baptized on 29 Apr 1832 St.Johns, Red River Settlement, (Manitoba) (HBCA-B.) (HBCR, E.4/1a, folio 88d.). He died before 1901.

16. Mary Jane Sutherland was born on 1 Nov 1848 St.Paul, (Manitoba) (MBS, C-14934.). She was baptized on 6 Dec 1848 St.Johns, (Manitoba) (Denney.). She married **William George Bird**, son of **George Bird** and **Mary Ann Thomas**, before 1868.

William George Bird was born in 1838 St.Paul, (Manitoba) (MBS, C-14934.). He was baptized on 6 Dec 1840 St.Johns, Red River Settlement, (Manitoba) (HBCR, E.4/1a, folio 169.).

17. Jessie Ann Sutherland was born on 23 Feb 1851 St.Paul, (Manitoba) (MBS, C-14931.). She married **Malcolm McLeod** before 1871.

Malcolm McLeod was born in 1841 Scotland (Denney.). He died on 6 Apr 1906 at sea (Ibid.).

18. Catherine Marie Sutherland was born on 18 Oct 1855 St.Paul, (Manitoba) (MBS, C-14934.). She married **Duncan Richard Setter**, son of **George Setter** and **Jessie Ellen Campbell**, before 1875.

Duncan Richard Setter was born on 23 Jul 1852 St.Andrews, (Manitoba) (Ibid.). He died on 3 May 1880 High Bluff, Manitoba, at age 27 (Denney.).

19. Charles John Sutherland was born on 16 Apr 1866 (HBC-PN , Poplar Point and High Bluff, #291.). He was baptized on 6 May 1866 St.Paul, (Manitoba) (Denney.). He married **Jemima Monkman**, daughter of **James Monkman** and **Margaret Halcrow**, before 1915. He died on 18 Jul 1921 Halcro, Saskatchewan, at age 55 (Ibid.).

Jemima Monkman was born on 25 Nov 1874 (Heather Hallett Research.).

Children of **Charles John Sutherland** and **Jemima Monkman** were as follows:

     i.   Jemima Sutherland.

     ii.   Bertha Sutherland.

     iii.   Ethel Sutherland.

     iv.   Sidney Sutherland died World War I, France (Denney.).

     v.   Charles Sutherland.

     vi.   Florence Ieleen Sutherland was born in Jun 1915 Halcro, Saskatchewan (Ibid.). She died on 4 Aug 1916 Halcro, Saskatchewan, at age 1 (Ibid.).

     vii.   Ida Lynd Sutherland was born circa Aug 1918 Halcro, Saskatchewan (Ibid.). She died on 22 Feb 1919 Halcro, Saskatchewan (Ibid.).

20. John George Sutherland was baptized on 24 Jul 1853 St.Paul, (Manitoba) (Ibid.). He married **Emma McLennan**, daughter of **Joseph Archibald McLennan** and **Mary Humphryville**, in 1874 St.Paul, Manitoba (Ibid.). He died on 22 Nov 1889 St.Paul, Manitoba, at age 36 (MB Vital Statistics, Death Reg. #1889,001073.).

Emma McLennan was born on 11 May 1857 (1901 Canada, page 5, Family 46, Line 43-46.). She married **Benjamin Isbister**, son of **John Isbister** and **Francis "Fanny" Sinclair**, on 10 Dec 1891 Winnipeg, Manitoba (MB Vital Statistics, Marriage Reg. #1891,001400.). She died on 3 May 1906 Winnipeg, Manitoba, at age 48 (Ibid., Death Reg. #1906,004279.).

Children of **John George Sutherland** and **Emma McLennan** were as follows:

   26   i.   Catherine Mary Sutherland, b. 1 Apr 1877 St.Paul, Manitoba.

     ii.   John R. J. Sutherland was born circa 1879 (1881 Canada, District 193-E, page 45, family 220.).

     iii.   Christie E. Sutherland was born circa Feb 1881 (Ibid.).

     iv.   Joseph Archibald Sutherland was born on 3 Mar 1886 St.Paul, Manitoba (MB Vital Statistics, Birth Reg. #1886,003925.).

     v.   Letitia Ann Sutherland was born on 11 Nov 1888 St.Paul, Manitoba (Ibid., Birth Reg. #1888,004768.).

21. Alfred William Sutherland was born on 18 Oct 1864 St.Paul, (Manitoba) (MBS, C-14933.) (1901 Canada, #11, R-1, page 4, family 110-111, line 7-13.). He married **Mary M. (--?--)** before 1892 (Ibid., #11, R-1, page 4, family 1110-111, line 7-13.).

Mary M. (--?--) was born on 28 Aug 1873 (Ibid., #11, R-1, page 4, family 110-111, line 7-13.).

Children of **Alfred William Sutherland** and **Mary M. (--?--)** were as follows:

     i.   Ernest S. Sutherland was born on 14 Jul 1892 (Ibid.).

     ii.   Alfred N. Sutherland was born in Jan 1897 (Ibid.).

     iii.   Eila A. Sutherland was born on 18 Mar 1899 (Ibid.).

22. Letitia Elizabeth Sutherland was born on 27 Apr 1869 St.Paul, (Manitoba) (MBS, C-14933.). She was baptized on 23 May 1869 St.Paul, (Manitoba) (Denney.). She married **Joseph Ballenden or Ballendine**, son of **John Ballenden** and **Ann Haywood**, before 1890 (1901 Canada, Dsitrict 11-r-1, page 4, family 112, line 14-18.).

Joseph Ballenden or Ballendine was born on 1 Jan 1863 (Denney.).

Generation Four

23. Alexander Sutherland was born in Dec 1859 (1911 Canada, District 43, page 8, family 82, line 25-31.). He married **Jane Auger**, daughter of **Toussaint Auger** and **Angelique (Indian)**, on 4 Jul 1892 Athabasca Landing, (Alberta) (ArchiviaNet, C-15005.).

Jane Auger was born in Mar 1872 Lac la Biche, (Alberta) (Ibid.).

Children of **Alexander Sutherland** and **Jane Auger** were as follows:

     i.   Alfred James Sutherland was born in Sep 1893 (1911 Canada, District 43, page 8, family 82, line 25-31.).

     ii.   Elizabeth Sutherland was born in Jul 1896 (Ibid.).

  iii. Norman Sutherland was born in May 1899 (Ibid.).

  iv. Mary Ann Sutherland was born before 1900 (ArchiviaNet, C-15005.). She died before 1900 (Ibid.).

  v. Robert Sutherland was born in Apr 1909 (1911 Canada, District 43, page 8, family 82, line 25-31.).

  vi. Roderick Sutherland was born in Jan 1910 (Ibid.).

24. Christie Alice Sutherland was born on 23 Mar 1866 Fort Pelly, (Saskatchewan) (1870C-MB, page 212, #239.) (ArchiviaNet, T-12030.). She married **Alexander Pruden**, son of **Louis Pruden** and **Fanny Isbister**, on 21 Jan 1886 St.Andrews, Manitoba (MB Vital Statistics, Marriage Reg. #1886,001264.). She married **John James Louis or Lewis**, son of **Peter Louis** and **Mary Ann Lillie**, on 25 Dec 1902 St.Clements, Manitoba (Ibid., Marriage Reg. #1903,003377.). She died on 1 Apr 1947 at age 81 (Rod Mac Quarrie, 20 May 2013.) (*Winnipeg Free Press*, Winnipeg, Manitoba, Wednesday, April 2, 1947, page 23.). She was buried on 3 Apr 1947.

 Alexander Pruden was born on 2 May 1866 St.Paul, (Manitoba) (Denney.). He was baptized on 27 May 1866 St.Andrews, (Manitoba) (Rod Mac Quarrie, B-467.). He died on 18 Dec 1900 R.M. of St.Clements, Manitoba, at age 34 (MB Vital Statistics, Death Reg. #1900,002944.).

 John James Louis or Lewis was born circa 1873 Manitoba (1916 Census of Canada from the National Archives of Canada (Transcription by ancestry.com), Ottawa, Canada, page 8, family 84.). He married **Christina Leblanc**, daughter of **Louis Leblanc** and **Elizabeth Fidler**, on 14 Jan 1899 Selkirk, Manitoba (MB Vital Statistics, Marriage Reg. #1902,003291.).

25. Peter Henry Sutherland was born on 30 Mar 1877 (1901 Canada, District 11-j-2, page 5-6, family 44, line 41-50, 1-4.). He was baptized on 16 Apr 1877 St.Paul, Manitoba (Denney.). He married **Daisy Mary Elizabeth Stevens**, daughter of **James Allan Stevens** and **Sarah Anna Caroline Smith**, on 24 Jun 1903 Selkirk, Manitoba (MB Vital Statistics, Marriage Reg. #1903,002803.).

 Daisy Mary Elizabeth Stevens was born on 7 Jul 1878 Bad Throat River (ArchiviaNet, C-15004.). She died on 25 Feb 1940 Winnipeg, Manitoba, at age 61 (MB Vital Statistics, Death Reg. #1940,008246.).

Children of **Peter Henry Sutherland** and **Daisy Mary Elizabeth Stevens** all born Selkirk, Manitoba, were as follows:

  i. Audrey Edith Sutherland was born on 29 May 1904 (Ibid., Birth Reg. #1904,009481.).

  ii. Lorne Henry Sutherland was born on 3 Aug 1905 (Ibid., Birth Reg. #1905,006230.) (Ibid., Birth Reg. #1905,006242.).

  iii. Wilfred Sutherland was born on 9 Jul 1907 (Ibid., Birth Reg. #1907,009477.).

  iv. Peter Stevens Sutherland was born on 30 Jan 1910 (Ibid., Birth Reg. #1910,005813.). He died on 22 Jun 1915 Selkirk, Manitoba, at age 5 (Ibid., Death Reg. #1915,180055.).

  v. Sophia May Sutherland was born on 7 Sep 1911 (Ibid., Birth Reg. #1911,009960.).

  vi. Allen John Sutherland was born on 3 Oct 1913 (Ibid., Birth Reg. #1913,062066#.).

26. Catherine Mary Sutherland was born on 1 Apr 1877 St.Paul, Manitoba (1901 Canada, page 5, Family 46, Line 43-46.). She was baptized on 13 May 1877 St.Paul, Manitoba (Denney.). She married **William J. Johnston** on 21 May 1904 Winnipeg, Manitoba (MB Vital Statistics, Marriage Reg. #1904,001642.).

 William J. Johnston was born circa 1882 Ontario.

Descendants of Peter Sutherland

Generation One

1. Peter Sutherland was born circa 1782 Quebec (1829C RRS HBCA E5/3 1829 Census of the Red River Settlement, HBCA E5/3, Hudson's Bay Company Archives, Provincial Archives, 200 Vaughan Street, Winnipeg, MB R3C 1T5, Canada., page 10.). He married **Angelique Assiniboine** before 1820.

Children of **Peter Sutherland** and **Angelique Assiniboine** were as follows:

  i. Marie Sutherland was born circa 1790 (1870C-MB 1870 Manitoba Census, National Archives of Canada, Ottawa, Ontario, Microfilm Reel Number C-2170., page 71, #2181.). She married (--?--) Paterson before 15 Jul 1870.

 2 ii. Genevieve Sutherland, b. circa 1801; m. Thomas Simpson; m. Richard Lane; m. Antoine Langevin; m. Michel Patenaude; d. 28 Dec 1872 St.Boniface, Manitoba; bur. 30 Dec 1872 St.Boniface, Manitoba.

 3 iii. Pierre Sutherland, b. 10 Jul 1820 Saskatchewan Valley; m. Suzanne McMillan; d. 10 Jan 1900 RM Ritchot, Manitoba; bur. 12 Jan 1900 St.Norbert, Manitoba.

Generation Two

2. Genevieve Sutherland was born circa 1801 (Ibid., page 71, #2182.). She was born circa 1806 (SB-Rozyk St. Boniface Roman Catholic Church, Manitoba, Canada, Baptisms, Marriages and Burials 1860-1875 Extractions, Compiled by Rosemary Rozyk, page 256, S-42.). She married according to the custom of the country **Thomas Simpson** before 1833. She married according to the custom of the country **Richard Lane**, son of **John Lane**, before 1840. She married **Antoine Langevin** before 1851. She married **Michel Patenaude**, son of **Michel Patenaude** and **Francoise Grosventre**, before 1871. She died on 28 Dec 1872 St.Boniface, Manitoba (MBS Scrip Applications, Original White Settlers & Halfbreeds residing in Manitoba on 15 July 1870, RG15-19, C-14933.) (SB-Rozyk, page 256, S-42.). She was buried on 30 Dec 1872 St.Boniface, Manitoba (MBS, C-14933.) (SB-Rozyk, page 256, S-42.).

 Richard Lane was born circa 1816 Sandgate, Kent, England (Ibid.) (*DCB-V10 Dictionary of Canadian Biography - Volume Ten*;Toronto, Ontario: University of Toronto Press, 2000).). He married **Mary McDermott**, daughter of **Andrew McDermott** and **Sarah McNab**, on 13 Jun 1846 (St.Johns), Upper Church, (Manitoba) (HBCA-B Hudson's Bay Company Archives - biographical sketches, Hudson's Bay Company Archives; Winnipeg, Manitoba, HBCA reference E4/2, fo. 98d.) (HBCR Hudson Bay Company Register of Anglican Church Baptisms, Marriages, and Burials for the Red River Settlement, 1821-1841; Hudson's Bay Company Archives, Winnipeg, Manitoba. Hereinafter cited as HBCR.). He married **Marguerite Walla Walla** circa 1854. He married **Mrs. Anna Gardiner** on 9 Dec 1858 (HBCA-B.). He died circa Mar 1877 The Dalles, Oregon (Ibid.).

 Antoine Langevin died before 1875.

 Michel Patenaude was born circa 1808 Fort des Prairie, Edmonton, (Alberta) (SFXI: 1834-1852 St.Francois Xavier 1834-1852 Register Index, B-151. Hereinafter cited as SFXI: 1835-1852.). He was baptized on 24 Jan 1837 St.Francois Xavier, (Manitoba) (Ibid.).

He married according to the custom of the country **Josephte Bourassa**, daughter of **Michel Bourassa** and **Marguerite Beaulieu**, before 1833. He married **Josephte Bourassa**, daughter of **Michel Bourassa** and **Marguerite Beaulieu**, on 24 Jan 1837 St.Francois Xavier, (Manitoba) (SFX: 1834-1850 St.Francois Xavier 1834-1851 Register, M-27. Hereinafter cited as SFX: 1834-1850.). He died on 12 Oct 1872 on the prairie (L1 Lebret Mission de St.Florent Roman Catholic Registre des Baptemes, Mariages & Seplutures, Qu'Appelle, Saskatchewan, 1868-1881., page 70, S-4. Hereinafter cited as L1.). He was buried on 19 Nov 1872 Lebret, (Saskatchewan) (Ibid.).

3. **Pierre Sutherland** was born on 10 Jul 1820 Saskatchewan Valley (MBS, C-14933.). He married **Suzanne McMillan**, daughter of **Pierre Alexander McMillan** and **Suzette Indian**, before 1841. He died on 10 Jan 1900 RM Ritchot, Manitoba, at age 79 (Manitoba Vital Statistics online, http://web2.gov.mb.ca, Death Reg. #1900,001107.) (St-N Cem *St.Norbert Parish Cemetery 1859-1906, We Remember*; Winnipeg, Manitoba, Canada: St.Norbert Parish-La Barriere Metis Council of the Metis Federation of Manitoba, 29 May 2010).). He was buried on 12 Jan 1900 St.Norbert, Manitoba (Ibid.).

Suzanne McMillan was born in Jul 1821 North West (MBS, C-14933.). She died on 22 Feb 1882 St.Norbert, Manitoba, at age 60 (SN2 Catholic Parish Register of St.Norbert, S-4. Hereinafter cited as SN2.). She was buried on 24 Feb 1882 St.Norbert, Manitoba (Ibid.).

Children of **Pierre Sutherland** and **Suzanne McMillan** were as follows:

4.   i.   Suzanne Sutherland, b. 14 Oct 1841 St.Boniface, (Manitoba); m. Francois Beriault.
5.   ii.   Pierre Sutherland, b. circa 15 Mar 1843 St.Boniface, (Manitoba); m. Marie Eulalie Galarneau.
6.   iii.   Elise Sutherland, b. 27 Jan 1845 St.Boniface, (Manitoba); m. Maxime Joseph Beriault; d. 23 May 1918 Ste.Anne, Manitoba.
7.   iv.   Antoine Sutherland, b. between 1847 and 1850 St.Boniface, (Manitoba); m. Elise Ritchot; d. before 1889.
    v.   Marie Sutherland was born circa 1851.
8.   vi.   Sarah Sutherland, b. circa 1852; m. Felix Cadotte; m. Louis Villebrun.
9.   vii.   Maurice Sutherland, b. circa 1852; m. Madeleine Dubois.
10.   viii.   Joseph Sutherland, b. Mar 1854 St.Boniface, (Manitoba); m. Sarah Vandal.
11.   ix.   Madeleine Sutherland, b. circa 1857; m. Louis Laliberte.
12.   x.   Christine Sutherland, b. 4 Jan 1857 St.Vital, (Manitoba); m. Leon Nault; m. (--?--) Beriault.
    xi.   Jean Sutherland was born circa 1860 (1870C-MB, page 71-72, #2208-2215.). He was buried on 21 Feb 1879 St.Norbert, Manitoba (SN2, S-5.).

Generation Three

4. **Suzanne Sutherland** was born on 14 Oct 1841 St.Boniface, (Manitoba) (MBS, C-14925.). She married **Francois Beriault**, son of **Gilbert Beriault** and **Suzanne Blondeau**, before 1858.
Francois Beriault was born on 12 Jul 1836 St.Boniface, (Manitoba) (Ibid.).

5. **Pierre Sutherland** was born circa 15 Mar 1843 St.Boniface, (Manitoba) (MBS, C-14933.) (1870C-MB, page 71, #2204.). He married **Marie Eulalie Galarneau**, daughter of **Joseph Galarneau** and **Marie St.Luc dit Repentigny**, on 22 Jan 1867 St.Boniface, (Manitoba) (SB-Rozyk, page 76, M-2.).

Marie Eulalie Galarneau was born on 14 Oct 1848 St.Boniface, (Manitoba) (MBS, C-14933.). She died on 17 Jul 1889 St.Norbert, Manitoba, at age 40 (St-N Cem.) (SN2, S-24.). She was buried on 19 Jul 1889 St.Norbert, Manitoba (St-N Cem.) (SN2, S-24.).

Children of **Pierre Sutherland** and **Marie Eulalie Galarneau** were as follows:

  i.   Anonyme Sutherland was born on 24 Oct 1867 (SB-Rozyk, page 97, S-26.). He/she died on 24 Oct 1867 (Ibid.). He/she was buried on 26 Oct 1867 St.Boniface, (Manitoba) (Ibid.).
  ii.   Joseph Sutherland was born on 28 Oct 1868 (Ibid., page 136, B-144.). He was baptized on 29 Oct 1868 St.Boniface, (Manitoba) (Ibid.). He married Placidie Breland, daughter of Thomas Breland and Philomene Page, on 26 Feb 1889 St.Francois Xavier, Manitoba (SFXI-Kipling St.Francois Xavier Register Index, 1834-1900; compiled by Clarence Kipling, M-6.) (MB Vital Statistics, Mar. Reg. #1889,001049.).
    Placidie Breland was born on 15 Jan 1871 Moose Jaw, (Saskatchewan) (HBS 1886-1901, 1906 Half-Breed Scrip Applications, RG15-21, Volume 1338, C-14952.). She was baptized on 24 Mar 1871 Lebret, (Saskatchewan) (Ibid.) (L1, page 31, B-13.).
  iii.   Damase Sutherland was baptized on 30 Jul 1870 St.Boniface, Manitoba (SB-Rozyk, page 190, B-69.). He married Marie Rosalie Smith, daughter of Alexandre Smith and Marie Rosalie Delorme, on 8 Nov 1910 St.Adolphe, Manitoba (SN2, B-51 (note).) (MB Vital Statistics, Marriage Reg. #1910,001213.).
    Marie Rosalie Smith was born on 7 Nov 1887 St.Norbert, Manitoba (SN2, B-51.). She was baptized on 10 Nov 1887 St.Norbert, Manitoba (Ibid.). She married **Charles Beaulieu**, son of **Timothee Beaulieu** and **Adele Rioux**, on 10 Nov 1919 (Ibid., B-51 (note).).
  iv.   Anonyme Sutherland was born circa 4 Aug 1872 St.Boniface, Manitoba. He/she died on 4 Aug 1872 St.Boniface, Manitoba (SB-Rozyk, page 247, S-31.). He/she was buried on 5 Aug 1872 St.Boniface, Manitoba (Ibid.).
  v.   Alphonse Albert Sutherland was born on 15 Jul 1873 St.Boniface, Manitoba (Ibid., page 284, B-61.). He was baptized on 15 Jul 1873 St.Boniface, Manitoba (Ibid.). He married Marie Rose Vermette, daughter of Maxime Vermette and Sophie McCarthy dit Mercredi, on 6 Feb 1902 St.Pierre Jolys, Manitoba (MM.).
    Marie Rose Vermette was born on 5 May 1883 R.M. of De Salaberry, Manitoba (Ibid., page 1278.) (MB Vital Statistics, Birth Reg. No. 1883,001777.).
  vi.   Alexandre Sutherland was born on 27 Jul 1875 St.Norbert, Manitoba (SN2, B-27.). He was baptized on 1 Aug 1875 St.Norbert, Manitoba (Ibid.).
  vii.   Marie Magdelaine Adelaide Sutherland was born on 22 May 1877 St.Norbert, Manitoba (Ibid., B-18.). She was baptized on 27 May 1877 St.Norbert, Manitoba (Ibid.).
  viii.   Baptiste Sutherland was born circa 1879 Manitoba (1881 Church of Latter Day Saints Census Transcription Project of Census Images from the National Archives of Canada, Ottawa, Canada, http://www.familysearch.org, District 184-E1, page 83, household 389.).

13   ix.   Marie Celina Sutherland, b. 8 Sep 1880 St.Norbert, Manitoba; m. Henry Vermette; d. 30 May 1907 DeSalaberry, Manitoba.

      x.   Joseph Julien Sutherland was born on 23 Aug 1882 St.Norbert, Manitoba (SN2, B-33.). He was baptized on 27 Aug 1882 St.Norbert, Manitoba (Ibid.). He married Marie Laure Delima Daoust on 11 Jun 1912 West Fort William, Ontario (Ibid.).

      xi.   Marie Eugenie Sutherland was born on 15 Apr 1884 RM St.Norbert, Manitoba (Ibid., B-22.) (MB Vital Statistics, Birth Reg. #1884,003201.). She was baptized on 28 Apr 1884 St.Norbert, Manitoba (SN2, B-22.). She died on 2 Feb 1889 St.Norbert, Manitoba, at age 4 (MB Vital Statistics, Death Reg. #1889,001061.) (SN2, S-7.). She was buried on 4 Feb 1889 St.Norbert, Manitoba (Ibid.).

      xii.   Marie Adeline Sutherland was born on 17 May 1886 St.Norbert, Manitoba (Ibid., B-21.). She was baptized on 19 May 1886 St.Norbert, Manitoba (Ibid.). She died on 11 Sep 1889 St.Norbert, Manitoba, at age 3 (MB Vital Statistics, Death Reg. #1889,002100.) (SN2, S-30.). She was buried on 13 Sep 1889 St.Norbert, Manitoba (Ibid.).

6. Elise Sutherland was born on 27 Jan 1845 St.Boniface, (Manitoba) (MBS, C-14925.). She married **Maxime Joseph Beriault**, son of **Gilbert Beriault** and **Suzanne Blondeau**, on 13 Jan 1863 St.Boniface, (Manitoba) (SB-Rozyk, page 98, M-2.) (RMSB *Repertoire des Mariages de Saint-Boniface (Manitoba) 1825-1983* compiled by Julien Hamelin S.C., (240, avenue Daly; Ottawa, Ontario K1N 6G2: Le Centre de Genealogie S. C., Publication #67, 1985), page 31.). She died on 23 May 1918 Ste.Anne, Manitoba, at age 73 (MB Vital Statistics, Death Reg. #1918,030245.).

   Maxime Joseph Beriault was born on 24 Mar 1839 St.Boniface, (Manitoba) (MBS, C-14925.). He died on 25 Mar 1922 Tache, Manitoba, at age 83 (MB Vital Statistics, Death Reg. #1922,010644.).

7. Antoine Sutherland was born between 1847 and 1850 St.Boniface, (Manitoba) (MBS, C-14933.) (1870C-MB, page 72, #2217.). He married **Elise Ritchot**, daughter of **Jean Baptiste Ritchot** and **Marie Anne Chatelain**, on 15 Nov 1870 St.Boniface, Manitoba (SB-Rozyk, page 197, M-32.). He died before 1889.

   Elise Ritchot was born on 28 Aug 1855 St.Vital, (Manitoba) (MBS, C-14933.). She married **Joseph Daunais**, son of **Jean Baptiste Daunais** and **Catherine Henry**, on 27 Aug 1889 (St.Norbert), Cartier, Manitoba (SN2, M-13.) (MB Vital Statistics, Marriage Reg. #1889,001525.).

Children of **Antoine Sutherland** and **Elise Ritchot** were as follows:

14   i.   Melanie Sutherland, b. 23 Jan 1872 St.Boniface, Manitoba; m. Elzear Daunais; m. James Phillips; d. 18 Dec 1916 St.Boniface, Manitoba.

      ii.   Marie Rose Sutherland was born on 15 Mar 1873 (SB-Rozyk, page 270-271, B-32.). She was baptized on 16 Mar 1873 St.Boniface, Manitoba (Ibid.). She died on 25 Jun 1873 (Ibid., page 282, S-42.). She was buried on 26 Jun 1873 St.Boniface, Manitoba (Ibid.).

      iii.   Bruno Sutherland was born on 1 Jul 1874 (Ibid., page 23, B-45.). He was baptized on 2 Jul 1874 St.Boniface, Manitoba (Ibid.). He married Marie Eleanore Morin, daughter of Jean Baptiste Morin and Sarah Letendre, on 24 Jul 1900 St.Boniface, Manitoba (RMSB, page 452.). He died on 30 Jan 1928 St.Boniface, Manitoba, at age 53 (Rod MacQuarrie Research, 16 Apr 2005.).

         Marie Eleanore Morin was born on 10 Nov 1881 Pembina County, Dakota Territory (AP Records of the Assumption Roman Catholic Church, Pembina, North Dakota: Baptisms, Marriages, Sepultures, 1848-1896; compiled by Reverend Father J. M. Belleau, 2 October 1944, page 193, B-35. Hereinafter cited as AP.). She was baptized on 12 Nov 1881 Assumption, Pembina, Pembina County, Dakota Territory (Ibid.).

      iv.   Marie Elise Sutherland was born on 22 Aug 1876 St.Norbert, Manitoba (SN2, B-28.). She was baptized on 22 Aug 1876 St.Norbert, Manitoba (Ibid.).

      v.   Justine Sutherland was born circa 1880 Cartier, Manitoba (1881 Canada, NA Film No. C-13283, District 184, Sub-district F, page 38, household 181.). She married Joseph Fridolin Harrison, son of Dolphis Harrison and Elise Cyr, on 3 Sep 1900 St.Boniface, Manitoba (RMSB, page 215.).

         Joseph Fridolin Harrison was baptized on 21 Mar 1871 Ste.Anne, Manitoba (IBMS.) (Rosemary Rozyk, 9 Jun 2009.) (INB, page 79.). He was born on 21 Mar 1871 Ste.Anne, Manitoba (Rosemary Rozyk, 9 Jun 2009.) (INB, page 79.). He married **Marie Catherine Falcon**, daughter of **Pierre Falcon** and **Marie Leveille,** on 9 Feb 1891 Ste.Anne, Manitoba (MM.).

      vi.   Louis Ignace Sutherland was born on 1 Feb 1882 Cartier, Manitoba (SN2, B-4.) (MB Vital Statistics, Birth Reg. #1882,001371.). He was baptized on 1 Feb 1882 St.Norbert, Manitoba (SN2, B-4.).

      vii.   Anne Sutherland was born on 15 Nov 1883 St.Norbert, Manitoba (MB Vital Statistics, Birth Reg. #1883,003591.) (SN2, B-41.). She was baptized on 15 Nov 1883 St.Norbert, Manitoba (Ibid.). She married Charles Harrison, son of Dolphis Harrison and Elise Cyr, on 5 Apr 1903 St.Boniface, Manitoba (RMSB.).

         Charles Harrison was born on 20 Dec 1873 Ste.Anne, Manitoba (Rosemary Rozyk, 9 Jun 2009.). He was baptized on 21 Dec 1873 Ste.Anne, Manitoba (IBMS.) (Rosemary Rozyk, 9 Jun 2009.) (INB, page 79.). He married **Marie Anorgele Cashawa**, daughter of **Alexandre Cashawa** and **Therese Welch,** on 22 Feb 1898 St.Boniface, Manitoba (RMSB.) (MB Vital Statistics, Marriage Reg. #1898,002069.).

      viii.   Phileas Sutherland was born on 19 Jul 1885 R.M. of Cartier, Manitoba (SN2, B-36.) (MB Vital Statistics, Birth Reg. #1885,005106.). He was baptized on 20 Jul 1885 St.Norbert, Manitoba (SN2, B-36.). He died on 7 Sep 1885 Cartier, Manitoba (Ibid., S-22.) (MB Vital Statistics, Death Reg. #1885,001586.). He was buried on 9 Sep 1885 St.Norbert, Manitoba (SN2, S-22.).

      ix.   Louis Robert Sutherland was born on 1 Sep 1886 St.Norbert, Manitoba (Ibid., B-42.). He was baptized on 2 Sep 1886 St.Norbert, Manitoba (Ibid.). He died on 10 Mar 1888 Cartier, Manitoba, at age 1 (MB Vital Statistics, Death Reg. #1888,001368.) (SN2, S-4.). He was buried on 12 Mar 1888 St.Norbert, Manitoba (Ibid.).

      x.   Pierre Robert Sutherland was born on 16 Jan 1888 Cartier, Manitoba (MB Vital Statistics, Birth Reg. #1888,003551.) (Ibid., Birth Reg. #1888,004801.) (SN2, B-7.). He was baptized on 20 Jan 1888 St.Norbert,

Manitoba (Ibid.). He married Marie Catherine Nolin, daughter of Thomas Nolin and Pauline Harrison, on 17 Oct 1910 Woodridge, Manitoba (MM.) (SN2, B-6.). He married Sophie Berthelet, daughter of Norbert Berthelet and Rosalie Colombe, on 26 Sep 1938 Woodbridge, Manitoba (Ibid., B-6 (note).) (MM, page 168 and 1199.).

Marie Catherine Nolin was born on 3 Oct 1891 Ste.Anne, Manitoba (1901 Canada, microfilm, T-6553, North Battleford, page 8, Family 76, line 38-43.) (MB Vital Statistics, Birth Reg. #1890,003511.).

Sophie Berthelet was born circa 1887.

    xi.   Joseph Antoine Arthur Sutherland was born on 1 May 1889 R.M. of Cartier, Manitoba (Ibid., Birth Reg. #1889,004023.) (SN2, B-23.). He was baptized on 4 May 1889 St.Norbert, Manitoba (Ibid.).

8. Sarah Sutherland was born circa 1852. She married **Felix Cadotte**, son of **Laurent Cadotte** and **Elisabeth Thomas**, on 28 Jan 1873 St.Norbert, Manitoba (SN1 Catholic Parish Register of St.Norbert 1857-1873, M-2. Hereinafter cited as SN1.). She married **Louis Villebrun**, son of **Louis Villebrun** and **Isabelle Berard**, on 21 Feb 1882 St.Norbert, Manitoba (SN2, M-4.).

Felix Cadotte was born in Sep 1849 St.Norbert, (Manitoba) (MBS, C-14926.). He died on 10 Feb 1878 St.Norbert, Manitoba, at age 28 (SN2, S-9.). He was buried on 12 Feb 1878 St.Norbert, Manitoba (Ibid.).

Louis Villebrun was born on 25 Oct 1856 St.Norbert, (Manitoba) (MBS, C-14934.). He married **Marie Rose Esther Pilon**, daughter of **Pierre Pilon** and **Helene Sauve**, before 1877. He died on 18 May 1920 St.Boniface, Manitoba, at age 63 (MB Vital Statistics, Death Reg. #1920,027055.).

9. Maurice Sutherland was born circa 1852. He married **Madeleine Dubois**, daughter of **Francois Dubois** and **Madeleine Laberge**, on 11 Nov 1873 St.Boniface, Manitoba (SB-Rozyk, page 295-296, M-19.).

Madeleine Dubois was born on 20 Apr 1860 (GI General Index to Manitoba and North-West Territories Half-Breeds and Original White Settlers who have preferred claims - April 1885, Microfilm Reel Number C-11878, National Archives of Canada, Ottawa, Ontario, page 38.). She married **Joseph Larence**, son of **Basile Larence** and **Agathe Iroquois**, on 20 May 1878 St.Boniface, Manitoba (RMSB, page 271.).

Children of **Maurice Sutherland** and **Madeleine Dubois** were as follows:

    15   i.   Maurice Sutherland, b. 14 Jan 1875 St.Boniface, Manitoba; m. Sara Jeanne Leany.
    16   ii.   Magdelaine Sutherland, b. 18 Oct 1876 St.Norbert, Manitoba; m. Joseph Ouellette.

10. Joseph Sutherland was born in Mar 1854 St.Boniface, (Manitoba) (MBS, C-14933.). He married **Sarah Vandal**, daughter of **Joseph Vandal** and **Louise Dupuis**, on 13 Feb 1877 Ste.Agathe, Manitoba (Ibid., C-14934.) (MM.) (Rod Mac Quarrie, 28 Dec 2011.).

Sarah Vandal was born on 22 Oct 1858 St.Norbert, (Manitoba) (MBS, C-14934.). She was baptized on 11 Nov 1858 Assumption, Pembina, Pembina County, Dakota Territory (AP, page 200, B-603.). She died on 18 Sep 1888 St.Jean-Baptiste, RM of Montcalm, Manitoba, at age 29 (MB Vital Statistics, Death Reg. #1888,002456.). She was buried on 20 Sep 1888 St.Jean-Baptiste, Manitoba (Rod Mac Quarrie, 28 Dec 2011.).

Children of **Joseph Sutherland** and **Sarah Vandal** were as follows:

    i.   Marie Alvina Sutherland was born on 22 Feb 1878 St.Norbert, Manitoba (SN2, B-10.). She was baptized on 24 Feb 1878 St.Norbert, Manitoba (Ibid.).
    ii.   Marie Claire Sutherland was born on 25 Jun 1880 St.Norbert, Manitoba (Ibid., B-30.). She was baptized on 26 Jun 1880 St.Norbert, Manitoba (Ibid.).
    iii.   Joseph Hector Sutherland was born on 1 Aug 1883 RM of Montcalm, Manitoba (MB Vital Statistics, Birth Reg. #1883,003987.).
    iv.   Joseph Louis Robert Sutherland was born on 9 Sep 1885 RM of Montcalm, Manitoba (Ibid., Birth Reg. #1885,001048.). He died on 6 Sep 1886 Montcalm, Manitoba (Ibid., Death Reg. #1886,001150.).
    v.   Marie Cleophee Sutherland was born on 23 Sep 1887 RM of Montcalm, Manitoba (Ibid., Birth Reg. #1887,001370.). She died on 14 Jan 1890 Montcalm, Manitoba, at age 2 (Ibid., Death Reg. #1890,002341.).

11. Madeleine Sutherland was born circa 1857. She married **Louis Laliberte**, son of **Antoine Laliberte** and **Marguerite Nadeau**, on 29 Jan 1878 St.Norbert, Manitoba (SN2, M-3.).

Louis Laliberte was born circa 1852 (1870C-MB, #1855, page 60.). He died on 14 Aug 1890 RM St.Norbert, Manitoba (MB Vital Statistics, Death Reg. #1890,001698.) (St-N Cem.) (SN2, S-26.). He was buried on 15 Aug 1890 St.Norbert, Manitoba (St-N Cem.) (SN2, S-26.).

12. Christine Sutherland was born on 4 Jan 1857 St.Vital, (Manitoba) (MBS, C-14931.). She married **Leon Nault**, son of **Benjamin Nault** and **Isabelle Hamelin**, on 12 Jan 1875 St.Norbert, Manitoba (SN2, M-2.). She married **(--?--) Beriault** before 1901 (HBS 1886-1901, 1906 Half-Breed Scrip Applications, RG15-21, Volume 1336; C-14949.).

Leon Nault was born circa 1855 Red River, (Manitoba) (1870C-MB, #465, page 16.). He died before 14 Aug 1901.

Generation Four

13. Marie Celina Sutherland was born on 8 Sep 1880 St.Norbert, Manitoba (SN2, B-47.). She was baptized on 12 Sep 1880 St.Norbert, Manitoba (Ibid.). She married **Henry Vermette**, son of **Maxime Vermette** and **Sophie McCarthy dit Mercredi**, on 29 Dec 1899 St.Pierre Jolys, Manitoba (MM.). She died on 30 May 1907 DeSalaberry, Manitoba, at age 26 (MB Vital Statistics, Death Reg. #1907,005308.).

Henry Vermette was born on 5 Apr 1875 St.Norbert, Manitoba (SN2, B-15.). He was baptized on 6 Apr 1875 St.Norbert, Manitoba (Ibid.). He married **Marie Lea Beaugrand dit Champage**, daughter of **David Beaugrand dit Champagne** and **Melanie Carriere**, on 7 Oct 1919 St.Boniface, Manitoba (RMSB.).

14. Melanie Sutherland was born on 23 Jan 1872 St.Boniface, Manitoba (SB-Rozyk, page 227, B-4.). She was baptized on 23 Jan 1872 St.Boniface, Manitoba (Ibid.). She married **Elzear Daunais**, son of **Joseph Daunais** and **Angelique Frobisher**, on 5 Jul 1892 St.Boniface, Manitoba (RMSB.). She married **James Phillips**, son of **Henry Phillips** and **Catherine Williams**, on 7 Mar 1902 Winnipeg, Manitoba (Rod Mac Quarrie, 8 Aug 2012.). She died on 18 Dec 1916 St.Boniface, Manitoba, at age 44 (Ibid.).

Elzear Daunais was born on 27 Oct 1867 St.Boniface, (Manitoba) (SB-Rozyk, page 97, B-94.). He was baptized on 27 Oct 1867 St.Boniface, (Manitoba) (Ibid.).

James Phillips was born circa 1851 Tavistock, Tevonshire, England (Rod Mac Quarrie, 8 Aug 2012.). He married Marie Zace, daughter of Alexis Zace and Angelique Ross, on 10 Jun 1884 St.Claude Mission, St.John, Rolette County, North Daktoa (Dominique Ritchot Research,, 26 Jan 2006.). He married Louise Victoire Ouellette, daughter of Francois Ouellette and Marguerite Dupuis, on 17 Aug 1917 Pentecostal Church, 133 Wolsley Avenue, Winnipeg, Manitoba (Rod Mac Quarrie, 8 Aug 2012.). He died on 28 May 1935 Deer Lodge Hospital, Winnipeg, Manitoba (Ibid.).

15. Maurice Sutherland was born on 14 Jan 1875 St.Boniface, Manitoba (SB-Rozyk, page 43, B-2.). He was baptized on 14 Jan 1875 St.Boniface, Manitoba (Ibid.). He married **Sara Jeanne Leany** before 1897.

Children of **Maurice Sutherland** and **Sara Jeanne Leany** are:

  i. Sara Jeanne Sutherland was born on 29 Apr 1897 St.Francois Xavier, Manitoba (SFXI-Kipling, B-20.).

16. Magdelaine Sutherland was born on 18 Oct 1876 St.Norbert, Manitoba (SN2, B-33.). She was baptized on 19 Oct 1876 St.Norbert, Manitoba (Ibid.). She married **Joseph Ouellette**, son of **Francois Ouellette** and **Marguerite Dupuis**, on 3 Feb 1892 St.Francois Xavier, Manitoba (SFXI-Kipling, M-3.).

Joseph Ouellette was born on 30 Sep 1868 St.Norbert, (Manitoba) (SN1, B-45.). He was baptized on 1 Oct 1868 St.Norbert, (Manitoba) (Ibid.).

Descendants of James Swain (b. c1775)

Generation One

1. James Swain was born circa 1775 St.Andrews, London, England (Denney Papers, Charles D. Denney, Glenbow Archives, Calgary, Alberta.) (HBCA-B Hudson's Bay Company Archives - biographical sketches, Hudson's Bay Company Archives; Winnipeg, Manitoba.). He married **Native Woman** before 1797. He died circa 1829 London, probably, England (Denney.).

Children of **James Swain** and **Native Woman** were as follows:

  i. Charlotte Swain was born circa 1797.
2 ii. James Swain, b. 14 Feb 1799 Hudson Bay; m. Margaret Racette; d. 9 Sep 1887 St.Clements, Manitoba.
3 iii. Thomas Swain, b. circa 1800 Red River, (Manitoba); m. Marguerite Dumais; d. 26 May 1873 Poplar Point, Manitoba; bur. 26 May 1873 St.Ann, Poplar Point, Manitoba.
4 iv. Sarah Swain, b. circa 1800; m. John McDonald; d. 7 Nov 1844.
5 v. Margaret Swain, b. 2 Apr 1802 Ruperts Land; m. Donald Gunn; d. 28 Nov 1870 St.Andrews, Manitoba.
6 vi. Mary Anne Swain, b. circa 1805; m. William Robert Smith.
  vii. Bridgette Swain was born circa 1814 (Ibid.). She was baptized on 25 Sep 1827 St.Johns, (Manitoba) (HBCR Hudson Bay Company Register of Anglican Church Baptisms, Marriages, and Burials for the Red River Settlement, 1821-1841; Hudson's Bay Company Archives, Winnipeg, Manitoba, E.4/1a, folio 66, #672. Hereinafter cited as HBCR.). She died on 13 Dec 1844 (Denney.).
7 viii. John Swain, b. circa 1818 Red River, (Manitoba); m. Marie Marguerite Allary.
8 ix. Elizabeth Swain, b. 1820 North West; m. John McLeod; d. 13 Feb 1895 RM. St.Clements, Manitoba.

Generation Two

2. James Swain was born on 14 Feb 1799 Hudson Bay (MBS Scrip Applications, Original White Settlers & Halfbreeds residing in Manitoba on 15 July 1870, RG15-19, C-14933.). He was baptized on 8 Jun 1823 St.Johns, Red River Colony, (Manitoba) (HBCA-B.) (HBCR, E.4/1a, folio 44.). He married **Margaret Racette**, daughter of **Charles Racette** and **Josephte "Cheoueninen" Sauteuse**, on 26 Oct 1826 St.Johns, (Manitoba) (Ibid., M-124.). He died on 9 Sep 1887 St.Clements, Manitoba, at age 88 (HBCA-B.) (Manitoba Vital Statistics online, http://web2.gov.mb.ca, Death Reg. #1887,002825.).

Margaret Racette was born in 1809 Lake Winnipeg (MBS, C-14933.).

Children of **James Swain** and **Margaret Racette** were as follows:

9 i. Margaret Swain, b. 25 Sep 1827 (St.Andrews), Rapids of Red River, (Manitoba); d. 1859.
  ii. Charlotte Swain was born on 6 Jan 1830 St.Andrews, (Manitoba) (Ibid., C-14934.). She was baptized on 4 Feb 1830 (St.Andrews), Rapids of Red River, (Manitoba) (HBCR, E.4/1a, folio 74d, #138.).
  iii. Daughter Swain was baptized on 29 May 1832 St.Johns, Red River Settlement, (Manitoba) (HBCA-B.) (HBCR, E.4/1a, folio 89d.).
10 iv. Elizabeth Swain, b. 20 Mar 1834 St.Andrews, (Manitoba); m. Michael Wagner.
  v. James Swain was baptized on 25 Nov 1834 (St.Andrews), Rapids of Red River, (Manitoba) (HBCA-B.) (HBCR, E.4/1a, folio 116.).
  vi. Charles Swain was baptized on 25 Jun 1839 St.Johns, Red River Settlement, (Manitoba) (HBCA-B.) (HBCR, E.4/1a, folio 161.). He was born circa 1840 St.Andrews, (Manitoba) (MBS, C-14933.). He married Frances McCorrister, daughter of Henry McCorrister and Marie Tait, on 2 Mar 1865 St.Andrews, (Manitoba) (Denney.).
    Frances McCorrister was born on 24 Jul 1847 St.Andrews, (Manitoba) (MBS, C-14933.). She was baptized on 22 Aug 1847 St.Andrews, (Manitoba) (Denney.).
  vii. John Swain was born circa 1841 (Manitoba) (1870C-MB 1870 Manitoba Census, National Archives of Canada, Ottawa, Ontario, Microfilm Reel Number C-2170., page 177, #5.).
  viii. Catherine Swain was baptized on 31 Dec 1842 St.Johns, (Manitoba) (HBCA-B.). She was buried on 1 Aug 1846 (Ibid.).
  ix. Ann Swain was baptized on 4 Apr 1845 St.Johns, (Manitoba) (Denney.). She was buried on 15 Aug 1846 (HBCA-B.).
11 x. Sarah Swain, b. 16 Jul 1846 St.Andrews, (Manitoba); m. George Flett; d. 23 Nov 1909 St.Clements, Manitoba.
  xi. Thomas Swain was baptized on 11 Dec 1849 St.Andrews, (Manitoba) (Denney.) (HBCA-B.). He died on 27 May 1865 St.Andrews, (Manitoba), at age 15 (Denney.).

12 xii. William Robert Swain, b. 17 Mar 1852 St.Andrews, (Manitoba); m. Sarah Omand; d. 25 Oct 1925 St.Clements, Manitoba.

13 xiii. Matilda Swain, b. Mar 1855 St.Andrews, (Manitoba); m. John Hourie; d. 20 Mar 1873 St.Andrews, Manitoba; bur. 23 Mar 1873 St.Andrews, Manitoba.

3. Thomas Swain was born circa 1800 Red River, (Manitoba) (1870C-MB, page 368, #1330.). He was born circa 1804 Ruperts Land (1838C RRS HBCA E5/9 1838 Census of the Red River Settlement, HBCA E5/9, Hudson's Bay Company Archives, Provincial Archives, 200 Vaughan Street, Winnipeg, MB R3C 1T5, Canada., page 27.). He married **Marguerite Dumais** before 1823. He married **Elizabeth Sabiston** on 14 Feb 1838 Red River Settlement, (Manitoba) (HBCR, No. 382.). He died on 26 May 1873 Poplar Point, Manitoba (MBS, C-14925.). He was buried on 26 May 1873 St.Ann, Poplar Point, Manitoba (Ibid.).

Children of **Thomas Swain** and **Marguerite Dumais** were:

14 i. Mary Swain, b. circa 1823 Swan River District; m. Antoine Allary.

Children of **Thomas Swain** and **Elizabeth Sabiston** were as follows:

15 i. Caroline Swain, b. Feb 1833; m. Joseph Vivier; d. 4 Aug 1885 Portage la Prairie, Manitoba.

ii. Margaret Swain was baptized on 30 Sep 1835 St.Johns, Red River Settlement, (Manitoba) (HBCR, E.4/1a, folio 123d.).

iii. Elizabeth Swain was born on 30 Sep 1835 St.Johns, Red River Settlement, (Manitoba) (Ibid.).

iv. Elizabeth Swain was born on 10 Jan 1837 Manitoba Post (MBS, C-14925.). She married David M. Brooks, son of John Brooks, on 15 Jul 1870 (Ibid.) (1870C-MB, page 368, #1322-1323.).
   David M. Brooks was born circa 1833 (Ibid., page 368, #1322.).

v. Thomas Swain was baptized on 6 Sep 1840 St.Johns, Red River Settlement, (Manitoba) (HBCR, E.4/1a, folio 168.).

vi. William Swain was baptized on 6 Jul 1845 St.Johns, (Manitoba) (Denney.). He died on 11 Jun 1851 St.Johns, (Manitoba), at age 5 (Ibid.).

4. Sarah Swain was born circa 1800 (Ibid.). She was baptized on 12 Jul 1825 St.Johns, Red River Settlement, (Manitoba) (HBCA-B.) (HBCR, E.4/1a, folio 56.). She married **John McDonald**, son of **Angus McDonald**, on 12 Jul 1825 St.Johns, (Manitoba) (Ibid., M-94.). She died on 7 Nov 1844 (Denney.).

John McDonald was born on 12 Nov 1791 Scotland (MBS, C-14930.).

5. Margaret Swain was born on 2 Apr 1802 Ruperts Land (MBS, C-14928.). She was baptized on 17 Jan 1826 St.Johns, (Manitoba) (HBCR, E.4/1a, folio 59.). She married **Donald Gunn**, son of **William Gunn**, on 17 Jan 1826 Red River Settlement, (Manitoba) (Ibid., M-108.). She died on 28 Nov 1870 St.Andrews, Manitoba, at age 68 (MBS, C-14928.).

Donald Gunn was born in Sep 1797 Halkirk, Caithnesshire, Scotland (Ibid.). He died on 30 Nov 1878 St.Andrews, Manitoba, at age 81 (Denney.).

6. Mary Anne Swain was born circa 1805 (Denney.). She was baptized on 12 Jul 1825 St.Johns, Red River Settlement, (Manitoba) (HBCA-B.) (HBCR, E.4/1a, folio 56.). She married **William Robert Smith**, son of **William Hart Smith** and **Hannah Woodman**, on 15 Jul 1825 St.Johns, (Manitoba) (Ibid., M-93.).

William Robert Smith was born circa 1795 England (1827C RRS HBCA E5/1 1827 Census of the Red River Settlement, HBCA E5/1, Hudson's Bay Company Archives, Provincial Archives, 200 Vaughan Street, Winnipeg, MB R3C 1T5, Canada., page 4.). He married **Ann Omand**, daughter of **James Omand** and **Jane Brown**, circa 1852. He died on 14 May 1869 Headingley, (Manitoba) (Denney.). He was buried in May 1869 St.Paul, Middlechurch, (Manitoba) (Ibid.).

7. John Swain was born circa 1818 Red River, (Manitoba) (1850Ci-MN *Minnesota Territorial Census, 1850*, Harpole, Patricia C. and Mary D. Nagle, ed., (St.Paul, Minnesota: Minnesota Historical Society, 1972), page 23; Dwelling 53; Family 53.). He was baptized on 25 Sep 1827 St.Johns, Red River Settlement, (Manitoba) (HBCR, E.4/1a, folio 66, #673.). He married **Marie Marguerite Allary**, daughter of **Michel Allary** and **Marguerite Saulteux**, on 18 Jan 1837 Red River Settlement, (Manitoba) (HBCA-B.) (HBCR, No. 331.).

Marie Marguerite Allary was born circa 1820 Red River, (Manitoba) (1850Ci-MN, page 23; Dwelling 53; Family 53.) (1870C-MB, page 291, #1554.). She married **Jean Baptiste Vasseur**, son of **Louis Vasseur** and **Marguerite Pelletier**, on 16 Jun 1851 Assumption, Pembina, Pembina County, Dakota Territory (AP-Reg Assumption Parish Register, Pembina, North Dakota, page 77, M-1. Hereinafter cited as Assumption Register.).

Children of **John Swain** and **Marie Marguerite Allary** were as follows:

i. John Swain was baptized on 29 Nov 1837 St.Johns, Red River Settlement, (Manitoba) (HBCR, E.4/1a, folio 147d.). He was buried on 1 Mar 1855 St.Francois Xavier, (Manitoba) (SFXI-Kipling St.Francois Xavier Register Index, 1834-1900; compiled by Clarence Kipling , S-12.).

16 ii. Thomas Swain, b. circa 1838 (Manitoba); m. Ellen Bremner; d. 29 Apr 1940 Langmeade, Saskatchewan.

17 iii. William Swain, b. circa Jul 1839 Red River, (Manitoba); m. Angelique Hamelin; m. Marie Laviolette.

18 iv. Therese Swain, b. circa 1848 Pembina County; m. Peter Fidler.

19 v. Alexander Swain, b. circa 1849 Pembina; m. Felicite Pelletier; d. before 9 Aug 1886.

20 vi. Elizabeth Swain, b. 7 Jun 1853; m. Cuthbert Pelletier.

21 vii. Elzear Swain, b. circa 1855; m. Justine Ducharme; m. Caroline Schmidt.

22 viii. Marguerite Swain, b. circa 1856; m. Charles Patenaude.

23 ix. Francois Swain, b. 1856; m. Sara Fagnant.

8. Elizabeth Swain was born in 1820 North West (MBS, C-14931.) (1870C-MB, page 179, #77.). She was baptized on 25 Sep 1827 St.Johns, Red River Settlement, (Manitoba) (HBCR, E.4/1a, folio 66, #674.). She married **John McLeod**, son of **Malcolm McLeod**, on 8 Sep 1829 St.Johns, Red River Settlement, (Manitoba) (Ibid., M-180.). She died on 13 Feb 1895 RM. St.Clements, Manitoba (MB Vital Statistics, Death Reg. #1895,001682.).

John McLeod was born in 1793 Uig, Scotland (MBS, C-14931.). He died in Sep 1873 St.Andrews, Manitoba (Ibid.).

Generation Three

9. Margaret Swain was baptized on 25 Sep 1827 (St.Andrews), Rapids of Red River, (Manitoba) (HBCR, E.4/1a, folio 65d, #667.). She married **John Favel**, son of **John James Favel** and **Isabelle Short,** on 13 May 1847 (St.Johns), Upper Church, Red River Settlement, (Manitoba) (Ibid., No. 404.). She died in 1859 (Rod Mac Quarrie, 16 May 2005.).

John Favel was born in 1825 above Palestime (MBS, C-14927.). He married **Mary Desmarais**, daughter of **Charles King Desmarais** and **Harriet Favel,** on 20 Sep 1869 St.Mary's Anglican Church, Portage la Prairie, (Manitoba) (SMACPLP St.Marys Anglican Church, Portage La Prairie, Manitoba, Baptisms, Marriages, Burials, 1855-1883, transcribed by Clarence Kipling , page 27, M-52.).

10. Elizabeth Swain was born on 20 Mar 1834 St.Andrews, (Manitoba) (MBS, C-14934.) (Denney.). She was baptized on 18 Apr 1837 St.Johns, (Manitoba) (Ibid.). She married **Michael Wagner**, son of **Panedie Wagner,** on 20 Jun 1861 St.Andrews, (Manitoba) (Ibid.).

Michael Wagner was born circa 1826 Germany (1870C-MB, page 225, #667.).

11. Sarah Swain was born on 16 Jul 1846 St.Andrews, (Manitoba) (MBS, C-14928.). She was baptized on 22 Aug 1847 St.Johns, (Manitoba) (Denney.) (HBCA-B.). She married **George Flett**, son of **George Flett** and **Charlotte Tourangeau,** on 22 Jan 1863 St.Andrews, (Manitoba) (Denney.). She died on 23 Nov 1909 St.Clements, Manitoba, at age 63 (Rod Mac Quarrie, 1 Oct 2006.).

George Flett was born on 24 Oct 1840 St.Andrews, (Manitoba) (MBS, C-14928.). He died on 20 Oct 1924 St.Clements, Manitoba, at age 83 (Rod Mac Quarrie, 1 Oct 2006.).

12. William Robert Swain was born on 17 Mar 1852 St.Andrews, (Manitoba) (MBS, C-14934.). He was baptized on 2 Apr 1852 St.Andrews, (Manitoba) (Denney.). He married **Sarah Omand**, daughter of **Thomas Omand** and **Sarah McDonald,** before 1881. He died on 25 Oct 1925 St.Clements, Manitoba, at age 73 (MB Vital Statistics, Death Regn No. 1925,043239.).

Sarah Omand was born on 3 Aug 1861 (MBS, C-14931.). She died on 23 Dec 1927 St.Andrews, Manitoba, at age 66 (MB Vital Statistics, Death Regn No. 1927,060209.).

Children of **William Robert Swain** and **Sarah Omand** were as follows:

    i. Sarah Margaret Swain was born on 15 Aug 1880 (1901 Canada, page 1, Family 1, Line 1-11.) (1881 Canada, District 185-B, page 8, family 36.). She married William George Flett, son of George Flett and Sarah Swain, on 3 Mar 1908 St.Clements, Manitoba (MB Vital Statistics, Mar Reg No. 1908,002772.).

       William George Flett was born on 10 Jun 1878 Manitoba (Rod Mac Quarrie, 1 Oct 2006.). He died on 22 Apr 1921 St.Clements, Manitoba, at age 42 (Ibid.).

    ii. John R. Swain was born on 10 Feb 1885 (1901 Canada, page 1, Family 1, Line 1-11.).

    iii. Catherine J. Swain was born on 1 Feb 1891 (Ibid.).

    iv. James Swain was born on 10 Mar 1892 (Ibid.).

    v. Alexander Swain was born on 14 Apr 1893 (Ibid.).

    vi. Emily Swain was born on 15 Mar 1894 (Ibid.).

    vii. Mary Swain was born on 27 Sep 1896 (Ibid.).

    viii. William L. Swain was born on 5 Nov 1898 (Ibid.).

    ix. Lawrence Swain was born on 29 Mar 1901 St.Clements, Manitoba (Ibid.).

13. Matilda Swain was born in Mar 1855 St.Andrews, (Manitoba) (MBS, C-14929.). She was baptized on 5 Apr 1855 St.Andrews, (Manitoba) (Denney.). She married **John Hourie**, son of **Robert Hourie** and **Christiana Anderson,** on 24 Jan 1870 St.Andrews, (Manitoba) (MBS, C-14929.). She died on 20 Mar 1873 St.Andrews, Manitoba (Ibid.). She was buried on 23 Mar 1873 St.Andrews, Manitoba (Ibid.).

John Hourie was born in Apr 1852 St.Andrews, (Manitoba) (Ibid.).

14. Mary Swain was born circa 1823 Swan River District (Ibid., C-14925.). She was born circa 1825 North West Territory (1870C-MB, page 297, #1736.). She was baptized on 9 Feb 1834 St.Johns, Red River Settlement, (Manitoba) (HBCR, E.4/1a, folio 106d.). She married **Antoine Allary**, son of **Antoine Allary** and **Josephte Caplette,** before 1853.

Antoine Allary was born circa 1817 North West Territory (1870C-MB, page 297, #1735.). He was born circa 1819 North West Territories (MBS, C-14925.). He was baptized on 19 May 1839 St.Francois Xavier, (Manitoba) (SFX: 1834-1850 St.Francois Xavier 1834-1851 Register, B-250. Hereinafter cited as SFX: 1834-1850.).

15. Caroline Swain was born in Feb 1833 (MBS, C-14934.). She was baptized on 12 Mar 1837 St.Johns, Red River Settlement, (Manitoba) (HBCR, E.4/1a, folio 139.). She married **Joseph Vivier**, son of **Alexis Vivier** and **Isabelle Short,** before 1856. She died on 4 Aug 1885 Portage la Prairie, Manitoba, at age 52 (MB Vital Statistics, Death Reg. #1885,001725.).

Joseph Vivier was born in 1825 St.Francois Xavier, (Manitoba) (MBS, C-14934.).

16. Thomas Swain was born on 6 Apr 1835 (CWLR *The Collected Writings Of Louis Riel*, 5 (University of Alberta Press, 1985), page 347.). He was born circa 1838 (Manitoba) (1870C-MB, page 292, #1567.). He was born circa 1845 Red River, (Manitoba) (1850Ci-MN, page 23; Dwelling 53; Family 53.). He was born in 1851 St.Andrews, (Manitoba) (MBS, C-14933.). He married **Ellen Bremner**, daughter of **Alexander Bremner** and **Elizabeth Twat,** on 21 Aug 1864 Holy Trinity, Headingley, (Manitoba) (Debbie Eden Research, 6 Jun 1993.). He died on 29 Apr 1940 Langmeade, Saskatchewan (Ibid.) (CWLR, page 347.).

Ellen Bremner was born in 1825 Headingley, (Manitoba) (MBS, C-14933.). She was born circa 1831 Headingley, (Manitoba) (Debbie Eden, 6 Jun 1993.). She was born in 1836 (1901 Canada, #205, D(1), page 3, family 20, line 34-36.). She was born circa 1841 Headingley, (Manitoba) (1881 Canada, District 192-2, page 33, household 160.). She and **Pierre Parenteau** met before 1860. She died on 18 Jul 1928 (Debbie Eden, 6 Jun 1993.). She was buried in Jul 1928 Langmeade, Saskatchewan (Ibid.).

Children of **Thomas Swain** and **Ellen Bremner** were as follows:

  24 i. Mary Ellen Swain, b. 1 Oct 1864; m. Andrew James McKay.

  25 ii. Ellen Harriet Swain, b. 6 Jan 1867 near, Saskatoon, (Saskatchewan); m. Archibald James Inkster; d. 20 Nov 1972 St.Catherines, Prince Albert District, Saskatchewan.

  26 iii. John Andrew Swain, b. 31 Jan 1868 Poplar Point, (Manitoba); m. Christine Inkster; d. 19 Mar 1967 Saskatchewan.

  27 iv. Sarah Elizabeth Swain, b. 25 Sep 1870 Winnipeg, Manitoba; m. Alexander Foulds; d. 22 Mar 1966 New Westminster, British Columbia.

17. William Swain was born circa 1838 Red River, (Manitoba) (1850Ci-MN, page 23; Dwelling 53; Family 53.). He was born circa Jul 1839 Red River, (Manitoba) (Denney.). He married **Angelique Hamelin**, daughter of **Joseph Hamelin** and **Therese Ducharme**, on 20 Nov 1857 St.Francois Xavier, (Manitoba) (SFXI-Kipling, M-43.). He and **Marie Laviolette** met circa 1868. He married **Marie Laviolette**, daughter of **Charles Laviolette** and **Elizabeth Montagnaise**, on 15 Jul 1888 Helena, Lewis & Clark, Montana (L&CCM Lewis & Clark County, Montana; Marriage Record Licenses and Certificates; 1865-1950; familysearch.org, Hereinafter cited as L&CCM.). He married **Marie Laviolette**, daughter of **Charles Laviolette** and **Elizabeth Montagnaise,** on 22 Jul 1888 St.Peter's Mission, Cascade County, Montana (SPMT St.Peter's Mission; Volume I; Marriage Register 1859-1895; Translated & Transcribed by Reverend Dale McFarlane, Archivist, Diocese of Great Falls-Billings, Montana; Spring 1981, page 49, #293.).

Angelique Hamelin was born in 1839 St.Boniface, (Manitoba) (MBS, C-14933.). She died in 1887 River Range, North Dakota (BIA-LS Bureau of Indian Affairs, Little Shell Enrollment Papers.).

Children of **William Swain** and **Angelique Hamelin** were as follows:

- i. John Swain was born on 17 Sep 1858 (SFXI-Kipling, B-298.). He was baptized on 19 Nov 1858 St.Francois Xavier, (Manitoba) (Ibid.) (INB *Index des Naissances and Baptemes* (St.Boniface, Manitoba: La Societe Historique de Saint-Boniface., c1995), page 174.). He died on 12 May 1885 Batoche, (Saskatchewan), at age 26 (BSAP Records of the Parish of Batoche, St.Antoine de Pudoue Roman Catholic Church: Register for Baptisms, Marriages, Deaths, Volume One, 1881-1909., page 33, S-19. Hereinafter cited as BSAP.). He was buried on 14 May 1885 Batoche, (Saskatchewan) (Ibid.).
- ii. Rosalie Swan was born on 11 Sep 1860 (INB, page 174.). She was baptized on 17 Sep 1860 St.Francois Xavier, (Manitoba) (SFXI-Kipling, B-88.) (INB, page 174.). She died on 23 Mar 1861 St.Francois Xavier, (Manitoba) (SFXI-Kipling, page 506, S-6.). She was buried on 25 Mar 1861 St.Francois Xavier, (Manitoba) (Ibid.).
- 28 iii. William Swain, b. circa Oct 1861; m. Marie Monias.
- 29 iv. Jean Baptiste Swain, b. 15 Mar 1864; m. Julienne Larence; m. Marie Madeline Gariepy; d. 15 Aug 1935 Harlem, Blaine County, Montana.
- 30 v. Marie Louise Swain, b. 6 Dec 1865; m. Cuthbert Lemire.
- 31 vi. David Swain, b. 24 May 1876 Musselshell, Musselshell County, Montana; m. Mary Boyer.
- vii. Pierre Swan was born on 27 Oct 1882 (DL Register of Sacre Coeur Roman Catholic Church, Duck Lake, Saskatchewan, 1870-1893, page 49, B-29. Hereinafter cited as DL.). He was baptized on 14 Nov 1882 Duck Lake, (Saskatchewan) (Ibid.).

Marie Laviolette was born circa 1835 (1870C-MB, #1097-1099.). She married **Joseph Chartier** on 4 Jun 1855 St.Francois Xavier, (Manitoba) (SFXI-Kipling, M-1.).

Children of **William Swain** and **Marie Laviolette** were as follows:

- 32 i. Alexandre Swain, b. 16 Nov 1868 Milk River, Montana; m. Flora Villebrun.
- 33 ii. Marie Florestine Swain, b. 23 Jul 1872 Fort Carlton, (Saskatchewan); m. Caleb Anderson; m. Henry Moran; d. 19 May 1947 Montana.
- iii. Betsy Swain was born on 15 Jan 1876 Cypress Hills, (Saskatchewan) (ArchiviaNet.). She died on 18 Jan 1876 Cypress Hills, (Saskatchewan) (Ibid.).
- iv. Thomas Swain was born on 18 Feb 1877 Lebret, (Saskatchewan) (L1 Lebret Mission de St.Florent Roman Catholic Registre des Baptemes, Mariages & Seplutures, Qu'Appelle, Saskatchewan, 1868-1881., page 208, B-83. Hereinafter cited as L1.). He was baptized on 19 Feb 1877 Lebret, (Saskatchewan) (Ibid.). He died in 1897 Havre, Montana (ArchiviaNet.).

18. Therese Swain was born in 1845 (Manitoba) (MBS, C-14927.). She was born circa 1848 Pembina County (1850Ci-MN, page 23; Dwelling 53; Family 53.). She was born circa 1850 (Manitoba) (1870C-MB, page 291, #1555.). She married **Peter Fidler**, son of **Charles Fidler** and **Ann Sanderson**, on 22 Feb 1871 Holy Trinity, Headingley, (Manitoba) (Denney.).

Peter Fidler was baptized on 18 Oct 1824 St.Johns, Red River Colony, (Manitoba) (HBCA-B, Biog. Leg. Lib.) (HBCR, E.4/1a, folio 51d.). He married **Jane Lambert**, daughter of **Etienne Lambert** and **Catherine Gaddy**, on 17 Feb 1860 Holy Trinity, Headingley, (Manitoba) (Debbie Eden, 6 Jun 1993.).

Children of **Therese Swain** and **Peter Fidler** were as follows:

- i. John Thomas Fidler.
- ii. Henry Fidler was born on 16 Feb 1874 Duck Lake, (Saskatchewan) (Edsel Bourque, 29 Sep 1995.).
- iii. Charles Fidler was born on 30 Sep 1875 (L1, page 183-184, B-110.). He was baptized on 2 Apr 1876 Lebret, (Saskatchewan) (Ibid.). He died on 24 May 1884 Prince Albert, (Saskatchewan), at age 8 (Denney.). He was buried on 26 May 1884 St.Catherines, Prince Albert District, (Saskatchewan) (Ibid.).
- iv. Margaret Jane Fidler was born on 14 Apr 1878 Regina, (Saskatchewan) (L1, page 222, B-5.) (Louis Verhagen.). She was baptized on 29 Apr 1878 Lebret, (Saskatchewan) (L1, page 222, B-5.). She married William Vezina, son of Moise Visignault or Vezina and Julie Pepin, on 12 May 1897 Prince Albert, (Saskatchewan). She died on 16 Sep 1970 St.Louis, Saskatchewan, at age 92 (Louis Verhagen.).

    William Vezina was born on 12 May 1874 Poplar Point, Manitoba (Rod Mac Quarrie, 29 Mar 2012.). He died on 2 May 1961 St.Louis, Saskatchewan, at age 86 (Edsel Bourque.).
- v. Betsy Fidler was born on 2 Oct 1882 Prince Albert, (Saskatchewan) (Denney.). She died in 1885 Prince Albert, (Saskatchewan) (Ibid.).
- vi. Alexander Peter Fidler was born in Sep 1883 Prince Albert, (Saskatchewan) (Louis Verhagen.). He was born in 1884 Prince Albert, (Saskatchewan) (ArchiviaNet.). He married Harriet Howse before 1907 Hardisty, (Alberta). He died in Apr 1966 Edmonton, Alberta (Louis Verhagen.). He was buried in Apr 1966 Elk Point, Alberta (Ibid.).

    Harriet Howse was born in 1885 High Bluff, (Manitoba). She married **Charles Grant**. Question: *Louis Verhagen says parents are Henry and Janet (Spence) Howse. This couple would have had a young child while still in their 80s.*

19. **Alexander Swain** was born circa 1849 Pembina (1850Ci-MN, page 23; Dwelling 53; Family 53.). He was born in Aug 1852 Headingley, (Manitoba) (MBS, C-14933.). He was baptized on 30 Apr 1870 Lebret, (Saskatchewan) (L1, page 20.). He married **Felicite Pelletier**, daughter of **Joseph Pelletier** and **Louise St.Denis**, on 2 May 1870 Lebret, (Saskatchewan) (Ibid., page 20, M-2.). He died before 9 Aug 1886 (L2 Lebret, Mission de St.Florent, Roman Catholic Registre des Baptemes, Mariages & Seplutures, Qu'Appelle, Saskatchewan, Book Two: 1881-1887, FHC microfilm 1032949., page 155, M-7. Hereinafter cited as L2.).

Felicite Pelletier was born on 24 Jul 1852 (SFXI 1851-1868 St.Francois Xavier 1852-1861 Register Index, B-27. Hereinafter cited as SFXI 1851-1868.). She was baptized on 29 Aug 1852 St.Francois Xavier, (Manitoba) (Ibid.). She married **Mathias Sansregret**, son of **Louis Pontbriand dit Sansregret** and **Genevieve Carriere**, on 9 Aug 1886 Lebret, (Saskatchewan) (L2, page 155, M-7.).

Children of **Alexander Swain** and **Felicite Pelletier** were as follows:

    i.   Marie Swan was born in Mar 1871 (INB, page 174.). She was baptized on 9 Jul 1871 St.Francois Xavier, Manitoba (SFXI-Kipling, B-55.). She married Exuper Desjarlais, son of Michel Desjarlais and Julie Bonneau, before 1890. She died on 12 Jan 1893 Qu'Appelle Mission, (Saskatchewan), at age 21 (Rod Mac Quarrie, 15 Mar 2007 extraction.). She was buried on 13 Jan 1893 Qu'Appelle Mission, (Saskatchewan) (Ibid.).

       Exuper Desjarlais was born on 23 Jul 1857 St.Francois Xavier, (Manitoba) (SFXI-Kipling, B-209.). He was baptized on 23 Jul 1857 St.Francois Xavier, (Manitoba) (Ibid.). He married **Marie Rose Cardinal**, daughter of **Charles Cardinal** and **Josephte Desmarais,** before 1898.

    ii. Pauline Swan was born on 30 Oct 1872 St.Laurent, (Saskatchewan) (SL-SK St.Laurent-de-Grandin Roman Catholic Registre des Baptemes, Mariages & Sepltures, St.Laurent, Saskatchewan, 1872-1896, page 12, B-32. Hereinafter cited as SL-SK.). She was baptized on 31 Oct 1872 St.Laurent-de-Grandin, (Saskatchewan) (Ibid.).

    iii. Florestine Swan was born on 10 Dec 1874 (L1, page 138, B-129.). She was baptized on 12 Dec 1874 Lebret, (Saskatchewan) (Ibid.). She died on 26 Jan 1875 (Ibid., page 140, S-2.). She was buried on 27 Jan 1875 Lebret, (Saskatchewan) (Ibid.).

    iv. Virginie Swan was born on 11 Dec 1875 (Ibid., page 184, B-120.). She was baptized on 1 Apr 1876 Lebret, (Saskatchewan) (Ibid.). She died on 15 Feb 1884 at age 8 (L2, page 93, S-5.). She was buried on 18 Feb 1884 Lebret, (Saskatchewan) (Ibid.).

    v.   Anonyme Swan was born on 16 Mar 1876 Lebret, (Saskatchewan) (L1, page 162, S-5.). She died on 17 Mar 1876 Lebret, (Saskatchewan) (Ibid.). She was buried on 20 Mar 1876 Lebret, (Saskatchewan) (Ibid.).

    vi. Joseph Swan was born on 4 May 1878 Qu'Appelle, (Saskatchewan) (Ibid., page 232, B-49.) (HBSI Index 1886-1901, 1906 Halfbreed Scrip Applications, RG15-21.). He was baptized on 10 Aug 1878 Lebret, (Saskatchewan) (L1, page 232, B-49.). He died on 15 Feb 1884 at age 5 (HBSI.) (ArchiviaNet, C-15001.).

    vii. Patrick Swan was born in Jan 1880 Willow Bunch, (Saskatchewan) (Ibid., C-15005.).

    viii. Justine Swan was born on 15 Jun 1883 (L2, page 66, B-40.). She was baptized on 18 Jun 1883 Lebret, (Saskatchewan) (Ibid.). She married Joseph Robillard on 10 Jan 1916 Lebret, Saskatchewan (Ibid.).

20. **Elizabeth Swain** was born on 7 Jun 1853 (AP Records of the Assumption Roman Catholic Church, Pembina, North Dakota: Baptisms, Marriages, Sepultures, 1848-1896; compiled by Reverend Father J. M. Belleau, 2 October 1944, page 92, B-43. Hereinafter cited as AP.). She was baptized on 2 Sep 1853 Assumption, Pembina, Pembina County, Dakota Territory (Ibid.). She married **Cuthbert Pelletier**, son of **Charles Pelletier** and **Suzanne Bercier,** on 31 Dec 1872 St-Laurent-de-Grandin, (Saskatchewan) (SL-SK, page 17, M-1.).

Cuthbert Pelletier was born circa 1846 Pembina (1850Ci-MN, page 27, Dwelling 90; Family 90.).

21. **Elzear Swain** was born circa 1855. He married **Justine Ducharme**, daughter of **Jean Baptiste Ducharme** and **Magdeleine Houle**, on 6 Apr 1874 Duck Lake, (Saskatchewan) (DL, page 21, M-10.). He married **Caroline Schmidt**, daughter of **Alfred 'Rabasca' Schmidt** and **Marguerite Lesperance**, on 5 Feb 1883 St.Laurent, (Saskatchewan) (Denney.).

Justine Ducharme was born on 22 Aug 1856 (SFXI-Kipling, B-135.). She was baptized on 30 Aug 1856 St.Francois Xavier, (Manitoba) (Ibid.). She died before 1883.

Children of **Elzear Swain** and **Justine Ducharme** were as follows:

    i.   Marie Swan was born on 7 May 1875 (L1, page 169, B-29.). She was baptized on 9 Aug 1876 Lebret, (Saskatchewan) (Ibid.).

    ii. John Thomas Swan was born in Jul 1875 Cypress Hills, (Saskatchewan) (Denney.) (L1, page 150, B-41.). He was baptized on 8 Aug 1875 Lebret, (Saskatchewan) (Ibid.). He married Margaret Boner in 1896 Prince Albert, (Saskatchewan) (ArchiviaNet, C-15005.).

    iii. Alexandre Swain was born on 23 Feb 1878 Cypress Hills, (Saskatchewan) (L1, page 228-229, B-40.) (HBSI.) (ArchiviaNet, C-15005.). He was baptized on 24 Feb 1878 Lebret, (Saskatchewan) (L1, page 228-229, B-40.). He died in 1898 Lake Manitoba, Manitoba (HBSI.) (ArchiviaNet, C-15005.).

    iv. Mary Swain was born on 22 Apr 1878 Cypress Hills, (Saskatchewan) (ArchiviaNet.). She married (--?--) Maveety before 1900.

    v.   Josephine Swan was born on 15 Apr 1879 Qu'Appelle, (Saskatchewan) (L1, page 247, B-26.). She was baptized on 31 May 1879 Lebret, (Saskatchewan) (Ibid.). She married Archibald Spence, son of Joseph Spence and Elizabeth Baby, in 1900 (ArchiviaNet, C-15004.).

       Archibald Spence was born circa 1871 Poplar Point, Manitoba (1881 Canada, District 186-F, page 10, house 37.).

    vi. Louis Swain was born on 2 Jan 1881 Cypress Hills, (Saskatchewan) (ArchiviaNet, C-15005.).

Caroline Schmidt was born on 10 Jan 1849 Red River, (Manitoba) (Denney.) (1870C-MB, #242, page 8.).

Children of **Elzear Swain** and **Caroline Schmidt** were as follows:

    i.   Edmund Swain was born circa Aug 1880 Prince Albert, (Saskatchewan) (ArchiviaNet, C-15005.).

    ii. Rose Yvonne Swain was born on 28 Nov 1883 Prince Albert, (Saskatchewan) (SK Vital Statistics, Birth Regn. #11580.) (ArchiviaNet, C-15005.).

iii. Frank Elzear Swain was born on 27 Jun 1885 Prince Albert, (Saskatchewan) (Ibid.) (SHC-PA-SK Sacred Heart Cathedral, Prince Albert, Saskatchewan, baptisms, marriages and burials, 1874-1900, B-5. Hereinafter cited as SHC-PA-SK.). He was baptized on 28 Jun 1885 Sacred Heart, Prince Albert, (Saskatchewan) (Ibid.). He married Madeline Card, daughter of George Card and Sarah Hall, on 5 May 1909 Fort Benton, Chouteau County, Montana (ChCM Chouteau County, Montana; Marriage Record Licenses and Certificates; 1865-1950; familysearch.org, Hereinafter cited as ChCM.).

Madeline Card was born circa 1889 Havre, Montana (Ibid.).

34 iv. Joseph Swain, b. 6 Jul 1887 (Saskatchewan); m. Margaret Allary; d. 10 Nov 1979 Rolette County, North Dakota.

v. Adele Swain was born circa 1888 (Saskatchewan) (1891 Census of Canada from the National Archives of Canada, Ottawa, Canada, page 7, family 26, line 13-21.).

vi. John Swain was born on 10 Feb 1889 (1901 Canada, #204-u, page 1, family 10, line 22-30.).

vii. Marie Swain was born circa Oct 1890 (Saskatchewan) (1891 Canada, page 7, family 26, line 13-21.).

viii. Eugenie Swain was born circa Oct 1890 (Saskatchewan) (Ibid.).

ix. Marguerite Swain was born on 16 May 1893 (1901 Canada, #204-u, page 1, family 10, line 22-30.).

22. Marguerite Swain was born circa 1853 (SFXI-Kipling, B-42.). She married Charles Patenaude, son of Michel Patenaude and Marguerite Montagnais, on 12 Jan 1874 St.Eustache, Manitoba (MM.) (ST-BSP.).

Charles Patenaude was born on 2 Aug 1838 (SFX: 1834-1850, B-202.). He was baptized on 17 Aug 1838 St.Francois Xavier, (Manitoba) (Ibid.). He married Rosalie Pritchard, daughter of William Pritchard and Marie Fleury, on 16 Aug 1863 St.Francois Xavier, (Manitoba) (SFXI-Kipling, M-15.).

23. Francois Swain was born in 1856 (HBC-PN , Poplar Point and High Bluff, #223.). He married Sara Fagnant, daughter of Jean Louis Fagnant and Josette St.Denis, on 30 Apr 1878 St.Eustache, Manitoba (ST-BSP, M-4.).

Sara Fagnant was born on 25 Jul 1860 (SFXI-Kipling, B-68.). She was baptized on 7 Aug 1860 St.Francois Xavier, (Manitoba) (Ibid.).

Children of Francois Swain and Sara Fagnant were as follows:

i. Francois Swain was born in Mar 1879 Wood Mountain, (Saskatchewan) (1889-TMC 1889 Census of Half Breed Chippewas residing in the vicinity of, but not on the Turtle Mountain Reservation, Dakota Territory, National Archives of the United States, Washington D.C., #545.) (L1, page 245, B-19.) (ArchiviaNet, C-15005.). He was baptized on 29 Apr 1879 Lebret, (Saskatchewan) (L1, page 245, B-19.).

35 ii. Marie Swain, b. Feb 1881 Manitoba; m. Josue Bercier.

iii. Roger Swain was born circa 1883 (1889-TMC-off, #547.). He was baptized on 10 Sep 1883 St.Claude, St.John, Rolette County, North Dakota (St.Claude BMD, Dominique Ritchot, page 14, B-67.).

iv. Rosalie Swain was born on 10 Jan 1886 Rolette County, North Dakota (Ibid., B-233, page 50.). She was baptized on 14 Feb 1886 St.Claude Mission, St.John, Rolette County, North Dakota (Ibid.).

v. Augustin Swain was baptized on 24 Apr 1887 St.Claude Mission, St.John, Rolette County, North Dakota (Ibid., B-327, page 65.).

36 vi. Julia Swain, b. circa Jun 1889; m. Alfred Pelletier.

Generation Four

24. Mary Ellen Swain was born on 1 Oct 1864 (HBC-PN , Headingly, #122.). She married Andrew James McKay, son of Alexander McKay and Catherine McCorrister, circa 1882.

Andrew James McKay was born on 8 Apr 1862 Headingley, (Manitoba) (Denney.). He died in Feb 1944 Horseshoe Bend, Saskatchewan, at age 81 (Ibid.).

25. Ellen Harriet Swain was born on 1 Oct 1866 (HBC-PN , Headingly, #123.). She was born on 6 Jan 1867 near, Saskatoon, (Saskatchewan) (Denney.) (SK Vital Statistics, #11465.). She married Archibald James Inkster, son of George Inkster and Elizabeth Regis Keziah Franks, on 8 Jan 1891 Prince Albert, (Saskatchewan) (Denney.). She died on 20 Nov 1972 St.Catherines, Prince Albert District, Saskatchewan, at age 105 (Ibid.).

Archibald James Inkster was born on 1 Jan 1865 (HBC-PN , Poplar Point and High Bluff, #121.). He was baptized on 18 Apr 1865 St.Johns, (Manitoba) (Denney.) (Rod Mac Quarrie, 16 Dec 2010.). He died on 24 Dec 1925 Prince Albert, Saskatchewan, at age 60 (Denney.).

26. John Andrew Swain was born on 31 Jan 1868 Poplar Point, (Manitoba) (Ibid.). He was born on 1 Oct 1868 (HBC-PN , Headingly, #124.). He married Christine Inkster, daughter of George Inkster and Elizabeth Regis Keziah Franks, on 11 Apr 1886 Prince Albert, Saskatchewan (Denney.). He died on 19 Mar 1967 Saskatchewan at age 99 (Ibid.) (Rod Mac Quarrie, 16 Dec 2010.).

Christine Inkster was born on 25 Jan 1872 Poplar Point, Manitoba (Denney.). She died on 19 Mar 1914 Paynton, Saskatchewan, at age 42 (Ibid.) (Rod Mac Quarrie, 16 Dec 2010.).

Children of John Andrew Swain and Christine Inkster were as follows:

i. Andrew Alexander George Swain was born on 4 Apr 1888 (Saskatchewan) (SK Vital Statistics, #12310.).

ii. Thomas E. J. Swain was born on 26 Sep 1889 (Saskatchewan) (1901 Canada, #205, Y-1, page 4, family 30, line 18-26.). He was born in Sep 1890 (Saskatchewan) (1911 Canada, #34, Twp 46, page 19, family 215, line 29-45.).

iii. Roderick Anthony Amond Swain was born on 15 Aug 1892 (Saskatchewan) (SK Vital Statistics, #8055.).

iv. Nellie Swain was born on 14 Oct 1894 (Saskatchewan) (1911 Canada, #34, Twp 46, page 19, family 215, line 29-45.) (1901 Canada, #205, Y-1, page 4, family 30, line 18-26.).

v. Vina Swain was born on 27 Aug 1895 (Saskatchewan) (Ibid.). She was born in Aug 1896 (Saskatchewan) (1911 Canada, #34, Twp 46, page 19, family 215, line 29-45.).

vi. Arabel Swain was born on 19 Apr 1899 (Saskatchewan) (Ibid.) (1901 Canada, #205, Y-1, page 4, family 30, line 18-26.).

vii. Helena Maude Elizabeth Swain was born on 19 Aug 1900 Prince Albert, (Saskatchewan) (SK Vital Statistics, #1861.). She married Franklin James Foulds, son of Alexander Foulds and Sarah Elizabeth Swain, on 22 May 1920 Fort-a-la-Corne, Saskatchewan (Rod Mac Quarrie, 15 May 2011.).

Franklin James Foulds was born on 23 May 1895 Prince Albert, (Saskatchewan) (SK Vital Statistics, #7066.).

    viii. Rowland Wilson Barnard Swain was born on 30 Jun 1903 Green Bluff, (Saskatchewan) (Ibid., #2813.).

    ix. Eunice Swain was born in Oct 1905 (Saskatchewan) (1911 Canada, #34, Twp 46, page 19, family 215, line 29-45.).

    x. Roy Swain was born in Oct 1908 Saskatchewan (Ibid.).

    xi. Ivy Swain was born in Oct 1909 Saskatchewan (Ibid.).

27. Sarah Elizabeth Swain was born on 25 Sep 1870 Winnipeg, Manitoba (HBSI.) (ArchiviaNet.). She married **Alexander Foulds**, son of **John Foulds** and **Mary Anne Adams**, on 28 Jul 1887 Prince Albert, (Saskatchewan) (Denney.). She died on 22 Mar 1966 New Westminster, British Columbia, at age 95 (Ibid.).

    Alexander Foulds was born on 12 Feb 1861 (HBC-PN , Poplar Point and High Bluff, #79.). He was baptized on 17 Mar 1861 St.James, (Manitoba) (SJAC, B-105.). He died on 20 Mar 1947 Meadow Lake, Saskatchewan, at age 86 (Denney.).

28. William Swain was born on 2 Jan 1861 North West Territories (MBS, C-14933.). He was born circa Oct 1861 (SFXI-Kipling, B-121.). He was baptized on 23 Nov 1861 St.Francois Xavier, (Manitoba) (Ibid.). He married **Marie Monias**, daughter of **Moise Monais** and **Magdeleine (--?--),** on 14 Jan 1885 Duck Lake, (Saskatchewan) (DL, page 62, M-1.).

    Children of **William Swain** and **Marie Monias** were:

    i. William Jean Swain was born in May 1886 (Ibid., page 71, B-9.). He was baptized on 20 Jun 1886 Duck Lake, (Saskatchewan) (Ibid.).

29. Jean Baptiste Swain was born on 15 Mar 1864 (SFXI-Kipling, B-51.). He was baptized on 30 Mar 1864 St.Francois Xavier, (Manitoba) (Ibid.). He married **Julienne Larence**, daughter of **Basile Larence** and **Marguerite Desjardins,** on 23 Oct 1888 St.Peter's Mission, Cascade County, Montana (SPMT , page 49, #295.). He married **Marie Madeline Gariepy**, daughter of **Elie Gariepy** and **Marie Larocque,** on 15 Aug 1919 Chinook, Blaine County, Montana (BCM Blaine County, Montana; Marriage Record Licenses and Certificates; 1865-1950; familysearch.org.). He died on 15 Aug 1935 Harlem, Blaine County, Montana, at age 71 (Ancestry.com, MT Death Index 1907-2002.).

    Julienne Larence was born in 1866 St.Albert, (Alberta) (NWHBS, C-14939.). She was born on 30 Aug 1875 McCloud, (Alberta). She married **Dieudonne Courtepatte**, son of **Jean-Baptiste Courtepatte dit LePoteau** and **Josephte Belcourt,** on 12 Jan 1886 St.Albert, (Alberta) (Denney.). She married **Peter Petit dit Thomas**, son of **Louis Petit** and **Angelic Grant,** on 15 Feb 1919 Cascade, Cascade County, Montana (1937-1987-LS Basic Roll Basic Membership Roll of the Landless Indians of Montana; 1937 Census Taken by Dr. Henry Roe Cloud; Edited c1987 to include official correspondence regarding 1937 membership; ** in Present Roll Number column indicates 1940s information added., #505.) (Ancestry.com, 1930 MT Census.) (CaCM Cascade County, Montana; Marriage Record Licenses and Certificates; 1865-1950; familysearch.org, Hereinafter cited as CaCM.).

    Children of **Jean Baptiste Swain** and **Julienne Larence** were as follows:

    i. Mary Rose Swan was born on 18 Nov 1888 St.Peter's Mission, Montana (1936-LS Henry Roe Cloud Roll 1936-1937, Pembina Band of Chippewa Indians Who Were Under the Leadership of Chief Thomas Little Shell, J. H. Dussome, Zortman, Montana and Vice-President: George SinClaire, Chinook, Montana, #__.). She married Carl Leroy Monroe, son of Carlton Leroy Monroe and Maria Belcourt, on 17 Nov 1904 Saypo, Teton County, Montana (TeCM Teton County, Montana; Marriage Record Licenses and Certificates; 1865-1950; familysearch.org, Hereinafter cited as TeCM.). She married Charles Barrows, son of John Barrows and Maggie Larence, on 15 Sep 1939 Great Falls, Cascade County, Montana (CaCM.). She died on 11 Jun 1944 Valley County, Montana, at age 55 (MT Death Montana State Genealogical Society Death Index.).

      Carl Leroy Monroe was born on 23 Jun 1883 Fort Benton, Choteau County, Montana (Denney.). He married **Sarah Baker**, daughter of **Benton Baker** and **Lucy Grossman,** on 10 Jul 1933 Great Falls, Cascade County, Montana (CaCM.). He died on 19 Jan 1979 Great Falls, Cascade County, Montana, at age 95 (SSDI.) (Ancestry.com, findagrave.com.).

      Charles Barrows was born on 13 Dec 1914 (CaCM.) (SSDI.). He married **Evelyn Adams**, daughter of **Charley Adams** and **Nettie Healy,** before 1936. He died in Nov 1971 at age 56 (Ibid.).

    ii. Victoria Swan was born in 1891 Choteau, Teton County, Montana. She married William Hamelin, son of Severe Hamelin and Domitille Lapierre, on 30 Dec 1909 Choteau, Teton County, Montana (TeCM.). She married Albert Bruno Sr., son of Cleophas "Joseph" Bruneau or Bruno and Euphrosine Hamelin, on 1 Jul 1919 Choteau, Teton County, Montana (Ibid.). She married John Davis Sinclair, son of Toussaint Samuel Sinclair and Susette Lasarte, on 19 Jun 1950 Teton County, Montana (Ibid.).

      William Hamelin was born in 1888 (Ibid.). He died on 1 Dec 1939 Choteau, Teton County, Montana (Brenda Snider Research, December 12, 2014.).

      Albert Bruno Sr was born on 15 Aug 1890 Tom Holmes ranch near Teton Mountains, Montana. He died on 21 Jan 1974 Choteau, Teton County, Montana, at age 83 (MT Death.).

      John Davis Sinclair was born on 6 Mar 1908 (SPMT , page 66, #263.). He was baptized on 13 Apr 1908 St.Peter's Mission, Cascade County, Montana (Ibid.).

    iii. Rainie Swan was born circa 1895 Montana (Ancestry.com, 1900 Census.).

    iv. Lucy Swan was born on 18 Jan 1901 (SPMT , page 39, #153.). She was baptized on 9 Jun 1901 St.Peter's Mission, Cascade County, Montana (Ibid.). She married Charles C. Twiggs, son of Robert Twiggs and Mary McCauley, on 27 Jun 1916 Great Falls, Cascade County, Montana (CaCM.).

      Charles C. Twiggs was born in 1887 Montana (Ibid.).

    v. Thomas Swan was born on 20 Jan 1904 Montana (SSDI.). He married Olive Desmarais, daughter of William John Desmarais and Olive "Babe" Larence, on 11 Feb 1942 Choteau, Teton County, Montana (1996-00LS 1996-2000 Little Shell Band of Chippewa Roll.) (Ardith "Ardi" Bryant Research: Aug 2006. Hereinafter cited as Ardith "Ardi" Bryant.) (TeCM.). He died on 3 Aug 1975 Teton County, Montana, at age 71 (SSDI.) (MT Death.).

Olive Desmarais was born on 16 Nov 1910 Montana (1996-00LS.). She married **Henry Joseph "Alex" Gervais**, son of **Daniel Gervais** and **Marguerite Swan**, on 19 Nov 1928 Great Falls, Cascade County, Montana (Ardith "Ardi" Bryant: Aug 2006.) (CaCM.). She married **Gilbert Meyers** in 1947 (Brenda Snider, Great Falls Tribune, 30 Jan 1981, 15 Sep 2013 email.). She died on 29 Jan 1981 Havre, Hill County, Montana, at age 70 (MT Death.) (SSDI.).

Marie Madeline Gariepy was born on 25 Mar 1887 Grassrange, Fergus County, Montana (1937-1987-LS Basic Roll, #495.). She married **Joseph Lee Laroque**, son of **Joseph Larocque** and **Mary Louise Klyne,** on 15 Aug 1910 Chinook, Blaine County, Montana (Kathie MacGregor Donahue Research.). She died on 13 Aug 1939 Ponoka, Alberta, at age 52 (Rod Mac Quarrie, 27 Mar 2013.).

Children of **Jean Baptiste Swain** and **Marie Madeline Gariepy** were as follows:

    i.   Gabriel Swan was born on 24 Sep 1918 (1936-LS, #495.).

    ii.   Rosemary Swan was born on 7 Sep 1920 Montana (Ibid.) (1937-1987-LS Basic Roll, #495.). She married Lawrence Guy Duncan, son of Thomas Oscar Duncan and Ellen Nesting, on 9 Feb 1935 Fergus County, Montana (FerCM Fergus County Courthouse, Montana; Marriage Record Licenses and Certificates, 1865-1950, familysearch.org., Hereinafter cited as FerCM.).

        Lawrence Guy Duncan was born in 1914 (Ibid.).

    iii.   Aloysius Swan was born on 4 Jul 1921 (1936-LS, #495.) (1937-1987-LS Basic Roll, #495.). He married Donna Fay Beaudry, daughter of Alfred Beaudry and Cora Belle Wagar, on 16 Mar 1951 Glasgow, Valley, Montana (VCM Valley County Courthouse, Glasgow, Montana; Marriage Record Licenses, 1865-1950, familysearch.org, Hereinafter cited as VCM.).

        Donna Fay Beaudry was born on 1 Jan 1933 (1936-LS, #77.) (1937-1987-LS Basic Roll, #77.). She married **Gilbert William Debray**, son of **William Mark Debray** and **Rose Klyne,** before 1958 (1987LS 1987-92 Little Shell Band of Chippewa Roll.).

    iv.   John Swan was born on 12 May 1924 (1936-LS, #495.) (1937-1987-LS Basic Roll, #495.).

    v.   Earl Norman Swan was born on 20 Oct 1925 Fort Belknap, Blaine County, Montana (1936-LS, #495.) (1996-00LS.) (1937-1987-LS Basic Roll, #495.). He died on 23 Sep 2007 Toppenish, Yakima County, Washington, at age 81 (SSDI.).

30. Marie Louise Swain was born on 6 Dec 1865 (SFXI-Kipling, B-111.). She was baptized on 15 Dec 1865 St.Francois Xavier, (Manitoba) (Ibid.). She married **Cuthbert Lemire**, son of **Pierre Lemire** and **Therese Pelletier,** on 3 Feb 1882 (St.Peter's Mission), Musselshell River, Montana (SPMT , page 32, #180.). She died on 6 May 1949 Havre, Montana, at age 83 (*HDN Havre Daily News*, Havre, Montana, Tuesday, 10 May 1949. Pg. 6. Hereinafter cited as HDN.).

Cuthbert Lemire was born on 30 Sep 1862 Devils Lake, Dakota Territory (SFXI-Kipling, B-27.). He was baptized on 24 Apr 1863 St.Francois Xavier, (Manitoba) (Ibid.). He died on 2 May 1941 Havre, Montana, at age 78 (*HDN*, Saturday, 3 May 1941. Pg. 3.) (Brenda Snider, 10 Apr 2015.).

31. David Swain was born circa 1874 near Roundup, Montana (1917 RB, #502.). He was born in 1876 Duck Lake, (Saskatchewan) (ArchiviaNet, C-15005.). He was born on 24 May 1876 Musselshell, Musselshell County, Montana (1937-1987-LS Basic Roll, #490.). He married **Mary Boyer**, daughter of **Joseph Boyer** and **Marguerite Pelletier,** before 1905 (1917 RB, #503.).

Mary Boyer was born circa 1888 (Ancestry.com, 1920 MT Census.).

Children of **David Swain** and **Mary Boyer** are as follows:

    i.   Adolph Swan was born circa 1905 Cypress Hills (1917 RB, #504.).

    ii.   Frank Swan was born circa 1909 Cypress Hills (Ibid., #505.).

    iii.   Albert Swan was born circa 1911 Gilford, Montana (Ibid., #506.).

    iv.   Edward Swan was born circa 1913 Browning, Glacier County, Montana (Ibid., #507.).

    v.   Elisabeth Swan was born circa Dec 1916 Rocky Boy Camp, Montana (Ibid., #508.).

    vi.   Nancy Swain was born circa 1918 Montana (Ancestry.com, 1920 MT Census.).

32. Alexandre Swain was born on 16 Nov 1868 Milk River, Montana (NWHBS, C-14941.). He married **Flora Villebrun**, daughter of **Guillaume Villebrun dit Ploufe** and **Flora Hope,** on 10 Jun 1890 St.Peter's Mission, Cascade County, Montana (SPMT , page 51, #310.).

Flora Villebrun was born on 23 Jan 1877 Lac la Biche, (Alberta) (LLBR1 Notre Dame des Tidoren, St.Paul Diocese, Lac La Biche, Registre des Baptemes, Mariages & Seplitures, Volume 1, 1853-1898., page 166, B-4. Hereinafter cited as LLBR1.). She was baptized on 25 Jan 1877 Lac la Biche, (Alberta) (Ibid.).

Children of **Alexandre Swain** and **Flora Villebrun** all born Montana are as follows:

    i.   Alfred P. Swan was born circa 1891 (Ancestry.com, 1900 Census.).

    ii.   John Swan was born circa 1895 (Ibid.).

    iii.   Mary Swan was born circa 1898 (Ibid.).

    iv.   Rosa Swan was born circa 1899 (Ibid.).

33. Marie Florestine Swain was born on 23 Jul 1872 Fort Carlton, (Saskatchewan) (HBS, Volume 1333; C-14945.). She was baptized on 29 Jul 1872 St.Laurent-de-Grandin, (Saskatchewan) (SL-SK, page 10, B-23.). She married **Caleb Anderson**, son of **Thomas Anderson** and **Fanny Pocha,** on 20 May 1889 St.Peter's Mission, Cascade County, Montana (SPMT , page 50, #300. Marriage record says mother is Fanny Beloy.). She married **Henry Moran**, son of **Jean Baptiste Morin** and **Marie Agnes Desjarlais,** before 1 Apr 1930. She died on 19 May 1947 Montana at age 74 (Ancestry.com, MT Death Index 1907-2002.).

Caleb Anderson was born on 18 May 1860 Portage la Prairie, (Manitoba) (MBS, C-14925.). He was baptized on 27 May 1860 St.Mary's Anglican Church, Portage la Prairie, (Manitoba) (SMACPLP, B-75.). He died in 1929.

Henry Moran was born on 27 Aug 1887 Malta, Valley County, Montana (1936-LS, #384.) (1937-1987-LS Basic Roll, #384.).

34. Joseph Swain was born on 6 Jul 1887 (Saskatchewan) (1891 Canada, page 7, family 26, line 13-21.) (1901 Canada, #204-u, page 1, family 10, line 22-30.). He was born on 5 Jun 1890 (ND Death Index.). He married **Margaret Allary**, daughter of **Francois Allary**

and **Eliza Patenaude**, before 1918 (1936-TMC, page 116.) (*1937-TMC*, page 484, Census No. 5648-5653.). He died on 10 Nov 1979 Rolette County, North Dakota, at age 92 (ND Death Index.).

   Margaret Allary was born on 17 Aug 1886 Wakopa, Manitoba (St.Claude BMD, Dominique Ritchot, B-281, page 57.). She was baptized on 5 Sep 1886 St.Claude Mission, St.John, Rolette County, North Dakota (Ibid.). She married **George Favel**, son of **Richard Favel** and **Marie Marguerite Sayer**, before 1906 (1936-TMC, page 116.). She died on 15 Jan 1977 Rolette County, North Dakota, at age 90 (ND Death Index.).

   Children of **Joseph Swain** and **Margaret Allary** are as follows:

     i.   Ida Swain was born on 10 Dec 1918 (*1937-TMC*, page 484, Census No. 5648-5653.).
     ii. Joseph Swain was born on 1 Apr 1921 (Ibid.).
     iii. Madeleine Swain was born on 5 Mar 1924 (Ibid.).
     iv. Zelma Swain was born on 17 Mar 1926 (Ibid.).
     v. John C. Swain was born on 26 Jun 1934 (Ibid.).

35. **Marie Swain** was born on 5 May 1879 Pilot Mound, Manitoba (1889-TMC-off, #546.) (Debbie Morin Ivers Research , 10 Mar 2000.). She was born in Feb 1881 Manitoba (1881 Canada, Film No. C-13283, District 186, Sub-district K, page 29, Household No. 135.). She married **Josue Bercier**, son of **Joseph Bercier** and **Flavie Falcon**, before 1913.

   Josue Bercier was born on 17 Apr 1876 St.Francois Xavier, Manitoba (SFXI-Kipling, B-12.). He was baptized 17 Apr 1876 St.Francois Xavier, Manitoba (Ibid.) (Rosemary Rozyk.).

36. **Julia Swain** was born circa Jun 1889 (1889-TMC-off, #550.). She married **Alfred Pelletier**, son of **Paul Pelletier** and **Lucie Gonneville**, before 1931 (1940C ND 1940 North Dakota, Sixteenth Census of the United States, National Archives of the United States, Washington, D.C., District 40-24B, page 6A.).

   Alfred Pelletier was born on 21 Mar 1887 North Dakota (1916-TMC, Census No. 2605.) (ND Death Index.). He died on 18 Aug 1950 Rolette, North Dakota, at age 63 (Ibid.).

Descendants of James Swain (b. c1808)

Generation One

1. **James Swain** was born circa 1808 Ruperts Land (1870C-MB 1870 Manitoba Census, National Archives of Canada, Ottawa, Ontario, Microfilm Reel Number C-2170., page 180, #101.). He was baptized on 5 May 1826 St.Johns, Red River Settlement, (Manitoba) (HBCR Hudson Bay Company Register of Anglican Church Baptisms, Marriages, and Burials for the Red River Settlement, 1821-1841; Hudson's Bay Company Archives, Winnipeg, Manitoba, E.4/1a, folio 128. Hereinafter cited as HBCR.). He was baptized on 10 Jan 1841 St.Johns, Red River Settlement, (Manitoba) (Ibid.). He married according to the custom of the country **Josephte Descoteaux**, daughter of **Pierre Descoteaux** and **Madeleine Dumille**, before 1822. He married **Josephte Descoteaux**, daughter of **Pierre Descoteaux** and **Madeleine Dumille**, on 7 Jan 1835 Red River Settlement, (Manitoba) (Ibid., No. 287.). He died circa 1848 (CWLR *The Collected Writings Of Louis Riel*, 5 (University of Alberta Press, 1985), page 347.).

   Josephte Descoteaux was born in May 1805 North West (MBS Scrip Applications, Original White Settlers & Halfbreeds residing in Manitoba on 15 July 1870, RG15-19, C-14929.). She was baptized on 10 Jan 1841 St.Johns, Red River Settlement, (Manitoba) (HBCR, E.4/1a, folio 128.). She married **Pierre Larocque**, son of **Francois Larocque dit Fontaine** and **Marie Anne Therese Cadieaux**, on 24 Oct 1853 St.Francois Xavier, (Manitoba) (SFXI-Kipling St.Francois Xavier Register Index, 1834-1900; compiled by Clarence Kipling , page 533, M-21.) (SFXI 1851-1868 St.Francois Xavier 1852-1861 Register Index, M-21. Hereinafter cited as SFXI 1851-1868.). She was buried on 17 Dec 1875 St.Boniface, (Manitoba) (IBMS *Index des Baptemes, Mariages et Sepultures* (La Societe Historique de Saint-Boniface).).

   Children of **James Swain** and **Josephte Descoteaux** were as follows:

  2   i.   James Swain, b. 1822 Red River, (Manitoba); m. Marie Arcand.
  3   ii. John Swain, b. 1829 Lake Manitoba, (Manitoba); m. Elise Laverdure.
  4   iii. Robert Swain, b. 9 Feb 1834 St.Johns, Red River Settlement, (Manitoba); m. Madeleine Lunn.
     iv. Mary Swain was baptized on 9 Feb 1834 St.Johns, (Manitoba) (Denney Papers, Charles D. Denney, Glenbow Archives, Calgary, Alberta.).
     v. George Swain was baptized on 9 Feb 1834 St.Johns, Red River Settlement, (Manitoba) (HBCR, E.4/1a, folio 106d.).
  5   vi. William Swain, b. circa Jul 1834 St.Charles, (Manitoba); m. Angelique Bruyere.
  6   vii. Marguerite Swain, b. 1835 St.Charles, (Manitoba); m. Olivier Larocque.
     viii. Antoine Jordy Swan was born circa Dec 1841 (AP Records of the Assumption Roman Catholic Church, Pembina, North Dakota: Baptisms, Marriages, Sepultures, 1848-1896; compiled by Reverend Father J. M. Belleau, 2 October 1944, page 7, B-11. Hereinafter cited as AP.). He was baptized on 28 Oct 1848 Assumption, Pembina, Pembina County, Minnesota Territory (Ibid.). He married Elizabeth Desmarais, daughter of Joseph Desmarais and Adelaide Clermont, on 17 May 1859 St.Francois Xavier, (Manitoba) (SFXI-Kipling, M-68.).

         Elizabeth Desmarais was born circa 1842 (1870C-MB, #918.). She married **Baptiste Assam** before 1885 (ArchiviaNet 1886-1901, 1906 Half-Breed Scrip Applications Index, RG15-21, Volume 1333 through 1371, Microfilm Reel Number C-14944 through C-15010, National Archives of Canada, Ottawa, Ontario, http://www.collectionscanada.gc.ca, C-15009.). Question: *Vivier, Charles; #1587, Address: Lacombe; for his deceased twin sisters: Philomene, born, 1874, on the Prairie; died, 1875, Salt Lake; Helen, born, 1874, on the Prairie; died, 1890, St. Peter's Mission;; Father: Charles Vivier (Métis) > Alexis Vivier; Mother: Betsy Desmarais (Métis) > Joseph Desmarais - Adelaide, 6 Aug 1900. Disallowed. Mother's name appears in books as wife of Bte. Assam. C-15009* (Ibid.).
  7   ix. Charles Swain, b. 20 Jan 1842 St.Johns, (Manitoba); m. Catherine Thibert; d. 1920.

x.   Thomas Swain was baptized on 23 Feb 1845 St.Johns, (Manitoba) (Denney.).

Generation Two

2. James Swain was born in 1822 Red River, (Manitoba) (NWHBSI Index 1885 Scrip Applications, North-West Halfbreeds residing outside Manitoba on 15 July 1870, RG15-20, page 76.). He was baptized on 9 Feb 1834 St.Johns, Red River Settlement, (Manitoba) (HBCR, E.4/1a, folio 106d.). He was baptized on 11 Feb 1851 St.Francois Xavier, (Manitoba) (SFX: 1834-1850 St.Francois Xavier 1834-1851 Register, B-891. Hereinafter cited as SFX: 1834-1850.). He married **Marie Arcand**, daughter of **Joseph Arcand** and **Marie Vestro dit Jeannotte or Jannot,** on 13 Feb 1851 St.Francois Xavier, (Manitoba) (Ibid., M-136.) (MM *Manitoba Marriages* in *Publication 45*, Volumes 1-3, compiled and edited by: Paul J. Lareau, Fr. Julien Hamelin, (240 Avenue Daly, Ottawa, Ontario K1N 6G2: Le Centre de Genealogie S.C., 1984), page 27.).

Marie Arcand was born in 1834 St.Francois Xavier, (Manitoba) (NWHBS 1885 Scrip Applications, North-West Halfbreeds residing outside Manitoba on 15 July 1870, RG15-20, C-14936.).

Children of **James Swain** and **Marie Arcand** were as follows:

8   i.   James Swain, b. 25 Oct 1851 St.Francois Xavier, (Manitoba); m. Josephte Azure; m. Elise Desnomme; d. 7 Aug 1913.

ii.   Romuald Swan was born on 20 Jan 1854 St.Francois Xavier, (Manitoba) (SFXI-Kipling, B-142.) (SFXI 1851-1868, B-142.). He was baptized on 20 Jan 1854 St.Francois Xavier, (Manitoba) (SFXI-Kipling, B-142.) (SFXI 1851-1868, B-142.). He died on 26 Oct 1855 St.Francois Xavier, (Manitoba), at age 1 (SFXI-Kipling, S-29.). He was buried on 27 Oct 1855 St.Francois Xavier, (Manitoba) (Ibid.).

9   iii. Adelaide Swain, b. 29 Dec 1856 St.Francois Xavier, (Manitoba); m. Alexander Azure; d. 11 Feb 1875; bur. 5 May 1875 Lebret, (Saskatchewan).

iv.   Isabelle Swain was born circa 1859 (Ibid., S-7.). She died on the prairie (Ibid.). She was buried on 4 Feb 1863 St.Francois Xavier, (Manitoba) (Ibid.) (SFXI: 1851-1869 St.Francois Xavier 1851-69 Register Index.).

10   v.   Marie Rose Swain, b. 3 Feb 1862 St.Francois Xavier, (Manitoba); m. Francois Xavier Lapierre; d. 2 Jul 1948 Montana.

11   vi.   Marie Christine Swain, b. 10 Dec 1872 Fort Benton, Choteau County, Montana; m. Pierre Pontbriand Sansregret; d. 26 Jul 1936 Augusta, Lewis and Clark County, Montana; bur. 29 Jul 1936 Augusta, Lewis & Clark County, Montana.

3. John Swain was born in 1829 Lake Manitoba, (Manitoba) (MBS, C-14933.). He was baptized on 9 Feb 1834 St.Johns, Red River Settlement, (Manitoba) (HBCR, E.4/1a, folio 106d.). He was baptized on 10 Jun 1855 St.Francois Xavier, (Manitoba) (SFXI-Kipling, B-49.). He married **Elise Laverdure**, daughter of **Joseph Laverdure** and **Nancy Maskegonne**, on 17 Feb 1857 St.Francois Xavier, (Manitoba) (Ibid., M-27.).

Elise Laverdure was born in 1826 (Ancestry.com Website, Death Index.). She was born on 12 Oct 1830 North West (MBS, C-14933.). She was born circa 1832 North West Territory (1870C-MB, page 240, #435.). She died on 5 Jul 1921 Old Round House, Lewistown, Fergus County, Montana, at age 90 (Ancestry.com, Death Index.) (Al Yerbury Research.).

Children of **John Swain** and **Elise Laverdure** were as follows:

i.   Nancy Swain was born on 17 Jan 1858.

ii.   John Swain was born circa 1859 St.Charles, (Manitoba) (MBS, C-14933.).

iii. Joseph Swan was born on 10 Oct 1860 St.Francois Xavier, (Manitoba) (SFXI-Kipling, B-96.). He was baptized on 12 Oct 1860 St.Francois Xavier, (Manitoba) (Ibid.). He married Veronique Laplante, daughter of Jean Baptiste Laplante and Madeleine Desfonds or Dufont, on 23 Jan 1877 St.Francois Xavier, Manitoba (Ibid., M-3.). He died on 23 Nov 1924 Lewistown, Fergus County, Montana, at age 64 (1936-LS Henry Roe Cloud Roll 1936-1937, Pembina Band of Chippewa Indians Who Were Under the Leadership of Chief Thomas Little Shell, J. H. Dussome, Zortman, Montana and Vice-President: George SinClaire, Chinook, Montana, #37.) (1937-1987-LS Basic Roll Basic Membership Roll of the Landless Indians of Montana; 1937 Census Taken by Dr. Henry Roe Cloud; Edited c1987 to include official correspondence regarding 1937 membership; ** in Present Roll Number column indicates 1940s information added., #501.).

Veronique Laplante was born on 27 Aug 1861 St.Francois Xavier, (Manitoba) (SFXI-Kipling, B-83.). She was baptized on 28 Aug 1861 St.Francois Xavier, (Manitoba) (Ibid.). She died on 6 Apr 1939 Lewistown, Fergus County, Montana, at age 77 (Al Yerbury.). She died on 6 Apr 1939 Lewistown, Fergus County, Montana, at age 77 (Ibid.).

iv.   Helene Swain was born on 1 Sep 1862 St.Charles, (Manitoba) (SB-Rozyk St. Boniface Roman Catholic Church, Manitoba, Canada, Baptisms, Marriages and Burials 1860-1875 Extractions, Compiled by Rosemary Rozyk, page 85, B-155.). She was baptized on 2 Sep 1862 St.Boniface, (Manitoba) (Ibid.). She died on 27 Oct 1863 at age 1 (Ibid., page 131, S-38.). She was buried on 5 Nov 1863 St.Boniface, (Manitoba) (Ibid.).

v.   William Swain was born circa 1864 (Ibid., page 58, S-31.). He died on 6 Aug 1866 (Ibid.). He was buried on 9 Aug 1866 St.Boniface, (Manitoba) (Ibid.).

vi.   Marie Swain was born on 14 Mar 1865 (Ibid., page 6, B-51.). She was baptized on 15 Mar 1865 St.Boniface, (Manitoba) (Ibid.).

12   vii. Marie Anne Swain, b. 19 Mar 1867; m. Julien Campion.

viii. Amable Swain was born on 7 Mar 1869.

13   ix.   Sarah Swain, b. circa 1870; m. Francois Sauve.

4. Robert Swain was baptized on 9 Feb 1834 St.Johns, Red River Settlement, (Manitoba) (HBCR, E.4/1a, folio 106d.). He married **Madeleine Lunn** before 1849.

Children of **Robert Swain** and **Madeleine Lunn** are:

14   i.   Frederic Swain, b. 1849 St.Charles, (Manitoba); m. Marguerite Monet dit Belhumeur.

5. **William Swain** was born circa Jul 1834 St.Charles, (Manitoba) (MBS, C-14933.). He was baptized on 22 Mar 1838 St.Johns, Red River Settlement, (Manitoba) (HBCR, E.4/1a, folio 150d.). He was baptized on 13 Jun 1852 St.Francois Xavier, (Manitoba) (SFXI 1851-1868, B-22.). He married **Angelique Bruyere**, daughter of **Jean Baptiste Bruyere** and **Angelique Guilbault,** on 20 Sep 1857 St.Francois Xavier, (Manitoba) (SFXI-Kipling, M-40.).

Angelique Bruyere was born on 7 Nov 1839 (SFX: 1834-1850, B-275.). She was baptized on 10 Nov 1839 St.Francois Xavier, (Manitoba) (Ibid.).

Children of **William Swain** and **Angelique Bruyere** were as follows:

    i.   Rose Swain was born on 20 Jul 1857 (SFXI-Kipling, B-203.). She was baptized on 13 Sep 1857 St.Francois Xavier, (Manitoba) (Ibid.) (INB *Index des Naissances and Baptemes* (St.Boniface, Manitoba: La Societe Historique de Saint-Boniface., c1995), page 174.). She died on 5 Dec 1871 St.Francois Xavier, Manitoba, at age 14 (SFXI-Kipling, S-45.). She was buried on 6 Dec 1871 St.Francois Xavier, Manitoba (IBMS.) (SFXI-Kipling, S-45.).

    ii.   William Swain was born on 22 Dec 1859 St.Charles, (Manitoba) (MBS, C-14933.) (SFXI-Kipling, B-19.) (INB, page 174.). He was baptized on 24 Apr 1860 St.Francois Xavier, (Manitoba) (SFXI-Kipling, B-19.).

    iii.   Isabelle Swain was born on 31 Mar 1862 (Ibid., B-49.). She was baptized on 26 May 1862 St.Francois Xavier, (Manitoba) (Ibid.).

    iv.   Marie Isabelle Swain was born on 5 Dec 1864 Baie St.Paul, (Manitoba) (Ibid., B-27.). She was baptized on 9 May 1865 St.Francois Xavier, (Manitoba) (Ibid.). She married Jean Baptiste Boyer, son of Isidore Boyer and Marguerite Allary, on 27 Jan 1880 St.Eustache, Manitoba (MM.) (ST-BSP St.Eustache (Baie St.Paul) 1877-1900 Register, M-1. Hereinafter cited as ST-BSP.). She died on 19 Dec 1884 at age 20 (Denney.).

        Jean Baptiste Boyer was born on 17 Jan 1857 Baie St.Paul, (Manitoba) (MBS, C-14925 (b. 20 Jan 1857).) (SFXI-Kipling, B-164.). He was baptized on 1 Feb 1857 St.Francois Xavier, (Manitoba) (Ibid.).

15   v.   Julie Swain, b. circa May 1866; m. Norbert Boyer; d. 21 Mar 1893 RM Ellice, Manitoba; bur. 23 Mar 1893 St.Lazare, Fort Ellice, Manitoba.

16   vi.   Veronique Swain, b. 21 Apr 1869 St.Francois Xavier, (Manitoba); m. Cuthbert Pelletier.

    vii.   Alexander Swan was born on 4 Oct 1871 (Ibid., B-80.). He was baptized on 2 Nov 1871 St.Francois Xavier, Manitoba (Ibid.) (INB, page 173.). He died in 1876 Wood Mountain, (Saskatchewan) (ArchiviaNet, C-15005.).

    viii.   Jean Swain was born on 13 Jul 1874 Swift Current, (Saskatchewan) (L1 Lebret Mission de St.Florent Roman Catholic Registre des Baptemes, Mariages & Seplutures, Qu'Appelle, Saskatchewan, 1868-1881., page 117, B-32. Hereinafter cited as L1.) (ArchiviaNet, C-15005.). He was baptized on 1 Aug 1874 Lebret, (Saskatchewan) (L1, page 117, B-32.).

    ix.   Marie Swain was born on 24 Apr 1877 Lebret, (Saskatchewan) (Ibid., page 211, B-101.). She was baptized on 24 Apr 1877 Lebret, (Saskatchewan) (Ibid.). She married Ambroise Bone before 30 May 1900 (Rod MacQuarrie Research, 15 Mar 2007 extraction.).

    x.   Philomene Swain was born on 22 May 1880 St.Francois Xavier, Manitoba (SFXI-Kipling, B-38.).

6. **Marguerite Swain** was born circa 1832 (SFX: 1834-1850, B-895.). She was born in 1835 St.Charles, (Manitoba) (MBS, C-14932.). She was baptized on 4 Mar 1851 St.Francois Xavier, (Manitoba) (SFX: 1834-1850, B-895.). She married **Olivier Larocque**, son of **Olivier Larocque** and **Madeleine Piche,** on 4 Mar 1851 St.Francois Xavier, (Manitoba) (Ibid., M-138.).

Olivier Larocque was born circa 1830 (Ibid.). He died before 25 May 1887 (St. Claude Mission, St. John, North Dakota, Baptisms, Marriages, Burials 1882-1888, 2006, Dominique Ritchot, S_, p. 60.). He was buried on 25 May 1887 St.Claude Mission, St.John, Rolette County, North Dakota (Ibid.).

7. **Charles Swain** was baptized on 20 Jan 1842 St.Johns, (Manitoba) (Denney.). He was born in Oct 1842 St.Charles, (Manitoba) (MBS, C-14933.). He was born circa 1843 (Ibid.). He was baptized on 28 Oct 1848 Assumption, Pembina, Pembina County, Minnesota Territory (AP, page 7, B-12.). He married **Catherine Thibert**, daughter of **Pierre Thibert** and **Julie Belcourt**, on 4 Sep 1864 St.Francois Xavier, (Manitoba) (SFXI-Kipling, M-9.). He died in 1920 (Lesa (Trotchie) Zimmerman Research, 19 Jun 2001.).

Catherine Thibert was born on 24 Dec 1846 North West (MBS, C-14933.).

Children of **Charles Swain** and **Catherine Thibert** were as follows:

    i.   Charles Swan was born on 7 Mar 1866 St.Charles, (Manitoba) (SB-Rozyk, page 45, B-32.). He was baptized on 11 Mar 1866 St.Boniface, (Manitoba) (Ibid.). He married Marie Anne Deschenaux, daughter of Joseph Descheneaux and Angelique Tanner, on 25 Apr 1892 St.Peter's Mission, Cascade County, Montana (SPMT , page 52, #314.). He married Millie Plante, daughter of Francois Xavier Plante and Madeleine Fisher, on 15 Mar 1906 Fergus County, Montana (familysearch.org Website, Montana Marriages.) (Brenda Snider Research, 16 Feb 2011.). He died on 14 Jul 1908 Montana at age 42 (MT Death.).

        Marie Anne Deschenaux was born on 4 Apr 1869 (1936-LS, #434.) (1937-1987-LS Basic Roll, #434.). She was born in 1871 St.Albert, (Alberta) (ArchiviaNet, C-15005.). She married **Johnny Gariepy**, son of **Pierre Gariepy** and **Marie Rose Grant,** on 5 Jun 1903 Columbia Falls, Flathead County, Montana (FlCM Flathead County, Montana; Marriage Record Licenses and Certificates; 1865-1950; familysearch.org, Hereinafter cited as FlCM.). She married **Johnny Gariepy**, son of **Pierre Gariepy** and **Marie Rose Grant,** on 15 Feb 1914 Lewistown, Fergus County, Montana (AYM Documentation of Metis Families of Red River and the Northwest Territories; Census, Biographical, and Historical: 1881 Census Qu'Appelle, Wood Mountain, Lac la Biche; History of the Turtle Mountain Band of Chippewas; Census for the Turtle Mountain Reservation 1884-1886; Pembina, Dakota Territory 1850 Census; Various Metis Census Records for Pembina County, ND 1910; compiled by Al Yerbery, 1996, Metis Marriages of Fergus County.) (FerCM Fergus County Courthouse, Montana; Marriage Record Licenses and Certificates, 1865-1950, familysearch.org., Hereinafter cited as FerCM.). She married **John Puynish** before 1936 (1936-LS, #434.).

        Millie Plante was born in 1888 Wood Mountain, (Saskatchewan) (Brenda Snider, 16 Feb 2011.).

ii. Pierre Swain was born on 11 Apr 1868 St.Francois Xavier, (Manitoba) (SFXI-Kipling, B-25.). He was baptized on 12 Apr 1868 St.Francois Xavier, (Manitoba) (Ibid.). He died on 11 Dec 1870 St.Francois Xavier, Manitoba, at age 2 (Ibid., S-32.). He was buried on 12 Dec 1870 St.Francois Xavier, Manitoba (Ibid.).

iii. Simeon Swan was born on 21 Jul 1870 St.Francois Xavier, Manitoba (Ibid., B-58.). He was baptized on 22 Jul 1870 St.Francois Xavier, Manitoba (Ibid.).

17 iv. Francois Xavier Swain, b. 8 Feb 1873 St.Francois Xavier, Manitoba; m. Marie Vitaline Breland; d. Oct 1937.

v. Madeleine Swan was born in Mar 1874 Qu'Appelle, (Saskatchewan) (HBSI.) (ArchiviaNet.). She was baptized on 23 Mar 1875 St.Boniface, Manitoba (IBMS.). She married Alexandre Landry, son of Moise Landry and Philomene Laframboise, on 22 Jan 1893 (St.Peter's Mission), Dearborn Canyon, Montana (SPMT , page 53, #319.). She died on 10 Dec 1944 Saskatoon, Saskatchewan, at age 70 (Lesa Zimmerman, 19 Jun 2001.).

Alexandre Landry was born on 6 Jul 1869 (SFXI-Kipling, B-61.). He was baptized on 15 Jul 1869 St.Francois Xavier, (Manitoba) (Ibid.). He died on 9 Dec 1940 Big River, Saskatchewan, at age 71 (Lesa Zimmerman, 19 Jun 2001.).

vi. Octavie Swan was born in Oct 1878 on the prairie (HBSI.) (ArchiviaNet.). She married Isidore Landry, son of Moise Landry and Philomene Laframboise, on 8 Oct 1896 Augusta, Lewis & Clark, Montana (L&CCM Lewis & Clark County, Montana; Marriage Record Licenses and Certificates; 1865-1950; familysearch.org, Hereinafter cited as L&CCM.). She died on 23 Apr 1972 Hardin, Big Horn County, Montana, at age 93 (Ginger Landrie Research, 27 Apr 1994.) (Social Security Death Index, . Hereinafter cited as SSDI.).

Isidore Landry was born on 31 Jul 1875 Duck Lake, (Saskatchewan) (HBSI.) (SL-SK St.Laurent-de-Grandin Roman Catholic Registre des Baptemes, Mariages & Sepltures, St.Laurent, Saskatchewan, 1872-1896, page 42, B-37. Hereinafter cited as SL-SK.). He was baptized on 31 Jul 1875 St.Laurent-de-Grandin, (Saskatchewan) (Ibid.). He died on 27 Mar 1962 Havre, Hill County, Montana, at age 86 (Ginger Landrie Research, 27 Apr 1994.).

18 vii. Rose Swain, b. Feb 1882 Wood Mountain, (Saskatchewan); m. Anton Schafer; m. Alexis Belgarde; d. before 1938.

viii. John Swan was born circa 1883 Barker, Montana (Al Yerbury, Fergus County Marriages.). He married Pauline Charette, daughter of Jean Baptiste Charette and Marie Beauchamp, on 12 Jan 1904 Lewistown, Fergus County, Montana (Ibid.) (FerCM.).

Pauline Charette was born in Aug 1887 Lewistown, Fergus County, Montana (Al Yerbury, Fergus County Marriages.) (1900C Fergus Co, MT Twelfth Census of the United States: 1900; Montana; Fergus County.).

Generation Three

8. **James Swain** was born on 25 Oct 1851 St.Francois Xavier, (Manitoba) (SFX: 1834-1850, B-903.). He was baptized on 26 Oct 1851 St.Francois Xavier, (Manitoba) (Ibid.). He married **Josephte Azure**, daughter of **Gabriel Azure** and **Cecile Laframboise,** on 12 Feb 1872 Lebret, (Saskatchewan) (L1, page 63-64, M-16.). He married **Elise Desnomme**, daughter of **Paul Desnomme** and **Marie Therese Desmarais,** on 13 Jul 1877 (St.Peter's Mission), Milk River, Montana Territory (SPMT , page 17, #87.). He died on 7 Aug 1913 at age 61 (Rod Mac Quarrie, 22 Dec 2009.).

Josephte Azure was born circa Dec 1852 (AP, page 89, B-73.). She was baptized on 1 May 1853 Assumption, Pembina, Pembina County, Dakota Territory (Ibid., page 89, B-74.). She died in Nov 1875 Qu'Appelle, (Saskatchewan) (NWHBS, C-14936.) (L1, page 162, S-2.). She was buried on 20 Mar 1876 Lebret, (Saskatchewan) (Ibid.).

Children of **James Swain** and **Josephte Azure** were as follows:

i. William Swan was born on 8 Jun 1873 Qu'Appelle Mission, (Saskatchewan) (Ibid., page 121, B-46.). He was baptized on 5 Sep 1873 Lebret, (Saskatchewan) (Ibid.). He married Josephine Bonneau, daughter of Michel Paul dit Bonneau and Eliza Boyer, on 4 Sep 1895 St.Peter's Mission, Cascade County, Montana (SPMT , page 2, #6.).

Josephine Bonneau was born circa 1881 Milk River, Montana (HBS 1886-1901, 1906 Half-Breed Scrip Applications, RG15-21, Volume 1337, C-14952.). She married **Joseph Napoleon Parenteau**, son of **Napoleon Parenteau** and **Rosalie Dubois**, on 26 May 1904 Havre, Chouteau County, Montana (ChCM Chouteau County, Montana; Marriage Record Licenses and Certificates; 1865-1950; familysearch.org, Hereinafter cited as ChCM.).

ii. Jacques Swain was born in May 1875 (Rod Mac Quarrie, 22 Dec 2009.). He died in May 1875 (Ibid.). He was buried on 5 Jun 1875 Qu'Appelle Mission, (Saskatchewan) (Ibid.).

Elise Desnomme was born on 29 May 1860 St.Francois Xavier, (Manitoba) (SFXI-Kipling, B-45.). She was baptized on 30 May 1860 St.Francois Xavier, (Manitoba) (Ibid.).

Children of **James Swain** and **Elise Desnomme** were as follows:

i. Marie Julia Swan was born on 28 Sep 1878 St.Peter's Mission, Cascade County, Montana (SPMT , page 117, #2486.). She was baptized on 28 Sep 1878 St.Peter's Mission, Cascade County, Montana (Ibid.). She died circa Nov 1878 White Mud River (ArchiviaNet, C-15005.).

ii. Marguerite Swan was born on 10 Oct 1878 St.Peter's Mission, Cascade County, Montana. She was born circa Oct 1879 Cypress Hills, (Saskatchewan) (HBSI.) (ArchiviaNet.). She married Daniel Gervais, son of Cleophas Gervais and Eliza McGillis, on 21 Jan 1898 Augusta, Lewis & Clark, Montana (SPMT , page 6, #24.) (L&CCM.). She died in 1920 Great Falls, Cascade County, Montana (BIA-LS.).

Daniel Gervais was born on 24 May 1874 Batoche, (Saskatchewan) (HBSI.) (INB.) (SL-SK, page 30, B-18.). He was baptized on 30 May 1874 St.Laurent-de-Grandin, (Saskatchewan) (Ibid.). He died in 1924 Augusta, Lewis and Clark County, Montana.

iii. Patrick Joseph Swan was born in Jan 1881 Cypress Hills, (Saskatchewan) (ArchiviaNet, C-15005.). He was born on 5 Jan 1882 St.Peter's Mission, Cascade County, Montana (David Courchane, Courchane/Courchene Family Research.). He married Josephine Falcon, daughter of Jean Baptiste 'Che-ma-nah' Falcon and Cecelia Courchene, on 2 Feb 1904 (St.Peter's Mission), Augusta, Montana (SPMT , page 8, #30.). He married Nancy Monroe, daughter of Francis Munroe and Nancy Boucher, before 1932. He died on 30 Sep 1968 Great Falls, Cascade County, Montana, at age 86 (D. Courchane.).

Josephine Falcon was born on 28 Jun 1884 St.Peter's Mission, Cascade County, Montana (Ibid.). She died on 27 Nov 1962 Seattle, King County, Washington, at age 78 (Ibid.).

Nancy Monroe was born circa 1908 Browning, Glacier County, Montana (CaCM Cascade County, Montana; Marriage Record Licenses and Certificates; 1865-1950; familysearch.org, Hereinafter cited as CaCM.) (1910C MT Thirteenth Census of the United States: 1910; Montana, National Archives of the United States, Washington D.C., District 125, page 1B, house 25, line 74.). She married **Jean Lemire**, son of **Pierre Lemire** and **Therese Pelletier,** on 27 Nov 1927 Great Falls, Cascade County, Montana (CaCM.).

19   iv.   Frank Swain, b. 23 Jan 1884 between Turtle Mountain and Cypress Hills, Montana; m. Mary Malaterre.

      v.   Elizabeth Swan was born in 1886 (1898 Louis & Clark County, Montana School Census; Courthouse, Helena, Montana: Superintendent of Schools.). She married Louis Doisi, son of Juilian Doisi and Mary Godard, on 4 May 1908 Augusta, Lewis & Clark, Montana (L&CCM.). She married Christian Nelsen, son of Mathias Nelsen and Marie Jensen, on 30 Oct 1919 Great Falls, Cascade County, Montana (CaCM.).

         Louis Doisi was born in 1881 (L&CCM.). He died before 30 Oct 1919 (CaCM.).

         Christian Nelsen was born in 1884 Denmark (Ibid.).

20   vi.   Peter Swain, b. 13 Jan 1892 Montana; m. Mary Ann Allen; d. 14 Jan 1965 Lewis and Clark County, Montana.

      vii.   Mary Sophie Swan was born on 2 Jun 1894. She married Charles Malaterre, son of Alexis Malaterre and Marie Jeanne Hamelin, on 28 Sep 1911 Augusta, Lewis & Clark, Montana (L&CCM.). She died on 29 Feb 1976 at age 81.

         Charles Malaterre was born on 13 Feb 1890 Choteau, Montana (Ibid.). He died on 31 Dec 1931 at age 41.

     viii.   Sam Swan was born circa 1896 (1898SC L&C Co, MT.).

      ix.   Cecilia Swan was born on 27 Sep 1897 Dearborn Canyon, Montana (SPMT , page 22, #88.). She was baptized on 4 Oct 1897 (St.Peter's Mission), Dearborn Canyon, Montana (Ibid.). She married John McGlaughlin on 9 Jan 1917 Augusta, Montana (Ibid., page 22, #88 (note).).

      x.   Daniel J. Swan was born on 16 Jan 1900 (Ancestry.com, WWI Draft Registration Cards.). He married Rosie Lafromboise, daughter of Francois Laframboise Jr. and Suzanne Rocheblave, before 1924 Montana (Ibid., 1930 MT Census.). He died on 18 Sep 1943 Montana at age 43 (Ibid., MT Death Index 1907-2002.).

         Rosie Lafromboise was born on 3 Oct 1900 Glasgow, Montana (Brenda Snider, 8 Feb 2012 (obit).). She married **Charles Garfield**, son of **James Garfield** and **Gray Hair (–?–),** on 30 May 1916 Oswego, Sheridan County, Montana (ShCM.). She died on 7 May 1960 Great Falls, Montana, at age 59 (MT Death.).

      xi.   Lucille Ursula Swan was born circa 1902 Montana (Ancestry.com, 1910 Census.). She married Joseph L. Azure, son of Antoine Azure Sr. and Julienne Collin, on 31 Jul 1920 Great Falls, Cascade County, Montana (CaCM.). She married David Henry, son of John (Dutch) Henry and Louise Trottier or Bluehorn, on 3 Aug 1929 Great Falls, Cascade County, Montana (Ibid.).

         Joseph L. Azure was born on 25 Dec 1891 Fort Belknap, Blaine County, Montana (1936-LS, #54.) (1937-1987-LS Basic Roll, #54.).

         David Henry was born circa 1892 (CaCM.).

9. Adelaide Swain was born on 29 Dec 1856 St.Francois Xavier, (Manitoba) (SFXI-Kipling, B-157.). She was baptized on 29 Dec 1856 St.Francois Xavier, (Manitoba) (Ibid.). She married **Alexander Azure**, son of **Gabriel Azure** and **Cecile Laframboise**, on 26 Nov 1872 Lebret, (Saskatchewan) (L1, page 82, M-4.). She died on 11 Feb 1875 at age 18 (Ibid., page 142, S-11.). She was buried on 5 May 1875 Lebret, (Saskatchewan) (Ibid.).

Alexander Azure was born on 28 Sep 1848 Pembina, Pembina County, Minnesota Territory (AP, page 7, B-9.). He was baptized on 29 Sep 1848 Assumption, Pembina, Pembina County, Minnesota Territory (Ibid.). He married **Marie Louise Morin**, daughter of **Antoine Morin** and **Louise Tanner,** on 10 Feb 1876 Lebret, (Saskatchewan) (L1, page 179, M-11.). He died in 1931 Alboridge, North Dakota (1936-LS, #8.).

10. Marie Rose Swain was born on 3 Feb 1862 St.Francois Xavier, (Manitoba) (SFXI-Kipling, B-12.). She was baptized on 7 Feb 1862 St.Francois Xavier, (Manitoba) (Ibid.). She married **Francois Xavier Lapierre**, son of **Antoine Lapierre** and **Catherine Gagnon,** on 25 Mar 1879 St.Peter's Mission, Montana Territory (SPMT , page 21, #107.). She died on 2 Jul 1948 Montana at age 86 (MT Death.).

Francois Xavier Lapierre was born on 19 Mar 1850 Pembina County, Minnesota Territory (AP-Reg Assumption Parish Register, Pembina, North Dakota, page 47, B-101. Hereinafter cited as Assumption Register.). He was baptized on 29 May 1850 Assumption, Pembina, Pembina County, Minnesota Territory (Ibid.). He married **Emma Hays** on 25 Sep 1871 Lewis & Clark County, Montana (L&CCM.). He died on 18 Jun 1928 Cascade County, Montana, at age 78 (MT Death.).

11. Marie Christine Swain was born on 10 Dec 1872 Fort Benton, Choteau County, Montana (L1, page 85, B-48.) (1937-1987-LS Basic Roll.). She was baptized on 14 Feb 1873 Lebret, (Saskatchewan) (L1, page 85, B-48.). She married **Pierre Pontbriand Sansregret,** son of **Pierre Sansregret dit Beaubrillant** and **Caroline Parenteau,** on 14 Oct 1889 St.Peter's Mission, Cascade County, Montana (SPMT , page 51, #308.) (familysearch.org, Montana Marriages.). She died on 26 Jul 1936 Augusta, Lewis and Clark County, Montana, at age 63 (Rod Mac Quarrie, 22 Dec 2009.). She was buried on 29 Jul 1936 Augusta, Lewis & Clark County, Montana (Ibid.).

Pierre Pontbriand Sansregret was born on 15 Mar 1867 Saskatoon, (Saskatchewan) (SFXI: 1834-1852 St.Francois Xavier 1834-1852 Register Index, B-37. Hereinafter cited as SFXI: 1835-1852.). He was baptized on 15 Mar 1867 St.Francois Xavier, (Manitoba) (Ibid.). He died on 11 Oct 1932 Augusta, Lewis and Clark County, Montana, at age 65 (Rod Mac Quarrie, 22 Dec 2009.) (MT Death.).

12. Marie Anne Swain was born on 19 Mar 1867 (SB-Rozyk, page 83, B-27.). She was baptized on 24 Mar 1867 St.Boniface, (Manitoba) (Ibid.). She married **Julien Campion**, son of **William Sapen dit Campion** and **Philomene Chalifoux,** on 17 Jan 1882 St.Peter's Mission, Cascade County, Montana Territory (SPMT , page 31, #170.).

Julien Campion was born on 13 Jun 1861 Lac Ste.Anne, (Alberta) (NWHBS, C-14937.) (Automated Genealogy 1901 Census Transcription Project and Census Images from the National Archives of Canada, http://www.automatedgenealogy.com, #202, g(2), page 7-8, family 74, line 49-50, 1-3.).

13. Sarah Swain was born circa 1870. She married **Francois Sauve**, son of **Norbert Sauve** and **Josephte St.Pierre**, on 26 Nov 1888 St.Peter's Mission, Montana (SPMT , page 49, #297.).

Francois Sauve was born on 21 Oct 1864 St.Boniface, (Manitoba) (NWHBS, C-14941.) (SFXI-Kipling, B-60.). He was baptized on 11 Nov 1864 St.Francois Xavier, (Manitoba) (Ibid.).

14. Frederic Swain was born in 1849 St.Charles, (Manitoba) (MBS, C-14933.). He married **Marguerite Monet dit Belhumeur**, daughter of **Michel Monet dit Belhumeur** and **Louise Gonneville**, on 10 Jun 1872 St.Francois Xavier, Manitoba (SFXI-Kipling, M-5.).

Marguerite Monet dit Belhumeur was born on 3 Oct 1848 St.Francois Xavier, (Manitoba) (SFX: 1834-1850, B-752.). She was baptized on 7 Oct 1848 St.Francois Xavier, (Manitoba) (Ibid.).

Children of **Frederic Swain** and **Marguerite Monet dit Belhumeur** were as follows:

   i. Domitilde Swan was born on 23 Jul 1873 St.Francois Xavier, Manitoba (SFXI-Kipling, B-49.). She was baptized on 27 Jul 1873 St.Francois Xavier, Manitoba (Ibid.) (INB, page 173.).

   ii. Marie Madeleine Swain was baptized on 11 Nov 1875 St.Eustache, Manitoba (IBMS.).

21   iii. Norman Swain, b. circa 1877; m. Marguerite (--?--).

   iv. Marguerite Swan was born on 26 Jul 1881 St.Francois Xavier, Manitoba (SFXI-Kipling, B-49.).

   v. Caroline Swan was born on 28 Apr 1884 Rolette County, North Dakota (St.Claude BMD, Dominique Ritchot, page 32, B-133.). She was baptized on 24 May 1884 St.Claude, St.John, Rolette County, North Dakota (Ibid.).

   vi. Charles Swan was born circa 1885 (1889-TMC-off, #539.).

22   vii. Patrice Swain, b. 27 Jun 1886 St.John, Rolette County, North Dakota; m. Agnes Gourneau; d. 6 Dec 1960 Rolette County, North Dakota.

   viii. Augustin Swain was born on 28 Apr 1889 St.John, Rolette County, North Dakota (ND Death Index.). He married Dora Gwin in 1928 Belcourt, Rolette County, North Dakota. He married Veronica Azure, daughter of Moise Azure and Marguerite Campion, on 14 Sep 1939 (BIA-TM Bureau of Indian Affairs, Turtle Mountain Enrollment and Probate Papers, Belcourt, North Dakota.). He died on 31 Mar 1982 Rolla, Rolette County, North Dakota, at age 92 (ND Death Index.). He was buried on 3 Apr 1982 St.Ann, Belcourt, Rolette County, North Dakota.

   Dora Gwin died in 1928.

   Veronica Azure was born on 14 Sep 1901 Rolette County, North Dakota (BIA-TM.). She died on 10 Jan 1981 Wolf Point, Roosevelt County, Montana, at age 79 (Ibid.). She was buried on 15 Jan 1981 St.Ann, Belcourt, Rolette County, North Dakota (Ibid.).

   ix. John Swain was born on 28 Apr 1889 St.John, Rolette County, North Dakota (1889-TMC-off, #542.).

15. Julie Swain was born circa May 1866 (SFXI-Kipling, B-109.). She was baptized on 28 Aug 1866 St.Francois Xavier, (Manitoba) (Ibid.). She married **Norbert Boyer**, son of **Joseph Boyer** and **Felicite Patenaude**, on 13 Apr 1884 Strathclair, Manitoba (Manitoba Vital Statistics online, http://web2.gov.mb.ca, Marriage Reg. #1884,001879.). She died on 21 Mar 1893 RM Ellice, Manitoba (HBS, Volume 1337, C-14952.) (MB Vital Statistics, Death Reg. #1896,002346.). She was buried on 23 Mar 1893 St.Lazare, Fort Ellice, Manitoba (HBS, Volume 1337, C-14952.).

Norbert Boyer was born on 31 Jan 1862 Indian Head (NWHBS, C-14936.). He was baptized on 22 May 1862 St.Francois Xavier, (Manitoba) (SFXI-Kipling, B-52.). He married **Elise Vivier**, daughter of **Michel Vivier** and **Elise Deschamps**, on 16 Jan 1921 St.Lazare, Fort Ellice, Manitoba (Denney.). He died on 17 Nov 1932 Ellice, Manitoba, at age 70 (MB Vital Statistics, Death Reg. #1932,044296.).

16. Veronique Swain was born on 21 Apr 1869 St.Francois Xavier, (Manitoba) (SFXI-Kipling, B-38.). She was baptized on 23 Apr 1869 St.Francois Xavier, (Manitoba) (Ibid.). She married **Cuthbert Pelletier**, son of **Jean Baptiste Pelletier** and **Madeleine Deschamps**, in 1888 (1900C-ND, House 293, page 306B.) (Michael K. Keplin Research, 22 March 2006.).

Cuthbert Pelletier was born in Jul 1864 (LLBR1 Notre Dame des Tidoren, St.Paul Diocese, Lac La Biche, Registre des Baptemes, Mariages & Sepltures, Volume 1, 1853-1898., page 59, B-314. Hereinafter cited as LLBR1.). He was baptized on 20 Sep 1864 Lac la Biche, (Alberta) (Ibid.).

17. Francois Xavier Swain was born on 8 Feb 1873 St.Francois Xavier, Manitoba (SFXI-Kipling, B-10.). He was baptized on 10 Feb 1873 St.Francois Xavier, Manitoba (Ibid.) (INB, page 173.). He married **Marie Vitaline Breland**, daughter of **Josue Breland** and **Marie Flavie Dauphinais**, on 22 Jan 1893 St.Peter's Mission, Cascade County, Montana (SPMT , page 52, #318.). He died in Oct 1937 at age 64 (Denney.).

Marie Vitaline Breland was born on 24 Apr 1876 St.Francois Xavier, Manitoba (SFXI-Kipling, B-16.) (MB Vital Statistics, Birth Reg. #1876,1535654 (10/02/1944).). She was baptized 25 Apr 1876 St.Francois Xavier, Manitoba (SFXI-Kipling, B-16.) (Rosemary Rozyk.). She died in Oct 1945 at age 69 (Denney.). She was buried in Oct 1945 Piapot (Ibid.).

Children of **Francois Xavier Swain** and **Marie Vitaline Breland** were as follows:

   i. Edward Swain.

   ii. Florence Swain.

   iii. Margaret Swain.

   iv. Peter Swain was born on 17 Feb 1894 (1901 Canada, District 204-n, page 1, family 7, line 12-17.).

   v. Frank Swain was born on 11 May 1896 (Ibid.).

   vi. Mary Victoria Anna Swain was born on 17 Apr 1898 (Saskatchewan) (Saskatchewan Vital Statistics online, http://vsgs.health.gov.sk.ca, #1333.).

   vii. George Peter Swain was born on 3 Sep 1900 (Saskatchewan) (Ibid., #2449.).

   viii. Marie Anne Suzanne Swain was born on 1 Aug 1902 (Saskatchewan) (Ibid., #2332.).

18. Rose Swain was born in Feb 1882 Wood Mountain, (Saskatchewan) (Denney.). She married **Anton Schafer**, son of **George Schafer** and **Paulina Sommer**, on 8 May 1901 Fort Benton, Chouteau County, Montana (ChCM.). She married **Alexis Belgarde**, son of **Gilbert Belgarde** and **Sophia Descoteaux**, before 1903 (1921 Turtle Mountain Chippewa Indian Census Roll, United States Indian Service Department of the Interior, Turtle Mountain Indian Agency, North Dakota, 30 June 1921 , Census No. 439-451.). She died before 1938 (1936-TMC, page 32.).

Anton Schafer was born circa 1862 Germany (ChCM.).

Alexis Belgarde was born on 13 Apr 1873 Grand Forks, North Dakota (L1, page 122, B-53.) (Turtle Mountain Star, Rolla, North Dakota, 3 Mar 1938.). He was baptized on 19 Sep 1873 Lebret, (Saskatchewan) (L1, page 122, B-53.). He died on 24 Feb 1938 Rolette County, North Dakota, at age 64 (ND Death Index.) (TM Star, 3 Mar 1938.). He was buried on 28 Feb 1938 St.Ann's, Belcourt, Rolette, North Dakota (Ibid.).

Generation Four

19. Frank Swain was born on 23 Jan 1884 between Turtle Mountain and Cypress Hills, Montana (1898SC L&C Co, MT.) (Ancestry.com, 1930 MT Census.) (Ibid., WWI Draft Registration Cards.) (ArchiviaNet, C-15005.). He married **Mary Malaterre**, daughter of **Alexis Malaterre** and **Marie Jeanne Hamelin**, on 21 Jan 1908 Augusta, Lewis & Clark, Montana (L&CCM.).

Mary Malaterre was born circa 1889 Chouteau County, Montana (Ibid.). She was born circa 1894 (1910C MT, page 5B.).

Children of **Frank Swain** and **Mary Malaterre** were as follows:

   i.   Florence Swan was born in 1913 Montana (Ancestry.com, 1930 MT Census.). She married Crispin Mango on 16 Feb 1929 Great Falls, Cascade County, Montana (CaCM.).
        Crispin Mango was born in 1906 Mexico (Ibid.).

   ii. Frances Charles Swan was born circa 1917 Montana (Ancestry.com, 1930 MT Census.). He died on 29 Aug 1932 Montana (MT Death.).

   iii. Josephine Swan was born on 23 Aug 1918 Augusta, Lewis and Clark County, Montana (1936-LS, #947.). She married Joseph Stanley, son of Jim Stanley and Mary Four Blanket, on 17 Feb 1934 Hill County, Montana (HCM Hill County, Montana; Marriage Record Licenses and Certificates; 1865-1950; familysearch.org, Hereinafter cited as HCM.). She died in Nov 1994 Great Falls, Cascade County, Montana, at age 76 (SSDI.).
        Joseph Stanley was born on 16 Jul 1908 Ronan, Montana (Ibid.). He died in Mar 1988 Havre, Hill County, Montana, at age 79 (Ibid.).

   iv. Margaret Swan was born circa 1922 Montana (Ancestry.com, 1920 MT Census.).

20. Peter Swain was born on 13 Jan 1892 Montana (1898SC L&C Co, MT.) (Ancestry.com, 1930 MT Census.) (Ibid., Death Index.) (Ibid., WWI Draft Registration Cards.). He married **Mary Ann Allen**, daughter of **Alexander Allan** and **Virginie "Jenny" Desnoyers dit Denny,** on 29 Apr 1922 Augusta, Lewis & Clark County, Montana (L&CCM.). He died on 14 Jan 1965 Lewis and Clark County, Montana, at age 73 (Ancestry.com, Death Index.).

Mary Ann Allen was born circa 1902 Butte, Silver Bow County, Montana (L&CCM.) (1930C MT.).

Children of **Peter Swain** and **Mary Ann Allen** were as follows:

   i.   Rose Mary Swan was born on 22 Apr 1920 Montana (SSDI.). She married Marvin J. Lapierre, son of John Rommell Lapierre and Mary Azure, on 27 Apr 1936 Great Falls, Cascade County, Montana (CaCM.). She married Clifford C. Mills, son of C. J. Mills and Anna Vennetta, on 11 Jan 1946 Great Falls, Cascade County, Montana (Ibid.). She died on 9 Mar 1997 Helena, Lewis & Clark County, Montana, at age 76 (MT Death.) (SSDI.).
        Marvin J. Lapierre was born on 27 Apr 1915 Augusta, Montana (Marriage Certificate.). He married **Caroline Rose Gladu**, daughter of **Philippe Gladu** and **Rosalie Gourneau,** on 12 Jan 1946 Great Falls, Cascade County, Montana (Brenda Snider, 25 May 2011.) (CaCM.). He died on 5 Jun 1976 Cascade County, Montana, at age 61 (MT Death.).
        Clifford C. Mills was born on 12 Jan 1918 (CaCM.) (SSDI.). He married **Elizabeth M. Ohmen**, daughter of **Elmer Ohmen** and **Bertha Miller,** on 19 Jun 1944 Conrad, Pondera County, Montana (PonCM Pondera County Courthouse, Montana; Marriage Record Licenses and Certificates; 1865-1950, familysearch.org, Hereinafter cited as PonCM.). He died on 5 Apr 2001 Helena, Lewis & Clark County, Montana, at age 83 (SSDI.).

   ii. Arthur Swan was born on 7 Aug 1921 Augusta, Lewis & Clark County, Montana (HCM.). He married Stella Parisian, daughter of Joseph Damase Parisien and Clara Gardipee, on 17 May 1945 Hill County, Montana (Ibid.). He and Stella Parisian obtained a marriage license on 17 May 1945 Hill County, Montana (Ibid.). He died on 31 Jul 1995 Lewis & Clark County, Montana, at age 73 (MT Death.).
        Stella Parisian was born on 31 Aug 1927 Lebret, Saskatchewan (HCM.). She married **Fred Hammons**, son of **Hedge Hammons** and **Anna Nelson,** on 9 Feb 1948 Hill County, Montana (Ibid.). She married **Franklin Flanagan** circa 1972 (Brenda Snider, 16 Dec 2014.). She died on 15 Nov 2011 Columbia Falls, Flathead County, Montana, at age 84 (Ibid.).

   iii. James Swan was born circa 1925 Montana (Ancestry.com, 1930 MT Census.).

21. Norman Swain was born circa 1877 (1889-TMC-off, #537.). He married **Marguerite (--?--)** before 1903 (1910C ND, District 153, page 12B, family 102.).

Marguerite (--?--) was born circa 1875 (Ibid.).

Children of **Norman Swain** and **Marguerite (--?--)** both born North Dakota are as follows:

   i.   Bernice Swain was born circa 1903 (Ibid.).

   ii. Lawrence Swain was born circa 1908 (Ibid.).

22. Patrice Swain was born on 27 Jun 1886 St.John, Rolette County, North Dakota (St.Claude BMD, Dominique Ritchot, B-270, page 56.). He was baptized on 30 Jun 1886 St.Claude Mission, St.John, Rolette County, North Dakota (Ibid.). He married **Agnes Gourneau**, daughter of **Louis Gourneau** and **Elise Marion,** before 1912. He died on 6 Dec 1960 Rolette County, North Dakota, at age 74 (ND Death Index.).

Agnes Gourneau was born on 23 Apr 1894 (1936-TMC, page 116.) (1923-TMC-ND 1923 Census of the Chippewa Indians of Turtle Mountain Agency, North Dakota, United States Indian Service Department of the Interior, Belcourt, North Dakota, superintendent H. J. McQuigg, 30 June 1923 , #3492-3497.).

Children of **Patrice Swain** and **Agnes Gourneau** were as follows:

   i.   Fred Swain was born on 3 Feb 1912 (1936-TMC, page 116.) (*1923-TMC-ND*, #3492-3497.). He married Ernestine Langer, daughter of Francois Langer and St.Ann Decouteau, before 1934. He died on 1 May 1958 Rolette County, North Dakota, at age 46 (ND Death Index.).

Ernestine Langer was born on 15 Aug 1916 (1936-TMC, page 144.) (ND Death Index.). She died on 27 Aug 1941 Rolette County, North Dakota, at age 25 (Ibid.).

ii. George Swain was born on 19 Feb 1914 (1936-TMC, page 116.) (*1923-TMC-ND*, #3492-3497.). He married Mary Rosine Frederick, daughter of Joseph Frederick Jr. and Rosalie Ladouceur, before 1936 (*1937-TMC*, page 483, Census No. 5645-5647.).

Mary Rosine Frederick was born on 12 Apr 1914 Rolette County, North Dakota (1936-TMC, page 94.) (1934-TMC Census of the Turtle Mountain Chippewa Indians, United States Indian Service Department of the Interior, Turtle Mountain Agency, North Dakota, 1 Apr 1934 , page 173, Census No. 2060-2063.). She married **James Edward Desjarlais**, son of **Patrice Desjarlais** and **Jessie Martin**, before 1939 Rolette County, North Dakota (1940C ND 1940 North Dakota, Sixteenth Census of the United States, National Archives of the United States, Washington, D.C., page 8A.).

iii. Eliza Swain was born on 11 Jun 1915 Rolette County, North Dakota (*1937-TMC*, page 25, Census No. 264-268.). She was born on 11 Jun 1917 Rolette County, North Dakota (*1923-TMC-ND*, #3492-3497.). She married John M. Azure, son of John Baptiste Azure No. 1 and Theresa (--?--), before 1934 Turtle Mountain Reservation, Rolette County, North Dakota (*1937-TMC*, page 25, Census No. 264-268.).

John M. Azure was born on 26 Jan 1909 Rolette County, North Dakota (BIA-TM.) (1919 Turtle Mountain Indian Census Roll, United States Indian Service Department of the Interior, Turtle Mountain Indian Agency, North Dakota, 30 June 1919 , #331-336.).

iv. Roderick Swain was born on 1 Jun 1918 (*1923-TMC-ND*, #3492-3497.).

v. Marie Z. V. Swain was born on 7 Sep 1920 (Ibid.).

Descendants of James Tait
Generation One

1. James Tait was born circa 1758 Stromness, Orphir, Orkney, Scotland (Denney Papers, Charles D. Denney, Glenbow Archives, Calgary, Alberta.) (HBCA-B Hudson's Bay Company Archives - biographical sketches, Hudson's Bay Company Archives; Winnipeg, Manitoba.). He married **Catherine Metisse** before 1792. He died on 2 Jan 1834 Stromness (Ibid., A.36/13, fos. 7-10.).

Children of **James Tait** and **Catherine Metisse** were as follows:

2 i. William Tait, b. 1792 Ruperts Land; m. Mary Bear (Cree); d. 12 Mar 1878 St.Ann, Poplar Point, Manitoba.

ii. Jane Tate was born circa 1795 (Denney.). She was baptized on 26 Nov 1820 St.Johns, Red River Settlement, (Manitoba) (HBCR Hudson Bay Company Register of Anglican Church Baptisms, Marriages, and Burials for the Red River Settlement, 1821-1841; Hudson's Bay Company Archives, Winnipeg, Manitoba, E.4/1a, folio 28. Hereinafter cited as HBCR.). She married according to the custom of the country John Spence, son of Magnus Spence and Christiana Cree, before 1815. She married John Spence, son of Magnus Spence and Christiana Cree, on 27 Nov 1820 (Fort Douglas), St.Johns, (Manitoba) (Ibid., M-4.).

John Spence was born circa 7 Apr 1793 Ruperts Land (Denney.). He was baptized on 20 Nov 1820 St.Johns, Red River Colony, (Manitoba) (Ibid.) (HBCR, E.4/1a, folio 28.). He married **Charlotte Whitford (Indian)** on 11 Sep 1848 (St.Andrews), The Rapids, Red River Settlement, (Manitoba) (Ibid., No. 172.). He was buried on 6 Dec 1869 St.Mary's Anglican Church, Portage la Prairie, (Manitoba) (SMACPLP St.Marys Anglican Church, Portage La Prairie, Manitoba, Baptisms, Marriages, Burials, 1855-1883, transcribed by Clarence Kipling , page 10, S-76.).

iii. James Tait was born circa 1810 (Denney.). He was baptized on 26 Nov 1820 St.Johns, Red River Settlement, (Manitoba) (HBCR, E.4/1a, folio 28.). He married Mary Lambert, daughter of Michel Lambert and Margaret 'Peggy' Favel, on 21 Feb 1837 Red River Settlement, (Manitoba) (Ibid., No. 338.).

Mary Lambert was born on 1 Mar 1822 North West (MBS Scrip Applications, Original White Settlers & Halfbreeds residing in Manitoba on 15 July 1870, RG15-19, C-14933.).

iv. Margaret Tate was born circa 1816. She married William Bear, son of White (Indian) Bear, on 3 Dec 1835 St.Johns, Red River Settlement, (Manitoba) (HBCR, No. 4.).

William Bear was born in 1810 North West (HBS 1886-1901, 1906 Half-Breed Scrip Applications, RG15-21, Volume 1335; C-14947.). He was baptized on 5 May 1833 St.Johns, Red River Settlement, (Manitoba) (HBCR, E.4/1a, folio 100.). He died in 1875 (HBS, Volume 1335; C-14947.).

Generation Two

2. William Tait was born in 1792 Ruperts Land (1828C RRS HBCA E5/2 1828 Census of the Red River Settlement, HBCA E5/2, Hudson's Bay Company Archives, Provincial Archives, 200 Vaughan Street, Winnipeg, MB R3C 1T5, Canada., page 2.) (1870C-MB 1870 Manitoba Census, National Archives of Canada, Ottawa, Ontario, Microfilm Reel Number C-2170., page 361, #1097.). He married **Mary Bear (Cree)** on 13 Feb 1829 St.Johns, (Manitoba) (*LHBCM List of Hudson Bay Company Marriages*; 139 Cook Street; Victoria, B.C.; V8V 3W8: Edited by Joanne J. Hughes, 1977.). He died on 12 Mar 1878 St.Ann, Poplar Point, Manitoba (Denney.). Question: *Marriage No. 154-177 in 1828-1829 are not found in the HBCA records.*

Children of **William Tait** and **Mary Bear (Cree)** were as follows:

3 i. Marie Tait, b. circa 1820 (Manitoba); m. Henry McCorrister; d. 22 Feb 1905 Little Britain, Manitoba.

ii. William Tate was born circa 1827 (Ibid.). He was baptized in Jan 1829 St.Johns, (Manitoba) (Ibid.). He married Catherine Cummings, daughter of Robert Cummings and Clementine Harper, on 15 Jan 1851 (Ibid.). He died before 15 Jul 1870.

Catherine Cummings was born on 19 Apr 1835 Behering River, North West (MBS, C-14932.). She was baptized on 17 Aug 1838 St.Johns, Berens River House, (Manitoba) (HBCR, E.4/1a, folio 153.). She married **Thomas Peebles**, son of **William Peebles** and **Nancy Indian**, before 15 Jul 1870.

4 iii. Philip Tait or Tate, b. 9 Oct 1827 Point Douglas; m. Mary Monkman; m. Eliza Steinhauer; m. Ann Fraser.

5 iv. Matilda Tait or Tate, b. circa 1829 St.Johns, (Manitoba); m. James Irwin; d. 1861.

6 v. John Tait or Tate, b. 23 Jul 1829; m. Catherine Cook; d. 3 Mar 1907 Portage la Prairie, Manitoba.

 vi. Robert Tate was baptized on 12 May 1830 St.Johns, (Manitoba) (Ibid., #174.).

7 vii. James Tait or Tate, b. 10 Jul 1831 St.Johns, Red River Settlement, (Manitoba); m. Margaret Paquin dit Pocha.

 viii. George Tate was baptized on 31 Mar 1833 St.Johns, Red River Settlement, (Manitoba) (Ibid., E.4/1a, folio 98.).

 ix. Peter Tate was baptized on 5 Mar 1835 St.Johns, Red River Settlement, (Manitoba) (Ibid., E.4/1a, folio 119.). He died on 27 Sep 1843 St.Johns, (Manitoba), at age 8 (Denney.).

 x. Magnus Tait was born on 6 Mar 1835 St.Johns, Red River Settlement, (Manitoba) (HBCR, E.4/1a, folio 119.).

 xi. Thomas Tate was baptized on 18 Dec 1835 St.Johns, Red River Settlement, (Manitoba) (Ibid., E.4/1a, folio 126.). He was buried on 29 Aug 1837 St.Johns, Red River Settlement, (Manitoba) (Ibid., Burial No. 220.).

8 xii. David Tait, b. circa 1837 Red River, (Manitoba); m. Elisabeth Jane Knight; d. 6 Feb 1873 Poplar Point, Manitoba.

 xiii. Joseph Tate was baptized on 12 Mar 1837 St.Johns, Red River Settlement, (Manitoba) (Ibid., E.4/1a, folio 139.).

9 xiv. Andrew Tait or Tate, b. 16 Jun 1839 St.Johns, Red River Settlement, (Manitoba); m. Elizabeth Anderson.

 xv. Charles Tate was born on 3 Jan 1841 (Denney.). He was baptized on 24 Jan 1841 St.Johns, Red River Settlement, (Manitoba) (HBCR, E.4/1a, folio 169d.).

 xvi. Frederick Tate was baptized on 14 Mar 1841 St.Johns, Red River Settlement, (Manitoba) (Ibid., E.4/1a, folio 170.).

 xvii. Mary Tait was baptized on 7 Aug 1842 St.Johns, (Manitoba) (Denney.).

 xviii. Jane Mary Tait was born on 8 Jan 1843 Point Douglas, (Manitoba) (Ibid.). She was baptized on 21 Apr 1844 St.Johns, (Manitoba) (Ibid.). She married John Whitford, son of Peter Whitford and Christiana Spence, in 1867 Fort Victoria, (Alberta) (NWHBS 1885 Scrip Applications, North-West Halfbreeds residing outside Manitoba on 15 July 1870, RG15-20, C-14942.).

  John Whitford was born in 1846 St.Andrews, (Manitoba) (Ibid.). He was baptized on 23 Aug 1846 St.Johns, (Manitoba) (HBCA-B, E.4/2, fo. 45.).

 xix. Elizabeth Tait was born in 1846 (Manitoba) (1870C-MB, page 113, #416.).

 xx. Ann Tait was born circa 1851 (Manitoba) (Ibid., page 114, #417.).

Generation Three

3. **Marie Tait** was born circa 1820 (Manitoba) (Ibid., page 178, #62.). She married **Henry McCorrister**, son of **Alexander McCorrister** and **Catherine Jones,** on 30 Nov 1843 (St.Johns), Upper Church, Red River Settlement, (Manitoba) (HBCR, No. _.). She died on 22 Feb 1905 Little Britain, Manitoba (Denney.).

Henry McCorrister was born in 1820 (Manitoba) (1870C-MB, page 178, #61.). He was baptized on 25 Sep 1827 (St.Andrews), Rapids of Red River, (Manitoba) (HBCR, E.4/1a, folio 66, #678.). He died circa 29 Jun 1879 St.Clements, Manitoba (Denney.).

4. **Philip Tait or Tate** was born on 9 Oct 1827 Point Douglas (NWHBS, C-14941.) (Automated Genealogy 1901 Census Transcription Project and Census Images from the National Archives of Canada, http://www.automatedgenealogy.com, #202 (n-1), page 23, family 219, line 23-26.). He married **Mary Monkman**, daughter of **James Monkman** and **Nancy Chaboyer**, on 7 Jun 1852 St.Johns, (Manitoba) (Denney.). He married **Eliza Steinhauer**, daughter of **Henry (Indian) Steinhauer** and **(--?--) Budd**, before 1869 (ArchiviaNet, C-15005.). He married **Ann Fraser**, daughter of **Colin Fraser** and **Nancy Gaudry**, in 1871 Edmonton, (Alberta) (NWHBS, C-14938.).

Mary Monkman was born circa 1832 (Denney.). She was baptized on 13 Apr 1835 St.Johns, Red River Settlement, (Manitoba) (HBCR, E.4/1a, folio 119d.). She died in 1865 Victoria, Alberta (Denney.).

Children of **Philip Tait or Tate** and **Mary Monkman** were as follows:

 i. Jane Mary Tate was born in 1854 Manitoba House (ArchiviaNet, C-15005.). She died in 1870 St.Cloud, Minnesota (Ibid.).

 ii. Charlotte Tate was born on 23 Dec 1856 Carlton, (Saskatchewan) (NWHBS, C-14941.). She died on 3 Mar 1875 Carlton, (Saskatchewan), at age 18 (Ibid.).

 iii. Eliza Tate was born on 10 Apr 1858 Carlton, (Saskatchewan) (Ibid., C-14942.). She married William McKay, son of William McKay and Mary Cook, on 3 Jan 1877 Asissipi Mission, Prince Albert, (Saskatchewan) (Denney.). She died on 9 Dec 1877 St.Marys, Prince Albert, (Saskatchewan), at age 19 (NWHBS, C-14942.).

  William McKay was born on 7 Sep 1852 (NWHBSI, page 55.). He was born on 17 Sep 1853 (1901 Canada, #250, u(1), page 13-14, family 101, line 49-49, 1-2.). He married **Maria Rowland**, daughter of **William Rowland** and **Betsy Ballendine**, on 8 Jan 1880 Battleford, (Saskatchewan). He died on 29 Aug 1932 Prince Albert, Saskatchewan, at age 79.

10 iv. Albert Tait or Tate, b. 29 Dec 1860 Carlton, (Saskatchewan); m. Sarah Garson.

 v. Charles Richard Tate was born on 7 Sep 1864 Victoria, (Alberta) (NWHBS, C-14941.) (SB-Rozyk St. Boniface Roman Catholic Church, Manitoba, Canada, Baptisms, Marriages and Burials 1860-1875 Extractions, Compiled by Rosemary Rozyk, page 178, B-22.). He was baptized on 21 Jan 1865 (Stony Lake), St.Boniface, (Manitoba) (Ibid.). He died circa Sep 1870 Victoria, (Alberta) (NWHBS, C-14941.).

Eliza Steinhauer was born in 1847 White Fish Lake, (Alberta) (ArchiviaNet, C-15005.). She died in 1869 Victoria, (Alberta) (Ibid.).

Ann Fraser was born on 9 Aug 1839 Jaspar House, (Alberta) (NWHBS, C-14938.) (1901 Canada, #202 (n-1), page 23, family 219, line 23-26.). She was baptized on 16 Apr 1846 Fort-des-Prairies (INB *Index des Naissances and Baptemes* (St.Boniface, Manitoba: La Societe Historique de Saint-Boniface., c1995), page 65.).

Children of **Philip Tait or Tate** and **Ann Fraser** were as follows:

 i. Anne Louisa Tate was born on 2 Aug 1872 Victoria, (Alberta) (ArchiviaNet, C-15005.). She married Alexander Monkman, son of Henry Monkman and Nancy Whitford, on 15 Jul 1900 Edmonton, (Alberta) (Denney.). She died in May 1939 at age 66 (Ibid.).

  Alexander Monkman was born on 29 Mar 1870 Manitoba House (HBSI.) (ArchiviaNet.). He was baptized on 15 May 1870 St.Mary's Anglican Church, Portage la Prairie, (Manitoba) (SMACPLP, page 43, B-341.). He died in 1941 (Denney.).

ii. Robert Edward Tate was born in 1874 Carlton, (Saskatchewan) (ArchiviaNet, C-15005.). He died in 1885 Edmonton, (Alberta) (Ibid.).

iii. George Tate was born on 18 Apr 1876 Fort Carlton, (Saskatchewan) (Ibid.).

iv. William Collin Tate was born in 1877 Carlton, (Saskatchewan) (Ibid.). He died in 1885 Edmonton, (Alberta) (Ibid.).

v. Henry Tate was born in 1880 Victoria, (Alberta) (Ibid.). He died in 1885 Edmonton, (Alberta) (Ibid.).

vi. Elise Jane Tate was born in 1884 Victoria, (Alberta) (Ibid.). She died in 1885 Edmonton, (Alberta) (Ibid.).

5. **Matilda Tait or Tate** was born circa 1829 St.Johns, (Manitoba) (Denney.). She married **James Irwin**, son of **James Irwine**, on 13 Nov 1848 (St.Johns), Upper Church, Red River Settlement, (Manitoba) (HBCR, No. 418.). She died in 1861 (MBS, C-14928.).

James Irwin was born circa 1817 England (1870C-MB, page 104, #100.). He was born in 1822 (HBCA-B.). He married **Nancy Johnston**, daughter of **Donald Johnston** and **Nancy Daniel**, in 1864 (MBS, C-14929.) (1870C-MB, page 186, #297.). He died on 24 Dec 1903 St.James, Manitoba (St.James Anglican Cemetery; Cemetery Transcription #121; Mavis and Maureen Smith, Unit "E," 1045 St.James Street, Winnipeg, Manitoba, Canada R3H 1B1: Manitoba Genealogical Society, Inc., 1983, page 86.).

6. **John Tait or Tate** was born on 23 Jul 1829 (1901 Canada, Family 24, Line 4-6.). He was baptized on 5 Aug 1829 St.Johns, Red River Settlement, (Manitoba) (HBCR, E.4/1a, folio 71.). He married **Catherine Cook**, daughter of **Joseph Cook** and **Catherine Sinclair**, on 18 Sep 1856 St.Johns, (Manitoba) (Denney.). He died on 3 Mar 1907 Portage la Prairie, Manitoba, at age 77 (MB Vital Statistics, Death Reg. #1907,001212.).

Catherine Cook was born circa 1831 Red River, (Manitoba) (1870C-MB, page 361, #1091.). She was born circa 1834 St.Peters, (Manitoba) (Denney.) (MBS, C-14934.). She was born on 25 Mar 1835 (1901 Canada, Family 24, Line 4-6.). She was baptized on 28 Jan 1839 (St.Peters), Indian Settlement on Red River, (Manitoba) (HBCR, E.4/1a, folio 118d.). She died on 12 Apr 1907 Portage la Prairie, Manitoba, at age 72 (MB Vital Statistics, Death Reg. #1907,001213.).

Children of **John Tait or Tate** and **Catherine Cook** were as follows:

i. Harriet Tate was baptized on 31 Mar 1833 St.Johns, Red River Settlement, (Manitoba) (HBCR, E.4/1a, folio 98.). She was baptized on 15 Feb 1857 St.Johns, (Manitoba) (Denney.). She died on 7 Feb 1870 Poplar Point, (Manitoba), at age 12 (Ibid.).

ii. Caroline Tate was born on 22 Nov 1858 (HBC-PN Public Notice of land claims of Half-Breed Children, Address: Provincial Archives of Manitoba, Winnipeg, Manitoba, File Reference: MG4D13 Box 1, Poplar Point and High Bluff, #323.). She was baptized on 24 Dec 1858 St.Johns, (Manitoba) (Denney.). She was born on 22 Nov 1859 (1901 Canada, #8, K-11, page 2, family 18, line 27-29.). She married Robert James Hallett, son of Henry Hallett and Helene 'Ellen' Eleanore McNab, on 1 Sep 1879 St.Anne's Anglican Church, Poplar Point, Manitoba (Children of the Rivers Volume 1, June 1999, page 137.). She married Alexander Smith, son of Angus Smith and Mary Inkster, on 9 May 1888 Portage la Prairie, Manitoba (MB Vital Statistics, Marriage Reg. #1888,001042.).

Robert James Hallett was born on 7 Dec 1856 St.Johns, (Manitoba) (MBS, C-14928.). He died on 4 Apr 1881 Poplar Point, Manitoba, at age 24 (Heather Hallett Research, 1 Feb 2008.) (Children of the Rivers -1, page 137.). He was buried on 6 Apr 1881 St.Anne's Anglican Church, Poplar Point, Manitoba (Ibid.).

Alexander Smith was born on 14 Mar 1861 Norway House (MBS, C-14933.).

iii. Philip Tate was born on 6 Feb 1860 Poplar Point, (Manitoba) (HBC-PN , Poplar Point and High Bluff, #324.). He was baptized on 20 Feb 1860 St.Mary's Anglican Church, Portage la Prairie, (Manitoba) (SMACPLP, page 12, B-93.).

iv. Mary Jane Tate was born Poplar Point, (Manitoba). She was baptized on 6 Dec 1863 St.Mary's Anglican Church, Portage la Prairie, (Manitoba) (Ibid., page 25, B-197.). She died on 1 Jan 1864 Ste.Anne, (Manitoba) (Denney.). She was buried on 3 Jan 1864 St.Mary's Anglican Church, Portage la Prairie, (Manitoba) (SMACPLP, page 4, S-27.).

v. Colin Tate was born on 6 Jan 1865 Poplar Point, (Manitoba) (HBC-PN , Poplar Point and High Bluff, #325.).

vi. Alfred H. Tate was born on 18 Apr 1867 Poplar Point, (Manitoba) (Ibid., Poplar Point and High Bluff, #326.).

vii. Margaret Tate was born on 19 Aug 1869 Poplar Point, (Manitoba) (Ibid., Poplar Point and High Bluff, #327.).

viii. Christopher Tate was born on 22 Nov 1874 (1901 Canada, Family 24, Line 4-6.). He married Mary Philomene Monkman on 22 Feb 1911 RM St.Laurent, Manitoba (MB Vital Statistics, Marriage Reg. #1911,001952.).

Mary Philomene Monkman was born circa 1887 (1916 Census of Canada from the National Archives of Canada (Transcription by ancestry.com), Ottawa, Canada, District 28-10, page 75, family 810.).

ix. Phoebe Tate was born circa 1877 Manitoba (1881 Church of Latter Day Saints Census Transcription Project of Census Images from the National Archives of Canada, Ottawa, Canada, http://www.familysearch.org, District 186-F, page 30, household 125.).

7. **James Tait or Tate** was baptized on 10 Jul 1831 St.Johns, Red River Settlement, (Manitoba) (HBCR, E.4/1a, folio 84.). He married **Margaret Paquin dit Pocha**, daughter of **Joseph Paquin** and **Marie Lapointe**, on 24 Sep 1857 St.Johns, (Manitoba) (Denney.).

Margaret Paquin dit Pocha was born in 1837 St.James, (Manitoba) (MBS, C-14934.). She was baptized on 27 Dec 1837 St.Johns, (Manitoba) (Denney.). She died on 21 Feb 1914 (Ibid.).

Children of **James Tait or Tate** and **Margaret Paquin dit Pocha** were as follows:

i. Mary Tait was baptized on 18 Jul 1858 St.Johns, (Manitoba) (Ibid.). She was buried on 21 Jun 1859 St.Mary's Anglican Church, Portage la Prairie, Manitoba (SMACPLP, page 2, S-14.).

ii. Catherine Tate was baptized on 13 Nov 1859 St.Mary's Anglican Church, Portage la Prairie, (Manitoba) (Ibid., page 8, B-62.).

iii. Antoine Tate was born circa 1860 (Manitoba) (1870C-MB, page 350, #758.).

iv. Joseph William Tate was born on 25 Jan 1861 High Bluff, (Manitoba) (HBC-PN , Poplar Point and High Bluff, #312.). He was baptized on 13 Dec 1862 St.Mary's Anglican Church, Portage la Prairie, (Manitoba) (SMACPLP, page 15, B-118.).

    v. Margaret Tate was born High Bluff, (Manitoba) (Ibid., page 21, B-164.). She was baptized on 9 Mar 1863 St.Mary's Anglican Church, Portage la Prairie, (Manitoba) (Ibid.). She died High Bluff, (Manitoba). She was buried on 5 Feb 1864 St.Mary's Anglican Church, Portage la Prairie, (Manitoba) (Ibid., S-31.).

    vi. Mary Matilda Tate was born circa 1864 (Manitoba) (1870C-MB, page 350, #754.). She died before 1875 (HBC-PN , Poplar Point and High Bluff, #313.).

    vii. James Tate was born on 11 Aug 1865 (Ibid., Poplar Point and High Bluff, #314.).

    viii. Ann Tate was born on 24 Nov 1867 (Ibid., Poplar Point and High Bluff, #315.).

    ix. Gilbert Tate was born on 26 Nov 1869 (Ibid., Poplar Point and High Bluff, #316.).

    x. John Tate was born circa 1872 High Bluff, Manitoba (1881 Canada, District 186-F, page 3, household 12.).

    xi. Caroline Tate was born on 20 May 1874 Minnedosa, Manitoba (ArchiviaNet.). She married Archibald Walker on 14 Dec 1901 Winnipeg, Manitoba (Ibid., C-15009.).

        Archibald Walker was born on 2 May 1875 (1901 Canada, District 12-d-2, page 4, family 29, line 23-26.).

8. David Tait was born circa 1837 Red River, (Manitoba) (1870C-MB, page 362, #1140.). He married **Elisabeth Jane Knight**, daughter of **William Knight** and **Margaret Cummings,** before 1868. He died on 6 Feb 1873 Poplar Point, Manitoba (Denney.).

  Elisabeth Jane Knight was born in 1851 St.Paul, (Manitoba) (MBS, C-14934.) (1870C-MB, page 362, #1141.). She was baptized on 18 Jul 1851 St.Paul, (Manitoba) (Denney.). She was born on 18 Jun 1852 (1901 Canada, #8, K-11, page 1, Family 2, Line 4-11.). She married **Lochlan McLean** on 22 Jun 1875 Poplar Point, Manitoba (Denney.).

Children of **David Tait** and **Elisabeth Jane Knight** both born Poplar Point, (Manitoba), were as follows:

    i. David James McKenzie Tait was born on 16 Jun 1868 (MBS, C-14932.). He died on 26 May 1871 Poplar Point, Manitoba, at age 2 (Ibid.). He was buried on 27 May 1871 St.Ann, Poplar Point, Manitoba (Ibid.).

    ii. Henry George Tait was born circa 1869 (1870C-MB, page 362, #1143.). He died on 5 Apr 1871 Poplar Point, Manitoba (Denney.).

9. Andrew Tait or Tate was born circa 7 Jun 1839 St.Johns, (Manitoba) (MBS, C-14933.). He was baptized on 16 Jun 1839 St.Johns, Red River Settlement, (Manitoba) (HBCR, E.4/1a, folio 161.). He married **Elizabeth Anderson**, daughter of **Thomas Anderson** and **Caroline Chenier,** on 7 Feb 1861 St.Mary's Anglican Church, Portage la Prairie, (Manitoba) (SMACPLP, page 8, M-15.).

  Elizabeth Anderson was born in 1842 St.Andrews, (Manitoba) (MBS, C-14934.).

Children of **Andrew Tait or Tate** and **Elizabeth Anderson** were as follows:

    i. Charles Tait was born on 22 Dec 1861 Poplar Point, (Manitoba) (Ibid., C-14933.). He was baptized on 19 Jan 1862 St.Mary's Anglican Church, Portage la Prairie, (Manitoba) (Ibid.) (SMACPLP, page 16, B-125.). He died on 19 Nov 1874 Poplar Point, Manitoba, at age 12 (MBS, C-14933.). He was buried on 19 Nov 1874 St.Ann, Poplar Point, Manitoba (Ibid.).

    ii. Catherine Tait was born on 29 Jun 1863 Poplar Point, (Manitoba) (Ibid.). She was baptized on 12 Jul 1863 St.Mary's Anglican Church, Portage la Prairie, (Manitoba) (Ibid.) (SMACPLP, page 23, B-179.).

11 iii. Maria Tait, b. 20 Aug 1865 Poplar Point, (Manitoba); m. James Anderson.

    iv. Thomas William Tait was born on 22 Apr 1867 Poplar Point, (Manitoba) (MBS, C-14933.). He was baptized on 24 Apr 1867 St.Ann, Poplar Point, (Manitoba) (Ibid.).

    v. Elizabeth Harriet Tait was born on 6 Feb 1869 Poplar Point, (Manitoba) (Ibid.). She was baptized on 18 Feb 1869 St.Ann, Poplar Point, (Manitoba) (Ibid.).

    vi. Alexander Tait was born on 2 Jun 1870 Poplar Point, (Manitoba) (Ibid.). He was baptized on 12 Jun 1870 St.Ann, Poplar Point, (Manitoba) (Ibid.).

    vii. Annie Tait was born in 1872 (Denney.). She died on 26 Jul 1880 Poplar Point, Manitoba (Ibid.).

12 viii. Eugene Tait, b. 21 Sep 1876; m. Maria Adams; d. 4 Jan 1919 Lindsay, Saskatchewan.

    ix. Clementine Tait was born in Mar 1879 (Ibid.). She died on 11 Jul 1879 Poplar Point, Manitoba (Ibid.).

    x. Mary Agnes Tait was born in May 1880 (Ibid.). She died on 27 Jul 1880 Poplar Point, Manitoba (Ibid.).

    xi. Clara Emma Tate was born on 26 Jun 1881 Qu'Appelle, (Saskatchewan) (ArchiviaNet, C-15005.).

    xii. Caroline Tate was born on 26 Jun 1881 Lindsay, (Saskatchewan) (Ibid.). She died on 27 Apr 1882 Lindsay, (Saskatchewan) (Ibid.).

    xiii. Rubina Ellen Tate was born on 26 Aug 1883 Lindsay, (Saskatchewan) (Ibid.). She died on 20 May 1884 Lindsay, (Saskatchewan) (Ibid.).

    xiv. Anne Tate was born on 27 Feb 1885 Lindsay, (Saskatchewan) (Ibid.). She died in May 1885 Lindsay, (Saskatchewan) (Ibid.).

Generation Four

10. Albert Tait or Tate was born on 29 Dec 1860 Carlton, (Saskatchewan) (Ibid.). He married **Sarah Garson**, daughter of **James Garson** and **Adelaide Crete,** on 14 Jun 1890 Lesser Slave Lake, (Alberta) (Ibid.).

  Sarah Garson was born on 14 Jun 1872 Norway House (HBCA-B.) (ArchiviaNet, C-15005.). She died in 1948 Edmonton, Alberta (Denney.).

Children of **Albert Tait or Tate** and **Sarah Garson** were as follows:

    i. George Kenneth Maxwell Tate was born on 11 Mar 1891 Lesser Slave Lake, (Alberta) (ArchiviaNet, C-15005.).

    ii. Francis Phillip Hardisty Tate was born on 9 Oct 1892 Fort Dunvegan, (Alberta) (Ibid.).

    iii. Louise Anne Tate was born on 24 Jun 1894 Fort Dunvegan, (Alberta) (Ibid.).

    iv. Eliza MacDonald Tate was born on 14 Jun 1896 Fort Dunvegan, (Alberta) (Ibid.).

    v. Colin Henry Fraser Tate was born on 25 Oct 1897 Fort Dunvegan, (Alberta) (Ibid.). He died in 1933 New York (Denney.).

    vi. Alexander Tate was born in Jun 1901 (Automated Genealogy 1911 Census Transcription Project and Census Images from the National Archives of Canada, http://www.automatedgenealogy.com, #55, page 1, family 10, line 38-46.).

      vii.   Fred Tate was born in Apr 1903 (Ibid.).

     viii.   Benjamin Tate was born in Nov 1905 (Ibid.).

11. Maria Tait was born on 20 Aug 1865 Poplar Point, (Manitoba) (MBS, C-14933.). She was baptized on 27 Aug 1865 St.Mary's Anglican Church, Portage la Prairie, (Manitoba) (SMACPLP, page 32, B-249.). She married **James Anderson**, son of **Henry Anderson** and **Sophia Harper,** before 1883.

    James Anderson was born on 14 Mar 1859 Portage la Prairie, (Manitoba) (Denney.). He was baptized on 5 Apr 1859 St.Mary's Anglican Church, Portage la Prairie, (Manitoba) (SMACPLP, page 6, B-48.).

12. Eugene Tait was born on 21 Sep 1876 (Denney.). He married **Maria Adams,** daughter of **James Adams** and **Elizabeth Bruce,** before 1901 (Ibid.). He died on 4 Jan 1919 Lindsay, Saskatchewan, at age 42 (Ibid.).

    Maria Adams was born on 2 Dec 1878 Poplar Point, Manitoba (Ibid.). She died on 27 Feb 1966 Lindsay, Saskatchewan, at age 87 (Ibid.).

Children of **Eugene Tait** and **Maria Adams** were as follows:

       i.   Bertha May Tate was born on 15 Nov (Ibid.). She died (Ibid.).

      ii.   Alma Lena Roberta Tate was born on 6 Oct 1901 (Ibid.). She died on 9 Jan 1923 at age 21 (Ibid.).

     iii.   Ethel Tate was born on 24 Feb 1903 (Ibid.).

     iv.   Lilly Violet Tate was born on 4 Mar 1904 (Ibid.). She died on 2 Mar 1923 at age 18 (Ibid.).

      v.   Andrew Tomlison Tate was born in 1905 (Ibid.). He died in 1905 (Ibid.).

     vi.   Nellie Elizabeth Tate was born on 14 Feb 1907 (Ibid.). She died on 19 Sep 1923 at age 16 (Ibid.). She was buried in Sep 1923 Qu'Appelle, Saskatchewan (Ibid.).

     vii.   Olive Irene Tate was born on 21 Apr 1909 (Ibid.).

    viii.   Eva Marie Tate was born on 15 Aug 1910 (Ibid.).

     ix.   Stuart Forest Tate was born on 20 May 1912 (Ibid.).

      x.   Leslie James Tate was born on 2 Dec 1913 (Ibid.). He died (Ibid.).

     xi.   Mary Ellen Tate was born on 17 Jan 1914 (Ibid.).

     xii.   Winnifred Tate was born on 21 Sep 1919 (Ibid.).

Descendants of John Tait

Generation One

1. John Tait, son of James Tait and Catherine, was born on 8 Jan 1801 Smythe, Ronaldshay, Orkney, Scotland (MBS Scrip Applications, Original White Settlers & Halfbreeds residing in Manitoba on 15 July 1870, RG15-19, C-14927.). He was born circa 1804 (1830C RRS HBCA E5/4 1830 Census of the Red River Settlement, HBCA E5/4, Hudson's Bay Company Archives, Provincial Archives, 200 Vaughan Street, Winnipeg, MB R3C 1T5, Canada., page 14.). He married **Elisabeth Brown**, daughter of **Joseph Brown** and **Elisabeth (--?--),** before 1827.

    Elisabeth Brown was born on 8 Sep 1803 North West (MBS, C-14933.). She died on 27 Jun 1882 St.Andrews, Manitoba, at age 78 (Manitoba Vital Statistics online, http://web2.gov.mb.ca, Death Reg. #1882,001866.).

Children of **John Tait** and **Elisabeth Brown** were as follows:

         i.   John Tate was baptized on 21 Dec 1827 St.Johns, (Manitoba) (HBCR Hudson Bay Company Register of Anglican Church Baptisms, Marriages, and Burials for the Red River Settlement, 1821-1841; Hudson's Bay Company Archives, Winnipeg, Manitoba, #710. Hereinafter cited as HBCR.).

  2   ii.   Joseph Tait, b. 14 Jun 1830 St.Johns, Red River Settlement, (Manitoba); m. Madeleine Corrigal; d. 29 May 1893 St.Andrews, Manitoba.

       iii.   Jane Tate was baptized on 14 Jun 1830 St.Johns, (Manitoba) (Ibid., E.4/1a, folio 77, #182.).

  3   iv.   Elizabeth Tait, b. 15 Mar 1832 St.Andrews, (Manitoba); m. Duncan McDonald.

        v.   James Tait was baptized on 4 Feb 1834 St.Johns, Red River Settlement, (Manitoba) (Ibid., E.4/1a, folio 95d.).

  4   vi.   Ann Tait, b. 24 Dec 1835 (St.Andrews), Rapids of Red River, (Manitoba); m. Alexander D. McDonald.

      vii.   John Tait was born on 25 Jan 1838 St.Johns, Red River Settlement, (Manitoba) (HBCA-B Hudson's Bay Company Archives - biographical sketches, Hudson's Bay Company Archives; Winnipeg, Manitoba, E.4/1, No. 1423.) (HBCR, E.4/1a, folio 149.).

     viii.   Mary Tait was baptized on 24 Jan 1840 St.Johns, Red River Settlement, (Manitoba) (HBCA-B, E.4/1, No. 1702.) (HBCR, E.4/1a, folio 164d.).

Generation Two

2. Joseph Tait was baptized on 14 Jun 1830 St.Johns, Red River Settlement, (Manitoba) (Ibid., E.4/1a, folio 77, #183.). He was born on 20 Jun 1831 St.Andrews, (Manitoba) (MBS, C-14933.). He married **Madeleine Corrigal,** daughter of **James Corrigal** and **Margaret Indian,** on 2 Feb 1854 St.Andrews, (Manitoba) (MBS.). He died on 29 May 1893 St.Andrews, Manitoba, at age 62 (MB Vital Statistics, Death Reg. #1893,002477.).

    Madeleine Corrigal was born on 14 Jan 1832 North West (MBS, C-14933.). She was baptized on 25 Oct 1836 St.Johns, Red River Settlement, (Manitoba) (HBCR, E.4/1a, folio 132d.). She died on 5 Jan 1915 St.Andrews, Manitoba, at age 82 (MB Vital Statistics, Death Reg. #1915,148446.).

Children of **Joseph Tait** and **Madeleine Corrigal** were as follows:

  5   i.   Mary Tait, b. 11 Sep 1857 St.Andrews, (Manitoba); d. 16 Mar 1926 Rockwood, Manitoba.

  6   ii.   Frances Jane Tait, b. 10 Feb 1859 St.Andrews, (Manitoba); m. John Cusitor.

      iii.   Robert Tait was born on 5 Jul 1863 St.Andrews, (Manitoba) (MBS, C-14933.). He was baptized on 20 Jul 1863 St.Andrews, (Manitoba) (Ibid.).

  iv. Eliza Margaret Tait was born on 20 Mar 1867 St.Andrews, (Manitoba) (Ibid.). She was baptized on 26 May 1867 St.Andrews, (Manitoba) (Ibid.).

  v. William Tait was born on 3 May 1869 St.Andrews, (Manitoba) (Ibid.). He was baptized on 30 May 1869 St.Andrews, (Manitoba) (Ibid.).

  vi. Alexander David Tait was born on 8 Oct 1871 St.Andrews, Manitoba (1881 Census of Canada from the National Archives of Canada, Ottawa, Canada, District 185-C-1, page 45, family 197.) (Automated Genealogy 1901 Census Transcription Project and Census Images from the National Archives of Canada, http://www.automatedgenealogy.com, District 11-1-2, page 3, family 26, line 31-32.).

3. Elizabeth Tait was born on 15 Mar 1832 St.Andrews, (Manitoba) (MBS, C-14930.). She married **Duncan McDonald**, son of **Donald 'Little' McDonald** and **Nancy Ferguson,** on 12 Feb 1852 St.Andrews, (Manitoba) (Denney Papers, Charles D. Denney, Glenbow Archives, Calgary, Alberta.).

Duncan McDonald was born in Sep 1825 St.Johns, (Manitoba) (MBS, C-14930.).

4. Ann Tait was baptized on 24 Dec 1835 (St.Andrews), Rapids of Red River, (Manitoba) (HBCA-B.) (HBCR, E.4/1a, folio 126.). She was born on 7 Dec 1836 St.Andrews, (Manitoba) (MBS, C-14930.). She married **Alexander D. McDonald**, son of **Donald "Big" (a) McDonald** and **Jane Beaudry,** on 26 Dec 1854 St.Andrews, (Manitoba) (Denney.).

Alexander D. McDonald was born on 6 Nov 1828 North West (MBS, C-14930.). He was baptized on 25 Dec 1834 (St.Andrews), Rapids of Red River, (Manitoba) (HBCA-B.) (HBCR, E.4/1a, folio 117d.).

Generation Three

5. Mary Tait was born on 11 Sep 1857 St.Andrews, (Manitoba) (MBS, C-14933.). She was baptized on 27 Sep 1857 St.Andrews, (Manitoba) (Ibid.). She married **Thomas Vincent**, son of **John Vincent** and **Mary Thomas,** before 1877. She died on 16 Mar 1926 Rockwood, Manitoba, at age 68 (MB Vital Statistics, Death Reg. #1926,013220.).

Thomas Vincent was born on 28 Apr 1853 St.Paul, (Manitoba) (1901 Canada, #11, H-2, page 7, family 35, line 13-23.). He was baptized on 30 Apr 1853 St.Paul, (Manitoba) (Denney.). He died on 12 Feb 1934 Winnipeg, Manitoba, at age 80 (MB Vital Statistics, Death Reg. #1934,008138.).

6. Frances Jane Tait was born on 10 Feb 1859 St.Andrews, (Manitoba) (MBS, C-14933.). She was baptized on 6 Mar 1859 St.Andrews, (Manitoba) (Ibid.). She married **John Cusitor**, son of **David Magnus Cusitor** and **Margaret Whitford,** on 1 May 1888 Portage la Prarie, Manitoba (MB Vital Statistics, Marriage Reg. #1889,001457.).

John Cusitor was born on 10 Sep 1857 Washington Territory (MBS, C-14926.). He and **Mary Mathilda Henderson** met before 1883.

Descendants of William Tait

Generation One

1. William Tait, son of James Tait and Catherine, was born circa 1795 Orkney, Scotland (1827C RRS HBCA E5/1 1827 Census of the Red River Settlement, HBCA E5/1, Hudson's Bay Company Archives, Provincial Archives, 200 Vaughan Street, Winnipeg, MB R3C 1T5, Canada., #8, page 1.). He married **Mary Auld**, daughter of **William Auld** and **Native Woman or Women**, on 10 Jul 1823 York Factory (HBCR Hudson Bay Company Register of Anglican Church Baptisms, Marriages, and Burials for the Red River Settlement, 1821-1841; Hudson's Bay Company Archives, Winnipeg, Manitoba, #65. Hereinafter cited as HBCR.). He was buried on 19 Nov 1872 Kildonan, Manitoba (MBS Scrip Applications, Original White Settlers & Halfbreeds residing in Manitoba on 15 July 1870, RG15-19, C-14933.).

Mary Auld was born circa 1804 (Denney Papers, Charles D. Denney, Glenbow Archives, Calgary, Alberta.). She was baptized on 10 Jul 1823 St.Johns, York Factory (HBCA-B Hudson's Bay Company Archives - biographical sketches, Hudson's Bay Company Archives; Winnipeg, Manitoba, E.4/1a, fo. 44d; E.4/1b. fo. 208d.) (HBCR, E.4/1a folio 44d.).

Children of **William Tait** and **Mary Auld** were as follows:

 2 i. Margaret Tait, b. 1824 Kildonan, (Manitoba); m. John 'Big John' Sutherland; d. 9 Feb 1901 North Dakota.

 3 ii. William Auld Tait Sr, b. 9 Dec 1826 Headingley, (Manitoba); m. Johanna Gunn; d. 3 Feb 1900 Assiniboia, Manitoba.

 4 iii. James Tait, b. 1 Oct 1827 Kildonan, (Manitoba); m. Ellen 'Nellie' Gunn; d. 24 Feb 1899 Assiniboia, Manitoba.

 5 iv. Robert Tait, b. 24 Apr 1830 Kildonan, (Manitoba); m. Jane Inkster; d. 1 Mar 1912 Winnipeg, Manitoba.

 6 v. John Tait, b. 8 Mar 1832 St.Johns, Red River Settlement, (Manitoba); m. Margaret Spence; d. 2 Feb 1916.

  vi. Joseph Tait was baptized on 23 Mar 1834 St.Johns, Red River Settlement, (Manitoba) (Ibid., E.4/1a, folio 108.).

  vii. David Tate was baptized on 15 Jul 1837 St.Johns, Red River Settlement, (Manitoba) (Ibid., E.4/1a, folio 142.). He died on 8 Feb 1873 St.Johns, Manitoba, at age 35 (Denney.).

 7 viii. George Tait, b. 1839 Kildonan, (Manitoba); m. Caroline Mary Spencer.

 8 ix. Charles Tait, b. 3 Jan 1841 Kildonan, (Manitoba); m. Barbara Flett.

  x. Mary Tait was born on 8 Jan 1843 Kildonan, (Manitoba) (MBS, C-14933.). She was baptized on 24 Jan 1843 St.Johns, (Manitoba) (Denney.).

  xi. Jane Tait was baptized on 15 Jan 1845 St.Johns, (Manitoba) (Ibid.). She married Thomas Reid, son of David Reid, on 26 Dec 1861 St.Johns, (Manitoba) (Ibid.).

   Thomas Reid was born circa 1825 (Ibid.).

  xii. Elizabeth Tait was born on 8 Feb 1847 Kildonan, (Manitoba) (MBS, C-14933.). She was baptized on 8 Feb 1847 St.Johns, (Manitoba) (Ibid.). She died on 26 Apr 1875 Kildonan, (Manitoba), at age 28 (Ibid.). She was buried on 26 Apr 1875 Kildonan, (Manitoba) (Ibid.).

 9 xiii. Sarah Tait, b. 8 Nov 1851 Kildonan, (Manitoba); m. George McKay; d. Dec 1931.

 10 xiv. Ann Tait, b. 21 Mar 1852 Kildonan, (Manitoba); m. Colin Inkster; d. 20 May 1925 RM West Kildonan, Manitoba.

Generation Two

2. Margaret Tait was born in 1824 Kildonan, (Manitoba) (Ibid.) (1870C-MB 1870 Manitoba Census, National Archives of Canada, Ottawa, Ontario, Microfilm Reel Number C-2170., page 245, #577.). She was baptized on 23 Jan 1825 St.Johns, Red River Colony, (Manitoba) (HBCR, E.4/1a, folio 53.). She married **John 'Big John' Sutherland**, son of **Robert Sutherland** and **Janet Matheson**, on 1 Apr 1847 (St.Johns), Upper Church, (Manitoba) (Ibid., No. 403.). She died on 9 Feb 1901 North Dakota (Denney.).

John 'Big John' Sutherland was born circa 1808 Scotland (1829C RRS HBCA E5/3 1829 Census of the Red River Settlement, HBCA E5/3, Hudson's Bay Company Archives, Provincial Archives, 200 Vaughan Street, Winnipeg, MB R3C 1T5, Canada., page 2.). He married **Catherine Matheson**, daughter of **Alexander 'Bon Homme' Matheson** and **Anne Matheson**, on 22 Jan 1829 St.Johns, (Manitoba) (Denney.). He married **Janet Polson**, daughter of **Alexander Polson** and **Catherine Matheson**, on 7 Feb 1837 Red River Settlement, (Manitoba) (HBCR, No. 335.). He died on 3 Feb 1891 (Denney.).

3. William Auld Tait Sr was born on 9 Dec 1826 Headingley, (Manitoba) (MBS, C-14933.). He was baptized on 31 Dec 1826 St.Johns, Red River Colony, (Manitoba) (HBCA-B, PAM, St.John's Baptisms, 1813-1828.) (HBCR, E.4/1a, folio 63.). He married **Johanna Gunn**, daughter of **John Gunn** and **Ann Sutherland**, on 18 Dec 1851 Kildonan, (Manitoba) (Denney.). He died on 3 Feb 1900 Assiniboia, Manitoba, at age 73 (Ibid.).

Johanna Gunn was born on 7 Aug 1829 (Automated Genealogy 1901 Census Transcription Project and Census Images from the National Archives of Canada, http://www.automatedgenealogy.com, #11, a-3, page 5, family 25. line 46-49.). She was baptized on 12 Aug 1829 St.Johns, Red River Settlement, (Manitoba) (HBCR, E.4/1a, folio 71.). She died on 21 May 1906 Winnipeg, Manitoba, at age 76 (Manitoba Vital Statistics online, http://web2.gov.mb.ca, Death Reg. #1906,004438.). She was buried in 1906 Headingley, Manitoba (Denney.).

Children of **William Auld Tait Sr.** and **Johanna Gunn** were as follows:

- 11   i.   John McCallum Tait, b. 24 Sep 1852 St.Johns, (Manitoba); m. Jane Ellen Clouston; d. 16 May 1911 Winnipeg, Manitoba.
-     ii.   William Tait Jr was born on 13 Oct 1854 St.Johns, (Manitoba) (MBS, C-14933.). He married Mary E. Affleck on 31 Mar 1881 Kildonan, Manitoba (Denney.).
  Mary E. Affleck was born in 1854.
-     iii.   Ann Tait was born on 5 Sep 1856 St.Johns, (Manitoba) (MBS, C-14933.). She was baptized on 25 Sep 1856 St.Johns, (Manitoba) (Denney.).
- 12   iv.   Robert William Tait, b. 16 Oct 1857 Headingley, (Manitoba); m. Martha Foulds; d. 2 Aug 1922 Prince Albert, Saskatchewan.
-     v.   Alexander Thomas Tait was baptized on 9 Sep 1860 Headingley, (Manitoba) (MBS, C-14933.).
-     vi.   Helen Jane Tait was born on 12 Mar 1861. She died on 29 Feb 1916 at age 54.
-     vii.   David James Tait was born on 2 Dec 1862 Headingley, (Manitoba) (Ibid.). He was baptized on 7 Dec 1862 (Ibid.). He died on 2 Mar 1922 at age 59 (Denney.). He was buried in 1922 Kildonan, (Manitoba) (Ibid.).
-     viii.   Alexander Thomas Tait was born on 13 Mar 1867 Headingley, (Manitoba) (MBS, C-14933.). He was baptized on 31 Mar 1867 (Ibid.). He married Flora Ann Taylor, daughter of John Taylor and Flora Campbell, on 23 Sep 1896 (Denney.).
  Flora Ann Taylor was born on 20 Jan 1867 Headingley, (Manitoba) (HBC-PN , Headingly, #161.).
-     ix.   George Tait was born on 17 Feb 1869 Headingley, (Manitoba) (MBS, C-14933.). He was baptized on 14 Mar 1870 (Ibid.).
-     x.   Henry Tait was born on 27 Jul 1874 Manitoba (1881 Church of Latter Day Saints Census Transcription Project of Census Images from the National Archives of Canada, Ottawa, Canada, http://www.familysearch.org, District 183A, page 35, house 142.) (1901 Canada, #11, a-3, page 5, family 25. line 46-49.).

4. James Tait was born in 1826 Kildonan, (Manitoba) (MBS, C-14933.). He was born on 1 Oct 1827 Kildonan, (Manitoba) (Denney.). He was baptized on 15 Oct 1828 St.Johns, (Manitoba) (Ibid.). He married **Ellen 'Nellie' Gunn**, daughter of **John Gunn** and **Ann Sutherland**, on 8 Mar 1854 Kildonan, (Manitoba) (Ibid.). He died on 24 Feb 1899 Assiniboia, Manitoba, at age 71 (MB Vital Statistics, Death Reg. #1899,001026.).

Question: *The baptism in 1828 was not found in the HBC records.*

Ellen 'Nellie' Gunn was baptized on 21 Mar 1825 St.Johns, Red River Settlement, (Manitoba) (HBCR, E.4/1a, folio 54.). She died on 19 Feb 1908 Assiniboia, Manitoba, at age 82 (MB Vital Statistics, Death Reg. #1908,001686.).

Children of **James Tait** and **Ellen 'Nellie' Gunn** were as follows:

-     i.   Mary Ann Tait was born on 13 Jun 1855 St.Johns, (Manitoba) (MBS, C-14933.) (1901 Canada, District 11-a-3, page 8, family 48, line 27-31.). She was baptized on 28 Jul 1855 (Denney.). She died on 4 Sep 1901 Winnipeg, Manitoba, at age 46 (MB Vital Statistics, Death Reg. #1901,001228.).
-     ii.   Joseph Tait was born on 12 Dec 1856 Kildonan, (Manitoba) (MBS, C-14933.). He was baptized on 19 Jan 1857 St.Johns, (Manitoba) (Denney.).
- 13   iii.   Margaret Tait, b. 24 Jun 1859 Headingley, (Manitoba); m. William A. Inkster; d. 30 Jun 1933 Stonewall, Manitoba.
-     iv.   John Gunn Tait was born on 9 Aug 1860 Headingley, (Manitoba) (MBS, C-14933.). He died on 23 Jul 1907 at age 46 (Denney.). He was buried in 1907 Headingley, (Manitoba) (Ibid.).
-     v.   William Tait was born on 21 Apr 1862 Headingley, (Manitoba) (MBS, C-14933.) (1901 Canada, District 11-a-3, page 8, family 48, line 27-31.). He was baptized on 26 May 1862 (MBS, C-14933.).
-     vi.   James Charles Tait was born on 5 Apr 1864 Headingley, (Manitoba) (Ibid.). He was baptized on 8 May 1864 (Ibid.).
-     vii.   Isabella Tait was born on 13 Jul 1866 Headingley, (Manitoba) (Ibid.). She was baptized on 5 Aug 1866 (Ibid.). She died on 11 Sep 1892 at age 26 (Denney.). She was buried in 1892 Headingley, Manitoba (Ibid.).
-     viii.   Jemima Ellen Tait was born on 1 Jan 1871 (1901 Canada, District 11-a-3, page 8, family 48, line 27-31.).

5. Robert Tait was born on 24 Apr 1830 Kildonan, (Manitoba) (MBS, C-14933.) (1901 Canada, #11, A-1, page 2, Family 16, Line 24-27.). He was baptized on 12 May 1830 St.Johns, Red River Settlement, (Manitoba) (HBCR, E.4/1a, folio 76d.). He married **Jane**

Inkster, daughter of **John Inkster** and **Mary Sinclair,** on 16 Feb 1858 St.Johns, (Manitoba) (Denney.). He died on 1 Mar 1912 Winnipeg, Manitoba, at age 81 (Ibid.) (CWLR *The Collected Writings Of Louis Riel*, 5 (University of Alberta Press, 1985), page 349.).

Jane Inkster was born on 17 Nov 1838 Kildonan, (Manitoba) (MBS, C-14933.) (1901 Canada, #11, A-1, page 2, Family 16, Line 24-27.). She was baptized on 16 Dec 1838 St.Johns, Red River Settlement, (Manitoba) (HBCR, E.4/1a, folio 158.). She died on 7 Aug 1926 St.James, Manitoba, at age 87 (MB Vital Statistics, Death Reg. #1926,038204.).

Children of **Robert Tait** and **Jane Inkster** were as follows:

    i. Thomas Herbert Tait was born on 11 Nov 1859 (MBS, C-14933.). He was baptized on 10 Dec 1859 St.Johns, (Manitoba) (Denney.). He married Margaret Jane (--?--) before 1888 (St.James Anglican Cemetery; Cemetery Transcription #121; Mavis and Maureen Smith, Unit "E," 1045 St.James Street, Winnipeg, Manitoba, Canada R3H 1B1: Manitoba Genealogical Society, Inc., 1983, page 97.). He married Mary Anabella Tait, daughter of John Tait and Margaret Spence, on 4 Apr 1893 St.James, Manitoba (Denney.) (MB Vital Statistics, Marriage Reg. #1893,001513.). He died on 28 Mar 1894 St.James, Manitoba, at age 34 (MGS: St.James Cemetery, page 97.).

        Margaret Jane (--?--) was born in Dec 1864 (Ibid.). She died on 8 Jun 1888 St.James, Manitoba, at age 23 (Ibid.).

        Mary Anabella Tait was born circa 1869 (Denney.).

    ii. Timoleon John Tait was born on 9 Nov 1861 (MBS, C-14933.). He was baptized on 16 Dec 1861 St.Johns, (Manitoba) (Denney.).

    iii. Colin Tait was born on 29 Nov 1862 St.James, (Manitoba) (MBS, C-14933.). He was baptized on 16 Dec 1862 St.James, (Manitoba) (SJAC St.James Anglican Church Extractions, Manitoba Genealogy Society, Winnipeg, Manitoba, B-134.). He died on 6 Jul 1871 St.James, (Manitoba), at age 8 (MBS, C-14934.) (MGS: St.James Cemetery, page 97.). He was buried on 8 Jul 1871 St.James, (Manitoba) (MBS, C-14934.).

14   iv. Ellen Harriet Tait, b. 13 Oct 1865 St.James, (Manitoba); m. George William Cumming; d. 1 Feb 1920 St.James, Manitoba.

    v. Mary Tait was born on 25 Nov 1867 St.James, (Manitoba) (Ibid., C-14933.). She was baptized on 27 Nov 1867 St.James, (Manitoba) (SJAC, B-192.) (MBS, C-14934.). She died on 25 Aug 1873 St.James, Manitoba, at age 5 (Ibid., C-14933.) (MGS: St.James Cemetery, page 97.). She was buried on 25 Aug 1873 St.James, Manitoba (MBS, C-14933.).

    vi. Margaret Tait was baptized on 14 Sep 1871 St.James, Manitoba (SJAC, B-244.). She died on 13 Dec 1872 St.Peters, Manitoba, at age 1 (MGS: St.James Cemetery, page 97.).

    vii. Adelaide Tait was born on 20 Jun 1872 Fort Garry, Manitoba (Denney.). She was baptized on 25 Aug 1872 St.James, Manitoba (SJAC, B-265.). She died on 1 Dec 1901 Winnipeg, Manitoba, at age 29 (MB Vital Statistics, Death Reg. #1901,001446.).

6. John Tait was baptized on 8 Mar 1832 St.Johns, Red River Settlement, (Manitoba) (HBCR, E.4/1a, folio 88.). He married **Margaret Spence**, daughter of **John Clarke Spence** and **Annabella McKenzie,** before 1869. He died on 2 Feb 1916 at age 83 (Denney.).

Margaret Spence was baptized on 27 Oct 1839 St.Johns, Red River Settlement, (Manitoba) (HBCR, E.4/1a, folio 42.).

Children of **John Tait** and **Margaret Spence** were:

    i. Mary Anabella Tait was born circa 1869 (Denney.). She married Thomas Herbert Tait, son of Robert Tait and Jane Inkster, on 4 Apr 1893 St.James, Manitoba (Ibid.) (MB Vital Statistics, Marriage Reg. #1893,001513.).

        Thomas Herbert Tait was born on 11 Nov 1859 (MBS, C-14933.). He was baptized on 10 Dec 1859 St.Johns, (Manitoba) (Denney.). He married **Margaret Jane (--?--)** before 1888 (MGS: St.James Cemetery, page 97.). He died on 28 Mar 1894 St.James, Manitoba, at age 34 (Ibid.).

7. George Tait was born in 1839 Kildonan, (Manitoba) (MBS, C-14933.). He was baptized on 20 Jan 1839 St.Johns, Red River Settlement, (Manitoba) (HBCR, E.4/1a, folio 158d.). He was born on 3 Jan 1842 (1901 Canada, #205 (z-1), page 2, family 15, line 37-42.). He married **Caroline Mary Spencer** before 1877.

Children of **George Tait** and **Caroline Mary Spencer** were as follows:

    i. William McMurray Tait was born on 2 Nov 1877 Prince Albert, (Saskatchewan) (Ibid.) (ArchiviaNet 1886-1901, 1906 Half-Breed Scrip Applications Index, RG15-21, Volume 1333 through 1371, Microfilm Reel Number C-14944 through C-15010, National Archives of Canada, Ottawa, Ontario, http://www.collectionscanada.gc.ca, C-15005.).

    ii. Colin Charles Tait was born on 16 Nov 1879 Prince Albert, (Saskatchewan) (Ibid.). He died on 11 Aug 1898 South Branch, (Saskatchewan), at age 18 (Ibid.).

    iii. Caroline Mary Tait was born on 20 Sep 1882 South Branch, (Saskatchewan) (Ibid.). She was born on 27 Oct 1882 (1901 Canada, #205 (z-1), page 2, family 15, line 37-42.).

    iv. Margaret Sarah Tait was born on 15 Oct 1884 South Branch, (Saskatchewan) (Ibid.) (ArchiviaNet, C-15005.).

    v. Arthur Tait was born on 6 Jun 1888 (1901 Canada, #205 (z-1), page 2, family 15, line 37-42.).

15   vi. Florence Catherine Tait, b. 10 May 1890 (Saskatchewan).

    vii. Arabella Dunlop Tait was born on 25 Dec 1892 (Saskatchewan) (Saskatchewan Vital Statistics online, http://vsgs.health.gov.sk.ca, Birth Reg. #7155.).

8. Charles Tait was born on 3 Jan 1841 Kildonan, (Manitoba) (MBS, C-14933.). He was baptized on 23 Nov 1845 St.Johns, (Manitoba) (Denney.). He married **Barbara Flett**, daughter of **Peter Flett** and **Euphemia Halcrow,** before 1865 (Ibid.).

Barbara Flett was born on 13 Apr 1839 St.Paul, (Manitoba) (MBS, C-14931.). She was baptized on 5 May 1839 St.Johns, Red River Settlement, (Manitoba) (HBCA-B, E.4/1a, folio 160d.). She married **James Clouston** before 1859. She married **Joseph McLennan**, son of **Joseph McLennan** and **Mary (--?--),** on 4 May 1868 St.Paul, (Manitoba) (Denney.). She died on 2 Sep 1873 St.Paul, Manitoba, at age 34 (MBS, C-14931.). She was buried on 2 Sep 1873 St.Paul, Manitoba (Ibid.).

Children of **Charles Tait** and **Barbara Flett** are:

i.   Martha Tait was born on 4 May 1865 St.Andrews, (Manitoba) (Ibid.). She was baptized on 4 Jun 1865 St.Andrews, (Manitoba) (Ibid.).

9. **Sarah Tait** was baptized on 10 Nov 1849 St.Johns, (Manitoba) (Denney.). She was born on 8 Nov 1851 Kildonan, (Manitoba) (MBS, C-14931.). She married **George McKay**, son of **James McKay** and **Marguerite Gladu,** on 20 Feb 1868 St.Johns, (Manitoba) (Denney.). She died in Dec 1931 at age 80 (Ibid.).

George McKay was born circa 1832 (SFX: 1834-1850 St.Francois Xavier 1834-1851 Register, B-179. Hereinafter cited as SFX: 1834-1850.). He was born in Nov 1833 North West Territories (MBS, C-14931.). He was baptized on 17 Sep 1837 St.Francois Xavier, (Manitoba) (SFX: 1834-1850, B-179.). He died in 1884 Prince Albert, (Saskatchewan). He was buried in 1884 Prince Albert, (Saskatchewan) (T. R. "Pat" McCloy, McKay Descendancy.).

10. **Ann Tait** was born on 21 Mar 1852 Kildonan, (Manitoba) (MBS, C-14929.). She married **Colin Inkster**, son of **John Inkster** and **Mary Sinclair,** on 16 Mar 1871 St.Johns, Manitoba (Denney.). She died on 20 May 1925 RM West Kildonan, Manitoba, at age 73 (MB Vital Statistics, Death Reg. #1925,022131.).

Colin Inkster was born on 3 Aug 1843 St.Johns, (Manitoba) (MBS, C-14929.). He was baptized on 13 Aug 1843 St.Johns, (Manitoba) (Denney.). He died on 28 Sep 1934 West Kildonan, Manitoba, at age 91 (MB Vital Statistics, Death Reg. #1934,036333.).

Generation Three

11. **John McCallum Tait** was born on 24 Sep 1852 St.Johns, (Manitoba) (MBS, C-14933.). He was baptized on 17 Oct 1852 St.Johns, (Manitoba) (Ibid.). He married **Jane Ellen Clouston**, daughter of **William Clouston** and **Catherine Campbell,** before 1879 (1881 Canada, District 183A, page 36, house 148.). He died on 16 May 1911 Winnipeg, Manitoba, at age 58 (MB Vital Statistics, Death Reg. #1911,003491.).

Jane Ellen Clouston was baptized on 12 Mar 1859 St.James, (Manitoba) (SJAC, B-77.). She was born on 12 Mar 1860 Headingley, (Manitoba) (MBS, C-14926.) (HBC-PN , Headingley, #32.).

Children of **John McCallum Tait** and **Jane Ellen Clouston** were as follows:

i.   Anne Tait was born circa 1879 Assiniboia, Manitoba (1881 Canada, District 183A, page 36, house 148.).

ii.   Johanah Eveline "Josie" Tait was born on 10 Jan 1882 Assiniboia, Manitoba (MB Vital Statistics, Birth Reg. #1882,002852.). She married John Lester Francis, son of Frederick Hanhurst Francis and Sarah Margaret Black, on 10 Jan 1907 Winnipeg, Manitoba (Ibid., Marriage Reg. #1907,002809.).

     John Lester Francis was born on 20 Apr 1875 (Denney.). He died on 5 Oct 1944 Winnipeg, Manitoba, at age 69 (MB Vital Statistics, Death Reg. #1944,040108.).

iii.   Mabel Tait was born on 27 Oct 1883 Assiniboia, Manitoba (Ibid., Birth Reg. #1883,003466.).

iv.   Edith Tait was born on 5 Nov 1885 (1901 Canada, #11, a-3, page 6, family 33. line 37-46.).

v.   Frank Tait was born on 1 Oct 1890 Assiniboia, Manitoba (MB Vital Statistics, Birth Reg. #1891,003156.).

vi.   John Tait was born on 8 Aug 1892 (1901 Canada, #11, a-3, page 6, family 33. line 37-46.).

vii.   Cyrille Tait was born on 4 Apr 1895 (Ibid.).

viii.   Cecil Tait was born on 14 Dec 1897 (Ibid.).

12. **Robert William Tait** was born on 10 Mar 1856 (Manitoba) (Ibid., #205, V-1, page 3, family 22, line 12-20.). He was born on 16 Oct 1857 Headingley, (Manitoba) (MBS, C-14933.). He married **Martha Foulds**, daughter of **John Foulds** and **Mary Anne Adams,** on 5 Apr 1883 Macdowall, Saskatchewan (Rod MacQuarrie Research, 15 May 2011.). He died on 2 Aug 1922 Prince Albert, Saskatchewan, at age 64 (Denney.) (Rod Mac Quarrie, 15 May 2011.).

Martha Foulds was born on 2 Jan 1863 High Bluff, (Manitoba) (HBC-PN , Poplar Point and High Bluff, #80.) (1901 Canada, #205, V-1, page 3, family 22, line 12-20.). She was baptized on 1 Feb 1863 St.James, (Manitoba) (SJAC, B-135.). She died on 6 Jul 1952 Prince Albert, Saskatchewan, at age 89 (Rod Mac Quarrie, 15 May 2011.).

Children of **Robert William Tait** and **Martha Foulds** were as follows:

i.   Frances Jessie Winnifred Tate was born on 17 Feb 1884 Prince Albert, (Saskatchewan) (ArchiviaNet, C-15005.). She married Alexander Douglas McDonald, son of John McDonald and Sarah Setter (Denney.).

     Alexander Douglas McDonald died on 6 May 1970 (Ibid.).

ii.   Aurora Tait was born on 25 Mar 1888 (Saskatchewan) (1901 Canada, #205, V-1, page 3, family 22, line 12-20.).

iii.   Mary Laura Evangaline Tait was born on 7 Jun 1889 (Saskatchewan) (SK Vital Statistics, #7954.).

iv.   Annie Tait was born on 8 Aug 1890 (Saskatchewan) (Ibid., #7985.).

v.   Irene Maude Gertrude Tait was born on 2 Jan 1893 (Saskatchewan) (1901 Canada, #205, V-1, page 3, family 22, line 12-20.) (SK Vital Statistics, #8068.).

vi.   Fred Tait was born on 30 Aug 1895 (Saskatchewan) (1901 Canada, #205, V-1, page 3, family 22, line 12-20.).

vii.   Christie Tait was born on 2 Mar 1897 (Saskatchewan) (Ibid.).

viii.   Robert William "Bert" Tait was born on 23 May 1899 (Saskatchewan) (Ibid.).

ix.   Rubina Tait was born in Jun 1903 (Automated Genealogy 1911 Census Transcription Project and Census Images from the National Archives of Canada, http://www.automatedgenealogy.com, District 9, page 19, family 166, line 3-11.).

x.   Gwendoline Tait was born in May 1905 (Ibid.).

13. **Margaret Tait** was born on 24 Jun 1859 Headingley, (Manitoba) (HBC-PN , Headingly, #150.). She married **William A. Inkster**, son of **John Inkster** and **Mary Fogarty,** in 1881 (Denney.). She died on 30 Jun 1933 Stonewall, Manitoba, at age 74 (Ibid.).

William A. Inkster was born on 7 Mar 1858 New Orleans, Louisiana (MBS, C-14929.). He died on 14 Oct 1938 Rockwood, Manitoba, at age 80 (MB Vital Statistics, Death Reg. #1938,044466.).

14. **Ellen Harriet Tait** was born on 13 Oct 1865 St.James, (Manitoba) (MBS, C-14933.) (1901 Canada, #95, D-1, page 11, family 126, line 11-15.). She was baptized on 12 Nov 1865 St.James, (Manitoba) (SJAC, B-169.) (MBS, C-14934.). She married **George William Cumming** on 2 Feb 1889 Winnipeg, Manitoba (MB Vital Statistics, Marriage Reg. #1889,001960.). She died on 1 Feb 1920 St.James, Manitoba, at age 54 (SJAC, page 50.).

George William Cumming died before 31 Mar 1901.

15. **Florence Catherine Tait** was born on 10 May 1890 (Saskatchewan) (SK Vital Statistics, Birth Reg. #7976.). She married **Henry George Donald**, son of **John Donald** and **Mary Ann Erasmus**, circa 1911 (1911 Canada, District 31, page 27, family 235, line 31-38.). **Henry George Donald** was born on 22 Jun 1884 South Branch, (Saskatchewan) (HBSI.) (ArchiviaNet.).

Descendants of John Falcon 'Shawshawwabanase' Tanner

Generation One

1. **John Falcon 'Shawshawwabanase' Tanner**, son of Rev. John Tanner, was born in 1781 (Denney Papers, Charles D. Denney, Glenbow Archives, Calgary, Alberta.). He married **Therese Indian**. He married **Sky Dawn** circa 1802 (Ibid.). He died in Jul 1846 (Ibid.).

Children of **John Falcon 'Shawshawwabanase' Tanner** and **Therese Indian** were as follows:

2   i.   John J. Tanner.
    ii.   Lucy Tanner.
3   iii.   Mary Elizabeth Tanner, d. 1883.
    iv.   Anonyme Tanner.
    v.   Anonyme Tanner.
4   vi.   Rev. James Tanner, b. circa 1805 below Fort Garry, (Manitoba); m. Marguerite Patrice; d. 30 Nov 1870 Poplar Point, Manitoba.
    vii.   Mary Tanner was born in 1809 (Rarihokwats Research, 26 Apr 1997.). She died in 1820 80 miles from Grand Prairie (Ibid.).
    viii.   Martha Ann Tanner was born in 1830 (Denney.). She was buried Mackinac Island, Michigan.

Children of **John Falcon 'Shawshawwabanase' Tanner** and **Sky Dawn** were as follows:

    i.   unnamed Tanner.
5   ii.   Thomas DeCorby Tanner dit Petitcho, m. Marie Neshotokoway Neukatek Ledoux; d. between 1872 and 1875.

Generation Two

2. **John J. Tanner.**

Children of **John J. Tanner** include:

    i.   John Tanner.

3. **Mary Elizabeth Tanner** died in 1883 (Ibid.).

Children of **Mary Elizabeth Tanner** and **(--?--) LaVogue** are as follows:

    i.   Joe LaVogue.
    ii.   George LaVogue.

Children of **Mary Elizabeth Tanner** and **Joseph Tall** are:

    i.   Joseph Tall.

4. **Rev. James Tanner** was born circa 1805 below Fort Garry, (Manitoba) (1870C-MB 1870 Manitoba Census, National Archives of Canada, Ottawa, Ontario, Microfilm Reel Number C-2170., page 361, #1111.) (Denney.). He married **Marguerite Patrice**, daughter of **Francois Patrice** and **Marie Charette**, before 15 Jul 1870. He died on 30 Nov 1870 Poplar Point, Manitoba (Ibid.).

Children of **Rev. James Tanner** include:

6   i.   Eliah Tanner.
7   ii.   Edward Tanner, b. circa 1832.
    iii.   John Tanner was born on 17 Aug 1837 Torch Lake, Lac du Flambeau, Wisconsin (Ibid.). He married Catherine Trottier, daughter of Joseph Trottier and Marie Sauteuse, on 14 Jul 1869 St.Mary's Anglican Church, Portage la Prairie, (Manitoba) (SMACPLP St.Marys Anglican Church, Portage La Prairie, Manitoba, Baptisms, Marriages, Burials, 1855-1883, transcribed by Clarence Kipling , page 25, M-52.).

> Catherine Trottier was born circa 1825 Red River, (Manitoba) (1870C-MB, page 361, #1115.). She was born circa 1830 Red River, (Manitoba) (1850Ci-MN *Minnesota Territorial Census, 1850*, Harpole, Patricia C. and Mary D. Nagle, ed., (St.Paul, Minnesota: Minnesota Historical Society, 1972), page 20; Dwelling 20, Family 20.). She married James Sinclair, son of **William Sinclair** and **Elizabeth Anderson**, before 1854.

Marguerite Patrice was born in 1830 Minnesota (MBS Scrip Applications, Original White Settlers & Halfbreeds residing in Manitoba on 15 July 1870, RG15-19, C-14927.) (1870C-MB, page 361, #1112.). She married **Jean Baptiste Desmarais**, son of **Francois Desmarais** and **Marie Suzette Saulteaux**, on 11 Sep 1871 St.Mary's Anglican Church, Portage la Prairie, Manitoba (SMACPLP, page 32, M-69.). She died in 1914 (Denney.).

5. **Thomas DeCorby Tanner dit Petitcho** married **Marie Neshotokoway Neukatek Ledoux**, daughter of **(--?--) Metis** and **Wehwasrh Indian**, in 1836 Turtle Mountain (HBSI Index 1886-1901, 1906 Halfbreed Scrip Applications, RG15-21.) (ArchiviaNet 1886-1901, 1906 Half-Breed Scrip Applications Index, RG15-21, Volume 1333 through 1371, Microfilm Reel Number C-14944 through C-15010, National Archives of Canada, Ottawa, Ontario, http://www.collectionscanada.gc.ca.). He died between 1872 and 1875 Qu'Appelle, (Saskatchewan).

Marie Neshotokoway Neukatek Ledoux was born in 1820 Turtle Mountain (HBSI.) (ArchiviaNet.). She married **Francois O Poh Tokahan Pettokahan Desmarais** before 1858. She married **Nahwahtcheweka-paw (--?--)** in 1862 (HBSI.) (ArchiviaNet.).

Children of **Thomas DeCorby Tanner dit Petitcho** and **Marie Neshotokoway Neukatek Ledoux** were as follows:

8   i.   Basile Pitchito Tanner, m. Elizabeth (--?--).
9   ii.   Suzanne Tanner, m. Thomas Saulteaux Page.
10   iii.   Joseph Tanner, b. 1822; m. Angelique Clermont.
11   iv.   Louise Tanner, b. circa 1832 Red Lake, Minnesota; m. Antoine Morin; m. Jacques Lagiri; d. before 1895.
12   v.   Thomas John Tanner, b. 1842; m. Elizabeth Betsy Mary Desmarais; d. 1936.

13   vi.   Alexis Tanner, b. circa 1843; m. Sara Kikiwik.

14   vii.   Angelique Tanner, b. circa Dec 1847; m. Joseph Descheneaux.

       viii.   John Tanner II was born circa 1851 (HBS 1886-1901, 1906 Half-Breed Scrip Applications, RG15-21, Volume 1335, C-14948; See Marguerite Belhumeur application.).

15   ix.   John Baptiste Tanner, b. 20 Aug 1853 Pembina, Minnesota Territory; m. Victoire Boyer.

16   x.   Marie Tanner, b. circa 1854; m. James Bone; m. Jean Belhumeur; d. 1924.

17   xi.   Anne Tanner, b. 2 Aug 1857 St.Mary's Anglican Church, Portage la Prairie, (Manitoba); m. Charles Descheneaux.

Generation Three

6. Eliah Tanner. Question: *Son of James Tanner?*

Children of **Eliah Tanner** include:

       i.   Edward Tanner was born circa 1862 Minnesota Territory (1870C-MB, page 361, #1113.).

7. Edward Tanner was born circa 1832.

Children of **Edward Tanner** include:

       i.   John Tanner.

8. Basile Pitchito Tanner married **Elizabeth (--?--).**

Children of **Basile Pitchito Tanner** and **Elizabeth (--?--)** were as follows:

18   i.   Sadie Tanner.

       ii.   Marie Pitchito was born in Jun 1872 (INB *Index des Naissances and Baptemes* (St.Boniface, Manitoba: La Societe Historique de Saint-Boniface., c1995), page 150.). She was baptized on 13 Aug 1872 St.Francois Xavier, Manitoba (IBMS *Index des Baptemes, Mariages et Sepultures* (La Societe Historique de Saint-Boniface).) (INB, page 150.).

       iii.   Basile Tanner was born on 10 Jul 1875 (L1 Lebret Mission de St.Florent Roman Catholic Registre des Baptemes, Mariages & Seplutures, Qu'Appelle, Saskatchewan, 1868-1881., page 156, B-70. Hereinafter cited as L1.). He was baptized on 17 Aug 1875 Lebret, (Saskatchewan) (Ibid.).

       iv.   Marie Petitot was born in May 1877 (Ibid., page 226, B-19.). She was baptized on 11 Dec 1877 Lebret, (Saskatchewan) (Ibid.).

9. Suzanne Tanner married **Thomas Saulteaux Page** on 30 May 1864 St.Francois Xavier, (Manitoba) (SFXI-Kipling St.Francois Xavier Register Index, 1834-1900; compiled by Clarence Kipling , M-2.). She married **Andre (Abe) Desjarlais** before 1870. She was enumerated in the census. *Is Suzanne the daughter of Thomas Tanner?*

10. Joseph Tanner was born in 1822 (Rarihokwats, 26 Apr 1996.). He was baptized on 10 Sep 1872 St.Laurent-de-Grandin, (Saskatchewan) (SL-SK St.Laurent-de-Grandin Roman Catholic Registre des Baptemes, Mariages & Seplutures, St.Laurent, Saskatchewan, 1872-1896, page 24, B-38. Hereinafter cited as SL-SK.). He married according to the custom of the country **Angelique Clermont** before 1840. Question: *Where does he fit? Did John Falcon Tanner have 10 children? Or did Julie name the wrong Tanner?*

Children of **Joseph Tanner** and **sister of Chief Yellow Quill** were as follows:

       i.   Anonyme Tanner.

       ii.   Anonyme Tanner.

19   iii.   Julie Tanner, b. 1849 Portage la Prairie, (Manitoba); m. John Wills.

Children of **Joseph Tanner** and **Angelique Clermont** were as follows:

20   i.   Marie Tanner, b. circa 1840; m. Jean Baptiste Nolin.

21   ii.   Joseph Tanner, b. circa 1841; m. Esqua-sis Indian; m. Francoise Delaronde.

       iii.   Thomas Pitcito was born circa 1844 (SFX: 1834-1850 St.Francois Xavier 1834-1851 Register, B-619. Hereinafter cited as SFX: 1834-1850.). He was baptized on 14 Jun 1846 St.Francois Xavier, (Manitoba) (Ibid.).

       iv.   Bazile Pitchito was born circa 1845 (Ibid., B-615.). He was baptized on 31 May 1846 St.Francois Xavier, (Manitoba) (Ibid.).

       v.   Marie Rose Tanner was born circa 1845 (SB-Rozyk, page 4, B-40.). She was baptized on 22 May 1865 St.Boniface, (Manitoba) (Ibid.).

11. Louise Tanner was born circa 1832 Red Lake, Minnesota (CWLR *The Collected Writings Of Louis Riel*, 5 (University of Alberta Press, 1985), page 349.) (SFX: 1834-1850, B-123.). She was baptized on 29 May 1836 St.Francois Xavier, (Manitoba) (Ibid.). She married **Antoine Morin**, son of **Antoine Morin** and **Therese Rocque**, on 19 Jun 1854 Assumption, Pembina, Pembina County, Dakota Territory (AP Records of the Assumption Roman Catholic Church, Pembina, North Dakota: Baptisms, Marriages, Sepultures, 1848-1896; compiled by Reverend Father J. M. Belleau, 2 October 1944, page 110-111, M-42. Hereinafter cited as AP.). She married **Jacques Lagiri** before 1868. She died before 1895.

Antoine Morin was born circa Aug 1830 Red River, (Manitoba) (CWLR, page 310.). He died on 23 Apr 1862 (SN1 Catholic Parish Register of St.Norbert 1857-1873 page 57, S-8. Hereinafter cited as SN1.). He was buried on 13 May 1862 St.Norbert, (Manitoba) (Ibid.).

12. Thomas John Tanner was born in 1842 (Denney.). He was baptized on 11 May 1856 St.Mary's Anglican Church, Portage la Prairie, (Manitoba) (SMACPLP, page 1, B-7.). He married **Elizabeth Betsy Mary Desmarais** before 1865. He died in 1936 (Denney.).

Children of **Thomas John Tanner** and **Elizabeth Betsy Mary Desmarais** were as follows:

       i.   Patrick Tanner was born in Aug 1865 (Manitoba) (NWHBS 1885 Scrip Applications, North-West Halfbreeds residing outside Manitoba on 15 July 1870, RG15-20, C-14941.). He was baptized on 27 Jun 1866 St.Mary's Anglican Church, Portage la Prairie, (Manitoba) (SMACPLP, B-269.).

       ii.   Henry Charles Tanner was baptized on 21 Nov 1866 St.Mary's Anglican Church, Portage la Prairie, (Manitoba) (Ibid., B-280.).

       iii.   Amelia Harriet Tanner was baptized on 23 Jul 1867 St.Mary's Anglican Church, Portage la Prairie, (Manitoba) (Ibid., B-292.). She married James Bird on 6 Oct 1882 Westbourne, Manitoba (MB Vital Statistics, Marriage Reg. #1883,001390.).

iv. Isabella Tanner was baptized on 18 May 1868 St.Mary's Anglican Church, Portage la Prairie, (Manitoba) (SMACPLP, B-310.). She was buried on 28 Jun 1868 St.Mary's Anglican Church, Portage la Prairie, (Manitoba) (Ibid., S-68.).

13. Alexis Tanner was born circa 1843. He married **Sara Kikiwik** before 1864.

Children of **Alexis Tanner** and **Sara Kikiwik** were as follows:

    i. Father Joseph Henri Kutensan was born in Nov 1864 (SB-Rozyk, page 8, B-60.). He was baptized on 21 Jun 1865 (Fort Alexandre), St.Boniface, (Manitoba) (Ibid.).

    ii. Marie Adelaide Pitchito was born in Feb 1865 (Ibid., page 5, B-45.). She was baptized on 27 May 1865 St.Boniface, (Manitoba) (Ibid.).

    iii. Job Pitchito was born in Jan 1867 (INB, page 150.). He was baptized on 13 Apr 1867 St.Francois Xavier, (Manitoba) (Ibid.) (IBMS.) (SFXI-Kipling, B-_.).

    iv. Jean Baptiste Pitchito was born on 1 Apr 1870 (INB, page 150.) (SFXI-Kipling, B-39.). He was baptized on 19 May 1870 St.Francois Xavier, (Manitoba) (INB, page 150.) (SFXI-Kipling, B-39.). He died on 15 Jan 1886 Lebret, (Saskatchewan), at age 15 (L2 Lebret, Mission de St.Florent, Roman Catholic Registre des Baptemes, Mariages & Seplutures, Qu'Appelle, Saskatchewan, Book Two: 1881-1887, FHC microfilm 1032949., page 132, S-4. Hereinafter cited as L2.). He was buried on 16 Jan 1886 Lebret, (Saskatchewan) (Ibid.).

    v. Virginie Kessisawen was born in Aug 1871 (SB-Rozyk, page 217, B-51.). She was baptized on 21 Aug 1871 St.Boniface, Manitoba (Ibid.).

    vi. Anonyme Pecheeto was born circa 1872 (L1, page 138, S-27.). He/she was buried on 1 Dec 1874 Lebret, (Saskatchewan) (Ibid.).

22 vii. Louise Tanner, b. 25 Mar 1874; m. Chrysostome Flamand.

    viii. Marie Tanner was born circa Apr 1875 (SL-SK, page 37, B-11.). She was baptized on 11 May 1875 St.Laurent-de-Grandin, (Saskatchewan) (Ibid.).

    ix. Alexandre Pitchito was born on 18 Jul 1875 (Ibid., page 44, B-49.). He was baptized on 30 Jul 1875 St.Laurent-de-Grandin, (Saskatchewan) (Ibid.).

    x. Joseph Tanner was born on 6 Aug 1876 (L1, page 210, B-98.). He was baptized on 13 Apr 1877 Lebret, (Saskatchewan) (Ibid.).

23 xi. Bella Tanner, b. 1879 Maple Creek, (Saskatchewan); m. Benoit Pepin.

14. Angelique Tanner was born circa Dec 1847 (AP, page 5, B-4.). She was baptized on 18 Aug 1848 Assumption, Pembina, Pembina County, Minnesota Territory (Ibid.). She married **Joseph Descheneaux**, son of **Pierre Descheneaux** and **Josephte Courchene**, on 11 May 1869 St.Boniface, (Manitoba) (SB-Rozyk, page 151, M-2.).
She was adopted in 1995.

Joseph Descheneaux was born on 7 Aug 1846 St.Norbert, (Manitoba) (HBSI.) (ArchiviaNet.). He married **Isabelle Lafournaise**, daughter of **Jerome Lafournaise dit Laboucane** and **Priscille Wills**, on 7 Oct 1901 St.Thomas, Duhamel, (Alberta) (DA Register of the Duhamel, Alberta Roman Catholic Church: 1881-1921, M-5. Hereinafter cited as DA.). He died on 5 Jun 1915 at age 68 (Denney.).

15. John Baptiste Tanner was born on 20 Aug 1853 Pembina, Minnesota Territory (AP, page 94, B-91.). He was baptized on 4 Sep 1853 Assumption, Pembina, Pembina County, Dakota Territory (Ibid.). He married **Victoire Boyer**, daughter of **Louis Boyer** and **Madeleine Trottier**, in 1875 Winnipeg, (Manitoba).

Victoire Boyer was born on 2 Aug 1854 St.Francois Xavier, (Manitoba) (SFXI-Kipling, B-151.) (SFXI 1851-1868 St.Francois Xavier 1852-1861 Register Index, B-151. Hereinafter cited as SFXI 1851-1868.). She was baptized on 3 Aug 1854 St.Francois Xavier, (Manitoba) (SFXI-Kipling, B-151.) (SFXI 1851-1868, B-151.). She died circa Apr 1880 south of Wood Mountain, (Saskatchewan) (L1, page 246, S-_.). She was buried on 15 May 1880 Lebret, (Saskatchewan) (Ibid.).

Children of **John Baptiste Tanner** and **Victoire Boyer** were as follows:

    i. Joseph Tanner was born circa 1869 (ArchiviaNet.).

    ii. Emelie Tanner was born on 22 Apr 1876 (L1, page 165, B-8.). She was baptized on 7 May 1876 Lebret, (Saskatchewan) (Ibid.). She died on 17 Jan 1881 St.Laurent, (Saskatchewan), at age 4 (SL-SK, page 47, S-1.). She was buried on 18 Jan 1881 St.Laurent-de-Grandin, (Saskatchewan) (Ibid.).

    iii. Amelia Tanner was born on 12 Apr 1880 Qu'Appelle, (Saskatchewan) (DL, page 36, B-40.). She was baptized on 28 Oct 1880 Duck Lake, (Saskatchewan) (Ibid.). She died circa 1880 Qu'Appelle, (Saskatchewan) (HBSI.).

16. Marie Tanner was born circa 1854 (HBS, Volume 1335, C-14948; See Marguerite Belhumeur application.). She was baptized on 11 May 1856 St.Mary's Anglican Church, Portage la Prairie, (Manitoba) (SMACPLP, page 1, B-8.). She married **James Bone**, son of **Yellowhead**, before 1874. She married **Jean Belhumeur**, son of **Andre Belhumeur** and **Marguerite Maron**, on 27 May 1874 Duck Lake, (Saskatchewan) (DL, page 22, M-11.). She died in 1924 (BIA-LS.).

James Bone died between 1873 and 1874.

Jean Belhumeur was born on 15 Sep 1832 St.Francois Xavier, (Manitoba) (MBS, C-14931.) (SB 1825-1834 St.Boniface Roman Catholic Registre des Baptemes, Mariages & Seplutures, 1825-1834, page 77, B-480. Hereinafter cited as SB 1825-1834.). He was baptized on 23 Sep 1832 St.Boniface, (Manitoba) (Ibid.). He married **Marie Malaterre**, daughter of **Jean Baptiste Malaterre** and **Angelique Adam**, on 10 Jan 1860 St.Francois Xavier, (Manitoba) (SFXI-Kipling, M-1.) (HBS, Volume 1335; C-14948.). He died on 5 Mar 1898 Ellice, Manitoba, at age 65 (Ibid.) (MB Vital Statistics, Death Reg. #1898,001522.). He was buried on 7 Mar 1898 (HBS, Volume 1335; C-14948.).

17. Anne Tanner was baptized on 2 Aug 1857 St.Mary's Anglican Church, Portage la Prairie, (Manitoba) (SMACPLP, page 5, B-33.). She was born in 1858 Portage la Prairie, (Manitoba) (ArchiviaNet, C-15005.). She was baptized on 6 Jul 1874 Duck Lake, (Saskatchewan) (DL, page 23, B-88.). She married **Charles Descheneaux**, son of **Pierre Descheneaux** and **Josephte Courchene**, on 7 Jul 1874 Duck Lake, (Saskatchewan) (Ibid., page 23, M-12.).

Charles Descheneaux was born in 1852 St.Norbert, (Manitoba) (NWHBS, C-14937.). He died on 23 Jun 1921 Duhamel, Alberta (Denney.). He was buried in Jun 1921 Duhamel, (Alberta) (Ibid.).

Generation Four

18. Sadie Tanner married **Colin Severight**.

19. Julie Tanner was born in 1849 Portage la Prairie, (Manitoba) (Ibid.). She married **John Wills**, son of **John Wills** and **Marie McKay**, on 15 Oct 1869 St.Francois Xavier, (Manitoba) (SFXI-Kipling, M-13.).

John Wills was born on 27 Dec 1848 St.Francois Xavier, (Manitoba) (SFX: 1834-1850, B-758.). He was baptized on 31 Dec 1848 St.Francois Xavier, (Manitoba) (Ibid.). He died on 19 Jan 1910 Eagle Hills, Saskatchewan, at age 61 (T. R. "Pat" McCloy, McKay Descendancy, McKay Descendancy.).

20. Marie Tanner was born circa 1840 (SFX: 1834-1850, B-620.). She was baptized on 14 Jun 1846 St.Francois Xavier, (Manitoba) (Ibid.). She married **Jean Baptiste Nolin**, son of **Joseph Nolin** and **Louise Frederic**, on 2 Sep 1861 St.Boniface, (Manitoba) (SB-Rozyk, page 31, M-31.).

Jean Baptiste Nolin was born circa 1834 Red River, (Manitoba) (1850Ci-MN, page 30, Dwelling 119, Family 119.). He was baptized on 16 Feb 1834 St.Boniface, (Manitoba) (SB-Rozyk, page 31, M-31 (note).). He was born in 1836 St.Vital, (Manitoba) (HBSI.) (ArchiviaNet.).

21. Joseph Tanner was born circa 1841. He married **Esqua-sis Indian** before 1862. He married **Francoise Delaronde**, daughter of **Louis Delaronde dit Laronde** and **Madeleine Boucher**, on 16 Oct 1873 St.Boniface, Manitoba (SB-Rozyk, page 293, M-18.).

Children of **Joseph Tanner** and **Esqua-sis Indian** were as follows:

    i.   Marie Joseph Jeanne Tanner was born circa 1862 (Ibid., page 4, B-41.). She was baptized on 22 May 1865 St.Boniface, (Manitoba) (Ibid.). She married Fulgence Boyer, son of Pierre Boyer and Genevieve Martin, before 1884. She married John Swain before 1901.

        Fulgence Boyer was born on 25 Mar 1852 St.Francois Xavier, (Manitoba) (MBSI Index Scrip Applications, Original White Settlers & Halfbreeds residing in Manitoba on 15 July 1870, RG15-19, C-14925 (25 Mar 1852).) (SFXI 1851-1868, B-11.). He was baptized on 28 Mar 1852 St.Francois Xavier, (Manitoba) (Ibid.). He died on 18 Jun 1888 St.Laurent, Manitoba, at age 36 (MB Vital Statistics, Death Reg. #1888,001811.).

    ii.   Marie Rose Tanner was born on 15 Jan 1872 Manitoba (1901 Canada, District 202-z, page 2, line 17.). She married Henri Delaronde, son of Etienne Delaronde or Laronde and Caroline Carriere, before 1896 (ArchiviaNet.).

        Henri Delaronde was born on 23 Dec 1866 St.Boniface, (Manitoba) (MBS, C-14929.) (SB-Rozyk, page 71, B-138.). He was baptized on 23 Dec 1866 St.Boniface, (Manitoba) (Ibid.).

    iii. Joseph Tanner was born in Dec 1877 Fort Walsh, (Saskatchewan) (HBSI.) (ArchiviaNet.). He died in Dec 1877 Fort Walsh, (Saskatchewan) (HBSI.) (ArchiviaNet.).

Francoise Delaronde was born in 1840 Red River Settlement, (Manitoba) (MBS, C-14929.).

22. Louise Tanner was born on 25 Mar 1874 (DL, page 20, B-78.). She was baptized on 1 Apr 1874 Duck Lake, (Saskatchewan) (Ibid.). She married **Chrysostome Flamand**, son of **Jean Baptiste Flamand** and **Marie Morand**, on 19 Jul 1897 Ellice, Manitoba (MB Vital Statistics, Marriage Reg. #1897,001449.).

Chrysostome Flamand was born on 25 Apr 1873 Fort Ellice, Manitoba (HBSI.) (L1, page 97-98, B-92.). He was baptized on 12 May 1873 Lebret, (Saskatchewan) (Ibid.).

23. Bella Tanner was born on 1 Dec 1878 (1901 Canada, #9, T-2, page 5, family 38, line 1-4.). She was born in 1879 Maple Creek, (Saskatchewan) (ArchiviaNet.). She married **Benoit Pepin**, son of **Narcisse Pepin** and **Marie Beaulieu**, on 29 Nov 1894 Fort Ellice, Manitoba (MB Vital Statistics, Marriage Reg. #1896,001020.).

Benoit Pepin was born on 30 Jun 1858 North West Territories (MBS, C-14932.). He married **Marie Christine Fleury**, daughter of **Michel Fleury** and **Marie Anne Piche**, on 25 Jan 1881 St.Eustache, Manitoba (ST-BSP, M-2.).

Descendants of George Taylor

Generation One

1. George Taylor was born circa 1760 Berwick-on-Tweed, England (HBCA-B Hudson's Bay Company Archives - biographical sketches, Hudson's Bay Company Archives; Winnipeg, Manitoba, A.32/3, fo. 179.). He married according to the custom of the country **Jane Native** before 1797.

Children of **George Taylor** and **Jane Native** were as follows:

  2   i.   Thomas Taylor, b. 1797; m. Marie Keith; d. 18 Dec 1879 home of his daughter Mr. Francis St.Denis, Pembroke, Ontario.

  3   ii. George Taylor II, b. circa 1799 Ruperts Land; m. Jane Prince; d. 18 Dec 1844 St.Andrews, (Manitoba).

  4   iii. Marguerite Taylor, b. 1805 Polar Sea; m. George Simpson; m. Louis Amable Hogue; d. 16 Dec 1885 Assiniboia, Manitoba.

  5   iv. Nancy Taylor, b. 1808 North West Territories; m. William Harper; m. John Cox; d. 16 Jul 1897 St.Andrews, Manitoba.

Generation Two

2. Thomas Taylor was born in 1797 (Denney Papers, Charles D. Denney, Glenbow Archives, Calgary, Alberta.). He was baptized on 12 Aug 1821 St.Johns, (Manitoba) (Ibid.). He was baptized on 12 Aug 1821 St.Johns, Red River Settlement, (Manitoba) (HBCR Hudson Bay Company Register of Anglican Church Baptisms, Marriages, and Burials for the Red River Settlement, 1821-1841; Hudson's Bay Company Archives, Winnipeg, Manitoba, E.4/1a, folio 35. Hereinafter cited as HBCR.). He married **Marie Keith**, daughter of **James Keith** and **Native Woman**, on 17 Aug 1831 St.Johns, Red River Settlement, (Manitoba) (HBCA-B, E.4/1b fo. 232.) (HBCR, M-218.). He died on 18 Dec 1879 home of his daughter Mr. Francis St.Denis, Pembroke, Ontario (HBCA-B, B.134/c/142, 140; A.1/180, fo. 17.).

Marie Keith was born circa 1814 (*DCB-V8 Dictionary of Canadian Biography - Volume Eight*;Toronto, Ontario: University of Toronto Press, 2000), Philip Goldring, page 454-455.). She was baptized on 1 Sep 1833 St.Johns, Red River Settlement, (Manitoba) (HBCR, E.4/1a, folio 104d.).

Children of **Thomas Taylor** and **Marie Keith** were as follows:

6 i. Thomas Taylor, b. 25 Aug 1831 North West; m. Elizabeth Margaret Kennedy; d. 1903 Lac Ste.Anne, (Alberta).

 ii. James Keith Taylor was baptized on 1 Sep 1833 St.Johns, Red River Settlement, (Manitoba) (Ibid.). He died on 1 Nov 1863 St.Johns, (Manitoba), at age 30 (Denney.).

 iii. Florence Taylor was born between 1835 and 1842. She died in 1882 (HBCA-B, E.4/1a, fos. 104d-105.).

7 iv. Jane Taylor, b. circa 1838.

8 v. George Taylor, b. 1838; m. Angelique Lafrance.

 vi. John Swanston Taylor was born in 1839 (HBCA-B.). He died in 1841 (Ibid.).

 vii. Albert Taylor was born before 1844. He died in 1844 (Ibid.).

9 viii. William Taylor, b. before 1848; m. Marie Louise Lafrance.

3. George Taylor II was born circa 1799 Ruperts Land (1843C RRS HBCA E5/11 1843 Census of the Red River Settlement, HBCA E5/11, Hudson's Bay Company Archives, Provincial Archives, 200 Vaughan Street, Winnipeg, MB R3C 1T5, Canada., page 22.). He married **Jane Prince**, daughter of **Mark Prince** and **Sarah**, on 11 Jan 1828 (York Factory), St.Johns, (Manitoba) (HBCR, M-147.). He died on 18 Dec 1844 St.Andrews, (Manitoba) (Denney.) (HBCA-B, A.16/48, fo. 142.).

Jane Prince was born circa 1810 Ruperts Land (1870C-MB 1870 Manitoba Census, National Archives of Canada, Ottawa, Ontario, Microfilm Reel Number C-2170., page 202, #800.). She was born in 1815 North West (MBS Scrip Applications, Original White Settlers & Halfbreeds residing in Manitoba on 15 July 1870, RG15-19, C-14934.). She married **Frederick Hemmingway** on 28 Sep 1848 (St.Andrews), The Rapids, Red River Settlement, (Manitoba) (HBCR, No. 173.).

Children of **George Taylor II** and **Jane Prince** were as follows:

10 i. Mary Taylor, b. circa 1827 North West; m. John Smith.

11 ii. Jane Taylor, b. 1 Feb 1829 North West; m. David Harcus.

12 iii. George Taylor III, b. 2 Aug 1833 St.Johns, Oxford House; m. Isabella Cooper.

13 iv. Victoria Taylor, b. 25 Feb 1834 North West Territories; m. Alexander 'Sandy' Thomas.

14 v. Robert Alexander Taylor, b. 9 Mar 1836 St.Johns, Red River Settlement, (Manitoba); m. Eliza Voller; d. 26 Mar 1919 St.Clements, Manitoba.

15 vi. Sarah Taylor, b. 1 Jun 1838 St.Johns, (Manitoba); m. Thomas McCorrister.

16 vii. Edward Prince Taylor, b. 1 Feb 1841 St.Johns, (Manitoba); m. Mary Sabiston; m. Sarah Stevens.

17 viii. Thomas Taylor, b. 1843 St.Andrews, (Manitoba); m. Mary Ann Young; d. 14 Jul 1875 St.Andrews, Manitoba.

4. Marguerite Taylor was born in 1805 Polar Sea (MBS, C-14928.). She was baptized on 7 Jul 1833 St.Johns, Red River Settlement, (Manitoba) (HBCR, E.4/1a, folio 102.). She married according to the custom of the country **George Simpson**, son of **George Simpson**, circa 1825. She married **Louis Amable Hogue**, son of **Louis Amable Hogue** and **Marie Anne Labelle**, on 24 Mar 1831 St.Johns, Red River Settlement, (Manitoba) (Ibid., M-215.). She died on 16 Dec 1885 Assiniboia, Manitoba (Manitoba Vital Statistics online, http://web2.gov.mb.ca, Death Reg. #1885,001556.).

George Simpson was born in 1786 Scotland (Denney.). He married according to the custom of the country **Elizabeth "Betsy" Sinclair**, daughter of **William Sinclair** and **Margaret Nahovway**, before 1822. He married according to the custom of the country **Mrs. (Keith's Indian wife) Keith** circa 1824. He married **Frances Ramsey Simpson**, daughter of **Geddes Mackenzie Simpson** and **Frances Hawkins**, on 24 Feb 1830 Bromley, Middlesex, England (Ibid.). He died on 7 Sep 1860 Lachine, Lower Canada (Ibid.) (*DCB-V8*, John S. Galbraith, page 812-817.).

Louis Amable Hogue was born on 14 Jul 1796 St-Vincent-de-Paul, Quebec (1835C RRS HBCA E5/8 1835 Census of the Red River Settlement, HBCA E5/8, Hudson's Bay Company Archives, Provincial Archives, 200 Vaughan Street, Winnipeg, MB R3C 1T5, Canada., page 9.) (Rod MacQuarrie Research, 19 Apr 2012.). He was baptized on 14 Jul 1796 St-Vincent-de-Paul, Quebec (Ibid.). He died on 26 Feb 1858 at age 61 (HBCA-B.).

5. Nancy Taylor was born in 1808 North West Territories (MBS, C-14926.). She was baptized on 20 Feb 1838 St.Johns, Red River Settlement, (Manitoba) (HBCR, E.4/1a, folio 149d.). She married **William Harper** on 17 May 1831 St.Johns, (Manitoba) (Denney.). She married **John Cox**, son of **John Cox**, on 11 Nov 1835 St.Johns, Red River Colony, (Manitoba) (HBCR, No. 1.). She died on 16 Jul 1897 St.Andrews, Manitoba (MB Vital Statistics, Death Reg. #1897,001043.).

William Harper. Question: *Entry not found in the HBCA marriage register.*

John Cox was born in 1795 Scotland (1870C-MB, page 199, #697.). He died on 16 Apr 1872 Little Britain, Manitoba (Denney.).

Generation Three

6. Thomas Taylor was born on 25 Aug 1831 North West (MBS, C-14933.) (SB 1825-1834, page 68, B-451.). He was baptized on 16 Jun 1832 St.Boniface, (Manitoba) (Ibid.). He was baptized on 1 Sep 1833 St.Johns, Red River Settlement, (Manitoba) (HBCA-B.) (HBCR, E.4/1a, folio 105.). He married **Elizabeth Margaret Kennedy**, daughter of **Philip Kennedy** and **Elizabeth 'Jessie' McKenzie**, on 10 Oct 1860 Fort Pelly, (Saskatchewan) (Denney.). He died in 1903 Lac Ste.Anne, (Alberta) (Ibid.).

Elizabeth Margaret Kennedy was born on 18 Mar 1843 St.Andrews, (Manitoba) (MBS, C-14933.). She was baptized on 22 Mar 1843 St.Johns, (Manitoba) (Denney.). She died on 1 Sep 1932 at age 89 (Ibid.).

Children of **Thomas Taylor** and **Elizabeth Margaret Kennedy** were as follows:

18 i. Caroline May Jessie Taylor, b. 15 Feb 1862 Touchwood Hills, (Saskatchewan); m. William Philip Beaupre.

 ii. Thomas Alexander Christy Taylor was born in 1866 Touchwood Hills, (Saskatchewan) (Ibid.). He was baptized on 20 Aug 1866 St.Johns, (Manitoba) (Ibid.).

 iii. Frances Emma Taylor was born in 1866 (Manitoba) (1870C-MB, page 183, #198.).

 iv. William Phillip Taylor was born in 1868 (Denney.). He married Annie Taylor on 11 Nov 1890 Wallace, Manitoba (MB Vital Statistics, Mar Reg. #1890,001611.).

 v. Edward Taylor was baptized on 19 Jun 1871 St.Andrews, Manitoba (Denney.).

19 vi. Margaret Taylor, b. circa 1873; m. Richard George Hardisty; d. 17 Jun 1901 Edmonton, (Alberta).

20 vii. Louisa Jane Taylor, b. 15 Jan 1875 Westbourne, Manitoba; m. Cecil Armistead.

viii. Frederick George Taylor was born on 1 Jan 1877 Westbourne, Manitoba (ArchiviaNet 1886-1901, 1906 Half-Breed Scrip Applications Index, RG15-21, Volume 1333 through 1371, Microfilm Reel Number C-14944 through C-15010, National Archives of Canada, Ottawa, Ontario, http://www.collectionscanada.gc.ca, C-15006.).

ix. Arthur Sydney Taylor was born on 9 Jan 1880 Carlton House, (Saskatchewan) (Ibid.). He was buried St.Marys, Prince Albert, (Saskatchewan) (Denney.).

x. Keith Swanston Taylor was born on 27 May 1882 Prince Albert, (Saskatchewan) (Saskatchewan Vital Statistics online, http://vsgs.health.gov.sk.ca, Birth Reg. #10796.).

7. Jane Taylor was born circa 1838 (PM Catholic Parish Register of Pembroke Mission, Ontario, Canada 1839-1842, 1856-1866, 1867-1878, page 11, M-3. Hereinafter cited as PM.). She married **Damase Gervais**, son of **Philippe Gervais** and **Flavie Boudreau**, on 2 Sep 1855 Notre-Dame-Du-Mont Carmel, LaPasse, Renfrew County, Ontario (Ibid.).

8. George Taylor was born in 1838 (HBCA-B.). He was baptized on 30 Sep 1867 LaPasse, Renfrew County, Ontario (Rod Mac Quarrie, 29 Dec 2011.). He married **Angelique Lafrance**, daughter of **Paul LaFrance dit Daragon** and **Suzanne Jeannot dit Bergeron**, on 30 Sep 1867 LaPasse, Renfrew County, Ontario (Lionel V. DeRagon Research.) (Rod Mac Quarrie, 29 Dec 2011.).

Angelique Lafrance was born on 9 Aug 1850 Ste.Marthe, Vaudreuil, Quebec (Lionel V. DeRagon.). She married **Joseph Follgenlogel**, son of **Michel Folgenlogel** and **Barbara Neighart**, on 20 Sep 1883 St.Eustache, Manitoba (MM.).

Children of **George Taylor** and **Angelique Lafrance** were as follows:

i. Mary Jane Taylor was born circa 1870 (1881 Canada, Film No. C-13283, District 186, Sub-district K, page 5, Household No. 21.).

ii. Fanny Taylor was born circa 1871 (Ibid.).

iii. Thomas Taylor was born circa 1873 (Ibid.).

9. William Taylor was born before 1848. He married **Marie Louise Lafrance**, daughter of **Paul LaFrance dit Daragon** and **Suzanne Jeannot dit Bergeron**, on 23 Oct 1869 Notre-Dame-du-Mont Carmel, LaPasse, Renfrew County, Ontario (Lionel V. DeRagon, 8 Dec 1992.) (PM, page 61, M-18.) (Rod Mac Quarrie, 29 Dec 2011.).

Marie Louise Lafrance was born on 11 Mar 1852 Rigaud, Vaudreuil, Quebec (Mary McClammy Research.). She married **Joseph Boucher**, son of **Calixte Boucher** and **Alice Lalonde**, on 16 Mar 1893 Pembroke, REN, Ontario (Lionel V. DeRagon, 8 Dec 1992.). She died Pembroke, REN, Ontario.

Children of **William Taylor** and **Marie Louise Lafrance** were:

i. William Taylor was born in Jan 1871 Quebec (Rod Mac Quarrie, 29 Dec 2011.).

10. Mary Taylor was born circa 1827 North West (1870C-MB, page 197, #651.). She was baptized on 16 Aug 1829 (York Factory), St.Johns, (Manitoba) (HBCR, #95.) (Ibid., E.4/1a, folio 71d, #95.). She married **John Smith**, son of **John James Smith** and **Mary Indian**, on 8 Apr 1847 (St.Andrews), Rapids Church, Red River Settlement, (Manitoba) (Ibid., No. 162.).

John Smith was born in 1821 North West (MBS, C-14934.). He was baptized on 12 Jul 1825 St.Johns, Red River Settlement, (Manitoba) (HBCR, E.4/1a, folio 56d.).

11. Jane Taylor was born on 1 Feb 1829 North West (MBS, C-14934.). She was baptized on 2 Aug 1833 St.Johns, Oxford House (HBCR, E.4/1a, folio 103.). She married **David Harcus**, son of **David Harcus** and **Margaret Richards**, on 12 Nov 1846 (St.Andrews), Rapids Church, (Manitoba) (Ibid., No. 151.).

David Harcus was baptized in Oct 1828 North West (MBS, C-14934.). He was baptized on 3 Oct 1837 St.Johns, Red River Settlement, (Manitoba) (HBCR, E.4/1a, folio 146.). He died on 18 Apr 1883 St.Andrews, Manitoba, at age 54 (MB Vital Statistics, Death Reg. #1883,001752.).

12. George Taylor III was born on 1 Oct 1829 York Factory (MBS, C-14933.). He was baptized on 2 Aug 1833 St.Johns, Oxford House (HBCA-B.) (HBCR, E.4/1a, folio 103d.). He married **Isabella Cooper**, daughter of **Charles Thomas Cooper** and **Catherine Thomas**, on 6 Mar 1854 St.Andrews, (Manitoba) (Denney.).

Isabella Cooper was born in 1835 North West (MBS, C-14934.).

Children of **George Taylor III** and **Isabella Cooper** were as follows:

21 i. George Taylor IV, b. 22 Feb 1855 St.Andrews, (Manitoba); m. Mary Rose Kirkness.

22 ii. Annabella Taylor, b. 3 Jan 1858 St.Andrews, (Manitoba); m. Robert Mowat.

23 iii. Catherine Jane Taylor, b. 2 Nov 1860 St.Andrews, (Manitoba).

iv. Thomas Richard Prince Taylor was born on 18 Apr 1862 St.Andrews, (Manitoba) (Ibid., C-14933.).

24 v. Louise Taylor, b. 2 Jul 1866 St.Andrews, (Manitoba); m. Amable Bouvette.

25 vi. Victoria Taylor, b. 3 Jun 1869 St.Andrews, (Manitoba); d. 28 Mar 1955 Melfort, Saskatchewan.

26 vii. William Richard Taylor, b. 12 Dec 1870 St.Andrews, Manitoba; m. Drusilla Child.

viii. James Taylor was born in 1881 Prince Albert, (Saskatchewan) (ArchiviaNet, C-15006.).

13. Victoria Taylor was born on 25 Feb 1834 North West Territories (Denney.). She was baptized on 11 Dec 1834 St.Johns, Red River Settlement, (Manitoba) (HBCA-B.) (HBCR, E.4/1a, folio 117.). She married **Alexander 'Sandy' Thomas** on 9 Oct 1851 St.Andrews, (Manitoba) (Denney.).

Alexander 'Sandy' Thomas died before 15 Jul 1870 (1870C-MB, page 191, #466.).

14. Robert Alexander Taylor was born in 1836 Fort of the Rockies (MBS, C-14933.) (Denney.). He was baptized on 9 Mar 1836 St.Johns, Red River Settlement, (Manitoba) (HBCA-B.) (HBCR, E.4/1a, folio 127d.). He married **Eliza Voller**, daughter of **James Voller** and **Nancy Birston**, on 27 Jun 1867 St.Andrews, (Manitoba) (HBCA-B.). He died on 26 Mar 1919 St.Clements, Manitoba, at age 83 (MB Vital Statistics, Death Reg. #1919,018439.).

Eliza Voller was born on 23 Jan 1849 St.Andrews, (Manitoba) (Denney.). She was baptized on 27 Mar 1849 St.Andrews, (Manitoba) (Ibid.). She died on 19 Feb 1921 R. M. of St.Clements, Manitoba, at age 72 (MB Vital Statistics, Death Reg. #1921,070502.).

Children of **Robert Alexander Taylor** and **Eliza Voller** were as follows:

27 i. Mary Ann Jane Taylor, b. 3 Jun 1868 St.Andrews, (Manitoba); m. Thomas Mowat; d. 26 Jan 1938 St.Andrews, Manitoba.

28 ii. Edward Taylor, b. 23 Aug 1870 St.Andrews, Manitoba; m. Clara Spence.

29   iii.   Caroline Taylor, b. 23 Oct 1871 St.Clements, Manitoba; m. James Frost.

15.   Sarah Taylor was born on 1 Jun 1838 St.Johns, (Manitoba) (MBS, C-14933.). She was baptized on 7 Jul 1838 St.Johns, Fort Garry, Red River Settlement, (Manitoba) (HBCA-B.) (HBCR, E.4/1a, folio 152.). She and **Thomas McCorrister** met before 1867.

Thomas McCorrister was born on 21 Jan 1847 St.Andrews, (Manitoba) (MBS, C-14930.). He married **Mary Stevens**, daughter of **William Richard Stevens** and **Mary Foulds**, on 1 Sep 1868 St.Andrews, (Manitoba) (Denney.). He died on 15 Mar 1896 St.Andrews, Manitoba, at age 49 (Ibid.).

16.   Edward Prince Taylor was baptized on 1 Feb 1841 St.Johns, (Manitoba) (Denney.). He married **Mary Sabiston**, daughter of **Alexander Sabiston** and **Nancy Campbell**, on 23 Jun 1862 St.Andrews, (Manitoba) (Ibid.). He married **Sarah Stevens**, daughter of **William Richard Stevens** and **Mary Foulds**, on 15 Jun 1871 St.Andrews, Manitoba (Ibid.).

Mary Sabiston was born in 1846 St.Andrews, (Manitoba) (Ibid.). She died before 15 Jul 1870 (1870C-MB, page 202, #793.).

Children of **Edward Prince Taylor** and **Mary Sabiston** all born St.Andrews, (Manitoba), were as follows:

30   i.   Edward Taylor, b. 3 Dec 1862; m. Sarah Ellen Monkman.
      ii.   Elizabeth Jane Taylor was baptized on 5 Jun 1864 (Denney.).
31   iii.   Mary Ann Taylor, b. 8 Sep 1866; m. Jeremiah Stevens; d. 1927.
      iv.   Victoria Taylor was baptized on 25 Oct 1868 (Ibid.).

Sarah Stevens was born on 19 Aug 1853 St.Andrews, (Manitoba) (MBS, C-14933.).

Children of **Edward Prince Taylor** and **Sarah Stevens** were as follows:

32   i.   Robert Taylor, b. 25 May 1873 Winnipeg, Manitoba; m. Christie Bell Monkman.
      ii.   Sarah Taylor was born on 26 Jul 1873 St.Andrews, Manitoba (Louis Verhagen Research.).
33   iii.   Catherine Taylor, b. 1875; m. Joseph Bird.
34   iv.   Priscilla Jane Taylor, b. 24 May 1877 Prince Albert, (Saskatchewan); m. Alex Spencer.
35   v.   Ellen Taylor, b. 1879 South Branch, (Saskatchewan); m. Alfred William Bird; d. 19 Jan 1899 Birch Hills, (Saskatchewan).
      vi.   Alice Margaret Taylor was born on 11 Jun 1881 Puckhan, (Saskatchewan) (HBSI Index 1886-1901, 1906 Halfbreed Scrip Applications, RG15-21.) (1901 Canada, microfilm, T-6553, Brancepeth, page 2, Family 8, line 7-9.) (ArchiviaNet, C-14998.). She married William Belcher Price, son of Joseph Harvey Price and Nancy Baillie, before 1901 (Ibid.).
            William Belcher Price was born on 4 Oct 1881 Battleford, (Saskatchewan) (1901 Canada, microfilm, T-6553, Brancepeth, page 2, Family 8, line 7-9.) (HBSI.) (ArchiviaNet, C-14998.).
      vii.   Eliza Taylor was born in 1882 Puckhan, (Saskatchewan) (ArchiviaNet.). She died on 12 May 1883 Puckhan, (Saskatchewan) (Ibid.).
      viii.   William Taylor was born on 15 Jan 1884 Puckhan, (Saskatchewan) (Ibid., C-15006.).
      ix.   Collin Taylor was born in 1886 (Louis Verhagen.).
      x.   Frederick Taylor was born in 1888 (Ibid.).
      xi.   Jessie Winnie Taylor was born on 20 Dec 1889 (Saskatchewan) (SK Vital Statistics, Birth Reg. #7978.).
      xii.   Edith Blanch Taylor was born on 25 Oct 1892 (Saskatchewan) (Ibid., Birth Reg. #7246.).
      xiii.   Caroline Emily Taylor was born on 8 Sep 1894 (Saskatchewan) (Ibid., Birth Reg. #7293.).
      xiv.   Mary Alexdra Lully Ann Taylor was born on 6 Jun 1896 (Saskatchewan) (Ibid., Birth Reg. #7451.).
      xv.   John Alexander Taylor was born on 16 Jul 1899 St.Sunany Parish, (Saskatchewan) (Ibid., Birth Reg. #1713.).

17.   Thomas Taylor was born in 1843 St.Andrews, (Manitoba) (MBS, C-14933.). He married **Mary Ann Young**, daughter of **James Young** and **Isabella Stevens**, before 1870. He died on 14 Jul 1875 St.Andrews, Manitoba (Ibid.).

Mary Ann Young was born in 1853 St.Andrews, (Manitoba) (Ibid., C-14934.).

Children of **Thomas Taylor** and **Mary Ann Young** both born St.Andrews, Manitoba, were as follows:

      i.   Victoria Jane Taylor was born on 13 Nov 1870 (Ibid., C-14933.).
36   ii.   Alexander Thomas Taylor, b. 17 Jun 1875; m. Harriet Jane Smith.

Generation Four

18.   Caroline May Jessie Taylor was born on 15 Feb 1862 Touchwood Hills, (Saskatchewan) (SK Vital Statistics, Birth Reg. #11400.). She was baptized on 29 Jun 1862 St.Peters, (Manitoba) (Denney.). She married **William Philip Beaupre**, son of **Philip Beaupre** and **Therese Denoyer**, circa 1883 Prince Albert, (Saskatchewan) (Ibid.).

William Philip Beaupre was born on 8 May 1852 Minnesota (1901 Canada, #202, g(2), page 1, family 4, line 18-28.).

19.   Margaret Taylor was born circa 1873. She married **Richard George Hardisty**, son of **Richard Charles Hardisty** and **Elizabeth Victoria (Eliza) McDougall**, on 21 Jul 1892 Edmonton, (Alberta) (Denney.) (ArchiviaNet.). She died on 17 Jun 1901 Edmonton, (Alberta) (Denney.).

Richard George Hardisty was born on 10 May 1871 Victoria, (Alberta) (HBSI.) (ArchiviaNet.). He died on 23 Jul 1943 at age 72 (Denney.).

20.   Louisa Jane Taylor was born on 15 Jan 1875 Westbourne, Manitoba (HBS, Volume 1334, C-14945.). She married **Cecil Armistead** before 1898 (Ibid.) (1901 Canada, #202, g(2), page 1, family 5, line 29-33.).

Cecil Armistead was born on 23 Jan 1874 (Ibid.).

21.   George Taylor IV was born on 22 Feb 1855 St.Andrews, (Manitoba) (MBS, C-14934.). He was baptized on 6 Mar 1855 St.Andrews, (Manitoba) (Denney.). He married **Mary Rose Kirkness** before 1879.

Mary Rose Kirkness was born on 29 May 1858 (1901 Canada, microfilm, T-6553, Brancepeth, page 1, Family 4, line 22-33.).

Children of **George Taylor IV** and **Mary Rose Kirkness** were as follows:

      i.   Thomas Richard Taylor was born on 16 Sep 1879 Puckhan, (Saskatchewan) (ArchiviaNet, C-15006.).
      ii.   Louisa Ann Taylor was born on 22 Oct 1881 Puckhan (1901 Canada, microfilm, T-6553, Brancepeth, page 1, Family 4, line 22-33.) (ArchiviaNet, C-15006.).
      iii.   Walter Alfred Taylor was born on 22 Oct 1883 Pickhan (Ibid., C-15005.). He died on 31 Mar 1891 at age 7 (Ibid.).

    iv. Jane Taylor was born on 20 Sep 1887 (1901 Canada, microfilm, T-6553, Brancepeth, page 1, Family 4, line 22-33.).

    v. Belinda Taylor was born on 24 Jul 1890 (Saskatchewan) (SK Vital Statistics, Birth Reg. #7981.).

    vi. William Fredrick Taylor was born on 16 Dec 1893 (Saskatchewan) (1901 Canada, microfilm, T-6553, Brancepeth, page 1, Family 4, line 22-33.) (SK Vital Statistics, Birth Reg. #8065.). He married Clara Pearl "Claribel" Lyons, daughter of James Lyons and Alice Christina Louise Folster, before 1916.

        Clara Pearl "Claribel" Lyons was born on 29 Sep 1896 Selkirk, Manitoba (MB Vital Statistics, Birth Reg. #1896,001079.). She died on 17 Mar 1985 Vancouver, British Columbia, at age 88.

    vii. Ida Martha Henrietta Taylor was born on 30 Oct 1894 (Saskatchewan) (1901 Canada, microfilm, T-6553, Brancepeth, page 1, Family 4, line 22-33.) (SK Vital Statistics, Birth Reg. #8134.).

    viii. Bentley A. Taylor was born on 25 Jan 1897 (Saskatchewan) (1901 Canada, microfilm, T-6553, Brancepeth, page 1, Family 4, line 22-33.) (SK Vital Statistics, Birth Reg. #8167.).

    ix. Mary V. Taylor was born on 18 May 1899 (Saskatchewan) (1901 Canada, microfilm, T-6553, Brancepeth, page 1, Family 4, line 22-33.) (SK Vital Statistics, Birth Reg. #1709.).

    x. Charlotte ELizabeth Taylor was born on 18 May 1899 (Saskatchewan) (1901 Canada, microfilm, T-6553, Brancepeth, page 1, Family 4, line 22-33.) (SK Vital Statistics, Birth Reg. #1710.).

22. Annabella Taylor was born on 3 Jan 1858 St.Andrews, (Manitoba) (MBS, C-14933.). She married **Robert Mowat**, son of **Robert Mowat** and **Charlotte Firth,** before 1880.

    Robert Mowat was born on 10 Apr 1857 St.Andrews, (Manitoba) (Ibid., C-14934.). He was baptized on 3 May 1857 St.Andrews, (Manitoba) (Denney.).

23. Catherine Jane Taylor was born on 2 Nov 1860 St.Andrews, (Manitoba) (MBS, C-14933.). She married **Henry George Young**, son of **James Young** and **Isabella Stevens,** before 1882.

    Henry George Young was born on 11 Nov 1855 St.Andrews, (Manitoba) (Ibid., C-14934.).

24. Louise Taylor was born on 2 Jul 1866 St.Andrews, (Manitoba). She married **Amable Bouvette**, son of **Francois Bouvette** and **Marguerite Marchand,** circa 1883 Prince Albert, (Saskatchewan) (HBS 1886-1901, 1906 Half-Breed Scrip Applications, RG15-21, Volume 1337, C-14951.).

    Amable Bouvette was born in Aug 1851 St.Johns, (Manitoba) (MBS, C-14925.). He married **Rachel Kirkness**, daughter of **John Kirkness** and **Elizabeth Cook**, on 15 May 1874 St.Boniface, Manitoba (SB-Rozyk, page 16-17, M-8.). He died on 21 Apr 1896 Dauphin, Manitoba, at age 44 (HBS, Volume 1337, C-14951.) (MB Vital Statistics, Reg. No. #1896,002447.).

25. Victoria Taylor was born on 3 Jun 1869 St.Andrews, (Manitoba) (MBS, C-14933.). She was baptized on 25 Jul 1869 St.Andrews, (Manitoba) (Denney.). She married **Miles Lyons**, son of **Thomas Lyons** and **Charlotte Pruden,** before 1889. She died on 28 Mar 1955 Melfort, Saskatchewan, at age 85.

    Miles Lyons was born in 1864 St.Clements, (Manitoba) (MBS, C-14930.). He was baptized on 9 Jul 1865 St.Peters, (Manitoba) (Denney.). He died on 4 Sep 1919 Saskatchewan (Rod Mac Quarrie, 29 May 2013.).

26. William Richard Taylor was born on 12 Dec 1870 St.Andrews, Manitoba (Rod Mac Quarrie, 28 Apr 2008.). He was baptized on 28 Jan 1871 St.Andrews, Manitoba (Ibid.). He married **Drusilla Child** before 1893 (Ibid.).

    Drusilla Child was born on 13 Jun 1864 England (Ibid.).

Children of **William Richard Taylor** and **Drusilla Child** were as follows:

    i. Adeline Drusilla Taylor was born on 13 Jun 1893 The Pas, (Saskatchewan) (MB Vital Statistics, Birth Reg. #1893,21217753.).

    ii. Victoria Elizabeth Taylor was born on 15 Sep 1894 The Pas, (Saskatchewan) (Ibid., Birth Reg. #1894,21317939.).

    iii. Amy Ruth Taylor was born on 19 Apr 1896 (Saskatchewan) (SK Vital Statistics, Birth Reg. #9646.).

    iv. Winnifred May Taylor was born on 4 May 1900 Birston, (Saskatchewan) (Ibid., Birth Reg. #1459.).

    v. Gertrude Ethel Taylor was born on 7 May 1900 Birston, (Saskatchewan) (Ibid., Birth Reg. #2042.).

    vi. Northcote William Taylor was born on 5 Aug 1902 Prince Albert, (Saskatchewan) (Ibid., Birth Reg. #2611.).

    vii. Cecil Randolph Taylor was born on 3 Aug 1905 The Pas, (Saskatchewan) (MB Vital Statistics, Birth Reg. #1905,19113535.).

27. Mary Ann Jane Taylor was born on 1 Jun 1868 (Manitoba) (1901 Canada, #11, (1-7), page 2, family 17, line 30-35.). She was born on 3 Jun 1868 St.Andrews, (Manitoba) (MBS, C-14933.). She was baptized on 6 Jul 1868 St.Andrews, (Manitoba) (Ibid.). She married **Thomas Mowat**, son of **Edward Mowat** and **Jane Norquay**, on 14 Jan 1886 St.Andrews, Manitoba (MB Vital Statistics, Mar Reg. #1886,001262.). She died on 26 Jan 1938 St.Andrews, Manitoba, at age 69 (Ibid., Death Reg. #1938,004382.).

    Thomas Mowat was born on 16 Jun 1865 St.Andrews, (Manitoba) (Denney.). He was born on 20 Jun 1865 St.Andrews, (Manitoba) (1901 Canada, #11, (1-7), page 2, family 17, line 30-35.). He was baptized on 14 Jul 1865 St.Andrews, (Manitoba) (Denney.).

28. Edward Taylor was born on 23 Aug 1870 St.Andrews, Manitoba (MBS, C-14933.). He married **Clara Spence**, daughter of **Alexander Spence** and **Ann Elizabeth Gardner,** on 4 Oct 1898 St.Clements, Manitoba (MB Vital Statistics, Reg. No. 1898,001707.).

    Clara Spence was born on 12 Mar 1880 St.Clements, Manitoba (1901 Canada, Family 3, Line 12-14.).

Children of **Edward Taylor** and **Clara Spence** are as follows:

    i. Lawrence Taylor was born on 7 Aug 1900 St.Clements, Manitoba (MB Vital Statistics, Reg. No. 1900-005685.).

    ii. Eliza Taylor was born on 25 Feb 1903 R.M. of St.Clements, Manitoba (Ibid., Birth Reg. #1903,008103.).

    iii. Edward Taylor was born on 22 Apr 1905 R.M. of St.Clements, Manitoba (Ibid., Birth Reg. #1905,004168.).

    iv. George Taylor was born on 26 Feb 1907 R.M. of St.Clements, Manitoba (Ibid., Birth Reg. #1907,006579.).

    v. William Taylor was born on 26 Feb 1907 R.M. of St.Clements, Manitoba (Ibid., Birth Reg. #1907,006580.).

29. Caroline Taylor was born on 23 Oct 1871 St.Clements, Manitoba (1901 Canada, Family 4, Line 15-19.). She married **James Frost** on 28 Feb 1894 Brandon, Manitoba (Ibid.) (MB Vital Statistics, Marriage Reg. #1894,98001187.).

    James Frost was born on 15 Apr 1870 (1901 Canada, Family 4, Line 15-19.).

30. **Edward Taylor** was baptized on 3 Dec 1862 St.Andrews, (Manitoba) (Denney.). He married **Sarah Ellen Monkman**, daughter of **Henry Monkman** and **Nancy Whitford,** before 1890.

Sarah Ellen Monkman was born on 4 Dec 1868 (1901 Canada, microfilm, T-6553, Brancepeth, page 3, Family 17, line 1-11.).

Children of **Edward Taylor** and **Sarah Ellen Monkman** were as follows:

      i.   Elise Taylor was born on 27 Jan 1890 (Saskatchewan) (SK Vital Statistics, Birth Reg. #7992.).

     ii.   Richard Henry Taylor was born on 16 Apr 1893 (Saskatchewan) (Ibid., Birth Reg. #7305.).

   iii.   Richard Stuart Taylor was born on 2 Oct 1893 (Saskatchewan) (Ibid., Birth Reg. #8127.).

   iv.   Evelina Mary Taylor was born on 30 Nov 1895 (Saskatchewan) (Ibid., Birth Reg. #7356.).

    v.   Hellen Taylor was born on 8 Sep 1899 Birch Hills, (Saskatchewan) (Ibid., Birth Reg. #1715.).

   vi.   John Charles Taylor was born on 5 Jun 1901 Brancepeth, (Saskatchewan) (Ibid., Birth Reg. #2620.).

31. **Mary Ann Taylor** was baptized on 8 Sep 1866 St.Andrews, (Manitoba) (Denney.). She married **Jeremiah Stevens**, son of **William Richard Stevens** and **Mary Foulds,** before 1884. She died in 1927 (Louis Verhagen.).

Jeremiah Stevens was born on 3 Aug 1861 St.Andrews, (Manitoba) (1901 Canada, microfilm, T-6553, Brancepeth, page 2, Family 9, line 10-20.) (1870C-MB, page 193, #516.). He died in 1923 Prince Albert, Saskatchewan (Louis Verhagen.).

32. **Robert Taylor** was born on 25 May 1873 Winnipeg, Manitoba (Ibid., Whitford Y(4), page 1, line 33-37, family 8.). He married **Christie Bell Monkman**, daughter of **Henry Monkman** and **Nancy Whitford,** on 19 Jul 1893 Clover Bar, Alberta (Denney.).

Christie Bell Monkman was born on 14 Jan 1874 Prince Albert, (Saskatchewan) (ArchiviaNet, C-15005.). She died on 5 Apr 1966 Edmonton, Alberta, at age 92 (Denney.). She was buried in Apr 1966 Soda Lake, Alberta (Ibid.).

Children of **Robert Taylor** and **Christie Bell Monkman** were as follows:

      i.   Glen Taylor.

     ii.   Thomas Taylor.

   iii.   Pearl Taylor.

   iv.   Nettie Taylor.

    v.   Eva Taylor was born on 13 May 1894 (Saskatchewan) (SK Vital Statistics, Birth Reg. #7274.).

   vi.   Gladys Clement Taylor was born on 29 Nov 1895 (Saskatchewan) (Ibid., Birth Reg. #7355.).

  vii.   Rose Taylor was born on 12 Dec 1897 (Saskatchewan) (Ibid., Birth Reg. #10064.).

 viii.   Mary Taylor was born on 24 Jan 1900 (1901 Canada, Whitford Y(4), page 1, line 33-37, family 8.).

33. **Catherine Taylor** was born in 1875 (Ibid., microfilm, T-6553, Birch Hills, page 2, Family 16, line 3-9.). She married **Joseph Bird** before 1894 (Ibid.).

Joseph Bird was born on 25 Mar 1871 (Ibid.).

34. **Priscilla Jane Taylor** was born on 24 May 1877 Prince Albert, (Saskatchewan) (Ibid., Birth Reg. #12075.) (ArchiviaNet, C-15004.). She married **Alex Spencer** before 1899 (Ibid.).

Alex Spencer was born on 22 Jul 1863 (1901 Canada, #205, n, page 6-7, family 57, line 49-50, 1.).

35. **Ellen Taylor** was born in 1879 South Branch, (Saskatchewan) (HBS, Volume 1336; C-14949.). She married **Alfred William Bird**, son of **Charles George Bird** and **Ann Halcrow,** before 1899. She died on 19 Jan 1899 Birch Hills, (Saskatchewan) (Ibid.).

Alfred William Bird was born on 22 May 1878 Halcro, (Saskatchewan) (Ibid.).

36. **Alexander Thomas Taylor** was born on 17 Jun 1875 St.Andrews, Manitoba (MBS, C-14933.). He was baptized on 16 Jul 1875 St.Andrews, Manitoba (Denney.). He married **Harriet Jane Smith**, daughter of **Jacob Smith** and **Catherine Loutit,** on 1 Dec 1897 St.Andrews, Manitoba (MB Vital Statistics, Marriage Reg. #1898,002415.).

Harriet Jane Smith was born on 7 Nov 1877 St.Andrews, Manitoba (1881 Census of Canada from the National Archives of Canada, Ottawa, Canada, District 185-C-1, page 23, household 109.) (1901 Canada, #11, L-7, page 3, family 28, line 24-25.).

Children of **Alexander Thomas Taylor** and **Harriet Jane Smith** were as follows:

      i.   Alexander Stanley Taylor was born on 28 Nov 1898 R. M. of St.Andrews, Manitoba (MB Vital Statistics, Birth Reg. #1898,001461.).

     ii.   Ella Taylor was born on 16 Aug 1900 R. M. of St.Andrews, Manitoba (Ibid., Birth Reg. #1900,005627.).

   iii.   John Edward Taylor was born on 24 Dec 1902 St.Andrews, Manitoba (Ibid., Birth Reg. #1903,008044.).

   iv.   Catherine Taylor was born on 7 Sep 1905 R. M. of St.Andrews, Manitoba (Ibid., Birth Reg. #1905,002135.).

    v.   Eva Mabel Taylor was born on 8 Feb 1907 R. M. of St.Andrews, Manitoba (Ibid., Birth Reg. #1907,006545.).

   vi.   Kathleen Taylor was born on 25 May 1909 R. M. of St.Andrews, Manitoba (Ibid., Birth Reg. #1909,004916.).

 37 vii.   Orton Erwin Taylor, b. 19 Feb 1911 R.M. of St.Andrews, Manitoba; d. 7 Apr 1983.

 viii.   Isabella Mary Ann Taylor was born in 1914 St.Andrews, Manitoba (1916 Census of Canada from the National Archives of Canada (Transcription by ancestry.com), Ottawa, Canada, 10-2, page 22, line 4-9.).

Generation Five

37. **Orton Erwin Taylor** was born on 19 Feb 1911 R.M. of St.Andrews, Manitoba (MB Vital Statistics, Birth Reg. #1911,005923.). He married **Gladys Irene Pruden**, daughter of **Cornelius Pruden** and **Elizabeth Jane Sinclair,** before 1935 (*Free Press*, September 10, 2003.). He died on 7 Apr 1983 at age 72 (Ibid.).

Gladys Irene Pruden was born on 9 Mar 1912 R.M. of St.Andrews, Manitoba (MB Vital Statistics, Birth Reg. #1912,002295.). She died on 8 Sep 2003 Lockport, Manitoba, at age 91 (*Free Press*, September 10, 2003.).

Children of **Orton Erwin Taylor** and **Gladys Irene Pruden** were:

      i.   Terrence "Terry" Taylor was born circa 1935. He died on 17 Nov 1985 (Ibid.).

Descendants of James Taylor

Generation One

1. James Taylor, son of Alexander Taylor, was born in 1789 (MBS Scrip Applications, Original White Settlers & Halfbreeds residing in Manitoba on 15 July 1870, RG15-19, C-14933.). He was born circa 1794 Morwick, Birsay, Orkney, Scotland (1829C RRS HBCA E5/3 1829 Census of the Red River Settlement, HBCA E5/3, Hudson's Bay Company Archives, Provincial Archives, 200 Vaughan Street, Winnipeg, MB R3C 1T5, Canada., page 5.) (HBCA-B Hudson's Bay Company Archives - biographical sketches, Hudson's Bay Company Archives; Winnipeg, Manitoba.). He married **Mary Inkster**, daughter of **James Inkster** and **Mary Cree**, on 9 Oct 1828 St.Johns, (Manitoba) (Denney Papers, Charles D. Denney, Glenbow Archives, Calgary, Alberta.) (*LHBCM List of Hudson Bay Company Marriages*; 139 Cook Street; Victoria, B.C.; V8V 3W8: Edited by Joanne J. Hughes, 1977.). He died on 4 Oct 1878 Poplar Point, Manitoba (Denney.).

Question: *Marriage No. 154-177 in 1828-1829 are not found in the HBCA records.*

Mary Inkster was born on 9 Jun 1811 North West (Ibid.). She was born in 1815 (MBS, C-14934.). She was baptized on 23 Jan 1821 (Brandon House), St.Johns, (Manitoba) (HBCA-B.) (HBCR Hudson Bay Company Register of Anglican Church Baptisms, Marriages, and Burials for the Red River Settlement, 1821-1841; Hudson's Bay Company Archives, Winnipeg, Manitoba, E.4/1a, folio 30d. Hereinafter cited as HBCR.). Question: *Mary seems to have had a dr. Lisette Josette b. 1826; m. to a Fr. Cdn. Francois Thibcault* (Denney.). Question: *This marriage is not found in the HBCA register.*

Children of **James Taylor** and **Mary Inkster** were as follows:

2   i.   James Taylor, b. 29 Jul 1829 St.Paul, (Manitoba); m. Phoebe Thomas; d. 14 Sep 1918 St.Paul, Manitoba.
3   ii.   William Taylor, b. 9 Oct 1831 St.Johns, Red River Settlement, (Manitoba); m. Margaret Gunn; d. 11 Jan 1868; bur. Jan 1868 St.Ann, Poplar Point, (Manitoba).
4   iii. John Taylor, b. 24 Jan 1834 St.Paul, (Manitoba); m. Flora Campbell; m. Frances Jane Brown; d. 2 Mar 1925 Headingley, Manitoba; bur. 5 Mar 1925 Headingley, Manitoba.
5   iv.   Mary Taylor, b. 1836 St.Paul, (Manitoba); m. George Bannerman; d. 27 May 1927 Winnipeg, Manitoba.
6   v.   Elizabeth "Betsy" Taylor, b. 20 May 1838 St.Paul, (Manitoba); m. Thomas James Slater; d. 15 Apr 1903 St.Paul, Manitoba.
7   vi.   Peter Taylor, b. 2 Aug 1840 St.Johns, Red River Settlement, (Manitoba); m. Catherine McDonald; d. 29 Jan 1944 St.Boniface, Manitoba.
8   vii. Alexander 'Sandy' Taylor, b. 8 Jan 1843 St.Paul, (Manitoba); m. Mary McDonald; d. 14 Aug 1910 Bresaylor, Saskatchewan.
9   viii. David Taylor, b. 1844 St.Paul, (Manitoba); m. Elizabeth Ann Spence; d. 27 Aug 1907 Bresaylor, Saskatchewan.
10   ix.   Ann Taylor, b. 27 Jan 1848 Headingley, (Manitoba); m. Alexander Roderick Chisholm; d. 1929 Paynton, Saskatchewan.
11   x.   Thomas Taylor, b. 1850 Poplar Point, (Manitoba); m. Florence Ladouceur.
12   xi.   Herbert Chapman Taylor, b. 10 Apr 1850 St.Paul, (Manitoba); m. Mary Ann McDonald; d. 19 Mar 1910 Montana.
     xii. Margaret Taylor was born circa 1852. She was buried on 23 Nov 1853 St.Paul, (Manitoba).

Generation Two

2. James Taylor was born on 29 Jul 1829 St.Paul, (Manitoba) (MBS, C-14934.) (Automated Genealogy 1901 Census Transcription Project and Census Images from the National Archives of Canada, http://www.automatedgenealogy.com, #11, R-1, page 4, family 117, line 35-39.). He was baptized on 12 Aug 1829 St.Johns, Red River Settlement, (Manitoba) (HBCA-B, E.4/1a fo. 71.) (HBCR, E.4/1a, folio 71.). He married **Phoebe Thomas**, daughter of **William Thomas** and **Eleanor Bunn**, on 10 Feb 1859 St.Paul, Middlechurch, (Manitoba) (Denney.). He died on 14 Sep 1918 St.Paul, Manitoba, at age 89 (Lesley Taylor Research, 9 Apr 2004 email.) (Manitoba Vital Statistics online, http://web2.gov.mb.ca, Death Reg. #1918,054206.).

Phoebe Thomas was born on 31 Mar 1833 St.Paul, (Manitoba) (MBS, C-14934.). She was baptized on 5 May 1833 St.Johns, Red River Settlement, (Manitoba) (HBCR, E.4/1a, folio 100.). She died on 1 Sep 1898 St.Paul, Manitoba, at age 65 (MB Vital Statistics, Death Reg. #1898,003106.).

Children of **James Taylor** and **Phoebe Thomas** were as follows:

13   i.   Mary Elizabeth Taylor, b. 25 May 1860 Red River, (Manitoba); m. Alfred Masters; d. 8 Jul 1908; bur. 10 Jul 1908 St.Paul, Middlechurch, Manitoba.
14   ii.   Sarah Ann Taylor, b. 5 May 1861; m. Thomas Buchanan.
     iii. Eleanor Harriet 'Nellie' Taylor was born on 15 Feb 1863 Red River, (Manitoba) (Denney.). She was baptized on 29 Mar 1863 St.Paul, (Manitoba) (Ibid.).
     iv.   Harriet Taylor was born on 15 Sep 1864 (Ibid.).
     v.   Flora Taylor was born on 27 Mar 1866 Middlechurch, (Manitoba) (Ibid.). She was baptized on 6 May 1866 St.Paul, (Manitoba) (Ibid.). She died on 20 Sep 1891 at age 25 (Ibid.).
15   vi.   Edward Thomas Taylor, b. 16 Apr 1868 Middlechurch, (Manitoba); m. Ida May Bowen.
     vii. Margaret Taylor was born on 19 Jan 1870 (Ibid.). She was baptized on 12 Feb 1870 St.Paul, (Manitoba) (Ibid.). She died on 7 Nov 1888 St.Paul, Middlechurch, Manitoba, at age 18 (Heather Hallett Research, 31 Mar 1995.).
16   viii. William Taylor, b. 17 Jul 1871 Middlechurch, Manitoba; m. Vina Gertrude Weigand.
17   ix.   Walter James Taylor, b. 21 Jul 1871 St.Paul, Manitoba; m. Ann Harriet Blaine.
     x.   Alfred Taylor was born on 1 May 1875 St.Paul, Manitoba (Ibid.) (1901 Canada, #11, R-1, page 4, family 117, line 35-39.). He was baptized on 6 Jun 1875 St.Paul, Manitoba (Heather Hallett, 31 Mar 1995.). He died on 1 Jan 1905 St.Paul, Middlechurch, Manitoba, at age 29 (Ibid.).
     xi.   Jemima Taylor was born on 5 Jun 1877 St.Paul, Manitoba (1901 Canada, #11, R-1, page 4, family 117, line 35-39.).

3. William Taylor was baptized on 9 Oct 1831 St.Johns, Red River Settlement, (Manitoba) (HBCA-B, E.4/1a fo. 85d.) (HBCR, E.4/1a, folio 85d.). He married **Margaret Gunn**, daughter of **Donald Gunn** and **Margaret Swain**, on 19 Feb 1856 Kildonan, (Manitoba) (Denney.). He died on 11 Jan 1868 at age 36 (Ibid.). He was buried in Jan 1868 St.Ann, Poplar Point, (Manitoba) (Ibid.).

Margaret Gunn was born on 6 Apr 1838 St.Johns, (Manitoba) (Ibid.). She was baptized on 15 May 1838 St.Johns, Red River Settlement, (Manitoba) (HBCR, E.4/1a, folio 151d.). She married **John Drain** before 1875.

Children of **William Taylor** and **Margaret Gunn** were as follows:

18   i.   Elizabeth Mary Taylor, b. 22 Jan 1857 St.Andrews, (Manitoba); m. Benjamin McKenzie Gunn; d. 4 Jan 1920 R.M. of St.Andrews, Manitoba.

19   ii.   George Taylor, b. 16 Oct 1858 St.Paul, (Manitoba); m. Clara Bremner; d. 1927.

     iii.   Margaret Taylor was born on 25 Jul 1860 Poplar Point, (Manitoba) (MBS, C-14933.). She was baptized on 2 Aug 1860 St.Mary's Anglican Church, Portage la Prairie, (Manitoba) (SMACPLP St.Marys Anglican Church, Portage La Prairie, Manitoba, Baptisms, Marriages, Burials, 1855-1883, transcribed by Clarence Kipling , page 10, B-79.). She married Henry Andrew Finley on 9 Feb 1878 St.Ann, Poplar Point, Manitoba (Denney.).

20   iv.   William Taylor, b. 7 Jun 1862 Poplar Point, (Manitoba); m. Marguerite Bremner; d. 31 Dec 1946 New Westminster, British Columbia.

     v.   Jane Taylor was born on 5 Apr 1864 Poplar Point, (Manitoba) (MBS, C-14933.). She was baptized on 13 Apr 1864 St.Mary's Anglican Church, Portage la Prairie, (Manitoba) (SMACPLP, page 28, B-221.).

21   vi.   Donald Herbert Taylor, b. 12 Mar 1868 Poplar Point, (Manitoba); m. Charlotte Shaw dit Ankenam or Akinam); d. 11 Oct 1953.

4.   **John Taylor** was born on 24 Jan 1834 St.Paul, (Manitoba) (MBS, C-14933.). He married **Flora Campbell**, daughter of **Colin Campbell** and **Elizabeth McGillivray**, on 23 Sep 1856 St.Johns, (Manitoba) (Denney.). He married **Frances Jane Brown**, daughter of **William Brown** and **Charlotte Omand**, on 31 Dec 1873 St.Johns, Manitoba (Ibid.). He died on 2 Mar 1925 Headingley, Manitoba, at age 91 (Ibid.). He was buried on 5 Mar 1925 Headingley, Manitoba (Ibid.).

Flora Campbell was born in 1833 North West (MBS, C-14933.). She was born on 7 Jan 1836 Middlechurch, (Manitoba) (Denney.). She died on 29 Dec 1872 Headingley, Manitoba (MBS, C-14933.). She was buried on 1 Jan 1873 Headingley, Manitoba (Ibid.).

Children of **John Taylor** and **Flora Campbell** were as follows:

     i.   James Colin Taylor was born on 22 Jul 1857 Headingley, (Manitoba) (Denney.). He was baptized on 2 Aug 1857 St.Paul, (Manitoba) (Ibid.). He was buried on 9 Jun 1860 Headingley, (Manitoba) (Ibid.).

22   ii.   John Taylor Jr, b. 23 Dec 1858 Headingley, (Manitoba); m. Frances Helen Beddome; d. 12 Feb 1927 (Headingley), RM Assiniboia, Manitoba.

     iii.   Alexander Taylor was born in 1860 Headingley, (Manitoba) (Ibid.). He died in 1862 Headingley, (Manitoba) (Ibid.).

     iv.   Mary Margaret Taylor was born on 19 Oct 1861 Headingley, (Manitoba) (HBC-PN Public Notice of land claims of Half-Breed Children, Address: Provincial Archives of Manitoba, Winnipeg, Manitoba, File Reference: MG4D13 Box 1, Headingly, #160.).

     v.   Thomas Campbell Taylor was born in 1863 Headingley, (Manitoba) (Denney.). He died on 2 Jan 1866 (Ibid.). He was buried on 3 Jan 1866 Headingley, (Manitoba) (Ibid.).

     vi.   Flora Ann Taylor was born on 20 Jan 1867 Headingley, (Manitoba) (HBC-PN , Headingly, #161.). She married Alexander Thomas Tait, son of William Auld Tait Sr. and Johanna Gunn, on 23 Sep 1896 (Denney.).

       Alexander Thomas Tait was born on 13 Mar 1867 Headingley, (Manitoba) (MBS, C-14933.). He was baptized on 31 Mar 1867 (Ibid.).

23   vii.   William Herbert Taylor, b. 16 Oct 1868 Headingley, (Manitoba); m. Lizzie Ellen Laird; d. 8 Jul 1925.

     viii.   Elizabeth Helena Taylor was born on 2 Jul 1871 Headingley, Manitoba (Denney.). She died on 25 Jan 1873 at age 1 (Ibid.). She was buried on 26 Jan 1873 Headingley, Manitoba (Ibid.).

Frances Jane Brown was born on 16 Feb 1855 St.Johns, (Manitoba) (MBS, C-14933.). She was baptized on 12 Mar 1855 St.Johns, (Manitoba) (Denney.). She died on 25 May 1925 Headingley, Manitoba, at age 70 (Ibid.).

Children of **John Taylor** and **Frances Jane Brown** all born Headingley, Manitoba, were as follows:

24   i.   Alice Ann Taylor, b. 16 Oct 1874; m. Richard Hamilton; d. 3 Mar 1943.

     ii.   Benjamin Taylor was born on 30 Nov 1875 (SJAC St.James Anglican Church Extractions, Manitoba Genealogy Society, Winnipeg, Manitoba, B-1.) (1901 Canada, #11, A-3, page 4, family 15, line 29-42.). He was baptized on 16 Jan 1876 St.James, Manitoba (SJAC, B-1.). He died on 9 Mar 1962 Headingley, Manitoba, at age 86 (Heather Hallett, 31 Mar 1995.).

25   iii.   Rupert Taylor, b. 7 Feb 1877; m. Alice Robina Dennison; d. 28 Feb 1957.

     iv.   Florence Mary Taylor was born on 26 Nov 1878 (1901 Canada, #11, A-3, page 4, family 15, line 29-42.). She died on 11 Oct 1957 at age 78 (Denney.).

     v.   Helen Charlotte Taylor was born on 20 Aug 1880 (1901 Canada, #11, A-3, page 4, family 15, line 29-42.). She died on 2 Jan 1960 at age 79 (Heather Hallett, 31 Mar 1995.).

     vi.   Frances Jane Taylor was born on 20 Apr 1882 (Denney.). She died on 26 May 1883 at age 1 (Ibid.). She was buried on 26 May 1883 Headingley, Manitoba (Ibid.).

     vii.   Jessie Taylor was born on 19 Nov 1883 (Heather Hallett, 31 Mar 1996.) (1901 Canada, #11, A-3, page 4, family 15, line 29-42.). She married Thomas Victor Ellaby on 30 Sep 1941 (Heather Hallett, 31 Mar 1996.). She was buried on 8 Sep 1969 (Ibid.).

     viii.   Frances Jane Taylor II was born on 18 Aug 1885 (1901 Canada, #11, A-3, page 4, family 15, line 29-42.). She died on 14 Mar 1958 at age 72 (Denney.).

     ix.   Margaret Ann Taylor was born on 30 Aug 1887 (1901 Canada, #11, A-3, page 4, family 15, line 29-42.).

     x.   James Brown Taylor was born on 17 Jun 1889 (Heather Hallett, 31 Mar 1995.) (1901 Canada, #11, A-3, page 4, family 15, line 29-42.). He married Irene Morris on 20 Apr 1921 (Heather Hallett, 31 Mar 1995.). He died on 10 Jul 1971 at age 82 (Ibid.). He was buried Headingley, Manitoba (Ibid.).

xi.   Archibald Bannerman Taylor was born on 25 Dec 1890 (1901 Canada, #11, A-3, page 4, family 15, line 29-42.). He died on 28 Aug 1956 at age 65 (Denney.).

xii.   Blanche Irene Taylor was born on 11 Dec 1892 (Heather Hallett, 31 Mar 1995.) (1901 Canada, #11, A-3, page 4, family 15, line 29-42.). She died on 14 Mar 1977 Headingley, Manitoba, at age 84 (Heather Hallett, 31 Mar 1995.).

26 xiii.   Agnes Schultz Taylor, b. 14 Nov 1894; m. Oswald Francis Montgomery; d. 20 Apr 1958.

xiv.   George Gray Taylor was born on 4 Apr 1897 (Denney.). He died on 22 Jun 1897 Headingley, Manitoba (Ibid.).

5. **Mary Taylor** was born in 1836 St.Paul, (Manitoba) (MBS, C-14925.) (HBCR, E.4/1a, folio 128.). She was baptized on 24 Jun 1836 St.Johns, Red River Settlement, (Manitoba) (HBCA-B, E.4/1a fo. 128.) (HBCR, E.4/1a, folio 128.). She married **George Bannerman**, son of **Alexander Bannerman** and **Janet McKay**, on 20 Jun 1861 St.Paul, Middlechurch, (Manitoba) (Denney.). She died on 27 May 1927 Winnipeg, Manitoba (MB Vital Statistics, Death Reg. #1927,024163.).

George Bannerman was born on 1 Aug 1834 Kildonan, (Manitoba). He was baptized on 30 Sep 1834 Red River Settlement, (Manitoba) (AI-Rozyk   Anglican Index of Baptisms, Marriages and Burials Extractions, Hudson Bay Company Archives, Winnipeg, Manitoba, Canada, Selected and Compiled by Rosemary Rozyk. Hereinafter cited as AI-Rozyk.) (HBCR, E.4/1a folio 111.). He died on 10 Aug 1885 Winnipeg, Manitoba, at age 51 (AI-Rozyk.) (MB Vital Statistics, Death Reg. #1885,001353.). He was buried on 11 Aug 1885 St.Johns, Manitoba (AI-Rozyk.).

6. **Elizabeth "Betsy" Taylor** was born on 20 May 1838 St.Paul, (Manitoba) (Ibid.). She was baptized on 24 Jun 1838 St.Johns, Red River Settlement, (Manitoba) (HBCA-B, E.4/1a fo. 151d.) (HBCR, E.4/1a, folio 151d.). She married **Thomas James Slater**, son of **James Slater** and **Mary Indian**, on 18 Dec 1856 St.Paul, Middlechurch, (Manitoba) (Denney.). She died on 15 Apr 1903 St.Paul, Manitoba, at age 64 (MB Vital Statistics, Death Reg. #1903,003548.).

Thomas James Slater was baptized on 23 Mar 1830 St.Johns, Red River Settlement, (Manitoba) (HBCR, E.4/1a, folio 76.). He died on 21 Feb 1894 St.Paul, Manitoba, at age 63 (MB Vital Statistics, Death Reg. #1894,001906.). He was buried on 21 Feb 1894 St.Paul, Middlechurch, Manitoba (Ibid.).

7. **Peter Taylor** was baptized on 2 Aug 1840 St.Johns, Red River Settlement, (Manitoba) (HBCA-B, E.4/1a fo. 168.) (HBCR, E.4/1a, folio 168.). He married **Catherine McDonald**, daughter of **Donald 'Little' McDonald** and **Nancy Ferguson**, on 31 Dec 1862 St.Andrews, (Manitoba) (Denney.). He died on 29 Jan 1944 St.Boniface, Manitoba, at age 103 (MB Vital Statistics, Death Reg. #1944,004067.).

Catherine McDonald was baptized on 25 Jul 1845 St.Johns, (Manitoba) (Denney.).

Children of **Peter Taylor** and **Catherine McDonald** were as follows:

27   i.   Eliza Taylor, b. 28 Oct 1863 Poplar Point, (Manitoba); m. Alexander Hunter Murray Setter; d. 1947; bur. 1947 Paynton, Saskatchewan.

ii.   John Taylor was born in Apr 1865 Poplar Point, (Manitoba) (Ibid.). He died on 11 Sep 1866 Poplar Point, (Manitoba), at age 1 (Ibid.).

28 iii.   Maurice Edward Taylor, b. 19 Jan 1867 Poplar Point, (Manitoba); m. Harriet Josephine McDonald; d. 19 Oct 1943 Paynton, Saskatchewan.

iv.   Flora Ann Taylor was born on 17 Sep 1868 Poplar Point, (Manitoba) (MBS, C-14933.). She was baptized on 28 Sep 1868 St.Ann, Poplar Point, (Manitoba) (Ibid.).

29 v.   Albert Scott Taylor, b. 7 May 1870 Poplar Point, (Manitoba); m. Rubana Bremner.

vi.   Victoria Taylor was born on 19 Aug 1872 (Denney.).

30 vii.   Walter David Taylor, b. 28 Mar 1874; d. 10 Oct 1955; bur. Burnaby, British Columbia.

viii.   Cuthbert 'Cubby' Taylor was born in 1876 (Heather Hallett, 31 Mar 1995.).

31 ix.   Catherine Jemima Taylor, b. 12 Nov 1877 Poplar Point, Manitoba; m. John Archibald Rowland; d. 12 Mar 1943 North Battleford, Saskatchewan; bur. Mar 1943 Battleford, Saskatchewan.

x.   Lochlin Alexander Taylor was born in 1879 (Denney.). He died in 1970 (Ibid.). He was buried in 1970 Paynton, Saskatchewan (Ibid.).

32 xi.   Mary Jane Maud Taylor, b. 22 Dec 1881 Prince Albert, Saskatchewan; m. Fred Kissack; d. 1972 North Battleford, Saskatchewan; bur. 1972 Woodlawn Cemetery, North Battleford, Saskatchewan.

xii.   Jessie Taylor was born on 1 Feb 1884 Bresaylor, (Saskatchewan) (ArchiviaNet 1886-1901, 1906 Half-Breed Scrip Applications Index, RG15-21, Volume 1333 through 1371, Microfilm Reel Number C-14944 through C-15010, National Archives of Canada, Ottawa, Ontario, http://www.collectionscanada.gc.ca, C-15006.). She died on 1 Mar 1884 Bresaylor, (Saskatchewan) (Ibid.).

xiii.   Ronald McDonald Taylor was born on 7 Feb 1885 Bresaylor, (Saskatchewan) (Ibid.). He died in 1964 Paynton, Saskatchewan (Heather Hallett, 31 Mar 1995.).

33 xiv.   Frederick Taylor, b. 2 Mar 1887; m. Hilda Larson.

xv.   Lydia Taylor was born on 20 Jun 1891 (Saskatchewan) (Saskatchewan Vital Statistics online, http://vsgs.health.gov.sk.ca, Death Reg. #6469.). She died on 21 Jun 1897 Bresaylor, (Saskatchewan), at age 6 (Heather Hallett, 31 Mar 1995.) (SK Vital Statistics, Death Reg. #1469.).

8. **Alexander 'Sandy' Taylor** was born on 8 Jan 1843 St.Paul, (Manitoba) (Denney.) (1901 Canada, microfilm T-6553, Bresaylor, page 3, family 27, line 28-40.). He was baptized on 29 Jan 1843 St.Johns, (Manitoba) (Denney.) (HBCA-B, E.4/12 fo. 23.). He married **Mary McDonald**, daughter of **Donald 'Little' McDonald** and **Nancy Ferguson,** on 16 Mar 1868 (Denney.). He died on 14 Aug 1910 Bresaylor, Saskatchewan, at age 67 (Heather Hallett, 31 Mar 1995.).

Mary McDonald was born on 8 Jan 1849 St.Andrews, (Manitoba) (Denney.). She was baptized on 6 Feb 1849 St.Andrews, (Manitoba) (Ibid.). She died on 8 Jan 1931 at age 82.

Children of **Alexander 'Sandy' Taylor** and **Mary McDonald** were as follows:

i.   Thomas Frederick Taylor was born on 22 Dec 1868 Poplar Point, (Manitoba) (MBS, C-14933.) (1901 Canada, microfilm T-6553, Bresaylor, page 3, family 27, line 28-40.). He was baptized on 10 Jan 1869 St.Ann, Poplar Point, (Manitoba) (MBS, C-14933.). He died on 20 Feb 1952 North Battleford, Saskatchewan, at age 83 (Denney.).

    ii.   Charles Taylor was born on 26 Mar 1870 Poplar Point, (Manitoba) (MBS, C-14933.). He was baptized on 24 Apr 1870 St.Ann, Poplar Point, (Manitoba) (Ibid.). He died on 18 Nov 1953 North Battleford, Saskatchewan, at age 83 (Denney.).

    iii.   John Taylor was born in Mar 1871 (Automated Genealogy 1911 Census Transcription Project and Census Images from the National Archives of Canada, http://www.automatedgenealogy.com, #34, Townships 46, page 6, family 82, line 24.). He was born in 1873 Poplar Point, Manitoba (Heather Hallett.). He died in 1937 North Battleford, (Saskatchewan) (Ibid.).

    iv.   William A. Taylor was born circa 1874 (1881 Church of Latter Day Saints Census Transcription Project of Census Images from the National Archives of Canada, Ottawa, Canada, http://www.familysearch.org, District 186-F, page 8, house 30.). He died circa 1950 (Heather Hallett, 31 Mar 1995.). He was buried circa 1950 Seattle, King County, Washington (Ibid.).

34   v.   Alice Taylor, b. 31 Aug 1875; m. Robert Leslie.

35   vi.   Mary Isabella 'Marabelle' Taylor, b. 12 Dec 1878 Poplar Point, Manitoba; m. Edward Emerson Mack; d. May 1950 Burnaby, British Columbia.

36   vii.   Margaret Jane 'Maggie' Taylor, b. 12 Dec 1878; m. Andre Gullion Pothier; d. 1962; bur. 1962 West Vancouver, British Columbia.

37   viii.   Cuthbert Francis 'Cubby' Taylor, b. 1 Sep 1880 Poplar Point, Manitoba; m. Annie Ross; d. 2 Nov 1966 North Battleford, Saskatchewan.

    ix.   Colin Taylor was born on 1 Aug 1882 Clark's Crossing, (Saskatchewan) (1901 Canada, microfilm T-6553, Bresaylor, page 3, family 27, line 28-40.) (ArchiviaNet, C-15005.). He died on 21 Apr 1950 North Battleford, Saskatchewan, at age 67 (Heather Hallett, 31 Mar 1995.).

38   x.   Ann Maria Taylor, b. 26 Apr 1884 Police Barracks, North Battleford, (Saskatchewan); m. Arthur Hayes; d. 1951; bur. 1951 Meota, Saskatchewan.

39   xi.   Allan Peterson Taylor, b. 23 Mar 1886 Bresaylor, Manitoba; m. Vera Hawley; d. 5 Sep 1936 North Battleford, Saskatchewan.

    xii.   David Livingston Taylor was born on 5 Jan 1888 Bresaylor, (Saskatchewan) (1901 Canada, microfilm T-6553, Bresaylor, page 3, family 27, line 28-40.). He died on 18 May 1963 North Battleford, Saskatchewan, at age 75 (Heather Hallett, 31 Mar 1995.).

    xiii.   Lillian Blanch 'Lilly' Taylor was born on 31 Aug 1890 Bresaylor, (Saskatchewan) (1901 Canada, microfilm T-6553, Bresaylor, page 3, family 27, line 28-40.) (SK Vital Statistics, Birth Reg. #6432.).

    xiv.   Edna G. Taylor was born on 1 Aug 1894 (Saskatchewan) (Ibid., Birth Reg. #6571.). She was born on 3 Aug 1894 Bresaylor, (Saskatchewan) (1901 Canada, microfilm T-6553, Bresaylor, page 3, family 27, line 28-40.).

9. David Taylor was born in 1844 St.Paul, (Manitoba) (Denney.). He was baptized on 29 Jun 1845 St.Johns, (Manitoba) (HBCA-B, E.4/2 fo. 37.). He was born on 10 Sep 1846 (1901 Canada, microfilm T-6553, Bresaylor, page 3, family 25, line 11-25.). He married **Elizabeth Ann Spence**, daughter of **Archibald James Spence** and **Elizabeth Ann Inkster,** in 1875 Headingley, Manitoba (Denney.). He died on 27 Aug 1907 Bresaylor, Saskatchewan (Ibid.).

Elizabeth Ann Spence was born on 13 Jan 1852 (1901 Canada, microfilm T-6553, Bresaylor, page 3, family 25, line 11-25.). She was born on 25 Jan 1857 (Denney.). She was baptized on 29 Jan 1857 St.Andrews, (Manitoba) (Ibid.). She died on 8 Jul 1938 Bresaylor, Saskatchewan, at age 81 (Ibid.).

Children of **David Taylor** and **Elizabeth Ann Spence** were as follows:

    i.   Roderick Taylor was born in 1876 Headingley, Manitoba (Heather Hallett, 31 Mar 1995.). He died on 21 Nov 1896 Battleford, (Saskatchewan) (Ibid.).

    ii.   Elizabeth Ann Taylor was born on 31 Oct 1876 (1901 Canada, microfilm T-6553, Bresaylor, page 3, family 25, line 11-25.).

40   iii.   Clarence Taylor, b. 11 Aug 1878 Headingley, (Manitoba); m. Margaret Ann Spence; d. 30 Oct 1961 Bresaylor, Saskatchewan.

41   iv.   Florence Mary Taylor, b. 12 Apr 1880 Headingley, Manitoba; m. William Joseph Goth; d. 4 Feb 1917.

    v.   James Taylor was born on 11 Jan 1881 (Heather Hallett, 31 Mar 1995.). He married Mary Mann in 1911 Bresaylor, Saskatchewan (Ibid.). He died on 24 Dec 1957 British Columbia at age 76 (Ibid.).

        Mary Mann was born in 1881 Scotland (Ibid.). She died on 5 Nov 1918 (Ibid.).

    vi.   Archibald Taylor was born on 12 Jan 1882 (1901 Canada, microfilm T-6553, Bresaylor, page 3, family 25, line 11-25.).

    vii.   Emma Jane Taylor was born on 19 Dec 1883 Bresaylor, (Saskatchewan) (Ibid.) (Ibid., District 202-f(2)-2, page 13, famiy 28, line 7-10.). She died on 15 Jul 1959 North Battleford, Saskatchewan, at age 75 (Denney.).

42   viii.   Jessie Ellen Taylor, b. 19 Nov 1885 Bresaylor, (Saskatchewan); m. James Brown; d. 28 Jan 1961.

43   ix.   Dora Jemima Taylor, b. 20 Sep 1887 Bresaylor, (Saskatchewan); m. Charles Henry Heapy; d. 7 Feb 1977.

44   x.   Minnie Taylor, b. 6 Dec 1889 Bresaylor, (Saskatchewan); m. John Murray Inman; d. 3 Apr 1935.

45   xi.   Andrew Stanley Taylor, b. 20 Oct 1891 Bresaylor, (Saskatchewan); m. Bertha Hazel Cowitz; d. 1982.

    xii.   Arthur David Taylor was born on 19 Oct 1893 Bresaylor, (Saskatchewan) (1901 Canada, microfilm T-6553, Bresaylor, page 3, family 25, line 11-25.) (SK Vital Statistics, Birth Reg. #6554.). He died on 10 Oct 1971 at age 77 (Heather Hallett, 31 Mar 1995.).

46   xiii.   Angus Chisholm Taylor, b. 7 Oct 1895 Bresaylor, (Saskatchewan); m. Marian Osborne; d. 31 Jan 1968 Calgary, Alberta.

47   xiv.   Charles Lindsay Taylor, b. 18 Oct 1897 Bresaylor, (Saskatchewan); m. Marian C. Gowan; d. 16 Aug 1974.

xv. Elsie Irene Taylor was born on 21 Oct 1899 Bresaylor, (Saskatchewan) (1901 Canada, microfilm T-6553, Bresaylor, page 3, family 25, line 11-25.) (SK Vital Statistics, Birth Reg. #1721.). She married Walter Gibson San Francisco, California.

xvi. Agnes Grace Taylor was born on 13 Sep 1902 Bresaylor, (Saskatchewan) (Denney.). She married Harold Mound San Francisco, California (Ibid.).

10. Ann Taylor was born on 27 Jan 1848 Headingley, (Manitoba) (HBC-PN , Poplar Point and High Bluff, #55.) (1901 Canada, microfilm T-6553, Bresaylor, page 3, family 28, line 41-47.). She was baptized on 20 Feb 1848 St.Johns, (Manitoba) (Denney.) (HBCA-B, E.4/2 fo. 55.). She married **Alexander Roderick Chisholm**, son of **Alexander Chisholm** and **Janet McDonald,** before 1873. She died in 1929 Paynton, Saskatchewan (Denney.).

Alexander Roderick Chisholm was born on 8 May 1843 Ontario (Ibid.) (1901 Canada, microfilm T-6553, Bresaylor, page 3, family 28, line 41-47.). He died in 1931 Paynton, Saskatchewan (Denney.).

11. Thomas Taylor was born in 1850 Poplar Point, (Manitoba) (ArchiviaNet, C-15006.). He married **Florence Ladouceur**, daughter of **Pierre Agapit Ladouceur** and **Marguerite Fraser,** on 28 Sep 1880 Lac la Biche, (Alberta) (LLBR1 Notre Dame des Tidoren, St.Paul Diocese, Lac La Biche, Registre des Baptemes, Mariages & Sepltures, Volume 1, 1853-1898., page 200, M-4. Hereinafter cited as LLBR1.).

Florence Ladouceur was born on 16 Jul 1864 (Ibid., page 58, B-311.). She was baptized on 31 Jul 1864 Lac la Biche, (Alberta) (Ibid.).

Children of **Thomas Taylor** and **Florence Ladouceur** were as follows:

i. Ida Taylor was born on 5 Mar 1884 (Alberta) (1901 Alberta Census Index, Alberta Genealogical Society, Edmonton, Alberta, www.agsedm.edmonton.ab.ca, page 1, line 28-37, Athabasca Landing.) (1901 Canada, microfilm T-6550, Athabaska Landing, page 1.).

ii. Alexandre Taylor was born on 25 Feb 1886 (Alberta) (1901C-AGSE, page 1, line 28-37, Athabasca Landing.) (1901 Canada, microfilm T-6550, Athabaska Landing, page 1.).

iii. Joseph Taylor was born on 25 Oct 1889 (Alberta) (1901C-AGSE, page 1, line 28-37, Athabasca Landing.) (1901 Canada, microfilm T-6550, Athabaska Landing, page 1.).

iv. Felix Taylor was born on 25 Jul 1893 (Alberta) (1901C-AGSE, page 1, line 28-37, Athabasca Landing.) (1901 Canada, microfilm T-6550, Athabaska Landing, page 1.).

v. George Taylor was born on 1 May 1895 (Alberta) (1901C-AGSE, page 1, line 28-37, Athabasca Landing.) (1901 Canada, microfilm T-6550, Athabaska Landing, page 1.).

vi. Caroline Taylor was born on 23 Jul 1897 Lac la Biche, (Alberta) (LLBR2 Notre Dame des Tidoren, St.Paul Diocese, Lac La Biche, Registre des Baptemes, Mariages & Sepltures, Volume 1, 1881-1907., B-19. Hereinafter cited as LLBR2.). She was baptized on 24 Jul 1897 Lac la Biche, (Alberta) (Ibid.).

vii. Louis Arti Taylor was born on 23 Jul 1897 Lac la Biche, (Alberta) (Ibid., B-18.). He was baptized on 24 Jul 1897 Lac la Biche, (Alberta) (Ibid.).

viii. Margaret Taylor was born on 27 May 1900 (Alberta) (1901 Canada, microfilm T-6550, Athabaska Landing, page 1.) (1901C-AGSE, page 1, line 28-37.).

12. Herbert Chapman Taylor was born on 10 Apr 1850 St.Paul, (Manitoba) (MBS, C-14934.). He was baptized on 19 May 1850 Middle Church, (Manitoba) (Rod MacQuarrie Research, 10 May 2001.). He married **Mary Ann McDonald**, daughter of **Duncan McDonald** and **Elizabeth Tait,** on 22 Feb 1871 (Denney.). He died on 19 Mar 1910 Montana at age 59 (Rod Mac Quarrie, 10 May 2001.).

Mary Ann McDonald was born on 2 Dec 1852 St.Andrews, (Manitoba) (MBS, C-14934.). She was baptized on 15 Dec 1852 St.Andrews, (Manitoba) (Denney.). She died on 2 Feb 1934 Phillips County, Montana, at age 81 (MT Death Montana State Genealogical Society Death Index.).

Children of **Herbert Chapman Taylor** and **Mary Ann McDonald** were as follows:

48   i. Peter Taylor, b. circa 11 Feb 1873 (Manitoba); m. Marie Marguerite Short; d. 27 Mar 1932 Kalispell, Flathead County, Montana.

ii. Duncan Alexander Taylor was born in 1874 (Heather Hallett, 31 Mar 1995.). He died on 25 Jul 1933 Deer Lodge County, Montana (MT Death.).

iii. Peter Taylor was born in 1876 Prince Albert, (Saskatchewan) (ArchiviaNet, C-15006.).

iv. Malcolm Taylor was born on 11 Sep 1876 Headingley, Manitoba (Heather Hallett, 31 Mar 1995.) (Ancestry.com Website, WWI Draft Registration.). He died on 27 Mar 1962 Cascade County, Montana, at age 85 (MT Death.).

49   v. Timolean Love Taylor, b. 16 May 1878 Manitoba; m. Vera Julia Johnson; m. Margaret Agnes Clark; d. 16 Aug 1939 Phillips County, Manitoba.

50   vi. Martha Louise Taylor, b. 1880; m. George DeFlyer; d. 29 Sep 1956 Stillwater County, Manitoba.

51   vii. Catherine Ann Taylor, b. 6 Jun 1882 Battleford, (Saskatchewan); m. Frank L. Godfrey; m. Bud J. Carter.

52   viii. Edith Taylor, b. 6 Mar 1885 Bresaylor, (Saskatchewan); m. Patrick Francis "Frank" Dardis; d. 20 Jan 1959 Warm Springs, Deer Lodge County, Montana.

53   ix. Harriet Elizabeth Taylor, b. May 1887; m. Israel McEwen; d. 17 Feb 1959 Phillips County, Montana.

x. Herbert Chapman Taylor was born on 26 Jun 1889 Battleford, (Saskatchewan) (1900C MT Twelfth Census of the United States: 1900; Montana, Sheet 4A, family 126, line 16-27.). He died on 2 Dec 1938 Phillips County, Montana, at age 49 (MT Death.).

xi. Hugh Richard Taylor was born on 20 Jun 1891 Bresaylor, (Saskatchewan) (SK Vital Statistics, Birth Reg. #6446.). He died on 27 Oct 1962 Phillips County, Montana, at age 71 (MT Death.).

xii. Hilda Esther Taylor was born on 20 Jan 1894 (Saskatchewan) (SK Vital Statistics, Birth Reg. #6556.). She married John A. McIntosh, son of Elmer McIntosh and Georgia Eckles, on 25 Oct 1927 Havre, Hill County, Montana (HCM Hill County, Montana; Marriage Record Licenses and Certificates; 1865-1950; familysearch.org: #2985, Hereinafter cited as HCM.). She died on 17 Jul 1973 Cascade County, Montana, at age 79 (MT Death.).

John A. McIntosh was born on 1 May 1885 Mercer, Missouri (HCM, #2985.). He and **Margaret Jane McIntosh** obtained a marriage license on 25 Oct 1927 Hill County, Montana (Ibid.). He died on 2 May 1960 Phillips County, Montana, at age 75 (MT Death.).

xiii.   Norman Taylor was born on 26 Mar 1897 Bresaylor, (Saskatchewan) (SK Vital Statistics, Birth Reg. #6793.) (Ancestry.com, WWI Draft Registration.). He died on 18 Nov 1923 Lincoln County, Montana, at age 26 (MT Death.).

Generation Three

13.   Mary Elizabeth Taylor was born on 25 May 1860 Red River, (Manitoba) (Heather Hallett, 31 Mar 1995.). She was baptized on 2 Jul 1860 St.Paul, (Manitoba) (Denney.). She married **Alfred Masters** on 11 Dec 1879 St.Paul, Middlechurch, Manitoba (Heather Hallett, 31 Mar 1995.). She died on 8 Jul 1908 at age 48 (Ibid.). She was buried on 10 Jul 1908 St.Paul, Middlechurch, Manitoba (Ibid.).

14.   Sarah Ann Taylor was born on 5 May 1861 (Ibid.). She was baptized in Sep 1861 St.Paul, (Manitoba) (Denney.). She married **Thomas Buchanan** on 7 Aug 1884 Assiniboia, Manitoba (MB Vital Statistics, Mar Reg. #1884,001248.).

15.   Edward Thomas Taylor was born on 16 Apr 1868 Middlechurch, (Manitoba) (Denney.) (1901 Canada, #11, R-1, page 4, family 114, line 22-26.). He was baptized on 17 May 1868 St.Paul, (Manitoba) (Denney.). He married **Ida May Bowen**, daughter of **Felix Bowen** and **Caroline Catherine Fidler**, on 8 Feb 1892 St.Paul, Manitoba (MB Vital Statistics, Mar Reg. #1892,001024.).

Ida May Bowen was born on 5 Apr 1875 St.Paul, Manitoba (Denney.) (1901 Canada, #11, R-1, page 4, family 114, line 22-26.).

Children of **Edward Thomas Taylor** and **Ida May Bowen** were as follows:

i.   James Alan Taylor was born on 30 Dec 1892 Middlechurch, Manitoba (Denney.) (1901 Canada, #11, R-1, page 4, family 114, line 22-26.).

ii.   Reuben Roy Taylor was born on 19 Aug 1895 Middlechurch, Manitoba (Denney.) (1901 Canada, #11, R-1, page 4, family 114, line 22-26.).

iii.   Sydney Taylor was born on 16 Sep 1897 Middlechurch, Manitoba (Denney.). He died on 13 Mar 1898 (Ibid.). He was buried on 16 Mar 1898 St.Paul, Middlechurch, Manitoba (Ibid.).

iv.   Lorne Taylor was born on 3 Mar 1899 St.Paul, Manitoba (1901 Canada, #11, R-1, page 4, family 114, line 22-26.).

v.   Ruby Alexandra Taylor was born on 15 Aug 1902 Middlechurch, Manitoba (Denney.).

vi.   Alfred Edward Taylor was born on 2 Apr 1905 Middlechurch, Manitoba (Ibid.).

vii.   Olive Laurenda Taylor was born on 6 Feb 1907 Middlechurch, Manitoba (Ibid.).

16.   William Taylor was born on 17 Jul 1871 Middlechurch, Manitoba (Heather Hallett, 31 Mar 1995.) (1901 Canada, #11, R-1, page 4, family 117, line 35-39.). He married **Vina Gertrude Weigand**, daughter of **Richard Weigand** and **Ella House,** on 3 Nov 1909 St.Paul, Middlechurch, Manitoba (Heather Hallett, 31 Mar 1995.).

Vina Gertrude Weigand was born in 1873 (Ibid.).

Children of **William Taylor** and **Vina Gertrude Weigand** are:

i.   Arthur Edmund Taylor was born on 14 Aug 1910 Middlechurch, Manitoba (Ibid.).

17.   Walter James Taylor was born on 21 Jul 1871 St.Paul, Manitoba (1901 Canada, #11, R-1, page 4, family 117, line 35-39.). He was baptized on 31 Aug 1872 St.Paul, Manitoba (Heather Hallett, 31 Mar 1995.). He married **Ann Harriet Blaine**, daughter of **Edward Blaine** and **Isabella Setter**, on 25 Jun 1903 St.Andrews, Manitoba (Ibid.).

Ann Harriet Blaine was born in 1880 (Ibid.).

Children of **Walter James Taylor** and **Ann Harriet Blaine** are as follows:

i.   Cecil Charles Taylor was born on 23 May 1904 (Ibid.).

ii.   Violet May Taylor was born on 21 Sep 1907 (Ibid.).

18.   Elizabeth Mary Taylor was born on 22 Jan 1857 St.Andrews, (Manitoba) (MBS, C-14933.). She was baptized on 1 Mar 1857 St.Paul, Middlechurch, (Manitoba) (Denney.). She married **Benjamin McKenzie Gunn**, son of **Alexander Gunn** and **Angelique McKenzie,** on 20 Feb 1878 St.Ann, Poplar Point, Manitoba (Ibid.). She died on 4 Jan 1920 R.M. of St.Andrews, Manitoba, at age 62 (MB Vital Statistics, Death Reg. #1920,006199.).

Benjamin McKenzie Gunn was born on 11 Dec 1854 St.Andrews, (Manitoba) (MBS, C-14934.). He was baptized on 9 Jan 1855 Kildonan, (Manitoba) (Denney.). He died on 14 Apr 1930 R.M. of St.Andrews, Manitoba, at age 75 (Joyce (Gunn) Anaka, *Donald Gunn Family History*, March 1996), G/S 1-4.) (MB Vital Statistics, Death Reg. #1930,020221.).

19.   George Taylor was born on 16 Oct 1858 St.Paul, (Manitoba) (MBS, C-14933.). He married **Clara Bremner**, daughter of **Charles Bremner** and **Emelie Wills,** before 1889. He died in 1927 (Denney.).

Clara Bremner was born on 8 Oct 1871 (Ibid.). She was baptized on 12 Oct 1871 (Ibid.). She died in 1940.

Children of **George Taylor** and **Clara Bremner** are as follows:

i.   Lena Taylor was born in 1889.

ii.   Allan Taylor was born in 1891 (Ibid.).

iii.   George W. Taylor was born on 17 Apr 1892 (Ibid.).

iv.   Annie Taylor was born on 13 Jun 1893 (Ibid.).

v.   Andrew Taylor was born on 25 Feb 1894 (Ibid.).

vi.   Charles Taylor was born in 1895 (Ibid.).

vii.   Eve Taylor was born in 1897 (Ibid.).

viii.   Rita Alice Taylor was born on 25 Jun 1898.

ix.   Ethel M. Taylor was born on 8 Jan 1900 (Ibid.).

20.   William Taylor was born on 7 Jun 1862 Poplar Point, (Manitoba) (MBS, C-14933.). He was baptized on 29 Jun 1862 St.Mary's Anglican Church, Portage la Prairie, (Manitoba) (SMACPLP, page 18, B-140.). He married **Marguerite Bremner**, daughter of **Charles Bremner** and **Emelie Wills,** before 1880. He died on 31 Dec 1946 New Westminster, British Columbia, at age 84 (Stan Hulme Research, 10 Mar 2000 e-mail, source: Reg #1946-09-013988 B.C. Archives Microfilm #B13192 and GSU Microfilm #2032424.).

Question: *Joyce Anaka says he died in 1949.*

Marguerite Bremner was born on 4 Jun 1863 St.Francois Xavier, (Manitoba) (SFXI-Kipling St.Francois Xavier Register Index, 1834-1900; compiled by Clarence Kipling , B-79.). She was born on 5 Jun 1863 Headingley, (Manitoba) (MBS, C-14926.). She was baptized on 7 Jun 1863 St.Francois Xavier, (Manitoba) (INB *Index des Naissances and Baptemes* (St.Boniface, Manitoba: La Societe Historique de Saint-Boniface., c1995), page 25.) (Rosemary Helga (Morrissette) Rozyk Research.). She died in Aug 1920 at age 57 (Denney.).

Children of **William Taylor** and **Marguerite Bremner** were as follows:

54 i. William Taylor, b. 25 Aug 1880; m. Winnifred Black; d. 1944; bur. 1944 Paynton, Saskatchewan.

55 ii. Mabel Amelia Taylor, b. 20 Dec 1884 Sturgeon River, (Alberta); m. George Kebblewhite; d. 1918.

56 iii. Ellen Harriet Taylor, b. Jun 1886 Sunnyside, (Alberta); m. William Milligan; d. Dec 1967 Edmonton, Alberta.

iv. Rev. Roy Charles Taylor was born on 11 Dec 1889 Sunnyside, (Alberta) (Ibid.). He married Edith Annie Batchelor on 3 Feb 1917 London, England (Ibid.). He died on 23 Jun 1963 Calgary, Alberta, at age 73 (Ibid.).

   Edith Annie Batchelor was born on 16 Sep 1890 England (Ibid.).

v. Ethel Helen Taylor was born in 1890 Sunnyside, (Alberta) (Ibid.). She died in 1959 (Ibid.).

vi. Mary Elizabeth Taylor was born in 1892 Sunnyside, (Alberta) (Ibid.). She married Cleland Swain (Ibid.). She died in 1918 (Ibid.).

   Cleland Swain married **Ruby Alice Taylor**, daughter of **William Taylor** and **Marguerite Bremner** (Ibid.).

vii. William Taylor was born in 1894 Sunnyside, (Alberta) (Ibid.). He died in 1927 (Ibid.).

viii. Ruby Alice Taylor was born in 1896 Sunnyside, (Alberta) (Ibid.). She married Cleland Swain (Ibid.). She died in 1931 (Ibid.).

   Cleland Swain married **Mary Elizabeth Taylor**, daughter of **William Taylor** and **Marguerite Bremner** (Ibid.).

57 ix. Rosy Christina Taylor, b. 1898 Peace River Crossing, (Alberta); m. Charles Gordon.

x. George Taylor was born on 9 Sep 1903 Sunnyside, (Alberta) (Ibid.). He married Mary Bremner Fort St.John, British Columbia.

xi. Esther Jane Taylor was born on 30 Jan 1905 Astleyville (Ibid.).

xii. Ruth Irene Taylor was born on 16 Jan 1909 Poplar Point, Manitoba (Ibid.).

xiii. Donald Gunn Taylor was born in 1912 (Heather Hallett, 31 Mar 1995.). He died on 21 Sep 1969 (Denney.).

21. **Donald Herbert Taylor** was born on 12 Mar 1868 Poplar Point, (Manitoba) (MBS, C-14933.) (HBCA-B.). He was baptized on 29 Mar 1868 St.Ann, Poplar Point, (Manitoba) (MBS, C-14933.). He married **Charlotte Shaw dit Ankenam or Akinam)**, daughter of **Felix Shaw dit Ankenam or Akinam** and **Caroline (--?--)**, before 1900 (HBCA-B.). He died on 11 Oct 1953 at age 85 (Denney.) (HBCA-B.).

Question: *Joyce Anaka says he died in 1955.*

Charlotte Shaw dit Ankenam or Akinam) was born circa 1878 (1901 Canada, #206, A-4, page 25, family 8, line 1-3.).

Children of **Donald Herbert Taylor** and **Charlotte Shaw dit Ankenam or Akinam)** are as follows:

i. Sandford Taylor.

ii. Dave Taylor.

iii. Charlie Taylor.

iv. Mabel Taylor married (--?--) Vogel (HBCA-B.).

v. Maggie Taylor married Claude Driver (Ibid.).

vi. Walter Taylor.

vii. Joan Taylor married (--?--) O'Neil (Ibid.).

viii. Henriette Taylor was born circa Sep 1900 (1901 Canada, #206, A-4, page 25, family 8, line 1-3.). She married Wes Yaeger (HBCA-B.).

22. **John Taylor Jr** was born on 23 Dec 1858 Headingley, (Manitoba) (HBC-PN , Headingly, #159.) (1901 Canada, District 11(a-3), page 3, famiy 8, line 39-46.). He married **Frances Helen Beddome**, daughter of **Henry Septimus Beddome M. D.** and **Frances Omand**, on 4 Feb 1880 St.Andrews, Manitoba (Denney.). He died on 12 Feb 1927 (Headingley), RM Assiniboia, Manitoba, at age 68 (MB Vital Statistics, Death Reg. #1927,010073.).

Frances Helen Beddome was born on 9 Jun 1860 York Factory (MBS, C-14925.) (1901 Canada, District 11(a-3), page 3, famiy 8, line 39-46.). She died on 28 Apr 1921 (Headingley), Assiniboia, Manitoba, at age 60 (MB Vital Statistics, Death Reg. #1921,023254.).

Children of **John Taylor Jr.** and **Frances Helen Beddome** were as follows:

i. George Campbell Taylor was born on 20 Oct 1880 Headingley, Manitoba (Denney.). He was buried on 9 Mar 1881 Headingley, Manitoba (Ibid.).

ii. John Edward Taylor was born on 7 Dec 1881 Prince Albert, (Saskatchewan) (ArchiviaNet, C-15005.). He died in Jun 1882 Prince Albert, (Saskatchewan) (Ibid.).

58 iii. Flora Ann Taylor, b. 29 Apr 1883 Prince Albert, (Saskatchewan); m. Charles Britton; d. 17 Jul 1930 RM Assiniboia, Manitoba.

59 iv. Frances Evelyn Taylor, b. 19 Oct 1884 Prince Albert, (Saskatchewan); m. David Alexander Campbell; d. 1956.

60 v. William Herbert Taylor, b. 4 Jul 1886; m. Jessie Chalmers; d. 1967.

61 vi. Henry Beddome 'Harry' Taylor, b. 9 Nov 1889 (Headingley), Assiniboia, Manitoba; m. Edith Isabelle Cann; d. 1961.

62 vii. Marguerite Ethel 'Daisy' Taylor, b. 23 Apr 1893 Headingley, Manitoba; m. James Puddifant.

viii. Kathleen Esther McLaurin Taylor was born on 31 Oct 1896 (Headingley), Assiniboia, Manitoba (MB Vital Statistics, Birth Reg. #1896,001239.). She died on 16 Mar 1897 Headingley, Manitoba (Denney.). She was buried on 17 Mar 1897 Headingley, Manitoba (Ibid.).

63 ix. Doris Mary Spencer Taylor, b. 27 Apr 1899 (Headingley), Assiniboia, Manitoba; m. Frederick Roy Britton.

23. **William Herbert Taylor** was born on 16 Oct 1868 Headingley, (Manitoba) (HBC-PN , Headingly, #162.). He married **Lizzie Ellen Laird** on 18 Jun 1896 Headingley, Manitoba (Denney.). He died on 8 Jul 1925 at age 56 (Ibid.).

Children of **William Herbert Taylor** and **Lizzie Ellen Laird** are:

64   i.   Colin Alexander Taylor, b. 20 Sep 1899 Headingley, Manitoba; m. Resi Elizabeth Clevenger.

24. Alice Ann Taylor was born on 16 Oct 1874 Headingley, Manitoba (Heather Hallett, 31 Mar 1995.). She married **Richard Hamilton**, son of **Joseph Hamilton** and **Mary Busby**, on 1 Mar 1899 Headingley, Manitoba (Denney.) (Heather Hallett, 31 Mar 1995.). She died on 3 Mar 1943 at age 68 (Ibid.).

Children of **Alice Ann Taylor** and **Richard Hamilton** both born Headingley, Manitoba, are as follows:
    i.   Florence May Hamilton was born on 14 Mar 1903 (Denney.).
    ii.   John Taylor Hamilton was born on 3 Jan 1905 (Ibid.).

25. Rupert Taylor was born on 7 Feb 1877 Headingley, Manitoba (Ibid.). He married **Alice Robina Dennison**, daughter of **William Dennison** and **Alice Ann McKay**, on 21 Dec 1904 (Ibid.). He died on 28 Feb 1957 Headingley, Manitoba, at age 80 (Ibid.).

Alice Robina Dennison was born on 13 Jun 1866 Kindonan, (Manitoba) (MBS, C-14927.). She married **Joseph Shep Quark**, son of **Andrew Quash** and **Charlotte Ship**, on 12 Sep 1886 St.James, Manitoba (Denney.).

Children of **Rupert Taylor** and **Alice Robina Dennison** were as follows:
65   i.   Reverend Rupert Leslie Taylor, b. 5 Dec 1905 Headingley, Manitoba; m. Gladys Russell Lyall; d. 20 Apr 1979.
    ii.   John Murray Taylor was born on 27 Jun 1908 Headingley, Manitoba (Ibid.). He died on 8 Jan 1927 at age 18 (Ibid.).
    iii.   Eric Morrison Taylor was born in Jul 1913 Headingley, Manitoba (Heather Hallett, 31 Mar 1995.). He died on 27 Sep 1913 Headingley, Manitoba (Ibid.).
    iv.   Catherine Frances Taylor was born on 20 Apr 1915 Headingley, Manitoba (Ibid.).
    v.   Kathleen Agnes Taylor was born on 15 Jun 1917 Headingley, Manitoba (Denney.).
    vi.   Kenneth Stewart Taylor was born on 2 May 1919 Winnipeg, Manitoba (Ibid.).
    vii.   Donald Allan Taylor was born on 29 Apr 1922 Headingley, Manitoba (Heather Hallett, 31 Mar 1995.). He died on 22 Jun 1944 at age 22 (Ibid.).

26. Agnes Schultz Taylor was born on 14 Nov 1894 Headingley, Manitoba (Ibid.) (1901 Canada, #11, A-3, page 4, family 15, line 29-42.). She married **Oswald Francis Montgomery**, son of **Oswald Montgomery** and **Elsie Spalding,** on 3 Sep 1919 Headingley, Manitoba (Heather Hallett, 31 Mar 1995.). She died on 20 Apr 1958 at age 63 (Ibid.).

Oswald Francis Montgomery was born in 1888 (Ibid.).

27. Eliza Taylor was born on 28 Oct 1863 Poplar Point, (Manitoba) (HBC-PN , Poplar Point and High Bluff, #328.). She was baptized on 8 Nov 1863 St.Mary's Anglican Church, Portage la Prairie, (Manitoba) (SMACPLP, page 24, B-192.). She married **Alexander Hunter Murray Setter**, son of **George Setter** and **Jessie Ellen Campbell,** on 2 Aug 1882 Battleford, (Saskatchewan) (Denney.). She died in 1947 (Ibid.). She was buried in 1947 Paynton, Saskatchewan (Ibid.).

Alexander Hunter Murray Setter was born on 6 May 1863 High Bluff, (Manitoba) (HBC-PN , Poplar Point and High Bluff, #246.). He died on 31 Dec 1933 Paynton, Saskatchewan, at age 70 (Denney.).

28. Maurice Edward Taylor was born on 19 Jan 1867 Poplar Point, (Manitoba). He was baptized on 24 Feb 1867 St.Ann, Poplar Point, (Manitoba) (MBS, C-14933.). He married **Harriet Josephine McDonald**, daughter of **John McDonald** and **Nancy McDonald**, on 16 Jan 1899 St.Andrews, Manitoba (Heather Hallett, 31 Mar 1995.). He died on 19 Oct 1943 Paynton, Saskatchewan, at age 76 (Ibid.).

Lily Coombs was born in 1895. She died in 1984. She was buried Paynton, (Saskatchewan).

Children of **Maurice Edward Taylor** and **Lily Coombs** were as follows:
66   i.   Kathleen Taylor, d. 1991.
    ii.   George Taylor died in 1974 (Ibid.).
    iii.   Jean Taylor died in 1982.
    iv.   Annie Taylor was born in 1919.

Harriet Josephine McDonald was born on 23 Feb 1868 (Manitoba) (Denney.). She was baptized on 13 Apr 1868 St.Andrews, (Manitoba) (Ibid.). She died in 1918 (Ibid.).

Children of **Maurice Edward Taylor** and **Harriet Josephine McDonald** were as follows:
    i.   Hazel Taylor was born on 8 Jan 1901 Battleford, (Saskatchewan) (Heather Hallett, 31 Mar 1995.).
    ii.   Anonyme Taylor was born in 1918 (Ibid.). She died in 1918 (Ibid.).

29. Albert Scott Taylor was born on 7 May 1870 Poplar Point, (Manitoba) (1870C-MB 1870 Manitoba Census, National Archives of Canada, Ottawa, Ontario, Microfilm Reel Number C-2170., page 355, #921.) (MB Vital Statistics, Birth Reg. #1870,1515299, registration date: 05/06/1942.). He married **Rubana Bremner**, daughter of **James Bremner** and **Letitia Fidler,** before 1894.

Rubana Bremner was born on 8 Apr 1869 Headingley, (Manitoba) (HBC-PN , Headingley, #14.). She was baptized on 18 Apr 1869 Headingley, (Manitoba) (Denney.).

Children of **Albert Scott Taylor** and **Rubana Bremner** were as follows:
    i.   Percy Taylor died circa 1909 Montana.
    ii.   Nora Isabella Taylor was born on 10 Mar 1894 (Saskatchewan) (SK Vital Statistics, Birth Reg. #6566.).

30. Walter David Taylor was born on 28 Mar 1874. He died on 10 Oct 1955 at age 81. He was buried Burnaby, British Columbia.

Martha Christianson was born on 1 Jan 1890. She died on 23 Feb 1969 at age 79.

Children of **Walter David Taylor** and **Martha Christianson** are as follows:
    i.   Archie Taylor was born in 1915 (Denney.).
    ii.   Ethel Taylor was born in 1917 (Heather Hallett, 31 Mar 1995.).

31. Catherine Jemima Taylor was born on 12 Nov 1877 Poplar Point, Manitoba (Denney.). She married **John Archibald Rowland**, son of **Alexander Rowland** and **Caroline Fraser,** on 28 Aug 1901 Battleford, (Saskatchewan) (Ibid.). She died on 12 Mar 1943 North Battleford, Saskatchewan, at age 65 (Ibid.). She was buried in Mar 1943 Battleford, Saskatchewan (Ibid.).

John Archibald Rowland was born on 18 Dec 1879 Victoria, (Saskatchewan) (ArchiviaNet, C-15000.). He died on 22 Jun 1953 North Battleford, Saskatchewan, at age 73 (Denney.).

32. Mary Jane Maud Taylor was born on 22 Dec 1881 Prince Albert, Saskatchewan (SK Vital Statistics, Birth Reg. #12046.) (ArchiviaNet, C-15006.). She married **Fred Kissack** in 1919 (Heather Hallett.). She died in 1972 North Battleford, Saskatchewan (Ibid.). She was buried in 1972 Woodlawn Cemetery, North Battleford, Saskatchewan (Ibid.).

Fred Kissack was born Minnesota. He was buried Woodlawn Cemetery, North Battleford, (Saskatchewan).

33. Frederick Taylor was born on 2 Mar 1887 (Ibid., 31 Mar 1995.). He married **Hilda Larson.**

Children of **Frederick Taylor** and **Hilda Larson** are as follows:

      i. Bernice Taylor.

      ii. Lloyd Taylor.

      iii. Evelyn Taylor.

34. Alice Taylor was born on 31 Aug 1875 (1901 Canada, microfilm T-6553, Bresaylor, page 3, family 27, line 28-40.). She married **Robert Leslie** before 1906.

Robert Leslie died circa 1931 Saskatchewan (Denney.).

35. Mary Isabella 'Marabelle' Taylor was born on 12 Dec 1878 Poplar Point, Manitoba (1901 Canada, microfilm T-6553, Bresaylor, page 3, family 27, line 28-40.) (Heather Hallett, 31 Mar 1995.). She married **Edward Emerson Mack** on 21 Oct 1902 parent's home, Bresaylor, (Saskatchewan) (Ibid.). She died in May 1950 Burnaby, British Columbia, at age 71 (Ibid.).

Edward Emerson Mack was born in 1872 Mill Village, Nova Scotia (Heather Hallett.). He died in 1962 (Ibid.).

36. Margaret Jane 'Maggie' Taylor was born on 12 Dec 1878 (1901 Canada, microfilm T-6553, Bresaylor, page 3, family 27, line 28-40.). She married **Andre Gullion Pothier** in 1912 (Denney.). She died in 1962 (Ibid.). She was buried in 1962 West Vancouver, British Columbia (Ibid.).

Andre Gullion Pothier was born in 1877 Nova Scotia. He died in 1956. He was buried West Vancouver, British Columbia.

37. Cuthbert Francis 'Cubby' Taylor was born on 1 Sep 1880 Poplar Point, Manitoba (1901 Canada, microfilm T-6553, Bresaylor, page 3, family 27, line 28-40.). He married **Annie Ross** in 1910 (Heather Hallett, 31 Mar 1995.). He died on 2 Nov 1966 North Battleford, Saskatchewan, at age 86 (Ibid.).

Annie Ross was born circa 1888 Scotland (Denney.). She died on 8 Feb 1961 North Battleford, Saskatchewan (Heather Hallett, 31 Mar 1995.).

Children of **Cuthbert Francis 'Cubby' Taylor** and **Annie Ross** are:

      i. Sidney Taylor was born on 2 Jun 1912 (Ibid.).

38. Ann Maria Taylor was born on 26 Apr 1884 Police Barracks, North Battleford, (Saskatchewan) (Ibid.) (1901 Canada, microfilm T-6553, Bresaylor, page 3, family 27, line 28-40.) (ArchiviaNet, C-15005.). She married **Arthur Hayes** in 1911 (Heather Hallett, 31 Mar 1995.). She died in 1951 (Ibid.). She was buried in 1951 Meota, Saskatchewan (Ibid.).

Arthur Hayes was born England (Ibid.). He died in 1963 (Ibid.). He was buried in 1963 Meota, Saskatchewan (Ibid.).

39. Allan Peterson Taylor was born on 23 Mar 1886 Bresaylor, Manitoba (1901 Canada, microfilm T-6553, Bresaylor, page 3, family 27, line 28-40.) (SK Vital Statistics, Birth Reg. #10949.). He married **Vera Hawley** before 1935. He died on 5 Sep 1936 North Battleford, Saskatchewan, at age 50 (Heather Hallett, 31 Mar 1995.).

Children of **Allan Peterson Taylor** and **Vera Hawley** are:

      i. Allan Taylor was born circa 1935 (Ibid.).

40. Clarence Taylor was born on 11 Aug 1878 Headingley, (Manitoba) (Denney.) (1901 Canada, microfilm T-6553, Bresaylor, page 3, family 25, line 11-25.). He married **Margaret Ann Spence**, daughter of **Edwin Spence** and **Jemima Cusitor,** before 1911 Prince Albert, Saskatchewan (Denney.). He died on 30 Oct 1961 Bresaylor, Saskatchewan, at age 83 (Ibid.).

Margaret Ann Spence was born on 4 Jan 1883 St.Catherines, Prince Albert District, (Saskatchewan) (ArchiviaNet, C-15004.). She died in 1945 (Denney.). Question: *From Charles Denney: b. 1881; f. Edwin* (Ibid.).

Children of **Clarence Taylor** and **Margaret Ann Spence** were as follows:

      i. Kenneth Taylor.

      ii. William Taylor.

      iii. Clarence Stanley Taylor was born in Jan 1911 (1911 Canada, District 34, page 7, family 92, line 14-16.) (1916 Census of Canada from the National Archives of Canada (Transcription by ancestry.com), Ottawa, Canada, District 18, page 11, family 112.).

      iv. Grace Irene Taylor was born in 1913 (Ibid.). She died in 1974 (Heather Hallett, 31 Mar 1995.).

      v. Gordon Elmer Taylor was born in 1915 (1916 Canada, District 18, page 11, family 112.). He died in 1985 (Heather Hallett, 31 Mar 1995.).

      vi. Edwin David 'Bud' Taylor was born in 1916 (1916 Canada, District 18, page 11, family 112.).

      vii. Ernest Taylor was born on 21 Oct 1918 (Heather Hallett, 31 Mar 1995.).

      viii. Myrtle Taylor was born circa 1920 (1921 Canada, District 215-26A, page 13.).

41. Florence Mary Taylor was born on 12 Apr 1880 Headingley, Manitoba (Denney.) (1901 Canada, microfilm T-6553, Bresaylor, page 3, family 25, line 11-25.). She married **William Joseph Goth**, son of **William Goth** and **Margaret McEwen,** on 8 Nov 1906 North Battleford, (Saskatchewan) (Denney.). She died on 4 Feb 1917 at age 36 (Ibid.).

William Joseph Goth was born on 17 Sep 1876 Lanark, Ontario (Ontario, Canada Births 1869-1913, ancestry.com, Hereinafter cited as ON Births.). He died on 5 Sep 1957 at age 80 (Denney.).

42. Jessie Ellen Taylor was born on 19 Nov 1885 Bresaylor, (Saskatchewan) (SK Vital Statistics, Birth Reg. #12360.) (ArchiviaNet, C-15006.). She married **James Brown** on 12 Jul 1911 Bresaylor, Saskatchewan (Heather Hallett.). She died on 28 Jan 1961 at age 75 (Denney.).

James Brown was born Cardiff, Ontario (Heather Hallett.). He died on 19 May 1930 (Ibid.).

43. Dora Jemima Taylor was born on 20 Sep 1887 Bresaylor, (Saskatchewan) (1901 Canada, microfilm T-6553, Bresaylor, page 3, family 25, line 11-25.) (SK Vital Statistics, Birth Reg. #12984.). She married **Charles Henry Heapy**, son of **Mathias Heapy** and **Lydia Lawson,** on 12 Jun 1907 Bresaylor, (Saskatchewan) (Denney.). She died on 7 Feb 1977 at age 89 (Ibid.).

Charles Henry Heapy was born Grafton, Walsh, North Dakota (Ibid.). He died Cranbrook, British Columbia (Ibid.).

44. Minnie Taylor was born on 6 Dec 1889 Bresaylor, (Saskatchewan) (1901 Canada, microfilm T-6553, Bresaylor, page 3, family 25, line 11-25.) (SK Vital Statistics, Birth Reg. #6499.). She married **John Murray Inman** before 1913 Bresaylor, Saskatchewan (Denney.). She died on 3 Apr 1935 at age 45 (Ibid.).

John Murray Inman was born Kilburn, New Brunswick. He died on 17 May 1967 North Battleford, (Saskatchewan).

45. Andrew Stanley Taylor was born on 20 Oct 1891 Bresaylor, (Saskatchewan) (1901 Canada, microfilm T-6553, Bresaylor, page 3, family 25, line 11-25.). He married **Bertha Hazel Cowitz**, daughter of **Albert Frank Cowitz** and **Margaret Billo,** on 20 Mar 1915 Calgary, Alberta (Denney.). He died in 1982 (Ibid.).

Bertha Hazel Cowitz was born Oklahoma.

Children of **Andrew Stanley Taylor** and **Bertha Hazel Cowitz** all born Bresaylor, Saskatchewan, were as follows:

    i. Kathleen Marjorie Taylor was born on 26 Dec 1915 (Ibid.). She died on 11 Dec 1972 at age 56 (Ibid.).
    ii. Beryl Jean Taylor was born on 19 Jul 1918 (Ibid.).
    iii. Leonard Ivan Taylor was born on 20 Aug 1919 (Ibid.).
    iv. Dorothy Hazel Taylor was born on 7 Feb 1923 (Ibid.). She died on 7 Feb 1924 Bresaylor, Saskatchewan, at age 1 (Ibid.).
    v. Ellis Roy Taylor was born on 22 Mar 1926 (Ibid.).
    vi. Mildred Elizabeth Taylor was born on 27 Jan 1928 (Ibid.).

46. Angus Chisholm Taylor was born on 7 Oct 1895 Bresaylor, (Saskatchewan) (1901 Canada, microfilm T-6553, Bresaylor, page 3, family 25, line 11-25.) (SK Vital Statistics, Birth Reg. #6658.). He married **Marian Osborne.** He died on 31 Jan 1968 Calgary, Alberta, at age 72 (Denney.).

Marian Osborne was born England.

Children of **Angus Chisholm Taylor** and **Marian Osborne** are as follows:

    i. Meryl Taylor.
    ii. Keith Taylor.
    iii. Lance Taylor.

47. Charles Lindsay Taylor was born on 18 Oct 1897 Bresaylor, (Saskatchewan) (1901 Canada, microfilm T-6553, Bresaylor, page 3, family 25, line 11-25.) (SK Vital Statistics, Birth Reg. #6833.). He married **Marian C. Gowan.** He died on 16 Aug 1974 at age 76 (Heather Hallett, 31 Mar 1995.).

Marian C. Gowan was born in 1905 Scotland (Ibid.). She died in 1955 (Ibid.).

Children of **Charles Lindsay Taylor** and **Marian C. Gowan** are:

    i. Jean Taylor.

48. Peter Taylor was born circa 11 Feb 1873 (Manitoba) (Ibid.). He married **Marie Marguerite Short**, daughter of **James Short** and **Mathilde McGillis,** on 25 Feb 1895 Malta, Valley County, Montana (VCM Valley County Courthouse, Glasgow, Montana; Marriage Record Licenses, 1865-1950, familysearch.org, Hereinafter cited as VCM.). He died on 27 Mar 1932 Kalispell, Flathead County, Montana (MT Death.).

Marie Marguerite Short was born on 7 Nov 1877 St.Laurent, (Saskatchewan) (SL-SK St.Laurent-de-Grandin Roman Catholic Registre des Baptemes, Mariages & Seplutres, St.Laurent, Saskatchewan, 1872-1896, page 5, B-47. Hereinafter cited as SL-SK.). She was baptized on 18 Nov 1877 St.Laurent-de-Grandin, (Saskatchewan) (Ibid.).

Children of **Peter Taylor** and **Marie Marguerite Short** were as follows:

  67 i. Frank Lee Taylor, b. 7 Jan 1908; m. Margaret A. Strand; d. 14 Feb 1988 Flathead County, Montana.
    ii. Mary Ann Taylor was born in Dec 1896 Malta, Valley County, Montana (1900 MT, Sheet 4A, family 127, line 28-32.). She married Edmond Gerhardt Doerr, son of Mathias B. Doerr and Mary Ann Clark, on 4 Jun 1917 Silver Bow County, Montana (SBCM Silver Bow County, Montana; Marriage Record Licenses and Certificates; 1865-1950; familysearch.org: #9626, Hereinafter cited as SBCM.).
        Edmond Gerhardt Doerr was born on 23 Mar 1895 Roslyn, Kittitas County, Washington (Ibid.) (Ancestry.com, WWI Draft Registration.). He died on 23 Oct 1950 South Prairie, Pierce County, Washington, at age 55 (Washington State Digital Archives, Secretary of State, State Archives, http://www.digitalcarchives.wa./gov, 960 Washington Street, Cheney, WA 99004.).
    iii. David Oliver Taylor was born in Feb 1897 Malta, Valley County, Montana (1900 MT, Sheet 4A, family 127, line 28-32.).
    iv. James Taylor was born in Nov 1898 Malta, Valley County, Montana (Ibid.).
  68 v. Alfred Taylor, b. circa 1900 Malta, Valley County, Montana; m. Winifred Messerly.
    vi. Alice Rose Taylor was born circa 1904 Malta, Phillips County, Montana (1910C MT Thirteenth Census of the United States: 1910; Montana, National Archives of the United States, Washington D.C., Sheet 10A, family 60, line 27-38.). She married Everett Henry, son of C. F. Henry and Josephine Burman, on 29 Oct 1926 Great Falls, Cascade County, Montana (CaCM Cascade County, Montana; Marriage Record Licenses and Certificates; 1865-1950; familysearch.org: #2993, Hereinafter cited as CaCM.). She and Everett Henry obtained a marriage license on 29 Oct 1926 Great Falls, Cascade County, Montana (Ibid.). She married Ray Russell Jorgensen on 9 Aug 1927 Choteau, Teton County, Montana (TeCM Teton County, Montana; Marriage Record Licenses and Certificates; 1865-1950; familysearch.org: #1497, Hereinafter cited as TeCM.). She and Ray Russell Jorgensen obtained a marriage license on 9 Aug 1927 Teton County, Montana (Ibid.).
        Everett Henry was born on 15 May 1893 Page, North Dakota (CaCM, #2993.) (Social Security Death Index, . Hereinafter cited as SSDI.). He died in Sep 1983 Glacier County, Montana, at age 90 (Ibid.).
        Ray Russell Jorgensen was born in 1903 Spokane, Spokane County, Washington (TeCM, #1497.).
  69 vii. Mervin Wallace Taylor, b. 25 Nov 1915 Malta, Valley County, Montana; m. Iva Rovina Webb; m. Anna Andrews; d. 21 Jun 2001 Lewiston, Nez Perce County, Idaho.

70   viii.   Lorna Taylor, b. 24 Jul 1919 Montana; m. George N. Stephens; m. Mac McMullen; m. Edwiin A. Peterson; m. Oscar C. Lein; d. 3 Oct 1987 Musselshell County, Montana.

49. **Timolean Love Taylor** was born on 16 May 1878 Manitoba (1901 Canada, microfilm T-6553, Bresaylor, page 3, family 26, line 26-27.) (Ancestry.com, WWI Draft Registration.). He married **Vera Julia Johnson** before 1911. He married **Margaret Agnes Clark** on 3 Dec 1938 Malta, Phillips County, Montana (PhCM   Phillips County Courthouse, Montana; Marriage Record Licenses and Certificates; 1865-1950, familysearch.org, Hereinafter cited as PhCM.). He died on 16 Aug 1939 Phillips County, Manitoba, at age 61 (MT Death.).

Vera Julia Johnson was born circa 1890 Nebraska (Ibid.) (1920C-MT   1920 Federal Census Montana, National Archives of the United States, Washington D.C., District 161, page 5B, line 69.). She died on 5 Sep 1926 Deer Lodge County, Montana (MT Death.).

Children of **Timolean Love Taylor** and **Vera Julia Johnson** were as follows:

      i.   George Wallace Taylor was born on 24 May 1911 Montana (SSDI.). He married Olga C. Reigstad on 5 May 1941 Glasgow, Valley County, Montana (VCM.). He died in Dec 1959 Great Falls, Cascade County, Nebraska, at age 48 (SSDI.).

          Olga C. Reigstad was born on 26 Aug 1911 (Ibid.). She died on 6 May 1977 Phillips County, Montana, at age 65 (Ibid.) (MT Death.).

      ii.   Hugh Richard Taylor was born on 16 Aug 1912 Montana (SSDI.). He married Lydia Gloria Lafond on 26 Jun 1937 Phillips County, Montana (PhCM.). He died on 5 Feb 1991 at age 78 (SSDI.).

          Lydia Gloria Lafond was born in 1920 (PhCM.).

      iii.   Doris L. Taylor was born circa 1914 Montana (1920C-MT, District 161, page 5B, line 69.) (PhCM.). She married Hugh S. Miller on 18 Aug 1932 Phillips County, Montana (Ibid.).

      iv.   Emory Johnson Taylor was born on 13 May 1915 Montana (SSDI.). He died in Nov 1980 Lebanon, Laclede, Missouri, at age 65 (Ibid.).

      v.   Carrie Marie Taylor was born in 1917 (Heather Hallett, 31 Mar 1995.).

Margaret Agnes Clark was born in 1901 (PhCM.).

50. **Martha Louise Taylor** was born in 1880 (1891 Census of Canada from the National Archives of Canada, Ottawa, Canada, District 200A, page 21, line 22.). She married **George DeFlyer**, son of **John DeFlyer** and **Matilda Fleming**, on 28 Mar 1901 Malta, Valley County, Montana (VCM.). She died on 29 Sep 1956 Stillwater County, Manitoba (MT Death.).

George DeFlyer was born on 2 Mar 1878 Illinois (Ancestry.com, WWI Draft Registration.). He died on 4 Nov 1953 Phillips County, Montana, at age 75.

51. **Catherine Ann Taylor** was born on 6 Jun 1882 Battleford, (Saskatchewan) (ArchiviaNet, C-15005.). She and **Frank L. Godfrey** obtained a marriage license on 9 Oct 1905 Valley County, Montana (VCM, No. 198.). She married **Frank L. Godfrey**, son of **Joseph Godfrey** and **Rebecca Monisey**, on 10 Oct 1905 Malta, Valley County, Montana (Ibid.). She married **Bud J. Carter** on 26 Apr 1921 Malta, Phillips County, Montana (PhCM.). She and **Bud J. Carter** obtained a marriage license on 26 Apr 1921 Malta, Phillips County, Montana (Ibid., #574.).

Frank L. Godfrey was born circa 1874 Alexander, Maine (VCM, M-193.).

Bud J. Carter was born in 1891 Wisconsin (PhCM.).

52. **Edith Taylor** was born on 6 Mar 1885 Bresaylor, (Saskatchewan) (ArchiviaNet, C-15005.). She married **Patrick Francis "Frank" Dardis**, son of **Patrick Dardis** and **Elizabeth Connery**, on 21 Jun 1912 Valier, Teton County, Montana (TeCM.). She died on 20 Jan 1959 Warm Springs, Deer Lodge County, Montana, at age 73 (MT Death.).

Patrick Francis "Frank" Dardis was born on 14 Dec 1883 Lawler, Chickasaw County, Iowa (SSDI.). He died on 6 Feb 1964 Conrad, Pondera County, Montana, at age 80 (Ibid.) (MT Death.).

53. **Harriet Elizabeth Taylor** was born in May 1887 (1900 MT, Sheet 4A, family 126, line 16-27.). She married **Israel McEwen**, son of **William McEwen** and **Martha Fox**, on 21 Apr 1910 Glasgow, Valley County, Montana (VCM.). She died on 17 Feb 1959 Phillips County, Montana, at age 71 (MT Death.).

Israel McEwen was born in 1867 (VCM.). He died on 17 Mar 1954 Phillips County, Montana (MT Death.).

Generation Four

54. **William Taylor** was born on 25 Aug 1880 (Heather Hallett, 31 Mar 1995.). He married **Winnifred Black** in 1912 (Ibid.). He died in 1944 (Ibid.). He was buried in 1944 Paynton, Saskatchewan (Ibid.).

Winnifred Black was born in 1892 England (Ibid.). She died in 1973 (Ibid.). She was buried in 1973 Paynton, Saskatchewan (Ibid.).

Children of **William Taylor** and **Winnifred Black** were as follows:

      i.   Winnifred Mary 'Molly' Taylor was born in 1913 Saskatchewan (Ibid.). She married George Webb on 24 Dec (Ibid.).

          George Webb was born England (Ibid.). He died in 1958 (Ibid.).

      ii.   Margaret 'Bessie' Taylor was born on 24 Aug 1914 Paynton, Saskatchewan (Ibid.). She married Vivian Rogers on 3 Apr 1938 Christ Church, Paynton, Saskatchewan (Ibid.).

          Vivian Rogers died on 16 May 1986 North Battleford, Saskatchewan (Ibid.).

      iii.   Edith Gwendolyne 'Gwen' Taylor was born in 1915 (Ibid.). She married Frank Andrews in 1947 (Ibid.).

      iv.   Cecil William Taylor was born on 25 May 1917 North Battleford, Saskatchewan (Ibid.). He married Evelyn Murphy on 3 Feb 1950 Notre Dame, North Battleford, Saskatchewan (Ibid.). He died on 23 Dec 1974 Saskatoon, Saskatchewan, at age 57 (Ibid.).

      v.   Marjorie Joyce Taylor was born in 1919 (Ibid.). She married George Button on 17 Jun 1939 (Ibid.).

          George Button died in Jun 1980 (Ibid.).

      vi.   Peter Roy Taylor was born in 1925 (Ibid.). He married June Wheeler, daughter of Ernest Wheeler and Ethel Parr, on 20 Oct 1948 St.Judes AC, Brantford, Ontario (Ibid.).

          June Wheeler was born on 30 Jun 1929 North Battleford, (Saskatchewan).

      vii.   Herbert Anderson Taylor was born on 13 May 1929 (Ibid.).

55. Mabel Amelia Taylor was born on 20 Dec 1884 Sturgeon River, (Alberta) (ArchiviaNet, C-15006.). She married **George Kebblewhite** in Mar 1903 Sunnyside, (Alberta) (Denney.). She died in 1918 (Ibid.).

George Kebblewhite was born on 18 Nov 1870 England (Ibid.). He died in Jun 1957 at age 86 (Ibid.). He was buried Edmonton, (Alberta).

56. Ellen Harriet Taylor was born in Jun 1886 Sunnyside, (Alberta) (Ibid.). She married **William Milligan** in 1905 (Ibid.). She died in Dec 1967 Edmonton, Alberta, at age 81 (Ibid.).

57. Rosy Christina Taylor was born in 1898 Peace River Crossing, (Alberta) (Ibid.). She married **Charles Gordon** Fort St.John (David Courchane, Courchane/Courchene Family Research.).

Charles Gordon was born circa 1882 Ireland. He died Manville, (Alberta).

58. Flora Ann Taylor was born on 29 Apr 1883 Prince Albert, (Saskatchewan) (ArchiviaNet, C-15005.). She married **Charles Britton** on 25 Sep 1906 Winnipeg, Manitoba (MB Vital Statistics, Marriage Reg. 1906,001842.). She died on 17 Jul 1930 RM Assiniboia, Manitoba, at age 47 (Ibid., Death Reg. #1930,035070.).

Charles Britton was born on 4 Apr 1876.

59. Frances Evelyn Taylor was born on 19 Oct 1884 Prince Albert, (Saskatchewan) (1901 Canada, District 11(a-3), page 3, famiy 8, line 39-46.) (ArchiviaNet, C-15005.). She married **David Alexander Campbell** on 10 Aug 1904 (Headingley), Assiniboia, Manitoba (MB Vital Statistics, Marriage Reg. #1904,002186.). She died in 1956 (Denney.).

David Alexander Campbell was born in Jan 1873 (1911 Canada, District 56, page 27-28, family 259, line 49-50, 1-2.).

60. William Herbert Taylor was born on 4 Jul 1886 (1901 Canada, District 11(a-3), page 3, famiy 8, line 39-46.). He married **Jessie Chalmers** before 1920. He died in 1967 (Denney.).

Children of **William Herbert Taylor** and **Jessie Chalmers** were:

     i. John Taylor died infant.

Children of **William Herbert Taylor** and **Doris (–?–)** are as follows:

     i. William Taylor.

     ii. David Chalmers Taylor was born on 6 Sep 1920 (Heather Hallett, 31 Mar 1995.).

     iii. Francis Beddome Taylor was born on 12 Sep 1922 (Ibid.).

61. Henry Beddome 'Harry' Taylor was born on 9 Nov 1889 (Headingley), Assiniboia, Manitoba (MB Vital Statistics, Birth Reg. #1889,001390.). He married **Edith Isabelle Cann** on 24 Jul 1912 Assiniboia, Manitoba (Ibid., Marriage Reg. #1912,004185.). He died in 1961 (Denney.).

Children of **Henry Beddome 'Harry' Taylor** and **Edith Isabelle Cann** are as follows:

     i. Henry Gordon Taylor.

     ii. Edward Taylor.

     iii. Helen Taylor.

     iv. Mabel Flora Taylor was born on 6 Mar 1913.

     v. John Kenneth Taylor was born in 1914.

62. Marguerite Ethel 'Daisy' Taylor was born on 23 Apr 1893 Headingley, Manitoba (1901 Canada, District 11(a-3), page 3, famiy 8, line 39-46.). She married **James Puddifant**, son of **James Lewis Puddifant** and **Edith Ingold,** on 14 Jul 1920 (Headingley), Assiniboia, Manitoba (MB Vital Statistics, Marriage Reg. #1920,037407.).

63. Doris Mary Spencer Taylor was born on 27 Apr 1899 (Headingley), Assiniboia, Manitoba (Ibid., Birth Reg. #1899,005108.). She married **Frederick Roy Britton**, son of **James Britton** and **Priscilla Robinson,** on 29 Mar 1922 Assiniboia, Manitoba (Ibid., Marriage Reg. #1922,013405.).

Frederick Roy Britton was born in 1893.

64. Colin Alexander Taylor was born on 20 Sep 1899 Headingley, Manitoba (Heather Hallett, 31 Mar 1995.). He married **Resi Elizabeth Clevenger.**

Children of **Colin Alexander Taylor** and **Resi Elizabeth Clevenger** are as follows:

     i. John Colin Taylor.

     ii. Edward Gustav Taylor.

65. Reverend Rupert Leslie Taylor was born on 5 Dec 1905 Headingley, Manitoba (Ibid.). He married **Gladys Russell Lyall** on 20 Apr 1931 (Ibid.). He died on 20 Apr 1979 at age 73 (Ibid.).

Children of **Reverend Rupert Leslie Taylor** and **Gladys Russell Lyall** are as follows:

     i. Patricia Sibbald Taylor.

     ii. John Rupert Lyall Taylor.

     iii. Hugh David Taylor was born on 7 May 1934 (Ibid.).

66. Kathleen Taylor died in 1991. She married **Jack Chaykoski.**

67. Frank Lee Taylor was born on 7 Jan 1908 (1987LS 1987-92 Little Shell Band of Chippewa Roll.). He married **Margaret A. Strand** on 28 Aug 1946 Malta, Phillips County, Montana (PhCM, #2428.). He died on 14 Feb 1988 Flathead County, Montana, at age 80 (SSDI.).

Margaret A. Strand was born on 20 Jul 1913 (PhCM.) (SSDI.). She married **Mathew John Moran**, son of **John Moran** and **Eleanor Plummer,** before 1931. She died on 28 Jun 2005 Columbia Falls, Flathead County, Montana, at age 91 (Ibid.).

Children of **Frank Lee Taylor** and **Margaret A. Strand** are as follows:

     i. Lee F. Taylor was born on 2 Mar 1951 (1987-92LS.).

     ii. Dave H. Taylor was born on 29 Jun 1952 (Ibid.).

68. Alfred Taylor was born circa 1900 Malta, Valley County, Montana (1910C MT, District 234, page 10A, line 27.). He married **Winifred Messerly** on 7 Jul 1928 Billings, Yellowstone County, Montana (YCM.).

Winifred Messerly was born in 1908 North Dakota.

Children of **Alfred Taylor** and **Winifred Messerly** are as follows:

     i. Douglas Duane Taylor was born on 31 Mar 1929 Malta, Valley County, Montana.

      ii. Margaret Ann Taylor was born in 1931 (Rod Mac Quarrie, 10 May 2011.). She married Ronald Raymond Jackson on 18 Aug 1958 Helena, Lewis & Clark County, Montana (Ibid.).

               Ronald Raymond Jackson was born in 1932 (Ibid.).

69. **Mervin Wallace Taylor** was born on 25 Nov 1915 Malta, Valley County, Montana (SSDI.). He married **Iva Rovina Webb**, daughter of **Ed Webb** and **Lillian Smith**, on 11 Dec 1937 Toole County, Montana (ToCM, #1733.). He married **Anna Andrews**, daughter of **Fred Andrews** and **Mary Medwedchuk**, on 15 Feb 1947 Missoula, Missoula County, Montana (MCM Missoula County, Montana; Marriage Record Licenses and Certificates; 1865-1950; familysearch.org: page 259, #6419, Hereinafter cited as MCM.). He died on 21 Jun 2001 Lewiston, Nez Perce County, Idaho, at age 85 (SSDI.).

  Iva Rovina Webb was born in 1914 (ToCM, #1733.).

  Children of **Mervin Wallace Taylor** and **Iva Rovina Webb** are:

      i. Beverly D. Taylor was born on 20 Aug 1938 Conrad, Montana (1987-92LS.).

  Anna Andrews was born on 30 Mar 1909 (MCM, page 259, #6419.) (SSDI.). She died in Nov 1970 Lewiston, Nez Perce County, Idaho, at age 61 (Ibid.).

70. **Lorna Taylor** was born on 24 Jul 1919 Montana (1920C-MT, District 161, page 5A, line 10.) (SSDI.). She married **George N. Stephens** on 14 Feb 1939 Cut Bank, Glacier County, Montana (GCM Glacier County, Montana; Marriage Record Licenses and Certificates; 1865-1950; familysearch.org, Hereinafter cited as GCM.). She married **Mac McMullen** before 1944 (1987-92LS.). She married **Edwin A. Peterson** on 17 Dec 1945 Livingston, Park County, Montana (PaCM Park County, Montana; Marriage Record Licenses and Certificates; 1865-1950; familysearch.org, Hereinafter cited as PaCM.). She married **Oscar C. Lein** on 5 Apr 1947 Great Falls, Cascade County, Montana (CaCM.). She died on 3 Oct 1987 Musselshell County, Montana, at age 68 (SSDI.) (MT Death.).

  Mac McMullen was born in 1906 (1987-92LS.).

Descendants of William Taylor

Generation One

1. **William Taylor** was born circa 1788 Birsay, Orkney, Scotland (1827C RRS HBCA E5/1 1827 Census of the Red River Settlement, HBCA E5/1, Hudson's Bay Company Archives, Provincial Archives, 200 Vaughan Street, Winnipeg, MB R3C 1T5, Canada., page 2.) (HBCA-B Hudson's Bay Company Archives - biographical sketches, Hudson's Bay Company Archives; Winnipeg, Manitoba.). He married according to the custom of the country **Sarah Sabiston**, daughter of **Peter Sabiston** and **Mary Asham**, before 1820. He married **Sarah Sabiston**, daughter of **Peter Sabiston** and **Mary Asham**, on 15 Oct 1827 St.Johns, (Manitoba) (HBCR Hudson Bay Company Register of Anglican Church Baptisms, Marriages, and Burials for the Red River Settlement, 1821-1841; Hudson's Bay Company Archives, Winnipeg, Manitoba, M-131. Hereinafter cited as HBCR.).

  Sarah Sabiston was born in 1800 North West (MBS Scrip Applications, Original White Settlers & Halfbreeds residing in Manitoba on 15 July 1870, RG15-19, C-14934.).

  Children of **William Taylor** and **Sarah Sabiston** were as follows:

  2 i. Elizabeth (Isabella) 'Lizette' Taylor, b. circa 1820 Red River, (Manitoba); m. Francois Morigeau dit Forgues; m. Patrick Finley; d. possibly, Ravalli, Missoula County, Montana.

  3 ii. James Taylor, b. 10 Jul 1825 St.Paul, (Manitoba); m. Amelia Bird; d. 18 Dec 1898 Portage la Prairie, Manitoba.

      iii. Charlotte Taylor was baptized on 10 Jul 1825 St.Johns, Red River Settlement, (Manitoba) (HBCR, E.4/1a, folio 56.).

      iv. George Taylor was baptized on 21 Oct 1829 St.Johns, Red River Settlement, (Manitoba) (Denney Papers, Charles D. Denney, Glenbow Archives, Calgary, Alberta.).

          Question: *The baptism for George was not found in the HBC Register Index.*

      v. Alexander Taylor was baptized on 8 May 1831 St.Johns, Red River Settlement, (Manitoba) (HBCR, E.4/1a, folio 81d.). He was buried on 28 Jun 1836 St.Johns, (Manitoba) (Denney.).

      vi. Catherine Taylor was baptized on 9 Dec 1832 St.Johns, Red River Settlement, (Manitoba) (HBCR, E.4/1a, folio 93d.). She was born in 1836 St.Paul, (Manitoba) (MBS, C-14930.).

  4 vii. David Taylor, b. 15 Nov 1835 St.Johns, Red River Settlement, (Manitoba); m. Jane Bird; m. Jane Hallett.

      viii. Margaret Taylor was baptized on 24 Nov 1840 St.Johns, Red River Settlement, (Manitoba) (HBCR, E.4/1a, folio169.).

Generation Two

2. **Elizabeth (Isabella) 'Lizette' Taylor** was born circa 1820 Red River, (Manitoba) (Denney.). She was baptized on 10 Jul 1825 St.Johns, Red River Settlement, (Manitoba) (HBCR, E.4/1a, folio 56.). She married **Francois Morigeau dit Forgues**, son of **Francois Forgues dit Monrougeau** and **Marie Genevieve Elie dit Breton**, before 1835. She married according to the custom of the country **Patrick Finley**, son of **Jacques Raphael 'Jocko' Finlay** and **Chippewa Spokane Pend d'Oreille Cree**, before 1836. She died possibly, Ravalli, Missoula County, Montana (David Courchane, Courchane/Courchene Family Research.).

  Francois Morigeau dit Forgues was baptized on 11 Jun 1793 (Bellechasse), Sts-Gervais and Protais, Quebec (PRDH online index, http://www.genealogic.umontreal.ca, No. 432084.). He was born on 11 Jun 1793 (Bellechasse), Sts-Gervais and Protais, Quebec (Ibid.). He was born circa 1795 St.Martin, Montreal, Quebec (D. Courchane.) (1860C-WA 1860 Washington Territorial Census, National Archives of the United States, Washington D.C., Line 1, House 1, Family 1, Sheet 159.) (Peter J. Gagne, *FCW-Gagne French-Canadians of the West, A Biographical Dictionary of French-Canadians and French Metis of the Western United States and Canada*;Pawtucket, Rhode Island: Quintin Publications, c1999), page 158.). He married according to the custom of the country **Plains Cree Woman** before 1827.

  Patrick Finley was born circa 1802 Fort Edmonton (D. Courchane.) (1860C-WA, Line 8, House 53, Family 50, Sheet 164.). He was baptized on 24 Nov 1842 Finley Camp, Porte d'Enfer, (Hellgate), Montana (D. Courchane.). He married according to the custom of the country **Margaret (--?--)** before 1819. He married according to the custom of the country **Marie Gaspar** before 1834 (Ibid.). He married according to the custom of the country **Mary Ashley**, daughter of **Jean-Pierre Asselin** and **Rosalie Cree**, before 1848. He died in Jan 1879 Montana Territory (Ibid.). He was buried on 9 Jan 1879 Frenchtown, Missoula County, Montana (Ibid.).

3. **James Taylor** was born on 10 Jul 1825 St.Paul, (Manitoba) (MBS, C-14933.). He was baptized on 10 Jul 1825 St.Johns, Red River Settlement, (Manitoba) (HBCR, E.4/1a, folio 56.). He married **Amelia Bird**, daughter of **Henry Bird** and **Harriet Calder,** on 13 Dec 1847 (St.Johns), Upper Church, Red River Settlement, (Manitoba) (Ibid., No. __.). He died on 18 Dec 1898 Portage la Prairie, Manitoba, at age 73 (Manitoba Vital Statistics online, http://web2.gov.mb.ca, Death Reg. #1899,001315.).

Amelia Bird was born in 1826 St.Paul, (Manitoba) (MBS, C-14933.). She was baptized on 21 Jun 1827 St.Johns, Red River Colony, (Manitoba) (AI-Rozyk   Anglican Index of Baptisms, Marriages and Burials Extractions, Hudson Bay Company Archives, Winnipeg, Manitoba, Canada, Selected and Compiled by Rosemary Rozyk. Hereinafter cited as AI-Rozyk.) (HBCR, E.4/1a, folio 63.). She died on 13 May 1898 Portage la Prairie, Manitoba (MB Vital Statistics, Death Reg. #1898,001674.).

Children of **James Taylor** and **Amelia Bird** were as follows:

   5   i.   George Taylor, b. 30 Aug 1848 St.Paul, (Manitoba); m. Mary Ann McNab; d. 13 Feb 1927 Portage la Prairie, Manitoba.

   6   ii.   William Taylor, b. 24 Sep 1849 St.Paul, (Manitoba); m. Jane Fidler.

   7   iii.   James Taylor, b. 24 Apr 1851 St.Paul, (Manitoba); m. Catherine Slater.

   8   iv.   Henry Taylor, b. 18 Oct 1852 St.Paul, (Manitoba); m. Harriet McNab.

   9   v.   Charlotte Taylor, b. 16 Aug 1854 St.Paul, (Manitoba); m. Donald Bruce; d. 12 Jul 1936 RM Woodlands, Manitoba.

      vi.   Alexander Taylor was born on 10 Mar 1856 (HBC-PN   Public Notice of land claims of Half-Breed Children, Address: Provincial Archives of Manitoba, Winnipeg, Manitoba, File Reference: MG4D13 Box 1, Poplar Point and High Bluff, #310.). He was baptized on 4 May 1856 St.Paul, Middlechurch, (Manitoba) (Denney.).

10   vii.   John Taylor, b. 17 Apr 1858 St.Paul, (Manitoba); m. Elizabeth Johnston; d. before 31 Mar 1901.

11   viii.   Elisabeth Taylor, b. 24 May 1860 St.Paul, (Manitoba); m. John Spencer Garton; d. 26 Aug 1930 RM Ochre River, Manitoba; bur. 1931 Poplar Point, Manitoba.

12   ix.   Alfred Taylor, b. 7 Apr 1862 St.Paul, (Manitoba); m. Elizabeth (--?--).

      x.   Benjamin Taylor was born on 9 Jun 1864 Poplar Point, (Manitoba) (MBS, C-14933.). He was baptized on 12 Jun 1864 St.Ann, Poplar Point, (Manitoba) (Ibid.).

      xi.   David Edwin Taylor was born on 29 Jun 1865 Poplar Point, (Manitoba) (Ibid.). He was baptized on 18 Jul 1866 St.Ann, Poplar Point, (Manitoba) (Ibid.). He died on 3 Nov 1871 Poplar Point, Manitoba, at age 6 (Ibid.). He was buried on 5 Nov 1871 St.Ann, Poplar Point, Manitoba (Ibid.).

13   xii.   Albert Taylor, b. 5 Jun 1867 Poplar Point, (Manitoba); m. Isabella Howse.

4. **David Taylor** was baptized on 15 Nov 1835 St.Johns, Red River Settlement, (Manitoba) (HBCR, E.4/1a, folio 124d.). He was born in 1837 St.Paul, (Manitoba) (MBS, C-14934.) (1870C-MB   1870 Manitoba Census, National Archives of Canada, Ottawa, Ontario, Microfilm Reel Number C-2170., page 358, #999.). He and **Jane Bird** met circa 1861. He and **Jane Hallett** met before 1864.

Question: *This is probably the David Taylor, he lived in the same town.   Did he actually have children with two Janes or not?*

Jane Bird was baptized on 14 Aug 1833 St.Johns, Red River Settlement, (Manitoba) (AI-Rozyk.) (HBCR, E.4/1a, folio 104.). She married **John Martin** before 19 Aug 1875 (MBS, C-14934.).

Children of **David Taylor** and **Jane Bird** were:

      i.   Charles George Bird was born on 28 Nov 1861 St.Paul, (Manitoba) (Ibid., C-14925.). He married Maria Robertson, daughter of William Robertson and Frances Lillie, before 1889.

          Maria Robertson was born on 14 Jan 1871 Carlton, (Saskatchewan) (HBS   1886-1901, 1906 Half-Breed Scrip Applications, RG15-21, Volume 1336; C-14950.).

Jane Hallett was baptized on 15 Dec 1839 St.Johns, Red River Settlement, (Manitoba) (HBCR, E.4/1a, folio 164.). She married **Joseph Spence**, son of **James Spence** and **Jane Morwick,** on 6 Jul 1857 St.Johns, (Manitoba) (Denney.). She married **Jean Baptiste Baby**, son of **Jean Baptiste Baby** and **Marie Courchene,** before 19 Aug 1875 (MBS, C-14934.).

Children of **David Taylor** and **Jane Hallett** both born Poplar Point, (Manitoba), were as follows:

      i.   Jane Taylor was born circa 1864 (1870C-MB, page 360, #1065.).

      ii.   Catherine Ann Taylor was born circa 1867 (Ibid., page 360, #1066.).

Generation Three

5. **George Taylor** was born on 30 Aug 1848 St.Paul, (Manitoba) (MBS, C-14934.). He was baptized on 24 Sep 1848 St.Johns, (Manitoba) (Denney.). He married **Mary Ann McNab**, daughter of **Thomas McNab** and **Harriet West,** before 15 Jul 1870 Poplar Point, Manitoba. He died on 13 Feb 1927 Portage la Prairie, Manitoba, at age 78 (MB Vital Statistics, Death Reg. #1927,009027.).

Mary Ann McNab was baptized on 24 Feb 1850 St.Johns, (Manitoba) (Denney.). She died on 14 Nov 1906 Portage la Prairie, Manitoba, at age 56 (MB Vital Statistics, Death Reg. #1906,003250.).

Children of **George Taylor** and **Mary Ann McNab** were:

      i.   Martha Taylor was born circa May 1872 (Denney.). She died on 22 Aug 1872 Poplar Point, Manitoba (Ibid.).

6. **William Taylor** was born on 24 Sep 1849 St.Paul, (Manitoba) (MBS, C-14934.). He was baptized on 21 Oct 1849 St.Johns, (Manitoba) (Denney.). He married **Jane Fidler**, daughter of **Clement Fidler** and **Charlotte Slater,** on 11 Jun 1878 (Ibid.).

Jane Fidler was baptized on 7 Nov 1850 St.Johns, (Manitoba) (Ibid.). She died before 1891.

Children of **William Taylor** and **Jane Fidler** were as follows:

      i.   Charles Edward Taylor was born on 1 Nov 1879 St.James, Manitoba (SJAC   St.James Anglican Church Extractions, Manitoba Genealogy Society, Winnipeg, Manitoba, B-419.). He was baptized on 1 Dec 1879 St.James, Manitoba (Ibid.).

      ii.   William Lawrence Taylor was born on 29 Mar 1882 (Ibid., B-451.). He was baptized on 7 May 1882 St.James, Manitoba (Ibid.).

      iii.   Ellen Harriet Taylor was born on 2 Jun 1884 Winnipeg, Manitoba (Ibid., B-489.) (MB Vital Statistics, Birth Reg. #1887,002361.). She was baptized on 10 Aug 1884 St.James, Manitoba (SJAC, B-489.).

iv. George Arthur Taylor was born on 26 Nov 1886 Winnipeg, Manitoba (Ibid., B-36.) (MB Vital Statistics, Birth Reg. #1887,002360.). He was baptized on 20 Feb 1887 St.James, Manitoba (SJAC, B-36.).

7. James Taylor was born on 24 Apr 1851 St.Paul, (Manitoba) (MBS, C-14934.). He was baptized on 8 Jun 1851 St.Paul, (Manitoba) (Denney.). He married **Catherine Slater**, daughter of **William Slater** and **Maria Rowland,** before 1873 (Automated Genealogy 1901 Census Transcription Project and Census Images from the National Archives of Canada, http://www.automatedgenealogy.com, #8, K-13, page 2, Family 17, Line 34-39.).

Catherine Slater was born on 16 Aug 1854 St.Paul, (Manitoba) (MBS, C-14934.) (1901 Canada, #8, K-13, page 2, Family 17, Line 34-39.).

Children of **James Taylor** and **Catherine Slater** were as follows:

i. Ellen Taylor was born circa 1873 Manitoba (1881 Church of Latter Day Saints Census Transcription Project of Census Images from the National Archives of Canada, Ottawa, Canada, http://www.familysearch.org, C-13283, District 186, Sub-district L, page 25, Household 118.).

ii. David J. Taylor was born on 2 Jul 1874 (1901 Canada, #8, K-13, page 2, Family 17, Line 34-39.).

iii. Edwin Taylor was born circa 1879 Manitoba (1881 Canada, C-13283, District 186, Sub-district L, page 25, Household 118.).

iv. Gilbert Taylor was born on 27 Feb 1883 Touchwood Hills, (Saskatchewan) (ArchiviaNet 1886-1901, 1906 Half-Breed Scrip Applications Index, RG15-21, Volume 1333 through 1371, Microfilm Reel Number C-14944 through C-15010, National Archives of Canada, Ottawa, Ontario, http://www.collectionscanada.gc.ca, C-15005.). He died on 25 Sep 1891 at age 8 (Ibid.).

v. Annie Taylor was born on 18 Mar 1885 Touchwood Hills, (Saskatchewan) (1901 Canada, #8, K-13, page 2, Family 17, Line 34-39.) (ArchiviaNet, C-15006.).

vi. Laura M. Taylor was born on 29 Jun 1892 (1901 Canada, #8, K-13, page 2, Family 17, Line 34-39.).

vii. Norman Taylor was born on 27 Nov 1893 Qu'Appelle, (Saskatchewan) (Ibid.) (Saskatchewan Vital Statistics online, http://vsgs.health.gov.sk.ca, Birth Reg. #13333.).

8. Henry Taylor was born on 18 Oct 1852 St.Paul, (Manitoba) (MBS, C-14934.). He was baptized on 12 Dec 1852 St.Paul, (Manitoba) (Denney.). He married **Harriet McNab**, daughter of **Thomas McNab** and **Harriet West,** before 1874.

Harriet McNab was baptized on 13 Feb 1853 St.Johns, (Manitoba) (Ibid.).

Children of **Henry Taylor** and **Harriet McNab** were as follows:

14 i. Martha Ann Taylor, b. 5 Jan 1875 Manitoba; m. James Cromarty.

ii. Angus Taylor was born circa 1876 Manitoba (1881 Canada, C-13283, District 186, Sub-district L, page 26, Household 120.).

iii. Robert Taylor was born on 18 Oct 1876 R.M. of Portage la Prairie, Manitoba (MB Vital Statistics, Birth Reg. #1883,002170.).

iv. Herbert Taylor was born circa 1878 Manitoba (1881 Canada, C-13283, District 186, Sub-district L, page 26, Household 120.).

v. Victoria Taylor was born in Apr 1880 Manitoba (Ibid.).

vi. John Taylor was born circa 1881 Manitoba (1891 Census of Canada from the National Archives of Canada, Ottawa, Canada.).

vii. Walter Taylor was born on 29 May 1886 R.M. of Woodlands, Manitoba (MB Vital Statistics, Birth Reg. #1886,004109.).

viii. Maud Taylor was born circa 1887 Manitoba (1891 Canada.).

9. Charlotte Taylor was born on 16 Aug 1854 St.Paul, (Manitoba) (MBS, C-14934.). She was baptized on 8 Oct 1854 St.Paul, (Manitoba) (Denney.). She married **Donald Bruce**, son of **James Bruce** and **Mary McNab**, on 11 Jan 1877 St.Ann's, Poplar Point, Manitoba (Rod MacQuarrie Research, 18 Oct 2010.). She died on 12 Jul 1936 RM Woodlands, Manitoba, at age 81 (MB Vital Statistics, Death Reg. #1936,028523.).

Donald Bruce was born on 2 Apr 1848 St.Johns, (Manitoba) (MBS, C-14925.). He married **Ann White**, daughter of **Thomas White** and **Mary Cunningham,** on 27 Apr 1871 St.Johns, Manitoba (Denney.). He died on 17 Jun 1926 Woodlands, Manitoba, at age 78 (MB Vital Statistics, Death Reg. #1926,028225.).

Children of **Charlotte Taylor** and **Donald Bruce** were as follows:

i. Catherine Ann Bruce was born on 8 Jun 1881 Woodlands, Manitoba (1891 Canada, District 6-S, page 13, line 7.) (1901 Canada, #11, page 5, family 55, line 32-38.).

ii. Elizabeth Victoria Emily Bruce was born on 27 Dec 1883 R.M. of Woodlands, Manitoba (1891 Canada, District 6-S, page 13, line 7.) (MB Vital Statistics, Birth Reg. #1884,003461.).

iii. Robert S. Bruce was born circa 1885 Woodlands, Manitoba (1891 Canada, District 6-S, page 13, line 7.).

iv. Roderick William Bruce was born on 2 Jan 1889 R.M. of Woodlands, Manitoba (MB Vital Statistics, Birth Reg. #1889,005628.).

v. James Douglas Bruce was born on 21 Mar 1890 R.M. of Woodlands, Manitoba (1891 Canada, District 6-S, page 13, line 7.) (MB Vital Statistics, Birth Reg. #1890,001170.).

vi. Lydia May Bruce was born on 16 Oct 1895 R.M. of Woodlands, Manitoba (Ibid., Birth Reg. #1895,001707.).

10. John Taylor was born on 17 Apr 1858 St.Paul, (Manitoba) (MBS, C-14933.). He was baptized on 6 Jun 1858 St.Paul, (Manitoba) (Denney.). He married **Elizabeth Johnston**, daughter of **Thomas James Johnston** and **Margaret Peebles,** on 10 May 1886 Winnipeg, Manitoba (MB Vital Statistics, Mar. Reg. #1886,001499.). He died before 31 Mar 1901 (1901 Canada, #8, K-13, page 2-3, Family 20, Line 45-50, 1-3.).

Elizabeth Johnston was born in Feb 1868 St.Andrews, (Manitoba) (HBC-PN , St.Andrews, #301.).

Children of **John Taylor** and **Elizabeth Johnston** were as follows:

i.   Ellen Harriet Taylor was born on 1 Apr 1887 Woodlands, Manitoba (MB Vital Statistics, Birth Reg. #1887,004391.).
ii. John Albert Taylor was born on 15 Aug 1888 St.Andrews, Manitoba (Ibid., Birth Reg. #1888,002304.).
iii. Rosa Ann Taylor was born on 10 Mar 1891 Woodlands, Manitoba (Ibid., Birth Reg. #1891,001282.).
iv. Flora Mildred Taylor was born on 26 Apr 1893 Portage la Prairie, Manitoba (Ibid., Birth Reg. #1893,004604.).
v.   Mabel Jane Taylor was born on 26 Apr 1893 Portage la Prairie, Manitoba (Ibid., Birth Reg. #1893,004605.).
vi. Walter George Taylor was born on 17 Feb 1895 Portage la Prairie, Manitoba (Ibid., Birth Reg. #1895,003188.).
vii. Archibald Clarence Taylor was born on 16 May 1900 Portage la Prairie, Manitoba (Ibid., Birth Reg. #1900,001381.).

11. **Elisabeth Taylor** was born on 24 May 1860 St.Paul, (Manitoba) (MBS, C-14933.). She was baptized on 1 Jul 1860 St.Paul, (Manitoba) (Ibid.). She married **John Spencer Garton**, son of **John Garton** and **Mary Spencer**, on 19 Jun 1879 Poplar Point, Manitoba (Denney.). She died on 26 Aug 1930 RM Ochre River, Manitoba, at age 70 (MB Vital Statistics, Death Reg. #1930,040158.). She was buried in 1931 Poplar Point, Manitoba (Denney.).

John Spencer Garton was born on 16 Jun 1857 (Ontario) (1901 Canada, Family 28, Line 20-26.). He was baptized on 26 Jun 1858 Moose Factory, (Ontario) (Denney.). He died on 13 Feb 1933 RM Portage la Prairie, Manitoba, at age 75 (MB Vital Statistics, Death Reg. #1933,012411.).

12. **Alfred Taylor** was born on 7 Apr 1862 St.Paul, (Manitoba) (MBS, C-14933.) (1901 Canada, #8, K-13, page 2, Family 11, Line 3-7.). He was baptized on 1 Jun 1864 St.Paul, (Manitoba) (MBS, C-14933.). He married **Elizabeth (--?--)** before 1890 (1901 Canada, #8, K-13, page 2, Family 11, Line 3-7.).

Elizabeth (--?--) was born on 2 Feb 1872 (Ibid.).

Children of **Alfred Taylor** and **Elizabeth (--?--)** were as follows:

i.   Alfred Edward Taylor was born on 11 Aug 1890 Portage la Prairie, Manitoba (Ibid.).
ii. David James Taylor was born on 2 May 1894 Portage la Prairie, Manitoba (Ibid.) (Automated Genealogy 1906 Census Transcription Project and Census Images from the National Archives of Canada, http://www.automatedgenealogy.com, District 4-18, page 14, family 111, line 12-17.).
iii. Catherine Jane Taylor was born on 27 Mar 1900 Portage la Prairie, Manitoba (1901 Canada, #8, K-13, page 2, Family 11, Line 3-7.).
iv. Erna Mary Taylor was born circa 1904 (1906 Canada, District 4-18, page 14, family 111, line 12-17.).

13. **Albert Taylor** was born on 5 Jun 1867 Poplar Point, (Manitoba) (MBS, C-14933.). He was born on 5 Jun 1868 Poplar Point, Manitoba (MB Vital Statistics, Birth Reg. #1868,13120764, registration date: 03/17/1938.). He married **Isabella Howse**, daughter of **Henry Howse** and **Elizabeth Nelly Inkster**, before 1892 (1901 Canada, #8, K-13, page 2, Family 12, Line 8-13.).

Isabella Howse was born on 10 May 1869 High Bluff, (Manitoba) (MBS, C-14929.). She was born on 10 May 1870 (1901 Canada, #8, K-13, page 2, Family 12, Line 8-13.).

Children of **Albert Taylor** and **Isabella Howse** were as follows:

i.   Curtis J. Taylor was born on 15 Jul 1892 Portage la Prairie, Manitoba (Ibid.).
ii. Frederick Scott Taylor was born on 24 Feb 1895 (Saskatchewan) (SK Vital Statistics, Birth Reg. #11694.).
iii. Myrtle I. Taylor was born on 7 Aug 1899 Portage la Prairie, Manitoba (1901 Canada, #8, K-13, page 2, Family 12, Line 8-13.).
iv. Mirum Taylor was born on 5 Nov 1900 Portage la Prairie, Manitoba (Ibid.).

Generation Four

14. **Martha Ann Taylor** was born on 5 Jan 1875 Manitoba (Ibid., District 8-k-13, page 1-2, family 10, line 48-50, 1-2.). She married **James Cromarty**, son of **James Cromarty Sr.** and **Nancy Inkster**, on 14 Dec 1898 Portage la Prairie, Manitoba (MB Vital Statistics, Marriage Reg. #1898,001513.).

James Cromarty was born on 22 Apr 1862 St.Andrews, (Manitoba) (MBS, C-14926.). He died on 7 Nov 1925 Portage la Prairie, Manitoba, at age 63 (MB Vital Statistics, Death Reg. #1925,048031.).

Ahnentafel between Francois Thibault and Louis Thibault

--- 1st Generation ---

1. **Francois Thibault** (HBCA-B Hudson's Bay Company Archives - biographical sketches, Hudson's Bay Company Archives; Winnipeg, Manitoba, E.353/2.) (Ibid.) was born circa 1802 at (William Henry Parish), Sorel, Quebec (Ibid.). He married **Mary Inkster** before 1825.

--- 2nd Generation ---

2. **Charles Thibault** (Ibid.) (PRDH online index, http://www.genealogic.umontreal.ca, #243049.) (Ibid.) was born on 27 Oct 1771 at LaPocatiere, Quebec (Ibid.). He was baptized on 28 Oct 1771 at LaPocatiere, Quebec (Ibid.). He married **Marie Madeleine Plourde**, daughter of **Augustin Plourde** and **Marie Madeleine Berube**, on 3 Oct 1796 at Riviere-Ouelle, Quebec (Ibid., #243050.).

--- 3rd Generation ---

4. **Michel Thibault** (Ibid., No. 352050.) (Ibid., #95802.) (Ibid., #163215.) was born on 11 Mar 1742 at L'Islet, Quebec (Ibid.). He was baptized on 11 Mar 1742 at L'Islet, Quebec (Ibid.). He married **Genevieve Judith Lemieux**, daughter of **Pierre-Augustin Lemieux** and **Marie-Genevieve Caron**, on 15 Feb 1762 at L'Islet, Quebec (Ibid.). He married **Marie Marthe Fortin**, daughter of **Julien Fortin** and **Elisabeth Caron**, on 30 Apr 1798 at St-Jean-Port-Joli, Quebec (Ibid.). He died on 27 Nov 1814 at St-Roche-des-Aulnaies, Quebec, at age 72 (Ibid.). He was buried on 28 Nov 1814 at St-Roche-des-Aulnaies, Quebec (Ibid.).

--- 4th Generation ---

8. **Jean-Francois Thibault** (Ibid., #95801.) (Ibid.) (Ibid.) was born on 4 Jan 1709 at L'Islet, Quebec (Ibid.). He was baptized on 4 Jan 1709 at L'Islet, Quebec (Ibid.). He married **Genevieve Cloutier**, daughter of **Jean-Baptitse Cloutier** and **Marie-Anne**

GERBERT, on 6 Nov 1736 at L'Islet, Quebec (Ibid., #95802.). He died on 27 Mar 1777 at L'Islet, Quebec, at age 68 (Ibid., #95801.). He was buried on 28 Mar 1777 at L'Islet, Quebec (Ibid.).

--- *5th Generation* ---

16. JEAN-FRANCOIS THIBAULT (DGFQ Jette, Rene, *Dictionnaire Genealogique des Familles du Quebec des Origines a 1730* (Montreal, Quebec, Canada: University of Montreal Press, 1983), page 1074.) (Ibid.) was born on 16 Dec 1675 at Cap-St-Ignace, Quebec (Ibid.) (PRDH online, No. 59311.). He was baptized on 20 Dec 1675 at Quebec, Quebec, Quebec (Ibid.) (DGFQ, page 1074.). A contract for the marriage to **MARIE-ANNE GUIMOND**, daughter of **CLAUDE GUIMOND** and **ANNE ROY**, was signed on 28 Jul 1704 (Ibid., page 1076.). He married **MARIE-ANNE GUIMOND**, daughter of **CLAUDE GUIMOND** and **ANNE ROY**, on 28 Jul 1704 at Cap-St-Ignace, Quebec (Ibid.). He married **MARIE-ANGELIQUE PROU**, daughter of **JEAN PROU** and **JACQUETTE FOURNIER**, on 12 Nov 1705 at Cap-St-Ignace, Quebec (Ibid.). A contract for the marriage to **MARIE-ANGELIQUE PROU**, daughter of **JEAN PROU** and **JACQUETTE FOURNIER**, was signed on 12 Mar 1706 (Ibid.).

--- *6th Generation* ---

32. FRANCOIS THIBAULT lived at at Ste-Catherine de LaFlotte, Re, La Rochelle, Aunis (Charente-Maritime) (Ibid., page 1074.). He was born between 1645 and 1648 (Ibid.). A contract for the marriage to **ELISABETH-AGNES LEFEBVRE**, daughter of **GUILLAUME LEFEBVRE** and **BARBE VIOT**, was signed on 3 Oct 1670 (Ibid.). He married **ELISABETH-AGNES LEFEBVRE**, daughter of **GUILLAUME LEFEBVRE** and **BARBE VIOT**, on 14 Oct 1670 at Beaupre, Quebec (Ibid.) (PRDH online, No. 28352.). He was buried on 10 Nov 1724 at Cap-St-Ignace, Quebec (Ibid., No. 27316.).

--- *7th Generation* ---

64. LOUIS THIBAULT married **RENEE GAUTHIER**.

Descendants of Francois Thibault

Generation One

1. Francois Thibault was born circa 1802 (William Henry Parish), Sorel, Quebec (HBCA-B Hudson's Bay Company Archives - biographical sketches, Hudson's Bay Company Archives; Winnipeg, Manitoba, E.353/2.). He married **Mary Inkster** before 1825.
Children of **Francois Thibault** and **Mary Inkster** were as follows:

> 2   i.   Francois Thibault, b. circa 1825; m. Helene Daignault.
> 3   ii.   Louise Thibault, b. 1826 St.Boniface, (Manitoba); m. Joseph Daigneault.

Generation Two

2. Francois Thibault was born circa 1825. He was born circa 1831 (Ibid., E.353/2; A.32/56 fo. 131-132.). He married **Helene Daignault**, daughter of **Joseph Daigneault** and **Genevieve 'Jennie' Cameron**, before 1856.
Question: *Son of a Native Woman?* (Ibid., E.353/2.).
Helene Daignault was born on 5 Nov 1832 St.Boniface, (Manitoba) (MBS Scrip Applications, Original White Settlers & Halfbreeds residing in Manitoba on 15 July 1870, RG15-19, C-14933.).
Children of **Francois Thibault** and **Helene Daignault** were as follows:

> 4   i.   Eulalie Mary Thibault, b. 13 Jan 1856 St.Boniface, (Manitoba); m. Francois Xavier Letendre dit Batoche.
>   ii.   Marguerite Thibault was born on 31 May 1859 St.Boniface, (Manitoba) (Ibid., C-14934.). She died on 1 Aug 1878 St.Boniface, Manitoba, at age 19 (Ibid.).
> 5   iii.   Francois Thibault, b. circa 1860; m. Virginie (--?--).
> 6   iv.   Helene Thibault, b. 25 Sep 1862 St.Boniface, (Manitoba); m. Jean Baptiste Jerome.
>   v.   Marie Adele Thibault was born on 5 Nov 1864 St.Boniface, (Manitoba) (SB-Rozyk St. Boniface Roman Catholic Church, Manitoba, Canada, Baptisms, Marriages and Burials 1860-1875 Extractions, Compiled by Rosemary Rozyk, page 166, B-108.). She was baptized on 5 Nov 1864 St.Boniface, (Manitoba) (Ibid.).
>   vi.   Marie Rose Thibault was born on 1 Sep 1866 (SFXI-Kipling St.Francois Xavier Register Index, 1834-1900; compiled by Clarence Kipling , B-114.). She was baptized on 27 Sep 1866 St.Francois Xavier, (Manitoba) (Ibid.). She died on 31 Aug 1867 St.Francois Xavier, (Manitoba) (Ibid., S-22.). She was buried on 2 Sep 1867 St.Francois Xavier, (Manitoba) (Ibid.).
>   vii.   Joseph Thibault was baptized on 15 Aug 1868 St.Laurent, (Manitoba) (IBMS *Index des Baptemes, Mariages et Sepultures* (La Societe Historique de Saint-Boniface).).
>   viii.   Marie Adele Thibault was born on 16 Sep 1870 St.Boniface, Manitoba (SB-Rozyk, page 194, B-82.). She was baptized on 17 Sep 1870 St.Boniface, Manitoba (Ibid.). She died on 11 Feb 1873 St.Boniface, Manitoba, at age 2 (Ibid., page 265, S-7.). She was buried on 12 Feb 1873 St.Boniface, Manitoba (Ibid.).

3. Louise Thibault was born in 1826 St.Boniface, (Manitoba) (MBS, C-14933.). She married **Joseph Daigneault**, son of **Joseph Daigneault** and **Genevieve 'Jennie' Cameron**, before 1849.
Joseph Daigneault was born on 4 Oct 1824 Red River Settlement (Ibid., C-14926.). He was born on 22 Oct 1825 (SB 1825-1834 St.Boniface Roman Catholic Registre des Baptemes, Mariages & Sepultures, 1825-1834, page 22, B-150. Hereinafter cited as SB 1825-1834.). He was baptized on 18 Dec 1825 (Winnipeg River), St.Boniface, (Manitoba) (Ibid.).

Generation Three

4. Eulalie Mary Thibault was born on 13 Jan 1856 St.Boniface, (Manitoba) (MBS, C-14930.). She married **Francois Xavier Letendre dit Batoche**, son of **Louis Letendre dit Batoche** and **Julie Delorme**, on 11 Apr 1875 Assumption, Pembina, Pembina County, Dakota Territory (AP Records of the Assumption Roman Catholic Church, Pembina, North Dakota: Baptisms, Marriages, Sepultures, 1848-1896; compiled by Reverend Father J. M. Belleau, 2 October 1944, M-4. Hereinafter cited as AP.).
Francois Xavier Letendre dit Batoche was born on 20 Jan 1851 Pembina, Pembina County, Dakota Territory (Ibid., page 51, B-14.). He was baptized on 21 Jan 1851 Assumption, Pembina, Pembina County, Dakota Territory (Ibid.).

5. Francois Thibault was born circa 1860. He married **Virginie (--?--)** before 1881.

Children of **Francois Thibault** and **Virginie (–?–)** were:

   i.   Helen Selina Thibault was born on 21 Aug 1881 Dakota Territory (Ibid., page 191, B-26.). She was baptized on 27 Aug 1881 Assumption, Pembina, Pembina County, Dakota Territory (Ibid.).

6. Helene Thibault was baptized on 25 Sep 1862 St.Boniface, (Manitoba) (SB-Rozyk, page 86, B-158.). She was born on 25 Sep 1862 St.Boniface, (Manitoba) (Ibid.). She married **Jean Baptiste Jerome**, son of **Andre Jerome** and **Marguerite Gosselin**, before 1889.

Jean Baptiste Jerome was born on 28 Jul 1857 Two Rivers, Kittson County, Minnesota (Ed Merck Research, 26 Apr 2010.). He died on 21 Mar 1926 Bemidji, Beltrami County, Minnesota, at age 68 (Ibid.).

Descendants of Pierre Thibert

Generation One

1. Pierre Thibert, son of Pierre Thibert and Philie Julie Maheux, was born circa 1812 Chateauguay, Quebec (HBCA-B Hudson's Bay Company Archives - biographical sketches, Hudson's Bay Company Archives; Winnipeg, Manitoba.). He was born on 10 May 1812 St.Joachim, Quebec (MBS Scrip Applications, Original White Settlers & Halfbreeds residing in Manitoba on 15 July 1870, RG15-19, C-14934.). He married according to the custom of the country **Julie Belcourt**, daughter of **Joseph Belcourt** and **Catherine L'Hirondelle**, before 1837. He married **Julie Belcourt**, daughter of **Joseph Belcourt** and **Catherine L'Hirondelle**, on 28 Oct 1841 Carlton House, Saskatchewan District (RTR Rundle, Reverend R. T., Journal of Baptisms & Marriages in Saskatchewan District, 1840 - 1848, M-21. Hereinafter cited as RTR.). He married **Julie Belcourt**, daughter of **Joseph Belcourt** and **Catherine L'Hirondelle**, on 1 Jun 1842 Fort-des-Prairies, (Alberta) (FDP Baptisms & Marriages Fort des Prairie, Saskatchewan District, C Kipling, M-1. Hereinafter cited as FDP.). He married **Louise Racette**, daughter of **Augustin Racette** and **Suzanne Groulx**, on 29 May 1865 St.Boniface, (Manitoba) (SB-Rozyk St. Boniface Roman Catholic Church, Manitoba, Canada, Baptisms, Marriages and Burials 1860-1875 Extractions, Compiled by Rosemary Rozyk, page 5, M-9.). He died on 29 Jul 1894 St.Francois Xavier, Manitoba, at age 82 (SFXI-Kipling St.Francois Xavier Register Index, 1834-1900; compiled by Clarence Kipling , S-10.).

Julie Belcourt was born circa 1822 (Ibid., S-2.). She was baptized on 1 Jun 1842 Fort-des-Prairies (INB *Index des Naissances and Baptemes* (St.Boniface, Manitoba: La Societe Historique de Saint-Boniface., c1995), page 13.). She died on 3 Mar 1862 St.Francois Xavier, (Manitoba) (SFXI-Kipling, S-2.). She was buried on 4 Mar 1862 St.Francois Xavier, (Manitoba) (Ibid.) (SFXI: 1851-1869 St.Francois Xavier 1851-69 Register Index.) (SFXI 1851-1868 St.Francois Xavier 1852-1861 Register Index, S-2. Hereinafter cited as SFXI 1851-1868.).

Children of **Pierre Thibert** and **Julie Belcourt** were as follows:

   2   i.   Marguerite Thibert, b. 29 Aug 1837 Moose Lake; m. Jean Baptiste Bercier.
   3   ii.   Francois Xavier Thibert, b. 21 Nov 1840 North West; m. Sophie Slater.
   4   iii. Charles Alphonse Thibert, b. 3 Apr 1844 North West; m. Elizabeth Slater; d. 3 Sep 1898 St.Francois Xavier, Manitoba.
   5   iv.   Catherine Thibert, b. 24 Dec 1846 North West; m. Charles Swain.
   6   v.   Elzear Thibert, b. 12 Jun 1849 North West; m. Elise Zace; d. 18 Apr 1917 RM Cartier, Manitoba.
       vi.   Elise Thibert was born circa 1851 (SFXI-Kipling, S-9.) (SFXI-1834-54.). She died on 30 Oct 1864 St.Francois Xavier, (Manitoba) (SFXI-Kipling, S-9.) (SFXI-1834-54.). She was buried on 31 Oct 1864 St.Francois Xavier, (Manitoba) (SFXI-Kipling, S-9.) (SFXI-1834-54.).
   7   vii. Marie Thibert, b. 19 Sep 1854 St.Francois Xavier, (Manitoba); m. Joseph Laplante; d. 22 May 1938 Cartier, Manitoba.
   8   viii. Philomene Thibert, b. 13 Apr 1858 St.Francois Xavier, (Manitoba); m. Francois Richard; d. 10 Nov 1921 Elie, Manitoba.
       ix.   Nancy Thibert was born on 1 Feb 1861 St.Francois Xavier, (Manitoba) (SFXI-Kipling, B-9.). She was baptized on 1 Feb 1861 St.Francois Xavier, (Manitoba) (Ibid.). She died on 18 Nov 1894 St.Francois Xavier, Manitoba, at age 33 (Ibid., S-22.).

Louise Racette was born circa 1833 (CCRPNW-V *Catholic Church Records of the Pacific Northwest, Vancouver, Volumes I and II and Stellamaris Mission* Translated by: Mikell de Lores Wormell Warner and Annotated by: Harriet Duncan Munnick, (St.Paul, Oregon: French Prairie Press, 1972), page 8, B-75.) (Ibid., page 10, M-12.). She was born in 1835 North West (MBS, C-14934.). She was baptized on 6 Sep 1838 Fort Edmonton (CCRPNW-V, page 8, B-75.). She died on 16 Sep 1878 St.Francois Xavier, Manitoba (SFXI-Kipling, S-45.).

Children of **Pierre Thibert** and **Louise Racette** both born St.Francois Xavier, (Manitoba), were as follows:

   9   i.   Elizabeth Thibert, b. 3 Mar 1866; m. Edwin Bourke; d. 18 Nov 1938.
   10 ii.   Pierre Thibert, b. 1 May 1868; m. Marie Mathilde Zace.

Generation Two

2. Marguerite Thibert was born on 29 Aug 1837 Moose Lake (MBS, C-14925.). She was baptized on 6 Jun 1841 Carlton House, Saskatchewan District (RTR, B-111.). She was baptized on 24 May 1842 (Fort Carlton), Fort-des-Prairies, (Saskatchewan) (FDP, B-4 and 5.). She married **Jean Baptiste Bercier**, son of **Jean Baptiste Bercier** and **Marie St.Pierre**, on 16 Jun 1857 St.Francois Xavier, (Manitoba) (SFXI-Kipling, M-30.).

Jean Baptiste Bercier was born in Jul 1832 St.Boniface, (Manitoba) (MBS, C-14925.).

3. Francois Xavier Thibert was born on 21 Nov 1840 North West (MBS, C-14934.). He was baptized on 6 Jun 1841 Carlton House, Saskatchewan District (RTR, B-112.). He was baptized on 24 May 1842 (Fort Carlton), Fort-des-Prairies, (Saskatchewan) (FDP, B-4 and 5.). He married **Sophie Slater**, daughter of **James Slater** and **Josephte Morissette**, on 7 Feb 1860 St.Francois Xavier, (Manitoba) (SFXI-Kipling, M-4.).

Sophie Slater was born on 11 May 1843 North West Territories (MBS, C-14934.).

Children of **Francois Xavier Thibert** and **Sophie Slater** were as follows:

      i.   Charles Simeon Thibert was born on 3 Nov 1860 St.Francois Xavier, (Manitoba) (SFXI-Kipling, B-100.). He was baptized on 5 Nov 1860 St.Francois Xavier, (Manitoba) (Ibid.). He died on 11 Sep 1862 St.Francois Xavier, (Manitoba), at age 1 (Ibid., S-14.). He was buried on 12 Sep 1862 St.Francois Xavier, (Manitoba) (Ibid.).

11   ii.   Marie Sophie Thibert, b. 2 Aug 1862 St.Francois Xavier, (Manitoba); m. Louis Allary.

     iii.   Eleonore Thibert was born on 29 May 1864 St.Francois Xavier, (Manitoba) (Ibid., B-23.). She was baptized on 30 May 1864 St.Francois Xavier, (Manitoba) (Ibid.). She was buried on 7 Feb 1866 St.Francois Xavier, (Manitoba) (IBMS *Index des Baptemes, Mariages et Sepultures* (La Societe Historique de Saint-Boniface).) (SFXI-Kipling, S-_.).

12   iv.   Pierre Thibert, b. 1 Jul 1866 St.Francois Xavier, (Manitoba); m. Marie Cecile Morin.

13   v.   Elise Thibert, b. 30 Aug 1868 St.Francois Xavier, (Manitoba).

     vi.   Charibaneu Thibert was born circa 1870 (St. Claude Mission, St. John, North Dakota, Baptisms, Marriages, Burials 1882-1888, 2006, Dominique Ritchot, page 5, B-32.). He was baptized in Jun 1882 St.Claude, St.John, Rolette County, North Dakota (Ibid.).

    vii.   Jonas Alphonse Thibert was born on 21 May 1871 St.Francois Xavier, Manitoba (SFXI-Kipling, B-45.). He was baptized on 22 May 1871 St.Francois Xavier, Manitoba (Ibid.) (INB, page 175.). He was buried on 12 Oct 1875 St.Francois Xavier, Manitoba (IBMS.) (SFXI-Kipling, S-34.).

   viii.   Charles Thibert was born on 15 Aug 1873 St.Francois Xavier, Manitoba (Ibid., B-54.). He was baptized on 17 Aug 1873 St.Francois Xavier, Manitoba (Ibid.) (INB, page 175.).

     ix.   Julie Thibert was born 9 Jul 1875 St.Eustache, Manitoba (Rosemary Rozyk.). She baptized on 9 Jul 1875 St.Eustache, Manitoba (IBMS.). She was buried on 17 Sep 1875 St.Eustache, Manitoba (Ibid.).

     x.   Xavier Thibert was born 4 Feb 1877 St.Eustache, Manitoba (Rosemary Rozyk.). He was baptized on 5 Feb 1877 St.Eustache, Manitoba (Ibid.)

     xi.   Joseph Thibert was born 8 Jul 1878 (Rosemary Rozyk.). He was baptized 18 Jul 1878 St.Eustache, Manitoba (Ibid.). He was buried on 29 Jun 1883 St.Claude Mission, St.John, Rolette County, North Dakota (Ibid.).

    xii.   Therese Thibert was born before 1 Jul 1884 (Ibid., S-24, p. 33.). She died on 1 Jul 1884 St.John, Rolette County, North Dakota (Ibid.). She was buried on 3 Jul 1884 St.Claude Mission, St.John, Rolette County, North Dakota (Ibid.).

14 xiii.   Marie Anne Thibert, b. 9 Dec 1886 St.Claude Mission, St.John, Rolette County, North Dakota; m. John Allard; d. 9 Aug 1934 Hutchinson Township, Rolette County, North Dakota; bur. 11 Aug 1934 Catholic Cemetery, St.John, Rolette County, North Dakota.

4. Charles Alphonse Thibert was born on 3 Apr 1844 North West (MBS, C-14934.). He married **Elizabeth Slater**, daughter of **James Slater** and **Josephte Morissette**, on 4 Sep 1864 St.Francois Xavier, (Manitoba) (SFXI-Kipling, M-8.). He died on 3 Sep 1898 St.Francois Xavier, Manitoba, at age 54 (Ibid., S-15.).

Elizabeth Slater was born in Oct 1846 North West Territories (MBS, C-14934.).

Children of **Charles Alphonse Thibert** and **Elizabeth Slater** were as follows:

      i.   Domitilde Thibert was born on 16 Sep 1865 St.Francois Xavier, (Manitoba) (Ibid.) (SFXI-Kipling, B-93.). She was baptized on 17 Sep 1865 St.Francois Xavier, (Manitoba) (MBS, C-14934.) (SFXI-Kipling, B-93.). She died on 30 Jan 1882 St.Francois Xavier, Manitoba, at age 16 (Ibid., S-4.).

     ii.   Jean Louis Thibert was born on 12 Apr 1867 St.Francois Xavier, (Manitoba) (Ibid., B-20.). He was baptized on 13 Apr 1867 St.Francois Xavier, (Manitoba) (Ibid.) (INB, page 175.). He died on 1 Mar 1872 St.Francois Xavier, Manitoba, at age 4 (SFXI-Kipling, S-7.). He was buried on 3 Mar 1872 St.Francois Xavier, Manitoba (IBMS.) (SFXI-Kipling, S-7.).

     iii.   Julie Thibert was born on 20 Apr 1869 St.Francois Xavier, (Manitoba) (Ibid., B-37.). She was baptized on 21 Apr 1869 St.Francois Xavier, (Manitoba) (Ibid.). She died on 21 Feb 1873 St.Francois Xavier, Manitoba, at age 3 (Ibid., S-23.). She was buried on 23 Feb 1873 St.Francois Xavier, Manitoba (Ibid.) (IBMS.).

15   iv.   Marie Thibert, b. 10 Jul 1871 St.Francois Xavier, Manitoba; m. Jean Plante.

     v.   Joseph Alphonse Dominique Thibert was born on 30 May 1873 St.Francois Xavier, Manitoba (SFXI-Kipling, B-40.). He was baptized on 2 Jun 1873 St.Francois Xavier, Manitoba (Ibid.). He died on 18 Aug 1873 St.Francois Xavier, Manitoba (Ibid., S-68.). He was buried on 20 Aug 1873 St.Francois Xavier, Manitoba (IBMS.) (SFXI-Kipling, S-68.).

     vi.   George Frederick Alphonse Thibert was born on 20 Jul 1874 St.Francois Xavier, Manitoba (Ibid., B-38.) (INB, page 175.). He was baptized on 20 Jul 1874 St.Francois Xavier, Manitoba (SFXI-Kipling, B-38.) (INB, page 175.). He died on 6 Nov 1875 St.Francois Xavier, Manitoba, at age 1 (SFXI-Kipling, S-35.). He was buried on 8 Nov 1875 St.Francois Xavier, Manitoba (IBMS.) (SFXI-Kipling, S-35.).

16 vii.   Louis Napoleon Thibert, b. 3 Aug 1876 St.Francois Xavier, Manitoba; m. Marie Jeanne Buckley.

   viii.   Louis Joseph Thibert was born on 27 Sep 1878 St.Francois Xavier, Manitoba (Ibid., B-29.). He died on 12 Mar 1880 St.Francois Xavier, Manitoba, at age 1 (Ibid., S-9.).

     ix.   Patrice Thibert was born on 30 Dec 1880 St.Francois Xavier, Manitoba (Ibid., B-70.). He died on 22 Jun 1890 St.Francois Xavier, Manitoba, at age 9 (Ibid., S-10.).

     x.   Marie Lucienne Josephine Alphonsine Thibert was born on 11 May 1883 St.Francois Xavier, Manitoba (Ibid., B-25.). She died on 23 Jul 1899 St.Francois Xavier, Manitoba, at age 16 (Ibid., S-3.).

     xi.   Joseph Julien Thibert was born on 19 Oct 1885 St.Francois Xavier, Manitoba (Ibid., B-52.). He died on 27 Dec 1886 St.Francois Xavier, Manitoba, at age 1 (Ibid., S-45.).

17 xii.   Rose Victoria Anne Thibert, b. 5 May 1889 St.Francois Xavier, Manitoba; m. Albert Breland.

5. Catherine Thibert was born on 24 Dec 1846 North West (MBS, C-14933.). She married **Charles Swain**, son of **James Swain** and **Josephte Descoteaux**, on 4 Sep 1864 St.Francois Xavier, (Manitoba) (SFXI-Kipling, M-9.).

Charles Swain was baptized on 20 Jan 1842 St.Johns, (Manitoba) (Denney Papers, Charles D. Denney, Glenbow Archives, Calgary, Alberta.). He was born in Oct 1842 St.Charles, (Manitoba) (MBS, C-14933.). He was born circa 1843 (Ibid.). He was baptized on 28 Oct 1848 Assumption, Pembina, Pembina County, Minnesota Territory (AP, page 7, B-12.). He died in 1920 (Lesa (Trotchie) Zimmerman Research, 19 Jun 2001.).

   6. Elzear Thibert was born on 12 Jun 1849 North West (MBS, C-14934.). He married **Elise Zace**, daughter of **Louis Gonzague Isaac Zace** and **Angelique Parisien,** on 28 Feb 1870 St.Francois Xavier, (Manitoba) (SFXI-Kipling, M-10.). He died on 18 Apr 1917 RM Cartier, Manitoba, at age 67 (MB Vital Statistics, Death Reg. #1917,024077.).

   Elise Zace was born on 26 Nov 1850 Pembina, Pembina County, Minnesota Territory (AP, page 46, B-117.). She was baptized on 27 Nov 1850 Assumption, Pembina, Pembina County, Minnesota Territory (Ibid.). She died on 10 Feb 1948 at age 97 (MBS.).

   Children of **Elzear Thibert** and **Elise Zace** were as follows:

      i.   Angelique Thibert was born on 19 Feb 1871 St.Francois Xavier, Manitoba (SFXI-Kipling, B-14.). She was baptized on 20 Feb 1871 St.Francois Xavier, Manitoba (Ibid.) (INB, page 175.). She died on 22 May 1930 at age 59.

18   ii.   Maxime Thibert, b. 22 Jan 1873 St.Francois Xavier, Manitoba; m. Isabelle Osite Desjardins; m. Marie Beatrice Plouffe; d. 13 Jan 1952.

     iii.   Alphonse Thibert was baptized on 15 Mar 1875 St.Eustache, Manitoba (Denney.). He married Marie Alice Paul, daughter of William Paul and Flavie Page, on 31 Jan 1905 St.Francois Xavier, Manitoba (MM *Manitoba Marriages* in *Publication 45*, Volumes 1-3, compiled and edited by: Paul J. Lareau, Fr. Julien Hamelin, (240 Avenue Daly, Ottawa, Ontario K1N 6G2: Le Centre de Genealogie S.C., 1984).). He died on 1 Mar 1910 St.Francois Xavier, Manitoba, at age 34 (Denney.).

        Marie Alice Paul was born on 4 Oct 1885 Baie St.Paul, Manitoba (Rosemary Helga (Morrissette) Rozyk Research, 28 Jan 1999 report.). She was baptized on 11 Oct 1885 St.Eustache, Manitoba (Ibid.). She married **Jean Baptiste Branconnier**, son of **Antoine Branconnier** and **Marie Sarah Celestine Bird,** on 22 Oct 1910 St.Francois Xavier, Manitoba (MB Vital Statistics, Mar. Reg. #1910,001365 (SFX).).

     iv.   Marie Anne Thibert was born on 16 Jul 1877 St.Francois Xavier, Manitoba (SFXI-Kipling, B-34.). She was baptized 18 Jul 1877 St.Francois Xavier, Manitoba (Ibid.) (Rosemary Rozyk.). She died on 30 Oct 1968 at age 91 (Denney.).

     v.   Hyacinthe Thibert was born on 14 Oct 1879 St.Francois Xavier, Manitoba (SFXI-Kipling, B-59.). He was baptized on 15 Oct 1879 St.Francois Xavier, Manitoba (Ibid.) (Rosemary Rozyk.). He died circa Jan 1882 (Ibid., S-3.).

     vi.   Marie Eleonore Thibert was born on 24 Feb 1881 St.Eustache, Manitoba (Rosemary Rozyk.) She was baptized on 25 Feb 1881 St.Eustache, Manitoba (Ibid.). She died on 17 Dec 1881 St.Francois Xavier, Manitoba (SFXI-Kipling, S-48.).

     vii.   Rosine Thibert was born on 8 Oct 1883 St.Francois Xavier, Manitoba (Ibid., B-43.). She died on 18 Dec 1886 St.Francois Xavier, Manitoba, at age 3 (Ibid., S-44.).

    viii.   Marie Rosalie Thibert was born on 8 Jul 1886 St.Francois Xavier, Manitoba (Ibid., B-28.).

     ix.   Alice Agnes Justine Thibert was born on 17 Sep 1889 St.Francois Xavier, Manitoba (Ibid., B-32.). She died on 3 May 1917 at age 27 (Denney.).

     x.   Elise Josephine Thibert was born on 14 Mar 1893 St.Francois Xavier, Manitoba (SFXI-Kipling, B-7.). She died on 13 Sep 1893 St.Francois Xavier, Manitoba (Ibid., S-18.).

     xi.   Marie Isabelle Victoire Thibert was born on 21 Jul 1894 St.Francois Xavier, Manitoba (Ibid., B-21.).

   7. Marie Thibert was born on 19 Sep 1854 St.Francois Xavier, (Manitoba) (Ibid., B-198.) (SFXI 1851-1868, B-198.) (Ibid., B-1.) (SFXI-Kipling, B-1.). She was baptized on 20 Sep 1854 St.Francois Xavier, (Manitoba) (Ibid., B-198.) (SFXI 1851-1868, B-198.) (SFXI-Kipling, B-1.) (SFXI 1851-1868, B-1.). She married **Joseph Laplante**, son of **Jean Baptiste Laplante** and **Madeleine Desfonds or Dufont,** on 1 Jul 1872 St.Francois Xavier, Manitoba (SFXI-Kipling, M-9.). She died on 22 May 1938 Cartier, Manitoba, at age 83 (MB Vital Statistics, Death Reg. #1938,024391.).

   Joseph Laplante was born on 31 Aug 1850 (Manitoba) (1870C-MB 1870 Manitoba Census, National Archives of Canada, Ottawa, Ontario, Microfilm Reel Number C-2170., page 270, #868.) (Automated Genealogy 1901 Census Transcription Project and Census Images from the National Archives of Canada, http://www.automatedgenealogy.com, District 11-n-5, page 3-4, family 26, line 50, 1-9.).

   8. Philomene Thibert was born on 13 Apr 1858 St.Francois Xavier, (Manitoba) (SFXI-Kipling, B-229.). She was baptized on 15 Apr 1858 St.Francois Xavier, (Manitoba) (Ibid.). She married **Francois Richard**, son of **Francois Xavier Richard** and **Anne Braconnier,** on 20 May 1884 St.Francois Xavier, Manitoba (Ibid., M-6.) (MB Vital Statistics, Marriage Reg. #1884,001874.). She died on 10 Nov 1921 Elie, Manitoba, at age 63 (Ibid., Death Reg. #1921,043285.).

   Francois Richard was born on 21 Jul 1864 St.Francois Xavier, (Manitoba) (SFXI-Kipling, B-29.) (MBS, C-14932.). He was baptized on 24 Jul 1864 St.Francois Xavier, (Manitoba) (SFXI-Kipling, B-29.) (MBS, C-14932.). He married **Rose Desjarlais**, daughter of **Louis Desjarlais** and **Julie Chartrand,** on 6 Aug 1923 St.Eustache, Manitoba (MM.).

   9. Elizabeth Thibert was born on 3 Mar 1866 St.Francois Xavier, (Manitoba) (Ibid.) (1901 Canada, #8, K-10, page 4, Family 42, Line 23-29.). She was baptized on 3 Mar 1866 St.Francois Xavier, (Manitoba) (SFXI-Kipling, B-15.). She married **Edwin Bourke**, son of **Andrew Bourke** and **Madeleine Lallemont dit Welsh,** on 2 Nov 1884 St.Francois Xavier, Manitoba (Ibid., M-9.) (MB Vital Statistics, Mar. Reg. #1884,001424.). She died on 18 Nov 1938 Portage la Prairie, Manitoba, at age 72 (Denney.).

   Edwin Bourke was born on 27 Aug 1863 St.James, (Manitoba) (MBS, C-14925.) (SB-Rozyk, page 134, B-177.) (1901 Canada, #8, K-10, page 4, Family 42, Line 23-29.). He was baptized on 30 Aug 1863 St.Boniface, (Manitoba) (SB-Rozyk, page 134, B-177.). He died on 9 Feb 1942 Portage la Prairie, Manitoba, at age 78 (Denney.).

   10. Pierre Thibert was born on 1 May 1868 St.Francois Xavier, (Manitoba) (SFXI-Kipling, B-31.). He was baptized on 1 May 1868 St.Francois Xavier, (Manitoba) (Ibid.). He married **Marie Mathilde Zace**, daughter of **Andre Zace** and **Mathilde Ross,** on 22 Nov 1887 St.Francois Xavier, Manitoba (Ibid., M-11.) (MB Vital Statistics, Mar. Reg. #1888,001100.) (Ibid., Mar. Reg. #1888,001591.).

Marie Mathilde Zace was born on 11 Dec 1870 St.Francois Xavier, Manitoba (MBS, C-14934.) (SFXI-Kipling, B-93.). She was baptized on 12 Dec 1870 St.Francois Xavier, Manitoba (MBS, C-14934.) (SFXI-Kipling, B-93.).

Children of **Pierre Thibert** and **Marie Mathilde Zace** were as follows:

    i.   Israel Honore Thibert was born on 15 Nov 1891 RM St.Francois Xavier, Manitoba (1901 Canada, MB, Selkirk, (#11), SFX, N-1, page 8, family 63, Line 9-15.) (MB Vital Statistics, Birth Reg. #1891,006122.). He married Mary Cleophee Nault, daughter of Joseph Nault and Olive Breland, on 23 Nov 1920 Ste.Rose du Lac, Manitoba (Ibid., Marriage Reg. #1920,056359.). He died in 1985 Ste.Rose du Lac, Manitoba (Rod MacQuarrie Research, 28 Dec 2011.).

          Mary Cleophee Nault was born on 12 Jan 1900 R.M. of Dauphin, Manitoba (MB Vital Statistics, Birth Reg. #1900,007535.). She died in 1980 Ste.Rose du Lac, Manitoba (Rod Mac Quarrie, 28 Dec 2011.).

    ii. Pierre Francois Xavier Thibert was born on 16 Dec 1893 St.Francois Xavier, Manitoba (SFXI-Kipling, B-27.).

    iii. Louis Gonzaque Thibert was born on 7 Sep 1895 St.Francois Xavier, Manitoba (Ibid., B-28.).

    iv. Marie Louise Emilienne Thibert was born on 21 Feb 1897 St.Francois Xavier, Manitoba (Ibid., B-8.). She married Arthur Nault, son of Joseph Nault and Olive Breland, on 25 Jul 1917 Lac Manitoba, Manitoba (Ibid., B-8 (note).) (MB Vital Statistics, Marriage Reg. #1917,040105.).

          Arthur Nault was born on 24 Jan 1889 Lac Dauphin, Manitoba (Ibid., Birth Reg. #1890,001344.).

    v. Jean Joseph Thibert was born on 27 Aug 1899 St.Francois Xavier, Manitoba (SFXI-Kipling, B-29.).

Generation Three

11. Marie Sophie Thibert was born on 2 Aug 1862 St.Francois Xavier, (Manitoba) (Ibid., B-67.). She was baptized on 3 Aug 1862 St.Francois Xavier, (Manitoba) (Ibid.). She married **Louis Allary**, son of **Pierre Allary** and **Genevieve Zace**, on 24 Jul 1876 St.Eustache, Manitoba (MM, page 16.) (ST-BSP St.Eustache (Baie St.Paul) 1877-1900 Register, M-2. Hereinafter cited as ST-BSP.).

Louis Allary was born on 21 Jan 1857 St.Francois Xavier, (Manitoba) (SFXI-Kipling, B-162.). He was baptized on 22 Jan 1857 St.Francois Xavier, (Manitoba) (Ibid.). He married **Elizabeth Allard**, daughter of **Michel Allard** and **Elizabeth Ross,** before 1902.

12. Pierre Thibert was born on 1 Jul 1866 St.Francois Xavier, (Manitoba) (SFXI-Kipling, B-90.). He was baptized on 1 Jul 1866 St.Francois Xavier, (Manitoba) (Ibid.). He married **Marie Cecile Morin**, daughter of **Francois Perreault dit Morin** and **Marguerite Robinson**, on 13 Nov 1883 St.Claude Mission, St.John, Rolette County, North Daktoa (Dominique Ritchot, 26 Jan 2006.) (St.Claude BMD, Dominique Ritchot, page 17, M-18.).

Marie Cecile Morin was born on 25 Nov 1863 St.Francois Xavier, (Manitoba) (SFXI-Kipling, B-103.). She was baptized on 25 Nov 1863 St.Francois Xavier, (Manitoba) (Ibid.). She died on 30 Jun 1922 Rolette County, North Dakota, at age 58 (ND Death Index.).

Children of **Pierre Thibert** and **Marie Cecile Morin** were as follows:

    i.   Adolphie Thibert was born on 10 Aug 1884 St.John, Rolette County, North Dakota (St.Claude BMD, Dominique Ritchot, page 31, B-122.). He was baptized on 17 Aug 1884 St.Claude, St.John, Rolette County, North Dakota (Ibid.).

    ii. Francois Abdala Thibert was baptized on 8 Apr 1886 St.Claude Mission, St.John, Rolette County, North Dakota (Ibid., B-242, page 52.). He was buried on 24 Dec 1887 St.Claude Mission, St.John, Rolette County, North Dakota (Ibid., S-61, p. 71.).

19 iii. Emilie Guillemine Thibert, b. 9 Jan 1888; m. Louis Langer; d. 20 Jul 1949 Bottineau County, North Dakota.

20 iv. Delima Rose Thibert, b. Nov 1889 North Dakota; m. Alexandre Lingan or Langan.

    v. Alfred Thibert was born in Nov 1891 North Dakota (1900C-ND, Sheet No. 10A, family 186, line 11-18.).

    vi. Rachel Thibert was born in Dec 1895 North Dakota (Ibid.).

21 vii. Flora Thibert, b. Jul 1897 North Dakota; m. Marcial Finley St.Germain.

    viii. John Thibert was born circa 1904 North Dakota (1910C ND Thirteenth Census of the United States: 1910; North Dakota, National Archives of the United States, Washington D.C., Sheet 28A, family 83, line 13-19.). He died on 20 Oct 1929 Rolette County, North Dakota (ND Death Index.).

22 ix. Arthur J. Thibert, b. 6 Mar 1905 North Dakota; m. Florestine Richard; d. 27 Jul 1980 Rolette, North Dakota.

13. Elise Thibert was born on 30 Aug 1868 St.Francois Xavier, (Manitoba) (INB, page 175.). She was baptized on 30 Aug 1868 St.Francois Xavier, (Manitoba) (Ibid.).

Children of **Elise Thibert** include:

    i.   Emily (--?--) was born circa 1887 (1889-TMC-off, #573.).

14. Marie Anne Thibert was baptized on 9 Dec 1886 St.Claude Mission, St.John, Rolette County, North Dakota (St.Claude BMD, Dominique Ritchot, B-310, page 63.). She married **John Allard**, son of **Michel Allard** and **Elizabeth Ross,** in Jun 1902 St.John, Rolette County, North Dakota (1930C ND, Sheet No. 1B, family 15, line 68-75.) (TM Star, 16 Aug 1934.). She died on 9 Aug 1934 Hutchinson Township, Rolette County, North Dakota, at age 47 (ND Death Index.) (TM Star, 16 Aug 1934.). She was buried on 11 Aug 1934 Catholic Cemetery, St.John, Rolette County, North Dakota (Ibid.).

John Allard was born on 3 Nov 1879 St.Francois Xavier, Manitoba (SFXI-Kipling, B-64.) (ND Death Index.). He was baptized 5 Nov 1879 St.Francois Xavier, Manitoba (SFXI-Kipling, B-64.) (Rosemary Rozyk.). He died on 6 Aug 1953 Rolette County, North Dakota, at age 73 (Ibid.).

15. Marie Thibert was born on 10 Jul 1871 St.Francois Xavier, Manitoba (SFXI-Kipling, B-56.). She was baptized on 11 Jul 1871 St.Francois Xavier, Manitoba (Ibid.) (INB, page 175.). She married **Jean Plante**, son of **Magloire Plante** and **Isabelle Lowe dit Nault,** on 3 Jan 1898 St.Francois Xavier, Manitoba (SFXI-Kipling, M-1.).

Jean Plante was born circa 1866 (Manitoba) (1870C-MB, page 251, #176.). He was born circa 1867 St.Albert, (Alberta) (SFXI-Kipling, M-1 (note).).

16. Louis Napoleon Thibert was born on 3 Aug 1876 St.Francois Xavier, Manitoba (SFXI-Kipling, B-29.). He married **Marie Jeanne Buckley**, daughter of **Patrick Buckley** and **Philomene Leclerc dit Leclair,** on 9 Jan 1900 St.Francois Xavier, Manitoba (Ibid., M-1.) (MB Vital Statistics, Marriage Reg. #1900,002154.).

Marie Jeanne Buckley was born in Dec 1880 Woodlands, Manitoba (SFXI-Kipling, M-1.) (1881 Canada, NA Film No. C-13283, District 186, Sub-district L, page 42, household 194+.).

Children of **Louis Napoleon Thibert** and **Marie Jeanne Buckley** are:

    i.   Marie E. Thibert was born on 8 Nov 1900 St.Francois Xavier, Manitoba (1901 Canada, MB, Selkirk, (#11), SFX, N-1, page 8, family 67, Line 31-36.).

17. **Rose Victoria Anne Thibert** was born on 5 May 1889 St.Francois Xavier, Manitoba (SFXI-Kipling, B-18.). She married **Albert Breland**, son of **Moise Breland** and **Philomene Page**, on 6 Mar 1905 St.Francois Xavier, Manitoba (MM.) (MB Vital Statistics, Mar. Reg. #1905,002667.).

  Albert Breland was born on 20 May 1879 St.Francois Xavier, Manitoba (SFXI-Kipling, B-28.). He was baptized 21 May 1879 St.Francios Xavier, Manitoba (Ibid.) (Rosemary Rozyk.).

18. **Maxime Thibert** was born on 22 Jan 1873 St.Francois Xavier, Manitoba (INB, page 175.). He was baptized on 24 Jan 1873 St.Francois Xavier, Manitoba (Ibid.) (SFXI-Kipling, B-5.). He married **Isabelle Osite Desjardins**, daughter of **Wenceslas Desjardins** and **Caroline Plante**, on 29 May 1900 St.Francois Xavier, Manitoba (Ibid., M-6.). He married **Marie Beatrice Plouffe**, daughter of **Georges Plouffe dit Gervais** and **Josephine Huppe**, on 9 Feb 1920 RM of Lawrence, Manitoba (MB Vital Statistics, Marriage Reg. #1920,0091335.). He died on 13 Jan 1952 at age 78 (Fort Garry St.Vital Roman Catholic Cemetery; Cemetery Transcription #42; Betty Atkinson, Lorne Harris Kathy Stokes, Unit E, 1045 St.James Street, Winnipeg, Manitoba, Canada %3H 1B1: Manitoba Genealogical Society, Inc., 1980-1981; update 1995, page 5.).

  Isabelle Osite Desjardins was born on 4 Jul 1880 St.Francois Xavier, Manitoba (SFXI-Kipling, B-40.).

Children of **Maxime Thibert** and **Isabelle Osite Desjardins** both born R.M. of St.Francois Xavier, Manitoba, are as follows:

    i.   Aime Henri Thibert was born on 13 Aug 1904 (1916 Census of Canada from the National Archives of Canada (Transcription by ancestry.com), Ottawa, Canada, District 2-1, page 11, line 40.) (MB Vital Statistics, Birth Reg. #1904,002665.). He married Marceline Georgiana Plouffe, daughter of Georges Plouffe dit Gervais and Josephine Huppe, on 14 Jun 1929 RM of Ste.Rose du Lac, Manitoba (Ibid., Marriage Reg. #1929,038432.).

        Marceline Georgiana Plouffe was born on 29 Jul 1910 St.Vital, Manitoba (Ibid., Birth Reg. #1910,005176.).

    ii. Valerie Diana Thibert was born on 1 Dec 1906 (1916 Canada, District 2-1, page 11, line 40.) (MB Vital Statistics, Birth Reg. #1906,002916.).

Marie Beatrice Plouffe was born on 3 Feb 1895 R.M. of La Broquerie, Manitoba (1901 Canada, #10, n-2, page 3, family 23, line 34-37.) (MB Vital Statistics, Birth Reg. #1895,002676.). She died in 1983 (Rod Mac Quarrie, 28 Dec 2011.).

Generation Four

19. **Emilie Guillemine Thibert** was born on 9 Jan 1888 (ND Death Index.). She was baptized on 10 Jan 1888 St.Claude Mission, St.John, Rolette County, North Dakota (St.Claude BMD, Dominique Ritchot, B-361, page 71.). She married **Louis Langer**, son of **Jean Baptiste Langer** and **Justine Malaterre**, before 1907 (1936-TMC, page 145.). She died on 20 Jul 1949 Bottineau County, North Dakota, at age 61 (ND Death Index.).

  Louis Langer was born on 10 Jan 1886 North Dakota (1919 Turtle Mountain Indian Census Roll, United States Indian Service Department of the Interior, Turtle Mountain Indian Agency, North Dakota, 30 June 1919 , Census No. 2022-2026.) (ND Death Index.). He died on 9 Oct 1953 Rolette County, North Dakota, at age 67 (Ibid.).

20. **Delima Rose Thibert** was born in Nov 1889 North Dakota (1900C-ND, Sheet No. 10A, family 186, line 11-18.). She married **Alexandre Lingan or Langan**, son of **Jean Baptiste Lingan** and **Angelique St.Germain,** before 1912.

  Alexandre Lingan or Langan was baptized on 10 Sep 1883 St.Claude, St.John, Rolette County, North Dakota (St.Claude BMD, Dominique Ritchot, page 14, B-68.).

21. **Flora Thibert** was born in Jul 1897 North Dakota (1900C-ND, Sheet No. 10A, family 186, line 11-18.). She married **Marcial Finley St.Germain**, son of **Francois St.Germain** and **Alphonsine "Rosine" Vivier,** before 1920 (*1937-TMC*, page 477-478, Census No. 5569-5576.).

  Marcial Finley St.Germain was born on 1 Feb 1898 North Dakota (1900C-ND, 424-424.) (1914-TMC 1914 Census of the Turtle Mountain Chippewa, North Dakota, National Archives of the United States, Washington D.C., Census No. 2823-2832.) (Ancestry.com Website, WWI Draft Registration.). He married **Mary Rose Allard**, daughter of **Elzear Allard** and **Julia Morin,** on 22 Feb 1944 Roosevelt County, Montana (RooCM Marriage Licenses and Certificates, Roosevelt County Courthouse, Wolf Point, Montana; FHC microfilm 1903324 and 1903325, Hereinafter cited as RooCM.).

22. **Arthur J. Thibert** was born on 6 Mar 1905 North Dakota (1910C ND, Sheet 28A, family 83, line 13-19.) (ND Death Index.). He married **Florestine Richard**, daughter of **Hyacinthe Chalifoux dit Richard** and **Bebienne Lingan,** before 1926. He died on 27 Jul 1980 Rolette, North Dakota, at age 75 (Ibid.).

  Florestine Richard was born on 30 Mar 1906 (1917-TMC 1917 Census of the Turtle Mountain Chippewa, North Dakota, National Archives of the United States, Washington D.C.).

Children of **Arthur J. Thibert** and **Florestine Richard** were as follows:

    i.   Arthur Lawrence Thibert Jr was born on 17 Apr 1926 (*1937-TMC*, page 486-487, Census No. 5677-5684.) (ND Death Index.). He died on 24 Dec 1992 Rolette, North Dakota, at age 66 (Ibid.).

    ii. Adolph Thibert was born on 9 Jul 1927 (*1937-TMC*, page 486-487, Census No. 5677-5684.).

    iii. Wanelda Thibert was born on 19 Sep 1928 (RLCM.) (*1937-TMC*, page 486-487, Census No. 5677-5684.). She married Joseph R. McGillis, son of William McGillis and Justine Richard, on 27 May 1947 Sidney, Richland County, Montana (RLCM.). She died on 25 Oct 1998 Williams County, North Dakota, at age 70 (ND Death Index.).

        Joseph R. McGillis was born on 9 Feb 1920 (1936-TMC, page 170.) (ND Death Index.). He died on 11 Nov 2008 Williams County, North Dakota, at age 88 (Ibid.).

    iv. Dorothy Thibert was born on 30 Oct 1929 (*1937-TMC*, page 486-487, Census No. 5677-5684.).

    v.   Elisabeth Thibert was born on 9 Mar 1932 (Ibid.).

    vi. Stella A. Thibert was born on 4 Jul 1933 (Ibid.).

    vii.   Alfred L. Thibert was born on 6 Nov 1935 (Ibid.).

    viii.   Evelyn Lucille Thibert was born on 20 Apr 1937 Rolette, North Dakota (1937-TMC-deaths Births & Deaths occurring between the dates of December 31, 1936 to Jan 1, 1938, United States Indian Service Department of the Interior, Belcourt, North Dakota, 1 January 1937.).

    ix.   Richard R. Thibert was born on 12 Jul 1938 (ND Death Index.). He died on 29 Jul 2006 Rolette, North Dakota, at age 68 (Ibid.).

Descendants of Basile Thifault

Generation One

1. Basile Thifault married **Marie Anne (--?--)** before 1811.

Marie Anne (--?--) died before 1832.

Children of **Basile Thifault** and **Marie Anne (--?--)** are:

    2   i.   Louis Thifault, b. before 1811; m. Isabelle Lyonnais.

Generation Two

2. Louis Thifault was born before 1811 (SB 1825-1834 St.Boniface Roman Catholic Registre des Baptemes, Mariages & Sepultures, 1825-1834, page 50, M-56 (father). Hereinafter cited as SB 1825-1834.). He married **Isabelle Lyonnais**, daughter of **Francois Lionais dit Delauney or Delaunay** and **Louise Sauteuse**, on 24 Jan 1832 St.Boniface, (Manitoba) (Ibid., page 50, M-56.).

Isabelle Lyonnais was born circa 1815 (Ibid.).

Children of **Louis Thifault** and **Isabelle Lyonnais** were as follows:

    3   i.   Louis Thifault, b. 1835; m. Francoise St.Pierre; m. Angelique Morissette; m. Suzanne Allary; d. 1892.

        ii.   Unnamed Thifault was born circa 1836. She died on 13 Jun 1855 Pembina, Pembina County, Dakota Territory (AP Records of the Assumption Roman Catholic Church, Pembina, North Dakota: Baptisms, Marriages, Sepultures, 1848-1896; compiled by Reverend Father J. M. Belleau, 2 October 1944, page 129, S-47. Hereinafter cited as AP.). She was buried on 13 Jun 1855 Assumption, Pembina, Pembina County, Dakota Territory (Ibid.).

    4   iii.   Thomas Thifault, b. circa 1844; m. Josephte Vivier; m. Veronique Ladouceur; d. 30 Apr 1884 Pembina County, Dakota Territory; bur. 1 May 1884 Assumption, Pembina, Pembina County, Dakota Territory.

    5   iv.   Marie Thifault, b. circa 1846; m. Johnny Hinghing.

        v.   Alexandre Thifault was born on 13 Nov 1853 Pembina, Pembina County, Dakota Territory (Ibid., page 98, B-106.). He was baptized on 15 Nov 1853 Assumption, Pembina, Pembina County, Dakota Territory (Ibid.).

Generation Three

3. Louis Thifault was born in 1835. He married **Francoise St.Pierre**, daughter of **Francois St.Pierre** and **Marie Laverdure**, on 5 Feb 1855 Assumption, Pembina, Pembina County, Dakota Territory (Ibid., M-51; page 124.). He married **Angelique Morissette**, daughter of **Narcisse Morissette** and **Julie Cardinal**, before 1874. He married **Suzanne Allary**, daughter of **Michel Allary** and **Marie Paquin**, before 1889. He died in 1892.

Francoise St.Pierre was born circa 1833.

Children of **Louis Thifault** and **Francoise St.Pierre** were as follows:

        i.   Anastasie Thifault was born on 18 Sep 1857 Pembina, Pembina County, Dakota Territory (Ibid., page 177, B-525.). She was baptized on 18 Sep 1857 Assumption, Pembina, Pembina County, Dakota Territory (Ibid.).

    6   ii.   Thomas Thifault, b. circa 1858; m. Margaret (--?--); m. Madeleine Decouteau; d. before 30 Jun 1925.

        iii.   Francois Thifault was born circa 1860 (1886-TMC 1886 Census of Half Breed Chippewas of Turtle Mountain, Dakota Territory, National Archives of the United States, Washington D.C., #411.).

    7   iv.   Mary Thifault, b. circa 1865; m. Israel Smith.

Angelique Morissette was baptized on 15 Jan 1847 Fort-des-Prairies, (Alberta) (INB *Index des Naissances and Baptemes* (St.Boniface, Manitoba: La Societe Historique de Saint-Boniface., c1995), page 130.). She died on 19 Dec 1884 Olga, Cavalier County, North Dakota, at age 37 (Olga Our Lady of the Sacred Heart, Olga, North Dakota 1882-1900, page 59, S-25. Hereinafter cited as Olga.). She was buried on 20 Dec 1884 Olga, Cavalier County, North Dakota (Ibid.).

Children of **Louis Thifault** and **Angelique Morissette** were as follows:

        i.   Joseph Thifault was born on 30 Mar 1874 (L1 Lebret Mission de St.Florent Roman Catholic Registre des Baptemes, Mariages & Seplutures, Qu'Appelle, Saskatchewan, 1868-1881., page 130, B-100. Hereinafter cited as L1.). He was baptized on 2 Apr 1874 Lebret, (Saskatchewan) (Ibid.).

        ii.   David Thifault was born in 1877 Dakota Territory.

    8   iii.   Louis Thifault, b. 19 Jan 1880 Wood Mountain, (Saskatchewan); m. Mary Rose Renville.

        iv.   Roger Jerome Thifault was born on 27 Apr 1883 Olga, Cavalier County, North Dakota (Olga, page 11, B-13.). He was baptized on 28 Apr 1883 Olga, Cavalier County, North Dakota (Ibid.). He died in 1899.

Suzanne Allary was born on 7 Apr 1849 Pembina County, Dakota Territory (AP, page 16, B-32.). She was baptized on 26 May 1849 Assumption, Pembina, Pembina County, Minnesota Territory (Ibid.). She married **Moise Delorme**, son of **Francois Delorme** and **Angelique Malaterre**, on 29 Aug 1865 St.Francois Xavier, (Manitoba) (SFXI-Kipling St.Francois Xavier Register Index, 1834-1900; compiled by Clarence Kipling , M-14.) (MM *Manitoba Marriages* in *Publication 45*, Volumes 1-3, compiled and edited by: Paul J. Lareau, Fr. Julien Hamelin, (240 Avenue Daly, Ottawa, Ontario K1N 6G2: Le Centre de Genealogie S.C., 1984), page 18.). She married **Antoine Lapierre** before 1882. She died in 1899 (BIA-TM Bureau of Indian Affairs, Turtle Mountain Enrollment and Probate Papers, Belcourt, North Dakota.).

4. Thomas Thifault was born circa 1839 (SJL-1 Register of Baptisms, Marriages, and Burials, St.Joseph, Leroy, North Dakota, Diocese of Saint Paul, Minnesota, 1870-1888, Book 1, page 133, S-131. Hereinafter cited as SJL-1.). He was born circa 1844. He married **Josephte Vivier** before 1868. He married **Veronique Ladouceur**, daughter of **Bazile Ladouceur** and **Angelique Martel**, circa

1871. He died on 30 Apr 1884 Pembina County, Dakota Territory (AP, page 225, S-1.). He was buried on 1 May 1884 Assumption, Pembina, Pembina County, Dakota Territory (Ibid.). Question: *Thomas is the probable son of Louis Thifault.*

Children of **Thomas Thifault** and **Josephte Vivier** are:

    i.   Justine Thyfault was born circa 1868 (SJL-1, page 153, M-81.). She married Louis Lecuyer, son of Francois Xavier Lecuyer and Josephte Vivier, on 8 Nov 1886 St.Joseph, Leroy, Pembina County, Dakota Territory (Ibid.).

        Louis Lecuyer was born in Feb 1864 (SFXI-Kipling, B-52.). He was baptized on 30 Mar 1864 St.Francois Xavier, (Manitoba) (Ibid.). He married **Judith Masson** before 1886 (Olga, page 98, S-8.).

Veronique Ladouceur was born in 1847 (NWHBSI Index 1885 Scrip Applications, North-West Halfbreeds residing outside Manitoba on 15 July 1870, RG15-20, page 47.). She was born circa 1854 (1889-TMC 1889 Census of Half Breed Chippewas of Turtle Mountain, Dakota Territory, National Archives of the United States, Washington D.C., #520-523.). She was born in Jun 1862 (1900C-ND 1900 United States Census, North Dakota, National Archives of the United States, Washington, D. C., 248-248.). She married **Joseph Houle**, son of **Antoine Houle** and **Genevieve St.Pierre**, on 17 May 1886 St.Joseph, Leroy, Pembina County, Dakota Territory (SJL-1, page 149, M-78.). She died circa 1900 (James D. Hartman Research, 8 Jan 2002.).

Children of **Thomas Thifault** and **Veronique Ladouceur** were as follows:

    i.   Henry Thifault was born on 23 Aug 1875 Pembina County, Dakota Territory (AP, B-24.). He was baptized on 27 Aug 1875 Assumption, Pembina, Pembina County, Dakota Territory (Ibid.).

    ii. Marie Celina Thifault was born on 9 Aug 1877 Dakota Territory (Ibid., B-30.). She was baptized on 25 Nov 1877 Assumption, Pembina, Pembina County, Dakota Territory (Ibid.). She married Henry Monet, son of Antoine Monet dit Belhumeur and Catherine Larivie, circa 1894.

        Henry Monet was born on 29 Aug 1873 Pembina, Pembina County, North Dakota (Ibid., page 83, B-3.). He was baptized on 8 Jan 1874 Assumption, Pembina, Pembina County, North Dakota (Ibid.).

    iii. Marie Jeanne Thifault was born on 10 Sep 1879 Dakota Territory (Ibid., page 163, B-30.). She was baptized on 28 Sep 1879 Assumption, Pembina, Pembina County, Dakota Territory (Ibid.).

    iv. Henry Thifault was born on 9 Mar 1882 Pembina, Pembina County, Dakota Territory (Ibid., page 204, B-23.). He was baptized on 2 Apr 1882 Assumption, Pembina, Pembina County, Dakota Territory (Ibid.).

5.   Marie Thifault was born circa 1846. She married **Toussaint Vallee**, son of **Joseph Vallee** and **Louise Page,** on 3 May 1862 Assumption, Pembina, Pembina County, Dakota Territory (Ibid., page 256, M-5.). She married **Johnny Hinghing** before 1874.

Toussaint Vallee was born on 8 Mar 1832 (SB 1825-1834, page 75, B-494.). He was baptized on 8 Sep 1832 St.Boniface, (Manitoba) (Ibid.).

Generation Four

6.   Thomas Thifault was born in 1850 (1936-TMC 1936 Tribal Roll, Turtle Mountain Indian Reservation, Office of Indian Affairs, received 28 Jan 1938, National Archives of the United States, Washington D.C., page 117.). He was born circa 1858. He was born in Aug 1859 North Dakota (1900C-ND, 394-394.). He was born in 1860 Dakota Territory. He married **Margaret (--?--)** before 1888. He married **Madeleine Decouteau**, daughter of **Norbert Decouteau** and **Rose Belgarde,** before 1909 (1936-TMC, page 117.). He died before 30 Jun 1925 (1925-TMC-ND 1925 Census of the Chippewa Indians of Turtle Mountain Agency, North Dakota, United States Indian Service Department of the Interior, Belcourt, North Dakota, superintendent H. J. McQuigg, 30 June 1925 , #3691-3698.).

Margaret (--?--) was born circa 1870.

Children of **Thomas Thifault** and **Margaret (--?--)** were as follows:

    i.   Vitaline Thifault was born circa Jun 1889 (1889-TMC, #1016.). She married Pierre Alexandre Dubois, son of Alexander Dubois and Marguerite Dease, before 1913 (1936-TMC, page 84.).

        Pierre Alexandre Dubois was born on 21 Jun 1888 Leroy, Pembina County, Dakota Territory (SJL-1, page 168, B-18.). He was baptized on 29 Jun 1888 St.Joseph, Leroy, Pembina County, Dakota Territory (Ibid.).

    ii. Raphael Thifault was born on 21 Mar 1890 (1936-TMC, page 117.) (1937-TMC Indian Census Roll of the Turtle Mountain Reservation, United States Indian Service Department of the Interior, Belcourt, North Dakota, J. E. Balmer, 1 January 1937 , page 488, Census No. 5697-5706.). He married Julie Poitras, daughter of Joseph Poitras and Alphonsine Belgarde, before 1914 (1936-TMC, page 117.).

        Julie Poitras was born on 25 May 1893 North Dakota (1900C-ND, House 435, page 323B.) (*1937-TMC*, page 488, Census No. 5697-5706.).

Madeleine Decouteau was born on 17 Sep 1889 (1890-TMC 1890 Census of Half Breed Chippewas of Turtle Mountain, Dakota Territory, National Archives of the United States, Washington D.C., #347.) (Rod MacQuarrie Research, 28 Dec 2012.). She married **Jean Baptiste Bruce**, son of **Joseph Bruce** and **Isabelle Ladouceur,** circa 1906 (1906-TMC 1906 Census of the Turtle Mountain Chippewa, United States Indian Service Department of the Interior, Belcourt, North Dakota, 30 June 1906.). She married **Joseph James Azure**, son of **James Azure** and **Marie Elise Delorme,** circa 1925 Turtle Mountain Reservation, Rolette County, North Dakota (*1937-TMC*, page 29, Census No. 314-318.). She died on 13 Mar 1966 Rolette County, North Dakota, at age 76 (ND Death Index.).

Children of **Thomas Thifault** and **Madeleine Decouteau** were as follows:

    i.   Paul Thifault was born on 19 Jan 1909 (BIA-TM-BMD Bureau of Indian Affairs, Turtle Mountain Death certificates: 1916-1952, extracted by Mary M. McClammy; Birth, Marriage, Death Records 1904-1950; Family record cards 1908; Family History Center; FHC Film #1249904, page 19.).

    ii. Clara Thifault was born on 19 Mar 1910 (1936-TMC, page 117.) (BIA-TM-BMD, page 35.).

    iii. Joseph A. Thiefault was born on 18 May 1912 (1936-TMC, page 117.) (BIA-TM-BMD, page 56.). He died on 27 Jan 1980 Belcourt, Rolette, North Dakota, at age 67 (Social Security Death Index, . Hereinafter cited as SSDI.) (ND Death Index.).

    iv. William Thifault was born on 20 May 1914 (1936-TMC, page 117.) (*1937-TMC*, page 487, Census No. 5692-5693.).

    v.   Agnes Thifault was born on 21 Apr 1917 Rolette County, North Dakota (Ibid., page 24, Census No. 252-255.). She married George Azure, son of James Azure and Marie Elise Delorme, circa 1934 (Ibid.).

George Azure was born on 10 May 1897 (BIA-TM.) (ND Death Index.). He was born in May 1898 North Dakota (1900C-ND, House 440, page 324A.). He was born on 5 May 1898 (1916-TMC 1916 Census of the Turtle Mountain Chippewa, North Dakota, National Archives of the United States, Washington D.C., Census No. 321.). He was born on 10 May 1898 Rolette County, North Dakota (*1937-TMC*, page 24, Census No. 252-255.). He married **Clarice Lafontaine**, daughter of **Agenore Lafontaine** and **Adele Amyotte**, before 1924 (Ibid., page 21, Census No. 224-226.). He died on 29 Feb 1952 Rolette County, North Dakota, at age 53 (ND Death Index.).

    vi.   Rose F. Thifault was born in 1919 (*1925-TMC-ND*, #3691-3698.).

    vii.   Eva Jane Thifault was born on 5 Sep 1920 (*1937-TMC*, page 371, Census No. 4380-4381.). She married John A. Morin, son of Andrew Morin and Sarah Gladu, before 1937.

        John A. Morin was born on 4 Jun 1901 (Ibid.). He died on 20 Aug 1990 Rolette, North Dakota, at age 89 (SSDI.) (ND Death Index.).

    viii.   Mildred F. Thifault was born in 1923 (*1925-TMC-ND*, #3691-3698.).

  7. Mary Thifault was born circa 1865 (1886-TMC, #410-416.). She was born in Jul 1874 North Dakota (1900C-ND, 310-310.). She married **Israel Smith**, son of **Joseph Smith** and **Charlotte Pelletier**, in 1889 (Ibid.).

  Israel Smith was born on 30 Jun 1861 Cypress Hills, (Saskatchewan). He was baptized on 18 Aug 1861 Assumption, Pembina, Pembina County, Dakota Territory (AP, page 245, B-220.). He married **Sara Champagne**, daughter of **Jean Baptiste Champagne Sr.** and **Elize Laverdure**, before 1903 (1936-TMC, page 110.). He died on 2 Nov 1924 Belcourt, Rolette County, North Dakota, at age 63 (ND Death Index.).

  8. Louis Thifault was born on 19 Jan 1880 Wood Mountain, (Saskatchewan) (1936-TMC, page 116.) (ArchiviaNet 1886-1901, 1906 Half-Breed Scrip Applications Index, RG15-21, Volume 1333 through 1371, Microfilm Reel Number C-14944 through C-15010, National Archives of Canada, Ottawa, Ontario, http://www.collectionscanada.gc.ca, C-15006.). He married **Mary Rose Renville**, daughter of **Octave Rainville** and **Josephte Montreuille**, before 1899 (1936-TMC, page 116.).

  Mary Rose Renville was born on 17 May 1882 (St. Claude Mission, St. John, North Dakota, Baptisms, Marriages, Burials 1882-1888, 2006, Dominique Ritchot, page 3, B-17.). She was baptized on 2 Jul 1882 St.Claude, St.John, Rolette County, North Dakota (Ibid.). She was born in Dec 1884 North Dakota (1900C-ND, House 273, page 304A.).

Children of **Louis Thifault** and **Mary Rose Renville** were as follows:

    i.   Louis Thifault was born in 1899 (1936-TMC, page 116.).

    ii.   Frank J. Thifault was born on 20 Jun 1905 (Ibid.). He married Mabel Morin, daughter of Alexander Morin and Marie Isabelle Belgarde, before 1928. He died on 14 Apr 1959 Seattle, King County, Washington, at age 53 (Washington State Digital Archives, Secretary of State, State Archives, http://www.digitalcarchives.wa./gov, 960 Washington Street, Cheney, WA 99004.).

        Mabel Morin was born on 14 Dec 1908 (Ancestry.com Website, U.S. Indian Census Schedules, 1885-1940.). She married **Joseph Paul St.Germaine**, son of **Elie St.Germain** and **Theresa Rainville,** on 19 Sep 1942 Sidney, Richland County, Montana (RLCM Richland County Courthouse, Montana; Marriage Record Licenses and Certificates; 1865-1950, familysearch.org, Hereinafter cited as RLCM.).

    iii.   Josephine Thifault was born in 1908 (1936-TMC, page 117.). She married Ralph Boe before 1927 (*1937-TMC*, page 71, Census No. 804-806.).

    iv.   St.Ann Thifault was born on 23 Feb 1910 (BIA-TM-BMD, page 33.) (1936-TMC, page 100.) (BIA-TM-BMD, page 34.). She married Marie Jules Gosselin, son of Joseph Gosselin and Marie Rose Fagnant, before 1934 (1936-TMC, page 100.).

        Marie Jules Gosselin was born on 18 Nov 1899 Willow Bunch, (Saskatchewan) (SIWB St.Ignace Roman Catholic Registre des Baptemes, Mariages & Sepltures, Willow Bunch, Saskatchewan, 1882-1917, FHC #1290091., B-21, page 35. Hereinafter cited as SIWB.). He was baptized on 19 Nov 1899 St.Ignace, Willow Bunch, (Saskatchewan) (Ibid.).

    v.   William J. Thifault (born on 18 May 1912 (ND Death Index.). He died on 20 May 1912 Rolette, North Dakota (Ibid.).

    vi.   Andrew Thifault was born on 26 Feb 1914 (1936-TMC, page 117.) (*1937-TMC*, page 487, Census No. 5694-5696.).

    vii.   John Thifault was born before 1915 (1936-TMC, page 117.). He died before 1938 (Ibid.).

Descendants of John Thomas

Generation One

  1. John Thomas was born circa 1751 London, England (HBCA-B Hudson's Bay Company Archives - biographical sketches, Hudson's Bay Company Archives; Winnipeg, Manitoba.). He married according to the custom of the country **Margaret (--?--)** before 1776. He died on 9 Jun 1822 Vaudreuil County, Quebec (Denney Papers, Charles D. Denney, Glenbow Archives, Calgary, Alberta.) (HBCA-B.). Question: *Are some of the last born children actually grandchildren?* (Ibid.).

Margaret (--?--) died on 31 Dec 1813 (Ibid.).

Children of **John Thomas** and **Margaret (--?--)** were as follows:

2	i.	Elizabeth Thomas, m. Richard Story Robins.
	ii.	Margaret Thomas.
	iii.	Frances Thomas married Andrew Stewart (Ibid., C.1/394.).
3	iv.	John Thomas Jr., b. circa 1776; m. Mary Indian; d. 3 Jun 1816 Moose Factory.
4	v.	Charlotte Thomas, b. 2 Jun 1778; m. John George McTavish; m. Peter Spence; d. 17 May 1843.
5	vi.	Eleanor Thomas, b. 22 Nov 1780; m. Peter Foy; m. Thomas Thomas; m. William Richards.

vii. Mary Thomas was born on 23 Jul 1791 (HBCA-B.). She died on 24 Oct 1802 at age 11 (Ibid.).

6 viii. Charles Thomas, b. 9 Sep 1793 Hudson's Bay.

7 ix. Ann Thomas, b. 29 Dec 1795 Moose Factory; m. Alexander Christie.

x. Edward Thomas was born on 5 Feb 1801 (Ibid.). He died on 25 Jul 1802 at age 1 (Ibid.).

xi. Richard Edward Thomas was born on 13 Feb 1803 (Ibid.). He died on 16 Dec 1803 (Ibid.).

xii. Jane Thomas was born on 29 Oct 1804 (Ibid.). She died on 1 Sep 1806 at age 1 (Ibid.).

xiii. Henry Thomas was born after 1805 (Ibid., A.32/3 fo. 156.).

Generation Two

2. Elizabeth Thomas married **Richard Story Robins** (Ibid., C.1/394.).

Children of **Elizabeth Thomas** and **Richard Story Robins** are:

i. Richard Story Robins married Hannah Schneider (HBCA-B.).

3. John Thomas Jr was born circa 1776. He married according to the custom of the country **Mary Indian** before 1814. He died on 3 Jun 1816 Moose Factory (Ibid., A.44/2.).

Mary Indian was born in 1800 Moose Factory. She was baptized on 27 Dec 1831 St.Johns, Red River Settlement, (Manitoba) (HBCR Hudson Bay Company Register of Anglican Church Baptisms, Marriages, and Burials for the Red River Settlement, 1821-1841; Hudson's Bay Company Archives, Winnipeg, Manitoba, E.4/1a, folio 86d. Hereinafter cited as HBCR.). She married according to the custom of the country **Richard Stevens**, son of **Henry Stevens**, circa 1819. She married **Richard Stevens**, son of **Henry Stevens**, on 27 Nov 1827 St.Johns, (Manitoba) (Ibid., M-135.).

Children of **John Thomas Jr.** and **Mary Indian** were:

8 i. Charles Thomas, b. 6 Feb 1814; m. Mary Bouvier; d. 28 Apr 1904 RM St.Andrews, Manitoba.

4. Charlotte Thomas was born on 2 Jun 1778 (HBCA-B.). She married according to the custom of the country **John George McTavish**, son of (--?--) **McTavish**, circa 1805 Moose Factory (Ibid., E. Mitchell, "Fort Timiscaming, p. 70, 74.) (*DCB-V7 Dictionary of Canadian Biography: Volume Seven*; Toronto, Ontario: University of Toronto Press, 2000.). She married **Peter Spence** on 8 Nov 1819 (HBCA-B.). She died on 17 May 1843 at age 64 (Ibid.).

John George McTavish was born circa 1778 Scotland (*DCB-V7.*). He married according to the custom of the country **Nancy McKenzie**, daughter of **Roderick McKenzie** and **Indian Woman,** circa 1813 (Denney.). He married **Catherine Turner** on 22 Feb 1830 (Ibid.) (HBCA-B.). He married **Elizabeth Cameron** in Mar 1843 (Denney.). He died on 20 Jul 1847 Montreal, Montreal, Quebec (Ibid.) (HBCA-B, Dec 1999.).

Peter Spence was born circa 1777 Brisay, Orkney, Scotland (HBCA-B.). He died on 2 Nov 1855 (Ibid.).

5. Eleanor Thomas was born on 22 Nov 1780 (Ibid.). She married **Peter Foy** (Ibid.). She married **Thomas Thomas** (Ibid.). She married **William Richards** before 1808 (Ibid.).

Question: *She also married Thomas Thomas, Children: Henry and Richard (Will, SF, Thomas John Sr.)* (Ibid.).

6. Charles Thomas was born on 9 Sep 1793 Hudson's Bay (Ibid.). He was baptized on 7 Apr 1828 St.Johns, Red River Colony, (Manitoba) (HBCR, E.4/1a, folio 69d.).

Children of **Charles Thomas** include:

i. Daniel Thomas was born in 1838 (HBCA-B, See R. L. Taylor, The Beaver, Dec. 1939, p. 35.). He died in 1942 (Ibid.).

7. Ann Thomas was born on 29 Dec 1795 Moose Factory (Denney.). She married **Alexander Christie** on 10 Feb 1835 St.Johns, Red River Settlement, (Manitoba) (HBCR, No. 293.).

Alexander Christie was born circa 1783 Aberdeen, Scotland (HBCA-B.). He died on 9 Dec 1872 Edinburgh, Scotland (Denney.) (HBCA-B, A.36/4.).

Generation Three

8. Charles Thomas was born on 6 Feb 1814 (Automated Genealogy 1901 Census Transcription Project and Census Images from the National Archives of Canada, http://www.automatedgenealogy.com, Family 31, Line 36-41.). He was born circa 1820 Nor-West (1870C-MB 1870 Manitoba Census, National Archives of Canada, Ottawa, Ontario, Microfilm Reel Number C-2170., page 136, #1153.). He was baptized on 7 Apr 1828 St.Johns, (Manitoba) (HBCR, HBC Baptisms; #740.). He married **Mary Bouvier**, daughter of **Jean Baptiste Bouvier** and **Marguerite Laurent or Crise**, before 1834. He died on 28 Apr 1904 RM St.Andrews, Manitoba, at age 90 (HBCA-B, A.12/S 525/1b f. 57.) (Manitoba Vital Statistics online, http://web2.gov.mb.ca, Death Reg. #1904,003543.).

Mary Bouvier was born circa 1817 Nor-West (1870C-MB, page 137, #1154.). She died on 8 Jul 1873 (Denney.). Question: *She was called the daughter of Patrick Bouvier in the 1870 census* (1870C-MB, page 136-137, #1153-1160.).

Children of **Charles Thomas** and **Mary Bouvier** were as follows:

10 i. Mary Thomas, b. 29 Sep 1834 North West; m. Richard William Thomas; d. 2 Nov 1896 St.Clements, Manitoba.

11 ii. Eleanor Thomas, b. 6 Sep 1838 North West; m. Donald McLean.

12 iii. Catherine Thomas, b. 12 Apr 1846 North West; m. Jeremiah Cooper; d. 12 Mar 1913 St.Andrews, Manitoba.

13 iv. Nancy Thomas, b. 8 Jul 1848; m. Louis Deschambault dit Fleury.

v. John Thomas was born on 29 Jul 1850 North West (MBS Scrip Applications, Original White Settlers & Halfbreeds residing in Manitoba on 15 July 1870, RG15-19, C-14934.).

14 vi. George Thomas, b. 17 Feb 1852 North West.

15 vii. Daniel Thomas, b. 12 Mar 1853 North West.

16 viii. Annabella Thomas, b. 27 Feb 1855 North West; m. William Sinclair dit McLeod.

ix. Henry Thomas was born in Nov 1856 North West (Ibid.). He married Anna Flett, daughter of John Flett and Nancy West, on 22 Mar 1882 St.Boniface, Manitoba (RMSB *Repertoire des Mariages de Saint-Boniface (Manitoba) 1825-1983* compiled by Julien Hamelin S.C., (240, avenue Daly; Ottawa, Ontario K1N 6G2: Le Centre de Genealogie S. C., Publication #67, 1985), page 461.).

x. Richard Thomas was born on 17 Feb 1858 North West (MBS, C-14934.).

9. Richard Thomas was born circa 1800 Albany, Hudsons Bay (1838C RRS HBCA E5/9 1838 Census of the Red River Settlement, HBCA E5/9, Hudson's Bay Company Archives, Provincial Archives, 200 Vaughan Street, Winnipeg, MB R3C 1T5, Canada., page 30.) (HBCA-B.). He was baptized on 13 Nov 1837 St.Johns, Red River Settlement, (Manitoba) (Ibid., E.4/1a, fo. 146d.) (HBCR, E.4/1a, folio 146d.). He married according to the custom of the country **Eleonore Thomas** before 1832. He married **Eleonore Thomas** on 21 Dec 1837 Red River Settlement, (Manitoba) (HBCA-B, E.4/1b, fo. 252d.) (HBCR, No. 374.).

Question: *Is Richard the son of Thomas and Eleanor Thomas?*

Eleonore Thomas was born circa 1807. She was baptized on 13 Nov 1837 (St.Peters), Red River Settlement, (Manitoba) (HBCA-B, E.4/1a, fo. 146d.) (HBCR, E.4/1a, folio 146d.).

Children of **Richard Thomas** and **Eleonore Thomas** were as follows:

17   i.   Louisa Thomas, b. 1832 North West; m. William Smith.

18   ii.   Richard William Thomas, b. 7 May 1834 North West; m. Mary Thomas; d. 2 Nov 1923 R.M. of St.Clements, Manitoba.

19   iii.   Margaret Thomas, b. 12 Mar 1837 St.Andrews, (Manitoba); m. Robert Peebles; m. Peter Hourie.

        iv.   Mathilda Thomas was baptized on 13 Nov 1837 St.Johns, Red River Settlement, (Manitoba) (HBCA-B, E.4/1a, fo. 146d.) (HBCR, E.4/1a, folio 146d.).

        v.   Charles Thomas was baptized on 13 Nov 1837 St.Johns, Red River Settlement, (Manitoba) (HBCA-B, E.4/1a, fo. 146d.) (HBCR, E.4/1a, folio 147d.).

        vi.   Alexander Thomas was baptized on 27 Nov 1837 St.Johns, Red River Settlement, (Manitoba) (Ibid.).

20   vii.   Nancy Thomas, b. 21 May 1845 St.Andrews, (Manitoba); m. John Favel; d. 20 Jan 1913 St.Andrews, Manitoba.

21   viii.   Henry Thomas, b. 9 Feb 1848 St.Andrews, (Manitoba); m. Charlotte Parisien.

Generation Four

10. Mary Thomas was born on 29 Sep 1834 North West (MBS, C-14934.). She married **Richard William Thomas**, son of **Richard Thomas** and **Eleonore Thomas,** before 1859. She died on 2 Nov 1896 St.Clements, Manitoba, at age 62 (MB Vital Statistics, Death Reg. #1896,001867.).

Richard William Thomas was born on 7 May 1834 North West (MBS, C-14934.). He was baptized on 13 Nov 1837 St.Johns, Red River Settlement, (Manitoba) (HBCA-B, E.4/1a, fo. 146d.) (HBCR, E.4/1a, folio 146d.). He died on 2 Nov 1923 R.M. of St.Clements, Manitoba, at age 89 (MB Vital Statistics, Death Reg. #1923,044442.).

Children of **Mary Thomas** and **Richard William Thomas** were as follows:

        i.   Catherine Thomas was born circa 1859 (Manitoba) (1870C-MB, page 136, #1149.).

22   ii.   Mathilda Thomas, b. 11 Mar 1862; m. Alexander Anderson.

23   iii.   John George Thomas, b. 5 Oct 1866.

24   iv.   Alexander Thomas, b. 10 Jun 1869 St.Andrews, (Manitoba); m. Helene Thomas.

        v.   James Henry Thomas was born on 28 Dec 1872 Grand Marais (ArchiviaNet 1886-1901, 1906 Half-Breed Scrip Applications Index, RG15-21, Volume 1333 through 1371, Microfilm Reel Number C-14944 through C-15010, National Archives of Canada, Ottawa, Ontario, http://www.collectionscanada.gc.ca, C-15006.). He married Catherine Mary Thomas, daughter of Daniel Thomas and Sophie Linklater, between 1895 and 1896 (Ibid.).

            Catherine Mary Thomas was born on 28 Jan 1879 Cumberland, (Saskatchewan) (Ibid.). She married **James Pritchard Dennett**, son of **Gilbert J. Dennett** and **Harriet Folster,** on 15 Feb 1904 Fort Alexandre, Manitoba (FTA Repertoire des Mariages du Fort Alexandre et Missions 1878-1955: Fort Alexandre (FTA), Manigotagan, Hole River; Compilation Agnes Labossiere, Verification Alfred Fortier; St.Boniface, Manitoba: La Cosiete Historique de Saint-Boniface, 1985.). She died in 1966.

        vi.   Mary Ann Thomas was born in 1874 Grand Marais (ArchiviaNet, C-15006.). She died in 1877 Grand Marais (Ibid.).

        vii.   Alice Thomas was born between Apr 1877 and Apr 1878 Grand Marais (Ibid.). She died between Jul 1877 and Jul 1878 Grand Marais (Ibid.).

        viii.   Louis Thomas was born circa Apr 1879 Grand Marais (Ibid.). He died circa Apr 1879 Grand Marais (Ibid.).

        ix.   William R. Thomas was born on 8 Apr 1882 Grand Marais (Ibid.) (1901 Canada, District 11-m-5, page 2, family 16, line 33-36.).

        x.   Phillip Thomas was born on 11 Apr 1885 R. M. of St.Clements, Manitoba (Ibid.) (MB Vital Statistics, Birth Reg. #1885,3919.).

11. Eleanor Thomas was born on 6 Sep 1838 North West (MBS, C-14931.). She married **Donald McLean**, son of **Donald McLean,** before 1858.

Donald McLean was born circa 1823 Scotland (1870C-MB, page 180, #116.).

12. Catherine Thomas was born on 12 Apr 1846 North West (MBS, C-14932.) (1901 Canada, Family 31, Line 36-39.). She married **Jeremiah Cooper**, son of **Charles Thomas Cooper** and **Catherine Thomas,** on 16 Jul 1863 St.Andrews, (Manitoba) (Denney.). She died on 12 Mar 1913 St.Andrews, Manitoba, at age 66 (MB Vital Statistics, Death Reg. #1913,015539.).

Jeremiah Cooper was born on 3 Feb 1842 St.Andrews, (Manitoba) (MBS, C-14926.) (1901 Canada, Family 31, Line 36-39.). He died on 29 Dec 1904 St.Andrews, Manitoba, at age 62 (MB Vital Statistics, Death Reg. #1904,001949.).

13. Nancy Thomas was born in 1846 Lac Caribou (NWHBS 1885 Scrip Applications, North-West Halfbreeds residing outside Manitoba on 15 July 1870, RG15-20, C-14942.). She was born on 8 Jul 1848 (SJCH Mission of St.Joseph, Cumberland House; Registre de Baptemes, de Mariages, et de Sepultures, B-7, page 2. Hereinafter cited as SJCH.). She was baptized on 16 Jun 1850 St.Joseph, Cumberland House, (Saskatchewan) (Ibid.). She married **Louis Deschambault dit Fleury**, son of **George Fleury Deschambault** and **Marguerite Loyer or McKenzie,** between 1864 and 1866 Fort Cumberland (NWHBS, C-14942.) (Ibid., C-14937.).

Louis Deschambault dit Fleury was born in 1844 McKenzie River (Ibid.).

14. George Thomas was born on 17 Feb 1852 North West (MBS, C-14934.). He married **Adelaide Moran**, daughter of **Pierre Moran** and **Genevieve Roy,** before 1873.

Adelaide Moran was born on 10 Mar 1857 (1901 Canada, District 11(m-5), page 2, famiy 18, line 40-43.).

Children of **George Thomas** and **Adelaide Moran** were as follows:

      i. Joseph George Thomas was born on 20 Dec 1873 Deer's Lake (ArchiviaNet, C-15006.). He died circa Apr 1875 St.Andrews, Manitoba (Ibid.).

25   ii. Pierre Richard "Peter" Thomas, b. Dec 1875 Devil's Lake; m. Elodie Bruyere.

26 iii. Helene Thomas, b. circa 1878; m. Joseph Morisseau; m. Alexander Thomas.

27 iv. Nancy Thomas, b. circa 1879; m. Louis Fontaine; m. Jean Baptiste Guimond.

      v. George Thomas Jr was born on 11 Jun 1881 Deer's Lake (Ibid.).

28 vi. Philip Thomas, b. 11 Jun 1881 Deer's Lake, Cumberland House, (Saskatchewan); m. Marguerite Nancy Thomas.

   vii. Josephine Thomas was born on 15 Apr 1883 Deer's Lake (Ibid.). She died in Aug 1885 Deer's Lake at age 2 (Ibid.).

29 viii. Mary Josephine Thomas, b. 12 Jun 1884 Deer's Lake; m. William Orvis.

    ix. Joseph Thomas was born in May 1901 (Automated Genealogy 1911 Census Transcription Project and Census Images from the National Archives of Canada, http://www.automatedgenealogy.com, District 29, page 3, family 12, line 23-27.).

15. Daniel Thomas was born circa 1838 Lac du Brochet (HBCA-B.). He was born on 12 Mar 1853 North West (MBS, C-14934.). He married **Sophie Linklater**, daughter of **Peter Linklater** and **Marie Morin,** before 1875.

Sophie Linklater was born circa 1861 (Automated Genealogy 1906 Census Transcription Project and Census Images from the National Archives of Canada, http://www.automatedgenealogy.com, District 8-6, page 64, family 489, line 7-12.).

Children of **Daniel Thomas** and **Sophie Linklater** were as follows:

      i. Thomas Thomas was born in 1875 Cumberland District, (Saskatchewan) (ArchiviaNet, C-15006.). He married Adeline Courchene, daughter of Maxime Courchene and Elise Bruyere, on 16 Feb 1897 Fort Alexandre, Manitoba (*Fort Alexandre Mariages*.). He died in 1900 Balsam Bay (ArchiviaNet, C-15006.).

         Adeline Courchene was born circa 1875 Manitoba (1881 Church of Latter Day Saints Census Transcription Project of Census Images from the National Archives of Canada, Ottawa, Canada, http://www.familysearch.org, Film #C-13283, District 186, Sub-district C, page #69, Household #334.). She married **Donald Sinclair,** son of **William Sinclair** and **(--?--) Dennet,** on 14 Jan 1902 Fort Alexandre, Manitoba (*Fort Alexandre Mariages*.).

     ii. Peter Thomas was born in Jun 1876 Cumberland, (Saskatchewan) (ArchiviaNet, C-15006.). He died in 1898 Balsam Bay (Ibid.).

   iii. Catherine Mary Thomas was born on 28 Jan 1879 Cumberland, (Saskatchewan) (Ibid.). She married James Henry Thomas, son of Richard William Thomas and Mary Thomas, between 1895 and 1896 (Ibid.). She married James Pritchard Dennett, son of Gilbert J. Dennett and Harriet Folster, on 15 Feb 1904 Fort Alexandre, Manitoba (*Fort Alexandre Mariages*.). She died in 1966.

         James Henry Thomas was born on 28 Dec 1872 Grand Marais (ArchiviaNet, C-15006.).

         James Pritchard Dennett was born in Oct 1881 Manitoba (1891 Census of Canada from the National Archives of Canada, Ottawa, Canada, page 5, family 19, line 6-8.) (1901 Canada, District 11-04-q(3), page 5, line 29.). He died in 1965.

30 iv. Edward Daniel Thomas, b. 14 Feb 1881 Devil's Lake; m. Eugenie Morisseau.

     v. Sophia Thomas was born on 2 Apr 1883 Cumberland, (Saskatchewan) (ArchiviaNet, C-15006.). She died in 1900 Balsam Bay (Ibid.).

31 vi. Marguerite Nancy Thomas, b. 15 Aug 1885 Cumberland District, (Saskatchewan); m. Philip Thomas.

   vii. Joseph Thomas was born circa 1893 (1911 Canada, District 8-6, page 64, family 489, line 7-12.).

32 viii. Virginie Thomas, b. circa 1893; m. Charles Fontaine.

33 ix. Sarah Thomas, b. circa 1896; m. John Georges Guimond.

     x. Marie Thomas was born circa 1904 (1906 Canada, District 8-6, page 64, family 489, line 7-12.). She married Peter Parisien, son of John Georges Parisien and Suzanne Guimond, on 18 Oct 1922 Fort Alexandre, Manitoba (*Fort Alexandre Mariages*.).

16. Annabella Thomas was born on 27 Feb 1855 North West (MBS, C-14934.). She married **William Sinclair dit McLeod,** son of **William Sinclair** and **Mathilda 'Hilda' Fidler,** circa 1876 (HBS 1886-1901, 1906 Half-Breed Scrip Applications, RG15-21, Volume 1338, C-14954.).

Children of **Annabella Thomas** include:

      i. Louisa Thomas was born in May 1876 Grand Marais, Manitoba (Ibid.). She was baptized on 9 Jun 1876 Netley Creek Mission (Ibid.). She married Arthur Henry Buckmaster on 20 Aug 1896 Whitemouth, Manitoba (Ibid.).

         Arthur Henry Buckmaster was born circa 1872 London, England (Ibid.).

William Sinclair dit McLeod was born on 15 Dec 1853 (Manitoba) (1901 Canada, District 11-q-2, page 17, family 159, line 4-13.). He was born on 15 Mar 1857 St.Clements, (Manitoba) (MBS, C-14933.).

17. Louisa Thomas was born circa 1828 (Manitoba) (1870C-MB, page 193, #524.). She was born in 1832 North West (MBS, C-14934.). She was baptized on 27 Nov 1837 St.Johns, Red River Settlement, (Manitoba) (HBCR, E.4/1a, folio 147d.). She married **William Smith,** son of **John James Smith** and **Mary Indian,** before 1867.

William Smith was born in 1823 North West (MBS, C-14934.). He was baptized on 12 Jul 1825 St.Johns, Red River Settlement, (Manitoba) (HBCR, E.4/1a, folio 56d.). He married **Charlotte Mowat,** daughter of **Edward Mowat** and **Margaret Indian,** on 12 Feb 1850 St.Andrews, (Manitoba) (Ibid., No. 194.). He died on 18 Apr 1884 St.Andrews, Manitoba (MB Vital Statistics, Death Reg. #1884,002480.).

18. Richard William Thomas was born on 7 May 1834 North West (MBS, C-14934.). He was baptized on 13 Nov 1837 St.Johns, Red River Settlement, (Manitoba) (HBCA-B, E.4/1a, fo. 146d.) (HBCR, E.4/1a, folio 146d.). He married **Mary Thomas,** daughter of

Charles Thomas and **Mary Bouvier,** before 1859. He died on 2 Nov 1923 R.M. of St.Clements, Manitoba, at age 89 (MB Vital Statistics, Death Reg. #1923,044442.).

Mary Thomas was born on 29 Sep 1834 North West (MBS, C-14934.). She died on 2 Nov 1896 St.Clements, Manitoba, at age 62 (MB Vital Statistics, Death Reg. #1896,001867.).

Children of **Richard William Thomas** and **Mary Thomas** were as follows:

    i.   Catherine Thomas, b. circa 1859 (Manitoba). (see previous).

    ii.   Mathilda Thomas, b. 11 Mar 1862; m. Alexander Anderson. (see # 22).

    iii.   John George Thomas, b. 5 Oct 1866. (see # 23).

    iv.   Alexander Thomas, b. 10 Jun 1869 St.Andrews, (Manitoba); m. Helene Thomas. (see # 24).

    v.   James Henry Thomas, b. 28 Dec 1872 Grand Marais; m. Catherine Mary Thomas. (see previous).

    vi.   Mary Ann Thomas, b. 1874 Grand Marais; d. 1877 Grand Marais. (see previous).

    vii.   Alice Thomas, b. between Apr 1877 and Apr 1878 Grand Marais; d. between Jul 1877 and Jul 1878 Grand Marais. (see previous).

    viii.   Louis Thomas, b. circa Apr 1879 Grand Marais; d. circa Apr 1879 Grand Marais. (see previous).

    ix.   William R. Thomas, b. 8 Apr 1882 Grand Marais. (see previous).

    x.   Phillip Thomas, b. 11 Apr 1885 R. M. of St.Clements, Manitoba. (see previous).

19. Margaret Thomas was born on 12 Mar 1837 St.Andrews, (Manitoba) (MBS, C-14929.). She was baptized on 22 Mar 1839 St.Johns, Red River Settlement, (Manitoba) (HBCR, E.4/1a, folio 159d.). She married **Robert Peebles,** son of **James Peebles** and **Nancy Ann Indian,** before 1861. She married **Peter Hourie,** son of **Robert Hourie** and **Christiana Anderson,** before 1875.

Robert Peebles was baptized on 29 Nov 1836 St.Johns, Red River Settlement, (Manitoba) (Ibid., E.4/1a, folio 134.).

Peter Hourie was born in 1849 St.Clements, (Manitoba) (MBS, C-14929.). He married **Nancy (--?--)** before 1871. He married **Elizabeth Sanderson,** daughter of **William Saunders or Sanderson** and **Mary McNab,** circa 1884.

20. Nancy Thomas was born on 21 May 1845 St.Andrews, (Manitoba) (MBS, C-14927.). She married **John Favel,** son of **Samuel Favel** and **Margaret Kipling,** before 1867. She died on 20 Jan 1913 St.Andrews, Manitoba, at age 67 (MB Vital Statistics, Death Reg. #1913,006373.).

John Favel was born in Aug 1843 (MBS, C-14927.). He was baptized on 15 Aug 1843 St.Johns, (Manitoba) (Denney.). He died on 22 Feb 1893 St.Andrews, Manitoba, at age 49 (MB Vital Statistics, Death Reg. #1893,002450.).

21. Henry Thomas was born on 9 Feb 1848 St.Andrews, (Manitoba) (MBS, C-14934.). He married **Charlotte Parisien,** daughter of **Baptiste Parisien** and **Margaret Destempt,** before 1870.

Charlotte Parisien was born in Oct 1848 St.Peters, (Manitoba) (Ibid.).

Children of **Henry Thomas** and **Charlotte Parisien** were as follows:

    i.   Margaret Jane Thomas was born on 22 May 1870 Little Britain, (Manitoba) (Ibid.). She was baptized on 22 May 1870 St.Andrews, (Manitoba) (Ibid.). She died on 22 May 1888 Manitoba at age 18 (Denney.). She was buried in May 1888 St.Jean Baptiste, Manitoba (Ibid.).

    ii.   Ellen Thomas was born circa 1873 (1881 Canada, District 185-C-2, page 24, house 128.).

    iii.   Louison Thomas was born circa 1874 (Ibid.).

34   iv.   Isabella Thomas, b. circa 1876; m. John George Thomas.

35   v.   Henry George Thomas, b. 15 Apr 1876 Grand Marais; m. Mary Ann Anderson.

    vi.   William Richard Thomas was born on 2 Feb 1880 Grand Marais (Ibid.) (ArchiviaNet, C-15006.).

36   vii.   Robert Alexander Tache Thomas, b. 30 Jun 1882 Grand Marais; m. Jessie Knott.

Generation Five

22. Mathilda Thomas was born circa 1860 (Manitoba) (1870C-MB, page 136, #1150.). She was born on 11 Mar 1862 (1901 Canada, District 11-M-5, page 2, family 13, line 12-23.). She married **Alexander Anderson,** son of **James Anderson** and **Elizabeth "Betsey" Isbister,** on 12 Feb 1883 St.Andrews, Manitoba (NWHBSI, page 101.) (MB Vital Statistics, Marriage Reg. #1883,001450.).

Alexander Anderson was born in 1862 (NWHBSI, page 101.). He was born on 12 Feb 1865 (1901 Canada, District 11-M-5, page 2, family 13, line 12-23.).

23. John George Thomas was born on 5 Oct 1866 (Ibid., District 11-q-3, page 2, family 14, line 4-11.). He married **Isabella Thomas,** daughter of **Henry Thomas** and **Charlotte Parisien,** in 1895 Grand Marais (ArchiviaNet, C-15006.).

Isabella Thomas was born circa 1876 (1881 Canada, District 185-C-2, page 24, house 128.) (1901 Canada, District 11-q-3, page 2, family 14, line 4-11.).

Children of **John George Thomas** and **Isabella Thomas** were as follows:

    i.   Anne Frances Thomas was born on 3 Dec 1895 R.M. of St.Clements, Manitoba (Ibid.) (MB Vital Statistics, Birth Reg. #1895,001182.).

    ii.   Alfred Thomas was born on 23 Aug 1898 R.M. of St.Clements, Manitoba (1901 Canada, District 11-q-3, page 2, family 14, line 4-11.) (MB Vital Statistics, Birth Reg. #1898,20616431; Reg. Date: 23/04/1958.).

    iii.   Alice Thomas was born on 9 Jun 1900 (1901 Canada, District 11-q-3, page 2, family 14, line 4-11.).

    iv.   Walter George Thomas was born on 25 Jun 1902 Balsam Bay, Manitoba (1911 Canada, District 29, page 3, family 10, line 5-14.) (MB Vital Statistics, Birth Reg. #1902,007993; Reg. Date: 22/07/1902.).

    v.   Charles Thomas was born on 30 Apr 1904 Grand Rapids, Manitoba (1911 Canada, District 29, page 3, family 10, line 5-14.) (MB Vital Statistics, Birth Reg. #1904,24323919; Reg. Date: 13/05/1968.).

    vi.   Arthur Thomas was born in May 1906 (1911 Canada, District 29, page 3, family 10, line 5-14.).

    vii.   Stanley Thomas was born on 11 Feb 1908 R.M. of St.Clements, Manitoba (Ibid.) (MB Vital Statistics, Birth Reg. #1908,004517.).

    viii.   Rachel Thomas was born on 3 Mar 1910 R.M. of St.Clements, Manitoba (1911 Canada, District 29, page 3, family 10, line 5-14.) (MB Vital Statistics, Birth Reg. #1910,010896.).

    ix.   Howard Thomas was born on 13 Jul 1912 R.M. of St.Clements, Manitoba (Ibid., Birth Reg. #1912,006281.).

24. Alexander Thomas was born on 10 Jun 1869 St.Andrews, (Manitoba) (1870C-MB, page 136, #1152.) (1901 Canada, District 11-m-5, page 2, family 16, line 33-36.). He married **Helene Thomas**, daughter of **George Thomas** and **Adelaide Moran,** on 15 Jan 1906 Fort Alexandre, Manitoba (*Fort Alexandre Mariages.*).

Helene Thomas was born circa 1878 (1906 Canada, District 8, page 108,family 79, lin4 2-11.). She married **Joseph Morisseau**, son of **Jacob Morisseau** and **Catherine Guimond,** on 17 Feb 1896 Fort Alexandre, Manitoba (*Fort Alexandre Mariages.*).

Children of **Alexander Thomas** and **Helene Thomas** are as follows:
     i. Phillip Thomas was born in Aug 1905 (1911 Canada, District 29, page 3, family 11, line 15-22.).
    ii. Matilda Thomas was born in Oct 1907 (Ibid.).
    iii. Alexander G. Thomas was born in Apr 1911 (Ibid.).

25. Pierre Richard "Peter" Thomas was born in Dec 1875 Devil's Lake (ArchiviaNet, C-15006.). He married **Elodie Bruyere**, daughter of **Jean Baptiste Bruyere** and **Agnes Greenleaf,** on 26 Apr 1897 Fort Alexandre, Manitoba (*Fort Alexandre Mariages.*).

Elodie Bruyere was born in Sep 1879 Balsam Bay (ArchiviaNet, C-15006.).

Children of **Pierre Richard "Peter" Thomas** and **Elodie Bruyere** are as follows:
     i. Johnny Thomas married Margaret Sinclair, daughter of Frederick Sinclair and Barbara McLeod, on 9 Jun 1921 Fort Alexandre, Manitoba (*Fort Alexandre Mariages.*).
        Margaret Sinclair was born on 30 Oct 1900 Grand Rapids, (Saskatchewan) (1901 Canada, Grand Rapids, page 1, Family 10, Line 46-50.).
    ii. Evangeline Thomas was born of Traverse Bay. She married Paul Alexandre Bruyere, son of Serge Bruyere and Sophie Courchene, on 29 Oct 1919 Fort Alexandre, Manitoba (*Fort Alexandre Mariages.*).
        Paul Alexandre Bruyere married **Josephine Potvin**, daughter of **Joseph Potvin** and **Catherine Sinclair,** on 7 Feb 1932 Fort Alexandre, Manitoba (Ibid.).

26. Helene Thomas was born circa 1878 (1906 Canada, District 8, page 108,family 79, lin4 2-11.). She married **Joseph Morisseau**, son of **Jacob Morisseau** and **Catherine Guimond,** on 17 Feb 1896 Fort Alexandre, Manitoba (*Fort Alexandre Mariages.*). She married **Alexander Thomas**, son of **Richard William Thomas** and **Mary Thomas,** on 15 Jan 1906 Fort Alexandre, Manitoba (Ibid.).

Alexander Thomas was born on 10 Jun 1869 St.Andrews, (Manitoba) (1870C-MB, page 136, #1152.) (1901 Canada, District 11-m-5, page 2, family 16, line 33-36.).

27. Nancy Thomas was born circa 1879 (Ibid., District 56, page 27, family 355, line 43-48.). She married **Louis Fontaine**, son of **Moise Fontaine** and **Francoise Guimond,** on 17 Apr 1896 Fort Alexandre, Manitoba (*Fort Alexandre Mariages.*). She married **Jean Baptiste Guimond**, son of **Andre Guimond** and **Therese Kent,** on 29 Nov 1926 Fort Alexandre, Manitoba (Ibid.).

Louis Fontaine was born circa 1873 (1911 Canada, District 56, page 27, family 355, line 43-48.).

Jean Baptiste Guimond was born on 9 May 1869 Fort Alexandre, (Manitoba) (SB-Rozyk, page 157, B-69.). He was baptized on 11 May 1869 (Fort Alexandre), St.Boniface, (Manitoba) (Ibid.). He married **Marie Chatelain**, daughter of **Jean Baptiste Chatelain** and **Marie Sinclair,** on 16 Jan 1890 Fort Alexandre, Manitoba (*Fort Alexandre Mariages.*).

28. Philip Thomas was born on 11 Jun 1881 Deer's Lake, Cumberland House, (Saskatchewan) (ArchiviaNet, C-15006.). He married **Marguerite Nancy Thomas**, daughter of **Daniel Thomas** and **Sophie Linklater,** on 29 Oct 1903 Fort Alexandre, Manitoba (*Fort Alexandre Mariages.*).

Marguerite Nancy Thomas was born on 15 Aug 1885 Cumberland District, (Saskatchewan) (ArchiviaNet, C-15006.).

Children of **Philip Thomas** and **Marguerite Nancy Thomas** are as follows:
     i. Eveline Thomas was born in Nov 1904 (1911 Canada, District 29, page 3, family 13, line 28-32.).
    ii. Laura Thomas was born in Mar 1908 (Ibid.).
    iii. Laurence Thomas was born in Apr 1910 (Ibid.).

29. Mary Josephine Thomas was born on 12 Jun 1884 Deer's Lake (ArchiviaNet, C-15006.). She married **William Orvis**, son of **John Benson Orvis** and **Isabella Irvine,** on 24 Jan 1906 Fort Alexandre, Manitoba (*Fort Alexandre Mariages.*).

William Orvis was born on 13 Apr 1885 Cooks Creek, Manitoba (1901 Canada, #11, m-5, page 1-2, family 9, line 43-50, 1-2.) (MB Vital Statistics, Birth Reg. #1885,1688826, Date: 03/03/1950.).

30. Edward Daniel Thomas was born on 14 Feb 1881 Devil's Lake (ArchiviaNet, C-15006.). He married **Eugenie Morisseau**, daughter of **Jean Baptiste Morisseau** and **Julie Guimond,** on 2 Jun 1902 Fort Alexandre, Manitoba (*Fort Alexandre Mariages.*).

Eugenie Morisseau was born circa 1879 (1906 Canada, District 8-6, page 64, family 490, line 13-17.).

Children of **Edward Daniel Thomas** and **Eugenie Morisseau** are as follows:
     i. Edward F. Thomas was born circa 1904 (Ibid.).
    ii. Eva Thomas was born circa Apr 1906 (Ibid.).

31. Marguerite Nancy Thomas was born on 15 Aug 1885 Cumberland District, (Saskatchewan) (ArchiviaNet, C-15006.). She married **Philip Thomas**, son of **George Thomas** and **Adelaide Moran,** on 29 Oct 1903 Fort Alexandre, Manitoba (*Fort Alexandre Mariages.*).

Philip Thomas was born on 11 Jun 1881 Deer's Lake, Cumberland House, (Saskatchewan) (ArchiviaNet, C-15006.).

Children of **Marguerite Nancy Thomas** and **Philip Thomas** are as follows:
     i. Eveline Thomas was born in Nov 1904 (1911 Canada, District 29, page 3, family 13, line 28-32.).
    ii. Laura Thomas was born in Mar 1908 (Ibid.).
    iii. Laurence Thomas was born in Apr 1910 (Ibid.).

32. Virginie Thomas was born circa 1893 (1906 Canada, District 8-6, page 64, family 489, line 7-12.). She married **Charles Fontaine**, son of **Charles Fontaine** and **Therese Charbonneau,** on 19 Feb 1917 Fort Alexandre, Manitoba (*Fort Alexandre Mariages.*).

33. Sarah Thomas was born circa 1896 (1906 Canada, District 8-6, page 64, family 489, line 7-12.). She married **John Georges Guimond**, son of **Pierre Guimond** and **Suzanne Finlayson,** on 8 Nov 1916 Fort Alexandre, Manitoba (*Fort Alexandre Mariages.*).

34. Isabella Thomas was born circa 1876 (1881 Canada, District 185-C-2, page 24, house 128.) (1901 Canada, District 11-q-3, page 2, family 14, line 4-11.). She married **John George Thomas**, son of **Richard William Thomas** and **Mary Thomas,** in 1895 Grand Marais (ArchiviaNet, C-15006.).

John George Thomas was born on 5 Oct 1866 (1901 Canada, District 11-q-3, page 2, family 14, line 4-11.).

35. **Henry George Thomas** was born on 15 Apr 1876 Grand Marais (1881 Canada, District 185-C-2, page 24, house 128.). He married **Mary Ann Anderson**, daughter of **Alexander Anderson** and **Mathilda Thomas**, in Aug 1901 Grand Marais (ArchiviaNet, C-15006.). **Mary Ann Anderson** was born on 21 Feb 1884 Grand Marais (Ibid.) (1901 Canada, District 11-M-5, page 2, family 13, line 12-23.).
Children of **Henry George Thomas** and **Mary Ann Anderson** are as follows:

    i.   Norman Thomas was born circa 1901 (1906 Canada, District 8-6, page 64, family 497, line 35-39.).

    ii. Emily Thomas was born circa 1904 (Ibid.).

36. **Robert Alexander Tache Thomas** was born on 30 Jun 1882 Grand Marais (ArchiviaNet, C-15006.). He married **Jessie Knott**, daughter of **Alexander Knott** and **Barbara Linklater**, on 8 Jan 1903 St.Clements, Manitoba (MB Vital Statistics, Marriage Reg. #1903,003375.).
Jessie Knott was born on 13 Dec 1881 Grand Marais (HBSI.) (ArchiviaNet.).
Children of **Robert Alexander Tache Thomas** and **Jessie Knott** all born R.M. of St.Clements, Manitoba, were as follows:

    i.   Colin Thomas was born on 7 Oct 1903 (MB Vital Statistics, Birth Reg. #1903,003978.).

    ii. Allan Thomas was born on 19 Oct 1905 (Ibid., Birth Reg. #1905,002182.).

    iii. Mary Maud Thomas was born on 3 Sep 1910 (Ibid., Birth Reg. #1911,005992.). She married Frederick Herbert William Taylor Lawrence Pruden, son of Thomas Pruden and Isabel Taylor, on 3 Sep 1928 Selkirk, Manitoba (Ibid., Marriage Reg. #1928,043326.).

        Frederick Herbert William Taylor Lawrence Pruden was born on 1 Apr 1899 Selkirk, Manitoba (Denney.). He died on 6 Feb 1980 Comax, British Columbia, at age 80 (British Columbia Archives: Vital Statistics, http://search.bcarchives.gov.bc.ca.).

Descendants of Thomas Thomas

Generation One

1. **Thomas Thomas** was born circa 1765 St.Andrew, Hoborn, London, England (1827C RRS HBCA E5/1 1827 Census of the Red River Settlement, HBCA E5/1, Hudson's Bay Company Archives, Provincial Archives, 200 Vaughan Street, Winnipeg, MB R3C 1T5, Canada., page 2.) (HBCA-B Hudson's Bay Company Archives - biographical sketches, Hudson's Bay Company Archives; Winnipeg, Manitoba.). He married according to the custom of the country **Sarah Cree** before 1795. He married **Sarah Cree** on 30 Mar 1821 St.Johns, (Manitoba) (HBCR Hudson Bay Company Register of Anglican Church Baptisms, Marriages, and Burials for the Red River Settlement, 1821-1841; Hudson's Bay Company Archives, Winnipeg, Manitoba, M-20. Hereinafter cited as HBCR.) (HBCA-B, E.4/1b, fo. 195d; E.4/1a, fo. 41; E.42, fo. 151.). He died on 24 Nov 1828 Red River Settlement, (Manitoba) (Denney Papers, Charles D. Denney, Glenbow Archives, Calgary, Alberta.) (HBCA-B.). He was buried in Nov 1828 St.Johns, (Manitoba) (Denney.).
Sarah Cree was born circa 1781 Ruperts Land (1831C RRS HBCA E5/5 1831 Census of the Red River Settlement, HBCA E5/5, Hudson's Bay Company Archives, Provincial Archives, 200 Vaughan Street, Winnipeg, MB R3C 1T5, Canada., page 15.). She was born circa 1786 Ruperts Land (Denney.). She was baptized on 10 Nov 1822 St.Johns, Red River Colony, (Manitoba) (HBCA-B, E.4/1b, fo. 195d; E.4/1a, fo. 41; E.42, fo. 151.) (HBCR, E.4/1a, folio 41.). She died on 18 Aug 1846 Red River Settlement (MBS Scrip Applications, Original White Settlers & Halfbreeds residing in Manitoba on 15 July 1870, RG15-19.) (HBCA-B, E.4/1b, fo. 195d; E.4/1a, fo. 41; E.42, fo. 151.). She was buried in Aug 1846 St.Johns, (Manitoba) (Denney.).
Children of **Thomas Thomas** and **Sarah Cree** were as follows:

  2   i.   Frances Thomas, b. circa 1795; m. Henry Buxton; d. before 1843 Oregon.

  3   ii.   Mary Ann Thomas, b. circa 1800; m. George Bird.

  4   iii. Sophia Thomas, b. circa 1805 Ruperts Land; m. Rev. William Mason; d. 1858.

  5   iv. Elisabeth Thomas, b. 27 Jan 1805 Swan River District; m. Joseph Bird; d. 1846.

  6   v.   William Thomas, b. 17 Jun 1806 North West; m. Eleanor Bunn; d. 13 Apr 1875 St.Paul, Manitoba; bur. 14 Apr 1875 St.Paul, Manitoba.

  7   vi. Sarah Thomas, b. circa 1808; m. James Beardy.

  8   vii. Catherine Thomas, b. 1810; m. John Bunn; d. 7 Jan 1834 St.Johns, (Manitoba).

  9   viii. Jane Thomas, b. circa 1816; m. Levi Bird; d. 1841.

  10 ix. Thomas Thomas, b. circa 1819 Ruperts Land; m. Harriet Stewart; d. 12 Mar 1859 St.Paul, (Manitoba).

Generation Two

2. **Frances Thomas** was born circa 1795 (Ibid.). She was baptized on 10 Nov 1822 St.Johns, Red River Settlement, (Manitoba) (HBCA-B, E.4/1a, fo. 41-41d.) (HBCR, E.4/1a, folio 41d.). She married **Henry Buxton** on 12 Jun 1828 St.Johns, Red River Church, (Manitoba) (Ibid., M-152.). She died before 1843 Oregon (HBCA-B.).
Henry Buxton was born circa 1792 Stavley, Derbyshire, Derbyshire, England (Ibid.). He married **Sarah Munger** in 1843 Oregon (Ibid.). He died in 1870 (Ibid.).
3. **Mary Ann Thomas** was born circa 1800 (Denney.). She was baptized on 1 Feb 1825 St.Johns, Red River Colony, (Manitoba) (HBCA-B, E.4/1a, fo. 53.) (HBCR, E.4/1a, folio 53.). She married according to the custom of the country **George Bird**, son of **James Curtis Bird** and **Mary Indian**, before 1821 (Denney.). She married **George Bird**, son of **James Curtis Bird** and **Mary Indian**, on 23 Aug 1825 Red River Settlement, (Manitoba) (HBCR, M-97.).
George Bird was born circa 1797 Ruperts Land (1827C RRS HBCA E5/1, #58, page 3.). He was buried on 28 Feb 1855 St.Paul, (Manitoba) (AI-Rozyk Anglican Index of Baptisms, Marriages and Burials Extractions, Hudson Bay Company Archives, Winnipeg, Manitoba, Canada, Selected and Compiled by Rosemary Rozyk. Hereinafter cited as AI-Rozyk.). Question: *His death date was given as 18 Oct 1856* (Documents Relating to the North West Company: A Biographical Dictionary of the Nor'Westers, M.A. W. Stewart Wallace, Volume XXII;Toronto, Ontario, Canada: The Champlain Society, 1934, Volume XXII, page 426.).

4. **Sophia Thomas** was born circa 1805 Ruperts Land (Ibid.). She was baptized on 10 Nov 1822 St.Johns, Red River Settlement, (Manitoba) (HBCA-B, E.4/1a, fo. 41-41d.) (HBCR, E.4/1a, folio 41d.). She married **Rev. William Mason** on 10 Aug 1843 (St.Paul), Middle Church, Red River Settlement, (Manitoba) (Ibid., No. 367.). She died in 1858 (Denney.).

Rev. William Mason was born England (Ibid.).

5. **Elisabeth Thomas** was born on 27 Jan 1805 Swan River District (Ibid.). She was baptized on 12 Jan 1826 St.Johns, Red River Settlement, (Manitoba) (HBCA-B, E.4/1a, fo. 58d.) (HBCR, E.4/1a, folio 58d.). She married **Joseph Bird**, son of **James Curtis Bird** and **Mary Indian**, on 30 Mar 1821 (Fort Douglas), St.Johns, (Manitoba) (Ibid., M-17.). She died in 1846.

Joseph Bird was born in 1800 Ruperts Land (MBS, C-14925.) (1827C RRS HBCA E5/1, #57, page 3; age 28.) (1870C-MB 1870 Manitoba Census, National Archives of Canada, Ottawa, Ontario, Microfilm Reel Number C-2170., page 359, #1028.). He was baptized on 12 Jan 1826 St.Johns, Red River, (Manitoba) (HBCR, E.4/1a, folio 58d.). He died on 9 Sep 1879 St.Ann, Poplar Point, Manitoba (Denney.).

6. **William Thomas** was born on 17 Jun 1806 North West (Ibid.). He was baptized on 10 Nov 1822 St.Johns, Red River Settlement, (Manitoba) (HBCA-B, E.4/1a, fo. 41-41d.) (HBCR, E.4/1a, folio 41d.). He married **Eleanor Bunn**, daughter of **Thomas Bunn** and **Phoebe Sinclair**, on 5 Feb 1829 St.Johns, (Manitoba) (Denney.). He died on 13 Apr 1875 St.Paul, Manitoba, at age 68 (MBS, C-14934.). He was buried on 14 Apr 1875 St.Paul, Manitoba (Ibid.).

Eleanor Bunn was born circa 1812 (Denney.). She was baptized on 9 Sep 1820 St.Johns, Rock Depot (HBCR, E.4/1a, folio 27.). She died on 15 Jun 1869 St.Paul, (Manitoba) (Denney.).

Children of **William Thomas** and **Eleanor Bunn** were as follows:

    i.   Daughter (Mary?) Thomas was baptized on 2 May 1831 St.Johns, Red River Settlement, (Manitoba) (HBCR, E.4/1a, folio 83d.).

11 ii.   William Thomas, b. 5 Dec 1831 St.Paul, (Manitoba); m. Isabella Dahl; m. Charlotte Rose; d. 2 Jan 1892 St.Paul, Manitoba.

12 iii. Phoebe Thomas, b. 31 Mar 1833 St.Paul, (Manitoba); m. James Taylor; d. 1 Sep 1898 St.Paul, Manitoba.

    iv. Thomas Thomas was baptized on 4 Nov 1834 St.Johns, Red River Settlement, (Manitoba) (Ibid., E.4/1a, folio 116.).

    v.   John Thomas was baptized on 12 Nov 1835 St.Johns, Red River Settlement, (Manitoba) (Ibid., E.4/1a, folio 124d.).

    vi. Catherine Thomas was born in 1837 (Ibid., Burial No. 316.). She was baptized on 15 Feb 1838 St.Johns, Red River Settlement, (Manitoba) (Ibid., E.4/1a, folio 149d.). She was buried on 20 Feb 1841 St.Johns, Red River Settlement, (Manitoba) (Ibid., Burial No. 316.).

13 vii. Charles Richard Thomas, b. 28 Apr 1839 St.Paul, (Manitoba); m. Charlotte Vincent; d. 25 Jan 1911 Winnipeg, Manitoba.

    viii. Sarah Elizabeth Thomas was baptized on 17 Jan 1841 St.Johns, Red River Settlement, (Manitoba) (Ibid., E.4/1a, folio 163.). She married James M. Eastman on 11 Jun 1879 St.Paul, Manitoba (Denney.). She died on 20 Sep 1925 Carberry, Manitoba, at age 84 (MB Vital Statistics, Death Reg. #1925,039196.).

         James M. Eastman was born on 25 Nov 1849 Ottawa, Ontario (Denney.) (1901 Canada, District 8-a-1, page 10, family 83, line 13-15.). He died on 27 Sep 1929 Winnipeg, Manitoba, at age 79 (MB Vital Statistics, Death Reg. #1929,044244.).

    ix. Harry James Thomas was baptized on 30 Oct 1842 St.Johns, (Manitoba) (Denney.). He died on 13 Dec 1842 St.Johns, (Manitoba) (Ibid.).

14 x.   Frances Jane Thomas, b. 18 Dec 1843 St.Paul, (Manitoba); m. Richard Duncan Campbell.

15 xi. Harriet Maria Thomas, b. 12 Mar 1846 St.Paul, (Manitoba); m. John Edward Harriott; d. 1 Oct 1871 St.Clements, Manitoba; bur. 3 Oct 1871 St.Clements, Manitoba.

    xii. Alfred Thomas was born on 11 Sep 1849 (Ibid.). He was baptized on 23 Sep 1849 St.Johns, (Manitoba) (Ibid.).

    xiii. James Thomas was baptized on 20 Apr 1852 St.Paul, (Manitoba) (Ibid.).

16 xiv. Edward Thomas, b. 8 Feb 1855; m. Elizabeth Jane McDonald; d. 5 May 1916 East St.Paul, Manitoba.

    xv. Eleanor Sophie Thomas was baptized on 29 Apr 1867 St.Johns, (Manitoba) (Ibid.).

7. **Sarah Thomas** was born circa 1808 (Ibid.). She married **James Beardy** before 1835.

Question: *Sarah is not mentioned in her father's will.*

James Beardy was born circa 1810. He was baptized on 23 Aug 1837 St.Johns, Red River Settlement, (Manitoba) (HBCR, E.4/1a, folio 145.).

8. **Catherine Thomas** was born in 1810 (Denney.). She was baptized on 10 Nov 1822 St.Johns, Red River Settlement, (Manitoba) (HBCA-B, E.4/1a, fo. 41-41d.) (HBCR, E.4/1a, folio 41d.). She married **John Bunn**, son of **Thomas Bunn** and **Sarah McNab**, on 23 Jul 1829 St.Johns, Red River Settlement, (Manitoba) (Ibid., M-179.). She died on 7 Jan 1834 St.Johns, (Manitoba) (Denney.) (HBCA-B.).

John Bunn was born between 1800 and 1803 Ruperts Land (1829C RRS HBCA E5/3 1829 Census of the Red River Settlement, HBCA E5/3, Hudson's Bay Company Archives, Provincial Archives, 200 Vaughan Street, Winnipeg, MB R3C 1T5, Canada., page 6.). He died on 31 May 1861 St.Johns, (Manitoba) (Denney.) (*DCB-V9 Dictionary of Canadian Biography - Volume Nine*;Toronto, Ontario: University of Toronto Press, 2000).) (HBCA-B.).

9. **Jane Thomas** was born circa 1816 (Denney.). She was baptized on 10 Nov 1822 St.Johns, Red River Settlement, (Manitoba) (HBCA-B, E.4/1a, fo. 41-41d.) (HBCR, E.4/1a, folio 41d.). She married **Levi Bird**, son of **James Curtis Bird** and **Elizabeth Montour**, on 9 Nov 1832 St.Johns, Red River Settlement, (Manitoba) (Ibid., M-247.). She died in 1841.

Levi Bird was born circa 1813 Ruperts Land (1833C RRS HBCA E5/7 1833 Census of the Red River Settlement, HBCA E5/7, Hudson's Bay Company Archives, Provincial Archives, 200 Vaughan Street, Winnipeg, MB R3C 1T5, Canada., page 4.). He died on 12 Jan 1864 (Denney.). He was buried circa Jan 1864 St.Johns, (Manitoba).

10. **Thomas Thomas** was born circa 1819 Ruperts Land (Denney.). He was baptized on 10 Nov 1822 St.Johns, Red River Settlement, (Manitoba) (HBCA-B, E.4/1a, fo. 41-41d.) (HBCR, E.4/1a, folio 41d.). He married **Harriet Stewart**, daughter of **David Ramsey**

Stewart and **Harriet Vincent,** on 21 Nov 1841 (St.Paul), Middle Church, Red River Settlement, (Manitoba) (Ibid., No. 361.). He died on 12 Mar 1859 St.Paul, (Manitoba) (Denney.).

Harriet Stewart was born on 30 Nov 1818 North West. She died on 18 Apr 1910 Rockwood, Manitoba, at age 91 (MB Vital Statistics, Death Reg. #1910,001558.).

Children of **Thomas Thomas** and **Harriet Stewart** were as follows:

17	i.	William George Thomas, b. 8 Jul 1843; m. Mary Ann Stevens.
18	ii.	Juliet Jane Thomas, b. 1 May 1845 St.Paul, (Manitoba); m. William Logan; d. 2 Feb 1935 Stonewall, Manitoba.
19	iii.	Harriet Sophia Thomas, b. 8 Aug 1847 Middlechurch, (Manitoba); m. James Graham; d. 6 Jul 1934 Stonewall, Manitoba.
	iv.	Thomas Charles Thomas was born on 5 Aug 1849 (Denney.). He was baptized on 14 Aug 1849 St.Johns, (Manitoba) (Ibid.). He died on 15 Dec 1849 St.Johns, (Manitoba) (Ibid.).
20	v.	Edwin Stewart Thomas, b. 7 Oct 1850; m. Mary Ann Allen; d. 7 Oct 1932.
21	vi.	David Henry Thomas, b. 24 Jan 1853; m. Ann Sarah Watts; d. 12 Aug 1917 Stonewall, Manitoba.
	vii.	William Mason Thomas was born on 22 May 1855 (Ibid.). He was baptized on 27 Jun 1855 St.Paul, (Manitoba) (Ibid.). He died on 2 Jan 1856 (Ibid.). He was buried in Jan 1865 St.Johns, (Manitoba).
22	viii.	John Thomas, b. 17 May 1857 St.Paul, (Manitoba); m. Elizabeth Jane Watts; d. 1947; bur. 1947 Hodgson Cemetery, Stonewall, Manitoba.

Generation Three

11. William Thomas was born on 5 Dec 1831 St.Paul, (Manitoba) (MBS, C-14934.). He was baptized on 29 Dec 1831 St.Johns, Red River Settlement, (Manitoba) (HBCR, E.4/1a, folio 86d.). He married **Isabella Dahl** on 5 Feb 1863 St.Paul, (Manitoba) (Denney.). He married **Charlotte Rose,** daughter of **William Rose** and **Nancy Sinclair,** on 20 Mar 1872 St.Johns, Manitoba (Ibid.). He died on 2 Jan 1892 St.Paul, Manitoba, at age 60 (MB Vital Statistics, Death Reg. #1892,001011.).

Isabella Dahl was born in 1845 (Denney.). She died on 13 Mar 1868 St.Paul, (Manitoba) (Ibid.).

Children of **William Thomas** and **Isabella Dahl** all born St.Paul, (Manitoba), were as follows:

i.	Edward John Thomas was born on 13 Nov 1863 (MBS, C-14934.). He was baptized on 13 Dec 1863 St.Paul, (Manitoba) (Ibid.).
ii.	William D. Thomas was born on 3 Dec 1865 (Ibid.).
iii.	Alexander Charles Thomas was baptized on 15 Mar 1868 (Denney.). He died on 14 Aug 1868 St.Paul, (Manitoba) (Ibid.).

Charlotte Rose was born in Oct 1849 St.Paul, (Manitoba) (Ibid.). She was baptized on 25 Nov 1849 St.Paul, (Manitoba) (Ibid.). She was born on 1 Jun 1850 St.Paul, (Manitoba) (MBS, C-14934.).

Children of **William Thomas** and **Charlotte Rose** were as follows:

i.	Eleanore Ann Thomas was baptized in Mar 1873 St.Paul, Manitoba (Denney.).
ii.	Sarah Elizabeth Thomas was born in 1874 Oak Point, Manitoba (HBS 1886-1901, 1906 Half-Breed Scrip Applications, RG15-21, Volume 1337, C-14952.). She was baptized on 29 Nov 1874 St.Paul, Manitoba (Denney.). She married Joseph Edwin Braid before 30 Nov 1901 St.Paul, Manitoba (HBS, Volume 1337, C-14952.).
iii.	Thomas James Thomas was baptized on 24 Dec 1876 St.Paul, Manitoba (Denney.). He died on 22 Mar 1877 St.Paul, Manitoba (Ibid.).
iv.	Harriet Maria Thomas was born circa 1877 (Rod Mac Quarrie, 24 Dec 2007 (source: 1881 Census).).
v.	Alfred Louis Thomas was born on 5 Sep 1880 St.Paul, Manitoba (1901 Canada, #11, R-1, page 4, family 119, line 41-46.).
vi.	Arthur Henry Thomas was born on 28 Feb 1883 RM St.Paul, Manitoba (MB Vital Statistics, Birth Reg. #1883,002591.). He died on 31 Aug 1883 St.Paul, Manitoba (Ibid., Death Reg. #1883,002529.).
vii.	Isabelle Thomas was born in 1884.
viii.	Margaret Jane Thomas was born on 19 Dec 1885 St.Paul, Manitoba (Ibid., Birth Reg. #1886,003918.). She died on 3 Sep 1896 St.Paul, Manitoba, at age 10 (Ibid., Death Reg. #1896,001900.).
ix.	Herbert Charles Thomas was born on 25 Mar 1889 St.Paul, Manitoba (Ibid., Birth Reg. #1889,005418.). He died on 22 Sep 1889 St.Paul, Manitoba (Ibid., Death Reg. #1889,002104.).
x.	Frances Louise Thomas was born on 20 May 1891 RM St.Paul, Manitoba (Ibid., Birth Reg. #1891,006027.).

12. Phoebe Thomas was born on 31 Mar 1833 St.Paul, (Manitoba) (MBS, C-14934.). She was baptized on 5 May 1833 St.Johns, Red River Settlement, (Manitoba) (HBCR, E.4/1a, folio 100.). She married **James Taylor,** son of **James Taylor** and **Mary Inkster,** on 10 Feb 1859 St.Paul, Middlechurch, (Manitoba) (Denney.). She died on 1 Sep 1898 St.Paul, Manitoba, at age 65 (MB Vital Statistics, Death Reg. #1898,003106.).

James Taylor was born on 29 Jul 1829 St.Paul, (Manitoba) (MBS, C-14934.) (1901 Canada, #11, R-1, page 4, family 117, line 35-39.). He was baptized on 12 Aug 1829 St.Johns, Red River Settlement, (Manitoba) (HBCA-B, E.4/1a fo. 71.) (HBCR, E.4/1a, folio 71.). He died on 14 Sep 1918 St.Paul, Manitoba, at age 89 (Lesley Taylor Research, 9 Apr 2004 email.) (MB Vital Statistics, Death Reg. #1918,054206.).

13. Charles Richard Thomas was born on 28 Apr 1839 St.Paul, (Manitoba) (MBS, C-14934.). He was baptized on 26 May 1839 St.Johns, Red River Settlement, (Manitoba) (HBCR, E.4/1a, folio 160d.). He married **Charlotte Vincent,** daughter of **John Vincent** and **Charlotte Thomas,** on 22 Jul 1869 St.Paul, (Manitoba) (Denney.). He died on 25 Jan 1911 Winnipeg, Manitoba, at age 71 (MB Vital Statistics, Death Reg. #1911,002841.).

Charlotte Vincent was born on 25 Nov 1849 St.Paul, (Manitoba) (MBS, C-14934.). She was baptized on 5 Dec 1849 St.Johns, (Manitoba) (Denney.). She died on 9 Apr 1902 Winnipeg, Manitoba, at age 52 (MB Vital Statistics, Death Reg. #1902,002081.).

Children of **Charles Richard Thomas** and **Charlotte Vincent** were as follows:

23	i.	Eleanor Harriet Thomas, b. 15 Aug 1871; m. John Isbister Anderson.
	ii.	John Edward Thomas was baptized on 16 Feb 1873 St.Paul, Manitoba (Denney.).

  iii. Catherine M. Thomas was born circa 1875 St.Paul, Manitoba (1881 Church of Latter Day Saints Census Transcription Project of Census Images from the National Archives of Canada, Ottawa, Canada, http://www.familysearch.org, NA Film #C-13283, District 185, Sub-district A, page 6, house 18.).

  iv. Charlotte Anne Thomas was baptized on 14 Sep 1876 St.Paul, Manitoba (Denney.).

  v. George William Thomas was born on 29 Jun 1878 St.Paul, Manitoba (1901 Canada, #12, f-3, page 1, family 9, line 33-40.).

  vi. Clara Thomas was born in Aug 1880 St.Paul, Manitoba (1881 Canada, NA Film #C-13283, District 185, Sub-district A, page 6, house 18.).

  vii. Mary J. Thomas was born on 25 Mar 1882 Manitoba (1901 Canada, #12, f-3, page 1, family 9, line 33-40.).

  viii. Juliet Jane Thomas was born on 9 Feb 1884 RM St.Paul, Manitoba (MB Vital Statistics, Birth Reg. #1884,003244.).

  ix. Florence Maud Thomas was born on 12 Mar 1886 St.Paul, Manitoba (1901 Canada, #12, f-3, page 1, family 9, line 33-40.) (MB Vital Statistics, Birth Reg. #1886,003924.).

  x. Walter Charles Thomas was born on 17 May 1891 RM St.Paul, Manitoba (Ibid., Birth Reg. #1891,006028.).

  xi. Alice Thomas was born on 14 May 1893 R.M. of Rockwood, Manitoba (Ibid., Birth Reg. #1893,005020.).

  xii. Thomas Walter Thomas was born on 17 May 1897 Manitoba (1901 Canada, #12, f-3, page 1, family 9, line 33-40.).

14. Frances Jane Thomas was born on 18 Dec 1843 St.Paul, (Manitoba) (MBS, C-14934.). She was baptized on 12 Jan 1844 St.Johns, (Manitoba) (Denney.). She married **Richard Duncan Campbell**, son of **Colin Campbell** and **Elizabeth McGillivray**, on 3 Aug 1865 St.Johns, (Manitoba) (Ibid.).

 Richard Duncan Campbell was born in 1842 Fort Chipewyan (MBS, C-14926.).

15. Harriet Maria Thomas was born on 12 Mar 1846 St.Paul, (Manitoba) (MBS, C-14928.). She was baptized on 1 Apr 1846 St.Johns, (Manitoba) (Ibid.). She married **John Edward Harriott**, son of **John Edward Harriott** and **Nancy Rowand**, on 13 Jul 1865 St.Paul, (Manitoba) (Denney.). She died on 1 Oct 1871 St.Clements, Manitoba, at age 25 (MBS, C-14928.). She was buried on 3 Oct 1871 St.Clements, Manitoba (Ibid.).

 John Edward Harriott was born on 29 Jun 1842 Fort Edmonton (Ibid.) (T. R. "Pat" McCloy, McKay Descendancy, McKay Descendancy.) (INB, page 79.). He was baptized on 30 Jun 1842 Fort-des-Prairies (Ibid.). He married **Jane Taylor**, daughter of **Samuel Taylor** and **Nancy McKay**, on 17 May 1871 St.Paul, (Manitoba) (T. R. McCloy, McKay Descendancy.). He died on 31 May 1924 St.Andrews, Manitoba, at age 81 (MB Vital Statistics, Death Reg. #1924,020518.). He was buried in 1924.

16. Edward Thomas was born on 8 Feb 1855 (Ibid.). He was baptized on 1 Mar 1855 St.Paul, (Manitoba) (Ibid.). He married **Elizabeth Jane McDonald**, daughter of **Alexander D. McDonald** and **Ann Tait**, on 29 Mar 1877 St.Paul, Manitoba (Ibid.). He died on 5 May 1916 East St.Paul, Manitoba, at age 61 (MB Vital Statistics, Death Reg. #1916,030312.).

 Elizabeth Jane McDonald was born on 23 Jan 1859 St.Andrews, (Manitoba) (MBS, C-14930.). She was baptized on 13 Feb 1859 St.Andrews, (Manitoba) (Ibid.). She died in 1949 (Denney.). She was buried in 1949 St.Paul, Middlechurch, Manitoba (Ibid.).

 Children of **Edward Thomas** and **Elizabeth Jane McDonald** were as follows:

  i. Jennie Thomas.

  ii. Dolly Thomas.

  iii. Sidney Thomas.

  iv. Mary Margaret Thomas was born in Sep 1880 St.Paul, Manitoba (1881 Canada, NA Film #C-13283, District 185, Sub-district A, page 5, house 17.).

  v. Frances Jane Thomas was born on 31 Jul 1882 RM of St.Paul, Manitoba (MB Vital Statistics, Birth Reg. #1882,17510101; Reg. Date: 07/02/1952.).

  vi. Edwin Stuart Thomas was born on 16 Aug 1886 RM St.Paul, Manitoba (Ibid., Birth Reg. #1886,001601.).

  vii. Elizabeth Pheobe Thomas was born on 29 Mar 1893 RM of St.Paul, Manitoba (Ibid., Birth Reg. #1893,27731063; Reg. Date: 03/05/1893.).

  viii. Gladys Thomas was born on 25 Mar 1897 St.Paul, Manitoba (1901 Canada, #11, r-2, page 1, family 2, line 2-7.).

17. William George Thomas was born on 8 Jul 1843 (Denney.). He was baptized on 30 Jul 1843 St.Johns, (Manitoba) (HBCR, #11.). He married **Mary Ann Stevens**, daughter of **John Stevens**, before 1867 (1870C-MB, page 115, #454.).

 Mary Ann Stevens was born circa 1849 (Manitoba) (Ibid.).

 Children of **William George Thomas** and **Mary Ann Stevens** were:

  i. John Thomas was born circa 1867 (Manitoba) (Ibid., page 115, #455.).

18. Juliet Jane Thomas was born on 1 May 1845 St.Paul, (Manitoba) (MBS, C-14930.). She was baptized on 22 Jun 1845 St.Johns, (Manitoba) (Denney.). She married **William Logan**, son of **Thomas Logan** and **Mary Anne Dease**, on 20 Sep 1864 St.Paul, (Manitoba) (Ibid.). She died on 2 Feb 1935 Stonewall, Manitoba, at age 89 (MB Vital Statistics, Death Reg. #1935,012271.).

 William Logan was born on 18 Dec 1841 St.Johns, (Manitoba) (MBS, C-14930.). He was baptized on 19 Dec 1841 St.Johns, (Manitoba) (Denney.). He died on 25 Mar 1922 Stonewall, Manitoba, at age 80 (MB Vital Statistics, Death Reg. #1922,010358.).

19. Harriet Sophia Thomas was born on 8 Aug 1847 Middlechurch, (Manitoba) (Denney.). She was baptized on 27 Sep 1847 St.Johns, (Manitoba) (Ibid.). She married **James Graham** on 5 Sep 1878 St.Paul, Manitoba (Ibid.). She died on 6 Jul 1934 Stonewall, Manitoba, at age 86 (Ibid.).

 James Graham was born on 29 Jan 1838 Ontario (Ibid.). He died in Jul 1888 at age 50 (Ibid.).

20. Edwin Stewart Thomas was born on 7 Oct 1850 (Denney.). He was baptized on 16 Nov 1850 St.Paul, (Manitoba) (Ibid.). He married **Mary Ann Allen**, daughter of **Robert Allen** and **Charlotte Scarbrough**, on 21 Jun 1883 Rockwood, Manitoba (MB Vital Statistics, Marriage Reg. #1883,001419.). He died on 7 Oct 1932 at age 82 (Denney.).

 Mary Ann Allen was born on 10 Aug 1846 Fort Dunvegan, (Alberta) (ArchiviaNet, C-15006.). She married **William Lucas Hardisty**, son of **Richard Hardisty** and **Margaret Sutherland**, in Aug 1857 Fort Simpson (Denney.). She died on 10 Jan 1930 Victoria at age 83 (Ibid.).

Children of **Edwin Stewart Thomas** and **Mary Ann Allen** were as follows:

 i. Ellen Florence Thomas was born on 1 Apr 1884 Rockwood, Manitoba (MB Vital Statistics, Birth Reg. #1884,002881.). She died on 7 Jan 1911 St.Laurent, Manitoba, at age 26 (Ibid., Death Reg. #1911,004934.).

 ii. Edwin James Thomas was born on 2 Dec 1888 R.M. of Rockwood, Manitoba (Ibid., Birth Reg. #1888,005028.). He died on 9 Nov 1898 Rockwood, Manitoba, at age 9 (Ibid., Death Reg. #1898,002984.).

 21. David Henry Thomas was born on 24 Jan 1853 (Denney.). He was baptized on 8 Mar 1853 St.Paul, (Manitoba) (Ibid.). He married **Ann Sarah Watts**, daughter of **Frederick Watts** and **Mary Sutherland,** on 28 Mar 1889 Rockwood, Manitoba (MB Vital Statistics, Marriage Reg. #1889,001028.). He died on 12 Aug 1917 Stonewall, Manitoba, at age 64 (Denney.).

 Ann Sarah Watts was born on 10 Jul 1869 (1901 Canada, District 11-h-3, page 5, family 43, line 43-50.). She died on 24 Feb 1950 Stonewall, Manitoba, at age 80 (Denney.).

Children of **David Henry Thomas** and **Ann Sarah Watts** were as follows:

 i. Frederick George Thomas was born on 10 Dec 1889 R.M. of Rockwood, Manitoba (MB Vital Statistics, Birth Reg. #1889,002496.).

 ii. Lillie Thomas was born on 12 Feb 1892 (1901 Canada, District 11-h-3, page 5, family 43, line 43-50.).

 iii. William Roy Thomas was born on 11 Dec 1894 R.M. of Rockwood, Manitoba (MB Vital Statistics, Birth Reg. #1895,003545.).

 iv. Florence Alvine Thomas was born on 24 Feb 1897 R.M. of Rockwood, Manitoba (Ibid., Birth Reg. #1897,006772.).

 v. Edith Mary Thomas was born on 17 Aug 1899 R.M. of Rockwood, Manitoba (Ibid., Birth Reg. #1899,003059.).

 22. John Thomas was born on 17 May 1857 St.Paul, (Manitoba) (Denney.). He married **Elizabeth Jane Watts**, daughter of **Frederick Watts** and **Mary Sutherland,** on 22 Jul 1886 Rockwood, Manitoba (MB Vital Statistics, Marriage Reg. #1886,001054.). He died in 1947 (Denney.). He was buried in 1947 Hodgson Cemetery, Stonewall, Manitoba (Ibid.).

 Elizabeth Jane Watts was born circa 1862 Mapleton, (Manitoba) (1870C-MB, page 158, #57.) (Denney.). She died on 3 Oct 1957 (Ibid.). She was buried in Oct 1957 Hodgson Cemetery, Stonewall, Manitoba (Ibid.).

Children of **John Thomas** and **Elizabeth Jane Watts** were as follows:

 i. Elizabeth Jane Thomas was born on 16 Apr 1887 R.M. of Rockwood, Manitoba (MB Vital Statistics, Birth Reg. #1887,003871.).

 ii. Martha Ann Thomas was born on 14 Nov 1888 R.M. of Rockwood, Manitoba (Ibid., Birth Reg. #1888,002083.).

 iii. Robert Henry Thomas was born on 25 Oct 1890 R.M. of Rockwood, Manitoba (Ibid., Birth Reg. #1890,003414.).

 iv. Florence Louisa Thomas was born on 15 Dec 1892 R.M. of Rockwood, Manitoba (Ibid., Birth Reg. #1892,003256.). She died on 20 Aug 1894 R.M. of Rockwood, Manitoba, at age 1 (Ibid., Death Reg. #1894,002823.).

 v. Adelaide Jane Thomas was born on 15 Dec 1896 R.M. of Rockwood, Manitoba (Ibid., Birth Reg. #1897,006748.).

 vi. Harriet Evelyn Thomas was born on 27 Mar 1899 R.M. of Rockwood, Manitoba (Ibid., Birth Reg. #1899,006528.).

 vii. William George Thomas was born on 22 Mar 1901 R.M. of St.Andrews, Manitoba (Ibid., Birth Reg. #1901,006342.).

 viii. John Frederick Thomas was born on 1 Aug 1904 R.M. of Rockwood, Manitoba (Ibid., Birth Reg. #1904,002001.).

Generation Four

 23. Eleanor Harriet Thomas was born on 15 Aug 1871 (1901 Canada, #12, f-3, page 1, family 9, line 33-40.). She was baptized on 24 Sep 1871 St.Paul, Manitoba (Denney.). She married **John Isbister Anderson**, son of **James Anderson** and **Elizabeth "Betsey" Isbister,** on 26 Jan 1888 St.Clements, Manitoba (1901 Canada, District 11-m-5, page 3, family 21, line 4-16.) (MB Vital Statistics, Marriage Reg. #1888,001087.).

 John Isbister Anderson was born in 1864 (NWHBSI, page 101.). He was born on 18 May 1867 North West Territory (1901 Canada, District 11-m-5, page 3, family 21, line 4-16.).

Ahnentafel between George Thorne Sr. and Abraham Thorn

--- 1st Generation ---

1. GEORGE THORNE SR. was born in 1797 at Sorel, Richelieu, Quebec. He married **MARIE LEMIRE**, daughter of **PIERRE LEMIRE** and **MARIE BLACKFOOT**, on 15 Sep 1828 at York Factory (*LHBCM List of Hudson Bay Company Marriages*; 139 Cook Street; Victoria, B.C.; V8V 3W8: Edited by Joanne J. Hughes, 1977.) (HBCR Hudson Bay Company Register of Anglican Church Baptisms, Marriages, and Burials for the Red River Settlement, 1821-1841; Hudson's Bay Company Archives, Winnipeg, Manitoba, #624. Hereinafter cited as HBCR.). Question: *Marriage No. 154-177 in 1828-1829 are not found in the HBCA records.* He died on 26 May 1887 at St.Francois Xavier, Manitoba (SFXI-Kipling St.Francois Xavier Register Index, 1834-1900; compiled by Clarence Kipling , S-20.).

--- 2nd Generation ---

2. JOHN THORNE (PRDH online index, http://www.genealogic.umontreal.ca, #220836.) (Ibid.) was born at Ireland. He was born circa 1759 at New Jersey (Ibid.). He was baptized on 14 Jun 1784 (Ibid.). He married **MARIE CHARLES COUILLAUD DIT LAROCQUE OR ROCBRUNE**, daughter of **FRANCOIS COUILLAUD DIT LAROCQUE OR LAROCQUEBRUNE** and **MARIE THERESE PINEAU**, on 29 Jul 1784 at General Hospital, Quebec, Quebec, Quebec (Ibid.).

--- 3rd Generation ---

4. ABRAHAM THORN (Ibid.) married **SUZANNE WEBSTER**.

Descendants of George Thorne Sr.

Generation One

1. George Thorne Sr was born in 1797 Sorel, Richelieu, Quebec. He married **Marie Lemire**, daughter of **Pierre Lemire** and **Marie Blackfoot,** on 15 Sep 1828 York Factory (*LHBCM List of Hudson Bay Company Marriages*; 139 Cook Street; Victoria, B.C.; V8V 3W8: Edited by Joanne J. Hughes, 1977.) (HBCR Hudson Bay Company Register of Anglican Church Baptisms, Marriages, and Burials for the Red River Settlement, 1821-1841; Hudson's Bay Company Archives, Winnipeg, Manitoba, #624. Hereinafter cited as HBCR.). He died on 26 May 1887 St.Francois Xavier, Manitoba (SFXI-Kipling St.Francois Xavier Register Index, 1834-1900; compiled by Clarence Kipling , S-20.).

Question: *Marriage No. 154-177 in 1828-1829 are not found in the HBCA records.*

Marie Lemire was born in 1805 North West (MBS Scrip Applications, Original White Settlers & Halfbreeds residing in Manitoba on 15 July 1870, RG15-19, C-14934.).

Children of **George Thorne Sr.** and **Marie Lemire** were as follows:

- 2   i.   Cecile Thorne, b. 7 Nov 1827 North West; m. Paul St.Denis.
- 3   ii.   George Thorne Jr, b. circa 1829 York Factory; m. Nancy McLeod.
-      iii. Genevieve Thorne was born circa 1830 (SB 1825-1834 St.Boniface Roman Catholic Registre des Baptemes, Mariages & Sepultures, 1825-1834, page 152, B-883. Hereinafter cited as SB 1825-1834.). She was baptized on 19 Oct 1834 St.Boniface, (Manitoba) (Ibid.). She died on 19 May 1879 St.Francois Xavier, Manitoba (SFXI-Kipling, S-11.) (MBS, C-14934.). She was buried on 21 May 1879 St.Francois Xavier, Manitoba (Ibid.).
-      iv.   Unnamed Thorne was born circa 1832 (SB 1825-1834, page 151-152, B-881.). He/she was baptized on 19 Oct 1834 St.Boniface, (Manitoba) (Ibid.).
- 4   v.   Angelique Thorne, b. 1835; m. Alexis Campbell.
- 5   vi.   Marie Thorne, b. circa 1837; m. Pierre Pelletier; m. Joseph Fleury; d. 30 Dec 1862 St.Francois Xavier, (Manitoba); bur. 31 Dec 1862 St.Francois Xavier, (Manitoba).
- 6   vii. David Thorne, b. 1 Dec 1839; m. Madeleine Auger; d. 13 Nov 1862 St.Francois Xavier, (Manitoba); bur. 14 Nov 1862 St.Francois Xavier, (Manitoba).
-      viii. Abraham Thorn was born on 23 Jan 1842 (SFX: 1834-1850 St.Francois Xavier 1834-1851 Register, B-393. Hereinafter cited as SFX: 1834-1850.). He was baptized on 25 Jan 1842 St.Francois Xavier, (Manitoba) (Ibid.). He died on 21 Mar 1843 at age 1 (Ibid., S-80.). He was buried on 24 Mar 1843 St.Francois Xavier, (Manitoba) (Ibid.).
- 7   ix.   John Francus Thorne, b. 16 Feb 1844 St.Francois Xavier, (Manitoba); m. Helene Demontigny.
- 8   x.   Nancy Thorne, b. Jul 1846 St.Francois Xavier, (Manitoba); m. Charles Demontigny; d. 11 Jan 1888 Rolette County, North Dakota.
- 9   xi.   Marie Thorne, b. 1 Feb 1849 St.Francois Xavier, (Manitoba); m. Louis Desjarlais; d. 29 Jun 1878 St.Francois Xavier, Manitoba.
- 10   xii. Elise Thorne, b. 11 Jan 1851 St.Francois Xavier, (Manitoba); m. Joseph L'Hirondelle; d. 7 Dec 1939 Calgary, Alberta.
-      xiii. Catherine Thorne was born on 3 Aug 1855 St.Francois Xavier, (Manitoba) (SFXI-Kipling, B-53.). She was baptized on 4 Aug 1855 St.Francois Xavier, (Manitoba) (Ibid.). She married Guillaume Ward, son of Joseph Ward and Angelique Welsh, on 10 Jan 1882 St.Francois Xavier, Manitoba (Ibid., M-1.).

      Question: *The groom was called William Bourke.*

      Guillaume Ward was born circa 1859.

Generation Two

2. Cecile Thorne was born on 7 Nov 1827 North West (MBS, C-14932.). She married **Paul St.Denis**, son of **Paul Gesson St.Denis** and **Catherine Gariepy,** on 1 Feb 1853 St.Francois Xavier, (Manitoba) (SFXI-Kipling, M-12.) (SFXI 1851-1868 St.Francois Xavier 1852-1861 Register Index, M-12. Hereinafter cited as SFXI 1851-1868.).

Paul St.Denis was born on 7 Jun 1832 St.Boniface, (Manitoba) (SB 1825-1834, page 66, B-441.). He was baptized on 8 Jun 1832 St.Boniface, (Manitoba) (Ibid.).

3. George Thorne Jr was born circa 1829 York Factory (NWHBS 1885 Scrip Applications, North-West Halfbreeds residing outside Manitoba on 15 July 1870, RG15-20, C-14942.) (SB 1825-1834, page 151, B-881.). He was baptized on 19 Oct 1834 St.Boniface, (Manitoba) (Ibid.). He married **Nancy McLeod**, daughter of **Joseph McLeod** and **Angelique Lacerte,** on 4 Jun 1855 St.Francois Xavier, (Manitoba) (SFXI-Kipling, M-3.).

Nancy McLeod was born on 20 Oct 1841 St.Boniface, (Manitoba) (MBS, C-14934.). She was buried on 18 Sep 1878 Lebret, (Saskatchewan) (L1 Lebret Mission de St.Florent Roman Catholic Registre des Baptemes, Mariages & Sepluutres, Qu'Appelle, Saskatchewan, 1868-1881., page 235, S-55. Hereinafter cited as L1.).

Children of **George Thorne Jr.** and **Nancy McLeod** were as follows:

-      i.   Julie Thorn was born circa Mar 1857 (SFXI-Kipling, B-199.). She was baptized on 7 Jun 1857 St.Francois Xavier, (Manitoba) (Ibid.). She married Pascal Gladu, son of Louis Gladu and Suzanne Desjarlais, on 6 Oct 1874 St.Eustache, Manitoba (MM.) (ST-BSP.). She died on 14 Apr 1875 St.Eustache, Manitoba (Denney Papers, Charles D. Denney, Glenbow Archives, Calgary, Alberta.). She was buried on 15 Apr 1875 St.Eustache, Manitoba (Ibid.).

      Pascal Gladu was born in 1847 St.Eustache, (Manitoba) (Jackie Gladue Jordan Research, 13 Jun 1998 Family group sheet.). He married **Sara Hogue**, daughter of **Amable Hogue** and **Betsy Morissette,** on 16 Apr 1880 St.Eustache, Manitoba (MM.) (ST-BSP, M-5.). He died on 25 Apr 1935 Portage la Prairie, Manitoba (MB Vital Statistics, Death Reg. #1935,024022.).
- 11   ii.   David Thorne, b. circa 1859 North West Territories; m. Harriet Anderson.
- 12   iii. George Thorne, b. circa 1859; m. Marie Rose Lillie.
-      iv.   John Thorne was born on 26 Apr 1861 (SFXI-Kipling, B-40.). He was baptized on 19 May 1861 St.Francois Xavier, (Manitoba) (Ibid.).

4. **Angelique Thorne** was born in 1835 (NWHBSI Index 1885 Scrip Applications, North-West Halfbreeds residing outside Manitoba on 15 July 1870, RG15-20, page 79.). She married **Alexis Campbell**, son of **Alexander Campbell** and **Louise Richard,** on 10 Jan 1856 St.Francois Xavier, (Manitoba) (SFXI-Kipling, M-10.).

Alexis Campbell was born in 1835 (NWHBSI, page 107.).

5. **Marie Thorne** was born circa 1837. She married **Pierre Pelletier**, son of **Charles Pelletier** and **Suzanne Bercier,** on 11 Jun 1855 St.Francois Xavier, (Manitoba) (SFXI-Kipling, M-4.). She married **Joseph Fleury**, son of **Louis Fleury** and **Josephte Belly,** on 3 Feb 1857 St.Francois Xavier, (Manitoba) (Ibid., M-26.). She died on 30 Dec 1862 St.Francois Xavier, (Manitoba) (Ibid., S-23.). She was buried on 31 Dec 1862 St.Francois Xavier, (Manitoba) (Ibid.).

Pierre Pelletier was born on 18 Mar 1829 (SB 1825-1834, page 25, B-552.). He was baptized on 21 Jun 1829 St.Boniface, (Manitoba) (Ibid.). He died in Jul 1855 at age 26 (SFXI: 1851-1869 St.Francois Xavier 1851-69 Register Index.). He was buried on 8 Feb 1856 St.Francois Xavier, (Manitoba) (SFXI-Kipling, S-42.) (SFXI-1834-54.).

Joseph Fleury was born in 1829 St.Boniface, (Manitoba) (MBS, C-14928.). He married **Madeleine Piche**, daughter of **Louis Piche** and **Charlotte Genthon dit Dauphinais**, on 7 Jan 1864 St.Francois Xavier, (Manitoba) (SFXI-Kipling, M-1.). He married **Julie Fosseneuve**, daughter of **Jean Baptiste Fosseneuve** and **Julie Morand,** on 7 Jan 1879 St.Francois Xavier, Manitoba (Ibid.).

6. **David Thorne** was born on 1 Dec 1839 (SFX: 1834-1850, B-279.). He was baptized on 4 Dec 1839 St.Francois Xavier, (Manitoba) (Ibid.). He married **Madeleine Auger**, daughter of **Antoine Auger** and **Marie Madeleine Klyne,** on 29 Jun 1858 St.Francois Xavier, (Manitoba) (SFXI-Kipling, M-51.). (MM, page 36.). He died on 13 Nov 1862 St.Francois Xavier, (Manitoba), at age 22 (SFXI-1834-54.). He was buried on 14 Nov 1862 St.Francois Xavier, (Manitoba) (SFXI-Kipling, S-18.) (SFXI-1834-54.).

Madeleine Auger was born in Jan 1838 (CCRPNW-V *Catholic Church Records of the Pacific Northwest, Vancouver, Volumes I and II and Stellamaris Mission* Translated by: Mikell de Lores Wormell Warner and Annotated by: Harriet Duncan Munnick, (St.Paul, Oregon: French Prairie Press, 1972), page 8, B-72.). She was baptized on 6 Sep 1838 Fort Edmonton (Ibid.). She died on 2 May 1863 at age 25 (SB-Rozyk St. Boniface Roman Catholic Church, Manitoba, Canada, Baptisms, Marriages and Burials 1860-1875 Extractions, Compiled by Rosemary Rozyk, page 110, S-12.). She was buried on 4 May 1863 St.Boniface, (Manitoba) (Ibid.).

Children of **David Thorne** and **Madeleine Auger** were as follows:

    13   i.   William Thorne, b. circa 1859 St.Boniface, (Manitoba); m. Julie Ross; m. Elise Ross; d. 10 Jun 1930 Batoche, Saskatchewan.

        ii.   Marie Thorne was born on 27 Dec 1862 St.Francois Xavier, (Manitoba) (INB, page 176.) (SFXI-Kipling, B-99.). She was baptized on 29 Dec 1862 St.Francois Xavier, (Manitoba) (INB, page 176.) (SFXI-Kipling, B-99.). She died on 18 Jun 1863 St.Francois Xavier, (Manitoba) (Ibid., S-19.). She was buried on 19 Jun 1863 St.Francois Xavier, (Manitoba) (Ibid.) (SFXI-1834-54.).

7. **John Francus Thorne** was born on 16 Feb 1844 St.Francois Xavier, (Manitoba) (SFX: 1834-1850, B-494.). He was baptized on 18 Feb 1844 St.Francois Xavier, (Manitoba) (Ibid.). He married **Helene Demontigny**, daughter of **Charles Demontigny** and **Marie Desjarlais,** on 17 Apr 1871 St.Francois Xavier, Manitoba (SFXI-Kipling, M-4.).

Helene Demontigny was baptized on 28 May 1853 St.Francois Xavier, (Manitoba) (Ibid., B-82.) (SFXI 1851-1868, B-82.).

Children of **John Francus Thorne** and **Helene Demontigny** were as follows:

        i.   John Thorn was born on 8 Jul 1872 St.Francois Xavier, Manitoba (SFXI-Kipling, B-61.) (INB, page 176.). He was baptized on 9 Jul 1872 St.Francois Xavier, Manitoba (SFXI-Kipling, B-61.) (INB, page 176.). He married Marguerite Rose Poitras in 1897 Boissevan (ArchiviaNet, C-15006.).

        ii.   Ernest Thorn was born on 28 Jul 1874 St.Eustache, Manitoba (INB, page 176.). He was baptized on 29 Jul 1874 St.Eustache, Manitoba (Ibid.). He married Josephine Paul, daughter of Pierre Paul and Adelaide Duboishue Breland, circa Oct 1900 Maryville, North Dakota (ArchiviaNet, C-15006.).

           Josephine Paul was born on 12 Feb 1881 St.Francois Xavier, Manitoba (SFXI-Kipling, B-8.) (ArchiviaNet, C-15006.).

        iii.   Paulin Thorne was born on 12 Oct 1876 St.Eustache, (Manitoba). (Rosemary Rozyk.). She was baptized 13 Oct 1876 St.Eustache, Manitoba (Ibid.)

    14   iv.   Marie Rose Thorne, b. 9 Mar 1879 St.Francois Xavier, Manitoba; m. Olivier Barron.

        v.   David Thorne was born on 20 Jun 1882 Rolette County, North Dakota (St. Claude Mission, St. John, North Dakota, Baptisms, Marriages, Burials 1882-1888, 2006, Dominique Ritchot, page 3, B-20.). He was baptized on 9 Jul 1882 St.Claude, St.John, Rolette County, North Dakota (Ibid.). He died in 1898 Boissevan (ArchiviaNet, C-15006.).

        vi.   Ellen Thorn was born in 1883 (Denney.). She died in 1896 (Ibid.).

        vii.   Alexander Thorn was born on 2 Jul 1884 St.John, Rolette County, North Dakota (ArchiviaNet, C-15006.). He was baptized on 4 Jul 1884 St.Claude, St.John, Rolette County, North Dakota (St.Claude BMD, Dominique Ritchot, page 33, B-140.).

        viii.   Philip Thorne was born on 13 Sep 1887 (1901 Canada, District 6-i(3), page 8, family 83, line 35-41.).

        ix.   Frances Thorne was born on 7 Jan 1890 (Ibid.).

    15   x.   James Thorne, b. 23 Sep 1893; m. Emma Dumont.

        xi.   Mary M. Thorne was born on 2 Sep 1896 (Ibid.).

8. **Nancy Thorne** was born in Jul 1846 St.Francois Xavier, (Manitoba) (SFX: 1834-1850, B-629.). She was baptized on 9 Aug 1846 St.Francois Xavier, (Manitoba) (Ibid.). She married **Charles Demontigny**, son of **Charles Demontigny** and **Marie Desjarlais,** on 3 Sep 1867 St.Francois Xavier, (Manitoba) (SFXI-Kipling, M-20.) (SFXI 1851-1868, M-20.). She died on 11 Jan 1888 Rolette County, North Dakota, at age 41 (AYM Documentation of Metis Families of Red River and the Northwest Territories; Census, Biographical, and Historical: 1881 Census Qu'Appelle, Wood Mountain, Lac la Biche; History of the Turtle Mountain Band of Chippewas; Census for the Turtle Mountain Reservation 1884-1886; Pembina, Dakota Territory 1850 Census; Various Metis Census Records for Pembina County, ND 1910; compiled by Al Yerbery, 1996, Death List of TMC Indians.).

Charles Demontigny was born on 28 May 1845 St.Francois Xavier, (Manitoba) (SFX: 1834-1850, B-573.). He was baptized on 29 May 1845 St.Francois Xavier, (Manitoba) (Ibid.). He married **Marie Rose Braconnier**, daughter of **Daniel Braconnier** and **Sarah Ducharme,** on 19 Apr 1905 St.Francois Xavier, Manitoba (MM, page 158.) (SFXI 1851-1868, M-20 (note).).

9. **Marie Thorne** was born on 1 Feb 1849 St.Francois Xavier, (Manitoba) (SFX: 1834-1850, B-766.). She was baptized on 4 Feb 1849 St.Francois Xavier, (Manitoba) (Ibid.). She married **Louis Desjarlais**, son of **Louis Desjarlais** and **Julie Chartrand,** on 3 Feb 1874 St.Francois Xavier, Manitoba (SFXI-Kipling, M-5.). She died on 29 Jun 1878 St.Francois Xavier, Manitoba, at age 29 (Ibid., S-40.).

Louis Desjarlais was born on 7 Apr 1855 Baie St.Paul, (Manitoba) (Ibid., B-32 and B-33.) (SFXI 1851-1868, B-32 and B-33.). He was baptized on 22 Apr 1855 St.Francois Xavier, (Manitoba) (Ibid.). He married **Marie Lucier**, daughter of **Joseph Lucier** and **Josephte Farquarhson dit Ferguson,** on 14 Oct 1879 St.Eustache, Manitoba (MM.) (ST-BSP, M-10.).

10. **Elise Thorne** was born on 11 Jan 1851 St.Francois Xavier, (Manitoba) (SFX: 1834-1850, B-877.). She was baptized on 12 Jan 1851 St.Francois Xavier, (Manitoba) (Ibid.). She married **Joseph L'Hirondelle**, son of **Joseph L'Hirondelle dit Nesotew** and **Marguerite Nepissing dit Commandant,** on 4 May 1868 St.Francois Xavier, (Manitoba) (SFXI-Kipling, M-5.). She died on 7 Dec 1939 Calgary, Alberta, at age 88 (Denney.).

Joseph L'Hirondelle was born on 3 Oct 1844 (INB, page 111.). He was baptized on 3 Oct 1844 Fort-des-Prairies, (Alberta) (Ibid.). He died on 5 Feb 1920 Calgary, Alberta, at age 75 (Denney.).

Generation Three

11. **David Thorne** was born circa 1859 North West Territories (Denney.). He was baptized on 7 Feb 1865 (Fort de la Montagne du Tondre), St.Boniface, (Manitoba) (SB-Rozyk, page 179, B-28.). He married **Harriet Anderson**, daughter of **David Anderson** and **Margaret Favel,** on 5 Jan 1884 Lebret, (Saskatchewan) (L2 Lebret, Mission de St.Florent, Roman Catholic Registre des Baptemes, Mariages & Seplutures, Qu'Appelle, Saskatchewan, Book Two: 1881-1887, FHC microfilm 1032949., page 76, M-1. Hereinafter cited as L2.).

Harriet Anderson was born in 1860 Qu'Appelle, (Saskatchewan) (HBS 1886-1901, 1906 Half-Breed Scrip Applications, RG15-21, Volume 1333; C-14945.). She married **Thomas Robillard**, son of **Jean Baptiste Robillard** and **Isabelle Comtois,** before 1894 (ArchiviaNet, C-14999.).

Children of **David Thorne** and **Harriet Anderson** were as follows:

    i.   Maria Thorne was born on 1 Apr 1882 Fort Qu'Appelle, (Saskatchewan) (L1, page 282, B-_.). She was baptized on 8 Apr 1882 Lebret, (Saskatchewan) (Ibid.).

    ii.   Antoine Thorn was born on 18 Feb 1884 Fort Qu'Appelle, (Saskatchewan) (L2, page 93, B-_.) (ArchiviaNet, C-15006.). He was baptized on 25 Feb 1884 Lebret, (Saskatchewan) (L2, page 93, B-_.).

    iii.   Marie Rose Thorne was born on 3 Dec 1885 (Ibid., page 155-156, B-57.). She was baptized on 18 Aug 1886 Lebret, (Saskatchewan) (Ibid.).

    iv.   May Robillard was born circa 1890 (Saskatchewan) (Automated Genealogy 1906 Census Transcription Project and Census Images from the National Archives of Canada, http://www.automatedgenealogy.com.).

    v.   Joseph Thorne was born on 20 Mar 1891 (Saskatchewan) (Saskatchewan Vital Statistics online, http://vsgs.health.gov.sk.ca, Birth Reg. #9034.).

12. **George Thorne** was born circa 1859 (SB-Rozyk, page 179, B-27.). He was baptized on 7 Feb 1865 (Fort de la Montagne du Tondre), St.Boniface, (Manitoba) (Ibid.). He married **Marie Rose Lillie**, daughter of **William Lillie** and **Eliza Gagnon,** on 20 Oct 1881 St.Francois Xavier, Manitoba (SFXI-Kipling, M-20.).

Marie Rose Lillie was born on 17 Dec 1867 St.Francois Xavier, (Manitoba) (Ibid., B-113.). She was baptized on 23 Dec 1867 St.Francois Xavier, (Manitoba) (Ibid.).

Children of **George Thorne** and **Marie Rose Lillie** were as follows:

    i.   Jeanne Thorne was born on 14 Nov 1880 Rock Lake (ArchiviaNet, C-15006.). She was born on 28 Nov 1883 Rolette County, North Dakota (St.Claude BMD, Dominique Ritchot, page 32, B-136.). She was baptized on 22 May 1884 St.Claude, St.John, Rolette County, North Dakota (Ibid.). She died on 6 May 1891 near Pilot Mound at age 7 (ArchiviaNet, C-15006.).

    ii.   William George Thorn was born on 3 Jul 1885 Rock Lake (1901 Canada, District 8(j-1), page 4, famiy 45, line 22-28.) (ArchiviaNet, C-15006.).

    iii.   Lisa A. Thorn was born on 12 Dec 1887 (1901 Canada, District 8(j-1), page 4, famiy 45, line 22-28.).

    iv.   Mary A. Thorn was born on 6 Dec 1890 (Ibid.).

    v.   Sarah M. Thorn was born on 1 Oct 1895 (Ibid.).

    vi.   William J. Thorn was born on 13 Jun 1899 (Ibid.).

13. **William Thorne** was born circa 1859 St.Boniface, (Manitoba) (MBS, C-14934.). He married **Julie Ross**, daughter of **Donald Ross** and **Catherine Delorme,** on 22 Feb 1881 St.Francois Xavier, Manitoba (SFXI-Kipling, M-7.). He married **Elise Ross**, daughter of **Donald Ross** and **Catherine Delorme,** on 18 Nov 1886 Batoche, (Saskatchewan) (BSAP Records of the Parish of Batoche, St.Antoine de Pudoue Roman Catholic Church: Register for Baptisms, Marriages, Deaths, Volume One, 1881-1909., page 52, M-2. Hereinafter cited as BSAP.). He died on 10 Jun 1930 Batoche, Saskatchewan (Denney.).

Julie Ross was born on 8 Mar 1862 St.Francois Xavier, (Manitoba) (SFXI-Kipling, B-19.). She was baptized on 9 Mar 1862 St.Francois Xavier, (Manitoba) (Ibid.). She died circa 15 May 1885 Batoche, (Saskatchewan) (BSAP, page 34, S-22.). She was buried on 16 May 1885 Batoche, (Saskatchewan) (Ibid.).

Children of **William Thorne** and **Julie Ross** were as follows:

    i.   Marie Elise Thorn was born on 21 Jun 1881 Fish Creek, (Saskatchewan) (Denney.).

    ii.   David Thorn was born on 1 Apr 1882 St.Francois Xavier, Manitoba (SFXI-Kipling, B-21.). He died on 4 Mar 1883 St.Francois Xavier, Manitoba (Ibid., S-5.).

    iii.   Marie Esilda Thorn was born on 22 May 1883 St.Francois Xavier, Manitoba (Ibid., B-28.). She died on 13 Feb 1900 Fish Creek, (Saskatchewan), at age 16 (Denney.).

    iv.   Alvina Thorn was born on 6 Mar 1884 Fish Creek, (Saskatchewan) (ArchiviaNet, C-15006.).

    v.   Asilda Thorn was born in May 1884 Fish Creek, (Saskatchewan) (Ibid.). She died on 13 Feb 1900 Fish Creek, (Saskatchewan), at age 15 (Ibid.).

    vi.   Anastasie Nancy Thorn was born on 1 Mar 1885 Fish Creek, (Saskatchewan) (BSAP, page 30, B-7.) (ArchiviaNet, C-15006.). She was baptized on 3 Mar 1885 Batoche, (Saskatchewan) (BSAP, page 30, B-7.).

Elise Ross was born on 14 Jun 1853 St.Francois Xavier, (Manitoba) (SFXI-Kipling, B-93.) (SFXI 1851-1868, B-93.). She was baptized on 19 Jun 1853 St.Francois Xavier, (Manitoba) (SFXI-Kipling, B-93.) (SFXI 1851-1868, B-93.). She married **Jean Baptiste Lefort**, son of **Francois Toussaint Lefort** and **Eliza Laplante**, on 13 Jan 1874 St.Francois Xavier, Manitoba (SFXI-Kipling, M-2.).

Children of **William Thorne** and **Elise Ross** were as follows:

    i.   Marie Elise Thorn was born on 21 Jun 1891 Batoche, (Saskatchewan) (BSAP, page 90, B-14.). She was baptized on 23 Jun 1891 Batoche, (Saskatchewan) (Ibid.).

    ii.   David Thorn was born on 23 Jun 1893 Batoche, (Saskatchewan) (Ibid., page 107, B-16.) (SK Vital Statistics, #7724.). He was baptized on 27 Jun 1893 Batoche, (Saskatchewan) (BSAP, page 107, B-16.). He died on 30 Mar 1894 Batoche, (Saskatchewan) (Ibid., page 114, S-6.). He was buried on 31 Mar 1894 Batoche, (Saskatchewan) (Ibid.).

    iii.   Nancy Thorn was born on 4 Mar 1895 Batoche, (Saskatchewan) (Ibid., page 122, B-7.) (SK Vital Statistics, #7816.). She was baptized on 11 Mar 1895 Batoche, (Saskatchewan) (BSAP, page 122, B-7.).

    iv.   David Thorn was born on 28 Jun 1897 (Saskatchewan) (SK Vital Statistics, #7919.).

14. Marie Rose Thorne was born on 9 Mar 1879 St.Francois Xavier, Manitoba (SFXI-Kipling, B-11.). She married **Olivier Barron**, son of **Charles Barron** and **Marie Comtois**, on 14 Jan 1901 (HBS, Volume 1334; C-14947.).

Olivier Barron was born on 22 Sep 1875 St.Francois Xavier, Manitoba (SFXI-Kipling, B-42.) (INB, page 10.). He was baptized on 23 Sep 1875 St.Francois Xavier, Manitoba (SFXI-Kipling, B-42.) (Rosemary Helga (Morrissette) Rozyk Research, 3 Nov 2006.) (INB, page 10.).

15. James Thorne was born on 23 Sep 1893 (1901 Canada, District 6-i(3), page 8, family 83, line 35-41.). He married **Emma Dumont**, daughter of **Basil Dumont** and **Mary Rose Azure**, before 1920 (1937-TMC Indian Census Roll of the Turtle Mountain Reservation, United States Indian Service Department of the Interior, Belcourt, North Dakota, J. E. Balmer, 1 January 1937 , page 493, Census No. 5761-5766.).

Emma Dumont was born on 10 Feb 1900 (1936-TMC, page 87.) (1918-TMC 1918 Census of the Turtle Mountain Chippewa, North Dakota, National Archives of the United States, Washington D.C.).

Children of **James Thorne** and **Emma Dumont** are as follows:

    i.   Lillian Thorne was born on 2 Dec 1920 (*1937-TMC*, page 493, Census No. 5761-5766.).

    ii.   Florence Thorne was born on 22 Sep 1922 (Ibid.).

    iii.   Rose Thorne was born on 14 Mar 1924 (Ibid.).

    iv.   Joseph Thorne was born on 7 Nov 1928 (Ibid.).

    v.   Bertha Thorne was born on 19 Dec 1931 (Ibid.).

Descendants of William Todd

Generation One

1. William Todd was born between 1784 and 1787 Dublin, Ireland (Denney Papers, Charles D. Denney, Glenbow Archives, Calgary, Alberta.) (*DCB-V8 Dictionary of Canadian Biography - Volume Eight*;Toronto, Ontario: University of Toronto Press, 2000), Arthur Ray, page 888-889.). He married according to the custom of the country **Marianne Ballantyne** circa 1822 (Denney.). He married according to the custom of the country **Isabelle Dennett**, daughter of **William Dennett** and **Sophia Indian or Ballantyne or Ballendine**, before 1825. He married **Isabelle Dennett**, daughter of **William Dennett** and **Sophia Indian or Ballantyne or Ballendine**, on 20 Aug 1839 (St.Andrews), Grand Rapids, Red River Settlement, (Manitoba) (*DCB-V8*, Arthur Ray, page 888-889.) (HBCA-B Hudson's Bay Company Archives - biographical sketches, Hudson's Bay Company Archives; Winnipeg, Manitoba, E./1a fo. 147, 161; E.4/1b fo. 262; E.4/2 fo. 140.) (HBCR Hudson Bay Company Register of Anglican Church Baptisms, Marriages, and Burials for the Red River Settlement, 1821-1841; Hudson's Bay Company Archives, Winnipeg, Manitoba, No. 418. Hereinafter cited as HBCR.) (Ibid.). He died on 22 Dec 1851 Red River, (Manitoba) (*DCB-V8*, Arthur Ray, page 888-889.).

Marianne Ballantyne died b 1830-1835 (Ibid.).

Children of **William Todd** and **Marianne Ballantyne** were as follows:

    i.   Marianne Todd was born circa Dec 1822 (HBCR, S-9.). She died in Mar 1823 York Factory (Ibid.). She was buried on 16 Mar 1823 York Factory (Ibid.).

  2 ii.   William Todd, b. 1823 York Factory; m. Sarah Jane Johnstone; m. Fanny Anne Hourie; d. 18 Jul 1871 St.Clements, Manitoba.

Isabelle Dennett was born circa 1804. She was baptized on 4 Jul 1839 St.Andrews, (Manitoba) (HBCA-B, E./1a fo. 147, 161; E.4/1b fo. 262; E.4/2 fo. 140.). She died on 4 Mar 1845 (Ibid.). Question: *Probable daughter of William Dennett and Sophia.*

Children of **William Todd** and **Isabelle Dennett** were as follows:

  3 i.   James Todd, b. 1825 York Factory; m. Josephine Deslauriers; d. 11 Jan 1887 St.Francois Xavier, Manitoba; bur. 13 Jan 1887 St.Francois Xavier, Manitoba.

    ii.   Samuel Todd was born circa Feb 1827 York Factory (Denney.). He was baptized on 24 Sep 1827 St.Johns, York Factory (HBCR, E.4/1a, folio 65d, #662.). He was buried on 9 Oct 1827 York Factory (HBCA-B, E.42 fo. 18.).

    iii.   Anne Todd was born in 1830 Brandon House (Denney.). She was baptized on 8 Jun 1830 St.Johns, (Manitoba) (HBCR, E.4/1a, folio 77d, #188.). She died on 8 May 1844 (Denney.). She was buried St.Johns, (Manitoba) (Ibid.).

       Question: *HBCA says daughter of Marianne Ballantyne.*

iv. Robert Todd was born in 1832 Brandon House (Ibid.). He was baptized on 30 May 1832 St.Johns, Brandon House, (Manitoba) (HBCA-B, E.4/1 fo. 90.) (HBCR, E.4/1a, folio 90.). He died in Dec 1905 Kamloops, British Columbia (Denney.).

4 v. John Todd, b. 24 Nov 1833 Fort Pelly; m. Magdeleine Ducharme; m. Matilda Williams; m. Marie Allary; d. 6 Feb 1896 Posen, Manitoba.

vi. Margaret Todd was born in 1835 Swan River (Ibid.). She was baptized on 5 Jul 1839 St.Johns, Red River Settlement, (Manitoba) (HBCA-B, E.4/1 fo. 161.) (HBCR, E.4/1a, folio 161.). She died on 2 Dec 1854 (Denney.). She was buried St.Johns, (Manitoba) (Ibid.).

5 vii. Donald Todd, b. 1837 Northwest Territories; m. Susanne Durand or Dumont; d. between 1886 and 1901.

6 viii. Mary Todd, b. 6 Aug 1839 St.Johns, Red River Settlement, (Manitoba); m. William Inkster; d. 15 Aug 1912 Kildonan, Manitoba.

ix. Charles Todd was born in 1841 (Ibid.). He died on 28 Apr 1875 (Ibid.). He was buried St.Johns, Manitoba (Ibid.).

7 x. Elizabeth 'Liza' Todd, b. 1843 Swan River; m. Joseph Corrigal; m. James Settee Jr; d. 1 Nov 1877.

Generation Two

2. William Todd was born in 1823 York Factory (Ibid.). He was baptized on 7 Sep 1823 St.Johns, York Factory (HBCA-B, E.4/1a fo. 45, 46d.) (HBCR, E.4/1a, folio 46d.). He married **Sarah Jane Johnstone** on 17 Sep 1849 (St.Andrews), The Rapids, Red River Settlement, (Manitoba) (Ibid., No. 188.). He married **Fanny Anne Hourie**, daughter of **John Hourie Jr.** and **Jessie Dennett**, circa 1870. He died on 18 Jul 1871 St.Clements, Manitoba (MBS Scrip Applications, Original White Settlers & Halfbreeds residing in Manitoba on 15 July 1870, RG15-19, C-14934.).

Sarah Jane Johnstone died circa 1869.

Children of **William Todd** and **Sarah Jane Johnstone** were as follows:

8 i. Albert Todd, b. circa 1847 (Manitoba); m. Mary McKay.

ii. Samuel Todd was baptized on 1 Feb 1850 St.Andrews, (Manitoba) (Denney.). He was buried on 11 Dec 1864 St.Johns, (Manitoba) (Ibid.).

iii. Isabelle Todd was born in 1852 British Columbia (NWHBS 1885 Scrip Applications, North-West Halfbreeds residing outside Manitoba on 15 July 1870, RG15-20, C-14942.). She married William Sinclair, son of Benjamin Sinclair and Marguerite Collins, in 1868 White Fish Lake, (Alberta) (Ibid., C-14941.) (Ibid., C-14942.). She married George Spence in 1876 Victoria, (Alberta) (Ibid.).

William Sinclair was born circa 1850 (Ibid., C-14941.). He died in 1875 Fort Victoria (Ibid.).

iv. William James Todd was born on 15 Jan 1853 St.Clements, (Manitoba) (MBS, C-14934.).

v. Donald Todd was born on 4 Aug 1855 North West Territories (Ibid.).

vi. Fanny Todd was born on 5 Jan 1857 North West Territories (Ibid.).

Fanny Anne Hourie was baptized on 13 Apr 1841 St.Johns, Red River Settlement, (Manitoba) (HBCR, E.4/1a, folio 172d.). She married **Narcisse Chatelain Sr.**, son of **Nicolas Chatelain** and **Anne Nanette Chartier,** before 12 Sep 1876 (MBS, C-14926.).

Children of **William Todd** and **Fanny Anne Hourie** were:

i. Mary Jane Todd was born on 27 Nov 1870 St.Clements, (Manitoba) (Ibid., C-14934.). She was baptized on 27 Nov 1870 St.Clements, (Manitoba) (Ibid.). She died on 19 Feb 1877 St.Clements, (Manitoba), at age 6 (Ibid.). She was buried on 19 Feb 1877 St.Clements, (Manitoba) (Ibid.).

3. James Todd was born in 1825 York Factory (NWHBS, C-14942.). He was baptized on 21 Aug 1825 St.Johns, York Fort, Hudson's Bay (HBCA-B, E.4/1a fo. 57.) (HBCR, E.4/1a, folio 57.). He married **Josephine Deslauriers**, daughter of **Antoine Deslauriers** and **Genevieve Gelinas dit Lacourse,** on 5 Aug 1852 St.Boniface, (Manitoba) (NWHBS, C-14942.) (Automated Genealogy 1901 Census Transcription Project and Census Images from the National Archives of Canada, http://www.automatedgenealogy.com, #11, N-3, page 2, Family 11, Line 3-5.). He died on 11 Jan 1887 St.Francois Xavier, Manitoba (Manitoba Vital Statistics online, http://web2.gov.mb.ca, Death Reg. #1887,001841.). He was buried on 13 Jan 1887 St.Francois Xavier, Manitoba (Denney.).

Josephine Deslauriers was born in 1837 (NWHBSI Index 1885 Scrip Applications, North-West Halfbreeds residing outside Manitoba on 15 July 1870, RG15-20, page 79, page 107.). She died on 31 Dec 1905 St.Francois Xavier, Manitoba (MB Vital Statistics, Death Reg. #1906,005457.).

Children of **James Todd** and **Josephine Deslauriers** were as follows:

i. Elizabeth Todd was born in Feb 1853 (NWHBS, C-14942.). She died in 1853 (Ibid.).

9 ii. William Todd, b. 1855; m. Mary Dufresne; d. between 1892 and 1895 Fort Pit, (Saskatchewan).

10 iii. Norbert Todd, b. 4 Feb 1857; m. Josephine Morin.

iv. James Alexis Todd was born circa 1861 (SB-Rozyk St. Boniface Roman Catholic Church, Manitoba, Canada, Baptisms, Marriages and Burials 1860-1875 Extractions, Compiled by Rosemary Rozyk, page _, B-_.). He was baptized on 20 Jun 1862 St.Boniface, (Manitoba) (Ibid.).

11 v. Peter Todd, b. 26 Oct 1863; m. Mary Jane Morin; d. 31 Mar 1908 Portage la Prairie, Manitoba; bur. 1908 St.Francois Xavier, Manitoba.

12 vi. Gilbert Todd, b. 13 Nov 1865 The Pas, Cumberland House, (Saskatchewan); m. Cleophee Lavallee.

13 vii. Norman Todd, b. 9 Nov 1868 York Factory; m. Marie Appoline Deslauriers; d. 1947.

14 viii. Gabriel Todd, b. 15 Mar 1871; m. Elise Lavallee.

15 ix. Alexander Todd, b. 26 Nov 1874; m. Marie Anne McDougall; d. 1938; bur. 1938 St.Francois Xavier, Manitoba.

4. John Todd was born on 24 Nov 1833 Fort Pelly (MBS, C-14934.). He was baptized on 22 Jul 1834 St.Johns, Red River Settlement, (Manitoba) (HBCA-B, E.4/1 fo. 110.) (HBCR, E.4/1a, folio 110.). He married **Magdeleine Ducharme** before 1854. He married **Matilda Williams**, daughter of **William Williams** and **Sarah "Sally" Fidler,** on 29 Mar 1855 St.Johns, (Manitoba) (Louis Verhagen Research.). He and **Marie Allary** met before 1859. He died on 6 Feb 1896 Posen, Manitoba, at age 62 (MB Vital Statistics, Death Reg. #1896,002529.).

Children of **John Todd** and **Magdeleine Ducharme** were:

    i.   John Todd was born on 10 May 1854 St.Charles, (Manitoba) (MBS, C-14934.). He married Rosalie Desjardins, daughter of Jean Baptiste Desjardins and Marguerite Hamelin, on 2 Jun 1874 Ste.Agathe, Manitoba (MM *Manitoba Marriages* in *Publication 45*, Volumes 1-3, compiled and edited by: Paul J. Lareau, Fr. Julien Hamelin, (240 Avenue Daly, Ottawa, Ontario K1N 6G2: Le Centre de Genealogie S.C., 1984).). He married Isabelle Bousquet, daughter of Michel Bousquet and Louise Vendette, on 28 Jan 1879 St.Vital, Battleford, (Saskatchewan) (SV St.Vital Roman Catholic Registre des Baptemes, Mariages & Sepltures, Battleford, Saskatchewan, 1878-1896, M-1, page 1. Hereinafter cited as SV.). He died on 10 Mar 1913 at age 58 (Denney.).

        Rosalie Desjardins was born on 5 Sep 1858 St.Norbert, (Manitoba) (SN1 Catholic Parish Register of St.Norbert 1857-1873, page 6, B-23. Hereinafter cited as SN1.). She was baptized on 6 Sep 1858 St.Norbert, (Manitoba) (Ibid.).

        Isabelle Bousquet was born circa 1841 Edmonton, (Alberta) (INB *Index des Naissances and Baptemes* (St.Boniface, Manitoba: La Societe Historique de Saint-Boniface., c1995), page 21.) (HBS 1886-1901, 1906 Half-Breed Scrip Applications, RG15-21, Volume 1337, C-14951.). She was baptized on 25 Apr 1845 Fort-des-Prairies (INB, page 21.). She married **Joseph Alexandre**, son of **Pash-ko-wagan Crin** and **Marie Indian,** circa 1860 St.Boniface, (Manitoba) (HBS, Volume 1337, C-14951.).

Matilda Williams was born in Aug 1821 North West Territories (MBS, C-14934.). She was baptized on 6 Aug 1822 St.Johns (HBCR, E.4/1a, folio 38d.).

Children of **John Todd** and **Matilda Williams** all born St.James, (Manitoba), were as follows:

    i.   Elizabeth Todd was born on 5 Dec 1855 (Denney.). She was baptized on 13 Jan 1856 St.James, (Manitoba) (SJAC St.James Anglican Church Extractions, Manitoba Genealogy Society, Winnipeg, Manitoba, B-37.). She died on 15 Sep 1886 St.James, Manitoba, at age 30 (Denney.).

    ii.   William Todd was born on 28 Feb 1857 (Ibid.). He was baptized on 22 Mar 1857 St.James, (Manitoba) (MBS, C-14934.) (SJAC, B-50.).

 16   iii.   Sarah Todd, b. 1 Dec 1858; m. Charles Oxford White.

    iv.   Maria Todd was born on 2 Feb 1861 (SJAC.). She was baptized on 3 Mar 1861 St.James, (Manitoba) (MBS, C-14934.) (SJAC, B-103.).

    v.   Robert Todd was born on 3 Dec 1863 (Denney.). He was baptized on 3 Jan 1864 St.James, (Manitoba) (SJAC, B-148.) (MBS, C-14934.). He married Flora Hallett, daughter of James Hallett and Mary Bourke, on 3 Jan 1885 Winnipeg, Manitoba (MB Vital Statistics, Marriage Reg. #1885,001657.). He died on 19 Apr 1899 St.James, Manitoba, at age 35 (St.James Anglican Cemetery; Cemetery Transcription #121; Mavis and Maureen Smith, Unit "E," 1045 St.James Street, Winnipeg, Manitoba, Canada R3H 1B1: Manitoba Genealogical Society, Inc., 1983, page 92.).

        Flora Hallett was born on 12 Feb 1864 St.James, (Manitoba) (MBS, C-14928.). She was baptized on 5 Mar 1865 St.James, (Manitoba) (Ibid., C-14934.) (SJAC, B-160.). She married **Liversedge Brandon** on 26 Nov 1913 (Denney.).

    vi.   Donald Todd was born on 14 Jun 1867 (SJAC.). He was baptized on 7 Jul 1867 St.James, (Manitoba) (Ibid., B-186.) (MBS, C-14934.).

Marie Allary was born circa 1830 Duck Bay, (Manitoba) (1870C-MB 1870 Manitoba Census, National Archives of Canada, Ottawa, Ontario, Microfilm Reel Number C-2170., page 363, #1169.). She and **Thomas Bremner** met before 1852 (Denney.). She and **William Bremner** met before 1865.

Children of **John Todd** and **Marie Allary** were:

 17   i.   Maria Todd, b. 1859 Sturgeon Creek, (Manitoba); m. Pierre Boucher.

5. Donald Todd was born in 1837 Northwest Territories (1881 Church of Latter Day Saints Census Transcription Project of Census Images from the National Archives of Canada, Ottawa, Canada, http://www.familysearch.org, District 192-R, page 1, family 2.). He was baptized on 4 Jul 1839 St.Johns, Red River Settlement, (Manitoba) (HBCA-B, E.4/1 fo. 161d.) (HBCR, E.4/1a, folio 161d.). He married **Susanne Durand or Dumont**, daughter of **Louis Durand** and **Marie "Okatshikew" Cree,** in 1875 Bears Hills, (Alberta) (NWHBS, C-14938.). He died between 1886 and 1901.

Susanne Durand or Dumont was born circa 1855 Beaver Hills Lake, (Alberta) (Ibid.) (1901 Canada, District 202-v(4), page 36, family 369, line 16-19.). She was born circa 1857 (MSJ-FA-E Register des Baptemes, Mariages & Sepultures 1858-1861 Mission St.Joachim, Fort Auguste, Fort des Prairies, Edmonton, No. 1, page 30, B-55. Hereinafter cited as MSJ-FA-E.). She was baptized on 28 Feb 1861 St.Joachim, Fort Edmonton, (Alberta) (Ibid.).

Children of **Donald Todd** and **Susanne Durand or Dumont** were as follows:

 18   i.   Harriet Todd, b. 15 Feb 1876 Tail Creek, (Alberta); m. Archibald Whitford.

    ii.   Samuel Todd was born in 1879 Battle River, (Alberta) (ArchiviaNet 1886-1901, 1906 Half-Breed Scrip Applications Index, RG15-21, Volume 1333 through 1371, Microfilm Reel Number C-14944 through C-15010, National Archives of Canada, Ottawa, Ontario, http://www.collectionscanada.gc.ca, C-15006.).

    iii.   Emma Todd was born on 1 Nov 1880 (Ibid.). She died on 20 Apr 1885 Beaver Hills, (Alberta), at age 4 (Ibid.).

    iv.   Daniel Todd was born in Nov 1881 Todd's Crossing, Battle River, (Alberta) (Ibid.).

    v.   Louis Todd was born in 1886 (1901 Canada, District 202-v(4), page 36, family 369, line 16-19.).

6. Mary Todd was baptized on 6 Aug 1839 St.Johns, Red River Settlement, (Manitoba) (HBCA-B, E.4/1 fo. 162d.) (HBCR, E.4/1a, folio 162d.). She was born on 17 Jul 1840 Fort Pelly (MBS, C-14929.). She married **William Inkster**, son of **John Inkster** and **Mary Sinclair,** on 5 Jun 1856 St.Johns, (Manitoba) (Denney.). She died on 15 Aug 1912 Kildonan, Manitoba, at age 73 (MB Vital Statistics, Death Reg. #1912,006346.).

William Inkster was born on 4 May 1836 Fort Garry, (Manitoba) (Denney.). He was baptized on 1 Jun 1836 St.Johns, Red River Settlement, (Manitoba) (HBCR, E.4/1a, folio 128d.). He died on 4 May 1869 St.Johns, (Manitoba), at age 33 (Denney.).

Children of **Mary Todd** and **William Inkster** all born St.Johns, (Manitoba), were as follows:

      vii. Alfred William Inkster was born on 19 Dec 1868 (MBS, C-14929.). He was baptized on 19 Jan 1869 St.Johns, (Manitoba) (Denney.). He died on 18 Oct 1896 at age 27 (Ibid.).

  7. Elizabeth 'Liza' Todd was born in 1843 Swan River (Ibid.). She was baptized on 15 Aug 1843 St.Johns, (Manitoba) (Ibid.) (HBCA-B, E.4/1 fo. 292.). She married **Joseph Corrigal**, son of **Jacob Corrigal,** on 20 Oct 1862 St.Johns, (Manitoba) (Denney.). She married **James Settee Jr.**, son of **James Settee (Cree)** and **Sarah "Sally" Cook,** on 5 Jul 1866 St.Paul, (Manitoba) (Ibid.) (HBCA-B, PAM St. Peters Marriages #110.). She died on 1 Nov 1877 (Denney.).

  Joseph Corrigal was born in 1839 (Ibid.).

  James Settee Jr was baptized on 30 Sep 1836 St.Johns, Red River Settlement, (Manitoba) (HBCA-B, E.4/1a fo. 21d.) (HBCR, E.4/1a, folio 131.).

Generation Three

  8. **Albert Todd** was born circa 1847 (Manitoba) (1870C-MB, page 164, #258.). He married **Mary McKay**, daughter of **William McKay** and **Susanne Versailles,** on 9 Nov 1874 Touchwood Hills, (Saskatchewan) (T. R. "Pat" McCloy, McKay Descendancy, McKay Descendancy.).

  Mary McKay was born on 20 Mar 1856 North West (MBS, C-14934.).

Children of **Albert Todd** and **Mary McKay** were as follows:

      i. Alfred Ernest Albert Todd was born on 18 Nov 1876 St.Francois Xavier, Manitoba (SFXI-Kipling St.Francois Xavier Register Index, 1834-1900; compiled by Clarence Kipling , B-7.) (MB Vital Statistics, Birth Reg. #1894,001906.). He was baptized on 7 Apr 1894 St.Francois Xavier, Manitoba (SFXI-Kipling, B-7.). He died on 26 Aug 1898 St.Boniface, Manitoba (ArchiviaNet, C-15006.). (MB Vital Statistics, Death Reg. #1898,002441) He was buried on 27 Aug 1898 St.Francois Xavier, Manitoba (SFXI-Kipling, S-16.). (Rosemary Rozyk.).

      ii. Samuel Absolam Todd was born on 13 Jun 1878 Qu'Appelle, (Saskatchewan). He died on 18 Apr 1881 Touchwood Hills, (Saskatchewan), at age 2 (ArchiviaNet, C-15007.).

      iii. William Todd was born in 1881 Qu'Appelle, (Saskatchewan) (Ibid., C-15006.).

  9. **William Todd** was born in 1855 (NWHBS, C-14942.). He married **Mary Dufresne**, daughter of **Edouard Dufresne** and **Marguerite Mondion,** before 1881 (Rod MacQuarrie Research, 6 Mar 2006.). He died between 1892 and 1895 Fort Pit, (Saskatchewan) (Eileen Horan Research, 6 March 2006.) (Rod Mac Quarrie, 6 Mar 2006.).

  Mary Dufresne was born on 13 Apr 1865 (Saskatchewan) (1901 Alberta Census Index, Alberta Genealogical Society, Edmonton, Alberta, www.agsedm.edmonton.ab.ca, page 2, line 8-13, Saddle Lake.) (Eileen Horan, 6 March 2006.). She was baptized on 27 May 1875 St.Laurent, (Saskatchewan) (Ibid.). She married **James Howse**, son of **Adam Howse** and **Margaret Favel,** before 1898 (1901C-AGSE, page 2, line 8-13, Saddle Lake.).

Children of **William Todd** and **Mary Dufresne** were as follows:

    19   i. James Todd, b. 3 May 1882 Fort Pitt District near present day Lloydminster, (Saskatchewan); m. Caroline Laframboise; d. 22 Oct 1967 Rossdale Flats Care Home, Edmonton, Alberta.

      ii. Ellen Todd was born in 1884 Bresaylor, (Saskatchewan) (ArchiviaNet.). She died circa Apr 1886 Fort Pitt, (Saskatchewan) (Ibid.).

      iii. Mary Todd was born on 17 Oct 1885 (1901 Canada, Egg Lake, page 6, Family 42, line 26-31.). She married John Lafournaise, son of Guillaume Lafournaise dit Laboucane and Caroline Gariepy, on 13 Jan 1903 St.Paul, (Alberta) (Stan Hulme Research, 5 Apr 2007.).

        John Lafournaise was born in 1880 Duck Lake, (Saskatchewan) (Ibid.). He was born in 1882 Duck Lake, (Saskatchewan) (ArchiviaNet.).

      iv. Isabelle Todd was born on 15 Nov 1887 (1901 Canada, Egg Lake, page 6, Family 42, line 26-31.). She was born in 1889 Manitoba (1901C-AGSE, page 2, line 8-13, Saddle Lake.).

  10. **Norbert Todd** was born on 4 Feb 1857 (1901 Canada, MB, Selkirk, (#11), SFX, N-1, page 2, family 19, Line 4-10.). He married **Josephine Morin**, daughter of **Jean Baptiste Comtois Morin** and **Josephte Lussier,** on 7 Jan 1885 St.Francois Xavier, Manitoba (SFXI-Kipling.) (MB Vital Statistics, Mar. Reg. #1889,001795.).

  Josephine Morin was born on 28 Mar 1869 St.Boniface, (Manitoba) (MBS, C-14931.) (SB-Rozyk, page 148, B-29.). She was baptized on 29 Mar 1869 St.Boniface, (Manitoba) (MBS, C-14931.) (SB-Rozyk, page 148, B-29.). She died in 1958 (Denney.).

Children of **Norbert Todd** and **Josephine Morin** were as follows:

      i. Anonyme Todd was born on 20 Nov 1885 Rabbit Point (HBSI.) (ArchiviaNet, C-15006.). He died on 5 Dec 1885 Rabbit Point (HBSI.) (ArchiviaNet, C-15006.). (Rosemary Rozyk.). He was buried on 7 Dec 1885 (Ibid.).

      ii. Jacques Norbert Todd was born on 6 Feb 1887 R.M. of St.Francois Xavier, Manitoba (MB Vital Statistics, Birth Reg. #1887,004199.). He was baptized on 8 Feb 1887 St.Francois Xavier, Manitoba (Rosemary Rozyk.). He died on 16 Jun 1887 St.Francois Xavier, Manitoba (Ibid., Death Reg. #1887,001852.). He was buried on 18 Jun 1887 St.Francois Xavier, Manitoba (Rosemary Rozyk.).

      iii. William Todd was born on 7 Jun 1888 R.M. of St.Francois Xavier, Manitoba (1901 Canada, MB, Selkirk, (#11), SFX, N-1, page 2, family 19, Line 4-10.) (MB Vital Statistics, Birth Reg. #1889,005448.). He married Barbara Tate in Oct 1922 (Denney.).

      iv. Marie Jeanne Todd was born on 7 Sep 1890 St.Francois Xavier, Manitoba (SFXI-Kipling, page 28, B-41.) (1901 Canada, MB, Selkirk, (#11), SFX, N-1, page 2, family 19, Line 4-10.) (MB Vital Statistics, Birth Reg. #1890,003607.).

      v. Marie Virginie Todd was born on 6 Aug 1892 St.Francois Xavier, Manitoba (SFXI-Kipling, B-37.) (MB Vital Statistics, Birth Reg. #1892,003427.). She was baptized on 7 Aug 1892 St.Francois Xavier, Manitoba (SFXI-Kipling, B-37) (Rosemary Rozyk.). She died on 7 Jun 1893 St.Francois Xavier, Manitoba (SFXI-Kipling, S-13.) (MB Vital Statistics, Death Reg. #1893,002566.). She was buried on 8 Jun 1893 St.Francois Xavier, Manitoba (SFXI-Kipling, S-13.) (Rosemary Rozyk.).

     vi. Joseph Todd was born on 9 May 1894 St.Francois Xavier, Manitoba (SFXI-Kipling, page 36, B-12.) (MB Vital Statistics, Birth Reg. #1894,001914.).

     vii. Marie Eleonore Todd was born on 29 Apr 1896 St.Francois Xavier, Manitoba (SFXI-Kipling, page 163, B-16.) (1901 Canada, MB, Selkirk, (#11), SFX, N-1, page 2, family 19, Line 4-10.) (MB Vital Statistics, Birth Reg. #1896,006046.).

     viii. Anonyme Todd was born on 10 May 1898 R.M. of St.Francois Xavier, Manitoba (Ibid., Birth Reg. #1899,006949.).

     ix. Louis Wilfred Todd was born on 14 Mar 1900 St.Francois Xavier, Manitoba (1901 Canada, MB, Selkirk, (#11), SFX, N-1, page 2, family 19, Line 4-10.).

     x. Etienne Todd was born on 30 Jul 1903 R.M. of St.Francois Xavier, Manitoba (MB Vital Statistics, Birth Reg. #1903,004014.).

11. Peter Todd was born on 26 Oct 1863 (SB-Rozyk, page 130, B-158.). He was baptized on 27 Oct 1863 St.Boniface, (Manitoba) (Ibid.). He married **Mary Jane Morin**, daughter of **Jean Baptiste Comtois Morin** and **Josephte Lussier,** on 29 Oct 1889 St.Francois Xavier, Manitoba (SFXI-Kipling, page 72, M-11.) (MB Vital Statistics, Mar. Reg. #1889,001797.). He died on 31 Mar 1908 Portage la Prairie, Manitoba, at age 44 (Denney.) (MB Vital Statistics, Death Reg. #1908,004815.). He was buried in 1908 St.Francois Xavier, Manitoba (Denney.).

Mary Jane Morin was born on 3 Feb 1873 St.Boniface, Manitoba (SB-Rozyk, page 264, B-20.). She was baptized on 4 Feb 1873 St.Boniface, Manitoba (Ibid.). She died circa 1958 Winnipeg, Manitoba (Denney.). She was buried circa 1958 Stonewall, Manitoba (Ibid.).

Children of **Peter Todd** and **Mary Jane Morin** were as follows:

     i. Antoine Frederic Modeste Todd was born on 16 Aug 1890 St.Francois Xavier, Manitoba (SFXI-Kipling, page 27, B-38.) (MB Vital Statistics, Birth Reg. #1890,003604.). He died on 13 Nov 1891 St.Francois Xavier, (Manitoba), at age 1 (SFXI-Kipling, page 129, S-20.) (MB Vital Statistics, Death Reg. #1891,002482.). He was buried 14 Nov 1891 St.Francois Xavier, Manitoba (SFXI-Kipling, page 129, S-20.) (Rosemary Rozyk.).

     ii. James William Todd was born on 23 Oct 1891 St.Francois Xavier, Manitoba (SFXI-Kipling, page 80, B-42.) (MB Vital Statistics, Birth Reg. #1891,006120.). He married Bridget Loretta Brynes on 5 May 1924 (Denney.). He died on 10 Sep 1969 Winnipeg, Manitoba, at age 77 (Ibid.).

     iii. Anonyme Todd was born and died on 14 Feb 1893 St.Francois Xavier, Manitoba. (Rosemary Rozyk.) He/she was buried on 16 Feb 1893 St.Francois Xavier, Manitoba (Ibid.).

     iv. Marie Alice Laura Todd was born on 6 Mar 1894 St.Francois Xavier, Manitoba (SFXI-Kipling, B-6.) (MB Vital Statistics, Birth Reg. #1894,001911.). She married Duncan A. McDougall on 30 Jun 1914 St.Marys, Winnipeg, Manitoba (SFXI-Kipling, B-6 (note).). She married Frederick Partner in Oct 1948 (Denney.).

       Frederick Partner died on 1 Jan 1972.

     v. Rosanna Todd was born on 17 Sep 1895 St.Francois Xavier, Manitoba (SFXI-Kipling, page 50, B-31.) (MB Vital Statistics, Birth Reg. #1895,001221.). She was baptized on 19 Sep 1895 St.Francois Xavier, Manitoba (Denney.).

     vi. Marie Josephine Helene Todd was born on 30 Apr 1897 St.Francois Xavier, Manitoba (SFXI-Kipling, page 178, B-22.) (MB Vital Statistics, Birth Reg. #1897,001294.). She married Valentine DeLacy Costello in 1917 Winnipeg, Manitoba (Denney.).

       Valentine DeLacy Costello was born on 14 Feb 1889 England. He died in 1973 Winnipeg, (Manitoba).

     vii. Pierre Ernest Todd was born on 11 Mar 1899 St.Francois Xavier, Manitoba (SFXI-Kipling, page 200, B-14.) (MB Vital Statistics, Birth Reg. #1899,006962.). He died in 1978 Stonewall, Manitoba (Denney.).

     viii. Louis Adelard Todd was born on 15 Dec 1900 R.M. of St.Francois Xavier, Manitoba (MB Vital Statistics, Birth Reg. #1901,006411.). He died in 1948 Vancouver, British Columbia (Denney.).

     ix. Lucien Todd was born on 4 Dec 1902 (Ibid.). He died in 1973 (Ibid.).

     x. Albert Adrien Todd was born on 18 Nov 1904 R.M. of St.Francois Xavier, Manitoba (MB Vital Statistics, Birth Reg. #1904,002695.). He died in 1956 (Denney.). He was buried in 1956 St.Francois Xavier, Manitoba (Ibid.).

     xi. Agnes Florence Todd was born on 28 Sep 1906 R.M. of St.Francois Xavier, Manitoba (MB Vital Statistics, Birth Reg. #1906,002898.). She died on 10 Oct 1980 at age 74 (Denney.). She was buried in Oct 1980 Stonewall, Manitoba (Ibid.).

     xii. Mary Victoria Todd was born on 27 May 1908. She died in 1926.

12. Gilbert Todd was born on 13 Nov 1865 The Pas, Cumberland House, (Saskatchewan) (NWHBS, C-14942.) (SB-Rozyk, page 62, B-101.). He was baptized on 15 Aug 1866 (The Pas), St.Boniface, (Manitoba) (Ibid.). He married **Cleophee Lavallee**, daughter of **Pierre Ayotte dit Lavallee** and **Marie Emerise Plante**, on 8 Jan 1895 St.Francois Xavier, Manitoba (SFXI-Kipling, M-10.) (MB Vital Statistics, Mar. Reg. #1895,002167.).

Cleophee Lavallee was born on 25 Nov 1871 St.Francois Xavier, Manitoba (SFXI-Kipling, B-84.) (INB, page 103.). She was baptized on 26 Nov 1871 St.Francois Xavier, Manitoba (SFXI-Kipling, B-84.) (INB, page 103.).

Children of **Gilbert Todd** and **Cleophee Lavallee** are as follows:

     i. Mary Todd.

     ii. Archibald Todd.

     iii. Victor Todd.

     iv. Pierre Todd married Stella Robidoux, daughter of Dieudonne Robidoux and Marie Anne Graziella Lamothe, on 26 May 1945 St.Francois Xavier, Starbuck, Manitoba (MM.).

     v. Joseph Todd.

     vi. Bertha Todd.

     vii. Delima Todd.

     viii. Vernon Todd.

ix. Angus Alfred Edouard Todd was born on 1 Dec 1895 St.Francois Xavier, Manitoba (SFXI-Kipling, B-40.) (MB Vital Statistics, Birth Reg. #1895,001225.).

x. Marie Claire Todd was born on 29 Dec 1896 St.Francois Xavier, Manitoba (SFXI-Kipling, B-1.) (MB Vital Statistics, Birth Reg. #1897,001290.).

xi. Marie Eleonore Todd was born on 5 Feb 1898 St.Francois Xavier, Manitoba (SFXI-Kipling, B-5.) (MB Vital Statistics, Birth Reg. #1898,003628.). She married C. Pierre Dauphinais on 22 Oct 1924 St.Pauls, Starbuck, Manitoba (SFXI-Kipling, B-5 (note).).

xii. Marie Agnes Delia Todd was born on 7 Mar 1913 R.M. of St.Francois Xavier, Manitoba (MB Vital Statistics, Birth Reg. #1913,018866.).

13. Norman Todd was born on 9 Nov 1868 York Factory (NWHBS, C-14942.). He married **Marie Appoline Deslauriers**, daughter of **Norbert Deslauriers dit Legault** and **Marie Frobisher,** on 9 Sep 1889 St.Francois Xavier, Manitoba (SFXI-Kipling, M-9.). He died in 1947 (Denney.).

Marie Appoline Deslauriers was born on 30 May 1868 St.Francois Xavier, (Manitoba) (SFXI-Kipling, B-68.). She was baptized on 30 May 1868 St.Francois Xavier, (Manitoba) (Ibid.). She died in 1953 (Denney.). She was buried in 1953 St.Francois Xavier, Manitoba (Ibid.).

Children of **Norman Todd** and **Marie Appoline Deslauriers** were as follows:

i. Alexina Todd was born on 4 Jan 1890 St.Francois Xavier, Manitoba (SFXI-Kipling, B-1.). She died on 20 Mar 1892 St.Francois Xavier, Manitoba, at age 2 (Ibid., S-10.) (MB Vital Statistics, Death Reg. #1892,001029.).

ii. Eleonore Todd was born on 9 Jul 1891 St.Francois Xavier, Manitoba (SFXI-Kipling, B-28.) (MB Vital Statistics, Birth Reg. #1891,006112.). She was baptized on 11 Jul 1891 St.Francois Xavier, Manitoba (SFXI-Kipling, B-28.) (Rosemary Rozyk.). She died on 10 Apr 1892 St.Francois Xavier, Manitoba (Ibid., Death Reg. #1892,001037.). She was buried on 12 Apr 1892 St.Francois Xavier, Manitoba (SFXI-Kipling, S-15.). (Rosemary Rozyk.).

iii. Marie Corinne Laura Todd was born on 5 Feb 1893 St.Francois Xavier, Manitoba (Ibid., B-5.) (MB Vital Statistics, Birth Reg. #1893,005219.). She married Louis Joseph Pierre Hogue, son of William Hogue and Virginie Lavallee, on 25 Nov 1913 St.Francois Xavier, Manitoba (MM.) (MB Vital Statistics, Mar. Reg. #1913,068209.).

Louis Joseph Pierre Hogue was born on 5 Apr 1885 St.Francois Xavier, Manitoba (SFXI-Kipling, B-10.) (MB Vital Statistics, Birth Reg. #1885,004012.).

iv. Norman Jacques Todd was born on 2 Oct 1894 St.Francois Xavier, Manitoba (SFXI-Kipling, B-29.) (MB Vital Statistics, Birth Reg. #1894,004896.).

v. Marie Louise Amanda Todd was born on 28 Jun 1896 St.Francois Xavier, Manitoba (SFXI-Kipling, B-23.) (MB Vital Statistics, Birth Reg. #1896,006050.). She married Eugene Alex Page, son of Jean Baptiste Page and Caroline Lavallee, on 11 Jan 1921 St.Francois Xavier, Manitoba (MM.).

Eugene Alex Page was born on 6 Jul 1892 St.Francois Xavier, Manitoba (SFXI-Kipling, B-31.).

vi. Albert Ernest Todd was born on 9 Jan 1898 St.Francois Xavier, Manitoba (Ibid., B-2.) (MB Vital Statistics, Birth Reg. #1898,003606.).

vii. Louis Octave Todd was born on 4 Sep 1899 St.Francois Xavier, Manitoba (SFXI-Kipling, B-32.) (MB Vital Statistics, Birth Reg. #1899,003431.).

viii. Louis Adelard Todd was born on 14 Jul 1901 R.M. of St.Francois Xavier, Manitoba (Ibid., Birth Reg. #1901,002717.). He married Marie Anne Stevenson on 7 Feb 1927 St.Francois Xavier, Manitoba (MM.). He died in 1937.

ix. Joseph Alexandre Todd was born on 18 Mar 1905 R.M. of St.Francois Xavier, Manitoba (MB Vital Statistics, Birth Reg. #1905,004209.).

x. William Todd was born circa 1907. He married Stella Deslauriers, daughter of Joseph William Deslauriers and Alice Cleophie A. Page, on 24 Mar 1935 St.Francois Xavier, Manitoba (MM.).

xi. Marie Georgeline Todd was born on 16 Mar 1907 R.M. of St.Francois Xavier, Manitoba (MB Vital Statistics, Birth Reg. #1907,006599.).

xii. Marie Bertha Irene Todd was born on 28 Jan 1911 R.M. of St.Francois Xavier, Manitoba (Ibid., Birth Reg. #1911,006050.).

14. Gabriel Todd was born on 15 Mar 1871 (SB-Rozyk, page 213, B-42.) (1901 Canada, #11, N-3, page 2, Family 11, Line 3-5.). He was baptized on 22 Jun 1871 St.Boniface, (Manitoba) (SB-Rozyk, page 213, B-42.). He married **Elise Lavallee**, daughter of **Pierre Martin Lavallee Sr.** and **Elise Deslauriers,** on 25 Nov 1901 St.Francois Xavier, Manitoba (MB Vital Statistics, Marriage Reg. #1901,001355.).

Elise Lavallee was born on 4 Dec 1876 St.Francois Xavier, Manitoba (SFXI-Kipling, B-45.). She was baptized 18 Dec 1876 St.Francois Xavier, Manitoba (Ibid.) (Rosemary Rozyk.).

Children of **Gabriel Todd** and **Elise Lavallee** were as follows:

i. Delia Todd.

ii. Marie Rose Todd was born on 1 Apr 1902 R.M. of St.Francois Xavier, Manitoba (MB Vital Statistics, Birth Reg. #1902,008047.).

iii. Joseph Albert Todd was born on 13 Feb 1904 R.M. of St.Francois Xavier, Manitoba (Ibid., Birth Reg. #1904,005358.).

iv. Peter Todd was born on 23 Dec 1905 R.M. of St.Francois Xavier, Manitoba (Ibid., Birth Reg. #1905,002215.). He died in 1950 (Denney.). He was buried in 1950 St.Francois Xavier, (Manitoba) (Ibid.).

v. Charles Edmund Todd was born on 2 Nov 1907 R.M. of St.Francois Xavier, Manitoba (MB Vital Statistics, Birth Reg. #1907,003806.).

vi. August Todd was born on 13 Oct 1910 (Denney.).

    vii.   Joseph Georges Arthur Todd was born on 22 Jun 1911 R.M. of St.Francois Xavier, Manitoba (MB Vital Statistics, Birth Reg. #1911,004148.).

    viii.   Marie Octavie Todd was born on 17 Apr 1913 R.M. of St.Francois Xavier, Manitoba (Ibid., Birth Reg. #1913,026791.).

15. Alexander Todd was born on 26 Nov 1874 (1901 Canada, #11, N-3, page 2, Family 11, Line 3-5.). He married **Marie Anne McDougall**, daughter of **John Peter McDougall** and **Elise Delorme**, on 14 Sep 1904 St.Francois Xavier, Manitoba (MM, page 859.) (MB Vital Statistics, Marriage Reg. #1904,002689.). He died in 1938 (Denney.). He was buried in 1938 St.Francois Xavier, Manitoba (Ibid.).

   Maria Anna McDougall was born on 8 Jul 1883 St.Francois Xavier, Manitoba (SFXI-Kipling, B-34.). She was baptized 9 Jul 1883 St.Francois Xavier, Manitoba (Ibid.) (Rosemary Rozyk.). She died in 1963 (Denney.). She was buried in 1963 St.Francois Xavier, Manitoba (Ibid.).

   Children of **Alexander Todd** and **Marie Anne McDougall** were as follows:

    i.   John Joseph Todd was baptized St.Francois Xavier, Manitoba. He was born on 18 Aug 1905 (Ibid.). He died in Aug 1976 Winnipeg, Manitoba (Ibid.).

    ii.   Josephine Todd was born on 4 Aug 1906 R.M. of St.Francois Xavier, Manitoba (MB Vital Statistics, Birth Reg. #1906,002902.). She married Harry Doherty (Rod Mac Quarrie, 16 April 2005.). She died on 17 Apr 1980 Winnipeg, Manitoba, at age 73 (Denney.).

    iii.   Joseph Todd was born on 10 Sep 1907 R.M. of St.Francois Xavier, Manitoba (MB Vital Statistics, Birth Reg. #1907,003802.).

    iv.   Bella Todd was baptized St.Francois Xavier, (Manitoba) (Denney.). She was born in Jun 1909 (Ibid.). She died in Jul 1959 Winnipeg, (Manitoba), at age 50 (Ibid.).

    v.   Leon Adelard Todd was born on 8 Sep 1910 R.M. of St.Francois Xavier, Manitoba (MB Vital Statistics, Birth Reg. #1910,005035.). He died in 1964 Winnipeg, Manitoba (Denney.).

    vi.   Louis Emile Todd was born on 11 Oct 1911 R.M. of St.Francois Xavier, Manitoba (MB Vital Statistics, Birth Reg. #1911,004169.).

    vii.   Jeanne Albina Todd was born on 16 Jan 1912 R.M. of St.Francois Xavier, Manitoba (Ibid., Birth Reg. #1913,011717.).

    viii.   Francois Xavier "Frank" Todd was born on 16 Apr 1914 R.M. of St.Francois Xavier, Manitoba (Ibid., Birth Reg. #1914,091870.). He died on 14 Aug 1950 Winnipeg, Manitoba, at age 36 (Denney.).

    ix.   Ida G. Todd was born on 16 Mar 1917 Chatfield, Manitoba (Ibid.).

    x.   Laura Todd was born on 12 Feb 1919 Chatfield, Manitoba (Ibid.).

    xi.   Donald Todd was born on 17 Mar 1923 Chatfield, Manitoba (Ibid.). He died in Jan 1961 Vancouver, British Columbia, at age 37 (Ibid.).

16. Sarah Todd was born on 1 Dec 1858 St.James, (Manitoba) (Ibid.). She was baptized on 26 Dec 1858 St.James, (Manitoba) (MBS, C-14934.) (SJAC, B-73.). She married **Charles Oxford White**, son of **(--?--) White**, before 1881.

   Charles Oxford White was born on 7 Oct 1847 England (1901 Canada, #12, C-5, page 12, Family 111, Line 23-28.).

17. Maria Todd was born in 1859 Sturgeon Creek, (Manitoba) (NWHBS, C-14936.). She was born circa 1864 Red River, (Manitoba) (1870C-MB, page 363, #1177.). She married **Pierre Boucher**, son of **Pierre Boucher** and **Marie Amable Bruneau**, on 26 Dec 1870 St.Joachim, Fort Edmonton, (Alberta) (MSJ-FA-E, page 71, M-4.).

   Pierre Boucher was born in Jan 1849 St.Albert, (Alberta) (NWHBS, C-14936.) (INB, page 19.). He was baptized on 3 Mar 1849 Fort-des-Prairies (Ibid.). He married **Isabelle Berland**, daughter of **Edouard "Vallah" or "Vallet" Berland** and **Genevieve Zan-yeo Matoos-kees Mondion**, in Nov 1866 Lac Ste.Anne, (Alberta) (NWHBS, C-14936.).

18. Harriet Todd was born on 15 Feb 1876 Tail Creek, (Alberta) (1901 Canada, District 202-v(4), page 36, family 370, line 20-23.) (ArchiviaNet, C-15010.). She married **Archibald Whitford**, son of **Francis Whitford** and **Jane Anderson**, before 1897 (1901 Canada, District 202-v(4), page 36, family 370, line 20-23.).

   Archibald Whitford was born on 16 Mar 1874 Buffalo Lake, (Alberta) (Ibid.) (ArchiviaNet, C-15009.).

Generation Four

19. James Todd was born on 3 May 1882 Fort Pitt District near present day Lloydminster, (Saskatchewan) (Eileen Horan, 6 March 2006.). He married **Caroline Laframboise**, daughter of **Louis Laframboise** and **Isabelle Cardinal**, circa Jan 1903 St.Thomas, St.Paul des Metis, (Alberta) (Ibid.). He died on 22 Oct 1967 Rossdale Flats Care Home, Edmonton, Alberta, at age 85 (Ibid.).

   Caroline Laframboise was born on 14 Jul 1885 (Alberta) (1901 Canada, District 202, x(3), page 15, family 126, line 38-43.). She died on 9 Sep 1964 Rossdale Flats Care Home, Edmonton, Alberta, at age 79 (Eileen Horan, 6 March 2006.).

   Children of **James Todd** and **Caroline Laframboise** were as follows:

    i.   Louis "Lorne" Todd was born on 24 Oct 1903 St.Paul des Metis, (Alberta) (Ibid.). He married Myrtle Therese Tough circa 1938 Tofield, Alberta (Ibid.). He died on 21 Oct 1981 at age 77 (Ibid.).

        Myrtle Therese Tough was born on 7 Sep 1910 Tolfield, Alberta (Ibid.). She died on 17 Dec 1997 Victoria, Vancouver Island, British Columbia, at age 87 (Ibid.).

    ii.   Alice Patricia Todd was born on 17 Mar 1906 St.Paul, Alberta (Ibid.). She married Ivan Walter Crowden circa 1925 Edmonton, Alberta (Ibid.). She died Edmonton, Alberta (Ibid.).

        Ivan Walter Crowden was born circa 1904 (Ibid.).

    iii.   Olive Todd was born on 18 Mar 1906 St.Paul, Alberta (Ibid.).

    iv.   William James "Jimmy" Todd was born in 1909 St.Paul, Alberta (Ibid.). He died in Sep 1920 St.Paul, Alberta (Ibid.).

    v.   Frank Todd was born circa 1911 St.Paul, Alberta (Ibid.). He died in 1970 (Ibid.).

    vi.   Ernest George Todd was born on 2 Feb 1912 St.Paul, Alberta (Ibid.). He married Judith Myrtle Sharpe in 1947 Calgary, Alberta (Ibid.). He died on 1 Dec 1972 at age 60 (Ibid.).

Judith Myrtle Sharpe was born on 26 Mar 1929 Calgary, Alberta (Ibid.). She died on 15 Nov 1997 at age 68 (Ibid.).

    vii.   Harvey Todd was born circa 1913 St.Paul, Alberta (Ibid.).

   viii.   Thelma Viola Todd was born circa 1915 St.Paul, Alberta (Ibid.). She died in 2000 (Ibid.).

    ix.   Gerry Todd was born circa 1917 St.Paul, Alberta (Ibid.).

     x.   Margaret Todd was born circa 1919 St.Paul, Alberta (Ibid.).

    xi.   Mary Todd was born circa 1921 St.Paul, Alberta (Ibid.).

   xii.   Elizabeth Todd was born circa 1923 St.Paul, Alberta (Ibid.).

   xiii.   Orville Victor Vincent "Mickey" Todd was born in 1925 St.Paul, Alberta (Ibid.). He married Miss Smith circa 1950 (Ibid.). He died in 1995 St.Paul, Alberta (Ibid.).

         Miss Smith was born circa 1927 (Ibid.).

   xiv.   Bessie Malvina Todd was born circa 1927 St.Paul, Alberta (Ibid.).

    xv.   Robert James "Bob" Todd was born circa 1929 St.Paul, Alberta (Ibid.). He married Violet (--?--) circa 1949 (Ibid.).

         Violet (--?--) was born circa 1931 (Ibid.).

Descendants of Jean Baptiste Tourangeau

Generation One

1. Jean Baptiste Tourangeau was born circa 1803 Montreal, Montreal, Quebec (HBCA-B Hudson's Bay Company Archives - biographical sketches, Hudson's Bay Company Archives; Winnipeg, Manitoba.). He married **Marie Vadnais**, daughter of **Joseph Vadnais,** before 1829.

Children of **Jean Baptiste Tourangeau** and **Marie Vadnais** were as follows:

     i.   Jean Baptiste Tourangeau was born circa 1829 Peace River District, North West (SFXI: 1834-1852 St.Francois Xavier 1834-1852 Register Index, B-34. Hereinafter cited as SFXI: 1835-1852.) (NWHBS 1885 Scrip Applications, North-West Halfbreeds residing outside Manitoba on 15 July 1870, RG15-20, C-14942.). He was baptized on 17 Aug 1834 St.Francois Xavier, (Manitoba) (SFXI: 1835-1852, B-34.). He married Nancy Omand, daughter of William Omand and Nancy Budd, in 1857 Athabasca, (Alberta) (NWHBS, C-14940.).

         Nancy Omand was born in 1835 Churchill, Hudson Bay (Ibid.).

  2 ii.   Antoine Tourangeau, b. circa 1830 Red River, (Manitoba); m. Madeleine Larocque.

  3 iii.   Sophie Tourangeau, b. 1834 Wabasca, Fort Chipewyan, (Alberta); m. Michel Lizotte; d. 28 Aug 1920 Fort Vermilion, Alberta.

  4 iv.   Francois Tourangeau, b. circa 1836; m. Isabel Cadieu.

  5 v.   Louis Tourangeau, b. 1838 Athabasca; m. Marie Alphonsine Laliberte.

  6 vi.   Catherine Tourangeau, b. circa 1848; m. Donald McDonald.

Generation Two

2. Antoine Tourangeau was born circa 1830 Red River, (Manitoba) (1870C-MB 1870 Manitoba Census, National Archives of Canada, Ottawa, Ontario, Microfilm Reel Number C-2170., #455, page 15.). He married **Madeleine Larocque**, daughter of **Charles Larocque** and **Catherine Macon,** before 1858.

Question: *Is he the son of Jean Baptiste Tourangeau and Marie Vadnais?*

Madeleine Larocque was born on 18 Aug 1834 St.Boniface, (Manitoba) (SB 1825-1834 St.Boniface Roman Catholic Registre des Baptemes, Mariages & Sepultures, 1825-1834, page 138, B-834. Hereinafter cited as SB 1825-1834.). She was baptized on 18 Aug 1834 St.Boniface, (Manitoba) (Ibid.).

Children of **Antoine Tourangeau** and **Madeleine Larocque** were as follows:

  7 i.   Beinvenne Tourangeau, b. circa 1858 Red River, (Manitoba); m. George Sanderson.

    ii.   Herminegilde Tourangeau was born circa 1858 Red River, (Manitoba) (1870C-MB, #458, page 15.).

  8 iii.   Amable Tourangeau, b. 26 Dec 1862 St.Boniface, (Manitoba); m. Lucia Desjardins.

  9 iv.   Jonas Tourangeau, b. circa 1863 Red River, (Manitoba); m. Isabelle Piche.

    v.   Catherine Tourangeau was born on 18 Mar 1869 Chipewyan, (Alberta) (ArchiviaNet 1886-1901, 1906 Half-Breed Scrip Applications Index, RG15-21, Volume 1333 through 1371, Microfilm Reel Number C-14944 through C-15010, National Archives of Canada, Ottawa, Ontario, http://www.collectionscanada.gc.ca, C-15007.).

  10 vi.   Louis Tourangeau, b. 15 Dec 1872 Chipewyan, (Alberta); m. Lucia Desjardins; m. Adele Lepine.

   vii.   Rose Tourangeau was born on 19 Jun 1876 Chipewyan, (Alberta) (Automated Genealogy 1901 Census Transcription Project and Census Images from the National Archives of Canada, http://www.automatedgenealogy.com, District 206-a(6), page 4, family 19, line 12-16.) (ArchiviaNet, C-15007.).

  viii.   Pierre Tourangeau was born circa 1881 (1901 Canada, District 206-a(6), page 4, family 19, line 12-16.).

3. Sophie Tourangeau was born in 1834 Wabasca, Fort Chipewyan, (Alberta) (ArchiviaNet.). She married **Michel Lizotte**, son of **Pierre-Nicolas Lizot** and **Marie Agathe Nadeau,** on 16 Oct 1850 Fort Chipewyan, (Alberta) (Ibid.). She died on 28 Aug 1920 Fort Vermilion, Alberta (Stan Hulme Research, 10 July 2006.).

Michel Lizotte was born on 6 Aug 1818 St-Michel, Yamaska, Yamaska, Quebec (Ibid.). He married according to the custom of the country **Angelique Sandovove** circa 1846. He died on 23 Aug 1917 Fort Vermilion, Alberta, at age 99 (Ibid.).

4. Francois Tourangeau was born circa 1836. He married **Isabel Cadieu** before 1876 (Ibid., C-15007.).

Question: *Is he the son of Jean Baptiste Tourangeau and Marie Vadnais?*

Children of **Francois Tourangeau** and **Isabel Cadieu** were as follows:

     i.   Sophie Tourangeau was born in Oct 1868 Fort Chipewyan, (Alberta) (1901 Canada, District 206-a(2), page 4, family 17, line 4-6.).

11   ii.   Isidore Tourangeau, b. 1876 Chipewyan, (Alberta); m. Isabel McKay.

12   iii.   Elise Tourangeau, b. 1876 Fort Chipewyan, (Alberta); m. Baptiste Lepine.

     iv.   Jean Baptiste Tourangeau was born in 1881 Athabasca District, (Alberta) (ArchiviaNet, C-15007.).

5. Louis Tourangeau was born in 1838 Athabasca (NWHBS, C-14942.). He married **Marie Alphonsine Laliberte**, daughter of **Antoine Laliberte** and **Marguerite Nadeau**, on 22 Nov 1864 St.Norbert, (Manitoba) (SN1 Catholic Parish Register of St.Norbert 1857-1873, page 113-114, M-5. Hereinafter cited as SN1.).

Marie Alphonsine Laliberte was born on 10 Jul 1838 (1901 Canada, #202, D-4, page 6, family 54, line 40-42.). She was born in 1848 Red River Settlement, (Manitoba) (NWHBS, C-14939.).

Children of **Louis Tourangeau** and **Marie Alphonsine Laliberte** were as follows:

     i.   Louis Tourangeau was born on 19 Nov 1865 St.Norbert, (Manitoba) (SN1, page 140, B-42.). He was baptized on 20 Nov 1865 St.Norbert, (Manitoba) (Ibid.). He died on 1 Dec 1865 St.Norbert, (Manitoba) (Ibid., page 143, S-41.). He was buried on 2 Dec 1865 St.Norbert, (Manitoba) (Ibid.).

13   ii.   Joseph Tourangeau, b. 12 Oct 1866 St.Norbert, (Manitoba); m. Sophia Bisson.

     iii.   Pierre Tourangeau was born on 25 Dec 1867 (NWHBSI Index 1885 Scrip Applications, North-West Halfbreeds residing outside Manitoba on 15 July 1870, RG15-20, page 80.). He was buried on 7 May 1893 St.Thomas, Duhamel, (Alberta) (DA Register of the Duhamel, Alberta Roman Catholic Church: 1881-1921, S-6. Hereinafter cited as DA.).

     iv.   Victoire Tourangeau was born circa Oct 1871 Fort Pitt, (Saskatchewan) (NWHBS, C-14942.) (SL-SK St.Laurent-de-Grandin Roman Catholic Registre des Baptemes, Mariages & Sepltures, St.Laurent, Saskatchewan, 1872-1896, page 1, B-_. Hereinafter cited as SL-SK.). He was baptized on 25 Oct 1871 St.Laurent-de-Grandin, (Saskatchewan) (Ibid.). He died on 26 Feb 1885 St.Albert, (Alberta) (NWHBS, C-14942.). He was buried on 27 Feb 1885 St.Albert, (Alberta) (Ibid.).

14   v.   Sara Tourangeau, b. 1873 St.Paul, (Alberta); m. Laurent L'Hirondelle.

     vi.   Henry Tourangeau was born in 1875 St.Albert, (Alberta) (ArchiviaNet, C-15007.). He died in 1886 St.Albert, (Alberta) (Ibid.).

     vii.   Elise Tourangeau was born in 1877 St.Albert, (Alberta) (Ibid.). She died in 1886 (Ibid.).

     viii.   Josue Tourangeau was born on 20 Sep 1880 St.Albert, (Alberta) (1901 Alberta Census Index, Alberta Genealogical Society, Edmonton, Alberta, www.agsedm.edmonton.ab.ca, page 6, line 40-42, St.Albert.) (1901 Canada, #202, D-4, page 6, family 54, line 40-42.).

     ix.   George Tourangeau was born on 24 Mar 1882 St.Albert, (Alberta) (ArchiviaNet, C-15007.).

     x.   Michel Tourangeau was born in 1885 St.Albert, (Alberta) (Ibid.). He died in 1886 St.Albert, (Alberta) (Ibid.).

6. Catherine Tourangeau was born circa 1848. She married **Donald McDonald** before 1866.

Question: *Is she the daughter of Jean Baptiste Tourangeau?*

Donald McDonald died circa 1895 Fort Chipewyan (HBS 1886-1901, 1906 Half-Breed Scrip Applications, RG15-21, Volume 1339, C-14955.).

Generation Three

7. Beinvenne Tourangeau was born circa 1858 Red River, (Manitoba) (1870C-MB, #457, page 15.). She married **George Sanderson**, son of **Henry Sanderson** and **Elizabeth Manger de Lard,** on 15 Jul 1881 Chipewyan (ArchiviaNet, C-15001.).

George Sanderson was born on 2 Dec 1878 Fort Resolution, (Northwest Territory) (Marie Beaupre.). He was baptized on 3 Dec 1878 Fort Resolution, (Northwest Territory) (Ibid.).

8. Amable Tourangeau was born on 26 Dec 1862 St.Boniface, (Manitoba) (SB-Rozyk St. Boniface Roman Catholic Church, Manitoba, Canada, Baptisms, Marriages and Burials 1860-1875 Extractions, Compiled by Rosemary Rozyk, page 95, B-176.). He was baptized on 26 Dec 1862 St.Boniface, (Manitoba) (Ibid.). He married **Lucia Desjardins**, daughter of **Baptiste Desjardins** and **Isabelle Madeleine Lafleur,** before 1889 (ArchiviaNet, C-15007.).

Lucia Desjardins was born on 15 Jul 1871 Isle-a-la-Crosse, (Saskatchewan) (Ibid.).

Children of **Amable Tourangeau** and **Lucia Desjardins** were as follows:

     i.   Baptiste Tourangeau was born in Jul 1889 (Automated Genealogy 1911 Census Transcription Project and Census Images from the National Archives of Canada, http://www.automatedgenealogy.com, District 45, page 1, family 4, line 15-19.).

     ii.   Adelaide Tourangeau was born in Jul 1897 (Ibid.).

     iii.   Sylvester Tourangeau was born in Jun 1907 (Ibid.).

9. Jonas Tourangeau was born circa 1863 Red River, (Manitoba) (1870C-MB, #460, page 15.). He married **Isabelle Piche**, daughter of **Charles Piche** and **Suzette Martin,** in 1886 Chipewyan, (Alberta) (ArchiviaNet, C-15007.).

Isabelle Piche was born in 1867 Chipewyan, (Alberta) (Ibid.).

Children of **Jonas Tourangeau** and **Isabelle Piche** are as follows:

     i.   Antoine Tourangeau was born circa 1890 (1901 Canada, District 206-a(6), page 7, family 35, line 9-14.).

     ii.   Louis Tourangeau was born circa 1893 (Ibid.).

     iii.   Isidore Tourangeau was born circa 1898 (Ibid.).

     iv.   Rose Tourangeau was born circa 1900 (Ibid.).

10. Louis Tourangeau was born on 15 Dec 1872 Chipewyan, (Alberta) (1911 Canada, page 14, Family 21, Line 3-8.) (ArchiviaNet, C-15007.). He married **Lucia Desjardins** before 1900 (1901 Canada, District 206-a(6), page 4, family 19, line 12-16.). He married **Adele Lepine**, daughter of **Baptiste Lepine** and **Madeleine Houle,** circa 1904 (1911 Canada, page 14, Family 21, Line 3-8.).

Lucia Desjardins was born circa 1883 (1901 Canada, District 206-a(6), page 4, family 19, line 12-16.).

Children of **Louis Tourangeau** and **Lucia Desjardins** are:

     i.   Marie Olive Tourangeau was born circa 1900 Athabaska, (Alberta) (Ibid.).

Adele Lepine was born in 1880 Big Island (HBSI.) (ArchiviaNet.). She married **Roderick Ross Flett**, son of **James Flett** and **Jane Lapee or Lepine,** on 6 Aug 1897 Fort Chipewyan, Athabasca, (Alberta) (Marriage Certificate.) (Alice Belgarde Jackson Collection.).

Children of **Louis Tourangeau** and **Adele Lepine** are as follows:

    i. Marie Tourangeau was born circa 1904 (1911 Canada, page 14, Family 21, Line 3-8.).

    ii. Celeste Tourangeau was born circa 1908 (Ibid.).

11. Isidore Tourangeau was born in 1876 Chipewyan, (Alberta) (ArchiviaNet, C-15007.). He married **Isabel McKay** before 1898. **Isabel McKay** was born in 1878 Mackenzie River District (HBSI.) (ArchiviaNet.).

Children of **Isidore Tourangeau** and **Isabel McKay** are:

    15 i. Veronique Tourangeau, b. circa 1898; m. Alexandre Beaulieu.

12. Elise Tourangeau was born in 1876 Fort Chipewyan, (Alberta) (Ibid., C-14984.). She married **Baptiste Lepine**, son of **Baptiste Lepine** and **Angelique Houle,** in 1893 Fort Chipewyan, (Alberta) (Ibid.).

Baptiste Lepine was born in 1871 Fort Simpson (ArchiviaNet.).

13. Joseph Tourangeau was born on 12 Oct 1866 St.Norbert, (Manitoba) (SN1, page 85, B-45.). He was baptized on 12 Oct 1866 St.Norbert, (Manitoba) (Ibid.). He married **Sophia Bisson**, daughter of **Baptiste Bisson** and **Pelagie Tastawitch,** in 1890 St.Albert, (Alberta) (ArchiviaNet, C-15007.).

Sophia Bisson was born in 1873 Dunvegan, (Alberta) (Ibid.).

Children of **Joseph Tourangeau** and **Sophia Bisson** were as follows:

    i. Adolphus Tourangeau was born in 1892 St.Albert, (Alberta) (Ibid.). He died in 1895 (Ibid.).

    ii. Henry Tourangeau was born in 1893 St.Albert, (Alberta) (Ibid.). He died in Jun 1900 Vermillion, (Alberta) (Ibid.).

    iii. Alexander Tourangeau was born in 1895 (Ibid.).

    iv. Marie Tourangeau was born in 1898 Vermillion, (Alberta) (Ibid.).

    v. Marie Tourangeau was born in 1898 Vermillion, (Alberta) (Ibid.).

    vi. Phillip Tourangeau was born in Apr 1900 Vermillion, (Alberta) (Ibid.).

14. Sara Tourangeau was born in 1873 St.Paul, (Alberta) (HBSI.). She married **Laurent L'Hirondelle**, son of **Alexis L'Hirondelle** and **Josephte Amyotte,** on 10 Oct 1891 (Denney.).

Laurent L'Hirondelle was born on 12 Aug 1860 Lac Ste.Anne, (Alberta) (NWHBS, C-14939.) (1901 Canada, #202, g(2), page 6, family 56, line 15-20.).

Generation Four

15. **Veronique Tourangeau** was born circa 1898 (Ibid., District 206-a(1), page 3, family 6, line 11-13.). She married **Alexandre Beaulieu**, son of **Joseph King Beaulieu Jr.** and **Flora Hope,** on 19 Jul 1916 Fort Resolution, (North West Territories) (Marie Beaupre.).

Ahnentafel between Joseph Tourond and Francois Touron

--- 1st Generation ---

1. JOSEPH TOUROND (PRDH online index, http://www.genealogic.umontreal.ca, #483484.) was born circa 1782 at Quebec, Quebec, Quebec (1870C-MB 1870 Manitoba Census, National Archives of Canada, Ottawa, Ontario, Microfilm Reel Number C-2170., 1786, page 58.). He was born circa 1791 at Quebec, Quebec, Quebec (MBS Scrip Applications, Original White Settlers & Halfbreeds residing in Manitoba on 15 July 1870, RG15-19, C-14934.). He was born on 8 Dec 1795 at St-Laurent, Quebec (PRDH online, #483484.). He was baptized on 8 Dec 1795 at St-Laurent, Quebec (Ibid.). He was born circa 1799 at St.Lawrence, Quebec (HBCA-B Hudson's Bay Company Archives - biographical sketches, Hudson's Bay Company Archives; Winnipeg, Manitoba.). He married **CHARLOTTE GLADU** before 1826. He married **ROSALIE LADEROUTE**, daughter of **JEAN PHILIBERT LADEROUTE** and **MARGUERITE PONTBRIAND DIT SANSREGRET,** before 1836 (SN1 Catholic Parish Register of St.Norbert 1857-1873, S-32. Hereinafter cited as SN1.). He died on 11 Jun 1873 at St.Norbert, Manitoba, at age 77 (MBS, C-14934.) (SN1, S-32.). He was buried on 13 Jun 1873 at St.Norbert, Manitoba (MBS, C-14934.) (SN1, S-32.).

--- 2nd Generation ---

2. JACQUES TOURON was baptized on 26 Sep 1760 at St-Vallier, Quebec (PRDH online, #83376.). He married **MARIE LOUISE LECOMPTE**, daughter of **JEAN-BAPTISTE LECOMTE** and **MARIE THERESE DUBOIS,** on 24 Apr 1780. He died on 19 Jun 1832 at Montreal, Montreal, Quebec, at age 71 (Ibid.). He was buried on 20 Jun 1832 at Montreal, Montreal, Quebec (Ibid.).

--- 3rd Generation ---

4. JACQUES TOURON was born on 30 Jul 1737 at Beauport, Quebec (Ibid., #156109.). He was baptized on 30 Jul 1737 at Beauport, Quebec (Ibid.). He married **MARIE DOROTHEE MONTIGNY**, daughter of **JEAN BAPTISTE MONTIGNY** and **DOROTHEE GAUTHIER,** on 24 Apr 1756 at St-Vallier, Quebec (Ibid.). He died on 6 Apr 1805 at Ste-Anne-des-Plaines, Quebec, at age 67 (Ibid.). He was buried on 8 Apr 1805 at Ste-Anne-des-Plaines, Quebec (Ibid.).

--- 4th Generation ---

8. PIERRE TOURON (Ibid., #96322.) (Ibid.) was baptized on 12 Dec 1705 at St-Georges, Le Vigeant, Poitiers, Poitou (Montmorillon, Vienne) (Ibid.). He married **MARIE-JEANNE DUBEAU**, daughter of **JACQUES DUBEAU** and **CATHERINE BEDARD,** on 7 Jan 1737 at Charlesbourg, Quebec. He died on 8 Jun 1788 at Ste-Rose, Quebec, at age 82 (Ibid.). He was buried on 10 Jun 1788 at Ste-Rose, Quebec (Ibid.).

--- 5th Generation ---

16. FRANCOIS TOURON married **CATHERINE CHARLAND**.

Descendants of Joseph Tourond

Generation One

1. **Joseph Tourond** was born circa 1782 Quebec, Quebec, Quebec (1870C-MB 1870 Manitoba Census, National Archives of Canada, Ottawa, Ontario, Microfilm Reel Number C-2170., 1786, page 58.). He was born circa 1791 Quebec, Quebec, Quebec (MBS Scrip Applications, Original White Settlers & Halfbreeds residing in Manitoba on 15 July 1870, RG15-19, C-14934.). He was born on 8 Dec 1795 St-Laurent, Quebec (PRDH online index, http://www.genealogic.umontreal.ca, #483484.). He was baptized on 8 Dec 1795 St-Laurent, Quebec (Ibid.). He was born circa 1799 St.Lawrence, Quebec (HBCA-B Hudson's Bay Company Archives - biographical sketches, Hudson's Bay Company Archives; Winnipeg, Manitoba.). He married **Charlotte Gladu** before 1826. He married **Rosalie Laderoute**, daughter of **Jean Philibert Laderoute** and **Marguerite Pontbriand dit Sansregret**, before 1836 (SN1 Catholic Parish Register of St.Norbert 1857-1873, S-32. Hereinafter cited as SN1.). He died on 11 Jun 1873 St.Norbert, Manitoba, at age 77 (MBS, C-14934.) (SN1, S-32.). He was buried on 13 Jun 1873 St.Norbert, Manitoba (MBS, C-14934.) (SN1, S-32.).

Charlotte Gladu was born circa 1800.

Children of **Joseph Tourond** and **Charlotte Gladu** were:

    2   i.   Joseph Tourond, b. Jul 1826 St.Boniface, (Manitoba); m. Josephte Paul.

Rosalie Laderoute was born in Sep 1816 North West (MBS, C-14934.).

Children of **Joseph Tourond** and **Rosalie Laderoute** were as follows:

    3   i.   Jacques Tourond, b. 8 Jul 1836 St.Boniface, (Manitoba); m. Marie Courchene.

    4   ii.   Jean Baptiste Tourond, b. 1 Jun 1838 St.Boniface, (Manitoba); m. Angelique Delorme; m. Regina Allard; d. 25 Apr 1891 Ritchot, Manitoba; bur. 27 Apr 1891 St.Norbert, Manitoba.

    5   iii.   Rosalie Tourond, b. circa 1845; m. Francois Delorme; d. 24 Feb 1865 St.Norbert, (Manitoba); bur. 26 Feb 1865 St.Norbert, (Manitoba).

    6   iv.   Isidore Tourond, b. 1847 St.Norbert, (Manitoba); m. Anne Vermette; d. 11 Feb 1923 LaBroquerie, Manitoba.

    7   v.   Elise Tourond, b. 15 Aug 1850; m. Toussaint Vermette; d. 26 Jan 1932 DeSalaberry, Manitoba.

        vi.   Joseph Damase Tourond was born on 21 May 1853 St.Norbert, (Manitoba) (Ibid.) (Automated Genealogy 1901 Census Transcription Project and Census Images from the National Archives of Canada, http://www.automatedgenealogy.com, #10, (a-2), page 5, family 43, line 21-22.). He married Marguerite Roy, daughter of Francois Roy and Isabelle Lafreniere, on 2 Feb 1875 St.Norbert, Manitoba (SN2 Catholic Parish Register of St.Norbert, M-5. Hereinafter cited as SN2.). He married Marie Louise Normand, daughter of Boniface Normand and Marie Rose Roy, on 5 Apr 1915 St.Boniface, Manitoba (RMSB *Repertoire des Mariages de Saint-Boniface (Manitoba) 1825-1983* compiled by Julien Hamelin S.C., (240, avenue Daly; Ottawa, Ontario K1N 6G2: Le Centre de Genealogie S. C., Publication #67, 1985), page 465.) (Manitoba Vital Statistics online, http://web2.gov.mb.ca, Marriage Reg. #1915,174021.). He died on 22 Feb 1922 R.M. of DeSalaberry, Manitoba, at age 68 (Ibid., Death Reg. #1922,007344.).

              Marguerite Roy was born on 12 Apr 1856 (1901 Canada, #10, (a-2), page 5, family 43, line 21-22.). She married **Daniel Larence**, son of **Norbert Larence** and **Josephte Parenteau**, on 29 Jan 1872 St.Norbert, Manitoba (SN1, M-5.). She died in Jan 1914 St.Pierre, Riviere Rat, Manitoba, at age 57 (Ibid.).

              Marie Louise Normand was born on 27 Mar 1873 St.Nobert, Manitoba (Ibid., B-21.). She was baptized on 28 Mar 1873 St.Nobert, Manitoba (Ibid.). She married **Charles Roger Delorme**, son of **Joseph Delorme** and **Angele Courchene**, on 28 Feb 1892 (Ritchot), St.Norbert, Manitoba (MM *Manitoba Marriages* in *Publication 45*, Volumes 1-3, compiled and edited by: Paul J. Lareau, Fr. Julien Hamelin, (240 Avenue Daly, Ottawa, Ontario K1N 6G2: Le Centre de Genealogie S.C., 1984), page 304, 936.) (SN2, M-3.) (MB Vital Statistics, #1892,001763.). She married **Ludger Genest**, son of **Zephirin Genest** and **Anna Bella Leblanc**, on 22 Jul 1922 St.Boniface, Manitoba (RMSB, page 189.).

    8   vii.   Henri Tourond, b. 16 Jun 1856 St.Norbert, (Manitoba); m. Louise Corrigal; d. 23 Sep 1904 De Salaberry, Manitoba.

Generation Two

2. **Joseph Tourond** was born in Jul 1826 St.Boniface, (Manitoba) (MBS, C-14934.). He married **Josephte Paul**, daughter of **Jean Baptiste Paul** and **Angelique Godin**, on 7 May 1850 St.Francois Xavier, (Manitoba) (SFX: 1834-1850 St.Francois Xavier 1834-1851 Register, M-126. Hereinafter cited as SFX: 1834-1850.).

Question: *Why wasn't he mentioned in scrip records as an heir to his father? Maybe there was more than one?*

Josephte Paul was born in Jul 1831 St.Francois Xavier, (Manitoba) (MBS, C-14934.) (1901 Canada, Batoche, page 1, Family 7, #42-46.). She died on 15 Dec 1928 at age 97 (David Courchane, Courchane/Courchene Family Research.).

Children of **Joseph Tourond** and **Josephte Paul** were as follows:

    9   i.   David Tourond, b. 12 Dec 1851 St.Francois Xavier, (Manitoba); m. Marie Virginie Fisher; d. 11 Sep 1890 Batoche, (Saskatchewan); bur. 15 Sep 1890 Batoche, (Saskatchewan).

    10   ii.   Calixte Tourond, b. 23 Apr 1853; m. Marguerite Ross; m. Josephte Gervais; d. 12 May 1885 Batoche, (Saskatchewan); bur. 14 May 1885 Batoche, (Saskatchewan).

    11   iii.   Pierre Tourond, b. 1 Feb 1855 St.Francois Xavier, (Manitoba); m. Catherine Gervais; d. 20 Mar 1887 Batoche, (Saskatchewan); bur. 22 Mar 1887 Batoche, (Saskatchewan).

    12   iv.   Patrice Tourond, b. 24 Mar 1857 St.Francois Xavier, (Manitoba); m. Marie Gervais; d. 28 Sep 1898 Batoche, Saskatchewan; bur. 30 Sep 1898 Batoche, Saskatchewan.

    13   v.   Elzear Tourond, b. 1 Sep 1859 St.Francois Xavier, (Manitoba); m. Ernestine Berland; d. 12 May 1885 Batoche, (Saskatchewan).

        vi.   Francois Tourond was born on 21 Aug 1861 St.Francois Xavier, (Manitoba) (SFXI-Kipling St.Francois Xavier Register Index, 1834-1900; compiled by Clarence Kipling , B-73.). He was baptized on 23 Aug 1861 St.Francois Xavier, (Manitoba) (Ibid.) (SFXI 1851-1868 St.Francois Xavier 1852-1861 Register Index, B-73. Hereinafter cited as SFXI 1851-1868.).

    vii. Charles Medard Tourond was born on 5 Oct 1863 St.Francois Xavier, (Manitoba) (SFXI-Kipling, B-92.). He was baptized on 6 Oct 1863 St.Francois Xavier, (Manitoba) (Ibid.). He died on 19 Jul 1885 Batoche, (Saskatchewan), at age 21 (BSAP Records of the Parish of Batoche, St.Antoine de Pudoue Roman Catholic Church: Register for Baptisms, Marriages, Deaths, Volume One, 1881-1909., page 37, S-34. Hereinafter cited as BSAP.). He was buried on 20 Jul 1885 Batoche, (Saskatchewan) (Ibid.).

14 viii. Marie Therese Tourond, b. 18 Jan 1866 St.Francois Xavier, (Manitoba); m. Joseph Napoleon Venne; d. 18 Aug 1891 Batoche, (Saskatchewan); bur. 20 Aug 1891 Batoche, (Saskatchewan).

15 ix. Elise Tourond, b. 18 Mar 1868 St.Francois Xavier, (Manitoba); m. Raphael Boyer.

    x. Hyacinthe Tourond was born on 28 Mar 1870 St.Francois Xavier, (Manitoba) (MBS, C-14934.) (SFXI-Kipling, B-10.). He was baptized on 29 Mar 1870 St.Francois Xavier, (Manitoba) (MBS, C-14934.) (SFXI-Kipling, B-10.). He died on 2 Feb 1873 St.Francois Xavier, Manitoba, at age 2 (Ibid., S-13.). He was buried on 3 Feb 1873 St.Francois Xavier, Manitoba (MBS, C-14934.) (SFXI-Kipling, S-13.).

3. Jacques Tourond was born on 8 Jul 1836 St.Boniface, (Manitoba) (MBS, C-14934.). He married **Marie Courchene**, daughter of **Francois Courchene** and **Francoise Beauchamp,** before 1856.

Marie Courchene was born in Mar 1831 St.Boniface, (Manitoba) (Ibid.). She died on 18 Aug 1917 Dumas, Saskatchewan, at age 86 (D. Courchane.). She was buried on 21 Aug 1917 Dumas, Saskatchewan (Ibid.).

Children of **Jacques Tourond** and **Marie Courchene** were as follows:

16 i. Jean Marie Tourond, b. 1856 Red River, (Manitoba); m. Marie Roy; d. 1949.

    ii. Marie Celina Tourond was born on 30 Sep 1858 St.Norbert, (Manitoba) (SN1, page 6, B-27.). She was baptized on 1 Oct 1858 St.Norbert, (Manitoba) (Ibid.). She died on 14 May 1863 St.Norbert, (Manitoba), at age 4 (Ibid., page 80, S-5.). She was buried on 15 May 1863 St.Norbert, (Manitoba) (Ibid.).

17 iii. Joseph Tourond, b. 14 Apr 1860 St.Norbert, (Manitoba); m. Rosalie Laberge; m. Marie Vermette.

    iv. Marie Rosalie Tourond was born on 28 Oct 1862 St.Norbert, (Manitoba) (Ibid., page 63, B-27.). She was baptized on 28 Oct 1862 St.Norbert, (Manitoba) (Ibid.). She died on 27 Oct 1863 St.Norbert, (Manitoba) (Ibid., page 89, S-15.). She was buried on 27 Oct 1863 St.Norbert, (Manitoba) (IBMS *Index des Baptemes, Mariages et Sepultures* (La Societe Historique de Saint-Boniface).).

18 v. Vincent-de-Paul Tourond dit Broquerie, b. 28 Jul 1864 St.Norbert, (Manitoba); m. Julienne Roy; m. Cecile Marion; d. May 1934 St.Lazare, Fort Ellice, Manitoba.

19 vi. Jean Baptiste Tourond, b. 18 Mar 1866; m. Marie Christine Monet dit Belhumeur.

20 vii. Joseph Clement Tourond, b. 30 Sep 1867 St.Norbert, (Manitoba); m. Marguerite Desjarlais; d. 21 Jan 1944 Grand Forks, North Dakota.

21 viii. Jacques Tourond, b. 30 Jul 1869 St.Norbert, (Manitoba); m. Marie Virginie Bruneau; d. 1954 Meadow Lake, Saskatchewan.

22 ix. Charles Frederic Joseph Albert Tourond, b. 26 Dec 1870 St.Norbert, Manitoba; m. Marjorie Florence Simpson; d. 20 Mar 1940 Beauchamp, Saskatchewan.

    x. Marie Rose Tourond was baptized on 24 Feb 1874 St.Norbert, Manitoba (SN2, B-12.). She was born on 24 Feb 1874 St.Norbert, Manitoba (Ibid.). She married James Mathew King on 28 Nov 1893 De Salaberry, Manitoba (MM.) (MB Vital Statistics, Marriage Reg. #1893,001048.).

4. Jean Baptiste Tourond was born on 1 Jun 1838 St.Boniface, (Manitoba) (MBS, C-14934.). He married **Angelique Delorme**, daughter of **Joseph Delorme** and **Brigitte Villebrun dit Plouf,** on 8 Jan 1861 St.Norbert, (Manitoba) (SN1, page 37-38, M-2.). He married **Regina Allard**, daughter of **Joseph Allard** and **Julie Langevin,** on 21 Oct 1889 St.Pierre Jolys, Manitoba (MM, page 22.). He died on 25 Apr 1891 Ritchot, Manitoba, at age 52 (MB Vital Statistics, Death Reg. #1891,002124.) (SN2, S-5.). He was buried on 27 Apr 1891 St.Norbert, Manitoba (St-N Cem *St.Norbert Parish Cemetery 1859-1906, We Remember*; Winnipeg, Manitoba, Canada: St.Norbert Parish-La Barriere Metis Council of the Metis Federation of Manitoba, 29 May 2010).) (SN2, S-5.).

Angelique Delorme was born in 1845 St.Norbert, (Manitoba) (MBS, C-14934.). She died before 1889.

Children of **Jean Baptiste Tourond** and **Angelique Delorme** were as follows:

23 i. Elise Tourond, b. 23 Feb 1862 St.Norbert, (Manitoba); m. Anaclet Lepine; d. 14 Nov 1894 Ritchot, Manitoba; bur. 16 Nov 1894 St.Norbert, Manitoba.

    ii. Jean Baptiste Noel Tourond was born on 25 Dec 1862 St.Norbert, (Manitoba) (SN1, page 69, B-44.). He was baptized on 25 Dec 1862 St.Norbert, (Manitoba) (Ibid.). He died on 30 Jan 1863 St.Norbert, (Manitoba) (Ibid., S-1.). He was buried on 31 Jan 1863 St.Norbert, (Manitoba) (Ibid., page 73, S-1.).

    iii. Joseph Tourond was born on 6 Jan 1864 St.Norbert, (Manitoba) (Ibid., page 94, B-4.). He was baptized on 6 Jan 1864 St.Norbert, (Manitoba) (Ibid.). He died on 3 Mar 1865 St.Norbert, (Manitoba), at age 1 (Ibid., page 125, S-5.). He was buried on 4 Mar 1865 St.Norbert, (Manitoba) (Ibid.).

24 iv. Rosalie Tourond, b. 31 Dec 1864 St.Norbert, (Manitoba); m. Pierre St.Germain; d. 3 May 1894 Ritchot, Manitoba; bur. 1 Jun 1894 St.Norbert, Manitoba.

    v. Jean Baptiste Regis Tourond was born on 23 Dec 1866 St.Norbert, (Manitoba) (Ibid., page 90, B-70.). He was baptized on 24 Dec 1866 St.Norbert, (Manitoba) (Ibid.).

    vi. Francois Tourond was born on 19 May 1868 St.Norbert, (Manitoba) (IBMS.) (SN1, B-20.). He was baptized on 19 May 1868 St.Norbert, (Manitoba) (Ibid.). He died on 10 Sep 1885 St.Norbert, Manitoba, at age 17 (SN2, S-23.) (MB Vital Statistics, Death Reg. #1885,001807.). He was buried on 12 Sep 1885 St.Norbert, Manitoba (SN2, S-23.).

    vii. Marie Josephine Tourond was born on 2 Sep 1869 St.Norbert, (Manitoba) (SN1, B-33.). She was baptized on 2 Sep 1869 St.Norbert, (Manitoba) (Ibid.). She married Joseph Pierre Parenteau, son of Pierre Parenteau and Nancy Farquarhson, on 10 Jul 1894 (Ritchot), St.Norbert, Manitoba (MM, page 965 & 1233.) (MB Vital Statistics, Marriage Reg. #1898,001519.).

Joseph Pierre Parenteau was born on 19 Aug 1863 St.Norbert, (Manitoba) (SN1, page 84, B-23.). He was baptized on 19 Aug 1863 St.Norbert, (Manitoba) (Ibid.). He died between 1900 and 1901.

viii. Joseph Theophile Tourond was born on 3 Jan 1871 St.Norbert, Manitoba (Ibid., page 138, B-2.). He was baptized on 4 Jan 1871 St.Norbert, Manitoba (Ibid.).

ix. Marie Caroline Josephine Agathe Tourond was born on 14 Jan 1873 St.Norbert, Manitoba (Ibid., B-2.). She was baptized on 15 Jan 1873 St.Norbert, Manitoba (Ibid.). She married Norbert Courchene, son of Antoine Courchene and Helene Delorme, on 2 Aug 1908 (Ritchot), St.Norbert, Manitoba (MM, page 1231.) (SN1, page 82, B-24 (note).) (MB Vital Statistics, Marriage Reg. #1908,001538.).

Norbert Courchene was born on 23 May 1866 St.Norbert, (Manitoba) (SN1, page 82, B-24.). He was baptized on 24 May 1866 St.Norbert, (Manitoba) (Ibid.). He married **Delia Laramee**, daughter of **Pierre Laramee** and **Marie Hamel**, on 16 Jan 1894 (St.Norbert), Ritchot, Manitoba (MM, page 277 & 722.) (MB Vital Statistics, Marriage Reg. #1898,001516.).

x. Jean Baptiste Tourond was baptized on 28 Sep 1874 St.Norbert, Manitoba (SN2, B-43.). He was born on 28 Sep 1874 St.Norbert, Manitoba (Ibid.). He died on 5 Feb 1883 RM Cartier, Manitoba, at age 8 (MB Vital Statistics, Death Reg. #1883,001257.) (SN2, S-6.). He was buried on 7 Feb 1883 St.Norbert, Manitoba (Ibid.).

xi. Francois Xavier Joseph Noel Tourond was born on 10 Aug 1876 St.Norbert, Manitoba (Ibid., B-25.). He was baptized on 11 Aug 1876 St.Norbert, Manitoba (Ibid.).

xii. Simeon Etienne Tourond was born on 26 Dec 1877 St.Norbert, Manitoba (Ibid., B-50.). He was baptized on 29 Dec 1877 St.Norbert, Manitoba (Ibid.).

xiii. Marie Celine Adeline Tourond was born on 26 Oct 1879 (Ibid., B-55.). She was baptized on 28 Oct 1879 St.Norbert, Manitoba (Ibid.).

xiv. Marie Louise Alvina Tourond was born on 25 May 1881 St.Norbert, Manitoba (Ibid., B-23.). She was baptized on 26 May 1881 St.Norbert, Manitoba (Ibid.). She died on 11 Jul 1888 St.Norbert, Manitoba, at age 7 (MB Vital Statistics, Death Reg. #1888,002643.). She was buried on 12 Jul 1888 St.Norbert, Manitoba (SN2, S-19.).

xv. Marie Elise Alphee Tourond was born on 1 Dec 1883 St.Norbert, Manitoba (Ibid., B-42.). She was baptized on 2 Dec 1883 St.Norbert, Manitoba (Ibid.). She died on 20 Mar 1884 St.Norbert, Manitoba (Ibid., S-11.). She was buried on 22 Mar 1884 St.Norbert, Manitoba (Ibid.).

5. Rosalie Tourond was born circa 1845 (SN1, page 123, S-3.). She married **Francois Delorme**, son of **Joseph Delorme** and **Brigitte Villebrun dit Plouf**, on 8 Jan 1861 St.Norbert, (Manitoba) (Ibid., page 37, M-1.). She died on 24 Feb 1865 St.Norbert, (Manitoba) (Ibid., page 123, S-3.). She was buried on 26 Feb 1865 St.Norbert, (Manitoba) (Ibid.).

Francois Delorme was born in 1833 St.Norbert, (Manitoba) (MBS, C-14927.). He married **Josephte St.Germain**, daughter of **Augustin St.Germain** and **Josephte Primeau**, on 7 Jan 1868 St.Norbert, (Manitoba) (SN2, M-3.). He died on 13 Jun 1900 RM Ritchot, Manitoba (MB Vital Statistics, Death Reg. #1900,001097.). He was buried on 15 Jun 1900 St.Norbert, Manitoba (St-N Cem.).

6. Isidore Tourond was born in 1847 St.Norbert, (Manitoba) (MBS, C-14934.). He married **Anne Vermette**, daughter of **Joseph Vermette** and **Angelique Laliberte**, on 5 Jan 1870 St.Norbert, (Manitoba) (SN1, M-3.). He died on 11 Feb 1923 LaBroquerie, Manitoba (MB Vital Statistics, Death Reg. #1923-008405.).

Anne Vermette was born in 1857 St.Norbert, (Manitoba) (MBS, C-14934.). She died on 8 Dec 1922 St.Boniface, Manitoba (MB Vital Statistics, Death Reg. #1922,046051.).

Children of **Isidore Tourond** and **Anne Vermette** were as follows:

25 i. Joseph Alexandre Tourond, b. 24 Nov 1871 St.Norbert, Manitoba; m. Marguerite Desjardins.

ii. Cyrille Tourond was born on 9 Oct 1873 (SN1, B-58.). He was baptized on 12 Oct 1873 St.Norbert, Manitoba (Ibid.).

iii. Cecile Tourond was born circa 1875 Manitoba (1881 Church of Latter Day Saints Census Transcription Project of Census Images from the National Archives of Canada, Ottawa, Canada, http://www.familysearch.org, District 184-D-1, page 20, household 84.). She married Henri Harel on 30 Jul 1894 De Salaberry, Manitoba (MM.) (MB Vital Statistics, Marriage Reg. #1894,002158.).

26 iv. Anne Octavie Tourond, b. 13 Aug 1875 St.Norbert, Manitoba; m. Cyrille Parisien; m. William Parisien.

v. Anne Tourond was born on 18 May 1877 St.Norbert, Manitoba (SN2, B-20.). She was baptized on 10 Jun 1877 St.Norbert, Manitoba (Ibid.). She married Charles Beaulieu, son of Timothee Beaulieu and Adele Rioux, on 23 Nov 1897 De Salaberry, Manitoba (MM, page 1231 & 916.) (MB Vital Statistics, Marriage Reg. #1897,001428.).

Charles Beaulieu was born Trois-Pistoles, Quebec (MM, page 916.). He married **Marie Rosalie Smith**, daughter of **Alexandre Smith** and **Marie Rosalie Delorme**, on 10 Nov 1919 (SN2, B-51 (note).).

27 vi. Alfred Tourond, b. 18 Jan 1880 Manitoba; m. Octavie Rougeau.

vii. Marcial Tourond was born in Jan 1881 Ste.Agathe, Manitoba (1881 Canada, District 184-D-1, page 20, household 84.).

viii. Josephine Tourond was born on 2 Nov 1884 Manitoba (1901 Canada, District 10, (e-7), page 3-4, line 49-50, 1-3.).

ix. Marie Eugenie Tourond was born on 28 Jan 1887 R.M. of De Salaberry, Manitoba (MB Vital Statistics, Birth Reg. #1887,003252.). She married Cyprien Rougeau on 25 Nov 1903 Broquerie, Manitoba (MM.).

28 x. Isidore Henri Baptiste Tourond, b. 19 Jul 1889 R.M. of De Salaberry, Manitoba; m. Marguerite Dubois.

7. Elise Tourond was born on 15 Aug 1850 (1901 Canada, District 10, (A-2), page 5, family 41, line 6-16.). She married **Toussaint Vermette**, son of **Joseph Vermette** and **Angelique Laliberte**, on 12 Jan 1872 St.Norbert, Manitoba (SN1, M-2.). She died on 26 Jan 1932 DeSalaberry, Manitoba, at age 81 (MB Vital Statistics, Death Reg. No. 1932,004235.).

Toussaint Vermette was born on 25 Dec 1848 (1901 Canada, District 10, (A-2), page 5, family 41, line 6-16.). He was born on 15 Jan 1849 St.Norbert, (Manitoba) (MBS, C-14934.). He died on 8 Aug 1930 DeSalaberry, Manitoba, at age 81 (MB Vital Statistics, Death Reg. No. 1930,045101.).

8. Henri Tourond was born on 16 Jun 1856 St.Norbert, (Manitoba) (MBS, C-14934.) (1901 Canada, #10, (a-2), page 5, family 42, line 17-20.). He married **Louise Corrigal**, daughter of **Edward Corrigal** and **Frances McGillivray,** on 11 Jul 1876 St.Norbert, Manitoba (SN2, M-4.). He died on 23 Sep 1904 De Salaberry, Manitoba, at age 48 (MB Vital Statistics, Death Reg. #1904,001480.).

Louise Corrigal was born on 12 May 1859 St.Andrews, (Manitoba) (MBS, C-14934.) (1901 Canada, #10, (a-2), page 5, family 42, line 17-20.).

Children of **Henri Tourond** and **Louise Corrigal** were as follows:

    i.   Lucie Tourond was born on 26 Jun 1886 Manitoba (MBS, C-14934.) (1901 Canada, #10, (a-2), page 5, family 42, line 17-20.). She married Alexandre St.Germain, son of Augustin St.Germain and Eulalie Perreault, on 6 Mar 1905 St.Pierre, De Salaberry, Manitoba (MB Vital Statistics, Mar. Reg. #1905,001125.) (MM.).

        Alexandre St.Germain was born on 30 Apr 1879 St.Norbert, Manitoba (SN2, B-23.). He was baptized on 30 Apr 1879 St.Norbert, Manitoba (Ibid.).

    ii.   Leon Georges Louis Henry Tourond was born on 26 May 1889 St.Norbert, Manitoba (Ibid., B-31.). He was baptized on 26 May 1889 St.Norbert, Manitoba (Ibid.). He died on 27 May 1889 St.Norbert, Manitoba (MB Vital Statistics, Death Reg. #1889,001056.) (SN2, S-19.). He was buried on 29 May 1889 St.Norbert, Manitoba (Ibid.).

Generation Three

9. David Tourond was born on 12 Dec 1851 St.Francois Xavier, (Manitoba) (SFX: 1834-1850, B-911.). He was baptized on 13 Dec 1851 St.Francois Xavier, (Manitoba) (Ibid.). He married **Marie Virginie Fisher**, daughter of **George Fisher** and **Emelie Boyer,** on 2 Feb 1875 St.Francois Xavier, Manitoba (SFXI-Kipling, M-4.). He died on 11 Sep 1890 Batoche, (Saskatchewan), at age 38 (BSAP, page 84, S-13.). He was buried on 15 Sep 1890 Batoche, (Saskatchewan) (Ibid.).

Marie Virginie Fisher was born on 22 Apr 1859 Qu'Appelle, (Saskatchewan) (MBS, C-14927.). She married **Leon Hamelin**, son of **Antoine Hamelin** and **Philomene Mathilde Perreault dit Morin,** on 22 Jun 1895 Lebret, (Saskatchewan) (Art Fisher Research.) (Joyce Black Research.) (Automated Genealogy 1906 Census Transcription Project and Census Images from the National Archives of Canada, http://www.automatedgenealogy.com, #15, (41), page 33, family 268, line 3-8.).

Children of **David Tourond** and **Marie Virginie Fisher** were as follows:

    i.   Joseph Tourond was born on 3 Sep 1876 Baie St.Paul, Manitoba (HBSI Index 1886-1901, 1906 Halfbreed Scrip Applications, RG15-21.) (ArchiviaNet 1886-1901, 1906 Half-Breed Scrip Applications Index, RG15-21, Volume 1333 through 1371, Microfilm Reel Number C-14944 through C-15010, National Archives of Canada, Ottawa, Ontario, http://www.collectionscanada.gc.ca.) (Denney.). He died on 16 Oct 1876 Baie St.Paul, Manitoba (HBSI.) (ArchiviaNet.) (Denney.).

    ii.   Joseph Marie Pierre Tourond was born on 20 Nov 1877 Baie St.Paul, Manitoba (ArchiviaNet.) (HBSI.). He died on 17 Mar 1882 St.Francois Xavier, Manitoba, at age 4 (SFXI-Kipling, S-9.) (MB Vital Statistics, Death Reg. #1882,001677.).

29   iii.   Marie Tourond, b. 20 Nov 1878 St.Eustache, Manitoba; m. Etienne Felix Adolphe-Henri Savage.

    iv.   Henry Alfred Tourond was born in 1881 Fish Creek, (Saskatchewan) (HBSI.) (ArchiviaNet.). He was born on 24 Aug 1881 St.Francois Xavier, Manitoba (SFXI-Kipling, B-42.). He died in 1894 (HBSI.) (ArchiviaNet.).

    v.   Jean Louis Tourond was born on 21 Sep 1883 Fish Creek, (Saskatchewan) (BSAP, page 18, B-23.). He was baptized on 30 Sep 1883 Batoche, (Saskatchewan) (Ibid.). He died on 16 Jul 1884 (ArchiviaNet.). He was buried St.Laurent, (Saskatchewan).

30   vi.   Marguerite Alexandrine Tourond, b. 30 Apr 1885 Batoche, (Saskatchewan); m. Paul Adolphe.

    vii.   Virginie Augustine Tourond was born circa 1887 (Art Fisher.). She died on 2 Apr 1901 (Saskatchewan) (Saskatchewan Vital Statistics online, http://vsgs.health.gov.sk.ca, Death Reg. #157.).

    viii.   Urbain Tourond was born in 1890 Qu'Appelle, (Saskatchewan) (1906 Canada, #15, (41), page 33, family 268, line 3-8.).

10. Calixte Tourond was born on 23 Apr 1853 (MBS, C-14934.) (SFXI-Kipling, B-64.) (SFXI 1851-1868, B-64.). He was baptized on 24 Apr 1853 St.Francois Xavier, (Manitoba) (SFXI-Kipling, B-64.) (SFXI 1851-1868, B-64.). He married **Marguerite Ross**, daughter of **Donald Ross** and **Catherine Delorme,** on 10 Feb 1874 St.Francois Xavier, Manitoba (SFXI-Kipling, M-7.). He married **Josephte Gervais**, daughter of **Alexis Gervais** and **Madeleine Fagnant,** on 4 Nov 1882 Batoche, (Saskatchewan) (BSAP, page 11, M-3.). He died on 12 May 1885 Batoche, (Saskatchewan), at age 32 (Ibid., page 33, S-17.). He was buried on 14 May 1885 Batoche, (Saskatchewan) (Ibid.).

Marguerite Ross was baptized on 27 Sep 1855 St.Francois Xavier, (Manitoba) (SFXI-Kipling, B-67.). She died on 6 Jun 1880 St.Francois Xavier, Manitoba, at age 24 (Ibid., S-20.). She was buried on 8 Jan 1880 St.Francois Xavier, Manitoba (Ibid.).

Children of **Calixte Tourond** and **Marguerite Ross** all born St.Francois Xavier, Manitoba, were as follows:

    i.   Agathe Tourond was born on 26 Dec 1874 (INB *Index des Naissances and Baptemes* (St.Boniface, Manitoba: La Societe Historique de Saint-Boniface., c1995), page 176.) (SFXI-Kipling, B-63.). She was baptized on 26 Dec 1874 St.Francois Xavier, Manitoba (Ibid.) (INB, page 176.). She died on 23 Feb 1889 Batoche, (Saskatchewan), at age 14 (BSAP, page 73, S-3.). She was buried on 25 Feb 1889 Batoche, (Saskatchewan) (Ibid.).

    ii.   Elzear Tourond was born on 19 Apr 1876 (SFXI-Kipling, B-15.). He was baptized on 24 Apr 1876 St.Francois Xavier, Manitoba (Ibid.) (Rosemary Rozyk.). He died on 15 Mar 1879 St.Francois Xavier, Manitoba, at age 2 (SFXI-Kipling., S-5.). He was buried on 17 Mar 1879 St.Francois Xavier, Manitoba (Ibid.) Rosemary Rozyk.).

    iii.   Elise Tourond was born on 14 Oct 1877 (Ibid., B-46.). She was baptized on 14 Oct 1877 St.Francois Xavier, Manitoba (Ibid.) (Rosemry Rozyk.). She died on 27 Mar 1879 St.Francois Xavier, Manitoba, at age 1 (Ibid., S-8.). She was buried on 29 Mar 1879 St.Francois Xavier, Manitoba (Ibid.) (Rosemary Rozyk.).

    iv.   Joseph Tourond was born on 13 Nov 1878 (Ibid., B-38.). He died on 30 Jan 1900 (Saskatchewan) at age 21 (SK Vital Statistics, Death Reg. No. 100.).

    v.   Domitilde Tourond was born on 14 Jan 1880 (SFXI-Kipling, B-2.). She died on 8 Aug 1880 St.Francois Xavier, Manitoba (Ibid., S-28.).

Josephte Gervais was born on 18 Aug 1851 St.Francois Xavier, (Manitoba) (SFX: 1834-1850, B-923.). She was baptized on 18 Aug 1851 St.Francois Xavier, (Manitoba) (Ibid.). She married **Leopold McGillis**, son of **Alexandre McGillis** and **Marguerite Bottineau,** on 10 Sep 1872 St.Francois Xavier, Manitoba (SFXI-Kipling, M-14.). She married **Boniface Lefort,** son of **Francois Toussaint Lefort** and **Eliza Laplante,** before 1888.

Children of **Calixte Tourond** and **Josephte Gervais** all born Fish Creek, (Saskatchewan), were as follows:

    i.   Jean Baptiste Tourond was born on 7 Sep 1883 (BSAP, page 17, B-19.) (ArchiviaNet, C-15007.). He was baptized on 9 Sep 1883 Batoche, (Saskatchewan) (BSAP, page 17, B-19.).

    ii.   Charles Tourond was born on 23 Oct 1884 (HBSI.). He died on 23 Oct 1884 Fish Creek, (Saskatchewan) (Ibid.).

    iii.   Marguerite Clemence Tourond was born on 30 Oct 1885 (BSAP, page 40, B-26.) (ArchiviaNet, C-15007.). She was baptized on 31 Oct 1885 Batoche, (Saskatchewan) (BSAP, page 40, B-26.).

11. Pierre Tourond was born on 1 Feb 1855 St.Francois Xavier, (Manitoba) (SFXI-Kipling, B-17.) (SFXI 1851-1868, B-17.). He was baptized on 3 Feb 1855 St.Francois Xavier, (Manitoba) (SFXI-Kipling, B-17.) (SFXI 1851-1868, B-17.). He married **Catherine Gervais,** daughter of **Alexis Gervais** and **Madeleine Fagnant,** on 17 Jan 1882 St.Francois Xavier, Manitoba (SFXI-Kipling, M-2.) (MB Vital Statistics, Marriage Reg. #1882,001392.). He died on 20 Mar 1887 Batoche, (Saskatchewan), at age 32 (HBSI.) (BSAP, page 55, S-5.). He was buried on 22 Mar 1887 Batoche, (Saskatchewan) (Ibid.).

Catherine Gervais was born on 22 May 1864 St.Francois Xavier, (Manitoba) (SFXI-Kipling, B-19.). She was baptized on 24 May 1864 St.Francois Xavier, (Manitoba) (Ibid.). She married **William Fidler,** son of **William Fidler** and **Marguerite McGillis,** circa 1890 (Denney.). She died on 9 Jun 1895 Batoche, (Saskatchewan), at age 31 (Ibid.) (BSAP, page 124, S-5.). She was buried on 11 Jun 1895 Batoche, (Saskatchewan) (Ibid.).

Children of **Pierre Tourond** and **Catherine Gervais** were as follows:

31   i.   Ambroise Tourond, b. 13 Jul 1883 Fish Creek, (Saskatchewan); m. Anne Thorn; d. 22 Sep 1912 Saskatchewan.

    ii.   Isidore Tourond was born on 14 Nov 1884 Fish Creek, (Saskatchewan) (Ibid., page 27, B-31.) (Denney.). He was baptized on 27 Nov 1884 Batoche, (Saskatchewan) (BSAP, page 27, B-31.).

    iii.   Solomon Eli Tourond was baptized on 12 Sep 1886 Batoche, (Saskatchewan) (Ibid., page 51, B-29.). He died on 8 Mar 1887 Batoche, (Saskatchewan) (Ibid., page 55, S-3.). He was buried on 9 Mar 1887 Batoche, (Saskatchewan) (Ibid.).

12. Patrice Tourond was baptized on 24 Mar 1857 St.Francois Xavier, (Manitoba) (SFXI-Kipling, B-171.). He was born on 24 Mar 1857 St.Francois Xavier, (Manitoba) (Ibid.). He married **Marie Gervais,** daughter of **Alexis Gervais** and **Madeleine Fagnant,** on 23 Nov 1885 Batoche, (Saskatchewan) (BSAP, page 41, M-1.). He died on 28 Sep 1898 Batoche, Saskatchewan, at age 41 (Ibid., S-8.). He was buried on 30 Sep 1898 Batoche, Saskatchewan (Ibid.).

Marie Gervais was born on 6 Feb 1866 St.Francois Xavier, (Manitoba) (SFXI-Kipling, B-13.). She was baptized on 7 Feb 1866 St.Francois Xavier, (Manitoba) (Ibid.).

Children of **Patrice Tourond** and **Marie Gervais** were as follows:

32   i.   Joseph Patrice Tourond, b. 3 Oct 1886 Batoche, (Saskatchewan); m. Nancy Victoria Batoche; d. 1964.

33   ii.   William Benedict Tourond, b. 17 Jan 1890; d. 5 Jun 1970.

    iii.   Marie E. Tourond was born on 23 Oct 1892 (Saskatchewan) (SK Vital Statistics, Birth Reg. No. 7769.).

    iv.   Louis David Victor Tourond was born on 13 Jun 1898 Saskatchewan (BSAP, B-14.) (SK Vital Statistics, Birth Reg. No. 1487.). He was baptized on 9 Jul 1898 Batoche, (Saskatchewan) (BSAP, B-14.).

13. Elzear Tourond was born on 1 Sep 1859 St.Francois Xavier, (Manitoba) (SFXI-Kipling, B-386.). He was baptized on 2 Sep 1859 St.Francois Xavier, (Manitoba) (Ibid.). He married **Ernestine Berland,** daughter of **Patrice Breland** and **Helene Dease,** on 6 Jun 1882 St.Francois Xavier, Manitoba (SFXI-Kipling, M-7.) (MB Vital Statistics, Marriage Reg. #1882,001397.). He died on 12 May 1885 Batoche, (Saskatchewan), at age 25 (BSAP, page 33, S-18.). He was bured on 14 May 1885 Batoche, (Saskatchewan) (Ibid.).

Ernestine Berland was born on 11 Jun 1863 St.Francois Xavier, (Manitoba) (SFXI-Kipling, B-53.). She was baptized on 11 Jun 1863 St.Francois Xavier, (Manitoba) (Ibid.) (SFXI 1851-1868, B-53.). She married **Olivier Robidoux** on 30 Aug 1887 St.Francois Xavier, Manitoba (SFXI-Kipling, M-8.) (MB Vital Statistics, Mar. Reg. #1887,001919.). She died on 7 Sep 1888 St.Francois Xavier, Manitoba, at age 25 (SFXI-Kipling, S-13.). She was buried 9 Sep 1888 St.Francois Xavier, Manitoba (Ibid.) (Rosemary Rozyk.).

Children of **Elzear Tourond** and **Ernestine Berland** both born Fish Creek, (Saskatchewan), were as follows:

    i.   Joseph Arthur Tourond was born on 8 Sep 1883 (BSAP, page 17, B-20.) (ArchiviaNet, C-15007.). He was baptized on 9 Sep 1883 Batoche, (Saskatchewan) (BSAP, page 17, B-20.).

    ii.   Marie Josephine Tourond was born on 17 Feb 1885 (Ibid., page 30, B-6.) (ArchiviaNet, C-15007.). She was baptized on 24 Feb 1885 Batoche, (Saskatchewan) (BSAP, page 30, B-6.). She married Robert Alcide Lesperance, son of Jean Lesperance and Emelie Lavallee, on 28 Nov 1911 St.Francois Xavier, Manitoba (MB Vital Statistics, Marriage Reg. #1911,001591.).

         Robert Alcide Lesperance was born on 4 Aug 1879 St.Francois Xavier, Manitoba (SFXI-Kipling, B-44.).

14. Marie Therese Tourond was born on 18 Jan 1866 St.Francois Xavier, (Manitoba) (Ibid., B-10.). She was baptized on 19 Jan 1866 St.Francois Xavier, (Manitoba) (Ibid.). She married **Joseph Napoleon Venne,** son of **Salomon Venne** and **Josephte St.Arnaud,** on 30 Jun 1887 Batoche, (Saskatchewan) (BSAP, page 59, M-6.). She died on 18 Aug 1891 Batoche, (Saskatchewan), at age 25 (Ibid., page 9, S-7.). She was buried on 20 Aug 1891 Batoche, (Saskatchewan) (Ibid.).

Joseph Napoleon Venne was born on 17 Oct 1864 St.Norbert, (Manitoba) (SN1, page 110, B-38.). He was baptized on 17 Oct 1864 St.Norbert, (Manitoba) (Ibid.). He married **Marie Louise Parenteau,** daughter of **Joseph Daudais Parenteau** and **Julie Houle,** on 16 Nov 1895 St.Vital, Battleford, (Saskatchewan) (SV St.Vital Roman Catholic Registre des Baptemes, Mariages & Sepltures, Battleford, Saskatchewan, 1878-1896, M-5. Hereinafter cited as SV.).

15. Elise Tourond was born on 18 Mar 1868 St.Francois Xavier, (Manitoba) (SFXI-Kipling, B-19.). She was baptized on 19 Mar 1868 St.Francois Xavier, (Manitoba) (Ibid.). She married **Raphael Boyer,** son of **William Boyer** and **Julienne Bousquet,** on 22 Oct 1894 Batoche, (Saskatchewan) (BSAP, page 119, M-4.) (Rosemary Helga (Morrissette) Rozyk Research, 27 Jan 1999.).

Raphael Boyer was born on 9 Sep 1867 St.Boniface, (Manitoba) (MBS, C-14925.) (SB-Rozyk St. Boniface Roman Catholic Church, Manitoba, Canada, Baptisms, Marriages and Burials 1860-1875 Extractions, Compiled by Rosemary Rozyk, page 93, B-78.). He was baptized on 10 Sep 1867 St.Boniface, (Manitoba) (MBS, C-14925.) (SB-Rozyk, page 93, B-78.).

16. **Jean Marie Tourond** was born in 1856 Red River, (Manitoba). He married **Marie Roy**, daughter of **Marcel Roy** and **Ursule Venne**, on 5 Apr 1880 St.Pierre Jolys, Manitoba (MM.). He died in 1949 (D. Courchane, 1992.).

Marie Roy was born on 8 Sep 1861 St.Norbert, (Manitoba) (SN1, page 47, B-32.). She was baptized on 8 Sep 1861 St.Norbert, (Manitoba) (Ibid.).

Children of **Jean Marie Tourond** and **Marie Roy** were as follows:

      i. Joseph Tourond was born in Mar 1881 Ste.Agathe, Manitoba (1881 Canada, District 184-D-1, page 27, household 122.).

  34 ii. Jean Patrice Amable Tourond, b. 2 May 1885; m. Rosalie Bruneau; d. 2 May 1962 Yorkton, Saskatchewan.

17. **Joseph Tourond** was born on 14 Apr 1860 St.Norbert, (Manitoba) (SN1, page 28, B-14.). He was baptized on 16 Apr 1860 St.Norbert, (Manitoba) (Ibid.). He married **Rosalie Laberge**, daughter of **Francois Laberge** and **Marguerite Gladu,** on 17 Nov 1885 De Salaberry, Manitoba (MM, page 1233.) (MB Vital Statistics, Marriage Reg. #1885,001433.). He married **Marie Vermette**, daughter of **Pierre Vermette** and **Caroline St.Denis,** on 28 Jul 1903 St.Norbert, Manitoba (MM, page 1233.).

Rosalie Laberge was born on 9 Jan 1869 (SFXI-Kipling, B-46.). She was baptized on 3 Jul 1869 St.Francois Xavier, (Manitoba) (Ibid.). She died on 27 Feb 1902 St.Boniface, Manitoba, at age 33 (MB Vital Statistics, Death Reg. #1902,001749.).

Children of **Joseph Tourond** and **Rosalie Laberge** were as follows:

  35 i. Patrice Tourond, b. 2 Sep 1886 Manitoba; m. Lydia Charpentier.

      ii. Louis Guillaume Tourond was born on 7 Aug 1888 (Olga Our Lady of the Sacred Heart, Olga, North Dakota 1882-1900, page 149, B-31. Hereinafter cited as Olga.). He was baptized on 12 Aug 1888 Olga, Cavalier County, North Dakota (Ibid.). He married Marie Emma Lumina Charette, daughter of Solomon Charette and Marie Azilda Carriere, on 13 Mar 1917 Winnipeg, Manitoba (MB Vital Statistics, Marriage Reg. #1917,015064.).

          Marie Emma Lumina Charette was born on 28 Mar 1898 R.M. of La Broquerie, Manitoba (Ibid., Birth Reg. #1898,002372.).

      iii. Pierre Tourond was born on 18 Mar 1890 Manitoba (1901 Canada, District 10, (e-5), page 4, family 33, line 35-43.).

      iv. Anna Tourond was born on 11 Sep 1892 Manitoba (Ibid.). She married Pierre Andre Gladu, son of Pierre Andre Gladu and Elise Parisien, on 14 Sep 1917 St.Boniface, Manitoba (RMSB, page 194.) (MB Vital Statistics, Mar. Reg. #1917,051013.).

          Pierre Andre Gladu was born on 4 Oct 1889 R.M. of De Salaberry, Manitoba (Ibid., Birth Reg. #1889,001876.).

      v. Marie Rosalie Anne Tourond was born on 12 Sep 1893 R.M. of De Salaberry, Manitoba (Ibid., Birth Reg. #1893,001983.).

      vi. Vincent de Paul Tourond was born on 20 Nov 1894 R.M. of De Salaberry, Manitoba (Ibid., Birth Reg. #1894,003358.). He married Rosa Vandal on 7 Jun 1922 St.Boniface, Manitoba (Ibid., Marriage Reg. #1922,021031.).

      vii. Marie Rose Tourond was born on 25 Jul 1896 Manitoba (1901 Canada, District 10, (e-5), page 4, family 33, line 35-43.). She married George Alfred Dumas, son of Michel Dumas and Veronique Ouellette, on 5 Nov 1917 St.Boniface, Manitoba (RMSB.) (MB Vital Statistics, Marriage Reg. #1917,063034.).

          George Alfred Dumas was born on 20 Dec 1889 R.M. Posen, Manitoba (1901 Canada, #8, 01, 0, page 3, family 24, Line 31-36.) (MB Vital Statistics, Birth Reg. #1889,005800.).

      viii. Dorothee Tourond was born on 8 Aug 1899 Manitoba (1901 Canada, District 10, (e-5), page 4, family 33, line 35-43.).

Marie Vermette was baptized on 9 Oct 1869 St.Norbert, (Manitoba) (SN1, B-37.). She was born on 9 Oct 1869 St.Norbert, (Manitoba) (Ibid.). She married **Norbert Spirilion Charette**, son of **Joseph Charette** and **Marie Gosselin,** on 5 Apr 1890 St.Norbert, Manitoba (SN2, M-4.).

Children of **Joseph Tourond** and **Marie Vermette** both born R.M. of La Broquerie, Manitoba, are as follows:

      i. Wilfrid Alphonse Tourond was born on 29 Nov 1905 (MB Vital Statistics, Birth Reg. #1905,007372.).

      ii. Alexandre Tourond was born on 19 Jul 1907 (Ibid., Birth Reg. #1907,002096.).

18. **Vincent-de-Paul Tourond dit Broquerie** was born on 28 Jul 1864 St.Norbert, (Manitoba) (SN1, page 105, B-35.). He was baptized on 29 Jul 1864 St.Norbert, (Manitoba) (Ibid.). He married **Julienne Roy**, daughter of **Augustin Roy** and **Pauline Normand,** on 26 Aug 1884 De Salaberry, Manitoba (MB Vital Statistics, Marriage Reg. #1884,001306.). He married **Cecile Marion** on 21 May 1906 St.Hebert, (Saskatchewan) (Denney.). He died in May 1934 St.Lazare, Fort Ellice, Manitoba, at age 69 (Ibid.).

Julienne Roy was baptized on 20 Jun 1868 St.Norbert, (Manitoba) (SN1, B-23.). She was born on 20 Jun 1868 St.Norbert, (Manitoba) (Ibid.). She died before 1906.

Children of **Vincent-de-Paul Tourond dit Broquerie** and **Julienne Roy** were as follows:

      i. Vincent Tourond was born on 12 Nov 1885 De Salaberry, Manitoba (MB Vital Statistics, Birth Reg. #1885,005297.).

      ii. Joseph Albert Henri Tourond was born on 17 Aug 1887 R.M. of De Salaberry, Manitoba (Ibid., Birth Reg. #1887,001075.).

      iii. Marguerite Tourond was born on 6 Jan 1889 De Salaberry, Manitoba (Ibid., Birth Reg. #1889,004433.). She died on 27 Jan 1899 R.M. of De Salaberry, Manitoba, at age 10 (Ibid., Death Reg. #1889,002724.).

      iv. Joseph Louis Damase Tourond was born either 9 Dec 1890 or 1891 R.M. of De Salaberry, Manitoba (Ibid., Birth Reg. #1890,002497.) (Ibid., Birth Reg. #1891,003494.). He married Marie Normand on 5 Apr 1915 St.Boniface, Manitoba (Ibid., Marriage Reg. #1915,174021.).

v. Anonyme Tourond was born on 12 Oct 1891 R.M. of De Salaberry, Manitoba (Ibid., Birth Reg. #1891,003520.). She died on 12 Oct 1891 De Salaberry, Manitoba (Ibid., Death Reg. #1891,00171.).

vi. Georges Augustin Tourond was born on 4 Jan 1893 R.M. of De Salaberry, Manitoba (Ibid., Birth Reg. #1893,006925.). He died on 1 Mar 1893 De Salaberry, Manitoba (Ibid., Death Reg. #1893,002030.).

vii. Joseph Toussaint Tourond was born on 8 May 1894 R.M. of De Salaberry, Manitoba (Ibid., Birth Reg. #1894,006345.). He died on 20 Aug 1894 De Salaberry, Manitoba (Ibid., Death Reg. #1894,002515.).

viii. Julienne Valentine Tourond was born on 25 Oct 1895 R.M. of De Salaberry, Manitoba (Ibid., Birth Reg. #1895,005358.).

ix. Lucy Tourond was born in Oct 1898 Manitoba (Automated Genealogy 1911 Census Transcription Project and Census Images from the National Archives of Canada, http://www.automatedgenealogy.com, District 27, page 21, line 9-18, family 222.).

x. Marie Marguerite Tourond was born on 25 Jun 1901 St.Pierre Jolys, Manitoba (MB Vital Statistics, Birth Reg. #1901,25125440, Reg. Date 16/07/1970.).

xi. Marie Bernadette Tourond was born on 8 Oct 1903 Forget, (Saskatchewan) (SK Vital Statistics, Birth Reg. #3991.).

Cecile Marion was born in Dec 1883 (1911 Canada, District 27, page 21, line 9-18, family 222.). She died on 11 May 1946 St-Rose-du-Lac, Manitoba, at age 62 (Denney.).

Children of **Vincent-de-Paul Tourond dit Broquerie** and **Cecile Marion** are as follows:

i. Angeline Cecile Tourond was born on 26 Apr 1907 High View, Saskatchewan (SK Vital Statistics, Birth Reg. No. 9451.).

ii. Anna Tourond was born in May 1909 Saskatchewan (1911 Canada, District 27, page 21, line 9-18, family 222.).

iii. Mary Rose Tourond was born in Apr 1910 Saskatchewan (Ibid.). She married Charles Hayden, son of Robert Joseph Hayden and Rosine Houle, on 25 Nov 1933 St.Lazare, Fort Ellice, Manitoba (Denney.).
   Charles Hayden was born in Jul 1907 (1911 Canada, District 9, page 2, family 18, line 29-37.).

iv. Edward Tourond was born in Jun 1911 Saskatchewan (Ibid., District 27, page 21, line 9-18, family 222.).

v. George Tourond was born in 1913 (1916 Census of Canada from the National Archives of Canada (Transcription by ancestry.com), Ottawa, Canada, District 16-26, page 8, line 33.).

vi. Eugene Tourond was born in 1915 (Ibid.).

19. Jean Baptiste Tourond was born on 18 Mar 1866 (SN1, page 82, B-23.). He was baptized on 29 Apr 1866 St.Norbert, (Manitoba) (Ibid.). He married **Marie Christine Monet dit Belhumeur**, daughter of **Jean Baptiste Monet dit Belhumeur** and **Julienne Petit**, before 1893.

Marie Christine Monet dit Belhumeur was born on 10 Nov 1876 (SJL-1 Register of Baptisms, Marriages, and Burials, St.Joseph, Leroy, North Dakota, Diocese of Saint Paul, Minnesota, 1870-1888, Book 1, page 74, B-24. Hereinafter cited as SJL-1.). She was baptized on 12 Nov 1876 St.Joseph, Leroy, Pembina County, Dakota Territory (Ibid.).

Children of **Jean Baptiste Tourond** and **Marie Christine Monet dit Belhumeur** were as follows:

i. Jean Baptiste Tourond was born on 21 Jul 1893 (Olga, page 224, B-_.). He was baptized on 30 Jul 1893 Olga, Cavalier County, North Dakota (Ibid.).

ii. Marie Rosalie Tourond was born on 23 Nov 1896 (Ibid., page 259, B-_.). She was baptized on 12 Dec 1896 Olga, Cavalier County, North Dakota (Ibid.).

iii. Marie Christina Florina Tourond was born on 9 Sep 1898 Olga, Cavalier County, North Dakota (Ibid., page 279, B-_.). She was baptized on 10 Sep 1898 Olga, Cavalier County, North Dakota (Ibid.).

iv. Marie Yvonne Tourond was baptized on 5 May 1901 Olga, Cavalier County, North Dakota (Ibid., page 308, B-_.). She was buried on 23 May 1901 Olga, Cavalier County, North Dakota (Ibid.).

v. Marie Ida Tourond was born on 31 Jul 1902 Olga, Cavalier County, North Dakota (Ibid., page 320, B-_.). She was baptized on 9 Aug 1902 Olga, Cavalier County, North Dakota (Ibid.).

vi. Jean Edward Tourond was born on 12 May 1904 Olga, Cavalier County, North Dakota (Ibid., page 335, B-_.). He was baptized on 31 May 1904 Olga, Cavalier County, North Dakota (Ibid.).

vii. Laurent Theodore Tourond was born on 25 Apr 1906 Olga, Cavalier County, North Dakota (Ibid., page 349, B-_.). He was baptized on 10 May 1906 Olga, Cavalier County, North Dakota (Ibid.).

viii. Charles Frederic Tourond was born on 4 Jun 1909 Olga, Cavalier County, North Dakota (Ibid., page 14, B-_.). He was baptized on 4 Jun 1909 Olga, Cavalier County, North Dakota (Ibid.).

20. Joseph Clement Tourond was born on 30 Sep 1867 St.Norbert, (Manitoba) (SN1, B-35.). He was baptized on 2 Oct 1867 St.Norbert, (Manitoba) (Ibid.). He married **Marguerite Desjarlais**, daughter of **Gregoire Desjarlais** and **Julie Pepin**, on 15 Jun 1897 Olga, Cavalier County, North Dakota (Olga, page 265, M-_.). He died on 21 Jan 1944 Grand Forks, North Dakota, at age 76 (North Dakota Department of Health Public Death Index.).

Marguerite Desjarlais was born on 16 Oct 1877 St.Eustache, Manitoba (Denney.). She was baptized on 17 Oct 1877 St.Eustache, Manitoba (Ibid.). She died on 19 Jan 1962 Cavalier County, North Dakota, at age 84 (ND Death Index.).

Children of **Joseph Clement Tourond** and **Marguerite Desjarlais** were as follows:

i. Marie Helene Tourond was born on 18 Mar 1898 Olga, Cavalier County, North Dakota (Olga, page 272, B-_.). She was baptized on 20 Mar 1898 Olga, Cavalier County, North Dakota (Ibid.). She died on 15 Jun 2002 Minnesota at age 104 (Social Security Death Index, . Hereinafter cited as SSDI.) (Minnesota Department of Health Public Death Index.).

ii. Joseph Francois Tourond was born on 2 Jan 1900 North Dakota (Olga, page 294, B-_.). He was baptized on 9 Feb 1900 Olga, Cavalier County, North Dakota (Ibid.).

iii. Joseph Edouard Clement Tourond was baptized on 26 Nov 1900 Olga, Cavalier County, North Dakota (Ibid., page 302, B-_.).

iv.   Joseph Edward Tourond was baptized on 26 Apr 1902 Olga, Cavalier County, North Dakota (Ibid., page 316, B-_.).

36   v.   Joseph William Tourond, b. 2 Jul 1903 Olga, Cavalier County, North Dakota; m. Joyce Ruth Solberg; d. 3 Aug 1997 Stearns County, Minnesota.

vi.   Joseph Francois Tourond was born on 4 Jul 1905 Olga, Cavalier County, North Dakota (Ibid., page 344, B-_.). He was baptized on 16 Jul 1905 Olga, Cavalier County, North Dakota (Ibid.). He died on 29 Aug 1994 Virginia at age 89.

vii.   Oscar Tourond was born on 31 Mar 1907 (1910C ND Thirteenth Census of the United States: 1910; North Dakota, National Archives of the United States, Washington D.C., District 63, page 13B, line 85.) (SSDI.). He died on 3 Aug 2000 Atlanta, Fulton County, Georgia, at age 93 (Ibid.).

viii.   Margaret Tourond was born on 9 Apr 1911 (1920 Turtle Mountain Chippewa Indian Census Roll, United States Indian Service Department of the Interior, Turtle Mountain Indian Agency, North Dakota, 30 June 1920 , District 235, page 8A, line 11.) (ND Death Index.). She died on 25 Jun 1933 Cavalier County, North Dakota, at age 22 (Ibid.).

37   ix.   Monica Mary Tourond, b. 10 Aug 1913 Langdon, Cavalier County, North Dakota; m. Leo Carl Fischer; d. 1 Dec 1988 Blaine County, Minnesota.

x.   Eugene Tourond was born circa 1917 (*1920 TMC*, District 235, page 8A, line 11.).

xi.   Michael John Tourond was born on 26 Jan 1919 (Ibid.) (SSDI.). He died on 1 Jul 2008 Minneapolis, Hennepin County, Minnesota, at age 89 (Ibid.).

21. **Jacques Tourond** was born on 30 Jul 1869 St.Norbert, (Manitoba) (SN1, B-29.). He was baptized on 31 Jul 1869 St.Norbert, (Manitoba) (Ibid.). He married **Marie Virginie Bruneau**, daughter of **Napoleon Bruneau** and **Marie Carriere**, on 1 Jan 1902 Olga, Cavalier County, North Dakota (Olga, page 314, M-_.). He died in 1954 Meadow Lake, Saskatchewan (Rod Mac Quarrie, 17 Jan 2013.). **Marie Virginie Bruneau** was born on 19 Dec 1882 Youville, Manitoba (MB Vital Statistics, Birth Reg. #1882,002483.). She died on 15 Feb 1960 Vancouver, British Columbia, at age 77 (Rod Mac Quarrie, 17 Jan 2013.).
Children of **Jacques Tourond** and **Marie Virginie Bruneau** were as follows:

i.   Jacob Amede Tourond was baptized on 11 Feb 1903 Olga, Cavalier County, North Dakota (Olga, page 324, B-_.). He died on 17 May 1904 at age 1 (Rod Mac Quarrie, 17 Jan 2013.).

ii.   Edmond Tourond was born on 7 May 1904 R.M. of La Broquerie, Manitoba (MB Vital Statistics, Birth Reg. #1904,003856.). He died in 1997 (Rod Mac Quarrie, 17 Jan 2013.).

38   iii.   Flavie Tourond, b. 1 Dec 1905 Olga, Cavalier County, North Dakota; m. Alcide Fortin; d. 22 Feb 1993.

iv.   Rosario Didace Joseph Tourond was born on 6 Oct 1907 Beauchamp, Saskatchewan (SK Vital Statistics, Birth Reg. No. 7752.). He died before 1916.

v.   Sophie Delores Tourond was born on 4 Nov 1909. She married Alex Thomas Hobbins (Rod Mac Quarrie, 17 Jan 2013.). She died on 9 Apr 1973 Langley, British Columbia, at age 63 (Ibid.).

39   vi.   Arthur Laurent Tourond, b. 3 Nov 1911 Spaulding, Saskatchewan; m. Carol Chew; d. 9 Apr 1973 Murrayville, British Columbia.

vii.   Robert Tourond was born in 1913 (1916 Canada, District 21-5, page 29, line 20.). He died in 1931 (Rod Mac Quarrie, 17 Jan 2013.).

40   viii.   Napoleon Pierre Tourond, b. 29 Nov 1915 Delisle, Saskatchewan; m. Barbara Lucille Grainger; d. 19 Jan 1977 Burns Lake, British Columbia; bur. 24 Jan 1977 Burns Lake, British Columbia.

22. **Charles Frederic Joseph Albert Tourond** was born on 26 Dec 1870 St.Norbert, Manitoba (SN1, page 137, B-55.). He was baptized on 28 Dec 1870 St.Norbert, Manitoba (Ibid.). He married **Virginie Nault**, daughter of **Napoleon Nault** and **Melanie Vandal**, on 26 Dec 1904 Olga, Cavalier County, North Dakota (Olga, page 339, M-_.). He married **Marjorie Florence Simpson** before 1940 (D. Courchane.). He died on 20 Mar 1940 Beauchamp, Saskatchewan, at age 69 (Rod Mac Quarrie, 28 Dec 2011.). **Virginie Nault** was born on 29 Aug 1882 Batoche, (Saskatchewan) (BSAP, page 9, B-16.). She was baptized on 30 Aug 1882 Batoche, (Saskatchewan) (Ibid.). She died in Sep 1968 Aysham, Saskatchewan, at age 86 (Rod Mac Quarrie, 28 Dec 2011.).
Children of **Charles Frederic Joseph Albert Tourond** and **Virginie Nault** were as follows:

i.   Philias Albert "Phillip" Tourond was born on 4 Oct 1905 Olga, Cavalier County, North Dakota (Olga, page 344, B-_.). He was baptized on 5 Oct 1905 Olga, Cavalier County, North Dakota (Ibid.).

41   ii.   Toby Tourond, b. 4 Aug 1907 Spalding, Saskatchewan.

iii.   Wilfred Tourond was born on 24 May 1909 Spalding, Saskatchewan (1911 Canada, District 13, page 2, line 47.) (Rod Mac Quarrie, 28 Dec 2011.).

42   iv.   Raymond Gilbert Tourond, b. 1 Jun 1911 Spalding, Saskatchewan; m. Edna Julia Lake; d. 11 Mar 1974 Squamish, British Columbia.

v.   Marie Rose Clara Tourond was born on 27 Nov 1915 Spalding, Saskatchewan (1916 Canada, District 18-39, page 7, line 10.) (Rod Mac Quarrie, 28 Dec 2011.). She married Joseph Stanislaw Lefebvre on 6 Nov 1934 (Ibid.). She died on 22 Jul 2003 at age 87 (Ibid.).
Joseph Stanislaw Lefebvre was born on 4 Apr 1910 (Ibid.). He died on 20 Jan 1996 at age 85 (Ibid.).

vi.   Rene Tourond was born on 26 Dec 1921 Spalding, Saskatchewan (Ibid.). He died on 3 Jul 1940 Spalding, Saskatchewan, at age 18 (Ibid.).

43   vii.   Alcide Tourond, b. 1924.

23. **Elise Tourond** was born on 23 Feb 1862 St.Norbert, (Manitoba) (SN1, page 54-55, B-5.). She was baptized on 23 Feb 1862 St.Norbert, (Manitoba) (Ibid.). She married **Anaclet Lepine**, son of **Jean Baptiste Lepine** and **Isabelle Parenteau,** on 27 Apr 1880 St.Norbert, Manitoba (SN2, M-5.). She died on 14 Nov 1894 Ritchot, Manitoba, at age 32 (MB Vital Statistics, Death Reg. #1898,002798.). She was buried on 16 Nov 1894 St.Norbert, Manitoba (St-N Cem.).

Anaclet Lepine was born circa 1858. He died on 3 Sep 1899 (Ritchot), St.Boniface, Manitoba (MB Vital Statistics, Death Reg. #1899,002270.) (Ibid., Death Reg. #1899,002750 at Ritchot.). He was buried on 5 Sep 1899 St.Norbert, Manitoba (St-N Cem.).

24. **Rosalie Tourond** was born on 31 Dec 1864 St.Norbert, (Manitoba) (SN1, page 118, B-1.). She was baptized on 1 Jan 1865 St.Norbert, (Manitoba) (Ibid.). She married **Pierre St.Germain**, son of **Augustin St.Germain** and **Josephte Primeau**, on 26 Nov 1890 St.Norbert, Manitoba (MM, page 1234 & 1180.) (MB Vital Statistics, Mar. Reg. #1890,001574.). She died on 3 May 1894 Ritchot, Manitoba, at age 29 (Ibid., Death Reg. #1898,002773.). She was buried on 1 Jun 1894 St.Norbert, Manitoba (St-N Cem.).

Pierre St.Germain was born circa 1858. He married **Adelaide Dumas**, daughter of **Michel Dumas** and **Henriette Landry**, on 11 Jan 1882 St.Boniface, Manitoba (RMSB, page 443.) (MB Vital Statistics, Mar. Reg. #1882,001421.). He died on 28 Mar 1922 St.Boniface, Manitoba (Ibid., Death Reg. #1922,010077.).

25. **Joseph Alexandre Tourond** was born on 24 Nov 1871 St.Norbert, Manitoba (SN1, page 152-153, B-58.). He was baptized on 25 Nov 1871 St.Norbert, Manitoba (Ibid.). He married **Marguerite Desjardins**, daughter of **Francois Desjardins** and **Marguerite Leclerc dit Leclair**, on 23 Nov 1897 De Salaberry, Manitoba (MM.) (MB Vital Statistics, Marriage Reg. #1897,001426.).

Marguerite Desjardins was born on 29 Mar 1875 Manitoba (1901 Canada, District 10, (e-5), page 2, family 13, line 9-12.).

Children of **Joseph Alexandre Tourond** and **Marguerite Desjardins** are as follows:

    i. Arthur Tourond married Elise Tourond, daughter of Alfred Tourond and Octavie Rougeau, on 24 May 1943 Woodridge, Manitoba (MM.).

    ii. Agnes Tourond was born on 16 Nov 1898 Manitoba (1901 Canada, District 10, (e-5), page 2, family 13, line 9-12.). She married Charles Durousel on 27 Apr 1919 (La Broquerie), Woodridge, Manitoba (MM.) (MB Vital Statistics, Marriage Reg. #1919,022073.).

    iii. Joseph Isidore Tourond was born on 8 Jul 1900 R.M. of La Broquerie, Manitoba (Ibid., Birth Reg. #1900,004388.).

    iv. Marie Marguerite Tourond was born on 22 Jan 1904 R.M. of La Broquerie, Manitoba (Ibid., Birth Reg. #1904,003844.).

    v. Alice Tourond was born in Apr 1906 Manitoba (1911 Canada, #24, page 2, family 19, line 16-23.).

    vi. Isidore Tourond was born in Jul 1908 Manitoba (Ibid.).

    vii. Francisa Tourond was born in May 1909 Manitoba (Ibid.).

26. **Anne Octavie Tourond** was born on 13 Aug 1875 St.Norbert, Manitoba (SN2, B-31.). She was baptized on 14 Aug 1875 St.Norbert, Manitoba (Ibid.). She married **Cyrille Parisien**, son of **Cyrille Parisien** and **Marie Cyr**, on 13 Oct 1896 St.Pierre Jolys, Manitoba (MM.). She married **William Parisien**, son of **Pierre Parisien** and **Marguerite Adam**, on 29 Apr 1915 (Sprague), Woodridge, Manitoba (Ibid.) (MB Vital Statistics, Marriage Reg. #1915,173085.).

Cyrille Parisien was born on 31 Dec 1873 St.Norbert, Manitoba (SN2, page 1, B-1.). He was baptized on 1 Jan 1874 St.Norbert, Manitoba (Ibid., B-1.). He married **Emma Berthelet**, daughter of **Francois Berthelet dit Savoyard** and **Melanie Ducharme**, on 12 Nov 1901 Broquerie, Manitoba (MM, page 967.) (MB Vital Statistics, Marriage Reg. # 1901,001066.). He died on 28 Jul 1914 St.Boniface, Manitoba, at age 40 (Ibid., Death Reg. #1914,113112.).

William Parisien was born on 14 Sep 1863 St.Norbert, (Manitoba) (SN1, page 86, B-28.). He was baptized on 14 Sep 1863 St.Norbert, (Manitoba) (Ibid.). He married **Elise Gladu**, daughter of **Pierre Gladu** and **Nancy Dease**, on 9 Jan 1883 (Salaberry), St.Pierre, Manitoba (MM.) (MB Vital Statistics, Marriage Reg. #1883,001281 (Salaberry).). He married **Marie Anne Bradley**, daughter of **James Bradley** and **Caroline Comtois**, on 15 Oct 1890 St.Norbert, Manitoba (Ibid., Marriage Reg. #1890,001573.) (SN2, M-8.). He died on 12 May 1929 LaBroquerie, Manitoba, at age 65 (MB Vital Statistics, Death Reg. #1929,060148.).

27. **Alfred Tourond** was born on 18 Jan 1880 Manitoba (1901 Canada, #10, (a-2), page 5, family 42, line 17-20.). He married **Octavie Rougeau** on 23 Jun 1913 (Sprague), Woodridge, Manitoba (MM.) (MB Vital Statistics, Marriage Reg. #1913,040132.).

Children of **Alfred Tourond** and **Octavie Rougeau** are as follows:

    i. Elise Tourond married Arthur Tourond, son of Joseph Alexandre Tourond and Marguerite Desjardins, on 24 May 1943 Woodridge, Manitoba (MM.).

44 ii. Georgette Tourond, m. Felix Parisien.

    iii. Aurise Tourond married Yvan Bain on 8 Jul 1961 Richer, Manitoba (Ibid.).

45 iv. Victoria Tourond, m. Joseph Alexandre Alfred Normand.

46 v. Leo Tourond, m. Adrienne Tourond.

    vi. James Tourond married Dolores Ducharme, daughter of Michel Ducharme and Lumina Lena Rougeau, on 17 Nov 1956 Richer, Manitoba (Ibid.).

    vii. Marie Anna Tourond was born circa 1913 (Ibid.). She married Paul Michel Lamirande, son of Alexis Lamirande and Marie Pilon, on 1 Jul 1940 St.Norbert, Manitoba (Ibid.) (SN2, B-4 (note).).

       Paul Michel Lamirande was born on 23 Jan 1875 St.Norbert, Manitoba (Ibid., B-4.). He was baptized on 25 Jan 1875 St.Norbert, Manitoba (Ibid.).

28. **Isidore Henri Baptiste Tourond** was born on 19 Jul 1889 R.M. of De Salaberry, Manitoba (MB Vital Statistics, Birth Reg. #1889,001867.). He married **Marguerite Dubois**, daughter of **Guillaume Dubois** and **Rose Trudeau**, on 25 May 1927 (Sprague), Woodridge, Manitoba (MM.) (MB Vital Statistics, Marriage Reg. #1927,028334.).

Children of **Isidore Henri Baptiste Tourond** and **Marguerite Dubois** are as follows:

    i. Isidore Tourond married Loretta Lepine, daughter of Joseph Hyacinthe Lepine and Agnes Harel, on 24 Feb 1962 Woodridge, Manitoba (MM.).

    ii. Adrien Tourond married Irene Gilberte Poiron on 22 Apr 1972 Woodridge, Manitoba (Ibid.).

47 iii. Adrienne Tourond, m. Leo Tourond.

Generation Four

29. **Marie Tourond** was baptized on 20 Nov 1878 St.Eustache, Manitoba (ST-BSP St.Eustache (Baie St.Paul) 1877-1900 Register. Hereinafter cited as ST-BSP.) (ArchiviaNet, C-15007.). She married **Etienne Felix Adolphe-Henri Savage** on 19 May 1902 Batoche, (Saskatchewan) (Denney.).

30. Marguerite Alexandrine Tourond was born on 30 Apr 1885 Batoche, (Saskatchewan) (HBSI.) (BSAP, page 33, B-16.). She was baptized on 2 May 1885 Batoche, (Saskatchewan) (Ibid.). She married **Paul Adolphe** before 1909.

31. Ambroise Tourond was born on 13 Jul 1883 Fish Creek, (Saskatchewan) (BSAP, page 16, B-15.). He was baptized on 15 Jul 1883 Batoche, (Saskatchewan) (Ibid.). He married **Anne Thorn** before 1905 (SK Vital Statistics, Birth Reg. No. 4931.). He died on 22 Sep 1912 Saskatchewan at age 29 (Ibid., Death Reg. No. 3626.).

Children of **Ambroise Tourond** and **Anne Thorn** are as follows:
  i. Joseph Fleury Tourond was born on 2 Nov 1905 Fish Creek, Saskatchewan (Ibid., Birth Reg. No. 4931.).
  ii. Eginor Tourond was born on 23 May 1908 Howell, Saskatchewan (Ibid., Birth Reg. #9150.).

32. Joseph Patrice Tourond was born on 3 Oct 1886 Batoche, (Saskatchewan) (BSAP, page 51, B-31.). He was baptized on 4 Oct 1886 Batoche, (Saskatchewan) (Ibid.). He married **Nancy Victoria Batoche.** He died in 1964 (Denney.).

Children of **Joseph Patrice Tourond** and **Nancy Victoria Batoche** are as follows:
  i. William Tourond.
  ii. Joseph Tourond.
  iii. Frances Tourond.
  iv. Jennie Tourond.
  v. Faye Tourond.

33. William Benedict Tourond was born on 17 Jan 1890 (Ibid.). He died on 5 Jun 1970 at age 80 (Ibid.).

Children of **William Benedict Tourond** and **Helen Borze** are as follows:
  i. Johnny Tourond.
  ii. Robert Tourond.
  iii. George Tourond.
  iv. Kathleen Tourond.
  v. Patrick Tourond.
  vi. James Tourond.
  vii. Elmira Tourond.
  viii. Zelda Tourond.
  ix. Lena Tourond.
  x. Marjorie Tourond.

34. Jean Patrice Amable Tourond was born on 2 May 1885. He was baptized on 9 Jun 1885 Olga, Cavalier County, North Dakota (Olga, page 73, B-30.). He married **Rosalie Bruneau**, daughter of **Napoleon Bruneau** and **Marie Carriere,** in Apr 1907 (Rod Mac Quarrie, 17 Jan 2013.). He died on 2 May 1962 Yorkton, Saskatchewan, at age 77 (Leah Tourond Research, 7 Oct 1992.).

Rosalie Bruneau was born on 15 Mar 1886 R.M. of DeSalaberry, Manitoba (MB Vital Statistics, Birth Reg. #1886,003019.). She died in 1957 Saskatoon, Saskatchewan (Rod Mac Quarrie, 17 Jan 2013.).

Children of **Jean Patrice Amable Tourond** and **Rosalie Bruneau** were as follows:
  i. Raphael Tourond was born on 13 May 1909 Olga, Cavalier County, North Dakota (Olga, page 12, B-_.). He was baptized on 29 May 1909 Olga, Cavalier County, North Dakota (Ibid.). He died on 5 Nov 1909 Olga, Cavalier County, North Dakota (Ibid., page 7, S-398.). He was buried on 5 Nov 1909 Our Lady of Sacred Heart, Olga, Cavalier County, North Dakota (Ibid.).
  ii. Raymond Frederick Tourond was born on 8 Jan 1911 (Ibid., page 33, B-_.). He was baptized on 4 Jun 1911 Olga, Cavalier County, North Dakota (Ibid.). He married Opal Marie Harrison before 1936 (D. Courchane.).
    Opal Marie Harrison was born on 4 Dec 1915.
  iii. Laura Tourond was born in 1912 (Rod Mac Quarrie, 17 Jan 2013.).
  iv. Eleonore Tourond was born in 1915 (Ibid.). She married Jean Baptiste Bouchard circa 1939.
  v. Lawrence Gilbert Tourond was born on 11 Sep 1921. He married Stella May Harrison before 1942. He died on 10 Jul 1975 at age 53.

35. Patrice Tourond was born on 2 Sep 1886 Manitoba (1901 Canada, District 10, (e-5), page 4, family 33, line 35-43.). He married **Lydia Charpentier** on 1 Apr 1913 (Sprague), Woodridge, Manitoba (MM.) (MB Vital Statistics, Marriage Reg. #1913,019114.).

Children of **Patrice Tourond** and **Lydia Charpentier** are as follows:
  i. Florida Tourond married Emery Berard on 29 Jan 1940 Richer, Manitoba (MM.).
  ii. Rosanna Tourond married Octave Herie on 23 Feb 1938 Richer, Manitoba (Ibid.).
  iii. William Tourond married Laura Lamontagne on 3 Aug 1946 Woodridge, Manitoba (Ibid.).
  iv. Agnes Tourond married Leo Prestidge on 26 Feb 1945 Woodridge, Manitoba (Ibid.).
  v. Elzire Tourond married Joseph Pierre Wilfred "William" Berthelet, son of Pierre Berthelet and Francoise Elmire Desmarais, on 17 Jun 1931 Woodridge, Manitoba (Ibid.).
    Joseph Pierre Wilfred "William" Berthelet was born on 17 Feb 1902 R.M. of Montcalm, Manitoba (1911 Canada, #23, page 3, family 19, line 8-12.) (MB Vital Statistics, Birth Reg. #1902,001285.).
  vi. Henri Tourond married Rita Goulet, daughter of Emile Goulet and Emma Ducharme, on 15 Jan 1940 Richer, Manitoba (MM.).
  vii. Olivine Tourond married Evangeliste Martel on 17 Oct 1936 Woodridge, Manitoba (Ibid.).
  viii. Rita Tourond married Roland Nolin, son of Frederic Nolin and Rose Bremner, on 8 Aug 1959 Richer, Manitoba (Ibid.).

36. Joseph William Tourond was born on 2 Jul 1903 Olga, Cavalier County, North Dakota (Olga, page 327, B-_.). He was baptized on 13 Jul 1903 Olga, Cavalier County, North Dakota (Ibid.). He married **Joyce Ruth Solberg** on 3 Jun 1940 Red Lakes Falls, Minnesota (Ibid., page 327, B-_ (note).). He died on 3 Aug 1997 Stearns County, Minnesota, at age 94 (MN Death Index.).

Joyce Ruth Solberg was born on 11 Mar 1918 (SSDI.). She died on 2 Jul 2010 Saint Cloud, Stearns County, Minnesota, at age 92 (Ibid.).

Children of **Joseph William Tourond** and **Joyce Ruth Solberg** are as follows:

      i.   Clement Peter Tourand was born on 25 Feb 1951 Kandiyohi County, Minnesota (Rod Mac Quarrie, 23 Dec 2012.). He married Diane Lenora Theis on 20 Sep 1975 Stearns County, Minnesota (Ibid.).

      ii.   Marsha Joy Tourand was born on 25 Jul 1954 Stearns County, Minnesota (Ibid.).

37. **Monica Mary Tourond** was born on 10 Aug 1913 Langdon, Cavalier County, North Dakota (*1920 TMC*, District 235, page 8A, line 11.) (SSDI.). She married **Leo Carl Fischer** on 15 Oct 1936 (Rod Mac Quarrie, 23 Dec 2012.). She died on 1 Dec 1988 Blaine County, Minnesota, at age 75 (SSDI.).

Leo Carl Fischer was born on 6 Mar 1906 (Rod Mac Quarrie, 23 Dec 2012.). He died on 14 Aug 1954 Langdon, Cavalier Couty, North Dakota, at age 48 (Ibid.).

38. **Flavie Tourond** was born on 1 Dec 1905 Olga, Cavalier County, North Dakota (D. Courchane.). She was baptized on 2 Dec 1905 Olga, Cavalier County, North Dakota (Olga, page 346, B-_.). She married **Alcide Fortin**. She died on 22 Feb 1993 at age 87 (D. Courchane.).

39. **Arthur Laurent Tourond** was born on 3 Nov 1911 Spaulding, Saskatchewan (Leah Tourond, 7 Oct 1992.). He married **Carol Chew** before 1954. He died on 9 Apr 1973 Murrayville, British Columbia, at age 61 (Ibid.).

Carol Chew was born on 11 Nov 1920.

Children of **Arthur Laurent Tourond** and **Carol Chew** are:

      i.   Leah Tourond was born on 6 Oct 1954 (D. Courchane.). She married Robert Koopman.

40. **Napoleon Pierre Tourond** was born on 29 Nov 1915 Delisle, Saskatchewan (Leah Tourond, 7 Oct 1992.). He married **Barbara Lucille Grainger** before 1949. He died on 19 Jan 1977 Burns Lake, British Columbia, at age 61 (Ibid.). He was buried on 24 Jan 1977 Burns Lake, British Columbia (Ibid.).

Children of **Napoleon Pierre Tourond** and **Barbara Lucille Grainger** are:

      i.   James Peter Tourond was born on 22 Jun 1949 (D. Courchane.). He married Leah Catherine Smith before 1978.

             Leah Catherine Smith was born on 30 Apr 1954 (Ibid.).

41. **Toby Tourond** was born on 4 Aug 1907 Spalding, Saskatchewan (1911 Canada, District 13, page 2, line 47.) (Rod Mac Quarrie, 28 Dec 2011.).

Children of **Toby Tourond** include:

      i.   Allen Tourond.

42. **Raymond Gilbert Tourond** was born on 1 Jun 1911 Spalding, Saskatchewan (1911 Canada, District 13, page 2, line 47.). He married **Edna Julia Lake** on 3 Jul 1937 (Rod Mac Quarrie, 28 Dec 2011.). He died on 11 Mar 1974 Squamish, British Columbia, at age 62 (Ibid.).

Edna Julia Lake was born on 26 Feb 1919 (Ibid.). She died on 1 Oct 1994 at age 75 (Ibid.).

Children of **Raymond Gilbert Tourond** and **Edna Julia Lake** are as follows:

      i.   Wayne Tourond.

      ii.   Doris Tourond.

      iii.   Donnie Tourond.

      iv.   Irma Tourond.

      v.   Pat Tourond.

      vi.   Mike Tourond.

43. **Alcide Tourond** was born in 1924 (D. Courchane, 1992.).

Marjorie Florence Simpson married **Charles Frederic Joseph Albert Tourond**, son of **Jacques Tourond** and **Marie Courchene**, before 1940 (D. Courchane.).

Children of **Alcide Tourond** and **Marjorie Florence Simpson** are as follows:

      i.   Laura Ellen Tourond was born in 1952 (Ibid.).

      ii.   Kevin Ian Tourond was born in 1956 (Ibid.).

44. **Georgette Tourond** married **Felix Parisien**, son of **Joseph Albert Parisien** and **Marie Albertine Delorme,** on 29 Oct 1943 Woodridge, Manitoba (MM.).

45. **Victoria Tourond** married **Joseph Alexandre Alfred Normand**, son of **Alfred Joseph Albert Normand** and **Helene Claire Lamirande,** on 5 Apr 1932 LaBroquerie, Manitoba (MB Vital Statistics, Marriage Reg. #1932,015276.).

Joseph Alexandre Alfred Normand was born on 6 Jun 1904 R.M. of LaBroquerie, Manitoba (1906 Canada, District 06, page 9, family 66, line 8-15.) (MB Vital Statistics, Birth Reg. #1904,008085.).

46. **Leo Tourond** married **Adrienne Tourond**, daughter of **Isidore Henri Baptiste Tourond** and **Marguerite Dubois,** on 31 Dec 1942 Woodridge, Manitoba (Ibid.).

Children of **Leo Tourond** and **Adrienne Tourond** are as follows:

      i.   May Tourond married Edward Klassen on 25 May 1974 Woodridge, Manitoba (Ibid.).

      ii.   Noel Tourond married Olga Maydaniuk on 23 Feb 1974 Woodridge, Manitoba (Ibid.).

47. **Adrienne Tourond** married **Leo Tourond**, son of **Alfred Tourond** and **Octavie Rougeau,** on 31 Dec 1942 Woodridge, Manitoba (Ibid.).

Children of **Adrienne Tourond** and **Leo Tourond** are as follows:

      i.   May Tourond married Edward Klassen on 25 May 1974 Woodridge, Manitoba (Ibid.).

      ii.   Noel Tourond married Olga Maydaniuk on 23 Feb 1974 Woodridge, Manitoba (Ibid.).

Descendants of William Edward Traill

Generation One

1. William Edward Traill, son of Thomas Traill and Catherine Parr Strickland, was born on 26 Jul 1844 near Lakefield, Ontario (T. R. "Pat" McCloy, McKay Descendancy, McKay Descendancy.) (HBCA-B Hudson's Bay Company Archives - biographical sketches, Hudson's Bay Company Archives; Winnipeg, Manitoba.) (Automated Genealogy 1901 Census Transcription Project and Census Images from the National Archives of Canada, http://www.automatedgenealogy.com, District 205-c(1), page 2, family 18, line 37-44.). He married **Harriet McKay**, daughter of **William McKay** and **Mary Cook**, on 1 Jun 1869 Fort Ellice, Manitoba (T. R. McCloy, McKay Descendancy.) (Denney Papers, Charles D. Denney, Glenbow Archives, Calgary, Alberta.). He died on 14 Jan 1917 Meskanaw, Saskatchewan, at age 72 (T. R. McCloy, McKay Descendancy.) (HBCA-B.).

Harriet McKay was born on 31 Dec 1846 Fort Pelly (T. R. McCloy, McKay Descendancy.) (ArchiviaNet 1886-1901, 1906 Half-Breed Scrip Applications Index, RG15-21, Volume 1333 through 1371, Microfilm Reel Number C-14944 through C-15010, National Archives of Canada, Ottawa, Ontario, http://www.collectionscanada.gc.ca.). She died on 5 Mar 1920 Meskanaw, Saskatchewan, at age 73 (T. R. McCloy, McKay Descendancy.).

Children of **William Edward Traill** and **Harriet McKay** were as follows:

- 2   i.   Walter Traill, b. 26 Feb 1870 Fort Pitt, (Saskatchewan); m. Harriet Ann McKay; d. 10 May 1957 Garrick, (Saskatchewan).
-    ii.   Catherine Parr Traill was born on 29 Nov 1871 Prince Albert, (Saskatchewan) (ArchiviaNet, C-15007.). She died on 18 Dec 1878 Lac la Biche, (Alberta), at age 7 (Ibid.).
-    iii.   Mary 'Molly' Traill was born on 18 Nov 1873 Prince Albert, (Saskatchewan) (Rarihokwats Research, 21 May 1997.) (ArchiviaNet, C-15007.). She died on 18 Aug 1874 Lac la Biche, (Alberta) (Rarihokwats, 21 May 1997.) (ArchiviaNet, C-15007.).
-    iv.   William McKay Traill was born on 25 Jun 1875 Lac la Biche, (Alberta) (1901 Canada, District 205-c(1), page 2, family 18, line 37-44.) (ArchiviaNet, C-15007.). He married Frances Eleanor Fortescue, daughter of Joseph Fortescue and Sarah Jane Mason, on 19 Dec 1909 Winnipeg, Manitoba (Manitoba Vital Statistics online, http://web2.gov.mb.ca, Marriage Reg. #1909,002873.). He died on 3 Jan 1969 Saanich, British Columbia, at age 93 (British Columbia Archives: Vital Statistics, http://search.bcarchives.gov.bc.ca.).
-    v.   Harry Traill was born on 20 Nov 1877 Lac la Biche, (Alberta) (ArchiviaNet, C-15007.). He died on 28 Dec 1878 Lac la Biche, (Alberta), at age 1 (Ibid.).
-    vi.   Ethel Traill was born on 9 Oct 1879 Fort Pitt, (Saskatchewan) (Ibid.). She married Frederick Johnstone Bigg on 26 Nov 1901 (Denney.). She died on 9 May 1914 at age 34 (Ibid.).
  - **Frederick Johnstone Bigg** was born in Jan 1875 England (Ibid.). He died on 3 Sep 1967 at age 92 (Ibid.).
-    vii.   Jessie Traill was born on 15 Nov 1881 Lesser Slave Lake, (Alberta) (Ibid.). She married William Rothney Drever, son of William Drever and Jane Eliza Still, on 26 Oct 1900 Prince Albert, (Saskatchewan) (Ibid.). She died on 22 Jan 1970 Burnaby, British Columbia, at age 88 (Ibid.).
  - **William Rothney Drever** was born on 1 May 1870 (Ibid.). He died in Jan 1961 Burnaby, British Columbia, at age 90 (Ibid.).
-    viii.   Mary Traill was born on 26 Nov 1883 Lesser Slave Lake, (Alberta) (Ibid.).
- 3   ix.   Maria Traill, b. 8 Feb 1886 Fort Vermilion, (Alberta); m. John McCloy; d. 9 Feb 1969.
-    x.   Harriet Traill was born on 12 Feb 1887 Fort Vermilion, (Alberta) (1901 Canada, District 205-c(1), page 2, family 18, line 37-44.). She died on 14 Sep 1930 at age 43 (Denney.).
-    xi.   Annie Traill was born on 28 Dec 1889 (1901 Canada, District 205-c(1), page 2, family 18, line 37-44.). She died on 27 Mar 1977 Victoria, British Columbia, at age 87 (Denney.).
-    xii.   Catherine Barbara Traill was born on 8 Mar 1892 (1901 Canada, District 205-c(1), page 2, family 18, line 37-44.). She married (--?--) Morrow on 18 Jun 1914 (Denney.).

Generation Two

2. Walter Traill was born on 26 Feb 1870 Fort Pitt, (Saskatchewan) (T. R. McCloy, McKay Descendancy.). He married **Harriet Ann McKay**, daughter of **John Dougall McKay** and **Harriet McKay**, on 9 Jan 1895 Prince Albert, (Saskatchewan) (Ibid.). He died on 10 May 1957 Garrick, (Saskatchewan), at age 87 (Ibid.).

Harriet Ann McKay was born on 18 Apr 1872 Portage la Prairie, Manitoba (Ibid.). She was baptized on 12 May 1872 St.Mary's Anglican Church, Portage la Prairie, Manitoba (SMACPLP St.Marys Anglican Church, Portage La Prairie, Manitoba, Baptisms, Marriages, Burials, 1855-1883, transcribed by Clarence Kipling, page 48, B-383.). She died on 9 Mar 1948 Victoria, British Columbia, at age 75 (T. R. McCloy, McKay Descendancy.).

Children of **Walter Traill** and **Harriet Ann McKay** were as follows:

-    i.   Allan D. Traill was born on 16 Jan 1897 Flett Springs, (Saskatchewan) (1901 Canada, Fletts Springs, page 2, Family 22, Line 31-36.).
-    ii.   Henry Magnus Traill was born on 5 May 1898 Flett Springs, (Saskatchewan) (Ibid.) (Saskatchewan Vital Statistics online, http://vsgs.health.gov.sk.ca, Birth Reg. #1458.).
-    iii.   Evelyn Traill was born on 7 Sep 1901 Kinistino, (Saskatchewan) (Ibid., Birth Reg. #2557.).
-    iv.   Catherine Parr Traill was born on 5 May 1903 18-44-21-2, (Saskatchewan) (Ibid., Birth Reg. #3161.).

3. Maria Traill was born on 8 Feb 1886 Fort Vermilion, (Alberta) (Denney.) (1901 Canada, District 205-c(1), page 2, family 18, line 37-44.). She married **John McCloy** in 1903 (Denney.). She died on 9 Feb 1969 at age 83 (Ibid.).

John McCloy was born on 1 Jan 1875 County Derry, Ireland (Ibid.). He died on 16 May 1965 Kinosota, Manitoba, at age 90 (Ibid.).

Children of **Maria Traill** and **John McCloy** were:

-    i.   Thomas Rennie 'Pat' McCloy was born in 1906. He married Noreen (--?--). He died on 9 Apr 1996 Calgary, Alberta (Geoff Burtonshaw Research.).

Ahnentafel between Andre Trottier and Gilles Trottier

--- *1st Generation* ---

1. ANDRE TROTTIER (PRDH online index, http://www.genealogic.umontreal.ca, No. 277474.) (Ibid.) was born on 27 Dec 1757 at Pointe-Claire, Quebec (1833C RRS HBCA E5/7 1833 Census of the Red River Settlement, HBCA E5/7, Hudson's Bay Company Archives, Provincial Archives, 200 Vaughan Street, Winnipeg, MB R3C 1T5, Canada., page 18.) (PRDH online, No. 277474.). He was baptized on 27 Dec 1757 at Pointe-Claire, Quebec (Ibid.). He married according to the custom of the country **LOUISE SAULTEAUX** before 1790.

--- *2nd Generation* ---

2. FRANCOIS TROTTIER DIT DESRUISSEAUX (DGFQ Jette, Rene, *Dictionnaire Genealogique des Familles du Quebec des Origines a 1730* (Montreal, Quebec, Canada: University of Montreal Press, 1983), page 1093.) (PRDH online, #13604.) (DGFQ, page 1093.) (Ibid.) was born circa 1715 (Ibid.). He married **MARIE-JOSEPHE BRUNET DIT BOURBONNAIS**, daughter of **LOUIS BRUNET DIT BOURBONNAIS** and **MARIE-MADELEINE GIRARD**, on 7 Jan 1739 at Pointe-Claire, Quebec (PRDH online, #85873.) (Ibid., No. 118039.). He died on 1 Jan 1764 at Pointe-Claire, Quebec (Ibid., #85873.) (Ibid., No. 278452.). He was buried on 2 Jan 1764 at Pointe-Claire, Quebec (Ibid., #85873.) (Ibid., No. 278452.).

--- *3rd Generation* ---

4. JOSEPH TROTTIER was baptized on 7 Nov 1689 at Montreal, Montreal, Quebec (DGFQ, page 1092.). A contract for the marriage to **CATHERINE MARTIN DIT LANGEVIN**, daughter of **FRANCOIS MARTIN DIT LANGEVIN** and **CATHERINE-BARBE GOYER**, was signed on 21 Nov 1712 at St-Paul, Lachine, Quebec (Ibid.) (PRDH online, No. 95134.). He married **JEANNE GALARNEAU**, daughter of **CHARLES GALARNEAU** and **GENEVIEVE GRESLON**, on 5 Jun 1736 at Pointe-Claire, Quebec (Ibid., #94414.).

--- *4th Generation* ---

8. JOSEPH TROTTIER (DGFQ, page 1092.) was also known as **BENJAMIN DIT JOSEPH TROTTIER** (Ibid.). He was born circa 1665 (Ibid.). A contract for the marriage to **MARIE-JEANNE ROBILLARD**, daughter of **CLAUDE ROBILLARD** and **MARIE GRANDIN**, was signed on 7 Nov 1688 (Ibid.). He married **MARIE-JEANNE ROBILLARD**, daughter of **CLAUDE ROBILLARD** and **MARIE GRANDIN**, on 9 Nov 1688 at Montreal, Montreal, Quebec (Ibid.). He died on 14 Sep 1722 at Lachine, Quebec (PRDH online.).

--- *5th Generation* ---

16. PIERRE TROTTIER was born in 1644 at St.Martin, Ige, Perche (DGFC Tanguay, Cyprien, *Dictionnaire Genealogique des Familles Canadiennes* (28 Felsmere Avenue, Pawtucket, Rhode Island 02861-2903: Quintin Publications, 1996 reprint), Volume 1, page 573.). A contract for the marriage to **SUZANNE MIGAUD** was signed on 18 Jan 1663 at Trois-Rivieres, Quebec (DGFQ, page 1092.) (DGFC, Volume 1, page 573.) (PRDH online, No. 94214.). He was buried on 8 Jan 1693 at Batiscan, Quebec (DGFQ, page 1092.) (DGFC, Volume 1, page 573.) (PRDH online, No. 8434.).

--- *6th Generation* ---

32. GILLES TROTTIER was born in 1590 at St.Martin, d'Ige, Perche (YACT Olivier, Reginald L., *Your Ancient Canadian Ties* (P. O. Box 368, Logan, Utah 84321: The Everton Publishers, Inc., 1972), page 316B.) (DGFC, Volume 1, page 573.). He married **CATHERINE LOISEAU** circa 1625 at Ige (DGFQ, page 1091.). He was buried on 10 May 1655 at Trois-Rivieres, Quebec (PRDH online, No. 89336.).

Descendants of Andre Trottier

Generation One

1. Andre Trottier was born on 27 Dec 1757 Pointe-Claire, Quebec (1833C RRS HBCA E5/7 1833 Census of the Red River Settlement, HBCA E5/7, Hudson's Bay Company Archives, Provincial Archives, 200 Vaughan Street, Winnipeg, MB R3C 1T5, Canada., page 18.) (PRDH online index, http://www.genealogic.umontreal.ca, No. 277474.). He was baptized on 27 Dec 1757 Pointe-Claire, Quebec (Ibid.). He married according to the custom of the country **Louise Saulteaux** before 1790.

Children of **Andre Trottier** and **Louise Saulteaux** were as follows:

    2   i.   Joseph Trottier, b. circa 1790 Pembina; m. Marie Sauteuse; bur. 30 Jan 1852 Assumption, Pembina, Pembina County, Dakota Territory.

    3   ii.   Andre Trottier, b. circa 1791 Ruperts Land; m. Marguerite Paquette; d. 24 Apr 1874 Lebret, (Saskatchewan); bur. 25 Apr 1874 Lebret, (Saskatchewan).

Children of **Andre Trottier** include:

    4   i.   Marguerite Trottier, b. circa 1796 Pembina County; m. (--?--) Jutras; m. Antoine Gingras; d. 8 Jun 1879 Leroy, Pembina County, Dakota Territory; bur. 9 Jun 1879 St.Joseph, Leroy, Pembina County, Dakota Territory.

       ii.   Adotte Trottier was born circa 1804.

Generation Two

2. Joseph Trottier was born circa 1790 Pembina (1850Ci-MN *Minnesota Territorial Census, 1850*, Harpole, Patricia C. and Mary D. Nagle, ed., (St.Paul, Minnesota: Minnesota Historical Society, 1972), page 20; Dwelling 20, Family 20.). He was baptized on 14 Jun 1841 St.Francois Xavier, (Manitoba) (SFX: 1834-1850 St.Francois Xavier 1834-1851 Register, B-355 and B-356. Hereinafter cited as SFX: 1834-1850.). He married according to the custom of the country **Marie Sauteuse** before 1822. He married **Marie Sauteuse** on 14 Jun 1841 St.Francois Xavier, (Manitoba) (Ibid., M-63.) (MM *Manitoba Marriages* in *Publication 45*, Volumes 1-3, compiled and edited by: Paul J. Lareau, Fr. Julien Hamelin, (240 Avenue Daly, Ottawa, Ontario K1N 6G2: Le Centre de Genealogie S.C., 1984), page 10.). He was buried on 30 Jan 1852 Assumption, Pembina, Pembina County, Dakota Territory (AP Records of the Assumption Roman Catholic Church, Pembina, North Dakota: Baptisms, Marriages, Sepultures, 1848-1896; compiled by Reverend Father J. M. Belleau, 2 October 1944, page 68, S-30. Hereinafter cited as AP.).

Marie Sauteuse was born circa 1786 (SFXI-Kipling St.Francois Xavier Register Index, 1834-1900; compiled by Clarence Kipling , S-37.). She was born circa 1790 Pembina County (1850Ci-MN, page 20; Dwelling 20, Family 20.). She was baptized on 14 Jun 1841 St.Francois Xavier, (Manitoba) (SFX: 1834-1850, B-355 and B-356.). She was buried on 8 Aug 1866 St.Francois Xavier, (Manitoba) (SFXI-Kipling, S-37.).

Children of **Joseph Trottier** and **Marie Sauteuse** were as follows:

5   i.   Scholastique Trottier, b. circa 1822 Pembina County; m. Antoine Blanc Gingras.

6   ii.   Jean Baptiste Trottier, b. circa 1824 Red River, (Manitoba); m. Isabelle Delorme; d. Mar 1871 on the prairie; bur. 15 May 1871 St.Joseph, Leroy, Dakota Territory.

     iii.   Marguerite Trottier was born circa 1828 Red River, (Manitoba) (1850Ci-MN, page 20; Dwelling 20, Family 20.).

7   iv.   Catherine Trottier, b. circa 1830 Red River, (Manitoba); m. James Sinclair; m. John Tanner.

     v.   Marie Trottier was born before 1833.

3.   **Andre Trottier** was born circa 1784 Pembina (1850C-MNT   1850 Minnesota Territory Census, Nation Archives of the United States, Washington D.C., page 26, Dwelling 84, Family 84.). He was born circa 1791 Ruperts Land (1833C RRS HBCA E5/7, page 23.). He married **Marguerite Paquette**, daughter of **Andre Paquette** and **Lizette Cree**, before 1812. He died on 24 Apr 1874 Lebret, (Saskatchewan) (L1   Lebret Mission de St.Florent Roman Catholic Registre des Baptemes, Mariages & Seplutures, Qu'Appelle, Saskatchewan, 1868-1881., page 112, S-7. Hereinafter cited as L1.). He was buried on 25 Apr 1874 Lebret, (Saskatchewan) (Ibid.).

   Marguerite Paquette was born circa 1788 St.Francois Xavier, (Manitoba) (MBS   Scrip Applications, Original White Settlers & Halfbreeds residing in Manitoba on 15 July 1870, RG15-19, C-14934.). She was born circa 1800 Red River, (Manitoba) (1850Ci-MN, page 26, Dwelling 84, Family 84.).

   Children of **Andre Trottier** and **Marguerite Paquette** were as follows:

8   i.   Josephte Trottier, b. Jul 1812 North West; m. Alexis Gonneville.

9   ii.   Andre Trottier, b. Nov 1816 Souris River; m. Isabelle Falcon dit Divertissant.

10   iii.   Bazile Trottier, b. circa 1819 Ruperts Land; m. Madeleine Fagnant; d. before 4 Aug 1844.

11   iv.   Madeleine Trottier, b. 1822 St.Andrews, (Manitoba); m. Louis Boyer; m. John Beaulieu.

12   v.   Jean Baptiste Trottier, b. circa 1825 Ruperts Land; m. Louise Chalifoux; d. circa 31 Mar 1855; bur. 24 Nov 1855 St.Francois Xavier, (Manitoba).

13   vi.   Marguerite Trottier, b. 1825 North West; m. Louis Fleury; d. 29 Oct 1902 RM Ellice, Manitoba.

14   vii.   Joseph Trottier, b. 1827 Oak Lake near Brandon, (Manitoba); m. Therese Vallee dit Laplante.

15   viii.   Marie Trottier, b. before 1831; m. Francois Laframboise; bur. 18 May 1867 St.Francois Xavier, (Manitoba).

     ix.   Catherine Trottier was born circa 1831 (SFXI: 1834-1852   St.Francois Xavier 1834-1852 Register Index, S-11. Hereinafter cited as SFXI: 1835-1852.). She was buried on 26 Nov 1834 St.Francois Xavier, (Manitoba) (Ibid.).

16   x.   Michel Trottier, b. 7 Jun 1832 St.Boniface, (Manitoba); m. Angelique Desjarlais; m. Marguerite (Indian) Landry; bur. 30 May 1885 Batoche, (Saskatchewan).

17   xi.   Antoine Trottier, b. 8 Dec 1834 St.Francois Xavier, (Manitoba); m. Angelique Laframboise.

     xii.   Francois Joseph Trottier was born on 4 Nov 1836 St.Francois Xavier, (Manitoba) (SFX: 1834-1850, B-140.). He was baptized on 5 Nov 1836 St.Francois Xavier, (Manitoba) (Ibid.).

18   xiii.   Charles Trottier, b. 4 Dec 1839 St.Francois Xavier, (Manitoba); m. Ursule Laframboise; m. Angelique Parenteau.

4.   **Marguerite Trottier** was born circa 1796 Pembina County (1850Ci-MN, page 21; Dwelling 28; Family 28.). She married according to the custom of the country (--?--) **Jutras** (unknown article title, *ACG American-Canadian Genealogist*, unknown location, Vol.18; #2; No.52; Spring; 1992; page 57.). She married according to the custom of the country **Antoine Gingras** before 1832. She died on 8 Jun 1879 Leroy, Pembina County, Dakota Territory (SJL-1   Register of Baptisms, Marriages, and Burials, St.Joseph, Leroy, North Dakota, Diocese of Saint Paul, Minnesota, 1870-1888, Book 1, page 94, S-18. Hereinafter cited as SJL-1.). She was buried on 9 Jun 1879 St.Joseph, Leroy, Pembina County, Dakota Territory (Ibid.).

Generation Three

5.   **Scholastique Trottier** was born circa 1822 Pembina County (1850Ci-MN, page 34, Dwelling 164, Family 164.). She married **Antoine Blanc Gingras**, son of **Antoine Gingras,** before 1839.

Question: *Scholastique's parents are unproven.*

   Antoine Blanc Gingras was born in 1821 Red River, (Manitoba) (Ibid.). He died on 26 Sep 1877 Leroy, Pembina County, Dakota Territory (SJL-1, page 83, S-8.). He was buried on 29 Sep 1877 St.Joseph, Leroy, Pembina County, Dakota Territory (Ibid.).

6.   **Jean Baptiste Trottier** was born circa 1824 Red River, (Manitoba) (1850Ci-MN, page 20; Dwelling 20, Family 20.). He married **Isabelle Delorme**, daughter of **Joseph Delorme** and **Isabelle Gourneau**, on 20 Aug 1855 Assumption, Pembina, Pembina County, Dakota Territory (AP, page 135, M-43.). He died in Mar 1871 on the prairie (SJL-1, page 10, S-6.). He was buried on 15 May 1871 St.Joseph, Leroy, Dakota Territory (Ibid.).

   Isabelle Delorme was born circa 1836 Red River, (Manitoba) (1850Ci-MN, page 28, Dwelling 96, Family 96.). She married **James Campbell**, son of **William Campbell** and **Elisabeth Ross**, on 17 Sep 1877 St.Joseph, Leroy, Pembina County, Dakota Territory (SJL-1, page 83, M-5.).

   Children of **Jean Baptiste Trottier** and **Isabelle Delorme** were as follows:

     i.   Marie Trottier was born on 3 Nov 1856 Dakota Territory (AP, page 169, B-493.). She was baptized on 15 May 1857 Assumption, Pembina, Pembina County, Dakota Territory (Ibid.).

19   ii.   Isabelle Trottier, b. 6 Apr 1858 Pembina County, Dakota Territory; m. Joseph Laframboise; d. 25 Jan 1949 Rolette County, North Dakota.

20   iii.   Joseph Trottier, b. 15 Jun 1860 Pembina, Pembina County, Dakota Territory; m. Helene Jerome; d. 4 Jul 1919 Belcourt, Rolette County, North Dakota; bur. 6 Jul 1919 St.Michaels Cemetery, Rolette County, North Dakota.

     iv.   Josephine Trottier was born on 28 Aug 1860 Pembina, Pembina County, Dakota Territory (Ibid., page 227, B-39.). She was baptized on 31 Aug 1860 Assumption, Pembina, Pembina County, Dakota Territory (Ibid.).

     v.   Sara Trottier was born circa 1865 (HBS 1886-1901, 1906 Half-Breed Scrip Applications, RG15-21, Volume 1339, C-14955.). She died on 11 Jun 1885 Leroy, Dakota Territory (Ibid.). She was buried on 12 Jun 1885 St.Joseph, Leroy, Dakota Territory (Ibid.).

     vi.   Patrice Trottier was born circa 1866 (Ibid.) (Ancestry.com Website, 1880 Census.). He died on 26 Jun 1880 Leroy, Pembina County, Dakota Territory (HBS, Volume 1339, C-14955.) (SJL-1, page 102, S-53.). He was buried on

29 Jun 1880 St.Joseph, Leroy, Pembina County, Dakota Territory (HBS, Volume 1339, C-14955.) (SJL-1, page 102, S-53.).

 vii. Rosalie Trottier was born circa 1869 (Olga Our Lady of the Sacred Heart, Olga, North Dakota 1882-1900, page 82, S-18. Hereinafter cited as Olga.). She died on 9 May 1885 Olga, Cavalier County, North Dakota (Ibid.). She was buried on 10 May 1885 Olga, Cavalier County, North Dakota (Ibid.). (SJL-D, page 16.).

 viii. Marie Marguerite Trottier was born on 26 Feb 1871 Wood Mountain, (Saskatchewan) (L1, page 42, B-67.). She was baptized on 27 Feb 1871 Lebret, (Saskatchewan) (Ibid.). She died on 11 Jan 1880 Leroy, Dakota Territory, at age 8 (HBS, Volume 1339, C-14955.). She was buried on 13 Jan 1880 St.Joseph, Leroy, Dakota Territory (Ibid.).

21 ix. Rose Trottier, b. Mar 1871 Dakota Territory; m. Joseph Grant; d. 27 Aug 1958 Rolette County, North Dakota.

7. Catherine Trottier was born circa 1825 Red River, (Manitoba) (1870C-MB, page 361, #1115.). She was born circa 1830 Red River, (Manitoba) (1850Ci-MN, page 20; Dwelling 20, Family 20.). She married **James Sinclair**, son of **William Sinclair** and **Elizabeth Anderson**, before 1854. She married **John Tanner**, son of **Rev. James Tanner**, on 14 Jul 1869 St.Mary's Anglican Church, Portage la Prairie, (Manitoba) (SMACPLP St.Marys Anglican Church, Portage La Prairie, Manitoba, Baptisms, Marriages, Burials, 1855-1883, transcribed by Clarence Kipling , page 25, M-52.).

James Sinclair was born circa 1829 (Ibid., S-58.) (1830C RRS HBCA E5/4 1830 Census of the Red River Settlement, HBCA E5/4, Hudson's Bay Company Archives, Provincial Archives, 200 Vaughan Street, Winnipeg, MB R3C 1T5, Canada., page 13.). He died on 31 Jan 1867 (Rod MacQuarrie Research, 28 Jan 2012.). He was buried on 15 Feb 1867 St.Mary's Anglican Church, Portage la Prairie, (Manitoba) (SMACPLP, page 8, S-58.).

John Tanner was born on 17 Aug 1837 Torch Lake, Lac du Flambeau, Wisconsin (Denney.).

8. Josephte Trottier was born in Jul 1812 North West (MBS, C-14928.). She married **William Sutherland**, son of **James Sutherland** and **Nancy Cook**, on 26 Dec 1834 St.Johns, Red River Settlement, (Manitoba) (HBCR Hudson Bay Company Register of Anglican Church Baptisms, Marriages, and Burials for the Red River Settlement, 1821-1841; Hudson's Bay Company Archives, Winnipeg, Manitoba, No. 289. Hereinafter cited as HBCR.). She married **Alexis Gonneville**, son of **Antoine Gonneville** and **Marguerite Labine dit Lacouture**, on 10 Jan 1837 St.Francois Xavier, (Manitoba) (SFXI: 1835-1852, M-26.).

William Sutherland was born before 1806 (HBCA-B Hudson's Bay Company Archives - biographical sketches, Hudson's Bay Company Archives; Winnipeg, Manitoba.). He was baptized on 27 May 1821 St.Johns, Red River Colony, (Manitoba) (HBCR, E.4/1a, folio 33d.).

Alexis Gonneville was born circa 1812 Ruperts Land (1843C RRS HBCA E5/11 1843 Census of the Red River Settlement, HBCA E5/11, Hudson's Bay Company Archives, Provincial Archives, 200 Vaughan Street, Winnipeg, MB R3C 1T5, Canada., page 26.). He was born circa 1817 St.Francois Xavier, (Manitoba) (MBS, C-14928.).

9. Andre Trottier was born in Nov 1816 Souris River (MBS, C-14934.). He married **Isabelle Falcon dit Divertissant**, daughter of **Pierre Falcon dit Divertissant** and **Marie Grant**, on 7 May 1839 St.Francois Xavier, (Manitoba) (SFX: 1834-1850, M-39.).

Isabelle Falcon dit Divertissant was born in Jun 1819 St.Francois Xavier, (Manitoba) (MBS, C-14934.).

Children of **Andre Trottier** and **Isabelle Falcon dit Divertissant** were as follows:

22 i. John Trottier, b. 1860 Carlton, North West Territories; m. Melanie Morin.

 ii. Alexandre Trottier was born in Oct 1863 North West Territories (Ibid.). He died on 11 Aug 1881 Lebret, (Saskatchewan), at age 17 (L2 Lebret, Mission de St.Florent, Roman Catholic Registre des Baptemes, Mariages & Seplutures, Qu'Appelle, Saskatchewan, Book Two: 1881-1887, FHC microfilm 1032949., page 10, S-19. Hereinafter cited as L2.). He was buried on 12 Aug 1881 Lebret, (Saskatchewan) (Ibid.).

10. Bazile Trottier was born circa 1819 Ruperts Land (Denney.). He married **Madeleine Fagnant**, daughter of **Jean Baptiste Fagnant** and **Josephte Monet dit Belhumeur**, on 8 Jan 1839 St.Francois Xavier, (Manitoba) (SFX: 1834-1850, M-35.). He died before 4 Aug 1844 (Ibid., B-528 (father).).

Madeleine Fagnant was born in 1825 St.Francois Xavier, (Manitoba) (MBS, C-14934.).

Children of **Bazile Trottier** and **Madeleine Fagnant** were as follows:

23 i. Jean Baptiste Trottier, b. 12 Sep 1841 St.Francois Xavier, (Manitoba); m. Rose McGillis; d. 1892.

24 ii. Julie Trottier, b. circa Apr 1844; m. Thomas Breland; d. 29 May 1866 St.Francois Xavier, (Manitoba); bur. 30 May 1866 St.Francois Xavier, (Manitoba).

11. Madeleine Trottier was born in 1822 St.Andrews, (Manitoba). She married **Louis Boyer**, son of **Pierre Boyer** and **Marguerite Bonneau**, on 13 Sep 1842 St.Francois Xavier, (Manitoba) (SFX: 1834-1850, M-72.). She married **John Beaulieu**, son of **Joseph Beaulieu** and **Marguerite Roussin**, on 30 Sep 1878 Lebret, (Saskatchewan) (L1, page 235, M-15.).

Louis Boyer was born circa 1821 Ruperts Land (1843C RRS HBCA E5/11, page 25.). He died circa 1855 on the prairie (SFXI-1834-54.). He was buried on 30 Mar 1858 St.Francois Xavier, (Manitoba) (SFXI-Kipling, S-75.) (SFXI-1834-54.).

John Beaulieu was born in 1820 Swan River District (NWHBS 1885 Scrip Applications, North-West Halfbreeds residing outside Manitoba on 15 July 1870, RG15-20, C-14936.). He was baptized on 8 Jun 1845 St.Francois Xavier, (Manitoba) (SFX: 1834-1850, B-575.). He married **Marie Gariepy**, daughter of **Louis Gariepy** and **Josephte Ducharme**, on 9 Jun 1845 St.Francois Xavier, (Manitoba) (Ibid., M-91.). He died on 25 Dec 1902 Lebret, (Saskatchewan) (Joyce Black Research.).

12. Jean Baptiste Trottier was born circa 1825 Ruperts Land (Denney.). He married **Louise Chalifoux**, daughter of **Michel Chalifoux dit Richard** and **Isabelle Collin**, on 12 Jan 1841 St.Francois Xavier, (Manitoba) (SFX: 1834-1850, M-55.). He died circa 31 Mar 1855 (SFXI-1834-54.). He was buried on 24 Nov 1855 St.Francois Xavier, (Manitoba) (SFXI-Kipling, S-35.).

Louise Chalifoux was born in 1818 North West (MBS, C-14934.). She was baptized on 4 Apr 1833 St.Boniface, (Manitoba) (SB 1825-1834 St.Boniface Roman Catholic Registre des Baptemes, Mariages & Sepultures, 1825-1834, page 96, B-562. Hereinafter cited as SB 1825-1834.).

Children of **Jean Baptiste Trottier** and **Louise Chalifoux** were as follows:

      i.   Louise Trottier was born on 2 Nov 1841 (SFX: 1834-1850, B-378.). She was baptized on 11 Nov 1841 St.Francois Xavier, (Manitoba) (Ibid.). She died in Mar 1857 at age 15 (SFXI-1834-54.). She was buried on 20 Apr 1857 St.Francois Xavier, (Manitoba) (SFXI-Kipling, S-65.).

25   ii.   Pascal Trottier, b. 7 Apr 1846; m. Rosalie St.Germain; bur. 22 Mar 1888 St.Claude Mission, St.John, Rolette County, North Dakota.

26   iii.   Rose Trottier, b. 1853; m. Alexandre Larocque; d. 14 Jun 1873 St.Francois Xavier, Manitoba; bur. 16 Jun 1873 St.Francois Xavier, Manitoba.

      iv.   Medard Trottier was born on 21 Mar 1855 St.Francois Xavier, (Manitoba) (Ibid., B-25.) (SFXI 1851-1868, B-25.). He was baptized on 22 Mar 1855 St.Francois Xavier, (Manitoba) (SFXI-Kipling, B-25.) (SFXI 1851-1868, B-25.).

27   v.   Vital Trottier, b. circa 1856 (Manitoba); m. Veronique Lingan.

13. Marguerite Trottier was born in 1825 North West (MBS, C-14928.). She married **Louis Fleury**, son of **Louis Fleury** and **Josephte Belly**, on 10 Jan 1843 St.Francois Xavier, (Manitoba) (SFX: 1834-1850, M-73.). She died on 29 Oct 1902 RM Ellice, Manitoba (MB Vital Statistics, Death Reg. #1902,001104.).

Louis Fleury was born circa 1813 Fort Alexander, (Manitoba) (1870C-MB, page 383, #386.). He was born in 1820 St.Francois Xavier, (Manitoba) (MBS, C-14928.). He died on 26 Nov 1897 Ellice, Manitoba (MB Vital Statistics, Death Reg. #1898,001515.).

14. Joseph Trottier was born in 1827 Oak Lake near Brandon, (Manitoba) (1850Ci-MN, page 26, Dwelling 84, Family 84.) (ArchiviaNet, C-15007.). He married **Therese Vallee dit Laplante**, daughter of **Antoine Vallee** and **Suzanne Lefebvre or Favel,** in 1852 St.Boniface, (Manitoba).

Therese Vallee dit Laplante was born circa 1830 Edmonton, (Alberta) (Ibid., C-15008.).

Children of **Joseph Trottier** and **Therese Vallee dit Laplante** were as follows:

      i.   Andre Trottier was born circa 1853 (SFXI-Kipling, S-26.). He died on 22 Jun 1871 St.Francois Xavier, Manitoba (Ibid.). He was buried on 24 Jun 1871 St.Francois Xavier, Manitoba (IBMS.) (SFXI-Kipling, S-26.).

      ii.   Julie Trottier was born circa May 1855 (Ibid., S-31.). She died on 19 Nov 1855 (Ibid.). She was buried on 21 Nov 1855 St.Francois Xavier, (Manitoba) (Ibid.).

      iii.   Joseph Trottier was born circa 1857 St.Francois Xavier, (Manitoba) (Denney.). He married Julie Grosseterre on 17 Aug 1879 Duck Lake, (Saskatchewan) (DL, page 27, M-3.).

          Julie Grosseterre married **Pierre Lapierre** before 1879.

28   iv.   Marguerite Trottier, b. 4 Oct 1857 near Fort Ellice, Manitoba; m. Bernard Paul.

      v.   Louis Trottier was born on 13 Jan 1859 (SFXI-Kipling, B-325.). He was baptized on 8 May 1859 St.Francois Xavier, (Manitoba) (Ibid.).

29   vi.   Albert Trottier, b. circa 1860 Fort Ellice, Manitoba; m. Isabelle Boudreau.

      vii.   Cuthbert Trottier was born on 25 May 1862 Fort Ellice, Manitoba (Ibid., B-65.). He was baptized on 5 Jun 1862 St.Francois Xavier, (Manitoba) (Ibid.).

30   viii.   Charles Trottier, b. 24 Apr 1865; m. Madeleine Okimasis.

      ix.   Marie Trottier was born on 27 Aug 1868 Brandon, (Manitoba) (Ibid., B-94.) (NWHBS, C-14942.). She was baptized on 4 Sep 1868 St.Francois Xavier, (Manitoba) (SFXI-Kipling, B-94.). She died between 1872 and 1873 Red Hill (NWHBS, C-14942.).

      x.   Adolphe Trottier was born on 21 Aug 1873 Duck Lake, (Saskatchewan) (DL, page 18, B-70.). He was baptized on 9 Nov 1873 Duck Lake, (Saskatchewan) (Ibid.). He died on 19 Mar 1874 Duck Lake, (Saskatchewan) (Ibid., page 21, S-5.). He was buried on 7 Apr 1874 Duck Lake, (Saskatchewan) (Ibid.).

15. Marie Trottier was born before 1831. She married **Francois Laframboise**, son of **Jean Baptiste Laframboise** and **Suzanne Beaudry or Gaudry,** circa 1849 St.Francois Xavier, (Manitoba) (NWHBS, C-14939.). She was buried on 18 May 1867 St.Francois Xavier, (Manitoba) (SFXI: 1835-1852, S-10.).

Francois Laframboise was born on 1 Nov 1827 Edmonton, (Alberta) (NWHBS, C-14939.). He was born on 24 Dec 1827 (1901 Canada, #204, v(2), page 1, family 2, line 4-5.). He and **Louise Chaboillez dit Chaboyer** met circa 1860. He married **Louise Chaboillez dit Chaboyer**, daughter of **Louis Chaboillez or Chaboyer** and **Louise Chartrand,** on 17 Jun 1867 St.Francois Xavier, (Manitoba) (SFXI-Kipling, M-16.). He married **Helene Rocheblave**, daughter of **Francois Rocheblave** and **Judith Desjarlais,** on 9 Dec 1871 St-Laurent-de-Grandin, (Saskatchewan) (SL-SK, page 1, M-_.) (Ibid., page 5-6, M-_.).

16. Michel Trottier was born in 1831 Red River, (Manitoba) (1850Ci-MN, page 26, Dwelling 84, Family 84.). He was born on 7 Jun 1832 St.Boniface, (Manitoba) (SB 1825-1834, page 66, B-442.). He was baptized on 8 Jun 1832 St.Boniface, (Manitoba) (Ibid.). He married **Angelique Desjarlais**, daughter of **Jean Baptiste Desjarlais** and **Marie Martin**, on 24 Nov 1857 St.Francois Xavier, (Manitoba) (SFXI-Kipling, M-44.). He married **Marguerite (Indian) Landry** before 1875. He was buried on 30 May 1885 Batoche, (Saskatchewan) (BSAP, page 35, S-25.).

Angelique Desjarlais was born circa 1838 (SFXI-Kipling, M-44.). She was buried on 5 Jan 1873 St.Laurent-de-Grandin, (Saskatchewan) (SL-SK, page 18, S-1.).

Children of **Michel Trottier** and **Angelique Desjarlais** were as follows:

      i.   Marie Trottier was born on 26 May 1859 Baie St.Paul, (Manitoba) (SFXI-Kipling, B-351.). She was baptized on 29 May 1859 St.Francois Xavier, (Manitoba) (Ibid.). She married John Martin, son of John Martin and Aima Gordon, on 30 Jan 1887 St.Eustache, Manitoba (MM.). She married Robert Thompson before 1900 (ArchiviaNet.).

          John Martin was born of, Montreal, Montreal, Quebec.

31   ii.   Andre Trottier, b. 10 Jan 1861 St.Francois Xavier, (Manitoba); m. Rose Laframboise.

32   iii.   Alexandre Trottier, b. 1 Jul 1862; m. Catherine Laframboise.

      iv.   Napoleon Trottier was born on 7 Nov 1863 St.Francois Xavier, (Manitoba) (SFXI-Kipling, B-101.). He was baptized on 8 Nov 1863 St.Francois Xavier, (Manitoba) (Ibid.).

    v.   Catherine Trottier was born circa Jan 1866 (Ibid., B-65.). She was baptized on 27 May 1866 St.Francois Xavier, (Manitoba) (Ibid.).

    vi.   Francois Trottier was born on 29 Jan 1869 St.Francois Xavier, (Manitoba) (Ibid., B-12.). He was baptized on 30 Jan 1869 St.Francois Xavier, (Manitoba) (Ibid.).

    vii.   Elise Trottier was born on 3 Jul 1871 (Ibid., B-54.). She was baptized on 6 Jul 1871 St.Francois Xavier, Manitoba (Ibid.) (INB, page 177.). She died on 16 Apr 1875 St.Eustache, Manitoba, at age 3 (Denney.). She was buried on 17 Apr 1875 St.Eustache, Manitoba (Ibid.).

Marguerite (Indian) Landry was born circa 1857 (1881 Canada, Film C-13285, District 192, page 12, Household 48.).

Children of **Michel Trottier** and **Marguerite (Indian) Landry** were as follows:

    i.   Michel Trottier was born in 1875 (ArchiviaNet, C-15007.). He married Marie Desjarlais in 1895 (Ibid.).

    ii.   Elzear Trottier was born on 7 Jan 1877 Crooked Lake Reserve, (Saskatchewan) (HBSI.) (L1, page 204, B-63.). He was baptized on 3 Feb 1877 Lebret, (Saskatchewan) (Ibid.). He died in 1886 Qu'Appelle Industrial School, (Saskatchewan) (HBSI.) (ArchiviaNet.).

    iii.   Adelaide Trottier was born circa 1879 (Saskatchewan) (1881 Canada, Film C-13285, District 192, page 12, Household 48.).

    iv.   Isidore Trottier was born in 1880 Crooked Lake Reserve, (Saskatchewan) (HBSI.) (ArchiviaNet.). He died on 28 Apr 1888 Qu'Appelle Industrial School, (Saskatchewan) (HBSI.) (ArchiviaNet.).

17. Antoine Trottier was born on 8 Dec 1834 St.Francois Xavier, (Manitoba) (SFXI-Kipling, B-56.) (SFXI: 1835-1852, B-56.). He was baptized on 9 Dec 1834 St.Francois Xavier, (Manitoba) (SFXI-Kipling, B-56.) (SFXI: 1835-1852, B-56.). He married **Angelique Laframboise**, daughter of **Jean Baptiste Laframboise** and **Suzanne Beaudry or Gaudry**, on 21 Sep 1857 St.Francois Xavier, (Manitoba) (SFXI-Kipling, M-39.).

Angelique Laframboise was born on 1 Jan 1830 (NWHBSI Index 1885 Scrip Applications, North-West Halfbreeds residing outside Manitoba on 15 July 1870, RG15-20, page 44.).

Children of **Antoine Trottier** and **Angelique Laframboise** were as follows:

    i.   Edouard Trottier was born on 11 Dec 1859 (SFXI-Kipling, B-28.). He was baptized on 12 May 1860 St.Francois Xavier, (Manitoba) (Ibid.). He was buried on 27 Feb 1866 St.Francois Xavier, (Manitoba) (Ibid., S-8.).

33   ii.   Norbert Trottier, b. 6 Mar 1861 Humboldt, (Saskatchewan); m. Eliza Fisher.

    iii.   Jean Trottier was born on 15 Jan 1863 (Ibid., B-37.). He was baptized on 10 May 1863 St.Francois Xavier, (Manitoba) (Ibid.).

    iv.   William Trottier was born on 7 Nov 1864 (Ibid., B-57.). He was baptized on 6 Aug 1865 St.Francois Xavier, (Manitoba) (Ibid.).

    v.   Francois Trottier was born on 1 Jan 1867 (SFXI: 1835-1852, B-40.). He was baptized on 18 May 1867 St.Francois Xavier, (Manitoba) (Ibid.). He married Emma Villebrun, daughter of Guillaume Villebrun dit Ploufe and Flora Hope, before 1900 (ArchiviaNet, C-15008.).

          Question: *Is Francois the widower of Emma Villebrun?* (Ibid.).

          Emma Villebrun was born on 19 Jun 1874 Lac la Biche, (Alberta) (LLBR1 Notre Dame des Tidoren, St.Paul Diocese, Lac La Biche, Registre des Baptemes, Mariages & Sepltures, Volume 1, 1853-1898., page 143, B-10. Hereinafter cited as LLBR1.). She was baptized on 21 Jun 1874 Lac la Biche, (Alberta) (Ibid.). She died between 1891 and 1894 Fort Benton, Montana (ArchiviaNet, C-15008.).

34   vi.   Marie Trottier, b. 24 Mar 1869; m. William Belcourt.

    vii.   Isabelle Trottier was born on 29 Dec 1870 (DL, page 6, B-22.). She was baptized on 23 Feb 1871 Duck Lake, (Saskatchewan) (Ibid.). She died between 1886 and 1887 Batoche, (Saskatchewan) (ArchiviaNet, C-15007.).

    viii.   Philomene Trottier was born on 6 Oct 1872 near, Saskatoon, (Saskatchewan) (Denney.) (SL-SK, page 12, B-31.). She was baptized on 26 Oct 1872 St.Laurent-de-Grandin, (Saskatchewan) (Ibid.). She died between 1893 and 1894 Havre, Hill County, Montana (ArchiviaNet, C-15007.).

18. Charles Trottier was born on 4 Dec 1839 St.Francois Xavier, (Manitoba) (SFX: 1834-1850, B-280.). He was baptized on 4 Dec 1839 St.Francois Xavier, (Manitoba) (Ibid.). He married **Ursule Laframboise**, daughter of **Jean Baptiste Laframboise** and **Suzanne Beaudry or Gaudry**, on 21 Aug 1860 St.Francois Xavier, (Manitoba) (SFXI-Kipling, M-14.). He and **Angelique Parenteau** met circa 1871 (ArchiviaNet, C-15007.).

Ursule Laframboise was born circa 1842.

Children of **Charles Trottier** and **Ursule Laframboise** were as follows:

35   i.   Remi Trottier, b. circa Jun 1861; m. Marie Madeleine Laframboise; d. 14 Mar 1938 Montana.

36   ii.   Isidore Trottier, b. 10 Jan 1863; m. Caroline Lemire.

37   iii.   Jean Baptiste Trottier, b. 5 Nov 1864; m. Caroline Lemire; d. 4 Nov 1963 Harlem, Montana; bur. 6 Nov 1963 Calvary Cemetery, Havre, Montana.

38   iv.   Helene Trottier, b. 20 Feb 1867; m. Hilaire Sansregret.

39   v.   Mathilde Trottier, b. 9 Feb 1869; m. Alphonse Caron.

    vi.   Charles Trottier was born on 6 Nov 1870 Saskatoon, (Saskatchewan) (Denney.) (DL, page 5, B-18.). He was baptized on 23 Feb 1871 Duck Lake, (Saskatchewan) (Ibid.). He died in Mar 1878 at age 7 (L1, page 220, B-17 [S-17].). He was buried on 16 Apr 1878 Lebret, (Saskatchewan) (Ibid.).

    vii.   Ursule Trottier was born on 3 Apr 1872 Saskatoon, (Saskatchewan) (HBSI.) (L1, page 54, B-18.). She was baptized on 24 Apr 1872 Lebret, (Saskatchewan) (Ibid.). She died on 17 Jun 1885 Batoche, (Saskatchewan), at age 13 (BSAP, page 36, S-31.). She was buried on 18 Jun 1885 Batoche, (Saskatchewan) (Ibid.).

40   viii.   Andre Trottier, b. 15 Apr 1873 near, Saskatoon, (Saskatchewan); m. Pauline "Susie" Wallace; d. 1 Feb 1937 Montana.

ix. Suzanne Trottier was born in Jun 1873 Saskatoon, (Saskatchewan) (Denney.) (DL, page 17, B-67.). She was baptized on 9 Nov 1873 Duck Lake, (Saskatchewan) (Ibid.).

x. Marie Rosine Trottier was born on 1 Apr 1876 Lebret, (Saskatchewan) (L1, page 184, B-111.). She was baptized on 2 Apr 1876 Lebret, (Saskatchewan) (Ibid.). She was buried on 21 Aug 1876 Lebret, (Saskatchewan) (Ibid., page 172, S-23.).

xi. Marie Cecilia Trottier was born on 3 May 1877 (SPMT , page 112, #2376.). She was baptized on 4 Jul 1877 (St.Peter's Mission), St.Peter's Mission, Montana Territory (Ibid.). She was buried on 16 Apr 1878 Lebret, (Saskatchewan) (L1, page 220, B-18 [S-18].).

Angelique Parenteau was born circa 1822 (1870C-MB, page 71, #2198.). She was born circa 1834 (1886-TMC 1886 Census of Half Breed Chippewas of Turtle Mountain, Dakota Territory, National Archives of the United States, Washington D.C., #188.). She was born in 1838 British Columbia (1880 Montana Census, National Archives of the United States, Washington D.C., page 343A, 217-226.). She married **Jean Baptiste Laframboise**, son of **Joseph "Leblanc" Laframboise** and **Cecile Dumont**, before 1860 (1900CI-ND-Rolette *1900 Turtle Mountain Indian Reservation Census Index, Rolette County, North Dakota* compiled by Mary Ann Quiring and Lily B. Zwolle, (n.p.: Mary Ann Quiring and Lily B. Zwolle, 1984).) (Rod Mac Quarrie, 22 Dec 2009.). She married **Moise Lapierre**, son of **Antoine Lapierre** and **Catherine Gagnon**, on 27 Feb 1871 Duck Lake, (Saskatchewan) (DL, page 7, M-3.).

Children of **Charles Trottier** and **Angelique Parenteau** were:

i. Marie Trottier was born circa 1871 (ArchiviaNet, C-15007.). She died circa 1888 St.John, North Dakota (Ibid.).

Generation Four

19. **Isabelle Trottier** was born on 6 Apr 1858 Pembina County, Dakota Territory (AP, page 189, B-572.). She was baptized on 25 Apr 1858 Assumption, Pembina, Pembina County, Dakota Territory (Ibid.). She married **Joseph Laframboise**, son of **Narcisse Laframboise** and **Josephte Cantara,** on 10 Jan 1878 St.Joseph, Leroy, Pembina County, Dakota Territory (SJL-1, page 85, M-1.). She died on 25 Jan 1949 Rolette County, North Dakota, at age 90 (ND Death Index.).

Joseph Laframboise was born on 11 Apr 1856 Dakota Territory (AP, page 148, B-413.). He was baptized on 26 May 1856 Assumption, Pembina, Pembina County, Dakota Territory (Ibid.). He died on 19 Sep 1938 Rolette County, Dakota Territory, at age 82 (ND Death Index.) (1937-TMC Indian Census Roll of the Turtle Mountain Reservation, United States Indian Service Department of the Interior, Belcourt, North Dakota, J. E. Balmer, 1 January 1937.).

20. **Joseph Trottier** was born on 15 Jun 1860 Pembina, Pembina County, Dakota Territory (AP, page 232-233, B-160.). He was baptized on 15 Jun 1860 Assumption, Pembina, Pembina County, Dakota Territory (Ibid.). He married **Helene Jerome**, daughter of **Louis Jerome** and **Angelique Boyer**, on 29 Feb 1892 St.Joseph, Leroy, Pembina County, North Dakota (SJL-2, M-3.). He died on 4 Jul 1919 Belcourt, Rolette County, North Dakota, at age 59 (BIA-TM-BMD.) (ND Death Index.). He was buried on 6 Jul 1919 St.Michaels Cemetery, Rolette County, North Dakota (BIA-TM-BMD.).

Helene Jerome was born on 11 Feb 1868 Pembina County, Dakota Territory (AP, page 31, B-3.). She was baptized on 11 Feb 1868 Assumption, Pembina, Pembina County, Dakota Territory (Ibid.). She married **Jacques Belgarde**, son of **Jean Baptiste Belgarde** and **Marie Emily Hamelin,** after 1918. She died on 31 Jan 1945 Rolette County, North Dakota, at age 76 (ND Death Index.).

Children of **Joseph Trottier** and **Helene Jerome** were as follows:

41   i. Joseph Trottier, b. 8 Mar 1897 North Dakota; m. Laura Clara Belgarde; d. 8 Feb 1964 Rolette County, North Dakota.

ii. Louise Trottier was born circa 1902 North Dakota (1910C ND Thirteenth Census of the United States: 1910; North Dakota, National Archives of the United States, Washington D.C., page 18B, family 106, line 35-40.).

42   iii. Martin Trottier, b. 23 Jan 1905 Belcourt, Rolette County, North Dakota; m. Clemence Marie Rose Belgarde; m. Mary Margaret Belgarde; d. 2 Jun 1936 Rolette County, North Dakota; bur. 5 Jun 1936 Belcourt, Rolette County, North Dakota.

iv. Mary Selma Trottier was born circa 1911 North Dakota (1930C ND Fifteenth Census of the United States: 1930; North Dakota, National Archives of the United States, Washington, D.C., page 1B, family 21, line 96-100.). She married Jerry August Lafrance, son of Joseph Lafrance and Mary DeTonnancour, on 14 Sep 1944 Glasgow, Valley County, Montana (familysearch.org Website, Montana Marriages.).

    Jerry August Lafrance was born in 1910 (Ibid.).

21. **Rose Trottier** was born in Mar 1871 Dakota Territory (1900C-ND, House 73, page 277B.). She married **Joseph Grant**, son of **Pierre Grant** and **Marie Vivier,** before 1890. She died on 27 Aug 1958 Rolette County, North Dakota, at age 87 (BIA-TM-BMD.) (ND Death Index.).

Joseph Grant was born in Feb 1871 North Dakota (1900C-ND, House 73, page 277B.).

22. **John Trottier** was born in 1860 Carlton, North West Territories (MBS, C-14934.). He married **Melanie Morin**, daughter of **Francois Perreault dit Morin** and **Marguerite Robinson,** on 29 Apr 1884 St.Claude Mission, St.John, Rolette County, North Daktoa (Dominique Ritchot Research,, 26 Jan 2006.).

Melanie Morin was born on 26 Oct 1859 (SFXI-Kipling, B-35.). She was baptized on 17 May 1860 St.Francois Xavier, (Manitoba) (Ibid.) (INB, page 128.).

Children of **John Trottier** and **Melanie Morin** were:

i. Marie-Anne Trottier was baptized on 20 Feb 1887 St.Claude Mission, St.John, Rolette County, North Dakota (St. Claude Mission, St. John, North Dakota, Baptisms, Marriages, Burials 1882-1888, 2006, Dominique Ritchot, B-304, page 62.).

23. **Jean Baptiste Trottier** was born on 12 Sep 1841 St.Francois Xavier, (Manitoba) (SFX: 1834-1850, B-366.). He was baptized on 12 Sep 1841 St.Francois Xavier, (Manitoba) (Ibid.). He married **Rose McGillis**, daughter of **Alexandre McGillis** and **Marguerite Bottineau,** on 5 Sep 1865 St.Francois Xavier, (Manitoba) (SFXI-Kipling, page 652, M-19.). He died in 1892 (1936-LS, #18.).

Rose McGillis was born on 10 Sep 1847 St.Francois Xavier, (Manitoba) (SFX: 1834-1850, B-706.). She was baptized on 12 Sep 1847 St.Francois Xavier, (Manitoba) (Ibid.). She died in 1929 (1936-LS, #18.).

Children of **Jean Baptiste Trottier** and **Rose McGillis** were as follows:

   i. Marie Rose Trottier was born on 2 Jan 1867 (SFXI: 1835-1852, B-43.). She was baptized on 19 May 1867 St.Francois Xavier, (Manitoba) (Ibid.).

43 ii. Patrice Trottier, b. 1 Nov 1868 Lake Pelchie, (Saskatchewan); m. Athalie Rose Whitford; d. after 1936 Val Marie, Saskatchewan.

44 iii. Rosalie Trottier, b. 25 May 1870 St.Francois Xavier, (Manitoba); m. Salomon 'Sam' Pritchard; d. 9 Sep 1942.

   iv. Jean Marie Trottier was born on 26 Apr 1872 Lebret, (Saskatchewan) (L1, page 66, B-74.). He was baptized on 27 Apr 1872 Lebret, (Saskatchewan) (Ibid.). He married Ernestine Lemire, daughter of Francois Lemire and Francoise Birston, before 1900.

    Ernestine Lemire was born on 10 May 1883 (L2, page 65, B-35.). She was baptized on 14 May 1883 Lebret, (Saskatchewan) (Ibid.).

45 v. Marie Anatalie Trottier, b. 3 Feb 1876 Saskatoon, (Saskatchewan); m. Antoine Caplette.

46 vi. Jean Baptiste Trottier, b. 3 Feb 1876 Saskatoon, (Saskatchewan); m. Rosalie Lemire; d. Willowfield.

47 vii. Ursule Trottier, b. 4 Feb 1877 Maple Creek, (Saskatchewan); m. Leon Parenteau; d. May 1970 Harlem, Blaine County, Montana.

48 viii. Andre Trottier, b. 1879 Maple Creek, (Saskatchewan); m. Rosalie Trottier; d. 1967 Saskatoon, Saskatchewan.

   ix. Helen Trottier was born in May 1883 Saskatoon, (Saskatchewan) (ArchiviaNet, C-15007.). She died circa Sep 1883 (Saskatchewan) (Ibid.).

   x. Joseph Trottier was born in Sep 1884 Swift Current, (Saskatchewan) (Ibid.). He died circa Oct 1884 (Saskatchewan) (Ibid.).

24. Julie Trottier was born circa Apr 1844 (SFX: 1834-1850, B-528.). She was baptized on 4 Aug 1844 St.Francois Xavier, (Manitoba) (Ibid.). She married **Thomas Breland,** son of **Pascal Breland** and **Maria Grant,** on 1 Feb 1864 St.Francois Xavier, (Manitoba) (SFXI-Kipling, M-5.) (SFXI 1851-1868, M-5.). She died on 29 May 1866 St.Francois Xavier, (Manitoba) (SFXI-Kipling, S-23.). She was buried on 30 May 1866 St.Francois Xavier, (Manitoba) (Ibid.).

Thomas Breland was born on 21 Sep 1842 St.Francois Xavier, (Manitoba) (SFX: 1834-1850, B-426.). He was baptized on 22 Sep 1842 St.Francois Xavier, (Manitoba) (Ibid.). He married **Philomene Page,** daughter of **Joseph Page** and **Genevieve Pelletier,** on 8 Jul 1867 St.Francois Xavier, (Manitoba) (SFXI-Kipling, M-18.). He married **Marie Rivet,** daughter of **Louis Rivet** and **Marguerite Gros Ventre Hamel,** on 24 Sep 1876 Lebret, (Saskatchewan) (L1, M-9, page 174-175.). He married **Therese Tanner,** daughter of **Thomas John Tanner** and **Louise Kee-na-we-pinai-si Saulteaux,** on 21 Aug 1879 Lebret, (Saskatchewan) (Ibid., page 251, M-3.). He married **Leonide Ritchot,** daughter of **Jean Baptiste Ritchot** and **Marie Anne Chatelain,** on 24 Jun 1894 (Ritchot), St.Norbert, Manitoba (MM, page 98.) (Ibid., page 1076.) (MB Vital Statistics, Mar. Reg. #1898,001517.).

25. Pascal Trottier was born on 7 Apr 1846 (SFX: 1834-1850, B-605.). He was baptized on 16 May 1846 St.Francois Xavier, (Manitoba) (Ibid.). He married **Rosalie St.Germain,** daughter of **Francois St.Germain** and **Louise Morand,** on 23 Aug 1870 St.Francois Xavier, Manitoba (SFXI-Kipling, M-14.). He was buried on 22 Mar 1888 St.Claude Mission, St.John, Rolette County, North Dakota (St.Claude BMD, Dominique Ritchot, S-68, p. 73.).

Rosalie St.Germain was born on 1 May 1853 St.Francois Xavier, (Manitoba) (SFXI-Kipling, B-68.) (SFXI 1851-1868, B-68.). She was baptized on 3 May 1853 St.Francois Xavier, (Manitoba) (Ibid.) (SFXI-Kipling, B-68.).

Children of **Pascal Trottier** and **Rosalie St.Germain** were as follows:

   i. Marie Rose Trottier was born on 1 Oct 1871 St.Francois Xavier, Manitoba (INB, page 177.) (SFXI-Kipling, B-74.). She was baptized on 1 Oct 1871 St.Francois Xavier, Manitoba (Ibid.) (INB, page 177.). She died on 31 Oct 1871 St.Francois Xavier, Manitoba (SFXI-Kipling, S-42.). She was buried on 1 Nov 1871 St.Francois Xavier, Manitoba (IBMS.) (SFXI-Kipling, S-42.).

   ii. Patrice Trottier was born on 16 May 1873 St.Francois Xavier, Manitoba (Ibid., B-37.). He was baptized on 17 May 1873 St.Francois Xavier, Manitoba (Ibid.) (INB, page 178.). He died on 2 Jul 1873 St.Francois Xavier, Manitoba (SFXI-Kipling, S-59.). He was buried on 4 Jul 1873 St.Francois Xavier, Manitoba (IBMS.) (SFXI-Kipling, S-59.).

   iii. Elise Trottier was born on 7 Aug 1874 St.Francois Xavier, Manitoba (Ibid., B-41.) (INB, page 177.). She was baptized on 9 Aug 1874 St.Francois Xavier, Manitoba (SFXI-Kipling, B-41.) (INB, page 177.). She died on 18 Feb 1875 St.Francois Xavier, Manitoba (SFXI-Kipling, S-6.). She was buried on 18 Feb 1875 St.Francois Xavier, Manitoba (IBMS.) (SFXI-Kipling, S-6.).

   iv. Melanie Trottier was born on 16 Feb 1876 St.Francois Xavier, Manitoba (Ibid., B-6.). She died on 21 Aug 1876 St.Francois Xavier, Manitoba (Ibid., S-19.).

   v. Natalie Rose Trottier was born on 27 Nov 1877 St.Francois Xavier, Manitoba (Ibid., B-53.). She was baptized 29 Nov 1877 St.Francois Xavier, Manitoba (Ibid.) (Rosemary Rozyk.). She died on 18 Mar 1880 St.Francois Xavier, Manitoba, at age 2 (Ibid., S-10.). She was buried 20 Mar 1880 St.Francois Xavier, Manitoba (Ibid.) (Rosemary Rozyk.).

49 vi. Napoleon "Paul" Trottier, b. 2 May 1880 St.Francois Xavier, Manitoba; m. Bibiane Eulalie Slater; d. 21 May 1942 Rolette County, North Dakota.

   vii. Moise Trottier was born on 27 Oct 1882 St.Francois Xavier, Manitoba (Ibid., B-55.) (ND Death Index.). He died on 1 Jan 1954 Rolette County, North Dakota, at age 71 (Ibid.).

50 viii. Elise Trottier, b. 22 Apr 1885 St.John, Rolette County, North Dakota; d. 27 Mar 1968 Rolette County, North Dakota.

   ix. Albert Trottier was baptized on 27 Mar 1888 St.Claude Mission, St.John, Rolette County, North Dakota (St.Claude BMD, Dominique Ritchot, B-369, page 74.).

26. Rose Trottier was born circa 1849 North West Territory (1870C-MB, page 261, #612.). She was born in 1853 (MBS, C-14929.) (SFXI-Kipling, S-57.). She married **Alexandre Larocque,** son of **Louis Larocque** and **Judith Guilbault,** on 25 May 1868 St.Francois

Xavier, (Manitoba) (Ibid., M-10.). She died on 14 Jun 1873 St.Francois Xavier, Manitoba (Ibid., S-57.). She was buried on 16 Jun 1873 St.Francois Xavier, Manitoba (MBS, C-14929.) (SFXI-Kipling, S-57.).

Alexandre Larocque was born on 13 Nov 1846 St.Francois Xavier, (Manitoba) (SFX: 1834-1850, B-636.). He was baptized on 15 Nov 1846 St.Francois Xavier, (Manitoba) (Ibid.). He married **Rose Sayer**, daughter of **Edouard Sayer** and **Madeleine Delorme,** on 1 Jul 1874 St.Francois Xavier, Manitoba (SFXI-Kipling, M-15.).

27.   **Vital Trottier** was born circa 1856 (Manitoba) (1870C-MB, page 262, #614.). He married **Veronique Lingan**, daughter of **Edouard Lingan** and **Marguerite Larocque,** on 6 Feb 1877 St.Francois Xavier, Manitoba (SFXI-Kipling, M-6.).

Veronique Lingan was born on 4 Mar 1861 St.Francois Xavier, (Manitoba) (Ibid., B-18.). She was baptized on 9 Mar 1861 St.Francois Xavier, (Manitoba) (Ibid.). She married **Joseph Houle**, son of **Joseph Houle** and **Catherine Lapierre,** on 22 Jan 1887 St.Claude Mission, St.John, Rolette County, North Daktoa (Dominique Ritchot, 26 Jan 2006.). She died on 18 Mar 1947 Rolette County, North Dakota, at age 86 (ND Death Index.).

Children of **Vital Trottier** and **Veronique Lingan** were as follows:

      i.   Joseph Trottier was born on 30 Mar 1878 St.Francois Xavier, Manitoba (SFXI-Kipling, B-13.). He was aptized 1 Apr 1878 St.Francois Xavier, Manitoba (Ibid.) (Rosemary Rozyk.). He died on 21 Feb 1881 St.Francois Xavier, Manitoba, at age 2 (Ibid., S-7.). He was buried 23 Feb 1881 St.Francois Xavier, Manitoba (Ibid.) (Rosemary Rozyk.)

51   ii. Rosine Trottier, b. 20 Nov 1879 St.Francois Xavier, Manitoba.

52   iii. Joseph Vital Trottier, b. 11 Sep 1881 St.Francois Xavier, Manitoba; m. LaRose Belgarde; d. 19 May 1974 Rolette, North Dakota.

      iv. Caroline Trottier was baptized on 7 Sep 1883 St.Claude, St.John, Rolette County, North Dakota (St.Claude BMD, Dominique Ritchot, page 14, B-66.).

28.   **Marguerite Trottier** was born on 4 Oct 1857 near Fort Ellice, Manitoba (SFXI-Kipling, B-242.) (HBSI.). She was baptized on 6 May 1858 St.Francois Xavier, (Manitoba) (SFXI-Kipling, B-242.). She married **Bernard Paul**, son of **Jean Baptiste Paul** and **Angelique Godin,** on 22 Jun 1885 Duck Lake, (Saskatchewan) (DL, page 67, M-7.).

Bernard Paul was born on 16 Jul 1848 St.Francois Xavier, (Manitoba) (SFX: 1834-1850, B-744.). He was baptized on 23 Jul 1848 St.Francois Xavier, (Manitoba) (Ibid.). He married **Marie Gervais**, daughter of **Bazile Gervais** and **Francoise Ledoux,** on 22 Nov 1870 St.Francois Xavier, Manitoba (SFXI-Kipling, M-18.).

29.   **Albert Trottier** was born circa 1860 Fort Ellice, Manitoba (SFXI-Kipling, B-51.). He was baptized on 22 May 1862 St.Francois Xavier, (Manitoba) (Ibid.). He married **Isabelle Boudreau**, daughter of **Alexandre Cayen dit Boudreau** and **Marie McGillis,** on 18 Oct 1886 Duck Lake, (Saskatchewan) (DL, page 73, M-9.).

Isabelle Boudreau was born on 10 Feb 1868 Carlton, (Saskatchewan) (SFXI-Kipling, B-35.) (HBSI.). She was baptized on 3 May 1868 St.Francois Xavier, (Manitoba) (SFXI-Kipling, B-35.).

Children of **Albert Trottier** and **Isabelle Boudreau** were as follows:

      i.   Emanuel Trottier was born in Jul 1888 (1901 Canada, #204, n(1), page 15, family 152, line 24-32.).

      ii. Napier Trottier was born in Jan 1890 (Ibid.).

      iii. Veronique Trottier was born in Nov 1890 (Ibid.).

      iv. Florence Trottier was born in Mar 1891 (Ibid.).

      v. Elizabeth Trottier was born in Oct 1892 (Ibid.).

      vi. Christian Trottier was born in Nov 1895 (Ibid.).

      vii. Louise Trottier was born in 1897 (Automated Genealogy 1911 Census Transcription Project and Census Images from the National Archives of Canada, http://www.automatedgenealogy.com, #39, page 24, family 266, line 19-32.).

      viii. Josephine Trottier was born in 1899 (Ibid.).

      ix. Mary Trottier was born in 1900 (Ibid.).

      x. Isabel Trottier was born in Jan 1900 (1901 Canada, #204, n(1), page 15, family 152, line 24-32.).

      xi. Alexandrine Trottier was born on 16 Jun 1907 Onion Lake, (Saskatchewan) (SK Vital Statistics, Birth Reg. #7723.).

      xii. Louis Trottier was born in 1909 (1911 Canada, #39, page 24, family 266, line 19-32.).

30.   **Charles Trottier** was born on 24 Apr 1865 (SFXI-Kipling, B-24.). He was baptized on 4 May 1865 St.Francois Xavier, (Manitoba) (Ibid.). He married **Madeleine Okimasis**, daughter of **Xavier Okemassis** and **Marie Therese Gladu,** on 13 Jun 1887 Duck Lake, (Saskatchewan) (DL, page 77, M-3.).

Madeleine Okimasis was born circa 1865 (Ibid., page 33, B-22.). She was born circa Apr 1869 near, Saskatoon, (Saskatchewan) (HBSI.). She was baptized on 6 May 1880 Duck Lake, (Saskatchewan) (DL, page 33, B-22.). She married **Jean Kananatenskupan** on 27 Jun 1885 Duck Lake, (Saskatchewan) (Ibid., page 66, M-5.).

Children of **Charles Trottier** and **Madeleine Okimasis** were as follows:

53   i.   Virginie Trottier, b. May 1885 Duck Lake, (Saskatchewan); m. William George Cunningham.

      ii. Marguerite Cecile Trottier was baptized on 29 May 1887 Duck Lake, (Saskatchewan) (Ibid., page 77, B-13.).

      iii. Marie Joseph Andre Trottier was born on 11 Sep 1889 Duck Lake, (Saskatchewan) (Ibid., page 88, B-19.) (SK Vital Statistics, Birth Reg. #7642.) (Ibid., Birth Reg. #7547.). He was baptized on 21 Sep 1889 Duck Lake, (Saskatchewan) (DL, page 88, B-19.).

      iv. Alphonsine Trottier was born on 28 Feb 1891 (Saskatchewan) (Ibid., S-15.) (SK Vital Statistics, Birth Reg. #8246.). She died on 2 Dec 1891 Duck Lake, (Saskatchewan) (DL, S-15.). She was buried on 4 Dec 1891 Duck Lake, (Saskatchewan) (Ibid.).

      v. Isabelle Marie Trottier was born on 20 Aug 1892 Duck Lake, (Saskatchewan) (Ibid., page 110, B-23.) (SK Vital Statistics, Birth Reg. #8212.). She was baptized on 30 Sep 1892 Duck Lake, (Saskatchewan) (DL, page 110, B-23.).

31. Andre Trottier was born on 10 Jan 1861 St.Francois Xavier, (Manitoba) (SFXI-Kipling, B-5.). He was baptized on 20 Jan 1861 St.Francois Xavier, (Manitoba) (Ibid.). He married **Rose Laframboise**, daughter of **Francois Laframboise** and **Marie Trottier,** circa 1881.

Rose Laframboise was born on 15 Nov 1857 (Ibid., B-234.). She was baptized on 25 Apr 1858 St.Francois Xavier, (Manitoba) (Ibid.). She married **Simon Pepin**, son of **Simon Pepin** and **Marie Parent**, in 1900 (Brenda Snider, 16 Feb 2011.). She married **Frank Baker or Guym**, son of **Fred Baker** and **B. Koontz**, on 9 Apr 1921 Hill County, Montana (Ibid.). She died on 20 Aug 1932 Havre, Montana, at age 74 (Ibid.). She was buried on 22 Aug 1932 Calvary Cemetery, Havre, Montana (Ibid.).

Children of **Andre Trottier** and **Rose Laframboise** were as follows:

    i.   William Trottier was born circa 1881 Cypress Hills, (Saskatchewan) (Rod Mac Quarrie, 24 May 2007.). He died circa 1881 Cypress Hills, (Saskatchewan) (Ibid.). He was buried circa 1881 Fort Walsh, (Saskatchewan) (Ibid.).

54   ii.   Florence Trottier, b. 25 Sep 1883 Maple Creek, (Saskatchewan); d. 20 Feb 1961 Havre, Hill County, Montana.

    iii.   Marie Veronique Trottier was born on 25 Jun 1885 Lebret, (Saskatchewan) (L2, page 116, B-70.). She was baptized on 25 Jun 1885 Lebret, (Saskatchewan) (Ibid.). She married Edward W. Filler, son of Josiah Filler and Lucinda Pratt, on 3 Aug 1904 Havre, Chouteau County, Montana (Brenda Snider, 16 Feb 2011.).

         Edward W. Filler was born in 1874 Watertown, Wisconsin (Ibid.).

    iv.   Rose Trottier was born in 1890 Montana (Ibid.).

    v.   Elizabeth Trottier was born in 1892 (Ibid.). She married Frank Meyers circa 1911 (Ibid.).

         Frank Meyers was born circa 1887 Illinois (Ibid.).

32. Alexandre Trottier was born on 1 Jul 1862 (SFXI-Kipling, B-71.). He was baptized on 15 Aug 1862 St.Francois Xavier, (Manitoba) (Ibid.). He married **Catherine Laframboise**, daughter of **Jean Baptiste Laframboise** and **Elise Thomas**, circa Oct 1884 Maple Creek, (Saskatchewan) (Denney.).

Catherine Laframboise was born in Aug 1864 White Mud River (SFXI-Kipling, B-49.) (SFXI 1851-1868, B-49.) (ArchiviaNet.). She was baptized on 5 Sep 1864 St.Francois Xavier, (Manitoba) (SFXI-Kipling, B-49.) (SFXI 1851-1868, B-49.).

Children of **Alexandre Trottier** and **Catherine Laframboise** were as follows:

    i.   Marie Rose Trottier was born in 1885 (SIWB St.Ignace Roman Catholic Registre des Baptemes, Mariages & Sepltures, Willow Bunch, Saskatchewan, 1882-1917, FHC #1290091., B-17, page 11. Hereinafter cited as SIWB.). She was baptized on 8 Mar 1886 St.Ignace, Willow Bunch, (Saskatchewan) (Ibid.).

55   ii.   Peter Trottier, b. circa 1890 (Saskatchewan); m. Justine Landry; d. circa 1965 Saskatoon, Saskatchewan.

    iii.   Roselenn Trottier was born circa 1894 (Saskatchewan) (Automated Genealogy 1906 Census Transcription Project and Census Images from the National Archives of Canada, http://www.automatedgenealogy.com, page 56, line 21-28.).

    iv.   Elizabeth Trottier was born circa 1898 (Saskatchewan) (Ibid.).

    v.   Delphine Trottier was born circa 1900 (Saskatchewan) (Ibid.).

    vi.   Patrick Trottier was born circa 1903 (Saskatchewan) (Ibid.). He was born on 8 Jan 1905 (Brenda Snider, 16 Feb 2011.). He died on 15 Oct 1952 Calgary, Alberta (Ibid.).

    vii.   Baby Trottier was born in 1906 (Saskatchewan) (1906 Canada, page 56, line 21-28.).

33. Norbert Trottier was born on 6 Mar 1861 Humboldt, (Saskatchewan) (NWHBS, C-14942.) (SFXI-Kipling, B-27.). He was baptized on 12 May 1861 St.Francois Xavier, (Manitoba) (Ibid.). He married **Eliza Fisher**, daughter of **John Fisher** and **Elizabeth Brabant,** on 26 Aug 1885 Lebret, (Saskatchewan) (L2, page 123, M-16.).

Eliza Fisher was born in 1858 near, Fort Qu'Appelle, (Saskatchewan). She married **Jean Baptiste "Bernard" Desmarais**, son of **Michel Desmarais** and **Josephte Rochon**, on 21 May 1876 Lebret, (Saskatchewan) (L1, page 161, M-_.).

Children of **Norbert Trottier** and **Eliza Fisher** were as follows:

    i.   Virginie Trottier was born on 4 Aug 1886 (L2, page 154-155, B-55.). She was baptized on 8 Aug 1886 Lebret, (Saskatchewan) (Ibid.).

56   ii.   Rosalie Trottier, b. circa 1888; m. Andre Trottier; d. 12 Oct 1973.

34. Marie Trottier was born on 24 Mar 1869 (SFXI-Kipling, B-35.). She was baptized on 1 May 1869 St.Francois Xavier, (Manitoba) (Ibid.). She married **William Belcourt**, son of **Joseph Belcourt** and **Madeleine Sapen dit Campion**, on 10 Oct 1888 St.Peter's Mission, Cascade County, Montana (SPMT , page 49, #294.).

William Belcourt was born on 21 Aug 1867 Edmonton, (Alberta) (NWHBS, C-14936.).

35. Remi Trottier was born circa Jun 1861 (SFXI-Kipling, B-75.). He was baptized on 25 Aug 1861 St.Francois Xavier, (Manitoba) (Ibid.). He married **Marie Madeleine Laframboise**, daughter of **Jean Baptiste Laframboise** and **Elise Thomas**, in 1892 Maple Creek, (Saskatchewan) (Denney.). He died on 14 Mar 1938 Montana (Ancestry.com, Montana Death Index.).

Marie Madeleine Laframboise was born in 1872 Saskatoon, (Saskatchewan) (Denney.). She was baptized on 10 May 1872 St.Laurent-de-Grandin, (Saskatchewan) (SL-SK, page 7, B-_.).

Children of **Remi Trottier** and **Marie Madeleine Laframboise** were as follows:

    i.   Edward Trotchie was born circa 1914 (Ancestry.com, Montana Death Index.). He died on 11 May 1971 Cascade County, Montana (Ibid.).

    ii.   Elizabeth Trotchie was born circa 1917 (Brenda Snider, 16 Feb 2011.).

36. Isidore Trottier was born on 10 Jan 1863 (SB-Rozyk, page 111, B-57.). He was baptized on 8 May 1863 St.Boniface, (Manitoba) (Ibid.). He married **Caroline Lemire**, daughter of **Francois Lemire** and **Francoise Birston,** on 17 Jul 1892 Havre, Chouteau County, Montana (Brenda Snider, 16 Feb 2011.) (familysearch.org, Montana Marriages.).

Caroline Lemire was born on 3 Feb 1872 (L1, page 52-53, B-13.). She was baptized on 23 Apr 1872 Lebret, (Saskatchewan) (Ibid.).

Children of **Isidore Trottier** and **Caroline Lemire** are as follows:

    i.   Selina Trottier was born circa 1897 (1911 Canada, family 190, line 5-16.).

    ii.   Elizabeth Trottier was born circa 1898 (Ibid.).

    iii.   Frank Trottier was born circa 1901 (Ibid.).

iv. Stan Trottier was born circa 1905 (Ibid.).

v. George Trottier was born on 13 Oct 1905 Lebret, (Saskatchewan) (Ibid.) (SK Vital Statistics, Birth Reg. #4923.).

vi. Charles Trottier was born circa 1907 (1911 Canada, family 190, line 5-16.).

vii. Anna Trottier was born on 19 Oct 1908 Dundurn, Saskatchewan (SK Vital Statistics, Birth Reg. #9208.).

viii. Joseph Trottier was born circa 1910 (1911 Canada, family 190, line 5-16.).

37. Jean Baptiste Trottier was born on 5 Nov 1864 (SFXI-Kipling, B-33.). He was baptized on 11 May 1865 St.Francois Xavier, (Manitoba) (Ibid.). He married **Caroline Lemire**, daughter of **Pierre Lemire** and **Therese Pelletier**, on 11 Oct 1892 Box Elder, Chouteau County, Montana (ChCM Chouteau County, Montana; Marriage Record Licenses and Certificates; 1865-1950; familysearch.org, Hereinafter cited as ChCM.). He died on 4 Nov 1963 Harlem, Montana, at age 98 (Brenda Snider, 22 Jan 2012.). He was buried on 6 Nov 1963 Calvary Cemetery, Havre, Montana (Ibid., 16 Feb 2011.).

Caroline Lemire was born on 10 Sep 1871 Long Lake, (Saskatchewan) (HBSI.) (L1, page 53, B-14.). She was baptized on 11 Apr 1872 Lebret, (Saskatchewan) (Ibid.). She died on 6 Jun 1933 Havre, Hill County, Montana, at age 61 (1937-1987-LS Basic Roll Basic Membership Roll of the Landless Indians of Montana; 1937 Census Taken by Dr. Henry Roe Cloud; Edited c1987 to include official correspondence regarding 1937 membership; ** in Present Roll Number column indicates 1940s information added., #511.).

Children of **Jean Baptiste Trottier** and **Caroline Lemire** were as follows:

57   i. Victoria B. Trottier, b. 15 Aug 1893 Fort Benton, Choteau County, Montana; d. Jun 1986 Havre, Hill County, Montana.

58   ii. Amelia Trottier, b. 1895 Montana; m. Clark C. Hawley.

59   iii. Celina Trottier, b. circa 1897 Havre, Hill County, Montana; m. William John Lemire.

60   iv. Rose Trottier, b. 28 Jan 1899 Havre, Hill County, Montana; m. Thomas R. Hunter.

61   v. John B. Trottier, b. 11 Jan 1901 Havre, Hill County, Montana; m. Sarah Allery; d. 23 May 1973 Great Falls, Cascade County, Montana.

62   vi. Michel Trottier, b. circa 1904 Montana; m. Eugenia Hamelin.

63   vii. Louis Trottier, b. 13 Mar 1905 Montana; m. Helen Isabelle Huntley; m. Mary Allery; d. 5 Oct 1971 Hill County, Montana.

64   viii. Louise Trottier, b. 19 Jun 1908 Havre, Hill County, Montana; m. Vance Victor Murphy; d. 6 Mar 1948 Havre, Hill County, Montana.

38. Helene Trottier was born on 20 Feb 1867 (SFXI: 1835-1852, B-39.). She was baptized on 17 May 1867 St.Francois Xavier, (Manitoba) (Ibid.). She married **Hilaire Sansregret**, son of **Pierre Sansregret dit Beaubrillant** and **Caroline Parenteau**, on 12 Jan 1886 St.Peter's Mission, Cascade County, Montana Territory (SPMT , page 45, #273.).

Hilaire Sansregret was born on 29 Jan 1863 (SFXI-Kipling, B-35.). He was baptized on 4 May 1863 St.Francois Xavier, (Manitoba) (Ibid.).

39. Mathilde Trottier was born on 9 Feb 1869 (SFXI-Kipling, B-32.). She was baptized on 25 Apr 1869 St.Francois Xavier, (Manitoba) (Ibid.). She married **Alphonse Caron**, son of **Pierre Carron** and **Petronilla Martin**, on 19 Apr 1887 (St.Peter's Mission), Willow Creek, Montana Territory (SPMT , page 47, #287.).

Alphonse Caron was born in Mar 1864.

40. Andre Trottier was born on 15 Apr 1873 near, Saskatoon, (Saskatchewan) (L1, page 91, B-68.). He was baptized on 3 May 1873 Lebret, (Saskatchewan) (Ibid.). He married **Pauline "Susie" Wallace**, daughter of **Francis Wallace** and **Madeleine Sauve**, on 18 Apr 1895 Havre, Chouteau County, Montana (ChCM.). He died on 1 Feb 1937 Montana at age 63 (Ancestry.com, Montana Death Index.).

Pauline "Susie" Wallace was born on 1 Aug 1879 (DL, page 27, B-24.). She was baptized on 3 Aug 1879 Duck Lake, (Saskatchewan) (Ibid.). She married **James Brown**, son of **James Brown** and **Alexandria Phillo**, on 12 Sep 1914 Havre, Hill County, Montana (HCM Hill County, Montana; Marriage Record Licenses and Certificates; 1865-1950; familysearch.org, Hereinafter cited as HCM.).

Children of **Andre Trottier** and **Pauline "Susie" Wallace** were as follows:

i. Delia Trottier was born circa 1897 (1906 Canada, #12, page 13, family 104, line 10-15.).

ii. Clara Trottier was born on 12 Apr 1901 (Ibid.) (Brenda Snider, 16 Feb 2011.). She married Fred Naples circa 1922 (Ibid.). She died on 15 Apr 1991 Soap Lake, Grant County, Washington, at age 90 (Ibid.).

iii. Ida Trottier was born on 3 Aug 1903 (1906 Canada, #12, page 13, family 104, line 10-15.) (Brenda Snider, 16 Feb 2011.). She died in Nov 1982 Ephrata, Grant County, Washington, at age 79 (Ibid.).

65   iv. George Andrew Trottier, b. 2 Dec 1905 Havre, Hill County, Montana; m. Mary Louise Briere; d. 31 Dec 1996 Havre, Hill County, Montana; bur. 3 Jan 1997 Kuper Memorial Cemetery.

v. Theresa Trotchie was born on 8 Aug 1908 Havre, Hill County, Montana (BIA-LS.). She married Robert E. Taylor before 1933 (1987LS 1987-92 Little Shell Band of Chippewa Roll.).

     Robert E. Taylor was born in 1903 Virginia (BIA-LS.).

vi. Clifford Trottier was born on 17 Nov 1910 Havre, Hill County, Montana (Brenda Snider, 16 Feb 2011.). He died on 16 May 1975 Seattle, King County, Washington, at age 64 (Ibid.) (Social Security Death Index, . Hereinafter cited as SSDI.).

Generation Five

41. Joseph Trottier was born on 8 Mar 1897 North Dakota (1910C ND, page 18B, family 106, line 35-40.) (ND Death Index.). He married **Laura Clara Belgarde**, daughter of **Jacques Belgarde** and **Cecile Laverdure**, circa 1921 North Dakota (1930C ND, page 1B, family 20, line 91-95.). He died on 8 Feb 1964 Rolette County, North Dakota, at age 66 (ND Death Index.).

Laura Clara Belgarde was born on 1 Jan 1898 North Dakota (1900C-ND, House 117, page 281A.) (*1937-TMC*, page 497-498, Census No. 5814-5819.) (ND Death Index.). She died on 7 Feb 1960 Rolette County, North Dakota, at age 62 (Ibid.).

Children of **Joseph Trottier** and **Laura Clara Belgarde** were as follows:

i. Alexander Joseph Trottier was born on 16 Nov 1921 North Dakota (1930C ND, page 1B, family 20, line 91-95.) (*1932-TMC*, page 434, Census No. 5121-5125.). He married Elizabeth Marie Picket, daughter of Thomas Picket and Margaret Winn, on 1 Jul 1944 Roosevelt County, Montana (RooCM Marriage Licenses and Certificates,

Roosevelt County Courthouse, Wolf Point, Montana; FHC microfilm 1903324 and 1903325, Hereinafter cited as RooCM.). He died on 4 Jun 1969 Roosevelt County, Montana, at age 47 (MT Death.).

Elizabeth Marie Picket was born in 1928 (RooCM.).

ii. Roy Joseph Trottier was born on 18 Feb 1923 North Dakota (1930C ND, page 1B, family 20, line 91-95.) (*1932-TMC*, page 434, Census No. 5121-5125.) (SSDI.). He died on 6 Jan 2002 Belcourt, Rolette County, North Dakota, at age 78 (Ibid.) (ND Death Index.).

iii. Mary Trottier was born on 7 Jan 1926 North Dakota (1930C ND, page 1B, family 20, line 91-95.) (*1932-TMC*, page 434, Census No. 5121-5125.).

iv. Eugene Harvey Trottier was born on 9 Apr 1930 North Dakota (Ibid.). He died on 28 Apr 2001 Yellowstone County, Montana, at age 71 (MT Death.).

v. Earl Trottier was born on 20 Dec 1933 (*1937-TMC*, page 497-498, Census No. 5814-5819.) (ND Death Index.). He died on 18 May 1940 Rolette County, North Dakota, at age 6 (Ibid.).

vi. Conrad Trottier was born circa 1934 (1940C ND 1940 North Dakota, Sixteenth Census of the United States, National Archives of the United States, Washington, D.C., page 8A.).

42. Martin Trottier was born on 23 Jan 1905 Belcourt, Rolette County, North Dakota (1930C ND, page 2A, family 28, line 38-40.) (1910C ND, page 18B, family 106, line 35-40.) (ND Death Index.) (TM Star, 2 Jan 1936.). He married **Clemence Marie Rose Belgarde**, daughter of **William Belgarde** and **Marie Therese Lavallee**, circa 1928 (1930C ND, page 2A, family 28, line 38-40.). He married **Mary Margaret Belgarde**, daughter of **Jean Baptiste Belgarde** and **Mary Vitaline Brunelle**, on 2 Jun 1936 Belcourt, Rolette County, North Dakota (1936-TMC, page 38.) (1930C ND, page 2A, family 28, line 38-40.) (TM Star, 4 Jan 1936.). He died on 2 Jun 1936 Rolette County, North Dakota, at age 31 (1936-TMC, page 38.) (ND Death Index.) (TM Star, 4 Jan 1936.). He was buried on 5 Jun 1936 Belcourt, Rolette County, North Dakota (Ibid.).

Clemence Marie Rose Belgarde was born in 1905 North Dakota (1936-TMC, page 38.) (1916-TMC 1916 Census of the Turtle Mountain Chippewa, North Dakota, National Archives of the United States, Washington D.C., Cenus No. 345-351.). She died on 1 Jan 1934 (1935-TMC Census of the Turtle Mountain Chippewa Indians, United States Indian Service Department of the Interior, Turtle Mountain Agency, North Dakota, Superintendant F. T. Scott, 1 Apr 1935 , 1934-1935 TMC Deaths.).

Children of **Martin Trottier** and **Clemence Marie Rose Belgarde** were as follows:

i. Mary Louise Trottier was born on 15 Sep 1929 North Dakota (1930C ND, page 2A, family 28, line 38-40.) (*1937-TMC*, page 498, Census No. 5822-5823.).

ii. Clifford Patrick Trottier was born on 3 May 1932 (Ibid.) (ND Death Index.). He died on 16 Dec 1981 Rolette, North Dakota, at age 49 (Ibid.).

Mary Margaret Belgarde was born on 6 Feb 1916 Rolette County, North Dakota (*1937-TMC*, page 53, Census No. 596-603.).

43. Patrice Trottier was born on 1 Nov 1868 Lake Pelchie, (Saskatchewan) (SFXI-Kipling, B-75.). He was baptized on 22 Aug 1869 St.Francois Xavier, (Manitoba) (Ibid.) (INB, page 178.). He married **Athalie Rose Whitford**, daughter of **James Francois 'Jimmy' Whitford** and **Marguerite Fagnant,** before 1894. He died after 1936 Val Marie, Saskatchewan (BIA-LS.).

Athalie Rose Whitford was born on 23 Mar 1866 St.Francois Xavier, (Manitoba) (SFXI-Kipling, B-20.). She was baptized on 25 Mar 1866 St.Francois Xavier, (Manitoba) (Ibid.). She died in 1933.

Children of **Patrice Trottier** and **Athalie Rose Whitford** were as follows:

i. John Baptiste Trottier was born on 12 Oct 1894 (Margaret Doney Dills Research, 31 March 2003; Source: 2 June 1985 letter to Margarite Doney from Louise Trottier.). He married Anastasia Gladue, daughter of Antoine Gladu and Marie Florestine Lemire, on 3 Jan 1924 Malta, Valley County, Montana (PhCM Phillips County Courthouse, Montana; Marriage Record Licenses and Certificates; 1865-1950, familysearch.org; #750, Hereinafter cited as PhCM.). He died on 3 Nov 1963 Blaine County, Montana, at age 69 (MT Death.).

Anastasia Gladue was born on 7 Apr 1906 Brookside, Montana. She died on 30 Aug 1989 Regina, Saskatchewan, at age 83 (Brenda Snider, 26 Aug 2015.) (*HDN Havre Daily News*, Havre, Montana, 1 Sep 1989. Hereinafter cited as HDN.).

ii. Marie Margaret Trottier was born on 31 Jan 1896 (Saskatchewan) (SK Vital Statistics, Birth Reg. #9969.).

iii. Marie Rose Trottier was born on 21 Oct 1896 (Margaret Doney Dills, 31 March 2003; Source: 2 June 1985 letter to Margarite Doney from Louise Trottier.) (1901 Canada, #204, 6, page 1, family 4, line 6-12.). She died in Apr 1980 at age 83 (Margaret Doney Dills, 31 March 2003; Source: 2 June 1985 letter to Margarite Doney from Louise Trottier.).

iv. Stella A. Trottier was born on 4 May 1897 Chinook, Blaine County, Montana (1937-1987-LS Basic Roll, #101.). She married Harry W. Bishop, son of William Bishop and Madeleine Cardinal, on 12 Mar 1936 Phillips County, Montana (1987-92LS.) (familysearch.org, Montana Marriages.). She died on 23 Aug 1964 Malta, Phillips County, Montana, at age 67 (Margaret Doney Dills, 31 March 2003; Source: 2 June 1985 letter to Margarite Doney from Louise Trottier.) (Brenda Snider, 26 Jan 2012.).

Harry W. Bishop was born in 1884 (1987-92LS.). He married **Madeline Merchied** on 14 Nov 1908 Dodson, Chouteau County, Montana (ChCM.). He married **Madeleine Emily**, daughter of **Jonas Hamelin** and **Marie Patenaude**, on 3 Oct 1914 Dodson, Blaine County, Montana (Rootsweb.com Website, Montana Marriage Index.). He died on 27 May 1961 Malta, Montana (MT Death.).

v. James Allen Trottier was born on 14 Oct 1898 (BIA-LS.) (Margaret Doney Dills, 31 March 2003; Source: 2 June 1985 letter to Margarite Doney from Louise Trottier.). He married Marie Philomene McGillis, daughter of William John McGillis and Marie Rose Ouellette, on 29 Dec 1921 Phillips County, Montana (PhCM.). He died on 29 Oct 1933 Montana at age 35 (Margaret Doney Dills, 31 March 2003; Source: 2 June 1985 letter to Margarite Doney from Louise Trottier.) (Ancestry.com, Montana Death Index.).

Marie Philomene McGillis was born on 8 May 1902 Willow Bunch, (Saskatchewan) (SIWB, B-12, page 40.) (SK Vital Statistics, Birth Reg. #1829.). She was baptized on 8 May 1902 St.Ignace, Willow Bunch,

(Saskatchewan) (SIWB, B-12, page 40.). She married **John Joseph Desmarais**, son of **John Robert Desmarais** and **Celina Petit,** on 31 Oct 1935 Phillips County, Montana (PhCM.). She died on 5 Nov 1998 Phillips County, Montana, at age 96 (Ancestry.com, Montana Death Index.).

vi. Maxime F. Trottier was born on 9 Jan 1900 (Saskatchewan) (BIA-LS.). He was born on 13 Jan 1900 (Margaret Doney Dills, 31 March 2003; Source: 2 June 1985 letter to Margarite Doney from Louise Trottier.). He married Alice Mary Doney, daughter of Jean Baptiste Delauney or Donais or Doney and Elizabeth Allery, on 28 Feb 1924 Phillips County, Montana (PhCM.). He died on 22 Dec 1969 Cascade, Phillips County, Montana, at age 69 (Margaret Doney Dills, 31 March 2003; Source: 2 June 1985 letter to Margarite Doney from Louise Trottier.) (Ancestry.com, Montana Death Index.) (familysearch.org.) (SSDI.).

    Alice Mary Doney was born on 15 Aug 1907 White Water, Phillips County, Montana (Margaret Doney Dills, 31 March 2003; Source: 2 June 1985 letter to Margarite Doney from Louise Trottier.). She died on 28 Jul 1948 Cascade County, Montana, at age 40 (MT Death.).

vii. Marie Edna Trottier was born on 4 May 1901 (Saskatchewan) (Margaret Doney Dills, 31 March 2003; Source: 2 June 1985 letter to Margarite Doney from Louise Trottier.) (SK Vital Statistics, Birth Reg. #2276.). She died in Jul 1974 at age 73 (Margaret Doney Dills, 31 March 2003; Source: 2 June 1985 letter to Margarite Doney from Louise Trottier.).

viii. Laura Trottier was born on 24 Feb 1902 (Ibid.). She died on 13 Jan 1933 at age 30 (Ibid.).

ix. Louise Trottier was born on 23 Sep 1904 Swift Current, (Saskatchewan) (Ibid.) (SK Vital Statistics, Birth Reg. #4813.). She married Patrick Baker, son of George Baker and Marie Josephine Frederick, circa 1921 North Dakota (1930C ND, page 2A, family 17-22, line 6-9.).

    Patrick Baker was born in Apr 1896 North Dakota (1900C-ND, House 201, page 294A.) (1936-TMC, page 30.). He married **Mary Rose Fournier**, daughter of **Norbert Fournier** and **Mary (--?--),** before 1918 (Ibid.).

x. Tillie Rose Trottier was born on 2 Apr 1906 Lake Pelchie, Saskatchewan (1937-1987-LS Basic Roll, #68.). She and Frank Azure obtained a marriage license on 6 Nov 1924 Roosevelt County, Montana (RooCM.). She married Frank Azure, son of Modeste Azure and Mathilde Short, on 6 Nov 1924 Justice of the Peace, Wolf Point, Roosevelt County, Montana (Ibid.). She died on 29 Sep 1949 Blaine County, Montana, at age 43 (Margaret Doney Dills, 31 March 2003; Source: 2 June 1985 letter to Margarite Doney from Louise Trottier.) (MT Death.).

    Frank Azure was born on 13 Sep 1903 Lodge Pole, Blaine County, Montana (1936-LS, #46.) (1937-1987-LS Basic Roll, #46.). He died on 9 Nov 1959 Great Falls, Cascade County, Montana, at age 56 (Brenda Snider, 29 Sep 2014, Great Falls Tribune.).

xi. Joseph Edward Patrice Trottier was born on 10 Oct 1907 Saskatchewan (Margaret Doney Dills, 31 March 2003; Source: 2 June 1985 letter to Margarite Doney from Louise Trottier.) (SK Vital Statistics, Birth Reg. #7755.). He married Agnes Doney, daughter of Jean Baptiste Delauney or Donais or Doney and Elizabeth Allery, on 16 Jul 1928 Malta, Valley County, Montana (PhCM, #1035.).

    Agnes Doney was born on 16 Sep 1909 (1936-TMC, page 83.) (BIA-TM-BMD, page 27.). She and **Frederick Parenteau** met before 1932.

44. Rosalie Trottier was born on 25 May 1870 St.Francois Xavier, (Manitoba) (SFXI-Kipling, B-50.). She was baptized on 27 May 1870 St.Francois Xavier, (Manitoba) (Ibid.). She married **Salomon 'Sam' Pritchard**, son of **John Pritchard** and **Rose Delorme,** on 28 Jul 1890 St.Vital, Battleford, (Saskatchewan) (SV St.Vital Roman Catholic Registre des Baptemes, Mariages & Sepltures, Battleford, Saskatchewan, 1878-1896, page 86, M-8. Hereinafter cited as SV.). She died on 9 Sep 1942 at age 72 (Denney.).

    Salomon 'Sam' Pritchard was born on 31 Jan 1869 Rocky Mountain House, North West Territories (Ibid.). He died on 11 Oct 1967 Lloydminster, British Columbia, at age 98 (Ibid.).

45. Marie Anatalie Trottier was born on 3 Feb 1876 Saskatoon, (Saskatchewan) (L1, page 179, B-75.) (HBS, Volume 1339, C-14955.). She was baptized on 9 Feb 1876 Lebret, (Saskatchewan) (L1, page 179, B-75.). She married **Antoine Caplette**, son of **Antoine Caplette** and **Seraphine Houle,** on 13 Feb 1893 St.Ignace, Willow Bunch, (Saskatchewan) (SIWB, M-1, page 112.).

    Antoine Caplette was born on 10 Jun 1865 (1901 Canada, #204, y(2), page 5, family 44, line 15-18.).

46. Jean Baptiste Trottier was born on 3 Feb 1876 Saskatoon, (Saskatchewan) (L1, page 179, B-74.) (HBS, Volume 1339, C-14955.). He was baptized on 9 Feb 1876 Lebret, (Saskatchewan) (L1, page 179, B-74.). He married **Rosalie Lemire**, daughter of **Pierre Lemire** and **Sara Delorme,** before 1901. He died Willowfield (Denney.).

    Rosalie Lemire was born on 6 Jun 1884 Touchwood Hills, (Saskatchewan) (HBSI.) (ArchiviaNet.).

    Children of **Jean Baptiste Trottier** and **Rosalie Lemire** are as follows:

i. Patrice Trottier was born on 1 Jun 1902 (Saskatchewan) (1906 Canada, #12, 04, page 2, family 11, line 24-29.) (SK Vital Statistics, Birth Reg. #2668.).

ii. John Trottier was born circa 1903 (Saskatchewan) (1906 Canada, #12, 04, page 2, family 11, line 24-29.).

iii. Leon Trottier was born circa 1904 (Saskatchewan) (Ibid.).

iv. Andrew Trottier was born circa 1905 (Saskatchewan) (Ibid.).

v. Marie Flora Trottier was born on 22 Nov 1908 Saskatoon, Saskatchewan (SK Vital Statistics, Birth Reg. #9220.).

47. Ursule Trottier was born on 4 Feb 1877 Maple Creek, (Saskatchewan) (HBSI.) (L1, page 206, B-73.) (ArchiviaNet.). She was baptized on 5 Feb 1877 Lebret, (Saskatchewan) (L1, page 206, B-73.). She married **Leon Parenteau**, son of **Isidore Parenteau** and **Judith Plante,** on 23 Aug 1897 Havre, Chouteau County, Montana (1987-92LS.) (familysearch.org, Montana Marriages.). She died in May 1970 Harlem, Blaine County, Montana, at age 93 (Denney.).

    Leon Parenteau was born on 8 Nov 1876 (1936-LS, #17.) (1937-1987-LS Basic Roll, #17.). He was born in 1877 Buffalo Lake, (Alberta) (HBSI.) (ArchiviaNet.).

48. Andre Trottier was born in 1879 Maple Creek, (Saskatchewan) (HBSI.). He married **Rosalie Trottier**, daughter of **Norbert Trottier** and **Eliza Fisher,** before 1906. He died in 1967 Saskatoon, Saskatchewan (Denney.).

Rosalie Trottier was born circa 1888. She died on 12 Oct 1973 Glasslen, Saskatchewan (Lesa (Trotchie) Zimmerman Research, 19 Jun 2001.).

Children of **Andre Trottier** and **Rosalie Trottier** were as follows:

    i.   Edward Trottier was born on 20 Apr 1906 Swift Current, Saskatchewan (Ibid.). He married Marie Jeanne Whitford, daughter of Jean Marie Whitford and Marguerite McGillis, on 20 Jan 1926 Red Pheasant, Saskatchewan (Ibid.). He died on 10 Oct 1961 North Battleford, Saskatchewan, at age 55 (Ibid.).

        Marie Jeanne Whitford was born on 26 Sep 1910 Willow Bunch, Saskatchewan (Ibid.). She died on 28 Jun 1972 Saskatoon, Saskatchewan, at age 61 (Ibid.).

    ii. David Trottier was born on 20 Aug 1907 Hanley, Saskatchewan (SK Vital Statistics, Birth Reg. #7739.).

49. Napoleon "Paul" Trottier was born on 2 May 1880 St.Francois Xavier, Manitoba (SFXI-Kipling, B-29.) (ND Death Index.). He married **Bibiane Eulalie Slater**, daughter of **James Slater** and **Marie Zace,** before 1905. He died on 21 May 1942 Rolette County, North Dakota, at age 62 (Ibid.).

Bibiane Eulalie Slater was born on 25 May 1883 St.John, Rolette County, North Dakota (St.Claude BMD, Dominique Ritchot, page 10, B-50.). She was baptized on 26 May 1883 St.Claude, St.John, Rolette County, North Dakota (Ibid.).

Children of **Napoleon "Paul" Trottier** and **Bibiane Eulalie Slater** were as follows:

    i.   Regina Trottier was born circa 1905 North Dakota (1920C-ND 1920 Federal Census North Dakota, National Archives of the United States, Washington D.C., page 5B, family 64, line 66-74.).

    ii. Patrick Trottier was born on 15 Apr 1907 North Dakota (Ibid.) (ND Death Index.). He married Mary Agnes Patenaude, daughter of Samson Patenaude and Placidie Jeannotte, before 1928. He died on 15 Feb 1985 Rolette, North Dakota, at age 77 (Ibid.).

        Mary Agnes Patenaude was born on 5 Sep 1911 (1936-TMC, page 186.) (BIA-TM-BMD, page 51.) (*1937-TMC*, page 499, Census No. 5830-5834.).

    iii. Eugene Trottier was born circa 1909 North Dakota (1920C-MTl, page 5B, family 64, line 66-74.).

    iv. James Trottier was born on 12 Sep 1910 (Ibid.) (ND Death Index.). He married Mary Agnes Wilkie, daughter of John Baptiste Joseph Wilkie and Mary Jane Belgarde, before 1934 (*1937-TMC*, Census No. 5839-5841.). He died on 4 Feb 1985 Rolette, North Dakota, at age 74 (ND Death Index.).

        Mary Agnes Wilkie was born on 20 May 1909 (1936-TMC, page 130.) (BIA-TM-BMD, page 25.). She married **James Russell Turcotte**, son of **Daniel Turcotte** and **Marie Rosine Delaunay,** before 1934.

    v.   Joseph R. Trottier was born on 9 Aug 1911 North Dakota (1920C-MTl, page 5B, family 64, line 66-74.) (ND Death Index.). He died on 22 Oct 1956 Rolette County, North Dakota, at age 45 (Ibid.).

    vi. William Trottier was born on 6 Oct 1915 North Dakota (1920C-MTl, page 5B, family 64, line 66-74.) (ND Death Index.). He married Evelyn Wilkie, daughter of Frederick Wilkie and Rosine Vivier, circa 1938. He married Cecelia Genevieve Gladue, daughter of Joseph Gladue and Rose Ann Lefloe or Lafloe, on 26 Jun 1952 Devils Lake, Ramsey County, North Dakota (TM Star.). He died on 27 May 2011 Rolette County, North Dakota, at age 95 (ND Death Index.).

        Evelyn Wilkie was born on 14 Feb 1921 (*1937-TMC*, page 526, Census No. 6153-6159.). She died in Aug 1982 at age 61 (*St.Ann's Centennial*, page 546-547.).

        Cecelia Genevieve Gladue was born on 16 Aug 1921 (1936-TMC, page 97.) (*1937-TMC*, page 193, Census No. 2308-2311.). She died on 2 Jul 2002 Devils Lake, Ramsey County, North Dakota, at age 80 (SSDI.).

    vii. Alice Grace Trottier was born on 25 Jun 1918 (Ibid.). She married Ferdinand Demontigny, son of Ambroise Demontigny and Mary Jane Wilkie, before 1935 (Ibid.) (*1937-TMC*, page 142, Census No. 1698-1699.). She died on 2 Dec 2006 Dunseith, Rolette County, North Dakota, at age 88 (SSDI.).

        Ferdinand Demontigny was born on 13 Jul 1910 Rolette County, North Dakota (1936-TMC, page 81.) (BIA-TM-BMD, page 37.) (ND Death Index.). He died on 29 Oct 1985 Rolla, Rolette County, North Dakota, at age 75 (Ibid.) (SSDI.).

    viii. Clara Trottier was born on 22 Feb 1920 (Ibid.). She married Michael Short, son of Daniel Short and Sara Larocque, before 1935. She died on 10 Dec 1993 Anaconda, Deer Lodge County, Montana, at age 73 (Ibid.).

        Michael Short was born on 29 Nov 1907 North Dakota (1910C ND, Sheet 13A, family 103, line 9-14.) (SSDI.). He died in Feb 1974 Albany, Linn County, Oregon, at age 66 (Ibid.).

    ix. Martin Trottier was born on 21 Feb 1922 (1930C ND, page 4A.) (SSDI.). He married Sylvia Lafournaise, daughter of James Lafournaise and Ernestine Vivier, on 6 Sep 1950 Belcourt, Rolette County, North Dakota (Rod Mac Quarrie, 27 Mar 2013.). He died on 14 Dec 1998 Rolla, Rolette County, North Dakota, at age 76 (SSDI.) (ND Death Index.).

        Sylvia Lafournaise was born on 15 Apr 1932 (*1937-TMC*, page 271, Census No. 3281-3284.). She died on 8 Oct 2000 Belcourt, Rolette County, North Dakota, at age 68 (SSDI.).

    x.   Arthur Trottier was born on 2 Nov 1923 (1930C ND, page 4A.) (SSDI.). He died on 17 Mar 1996 Sacramento, Sacramento, California, at age 72 (Ibid.).

    xi. Violet Trottier was born circa 1927 (1930C ND, page 4A.).

50. Elise Trottier was born on 22 Apr 1885 St.John, Rolette County, North Dakota (St.Claude BMD, Dominique Ritchot, page 43, B-196.). She was baptized on 29 Apr 1885 St.Claude, St.John, Rolette County, North Dakota (Ibid.). She married **Jean Baptiste Slater**, son of **James Slater** and **Marie Zace,** circa 1902 (1910C ND, Sheet 28A, family 82, line 5-12.). She died on 27 Mar 1968 Rolette County, North Dakota, at age 82 (ND Death Index.).

Jean Baptiste Slater was born on 17 Jun 1881 (Denney.) (1910C ND, Sheet 28A, family 82, line 5-12.). He died on 1 Mar 1963 Rolette County, North Dakota, at age 81 (ND Death Index.).

51. Rosine Trottier was born on 20 Nov 1879 St.Francois Xavier, Manitoba (SFXI-Kipling, B-68.). She married **Joseph Vivier**, son of **Charles Vivier** and **Marguerite Parenteau,** before 1898.

Joseph Vivier was born on 30 Jun 1879 Manitoba (1881 Canada, C-13283, District 186, Sub-district L, page 25, Household 114.) (ND Death Index.). He died on 1 Jun 1940 Belcourt, Rolette County, North Dakota, at age 60 (Ibid.).

52. Joseph Vital Trottier was born on 11 Sep 1881 St.Francois Xavier, Manitoba (SFXI-Kipling, B-47.). He married **LaRose Belgarde**, daughter of **Jean Baptiste Belgarde** and **Marie Emily Hamelin,** before 1903 (1936-TMC, page 120.). He died on 19 May 1974 Rolette, North Dakota, at age 92 (ND Death Index.).

LaRose Belgarde was born in Dec 1886 North Dakota (1900C-ND, House 116, page 283A.). She died before 1920 (1921 Turtle Mountain Chippewa Indian Census Roll, United States Indian Service Department of the Interior, Turtle Mountain Indian Agency, North Dakota, 30 June 1921 , Census No. 3347-3352.).

Children of **Joseph Vital Trottier** and **LaRose Belgarde** all born North Dakota were as follows:

    i.   Mary Florestine Trottier was born on 28 Apr 1904 (1936-TMC, page 120.) (*1921 TMC*, Census No. 3347-3352.). She married Peter Jaqmaret, son of (--?--) Jaqmaret and Marie Julie McGillis, before 1926 (*1937-TMC*, page 235, Census No. 2832-2836.).

        Peter Jaqmaret was born on 7 Aug 1900 (*1909-TMC*, Census No. 1012-1020.).

    ii. Raphael Trottier was born on 15 Apr 1906 (1936-TMC, page 120.) (*1921 TMC*, Census No. 3347-3352.) (SSDI.). He married Marie Rose Ladouceur, daughter of Joseph Ladouceur and Clemence Charette, before 1930. He married Marie Olive Brunelle, daughter of Henry Ernest Brunelle and Betsy Delorme, before 1952. He died on 9 Oct 1969 Belcourt, Rolette County, North Dakota, at age 63 (Ibid.) (ND Death Index.).

        Marie Rose Ladouceur was born on 28 Feb 1913 Rolette County, North Dakota (Ancestry.com, 30 Jun 1919 Indian Census.).

        Marie Olive Brunelle was born on 20 Aug 1923 Rolette County, North Dakota (*1937-TMC*, page 88, Census No. 1006-1017.).

    iii. Patrice Trottier was born on 15 Apr 1908 (1936-TMC, page 120.) (*1932-TMC*, page 434, Census No. 5118-5120.) (*1921 TMC*, Census No. 3347-3352.) (*1937-TMC*, page 490, Census No. 5827-5829.). He married Delia Celina Brunelle, daughter of John Brunelle Jr. and Marie Claudia Petit, before 1937 (Ibid., page 499, Census No. 5827-5829.). He died on 2 Jan 1989 Rolette, North Dakota, at age 80 (ND Death Index.).

        Delia Celina Brunelle was born on 20 Jan 1911 Rolette County, North Dakota (1936-TMC, page 51.) (BIA-TM-BMD, page 44.) (*1919 Turtle Mountain*, Census No. 736-743.). She died on 9 May 1970 Rolette County, North Dakota, at age 59 (ND Death Index.).

    iv. Lillian Trottier was born on 17 May 1910 (1936-TMC, page 120.) (BIA-TM-BMD, page 36.). She married Louis Alphonse Leduc, son of Francis Leduc and Louise Belland, before 1937 (*1937-TMC*, page 319, Census No. 3870.).

        Louis Alphonse Leduc was born on 20 Apr 1905 (ND Death Index.). He died on 13 Dec 1979 Bottineau County, North Dakota, at age 74 (SSDI.) (ND Death Index.).

    v. John Baptiste Trottier was born on 6 Aug 1912 (1936-TMC, page 120.) (BIA-TM-BMD, page 61.) (*1932-TMC*, page 434, Census No. 5118-5120.) (*1921 TMC*, Census No. 3347-3352.). He married Blanche Martin, daughter of Frank Martin and Julia Caribou, on 24 Apr 1940 Devils Lake, Ramsey County, North Dakota (Rod Mac Quarrie, 27 Mar 2013.) (TM Star, 8 Sep 2008, page 3.). He died on 8 Jun 2005 Heartland Care Center, Devils Lake, Ramsey County, North Dakota, at age 92 (ND Death Index.) (SSDI.).

        Blanche Martin was born on 21 Jul 1917 Rolla, Rolette County, North Dakota (1920C-MTl, page 9A.) (TM Star, 8 Sep 2008, page 3.). She died on 2 Sep 2008 Devils Lake, Ramsey County, North Dakota, at age 91 (ND Death Index.).

    vi. Mary Trottier was born on 14 Mar 1915 (1936-TMC, page 120.) (*1921 TMC*, Census No. 3347-3352.). She died before 30 Jun 1921 North Dakota (Ibid.).

53. Virginie Trottier was born in May 1885 Duck Lake, (Saskatchewan) (ArchiviaNet, C-15007.). She married **William George Cunningham**, son of **James Cunningham** and **Mary Hodgson,** before 1906 Onion Lake, (Saskatchewan) (Denney.).

William George Cunningham was born on 28 May 1884 St.Albert, (Alberta) (1901 Canada, District 202-f(4), page 4, line 33.).

54. Florence Trottier was born on 25 Sep 1883 Maple Creek, (Saskatchewan) (BIA-LS.) (familysearch.org, Montana Marriages.). She married **John Jack Wallace**, son of **Francis Wallace** and **Madeleine Sauve,** on 25 Dec 1906 Havre, Chouteau County, Montana (BIA-LS.) (familysearch.org, Montana Marriages.). She died on 20 Feb 1961 Havre, Hill County, Montana, at age 77 (BIA-LS.) (Brenda Snider, 16 Feb 2011.).

John Jack Wallace was born on 2 Jan 1885 Prince Albert, (Saskatchewan) (BIA-LS.) (familysearch.org, Montana Marriages.). He died on 23 Mar 1959 Musselshell County, Montana, at age 74 (MT Death.).

55. Peter Trottier was born circa 1890 (Saskatchewan) (1906 Canada, page 56, line 21-28.). He married **Justine Landry**, daughter of **Moise Landry** and **Philomene Laframboise,** before 1908. He died circa 1965 Saskatoon, Saskatchewan (Brenda Snider, 16 Feb 2011.).

Justine Landry was born on 28 Feb 1885 Augusta, Lewis and Clark County, Montana (Denney.). She died on 28 Feb 1968 Saskatoon, Saskatchewan, at age 83 (Ibid.).

Children of **Peter Trottier** and **Justine Landry** were as follows:

    i.   Bob Trotchie.

    ii. Louise Trotchie.

    iii. Alexander Trottier was born on 23 Aug 1908 Dundurn, Saskatchewan (SK Vital Statistics, Birth Reg. #9186.).

    iv. Vi Trotchie was born on 6 Jan 1918 (Brenda Snider, 16 Feb 2011.).

    v. Clarence Trotchie was born on 14 Oct 1923 Round Prairie, Saskatchewan (Ibid.). He died on 10 Apr 1987 Saskatoon, Saskatchewan, at age 63 (Ibid.).

56. Rosalie Trottier was born circa 1888. She married **Andre Trottier**, son of **Jean Baptiste Trottier** and **Rose McGillis,** before 1906. She died on 12 Oct 1973 Glasslen, Saskatchewan (Lesa Zimmerman, 19 Jun 2001.).

Andre Trottier was born in 1879 Maple Creek, (Saskatchewan) (HBSI.). He died in 1967 Saskatoon, Saskatchewan (Denney.).

Children of **Rosalie Trottier** and **Andre Trottier** were as follows:

    i.   Edward Trottier was born on 20 Apr 1906 Swift Current, Saskatchewan (Lesa Zimmerman, 19 Jun 2001.). He married Marie Jeanne Whitford, daughter of Jean Marie Whitford and Marguerite McGillis, on 20 Jan 1926 Red Pheasant, Saskatchewan (Ibid.). He died on 10 Oct 1961 North Battleford, Saskatchewan, at age 55 (Ibid.).

        Marie Jeanne Whitford was born on 26 Sep 1910 Willow Bunch, Saskatchewan (Ibid.). She died on 28 Jun 1972 Saskatoon, Saskatchewan, at age 61 (Ibid.).

    ii.   David Trottier was born on 20 Aug 1907 Hanley, Saskatchewan (SK Vital Statistics, Birth Reg. #7739.).

57. Victoria B. Trottier was born on 15 Aug 1893 Fort Benton, Choteau County, Montana (SSDI.). She married **Clarence Brough**, son of **Alvin M. Brough** and **Sarah J. Stucker**, on 3 Apr 1914 Glasgow, Valley, Montana ((VCM Valley County Courthouse, Glasgow, Montana; Marriage Record Licenses, 1865-1950, familysearch.org: Volume 3, Hereinafter cited as VCM.). She and **Clarence Brough** obtained a marriage license on 3 Apr 1914 Valley County, Montana (Ibid.). She died in Jun 1986 Havre, Hill County, Montana, at age 92 (SSDI.) (MT Death.).

Clarence Brough was born on 19 Nov 1875 Port Washington. He died in 1959 Havre, Hill County, Montana.

58. Amelia Trottier was born on 30 May 1891 Havre, Hill County, Montana (1937-1987-LS Basic Roll, #274.). She was born in 1895 Montana (1910C MT Thirteenth Census of the United States: 1910; Montana, National Archives of the United States, Washington D.C., page 4B, family 43, line 83-92.). She married **Clark C. Hawley**, son of **Charles Hawley** and **C. A. Grant**, on 9 Feb 1915 Havre, Hill County, Montana (familysearch.org, Montana Marriages.).

Clark C. Hawley was born circa 1886 Fort Benton, Montana (Ibid.). He died before 1937.

59. Celina Trottier was born circa 1897 Havre, Hill County, Montana (1917 RB Tentative Roll of Rocky Boy Indians, 30 May 1917, Copied by Verne Dusenbery, 15 Apr 1953, Rocky Boy Agency, Montana, #306.) (familysearch.org, Montana Marriages.). She married **William John Lemire**, son of **Cuthbert Lemire** and **Marie Louise Swain**, on 19 Apr 1916 Havre, Hill County, Montana (1917 RB, #306.) (HCM.).

William John Lemire was born on 15 Jun 1891 Box Elder, Hill County, Montana.

60. Rose Trottier was born on 28 Jan 1899 Havre, Hill County, Montana (1937-1987-LS Basic Roll, #282.) (Ibid., #511.). She married **Thomas R. Hunter** on 16 Sep 1929 Hill County, Montana (1910C MT, page 4B, family 43, line 83-92.).

Thomas R. Hunter was born circa 1905 North Dakota.

61. John B. Trottier was born on 11 Jan 1901 Havre, Hill County, Montana (1936-LS, #512.) (1937-1987-LS Basic Roll, #512.). He married **Sarah Allery**, daughter of **Joseph Allary** and **Marguerite Hamelin**, on 17 Jul 1924 Hill County, Montana (HCM.). He died on 23 May 1973 Great Falls, Cascade County, Montana, at age 72 (MT Death.).

Sarah Allery was born in 1902 (1936-TMC, page 19.). She died on 25 Mar 1980 Cascade County, Montana (MT Death.).

Children of **John B. Trottier** and **Sarah Allery** were as follows:

    i.   John Julius "Jack" Trotchie was born on 27 Mar 1927 (1936-LS, #512.) (1937-1987-LS Basic Roll, #512.) (SSDI.). He died on 19 Mar 2005 Great Falls, Cascade, Montana, at age 77 (Ibid.).

    ii.   Lorraine Barbara Trotchie was born on 10 Nov 1929 (1936-LS, #512.) (1937-1987-LS Basic Roll, #512.). She married Kenneth Mee before 1987. She died on 11 Sep 2011 Great Falls, Cascade, Montana, at age 81 (SSDI.).

    iii.   Walter Trotchie was born on 2 Apr 1932 (1936-LS, #512.) (1937-1987-LS Basic Roll, #512.).

    iv.   Maxim Michael Trotchie was born on 5 Feb 1934 (1936-LS, #512.) (1937-1987-LS Basic Roll, #512.). He married Unknown (--?--) circa 1956. He married Eleanor Ramos, daughter of Narciso Ramos and Emma Daisy Lapierre, on 10 Mar 1972 Lethbridge, Alberta (Brenda Snider, 2 June 2006 email.).

        Eleanor Ramos was born on 16 Sep 1923 Sand Coulee, Cascade County, Montana (Ibid.). She married **(--?--) Wilson** circa 1942. She died on 19 Nov 2003 Great Falls, Cascade County, Montana, at age 80 (Ibid.) (SSDI.).

    v.   Laura Trotchie was born on 22 Aug 1936 (1936-LS, #512.) (1937-1987-LS Basic Roll, #512.). She married Joseph Marvin Rocheleau, son of Joseph Rocheleau and Ada O. Wells, before 1954 (Brenda Snider, 20 Oct 2014.).

        Joseph Marvin Rocheleau was born on 7 Oct 1932 Lewistown, Fergus County, Montana (Rod Mac Quarrie, 14 Aug 2012.). He died on 11 Oct 1971 Lewis & Clark County, Montana, at age 39 (MT Death.).

    vi.   Raymond Adolph Trotchie was born on 18 Nov 1938 (1900-1960 Cascade County, Montana School Census; Courthouse, Great Falls, Montana: Superintendent of Schools, Cascade County.). He died on 3 Jun 2012 Great Falls, Cascade, Montana, at age 73 (SSDI.).

    vii.   Larry E. Trotchie was born on 27 Sep 1941 (1900-60 SC Cascade Co, MT.).

62. Michel Trottier was born circa 1904 Montana (1920C-MT, Sheet 1A, family 6, line 31-39.). He married **Eugenia Hamelin**, daughter of **Louis Hamelin** and **Mathilde Laverdure**, on 17 Jul 1924 Hill County, Montana (familysearch.org, Montana Marriages.).

Eugenia Hamelin was born on 25 Nov 1904 Free Water, Montana (1937-1987-LS Basic Roll, #116.).

Children of **Michel Trottier** and **Eugenia Hamelin** are as follows:

    i.   Alice May Trotchie was born on 26 May 1926 (1936-LS, #89.) (1937-1987-LS Basic Roll, #116.).

    ii.   Marvin Trotchie was born on 4 Sep 1929 (1936-LS, #89.) (1937-1987-LS Basic Roll, #116.).

    iii.   Rita Trotchie was born on 26 Sep 1931 (1936-LS, #89.) (1937-1987-LS Basic Roll, #116.).

63. Louis Trottier was born on 13 Mar 1905 Montana (Ibid., #513.). He married **Helen Isabelle Huntley**, daughter of **Harold Fred Huntley** and **Marie Bonneau**, on 21 Jan 1925 Hill County, Montana (HCM.). He married **Mary Allery**, daughter of **Joseph Allary** and **Marguerite Hamelin**, in 1934 Havre, Hill County, Montana (Brenda Snider, 11 Apr 2014.). He died on 5 Oct 1971 Hill County, Montana, at age 66 (MT Death.) (SSDI.).

Helen Isabelle Huntley was born circa 1912 Montana (1920C-MT, page 16B, line 72.). She married **Elmer Francis Racette**, son of **Joseph Racette** and **Sarah Jane Jocko or Miron**, on 22 Oct 1944 Hill County, Montana (HCM.). She married **Howard Allen Sinclair**, son of **Jeremiah Sinclair** and **Eliza Racette**, on 5 Feb 1953 Conrad, Pondera County, Montana (PonCM Pondera County Courthouse, Montana; Marriage Record Licenses and Certificates; 1865-1950, familysearch.org, Hereinafter cited as PonCM.).

Children of **Louis Trottier** and **Helen Isabelle Huntley** are:

i. Viola Trotchie was born on 14 Mar 1929 Havre, Hill County, Montana (1937-1987-LS Basic Roll, #513.). She married James L. Staples before 1946 (1987-92LS.).

James L. Staples was born in 1919 (Ibid.).

Mary Allery was born on 29 Apr 1896 (1936-TMC, page 19.) (1925-TMC-ND 1925 Census of the Chippewa Indians of Turtle Mountain Agency, North Dakota, United States Indian Service Department of the Interior, Belcourt, North Dakota, superintendent H. J. McQuigg, 30 June 1925 , Census No. 249.) (SSDI.). She was born in Sep 1898 North Dakota (1900C-ND, House 132, page 285A.). She married **William Fanning** on 21 Feb 1918 Phillips County, Montana (PhCM.). She married **Edward Michael Lemire**, son of **Cuthbert Lemire** and **Marie Louise Swain,** on 15 Apr 1922 Hill County, Montana (HCM.) (Brenda Snider, 11 Apr 2014.). She died on 22 Jun 1981 Havre, Hill County, Montana, at age 85 (SSDI.) (Brenda Snider, 11 May 2014.).

64. Louise Trottier was born on 19 Jun 1908 Havre, Hill County, Montana (1936-LS, #381.) (1937-1987-LS Basic Roll, #391.). She married **Vance Victor Murphy**, son of **Jack Murphy** and **Emma Tegan,** on 9 Jun 1933 Chinook, Blaine County, Montana (1987-92LS.) (familysearch.org, Montana Marriages.). She died on 6 Mar 1948 Havre, Hill County, Montana, at age 39.

Vance Victor Murphy was born on 15 Apr 1912 Montana (SSDI.) (familysearch.org, Montana Marriages.). He married **Olive Katherine Christopherson**, daughter of **Andrew Christopherson** and **Johanna Hoem,** on 15 Jan 1947 Roosevelt County, Montana (Ibid.). He died on 9 Apr 2010 Havre, Montana, at age 97 (SSDI.).

65. George Andrew Trottier was born on 2 Dec 1905 Havre, Hill County, Montana (1936-LS, #510.) (1937-1987-LS Basic Roll, #510.) (SSDI.). He married **Mary Louise Briere**, daughter of **Gregoire Bruyere** and **Marie Alphonsine Allary,** on 2 Nov 1929 Chinook, Blaine County, Montana (BCM.). He died on 31 Dec 1996 Havre, Hill County, Montana, at age 91 (SSDI.) (MT Death.). He was buried on 3 Jan 1997 Kuper Memorial Cemetery.

Mary Louise Briere was born on 10 Apr 1911 (BIA-TM-BMD, page 61.) (*1923-TMC-ND*, Census No. 756-761.) (*1937-TMC*, page 497, Census No. 5807-5811.). She died in Nov 1982 Havre, Montana, at age 71 (SSDI.) (*HDN*, Nov 1982.).

Children of **George Andrew Trottier** and **Mary Louise Briere** were as follows:

i. Georgia Marie Trotchie married (--?--) Brunette.

ii. Patricia Jacqueline 'Jackie' Trotchie.

iii. Deanna Louise Trotchie.

iv. Jackie Trotchie.

v. Clara Rose Trotchie married (--?--) Anderson.

vi. Florence Mae Trotchie was born on 20 May 1928 Montana (1936-LS, #510.) (1937-1987-LS Basic Roll, #510.) (*1937-TMC*, page 497, Census No. 5807-5811.). She married Norman Alfred Mutchler, son of Jacob Alva Mutchler and Lela Grows, on 18 Mar 1947 Malta, Hill County, Montana (HCM.).

Norman Alfred Mutchler was born circa 1920 (familysearch.org, Montana Marriages.).

vii. Pauline Faye Trotchie was born on 17 Aug 1930 (1936-LS, #510.) (1937-1987-LS Basic Roll, #510.) (*1937-TMC*, page 497, Census No. 5807-5811.). She married (--?--) Fellows.

viii. Albert Trothier was born on 28 Apr 1933 (Ibid.). He died on 16 Apr 1936 at age 2 (Ibid.).

ix. Alice Faye Trotchie was born on 4 Jul 1936 (1936-LS, #510.) (1937-1987-LS Basic Roll, #510.) (*1937-TMC*, page 497, Census No. 5807-5811.).

x. Joseph Andrew Trotchie was born on 22 Jul 1939 Montana (familysearch.org, Montana Marriages.). He married Julie Beckert on 8 Oct 1958 Townsend, Broadwater County, Montana (Ibid.). He died on 6 Oct 2011 Missoula, Missoula, Montana, at age 72 (SSDI.).

Descendants of Mathew Truthwaite

Generation One

1. Mathew Truthwaite, son of John Truthwaite, was born circa 1753 Saint Marylebone, Middlesex, England (HBCA-B Hudson's Bay Company Archives - biographical sketches, Hudson's Bay Company Archives; Winnipeg, Manitoba.). He married according to the custom of the country **Elizabeth Indian** before 1790. He died on 18 Feb 1793 (Ibid., B.3/b/30 fos. 21d-22d.).

Elizabeth Indian was born circa 1770.

Children of **Mathew Truthwaite** and **Elizabeth Indian** were as follows:

2 i. Jacob Truthwaite, b. circa 1790 Ruperts Land; m. Elizabeth Vincent; d. 8 Jan 1873 St.Andrews, Manitoba; bur. 11 Jan 1873 St.Andrews, Manitoba.

ii. Edward Truthwaite was born before 1793.

3 iii. Mary Truthwaite, b. circa 1793; m. George Moore.

Generation Two

2. Jacob Truthwaite was born circa 1786 (HBCA-B.). He was born circa 1790 Ruperts Land (1830C RRS HBCA E5/4 1830 Census of the Red River Settlement, HBCA E5/4, Hudson's Bay Company Archives, Provincial Archives, 200 Vaughan Street, Winnipeg, MB R3C 1T5, Canada., page 14.) (1870C-MB 1870 Manitoba Census, National Archives of Canada, Ottawa, Ontario, Microfilm Reel Number C-2170., page 194, #543.). He was baptized on 12 Mar 1830 St.Johns, Red River Settlement, (Manitoba) (HBCR Hudson Bay Company Register of Anglican Church Baptisms, Marriages, and Burials for the Red River Settlement, 1821-1841; Hudson's Bay Company Archives, Winnipeg, Manitoba, E.4/1a, folio 75d. Hereinafter cited as HBCR.). He married according to the custom of the country **Elizabeth Vincent**, daughter of **Thomas Vincent** and **Jane Renton,** before 1816. He married **Elizabeth Vincent**, daughter of **Thomas Vincent** and **Jane Renton,** on 12 Mar 1830 Red River Settlement, (Manitoba) (Ibid., M-196.) (HBCA-B, E.4/1a fo. 75d; E.4/1b, fo. 227.). He died on 8 Jan 1873 St.Andrews, Manitoba (MBS Scrip Applications, Original White Settlers & Halfbreeds residing in Manitoba on 15 July 1870, RG15-19, C-14934.). He was buried on 11 Jan 1873 St.Andrews, Manitoba (Ibid.).

Elizabeth Vincent was born in 1802 (Ibid.). She was baptized on 17 Sep 1809 Albany (HBCA-B, B.3/a/112; MS311 #2, MS 161, Ontario Archives; A.36/14; A.44/2, p. 57.). She was baptized on 12 Mar 1830 St.Johns, Red River Settlement, (Manitoba) (HBCR,

E.4/1a, folio 75d.). She died on 6 Jul 1875 St.Andrews, Manitoba (MBS, C-14934.). She was buried on 8 Jul 1875 St.Andrews, Manitoba (Denney Papers, Charles D. Denney, Glenbow Archives, Calgary, Alberta.).

Children of **Jacob Truthwaite** and **Elizabeth Vincent** were as follows:

4   i.   Jane Truthwaite, b. circa 1816; m. James Anderson; d. 1843.

5   ii.   Isabella Truthwaite, b. circa 1818; m. John Norquay; d. 18 Oct 1843.

6   iii.   Thomas Truthwaite Sr, b. 18 Mar 1820 Albany; m. Catherine McDermott; d. 13 Jul 1899 St.Andrews, Manitoba.

7   iv.   Elizabeth Truthwaite, b. 1825 North West; m. James Richards; d. Jan 1875 St.Andrews, Manitoba.

8   v.   Mary Truthwaite, b. 12 Mar 1830 St.Johns, Red River Settlement, (Manitoba); m. Thomas Mowat.

   vi.   Harriet Truthwaite was born on 31 Jan 1831 St.Johns, Red River Settlement, (Manitoba) (HBCA-B, E.4/1a fo. 82.) (HBCR, E.4/1a, folio 82.).

9   vii.   Sarah Truthwaite, b. 20 Dec 1833 St.Johns, Red River Settlement, (Manitoba); m. William Pruden; d. 8 Apr 1900 Selkirk, Manitoba.

10   viii.   Nancy "Ann" Truthwaite, b. 17 Jan 1839 St.James, (Manitoba); m. Andrew McDermott; d. 11 Dec 1896 St.James, Manitoba.

3. Mary Truthwaite was born circa 1793. She was born in 1800 North West (MBS, C-14931.). She was born circa 1810 Ruperts Land (1870C-MB, page 190, #406.). She married **George Moore** before 1818.

George Moore died before 1870.

Generation Three

4. Jane Truthwaite was born circa 1816 (Denney.). She was baptized on 12 Mar 1830 St.Johns, Red River Settlement, (Manitoba) (HBCA-B, E.4/1a fo. 75d.) (HBCR, E.4/1a, folio 75d.). She married **James Anderson**, son of **James Anderson** and **Mary Saulteaux**, on 21 Feb 1832 St.Johns, Red River Settlement, (Manitoba) (Ibid., M-234.). She died in 1843 (Denney.).

James Anderson was born in 1808 North West Territory (MBS, C-14925.). He was baptized on 23 Jan 1821 Brandon House (HBCA-B, E.4/1a fo. 29d #46.) (HBCR, E.4/1a folio 29d.). He married **Harriet Smith**, daughter of **John James Smith** and **Mary Indian**, on 31 Aug 1844 (St.Andrews), Grand Rapids, (Manitoba) (Ibid., page 91, No. 128.). He died on 19 Jan 1896 R.M. of St.Andrews, Manitoba (MB Vital Statistics, Death Reg. #1896,002666.).

5. Isabella Truthwaite was born circa 1818. She was baptized on 12 Mar 1830 St.Johns, Red River Settlement, (Manitoba) (HBCA-B, E.4/1a fo. 75d.) (HBCR, E.4/1a, folio 75d.). She married **John Norquay**, son of **Oman Norquay** and **Jane Morwick**, on 21 Feb 1832 St.Johns, Red River Settlement, (Manitoba) (Ibid., M-235.) (HBCA-B, E.4/1b fo. 234.). She died on 18 Oct 1843 (Ibid., E.4/2 fo. 131d.).

John Norquay was born circa 1810 Ruperts Land (1832C RRS HBCA E5/6 1832 Census of the Red River Settlement, HBCA E5/6, Hudson's Bay Company Archives, Provincial Archives, 200 Vaughan Street, Winnipeg, MB R3C 1T5, Canada., page 14.). He was baptized on 17 Jun 1822 St.Johns, Red River Colony, (Manitoba) (HBCR, E.4/1a, folio 28.) (HBCA-B.). He married **Nancy Ward**, daughter of **John Ward** and **Angelique Bruyere**, on 9 Oct 1845 (St.Andrews), Rapids Church, (Manitoba) (Ibid.) (HBCR, No. 142.). He died in Jun 1849 St.Johns, (Manitoba) (Denney.) (HBCA-B.). He was buried on 10 Jun 1849 St.Johns, (Manitoba) (Ibid., E.4/2 fo. 158.).

6. Thomas Truthwaite Sr was born on 18 Mar 1820 Albany (Denney.). He was baptized on 12 Mar 1830 St.Johns, Red River Settlement, (Manitoba) (HBCA-B, E.4/1a fo. 75d.) (HBCR, E.4/1a, folio 75d.). He married **Catherine McDermott**, daughter of **Andrew McDermott** and **Sarah McNab**, on 18 Dec 1845 (St.Johns), Upper Church, (Manitoba) (HBCA-B, HBCA reference E4/2, fo. 157d.) (HBCR.). He died on 13 Jul 1899 St.Andrews, Manitoba, at age 79 (MB Vital Statistics, Death Reg. #1899,002820.).

Catherine McDermott was born on 10 Jun 1827 St.Johns, (Manitoba) (MBS, C-14934.) (Automated Genealogy 1901 Census Transcription Project and Census Images from the National Archives of Canada, http://www.automatedgenealogy.com, Family 35, Line 15-22, page 4.). She died on 13 Sep 1907 St.Andrews, Manitoba, at age 80 (Denney.).

Children of **Thomas Truthwaite Sr.** and **Catherine McDermott** all born St.Andrews, (Manitoba), were as follows:

11   i.   Thomas Truthwaite Jr, b. 27 Jul 1847; m. Cecile Robert; m. Caroline Pruden; d. 3 Sep 1876.

12   ii.   Andrew Truthwaite, b. 20 Sep 1849; m. Hannah McDonald; d. 5 Jul 1936.

13   iii.   Sarah Ann Elizabeth Truthwaite, b. 5 May 1851; m. Charles A. Spencer; m. John MacDougall.

   iv.   Jane Mary Truthwaite was born on 14 Jun 1853 (1901 Canada, Family 35, Line 15-22, page 4.). She was baptized on 4 Jul 1853 St.Andrews, (Manitoba) (MBS, C-14934.). She died on 18 Nov 1934 R.M. of St.Andrews, Manitoba, at age 81 (MB Vital Statistics, Death Reg. #1934,044405.).

14   v.   Jacob Truthwaite, b. 27 Jul 1855; m. Jane (--?--); m. Sarah Swanson McDonald; d. 7 Jan 1940.

15   vi.   Harriet Marie Truthwaite, b. 12 Jan 1858; m. Thomas Sinclair; m. Malcolm Ross; d. 27 Jan 1949.

   vii.   Alexander Truthwaite was baptized on 12 Dec 1861 (Denney.). He died on 16 Oct 1864 St.Andrews, (Manitoba), at age 2.

7. Elizabeth Truthwaite was born in 1825 North West (MBS, C-14932.). She was baptized on 12 Mar 1830 St.Johns, Red River Settlement, (Manitoba) (HBCA-B, E.4/1a fo. 75d.) (HBCR, E.4/1a, folio 75d.). She married **James Richards**, son of **Jean Baptiste Richards** and **Margaret (--?--)**, on 6 Feb 1845 (St.Andrews), Grand Rapids, (Manitoba) (Ibid., No. 139.). She died in Jan 1875 St.Andrews, Manitoba (MBS, C-14932.).

James Richards was born circa 1820 (Denney.). He died on 4 Jan 1870 St.Andrews, (Manitoba) (Ibid.).

8. Mary Truthwaite was baptized on 12 Mar 1830 St.Johns, Red River Settlement, (Manitoba) (HBCA-B, E.4/1a fo. 75d.) (HBCR, E.4/1a, folio 75d.). She married **Thomas Mowat**, son of **Edward Mowat** and **Margaret Indian**, on 6 Feb 1845 (St.Andrews), Grand Rapids, (Manitoba) (Ibid., No. 138.).

Thomas Mowat was born in 1821 Nelson River, Ruperts Land (MBS, C-14931.). He was baptized on 19 Apr 1834 (St.Andrews), Rapids of Red River, (Manitoba) (HBCA-B.) (HBCR, E.4/1a, folio 114.).

9. Sarah Truthwaite was baptized on 20 Dec 1833 St.Johns, Red River Settlement, (Manitoba) (HBCA-B, E.4/1a fo. 106.) (HBCR, E.4/1a, folio 106.). She was born on 22 Nov 1835 St.Andrews, (Manitoba) (MBS, C-14932.). She married **William Pruden**, son of

Peter Pruden and **Josephte Jolicoeur**, on 29 Mar 1854 St.Andrews, (Manitoba) (Denney.). She died on 8 Apr 1900 Selkirk, Manitoba, at age 66 (MB Vital Statistics, Death Reg. #1900,003648.).

William Pruden was born on 14 Jan 1833 Fort Mackenzie (Denney.). He was baptized on 7 Jul 1836 (St.Andrews), Rapids of Red River, (Manitoba) (HBCR, E.4/1a, folio 129d.). He married **Mary Hart** on 2 Jul 1908 Selkirk, Selkirk, Manitoba (MB Vital Statistics, Marriage Reg. #1908,001111.). He died on 16 May 1914 Selkirk, Manitoba, at age 81 (Ibid., Death Reg. #1914,097061.). He was buried in May 1917 St.Clements, Manitoba.

10. **Nancy "Ann" Truthwaite** was born on 17 Jan 1839 St.James, (Manitoba) (MBS, C-14930.). She was baptized on 26 Feb 1839 St.Johns, Red River Settlement, (Manitoba) (HBCA-B, E.4/1a fo. 129d.) (HBCR, E.4/1a, folio 159d.). She married **Andrew McDermott**, son of **Andrew McDermott** and **Sarah McNab**, on 6 Apr 1860 St.Andrews, (Manitoba) (Denney.). She died on 11 Dec 1896 St.James, Manitoba, at age 57 (St.James Anglican Cemetery; Cemetery Transcription #121; Mavis and Maureen Smith, Unit "E," 1045 St.James Street, Winnipeg, Manitoba, Canada R3H 1B1: Manitoba Genealogical Society, Inc., 1983, page 45.).

Andrew McDermott was born on 10 Aug 1838 St.Johns, (Manitoba) (MBS, C-14930.) (1901 Canada, #11, A-1, page 4, Family 26, Line 3-8.). He died on 27 Dec 1908 Assiniboia, Manitoba, at age 70 (MGS: St.James Cemetery, page 45.) (MB Vital Statistics, Death Reg. #1908,003878 (Winnipeg).) (Ibid., Death Reg. #1908,004137 (Assiniboia).).

Generation Four

11. **Thomas Truthwaite Jr** was born on 27 Jul 1847 St.Andrews, (Manitoba) (Denney.). He was baptized on 17 Oct 1847 St.Johns, (Manitoba) (Ibid.). He and **Cecile Robert** met before 1868. He married **Caroline Pruden**, daughter of **John Peter Pruden** and **Sarah Ross,** on 25 Jun 1874 St.Andrews, Manitoba (Ibid.). He died on 3 Sep 1876 at age 29.

Cecile Robert was born circa 1846 (Manitoba) (1870C-MB, page 170, #477.).

Children of **Thomas Truthwaite Jr.** and **Cecile Robert** were:

    i.   Margaret Truthwaite was born circa 1868 (Manitoba) (Ibid., page 170, #478.). She married John Macdougall in 1888 (Denney.). She died on 28 Aug 1915 St.Andrews, Manitoba (Ibid.).

Caroline Pruden was born on 27 Dec 1853 St.Andrews, (Manitoba) (MBS, C-14934.). She was baptized on 24 Jan 1854 St.Andrews, (Manitoba) (Denney.). She died on 30 Nov 1924 St.Andrews, Manitoba, at age 70 (MB Vital Statistics, Death Reg. #1924,044399.).

Children of **Thomas Truthwaite Jr.** and **Caroline Pruden** were:

    i.   John Thomas Truthwaite was born circa Sep 1875. He died on 21 May 1876 St.Andrews, Manitoba.

12. **Andrew Truthwaite** was born on 20 Sep 1849 St.Andrews, (Manitoba) (MBS, C-14934.). He was baptized on 19 Oct 1849 St.Andrews, (Manitoba) (Denney.). He married **Hannah McDonald**, daughter of **Duncan McDonald** and **Elizabeth Tait,** before 1878. He died on 5 Jul 1936 St.Andrews, Manitoba, at age 86 (MB Vital Statistics, Death Reg. #1936,036447.).

Hannah McDonald was born on 18 Apr 1858 St.Andrews, (Manitoba) (Denney.). She was baptized on 18 Apr 1858 St.Andrews, (Manitoba) (Ibid.). She died on 16 Apr 1935 R.M. of St.Andrews, Manitoba, at age 76 (MB Vital Statistics, Death Reg. #1935,016432.).

Children of **Andrew Truthwaite** and **Hannah McDonald** were as follows:

    i.   Florence M. Truthwaite was born on 23 Mar 1878 St.Andrews, Manitoba (1901 Canada, #11, 1-7, page 9, family 79, line 1-12.).

    ii.   Andrew T. Truthwaite was born on 31 Jan 1880 St.Andrews, Manitoba (Ibid.).

    iii.   Catherine R. Truthwaite was born on 3 Oct 1881 St.Andrews, Manitoba (Ibid.).

  16 iv.   Alfred Truthwaite, b. 21 Jul 1883 R.M. of St.Andrews, Manitoba; m. Matilda Ann Harriott; d. 2 Aug 1930.

  17 v.   Charles William Truthwaite, b. 28 Mar 1887 R.M. of St.Andrews, Manitoba; m. Mabel Harriet Campbell; d. 18 Jan 1949 Cloverdale, Manitoba.

    vi.   Alexander Truthwaite was born on 9 Sep 1889 St.Andrews, Manitoba (Ibid.).

    vii.   Jessie Truthwaite was born on 21 Jan 1892 R.M. of Springfield, Manitoba (Ibid.) (MB Vital Statistics, Birth Reg. #1892,006075.).

    viii.   Alice Truthwaite was born on 4 Oct 1894 R.M. of St.Andrews, Manitoba (1901 Canada, #11, 1-7, page 9, family 79, line 1-12.) (MB Vital Statistics, Birth Reg. #1894,004798.).

    ix.   Victor Henry Truthwaite was born on 24 May 1897 R.M. of St.Andrews, Manitoba (1901 Canada, #11, 1-7, page 9, family 79, line 1-12.) (MB Vital Statistics, Birth Reg. #1897,001215.).

    x.   Myles McDermot Truthwaite was born on 21 Jul 1900 St.Andrews, Manitoba (1901 Canada, #11, 1-7, page 9, family 79, line 1-12.) (MB Vital Statistics, Birth Reg. #1900,005624.).

    xi.   John Harold Truthwaite was born on 30 Jan 1903 R.M. of St.Andrews, Manitoba (Ibid., Birth Reg. #1903,008050.).

13. **Sarah Ann Elizabeth Truthwaite** was born on 5 May 1851 St.Andrews, (Manitoba) (1901 Canada, Family 33, Line 1-11, page 4.). She married **Charles A. Spencer**, son of **John Hodges Spencer** and **Anne Sinclair**, on 17 Feb 1871 St.Johns, Manitoba (Denney.). She married **John MacDougall** in 1874 (Ibid.).

Charles A. Spencer was born circa 1845 (Manitoba) (1870C-MB, page 199, #686.). He died on 30 Jun 1872 St.Andrews, Manitoba (Denney.).

John MacDougall was born on 2 Feb 1846 Scotland (1901 Canada, Family 33, Line 1-11, page 4.).

14. **Jacob Truthwaite** was born on 27 Jul 1855 St.Andrews, (Manitoba) (MBS, C-14934.). He was baptized on 26 Aug 1855 St.Andrews, (Manitoba) (Denney.). He married **Jane (--?--)** before 1878 (1881 Canada, District 185-C-1, page 22, house 104.). He married **Sarah Swanson McDonald**, daughter of **Duncan McDonald** and **Elizabeth Tait**, on 29 Jul 1884 St.Andrews, Manitoba (MB Vital Statistics, Marriage Reg. #1884,001414.). He died on 7 Jan 1940 RM Fisher Branch, Manitoba, at age 84 (Ibid., Death Reg. #1940,004354.).

Jane (--?--) was born circa 1857 (1881 Canada, District 185-C-1, page 22, house 104.).

Children of **Jacob Truthwaite** and **Jane (--?--)** were as follows:

  18 i.   Catherine Ann Truthwaite, b. 7 May 1877; m. Samuel L. Vincent; d. 6 May 1943.

    ii.   Sarah Jane Truthwaite was born circa 1879 (Ibid.).

Sarah Swanson McDonald was born on 11 May 1863 St.Andrews, (Manitoba) (Denney.). She was baptized on 11 May 1863 St.Andrews, (Manitoba) (Ibid.).

Children of **Jacob Truthwaite** and **Sarah Swanson McDonald** were as follows:

 i. Elizabeth Truthwaite was born circa Feb 1885 (MB Vital Statistics, Death Reg. #1886,001386.). She died on 8 Sep 1886 St.Andrews, Manitoba (Ibid.).

 ii. Duncan Truthwaite was born on 19 Jun 1887 R.M. of St.Andrews, Manitoba (1901 Canada, Family 36, Line 23-30, page 4.) (MB Vital Statistics, Birth Reg. #1887,001824.). He married Marie Rosalie Houde, daughter of Hercule Celestin Houde and Philomene Morissette, after 1901 (Rosemary Helga (Morrissette) Rozyk Research, 1 Nov 2006.).

  Marie Rosalie Houde was born on 8 Jun 1893 R.M. of Dufferin, Manitoba (SFXI-Kipling St.Francois Xavier Register Index, 1834-1900; compiled by Clarence Kipling , B-8.) (MB Vital Statistics, Birth Reg. #1894,006426.). She was baptized on 12 Apr 1894 St.Francois Xavier, Manitoba (SFXI-Kipling, B-8.) (Rosemary Rozyk, 11 Nov 2006.). She married **Jean Pierre Ouellette** on 17 Feb 1919 Sacre-Coeur, Winnipeg, Manitoba (SFXI-Kipling, B-8 (note).) (Rosemary Rozyk, 11 Nov 2006.).

 iii. Unnamed Truthwaite was born on 24 May 1889 R.M. of St.Andrews, Manitoba (MB Vital Statistics, Birth Reg. #1889,005306.).

 iv. Thomas Truthwaite was born on 23 Aug 1890 Little Britain, Manitoba (Ibid., Birth Reg. #1890,19414195, Reg. Date: 17/11/1955.).

 v. Horace Truthwaite was born on 7 Mar 1893 R.M. of St.Andrews, Manitoba (1901 Canada, Family 36, Line 23-30, page 4.) (MB Vital Statistics, Birth Reg. #1893,005127.).

 vi. Mary Truthwaite was born on 3 Jul 1895 R.M. of St.Andrews, Manitoba (1901 Canada, Family 36, Line 23-30, page 4.) (MB Vital Statistics, Birth Reg. #1895,001116.).

 vii. Hector Henry Truthwaite was born on 19 Dec 1897 R.M. of St.Andrews, Manitoba (1901 Canada, Family 36, Line 23-30, page 4.) (MB Vital Statistics, Birth Reg. #1898,003505.).

 viii. Elizabeth Truthwaite was born on 31 Jul 1900 R.M. of St.Andrews, Manitoba (1901 Canada, Family 36, Line 23-30, page 4.) (MB Vital Statistics, Birth Reg. #1900,005625.).

 ix. Jacob Truthwaite was born on 30 Sep 1902 R.M. of St.Andrews, Manitoba (Ibid., Birth Reg. #1902,007954.).

15. **Harriet Marie Truthwaite** was born on 12 Jan 1858 St.Andrews, (Manitoba) (Denney.). She was baptized on 17 Jan 1858 St.Andrews, (Manitoba) (Ibid.). She married **Thomas Sinclair**, son of **Thomas Sinclair** and **Hannah Cummings**, on 5 Apr 1882 St.Andrews, Manitoba (MB Vital Statistics, Marriage Reg. #1882,001456.). She married **Malcolm Ross**, son of **George Ross** and **Catherine Berland**, on 26 Jan 1898 St.Andrews, Manitoba (Ibid., Marriage Reg. #1898,002416.). She died on 27 Jan 1949 at age 91 (Denney.).

Thomas Sinclair was born on 9 Apr 1841 St.Andrews, (Manitoba) (MBS, C-14934.). He was baptized on 10 May 1841 St.Johns, Red River Settlement, (Manitoba) (HBCR, E.4/1a, folio 173.). He married **Alice Mathilda Davis**, daughter of **George Davis** and **Catherine Birston**, on 30 Sep 1875 St.Andrews, Manitoba (Denney.). He died on 8 Mar 1888 Selkirk, Manitoba, at age 46 (MB Vital Statistics, Death Reg. #1888,001283.).

Malcolm Ross was born on 30 Jan 1847 St.Andrews, (Manitoba) (MBS, Supplementary Returns; C-14934.) (1901 Canada, District 11-8-3, page 18, family 179, line 33-37.). He was baptized on 20 Feb 1847 St.Andrews, (Manitoba) (MBS, Supplementary Returns; C-14934.). He married **Jane Anderson**, daughter of **Thomas Anderson** and **Louisa Cooper,** on 24 Mar 1881 St.Andrews, Manitoba (Denney.). He died on 3 Feb 1909 Springfield, Manitoba, at age 62 (MB Vital Statistics, Death Reg. #1909,005008.).

Generation Five

16. **Alfred Truthwaite** was born on 21 Jul 1883 R.M. of St.Andrews, Manitoba (Ibid., #11, 1-7, page 9, family 79, line 1-12.) (MB Vital Statistics, Birth Reg. #1883,004411.). He married **Matilda Ann Harriott**, daughter of **John Edward Harriott** and **Jane Taylor,** on 30 Oct 1912 St.Andrews, Manitoba (Ibid., Marriage Reg. #1912,004722.). He died on 2 Aug 1930 at age 47.

Matilda Ann Harriott was born on 4 Mar 1889 R.M. of St.Andrews, Manitoba (1901 Canada, #11, 1-6, page 3, family 18, line 3-14.) (MB Vital Statistics, Birth Reg. #1889,005297.). She died on 14 Nov 1918 St.Andrews, Manitoba, at age 29 (Ibid., Death Reg. #1918,066349.).

Children of **Alfred Truthwaite** and **Matilda Ann Harriott** are:

 i. Irene Truthwaite was born circa 1915 (1916 Census of Canada from the National Archives of Canada (Transcription by ancestry.com), Ottawa, Canada, District 10-2, page 16, line 17.).

17. **Charles William Truthwaite** was born on 28 Mar 1887 R.M. of St.Andrews, Manitoba (1901 Canada, #11, 1-7, page 9, family 79, line 1-12.) (MB Vital Statistics, Birth Reg. #1887,004075.). He married **Mabel Harriet Campbell**, daughter of **Malcolm John Campbell** and **Anna Maria Harriott**, on 28 Jan 1914 St.Andrews, Manitoba (Ibid., Marriage Reg. #1914,077158.). He died on 18 Jan 1949 Cloverdale, Manitoba, at age 61 (*Free Press*, Friday, January 21, 1949, page 6.) (Ibid., Saturday, January 22, 1949, page 28.).

Mabel Harriet Campbell was born on 19 Dec 1888 R.M. of St.Andrews, Manitoba (MB Vital Statistics, Birth Reg. #1889,005279.) (Ibid., Marriage Reg. #1914,077158.). She died on 18 Jan 1940 Selkirk, Manitoba, at age 51 (Ibid., Death Reg. #1940,004294.).

Children of **Charles William Truthwaite** and **Mabel Harriet Campbell** were as follows:

 i. Malcolm Allan Truthwaite was born on 15 Sep 1914 R.M. of St.Andrews, Manitoba (Ibid., Birth Reg. #1914,124762.).

 ii. Helen Marie Truthwaite was born on 13 Apr 1916. She died on 29 Mar 2005 Betel Home, Selkirk, Manitoba, at age 88.

 iii. Charles Harry Truthwaite was born in 1918 (Ibid., Death Reg. #1923,028388.). He died on 12 Jul 1923 St.Andrews, Manitoba (Ibid.).

18. **Catherine Ann Truthwaite** was born on 7 May 1877 (1901 Canada, Family 35, Line 15-22, page 4.). She married **Samuel L. Vincent**, son of **William Thomas Vincent** and **Catherine Ross,** on 10 Jul 1907 St.Andrews, Manitoba (MB Vital Statistics, Marriage Reg. #1907,002585.). She died on 6 May 1943 at age 65 (Denney.).

Samuel L. Vincent was born on 15 May 1881 (Ibid.). He died on 31 Jan 1944 Winnipeg, Manitoba, at age 62 (MB Vital Statistics, Death Reg. #1944,008090.).

Ahnentafel between Vital Turcotte and Francois Turcot

--- 1st Generation ---

1. VITAL TURCOTTE was born circa 1818 at North West (1870C-MB 1870 Manitoba Census, National Archives of Canada, Ottawa, Ontario, Microfilm Reel Number C-2170., #1, St.Boniface; page 1.). He was baptized on 21 Apr 1832 at St.Boniface, (Manitoba) (SB 1825-1834 St.Boniface Roman Catholic Registre des Baptemes, Mariages & Sepultures, 1825-1834, page 60, B-423. Hereinafter cited as SB 1825-1834.). He married **MADELEINE CAPLETTE**, daughter of **JOSEPH CAPLETTE** and **ANGELIQUE GUIBOCHE**, before 1837. He married **MARGUERITE HAMEL** before 1872. He died on 1 Jan 1882 at St.Francois Xavier, Manitoba (SFXI-Kipling St.Francois Xavier Register Index, 1834-1900; compiled by Clarence Kipling , S-1.).

--- 2nd Generation ---

2. JEAN BAPTISTE TURCOTTE (PRDH online index, http://www.genealogic.umontreal.ca, #44908.) (Ibid.) was born on 8 Apr 1774 at St-Cuthbert, Quebec (Ibid., No. 489944.). He was baptized on 9 Apr 1774 at St-Cuthbert, Quebec (Ibid.) (Rod MacQuarrie Research, 26 Oct 2012.). He was born circa 1775 at Quebec (1829C RRS HBCA E5/3 1829 Census of the Red River Settlement, HBCA E5/3, Hudson's Bay Company Archives, Provincial Archives, 200 Vaughan Street, Winnipeg, MB R3C 1T5, Canada., page 13.). He was born circa 1784 at Quebec (1840C RRS HBCA E5/10 1840 Census of the Red River Settlement, HBCA E5/10, Hudson's Bay Company Archives, Provincial Archives, 200 Vaughan Street, Winnipeg, MB R3C 1T5, Canada., page 27.). He was contracted as a voyageur in 1804 at Fort des Prairies *1804 NWCo voyageur-contre-maitre at Fort des Prairies, after fusion of 1804 (Masson, Les Bourgeois, p. 397* (Rod Mac Quarrie, 26 Oct 2012.). He married **SUSANNE DUBEY (METISSE)** circa 1818.

--- 3rd Generation ---

4. JEAN BAPTISTE TURCOT (PRDH online, #44908.) (Ibid., No. 103106.) (Ibid.) was born on 26 Oct 1743 at L'Ile-Dupas, Quebec (Ibid.). He was baptized on 26 Oct 1743 at L'Ile-Dupas, Quebec (Ibid.). He married **MARIE PELAGIE GRIGNON DIT DUCHICOT**, daughter of **PIERRE GRIGNON DIT DUCHICOT** and **JOSEPHE-MARGUERITE CHEVALIER**, on 11 Nov 1768 at Berthier-en-Haut, Quebec (Ibid., #44908.). He married **MARIE LOUISE MINIER DIT LAGACE**, daughter of **CHARLES MINIER DIT LAGACE** and **MARIE-LOUISE DUCROS**, on 22 Apr 1793 at St-Cuthbert, Quebec (Ibid., #190149.). He died on 30 Aug 1832 at St-Cuthbert, Quebec, at age 88 (Ibid., #117365.). He was buried on 31 Aug 1832 at St-Cuthbert, Quebec (Ibid.).

--- 4th Generation ---

8. ALEXIS TURCOT (Ibid., No. 103106.) (Ibid., #117309.) (Ibid.) was born on 6 May 1713 at Sorel, Richelieu, Quebec (Ibid.) (DGFQ Jette, Rene, *Dictionnaire Genealogique des Familles du Quebec des Origines a 1730* (Montreal, Quebec, Canada: University of Montreal Press, 1983), page 1100.). He was baptized on 10 May 1713 at Sorel, Quebec (PRDH online, #117309.) (DGFQ, page 1100.). A contract for the marriage to **MARIE-MADELEINE DUTEAU**, daughter of **JACQUES DUTEAU** and **MARGUERITE DUCLOS**, was signed on 20 Feb 1740. He died on 16 Oct 1802 at St-Cuthbert, Quebec, at age 89 (PRDH online, #117309.). He was buried on 18 Oct 1802 at St-Cuthbert, Quebec (Ibid.).

--- 5th Generation ---

16. ALEXIS TURCOT (Ibid.) (Ibid., #10358.) (DGFQ, page 1099.) (PRDH online, #10358.) (DGFQ, page 1099.) was born on 21 Mar 1682 at Champlain, Quebec (Ibid.). He was baptized on 24 Mar 1682 at Champlain, Quebec (Ibid.). A contract for the marriage to **MARIE-MADELEINE DUBORD DIT FONTAINE**, daughter of **JULIEN OR GUILLIAN DUBORD DIT LAFONTAINE** and **CATHERINE GUERARD**, was signed on 7 Jan 1709 (Ibid., page 1100.). He married **MARIE-MADELEINE DUBORD DIT FONTAINE**, daughter of **JULIEN OR GUILLIAN DUBORD DIT LAFONTAINE** and **CATHERINE GUERARD**, on 12 Jan 1709 at Champlain, Quebec (PRDH online, #10358.) (DGFQ, page 1100.). He was buried on 4 Apr 1731 at Berthierville, Quebec (PRDH online, #71423.).

--- 6th Generation ---

32. JACQUES TURCOT (DGFQ, page 1099.) (Ibid.) (Ibid.) was baptized on 4 Sep 1652 at Trois-Rivieres, Quebec (Ibid.). A contract for the marriage to **ANNE DESROSIERS**, daughter of **ANTOINE DESROSIERS** and **ANNE LENEUF**, was signed on 4 Apr 1674 at Champlain, Quebec (Ibid.).

--- 7th Generation ---

64. JEAN TURCOT lived at at Fontenay-le-Comte, Maillezais, Poitou (Vendee) (Ibid.). A contract for the marriage to **FRANCOISE CAPEL**, daughter of **JULIEN CAPEL** and **LAURENCE LECOMPTE**, was signed on 25 Apr 1651 at Trois-Rivieres, Quebec (Ibid.) (PRDH online, No. 94125.). He died on 19 Aug 1652 at Trois-Rivieres, Quebec (DGFQ, page 1099.).

--- 8th Generation ---

128. FRANCOIS TURCOT married **JOSEPHE PUINANDEAU**.

Descendants of Vital Turcotte

Generation One

1. Vital Turcotte was born circa 1818 North West (1870C-MB 1870 Manitoba Census, National Archives of Canada, Ottawa, Ontario, Microfilm Reel Number C-2170., #1, St.Boniface; page 1.). He was baptized on 21 Apr 1832 St.Boniface, (Manitoba) (SB 1825-1834 St.Boniface Roman Catholic Registre des Baptemes, Mariages & Sepultures, 1825-1834, page 60, B-423. Hereinafter cited as SB 1825-1834.). He married **Madeleine Caplette**, daughter of **Joseph Caplette** and **Angelique Guiboche,** before 1837. He married **Marguerite Hamel** before 1872. He died on 1 Jan 1882 St.Francois Xavier, Manitoba (SFXI-Kipling St.Francois Xavier Register Index, 1834-1900; compiled by Clarence Kipling , S-1.).

Madeleine Caplette was born in 1818 North West Territories (MBS Scrip Applications, Original White Settlers & Halfbreeds residing in Manitoba on 15 July 1870, RG15-19, C-14934.) (SB 1825-1834, page 102, B-591.). She was baptized on 25 May 1833 St.Boniface, (Manitoba) (Ibid.). She died on 21 Nov 1906 St.Francois Xavier, Manitoba (Manitoba Vital Statistics online, http://web2.gov.mb.ca, Death Reg. #1906,003548.).

Children of **Vital Turcotte** and **Madeleine Caplette** were as follows:

2   i.   Jean Baptiste Turcotte, b. 22 Feb 1837 St.Boniface, (Manitoba); m. Angelique Paquin; m. Marguerite Descoteaux; d. circa 1902 Belcourt, Rolette County, North Dakota.

3   ii.   Pelagie Turcotte, b. 24 Apr 1843 St.James, (Manitoba); m. Joseph Hogue; d. 13 Nov 1928 St.Boniface, Manitoba.

4   iii.   Genevieve Turcotte, b. Oct 1846 St.Boniface, (Manitoba); m. Louis Lesperance; m. Antoine Vandal; d. 2 Jan 1894 Montcalm, Manitoba.

5   iv.   Joseph Turcotte, b. 30 Aug 1849 Headingley, (Manitoba); m. Sarah McMillan.

6   v.   Julie Turcotte, b. 9 Jan 1851 St.James, (Manitoba); m. Louis Hogue; d. 29 Aug 1927 St.Francois Xavier, Manitoba.

7   vi.   Marguerite Turcotte, b. 23 Dec 1853 St.Boniface, (Manitoba); m. Peter Bremner; m. Joseph Branconnier.

8   vii.   Norbert Turcotte, b. 12 Jun 1855 St.Boniface, (Manitoba); m. Josephte Lepine.

9   viii.   Pascal Turcotte, b. 23 Aug 1857 St.Boniface, (Manitoba); m. Mary Daisy Wells.

10   ix.   Modeste Turcotte, b. 4 Mar 1860 St.Boniface, (Manitoba); m. Caroline Allary dit Henry; m. Madeleine Jobin.

     x.   Clara Turcotte was born on 11 Nov 1861 St.Boniface, (Manitoba) (MBS, C-14934.) (SB-Rozyk   St. Boniface Roman Catholic Church, Manitoba, Canada, Baptisms, Marriages and Burials 1860-1875 Extractions, Compiled by Rosemary Rozyk, page 37, B-143.). She was baptized on 11 Nov 1861 St.Boniface, (Manitoba) (MBS, C-14934.) (SB-Rozyk, page 37, B-143.). She married David C. McDaniels, son of Calvin McDaniels and Marie Joan (--?--), on 9 Jan 1879 Fort Walsh, (Saskatchewan) (SPMT St.Peter's Mission; Volume I; Marriage Register 1859-1895; Translated & Transcribed by Reverend Dale McFarlane, Archivist, Diocese of Great Falls-Billings, Montana; Spring 1981.). She married David C. McDaniels, son of Calvin McDaniels and Marie Joan (--?--), on 19 Feb 1879 Fort Benton, Choteau County, Montana Territory (Ibid.).

     xi.   James Patrice McKenzie Turcotte was born on 18 Dec 1864 St.Boniface, (Manitoba) (MBS, C-14934.) (SB-Rozyk, page 170, B-121.). He was baptized on 20 Dec 1864 St.Boniface, (Manitoba) (MBS, C-14934.) (SB-Rozyk, page 170, B-121.). He died on 7 Mar 1874 St.Boniface, Manitoba, at age 9 (MBS, C-14934.) (SB-Rozyk, page 10, S-13.). He was buried on 8 Mar 1874 St.Boniface, Manitoba (MBS, C-14934.) (SB-Rozyk, page 10, S-13.).

     xii.   Caroline Turcotte was born circa 1866.

Children of **Vital Turcotte** and **Marguerite Hamel** were:

11   i.   Henrietta Turcotte, b. 1872 Wood Mountain, (Saskatchewan); m. Charles Houle; m. John Baptiste Grant.

Generation Two

2. Jean Baptiste Turcotte was born on 22 Feb 1837 St.Boniface, (Manitoba). He was born in Jan 1838 (1900C-ND 1900 United States Census, North Dakota, National Archives of the United States, Washington, D. C., House 252, page 301A.). He married **Angelique Paquin**, daughter of **Jean Baptiste Paquin** and **Gevevieve Laterregrasse**, in 1858 St.Boniface, (Manitoba). He married **Marguerite Descoteaux**, daughter of **Louis Decouteau Sr.** and **Isabelle Laverdure**, on 15 Sep 1884 St.Claude Mission, St.John, Rolette County, North Daktoa (Dominique Ritchot Research,, 26 Jan 2006.). He died circa 1902 Belcourt, Rolette County, North Dakota.

Angelique Paquin was born between 1840 and 1845 near, Red Lake, Minnesota. She died in 1884 St.John, Rolette County, North Dakota (St. Claude Mission, St. John, North Dakota, Baptisms, Marriages, Burials 1882-1888, 2006, Dominique Ritchot, S-21, p. 28.). She was buried on 3 Mar 1884 St.Claude Mission, St.John, Rolette County, North Dakota (Ibid.).

Children of **Jean Baptiste Turcotte** and **Angelique Paquin** were as follows:

12   i.   Vital Turcotte, b. 15 Jan 1858 Pembina, Pembina County, Dakota Territory; d. 1918 Hays, Blaine County, Montana.

     ii.   Jean Baptiste Turcotte was born in 1860 on the plains. He died in Dec 1873 Wood Mountain, (Saskatchewan).

13   iii.   Napoleon Turcotte, b. 1861 Turtle Mountain, Dakota Territory.

14   iv.   Marie Turcotte, b. 4 Sep 1861 Pembina County, Dakota Territory; m. Francois Laverdure; d. circa 1888 Lewistown, Fergus County, Montana.

     v.   Norbert Turcotte was born in 1862 on the plains. He died in Jul 1877 Wood Mountain, (Saskatchewan).

     vi.   William Turcotte was born in 1864 on the plains. He was baptized on 9 Feb 1864. He died in Jun 1879 Cypress Hills, (Saskatchewan).

15   vii.   Suzanne Turcotte, b. 1868 St.Joe, Pembina County, Dakota Territory; m. William Frederick; d. 18 Apr 1946 Rolette County, North Dakota.

     viii.   Adele Turcotte was born on 19 Oct 1870 Pembina, Pembina County, Dakota Territory (AP Records of the Assumption Roman Catholic Church, Pembina, North Dakota: Baptisms, Marriages, Sepultures, 1848-1896; compiled by Reverend Father J. M. Belleau, 2 October 1944, page 45, B-19. Hereinafter cited as AP.). She was baptized on 19 Oct 1870 Assumption, Pembina, Pembina County, Dakota Territory (Ibid.).

16   ix.   Daniel Turcotte, b. 5 Aug 1873; m. Marie Rosine Delaunay; d. 30 Aug 1951 Williams County, North Dakota.

     x.   Anastasie Turcotte was born circa 1875 (1885-TMC 1885 Census of Half Breed Chippewas of Turtle Mountain, Dakota Territory, National Archives of the United States, Washington D.C., #228.).

     xi.   Patrice Turcotte was baptized on 13 Mar 1876 Lebret, (Saskatchewan) (L1 Lebret Mission de St.Florent Roman Catholic Registre des Baptemes, Mariages & Seplutures, Qu'Appelle, Saskatchewan, 1868-1881., page 181, B-80. Hereinafter cited as L1.). He died circa 15 Jun 1878 (Ibid., page 235, S-53.). He was buried on 12 Sep 1878 Lebret, (Saskatchewan) (Ibid.).

     xii.   Angelique Turcotte was born on 16 Mar 1877 (Ibid., page 284, B-_.). She was baptized on 13 Jun 1879 Lebret, (Saskatchewan) (Ibid.).

17   xiii.   Angelique Turcotte, b. 9 Mar 1878 Milk River, Montana; m. Francois Davis; d. 28 Oct 1952 Rolette County, North Dakota.

     xiv.   William Delonais Turcotte was born on 15 Jul 1881 North Dakota (1915-TMC 1915 Census of the Turtle Mountain Chippewa, North Dakota, National Archives of the United States, Washington D.C.). He married Mary Matilda Laframboise, daughter of Joseph Laframboise and Marie Rose Parenteau, on 10 Apr 1917 (Rod

MacQuarrie Research, 22 Dec 2009.). He died on 13 Dec 1958 Rolette County, North Dakota, at age 77 (North Dakota Department of Health Public Death Index.).

Mary Matilda Laframboise was born on 28 Jan 1898 Belcourt, Rolette County, North Dakota (1900C-ND, House 233, page 298B.) (1898-TMC 1898 Census of Half Breed Chippewas of Turtle Mountain, North Dakota, National Archives of the United States, Washington D.C.) (1937-TMC Indian Census Roll of the Turtle Mountain Reservation, United States Indian Service Department of the Interior, Belcourt, North Dakota, J. E. Balmer, 1 January 1937 , page 503, Census No. 5890-5891.). She married **Arnold Hall** before 1917.

Marguerite Descoteaux was born on 1 Mar 1852 (AP, page 69, B-6.). She was baptized on 22 Mar 1852 Assumption, Pembina, Pembina County, Dakota Territory (Ibid.). She married **Francois Delauney dit Daunais**, son of **Joseph Delauney** and **Josephte Henry**, on 4 Sep 1871 St.Joseph, Leroy, Dakota Territory (SJL-1 Register of Baptisms, Marriages, and Burials, St.Joseph, Leroy, North Dakota, Diocese of Saint Paul, Minnesota, 1870-1888, Book 1, page 14, M-4. Hereinafter cited as SJL-1.). She died on 25 Oct 1945 Trenton, Williams County, North Dakota, at age 93 (ND Death Index.).

Children of **Jean Baptiste Turcotte** and **Marguerite Descoteaux** were as follows:

18　i.　Celina Turcotte, b. 2 Feb 1883 North Dakota; m. John Brunelle Jr; m. Gabriel Beauchman; d. 25 Jul 1949 Roosevelt County, Montana.
19　ii.　Pierre 'Peter' Turcotte, b. 28 Nov 1883 North Dakota; m. Elise Zaste; d. 24 Oct 1949 Belcourt, Rolette County, North Dakota.
20　iii.　Collin Turcotte, b. 2 Jul 1887 North Dakota; m. Christine Jeannotte; d. Apr 1969 Lansing, Ingham, Michigan.
21　iv.　Mary Jane Turcotte, b. 17 Oct 1889; m. Louis Brunelle; d. Jan 1984.
22　v.　Sarah Turcotte, b. Dec 1893 North Dakota; m. Joseph Beauchman.

3. Pelagie Turcotte was born on 24 Apr 1843 St.James, (Manitoba) (MBS, C-14929.). She married **Joseph Hogue**, son of **Louis Amable Hogue** and **Marguerite Taylor**, on 11 Jan 1859 St.Boniface, (Manitoba) (Treasure of Time: The Rural Municipality of Cartier: 1914-1984; n.p.: n.pub., 1984, page 373.) (*Winnipeg Free Press*, Winnipeg, Manitoba, 12 Jan 1915.). She died on 13 Nov 1928 St.Boniface, Manitoba, at age 85 (MB Vital Statistics, Death Reg. #1928,059062.).

Joseph Hogue was born on 30 Dec 1835 St.James, (Manitoba) (MBS, C-14928.). He died on 31 Mar 1924 Assiniboia, Manitoba, at age 88 (MB Vital Statistics, Death Reg. #1924,012248.). He was buried on 2 Apr 1924 St.Charles, Manitoba (Rosemary Helga (Morrissette) Rozyk Research, 20 Sep 2009, Free Press.).

4. Genevieve Turcotte was born in Oct 1846 St.Boniface, (Manitoba). She married **Louis Lesperance**, son of **Alexis Bonami Lesperance** and **Marguerite Grenon**, on 13 Jan 1863 St.Boniface, (Manitoba) (SB-Rozyk, page 98, M-3.). She married **Antoine Vandal**, son of **Antoine Vandal** and **Marguerite Savoyard dit Berthelet**, on 20 Jun 1887 St.Francois Xavier, Manitoba (SFXI-Kipling, M-6.). She died on 2 Jan 1894 Montcalm, Manitoba, at age 47 (MB Vital Statistics, Death Reg. #1894,001631.).

Louis Lesperance was born circa 1840 (SB-Rozyk, page 82, S-8.). He died on 15 Mar 1867 (Ibid.). He was buried on 18 Mar 1867 St.Boniface, (Manitoba) (Ibid.).

Antoine Vandal was born circa 1833 St.Norbert, (Manitoba) (MBS, C-14934.). He married **Scholastique Frobisher**, daughter of **Thomas Frobisher** and **Scholastique Pilon**, on 10 Jan 1860 St.Norbert, (Manitoba) (SN1, M-8, page 25.). He married **Marguerite St.Denis**, daughter of **Jacques St.Denis** and **Charlotte Rocheleau**, on 21 Jan 1879 St.Jean Baptiste, Manitoba (MM.). He married **Sarah McMillan**, daughter of **William McMillan** and **Margaret Dease,** on 18 Jul 1898 Assiniboia, Manitoba (MB Vital Statistics, Marriage Reg. #1899,001956.).

5. Joseph Turcotte was born on 30 Aug 1849 Headingley, (Manitoba) (MBS, C-14934.). He married **Sarah McMillan**, daughter of **William McMillan** and **Margaret Dease**, on 26 Jan 1870 St.Boniface, (Manitoba) (SB-Rozyk, page 172, M-4.).

Sarah McMillan was born on 5 Mar 1854 St.Vital, (Manitoba) (MBS, C-14934.). She married **Pierre Jobin**, son of **Ambroise Jobin** and **Marguerite Mandeville**, on 22 Jan 1884 Assiniboia, Manitoba (MB Vital Statistics, Marriage Reg. #1884,001694.). She married **Antoine Vandal**, son of **Antoine Vandal** and **Marguerite Savoyard dit Berthelet**, on 18 Jul 1898 Assiniboia, Manitoba (Ibid., Marriage Reg. #1899,001956.).

Children of **Joseph Turcotte** and **Sarah McMillan** were as follows:

　　i.　Alfred Turcotte was born circa 1871 (1881 Canada, District 183A, page 57, house 230+.).
23　ii.　Joseph Turcotte, b. 4 Nov 1872 Manitoba; m. Alvina Vandal; d. 22 Apr 1955 Kenora, Ontario.
24　iii.　Leonide Turcotte, b. 20 Apr 1874 Manitoba; m. Marie Virginie Alexandrine Ranger.
　　iv.　Archie Turcotte was born on 5 Aug 1879 Manitoba (1901 Canada, #11, 1-2, page 11, family 89, line 12-18.).

6. Julie Turcotte was born on 9 Jan 1851 St.James, (Manitoba) (MBS, C-14928.). She married **Louis Hogue**, son of **Louis Amable Hogue** and **Marguerite Taylor**, on 14 Jan 1868 St.Boniface, (Manitoba) (SB-Rozyk, page 104, M-2.). She died on 29 Aug 1927 St.Francois Xavier, Manitoba, at age 76 (MB Vital Statistics, Death Reg. #1926,040186.).

Louis Hogue was born in 1846 St.James, (Manitoba) (MBS, C-14928.). He died on 10 Mar 1937 Belcourt, Manitoba (Treasure of Time, page 373.). He was buried in 1937 St.Eustache, Manitoba (Ibid.).

7. Marguerite Turcotte was born on 23 Dec 1853 St.Boniface, (Manitoba) (MBS, C-14925.). She married **Peter Bremner**, son of **William Bremner** and **Marie Gariepy**, on 17 Jan 1870 St.Boniface, (Manitoba) (SB-Rozyk, page 172, M-3.). She married **Joseph Branconnier**, son of **Antoine Branconnier** and **Marie Sarah Celestine Bird**, on 21 Oct 1894 St.Francois Xavier, Manitoba (MB Vital Statistics, Marriage Reg. #1894,002128.).

Peter Bremner was born on 14 Dec 1845 St.Francois Xavier, (Manitoba) (MBS, C-14925.). He was baptized on 26 Dec 1845 St.Johns, (Manitoba) (Denney.). He died on 18 Dec 1886 Assiniboia, Manitoba, at age 41 (MB Vital Statistics, Death Reg. #1886,002543.).

Joseph Branconnier was born on 6 Jan 1863 St.Charles, (Manitoba) (SB-Rozyk, page 112, B-64.). He was baptized on 6 Jan 1863 (St.Charles), St.Boniface, (Manitoba) (Ibid.). He married **Marguerite Piche**, daughter of **Louis Piche** and **Angelique Lepine**, on 16 Feb 1885 St.Francois Xavier, Manitoba (SFXI-Kipling, M-8.). He died on 16 Jul 1911 RM St.Francois Xavier, Manitoba, at age 48 (MB Vital Statistics, Death Reg. #1911,002052.).

8. Norbert Turcotte was born on 12 Jun 1855 St.Boniface, (Manitoba) (MBS, C-14934.). He married **Josephte Lepine**, daughter of **Maxime Lepine** and **Josephte Lavallee**, on 17 Jan 1876 St.Francois Xavier, Manitoba (SFXI-Kipling, M-2.).

Josephte Lepine was born circa 1858 (Manitoba) (1870C-MB, page 248, #78.).

Children of **Norbert Turcotte** and **Josephte Lepine** were as follows:

- i. Maxime Adrien Turcotte was born on 15 May 1877 St.Francois Xavier, Manitoba (SFXI-Kipling, B-25.). He was baptized on 16 May 1877 St.Francois Xavier, Manitoba (Ibid.) (Rosemary Rozyk.). He died on 26 Jan 1878 St.Francois Xavier, Manitoba (Ibid., S-2.). He was buried on 28 Jan 1878 St.Francois Xavier, Manitoba (Ibid.) (Rosemary Rozyk.).
- 25 ii. Alexina Turcotte, b. 27 Dec 1878 St.Francois Xavier, Manitoba; m. Ambroise Chalifoux dit Richard.
- iii. Albert Ulric Turcotte was born on 3 Feb 1881 St.Francois Xavier, Manitoba (Ibid., B-6.). He was baptized 6 Feb 1881 St.Francois Xavier, Manitoba (Ibid.) (Rosemary Rozyk.).
- iii. Anonyme Turcotte was born and died on 28 Feb 1883 St.Francois Xavier, Manitoba (Rosemary Rozyk.). (He/she was buried on 2 Mar 1881 St.Francois Xavier, Manitoba (Ibid.).
- iv. Michel Turcotte was born on 17 Jul 1884 St.Laurent, (Saskatchewan) (ArchiviaNet 1886-1901, 1906 Half-Breed Scrip Applications Index, RG15-21, Volume 1333 through 1371, Microfilm Reel Number C-14944 through C-15010, National Archives of Canada, Ottawa, Ontario, http://www.collectionscanada.gc.ca, C-15007.).
- v. Zenaide Turcotte was born on 27 Dec 1885 St.Louis, (Saskatchewan) (Ibid.).
- vi. Lucie Georgina Turcotte was born on 21 Dec 1886. She was christened on 3 Jan 1887 St.Laurent, (Saskatchewan).
- vii. Xerine Alice Turcotte was christened on 27 Nov 1888 St.Laurent, (Saskatchewan). She married William Charles Kember on 23 Jun 1912 Duck Lake, (Saskatchewan).
- viii. Acilda Turcotte was born on 5 Dec 1891 (Saskatchewan) (1901 Canada, District 205-a(2), page 1, family 5, line 26-34.).
- ix. Oroville Turcotte was born on 28 Dec 1892 (Saskatchewan) (Ibid.).
- x. Jane Turcotte was born on 27 Sep 1894 (Saskatchewan) (Ibid.).
- xi. Martha Turcotte was born on 15 Nov 1896 (Saskatchewan) (Ibid.).
- xii. Marie Alexandrine Turcotte was born on 27 Jul 1902 Duck Lake, (Saskatchewan) (Saskatchewan Vital Statistics online, http://vsgs.health.gov.sk.ca, Birth Reg. #2697.).
- xiii. Albert Turcotte was born on 14 Dec 1903 Duck Lake, (Saskatchewan) (Ibid., Birth Reg. #3264.).

9. Pascal Turcotte was born on 23 Aug 1857 St.Boniface, (Manitoba) (MBS, C-14934.). He was born circa 1876 Dakota Territory (AYM Documentation of Metis Families of Red River and the Northwest Territories; Census, Biographical, and Historical: 1881 Census Qu'Appelle, Wood Mountain, Lac la Biche; History of the Turtle Mountain Band of Chippewas; Census for the Turtle Mountain Reservation 1884-1886; Pembina, Dakota Territory 1850 Census; Various Metis Census Records for Pembina County, ND 1910; compiled by Al Yerbery, 1996, Fergus County Marriages.). He married **Mary Daisy Wells**, daughter of **Daniel Wells** and **Louise Collin**, before 1879.

Mary Daisy Wells was born circa 1863 Montana (Al Yerbury Research, Fergus County Marriages.). She married **Norbert Laverdure**, son of **Francois Xavier Laverdure** and **Marguerite Pelletier**, on 5 Nov 1888 Fergus County, Montana (Ibid., Metis Marriages of Fergus Co., MT; p.8; Norbert Laverdure (Ganaza & Marguerite LaFountain) age 24; b.p. Montana to Mary Wells (David & Louis ?) age 25; b.p. Montana married 5 Nov 1888.) (FerCM Fergus County Courthouse, Montana; Marriage Record Licenses and Certificates, 1865-1950, familysearch.org., Hereinafter cited as FerCM.). She died on 15 Apr 1923 Lewistown, Fergus County, Montana (Al Yerbury, From Creel Funeral Home Records: Mary Daisy Laverdure, age 63, b. 1860, d. 15 Apr 1923, parents: Dan Wells & Louise Collins.).

Children of **Pascal Turcotte** and **Mary Daisy Wells** were as follows:

- i. Modeste Turcotte was born on 1 Aug 1881 Maple Creek, (Saskatchewan) (ArchiviaNet, C-15007.). He died on 1 Aug 1881 Maple Creek, (Saskatchewan) (Ibid.).
- ii. James Turcotte was born on 19 Nov 1881 North Dakota (1937-1987-LS Basic Roll Basic Membership Roll of the Landless Indians of Montana; 1937 Census Taken by Dr. Henry Roe Cloud; Edited c1987 to include official correspondence regarding 1937 membership; ** in Present Roll Number column indicates 1940s information added., #516.). He married Justine Berger, daughter of Isaie Berger and Clemence Gourneau, on 3 May 1903 Lewistown, Fergus County, Montana (AYM, Fergus County Marriages.) (FerCM.). He died on 6 Jul 1967 Billings, Yellowstone County, Montana, at age 85 (Rod Mac Quarrie, 22 Dec 2009.).
  - **Justine Berger** was born on 23 Jan 1884 Lewistown, Fergus County, Montana (1937-1987-LS Basic Roll, #520.). She died on 2 May 1968 Fergus County, Montana, at age 84 (Rod Mac Quarrie, 22 Dec 2009.).
- iii. Joseph Turcotte was born in Dec 1883 Fort Walsh, (Saskatchewan) (ArchiviaNet.). He was born on 18 Dec 1885 North Dakota (Social Security Death Index, . Hereinafter cited as SSDI.). He married Marguerite Berger, daughter of Isaie Berger and Clemence Gourneau, on 17 Oct 1910 Lewistown, Fergus County, Montana (Al Yerbury, Fergus County Marriages.) (FerCM.). He died on 24 Nov 1966 Lewistown, Fergus County, Washington, at age 82 (MT Death Montana State Genealogical Society Death Index.) (SSDI.).
  - **Marguerite Berger** was born on 2 Feb 1875 (L1, page 148, B-35.). She was baptized on 8 Feb 1875 Lebret, (Saskatchewan) (Ibid.). She married **Jean James Wills**, son of **Edouard Wills** and **Isabelle McGillis**, on 7 Apr 1896 Lewistown, Fergus County, Montana (Al Yerbury, Fergus County Marriages.) (FerCM.). She died on 7 May 1936 Lewistown, Fergus County, Montana, at age 61 (Al Yerbury.) (Rod Mac Quarrie, 28 Oct 2012.) (MT Death.).
- 26 iv. Zilda Turcotte, b. 13 May 1884 Peltiere Lake; m. Dwight Luther Beatty; m. Roscoe Bozarth.

10. Modeste Turcotte was born on 4 Mar 1860 St.Boniface, (Manitoba) (MBS, C-14934.). He married **Caroline Allary dit Henry**, daughter of **Pierre Henry dit Allary** and **Angelique Parisien**, before 1878 (Lynn Marion Research, 13 May 2005.). He married **Madeleine Jobin**, daughter of **Ambroise Jobin** and **Marguerite Mandeville**, on 18 Feb 1882 Assiniboia, Manitoba (MB Vital Statistics, Marriage Reg. #1882,001643.).

Caroline Allary dit Henry was born circa 1858 (1870C-MB, page 1-2, #28-34.). She married **Jean Baptiste Pelletier**, son of **Antoine Pelletier** and **Julie Fournier**, on 24 Feb 1879 St.Boniface, Manitoba (RMSB.) (Rosemary Rozyk, 22 Mar 2008.).

Children of **Modeste Turcotte** and **Caroline Allary dit Henry** were:

27   i.   Marie Rose Turcotte, b. 1878 Cypress Hills, (Saskatchewan); m. Elzear Lafontaine; d. 29 May 1963 Lewistown, Fergus County, Montana.

Madeleine Jobin was born on 18 Nov 1856 St.Boniface, (Manitoba) (MBS, C-14929.). She married **Basile Belgarde**, son of **Alexis Belgarde** and **Suzanne Gourneau,** before Jul 1899. She died before Jul 1901 (1901-TMC 1901 Census of Half Breed Chippewas of Turtle Mountain, North Dakota, National Archives of the United States, Washington D.C.).

Children of **Modeste Turcotte** and **Madeleine Jobin** were as follows:

     i.   Emma Louise Turcotte was born on 21 Feb 1883 Illet de Bois, Manitoba (SFXI-Kipling, B-18.).

     ii.   Marie Turcotte was born circa 1887 (1890-TMC 1890 Census of Half Breed Chippewas of Turtle Mountain, Dakota Territory, National Archives of the United States, Washington D.C., #1128.).

28   iii.   Lena Jennie Turcotte, b. circa 1888; d. 4 Aug 1965 Coffeyville, Kansas.

29   iv.   Wilhelmina Turcotte, b. circa 1892; m. Neil Jones; d. 3 Dec 1973 San Francisco, San Francisco County, California.

     v.   Emily Turcotte was born circa 1896 Rolette County, North Dakota (1899-TMC 1899 Census of Half Breed Chippewas of Turtle Mountain, North Dakota, National Archives of the United States, Washington D.C.).

11. Henrietta Turcotte was born in 1872 Wood Mountain, (Saskatchewan) (ArchiviaNet.). She married **Charles Houle**, son of **Antoine Houle** and **Genevieve St.Pierre,** circa Jun 1886 (1884-TMC 1884-1886 Census of Half Breed Chippewas of Turtle Mountain, Dakota Territory, National Archives of the United States, Washington D.C.). She married **John Baptiste Grant**, son of **Pierre Grant** and **Marie Vivier,** circa 1929 (BIA-TM Bureau of Indian Affairs, Turtle Mountain Enrollment and Probate Papers, Belcourt, North Dakota, John Baptiste Grant Probate.).

Charles Houle was born on 5 Sep 1861 Pembina County, Dakota Territory (AP, page 246, B-225.). He was baptized on 7 Sep 1861 Assumption, Pembina, Pembina County, Dakota Territory (Ibid.). He died on 10 Jun 1926 Rolette County, North Dakota, at age 64 (ND Death Index.).

John Baptiste Grant was born in Jun 1864 North Dakota (1900C-ND, House 227, page 297B.). He married **Margaret Azure**, daughter of **Pierre Azure** and **Marie Marthe Breland,** in 1882 (Ibid.). He died on 4 Mar 1942 Rolette County, North Dakota, at age 77 (BIA-TM, John Baptiste Grant Probate.) (ND Death Index.).

Generation Three

12. Vital Turcotte was born on 15 Jan 1858 Pembina, Pembina County, Dakota Territory (AP, page 184, B-562.). He was baptized on 15 Jan 1858 Assumption, Pembina, Pembina County, Dakota Territory (Ibid.). He married **Adele Berger**, daughter of **Pierre Berger** and **Judith Wilkie,** on 29 Jan 1878 (St.Peter's Mission), Milk River, Montana Territory (SPMT , page 19, #94.). He died in 1918 Hays, Blaine County, Montana.

Adele Berger was born on 16 May 1859 Pembina County, Dakota Territory (AP, page 216, B-126.). She was baptized on 16 May 1859 Assumption, Pembina, Pembina County, Dakota Territory (Ibid.). She died on 17 Nov 1948 Rolette County, North Dakota, at age 89 (ND Death Index.).

Children of **Vital Turcotte** and **Adele Berger** were as follows:

     i.   Joseph Turcotte was born on 11 Dec 1878 St.Peter's Mission, Montana (SPMT , page 118, #2506.). He was baptized on 12 Dec 1878 St.Peter's Mission, Montana (Ibid.).

     ii.   Christine Turcotte was born circa 1881 Lewistown, Fergus County, Montana (FerCM.). She married Jean Baptiste Lariviere, son of Francois Lariviere and Marie Delorme, on 29 Aug 1898 Choteau County, Montana (ChCM Chouteau County, Montana; Marriage Record Licenses and Certificates; 1865-1950; familysearch.org, Hereinafter cited as ChCM.).

        Jean Baptiste Lariviere was born on 31 Dec 1874 (INB, page 100.). He was baptized on 1 Jan 1875 St.Eustache, Manitoba (IBMS *Index des Baptemes, Mariages et Sepultures* (La Societe Historique de Saint-Boniface).) (INB, page 100.).

30   iii.   John Turcotte, b. 24 Dec 1882 Lewistown, Fergus County, Montana; m. Julia McConnell; d. 24 Oct 1960 Powell County, Montana.

     iv.   Patrice Turcotte was born circa 1884 (1892 Oct 1 McCumber Census of the Turtle Mountain band of Chippewa Indians, Belcourt, North Dakota, National Archives of the United States, Washington D.C., Document No. 229, Family 74, #355-362.).

31   v.   Charles Turcotte, b. 6 Jul 1886 Lewistown, Fergus County, Montana; m. Evelyn Larocque.

32   vi.   Marie Turcotte, b. 4 Feb 1887 Lewistown, Fergus County, Montana; m. James C. Doney; d. 30 Oct 1956 Blaine County, Montana.

     vii.   Cecelia Turcotte was born circa 1888 (Ibid.).

     viii.   Lucy Theresa Turcotte was born on 6 Sep 1890 Lewistown, Fergus County, Montana (SSDI.) (GCM Glacier County, Montana; Marriage Record Licenses and Certificates; 1865-1950; familysearch.org, Hereinafter cited as GCM.). She married Justus Sharp, son of William Sharp and Rose Miller, on 9 Aug 1919 Cut Bank, Glacier Couty, Montana (Ibid.). She died on 11 Mar 1981 Libby, Lincoln County, Montana, at age 90 (MT Death.) (SSDI.). She died on 12 Mar 1981 at age 90 (Brenda Snider Research, 9 Oct 2014.).

        Justus Sharp was born on 12 Aug 1900 Browning, Glacier Couty, Montana (SSDI.). He died on 1 Jun 1970 Browning, Glacier Couty, Montana, at age 69 (Ibid.) (MT Death.).

     ix.   Modeste Turcotte was born on 24 Jan 1893 Lewistown, Fergus County, Montana (1937-1987-LS Basic Roll, #521.).

33   x.   Rebecca Alma Turcotte, b. 8 Feb 1894 St.Pauls, Montana; m. Frank Halverson; m. Adolph Carl Weedman.

     xi.   Madeline Turcotte was born on 29 Sep 1894 Lewistown, Fergus County, Montana (Death Certificate, State File No. 15225, 6-17-1952.). She was born circa 1896 (1906-TMC 1906 Census of the Turtle Mountain Chippewa, United States Indian Service Department of the Interior, Belcourt, North Dakota, 30 June 1906 , Census No. 2223-2229.). She and Lawrence Azure obtained a marriage license on 23 Jun 1930 Phillips County, Montana (PhCM Phillips County Courthouse, Montana; Marriage Record Licenses and Certificates; 1865-1950, familysearch.org,

Hereinafter cited as PhCM.). She died on 7 May 1952 Montana State Hospital, Warm Springs Township, Deer Lodge County, Montana (Death Cert., State File No. 15225, 6-17-1952.).

Lawrence Azure was born circa 1878 Montana (1930C MT 1930 Montana, Fifteenth Census of the United States, National Archives of the United States, Washington, D.C., Sheet 2B, Family 33, line 67-70.). He married **Matilda (--?--)** before 1916 (1920C-MT 1920 Federal Census Montana, National Archives of the United States, Washington D.C., page 1A.). He died on 11 Aug 1936 Blaine County, Montana (MT Death.).

xii. Sarah Turcotte was born circa 1898 (*1906-TMC*, Census No. 2223-2229.).

xiii. Joseph Turcotte was born on 11 Jul 1902 St.Pauls Mission, Hays, Blaine County, Montana (MT Death.) (Brenda Snider, 5 Oct 2014, obituary.). He died on 22 May 1968 Great Falls, Cascade County, Montana, at age 65 (MT Death.).

13. Napoleon Turcotte was born in Oct 1857 North Dakota (1900C-ND, 262-262.). He was born in 1861 Turtle Mountain, Dakota Territory (NWHBS 1885 Scrip Applications, North-West Halfbreeds residing outside Manitoba on 15 July 1870, RG15-20, C-14942.). He married **Madeleine Deschamps**, daughter of **Jean Baptiste Deschamps** and **Isabelle Allary**, on 7 May 1883 St.Ignace, Willow Bunch, (Saskatchewan) (SIWB St.Ignace Roman Catholic Registre des Baptemes, Mariages & Sepltures, Willow Bunch, Saskatchewan, 1882-1917, FHC #1290091., page 110, M-5. Hereinafter cited as SIWB.).

Madeleine Deschamps was born in 1858 Turtle Mountain Reservation, North Dakota (BIA-TM-BMD.). She was born in 1859 St.Francois Xavier, (Manitoba). She was born circa 1862 (Manitoba) (1870C-MB, page 320, #2471.). She died on 1 Jun 1919 (BIA-TM-BMD.) (ND Death Index.).

Children of **Napoleon Turcotte** and **Madeleine Deschamps** were as follows:

34 i. Marie Louise Turcotte, b. 28 Jun 1883 between, Regina and Wood Mountain, (Saskatchewan); m. Louis Desjarlais.

35 ii. Antoine Turcotte, b. circa Feb 1885; m. Hiemyaw or Wisimyan (--?--); m. Adele Peltier.

14. Marie Turcotte was born on 4 Sep 1861 Pembina County, Dakota Territory (AP, page 246, B-223.). She was baptized on 5 Sep 1861 Assumption, Pembina, Pembina County, Dakota Territory (Ibid.). She married **Francois Laverdure**, son of **Pierre Laverdure** and **Catherine Charette**, on 15 Jan 1879 St.Peter's Mission, Montana Territory (SPMT, page 20, #101.). She died circa 1888 Lewistown, Fergus County, Montana (Historical Data Project, Bismarck, North Dakota;. Hereinafter cited as "HDP.").

Francois Laverdure was born on 11 Mar 1853 (AP, page 85, B-60.). He was baptized on 18 Apr 1853 Assumption, Pembina, Pembina County, Dakota Territory (Ibid.). He died in 1888 Lewistown, Fergus County, Montana.

15. Suzanne Turcotte was born in 1868 St.Joe, Pembina County, Dakota Territory (HDP, received from Doris Turcotte.). She was baptized on 16 Jun 1868 (NWHBSI Index 1885 Scrip Applications, North-West Halfbreeds residing outside Manitoba on 15 July 1870, RG15-20, page 79.). She married **William Frederick**, son of **Joseph Frederick dit Langis or Langer** and **Marie Anne Keplin**, on 26 Jun 1885 Belcourt, Rolette County, North Dakota (HDP, Liberty Memorial Building, Bismarck, ND; from Al Yerbury; 6 Feb 1997.). She died on 18 Apr 1946 Rolette County, North Dakota (ND Death Index.).

William Frederick was born on 31 Jul 1868 White Bear Lake, Minnesota (HDP, Liberty Memorial Building, Bismarck, ND; from Al Yerbury; 6 Feb 1997.). He was born in 1869 (1936-TMC, page 94.). He died on 8 Dec 1937 Rolette County, North Dakota, at age 69 (ND Death Index.).

16. Daniel Turcotte was born on 5 Aug 1873 (L1, page 98, B-24.). He was baptized on 10 Aug 1873 Lebret, (Saskatchewan) (Ibid.). He married **Marie Rosine Delaunay**, daughter of **Francois Delauney dit Daunais** and **Marguerite Descoteaux**, on 12 Apr 1890 (BIA-TM.). He died on 30 Aug 1951 Williams County, North Dakota, at age 78 (ND Death Index.).

Marie Rosine Delaunay was born on 25 Dec 1869 Mouse River, Dakota Territory (BIA-TM.). She was born on 25 Dec 1873 (L1, page 126, B-79.). She was baptized on 26 Dec 1873 Lebret, (Saskatchewan) (Ibid.). She died on 8 Jan 1960 Williams County, North Dakota, at age 86 (ND Death Index.). Question: *She is called Rosine Dubois in 1937 (1937-TMC*, page 501, Census No. 5864-5866.).

Children of **Daniel Turcotte** and **Marie Rosine Delaunay** were as follows:

36 i. Daniel Turcotte Jr, b. 29 Jan 1892 Belcourt, North Dakota; m. Clara Burns.

37 ii. John B. Turcotte, b. 1893; m. Margaret Latreille.

38 iii. Mary Josephine Turcotte, b. 23 Feb 1895 North Dakota; m. Job Peter Joseph Falcon; d. 16 Mar 1969 Trenton, Williams County, North Dakota.

iv. William Turcotte was born on 7 Sep 1898 Belcourt, Rolette County, North Dakota (HDP.). He died in 1917 Trenton, Williams, North Dakota (Ibid.).

39 v. Marie Claudia Turcotte, b. 1900; m. Guy Otis Shanks; d. 6 Jan 1929 Portland, Multnomah, Oregon.

vi. Joseph Turcotte was born on 3 Sep 1899 (Ibid.). He was born in 1904 (1936-TMC, page 121.). He and Josephine St.Germain obtained a marriage license on 8 Dec 1923 Roosevelt County, Montana (RooCM Marriage Licenses and Certificates, Roosevelt County Courthouse, Wolf Point, Montana; FHC microfilm 1903324 and 1903325, Hereinafter cited as RooCM.). He married Josephine St.Germain, daughter of Francois St.Germain and Elizabeth Geddies, on 9 Dec 1923 Justice of the Peace, Wolf Point, Roosevelt County, Montana (Ibid.).

Josephine St.Germain was born on 28 Aug 1905 Poplar, Roosevelt County, Montana (Ibid.).

40 vii. Robert Ruben Turcotte, b. 4 Sep 1907; m. Emma Laura Slater; d. 2 May 1972 Trenton, Williams County, North Dakota.

viii. Mary Florestine Turcotte was born on 5 Jul 1910 (HDP.) (BIA-TM-BMD, page 48.). She married Pete Barnachia, son of Jaime Barnachia and Pauline Bocsit, on 28 Oct 1935 Sidney, Richland County, Montana (RLCM Richland County Courthouse, Montana; Marriage Record Licenses and Certificates; 1865-1950, familysearch.org, Hereinafter cited as RLCM.). She married Lloyd Williams before 1937 (*1937-TMC*, page 533, Census No. 6366.).

Pete Barnachia was born in 1911 (RLCM.).

ix. James Russell Turcotte was born on 9 Feb 1913 North Dakota (*1937-TMC*, page 501, Census No. 5864-5866.). He married Mary Agnes Wilkie, daughter of John Baptiste Joseph Wilkie and Mary Jane Belgarde, before 1934.

Mary Agnes Wilkie was born on 20 May 1909 (1936-TMC, page 130.) (BIA-TM-BMD, page 25.). She married **James Trottier**, son of **Napoleon "Paul" Trottier** and **Bibiane Eulalie Slater,** before 1934 (*1937-TMC*, Census No. 5839-5841.).

    41   x.   Clarence Walter Turcotte, b. 9 May 1916 Trenton, Williams, North Dakota; m. Flora Katherine Falcon; m. Doris Louise Morin; d. 6 Feb 1980 Trenton, Williams, North Dakota; bur. Feb 1980 Trenton, Williams, North Dakota.

  17. Angelique Turcotte was born on 9 Mar 1878 Milk River, Montana (SPMT , page 116, #2461.). She was baptized on 10 Mar 1878 (St.Peter's Mission), Milk River, Montana (Ibid.). She married **Francois Davis**, son of **William Davis Sr.** and **Marie Vallee,** before 30 Jun 1893 North Dakota (1900C-ND, House 402, page 318B.) (1893-TMC 1893 Census of Half Breed Chippewas of Turtle Mountain, Dakota Territory, National Archives of the United States, Washington D.C., page 15, Census No. 394-395.). She died on 28 Oct 1952 Rolette County, North Dakota, at age 74 (ND Death Index.).

  Francois Davis was born on 1 Nov 1869 (Ibid.). He was born in 1873 Minnesota (1936-TMC, page 61.) (1880C MT, page 428, #40-41.). He was born in Feb 1875 North Dakota (1900C-ND, House 402, page 318B.). He died on 22 Sep 1947 Rolette County (ND Death Index.).

  18. Celina Turcotte was born on 2 Feb 1883 North Dakota (1918-TMC 1918 Census of the Turtle Mountain Chippewa, North Dakota, National Archives of the United States, Washington D.C., Census No. 424-431.). (BIA-TM, Gabriel L. Beachman, Jr. Family history card.). She married **Gabriel Beauchman**, son of **Gabriel Beauchman** and **Marguerite Azure,** on 30 Jan 1901 (Ibid., Gabriel L. Beachman Probate.). She died on 25 Jul 1949 Roosevelt County, Montana, at age 66 (Ibid., Celina Turcotte Beachman Individual history card.) (MT Death.).

  John Brunelle Jr was born on 22 Aug 1879 Grand Forks, Minnesota (*St.Ann's Centennial.*). He married **Marie Claudia Petit**, daughter of **Joseph Petit dit Thomas** and **Catherine Vivier**, in 1899 Belcourt, Rolette County, North Dakota (1900C-ND, House 383, page 316B.). He died on 31 Jul 1954 Belcourt, Rolette County, North Dakota, at age 74 (ND Death Index.).

  Gabriel Beauchman was born on 28 Jan 1878 Milk River, Montana Territory (SPMT , page 115, #2458.). He was baptized on 28 Jan 1878 (St.Peter's Mission), Milk River, Montana Territory (Ibid.). He was baptized on 2 Feb 1878 Lebret, (Saskatchewan) (L1, page 284, B-_.). He died on 3 Aug 1971 Poplar, Roosevelt County, Montana, at age 93 (MT Death.).

  19. Pierre 'Peter' Turcotte was born on 28 Nov 1883 North Dakota (ND Death Index.). He was born in Sep 1886 North Dakota (1900C-ND, 253-253.). He married **Elise Zaste**, daughter of **Elzear Zaste** and **Adele Blackbird**, in Jun 1918 Belcourt, Rolette County, North Dakota (*St.Ann's Centennial*, page 548.). He died on 24 Oct 1949 Belcourt, Rolette County, North Dakota, at age 65 (Ibid.) (ND Death Index.).

  Elise Zaste was born on 16 Aug 1902 Belcourt, Rolette County, North Dakota (1936-TMC, page 121.) (*St.Ann's Centennial*, page 548.). She married **Frederick Wilkie**, son of **Antoine Alexander Wilkie** and **Magdeleine Bercier,** on 8 Oct 1971 Belcourt, Rolette County, North Dakota (Ibid.). She died on 22 Oct 1982 Belcourt, Rolette County, North Dakota, at age 80 (Ibid.) (ND Death Index.).

  Children of **Pierre 'Peter' Turcotte** and **Elise Zaste** are as follows:

       i.   Joseph Ernest Turcotte was born on 24 Mar 1923 (*1937-TMC*, page 503, Census No. 5879-5884.).
      ii.   Georgeline R. Turcotte was born on 4 Aug 1925 (Ibid.).
     iii.   Louis P. Turcotte was born on 7 Mar 1928 (Ibid.).
     iv.   Delores Turcotte was born circa 1930.
      v.   Audrey Vitaline Turcotte was born on 3 Feb 1932 (Ibid.).

  20. Collin Turcotte was born on 2 Jul 1887 North Dakota (SSDI.). He married **Christine Jeannotte**, daughter of **Gregoire Frederic Jeannotte** and **Marie Rose Desjarlais,** before 1911. He died in Apr 1969 Lansing, Ingham, Michigan, at age 81 (Ibid.).

  Christine Jeannotte was born in Mar 1892 North Dakota (1900C-ND, House 90, page 279B.).

  Children of **Collin Turcotte** and **Christine Jeannotte** were as follows:

       i.   LaRose Turcotte was born on 8 May 1911 (1936-TMC, page 121.) (BIA-TM-BMD, page 47.).
      ii.   Fred Turcotte was born on 26 Aug 1912 (1936-TMC, page 121.) (BIA-TM-BMD, page 59.).
     iii.   Louis Turcotte was born on 27 Aug 1912 (1936-TMC, page 121.) (BIA-TM-BMD, page 59.). He died before 1936 (1936-TMC, page 121.).
     iv.   Louis A. Turcotte was born in 1915 (Ibid.).
  42   v.   Marie Cecelia Turcotte, b. 23 Apr 1916; m. Gordon Obadiah Smith; d. 24 Jan 2009.
     vi.   Andrew Turcotte was born on 14 Mar 1917 (Ibid.) (*1937-TMC*, page 501, Census No. 5851-5863.).
  43 vii.   William James Turcotte, b. 6 Mar 1919; m. Helene Margarete Bauchsch.
    viii.   Edna Pearl Turcotte was born on 7 Mar 1921 (1936-TMC, page 121.) (*1937-TMC*, page 501, Census No. 5851-5863.).
     ix.   Josephine Grace Turcotte was born in 1922 (1936-TMC, page 121.). She died before 1929.
     x.   Alvina Elizabeth Turcotte was born on 7 Nov 1922 (Ibid.) (*1937-TMC*, page 501, Census No. 5851-5863.).
     xi.   Lawrence Turcotte was born on 30 Oct 1923 (Ibid.).
     xii.   Irene Turcotte was born on 17 Aug 1925 (Ibid.).
    xiii.   Stanley Turcotte was born on 8 Nov 1926 (Ibid.).
    xiv.   Henry Turcotte was born on 2 Jul 1929 (Ibid.).
     xv.   Rita Turcotte was born on 2 Apr 1931 (Ibid.).
    xvi.   Juanita Turcotte was born on 3 May 1933 (Ibid.).

  21. Mary Jane Turcotte was born on 17 Oct 1889 (Cindy Charlebois Research.). She married **Louis Brunelle**, son of **John Brunelle** and **Julia Montreuille,** on 15 May 1906 St.Ann, Belcourt, Rolette County, North Dakota (Ibid.). She died in Jan 1984 at age 94 (Ibid.).

  Louis Brunelle was born in May 1886 North Dakota (1900C-ND, House 272, page 304A.) (1936-TMC, page 51.). He died on 6 Aug 1957 Rolette County, North Dakota, at age 71 (Cindy Charlebois.) (ND Death Index.).

  22. Sarah Turcotte was born in Dec 1893 North Dakota (1918-TMC, Census No. 419-423.). She married **Joseph Beauchman**, son of **Gabriel Beauchman** and **Marguerite Azure,** before 1911.

  Joseph Beauchman was born on 16 Aug 1890 Rolette County, North Dakota (*1921 TMC*, Census No. 430-436.).

23. **Joseph Turcotte** was born on 4 Nov 1872 Manitoba (1901 Canada, #10, f-2, page 1, family 5, line 35-37.). He married **Alvina Vandal**, daughter of **Antoine Vandal** and **Marguerite St.Denis**, on 15 Oct 1900 (St.Jean Baptiste), Montcalm, Manitoba (MM.) (MB Vital Statistics, Marriage Reg. #1900,001102 (Montcalm).). He died on 22 Apr 1955 Kenora, Ontario, at age 82 (Rod Mac Quarrie, 28 Dec 2011.).

Alvina Vandal was born on 8 Dec 1881 Manitoba (1901 Canada, #10, f-2, page 1, family 5, line 35-37.). She died on 12 Nov 1948 Kenora, Ontario, at age 66 (Rod Mac Quarrie, 28 Dec 2011.).

Children of **Joseph Turcotte** and **Alvina Vandal** were as follows:

    i.   Robert Joseph Edmond Turcotte was born on 24 Feb 1901 R.M. of Montcalm, Manitoba (1901 Canada, #10, f-2, page 1, family 5, line 35-37.) (MB Vital Statistics, Birth Reg. #1901,005333.).

    ii.   William John Turcotte was born on 12 Feb 1902 Assiniboia, Manitoba (Ibid., Birth Reg. #1902,001194.).

    iii.   Marie Mabel Albina Turcotte was born on 28 Jul 1903 Assiniboia, Manitoba (Ibid., Birth Reg. #1903,001704.). She married Joseph Paul Adelard Landry, son of Joseph Landry and Elise Roy, on 25 Nov 1925 St.Jean Baptiste, Manitoba (MM.) (MB Vital Statistics, Marriage Reg. #1925,047416.).

          Joseph Paul Adelard Landry was born on 6 Dec 1901 RM of Montcalm, Manitoba (Ibid., Birth Reg. #1901,001688.).

    iv.   Marcel Turcotte was born circa Apr 1904 St.Charles, Manitoba (MM.) (1906 Canada, District 4-13, page 17, line 22.) (1911 Canada, District 53, page 3, line 31.). He married Marie Cecile Sabourin on 10 Sep 1944 St.Jean Baptiste, Manitoba (MM.).

    v.   Henri Turcotte was born in Feb 1906 (1906 Canada, District 4-13, page 17, line 22.). He married Irene Beaudette on 30 Sep 1931 St.Jean Baptiste, Manitoba (MM.).

    vi.   Effie Turcotte was born circa Jul 1906 (1911 Canada, District 53, page 3, line 31.).

    vii.   Josephine Turcotte was born on 20 Apr 1907 Winnipeg, Manitoba (MB Vital Statistics, Birth Reg. #1907,25225737.). She married Ovide Fontaine on 25 Apr 1928 St.Jean Baptiste, RM of Montcalm, Manitoba (MM.) (MB Vital Statistics, Marriage Reg. #1928,023272.).

    viii.   Horace Turcotte was born circa Apr 1909 (1911 Canada, District 53, page 3, line 31.).

    ix.   Antoine Turcotte was born on 5 Mar 1910 St.Jean-Baptiste, Manitoba (Ibid.) (Rod Mac Quarrie, 28 Dec 2011.). He died on 24 Feb 1977 Winnipeg, Manitoba, at age 66 (Ibid.).

    x.   Ernest Turcotte was born circa 1912 (1916 Census of Canada from the National Archives of Canada (Transcription by ancestry.com), Ottawa, Canada, District 9-10, page 13, line 35.).

    xi.   Rolland Turcotte was born circa 1913 (Ibid.).

    xii.   Eugene Turcotte was born circa 1915 (Ibid.). He married Fernande Lagace on 11 Jun 1942 Lasalle, Manitoba (MM.).

24. **Leonide Turcotte** was born on 20 Apr 1874 Manitoba (1901 Canada, #11, 1-2, page 11, family 89, line 12-18.). He married **Marie Virginie Alexandrine Ranger**, daughter of **Joseph Ranger** and **Marguerite Larocque**, on 25 Jan 1905 St.Boniface, Manitoba (RMSB, page 471.) (MB Vital Statistics, Marriage Reg. #1905,002091.).

Marie Virginie Alexandrine Ranger was born on 22 Dec 1885 St.Boniface, Manitoba (1901 Canada, District 10-n-1, page 5, family 38, line 35-41.) (MB Vital Statistics, Birth Reg. #1885,004908.).

Children of **Leonide Turcotte** and **Marie Virginie Alexandrine Ranger** are as follows:

    i.   Maggie Turcotte was born in Nov 1905 (1911 Canada, District 53, page 3, line 42.).

    ii.   Marie Blanche Turcotte was born on 5 Nov 1906 St.Charles, Manitoba (MB Vital Statistics, Birth Reg. #1906,23622557, Reg. Date: 19/05/1966.). She married Marius Goulet, son of Albert Goulet and Marie Louise Parenteau, on 10 Oct 1923 St.Boniface, Manitoba (RMSB.).

    iii.   Pauline Turcotte was born in Dec 1907 (1911 Canada, District 53, page 3, line 42.).

25. **Alexina Turcotte** was born on 26 Dec 1878 St.Francois Xavier, Manitoba (SFXI-Kipling, B-50.). She was baptized 27 Dec 1878 St.Francois Xavier, Manitoba (Ibid.) (Rosemary Rozyk.). She married **Ambroise Chalifoux dit Richard**, son of **Antoine Chalifoux dit Richard** and **Elizabeth Fidler**, circa 1900.

Ambroise Chalifoux dit Richard was baptized on 8 Jul 1875 St.Eustache, Manitoba (IBMS.).

26. **Zilda Turcotte** was born on 13 May 1884 Peltiere Lake (ArchiviaNet.). She married **Dwight Luther Beatty**, son of **Oliver R. Beatty** and **Ina Pearson**, on 7 May 1906 Lewistown, Fergus County, Montana (FerCM.). She married **Roscoe Bozarth** before 1920 (1920C-MT, page 5A.).

Dwight Luther Beatty was born on 14 Aug 1884 Fort Dodge, Iowa (FerCM.) (Ancestry.com, WWI Draft Registration.).

Roscoe Bozarth was born on 18 Feb 1886 Washington (1920C-MT, page 5A.) (Ancestry.com, WWI Draft Registration.).

27. **Marie Rose Turcotte** was born in 1878 Cypress Hills, (Saskatchewan) (ArchiviaNet.). She married **Elzear Lafontaine**, son of **Antoine Faillant dit Lafontaine** and **Madeleine Ross**, circa 1895 Turtle Mountain, North Dakota (1902-1930 Fergus County, Montana School Census; Courthouse, Lewistown, Montana: Superintendent of Schools, Fergus County.) (1900C-ND, House 405, page 319A.). She died on 29 May 1963 Lewistown, Fergus County, Montana (BIA-LS Bureau of Indian Affairs, Little Shell Enrollment Papers.).

Elzear Lafontaine was born on 9 Nov 1871 Saskatoon, (Saskatchewan) (HBSI.) (ArchiviaNet.). He was born in Aug 1872 North Dakota (1900C-ND, House 405, page 319A.). He died on 12 Jan 1949 Lewistown, Fergus County, Montana, at age 77 (Al Yerbury, Creel Funeral Home Records.) (Turtle Mountain Reservation Probate Record, #1585, Branch of Trust & Natural Resources.) (MT Death.).

28. **Lena Jennie Turcotte** was born circa 1888 (1890-TMC, #1129.). She married **Clifton Wilson** on 23 Jun 1909 Lawrence, Douglas County, Kansas (1936-TMC, page 133.) (Marriage Certificate.). She died on 4 Aug 1965 Coffeyville, Kansas.

Clifton Wilson was born in 1888 (1936-TMC, page 133.).

29. **Wilhelmina Turcotte** was born circa 1892 (1936-TMC, page 127.) (*1937-TMC*, page 250, Census No. 3007-3013.). She married **Neil Jones** on 31 May 1913 Fort Sill, Comanche County, Oklahoma (Marr. Cert.). She died on 3 Dec 1973 San Francisco, San Francisco County, California.

Neil Jones was born on 19 Jun 1892 Pennsylvania (1936-TMC, page 127.) (1940C CA 1940 California, Sixteenth Census of the United States, National Archives of the United States, Washington, D.C., page 3A.) (WIS Birth Wisconsin Birth/Christening Index.). He died on 25 Jun 1962 Shasta County, California, at age 70 (Ibid.).

Generation Four

30. John Turcotte was born circa 1880 (1892C-TMC , Family 74, #355-362.). He was born on 24 Dec 1882 Lewistown, Fergus County, Montana (1937-1987-LS Basic Roll, #517.). He married **Julia McConnell**, daughter of **Ira McConnell** and **Mary (--?--)**, on 19 Jun 1906 Chouteau County, Montana (ChCM.). He died on 24 Oct 1960 Powell County, Montana, at age 77 (MT Death.).
Julia McConnell was born circa 1890 Montana (1910C MT.).
Children of **John Turcotte** and **Julia McConnell** were as follows:

i. Matilda "Mattie" "Maza-si-na-to" Turcotte was born circa 1907 (MT Death.). She married Louis Turntoes on 1 Sep 1929 St.Paul's Mission, Blaine County, Montana (BCM Blaine County, Montana; Marriage Record Licenses and Certificates; 1865-1950; familysearch.org.). She died on 3 Jun 1975 Hill County, Montana (MT Death.).
Louis Turntoes was born in 1905 (BCM.).

ii. Eva Theresa "Ah-bi-do-th" Turcotte was born circa Dec 1908 Fort Belknap, Chouteau County, Montana (1910C MT.). She married Cecil Jones, son of Eb Jones and Juliann Fanglaye, on 27 Aug 1928 St.Pauls Mission, Blaine County, Montana (BCM.). She died on 29 May 1992 Havre, Hill County, Montana (MT Death.).
Cecil Jones was born in 1908 Leslie, South Dakota (BCM.).

iii. Mary Ann "Ni-ah-do-th" Turcotte was born on 29 May 1911 Hays, Blaine County, Montana (1923-Fort Belknap Census of the Assiniboine Indians of Fort Belknap, Montana, United States Indian Service Department of the Interior, Fort Belknap Agency, Montana, Superintendant J. T. Marshall, 30 Jun 1923 , Census No. 524-530.) (BCM.). She married Jones McGuire on 24 Dec 1931 Phillips County, Montana (PhCM.). She married Frank R. Fox, son of George Fox and Emma Seely, on 15 Apr 1944 Blaine County, Wisconsin (BCM.). She died on 12 Feb 1964 Hays, Blaine County, Montana, at age 52 (MT Death.).
Frank R. Fox was born on 23 Jan 1897 Wautoma, Wisconsin (BCM.). He died on 30 Aug 1971 Phillips County, Montana, at age 74 (SSDI.) (MT Death.).

iv. Cynthia Alma Turcotte was born in 1914 Fort Belknap Indian Reservation, Montana (1923-Fort Belknap, Census No. 524-530.).

v. Norbert "Da-ce-ces" Turcotte was born on 17 May 1915 Hays, Blaine County, Montana (BCM.). He married Joyce Carlson, daughter of Charles Carlson and Belle Martin, on 11 Sep 1940 Chinook, Blaine County, Montana (Ibid.). He died on 7 Jul 1987 Blaine County, Montana, at age 72 (MT Death.).
Joyce Carlson was born on 29 Jul 1918 Wadena, Minnesota (BCM.).

vi. Earl Turcotte was born on 2 May 1920 Fort Belknap Indian Reservation, Montana (1923-Fort Belknap, Census No. 524-530.). He died on 31 Aug 1924 Fort Belknap, Blaine County, Montana, at age 4 (1925-Fort Belknap 1925 Indian Census Roll of the Fort Belknap Reservation, United States Indian Service Department of the Interior, Fort Belknap Agency, Montana, 30 jun 1925 , Census No. 539-544.).

vii. Irma May Turcotte was born on 8 Apr 1929 Hays, Blaine County, Montana (1934-FB 1934 Census of the Fort Belknap, Montana, United States Indian Service Department of the Interior, Washington D.C., 1 Apr 1934 , Census No. 1274-1279.). She married Raymond Thomas Gone, son of Fred Gone and Mary John, on 2 Jul 1948 St.Paul's Mission, Hays, Blaine County, Montana (BCM.). She died on 24 Nov 1988 Blaine County, Montana, at age 59 (MT Death.).
Raymond Thomas Gone was born on 6 Jun 1926 Hays, Blaine County, Montana (BCM.). He died on 9 Sep 1978 Valley County, Montana, at age 52 (SSDI.) (MT Death.).

31. Charles Turcotte was born on 6 Jul 1886 Lewistown, Fergus County, Montana (Ancestry.com, WWI Draft Registration.) (MT Death.). He married **Evelyn Larocque**, daughter of **Joseph Larocque** and **Mary Louise Klyne**, on 29 Sep 1921 Phillips County, Montana (PhCM, #599.). He died on 21 Jun 1972 Cut Bank, Glacier County, Montana, at age 85 (SSDI.) (MT Death.).
Evelyn Larocque was born on 22 May 1904 Lewistown, Fergus County, Montana (Death Cert., State File No. 5018, 11-6-1929.). She died on 29 Oct 1929 Montana State Hospital, Warm Springs Township Galen, Deer Lodge County, Montana, at age 25 (Ibid.).
Children of **Charles Turcotte** and **Evelyn Larocque** were as follows:

i. Adelma Turcotte was born on 20 May 1923 (1937-1987-LS Basic Roll, #515.). She married Robert Allison, son of Wendell Allison and Lydie Harlan, on 4 Jun 1941 Whitefish, Flathead County, Montana (FlCM Flathead County, Montana; Marriage Record Licenses and Certificates; 1865-1950; familysearch.org, Hereinafter cited as FlCM.). She married Michael F. McGrath, son of Thomas McGrath and Theresa McNanna, on 22 Sep 1949 Conrad, Pondera County, Montana (PonCM Pondera County Courthouse, Montana; Marriage Record Licenses and Certificates; 1865-1950, familysearch.org, Hereinafter cited as PonCM.).
Robert Allison was born in 1919 (FlCM.).
Michael F. McGrath was born on 13 Aug 1914 Butte, Montana (PonCM.) (SSDI.) (Brenda Snider, 8 Oct 2014, obituary.). He married **Bertie Ross** on 23 Aug 1958 Yakima, Yakima County, Washingtron (Ibid.). He died on 7 Dec 1977 Ellensburg, Kittitas County, Washington, at age 63 (SSDI.) (Washington State Digital Archives, Secretary of State, State Archives, http://www.digitalcarchives.wa./gov, 960 Washington Street, Cheney, WA 99004.).

ii. Benjamin Turcotte was born on 4 Sep 1924 (SSDI.). He died on 22 Aug 1997 Great Falls, Cascade County, Montana, at age 72 (Ibid.) (MT Death.).

iii. Mary Bernice Turcotte was born on 13 Mar 1927 Hays, Blaine County, Montana (1987LS 1987-92 Little Shell Band of Chippewa Roll.) (1937-1987-LS Basic Roll, #515.). She married Robert King before 1952 (1987-92LS.). She married John G. Buck before 1965 (Ibid.).
Robert King was born circa 1927.

John G. Buck was born circa 1927.

iv. Theresa Mary Turcotte was born on 1 Feb 1929 Hays, Blaine County, Montana (SSDI.). She married Jack Heavy Runner, son of Jack Heavy Runner and Irene Wolf Chief, on 16 Sep 1946 Cut Bank, Glacier Couty, Montana (GCM.). She married Joseph J. Larocque, son of Raphael Larocque and Isabelle Petit dit Thomas, before 1953 (1987-92LS.). She died on 20 Apr 2001 Chinook, Blaine County, Montana, at age 72 (SSDI.) (MT Death.).

Jack Heavy Runner was born on 3 Feb 1924 Browning, Glacier County, Montana (SSDI.). He died on 8 Dec 2008 Browning, Glacier County, Montana, at age 84 (Ibid.).

Joseph J. Larocque was born circa 1922 (1930C MT, District 14-37, page 1B, line 69.). He was born on 3 Mar 1926 Lewistown, Fergus County, Montana (BIA-LS.).

32. Marie Turcotte was born on 4 Feb 1887 Lewistown, Fergus County, Montana (1937-1987-LS Basic Roll, #186.). She married **James C. Doney**, son of **John Marie Delauney dit Doney** and **Virginie Lafontaine**, on 13 Jan 1906 Choteau, Teton County, Montana (TeCM.). She died on 30 Oct 1956 Blaine County, Montana, at age 69 (MT Death.).

James C. Doney was born on 11 Aug 1883 (1987-92LS.). He died on 13 Nov 1959 Blaine County, Montana, at age 76 (MT Death.).

33. Rebecca Alma Turcotte was born on 8 Feb 1894 St.Pauls, Montana (RooCM.). She married **Frank Halverson** before 1918 (1987-92LS.). She and **Adolph Carl Weedman** obtained a marriage license on 9 Nov 1931 Roosevelt County, Montana (RooCM.). She married **Adolph Carl Weedman**, son of **Carl Weedman** and **Paulina Kerbes,** on 9 Nov 1931 Justice of the Peace, Wolf Point, Roosevelt County, Montana (Ibid.).

Frank Halverson was born circa 1898. He died before Nov 1931.

34. Marie Louise Turcotte was born on 28 Jun 1883 between, Regina and Wood Mountain, (Saskatchewan) (L2 Lebret, Mission de St.Florent, Roman Catholic Registre des Baptemes, Mariages & Seplutures, Qu'Appelle, Saskatchewan, Book Two: 1881-1887, FHC microfilm 1032949., page 75, B-_. Hereinafter cited as L2.). She was baptized on 14 Jul 1883 Lebret, (Saskatchewan) (Ibid.) (Ibid., page 70, B-35.). She married **Louis Desjarlais**, son of **Francois Xavier Desjarlais** and **Rachel St.Pierre,** in 1899 (1900C-ND, House 362, page 314A.).

Louis Desjarlais was born on 23 Mar 1877 Cypress Hills, (Saskatchewan) (HBSI.) (SPMT , page 106, #2315.). He was baptized on 26 Apr 1877 (St.Peter's Mission), Fort Benton, Montana Territory (Ibid.). He died on 6 Jan 1953 Rolette County, North Dakota, at age 75 (ND Death Index.).

35. Antoine Turcotte was born circa Feb 1885 (NWHBS, C-14937.). He married **Hiemyaw or Wisimyan (--?--)** before 1910 (BIA-TM-BMD, page 35.). He married **Adele Peltier** before 1922 (1936-TMC, page 121.).

Children of **Antoine Turcotte** and **Hiemyaw or Wisimyan (--?--)** are as follows:

i. Celina Turcotte was born on 15 Mar 1910 (Ibid., page 122.) (BIA-TM-BMD, page 35.) (*1937-TMC*, page 500, Census No. 5842-5848.).

ii. Mary Turcotte was born on 31 Jul 1915 Rolette County, North Dakota (1930C ND Fifteenth Census of the United States: 1930; North Dakota, National Archives of the United States, Washington, D.C., Sheet No. 3-B & 4-A, Family 55, line 95-100, 1.) (*1937-TMC*, page 500, Census No. 5842-5848.).

Adele Peltier was born in 1888 (1936-TMC, page 122.). She and **Standing in the Sky "Kijikoukanipawit" (--?--)** met before 1906 (BIA-TM-BMD, page 21.).

Children of **Antoine Turcotte** and **Adele Peltier** all born Rolette County, North Dakota, are as follows:

i. Vitaline Turcotte was born on 19 Jan 1922 (1930C ND, Sheet No. 3-B & 4-A, Family 55, line 95-100, 1.) (*1937-TMC*, page 500, Census No. 5842-5848.).

ii. Albert Turcotte was born on 23 Feb 1924 (1930C ND, Sheet No. 3-B & 4-A, Family 55, line 95-100, 1.) (*1937-TMC*, page 500, Census No. 5842-5848.).

iii. Alfred Turcotte was born on 27 Nov 1926 (1930C ND, Sheet No. 3-B & 4-A, Family 55, line 95-100, 1.) (*1937-TMC*, page 500, Census No. 5842-5848.).

iv. Alvina Turcotte was born on 8 Feb 1929 (1930C ND, Sheet No. 3-B & 4-A, Family 55, line 95-100, 1.) (*1937-TMC*, page 500, Census No. 5842-5848.).

36. Daniel Turcotte Jr was born on 29 Jan 1892 Belcourt, North Dakota (HDP.). He was born on 26 Nov 1893 Belcourt, North Dakota (RooCM.). He and **Clara Burns** obtained a marriage license on 2 Jun 1921 Roosevelt County, Montana (Ibid.). He married **Clara Burns**, daughter of **Simon Burns** and **Annie Komner,** on 29 Jun 1921 Justice of the Peace, Bainville, Montana (Ibid.).

Clara Burns was born on 8 Dec 1901 Minnesota (Ibid.).

Children of **Daniel Turcotte Jr.** and **Clara Burns** were as follows:

i. Joseph Turcotte was born on 20 Mar 1922 (*1937-TMC*, page 502, Census No. 5867-5873.).

ii. Edna Turcotte was born on 12 Feb 1924 (Ibid.). She married Cesar Belmonte, son of Pedro Belmonte and Marciana Palagonas, on 31 Aug 1938 Sidney, Richland County, Montana (RLCM.).

Cesar Belmonte was born on 25 Feb 1913 (Ibid.) (SSDI.). He died in Jun 1986 Somerton, Yuma County, Arizona, at age 73 (Ibid.).

iii. Evelyn Turcotte was born on 16 Apr 1926 (*1937-TMC*, page 502, Census No. 5867-5873.). She married Louis Acosta Ortiz, son of Eulozio Ortiz and Juliana Acosta, on 8 Jun 1942 Sidney, Richland County, Montana (RLCM.). She died on 15 Nov 2010 Williston, Williams County, North Dakota, at age 84 (SSDI.).

Louis Acosta Ortiz was born on 14 Aug 1914 Philippines (RLCM.) (WIS Birth.). He died on 16 Nov 1984 Salinas, Monterey County, California, at age 70 (SSDI.) (WIS Birth.).

iv. Viola Turcotte was born on 6 Oct 1929 (*1937-TMC*, page 502, Census No. 5867-5873.).

v. Angela Turcotte was born on 12 Feb 1934 (Ibid.).

vi. Glen Turcotte was born on 24 Dec 1935 (Ibid.).

37. John B. Turcotte was born in 1893 (1936-TMC, page 120.) (1912-TMC 1912 Census of the Turtle Mountain Chippewa, United States Indian Service Department of the Interior, Turtle Mountain Agency, North Dakota, 30 June 1912 , Census No. 2679.). He was born on 26 Dec 1896 (HDP.). He married **Margaret Latreille**, daughter of **Louis Napoleon Latreille** and **Sara Azure,** on 8 Jun 1912 (1936-TMC, page 120.) (BIA-TM-BMD, page 63.).

Margaret Latreille was born on 20 Aug 1894 North Dakota (1900C-ND, 342-342.) (SSDI.). She married **Michael Salo** before 1921 (*1937-TMC*, page 450, Census No. 5354-5358.). She died in Oct 1985 Spokane, Spokane County, Washington, at age 91 (SSDI.).

Children of **John B. Turcotte** and **Margaret Latreille** are as follows:

    i. John A. Turcotte was born on 25 Jan 1913 (1936-TMC, page 120.) (BIA-TM-BMD, page 63.) (*1937-TMC*, page 502, Census No. 5874-5876.).

    ii. Elmer Marion Turcotte was born on 30 Jul 1914 (1936-TMC, page 120.) (*1937-TMC*, page 502, Census No. 5874-5876.).

    iii. Lous N. Turcotte was born on 25 Aug 1918 (1930C ND, page 9B.) (*1937-TMC*, page 502, Census No. 5874-5876.).

38. Mary Josephine Turcotte was born on 23 Feb 1895 North Dakota (HDP.) (1936-TMC, page 92.) (1916-TMC, Census No. 1264-1265.). She married **Job Peter Joseph Falcon**, son of **Job Falcon** and **Marie Larocque,** before 1913. She died on 16 Mar 1969 Trenton, Williams County, North Dakota, at age 74 (ND Death Index.).

Job Peter Joseph Falcon was born on 5 Apr 1893 North Dakota (1916-TMC, Census No. 1264-1265.) (ND Death Index.) (SSDI.). He died on 30 Dec 1966 Trenton, Williams County, North Dakota, at age 73 (ND Death Index.) (SSDI.).

39. Marie Claudia Turcotte was born in Nov 1897 (HDP.). She was born in 1900 (1936-TMC, page 121.) (*1937-TMC*, page 458, Census No. 5436-5439.). She married **Guy Otis Shanks** before 1919 (Ibid.). She died on 6 Jan 1929 Portland, Multnomah, Oregon (HDP.).

40. Robert Ruben Turcotte was born on 4 Sep 1907 (HDP.) (ND Death Index.) (SSDI.). He married **Emma Laura Slater**, daughter of **Jean Baptiste Slater** and **Elise Trottier,** on 28 Oct 1928. He died on 2 May 1972 Trenton, Williams County, North Dakota, at age 64 (Ibid.) (ND Death Index.).

Emma Laura Slater was born on 6 May 1910 (SSDI.). She died on 8 Oct 1996 Trenton, Williams County, North Dakota, at age 86 (Ibid.).

Children of **Robert Ruben Turcotte** and **Emma Laura Slater** are as follows:

    i. Claudine Turcotte was born circa Jan 1929 (1930C ND, page 3A.).

    ii. June Mary Turcotte was born on 4 Jun 1930 (*1937-TMC*, page 503, Census No. 5885-5889.).

    iii. Joan Turcotte was born on 4 Jun 1931 (Ibid.).

    iv. Lawrence Turcotte was born on 30 Jan 1933 (Ibid.).

    v. Dina Lou Turcotte was born on 4 May 1936 (Ibid.).

41. Clarence Walter Turcotte was born on 9 May 1916 Trenton, Williams, North Dakota (*1921 TMC*, Census No. 3353-3360.). He married **Flora Katherine Falcon**, daughter of **Alphonse "Alfred" Falcon** and **Louise 'Elise' Levay,** on 24 Jul 1935 St.Joseph's Catholic Church, Williston, Williams County, North Dakota (Rod Mac Quarrie, 27 Mar 2013.). He married **Doris Louise Morin**, daughter of **Joseph Andrew Morin** and **Isabell Harriet Baney,** circa 1945 Wolf Point, Roosevelt County, Montana. He died on 6 Feb 1980 Trenton, Williams, North Dakota, at age 63 (ND Death Index.) (SSDI.). He was buried in Feb 1980 Trenton, Williams, North Dakota.

Flora Katherine Falcon was born on 2 Feb 1914 (1936-TMC, page 91.) (ND Death Index.). She died on 27 Jun 2001 Williston, Williams County, North Dakota, at age 87 (Ibid.) (SSDI.).

Children of **Clarence Walter Turcotte** and **Flora Katherine Falcon** were as follows:

    i. Gloria Bell Turcotte was born on 27 Sep 1936 Poplar, Roosevelt County, Montana (MT Death.). She died on 29 Sep 1936 Poplar, Roosevelt County, Montana (Ibid.).

    ii. William Clarence Turcotte was born on 30 Dec 1957 Williams County, North Dakota (ND Death Index.). He died on 13 Sep 1959 Williams County, North Dakota, at age 1 (Ibid.).

    iii. Gary Turcotte was born on 25 Jul 1959 (Minot Daily News, Minot, North Dakota, 5 Mar 2014.). He died on 26 Feb 2014 Denver, Colorado, at age 54 (Ibid.). Question: *He was survived by his mother Rena Falcon.*

Doris Louise Morin was born on 10 Apr 1920 Medicine Lake, Sheridan County, Montana. She married **Joseph Wilfred 'Jack' Brien**, son of **Joseph Alexander Brien** and **Louise 'Elise' Levay,** on 4 May 1939 Wolf Point, Roosevelt County, Montana (RooCM.). She and **Joseph Wilfred 'Jack' Brien** obtained a marriage license on 4 May 1939 Wolf Point, Roosevelt County, Montana (Ibid.). She married **Frank Costa** circa 1965 Carson City, Nevada. She died on 30 Apr 2000 Williston, Williams County, North Dakota, at age 80 (ND Death Index.).

Children of **Clarence Walter Turcotte** and **Doris Louise Morin** are as follows:

    i. Clarence Donald Turcotte was born on 30 Nov 1945 Santa Cruz, Santa Cruz, California. He married Cheryl (--?--).

    ii. Gary Turcotte was born on 9 May 1947 Salinas, California. He married Karen Heflin.

42. Marie Cecelia Turcotte was born on 23 Apr 1916 (1936-TMC, page 121.) (TM Star, 2 Feb 2009.) (*1937-TMC*, page 466, Census No. 6437-6438.). She married **Gordon Obadiah Smith** on 23 Jul 1936 Detroit, Michigan (TM Star, 2 Feb 2009.). She died on 24 Jan 2009 Mount Pleasant, Michigan, at age 92 (Ibid.).

43. William James Turcotte was born on 6 Mar 1919 (1936-TMC, page 121.) (Ancestry.com, 1938-1946 WWII Army Enlistment Records.) (*1937-TMC*, page 501, Census No. 5851-5863.). He married **Helene Margarete Bauchsch.**

Descendants of Joseph Turner

Generation One

1. Joseph Turner, son of Philip Turner and an Eskimo woman, was born circa 1783 Moose Factory (HBCA-B Hudson's Bay Company Archives - biographical sketches, Hudson's Bay Company Archives; Winnipeg, Manitoba.). He married according to the custom of the country **Emma (--?--)** circa 1812. He died on 16 Mar 1865 (Ibid.).

Emma (--?--) was born circa 1790 (Denney Papers, Charles D. Denney, Glenbow Archives, Calgary, Alberta.). She died in 1873 (Ibid.).

Children of **Joseph Turner** and **Emma (--?--)** were as follows:

2.   i.   Philip Turner, b. circa 1812; m. Jane Chisholm Boland; d. 1882.
3.   ii.   Joseph Turner, b. circa 1816 Moose Factory; m. Sarah Humphryville; d. 21 Apr 1885.
4.   iii.   Richard Turner, b. circa 1820; m. Jane Margaret Brown; d. 1869.
    iv.   Elizabeth Turner was born circa 1823 (Ibid.). She married William Isbister on 18 Jun 1840 Moose Factory.
    v.   Alexander Turner was baptized on 21 Nov 1826 Moose Factory (Ibid.).
5.   vi.   Charlotte Turner, b. 11 Jul 1828 Ruperts Land; m. James Harper; d. 24 Dec 1909 Selkirk, Manitoba.
    vii.   Matilda Turner was baptized on 17 Jul 1832 Moose Factory (Ibid.).
    viii.   Jane Turner was baptized on 7 Apr 1835 Moose Factory (Ibid.).

Generation Two

2. Philip Turner was born circa 1812 (HBCA-B.). He married **Jane Chisholm Boland** on 10 May 1837 Moose Factory (Denney.). (Edited by Pearl L. Weston, *Across the River: A History of the Turner, Thomson, Campbell Families*; 620-8th Ave. NE; Swift Current, SK S9H 2R3: n.pub., 1995.). He died in 1882 (HBCA-B.).

Children of **Philip Turner** and **Jane Chisholm Boland** were as follows:

6.   i.   Joseph Alexander Turner, b. 5 Dec 1838 Moose Factory; m. Jane Whitford; d. 14 Nov 1912 Fort Saskatchewan, Alberta.
    ii.   Mary Turner was born in Sep 1840 (Denney.). She died on 17 Dec 1843 Moose Factory at age 3 (Ibid.).
    iii.   Elizabeth Turner was born in 1843 (HBCA-B.).
    iv.   Barbara Turner was born in 1845 (Ibid.).
7.   v.   Robert Turner, b. 19 Jan 1848 Moose Factory; m. Jemima Agnes.
8.   vi.   Samuel Turner, b. circa 1850; m. Margaret (--?--).
9.   vii.   George Turner, b. 12 Jul 1853 Moose Factory; m. Rose (--?--).
    viii.   Margaret Turner was born on 22 Apr 1856 Moose Factory (Denney.).
    ix.   Genevieve Turner was born circa 1859 (Ibid.). She died on 21 Dec 1871 (Ibid.). She was buried Moose Factory.
    x.   Thomas Turner was baptized on 16 Aug 1859 Moose Factory (Ibid.).
    xi.   Ella Jane Turner was baptized on 26 Aug 1865 Moose Factory (Ibid.).

3. Joseph Turner was born circa 1816 Moose Factory (HBCA-B.). He was born circa 1822 (SL-SK St.Laurent-de-Grandin Roman Catholic Registre des Baptemes, Mariages & Sepltures, St.Laurent, Saskatchewan, 1872-1896, page 24, B-38. Hereinafter cited as SL-SK.). He married **Sarah Humphryville**, daughter of **Thomas Humphryville or Humpherville** and **Hannah or Annie Turner**, on 1 Apr 1838 Cumberland House, (Saskatchewan) (NWHBS 1885 Scrip Applications, North-West Halfbreeds residing outside Manitoba on 15 July 1870, RG15-20, C-14942.). He died on 21 Apr 1885 (Denney.).

Sarah Humphryville was born circa 1822 The Pas, (Saskatchewan) (NWHBS, C-14942.). She was baptized on 31 May 1836 St.Johns, Red River Colony, (Manitoba) (HBCR Hudson Bay Company Register of Anglican Church Baptisms, Marriages, and Burials for the Red River Settlement, 1821-1841; Hudson's Bay Company Archives, Winnipeg, Manitoba, E.4/1a, folio 128d. Hereinafter cited as HBCR.). She died on 15 Jul 1882 Fort-a-la-Corne, (Saskatchewan) (NWHBS, C-14942.).

Children of **Joseph Turner** and **Sarah Humphryville** were as follows:

10.   i.   Philip Turner, b. 9 Nov 1839 Cumberland House, (Saskatchewan); m. Harriet Anderson; m. Mary Hourie; d. 23 Apr 1919 Butler, Saskatchewan.
11.   ii.   Emma Turner, b. 27 Sep 1841 Cumberland, (Saskatchewan); m. John Thompson.
    iii.   Elizabeth Turner was born on 27 Aug 1843. She died in 1843.
    iv.   Charlotte Turner was born on 14 Sep 1844. She died on 23 Jan 1854 at age 9.
    v.   Joseph Turner was born on 18 Sep 1846. He died on 9 Nov 1846.
12.   vi.   Sarah Turner, b. 18 Sep 1847 Cumberland House, (Saskatchewan); m. George Goodfellow.
13.   vii.   Nancy Turner, b. 20 Nov 1849 Cumberland, North West Territories; m. John Alexander McDonald.
14.   viii.   John Turner, b. 27 Jul 1851 Cumberland House, (Saskatchewan); m. Margaret McKay; d. 16 Sep 1926 Clouston, Saskatchewan.
15.   ix.   Peter Turner, b. 20 Jul 1853 Fort-a-la-Corne, (Saskatchewan); m. Mary Ann Beads; d. 26 Sep 1924 Clouston, Saskatchewan.
16.   x.   Mary Turner, b. 28 Jul 1855 Fort-a-la-Corne, (Saskatchewan); m. James Goodlad; d. 15 Jan 1943 Fort-a-la-Corne, (Saskatchewan).
    xi.   Jane Turner was born on 7 Dec 1857. She died on 25 Oct 1859 at age 1.
17.   xii.   Hannah Turner, b. 20 Oct 1859; m. William Henry Bartlett; d. 8 May 1900 (Saskatchewan).
    xiii.   Eliza Turner was born on 26 Aug 1863 (Heather Hallett Research.). She died on 1 Aug 1865 at age 1 (Ibid.).
18.   xiv.   Frances Matilda 'Fanny' Turner, b. 28 Oct 1865 Fort-a-la-Corne, (Saskatchewan); m. Charles Woodman; d. 18 Nov 1918.
19.   xv.   Harriet Turner, b. 5 Sep 1870 Fort-a-la-Corne, (Saskatchewan); m. Thomas Exley Parker.

4. Richard Turner was born circa 1820 (MBS Scrip Applications, Original White Settlers & Halfbreeds residing in Manitoba on 15 July 1870, RG15-19, C-14934.). He married **Jane Margaret Brown** before 1851. He died in 1869 (Ibid.).

Question: *Assumed son of Joseph Turner* (Denney.).

Jane Margaret Brown died in 1867.

Children of **Richard Turner** and **Jane Margaret Brown** were as follows:

    i.   Barbara Mary Turner was born on 5 Sep 1851 North West (Ibid.). She married Robert McDonald, son of William McDonald and Margaret Mowat, on 3 Jul 1873 St.Andrews, (Manitoba) (Ibid.).

Robert McDonald was born on 10 Oct 1848 St.Andrews, (Manitoba) (MBS, Supplementary Returns: C-14934.). He was baptized on 18 Oct 1848 St.Andrews, (Manitoba) (Denney.).

- ii. Joseph Turner was born in 1856 (MBS, C-14934.). He died in 1875 (Ibid.).
- iii. Nancy Turner was born on 11 Jul 1856 St.Andrews, (Manitoba) (Ibid.).
- iv. Elizabeth Turner was born in 1858 St.Andrews, (Manitoba) (Ibid.).
- 20 v. John Turner, b. 29 Jan 1861 St.Andrews, (Manitoba).
- vi. Alexander Turner was born in 1863 St.Andrews, (Manitoba) (Ibid.). He was baptized on 25 Jan 1863 St.Andrews, (Manitoba) (Ibid.).

5. Charlotte Turner was born on 11 Jul 1828 Ruperts Land (Ibid., C-14928.). She was baptized on 26 Jun 1844 Moose Factory (Denney.). She married **James Harper**, son of **William Harper** and **Mary Indian,** on 17 Oct 1844 (St.Andrews), Grand Rapids, (Manitoba) (HBCR, page 91, No. 129.). She died on 24 Dec 1909 Selkirk, Manitoba, at age 81 (Manitoba Vital Statistics online, http://web2.gov.mb.ca, Death Reg. #1909,002039.).

James Harper was born on 16 Dec 1810 Ruperts Land (MBS, C-14928.). He died on 7 Apr 1887 St.Andrews, Lisgar, Manitoba, at age 76 (MB Vital Statistics, Death Reg. #1887,001758.).

Generation Three

6. Joseph Alexander Turner was born on 5 Dec 1838 Moose Factory (Denney.) (ArchiviaNet, C-15007.). He married **Jane Whitford**, daughter of **Samuel Whitford** and **Mary Henderson,** on 9 Jan 1862 St.Mary's Anglican Church, Portage la Prairie, (Manitoba) (SMACPLP St.Marys Anglican Church, Portage La Prairie, Manitoba, Baptisms, Marriages, Burials, 1855-1883, transcribed by Clarence Kipling , page 10, M-19.). He died on 14 Nov 1912 Fort Saskatchewan, Alberta, at age 73 (Denney.).

Jane Whitford was born on 18 Nov 1845 (Manitoba) (Ibid.). She was baptized on 4 Dec 1845 St.Andrews, (Manitoba) (Ibid.). She died on 15 Dec 1928 Fort Saskatchewan, Alberta, at age 83 (Ibid.).

Children of **Joseph Alexander Turner** and **Jane Whitford** were as follows:

- 21 i. Mary Jane Turner, b. 13 Mar 1863 Portage la Prairie, (Manitoba); m. George Ferguson.
- 22 ii. Elizabeth Margaret Turner, b. 27 May 1865 Portage la Prairie, (Manitoba); m. Joseph Chabot.
- iii. Eliza Turner was born on 22 Nov 1867 (NWHBSI Index 1885 Scrip Applications, North-West Halfbreeds residing outside Manitoba on 15 July 1870, RG15-20, page 80.). She died on 18 Nov 1949 at age 81 (Denney.).
- 23 iv. Robert William Turner, b. 17 Feb 1870 Victoria, (Alberta).
- 24 v. Philip Richard Turner, b. 6 May 1872 Victoria, (Alberta); m. Mary Margaret Coutts.
- vi. Annabella Turner was born on 13 Dec 1874 Fort Victoria, (Alberta) (ArchiviaNet, C-15007.) (Denney.). She died on 14 Mar 1886 Fort Saskatchewan, (Alberta), at age 11 (Ibid.) (ArchiviaNet, C-15007.).
- vii. Henry George Turner was born on 14 Feb 1877 Victoria, (Alberta) (Ibid.) (Denney.). He died on 16 Mar 1886 Fort Saskatchewan, (Alberta), at age 9 (Ibid.) (ArchiviaNet, C-15007.).
- viii. John Frederick Turner was born on 23 Aug 1879 Fort Victoria (Ibid.).
- ix. Archibald Turner was born on 13 Aug 1881 Victoria (Ibid.). He died on 27 Jun 1957 Fort Saskatchewan at age 75 (Denney.).
- x. Barbara Ellen Turner was born on 2 Dec 1884 Fort Saskatchewan, (Alberta) (ArchiviaNet, C-15007.). She died in 1886 Fort Saskatchewan, (Alberta) (Ibid.).

7. Robert Turner was born on 19 Jan 1848 Moose Factory (Edited by Pearl L. Weston, *Across the River*.). He married **Jemima Agnes** before 1878.

Jemima Agnes was born in 1862. She died on 27 Jan 1892 Moose Factory.

Children of **Robert Turner** and **Jemima Agnes** all born Moose Factory were as follows:

- i. John Henry George Turner was baptized on 28 Jul 1878 (Denney.).
- ii. Thomas Hamilton Turner was baptized on 26 Sep 1880 (Ibid.).
- iii. Philip Andrew Turner was baptized on 22 Oct 1882 (Ibid.). He died on 23 May 1898 at age 15 (Ibid.).
- iv. Joseph Walter Turner was baptized on 28 Dec 1884 (Ibid.).
- v. Robert Franklin Turner was baptized on 25 Dec 1886 (Ibid.). He died on 21 Apr 1916 Rupert's House at age 29 (HBCA-B.).
- vi. William Frederick Turner was baptized on 30 Jun 1889 (Denney.).
- vii. Jemima Agnes Turner was baptized on 20 Dec 1891 (Ibid.). She died on 6 Jun 1892 (Ibid.).

8. Samuel Turner was born circa 1850. He married **Margaret (--?--)** before 1875.

Margaret (--?--) was born in 1837. She died on 15 May 1886 Moose Factory.

Children of **Samuel Turner** and **Margaret (--?--)** all born Moose Factory were as follows:

- i. Mary Turner was baptized on 12 Dec 1875 (Ibid.).
- ii. Samuel Turner was baptized on 16 Sep 1877 (Ibid.).
- iii. Barbara Ann Turner was baptized on 7 Apr 1882 (Ibid.).
- iv. William Orange Turner was baptized on 30 Nov 1884 (Ibid.).

Children of **Samuel Turner** and **Hannah (--?--)** all born Moose Factory were as follows:

- i. Emma Turner was baptized on 4 Aug 1889 (Ibid.).
- ii. Elizabeth Ann Turner was baptized on 18 May 1891 (Ibid.).
- iii. John Oak Turner was baptized on 30 Apr 1893 (Ibid.).

9. George Turner was baptized on 12 Jul 1853 Moose Factory (Ibid.). He married **Rose (--?--)** before 1882.

Children of **George Turner** and **Rose (--?--)** all born Moose Factory were as follows:

- i. Robert Alexander Turner was baptized on 22 Oct 1882 (Ibid.). He died on 25 Nov 1900 Moose Factory at age 18 (Ibid.).
- ii. James Frederick Turner was baptized on 26 Oct 1884 (Ibid.).
- iii. Jane Barbara Turner was baptized on 13 Jan 1889 (Ibid.).

      iv.   Herbert Hamilton Turner was baptized on 20 Dec 1891 (Ibid.). He died on 7 Jun 1892 Moose Factory (Ibid.).

10. **Philip Turner** was born on 9 Nov 1839 Cumberland House, (Saskatchewan) (NWHBS, C-14942.) (1901 Canada, microfilm, T-6553, Butler, page 3, Family 29, line 23-29.). He married **Harriet Anderson**, daughter of **John Anderson** and **Mary Anne Desmarais**, on 25 Apr 1864 Fort-a-la-Corne, (Saskatchewan) (NWHBS, C-14942.). He married **Mary Hourie**, daughter of **Thomas Hourie** and **Agnes Bird**, in 1896 (Ibid.). He died on 23 Apr 1919 Butler, Saskatchewan, at age 79 (HBCA-B.).

    Harriet Anderson was born in 1849 Winnipeg, (Manitoba) (NWHBS, C-14942.). She was baptized on 27 May 1849 St.Andrews, (Manitoba) (AI-Rozyk Anglican Index of Baptisms, Marriages and Burials Extractions, Hudson Bay Company Archives, Winnipeg, Manitoba, Canada, Selected and Compiled by Rosemary Rozyk. Hereinafter cited as AI-Rozyk.).

    Children of **Philip Turner** and **Harriet Anderson** were as follows:

  25   i.   Mary Turner, b. 18 Dec 1866 Pakan, (Alberta); m. William Stevens Jr.

       ii.   Sarah Turner was born on 15 Sep 1868 Carlton, (Saskatchewan) (NWHBS, C-14941.).

  26   iii.   John Turner, b. 6 Nov 1871 Fort-a-la-Corne, (Saskatchewan); m. Susan Agnes Deschambault.

       iv.   Peter Turner was born on 1 Mar 1873 Prince Albert, (Saskatchewan) (Ibid., C-14942.) (ArchiviaNet, C-15007.). He died on 29 Nov 1873 Prince Albert, (Saskatchewan) (NWHBS, C-14942.) (ArchiviaNet, C-15007.).

  27   v.   Margaret Turner, b. 1 Jul 1874 Prince Albert, (Saskatchewan); m. Donald McDonald.

  28   vi.   Francis Henry Turner, b. 5 Dec 1876 Prince Albert, (Saskatchewan); m. Maude Eveline Ballendine; d. 20 Mar 1907 Coxby, (Saskatchewan).

      vii.   Elisabeth Harriet Turner was born on 9 Jul 1877 Prince Albert, (Saskatchewan) (NWHBS, C-14942.) (ArchiviaNet, C-15007.). She died on 29 Aug 1878 Prince Albert, (Saskatchewan), at age 1 (NWHBS, C-14942.) (ArchiviaNet, C-15007.).

   viii.   Colin George Turner was born on 12 Nov 1878 Prince Albert, (Saskatchewan) (NWHBS, C-14942.) (Saskatchewan Vital Statistics online, http://vsgs.health.gov.sk.ca, Birth Reg. #11185.) (ArchiviaNet, C-15007.). He married Lena McKay, daughter of William Edward 'Billy' McKay and Justine 'Christina' Cayen dit Boudreau, on 25 Jun 1911 Medicine Hat, (Alberta) (T. R. "Pat" McCloy, McKay Descendancy, McKay Descendancy.).

       ix.   Philip Turner Jr was born on 20 Jan 1880 Prince Albert, (Saskatchewan) (NWHBS, C-14942.) (ArchiviaNet, C-15007.).

       x.   Catherine Jane Turner was born on 11 Jun 1881 Prince Albert, (Saskatchewan) (NWHBS, C-14942.) (ArchiviaNet, C-15007.). She died on 27 Jan 1893 Butler's Settlement, (Saskatchewan), at age 11 (T. R. McCloy.) (ArchiviaNet, C-15007.).

       xi.   Alexander James Stewart Turner was born on 22 May 1883 Prince Albert, (Saskatchewan) (NWHBS, C-14942.) (ArchiviaNet, C-15007.).

      xii.   Charles Thomas Turner was born on 21 Oct 1885 Fort-a-la-Corne, (Saskatchewan) (T. R. McCloy.) (ArchiviaNet, C-15007.).

Mary Hourie was born on 18 May 1879 (1901 Canada, microfilm, T-6553, Butler, page 3, Family 29, line 23-28.).

Children of **Philip Turner** and **Mary Hourie** were as follows:

       i.   Lawrence Wilfred Turner was born on 1 Sep 1897 Butler, (Saskatchewan) (Ibid.).

       ii.   Ellen Harriet Turner was born on 14 Jul 1899 Butler, (Saskatchewan) (Ibid.).

      iii.   Emma Gertrude Turner was born in Feb 1903 (Automated Genealogy 1911 Census Transcription Project and Census Images from the National Archives of Canada, http://www.automatedgenealogy.com, District 20, page 3, family 38, line 19-23.).

       iv.   Florence Turner was born in Jul 1907 (Ibid.).

11. **Emma Turner** was born on 27 Sep 1841 Cumberland, (Saskatchewan) (Edited by Pearl L. Weston, *Across the River*.). She married **John Thompson** in 1859 Fort-a-la-Corne, (Saskatchewan) (NWHBS, C-14942.).

    John Thompson was born Scotland.

12. **Sarah Turner** was born on 18 Sep 1847 Cumberland House, (Saskatchewan) (NWHBSI.) (1901 Canada, #205-e(1); page 3, family 27, line 45-49.) (ArchiviaNet, C-15007.). She married **George Goodfellow** in 1865 Fort-a-la-Corne, (Saskatchewan) (NWHBSI.).

    George Goodfellow was born on 12 Aug 1842 Scotland (1901 Canada, #205-e(1); page 3, family 27, line 45-49.).

13. **Nancy Turner** was born on 20 Nov 1849 Cumberland, North West Territories (NWHBS, C-14940.). She married **John Alexander McDonald**, son of **William McDonald** and **Catherine Gunn**, on 1 Apr 1870 Prince Albert, (Saskatchewan) (Ibid.).

    John Alexander McDonald was born on 16 Jun 1842 Kildonan, (Manitoba) (MBS, C-14930.). He was baptized on 26 Jun 1842 St.Johns, (Manitoba) (Ibid.).

14. **John Turner** was born on 27 Jul 1851 Cumberland House, (Saskatchewan) (T. R. McCloy, McKay Descendancy.). He married **Margaret McKay**, daughter of **Alexander McKay** and **Catherine McCorrister**, on 2 Dec 1875 Prince Albert, (Saskatchewan) (Denney.) (T. R. McCloy, McKay Descendancy.). He died on 16 Sep 1926 Clouston, Saskatchewan, at age 75 (Ibid.).

    Margaret McKay was born circa 1858 North West Territory (1870C-MB, page 287, #1424.).

    Children of **John Turner** and **Margaret McKay** were as follows:

       i.   Harriet Turner.

  29   ii.   Maria Maud Turner, m. Rudolph Thomas Inkster.

      iii.   Sarah Catherine Turner was born on 30 Mar 1877 Prince Albert, (Saskatchewan) (ArchiviaNet, C-15007.). She died on 20 May 1881 Prince Albert, (Saskatchewan), at age 4 (Ibid.).

       iv.   Margaret Bell Turner was born on 6 May 1900 Prince Albert, (Saskatchewan) (SK Vital Statistics, Birth Reg. #2095.).

15. **Peter Turner** was born on 20 Jul 1853 Fort-a-la-Corne, (Saskatchewan) (1901 Canada, #205, e(1), page 4, family 29, line 1-9.). He married **Mary Ann Beads**, daughter of **Jacob Beads** and **Charlotte Adhemar**, on 2 Dec 1875 St.Marys, Prince Albert, (Saskatchewan) (Denney.). He died on 26 Sep 1924 Clouston, Saskatchewan, at age 71 (Ibid.).

Mary Ann Beads was born on 10 Mar 1859 (1901 Canada, #205, e(1), page 4, family 29, line 1-9.). She was baptized on 3 Apr 1859 St.Andrews, (Manitoba) (HBCA-B, HBCA Reference: PAM, St. Andrews Bapt. 780.).

Children of **Peter Turner** and **Mary Ann Beads** were as follows:

    i.   Margaret Turner was born on 27 Sep 1878 Prince Albert, (Saskatchewan) (1901 Canada, #205, e(1), page 4, family 29, line 1-9.) (ArchiviaNet, C-15007.).

    ii.   James Turner was born on 6 Dec 1880 Fort-a-la-Corne, (Saskatchewan) (Ibid.). He died on 6 Jan 1881 Fort-a-la-Corne, (Saskatchewan) (Ibid.).

    iii.   Elizabeth Turner was born in Dec 1881 Fort-a-la-Corne, (Saskatchewan) (Ibid.). She died in Dec 1881 Fort-a-la-Corne, (Saskatchewan) (Ibid.).

    iv.   Sarah Turner was born on 23 Nov 1882 Fort-a-la-Corne, (Saskatchewan) (NWHBSI.) (ArchiviaNet, C-15007.).

    v.   Lilly Turner was born on 23 Nov 1883 Fort-a-la-Corne, (Saskatchewan) (1901 Canada, #205, e(1), page 4, family 29, line 1-9.).

    vi.   Peter Turner was born on 24 Sep 1885 Fort-a-la-Corne, (Saskatchewan) (ArchiviaNet, C-15007.). He died in Jan 1896 Fort-a-la-Corne, (Saskatchewan), at age 10 (Ibid.).

    vii.   Thomas William Turner was born on 27 Nov 1887 Fort-a-la-Corne, (Saskatchewan) (1901 Canada, #205, e(1), page 4, family 29, line 1-9.).

    viii.   Joseph Edward Turner was born on 25 Mar 1890 Fort-a-la-Corne, (Saskatchewan) (Ibid.).

    ix.   Arthur Norman Turner was born on 27 Jul 1892 Fort-a-la-Corne, (Saskatchewan) (Ibid.) (SK Vital Statistics, Birth Reg. #7195.).

    x.   Frederick P. Osborne Turner was born on 20 Jan 1898 Fort-a-la-Corne, (Saskatchewan) (1901 Canada, #205, e(1), page 4, family 29, line 1-9.).

    xi.   John Henry Edward Turner was born on 3 Feb 1901 Fort-a-la-Corne, (Saskatchewan) (Ibid.).

16. **Mary Turner** was born on 28 Jul 1855 Fort-a-la-Corne, (Saskatchewan) (NWHBS, C-14938.) (Denney.). She married **James Goodlad** on 10 Jul 1876 Fort-a-la-Corne, (Saskatchewan) (NWHBS, C-14938.) (Denney.). She died on 15 Jan 1943 Fort-a-la-Corne, (Saskatchewan), at age 87.

James Goodlad died in 1902.

17. **Hannah Turner** was born on 20 Oct 1859 (Edited by Pearl L. Weston, *Across the River*.). She married **William Henry Bartlett**, son of **John Bartlett,** on 14 Feb 1877 Fort-a-la-Corne, (Saskatchewan) (Ibid.). She died on 8 May 1900 (Saskatchewan) at age 40 (SK Vital Statistics, Death Reg. #85.).

William Henry Bartlett was born circa 1851 England (1881 Canada, District 192-2, page 14, household 74.). He died on 5 Jun 1894 (Saskatchewan) (SK Vital Statistics, Death Reg. #587.).

18. **Frances Matilda 'Fanny' Turner** was born on 28 Oct 1865 Fort-a-la-Corne, (Saskatchewan) (NWHBS, C-14942.). She married **Charles Woodman** before 1888. She died on 18 Nov 1918 at age 53 (Edited by Pearl L. Weston, *Across the River*.).

19. **Harriet Turner** was born on 5 Sep 1870 Fort-a-la-Corne, (Saskatchewan) (ArchiviaNet.). She married **Thomas Exley Parker** before 1899.

20. **John Turner** was born on 29 Jan 1861 St.Andrews, (Manitoba) (MBS, C-14934.). He was baptized on 17 Mar 1861 St.Andrews, (Manitoba) (Ibid.). He married **Lucille Anderson**, daughter of **John Gilbert Anderson** and **Marie Charon dit Ducharme,** in May 1884 Edmonton, (Alberta) (NWHBS, C-14942.).

Lucille Anderson was born on 17 Oct 1869 Edmonton, (Alberta) (Ibid.). She was baptized on 5 Dec 1869 St.Joachim, Fort Edmonton, (Alberta) (MSJ-FA-E Register des Baptemes, Mariages & Sepultures 1858-1861 Mission St.Joachim, Fort Auguste, Fort des Prairies, Edmonton, No. 1, page 68, B-_. Hereinafter cited as MSJ-FA-E.).

Children of **John Turner** and **Lucille Anderson** were as follows:

    i.   Mary Margaret Turner was born on 10 Feb 1885 Miner's Flat, (Alberta) (ArchiviaNet, C-15007.). She died on 15 Dec 1886 Miner's Flat, (Alberta), at age 1 (Ibid.).

    ii.   Edward Turner was born on 6 Feb 1890 (1901 Canada, #202-n(1); page 30, family 282, line 3-10.).

    iii.   John Richard Turner was born on 3 Apr 1892 (Ibid.).

    iv.   Ernest Turner was born on 6 Feb 1894 (Ibid.).

    v.   James Turner was born on 9 Apr 1896 (Ibid.).

    vi.   Barbara Turner was born on 6 Apr 1898 (Ibid.).

    vii.   Mary Florence Turner was born on 6 Apr 1900 (Ibid.).

    viii.   Mabel Turner was born in May 1903 (1911 Canada, District 62, page 1-2, family 12, line 42-50, 1.).

    ix.   William Turner was born in Apr 1906 (Ibid.).

    x.   Stanley Turner was born in Nov 1908 (Ibid.).

Generation Four

21. **Mary Jane Turner** was born on 13 Mar 1863 Portage la Prairie, (Manitoba) (Denney.). She was baptized on 12 Apr 1863 St.Mary's Anglican Church, Portage la Prairie, (Manitoba) (SMACPLP, page 21, B-168.). She married **George Ferguson** before 1885.

22. **Elizabeth Margaret Turner** was born on 27 May 1865 Portage la Prairie, (Manitoba) (NWHBS, C-14942.) (ArchiviaNet, C-15007.). She was baptized on 4 Jun 1865 St.Mary's Anglican Church, Portage la Prairie, (Manitoba) (SMACPLP, page 31, B-248.). She married **Joseph Chabot** on 24 Sep 1885 Fort Saskatchewan, (Alberta) (ArchiviaNet, C-15007.).

Joseph Chabot was born on 13 Jun 1861 (1901 Canada, #202-q(1))-1, page 8, family 97, line 16-24.).

23. **Robert William Turner** was born on 17 Feb 1870 Victoria, (Alberta) (NWHBS, C-14942.). He married **Catherine Brown**, daughter of **Magnus Brown** and **Bella Dog-Rib Indian**, before 1899 (ArchiviaNet, C-15007.) (1901 Canada, #202-q(1))-1, page 1, family 13, line 35-37.).

Catherine Brown was born on 17 Sep 1872 Fort Simpson, Athabasca, (Alberta) (ArchiviaNet, C-15007.) (1901 Canada, #202-q(1))-1, page 1, family 13, line 35-37.).

Children of **Robert William Turner** and **Catherine Brown** were:

i. Florence Turner was born on 26 Jan 1899 Fort Saskatchewan, (Alberta) (Ibid.).

24. Philip Richard Turner was born on 6 May 1872 Victoria, (Alberta) (Ibid., #202-q(1)-1; page 5, family 76, line 26-28.) (ArchiviaNet, C-15007.). He married **Mary Margaret Coutts,** daughter of **Peter Coutts** and **Amelia Henderson,** before 1900 (1911 Canada, District 27, page 4, family 42, line 23-32.).

Mary Margaret Coutts was born on 27 Aug 1883 Fort Saskatchewan, (Saskatchewan) (ArchiviaNet, C-15007.).

Children of **Philip Richard Turner** and **Mary Margaret Coutts** were as follows:

i. Richard E. Turner was born in Dec 1900 (1911 Canada, District 27, page 4, family 42, line 23-32.).

ii. Edna Turner was born in May 1901 (Ibid.).

iii. Reginald Turner was born in Oct 1902 (Ibid.).

iv. Katherine Turner was born in Aug 1905 (Ibid.).

v. Phillip Turner was born in Jul 1908 (Ibid.).

vi. Peter Turner was born in Mar 1910 (Ibid.).

vii. Mamie Turner was born circa 1912 (1921 Census of Canada from the National Archives of Canada (Transcription by ancestry.com), Ottawa, Canada, District 11-38, page 12.).

viii. Karl Turner was born circa 1914 (Ibid.).

ix. Bennie Turner was born circa 1917 (Ibid.).

x. Margaret Turner was born in 1920 (Ibid.).

25. Mary Turner was born on 18 Dec 1866 Pakan, (Alberta) (NWHBS, C-14941.) (1901 Canada, District 205-g, page 3, family 28, line 38-46.). She married **William Stevens Jr.,** son of **William Richard Stevens** and **Mary Foulds,** in 1884 Pakan, (Alberta) (NWHBS, C-14941.).

William Stevens Jr was born on 18 Oct 1865 St.Andrews, (Manitoba) (1870C-MB, page 193, #517.) (1901 Canada, District 205-g, page 3, family 28, line 38-46.).

26. John Turner was born on 6 Nov 1871 Fort-a-la-Corne, (Saskatchewan) (NWHBS, C-14942.) (1901 Canada, microfilm, T-6553, Butler, page 3, Family 30, line 29-35.) (ArchiviaNet, C-15007.). He married **Susan Agnes Deschambault,** daughter of **Louis Deschambault dit Fleury** and **Nancy Thomas,** before 1892.

Susan Agnes Deschambault was born on 1 Mar 1876 Cumberland, (Saskatchewan) (ArchiviaNet.) (1901 Canada, microfilm, T-6553, Butler, page 3, Family 30, line 29-35.).

Children of **John Turner** and **Susan Agnes Deschambault** were as follows:

i. George F. L. Turner was born on 25 Feb 1892 Butler, (Saskatchewan) (Ibid.).

ii. Philip Turner was born on 15 Apr 1894 Butler, (Saskatchewan) (Ibid.).

iii. Sarah Nancy Turner was born on 22 Jun 1896 Butler, (Saskatchewan) (Ibid.) (SK Vital Statistics, Birth Reg. #7427.).

iv. Thomas Howard Turner was born on 30 Jan 1899 Butler, (Saskatchewan) (1901 Canada, microfilm, T-6553, Butler, page 3, Family 30, line 29-35.) (SK Vital Statistics, Birth Reg. #2066.).

v. John Arthur Turner was born on 22 Feb 1901 Butler, (Saskatchewan) (1901 Canada, microfilm, T-6553, Butler, page 3, Family 30, line 29-35.).

vi. Virginia Catherine Turner was born on 2 Jul 1903 (Saskatchewan) (SK Vital Statistics, Birth Reg. #3580.).

vii. Mary Margaret Turner was born on 5 Mar 1908 Coxby, Saskatchewan (Ibid., Birth Reg. #9235.).

viii. Lawrence Turner was born in Jun 1910 (1911 Canada, District 20, page 3, family 39, line 24-33.).

27. Margaret Turner was born on 1 Jul 1874 Prince Albert, (Saskatchewan) (NWHBS, C-14942.) (ArchiviaNet.). She married **Donald McDonald,** son of **John "D" McDonald** and **Charlotte Inkster,** before 1893.

Donald McDonald was born circa 1863 North West (1870C-MB, page 129, #929.).

28. Francis Henry Turner was born on 5 Dec 1876 Prince Albert, (Saskatchewan) (NWHBS, C-14942.) (1901 Canada, microfilm, T-6553, Butler, page 3, Family 26, line 9-12.). He married **Maude Eveline Ballendine,** daughter of **Robert "A" Ballendine** and **Flora Budd,** before 1900. He died on 20 Mar 1907 Coxby, (Saskatchewan), at age 30 (Edited by Pearl L. Weston, *Across the River.*) (SK Vital Statistics, Death Reg. # 227.).

Maude Eveline Ballendine was born on 17 Feb 1879 Devon, Cumberland District (ArchiviaNet.) (Denney.).

Children of **Francis Henry Turner** and **Maude Eveline Ballendine** were as follows:

i. Myra Turner was born on 20 Feb 1900 Butler, (Saskatchewan) (1901 Canada, microfilm, T-6553, Butler, page 3, Family 26, line 9-12.).

ii. Robert Chester Turner was born on 19 Feb 1901 Butler, (Saskatchewan) (Ibid.).

iii. Gordon Tumey Turner was born on 20 Feb 1903 Coxby, (Saskatchewan) (SK Vital Statistics, Birth Reg. #3254.).

iv. Florence Margaret Turner was born on 9 Jan 1905 Coxby, (Saskatchewan) (Ibid., Birth Reg. #4945.).

v. Edith Diana Turner was born on 4 Jan 1906 (Saskatchewan) (Ibid., Birth Reg. #6241.).

29. Maria Maud Turner married **Rudolph Thomas Inkster,** son of **Archibald James Inkster** and **Ellen Harriet Swain,** on 31 Aug 1926 Prince Albert, (Saskatchewan) (Denney.).

Rudolph Thomas Inkster was born on 30 Nov 1895 (Saskatchewan) (SK Vital Statistics, Birth Reg. #10799.). He died in 1969 (Denney.).

Descendants of Antoine Vallee

Generation One

1. Antoine Vallee married according to the custom of the country **Suzanne Lefebvre or Favel** before 1811.

Children of **Antoine Vallee** and **Suzanne Lefebvre or Favel** were as follows:

2   i. Louise Vallee, b. 1817; m. Olivier "Carlouche" Vivier.

3   ii.   Helene Vallee, b. 1818; m. Francois Villeneuve dit la Fourche; d. before 21 Feb 1870.

4   iii.   Angelique Vallee, b. circa 1820; m. Louis Leblanc; m. Basile Hebert.

5   iv.   Louis Vallee, b. circa 1821; m. Louise Durand; d. before 1867.

6   v.   Marie Vallee, b. 1825 North West Territories; m. Charles Ducharme.

7   vi.   Therese Vallee dit Laplante, b. circa 1830 Edmonton, (Alberta); m. Joseph Trottier.

Generation Two

2. Louise Vallee was born in 1817. She married **Olivier "Carlouche" Vivier**, son of **Alexis Vivier** and **Marie Anne Assiniboine**, on 27 Sep 1842 Fort-des-Prairies, (Alberta) (FDP Baptisms & Marriages Fort des Prairie, Saskatchewan District, C Kipling, M-24. Hereinafter cited as FDP.). She married **Olivier "Carlouche" Vivier**, son of **Alexis Vivier** and **Marie Anne Assiniboine**, before 1853. **Olivier "Carlouche" Vivier** was born circa 1821.

3. Helene Vallee was born in 1818. She married according to the custom of the country **Francois Villeneuve dit la Fourche**, son of **Augustin Amiot dit Villeneuve** and **Marguerite Proulx dit Clement**, before 1836. She married **Francois Villeneuve dit la Fourche**, son of **Augustin Amiot dit Villeneuve** and **Marguerite Proulx dit Clement**, on 12 Sep 1842 Fort-des-Prairies, (Alberta) (FDP, M-10.). She died before 21 Feb 1870 (SN1 Catholic Parish Register of St.Norbert 1857-1873, M-6. Hereinafter cited as SN1.).

Francois Villeneuve dit la Fourche was baptized on 28 Sep 1811 St.Eustache, Quebec (Rod MacQuarrie Research, 16 Oct 2009, Source: Drouin.). He was born on 28 Sep 1811 St.Eustache, Quebec (Ibid.). He married **Angelique Houle**, daughter of **Charles Houle** and **Madeleine Breland**, before 1858.

4. Angelique Vallee was born circa 1820 (Ibid., C-14942.). She married according to the custom of the country **Louis Leblanc** before 1834. She married **Louis Leblanc** on 18 Jul 1842 Fort-des-Prairies, (Alberta) (FDP, M-7.). She married **Basile Hebert**, son of **Pierre Hebert** and **Agathe Vanasse**, on 14 Oct 1861 St.Joachim, Fort Edmonton, (Alberta) (MSJ-FA-E Register des Baptemes, Mariages & Sepultures 1858-1861 Mission St.Joachim, Fort Auguste, Fort des Prairies, Edmonton, No. 1, page 38, M-5. Hereinafter cited as MSJ-FA-E.).

Louis Leblanc was born circa 1806.

Basile Hebert married **Isabelle Piche**, daughter of **Baptiste Ka-kee-tis-taw Piche** and **Rosalie Blandion**, in 1871 (HBSI.).

5. Louis Vallee was born circa 1821. He married **Louise Durand**, daughter of **Paul dit Nabais Durand dit Dumond** and **Marie Ahs-Ke-Kah-um-ah-taht Metisse**, on 15 Jan 1844 Fort-des-Prairies, (Alberta) (FDP, M-29.). He died before 1867 (SB-Rozyk St. Boniface Roman Catholic Church, Manitoba, Canada, Baptisms, Marriages and Burials 1860-1875 Extractions, Compiled by Rosemary Rozyk, page 80, B-18.).

Louise Durand was born between 1821 and 1824. She was baptized on 15 Oct 1841 Rocky Mountain House, Saskatchewan District (RTR, B-138.). She was baptized on 29 Jul 1842 Fort-des-Prairies (INB, page 57.). She died on 4 Jul 1871 Pembina, Pembina County, Dakota Territory (MBS, C-14934.). She was buried on 5 Jul 1871 Pembina, Pembina County, Dakota Territory (Ibid.).

Children of **Louis Vallee** and **Louise Durand** were as follows:

8   i.   Suzanne Vallee, b. circa 1845; m. Theodore Carriere; d. circa 1870.

9   ii.   Judith Vallee, b. circa 1852; m. Francois Xavier Robert Stoffengen; m. Christopher Reggin; d. 19 Dec 1875; bur. 21 Dec 1875.

10   iii.   Rosalie Vallee, b. 17 Dec 1852; m. Francois Montreuille; d. before 1877.

     iv.   Marie Vallee was born on 12 Jan 1855 (SFXI 1851-1868 St.Francois Xavier 1852-1861 Register Index, B-34. Hereinafter cited as SFXI 1851-1868.). She was baptized on 25 Apr 1855 St.Francois Xavier, (Manitoba) (SFXI-Kipling St.Francois Xavier Register Index, 1834-1900; compiled by Clarence Kipling , B-34.) (SFXI 1851-1868, B-34.).

     v.   Louis Alphonse Vallee was born on 14 Sep 1856 (SFXI-Kipling, B-140.). He was baptized on 20 Sep 1856 St.Francois Xavier, (Manitoba) (Ibid.).

     vi.   Helene Vallee was born before 1867. She died before 1877.

6. Marie Vallee was born in 1825 North West Territories (MBS, C-14934.). She married **Charles Ducharme**, son of **Nicolas Ducharme dit Charon** and **Genevieve Cree**, on 17 May 1847 Fort-des-Prairies, (Alberta) (FDP, M-115.).

Charles Ducharme was born before 1813 Ruperts Land (1835C RRS HBCA E5/8 1835 Census of the Red River Settlement, HBCA E5/8, Hudson's Bay Company Archives, Provincial Archives, 200 Vaughan Street, Winnipeg, MB R3C 1T5, Canada., page 25.) (SFXI: 1834-1852 St.Francois Xavier 1834-1852 Register Index, M-7. Hereinafter cited as SFXI: 1835-1852.). He married **Angelique Pangman**, daughter of **Pierre 'Bostonais' Pangman** and **Marguerite Sauteuse**, on 4 Feb 1834 St.Francois Xavier, (Manitoba) (Ibid.). He died before 1870.

7. Therese Vallee dit Laplante was born circa 1830 Edmonton, (Alberta) (ArchiviaNet, C-15008.). She married **Joseph Trottier**, son of **Andre Trottier** and **Marguerite Paquette**, in 1852 St.Boniface, (Manitoba).

Joseph Trottier was born in 1827 Oak Lake near Brandon, (Manitoba) (1850Ci-MN *Minnesota Territorial Census, 1850*, Harpole, Patricia C. and Mary D. Nagle, ed., (St.Paul, Minnesota: Minnesota Historical Society, 1972), page 26, Dwelling 84, Family 84.) (ArchiviaNet, C-15007.).

Generation Three

8. Suzanne Vallee was born circa 1845. She married **Theodore Carriere**, son of **Alexis Carriere** and **Suzanne Ducharme**, on 27 Jan 1863 St.Boniface, (Manitoba) (SB-Rozyk, page 101, M-7.). She died circa 1870.

Theodore Carriere was born between 1835 and 1838. He married **Angelique Dorion**, daughter of **John Dorion** and **Therese Constant**, in 1864 Grand Rapids, (Saskatchewan) (ArchiviaNet.). He died on 20 Jun 1875 Lake Winnipeg, Manitoba (MBS, C-14926.).

9. Judith Vallee was born circa 1852. She married **Francois Xavier Robert Stoffengen** on 31 Aug 1869 St.Boniface, (Manitoba) (SB-Rozyk, page 161, M-6.). She married **Christopher Reggin** before 1873. She died on 19 Dec 1875 Pembina County, Dakota Territory (MBS, C-14934.). She was buried on 21 Dec 1875 Pembina County, Dakota Territory (Ibid.).

10. Rosalie Vallee was born on 17 Dec 1852 (SFXI-Kipling, B-_.) (SFXI 1851-1868, B-66.). She was baptized on 1 May 1853 St.Francois Xavier, (Manitoba) (SFXI-Kipling, B-_.) (SFXI 1851-1868, B-66.). She married **Francois Montreuille**, son of **Joseph**

Montreuille and **Isabelle Mi-ji-gi-si Bottineau,** on 6 Aug 1872 Assumption, Pembina, Pembina County, Dakota Territory (AP, page 70, M-3.). She died before 1877 (MBS, C-14934.).

Francois Montreuille was born circa 1840 Pembina County (1850Ci-MN, page 26, Dwelling 79, Family 79.).

Descendants of (--?--) Vallee

Generation One

1. **(--?--) Vallee** married according to the custom of the country **Cree Indian Woman** before 1810. He married **Marie Anne (--?--)** before 1811.

Children of **(--?--) Vallee** include:

    2   i.   Pierre Pissikossis Vallee, m. Marie Fleury.

    3   ii. Louis Vallee, b. circa 1801 Ruperts Land; m. Louise Martel; d. Apr 1861 on the prairie; bur. 8 May 1861 St.Francois Xavier, (Manitoba).

Children of **(--?--) Vallee** and **Cree Indian Woman** are:

    4   i.   Jean Baptiste Vallee, b. 1810 Red River, (Manitoba); m. Marie Kipling; d. before 29 Aug 1882.

Children of **(--?--) Vallee** and **Marie Anne (--?--)** were:

    5   i.   Joseph Vallee, b. circa 1811 Ruperts Land; m. Louise Page; d. 3 Jan 1889 Rolette County, North Dakota.

Generation Two

2. **Pierre Pissikossis Vallee** married **Marie Fleury,** daughter of **(--?--) Fleury** and **Wappi-mostiosnos (--?--),** in 1852 Fort Pitt, (Saskatchewan) (HBSI Index 1886-1901, 1906 Halfbreed Scrip Applications, RG15-21.) (ArchiviaNet 1886-1901, 1906 Half-Breed Scrip Applications Index, RG15-21, Volume 1333 through 1371, Microfilm Reel Number C-14944 through C-15010, National Archives of Canada, Ottawa, Ontario, http://www.collectionscanada.gc.ca.).

Marie Fleury was born in 1836 Fort Pitt, (Saskatchewan) (HBSI.) (ArchiviaNet.). She married **Francois Desjarlais,** son of **Joseph Desjarlais** and **Josephte Cardinal,** in 1874 Red Deer River, (Alberta) (HBSI.) (ArchiviaNet.).

Children of **Pierre Pissikossis Vallee** and **Marie Fleury** were as follows:

    i.   Suzanne Vallee.

    ii. John Vallee was born in 1860 Fort Pitt, (Saskatchewan) (HBSI.) (ArchiviaNet.). He died in 1874 Fort Pitt, (Saskatchewan) (HBSI.) (ArchiviaNet.).

    iii. Baptiste Vallee was born in 1862 Fort Pitt, (Saskatchewan) (HBSI.). He died in 1874 Fort Pitt, (Saskatchewan) (Ibid.).

    iv. Marguerite Vallee was born in 1867 Fort Pitt, (Saskatchewan) (ArchiviaNet, C-15008.).

3. **Louis Vallee** was born circa 1801 Ruperts Land (1832C RRS HBCA E5/6 1832 Census of the Red River Settlement, HBCA E5/6, Hudson's Bay Company Archives, Provincial Archives, 200 Vaughan Street, Winnipeg, MB R3C 1T5, Canada., page 18.). He married **Louise Martel,** daughter of **Jean Baptiste Martel** and **Marguerite Dion,** before 1829. He died in Apr 1861 on the prairie (SFXI: 1851-1869 St.Francois Xavier 1851-69 Register Index.). He was buried on 8 May 1861 St.Francois Xavier, (Manitoba) (SFXI-Kipling St.Francois Xavier Register Index, 1834-1900; compiled by Clarence Kipling , S-9.) (SFXI-1834-54.).

Louise Martel was born circa 1810. She died before 18 Jan 1871 (L1 Lebret Mission de St.Florent Roman Catholic Registre des Baptemes, Mariages & Seplutures, Qu'Appelle, Saskatchewan, 1868-1881., page 41, M-6. Hereinafter cited as L1.).

Children of **Louis Vallee** and **Louise Martel** were as follows:

    6   i.   Louise Vallee, b. 21 Jul 1829 St.Boniface, (Manitoba); m. Joseph Vandal; d. 17 Jul 1887 Lebret, (Saskatchewan); bur. 19 Jul 1887 Lebret, (Saskatchewan).

    7   ii. Moise Vallee, b. 10 Apr 1832; m. Reine Davis; d. 1888.

    8   iii. Louis Vallee, b. 26 Apr 1832; m. Julie Fosseneuve; d. 5 Jan 1873 St.Francois Xavier, Manitoba; bur. 7 Jan 1873 St.Francois Xavier, Manitoba.

    9   iv. Suzanne Vallee, b. 1833 Pembina County, Minnesota Territory; m. Joseph Lafournaise; d. 10 Dec 1919 Belcourt, Rolette County, North Dakota; bur. 13 Dec 1919 St.Ann, Belcourt, Rolette County, North Dakota.

   10 v. Marie Vallee, b. 1837 St.Boniface, (Manitoba); m. Joseph Gosselin; m. Michel Klyne.

   11 vi. Marguerite Vallee, b. circa 1846; m. Joseph Assiniboine dit Desmarais.

   12 vii. Joseph Vallee, b. Mar 1846 Assiniboia Settlement; m. Marie Villebrun; d. 29 Apr 1892 St.Boniface, Manitoba.

4. **Jean Baptiste Vallee** was born in 1810 Red River, (Manitoba) (NWHBSI Index 1885 Scrip Applications, North-West Halfbreeds residing outside Manitoba on 15 July 1870, RG15-20, page 84.) (1850Ci-MN *Minnesota Territorial Census, 1850,* Harpole, Patricia C. and Mary D. Nagle, ed., (St.Paul, Minnesota: Minnesota Historical Society, 1972), page 29, Dwelling 117, Family 117.). He married **Marie Kipling,** daughter of **John James Kipling** and **Marguerite Okkanens Saulteaux,** before 1837. He died before 29 Aug 1882 (SJL-1 Register of Baptisms, Marriages, and Burials, St.Joseph, Leroy, North Dakota, Diocese of Saint Paul, Minnesota, 1870-1888, Book 1, page 120, M-41. Hereinafter cited as SJL-1.).

Marie Kipling was born circa 1819 Red River, (Manitoba) (1850Ci-MN, page 29, Dwelling 117, Family 117.). She died on 5 Jul 1878 (SJL-1, page 88, S-4.). She died on 5 Jul 1878 (Ibid.). She was buried on 8 Jul 1878 St.Joseph, Leroy, Pembina County, Dakota Territory (Ibid.). She was buried on 8 Jul 1878 St.Joseph, Leroy, Pembina County, Dakota Territory (Ibid.). Question: *is she the daughter of John J. Kipling?*

Children of **Jean Baptiste Vallee** and **Marie Kipling** were as follows:

   13 i.   Louise Vallee, b. circa Feb 1837 on the plains; m. Joseph Bottineau.

   14 ii. Jean Baptiste Vallee, b. 27 Jan 1839; m. Elizabeth Martel; m. Sophia Descoteaux; d. before 1 Jun 1900.

        iii. Eliza Vallee was born on 5 Mar 1841 (SFX: 1834-1850 St.Francois Xavier 1834-1851 Register, B-352. Hereinafter cited as SFX: 1834-1850.). She was baptized on 23 May 1841 St.Francois Xavier, (Manitoba) (Ibid.).

iv.   Marie Vallee was born in Dec 1842 (Ibid., B-457.). She was baptized on 21 May 1843 St.Francois Xavier, (Manitoba) (Ibid.). She died on 25 May 1857 Pembina County, Dakota Territory, at age 14 (AP Records of the Assumption Roman Catholic Church, Pembina, North Dakota: Baptisms, Marriages, Sepultures, 1848-1896; compiled by Reverend Father J. M. Belleau, 2 October 1944, page 170, S-71. Hereinafter cited as AP.). She was buried on 25 May 1857 Assumption, Pembina, Pembina County, Dakota Territory (Ibid.).

v.   Alexandre Vallee was born on 19 Mar 1845 (SFX: 1834-1850, B-567.). He was baptized on 4 May 1845 St.Francois Xavier, (Manitoba) (Ibid.).

15   vi.   Antoine Vallee, b. circa Apr 1847; m. Esther Lariviere; d. 15 Aug 1882 Leroy, Pembina County, Dakota Territory; bur. 17 Aug 1882 St.Joseph, Leroy, Pembina County, Dakota Territory.

vii.   Abraham Vallee was born circa 1849 Red River, (Manitoba) (1850Ci-MN, page 29, Dwelling 117, Family 117.). He died on 18 Jan 1876 (SJL-1, page 66, S-2.). He was buried on 20 Jan 1876 St.Joseph, Leroy, Pembina County, Dakota Territory (Ibid.).

16   viii.   Jean Baptiste Vallee, b. 9 Jan 1852; m. Julienne Petit; d. 19 Mar 1931 Belcourt, Rolette County, North Dakota.

ix.   Toussaint Vallee was born on 20 Feb 1854 Dakota Territory (AP, page 105, B-281.). He was baptized on 22 Apr 1854 Assumption, Pembina, Pembina County, Dakota Territory (Ibid.).

x.   Marie Vallee was born on 6 Jun 1856 Pembina County, Dakota Territory (Ibid., page 150, B-422.). She was baptized on 9 Jun 1856 Assumption, Pembina, Pembina County, Dakota Territory (Ibid.). She died on 28 Dec 1856 Pembina, Pembina County, Dakota Territory (Ibid., page 162, S-66.). She was buried on 29 Dec 1856 Assumption, Pembina, Pembina County, Dakota Territory (Ibid.).

xi.   Caroline Vallee was born on 26 Apr 1859 Pembina, Pembina County, Dakota Territory (Ibid., page 216, B-122.). She was baptized on 26 Apr 1859 Assumption, Pembina, Pembina County, Dakota Territory (Ibid.).

17   xii.   Marguerite Vallee, b. Nov 1862 North Dakota; m. Michel Laframboise; m. Louis Vallee; d. 4 Feb 1934 Belcourt, Rolette, North Dakota; bur. 5 Feb 1934 St.Ann's, Belcourt, Rolette, North Dakota.

18   xiii.   Caroline Vallee, b. circa 1863; m. Jean Baptiste Cloutier.

5. Joseph Vallee was born circa 1811 Ruperts Land (1833C RRS HBCA E5/7 1833 Census of the Red River Settlement, HBCA E5/7, Hudson's Bay Company Archives, Provincial Archives, 200 Vaughan Street, Winnipeg, MB R3C 1T5, Canada., page 23.). He was born in 1814 Red River, (Manitoba) (1850Ci-MN, page 26-27, Dwelling 87, Family 87.). He married **Louise Page**, daughter of **Joseph Page** and **Marguerite Poitras,** before 1832. He died on 3 Jan 1889 Rolette County, North Dakota (AYM Documentation of Metis Families of Red River and the Northwest Territories; Census, Biographical, and Historical: 1881 Census Qu'Appelle, Wood Mountain, Lac la Biche; History of the Turtle Mountain Band of Chippewas; Census for the Turtle Mountain Reservation 1884-1886; Pembina, Dakota Territory 1850 Census; Various Metis Census Records for Pembina County, ND 1910; compiled by Al Yerbery, 1996, Death List of TMC Indians.).

Louise Page was born circa 1820 Red River, (Manitoba) (1850Ci-MN, page 26-27, Dwelling 87, Family 87.).

Children of **Joseph Vallee** and **Louise Page** were as follows:

19   i.   Toussaint Vallee, b. 8 Mar 1832; m. Marie Thifault.

20   ii.   Marie Vallee, b. 16 Apr 1835 St.Francois Xavier, (Manitoba); m. William Davis Sr.

iii.   Madeleine Vallee was born in Jul 1835 North Dakota (1900C-ND 1900 United States Census, North Dakota, National Archives of the United States, Washington, D. C., 179-179.). She married Jean Baptiste Champagne Sr., son of Emmanuel Beaugrand dit Champagne and Marguerite Larocque, on 17 Apr 1884 St.Claude Mission, St.John, Rolette County, North Daktoa (NWHBSI, page 108.) (Dominique Ritchot Research,, 26 Jan 2006.).

    Question: *Is Madeleine Vallee the daughter of Joseph Valle and Louise Page?*

    Jean Baptiste Champagne Sr was born in Feb 1831 Pembina, Minnesota Territory (1900C-ND, House 179, page 291B.). He married **Isabelle Parisien**, daughter of **Jean Baptiste Parisien** and **Charlotte Nolin,** on 10 Mar 1856 Assumption, Pembina, Pembina County, Dakota Territory (AP, page 144, M-49.). He married **Elize Laverdure**, daughter of **Joseph Laverdure** and **Therese Villebrun**, circa 1870. He died before 1938 (1936-TMC 1936 Tribal Roll, Turtle Mountain Indian Reservation, Office of Indian Affairs, received 28 Jan 1938, National Archives of the United States, Washington D.C., page 54.).

21   iv.   Rosalie Vallee, b. 28 Feb 1841; m. Francois Langer.

v.   Charles Vallee was born on 4 Apr 1844 (SFX: 1834-1850, B-512.). He was baptized on 4 May 1844 St.Francois Xavier, (Manitoba) (Ibid.). He was buried on 21 Apr 1845 St.Francois Xavier, (Manitoba) (Ibid., S-126.).

22   vi.   Francois Vallee, b. 13 Mar 1846; m. Marie Sioux; m. Josephine Cook.

vii.   Philomene Vallee was born on 4 Mar 1849 (Ibid., B-779.). She was baptized on 8 Jun 1849 St.Francois Xavier, (Manitoba) (Ibid.).

viii.   Louise Vallee was born on 20 Aug 1853 (AP, page 93, B-86.). She was baptized on 2 Sep 1853 Assumption, Pembina, Pembina County, Dakota Territory (Ibid.).

Generation Three

6. Louise Vallee was born on 21 Jul 1829 St.Boniface, (Manitoba) (SB 1825-1834 St.Boniface Roman Catholic Registre des Baptemes, Mariages & Sepultures, 1825-1834, page 28, B-565. Hereinafter cited as SB 1825-1834.). She was baptized on 22 Jul 1829 St.Boniface, (Manitoba) (Ibid.). She married **Antoine Desjarlais dit Morel**, son of **Antoine Desjarlais** and **Susanna (--?--),** before 1850. She married **Joseph Vandal**, son of **Antoine Vandal** and **Angelique Sauteuse,** on 28 Aug 1860 Assumption, Pembina, Pembina County, Dakota Territory (AP, page 234-235, M-89.). She died on 17 Jul 1887 Lebret, (Saskatchewan), at age 57 (L2 Lebret, Mission de St.Florent, Roman Catholic Registre des Baptemes, Mariages & Sepultures, Qu'Appelle, Saskatchewan, Book Two: 1881-1887, FHC microfilm 1032949., page 186, S-17. Hereinafter cited as L2.). She was buried on 19 Jul 1887 Lebret, (Saskatchewan) (Ibid.).

Antoine Desjarlais dit Morel was born circa 1825 Red River, (Manitoba) (1850Ci-MN, page 18, Dwelling 5, Family 5.).

Joseph Vandal was born circa 1817. He was born circa 1820 Red River, (Manitoba). He married **Louise Dupuis**, daughter of **Jean Baptiste Dupuis** and **Marie Corbeau dit Hughes,** before 1842. He died on 12 May 1885 Batoche, (Saskatchewan) (BSAP Records of the Parish of Batoche, St.Antoine de Pudoue Roman Catholic Church: Register for Baptisms, Marriages, Deaths, Volume One, 1881-1909., page 33, S-21. Hereinafter cited as BSAP.). He was buried on 14 May 1885 Batoche, (Saskatchewan) (Ibid.). Question: *Is he the one?*

Children of **Louise Vallee** and **Joseph Vandal** were as follows:

    i.   Virginie Vandal was born on 8 Jul 1861 (SN1, page 45, B-22.). She was baptized on 21 Jul 1861 St.Norbert, (Manitoba) (Ibid.). She married Charles Desjarlais, son of Antoine Desjarlais dit Morel and Louise Vallee, before 1882 (1901 Canada, 203, d(1), page 5, family 54, line 24-29.).

        Charles Desjarlais was born on 26 Apr 1852 (AP, page 73, B-23.). He was baptized on 28 May 1852 Assumption, Pembina, Pembina County, Dakota Territory (Ibid.). He was baptized on 10 Jun 1852 Assumption, Pembina, Pembina County, Dakota Territory (Ibid., page 73, B-25.).

    ii.   Veronique Vandal was born circa 1864 on the plains, Dakota Territory.

    iii.   Joseph Vandal was born on 5 Jan 1864 (SN1, page 96, B-6.). He was baptized on 10 Jan 1864 St.Norbert, (Manitoba) (Ibid.).

    iv.   Napoleon Vandal was born on 15 Mar 1868 Lac Ste.Anne, (Alberta) (ArchiviaNet, C-15008.).

7. Moise Vallee was born on 10 Apr 1832 (Joyce Black Research.). He married **Reine Davis**, daughter of **Jean Baptiste Davis** and **Julie Desnomme or Dussomme,** before 1867. He died in 1888 (Kevin Veenstra, e-mail, 31 May 1998.).

Reine Davis was born on 20 Jul 1847 St.Boniface, (Manitoba) (MBS Scrip Applications, Original White Settlers & Halfbreeds residing in Manitoba on 15 July 1870, RG15-19, C-14926.). She died in 1918 St.Dolphin, Ituna, Saskatchewan (Joyce Black.).

Children of **Moise Vallee** and **Reine Davis** were as follows:

    i.   Virginie Vallee was born circa 1867 (Saskatchewan) (L2, page 154, S-45.) (1881 Church of Latter Day Saints Census Transcription Project of Census Images from the National Archives of Canada, Ottawa, Canada, http://www.familysearch.org, Film No. C-13285, district 192, page 19, household 76.). She died on 26 Jul 1886 (L2, page 154, S-45.). She was buried on 28 Jul 1886 Lebret, (Saskatchewan) (Ibid.).

    ii.   Anonyme Vallee was born on 4 Jun 1868 St.Boniface, (Manitoba) (SB-Rozyk St. Boniface Roman Catholic Church, Manitoba, Canada, Baptisms, Marriages and Burials 1860-1875 Extractions, Compiled by Rosemary Rozyk, page 119, S-15.). He/she died on 4 Jun 1868 St.Boniface, (Manitoba) (Ibid.). He/she was buried on 5 Jun 1868 St.Boniface, (Manitoba) (Ibid.).

23   iii.   Isidore Vallee, b. 16 Jul 1869; m. Caroline Beaulieu; d. Jun 1942 North Battleford, Saskatchewan.

    iv.   Julie Alphonsine Vallee was born on 21 Dec 1870 Lebret, (Saskatchewan) (L1, page 40-41, B-58.). She was baptized on 24 Dec 1870 Lebret, (Saskatchewan) (Ibid.). She was buried on 15 Apr 1871 Lebret, (Saskatchewan) (Ibid., page 33, S-5.).

    v.   Jean Baptiste Vallee was born on 9 Feb 1872 Lebret, (Saskatchewan) (Ibid., page 50, B-4.). He was baptized on 9 Feb 1872 Lebret, (Saskatchewan) (Ibid.). He died on 24 Apr 1874 Lebret, (Saskatchewan), at age 2 (Ibid., page 112, S-_.). He was buried on 25 Apr 1874 Lebret, (Saskatchewan) (Ibid.).

    vi.   Jean Baptiste Vallee was born circa 1873 (L2, page 76, S-2.) (1881 Canada, Film No. C-13285, district 192, page 19, household 76.). He died on 17 Jan 1884 Lebret, (Saskatchewan) (L2, page 76, S-2.). He was buried on 18 Jan 1884 Lebret, (Saskatchewan) (Ibid.).

    vii.   Charles Vallee was born on 20 Jun 1873 Lebret, (Saskatchewan) (L1, page 95, B-84.). He was baptized on 20 Jun 1873 Lebret, (Saskatchewan) (Ibid.). He was buried on 10 Oct 1873 Lebret, (Saskatchewan) (Ibid., page 101, S-16.).

    viii.   Jerome Vallee was born on 1 Feb 1875 (Ibid., page 152, B-50.). He was baptized on 18 Mar 1875 Lebret, (Saskatchewan) (Ibid.).

24   ix.   Alexander Vallee, b. 5 Aug 1876; m. Cecile Marie Beaulieu; d. circa 1950.

    x.   Anonyme Vallee was born on 18 Feb 1878 Qu'Appelle, (Saskatchewan). She died on 18 Feb 1878 Qu'Appelle, (Saskatchewan).

    xi.   Augustin Vallee was born on 8 Dec 1879 Lebret, (Saskatchewan) (Ibid., page 254, B-52.). He was baptized on 10 Dec 1879 Lebret, (Saskatchewan) (Ibid.).

    xii.   Moise Vallee was born on 7 Oct 1881 Lebret, (Saskatchewan) (L2, page 14, B-57.). He was baptized on 10 Oct 1881 Lebret, (Saskatchewan) (Ibid.).

    xiii.   Jean Edouard Vallee was born on 13 Feb 1883 (Saskatchewan) (Ibid., page 59, B-15.). He was baptized on 15 Feb 1883 Lebret, (Saskatchewan) (Ibid.). He died on 2 Apr 1883 (Ibid., page 61, S-5.). He was buried on 3 Apr 1883 Lebret, (Saskatchewan) (Ibid.).

    xiv.   Louisa Vallee was born on 27 Feb 1884 Lebret, (Saskatchewan) (Ibid., page 79, B-12.). She was baptized on 2 Mar 1884 Lebret, (Saskatchewan) (Ibid.).

    xv.   Marie Celina Vallee was born on 23 May 1886 Lebret, (Saskatchewan) (Ibid., page 151, B-47.). She was baptized on 23 May 1886 Lebret, (Saskatchewan) (Ibid.). She married William Malboeuf, son of Pierre Malboeuf and Marie Celina Ross, on 3 Feb 1909 Ste.Delphine (Denney.).

        William Malboeuf was born circa 1878 (1889-TMC 1889 Census of Half Breed Chippewas residing in the vicinity of, but not on the Turtle Mountain Reservation, Dakota Territory, National Archives of the United States, Washington D.C., #414.).

8. Louis Vallee was born on 26 Apr 1832 (SB 1825-1834, page 61, B-427.). He was baptized on 29 Apr 1832 St.Boniface, (Manitoba) (Ibid.). He married **Julie Fosseneuve**, daughter of **Jean Baptiste Fosseneuve** and **Julie Morand,** on 8 Jan 1852 St.Francois Xavier, (Manitoba) (SFXI 1851-1868 St.Francois Xavier 1852-1861 Register Index, M-1. Hereinafter cited as SFXI 1851-1868.). He died on 5 Jan 1873 St.Francois Xavier, Manitoba, at age 40 (MBS, C-14934.) (SFXI-Kipling, S-3.). He was buried on 7 Jan 1873 St.Francois Xavier, Manitoba (Ibid.) (MBS, C-14934.).

Julie Fosseneuve was born in Jan 1837 Pembina County, Minnesota Territory (Ibid.). She married **Joseph Fleury**, son of **Louis Fleury** and **Josephte Belly**, on 7 Jan 1879 St.Francois Xavier, Manitoba (SFXI-Kipling, M-1.).

Children of **Louis Vallee** and **Julie Fosseneuve** were as follows:

      i.   Therese Vallee was born circa Feb 1853 (Ibid., B-89.) (Ibid.). She was baptized on 5 Jun 1853 St.Francois Xavier, (Manitoba) (Ibid.) (Ibid.). She died on 11 Oct 1853 St.Francois Xavier, (Manitoba) (Ibid., S-21.) (SFXI 1851-1868, S-21.). She was buried on 12 Oct 1853 St.Francois Xavier, (Manitoba) (SFXI-Kipling, S-21.) (SFXI 1851-1868, S-21.).

25 ii.   Josephte Vallee, b. 18 Aug 1854 St.Francois Xavier, (Manitoba); m. Louis Chalifoux; m. Bernard Delorme; d. 29 Jan 1938 Rolette County, North Dakota.

26 iii. Louis Vallee, b. 16 Jan 1857; m. Catherine Ross; m. Julienne Pepin; m. Marguerite Vallee.

      iv. Cuthbert Vallee was born on 25 Dec 1858 St.Francois Xavier, (Manitoba) (SFXI-Kipling, B-302.). He was baptized on 28 Dec 1858 St.Francois Xavier, (Manitoba) (Ibid.). He died on 25 Jan 1873 St.Francois Xavier, Manitoba, at age 14 (Ibid., S-8.). He was buried on 27 Jan 1873 St.Francois Xavier, Manitoba (IBMS *Index des Baptemes, Mariages et Sepultures* (La Societe Historique de Saint-Boniface).) (SFXI-Kipling, S-8.).

27 v.   Catherine Vallee, b. 22 Apr 1861 St.Francois Xavier, (Manitoba); m. Andre Fleury.

      vi. Philomene Vallee was born circa 1862.

      vii. Joseph Vallee was born circa 1864.

      viii. Clemence Vallee was born circa Jul 1864 (Ibid., S-7.) (SFXI-1834-54.). He died on 16 Feb 1865 St.Francois Xavier, (Manitoba) (SFXI-Kipling, S-7.) (SFXI-1834-54.). He was buried on 17 Feb 1865 St.Francois Xavier, (Manitoba) (SFXI-Kipling, S-7.) (SFXI-1834-54.).

      ix. Napoleon Vallee was born on 6 Jan 1866 St.Francois Xavier, (Manitoba) (SFXI-Kipling, B-9.). He was baptized on 10 Jan 1866 St.Francois Xavier, (Manitoba) (Ibid.). He died on 20 Nov 1866 St.Francois Xavier, (Manitoba) (Ibid., S-51.). He was buried on 22 Nov 1866 St.Francois Xavier, (Manitoba) (Ibid.).

      x.   Veronique Vallee was born on 6 Oct 1867 St.Francois Xavier, (Manitoba) (Ibid., B-100.). She was baptized on 11 Oct 1867 St.Francois Xavier, (Manitoba) (Ibid.). She died on 21 Mar 1868 St.Francois Xavier, (Manitoba) (Ibid., S-6.). She was buried on 23 Mar 1868 St.Francois Xavier, (Manitoba) (Ibid.).

      xi. Bernard Vallee was born on 5 Feb 1869 St.Francois Xavier, (Manitoba) (Ibid., B-15.). He was baptized on 6 Feb 1869 St.Francois Xavier, (Manitoba) (Ibid.). He died on 21 Mar 1869 St.Francois Xavier, (Manitoba) (Ibid., S-5.). He was buried on 22 Mar 1869 St.Francois Xavier, (Manitoba) (Ibid.).

      xii. Marie Vallee was born on 15 Feb 1870 St.Francois Xavier, (Manitoba) (Ibid., B-6.). She was baptized on 22 Feb 1870 St.Francois Xavier, (Manitoba) (Ibid.). She died on 29 Apr 1871 St.Francois Xavier, Manitoba, at age 1 (Ibid., S-9.) (MBS, C-14934.). She was buried on 30 Apr 1871 St.Francois Xavier, Manitoba (SFXI-Kipling, S-9.) (MBS, C-14934.).

28 xiii. Melanie Vallee, b. 13 Jul 1873; m. James William Lillie; d. 7 Nov 1890 Rock Lake, (Manitoba).

9. Suzanne Vallee was born in 1833 Pembina County, Minnesota Territory. She married **Joseph Lafournaise**, son of **Joseph Lafournaise dit Laboucane** and **Susanne Leclair or Leclerc**, in 1852 (NWHBSI, page 84.) (Ibid., page 111.). She died on 10 Dec 1919 Belcourt, Rolette County, North Dakota. She was buried on 13 Dec 1919 St.Ann, Belcourt, Rolette County, North Dakota.

Joseph Lafournaise was born in 1826 (Ibid.).

10. Marie Vallee was born in 1837 St.Boniface, (Manitoba) (NWHBS, C-14942.). She married **Joseph Gosselin**, son of **Michel Gosselin dit Commis** and **Josette Deschamps**, on 16 Jun 1856 Assumption, Pembina, Pembina County, Dakota Territory (AP, page 152-153, M-53.). She married **Michel Klyne**, son of **Michel Klyne** and **Madeleine Millet dit Beauchemin,** on 14 Aug 1876 Lebret, (Saskatchewan) (L1, page 171, M-4.).

Joseph Gosselin was born circa 1834 (Ibid., page 33, S-4.) (NWHBS, C-14938.). He died on 13 Feb 1871 Wood Mountain, (Saskatchewan) (L1, page 33, S-4.). He was buried on 15 Apr 1871 Lebret, (Saskatchewan) (Ibid.).

Michel Klyne was born on 18 Dec 1839 (SFX: 1834-1850, B-282.). He was baptized on 22 Dec 1839 St.Francois Xavier, (Manitoba) (Ibid.). He married **Helene Davis**, daughter of **Jean Baptiste Davis** and **Julie Desnomme or Dussomme,** before 1864.

11. Marguerite Vallee was born circa 1846 (L1, page 68 (confirmation).). She married **Joseph Assiniboine dit Desmarais**, son of **Francois Desmarais** and **Josephte Martin**, on 18 Jan 1871 Lebret, (Saskatchewan) (Ibid., page 41, M-6.).

Children of **Marguerite Vallee** include:

      i.   Marie Angelique Vallee was born on 24 Jun 1883 (L2, page 69, B-48.). She was baptized on 22 Jul 1883 Lebret, (Saskatchewan) (Ibid.).

Joseph Assiniboine dit Desmarais was born circa 1839 (SFXI-Kipling, B-114.). He was baptized on 18 May 1856 St.Francois Xavier, (Manitoba) (Ibid.).

12. Joseph Vallee was born in Mar 1846 Assiniboia Settlement (MBS, C-14934.). He married **Marie Villebrun**, daughter of **Louis Villebrun** and **Louise Collin**, on 10 Feb 1863 St.Boniface, (Manitoba) (SB-Rozyk, page 103, M-13.). He died on 29 Apr 1892 St.Boniface, Manitoba, at age 46 (Manitoba Vital Statistics online, http://web2.gov.mb.ca, Death Reg. #1892,002662.).

Marie Villebrun was born on 22 May 1832 St.Boniface, (Manitoba) (MBS, C-14934.). She was baptized on 25 May 1832 St.Boniface, (Manitoba) (SB 1825-1834, page 65, B-437.). She and **Jean Baptiste Flamand** met before 1854.

Children of **Joseph Vallee** and **Marie Villebrun** were as follows:

29 i.   Philomene Vallee, b. 9 Apr 1863 St.Boniface, (Manitoba); m. Patrice Parenteau; d. 23 Mar 1953 Vancouver, British Columbia.

      ii. Joseph Vallee was born in 1865 (MBS, C-14934.) (SB-Rozyk, page 280, S-39.). He died on 14 Jun 1873 St.Boniface, Manitoba (Ibid.). He was buried on 15 Jun 1873 St.Boniface, Manitoba (Ibid.).

13. Louise Vallee was born circa Feb 1837 on the plains (SFX: 1834-1850, B-196.). She was baptized on 4 Jun 1838 St.Francois Xavier, (Manitoba) (Ibid.). She married **Joseph Bottineau**, son of **Joseph Bottineau** and **Angelique Cardinal,** circa 1866 St.Joseph, Pembina County, Dakota Territory (NWHBS, C-14936.).

Joseph Bottineau was born on 24 Mar 1841 St.Francois Xavier, (Manitoba) (SFX: 1834-1850, B-347.). He was baptized on 24 Mar 1841 St.Francois Xavier, (Manitoba) (Ibid.).

14. **Jean Baptiste Vallee** was born on 27 Jan 1839 (SFX: 1834-1850, B-232.). He was baptized on 31 Jan 1839 St.Francois Xavier, (Manitoba) (Ibid.). He married **Elizabeth Martel**, daughter of **Jean Baptiste Martel** and **Josephte Godon,** before 1868 (SJL-1, page 115, M-37.) (Ibid., page 120, S-90.). He married **Sophia Descoteaux**, daughter of **Louis Decouteau Sr.** and **Isabelle Laverdure,** on 29 Nov 1881 St.Joseph, Leroy, Pembina County, Dakota Territory (Ibid., page 115, M-37.). He died before 1 Jun 1900 (1900C-ND, 184-184.).

Elizabeth Martel was born circa 1849 Red River, (Manitoba) (1850Ci-MN, page 22, Dwelling 40, Family 40.). She was born circa 1850 (SJL-1, page 46, S-5.). She died on 24 May 1874 Leroy, Pembina County, Dakota Territory (Ibid.). She was buried on 25 May 1874 St.Joseph, Leroy, Pembina County, Dakota Territory (Ibid.).

Children of **Jean Baptiste Vallee** and **Elizabeth Martel** were as follows:

     i.   Domitilde Vallee was born circa 1868 (1886-TMC, #809.). She married Isidore Edward Rainville, son of Joseph Rainville and Euphrosine Belgarde, on 12 Mar 1885 St.Claude Mission, St.John, Rolette County, North Daktoa (Dominique Ritchot, 26 Jan 2006.).

         Isidore Edward Rainville was born circa 1859 Dakota Territory (*1860-DT-Inx Index to 1860 Census of Dakota Territory*, Rogers-Patton Researchers; P. O. Box 64, Hill City, S.D. 57701: Rogers-Patton Researchers, page 46.).

     ii. Marie Rose Vallee was born circa 1868 (SJL-1, page 120, S-90.). She died on 1 Oct 1882 Leroy, Pembina County, Dakota Territory (Ibid.). She was buried on 2 Oct 1882 St.Joseph, Leroy, Pembina County, Dakota Territory (Ibid.).

     iii. Charles Vallee was born on 18 Mar 1872 (Ibid., page 24, B-9.). He was baptized on 21 Mar 1872 St.Joseph, Leroy, Dakota Territory (Ibid.). He died on 30 Sep 1875 Leroy, Pembina County, Dakota Territory, at age 3 (Ibid., page 60, S-9.). He was buried on 1 Oct 1875 St.Joseph, Leroy, Pembina County, Dakota Territory (Ibid.).

     iv. Marie Virginie Vallee was born on 27 Apr 1874 Leroy, Pembina County, Dakota Territory (Ibid., page 46, B-13.). She was baptized on 28 Apr 1874 St.Joseph, Leroy, Dakota Territory (Ibid.). She died on 20 Jul 1874 Leroy, Pembina County, Dakota Territory (Ibid., page 49, S-11.). She was buried on 21 Jul 1874 St.Joseph, Leroy, Pembina County, Dakota Territory (Ibid.).

Sophia Descoteaux was born circa 1843. She married **Gilbert Belgarde**, son of **Alexis Belgarde** and **Marguerite Dufort,** before 1866 (L1, page 122, B-53 (parents).).

Children of **Jean Baptiste Vallee** and **Sophia Descoteaux** were as follows:

     i.   Marie Vallee was born in Jan 1880 North Dakota (1900C-ND, 344-344.). She was born circa 1881. She was born circa 1882 (1885-TMC 1885 Census of Half Breed Chippewas of Turtle Mountain, Dakota Territory, National Archives of the United States, Washington D.C., #405.).

   30 ii. Marie Caroline Vallee, b. 28 Nov 1882; m. Adolphe Pelletier; m. (--?--) Klyne.

   31 iii. John Baptist Vallee, b. circa 1884 Bellmont, South Dakota; m. Mabel Laverdure; d. 18 Jan 1958 Yellowstone County, Montana.

   32 iv. Abraham Vallee, b. circa 1886; m. Liza Caplette; d. 21 May 1957 Hill County, Montana.

       v.   Mary Vallee was born in 1888 (1936-TMC, page 45.).

15. **Antoine Vallee** was born circa Apr 1847 (SFX: 1834-1850, B-702.). He was baptized on 22 Aug 1847 St.Francois Xavier, (Manitoba) (Ibid.). He married **Esther Lariviere**, daughter of **Francois Lariviere** and **Catherine Landry,** on 20 Jun 1877 St.Boniface, (Manitoba). He died on 15 Aug 1882 Leroy, Pembina County, Dakota Territory (SJL-1, page 120, S-88.). He was buried on 17 Aug 1882 St.Joseph, Leroy, Pembina County, Dakota Territory (Ibid.).

Esther Lariviere was born circa 1842 Red River, (Manitoba) (1870C-MB, #316-318, page 11.). She and **Francois Welsh** met circa 1866. She married **Roger Henault**, son of **Pierre Henault** and **Marguerite Larocque,** on 7 Sep 1885 St.Boniface, Manitoba (RMSB *Repertoire des Mariages de Saint-Boniface (Manitoba) 1825-1983* compiled by Julien Hamelin S.C., (240, avenue Daly; Ottawa, Ontario K1N 6G2: Le Centre de Genealogie S. C., Publication #67, 1985).).

Children of **Antoine Vallee** and **Esther Lariviere** were as follows:

     i.   Alexandre Georges Landry was born on 30 Apr 1869 (SB-Rozyk, page 151, B-43.). He was baptized on 4 May 1869 St.Boniface, (Manitoba) (Ibid.).

   33 ii. William Vallee, b. circa 1873; m. Marie Sara Parisien; m. Sophie Henault dit Canada.

     iii. Hormidas Vallee was born on 3 Sep 1882 Pembina, Pembina County, Dakota Territory (AP, page 207, B-39.). He was baptized on 4 Sep 1882 Assumption, Pembina, Pembina County, Dakota Territory (Ibid.). He died on 6 Nov 1882 Leroy, Pembina County, Dakota Territory (SJL-1, page 121, S-93.). He was buried on 7 Nov 1882 St.Joseph, Leroy, Pembina County, Dakota Territory (Ibid.).

16. **Jean Baptiste Vallee** was born on 9 Jan 1852 (AP, page 71, B-13.). He was baptized on 13 May 1852 Assumption, Pembina, Pembina County, Dakota Territory (Ibid.). He married **Julienne Petit**, daughter of **Louis Petit** and **Marguerite Frederic,** circa 1886. He died on 19 Mar 1931 Belcourt, Rolette County, North Dakota, at age 79 (*St.Ann's Centennial, 100 Years of Faith - 1885-1985*; Belcourt, North Dakota: St.Ann Parish, 1985), page 537-538.) (ND Death Index.).

Question: *Jane, Victoria and Joseph may be Monette grandchildren.*

Julienne Petit was born on 17 Jan 1859 Pembina County, Dakota Territory (AP, page 203, B-610.). She was baptized on 18 Jan 1859 Assumption, Pembina, Pembina County, Dakota Territory (Ibid.). She married **Jean Baptiste Monet dit Belhumeur**, son of **Michel Monet dit Belhumeur** and **Josephte Bruyere,** on 25 Jan 1876 St.Joseph, Leroy, Pembina County, Dakota Territory (SJL-1, page 67, M-3.). She died on 29 Mar 1925 Rolette, North Dakota, at age 66 (ND Death Index.).

Children of **Jean Baptiste Vallee** and **Julienne Petit** were as follows:

   34 i.   John Baptiste Vallee, b. 18 Dec 1886; m. Mary Jane Lafontaine; d. 21 Aug 1969 Belcourt, Rolette County, North Dakota.

     ii. Virginia Vallee was born in Feb 1888 North Dakota (1900C-ND, House 250, page 300B.).

      iii.   Joseph Vallee was born in Nov 1890 North Dakota (Ibid.).

35   iv.   Julie Ann Vallee, b. 13 Feb 1894 Rolette County, North Dakota; m. Jerome Laframboise; d. 11 Apr 1944 Rolette County, North Dakota.

36   v.   Eliza Vallee, b. 15 Sep 1896; m. Francois Decouteau; d. 17 Oct 1967 Ward County, North Dakota.

37   vi.   Emma Vallee, b. Jun 1898 North Dakota; m. Albert Laframboise; m. Napoleon Decouteau; m. Telesphore Joseph Renault; d. 18 Jan 1986 Dunseith, Rolette County, North Dakota.

38   vii.   Jane Evelin Vallee, b. 1901; m. Michael Bercier; m. Francis Poitras.

39   viii.   Victoria "Jane" Vallee, b. 1903; m. Louis Daniel Champagne; d. 12 Dec 1969 Rolette County, North Dakota.

      ix.   Joseph Vallee was born circa 1905 (1936-TMC, page 122.). He died before 1936 (Ibid.).

17. Marguerite Vallee was born in Nov 1862 North Dakota (1900C-ND, 286-286.). She was born in 1863 (NWHBSI, page 83.). She married **Michel Laframboise**, son of **Narcisse Laframboise** and **Josephte Cantara**, on 29 Aug 1882 St.Joseph, Leroy, Pembina County, Dakota Territory (SJL-1, page 120, M-41.). She married **Louis Vallee**, son of **Louis Vallee** and **Julie Fosseneuve**, circa 1932 (Turtle Mountain Star, Rolla, North Dakota, 26 Oct 1933.). She died on 4 Feb 1934 Belcourt, Rolette, North Dakota, at age 71 (1934-TMC Census of the Turtle Mountain Chippewa Indians, United States Indian Service Department of the Interior, Turtle Mountain Agency, North Dakota, 1 Apr 1934.) (ND Death Index.) (TM Star, 8 Feb 1934.). She was buried on 5 Feb 1934 St.Ann's, Belcourt, Rolette, North Dakota (Ibid.).

   Michel Laframboise was born on 26 Jul 1858 Dakota Territory (AP, page 195, B-592.). He was baptized on 1 Sep 1858 Assumption, Pembina, Pembina County, Dakota Territory (Ibid.). He died on 16 Nov 1925 Belcourt, Rolette County, North Dakota, at age 67 (BIA-TM-BMD.) (ND Death Index.). He was buried on 19 Nov 1925 Belcourt, Rolette County, North Dakota (BIA-TM-BMD.).

   Louis Vallee was born on 16 Jan 1857 (SFXI-Kipling, B-163.). He was baptized on 25 Jan 1857 St.Francois Xavier, (Manitoba) (Ibid.). He married **Catherine Ross**, daughter of **Hugh Ross** and **Sarah Short**, on 19 Feb 1878 St.Francois Xavier, Manitoba (Ibid., M-6.). He married **Julienne Pepin**, daughter of **Narcisse Pepin** and **Marie Beaulieu**, circa 1922.

18. Caroline Vallee was born circa 1863. She married **Jean Baptiste Cloutier**, son of **Jean Baptiste Cloutier** and **Marie Langer**, on 30 Jan 1883 Olga, Cavalier County, North Dakota (Olga Our Lady of the Sacred Heart, Olga, North Dakota 1882-1900, page 8, M-4. Hereinafter cited as Olga.).

   Jean Baptiste Cloutier was born on 18 Dec 1857 Ste.Agathe, (Manitoba) (MBS, C-14926.). He died on 20 Dec 1900 Walhalla, North Dakota, at age 43 (SJL-D, page 10.). He was buried on 22 Dec 1900 St.Boniface, Walhalla, North Dakota (Ibid.).

19. Toussaint Vallee was born on 8 Mar 1832 (SB 1825-1834, page 75, B-494.). He was baptized on 8 Sep 1832 St.Boniface, (Manitoba) (Ibid.). He married **Marie Thifault**, daughter of **Louis Thifault** and **Isabelle Lyonnais**, on 3 May 1862 Assumption, Pembina, Pembina County, Dakota Territory (AP, page 256, M-5.).

   Marie Thifault was born circa 1846. She married **Johnny Hinghing** before 1874.

   Children of **Toussaint Vallee** and **Marie Thifault** were as follows:

      i.   Roger Vallee was born on 1 Oct 1864 St.Joseph, Dakota Territory (SN1, page 130, B-27.) (AP, page 16, B-_.). He was baptized on 28 Jul 1865 St.Norbert, (Manitoba) (SN1, page 130, B-27.). He was baptized on 28 Jul 1865 Assumption, Pembina, Pembina County, Dakota Territory (AP, page 16, B-_.).

40   ii.   Marie Madeleine Vallee, b. 11 Nov 1867; m. Pierre McLeod; d. 18 Aug 1957 Belcourt, Rolette County, North Dakota.

20. Marie Vallee was born on 16 Apr 1835 St.Francois Xavier, (Manitoba) (SFX: 1834-1850, B-89.). She was baptized on 16 Apr 1835 St.Francois Xavier, (Manitoba) (Ibid.). She married **William Davis Sr.**, son of **Jean Baptiste Davis** and **Josephte Saulteuse**, on 21 Aug 1862 Assumption, Pembina, Pembina County, Dakota Territory (AP, page 260, M-13.).

   William Davis Sr was born circa 1823 Red River, (Manitoba) (1850Ci-MN, page 33, Dwelling 149 Family 149.). He was born in Sep 1823 North Dakota (1900C-ND, House 129, page 284B.). He was born circa 1824 Pembina County (1850Ci-MN, page 29, Dwelling 116, Family 116.). He married **Marie Henault**, daughter of **Charles Henault** and **Marie Iris**, before 1844. He married **Madeleine Gonneville**, daughter of **Antoine Gonneville** and **Marguerite Labine dit Lacouture**, in 1890 (1900C-ND, House 129, page 284B.).

21. Rosalie Vallee was born on 28 Feb 1841 (SFX: 1834-1850, B-345.). She was baptized on 2 Mar 1841 St.Francois Xavier, (Manitoba) (Ibid.). She married **Francois Langer**, son of **Francois Langer** and **Marguerite George**, on 8 Mar 1859 Assumption, Pembina, Pembina County, Dakota Territory (AP, page 204-205, M-78.).

   Francois Langer was born circa 1838.

22. Francois Vallee was born on 13 Mar 1846 (SFX: 1834-1850, B-606.). He was baptized on 17 May 1846 St.Francois Xavier, (Manitoba) (Ibid.). He married **Marie Sioux** in 1878. He married **Josephine Cook** before 1907 (1907-Sioux 1907 Indian Census Roll of the Sioux Reservation, United States Indian Service Department of the Interior, Devils Lake Agency, North Dakota, 30 Jun 1907.).

   Children of **Francois Vallee** include:

      i.   Marie Rose Vallee was born circa 1873 (1885-TMC, #122.).

   Marie Sioux was born circa 1846 (Ibid., #121.).

   Children of **Francois Vallee** and **Marie Sioux** were as follows:

      i.   Seraphine Vallee was born circa 1881 (Ibid., #123.).

      ii.   Adele Vallee was born circa 1883 (1888-TMC, #979.).

      iii.   Emma Celina Vallee was born on 1 Nov 1884 Rolette County, North Dakota (St.Claude BMD, Dominique Ritchot, page 36, B-155.). She was baptized on 27 Dec 1884 St.Claude, St.John, Rolette County, North Dakota (Ibid.).

   Josephine Cook was born circa 1855 (1901-Sioux 1901 Indian Census Roll of the Sioux Reservation, United States Indian Service Department of the Interior, Devils Lake Agency, North Dakota, 30 Jun 1901, Census No. 452-454.). She married **Francois Xavier Cadotte**, son of **Joseph Cadotte** and **Genevieve Picard**, before 1889.

Generation Four

23. Isidore Vallee was born on 16 Jul 1869 (L1, page 9, B-26.). He was baptized on 16 Jul 1869 Lebret, (Saskatchewan) (Ibid.). He married **Caroline Beaulieu**, daughter of **Thomas Beaulieu dit Sinclair** and **Marguerite Fisher**, on 26 May 1896 Lebret, (Saskatchewan)

(Art Fisher Research, 1994; From Genealogy of Joyce Black, 1981.) (Eileen Horan, 4 Jun 2012.). He died in Jun 1942 North Battleford, Saskatchewan, at age 72 (Art Fisher, 1994; From Genealogy of Joyce Black, 1981.).

Caroline Beaulieu was born on 10 Jan 1876 (L1, page 167, B-23.). She was baptized on 29 Jul 1876 Lebret, (Saskatchewan) (Ibid.).

Children of **Isidore Vallee** and **Caroline Beaulieu** were as follows:

    i. Thomas Vallee.

    ii. Frederick John Vallee married Dora Hosker (Art Fisher, Jan 1998; From Genealogy of Joyce Black, 1981.).

    iii. George Morris Vallee married Lena Pinay (Ibid.).

    iv. Anonyme Vallee.

    v. Marie Alexandrine Vallee was born on 16 May 1897 (1901 Canada, District 203-x, page 1, family 6, line 26-29.). She married Earl Way (Art Fisher, Jan 1998; From Genealogy of Joyce Black, 1981.).

    vi. Marie Artemise Vallee was born on 22 Aug 1899 (1901 Canada, District 203-x, page 1, family 6, line 26-29.). She married Mel Lander Way (Art Fisher, Jan 1998; From Genealogy of Joyce Black, 1981.).

    vii. Annie Vallee was born circa 1902 (Automated Genealogy 1906 Census Transcription Project and Census Images from the National Archives of Canada, http://www.automatedgenealogy.com, District 15-41, page 18-19, family 151, line 38-40, 1-3.).

41 viii. Alice Virginia Vallee, b. circa 1904; m. William Cheviel.

24. Alexander Vallee was born on 5 Aug 1876 (L1, page 170, B-34.). He was baptized on 16 Aug 1876 Lebret, (Saskatchewan) (Ibid.). He married **Cecile Marie Beaulieu**, daughter of **John Beaulieu dit Sinclair** and **Eliza Fisher,** before 1900 (HBS 1886-1901, 1906 Half-Breed Scrip Applications, RG15-21, Volume 1335; C-14947.) (Kevin Veenstra, e-mail, 31 May 1998.). He died circa 1950 (Ibid.).

Cecile Marie Beaulieu was born on 5 Apr 1879 Katepwe (HBS, Volume 1335; C-14947.). She was baptized on 9 Apr 1879 Lebret, (Saskatchewan) (L1, page 242, B-11.) (HBS, Volume 1335; C-14947.).

Children of **Alexander Vallee** and **Cecile Marie Beaulieu** are:

    i. Marie Evelyn Vallee was born in 1903 (Kevin Veenstra, e-mail, 31 May 1998.).

25. Josephte Vallee was born on 18 Aug 1854 St.Francois Xavier, (Manitoba) (SFXI-Kipling, B-180.) (SFXI 1851-1868, B-180.). She was baptized on 19 Aug 1854 St.Francois Xavier, (Manitoba) (Ibid.). She married **Louis Chalifoux**, son of **Michel Chalifoux dit Richard** and **Francoise Piche**, on 3 Feb 1874 St.Francois Xavier, Manitoba (SFXI-Kipling, M-4.). She married **Bernard Delorme**, son of **Joseph Delorme** and **Isabelle Gourneau**, on 30 Jan 1884 St.Claude Mission, St.John, Rolette County, North Dakota (1887-TMC 1887 Census of Half Breed Chippewas of Turtle Mountain, Dakota Territory, National Archives of the United States, Washington D.C., #218.) (Dominique Ritchot, 18 Jan 2006, source: St.Claude Mission Index 1882-1887.) (St.Claude BMD, Dominique Ritchot, page 21, M-22.). She died on 29 Jan 1938 Rolette County, North Dakota, at age 83 (ND Death Index.).

Louis Chalifoux was born on 25 Sep 1852 (SFXI 1851-1868, B-37.). He was baptized on 4 Oct 1852 St.Francois Xavier, (Manitoba) (Ibid.). He died on 4 Jun 1882 St.Francois Xavier, Manitoba, at age 29 (SFXI-Kipling, S-22.).

Bernard Delorme was born on 20 Dec 1855 (AP, page 157, B-338.). He was baptized on 7 Sep 1856 Assumption, Pembina, Pembina County, Dakota Territory (Ibid.). He married **Christine Robinson**, daughter of **Francois Galipeau dit Wabicier Robertson or Robinson** and **Angelique Bruyere,** in 1895 (1900C-ND, House 281, page 305A.). He died on 8 Aug 1935 Rolette County, North Dakota, at age 79 (ND Death Index.).

26. Louis Vallee was born on 16 Jan 1857 (SFXI-Kipling, B-163.). He was baptized on 25 Jan 1857 St.Francois Xavier, (Manitoba) (Ibid.). He married **Catherine Ross**, daughter of **Hugh Ross** and **Sarah Short**, on 19 Feb 1878 St.Francois Xavier, Manitoba (Ibid., M-6.). He married **Julienne Pepin**, daughter of **Narcisse Pepin** and **Marie Beaulieu**, circa 1922. He married **Marguerite Vallee**, daughter of **Jean Baptiste Vallee** and **Marie Kipling,** circa 1932 (TM Star, 26 Oct 1933.).

Catherine Ross was born on 17 May 1848 St.Francois Xavier, (Manitoba) (SFX: 1834-1850, B-735.). She was baptized on 21 May 1848 St.Francois Xavier, (Manitoba) (Ibid.). She married **Jean Baptiste Allard**, son of **Ambroise Allard** and **Marguerite Chalifoux,** on 21 Jan 1867 St.Francois Xavier, (Manitoba) (SFXI-Kipling, M-3.) (MM *Manitoba Marriages* in *Publication 45*, Volumes 1-3, compiled and edited by: Paul J. Lareau, Fr. Julien Hamelin, (240 Avenue Daly, Ottawa, Ontario K1N 6G2: Le Centre de Genealogie S.C., 1984), page 20.).

Children of **Louis Vallee** and **Catherine Ross** were as follows:

    i. Agathe Vallee was born on 27 Nov 1878 Fort Severin, Boissevain, Manitoba (ArchiviaNet, C-15008.). She died on 31 Dec 1878 Boissevain, Manitoba (Ibid.).

    ii. Apolline Vallee was born on 28 Nov 1878 St.Francois Xavier, Manitoba (SFXI-Kipling, B-41.). She died on 31 Dec 1878 St.Francois Xavier, Manitoba, at age 1 (Ibid., S-1.).

    iii. Justine Vallee was born on 18 Apr 1880 St.Francois Xavier, Manitoba (Ibid., B-26.). She died in 1899 Killarney, Manitoba (ArchiviaNet, C-15008.).

42 iv. Andre Vallee, b. 18 Apr 1885 St.Claude, St.John, Rolette County, North Dakota; m. Madeleine Rose Dillon.

    v. Julie Vallee was born on 9 Aug 1887 Rolette County, North Dakota (St.Claude BMD, Dominique Ritchot, B-342, page 68.). She was baptized on 22 Aug 1887 St.Claude Mission, St.John, Rolette County, North Dakota (Ibid.).

Julienne Pepin was born on 12 Apr 1865 North West Territories (MBS, C-14932.). She was born on 20 Jun 1865 Fort Resolution, (Northwest Territory) (Marie Beaupre Extractions.). She was baptized on 21 Jun 1865 Fort Resolution, (Northwest Territory) (Ibid.). She married **Joseph Smith**, son of **Joseph Smith** and **Charlotte Pelletier**, on 22 Jan 1883 Olga, Cavalier County, North Dakota (NWHBS, C-14941.) (Olga, page 9, M-1.). She died on 14 Feb 1931 Belcourt, Rolette, North Dakota, at age 65 (ND Death Index.). She was buried on 17 Feb 1931 St.Ann's, Belcourt, Rolette County, North Dakota (TM Star, 19 February 1931, page 2.).

Marguerite Vallee was born in Nov 1862 North Dakota (1900C-ND, 286-286.). She was born in 1863 (NWHBSI, page 83.). She married **Michel Laframboise**, son of **Narcisse Laframboise** and **Josephte Cantara**, on 29 Aug 1882 St.Joseph, Leroy, Pembina County, Dakota Territory (SJL-1, page 120, M-41.). She died on 4 Feb 1934 Belcourt, Rolette, North Dakota, at age 71 (*1934-TMC.*) (ND Death Index.) (TM Star, 8 Feb 1934.). She was buried on 5 Feb 1934 St.Ann's, Belcourt, Rolette, North Dakota (Ibid.).

27. **Catherine Vallee** was born on 22 Apr 1861 St.Francois Xavier, (Manitoba) (SFXI-Kipling, B-23.). She was baptized on 24 Apr 1861 St.Francois Xavier, (Manitoba) (Ibid.). She married **Andre Fleury**, son of **Joseph Fleury** and **Marie Thorne**, on 15 Jul 1879 St.Francois Xavier, Manitoba (Ibid., M-10.).

Andre Fleury was born on 19 Oct 1860 St.Francois Xavier, (Manitoba) (Ibid., B-97.). He was baptized on 21 Oct 1860 St.Francois Xavier, (Manitoba) (MBS, C-14928.) (SFXI-Kipling, B-97.).

Children of **Catherine Vallee** and **Andre Fleury** are:

    i. Agatha Fleury was born circa 1884 (1889-TMC-off, #173.).

28. **Melanie Vallee** was born on 13 Jul 1873 (SFXI-Kipling, B-47.) (INB, page 179.). She was baptized on 14 Jul 1873 St.Francois Xavier, Manitoba (SFXI-Kipling, B-47.) (INB, page 179.). She married **James William Lillie**, son of **William Lillie** and **Eliza Gagnon**, on 7 Aug 1886 St.Claude Mission, St.John, Rolette County, North Dakota (HBSI.) (ArchiviaNet.) (Dominique Ritchot, 26 Jan 2006.). She died on 7 Nov 1890 Rock Lake, (Manitoba), at age 17 (HBSI.) (ArchiviaNet.).

James William Lillie was born on 18 Aug 1865 St.Francois Xavier, (Manitoba) (SFXI-Kipling, B-70.). He was baptized on 20 Aug 1865 St.Francois Xavier, (Manitoba) (Ibid.).

29. **Philomene Vallee** was born on 9 Apr 1863 St.Boniface, (Manitoba) (SB-Rozyk, page 109, B-49.). She was baptized on 9 Apr 1863 St.Boniface, (Manitoba) (Ibid.). She married **Patrice Parenteau**, son of **Pierre Parenteau** and **Helene Normand**, on 20 Jan 1880 St.Boniface, Manitoba (RMSB.). She died on 23 Mar 1953 Vancouver, British Columbia, at age 89 (Rod Mac Quarrie, 30 Aug 2012.).

Patrice Parenteau was born on 7 Oct 1862 (SN1, page 64, B-31.). He was baptized on 9 Nov 1862 St.Norbert, (Manitoba) (MBS, C-14931.) (SN1, page 64, B-31.). He died on 9 Jan 1904 Batoche, (Saskatchewan), at age 41 (BSAP, page 225, S-16.). He was buried on 11 Jan 1904 Batoche, (Saskatchewan) (Ibid.).

30. **Marie Caroline Vallee** was born on 28 Nov 1882 (Olga, page 8, B-12.). She was baptized on 28 Dec 1882 Olga, Cavalier County, North Dakota (Ibid.). She married **Adolphe Pelletier**, son of **Jean Baptiste Pelletier** and **Madeleine Deschamps**, in 1898 (1900C-ND, House 357, page 313B.). She married **(--?--) Klyne** before 1915 (1936-TMC, page 192.).

Adolphe Pelletier was born on 12 Jun 1868 (L1, page 8, B-19.). He was baptized on 23 May 1869 Lebret, (Saskatchewan) (Ibid.).

31. **John Baptist Vallee** was born circa 1884 Bellmont, South Dakota (BHCM Big Horn County, Montana; Marriage Record Licenses and Certificates; 1865-1950; familysearch.org, Hereinafter cited as BHCM.) (1885-TMC, #398-406.). He married **Mabel Laverdure**, daughter of **Frank Laverdure** and **Rose Wells**, on 3 Apr 1923 St.Xavier, Big Horn, Montana (BHCM.). He died on 18 Jan 1958 Yellowstone County, Montana (MT Death.).

Mabel Laverdure was born on 10 Jun 1905 Grass Range, Montana (SSDI.) (BHCM.). She was baptized on 9 Jul 1905 St.Leo's, Lewistown, Fergus County, Montana (St.Leo's Roman Catholic Church: Baptisms and Marriages, Lewistown, Montana.). She married **Alfred Myron Shibley Sr.**, son of **Clarence Bertrom Shibley** and **Lula Maude Boone**, before 1937 (1987LS 1987-92 Little Shell Band of Chippewa Roll.). She died on 5 Jun 1996 Billings, Yellowstone County, Montana, at age 90 (SSDI.) (MT Death.).

Children of **John Baptist Vallee** and **Mabel Laverdure** are:

    i. Aloysius Vallee was born on 25 Mar 1924 (*1937-TMC*, page 505, Census No. 5904-5905.).

32. **Abraham Vallee** was born circa 1886. He was born in 1887 (1937-1987-LS Basic Roll Basic Membership Roll of the Landless Indians of Montana; 1937 Census Taken by Dr. Henry Roe Cloud; Edited c1987 to include official correspondence regarding 1937 membership; ** in Present Roll Number column indicates 1940s information added., #523.) (Ibid.). He married **Liza Caplette**, daughter of **Jean Baptiste Caplette** and **Josephine Gagnon**, before 1916 (1917 RB, #595.). He died on 21 May 1957 Hill County, Montana (MT Death.).

Liza Caplette was born on 1 May 1899 Malta, Valley County, Montana (1917 RB, #595.) (BIA-LS Bureau of Indian Affairs, Little Shell Enrollment Papers.) (1937-1987-LS Basic Roll, #523.). She died on 11 Feb 1952 Big Horn County, Montana, at age 52 (MT Death.).

Children of **Abraham Vallee** and **Liza Caplette** are as follows:

    i. Abraham Vallee Jr was born on 4 Jul 1916 Crow Reservation, Montana (1917 RB, #596.).

    ii. Charlie Vallee was born on 19 Sep 1919 (1936-LS Henry Roe Cloud Roll 1936-1937, Pembina Band of Chippewa Indians Who Were Under the Leadership of Chief Thomas Little Shell, J. H. Dussome, Zortman, Montana and Vice-President: George SinClaire, Chinook, Montana, #523.) (1937-1987-LS Basic Roll, #523.).

    iii. Alex Vallee was born on 20 Apr 1922 (1936-LS, #523.) (1937-1987-LS Basic Roll, #523.).

    iv. Mary Vallee was born on 19 Sep 1923 (1936-LS, #523.) (1937-1987-LS Basic Roll, #523.).

    v. Frank Vallee was born on 29 Oct 1926 (1936-LS, #523.) (1937-1987-LS Basic Roll, #523.).

    vi. Emma Vallee was born on 19 Aug 1932 (1936-LS, #523.) (1937-1987-LS Basic Roll, #523.).

    vii. George Vallee was born on 15 Mar 1935 (1936-LS, #523.).

33. **William Vallee** was born circa 1873 (MM.). He married **Marie Sara Parisien**, daughter of **Alexis Parisien** and **Marguerite Comtois**, on 28 Nov 1893 St.Norbert, Manitoba (Ibid.). He married **Sophie Henault dit Canada**, daughter of **Pierre Henault** and **Marguerite Larocque**, on 30 Oct 1899 St.Boniface, Manitoba (1901 Canada, District 10-i-2, page 6, line 1.) (RMSB, page 475.).

Marie Sara Parisien was born on 1 Oct 1871 St.Norbert, Manitoba (SN1, page 152, B-53.). She was baptized on 2 Oct 1871 St.Norbert, Manitoba (Ibid.).

Children of **William Vallee** and **Marie Sara Parisien** were as follows:

    i. Albert Vallee was born circa Nov 1894 (St-N Cem *St.Norbert Parish Cemetery 1859-1906, We Remember*; Winnipeg, Manitoba, Canada: St.Norbert Parish-La Barriere Metis Council of the Metis Federation of Manitoba, 29 May 2010.). He died on 21 Feb 1895 Ritchot, Manitoba (Ibid.) (MB Vital Statistics, Death Reg. #1898,002811.). He was buried on 23 Feb 1895 St.Norbert, Manitoba (St-N Cem.).

    ii. Joseph Vallee was born on 21 Jul 1896 (Rod Mac Quarrie, 17 Jan 2013.).

Sophie Henault dit Canada was baptized on 1 Oct 1862 St.Boniface, (Manitoba) (SB-Rozyk, page 86, B-160.). She was born on 1 Oct 1862 St.Boniface, (Manitoba) (Ibid.). She married **Joseph Roussin**, son of **Francois Roussin** and **Elise Courchene**, on 29 Jan 1878 Ste.Anne, Manitoba (MM.).

Children of **William Vallee** and **Sophie Henault dit Canada** were as follows:

      i.   Pierre William Rosario Vallee was born on 28 Oct 1900 St.Boniface, Manitoba (1901 Canada, District 10-i-2, page 6, line 1.) (MB Vital Statistics, Birth Reg. #1900,003581.). He married Christina Jestadt, daughter of Joseph Jestadt and Caroline Yast, on 12 Feb 1937 St.Boniface, Manitoba (RMSB, page 475.).

     ii.   Rosa Vallee was born circa 1901 (1906 Canada, District 7-19-B, page 37, line 27.).

    iii.   Alexandre Vallee was born circa 1905 (Ibid.). He married Marguerite Johnson, daughter of James Johnson and Barbara McGee, on 30 Jun 1926 St.Boniface, Manitoba (RMSB, page 476.).

34. John Baptiste Vallee was born on 18 Dec 1886 (*St.Ann's Centennial*, page 537.). He was born on 15 Nov 1888 North Dakota (SSDI.). He married **Mary Jane Lafontaine**, daughter of **Pierre Frederic Lafontaine** and **Isabelle Delaunay**, before 1916. He died on 21 Aug 1969 Belcourt, Rolette County, North Dakota, at age 82 (*St.Ann's Centennial*, page 537.) (SSDI.).

   Mary Jane Lafontaine was born on 27 Feb 1896 North Dakota (1900C-ND, 287-287.) (SSDI.). She died on 15 Mar 1970 Belcourt, Rolette County, North Dakota, at age 74 (Ibid.).

Children of **John Baptiste Vallee** and **Mary Jane Lafontaine** were as follows:

      i.   Rose Delphine Vallee was born on 14 Jan 1916 (*St.Ann's Centennial*, page 537.). She died after 30 Jun 1926.

     ii.   Francis Vallee was born on 10 Jul 1917 (Ibid.). He died on 1 Nov 1918 at age 1 (1933-TMC Census of the Turtle Mountain Chippewa Indians, United States Indian Service Department of the Interior, Turtle Mountain Agency, North Dakota, 1 Apr 1933 , page 450, Census No. 5393-5401.).

    iii.   Emil Vallie was born on 6 Jun 1919 (*St.Ann's Centennial*, page 537.) (*1937-TMC*, page 504, Census No. 5895-5903.). He married Dorothy Parisien, daughter of David Parisien and Josephte Page, before 1953. He died on 6 Jan 1995 Belcourt, Rolette County, North Dakota, at age 75 (ND Death Index.).

          Dorothy Parisien was born on 13 Aug 1923 (Rod Mac Quarrie, 17 Jan 2013.). She died on 9 Nov 1987 Rolette County, North Dakota, at age 64 (ND Death Index.).

    iv.   Eleanor Vallee was born on 6 Nov 1920 (*St.Ann's Centennial*, page 537.) (*1937-TMC*, page 504, Census No. 5895-5903.).

     v.   Joseph William Vallie was born on 28 Feb 1924 (*St.Ann's Centennial*, page 537.) (*1937-TMC*, page 504, Census No. 5895-5903.). He married Norine Poitra, daughter of Severe Poitras and Helen "Ellen" Pelletier, on 5 Jan 1944 Belcourt, Rolette County, North Dakota (TM Star.). He died on 22 Jul 2011 Valley Elder Care, Grand Forks, North Dakota, at age 87 (Ibid.).

          Norine Poitra was born on 2 Apr 1926 (1936-TMC, page 101.) (*1937-TMC*, page 431-432, Census No. 5128-5136.). She died on 5 Feb 1998 Aberdeen, Brown, South Dakota, at age 71 (SSDI.).

    vi.   Mary Jane Vallee was born on 16 Dec 1925 (*St.Ann's Centennial*, page 537.) (*1937-TMC*, page 504, Census No. 5895-5903.).

   vii.   Louis Daniel Vallee was born on 9 May 1927 (*St.Ann's Centennial*, page 537.) (*1937-TMC*, page 504, Census No. 5895-5903.).

  viii.   Helen Vallee was born on 14 Mar 1929 (Ibid.).

    ix.   Cecelia Vallee was born on 17 Mar 1931 (1936-TMC, page 122.) (*1937-TMC*, page 504, Census No. 5895-5903.).

35. Julie Ann Vallee was born on 13 Feb 1894 Rolette County, North Dakota (*St.Ann's Centennial*, page 537.) (ND Death Index.). She married **Jerome Laframboise**, son of **Michel Laframboise** and **Marguerite Vallee**, in Aug 1919 (*St.Ann's Centennial*, page 537.). She died on 11 Apr 1944 Rolette County, North Dakota, at age 50 (ND Death Index.).

   Jerome Laframboise was born on 10 Feb 1891 North Dakota (Rod Mac Quarrie, 22 Dec 2009.). He died on 16 Apr 1971 Rolette County, North Dakota, at age 80 (ND Death Index.).

36. Eliza Vallee was born on 15 Sep 1896 (1936-TMC, page 67.) (*1937-TMC*, page 125-126, Census No. 1473-1485.) (ND Death Index.). She married **Francois Decouteau**, son of **Elzear Decouteau** and **Marie Rose Lafontaine**, before 1915 (1936-TMC, page 67.). She died on 17 Oct 1967 Ward County, North Dakota, at age 71 (ND Death Index.).

   Francois Decouteau was born on 11 Jul 1893 North Dakota (1936-TMC, page 67.) (1893-TMC, page 15, Census No. 381-383.) (*1937-TMC*, page 125-126, Census No. 1473-1485.). He died on 11 Sep 1972 Belcourt, Rolette County, North Dakota, at age 79 (SSDI.) (ND Death Index.).

37. Emma Vallee was born in Jun 1898 North Dakota (1900C-ND, House 250, page 300B.). She married **Albert Laframboise**, son of **Michel Laframboise** and **Marguerite Vallee**, before 1919 (1936-TMC, page 140.). She married **Napoleon Decouteau**, son of **Norbert Decouteau** and **Rose Belgarde**, circa 1920. She married **Telesphore Joseph Renault**, son of **Jean Renaud** and **Angelique Azure**, circa 1928. She died on 18 Jan 1986 Dunseith, Rolette County, North Dakota, at age 87 (SSDI.) (ND Death Index.).

   Albert Laframboise was born on 5 Feb 1895 Rolette County, North Dakota (1900C-ND, House 326, page 305B.) (ND Death Index.). He married **Mary Vitaline Allery**, daughter of **Joseph Lawrence Allery** and **Justine Nadeau**, before 1937 (*1937-TMC*, page 277, Census No. 3352-3353.). He married **Mary Lucas** before 1947. He died on 3 Mar 1964 Rolette County, North Dakota, at age 69 (ND Death Index.).

   Napoleon Decouteau was born in 1899 (1936-TMC, page 70.) (1924-TMC-ND 1924 Census of the Chippewa Indians of Turtle Mountain Agency, North Dakota, United States Indian Service Department of the Interior, Belcourt, North Dakota, superintendent H. J. McQuigg, 30 June 1924 , Census No. 1101-1103.). He was born in Jun 1900 North Dakota (1900C-ND, House 181, page 291B.). He died on 11 Dec 1922 Rolette County, North Dakota (ND Death Index.) (*1924-TMC-ND*, Census No. 1101-1103.).

   Telesphore Joseph Renault was born on 8 Apr 1882 Montana Territory (1936-TMC, page 104.). He married **Marie Alexandrine Roussin**, daughter of **Eustache Roussin** and **Madeleine Champagne**, before 1905. He married **Elise Delorme**, daughter of **Joseph Delorme** and **Angelique Gingras**, before 1921. He died on 26 Feb 1964 Houston, Harris County, Texas, at age 81 (SSDI.).

38. Jane Evelin Vallee was born in 1901 (1936-TMC, page 38.). She married **Michael Bercier**, son of **Cuthbert Bercier** and **Justine Lafreniere**, before 1919. She and **Francis Poitras** met before 1925.

   Michael Bercier was born in Mar 1892 North Dakota (1900C-ND, House 489, page 331A.). He married **Florestine Azure**, daughter of **Francois Azure** and **Marie Berger**, before 1934 (*1937-TMC*, page 65, Census No. 1357, 6513, 5372, 6512, 738-741.). He died on

21 Sep 1962 Hospital, Minot, North Dakota, at age 70 (ND Death Index.). He was buried on 24 Sep 1962 St.Ann's Cemetery, Belcourt, Rolette County, North Dakota (TM Star, 27 Sep 1962.).

Francis Poitras was born on 28 Jun 1904 Belcourt, Rolette County, North Dakota (*1937-TMC*, page 420, Census No. 4977.). He and **Ernestine Lafournaise** met before 1934 (Ibid., page 8, Census No. 83-85.). He married **Mathilda Azure**, daughter of **William Azure** and **Josephine Dumont**, on 26 Dec 1938 St.Ann, Belcourt, Rolette County, North Dakota (*St.Ann's Centennial*, page 496.). He died on 22 Jun 1974 Rolette County, North Dakota, at age 69 (ND Death Index.).

39. **Victoria "Jane" Vallee** was born in 1903 (1936-TMC, page 122.). She married **Louis Daniel Champagne**, son of **Louis Champagne** and **Marie Rose Poitras**, before 1925 (*St.Ann's Centennial*, page 538.). She died on 12 Dec 1969 Rolette County, North Dakota (ND Death Index.).

Louis Daniel Champagne was born on 25 Jan 1900 Rolette County, North Dakota (1900C-ND, House 180, page 291B.) (1936-TMC, page 55.) (ND Death Index.). He died on 27 Aug 1961 Rolette County, North Dakota, at age 61 (Ibid.).

40. **Marie Madeleine Vallee** was born on 11 Nov 1867 (1888-TMC, #702-706.) (ND Death Index.). She married **Pierre McLeod**, son of **Joseph McLeod** and **Angelique Lacerte**, in 1888 (1900C-ND, 265-265.). She died on 18 Aug 1957 Belcourt, Rolette County, North Dakota, at age 89 (ND Death Index.).

Pierre McLeod was born on 2 Oct 1843 Baie St.Paul, (Manitoba) (MBS, C-14931.). He married **Rose Delima Delorme**, daughter of **Francois Delorme** and **Angelique Malaterre**, on 22 Jan 1867 St.Francois Xavier, (Manitoba) (SFXI-Kipling, M-4.). He married **Sara Emond**, daughter of **Seraphin Emond** and **Marie Lapierre**, on 12 Jan 1875 St.Francois Xavier, Manitoba (Ibid., M-3.). He died on 10 Feb 1926 Rolette County, North Dakota, at age 82 (ND Death Index.).

Generation Five

41. **Alice Virginia Vallee** was born circa 1904 (1906 Canada, District 15-41, page 18-19, family 151, line 38-40, 1-3.). She married **William Cheviel** (Art Fisher, Jan 1998; From Genealogy of Joyce Black, 1981.).

42. **Andre Vallee** was baptized on 18 Apr 1885 St.Claude, St.John, Rolette County, North Dakota (St.Claude BMD, Dominique Ritchot, page 42, B-189.). He and **Madeleine Rose Dillon** obtained a marriage license on 14 Feb 1924 Roosevelt County, Montana (RooCM.). He married **Madeleine Rose Dillon**, daughter of **John R. Dillon** and **Cecile Deschamps**, on 15 Feb 1924 Justice of the Peace, Wolf Point, Roosevelt County, Montana (Ibid.).

Madeleine Rose Dillon was born in Dec 1880 Cypress Hills, (Saskatchewan) (ArchiviaNet.) (HBSI.) (1881 Canada, Film C-13285, District 192, page 9, Household 32.). She was born circa 1885 Glasgow, Valley County, Montana (VCM Valley County Courthouse, Glasgow, Montana; Marriage Record Licenses, 1865-1950, familysearch.org: Volume 2; #897, Hereinafter cited as VCM.). She married **Isidore Larocque**, son of **Jean Baptiste Larocque** and **Julie Lemire**, before 1898. She and **William Decouteau** obtained a marriage license on 28 Sep 1911 Valley County, Montana (Ibid.). She married **William Decouteau**, son of **Louis Decouteau** and **Genevieve Amyotte**, on 20 Jul 1913 Poplar, Montana (Ibid.). She married **Charles Carson**, son of **Edward Carson** and **Bell Wambles**, before 1987.

Children of **Andre Vallee** include:

    i.   Vida Vallee was born on 24 Aug 1926 (1937-1987-LS Basic Roll, #522.).

    ii.   Rainey Vallee was born on 18 Feb 1928 (Ibid.).

Descendants of Pierre Vanasse dit Anas

Generation One

1. **Pierre Vanasse dit Anas** married **Julie Parisien**, daughter of **Baptiste Parisien** and **Suzanne Stony Indian**, before 1833.

Julie Parisien was born circa 1810 Pembina. She was born in 1818 Edmonton, (Alberta) (NWHBS 1885 Scrip Applications, North-West Halfbreeds residing outside Manitoba on 15 July 1870, RG15-20, C-14942.). She was born circa 1820 Pembina County (1850Ci-MN *Minnesota Territorial Census, 1850*, Harpole, Patricia C. and Mary D. Nagle, ed., (St.Paul, Minnesota: Minnesota Historical Society, 1972), page 31, Dwelling 129, Family 129.). She married **Antoine Houle**, son of **Antoine Houle** and **Elise Indian**, circa 1836 St.Boniface, (Manitoba). She died in 1872 near, Carlton, (Saskatchewan).

Children of **Pierre Vanasse dit Anas** and **Julie Parisien** were:

  2   i.   Jean Baptiste Vanasse, b. circa Sep 1833; m. Catherine Cardinal; d. 13 Mar 1920 Tail Creek, Alberta.

Generation Two

2. **Jean Baptiste Vanasse** was born circa Sep 1833 (SB 1825-1834 St.Boniface Roman Catholic Registre des Baptemes, Mariages & Sepultures, 1825-1834, page 134, B-818. Hereinafter cited as SB 1825-1834.). He was baptized on 13 Jul 1834 St.Boniface, (Manitoba) (Ibid.). He married **Catherine Cardinal**, daughter of **Antoine Cardinal** and **Marie Comtois**, in 1855 Jaspar House, (Alberta) (Denney Papers, Charles D. Denney, Glenbow Archives, Calgary, Alberta.). He died on 13 Mar 1920 Tail Creek, Alberta (Ibid.).

Catherine Cardinal was born circa Feb 1838 (CCRPNW-V *Catholic Church Records of the Pacific Northwest, Vancouver, Volumes I and II and Stellamaris Mission* Translated by: Mikell de Lores Wormell Warner and Annotated by: Harriet Duncan Munnick, (St.Paul, Oregon: French Prairie Press, 1972), page 11, B-98.). She was baptized on 3 Oct 1838 Jaspar House, (Alberta) (Ibid.). She died on 5 Dec 1905 Tail Creek, Alberta (Denney.).

Children of **Jean Baptiste Vanasse** and **Catherine Cardinal** were as follows:

  3   i.   Philomene Vanasse, b. Oct 1856 Rocky Mountains; m. Jean Baptiste Dumont.

  4   ii.   Jean Baptiste Vanasse dit Anas, b. 19 Sep 1857 Fort-des-Prairies; m. Emelie Calder; d. 1 Apr 1947 Onion Lake, Saskatchewan.

    iii. Narcisse Vanasse was born in 1860. He died circa 1860.

    iv. Charles Anas was born on 3 May 1861 (MSJ-FA-E Register des Baptemes, Mariages & Sepultures 1858-1861 Mission St.Joachim, Fort Auguste, Fort des Prairies, Edmonton, No. 1, page 34, B-78. Hereinafter cited as MSJ-FA-E.). He was baptized on 10 May 1861 St.Joachim, Fort Edmonton, (Alberta) (Ibid.). He died in Oct 1870 on the plains at age 9 (ArchiviaNet 1886-1901, 1906 Half-Breed Scrip Applications Index, RG15-21, Volume 1333 through 1371, Microfilm Reel Number C-14944 through C-15010, National Archives of Canada, Ottawa, Ontario, http://www.collectionscanada.gc.ca, C-15008.).

5   v.   Marguerite Vanasse dit Anas, b. 10 Sep 1863 Victoria, (Alberta); m. Modeste Loyer.

6   vi.   Julienne Vanasse, b. 30 Aug 1867 St.Boniface, (Manitoba); m. Louis Rousselle Jr.

7   vii.   Pauline Vanasse, b. 30 Aug 1867 St.Boniface, (Manitoba); m. Daniel Belcourt.

   viii.   William Vanasse dit Anas was born in Jun 1870 Saskatchewan River, North West Territories (NWHBS, C-14942.).

   ix.   Marie Catherine Vanasse was born on 7 Apr 1872 (MSJ-FA-E, page 77, B-6.). She was baptized on 18 Apr 1872 (Fort la Montagne) St.Joachim, Fort Edmonton, (Alberta) (Ibid.).

8   x.   Adelaide Vanasse, b. circa Feb 1874 Rocky Mountain House, (Alberta); m. Camille Miquelon.

9   xi.   Eleanore Vanasse, b. 28 Apr 1876 Calgary, (Alberta); m. Adolphus L'Hirondelle.

   xii.   Isabelle Vanasse was born on 20 Oct 1878 Calgary, (Alberta) (HBSI Index 1886-1901, 1906 Halfbreed Scrip Applications, RG15-21.) (ArchiviaNet.). She married John A. McFadden before 1899.

   xiii.   Melanie Anasse was born on 6 Sep 1883 Calgary, (Alberta) (HBS 1886-1901, 1906 Half-Breed Scrip Applications, RG15-21, Volume 1333; C-14944.). She was baptized on 9 Sep 1883 Calgary, (Alberta) (Ibid.).

Generation Three

3. Philomene Vanasse was born in Oct 1856 Rocky Mountains (NWHBS, C-14938.). She married **Jean Baptiste Dumont**, son of **Jean Baptiste Dumont** and **Isabelle Gray**, on 22 Apr 1872 (Fort la Montagne) St.Joachim, Fort Edmonton, (Alberta) (Ibid.) (MSJ-FA-E, page 77, M-2.).

Jean Baptiste Dumont was baptized on 26 Jun 1851 Fort-des-Prairies (INB *Index des Naissances and Baptemes* (St.Boniface, Manitoba: La Societe Historique de Saint-Boniface., c1995), page 56.). He was born on 26 Jun 1851 Slave Lake, (Alberta) (NWHBS, C-14938.) (INB, page 56.). He married **Nancy Gladu**, daughter of **John Quinn or Gladu** and **Julie Batoche,** before 1897 (HBSI.) (Automated Genealogy 1901 Census Transcription Project and Census Images from the National Archives of Canada, http://www.automatedgenealogy.com, Egg Lake, page 7, Family 50, line 17-22.). Question: *Did Jean Baptiste Dumont have a second wife and family?*

4. Jean Baptiste Vanasse dit Anas was baptized on 19 Sep 1857 Fort-des-Prairies (INB, page 6.). He was born in Nov 1857 Edmonton, (Alberta) (NWHBS, C-14942.). He married **Emelie Calder**, daughter of **Peter Calder** and **Isabelle Lussier,** circa 1876 Calgary, (Alberta) (Ibid.). He died on 1 Apr 1947 Onion Lake, Saskatchewan, at age 89 (Denney.).

Emelie Calder was born on 10 Jul 1850 (INB, page 28.). She was baptized on 14 Jul 1850 Fort-des-Prairies (Ibid.).

Children of **Jean Baptiste Vanasse dit Anas** and **Emelie Calder** were as follows:

   i.   Peter Anasse was born in 1877 Calgary, (Alberta) (HBS, Volume 1333; C-14944.).

10   ii.   Emelia Vanasse, b. 1 Jan 1877 Calgary, (Alberta); m. Augustin Eustache Hamelin.

   iii.   Isabella Catherine Anasse was born in 1879 Calgary, (Alberta) (Ibid.).

11   iv.   Justine Vanasse, b. circa Dec 1881 Calgary, (Alberta); m. John Rousselle.

   v.   James Baptiste Anasse was born in Mar 1882 Calgary, (Alberta) (Ibid.).

   vi.   Mary Anasse was born in Dec 1884 Calgary, (Alberta) (Ibid.).

   vii.   Daniel Anasse was born on 19 Jul 1885 Calgary, (Alberta) (Ibid.). He married Anna Dufresne, daughter of Francois Dufresne and Catherine Piche dit Morin or Mijawabemen, before 1917 (Bruce Dumont Research, 11 Jul 1998.).

      Anna Dufresne was born after 1885.

   viii.   Eliza Anasse was born on 12 Sep 1886 Calgary, (Alberta) (HBS, Volume 1333; C-14944.).

   ix.   Sophia Vanesse was born on 18 Apr 1892 Hobbema, (Alberta). She married Arthur Joseph Lewis on 14 Sep 1915 Mirror, (Alberta). She died on 26 Mar 1963 Calgary, (Alberta), at age 70.

5. Marguerite Vanasse dit Anas was born on 10 Sep 1863 Victoria, (Alberta) (NWHBS, C-14940.). She married **Modeste Loyer**, son of **Louis Loyer** and **Isabelle Gray**, on 30 Oct 1882 St.Mary's, Calgary, (Alberta) (E/C-M Repertoire des Mariages de la Paroisse Saint-Joachim Edmonton, Sainte-Famille, St.Mary's Calgary; J. Hamelin S. C. and H. Houle C.; 2244, Rue Fullum, Montreal, Qc H2K 3N9: Le Centre de Genealogie S. C., 1990, Publication Number 130, page 2.).

Modeste Loyer was born on 5 Oct 1853 Lac Ste.Anne, (Alberta) (NWHBS, C-14940.). He was baptized on 30 Oct 1853 Fort-des-Prairies (INB, page 112.). He married **Eliza Maskote-Pwan** in 1877 St.Albert, (Alberta) (NWHBS, C-14940.).

6. Julienne Vanasse was born on 30 Aug 1867 St.Boniface, (Manitoba) (SB-Rozyk St. Boniface Roman Catholic Church, Manitoba, Canada, Baptisms, Marriages and Burials 1860-1875 Extractions, Compiled by Rosemary Rozyk, page 92-93, B-74.). She was baptized on 30 Aug 1867 St.Boniface, (Manitoba) (Ibid.). She married **Louis Rousselle Jr.**, son of **Louis Rousselle Sr.** and **Angelique Tessier,** on 23 Nov 1881 St.Mary's, Calgary, (Alberta) (NWHBS, C-14941.) (*E/C-M*, page 2.).

Louis Rousselle Jr was born on 1 Feb 1860 Fort Edmonton, (Alberta) (MSJ-FA-E, page 23, B-26.). He was baptized on 1 Feb 1860 St.Joachim, Fort Edmonton, (Alberta) (Ibid.).

7. Pauline Vanasse was born on 30 Aug 1867 St.Boniface, (Manitoba) (SB-Rozyk, page 92-93, B-73.). She was baptized on 30 Aug 1867 St.Boniface, (Manitoba) (Ibid.). She married **Daniel Belcourt**, son of **Joseph Belcourt** and **Madeleine Sapen dit Campion**, on 14 Aug 1882 St.Mary's, Calgary, (Alberta) (NWHBS, C-14936.) (NWHBSI Index 1885 Scrip Applications, North-West Halfbreeds residing outside Manitoba on 15 July 1870, RG15-20, page 83.) (*E/C-M*, page 2.).

Daniel Belcourt was born on 22 Dec 1857 St.Albert, (Alberta) (NWHBS, C-14936.) (INB, page 13.). He was baptized on 22 Dec 1857 Fort-des-Prairies (Ibid.).

8. Adelaide Vanasse was born circa Feb 1874 Rocky Mountain House, (Alberta) (HBSI.) (MSJ-FA-E, page 83, B-5.). She was baptized on 22 May 1874 St.Joachim, Fort Edmonton, (Alberta) (Ibid.). She married **Camille Miquelon**, son of **Zoel Miquelon** and **Nancy Darning**, on 17 May 1894 St.Mary's, Calgary, (Alberta) (*E/C-M*, page 2.).

Camille Miquelon was born on 10 Nov 1871 (1901 Canada, District 202-q(3), page 2, family 15, line 21-25.).

9. Eleanore Vanasse was born on 28 Apr 1876 Calgary, (Alberta) (ArchiviaNet.). She married **Adolphus L'Hirondelle**, son of **Andre L'Hirondelle** and **Eliza Delorme,** before 1900.

Adolphus L'Hirondelle was born on 27 Jan 1877 St.Albert, (Alberta) (Ibid.) (1901 Canada, #202, g(2), page 8, family 78, line 12-14.).

Generation Four

10. Emelia Vanasse was born on 1 Jan 1877 Calgary, (Alberta) (ArchiviaNet.). She married **Augustin Eustache Hamelin**, son of **Augustin Hamelin dit Azure** and **Marie Desjarlais,** on 16 Apr 1895 Bears Hills, (Alberta) (HBSI.) (ArchiviaNet.).

Augustin Eustache Hamelin was born circa Jun 1872 (MSJ-FA-E, page 78, B-9.). He was baptized on 21 Jul 1872 St.Joachim, Fort Edmonton, (Alberta) (Ibid.). He was born in May 1873 Red Deer, (Alberta) (HBSI.) (ArchiviaNet.).

11. Justine Vanasse was born circa Dec 1881 Calgary, (Alberta). She married **John Rousselle**, son of **Louis Rousselle Sr.** and **Angelique Tessier,** before 1890.

John Rousselle was born on 20 Oct 1864 Fort Edmonton, (Alberta) (MSJ-FA-E, page 56, B-167.). He was baptized on 22 Oct 1864 St.Joachim, Fort Edmonton, (Alberta) (Ibid.).

Descendants of Pierre Vanasse dit Anas

Generation One

1. Pierre Vanasse dit Anas married **Julie Parisien**, daughter of **Baptiste Parisien** and **Suzanne Stony Indian,** before 1833.

Julie Parisien was born circa 1810 Pembina. She was born in 1818 Edmonton, (Alberta) (NWHBS 1885 Scrip Applications, North-West Halfbreeds residing outside Manitoba on 15 July 1870, RG15-20, C-14942.). She was born circa 1820 Pembina County (1850Ci-MN *Minnesota Territorial Census, 1850*, Harpole, Patricia C. and Mary D. Nagle, ed., (St.Paul, Minnesota: Minnesota Historical Society, 1972), page 31, Dwelling 129, Family 129.). She married **Antoine Houle**, son of **Antoine Houle** and **Elise Indian,** circa 1836 St.Boniface, (Manitoba). She died in 1872 near, Carlton, (Saskatchewan).

Children of **Pierre Vanasse dit Anas** and **Julie Parisien** were:

    2   i.   Jean Baptiste Vanasse, b. circa Sep 1833; m. Catherine Cardinal; d. 13 Mar 1920 Tail Creek, Alberta.

Generation Two

2. Jean Baptiste Vanasse was born circa Sep 1833 (SB 1825-1834 St.Boniface Roman Catholic Registre des Baptemes, Mariages & Sepultures, 1825-1834, page 134, B-818. Hereinafter cited as SB 1825-1834.). He was baptized on 13 Jul 1834 St.Boniface, (Manitoba) (Ibid.). He married **Catherine Cardinal**, daughter of **Antoine Cardinal** and **Marie Comtois,** in 1855 Jaspar House, (Alberta) (Denney Papers, Charles D. Denney, Glenbow Archives, Calgary, Alberta.). He died on 13 Mar 1920 Tail Creek, Alberta (Ibid.).

Catherine Cardinal was born circa Feb 1838 (CCRPNW-V *Catholic Church Records of the Pacific Northwest, Vancouver, Volumes I and II and Stellamaris Mission* Translated by: Mikell de Lores Wormell Warner and Annotated by: Harriet Duncan Munnick, (St.Paul, Oregon: French Prairie Press, 1972), page 11, B-98.). She was baptized on 3 Oct 1838 Jaspar House, (Alberta) (Ibid.). She died on 5 Dec 1905 Tail Creek, Alberta (Denney.).

Children of **Jean Baptiste Vanasse** and **Catherine Cardinal** were as follows:

    3   i.   Philomene Vanasse, b. Oct 1856 Rocky Mountains; m. Jean Baptiste Dumont.

    4   ii.   Jean Baptiste Vanasse dit Anas, b. 19 Sep 1857 Fort-des-Prairies; m. Emelie Calder; d. 1 Apr 1947 Onion Lake, Saskatchewan.

        iii.   Narcisse Vanasse was born in 1860. He died circa 1860.

        iv.   Charles Anas was born on 3 May 1861 (MSJ-FA-E Register des Baptemes, Mariages & Sepultures 1858-1861 Mission St.Joachim, Fort Auguste, Fort des Prairies, Edmonton, No. 1, page 34, B-78. Hereinafter cited as MSJ-FA-E.). He was baptized on 10 May 1861 St.Joachim, Fort Edmonton, (Alberta) (Ibid.). He died in Oct 1870 on the plains at age 9 (ArchiviaNet 1886-1901, 1906 Half-Breed Scrip Applications Index, RG15-21, Volume 1333 through 1371, Microfilm Reel Number C-14944 through C-15010, National Archives of Canada, Ottawa, Ontario, http://www.collectionscanada.gc.ca, C-15008.).

    5   v.   Marguerite Vanasse dit Anas, b. 10 Sep 1863 Victoria, (Alberta); m. Modeste Loyer.

    6   vi.   Julienne Vanasse, b. 30 Aug 1867 St.Boniface, (Manitoba); m. Louis Rousselle Jr.

    7   vii.   Pauline Vanasse, b. 30 Aug 1867 St.Boniface, (Manitoba); m. Daniel Belcourt.

        viii.   William Vanasse dit Anas was born in Jun 1870 Saskatchewan River, North West Territories (NWHBS, C-14942.).

        ix.   Marie Catherine Vanasse was born on 7 Apr 1872 (MSJ-FA-E, page 77, B-6.). She was baptized on 18 Apr 1872 (Fort la Montagne) St.Joachim, Fort Edmonton, (Alberta) (Ibid.).

    8   x.   Adelaide Vanasse, b. circa Feb 1874 Rocky Mountain House, (Alberta); m. Camille Miquelon.

    9   xi.   Eleanore Vanasse, b. 28 Apr 1876 Calgary, (Alberta); m. Adolphus L'Hirondelle.

        xii.   Isabelle Vanasse was born on 20 Oct 1878 Calgary, (Alberta) (HBSI Index 1886-1901, 1906 Halfbreed Scrip Applications, RG15-21.) (ArchiviaNet.). She married John A. McFadden before 1899.

        xiii.   Melanie Anasse was born on 6 Sep 1883 Calgary, (Alberta) (HBS 1886-1901, 1906 Half-Breed Scrip Applications, RG15-21, Volume 1333; C-14944.). She was baptized on 9 Sep 1883 Calgary, (Alberta) (Ibid.).

Generation Three

3. Philomene Vanasse was born in Oct 1856 Rocky Mountains (NWHBS, C-14938.). She married **Jean Baptiste Dumont**, son of **Jean Baptiste Dumont** and **Isabelle Gray**, on 22 Apr 1872 (Fort la Montagne) St.Joachim, Fort Edmonton, (Alberta) (Ibid.) (MSJ-FA-E, page 77, M-2.).

Jean Baptiste Dumont was baptized on 26 Jun 1851 Fort-des-Prairies (INB *Index des Naissances and Baptemes* (St.Boniface, Manitoba: La Societe Historique de Saint-Boniface., c1995), page 56.). He was born on 26 Jun 1851 Slave Lake, (Alberta) (NWHBS, C-14938.) (INB, page 56.). He married **Nancy Gladu**, daughter of **John Quinn or Gladu** and **Julie Batoche,** before 1897 (HBSI.) (Automated Genealogy 1901 Census Transcription Project and Census Images from the National Archives of Canada, http://www.automatedgenealogy.com, Egg Lake, page 7, Family 50, line 17-22.). Question: *Did Jean Baptiste Dumont have a second wife and family?*

4. Jean Baptiste Vanasse dit Anas was baptized on 19 Sep 1857 Fort-des-Prairies (INB, page 6.). He was born in Nov 1857 Edmonton, (Alberta) (NWHBS, C-14942.). He married **Emelie Calder**, daughter of **Peter Calder** and **Isabelle Lussier**, circa 1876 Calgary, (Alberta) (Ibid.). He died on 1 Apr 1947 Onion Lake, Saskatchewan, at age 89 (Denney.).

Emelie Calder was born on 10 Jul 1850 (INB, page 28.). She was baptized on 14 Jul 1850 Fort-des-Prairies (Ibid.).

Children of **Jean Baptiste Vanasse dit Anas** and **Emelie Calder** were as follows:

    i. Peter Anasse was born in 1877 Calgary, (Alberta) (HBS, Volume 1333; C-14944.).

10 ii. Emelia Vanasse, b. 1 Jan 1877 Calgary, (Alberta); m. Augustin Eustache Hamelin.

    iii. Isabella Catherine Anasse was born in 1879 Calgary, (Alberta) (Ibid.).

11 iv. Justine Vanasse, b. circa Dec 1881 Calgary, (Alberta); m. John Rousselle.

    v. James Baptiste Anasse was born in Mar 1882 Calgary, (Alberta) (Ibid.).

    vi. Mary Anasse was born in Dec 1884 Calgary, (Alberta) (Ibid.).

    vii. Daniel Anasse was born on 19 Jul 1885 Calgary, (Alberta) (Ibid.). He married Anna Dufresne, daughter of Francois Dufresne and Catherine Piche dit Morin or Mijawabemen, before 1917 (Bruce Dumont Research, 11 Jul 1998.).

     Anna Dufresne was born after 1885.

    viii. Eliza Anasse was born on 12 Sep 1886 Calgary, (Alberta) (HBS, Volume 1333; C-14944.).

    ix. Sophia Vanesse was born on 18 Apr 1892 Hobbema, (Alberta). She married Arthur Joseph Lewis on 14 Sep 1915 Mirror, (Alberta). She died on 26 Mar 1963 Calgary, (Alberta), at age 70.

5. Marguerite Vanasse dit Anas was born on 10 Sep 1863 Victoria, (Alberta) (NWHBS, C-14940.). She married **Modeste Loyer**, son of **Louis Loyer** and **Isabelle Gray**, on 30 Oct 1882 St.Mary's, Calgary, (Alberta) (E/C-M Repertoire des Mariages de la Paroisse Saint-Joachim Edmonton, Sainte-Famille, St.Mary's Calgary; J. Hamelin S. C. and H. Houle S. C.; 2244, Rue Fullum, Montreal, Qc H2K 3N9: Le Centre de Genealogie S. C., 1990, Publication Number 130, page 2.).

Modeste Loyer was born on 5 Oct 1853 Lac Ste.Anne, (Alberta) (NWHBS, C-14940.). He was baptized on 30 Oct 1853 Fort-des-Prairies (INB, page 112.). He married **Eliza Maskote-Pwan** in 1877 St.Albert, (Alberta) (NWHBS, C-14940.).

6. Julienne Vanasse was born on 30 Aug 1867 St.Boniface, (Manitoba) (SB-Rozyk St. Boniface Roman Catholic Church, Manitoba, Canada, Baptisms, Marriages and Burials 1860-1875 Extractions, Compiled by Rosemary Rozyk, page 92-93, B-74.). She was baptized on 30 Aug 1867 St.Boniface, (Manitoba) (Ibid.). She married **Louis Rousselle Jr.**, son of **Louis Rousselle Sr.** and **Angelique Tessier**, on 23 Nov 1881 St.Mary's, Calgary, (Alberta) (NWHBS, C-14941.) (E/C-M, page 2.).

Louis Rousselle Jr was born on 1 Feb 1860 Fort Edmonton, (Alberta) (MSJ-FA-E, page 23, B-26.). He was baptized on 1 Feb 1860 St.Joachim, Fort Edmonton, (Alberta) (Ibid.).

7. Pauline Vanasse was born on 30 Aug 1867 St.Boniface, (Manitoba) (SB-Rozyk, page 92-93, B-73.). She was baptized on 30 Aug 1867 St.Boniface, (Manitoba) (Ibid.). She married **Daniel Belcourt**, son of **Joseph Belcourt** and **Madeleine Sapen dit Campion**, on 14 Aug 1882 St.Mary's, Calgary, (Alberta) (NWHBS, C-14936.) (NWHBSI Index 1885 Scrip Applications, North-West Halfbreeds residing outside Manitoba on 15 July 1870, RG15-20, page 83.) (E/C-M, page 2.).

Daniel Belcourt was born on 22 Dec 1857 St.Albert, (Alberta) (NWHBS, C-14936.) (INB, page 13.). He was baptized on 22 Dec 1857 Fort-des-Prairies (Ibid.).

8. Adelaide Vanasse was born circa Feb 1874 Rocky Mountain House, (Alberta) (HBSI.) (MSJ-FA-E, page 83, B-5.). She was baptized on 22 May 1874 St.Joachim, Fort Edmonton, (Alberta) (Ibid.). She married **Camille Miquelon**, son of **Zoel Miquelon** and **Nancy Darning**, on 17 May 1894 St.Mary's, Calgary, (Alberta) (E/C-M, page 2.).

Camille Miquelon was born on 10 Nov 1871 (1901 Canada, District 202-q(3), page 2, family 15, line 21-25.).

9. Eleanore Vanasse was born on 28 Apr 1876 Calgary, (Alberta) (ArchiviaNet.). She married **Adolphus L'Hirondelle**, son of **Andre L'Hirondelle** and **Eliza Delorme**, before 1900.

Adolphus L'Hirondelle was born on 27 Jan 1877 St.Albert, (Alberta) (Ibid.) (1901 Canada, #202, g(2), page 8, family 78, line 12-14.).

Generation Four

10. Emelia Vanasse was born on 1 Jan 1877 Calgary, (Alberta) (ArchiviaNet.). She married **Augustin Eustache Hamelin**, son of **Augustin Hamelin dit Azure** and **Marie Desjarlais**, on 16 Apr 1895 Bears Hills, (Alberta) (HBSI.) (ArchiviaNet.).

Augustin Eustache Hamelin was born circa Jun 1872 (MSJ-FA-E, page 78, B-9.). He was baptized on 21 Jul 1872 St.Joachim, Fort Edmonton, (Alberta) (Ibid.). He was born in May 1873 Red Deer, (Alberta) (HBSI.) (ArchiviaNet.).

11. Justine Vanasse was born circa Dec 1881 Calgary, (Alberta). She married **John Rousselle**, son of **Louis Rousselle Sr.** and **Angelique Tessier**, before 1890.

John Rousselle was born on 20 Oct 1864 Fort Edmonton, (Alberta) (MSJ-FA-E, page 56, B-167.). He was baptized on 22 Oct 1864 St.Joachim, Fort Edmonton, (Alberta) (Ibid.).

Ahnentafel between Antoine Vandal and Etienne Vandal

--- 1st Generation ---

1. ANTOINE VANDAL (PRDH online index, http://www.genealogic.umontreal.ca, No. 695530.) (Ibid.). Question: *Probable son of Antoine Vandal and Marie Charlotte Mandeville.* He was born circa 1781 at Lower Canada (1850Ci-MN *Minnesota Territorial Census, 1850*, Harpole, Patricia C. and Mary D. Nagle, ed., (St.Paul, Minnesota: Minnesota Historical Society, 1972), page 30, Dwelling 118, Family 118.). He was born circa 1783 at Quebec (1827C RRS HBCA E5/1 1827 Census of the Red River Settlement, HBCA E5/1, Hudson's Bay Company Archives, Provincial Archives, 200 Vaughan Street, Winnipeg, MB R3C 1T5, Canada., page 6.). He was baptized on 18 Apr 1785 at Sorel, Quebec (PRDH online, No. 695530.). He was born on 18 Apr 1785 at Sorel, Quebec (Ibid.). He married **ANGELIQUE SAUTEUSE** before 1809. As of 1829, he was also known as **TWENICHE VANDALE** (1829C RRS HBCA E5/3 1829 Census of the Red River Settlement, HBCA E5/3, Hudson's Bay Company Archives, Provincial Archives, 200 Vaughan Street, Winnipeg,

MB R3C 1T5, Canada., page 2.). He died on 18 Dec 1870 at St.Norbert, Manitoba, at age 85 (SN1 Catholic Parish Register of St.Norbert 1857-1873, page 136, S-6. Hereinafter cited as SN1.). He was buried on 19 Dec 1870 at St.Norbert, Manitoba (Ibid.).

--- 2nd Generation ---

2. ANTOINE VANDAL was born on 26 Oct 1752 at Sorel, Richelieu, Quebec (PRDH online, #120717.). He was baptized on 27 Oct 1752 at Sorel, Richelieu, Quebec (Ibid.). He married MARIE CHARLOTTE MANDEVILLE, daughter of ALEXIS MANDEVILLE and FRANCOISE HUS, on 11 Feb 1771 at Sorel, Quebec (Ibid., No. 226165.). He died on 30 Apr 1824 at Sorel, Richelieu, Quebec, at age 71 (Ibid., #120717.). He was buried on 1 May 1824 at Sorel, Richelieu, Quebec (Ibid.).

--- 3rd Generation ---

4. JACQUES VANDAL (DGFQ Jette, Rene, *Dictionnaire Genealogique des Familles du Quebec des Origines a 1730* (Montreal, Quebec, Canada: University of Montreal Press, 1983), page 1112.) (Ibid.) (Ibid.) was baptized on 8 Oct 1725 at Neuville, Quebec (Ibid.). He married MARIE ANTOINETTE BEAUGRAND DIT CHAMPAGNE, daughter of ANTOINE BEAUGRAND DIT CHAMPAGNE and MARIE JOSEPHE COUTU, on 15 Jan 1748 at Lanoraie, Quebec (PRDH online.). He married MARIE THERESE VENNE, daughter of LOUIS VENNE and LOUISE MARIE THERESE DESAUTELS DIT LAPOINTE, on 14 Feb 1757 at Sorel, Quebec (Ibid., No. 321957.). He died on 20 Jan 1779 at Sorel, Quebec, at age 53 (Ibid., No. 377577.). He was buried on 21 Jan 1779 at Sorel, Quebec (Ibid.).

--- 4th Generation ---

8. FRANCOIS VANDAL was born on 3 Feb 1682 at Neuville, Quebec (DGFQ, page 1112.) (PRDH online, No. 53621.). He was baptized on 8 Feb 1682 at Neuville, Quebec (DGFQ, page 1112.) (PRDH online, No. 53621.). He married MARIE-ANTOINETTE RIPAULT, daughter of ROCH RIPAULT DIT ROLET OR ROLLET and MARIE-ANNE AUBERT, on 10 Feb 1716 at Grondines, Quebec (DNCF *Dictionnaire National des Canadiens-Francais Tome I & II* Gabriel Drouin, editor (revised 1985; Siege Social, 4184, rue St-Denis, Montreal, Canada: l'Institut Genealogique Drouin, 1979), page 1325.) (DGFQ, page 1112.) (PRDH online, No. 56137.). A contract for the marriage to MARIE-ANTOINETTE RIPAULT, daughter of ROCH RIPAULT DIT ROLET OR ROLLET and MARIE-ANNE AUBERT, was signed on 16 Feb 1716 (DGFQ, page 1112.). He was buried on 22 Feb 1742 at Neuville, Quebec (PRDH online, No. 156598.).

--- 5th Generation ---

16. FRANCOIS VANDAL lived at at Verantes, Saumur, Angers, Anjou (Maine-et-Loire) (DNCF, page 1325.) (DGFQ, page 1112.). He was also known as FRANCOIS VANDALE (DNCF, page 1239.). He was born between 1645 and 1651 (DGFQ, page 1112.). He married MARIE-MADELEINE PINEL, daughter of GILLES PINEL and ANNE LEDET, on 19 Mar 1680 at Neuville, Quebec (Ibid.). He was buried on 6 Dec 1697 at Neuville, Quebec (Ibid.).

--- 6th Generation ---

32. ETIENNE VANDAL married JULIENNE GROLE.

Descendants of Antoine Vandal

Generation One

1. **Antoine Vandal** was born on 26 Oct 1752 Sorel, Richelieu, Quebec (PRDH online index, http://www.genealogic.umontreal.ca, #120717.). He was baptized on 27 Oct 1752 Sorel, Richelieu, Quebec (Ibid.). He married **Marie Charlotte Mandeville**, daughter of **Alexis Mandeville** and **Francoise Hus**, on 11 Feb 1771 Sorel, Quebec (Ibid., No. 226165.). He died on 30 Apr 1824 Sorel, Richelieu, Quebec, at age 71 (Ibid., #120717.). He was buried on 1 May 1824 Sorel, Richelieu, Quebec (Ibid.).

Marie Charlotte Mandeville was born on 28 Aug 1752 Sorel, Richelieu, Quebec (Ibid., #120796.). She was baptized on 28 Aug 1752 Sorel, Richelieu, Quebec (Ibid.). She died on 11 Jun 1828 Sorel, Richelieu, Quebec, at age 75 (Ibid.). She was buried on 13 Jun 1828 Sorel, Richelieu, Quebec (Ibid.).

Children of **Antoine Vandal** and **Marie Charlotte Mandeville** all born Sorel, Quebec, were as follows:

    i. Antoine Vandal was born on 25 Feb 1772 (Ibid., No. 694784.). He was baptized on 25 Feb 1772 Sorel, Quebec (Ibid.). He died on 23 Aug 1772 Sorel, Quebec (Ibid., No. 560360.). He was buried on 24 Aug 1772 Sorel, Quebec (Ibid.).

    ii. Genevieve Vandal was born on 4 Nov 1773 (Ibid., No. 694880.). She was baptized on 4 Nov 1773 Sorel, Quebec (Ibid.).

    iii. Marie Vandal was born on 1 Jun 1777 (Ibid., No. 695060.). She was baptized on 3 Jun 1777 Sorel, Quebec (Ibid.). She was buried on 7 Aug 1777 Sorel, Quebec (Ibid., No. 560529.).

    iv. Jean Baptiste Vandal was born on 5 Dec 1778 (Ibid., No. 695154.). He was baptized on 5 Dec 1778 Sorel, Quebec (Ibid.). He died on 17 Apr 1779 Sorel, Quebec (Ibid., No. 560578.). He was buried on 18 Apr 1779 Sorel, Quebec (Ibid.).

  2 v. Antoine Vandal, b. 18 Apr 1785; m. Angelique Sauteuse; d. 18 Dec 1870; bur. 19 Dec 1870.

  3 vi. Pierre Vandal, b. 29 Jun 1787.

    vii. Elionard Vandal was born on 4 Dec 1793 (Ibid., No. 696098.). He was baptized on 5 Dec 1793 Sorel, Quebec (Ibid.).

    viii. Marguerite Vandal was born on 4 Mar 1798 (Ibid., No. 696387.). She was baptized on 5 Mar 1798 Sorel, Quebec (Ibid.).

Generation Two

2. **Antoine Vandal** was born circa 1781 Lower Canada (1850Ci-MN *Minnesota Territorial Census, 1850*, Harpole, Patricia C. and Mary D. Nagle, ed., (St.Paul, Minnesota: Minnesota Historical Society, 1972), page 30, Dwelling 118, Family 118.). He was born circa 1783 Quebec (1827C RRS HBCA E5/1 1827 Census of the Red River Settlement, HBCA E5/1, Hudson's Bay Company Archives, Provincial Archives, 200 Vaughan Street, Winnipeg, MB R3C 1T5, Canada., page 6.). He was born on 18 Apr 1785 Sorel, Quebec (PRDH online, No. 695530.). He was baptized on 18 Apr 1785 Sorel, Quebec (Ibid.). He married **Angelique Sauteuse** before 1809. He died on 18 Dec 1870 St.Norbert, Manitoba, at age 85 (SN1 Catholic Parish Register of St.Norbert 1857-1873, page 136, S-6. Hereinafter cited as SN1.). He was buried on 19 Dec 1870 St.Norbert, Manitoba (Ibid.).

Question: *Probable son of Antoine Vandal and Marie Charlotte Mandeville.* He was contracted as a voyageur in 1804 Lake Winnipeg *a voyageur for the North West Company* (Denney Papers, Charles D. Denney, Glenbow Archives, Calgary, Alberta.). He was contracted as a voyageur after 1804 Athabasca District *a voyageur for the North West Company* (Ibid.).

Angelique Sauteuse was born circa 1780.

Children of **Antoine Vandal** and **Angelique Sauteuse** were as follows:

4	i.	Isabelle Vandal, b. circa 1809 North West Territory; m. Salomon Hamelin; d. 27 May 1896 Dauphin, Manitoba.
5	ii.	Antoine Vandal, b. Dec 1809 North West; m. Marguerite Savoyard dit Berthelet; d. 25 Aug 1882 Montcalm, Manitoba; bur. 26 Aug 1882 St-Jean Baptiste, Manitoba.
6	iii.	Pierre Vandal, b. 1813 North West Territory; m. Rosalie Hamelin; bur. 4 Nov 1904 St.Boniface, Walhalla, Pembina County, North Dakota.
7	iv.	Joseph Vandal, b. circa 1817; m. Louise Dupuis; m. Louise Vallee; d. 12 May 1885 Batoche, (Saskatchewan); bur. 14 May 1885 Batoche, (Saskatchewan).
8	v.	Benjamin Vandal, b. circa 1820 Red River, (Manitoba); m. Marguerite Allary; m. Victoire Cyr; d. circa Oct 1870 St.Albert, (Alberta); bur. circa Oct 1870 St.Albert, (Alberta).

3. Pierre Vandal was born on 29 Jun 1787 Sorel, Quebec (PRDH online, No. 695687.). He was baptized on 29 Jun 1787 Sorel, Quebec (Ibid.). He married **Charlotte Hughes**, daughter of **James Hughes** and **Nan-touche Corbeau,** before 1818.

Charlotte Hughes was born in 1796 (SB 1825-1834 St.Boniface Roman Catholic Registre des Baptemes, Mariages & Sepultures, 1825-1834, page 149-150, B-876. Hereinafter cited as SB 1825-1834.). She was baptized on 30 Sep 1834 St.Boniface, (Manitoba) (Ibid.). She died on 15 Feb 1872 St.Norbert, Manitoba (MBS Scrip Applications, Original White Settlers & Halfbreeds residing in Manitoba on 15 July 1870, RG15-19, C-14934.) (SN1, S-12.). She was buried on 17 Feb 1872 St.Norbert, Manitoba (MBS, C-14934.) (SN1, S-12.).

Children of **Pierre Vandal** and **Charlotte Hughes** were as follows:

9	i.	Antoine Vandal, b. circa 1819 North West; m. Isabelle Beauchemin.
	ii.	Joseph Vandal was born circa 1824 (1870C-MB 1870 Manitoba Census, National Archives of Canada, Ottawa, Ontario, Microfilm Reel Number C-2170., #628, page 21.). He died on 1 Nov 1873 St.Norbert, Manitoba (MBS, Extraction; C-14934.) (SN1, S-35.). He was buried on 2 Nov 1873 St.Norbert, Manitoba (MBS, Extraction; C-14934.) (SN1, S-35.).
10	iii.	Augustin Vandal, b. circa 1826 Red River, (Manitoba); m. Marie Dupuis; d. 6 Jan 1862 St.Norbert, (Manitoba); bur. 8 Jan 1862 St.Norbert, (Manitoba), England.
	iv.	Pierre Vandal was born circa 1828 (SB 1825-1834, page 130, B-797.). He was baptized on 8 Jul 1834 St.Boniface, (Manitoba) (Ibid.). He died on 22 Aug 1834 St.Boniface, (Manitoba) (Ibid., page 140, S-69.). He was buried on 22 Aug 1834 St.Boniface, (Manitoba) (Ibid.).
	v.	Marguerite Vandal was born in 1822 Red River (1870C-MB, #627, page 21.). She was born circa 1829 (SB 1825-1834, page 130-131, B-798.). She was baptized on 8 Jul 1834 St.Boniface, (Manitoba) (Ibid.).
11	vi.	Jean Baptiste Vandal, b. circa 1832; m. Marie Primeau; d. 22 Feb 1888 Batoche, (Saskatchewan); bur. 24 Feb 1888 Batoche, (Saskatchewan).

Generation Three

4. Isabelle Vandal was born circa 1809 North West Territory (MBS, C-14928.). She married **Salomon Hamelin**, son of **Jacques Hamelin** and **Angelique Tourangeau**, on 9 Feb 1831 St.Boniface, Manitoba (*Winnipeg Free Press*, Winnipeg, Manitoba, 10 Feb 1886, page 4.) (Rod MacQuarrie Research, 4 May 2009.). She died on 27 May 1896 Dauphin, Manitoba (Manitoba Vital Statistics online, http://web2.gov.mb.ca, Death Reg. #1899,002448.).

Salomon Hamelin was born on 6 Apr 1810 Red River Settlement, (Manitoba) (MBS, C-14928.). He died on 30 Sep 1893 St.Rose-du-Lac, Manitoba, at age 83 (Jan Evans Research.).

5. Antoine Vandal was born in Dec 1809 North West (MBS, C-14934.). He was born circa 1813 Ruperts Land (1835C RRS HBCA E5/8 1835 Census of the Red River Settlement, HBCA E5/8, Hudson's Bay Company Archives, Provincial Archives, 200 Vaughan Street, Winnipeg, MB R3C 1T5, Canada., page 21.). He married **Marguerite Savoyard dit Berthelet**, daughter of **Toussaint Savoyard dit Berthelet** and **Marguerite Sauteuse**, on 28 Jan 1834 St.Boniface, (Manitoba) (Rosemary Helga (Morrissette) Rozyk Research, 18 Sep 2009.). He died on 25 Aug 1882 Montcalm, Manitoba, at age 72 (Ibid., 13 Nov 2006.) (MB Vital Statistics, Death Reg. #1882,001562.). He was buried on 26 Aug 1882 St-Jean Baptiste, Manitoba (Rosemary Rozyk, 13 Nov 2006.).

Marguerite Savoyard dit Berthelet was born in 1817 USA (MBS, C-14934.).

Children of **Antoine Vandal** and **Marguerite Savoyard dit Berthelet** were as follows:

	i.	Justine Vandal was born circa 1827 (SN1, page 51, S-1.). She died on 6 Jan 1862 (Ibid.). She was buried on 8 Jan 1862 St.Norbert, (Manitoba) (Ibid.).
12	ii.	Antoine Vandal, b. circa 1833 St.Norbert, (Manitoba); m. Scholastique Frobisher; m. Marguerite St.Denis; m. Genevieve Turcotte; m. Sarah McMillan.
13	iii.	Joseph Vandal, b. 1839 St.Norbert, (Manitoba); m. Julienne Braconnier.
	iv.	Catherine Vandal was born in Mar 1842 St.Norbert, (Manitoba) (MBS, C-14934.).
14	v.	Francois Vandal, b. circa 1843; m. Genevieve St.Germain; d. 9 Jan 1892 Oak Lake, Manitoba.
15	vi.	Gabriel Vandal, b. circa 1846; m. Sarah Turner; m. Marie Chatelain or Mos-es-skay-pec.
16	vii.	Roger Vandal, b. circa 1849; m. Isabelle Braconnier; d. 31 Oct 1888 St.Boniface, Manitoba.
17	viii.	Louis Vandal, b. 1849 St.Norbert, (Manitoba); m. Reine Victoria Ducharme; d. 8 Dec 1913 La Broquerie, Manitoba.
18	ix.	Melanie Vandal, b. 1 May 1853 St.Norbert, (Manitoba); m. Napoleon Nault; d. Nov 1898 Olga, Cavalier County, North Dakota; bur. 6 Nov 1898 Olga, Cavalier County, North Dakota.

      x.   Moise Vandal was born in 1854 (Ibid.) (SN1, page 145-146, S-8.). He died on 22 May 1871 St.Norbert, Manitoba (MBS, C-14934.) (SN1, page 145-146, S-8.). He was buried on 24 May 1871 St.Norbert, Manitoba (MBS, C-14934.) (SN1, page 145-146, S-8.).

6. Pierre Vandal was born circa 1812 (Manitoba) (SJL-D St.Joseph Leroy, North Dakota, Record of Interments 1888-1932, page 15.). He was born in 1813 North West Territory (MBS, C-14934.). He was born circa 1814 Red River, (Manitoba) (1850Ci-MN, page 32, Dwelling 139, Family 139.). He married **Rosalie Hamelin**, daughter of **Jacques Hamelin** and **Angelique Tourangeau**, before 1836. He was buried on 4 Nov 1904 St.Boniface, Walhalla, Pembina County, North Dakota (SJL-D, page 15.).

   Rosalie Hamelin was born in 1818 North West Territory (MBS, C-14934.). She was born circa 1820 Red River, (Manitoba) (1850Ci-MN, page 32, Dwelling 139, Family 139.).

Children of **Pierre Vandal** and **Rosalie Hamelin** were as follows:

     19   i.   Pierre Vandal, b. circa 1836 Red River, (Manitoba); m. Euphrosine Langer; bur. 14 Apr 1903 St.Boniface, Walhalla, Pembina County, North Dakota.

     20   ii.   Nancy Vandal, b. circa 1838 Red River, (Manitoba); m. Jean Baptiste Langer; bur. 29 Dec 1904 St.Boniface, Walhalla, Pembina County, North Dakota.

          iii.   Rosalie Vandal was born circa 1840 Red River, (Manitoba) (Ibid.).

     21   iv.   Marguerite Vandal, b. 24 Apr 1844 Ste.Agathe, (Manitoba); m. Gabriel Houle.

     22   v.   John Baptiste Vandal, b. 12 May 1848 St.Vital, (Manitoba); m. Marguerite Vivier; m. Madeleine Jeannotte; m. Sarah Morin; d. 12 Nov 1937 Rolette, North Dakota; bur. 16 Nov 1937 St. Ann's Catholic Cemetery, Belcourt, Rolette, North Dakota.

     23   vi.   Francois Vandal, b. 25 Sep 1849; m. Marie Ouellette; d. 1 Apr 1935 Pembina County, North Dakota.

     24   vii.   Joseph Vandal, b. 25 Apr 1852 Pembina, Pembina County, Dakota Territory; m. Josephine Berthelet; d. 9 Nov 1927 Walhalla, Pembina County, North Dakota; bur. 11 Nov 1927 St.Boniface, Walhalla, Pembina County, North Dakota.

          viii.   Josephine Vandal was born on 19 Dec 1855 Pembina, Pembina County, Dakota Territory (AP Records of the Assumption Roman Catholic Church, Pembina, North Dakota: Baptisms, Marriages, Sepultures, 1848-1896; compiled by Reverend Father J. M. Belleau, 2 October 1944, page 140, B-395. Hereinafter cited as AP.). She was baptized on 20 Dec 1855 Assumption, Pembina, Pembina County, Dakota Territory (Ibid.).

     25   ix.   Elzear Vandal, b. 16 May 1857 Pembina, Pembina County, Dakota Territory; m. Marie Langer; bur. 23 Aug 1904 St.Boniface, Walhalla, Pembina County, North Dakota.

     26   x.   Bernard Vandal, b. 19 Jun 1860 Ste.Agathe, (Manitoba); m. Euphrosine Langer; m. Marie Camelin; d. 1 May 1947 Pembina County, North Dakota.

          xi.   Philomene Vandal was born on 25 Mar 1864 (SN1, page 102, B-23.). She was baptized on 16 Apr 1864 St.Norbert, (Manitoba) (Ibid.). She died on 15 Nov 1865 St.Norbert, (Manitoba), at age 1 (Ibid., page 140, S-33.). She was buried on 17 Nov 1865 St.Norbert, (Manitoba) (Ibid.).

7. Joseph Vandal was born circa 1817. He was born circa 1820 Red River, (Manitoba). He married **Louise Dupuis**, daughter of **Jean Baptiste Dupuis** and **Marie Corbeau dit Hughes,** before 1842. He married **Louise Vallee**, daughter of **Louis Vallee** and **Louise Martel**, on 28 Aug 1860 Assumption, Pembina, Pembina County, Dakota Territory (AP, page 234-235, M-89.). He died on 12 May 1885 Batoche, (Saskatchewan) (BSAP Records of the Parish of Batoche, St.Antoine de Pudoue Roman Catholic Church: Register for Baptisms, Marriages, Deaths, Volume One, 1881-1909., page 33, S-21. Hereinafter cited as BSAP.). He was buried on 14 May 1885 Batoche, (Saskatchewan) (Ibid.).

   Question: *Is he the one?*

   Louise Dupuis was born circa 1822 Red River, (Manitoba) (1850Ci-MN, page 30, Dwelling 125, Family 125.). She died before 1860.

Children of **Joseph Vandal** and **Louise Dupuis** were as follows:

          i.   Clouie Vandal was born in 1842 Red River, (Manitoba) (Ibid.).

     27   ii.   Jean Baptiste Vandal, b. 1 Jan 1846 St.Boniface, (Manitoba); m. Henriette Braconnier.

     28   iii.   Catherine Vandal, b. 25 May 1846; m. Jean Baptiste Deschamps.

     29   iv.   Francois Vandal, b. 20 Sep 1848 Dakota Territory; m. Isabelle Deschamps.

     30   v.   Elise Vandal, b. 5 Feb 1850; m. Felix Marcellais.

     31   vi.   Sarah Vandal, b. 22 Oct 1858 St.Norbert, (Manitoba); m. Joseph Sutherland; d. 18 Sep 1888 St.Jean-Baptiste, RM of Montcalm, Manitoba; bur. 20 Sep 1888 St.Jean-Baptiste, Manitoba.

   Louise Vallee was born on 21 Jul 1829 St.Boniface, (Manitoba) (SB 1825-1834, page 28, B-565.). She was baptized on 22 Jul 1829 St.Boniface, (Manitoba) (Ibid.). She married **Antoine Desjarlais dit Morel**, son of **Antoine Desjarlais** and **Susanna (--?--)**, before 1850. She died on 17 Jul 1887 Lebret, (Saskatchewan), at age 57 (L2 Lebret, Mission de St.Florent, Roman Catholic Registre des Baptemes, Mariages & Seplutures, Qu'Appelle, Saskatchewan, Book Two: 1881-1887, FHC microfilm 1032949., page 186, S-17. Hereinafter cited as L2.). She was buried on 19 Jul 1887 Lebret, (Saskatchewan) (Ibid.).

Children of **Joseph Vandal** and **Louise Vallee** were as follows:

     32   i.   Virginie Vandal, b. 8 Jul 1861; m. Charles Desjarlais.

          ii.   Veronique Vandal was born circa 1864 on the plains, Dakota Territory.

          iii.   Joseph Vandal was born on 5 Jan 1864 (SN1, page 96, B-6.). He was baptized on 10 Jan 1864 St.Norbert, (Manitoba) (Ibid.).

          iv.   Napoleon Vandal was born on 15 Mar 1868 Lac Ste.Anne, (Alberta) (ArchiviaNet 1886-1901, 1906 Half-Breed Scrip Applications Index, RG15-21, Volume 1333 through 1371, Microfilm Reel Number C-14944 through C-15010, National Archives of Canada, Ottawa, Ontario, http://www.collectionscanada.gc.ca, C-15008.).

8. Benjamin Vandal was born circa 1820 Red River, (Manitoba) (1870C-MB, page 364, #1192.). He was born in 1831 Red River, (Manitoba) (NWHBS 1885 Scrip Applications, North-West Halfbreeds residing outside Manitoba on 15 July 1870, RG15-20, C-14942.). He married **Marguerite Allary**, daughter of **Antoine Allary** and **Josephte Caplette**, circa 1854 St.Boniface, (Manitoba) (HBS 1886-

1901, 1906 Half-Breed Scrip Applications, RG15-21, Volume 1333; C-14944.). He and **Victoire Cyr** met before 1861. He died circa Oct 1870 St.Albert, (Alberta) (NWHBS, C-14942.). He was buried circa Oct 1870 St.Albert, (Alberta) (Ibid.).

Marguerite Allary was born circa Jul 1836 St.Charles, (Manitoba) (MBS, C-14934.). She married **Louis Bruneau dit Montagnais**, son of **Michel Joachim Bruneau** and **Catherine Ladouceur**, on 26 Dec 1870 St.Joachim, Fort Edmonton, (Alberta) (MSJ-FA-E Register des Baptemes, Mariages & Sepultures 1858-1861 Mission St.Joachim, Fort Auguste, Fort des Prairies, Edmonton, No. 1, page 70, M-2. Hereinafter cited as MSJ-FA-E.). She died on 20 Oct 1918 Lake Eliza, Alberta (The New Nation - Christ's Chosen People, by Mary Madeleine Lee; 1987, page 159.). She was buried in Oct 1918 St.Paul, Alberta (Denney.).

Children of **Benjamin Vandal** and **Marguerite Allary** were as follows:

    33   i.   Norman Vandal, b. 15 Feb 1857; m. Julie Munroe.

           ii.   Philomene Vandal was born on 15 Jul 1863 St.Boniface, (Manitoba) (SB-Rozyk, page 122, B-105.). She was baptized on 16 Jul 1863 St.Boniface, (Manitoba) (Ibid.).

Victoire Cyr was born on 5 Aug 1843 (SFX: 1834-1850, B-464.). She was baptized on 6 Aug 1843 St.Francois Xavier, (Manitoba) (Ibid.). She married **Paul Maskegonne**, son of **Paul Maskegonne** and **Marie Desjarlais**, on 13 Jul 1864 (La Riviere Sturgeon), St.Boniface, Manitoba (SB-Rozyk, page 156, M-12.).

Children of **Benjamin Vandal** and **Victoire Cyr** were:

    34   i.   Sarah Vandal, b. 15 Jun 1861; m. Etienne Pepin; d. 1893.

9. Antoine Vandal was born circa 1819 North West (MBS, C-14934.). He was born on 10 Dec 1822 (1901 Canada, microfilm, T-6553, Bellevue, page 8, Family 74, line 9-17.). He married **Isabelle Beauchemin**, daughter of **Benjamin Beauchemin** and **Marie Parenteau**, before 1848.

Isabelle Beauchemin was born circa Jun 1828 St.Boniface, (Manitoba) (MBS, C-14934.). She died on 26 Aug 1878 St.Norbert, Manitoba (St-N Cem *St.Norbert Parish Cemetery 1859-1906, We Remember*; Winnipeg, Manitoba, Canada: St.Norbert Parish-La Barriere Metis Council of the Metis Federation of Manitoba, 29 May 2010).) (SN2, S-36.). She was buried on 27 Aug 1878 St.Norbert, Manitoba (St-N Cem.) (SN2, S-36.).

Children of **Antoine Vandal** and **Isabelle Beauchemin** were as follows:

    35   i.   Pierre Vandal, b. 15 Jan 1848; m. Louise Poitras.

    36   ii.   Antoine Vandal, b. 10 Jul 1849; m. Alphosine Henry.

          iii.   Anonyme Vandal was born on 1 Aug 1850 (AP, page 43, S-13.). She died on 7 Aug 1850 (Ibid.). She was buried on 11 Aug 1850 Assumption, Pembina, Pembina County, Dakota Territory (Ibid.).

    37   iv.   Isabelle Vandal, b. 25 Dec 1852 St.Norbert, (Manitoba); m. Maurice Henry; bur. 15 Jul 1882 Lebret, (Saskatchewan).

    38   v.   Joseph Vandal, b. 29 Oct 1856 St.Norbert, (Manitoba); m. Rosalie Rocheleau; d. 19 Jan 1879 St.Norbert, Manitoba; bur. 21 Jan 1879 St.Norbert, Manitoba.

    39   vi.   Melanie Vandal, b. 11 Apr 1859 St.Norbert, (Manitoba); m. Jean Baptiste Rocheleau; d. 3 Jun 1885 Batoche, (Saskatchewan); bur. 5 Jun 1885 Batoche, (Saskatchewan).

          vii.   Marie Vandal was born on 29 Oct 1861 St.Norbert, (Manitoba) (SN1, page 48, B-36.). She was baptized on 30 Oct 1861 St.Norbert, (Manitoba) (Ibid.). She died on 13 Mar 1880 St.Norbert, Manitoba, at age 18 (SN2, S-6.). She was buried on 15 Mar 1880 St.Norbert, Manitoba (Ibid.).

          viii.   Francois Vandal was born on 29 Oct 1861 St.Norbert, (Manitoba) (SN1, page 48, B-35.). He was baptized on 30 Oct 1861 St.Norbert, (Manitoba) (Ibid.). He died on 23 Feb 1862 St.Norbert, (Manitoba) (Ibid., page 55, S-3.). He was buried on 24 Feb 1862 St.Norbert, (Manitoba) (Ibid.).

          ix.   Jean Baptiste Vandal was born on 8 May 1864 St.Norbert, (Manitoba) (MBS, C-14934.) (SN1, page 104, B-29.). He was baptized on 5 Sep 1864 St.Norbert, (Manitoba) (Ibid.). He died on 25 Dec 1872 St.Norbert, Manitoba, at age 8 (MBS, C-14934.) (SN1, S-20.). He was buried on 27 Dec 1872 St.Norbert, Manitoba (MBS, C-14934.) (SN1, S-20.).

          x.   Sara Vandal was born on 6 Nov 1866 (Ibid., page 88, B-62.). She was baptized on 25 Nov 1866 St.Norbert, (Manitoba) (Ibid.). She died on 6 Jun 1867 (Ibid., S-11.). She was buried on 8 Jun 1867 St.Norbert, (Manitoba) (Ibid.).

          xi.   Philomene Vandal was born on 16 Jul 1868 St.Norbert, (Manitoba) (Ibid., B-27.). She was baptized on 19 Jul 1868 St.Norbert, (Manitoba) (Ibid.). She died on 24 Jan 1885 Batoche, (Saskatchewan), at age 16 (BSAP, page 29, S-2.). She was buried on 26 Jan 1885 Batoche, (Saskatchewan) (Ibid.).

          xii.   Alexandre Vandal was born on 25 Aug 1871 St.Norbert, Manitoba (SN1, page 150, B-44.). He was baptized on 26 Aug 1871 St.Norbert, Manitoba (Ibid.). He died on 24 Dec 1889 Fish Creek, (Saskatchewan), at age 18 (Denney.) (BSAP, page 78, S-11.). He was buried on 25 Dec 1889 Batoche, (Saskatchewan) (Ibid.).

          xiii.   Marie Therese Vandal was born on 6 May 1874 St.Norbert, Manitoba (SN2, B-21.). She was baptized on 7 May 1874 St.Norbert, Manitoba (Ibid.). She died on 11 Sep 1874 St.Norbert, Manitoba (Ibid., S-25.). She was buried on 12 Sep 1874 St.Norbert, Manitoba (Ibid.).

10. Augustin Vandal was born circa 1826 Red River, (Manitoba) (1850Ci-MN, page 30, Dwelling 118, Family 118.). He married **Marie Dupuis**, daughter of **Jean Baptiste Dupuis** and **Marie Corbeau dit Hughes**, before 1857. He died on 6 Jan 1862 St.Norbert, (Manitoba) (SN1, S-1.). He was buried on 8 Jan 1862 St.Norbert, (Manitoba), England (Ibid.).

Marie Dupuis was born in 1831 St.Boniface, (Manitoba) (MBS, C-14930.). She and **John Logan** met before 15 Jul 1870.

Children of **Augustin Vandal** and **Marie Dupuis** were as follows:

    40   i.   Augustin Vandal, b. Jul 1857 St.Norbert, (Manitoba); m. Sophie Parisien; d. before 1895.

          ii.   Marie Vandal was born circa 1858 (SN1, page 63, S-11.). She died on 6 Oct 1862 (Ibid.). She was buried on 8 Oct 1862 St.Norbert, (Manitoba) (Ibid.).

          iii.   Isabelle Vandal was born circa 1858 (Ibid., page 61, S-10.). She died on 11 Sep 1862 (Ibid.). She was buried on 13 Sep 1862 St.Norbert, (Manitoba) (Ibid.).

41 iv. Melanie Vandal, b. 25 Dec 1858; m. John Henry.

   v. Marie Jane Vandal was born on 29 Mar 1862 St.Norbert, (Manitoba) (Ibid., page 56, B-8.). She was baptized on 30 Mar 1862 St.Norbert, (Manitoba) (Ibid.).

11. Jean Baptiste Vandal was born in Jul 1830 Edmonton, (Alberta) (MBS, C-14934.). He was born circa 1832 (SB 1825-1834, page 131, B-799.). He was baptized on 8 Jul 1834 St.Boniface, (Manitoba) (Ibid.). He married **Marie Primeau**, daughter of **Joseph Primeau** and **Marguerite Stevenson**, circa 1857. He died on 22 Feb 1888 Batoche, (Saskatchewan) (BSAP, page 65, S-1.). He was buried on 24 Feb 1888 Batoche, (Saskatchewan) (Ibid.).

Marie Primeau was born in 1839 Fort Alexandre (MBS, C-14934.). She was born in 1840 (Manitoba) (1901 Canada, page 5, Family 37, #32.).

Children of **Jean Baptiste Vandal** and **Marie Primeau** were as follows:

42 i. Joseph Vandal, b. circa 1857 (Manitoba); m. Elizabeth Champagne; d. 20 Dec 1885 Batoche, (Saskatchewan); bur. 22 Dec 1885 Batoche, (Saskatchewan).

43 ii. Rosalie Vandal, b. 22 Aug 1859 St.Norbert, (Manitoba); m. Charles Pruden; d. before 1901.

44 iii. William Vandal, b. 15 Aug 1861; m. Virginie Boyer.

   iv. Anne Vandal was born on 26 Sep 1863 St.Norbert, (Manitoba) (SN1, page 87, B-32.). She was baptized on 27 Sep 1863 St.Norbert, (Manitoba) (Ibid.). She died on 30 Dec 1885 Batoche, (Saskatchewan), at age 22 (BSAP, page 42, S-28.). She was buried on 31 Dec 1885 Batoche, (Saskatchewan) (Ibid.).

45 v. Pierre Modeste Vandal, b. 1 Feb 1866 St.Norbert, (Manitoba); m. Adelaide Parenteau.

46 vi. Norbert Vandal, b. circa Dec 1868; m. Virginie Carriere.

47 vii. Marie Louise Vandal, b. 2 Mar 1873 Batoche, (Saskatchewan); m. Joseph Fisher.

48 viii. Eulalie Vandal, b. 8 Nov 1878 Batoche, (Saskatchewan); m. Louis Gervais.

Generation Four

12. Antoine Vandal was born circa 1833 St.Norbert, (Manitoba) (MBS, C-14934.). He married **Scholastique Frobisher**, daughter of **Thomas Frobisher** and **Scholastique Pilon**, on 10 Jan 1860 St.Norbert, (Manitoba) (SN1, M-8, page 25.). He married **Marguerite St.Denis**, daughter of **Jacques St.Denis** and **Charlotte Rocheleau**, on 21 Jan 1879 St.Jean Baptiste, Manitoba (MM.). He married **Genevieve Turcotte**, daughter of **Vital Turcotte** and **Madeleine Caplette**, on 20 Jun 1887 St.Francois Xavier, Manitoba (SFXI-Kipling, M-6.). He married **Sarah McMillan**, daughter of **William McMillan** and **Margaret Dease,** on 18 Jul 1898 Assiniboia, Manitoba (MB Vital Statistics, Marriage Reg. #1899,001956.).

Scholastique Frobisher was born circa 1843 St.Norbert, (Manitoba) (MBS, C-14934.).

Children of **Antoine Vandal** and **Scholastique Frobisher** were as follows:

49 i. Nancy Vandal, b. 21 Feb 1861; m. William Vermette; d. 14 Dec 1899 Ritchot, Manitoba; bur. 16 Dec 1899 St.Norbert, Manitoba.

50 ii. Virginie Vandal, b. 26 Apr 1862 St.Norbert, (Manitoba); m. Napoleon Gregoire; d. 6 Dec 1954.

51 iii. Marie Rose Vandal, b. 18 Aug 1863 St.Norbert, (Manitoba); m. Adelard Breton; d. 10 Mar 1900 Montcalm, Manitoba.

52 iv. Frederic Vandal, b. 22 Dec 1864 St.Norbert, (Manitoba); m. Marie Virginie Vermette.

53 v. Eliza Vandal, b. 6 Nov 1866; m. Martin Nault; d. 15 Jul 1893 Montcalm, Manitoba; bur. 17 Jul 1893 St.Jean-Baptiste, Manitoba.

   vi. Julienne Vandal was baptized on 3 Sep 1868 St.Norbert, (Manitoba) (SN1, B-42.). She was born on 3 Sep 1868 St.Norbert, (Manitoba) (Ibid.). She died on 7 Dec 1880 St-Jean-Baptiste, Manitoba, at age 12 (Rod Mac Quarrie, 28 Dec 2011.). She was buried on 9 Dec 1880 St-Jean-Baptiste, Manitoba (Ibid.).

   vii. Marie Jeanne Vandal was born on 14 Feb 1871 (SN1, page 145, B-25.). She was baptized on 7 May 1871 St.Norbert, Manitoba (Ibid.). She died on 6 Dec 1872 Ste.Agathe, Manitoba, at age 1 (Rod Mac Quarrie, 28 Dec 2011.). She was buried on 8 Dec 1872 Ste.Agathe, Manitoba (Ibid.).

54 viii. Patrice Vandal, b. 11 Oct 1872 Manitoba; m. Vitaline Anne Jerome; d. after 1943.

   ix. Alfred Vandal was born on 28 May 1874 Manitoba (1881 Church of Latter Day Saints Census Transcription Project of Census Images from the National Archives of Canada, Ottawa, Canada, http://www.familysearch.org, Film No. C-13282, District 184, Sub-district A, page 21, Household No. 88.) (Rod Mac Quarrie, 28 Dec 2011.).

   x. Marie Octavie Vandal was born on 24 Mar 1876 Riviere-aux-Prunes, Manitoba (Ibid.). She was baptized on 24 Mar 1876 Ste.Agathe, Manitoba (Ibid.). She died on 30 Oct 1880 St-Jean-Baptiste, Manitoba, at age 4 (Ibid.). She was buried on 1 Nov 1880 St-Jean-Baptiste, Manitoba (Ibid.).

Marguerite St.Denis was born on 1 Dec 1860 St.Norbert, (Manitoba) (SN1, page 35, B-46.). She was baptized on 1 Dec 1860 St.Norbert, (Manitoba) (Ibid.). She died on 30 Apr 1884 Montcalm, Provencher, Manitoba, at age 23 (MB Vital Statistics, Death Reg. #1884,002283.).

Children of **Antoine Vandal** and **Marguerite St.Denis** were as follows:

   i. Joseph Alexandre Vandal was born on 8 Jan 1880 St-Jean-Baptiste, Manitoba (Rod Mac Quarrie, 28 Dec 2011.). He was baptized on 13 Jan 1880 St-Jean-Baptiste, Manitoba (Ibid.). He died on 10 Feb 1880 St-Jean-Baptiste, Manitoba (Ibid.). He was buried on 11 Feb 1880 St-Jean-Baptiste, Manitoba (Ibid.).

55 ii. Alvina Vandal, b. 8 Dec 1881 Manitoba; m. Joseph Turcotte; d. 12 Nov 1948 Kenora, Ontario.

   iii. Marie Octavie Vandal was born on 10 Jan 1884 R.M. of Montcalm, Manitoba (MB Vital Statistics, Birth Reg. #1884,002610.). She was baptized on 11 Jan 1884 St-Jean-Baptiste, Manitoba (Rod Mac Quarrie, 28 Dec 2011.). She died on 20 Jun 1884 St-Jean-Baptiste, Manitoba (Ibid.). She was buried on 21 Jun 1884 St-Jean-Baptiste, Manitoba (Ibid.).

Genevieve Turcotte was born in Oct 1846 St.Boniface, (Manitoba). She married **Louis Lesperance**, son of **Alexis Bonami Lesperance** and **Marguerite Grenon**, on 13 Jan 1863 St.Boniface, (Manitoba) (SB-Rozyk, page 98, M-3.). She died on 2 Jan 1894 Montcalm, Manitoba, at age 47 (MB Vital Statistics, Death Reg. #1894,001631.).

Sarah McMillan was born on 5 Mar 1854 St.Vital, (Manitoba) (MBS, C-14934.). She married **Joseph Turcotte**, son of **Vital Turcotte** and **Madeleine Caplette**, on 26 Jan 1870 St.Boniface, (Manitoba) (SB-Rozyk, page 172, M-4.). She married **Pierre Jobin**, son of **Ambroise Jobin** and **Marguerite Mandeville**, on 22 Jan 1884 Assiniboia, Manitoba (MB Vital Statistics, Marriage Reg. #1884,001694.).

13. Joseph Vandal was born in 1839 St.Norbert, (Manitoba) (MBS, C-14934.). He married **Julienne Braconnier**, daughter of **Amable Branconnier** and **Elizabeth Stevenson**, on 17 Apr 1866 St.Norbert, Manitoba (MM.) (SN1, page 81, M-2.).

Julienne Braconnier was born on 17 Apr 1850 St.Vital, (Manitoba) (MBS, C-14934.). She died on 13 Dec 1935 at age 85 (Rosemary Rozyk, 28 Jan 1999 report.). She was buried on 15 Dec 1935 St.Jean Baptiste, Manitoba (Ibid.).

Children of **Joseph Vandal** and **Julienne Braconnier** are:

 i. Marie Vandal was born circa 1877 (1886-TMC 1886 Census of Half Breed Chippewas of Turtle Mountain, Dakota Territory, National Archives of the United States, Washington D.C., #450.).

14. Francois Vandal was born in 1832 St.Norbert, (Manitoba) (MBS, C-14934.). He was born circa 1843 (1870C-MB, #1920, page 62.). He married **Genevieve St.Germain**, daughter of **Pierre St.Germain** and **Genevieve Gosselin**, on 15 Feb 1870 St.Norbert, (Manitoba) (SN1, M-4.). He died on 9 Jan 1892 Oak Lake, Manitoba (Rod Mac Quarrie, 28 Dec 2011.).

Genevieve St.Germain was born on 12 Oct 1852 St.Norbert, (Manitoba) (MBS, C-14934.). She married **Martial Payette**, son of **Jean Baptiste Payette** and **Angele Lafleur**, on 24 Jul 1901 (St.Norbert), Ritchot, Manitoba (MM, page 982 (St.Norbert).) (MB Vital Statistics, Marriage Reg. #1902,002524 (Ritchot).) (SN2, M-7.). She died on 15 May 1917 RM Sprague, Manitoba, at age 64 (MB Vital Statistics, Death Reg. #1917,030212.).

Children of **Francois Vandal** and **Genevieve St.Germain** were as follows:

 i. Jean Francois Vandal was born on 27 Dec 1870 St.Norbert, Manitoba (IBMS *Index des Baptemes, Mariages et Sepultures* (La Societe Historique de Saint-Boniface).) (SN1, page 137, B-54.). He was baptized on 28 Dec 1870 St.Norbert, Manitoba (Ibid.). He died on 8 Nov 1874 St.Norbert, Manitoba, at age 3 (SN2, S-34.). He was buried on 9 Nov 1874 St.Norbert, Manitoba (Ibid.).

 ii. Marie Louise Vandal was born on 12 Aug 1872 St.Norbert, Manitoba (SN1, B-35.). She was baptized on 14 Aug 1872 St.Norbert, Manitoba (Ibid.).

 iii. Victoria Vandal was born on 12 Apr 1874 (1901 Canada, District 10-h-1, page 6, family 46, line 18-26.).

 iv. Alexandre Vandal was born in Aug 1875 (SL-SK St.Laurent-de-Grandin Roman Catholic Registre des Baptemes, Mariages & Seplitures, St.Laurent, Saskatchewan, 1872-1896, page 45, B-52. Hereinafter cited as SL-SK.). He was baptized on 22 Aug 1875 St.Laurent-de-Grandin, (Saskatchewan) (Ibid.). He died on 17 Dec 1894 Ritchot, Manitoba, at age 19 (St-N Cem.) (MB Vital Statistics, Death Reg. #1898,002802.). He was buried on 19 Dec 1894 St.Norbert, Manitoba (St-N Cem.).

56 v. Marguerite Vandal, b. 20 Mar 1878 St.Norbert, Manitoba; m. Francois Xavier Desmarais.

57 vi. Adeline Vandal, b. 15 Jun 1880; m. Joseph Gustave Bruce; m. Joseph Alfred Sauve.

 vii. Adolphe Vandal was born on 22 Jul 1882 St.Nobert, Manitoba (MB Vital Statistics, Birth Reg. #1882,002075.) (SN2, B-26.). He was baptized on 23 Jul 1882 St.Norbert, Manitoba (Ibid.). He married Marie Adele Parisien, daughter of Roger Parisien and Marie Laramee, on 25 Aug 1917 St.Boniface, Manitoba (MB Vital Statistics, Marriage Reg. #1917,045021.).

  Marie Adele Parisien was born on 13 Jan 1892 R.M. of Ritchot, Manitoba (Ibid., Birth Reg. #1892,003223.) (SN2, B-3.).

 viii. Nancy Josephine Vandal was born on 15 Dec 1884 St.Nobert, Manitoba (MB Vital Statistics, Birth Reg. #1884,001278.) (SN2, B-66.). She was baptized on 16 Dec 1884 St.Norbert, Manitoba (Ibid.). She married Joseph Alexandre Gustave Dubois on 27 Sep 1915 Woodridge, Manitoba (MM.) (SN2, B-66 (note).).

  Joseph Alexandre Gustave Dubois was born on 23 Apr 1893 R.M. of La Broquerie, Manitoba (MB Vital Statistics, Birth Reg. #1893,004124.) (Ibid., Birth Reg. #1893,002296.).

 ix. Marie Louise Anna Vandal was born on 14 Jun 1887 R.M. of Tache, Manitoba (Ibid., Birth Reg. #1887,004340.). She married Samuel Leblanc on 1 Oct 1907 Woodridge, Manitoba (MM.).

 x. Adolphe Antoine Frederic Vandal was born on 20 Feb 1889 Lorette, Manitoba (St-N Cem.) (Rod Mac Quarrie, 28 Dec 2011.). He was baptized on 24 Feb 1889 Lorette, Manitoba (Ibid.). He died on 19 Aug 1889 St.Norbert, Manitoba (St-N Cem.) (MB Vital Statistics, Death Reg. #1889,002098.) (SN2, S-29.). He was buried on 21 Aug 1889 St.Norbert, Manitoba (St-N Cem.) (SN2, S-29.).

 xi. Marie Lucie Amanda Vandal was born on 22 Sep 1891 St.Nobert, Manitoba (MB Vital Statistics, Birth Reg. #1891,005219.) (SN2, B-59.). She was baptized on 23 Sep 1891 St.Norbert, Manitoba (Ibid.).

15. Gabriel Vandal was born circa 1846. He married **Sarah Turner**, daughter of **John Turner** and **Anne Constant**, on 5 Apr 1873 St.Norbert, Manitoba (SN1, M-5.). He married **Marie Chatelain or Mos-es-skay-pec**, daughter of **John Meshaskepip Chatelain** and **Emma (--?--) (Metis)**, circa Jul 1876 St.Laurent, (Saskatchewan) (HBSI Index 1886-1901, 1906 Halfbreed Scrip Applications, RG15-21.). Question: *Who are Marie and William born born 1896?*

Sarah Turner was born circa 1846 (SN2, S-22.). She was baptized on 5 Apr 1873 St.Norbert, Manitoba (IBMS.) (SN1, B-22.). She died on 3 Sep 1874 St.Norbert, Manitoba, at age 1 (SN2, S-22.). She was buried on 4 Sep 1874 St.Norbert, Manitoba (Ibid.).

Children of **Gabriel Vandal** and **Sarah Turner** were as follows:

 i. Frederic Vandal was born in 1868 on the prairie (MBS, C-14934.) (SN2, S-38.). He died on 26 Jun 1874 St.Norbert, Manitoba (MBS, C-14934.) (SN2, S-38.). He was buried on 27 Jun 1874 St.Norbert, Manitoba (MBS, C-14934.) (SN2, S-38.).

 ii. Marguerite Vandal was born on 14 Jun 1871 (DL Register of Sacre Coeur Roman Catholic Church, Duck Lake, Saskatchewan, 1870-1893, page 12, B-45. Hereinafter cited as DL.). She was baptized on 9 Jul 1871 Duck Lake, (Saskatchewan) (Ibid.). She died on 28 Aug 1875 St.Norbert, Manitoba, at age 4 (MBS, C-14934.) (SN2, S-21.). She was buried on 29 Aug 1875 St.Norbert, Manitoba (MBS, C-14934.) (SN2, S-21.).

      iii.   Alexandre Vandal was born on 5 Oct 1872 St.Norbert, Manitoba (SN1, B-44.). He was baptized on 6 Oct 1872 St.Norbert, Manitoba (Ibid.). He died on 1 Nov 1874 St.Norbert, Manitoba, at age 2 (SN2, S-33.). He was buried on 2 Nov 1874 St.Norbert, Manitoba (Ibid.).

      iv.   Napasis Vandal was born before 1874 (ArchiviaNet, C-15008.). He died before 1874 (Ibid.).

Marie Chatelain or Mos-es-skay-pec was born circa 1860 (SL-SK, page 41, B-35.). She was born in 1866 near, Carlton, (Saskatchewan). She was baptized on 30 Jun 1875 St.Laurent-de-Grandin, (Saskatchewan) (Ibid.).

Children of **Gabriel Vandal** and **Marie Chatelain or Mos-es-skay-pec** were as follows:

58   i.   Patrice Vandal, b. 30 May 1876 St.Laurent, (Saskatchewan); m. Marie (--?--).

      ii.   Marie Vandal was born circa 1877 (Saskatchewan) (1881 Canada, C-13285, District 192-1, page 13, household 61.).

      iii.   Catherine Vandal was born circa 1879 (SL-SK, page 63, S-23.). She was buried on 19 Dec 1882 St-Laurent-de-Grandin, (Saskatchewan) (Ibid.).

      iv.   Rosalie Vandal was born on 17 May 1882 Duck Lake, (Saskatchewan) (DL, page 47, B-17.). She was baptized on 17 May 1882 Duck Lake, (Saskatchewan) (Ibid.).

      v.   John Vandal was born circa Mar 1884 (1901 Canada, microfilm, T-6553, Devil Lake, page 3, Family 18, line 6-15.) (Rod Mac Quarrie, 28 Dec 2011.). He was baptized on 8 Jun 1884 Duck Lake, (Saskatchewan) (Ibid.).

      vi.   Alfred Frederic Vandal was born on 25 Dec 1885 Sandy Lake, (Saskatchewan) (DL, page 71, B-8.) (ArchiviaNet, C-15008.). He was baptized on 11 Jun 1886 Duck Lake, (Saskatchewan) (DL, page 71, B-8.).

59   vii.   Maria Vandal, b. 5 Mar 1896 (Saskatchewan); m. Edward Campbell; d. 1950 Big River Hospital, Saskatchewan.

     viii.   William Vandal was born on 3 Jun 1897 (1901 Canada, microfilm, T-6553, Devil Lake, page 3, Family 18, line 6-15.).

16. Roger Vandal was born circa 1849. He married **Isabelle Braconnier**, daughter of **Amable Branconnier** and **Elizabeth Stevenson**, on 11 Nov 1873 Ste.Agathe, Manitoba (MM.). He died on 31 Oct 1888 St.Boniface, Manitoba (Rod Mac Quarrie, 28 Dec 2011.).

Isabelle Braconnier was born on 15 Aug 1855 (Rosemary Rozyk, 28 Jan 1999 report.). She married **Etienne Desmarais**, son of **Severe Desmarais** and **Marguerite Desjardins**, on 7 Sep 1890 Montcalm, Manitoba (MB Vital Statistics, Mar. Reg. #1890,001457.). She died on 5 Dec 1936 at age 81 (Rosemary Rozyk, 28 Jan 1999 report.). She was buried on 9 Dec 1936 St.Jean Baptiste, Manitoba (Ibid.).

Children of **Roger Vandal** and **Isabelle Braconnier** were as follows:

60   i.   Marie Isabelle Vandal, b. 26 Jan 1876; m. Joseph Norbert Berthelet; d. 1961.

61   ii.   Joseph Roger Vandal, b. 5 Feb 1878 Qu'Appelle Mission, (Saskatchewan); m. Emma Victoria Melanie Laplante.

62   iii.   Marie Adeline Vandal, b. 1 Feb 1880 Manitoba; m. Jean Baptiste Berthelet.

63   iv.   Marie Alvina Vandal, b. 16 Jan 1882 R.M. of Montcalm, Manitoba; m. Joseph Alexandre Berthelet.

      v.   Louis Vandal was born on 27 Jun 1883 Fish Creek, (Saskatchewan) (ArchiviaNet, C-15008.). He died on 28 Jun 1883 Fish Creek, (Saskatchewan) (Ibid.).

      vi.   Marie Amanda "Maude" Vandal was born on 13 Apr 1884 (BSAP, page 21, B-9.). She was baptized on 19 Apr 1884 Batoche, (Saskatchewan) (Ibid.). She married Julien Larocque, son of Antoine Larocque and Elise Delorme, on 29 Feb 1916 St.Jean Baptiste, Manitoba (MM.). She died on 8 Sep 1944 Winnipeg, Manitoba, at age 60 (Rod Mac Quarrie, 28 Dec 2011.). She was buried on 11 Sep 1944 St.Boniface, Manitoba (Ibid.).

          Julien Larocque was born on 24 Feb 1889 Manitoba (SN2, B-12.). He was baptized on 1 Mar 1899 St.Norbert, Manitoba (Ibid.). He married **Adeline Flamand**, daughter of **Jean Flamand** and **Alphonsine Bruce**, on 14 Jan 1908 Ste.Anne, Manitoba (MM.). He married **Margaret Ann Conibear** on 9 Feb 1956 St.Norbert, Manitoba (Ibid.). He died on 5 Mar 1969 General Hospital, Winnipeg, Manitoba, at age 80 (*Free Press*, 8 Mar 1969, page 33.).

      vii.   Isaac Vandal was born on 19 Jun 1886 Batoche, (Saskatchewan) (BSAP, page 49, B-20.). He was baptized on 21 Jun 1886 Batoche, (Saskatchewan) (Ibid.). He died on 12 Mar 1892 St. Jean-Baptiste, Manitoba, at age 5 (Rod Mac Quarrie, 28 Dec 2011.). He was buried on 14 Mar 1892 St. Jean-Baptiste, Manitoba (Ibid.).

17. Louis Vandal was born in 1849 St.Norbert, (Manitoba) (MBS, C-14934.). He was born on 10 Apr 1850 (Manitoba) (1901 Canada, District 10, E-5, page 5, line 6-11, family 38.). He married **Reine Victoria Ducharme**, daughter of **Prosper Charron dit Ducharme** and **Marianne Monet dit Belhumeur**, on 6 May 1873 St.Norbert, Manitoba (SN1, M-6.). He died on 8 Dec 1913 La Broquerie, Manitoba (MB Vital Statistics, Death Reg. #1913,072245.).

Reine Victoria Ducharme was born on 22 Dec 1851 St.Boniface, (Manitoba) (MBS, C-14927.). She was born on 23 Dec 1853 (Manitoba) (1901 Canada, District 10, E-5, page 5, line 6-11, family 38.).

Children of **Louis Vandal** and **Reine Victoria Ducharme** were as follows:

64   i.   Joseph Louis Vandal, b. 9 Jul 1875 Manitoba; m. Marie Alvina St.Germain.

65   ii.   Julien Vandal, b. 28 Oct 1878 Manitoba; m. Cleophee Berthelet; d. 7 Aug 1936 St.Boniface, Manitoba.

      iii.   Marie Rose Anna Vandal was born on 22 Dec 1879 St-Jean-Baptiste, Manitoba (Rod Mac Quarrie, 28 Dec 2011.). She was baptized on 23 Dec 1879 St-Jean-Baptiste, Manitoba (Ibid.). She died on 23 May 1881 St-Jean-Baptiste, Manitoba, at age 1 (Ibid.). She was buried on 24 May 1881 St-Jean-Baptiste, Manitoba (Ibid.).

      iv.   Louis David Avila Vandal was born on 14 Jul 1883 Woodridge, R.M. of Montcalm, Manitoba (MB Vital Statistics, Birth Reg. #1883,003984.). He married Marie Mathilde Sauve, daughter of Joseph Sauve and Eulalie Carriere, on 31 Mar 1912 Woodridge, Manitoba (MM.).

          Marie Mathilde Sauve was born on 20 Dec 1894 RM of De Salaberry, Manitoba (1901 Canada, #10, e-7, page 3, family 22, line 17-20.) (MB Vital Statistics, Birth Reg. #1894,003366.).

66   v.   Marie Olivine Vandal, b. 24 Sep 1885 R.M. of Montcalm, Manitoba; m. William Sauve; m. Napoleon Hebert.

      vi.   Delia Vandal was born on 25 Jan 1888 R.M. of Montcalm, Manitoba (Ibid., Birth Reg. #1888,004174.). She married Albert Lambert on 25 Jun 1907 Woodridge, Manitoba (MM.).

    vii. Joseph Adelard Celestin Vandal was born on 23 Feb 1890 R.M. of Montcalm, Manitoba (MB Vital Statistics, Birth Reg. #1890,005503.). He was baptized on 24 Feb 1890 St-Jean-Baptiste, Manitoba (Rod Mac Quarrie, 28 Dec 2011.). He died on 7 Feb 1895 St-Jean-Baptiste, Manitoba, at age 4 (Ibid.). He was buried on 10 Feb 1895 St-Jean-Baptiste, Manitoba (Ibid.).

67 viii. Marie Louise Eva Vandal, b. 19 Mar 1892 R.M. of Montcalm, Manitoba; m. Alfred Nault.

    ix. Marie Anna Vandal was born on 29 Jan 1896 R.M. of Montcalm, Manitoba (MB Vital Statistics, Birth Reg. #1896,004877.). She was baptized on 9 Feb 1896 St-Jean-Baptiste, Manitoba (Rod Mac Quarrie, 28 Dec 2011.). She died on 6 May 1897 St-Jean-Baptiste, Manitoba, at age 1 (Ibid.). She was buried on 7 May 1897 St-Jean-Baptiste, Manitoba (Ibid.).

18. Melanie Vandal was born on 1 May 1853 St.Norbert, (Manitoba) (MBS, C-14934.). She married **Napoleon Nault**, son of **Andre Nault** and **Anastasie Landry**, on 12 Feb 1877 St.Norbert, Manitoba (SN2, M-4.). She died in Nov 1898 Olga, Cavalier County, North Dakota, at age 45 (Olga Our Lady of the Sacred Heart, Olga, North Dakota 1882-1900, page 280, S-_. Hereinafter cited as Olga.). She was buried on 6 Nov 1898 Olga, Cavalier County, North Dakota (Ibid.).

Napoleon Nault was born on 17 Sep 1858 St.Vital, (Manitoba) (MBS, C-14931.). He married **Louise Boucher**, daughter of **Emelien Boucher** and **Suzanne Desjarlais Collin**, before 1901. He married **Harriet "Hattie" Jarvis**, daughter of **Elie Jarvis**, on 3 Jan 1908 Glasgow, Valley County, Montana (VCM Valley County Courthouse, Glasgow, Montana; Marriage Record Licenses, 1865-1950, familysearch.org: M-335, Hereinafter cited as VCM.). He and **Harriet "Hattie" Jarvis** obtained a marriage license on 3 Jan 1908 Valley County, Montana (VCM.). He died on 12 Apr 1931 Havre, Hill County, Montana, at age 72 (Rod Mac Quarrie, 28 Dec 2011.) (MT Death Montana State Genealogical Society Death Index.).

19. Pierre Vandal was born circa 1836 Red River, (Manitoba) (1850Ci-MN, page 32, Dwelling 139, Family 139.). He married **Euphrosine Langer**, daughter of **Francois Langer** and **Marguerite George**, on 10 May 1858 Assumption, Pembina, Pembina County, Dakota Territory (AP, page 189-190, M-67.). He was buried on 14 Apr 1903 St.Boniface, Walhalla, Pembina County, North Dakota (SJL-D, page 14.).

Euphrosine Langer was born on 21 Dec 1837 (SFX: 1834-1850, B-190.). She was baptized on 8 Jan 1838 St.Francois Xavier, (Manitoba) (Ibid.).

Children of **Pierre Vandal** and **Euphrosine Langer** were as follows:

68 i. Josephine Vandal, b. 18 May 1860 Pembina, Pembina County, Dakota Territory; m. Emile Wendt; d. 7 Jul 1947 Walhalla, Pembina County, North Dakota.

69 ii. Marie Octavie Vandal, b. 5 Apr 1863 Dakota Territory; m. Francois Gervais; d. circa 18 Feb 1903 Walhalla, Pembina County, North Dakota; bur. 18 Feb 1903 St.Boniface, Walhalla, Pembina County, North Dakota.

    iii. Sarah Vandal was born on 17 May 1866 Dakota Territory (Rod Mac Quarrie, 28 Dec 2011.). She married Baptiste Cloutier on 19 Jul 1886 Walhalla, Pembina County, North Dakota (Ibid.).

70 iv. Hormidas Vandal, b. circa 1868 Dakota Territory; m. Marie Anne Catherine Houle.

71 v. Clemence Vandal, b. 16 Jun 1869 Dakota Territory; m. William Petit dit Thomas; d. circa 26 Apr 1917 Walhalla, Pembina County, North Dakota; bur. 26 Apr 1917 St.Boniface, Walhalla, Pembina County, Dakota Territory.

    vi. Marie Veronique Vandal was born on 23 May 1875 (Ibid.).

72 vii. Joseph Vandal, b. 8 Sep 1879 Pembina County, Dakota Territory; m. Mary (--?--).

20. Nancy Vandal was born circa 1838 Red River, (Manitoba) (1850Ci-MN, page 32, Dwelling 139, Family 139.) (SJL-D, page 15.). She married **Jean Baptiste Langer**, son of **Francois Langer** and **Marguerite George**, on 8 Jan 1856 Assumption, Pembina, Pembina County, Dakota Territory (AP, page 142, M-47.). She was buried on 29 Dec 1904 St.Boniface, Walhalla, Pembina County, North Dakota (SJL-D, page 15.).

Jean Baptiste Langer was born circa 1821. He was born circa 1822 La Fourche, (Manitoba) (Ibid., page 17.). He was born circa 1827 Red River, (Manitoba) (1850Ci-MN, page 34, Dwelling 166, Family 166.). He died on 21 Sep 1906 Walhalla, Pembina County, North Dakota (SJL-D, page 17.). He was buried on 23 Sep 1906 St.Boniface, Walhalla, Pembina County, North Dakota (Ibid.).

21. Marguerite Vandal was born on 24 Apr 1844 Ste.Agathe, (Manitoba) (MBS, C-14929.). She married **Gabriel Houle**, son of **Charles Houle** and **Catherine Falardeau**, on 3 Sep 1867 St.Norbert, (Manitoba) (SN1, M-11.).

Gabriel Houle was born between 1844 and 1845 Red River, (Manitoba) (1850Ci-MN, page 33-34, Dwelling 162, Family 162.). He was born on 26 Oct 1845 Ste.Agathe, (Manitoba) (MBS, C-14929.).

22. John Baptiste Vandal was born on 12 May 1848 St.Vital, (Manitoba) (MBS, C-14934.). He married **Marguerite Vivier**, daughter of **Francois Vivier** and **Josephte Dubois**, before 1870. He married **Madeleine Jeannotte**, daughter of **Francois Jeannotte** and **Madeleine Falcon dit Divertissant**, between 1922 and 1924. He married **Sarah Morin** in 1932 (Turtle Mountain Star, Rolla, North Dakota, 18 Nov 1937.). He died on 12 Nov 1937 Rolette, North Dakota, at age 89 (Ibid.) (ND Death Index.). He was buried on 16 Nov 1937 St. Ann's Catholic Cemetery, Belcourt, Rolette, North Dakota (TM Star, 18 Nov 1937.).

Marguerite Vivier was born on 1 Apr 1852 St.Vital, (Manitoba) (AP, page 73, B-20.) (MBS, C-14934.). She was baptized on 23 May 1852 Assumption, Pembina, Pembina County, Dakota Territory (AP, page 73, B-20.). She died on 12 Mar 1919 North Dakota at age 66 (TM Star, 18 Nov 1937.). She died circa Feb 1921 (1921 Turtle Mountain Chippewa Indian Census Roll, United States Indian Service Department of the Interior, Turtle Mountain Indian Agency, North Dakota, 30 June 1921.).

Children of **John Baptiste Vandal** and **Marguerite Vivier** were as follows:

    i. Monique Vandal was born circa 1870 Red River, (Manitoba) (1870C-MB, #1401, page 46.) (1886-TMC, #487.).

73 ii. Marie Rose Vandal, b. 7 Aug 1872 North Dakota; m. Patrice Gourneau; m. William Laverdure; d. 2 Feb 1946 Rolette County, North Dakota.

74 iii. Francois Joseph "Frank" Vandal, b. 11 Oct 1875 Walhalla, North Dakota; m. Marie McLeod; m. Georgianna Houle; d. 15 Oct 1962 Mercy Hospital, Williston, Williams County, North Dakota; bur. 19 Oct 1962 Trenton, Williams County, North Dakota.

75 iv. Angelique Vandal, b. 15 Apr 1878 North Dakota; m. Edward Norman Petit dit Thomas; m. Pierre Herman; d. 25 May 1923 Belcourt, Rolette County, North Dakota.

76   v.   Celina Vandal, b. 30 Nov 1880 North Dakota; m. Albert Wilkie; d. between 1918 and 1919.

77   vi.   Marie Henriette Vandal, b. 6 Jun 1883 Leroy, Pembina County, Dakota Territory; m. Joseph Robert Azure.

78   vii.   John Baptiste Vandal, b. 11 Sep 1885; m. Eliza Jane Gourneau; d. 22 Feb 1976 Belcourt, Rolette County, North Dakota.

79   viii.   Patrice Vandal, b. 3 Aug 1887 North Dakota; m. Marie Clara Monette; d. 27 Nov 1920 Belcourt, Rolette, North Dakota.

80   ix.   Joseph Vandal, b. 13 Mar 1891; m. Agatha Rose Lafontaine; d. 18 May 1952 Ward County, North Dakota.

81   x.   St.Ann Vandal, b. 7 Sep 1893 North Dakota; m. Alcide Nicolas St.Arnaud; d. 9 Feb 1923 Rolette County, North Dakota.

82   xi.   Mary Jane Vandal, b. 27 Jun 1897 North Dakota; m. John Baptiste Decouteau; d. 8 Nov 1974 McLean County, North Dakota.

Madeleine Jeannotte was born on 22 Jul 1840 North West Territories (SFXI-Kipling.) (SFX: 1834-1850, B-316.). She was baptized on 9 Aug 1840 St.Francois Xavier, (Manitoba) (Ibid.). She married **Antoine Bouvier**, son of **Jean Baptiste Bouvier** and **Marguerite Laurent or Crise**, on 7 Jan 1859 St.Francois Xavier, (Manitoba) (SFXI-Kipling, M-62.). She married **Charles Cuthbert Grant**, son of **Cuthbert Grant** and **Marie McGillis**, before 1893. She died on 7 Sep 1931 Belcourt, Rolette County, North Dakota, at age 91 (TM Star, Thurs, Sep 10, 1931, page 8.). She was buried on 10 Sep 1931 St.Ann's Cemetery, Belcourt, Rolette County, North Dakota (Ibid.).

Sarah Morin was born on 28 May 1863 (ND Death Index.). She married **Leon Jeannotte or Jannot**, son of **Alexander Jeannotte** and **Marguerite Page**, before 1924. She married **Pierre Herman**, son of **Edouard Herman** and **Marguerite Dauphinais**, before 30 Jun 1924 (1924-TMC-ND 1924 Census of the Chippewa Indians of Turtle Mountain Agency, North Dakota, United States Indian Service Department of the Interior, Belcourt, North Dakota, superintendent H. J. McQuigg, 30 June 1924 , Census No. 1837-1844.). She died on 1 Dec 1939 Rolette, North Dakota, at age 76 (ND Death Index.).

23. Francois Vandal was born on 25 Sep 1849 (AP, page 24, B-58.). He was baptized on 20 Jan 1850 Assumption, Pembina, Pembina County, Minnesota Territory (Ibid.). He married **Marie Ouellette**, daughter of **Pierre Ouellette** and **Marguerite Grandbois**, on 1 Oct 1872 St.Norbert, Manitoba (SN1, M-14.). He died on 1 Apr 1935 Pembina County, North Dakota, at age 85 (ND Death Index.).

Marie Ouellette was born circa 1857. She died on 20 Jun 1933 Pembina County, North Dakota (Ibid.).

Children of **Francois Vandal** and **Marie Ouellette** were as follows:

    i.   Marguerite Vandal was born on 1 Sep 1873 (SN1, B-49.). She was baptized on 9 Sep 1873 St.Norbert, Manitoba (Ibid.). She was buried on 4 Jul 1877 Ste.Agathe, Manitoba (MGS: St.Agathe Cemetery, page 9.).

    ii.   Marie Anne Vandal was born on 10 Mar 1875 Manitoba (1880 U. S. Census, Dakota Territory, National Archives of the United States, Washington D.C., page 14; SD.15; ED.76; 112.) (Rod Mac Quarrie, 28 Dec 2011.). She married Jean Baptiste Jerome, son of Joseph Jerome and Marguerite Smith, before 1895. She died on 28 Feb 1900 Walhalla, North Dakota, at age 24 (SJL-D, page 10.). She was buried on 3 Mar 1900 St.Boniface, Walhalla, North Dakota (Ibid.).

          Jean Baptiste Jerome was born on 15 Nov 1867 Pembina, Pembina County, Dakota Territory (AP, page 27, B-10.). He was baptized on 3 Dec 1867 Assumption, Pembina, Pembina County, Dakota Territory (Ibid.). He died on 15 Nov 1895 Walhalla, Pembina County, North Dakota, at age 28 (SJL-D, page 5.). He was buried on 17 Nov 1895 St.Boniface, Walhalla, Pembina County, North Dakota (Ibid.).

    iii.   Peter Vandal was born circa 1877 (1880 U.S., Dakota Territory, Pembina, , page 14; SD.15; ED.76; 112.).

    iv.   Louise Vandal was born on 9 Nov 1879 (SJL-1, page 96, B-70.). She was baptized on 16 Nov 1879 St.Joseph, Leroy, Pembina County, Dakota Territory (Ibid.).

    v.   Bernard Vandal was born circa 1882 (1885 U. S. Census, Dakota Territory, Rolette County, National Archives of the United States, Washington D.C., District 37, page 76, line 29.).

    vi.   Joseph Vandal was born in 1884 (Ibid.). He died on 20 Aug 1885 Walhalla, North Dakota (Rod Mac Quarrie, 28 Dec 2011.). He was buried on 14 Mar 1886 Walhalla, North Dakota (Ibid.).

    vii.   Ancelet Vandal was born on 10 Jul 1886 (Ibid.).

    viii.   Clemence Vandal was born on 10 Oct 1888 (Ibid.).

    ix.   Francois Vandal was born on 11 Jun 1894 Walhalla, North Dakota (SJL-D, page 15.) (Olga, page 232, B-_.). He was baptized on 4 Jul 1894 Olga, Cavalier County, North Dakota (Ibid.). He was buried on 17 Oct 1904 St.Boniface, Walhalla, Pembina County, North Dakota (SJL-D, page 15.).

24. Joseph Vandal was born on 25 Apr 1852 Pembina, Pembina County, Dakota Territory (AP, page 70, B-9.). He was baptized on 25 Apr 1852 Assumption, Pembina, Pembina County, Dakota Territory (Ibid.). He married **Josephine Berthelet**, daughter of **Joseph Berthelet** and **Marguerite Dubois**, on 7 Jan 1874 Ste.Agathe, Manitoba (MM, page 1262.). He died on 9 Nov 1927 Walhalla, Pembina County, North Dakota, at age 75 (W-D St.Boniface, Walhalla, North Dakota, Death Register 1913-1931.). He was buried on 11 Nov 1927 St.Boniface, Walhalla, Pembina County, North Dakota (Ibid.).

Josephine Berthelet was born circa 1857.

Children of **Joseph Vandal** and **Josephine Berthelet** were as follows:

    i.   Marie Vandal was born in Sep 1875 (Rod Mac Quarrie, 28 Dec 2011.). She died in Sep 1875 (Ibid.). She was buried on 7 Sep 1875 Ste.Agathe, Manitoba (Ibid.).

    ii.   Marie Adeline Vandal was born on 5 Oct 1876 Ste.Agathe, Manitoba (1880 U.S., Dakota Territory, Pembina, , page 14; SD.15; ED.76; 113.) (Rod Mac Quarrie, 28 Dec 2011.). She was baptized on 6 Oct 1876 Ste.Agathe, Manitoba (Ibid.). She died on 12 Mar 1886 Walhalla, North Dakota, at age 9 (Ibid.). She was buried on 16 Mar 1886 Walhalla, North Dakota (Ibid.).

    iii.   Joseph Vandal was born on 18 Feb 1880 Leroy, Pembina County, Dakota Territory (SJL-1, page 98, B-83.). He was baptized on 21 Feb 1880 St.Joseph, Leroy, Pembina County, Dakota Territory (Ibid.). He died on 1 Feb 1883 Olga, Cavalier County, North Dakota, at age 2 (Olga, page 11, S-1.). He was buried on 3 Feb 1883 Olga, Cavalier County, North Dakota (Ibid.).

83   iv.   Ernestine Vandal, b. circa 1881; m. Joseph Frederick Ouellette.

       v.   Jean Baptiste Vandal was born on 8 Feb 1882 Leroy, Pembina County, Dakota Territory (SJL-1, page 116, B-205.). He was baptized on 26 Feb 1882 St.Joseph, Leroy, Pembina County, Dakota Territory (Ibid.). He died on 6 Jun 1883 Leroy, Pembina County, Dakota Territory, at age 1 (Ibid., page 126, S-114.). He was buried on 8 Jun 1883 St.Joseph, Leroy, Pembina County, Dakota Territory (Ibid.).

84   vi.   Sara Vandal, b. 3 Apr 1884 Walhalla, North Dakota; m. Daniel Dauphinais; bur. 10 Nov 1918 St.Boniface, Walhalla, Pembina County, North Dakota.

     vii.   Annie Vandal was born in Jul 1885 North Dakota (1900C ND, District 45, page 15A, family 2, line 5-10.).

   viii.   Anne Sara Vandal was born on 23 Jul 1886 (Rod Mac Quarrie, 28 Dec 2011.).

     ix.   Marie Vandal was born on 2 Nov 1890 Walhalla, North Dakota (Ibid.).

      x.   Flora Vandal was born on 24 Mar 1892 (Ibid.).

25. Elzear Vandal was born on 11 May 1857 St.Joseph, Pembina County, Dakota Territory (MBS, C-14934.). He was born on 16 May 1857 Pembina, Pembina County, Dakota Territory (AP, page 169, B-496.). He was baptized on 16 May 1857 Assumption, Pembina, Pembina County, Dakota Territory (Ibid.). He married **Marie Langer**, daughter of **Edouard Langer** and **Marguerite Coulombe**, on 4 Aug 1879 St.Joseph, Leroy, Pembina County, Dakota Territory (SJL-1, page 94, M-8.). He was buried on 23 Aug 1904 St.Boniface, Walhalla, Pembina County, North Dakota (SJL-D, page 15.).

Marie Langer was born circa 1855 (SJL-1, page 94, M-8.).

Children of **Elzear Vandal** and **Marie Langer** were as follows:

       i.   Bernard Vandal was born on 2 Jun 1880 (Ibid., page 101, B-101.). He was baptized on 8 Jun 1880 St.Joseph, Leroy, Pembina County, Dakota Territory (Ibid.).

      ii.   Marie Adele Delphine Vandal was born in Jun 1882 (Ibid., page 119, B-225.). She was baptized on 10 Jul 1882 St.Joseph, Leroy, Pembina County, Dakota Territory (Ibid.).

     iii.   Joseph Vandal was born in 1883 (Rod Mac Quarrie, 28 Dec 2011.). He died on 29 Dec 1885 (Ibid.). He was buried on 14 Mar 1886 Walhalla, North Dakota (Ibid.).

     iv.   Moise Vandal was born on 8 Aug 1885 Walhalla, North Dakota (Ibid.). He was baptized on 16 Aug 1885 Walhalla, North Dakota (Ibid.). He died on 13 Mar 1886 Walhalla, North Dakota (Ibid.). He was buried on 14 Mar 1886 Walhalla, North Dakota (Ibid.).

85   v.   Alexandre Vandal, b. 30 Mar 1887 North Dakota; m. Angelique Langer; m. Delia Laferte; d. 7 Dec 1971 Pembina County, North Dakota.

86   vi.   Peter Vandal, b. 27 Sep 1890 Walhalla, North Dakota; m. Delia Houle; d. 18 Dec 1957 Pembina County, North Dakota.

    vii.   Frederic Vandal was born on 9 Jul 1892 (Ibid.).

26. Bernard Vandal was born on 19 Jun 1860 Ste.Agathe, (Manitoba) (MBS, C-14934.) (AP, page 234, B-166.). He was baptized on 17 Aug 1860 Assumption, Pembina, Pembina County, Dakota Territory (Ibid.). He married **Euphrosine Langer**, daughter of **Edouard Langer** and **Marguerite Coulombe**, on 22 Feb 1881 St.Joseph, Leroy, Pembina County, Dakota Territory (SJL-1, page 108, M-23.). He married **Marie Camelin**, daughter of **Francois Camelin** and **Marguerite Trottier**, on 1 Jun 1884 Olga, Cavalier County, North Dakota (Olga, page 45, M-8.). He died on 1 May 1947 Pembina County, North Dakota, at age 86 (ND Death Index.).

Euphrosine Langer was baptized on 25 Oct 1858 Assumption, Pembina, Pembina County, Dakota Territory (AP, page 199-200, B-600.). She was born on 25 Oct 1858 Pembina, Pembina County, Dakota Territory (Ibid.). She died on 24 Feb 1883 at age 24 (Olga, page 12, S-4.). She was buried on 27 Feb 1883 Olga, Cavalier County, North Dakota (Ibid.).

Children of **Bernard Vandal** and **Euphrosine Langer** were:

       i.   Marie Therese Vandal was born on 11 Dec 1881 Leroy, Pembina County, Dakota Territory (SJL-1, page 115, B-195.). She was baptized on 26 Dec 1881 St.Joseph, Leroy, Pembina County, Dakota Territory (Ibid.).

27. Jean Baptiste Vandal was born circa 1844 Red River, (Manitoba) (1850Ci-MN, page 30, Dwelling 125, Family 125.). He was born on 1 Jan 1846 St.Boniface, (Manitoba) (MBS, C-14934.). He married **Henriette Braconnier**, daughter of **Amable Branconnier** and **Elizabeth Stevenson**, on 3 Jun 1867 St.Norbert, (Manitoba) (SN1, M-9.).

Henriette Braconnier was born circa Jul 1843 St.Norbert, (Manitoba) (MBS, C-14934.).

Children of **Jean Baptiste Vandal** and **Henriette Braconnier** were as follows:

       i.   Antoine Vandal was born on 1 Nov 1873 Qu'Appelle, (Saskatchewan) (ArchiviaNet, C-15008.). He died in 1886 St.Laurent, (Saskatchewan) (Ibid.).

      ii.   Maria Vandal was born on 30 Oct 1876 (1901 Canada, Fish Creek, page 2, Family 15, Line 14-15.). She married Baptiste Deschamps, son of Baptiste Deschamps dit Rabaska and Marguerite Berard, before 1901 (Ibid.).

             Baptiste Deschamps was born on 3 May 1872 St.Albert, (Alberta) (MSJ-FA-E, page 77, B-5.) (HBSI.). He was baptized on 4 May 1872 St.Joachim, Fort Edmonton, (Alberta) (MSJ-FA-E, page 77, B-5.).

28. Catherine Vandal was born circa 1846 Red River, (Manitoba) (1850Ci-MN, page 30, Dwelling 125, Family 125.). She was born on 25 May 1846 (1901 Canada, Fish Creek, page 2, Family 21, Line 32-39.). She married **Jean Baptiste Deschamps**, son of **Jean Baptiste Deschamps** and **Isabelle Allary**, before 1871.

Jean Baptiste Deschamps was born on 15 May 1846 (Ibid.). He was born circa 1849 (Manitoba) (1870C-MB, page 320, #2466.).

29. Francois Vandal was born on 20 Sep 1848 Dakota Territory (1901 Canada, Fish Creek, page 2, Family 20, Line 28-31.). He was born circa 1853 (1886-TMC, #460-466.). He married **Isabelle Deschamps**, daughter of **Jean Baptiste Deschamps** and **Isabelle Allary**, circa 1872.

Isabelle Deschamps was born circa 1843 (Ibid., #461.). She was born on 12 Jan 1846 (1901 Canada, Fish Creek, page 2, Family 20, Line 28-31.). She married **Jean Baptiste Parisien**, son of **Baptiste Parisien** and **Sophie Blayonne**, before 1859.

Children of **Francois Vandal** and **Isabelle Deschamps** were as follows:

       i.   Cecile Vandal was born on 26 Aug 1872 Edmonton, (Alberta) (ArchiviaNet, C-15008.). She was baptized on 22 Sep 1872 St.Albert, (Alberta) (Rod Mac Quarrie, 28 Dec 2011.). She died on 28 Jul 1874 Edmonton, (Alberta), at age 1 (ArchiviaNet, C-15008.). She was buried on 29 Jul 1874 St.Albert, (Alberta) (Rod Mac Quarrie, 28 Dec 2011.).

87   ii.   Veronique Vandal, b. Jul 1874 Edmonton, (Alberta); m. Emilien Dumas or Dumais.

    iii.   Charles Albert Vandal was born on 13 Apr 1876 Edmonton, (Alberta) (ArchiviaNet, C-15008.). He was baptized on 23 May 1876 St.Albert, (Alberta) (Rod Mac Quarrie, 28 Dec 2011.). He died on 28 Aug 1894 Fish Creek, (Saskatchewan), at age 18 (ArchiviaNet, C-15008.). He was buried on 28 Aug 1884 St.Laurent, (Saskatchewan) (Rod Mac Quarrie, 28 Dec 2011.).

    iv.   Henriette Vandal was born on 16 Mar 1878 Edmonton, (Alberta) (ArchiviaNet, C-15008.).

    v.   Moise Vandal was born in 1881 Willow Bunch, (Saskatchewan) (Ibid.). He died in 1882 north of Willow Bunch, (Saskatchewan) (Ibid.).

    vi.   Domitilde Vandal was born on 3 Jan 1885 Fish Creek, (Saskatchewan) (BSAP, page 29, B-1.) (ArchiviaNet, C-15008.). She was baptized on 5 Jan 1885 Batoche, (Saskatchewan) (BSAP, page 29, B-1.) (Rod Mac Quarrie, 28 Dec 2011.).

30.   **Elise Vandal** was born on 5 Feb 1850 (AP, page 37, B-103.). She was baptized on 2 Jun 1850 Assumption, Pembina, Pembina County, Minnesota Territory (Ibid.). She married **Felix Marcellais**, son of **Louis Marcellais** and **Sophie Indian,** on 26 Oct 1869 St.Norbert, (Manitoba) (SN1, M-4.).

    Felix Marcellais was born on 4 Mar 1847 St.Boniface, (Manitoba) (MBS, C-14930.). He died on 14 Jan 1890 St.Norbert, Manitoba, at age 42 (MB Vital Statistics, Death Reg. #1890, 002599.) (SN2, S-2.). He was buried on 16 Jan 1890 St.Norbert, Manitoba (Ibid.).

31.   **Sarah Vandal** was born on 22 Oct 1858 St.Norbert, (Manitoba) (MBS, C-14934.). She was baptized on 11 Nov 1858 Assumption, Pembina, Pembina County, Dakota Territory (AP, page 200, B-603.). She married **Joseph Sutherland**, son of **Pierre Sutherland** and **Suzanne McMillan,** on 13 Feb 1877 Ste.Agathe, Manitoba (MBS, C-14934.) (MM.) (Rod Mac Quarrie, 28 Dec 2011.). She died on 18 Sep 1888 St.Jean-Baptiste, RM of Montcalm, Manitoba, at age 29 (MB Vital Statistics, Death Reg. #1888,002456.). She was buried on 20 Sep 1888 St.Jean-Baptiste, Manitoba (Rod Mac Quarrie, 28 Dec 2011.).

    Joseph Sutherland was born in Mar 1854 St.Boniface, (Manitoba) (MBS, C-14933.).

32.   **Virginie Vandal** was born on 8 Jul 1861 (SN1, page 45, B-22.). She was baptized on 21 Jul 1861 St.Norbert, (Manitoba) (Ibid.). She married **Charles Desjarlais**, son of **Antoine Desjarlais dit Morel** and **Louise Vallee,** before 1882 (1901 Canada, 203, d(1), page 5, family 54, line 24-29.).

    Charles Desjarlais was born on 26 Apr 1852 (AP, page 73, B-23.). He was baptized on 28 May 1852 Assumption, Pembina, Pembina County, Dakota Territory (Ibid.). He was baptized on 10 Jun 1852 Assumption, Pembina, Pembina County, Dakota Territory (Ibid., page 73, B-25.).

33.   **Norman Vandal** was born on 15 Feb 1857 (AP, page 170, B-498.). He was baptized on 5 Jun 1857 Assumption, Pembina, Pembina County, Dakota Territory (Ibid.). He married **Julie Munroe**, daughter of **Felix Munroe** and **Louise Seguin dit Laderoute,** on 2 Sep 1874 Bulls Lake on the plains (NWHBS, C-14940.) (Rod Mac Quarrie, 28 Dec 2011.).

    Julie Munroe was born on 25 Aug 1856 St.Albert, (Alberta) (INB, page 130.) (NWHBS, C-14940.). She was baptized on 10 Sep 1856 Fort-des-Prairies, (Alberta) (INB, page 130.).

Children of **Norman Vandal** and **Julie Munroe** were as follows:

    i.   Marguerite Vandal was born on 15 Dec 1875 Tail Creek, (Alberta) (NWHBS, C-14940.) (1901 Canada, #202, g, page 1-2, family 11, line 46-49, 1-9.). She married Bartel Meziere after 1901 (Rod Mac Quarrie, 28 Dec 2011.).

    ii.   Julie Vandal was born in 1877 Tail Creek, (Alberta) (NWHBS, C-14940.) (ArchiviaNet, C-15008.). She died in 1877 Tail Creek, (Alberta) (NWHBS, C-14940.) (ArchiviaNet, C-15008.).

    iii.   Antoine Vandal was born in 1879 Tail Creek, (Alberta) (NWHBS, C-14940.) (ArchiviaNet, C-15008.). He died on 4 Sep 1881 St.Albert, (Alberta) (NWHBS, C-14940.) (ArchiviaNet, C-15008.). He was buried on 5 Sep 1881 St.Albert, (Alberta) (Ibid.) (Rod Mac Quarrie, 28 Dec 2011.).

88   iv.   Maggie Vandal, b. 10 Mar 1882; m. Raoul Leontz Moser; d. 28 Aug 1968 Leduc, Alberta.

    v.   Adelaide Vandal was born on 16 Aug 1884 Edmonton, (Alberta) (MSJ-FA-E, page 100, B-12.). She was baptized on 17 Aug 1884 St.Joachim, Edmonton, (Alberta) (Ibid.).

    vi.   Louise Vandal was born on 10 Apr 1885 Edmonton, (Alberta) (1901 Canada, #202, g, page 1-2, family 11, line 46-49, 1-9.) (ArchiviaNet, C-15008.).

    vii.   Magloire Vandal was born on 21 Dec 1889 (MSJ-FA-E, page 132, B-16.). He was baptized on 25 Dec 1889 St.Joachim, Edmonton, (Alberta) (Ibid.).

    viii.   Benjamin Vandal was born on 8 Jul 1891 (1901 Canada, #202, g, page 1-2, family 11, line 46-49, 1-9.). He was born on 25 Jun 1892 (Denney.). He was baptized on 30 Jun 1892 (Ibid.). He married Hermine Calliou circa 1914 (Rod Mac Quarrie, 28 Dec 2011.).

        Hermine Calliou was born in 1889 (Ibid.).

    ix.   Helene Vandal was born on 23 Mar 1894 (Denney.). She was baptized on 29 Mar 1894 (Ibid.).

    x.   Flora Elizabeth Vandal was born on 4 Apr 1896 (Ibid.). She was baptized on 18 Apr 1896 (Ibid.).

    xi.   Jerome Vandal was born on 1 Nov 1899 (1901 Canada, #202, g, page 1-2, family 11, line 46-49, 1-9.).

    xii.   Mary Clara Vandal was born circa 1901 (Denney.). She married Paul Stanley Brown on 11 Nov 1924 Vancouver, British Columbia (Rod Mac Quarrie, 28 Dec 2011.).

        Paul Stanley Brown was born on 14 Jan 1895 Portland, Oregon (Ibid.).

34.   **Sarah Vandal** was born on 15 Jun 1861 (MBS, C-14934.). She married **Etienne Pepin**, son of **Antoine Pepin** and **Marguerite Davis,** on 24 Jan 1883 St.Eustache, Manitoba (MM.). She died in 1893 (Rod Mac Quarrie, 28 Dec 2011.).

    Etienne Pepin was born on 30 Jul 1857 Dakota Territory (AP, page 173-174, B-511.). He was baptized on 5 Aug 1857 Assumption, Pembina, Pembina County, Dakota Territory (Ibid.). He married **Margaret Day After Day** in 1893 (1900C-ND 1900 United States Census, North Dakota, National Archives of the United States, Washington, D. C., House 144, page 286B.). He died on 25 Oct 1904 at age 47 (BIA-TM-BMD Bureau of Indian Affairs, Turtle Mountain Death certificates: 1916-1952, extracted by Mary M. McClammy;

Birth, Marriage, Death Records 1904-1950; Family record cards 1908; Family History Center; FHC Film #1249904, Deceased Allottees 1909-1911, page 8.).

35. Pierre Vandal was born on 15 Jan 1848 (1901 Canada, Fish Creek, page 1, Family 5, Line 13-24.). He married **Louise Poitras**, daughter of **Ignace Poitras** and **Helene McGillis**, on 9 Jun 1874 St.Francois Xavier, Manitoba (SFXI-Kipling, M-11.).

Louise Poitras was born on 1 Jul 1857 (Ibid., B-217.). She was baptized on 6 Sep 1857 St.Francois Xavier, (Manitoba) (Ibid.) (INB, page 152.).

Children of **Pierre Vandal** and **Louise Poitras** were as follows:

    i.   Marie Philomene Vandal was born on 24 Apr 1875 (Denney.) (INB.) (SL-SK, page 37, B-9.). She was baptized on 26 Apr 1875 St.Laurent-de-Grandin, (Saskatchewan) (Ibid.). She died on 15 Jan 1893 Fish Creek, (Saskatchewan), at age 17 (Denney.) (BSAP, page 103, S-1.). She was buried on 16 Jan 1893 Batoche, (Saskatchewan) (Ibid.).

    ii.   Pierre Louis Vandal was born on 16 Oct 1876 Batoche, (Saskatchewan) (ArchiviaNet, C-15008.). He died circa 16 Nov 1878 (SL-SK, page 23, S-21.). He was buried on 16 Nov 1878 St.Laurent-de-Grandin, (Saskatchewan) (Ibid.).

89   iii.   Marie Rose Vandal, b. 24 Sep 1877 Batoche, (Saskatchewan); m. Clovis Nogier.

    iv.   Marie Emelie Vandal was born on 24 Dec 1878 (Ibid., page 24, B-57.). She was baptized on 24 Dec 1878 St.Laurent-de-Grandin, (Saskatchewan) (Ibid.). She died on 14 Jun 1900 Fish Creek, (Saskatchewan), at age 21 (SK Vital Statistics, Death Reg. #235.) (ArchiviaNet, C-15008.).

    v.   Etienne Vandal was born on 17 Jan 1880 Duck Lake, (Saskatchewan) (DL, page 30, B-1.). He was baptized on 19 Jan 1880 Duck Lake, (Saskatchewan) (Ibid.).

90   vi.   Rose Germaine Vandal, b. 8 Feb 1881 Batoche, (Saskatchewan); m. Alexandre Lavallee.

    vii.   William Vandal was born on 11 Oct 1882 Fish Creek, (Saskatchewan) (BSAP, page 10, B-24.) (ArchiviaNet, C-15008.). He was baptized on 12 Oct 1882 Batoche, (Saskatchewan) (BSAP, page 10, B-24.). He married Alvina Parenteau, daughter of Louis Parenteau and Rosalie Letendre, on 21 Feb 1911 Batoche, Saskatchewan (Denney.).
           Alvina Parenteau was born on 30 Mar 1891 Batoche, (Saskatchewan) (BSAP, page 88, B-6.) (SK Vital Statistics, Birth Reg. #7600.). She was baptized on 30 Mar 1891 Batoche, (Saskatchewan) (BSAP, page 88, B-6.).

    viii.   Eulalie Vandal was born on 25 Mar 1884 Fish Creek, (Saskatchewan) (Ibid., page 20, B-6.). She was baptized on 26 Mar 1884 Batoche, (Saskatchewan) (Ibid.).

    ix.   Simon Vandal was born on 4 Dec 1886 Fish Creek, (Saskatchewan) (ArchiviaNet, C-15008.). He was baptized on 5 Dec 1886 Batoche, (Saskatchewan) (Denney.).

    x.   Josephine Vandal was born on 4 Mar 1888 Batoche, (Saskatchewan) (BSAP, page 65, B-6.). She was baptized on 5 Mar 1888 Batoche, (Saskatchewan) (Ibid.).

    xi.   Florentine Vandal was born on 9 Nov 1889 Fish Creek, (Saskatchewan) (1901 Canada, Fish Creek, page 1, Family 5, Line 13-24.).

    xii.   Virginie Vandal was born on 16 Nov 1891 Fish Creek, (Saskatchewan) (BSAP, page 91, B-18.). She was baptized on 23 Nov 1891 Batoche, (Saskatchewan) (Ibid.). She married Pierre Lavallee on 29 Jul 1913 Batoche, Saskatchewan (Denney.).

    xiii.   Louis David Vandal was born on 18 Dec 1893 Fish Creek, (Saskatchewan) (BSAP, page 112, B-32.). He was baptized on 19 Dec 1893 Batoche, (Saskatchewan) (Ibid.). He died on 28 Oct 1894 Fish Creek, (Saskatchewan) (Ibid., page 119, S-12.). He was buried on 30 Oct 1894 Batoche, (Saskatchewan) (Ibid.).

    xiv.   Napoleon Norbert Vandal was born on 1 Jun 1895 Fish Creek, (Saskatchewan) (Ibid., page 124, B-15.). He was baptized on 2 Jun 1895 Batoche, (Saskatchewan) (Ibid.).

    xv.   Joseph Albert Vandal was born on 18 Dec 1897 Fish Creek, (Saskatchewan) (1901 Canada, Fish Creek, page 8, Family 5, Line 13-24.).

    xvi.   Elmira Vandal was born on 9 Mar 1899 Fish Creek, (Saskatchewan) (Ibid.).

36. Antoine Vandal was born on 10 Jul 1849 (Ibid., microfilm, T-6553, Bellevue, page 8, Family 74, line 9-17.). He was born circa 1850 Red River, (Manitoba). He married **Alphosine Henry**, daughter of **Alexis Henry** and **Marie Daunais dit Lyonnaise,** on 16 Jan 1872 St.Norbert, Manitoba (SN1, M-3.).

Alphosine Henry was born on 10 Aug 1851 St.Vital, (Manitoba) (MBS, C-14934.) (1901 Canada, microfilm, T-6553, Bellevue, page 8, Family 74, line 9-17.).

Children of **Antoine Vandal** and **Alphosine Henry** were as follows:

    i.   Emelie Cecile Vendale was born on 23 May 1873 St.Norbert, Manitoba (SN1, B-31.). She was baptized on 24 May 1873 St.Norbert, Manitoba (Ibid.). She died on 4 May 1874 St.Norbert, Manitoba (SN2, S-9.). She was buried on 6 May 1874 St.Norbert, Manitoba (Ibid.).

    ii.   Joseph Elzear Vendal was born on 10 Mar 1874 St.Norbert, Manitoba (Ibid., B-13.). He was baptized on 11 Mar 1874 St.Norbert, Manitoba (Ibid.). He died on 3 Dec 1876 St.Norbert, Manitoba, at age 2 (Ibid., S-13.). He was buried on 4 Dec 1876 St.Norbert, Manitoba (Ibid.).

    iii.   Pierre Maxime Vandal was born on 28 Jun 1875 St.Norbert, Manitoba (Ibid., B-22.). He was baptized on 28 Jun 1875 St.Norbert, Manitoba (Ibid.). He died on 28 Jun 1875 St.Norbert, Manitoba (Ibid., S-16.). He was buried on 29 Jun 1875 St.Norbert, Manitoba (Ibid.).

    iv.   Virginie Vandal was born circa Apr 1876 (Ibid., S-7.). She died on 18 May 1876 St.Norbert, Manitoba (Ibid.). She was buried on 19 May 1876 St.Norbert, Manitoba (Ibid.).

91   v.   Marie Emelie Vandal, b. 27 May 1877 St.Norbert, Manitoba; m. Joseph Ross.

92   vi.   Frederick Vandal, b. 17 Jun 1879; m. Sophia Mary Fiddler; d. 26 Sep 1964 Prince Albert, Saskatchewan; bur. 30 Sep 1964 South Hill, Prince Albert, Saskatchewan.

93   vii.   Mathilde Vandal, b. 27 Jan 1881 Montagne la Bosse; m. John Fidler; m. Louis Grassick; d. 22 Jan 1958 Cudworth, Saskatchewan.

94   viii.   Francois Vandal, b. 2 Jan 1883 Batoche, (Saskatchewan); m. Anna (Skierra) Skarra; d. 1 Nov 1918 Cudworth, Saskatchewan.

    ix.   Leon Salomon Vandal was born on 9 Feb 1885 Batoche, (Saskatchewan) (BSAP, page 29, B-2.). He was baptized on 16 Feb 1885 Batoche, (Saskatchewan) (Ibid.).

    x.   Theodore Vandal was born on 27 Jan 1886 Batoche, (Saskatchewan) (Ibid., page 43, B-2.). He was baptized on 28 Jan 1886 Batoche, (Saskatchewan) (Ibid.).

    xi.   Helene Vandal was born on 11 Feb 1888 Batoche, (Saskatchewan) (Ibid., page 65, B-5.). She was baptized on 13 Feb 1888 Batoche, (Saskatchewan) (Ibid.).

    xii.   Patrice Vandal was born on 4 May 1891 Batoche, (Saskatchewan) (Ibid., page 89, B-11.). He was baptized on 5 May 1891 Batoche, (Saskatchewan) (Ibid.). He died on 8 Jun 1891 Batoche, (Saskatchewan) (Ibid., page 90, S-8.). He was buried on 9 Jun 1891 Batoche, (Saskatchewan) (Ibid.).

37. Isabelle Vandal was born on 25 Dec 1852 St.Norbert, (Manitoba) (MBS, C-14929.). She married **Maurice Henry**, son of **Alexis Henry** and **Marie Daunais dit Lyonnaise**, on 16 Jan 1872 St.Norbert, Manitoba (SN1, M-4.). She was buried on 15 Jul 1882 Lebret, (Saskatchewan) (L2, page 38, S-14.).

Maurice Henry was born on 8 Jan 1847 St.Norbert, (Manitoba) (MBS, C-14929.). He married **Blandine Ross**, daughter of **Donald Ross** and **Catherine Delorme**, on 18 Feb 1884 Batoche, (Saskatchewan) (BSAP, page 19, M-1.). He died on 1 Apr 1934 at age 87.

38. Joseph Vandal was born on 29 Oct 1856 St.Norbert, (Manitoba) (MBS, C-14934.). He married **Rosalie Rocheleau**, daughter of **Jean Baptiste Rocheleau** and **Marie Anne Carriere**, on 10 Oct 1876 St.Norbert, Manitoba (SN2, M-6.). He died on 19 Jan 1879 St.Norbert, Manitoba, at age 22 (Ibid., S-3.). He was buried on 21 Jan 1879 St.Norbert, Manitoba (Ibid.).

Rosalie Rocheleau was born circa 1855 Fort Ellice, Manitoba (Denney.). She married **Joseph Nault**, son of **Andre Nault** and **Anastasie Landry**, on 16 Feb 1874 St.Norbert, Manitoba (SN2, M-3.). She married **Napoleon Carriere**, son of **Elie Carriere** and **Elmire Landry**, on 27 May 1883 Batoche, (Saskatchewan) (BSAP, page 15, M-2.).

Children of **Joseph Vandal** and **Rosalie Rocheleau** all born St.Norbert, Manitoba, were as follows:

    i.   Patrice Vandal was born on 31 Jul 1877 (SN2, B-28.). He was baptized on 31 Jul 1877 St.Norbert, Manitoba (Ibid.). He died on 29 Apr 1878 St.Norbert, Manitoba (Ibid., S-21.). He was buried on 5 May 1878 St.Norbert, Manitoba (Ibid.).

    ii.   Marie Alvina Vandal was born on 31 Jul 1877 (Ibid., B-29.). She was baptized on 31 Jul 1877 St.Norbert, Manitoba (Ibid.). She died on 31 Jan 1878 St.Norbert, Manitoba (Ibid., S-6.). She was buried on 2 Feb 1878 St.Norbert, Manitoba (Ibid.).

95   iii.   Marie Virginie Vandal, b. 13 May 1879; m. William Sauve; d. 12 Apr 1904.

39. Melanie Vandal was born on 11 Apr 1859 St.Norbert, (Manitoba) (SN1, page 9-10, B-9.). She was baptized on 12 Apr 1859 St.Norbert, (Manitoba) (Ibid.). She married **Jean Baptiste Rocheleau**, son of **Jean Baptiste Rocheleau** and **Marie Anne Carriere**, on 10 Oct 1876 St.Norbert, Manitoba (SN2, M-5.). She died on 3 Jun 1885 Batoche, (Saskatchewan), at age 26 (BSAP, page 35, S-29.). She was buried on 5 Jun 1885 Batoche, (Saskatchewan) (Ibid.).

Jean Baptiste Rocheleau was born on 8 Jan 1851 St.Norbert, (Manitoba) (1870C-MB, #1959, page 64.) (1901 Canada, Fish Creek, page 1, Family 10, Line 42-46.) (MBS, Reel T-12030.).

40. Augustin Vandal was born in Jul 1857 St.Norbert, (Manitoba) (MBS, C-14934.). He married **Sophie Parisien**, daughter of **Andre Parisien** and **Julie Zace**, on 8 Jan 1885 St.Norbert, Manitoba (SN2, M-3.). He died before 1895.

Sophie Parisien was born on 18 Nov 1862 St.Norbert, (Manitoba) (SN1, page 65, B-34.). She was baptized on 18 Nov 1862 St.Norbert, (Manitoba) (Ibid.). She married **Andre Morisseau**, son of **Andre Morisseau** and **Cecile Monet dit Belhumeur**, on 29 Jul 1895 Ste.Rose, Manitoba (MM.).

Children of **Augustin Vandal** and **Sophie Parisien** were as follows:

    i.   Toussaint Vandal was born on 1 Nov 1885 St.Norbert, Manitoba (SN2, B-53.) (MB Vital Statistics, Birth Reg. #1885,0016391.). He was baptized on 2 Nov 1885 St.Norbert, Manitoba (SN2, B-53.). He died on 30 Mar 1887 St.Norbert, Manitoba, at age 1 (Ibid., S-6.) (MB Vital Statistics, Death Reg. #1887,001827.). He was buried on 1 Apr 1887 St.Norbert, Manitoba (SN2, S-6.).

    ii.   Joseph Jeremie Vandal was born on 22 Jan 1887 RM of St.Nobert, Manitoba (MB Vital Statistics, Birth Reg. #1887,004181.) (SN2, B-8.). He was baptized on 25 Jan 1887 St.Norbert, Manitoba (Ibid.).

    iii.   Ursule Vandal was born on 8 Apr 1889 St.Nobert, Manitoba (MB Vital Statistics, Birth Reg. #1889,005395.) (SN2, B-20.). She was baptized on 9 Apr 1889 St.Norbert, Manitoba (Ibid.).

    iv.   Joseph Philias Vandal was born on 10 May 1891 R.M. of Turtle Mountain, Manitoba (MB Vital Statistics, Birth Reg. #1891,001670.). He married Ema Pelter on 15 Feb 1926 RM of Lawrence, Manitoba (Ibid., Marriage Reg. #1926,007266.).

    v.   Adolphus Vandal was born on 29 Jun 1893 (1901 Canada, District 9-1-1, page 11, family 88, line 2-9.) (Rod Mac Quarrie, 28 Dec 2011.).

41. Melanie Vandal was born on 25 Dec 1858 (SN1, page 9, B-5.). She was baptized on 5 Mar 1859 St.Norbert, (Manitoba) (Ibid.). She married **John Henry**, son of **John Henry** and **Josephte Parisien**, on 9 Feb 1880 St.Norbert, Manitoba (SN2, M-2.).

John Henry was born on 7 Apr 1851 St.Norbert, (Manitoba) (MBS, C-14928.).

42. Joseph Vandal was born circa 1857 (Manitoba) (1881 Canada, C-13285, District 192-1, page 24, household 109.). He married **Elizabeth Champagne**, daughter of **Emmanuel Champagne** and **Marie Letendre**, on 14 Jul 1879 St.Boniface, Manitoba (RMSB.). He died on 20 Dec 1885 Batoche, (Saskatchewan) (BSAP, page 41, S-37.). He was buried on 22 Dec 1885 Batoche, (Saskatchewan) (Ibid.).

Elizabeth Champagne was born on 30 Aug 1853 Pine Creek, (Manitoba) (MBS, C-14925.). She married **Joseph Azure**, son of **Joseph Azure** and **Angelique Martel**, on 29 Dec 1873 Lebret, (Saskatchewan) (L1, page 127, M-9.). She married **Thomas Petit**, son of **Thomas Petit** and **Josephte Ouellette**, on 24 Jan 1888 Batoche, (Saskatchewan) (BSAP, page 64, M-1.).

Children of **Joseph Vandal** and **Elizabeth Champagne** were as follows:

- i. Joseph Vandal was born on 4 Jun 1880 Batoche, (Saskatchewan) (ArchiviaNet, C-15008.). He was baptized on 5 Jun 1880 Duck Lake, (Saskatchewan) (DL, page 31, B-8.).
- 96 ii. Elise Vandal, b. 8 Jun 1882 Batoche, (Saskatchewan); m. Chrysostome Boyer.
- iii. Marie Adelaide Vandal was born on 3 Nov 1884 Battleford, (Saskatchewan) (SV St.Vital Roman Catholic Registre des Baptemes, Mariages & Sepltures, Battleford, Saskatchewan, 1878-1896, B-29. Hereinafter cited as SV.). She was baptized on 4 Nov 1884 St.Vital, Battleford, (Saskatchewan) (Ibid.). She married Francois Villeneuve on 24 Nov 1903 Fish Creek, (Saskatchewan) (Heather Hallett Research, 22 Jan 2002.).

43. Rosalie Vandal was born on 22 Aug 1859 St.Norbert, (Manitoba) (SN1, B-27, page 18.). She was baptized on 23 Aug 1859 St.Norbert, (Manitoba) (Ibid.). She married **Charles Pruden**, son of **James Pruden** and **Genevieve Desjarlais**, on 7 Jan 1880 Duck Lake, (Saskatchewan) (DL, page 31, M-1.). She died before 1901 (1901 Canada, District 205-u(1), pare 11, line 33.).

Charles Pruden was born on 7 Feb 1856 McKenzie River (Denney.). He died on 14 Jan 1917 Prince Albert, Saskatchewan, at age 60 (Ibid.).

44. William Vandal was born on 15 Aug 1861 (SB-Rozyk, page 27, B-105.). He was baptized on 17 Aug 1861 St.Boniface, (Manitoba) (Ibid.). He married **Virginie Boyer**, daughter of **Jean Baptiste Boyer** and **Elizabeth Bousquet**, on 7 Feb 1882 St-Laurent-de-Grandin, (Saskatchewan) (SL-SK, page 56-57, M-2.).

Virginie Boyer was born on 24 Jan 1865 St.Boniface, (Manitoba) (SB-Rozyk, page 175, B-8.). She was baptized on 24 Jan 1865 St.Boniface, (Manitoba) (Ibid.).

Children of **William Vandal** and **Virginie Boyer** were as follows:

- i. William Vandal was born on 3 Dec 1882 St.Laurent, (Saskatchewan) (SL-SK, page 62, B-22.). He was baptized on 4 Dec 1882 St.Laurent, (Saskatchewan) (Ibid.). He died on 5 Jan 1905 Batoche, (Saskatchewan), at age 22 (BSAP, page 231, S-1.). He was buried on 17 Jan 1905 Batoche, (Saskatchewan) (Ibid.).
- ii. Virginie Vandal was born on 11 May 1884 St.Laurent, (Saskatchewan) (ArchiviaNet, C-15008.). She was baptized on 12 May 1884 St.Laurent, (Saskatchewan) (Denney.). She died on 5 Feb 1885 Batoche, (Saskatchewan) (ArchiviaNet, C-15008.).
- iii. Jean Baptiste Vandal was born on 27 Feb 1886 Batoche, (Saskatchewan) (BSAP, page 44, B-6.). He was baptized on 28 Feb 1886 Batoche, (Saskatchewan) (Ibid.).
- iv. Marie Vandal was born on 17 Jan 1888 Batoche, (Saskatchewan) (Ibid., page 64, B-3.). She was baptized on 18 Jan 1888 Batoche, (Saskatchewan) (Ibid.). She died on 16 Mar 1890 Batoche, (Saskatchewan), at age 2 (Ibid., page 81, S-7.). She was buried on 17 Mar 1890 Batoche, (Saskatchewan) (Ibid.).
- v. Joseph Aimie Vandal was born on 6 May 1890 Batoche, (Saskatchewan) (Ibid., page 82, B-12.). He was baptized on 7 May 1890 Batoche, (Saskatchewan) (Ibid.).
- vi. George Alfred Vandal was born on 19 Jan 1892 St.Laurent, (Saskatchewan) (Denney.). He was baptized on 20 Jan 1892 St.Laurent, (Saskatchewan) (Ibid.).
- vii. Norbert Vandal was born on 28 May 1894 (BSAP, page 115, B-10.). He was baptized on 2 Jun 1894 Batoche, (Saskatchewan) (Ibid.).
- viii. Alcide Vandal was born in Jul 1896 (Denney.). He was baptized on 8 Oct 1896 Batoche, (Saskatchewan) (Ibid.).
- ix. Marguerite Eudore Vandal was born on 6 Nov 1898 (Ibid.). She was baptized on 18 Dec 1898 Batoche, (Saskatchewan) (Ibid.). She married M. Birmingham on 27 Aug 1920 Saskatoon, Saskatchewan (Ibid.).
  M. Birmingham was born of, Saskatoon, (Saskatchewan).
- x. Henri Vandal was baptized Batoche, (Saskatchewan) (Ibid.). He was born on 29 Jul 1900 (Ibid.).

45. Pierre Modeste Vandal was born on 1 Feb 1866 St.Norbert, (Manitoba) (SN1, page 78-79, B-7.). He was baptized on 3 Feb 1866 St.Norbert, (Manitoba) (Ibid.). He married **Adelaide Parenteau**, daughter of **Pierre Parenteau** and **Marie Anne Caron**, on 26 Apr 1887 Batoche, (Saskatchewan) (BSAP, page 57, M-4.).

Adelaide Parenteau was born on 3 Nov 1868 St.Norbert, (Manitoba) (SN1, B-51.). She was baptized on 3 Nov 1868 St.Norbert, (Manitoba) (Ibid.).

Children of **Pierre Modeste Vandal** and **Adelaide Parenteau** were as follows:

- i. Anne Vandal was born on 29 Jul 1888 Batoche, (Saskatchewan) (BSAP, page 69, B-12.). She was baptized on 29 Jul 1888 Batoche, (Saskatchewan) (Ibid.).
- ii. Modeste Vandal was born on 7 May 1891 Batoche, (Saskatchewan) (Ibid., page 89, B-12.). He was baptized on 10 May 1891 Batoche, (Saskatchewan) (Ibid.).
- iii. Joseph Norbert Vandal was born on 2 Jun 1893 Batoche, (Saskatchewan) (Ibid., page 107, B-14.). He was baptized on 3 Jun 1893 Batoche, (Saskatchewan) (Ibid.). He died on 25 Mar 1894 Batoche, (Saskatchewan) (Ibid., page 114, S-5.). He was buried Batoche, (Saskatchewan). He was buried on 26 Mar 1894 Batoche, (Saskatchewan) (Ibid.).
- iv. Marie Louise Vandal was born in Jun 1895. She died on 7 Aug 1896 Batoche, (Saskatchewan), at age 1.
- v. Marie Ernestine Emelie Vandal was born in 1897. She died on 21 Aug 1897 Prince Albert, (Saskatchewan). She was buried Batoche, (Saskatchewan).

46. Norbert Vandal was born circa Dec 1868 (SB-Rozyk, page 155, B-59.). He was baptized on 2 Jul 1869 St.Boniface, (Manitoba) (Ibid.). He married **Virginie Carriere**, daughter of **Charles Toussaint Carriere** and **Cecile Beauchemin**, on 24 Sep 1895 Batoche, (Saskatchewan) (BSAP, page 127, M-5.).

Virginie Carriere was born on 11 Sep 1875 St.Norbert, Manitoba (SN2, B-38.). She was baptized on 12 Sep 1875 St.Norbert, Manitoba (Ibid.).

Children of **Norbert Vandal** and **Virginie Carriere** were as follows:

 i.   Marie Louise Vandal was born on 21 May 1897 Batoche, (Saskatchewan) (SK Vital Statistics, Birth Reg. #7915.). She died on 6 Jul 1897 Batoche, (Saskatchewan) (Ibid., Death Reg. #1281.).

 ii.   Emma Vandal was born on 2 Aug 1897 Batoche, (Saskatchewan) (1901 Canada, Fish Creek, page 16, Family 169, Line 28-31.) (SK Vital Statistics, Birth Reg. #1521.).

 iii.   Alice Vandal was born on 9 Dec 1898 Fish Creek, (Saskatchewan) (1901 Canada, Fish Creek, page 16, Family 169, Line 28-31.) (SK Vital Statistics, Birth Reg. #2119.).

 iv.   Georgine Vandal was born in Aug 1908 (Automated Genealogy 1911 Census Transcription Project and Census Images from the National Archives of Canada, http://www.automatedgenealogy.com, District 10, page 6, family 80, line 23-28.).

 v.   William Vandal was born in Feb 1911 (Ibid.).

47.   **Marie Louise Vandal** was born on 2 Mar 1873 Batoche, (Saskatchewan) (HBSI.) (SL-SK, page 18, B-8.). She was baptized on 21 Mar 1873 St.Laurent-de-Grandin, (Saskatchewan) (Ibid.). She married **Joseph Fisher**, son of **George Fisher** and **Emelie Boyer,** on 10 May 1892 Lebret, (Saskatchewan) (Art Fisher Research, From Joyce Black Genealogy, 1981.).

 Joseph Fisher was born on 16 Sep 1870 St.Boniface, Manitoba (SB-Rozyk, page 194, B-80.). He was baptized on 16 Sep 1870 St.Boniface, Manitoba (Ibid.). He died on 8 Aug 1922 Saskatoon, Saskatchewan, at age 51 (Joyce Black Research.).

48.   **Eulalie Vandal** was born on 8 Nov 1878 Batoche, (Saskatchewan) (HBSI.) (ArchiviaNet.) (SL-SK, page 23, B-55.). She was baptized on 12 Nov 1878 St.Laurent-de-Grandin, (Saskatchewan) (Ibid.). She married **Louis Gervais**, son of **Alexis Gervais** and **Madeleine Fagnant,** on 17 May 1899 Batoche, (Saskatchewan) (Denney.).

 Louis Gervais was born on 1 Jun 1875 Fish Creek, (Saskatchewan) (HBSI.) (ArchiviaNet.).

Generation Five

49.   **Nancy Vandal** was born on 21 Feb 1861 (SN1, page 41, B-6.). She was baptized on 22 Feb 1861 St.Norbert, (Manitoba) (Ibid.). She married **William Vermette**, son of **Antoine Vermette** and **Cecile Rocque,** on 11 Nov 1879 St.Jean Baptiste, Manitoba (MM.). She died on 14 Dec 1899 Ritchot, Manitoba, at age 38 (St-N Cem.) (MB Vital Statistics, Death Reg. #1899,002690.). She was buried on 16 Dec 1899 St.Norbert, Manitoba (St-N Cem.).

 William Vermette was born on 25 Jan 1861 St.Norbert, (Manitoba) (SN1, page 40, B-3.). He was baptized on 25 Jan 1861 St.Norbert, (Manitoba) (Ibid., B-3.). He married **Nancy Frobisher**, daughter of **Thomas Frobisher** and **Scholastique Pilon**, on 30 Nov 1900 (Ritchot), St.Norbert, Manitoba (MB Vital Statistics, Marriage Reg. #1900,001265.). He died on 20 Dec 1925 St.Vital, Manitoba, at age 64 (Ibid., Death Reg. No. 1925,052409.).

50.   **Virginie Vandal** was born on 26 Apr 1862 St.Norbert, (Manitoba) (SN1, page 57, B-9.). She was baptized on 27 Apr 1862 St.Norbert, (Manitoba) (Ibid.). She married **Napoleon Gregoire**, son of **Leon Gregoire** and **Olive Savoie,** on 4 Nov 1884 St.Jean-Baptiste, Montcalm, Manitoba (MM.) (MB Vital Statistics, Marriage Reg. #1884,001346.). She died on 6 Dec 1954 at age 92 (Rod Mac Quarrie, 28 Dec 2011.). She was buried in 1911 4-2-E, Provencher, Manitoba (1911 Canada, District 19, page 5, line 28.).

 Napoleon Gregoire was born on 16 Apr 1862 St.Cuthbert, Berthier, Quebec (Rod Mac Quarrie, 28 Dec 2011.). He was baptized on 17 Apr 1862 St.Cuthbert, Berthier, Quebec (Ibid.). He died on 28 Nov 1936 St.Jean-Baptiste, RM Montcalm, Manitoba, at age 74 (MB Vital Statistics, Death Reg. #1936,048427.).

51.   **Marie Rose Vandal** was born on 4 May 1863 (HBC-PN , Ste.Agathe, #265.). She was born on 18 Aug 1863 St.Norbert, (Manitoba) (SN1, page 83-84, B-22.). She was baptized on 18 Aug 1863 St.Norbert, (Manitoba) (Ibid.). She married **Adelard Breton**, son of **Gaspard Breton** and **Philomene Belanger,** on 7 Jan 1884 St.Jean-Baptiste, Montcalm, Manitoba (MB Vital Statistics, Marriage Reg. #1884,001785.). She died on 10 Mar 1900 Montcalm, Manitoba, at age 36 (Ibid., Death Reg. #1900,004124.).

 Adelard Breton was born on 9 May 1858 St.Vallier, Bellechasse, Quebec (Rod Mac Quarrie, 28 Dec 2011.). He was baptized on 10 May 1858 St.Vallier, Bellechasse, Quebec (Ibid.). He died on 19 Dec 1904 Winnipeg, Manitoba, at age 46 (MB Vital Statistics, Death Reg. #1904,001063.).

52.   **Frederic Vandal** was born on 22 Dec 1864 St.Norbert, (Manitoba) (SN1, page 115, B-51.). He was baptized on 22 Dec 1864 St.Norbert, (Manitoba) (Ibid.). He married **Marie Virginie Vermette**, daughter of **Louis Vermette** and **Julie Cadotte,** on 19 Jan 1886 St.Jean Baptiste, RM of Montcalm, Manitoba (MB Vital Statistics, Marriage Reg. #1886,001195.).

 Marie Virginie Vermette was born on 25 Feb 1866 St.Norbert, (Manitoba) (INB.). She was baptized on 25 Feb 1866 St.Norbert, (Manitoba) (Ibid.). She died after 9 Jan 1893.

Children of **Frederic Vandal** and **Marie Virginie Vermette** all born R.M. of Montcalm, Manitoba, were as follows:

 i.   Marie Antonia Vandal was born on 15 Apr 1887 (MB Vital Statistics, Birth Reg. #1887,003577.).

 ii.   Rosanna Vandal was born on 24 Jan 1888 (Ibid., Birth Reg. #1888,001773.). She died on 27 Jan 1889 Montcalm, Manitoba, at age 1 (Ibid., Death Reg. #1889,002814.). She was buried on 28 Jan 1889 St.Jean-Baptiste, Manitoba (Rod Mac Quarrie, 28 Dec 2011.).

 iii.   Marie Adele Victoria Vandal was born on 1 Nov 1889 (MB Vital Statistics, Birth Reg. #1889,002221.). She died on 24 Nov 1890 St.Jean-Baptiste, Manitoba, at age 1 (Rod Mac Quarrie, 28 Dec 2011.). She was buried on 26 Nov 1890 St.Jean-Baptiste, Manitoba (Ibid.).

 iv.   Joseph Louis Frederic David Vandal was born on 9 Jan 1893 (MB Vital Statistics, Birth Reg. #1893,004314.).

53.   **Eliza Vandal** was born on 6 Nov 1866 (SN1, page 88, B-60.). She was baptized on 11 Nov 1866 St.Norbert, (Manitoba) (Ibid.). She married **Martin Nault**, son of **Andre Nault** and **Anastasie Landry,** on 29 Jun 1891 St.Jean Baptiste, Montcalm, Manitoba (MM.) (MB Vital Statistics, Mar. Reg. #1893,001049.). She died on 15 Jul 1893 Montcalm, Manitoba, at age 26 (Ibid., Death Reg. #1893,001144.). She was buried on 17 Jul 1893 St.Jean-Baptiste, Manitoba (Rod Mac Quarrie, 28 Dec 2011.).

 Martin Nault was born on 6 May 1865 St.Vital, (Manitoba) (MBS, C-14931.) (SB-Rozyk, page 3, B-33.). He was baptized on 7 May 1865 St.Boniface, (Manitoba) (Ibid.). He and **Josephine Blondin** met circa 1884. He married **Sarah Gariepy**, daughter of **Joseph Gariepy** and **Cecilia Wilkie,** on 12 Nov 1895 Olga, Cavalier County, North Dakota (Olga, page 246, M-_.).

54. **Patrice Vandal** was born on 11 Oct 1872 Manitoba (1881 Canada, Film No. C-13282, District 184, Sub-district A, page 21, Household No. 88.) (Rod Mac Quarrie, 28 Dec 2011.). He married **Vitaline Anne Jerome**, daughter of **Martin Jerome** and **Leocadie Carriere,** on 1 Feb 1897 St.Pierre Jolys, Manitoba (MB Vital Statistics, Marriage Reg. #1897,002182.). He died after 1943.

   Vitaline Anne Jerome was born on 26 Jul 1874 St.Norbert, Manitoba (SN2, B-36.). She was baptized on 26 Jul 1874 St.Norbert, Manitoba (Ibid.). She died on 23 Nov 1943 St.Boniface, Manitoba, at age 69 (Rod Mac Quarrie, 28 Dec 2011.).

   Children of **Patrice Vandal** and **Vitaline Anne Jerome** were as follows:

   i. Joseph Vandal was born on 7 Nov 1897 R.M. of Montcalm, Manitoba (MB Vital Statistics, Birth Reg. #1897,003149.). He died on 7 Nov 1897 Montcalm, Manitoba (Ibid., Death Reg. #1897,002765.). He was buried on 8 Nov 1897 St.Jean-Baptiste, Manitoba (Rod Mac Quarrie, 28 Dec 2011.).

   ii. Marie Anne Ida Vandal was born on 8 Nov 1898 R.M. of Montcalm, Manitoba (MB Vital Statistics, Birth Reg. #1898,005835.).

   iii. Joseph Patrice Alexander Vandal was born on 6 May 1900 R.M. of Montcalm, Manitoba (Ibid., Birth Reg. #1900,001096.). He was baptized on 8 May 1900 St.Jean-Baptiste, Manitoba (Rod Mac Quarrie, 28 Dec 2011.). He died on 26 Mar 1901 St.Jean-Baptiste, Manitoba (Ibid.). He was buried on 27 Mar 1901 St.Jean-Baptiste, Manitoba (Ibid.).

   iv. Marie Louise Amanda Vandal was born on 17 Dec 1901 R.M. of Montcalm, Manitoba (MB Vital Statistics, Birth Reg. #1902,1617279.). She married Timothee Laforme on 20 Jan 1920 St.Jean Baptiste, R.M. of Montcalm, Manitoba (MM.) (MB Vital Statistics, Marriage Reg. #1920,004043.).

   v. Marie Ida Vandal was born on 26 Jul 1903 R.M. of Montcalm, Manitoba (Ibid., Birth Reg. #1903,002732.).

   vi. Joseph Edouard William Vandal was born on 4 Jan 1905 R.M. of Montcalm, Manitoba (Ibid., Birth Reg. #1905,002807.).

   vii. Marie Isabelle Marguerite Vandal was born on 7 Oct 1906 R.M. of Montcalm, Manitoba (Ibid., Birth Reg. #1906,001591.).

   viii. Eugene Vandal was born in Jun 1907 (1911 Canada, District 19, page 5, line 40.). He married Alphonsine St.Godard, daughter of Albert St.Godard and Marie-Anne Baril, on 28 Apr 1936 St.Jean Baptiste, Manitoba (MM.).

   ix. Joseph Maurice Felix Vandal was born on 12 Sep 1910 RM of Montcalm, Manitoba (1911 Canada, District 19, page 5, line 40.) (MB Vital Statistics, Birth Reg. #1910,003699.). He married Dorilda Richard on 17 Dec 1938 St.Jean Baptiste, Manitoba (MM.).

   x. Germain Vandal was born on 9 Aug 1912 St.Jean-Baptiste, Manitoba (Ibid.) (Rod Mac Quarrie, 28 Dec 2011.). He married Flora St.Godard, daughter of Albert St.Godard and Marie-Anne Baril, on 21 Oct 1940 St.Jean Baptiste, Manitoba (MM, page 1181.). He died on 13 Aug 2000 St.Boniface, Manitoba, at age 88 (Rod Mac Quarrie, 28 Dec 2011.).

55. **Alvina Vandal** was born on 8 Dec 1881 Manitoba (1901 Canada, #10, f-2, page 1, family 5, line 35-37.). She married **Joseph Turcotte**, son of **Joseph Turcotte** and **Sarah McMillan**, on 15 Oct 1900 (St.Jean Baptiste), Montcalm, Manitoba (MM.) (MB Vital Statistics, Marriage Reg. #1900,001102 (Montcalm).). She died on 12 Nov 1948 Kenora, Ontario, at age 66 (Rod Mac Quarrie, 28 Dec 2011.).

   Joseph Turcotte was born on 4 Nov 1872 Manitoba (1901 Canada, #10, f-2, page 1, family 5, line 35-37.). He died on 22 Apr 1955 Kenora, Ontario, at age 82 (Rod Mac Quarrie, 28 Dec 2011.).

56. **Marguerite Vandal** was born on 20 Mar 1878 St.Norbert, Manitoba (SN2, B-13.). She was baptized on 21 Mar 1878 St.Norbert, Manitoba (Ibid.). She married **Francois Xavier Desmarais**, son of **Severe Desmarais** and **Marguerite Desjardins,** on 19 Nov 1900 (Ritchot), St.Norbert, Manitoba (MM.) (MB Vital Statistics, Marr. Reg. #1900,001264.).

   Francois Xavier Desmarais was born in May 1878 (1911 Canada, #24, page 2, family 16, line 6-12.).

57. **Adeline Vandal** was born on 15 Jun 1880 (1901 Canada, St.Boniface, Family 17, Line 1-8, page 3.). She married **Joseph Gustave Bruce**, son of **Hermenegilde Bruce** and **Adele Lacerte,** on 7 Nov 1899 St.Norbert, Manitoba (MM.). She married **Joseph Alfred Sauve**, son of **Joseph Sauve** and **Eulalie Carriere,** on 8 Jul 1929 St.Boniface, Manitoba (RMSB, page 429.).

   Joseph Gustave Bruce was born on 22 Feb 1875 St.Norbert, Manitoba (SN2, B-10.). He was baptized on 28 Feb 1875 St.Norbert, Manitoba (Ibid.). He died on 1 Apr 1916 St.Boniface, Manitoba, at age 41 (MB Vital Statistics, Death Reg. #1916,00023031.).

   Joseph Alfred Sauve was born on 4 Apr 1882 Cartier, Manitoba (SN2, B-13.) (MB Vital Statistics, Birth Reg. #1882,001376.) (1901 Canada, #10, a-3, page 13, family 101, line 12-13.). He was baptized on 4 Apr 1882 St.Norbert, Manitoba (SN2, B-13.). He married **Helene Klyne**, daughter of **John Georges Klyne** and **Catherine Rosalie Perreault dit Morin,** on 26 Feb 1906 Woodridge, Manitoba (MM, page 640 & 1141.).

58. **Patrice Vandal** was born on 30 May 1876 St.Laurent, (Saskatchewan) (SL-SK, page 59, B-17.). He was baptized on 31 May 1876 St.Laurent-de-Grandin, (Saskatchewan) (Ibid.). He married **Marie (--?--)** before 1900 (1901 Canada, microfilm, T-6553, Devil Lake, page 3, Family 18, line 6-15.).

   Marie (--?--) was born on 21 Dec 1881 (Ibid.).

   Children of **Patrice Vandal** and **Marie (--?--)** are:

   i. Philomene Vandal was born on 24 Mar 1900 (Ibid.).

59. **Maria Vandal** was born on 5 Mar 1896 (Saskatchewan) (Ibid.) (SK Vital Statistics, Birth Reg. #8642.). She married **Edward Campbell**, son of **Archibald Campbell** and **Mary Ma-miskottash-ke-ne-ka,** circa 1916. She died in 1950 Big River Hospital, Saskatchewan (Rod Mac Quarrie, 28 Dec 2011.).

   Edward Campbell was born on 28 Jan 1881 Lily Plain, (Saskatchewan) (HBS, Volume 1339, C-14955.). He died circa 1932 Park Valley, Saskatchewan (Rod Mac Quarrie, 28 Dec 2011.).

60. **Marie Isabelle Vandal** was born on 26 Jan 1876 (Ibid.). She married **Joseph Norbert Berthelet**, son of **Norbert Berthelet** and **Rosalie Colombe,** on 6 Feb 1900 (Ste.Agathe), Morris, Manitoba (MM.) (MB Vital Statistics, Marriage Reg. #1900,001993.). She died in 1961 (Rod Mac Quarrie, 28 Dec 2011.).

Joseph Norbert Berthelet was born on 27 Sep 1875 (Rosemary Rozyk, 28 Jan 1999 report.) (INB, page 16.). He was baptized on 7 Oct 1875 Ste.Agathe, Manitoba (Rosemary Rozyk, 28 Jan 1999 report.) (INB, page 16.).

61. **Joseph Roger Vandal** was born on 5 Feb 1878 Qu'Appelle Mission, (Saskatchewan) (ArchiviaNet, C-15008.). He married **Emma Victoria Melanie Laplante**, daughter of **Patrice Laplante** and **Monique Grandbois,** on 22 Nov 1904 Aubigny, Manitoba (MM.).

Emma Victoria Melanie Laplante was born on 28 Jul 1885 Leroy, Pembina County, Dakota Territory (SJL-1, page 144, B-423.). She was baptized on 30 Jul 1885 St.Joseph, Leroy, Pembina County, Dakota Territory (Ibid.).

Children of **Joseph Roger Vandal** and **Emma Victoria Melanie Laplante** are as follows:
- i. Marie Regina Eva Vandal was born on 18 May 1907 RM of Montcalm, Manitoba (MB Vital Statistics, Birth Reg. #1907,005319.).
- ii. Marie Bernadette Eeaerina Vandal was born on 20 Jan 1909 Morris, Manitoba (Ibid., Birth Reg. #1909,013644.).
- iii. David Vandal was born circa 1913 (1916 Canada, District 9-20, page 30, line 8.).
- iv. Edward Vandal was born circa Feb 1916 (Ibid.).

62. **Marie Adeline Vandal** was born on 1 Feb 1880 Manitoba (Rod Mac Quarrie, 28 Dec 2011.). She married **Jean Baptiste Berthelet**, son of **Norbert Berthelet** and **Rosalie Colombe,** on 14 Jul 1903 St.Jean Baptiste, Manitoba (MM.).

Jean Baptiste Berthelet was born on 3 Oct 1880 Ste.Agathe, Manitoba (1881 Canada, District 184-D-1, page 5, household 20.) (1901 Canada, #10, g, page 9, family 81, line 33-39.).

63. **Marie Alvina Vandal** was born on 16 Jan 1882 R.M. of Montcalm, Manitoba (MB Vital Statistics, Birth Reg. #1882,001686.). She married **Joseph Alexandre Berthelet**, son of **Joseph Berthelet** and **Francoise Caron,** on 7 Jan 1903 St.Jean Baptiste, Manitoba (MM.).

Joseph Alexandre Berthelet was born on 6 Aug 1881 Ritchot, Manitoba (MB Vital Statistics, Birth Reg. #1881,13421475, Date: 21/08/1939.) (1901 Canada, #10, g-1, page 3, family 23, line 33-36.).

64. **Joseph Louis Vandal** was born on 9 Jul 1875 Manitoba (1901 Canada, District 10, E-5, page 5, line 12-14, family 39.). He married **Marie Alvina St.Germain**, daughter of **Pierre St.Germain** and **Emelie Gaudry,** on 10 Apr 1899 St.Norbert, Manitoba (MM.) (MB Vital Statistics, Mar. Reg. #1899,002212.).

Marie Alvina St.Germain was born on 7 Mar 1881 St.Norbert, Manitoba (SN2, B-9.). She was baptized on 8 Mar 1881 St.Norbert, Manitoba (Ibid.).

Children of **Joseph Louis Vandal** and **Marie Alvina St.Germain** are as follows:
- i. Marie Anna Victoria Vandal was born on 7 Feb 1900 R.M. of Montcalm, Manitoba (1901 Canada, District 10, E-5, page 5, line 12-14, family 39.) (MB Vital Statistics, Birth Reg. #1900,001061.). She married Augustin Hebert on 9 Nov 1920 Woodridge, Manitoba (MM.) (MB Vital Statistics, Marriage Reg. #1920,056198.).
- ii. Rose Emelie Vandal was born on 25 Nov 1901 RM of LaBroquerie, Manitoba (Ibid., Birth Reg. #1901,001381.).
- iii. Joseph Julien Vandal was born on 15 Jun 1904 R.M. of La Broquerie, Manitoba (Ibid., Birth Reg. #1904,003865.).
- iv. Theodore Vandal was born on 15 Jun 1904 RM of LaBroquerie, Manitoba (Ibid.).
- v. Florida Evangeline Vandal was born on 29 Aug 1907 RM of LaBroquerie, Manitoba (Ibid., Birth Reg. #1907,002098.).

65. **Julien Vandal** was born on 28 Oct 1878 Manitoba (1901 Canada, District 10, E-5, page 5, line 4-5, family 37.). He married **Cleophee Berthelet**, daughter of **Norbert Berthelet** and **Rosalie Colombe,** on 2 Jul 1900 St.Jean Baptiste, Manitoba (MM.). He died on 7 Aug 1936 St.Boniface, Manitoba, at age 57 (Rod Mac Quarrie, 28 Dec 2011.).

Cleophee Berthelet was born on 26 Jan 1885 Manitoba (1901 Canada, District 10, E-5, page 5, line 4-5, family 37.).

Children of **Julien Vandal** and **Cleophee Berthelet** were as follows:
- i. Jules Adelard Vandal was born on 24 Jun 1900 RM of LaBroquerie, Manitoba (MB Vital Statistics, Birth Reg. #1901,001385.). He was baptized on 25 Jun 1901 St.Jean-Baptiste, Manitoba (Rod Mac Quarrie, 28 Dec 2011.). He died on 17 Aug 1901 St.Jean-Baptiste, Manitoba, at age 1 (Ibid.). He was buried on 19 Aug 1901 St.Jean-Baptiste, Manitoba (Ibid.).
- ii. Arthur Vandal was born circa 1905. He married Leontine Huppe, daughter of Daniel Huppe and Julie Ducharme, on 19 Feb 1930 Woodridge, Manitoba (MM.) (MB Vital Statistics, Marriage Reg. #1930,062004.).
    Leontine Huppe was born on 24 Sep 1911 RM of LaBroquerie, Manitoba (Ibid., Birth Reg. #1911,002204.). She died on 3 Oct 2000 Seven Oaks Hospital, Winnipeg, Manitoba, at age 89 (Rod Mac Quarrie, 28 Dec 2011.).
- iii. Ethel Vandal was born on 2 May 1906 (1911 Canada, District 24, page 2, line 48.). She married Joseph Isidore Pierre Girouard, son of Isidore Girouard and Madeleine Durand, on 15 Apr 1925 Woodridge, Manitoba (MM, page 510.). She died on 27 Oct 1962 St.Boniface, Manitoba, at age 56 (1911 Canada, District 24, page 2, line 48.).
    Joseph Isidore Pierre Girouard was born on 22 Oct 1899 RM of LaBroquerie, Manitoba (MB Vital Statistics, Birth Reg. #1899,002166.). He died on 21 Jan 1960 St.Boniface, Manitoba, at age 60 (Rod Mac Quarrie, 28 Dec 2011.).
- iv. Marie Etiennette Vandal was born on 27 May 1907 RM of Montcalm, Manitoba (MB Vital Statistics, Birth Reg. #1907,005321.).
- v. Eveline Vandal was born circa 1915. She married William Sauve, son of Joseph Alfred Sauve and Helene Klyne, on 18 Sep 1933 Woodridge, Manitoba (MM.).
    William Sauve was born circa 1913 (1916 Canada, District 9-4, page 15, line 36.) (Ibid., District 9-5, page 16, line 6.).
- vi. Antoinette Vandal was born circa 1917. She married Alfred Augustin "Leo" Sauve, son of Joseph Alfred Sauve and Helene Klyne, on 13 Jan 1936 Woodridge, Manitoba (MM.).
    Alfred Augustin "Leo" Sauve was born on 20 May 1911 LaBroquerie, Manitoba (1911 Canada, District 24, page 3, line 2.) (MB Vital Statistics, Birth Reg. #1911,014631.).

66. **Marie Olivine Vandal** was born on 24 Sep 1885 R.M. of Montcalm, Manitoba (Ibid., Birth Reg. #1885,001051.). She married **William Sauve**, son of **Joseph Sauve** and **Eulalie Carriere,** on 25 Sep 1905 Woodridge, Manitoba (MM.). She married **Napoleon**

Hebert, son of **Jean Hebert** and **Marie Beaudin,** on 27 Nov 1916 (Woodridge, LaBroquerie, Manitoba (Ibid., page 582.) (MB Vital Statistics, Marriage Reg. #1916,064069.).

William Sauve was born on 16 Feb 1879 (Saskatchewan) (1901 Canada, #10, a-3, page 13, family 101, line 12-13.) (SL-SK, page 27, B-2.). He was baptized on 16 Feb 1879 St.Laurent-de-Grandin, (Saskatchewan) (Ibid.). He married **Marie Virginie Vandal,** daughter of **Joseph Vandal** and **Rosalie Rocheleau,** on 20 Jan 1902 St.Malo, DeSalaberry, Manitoba (MM.) (MB Vital Statistics, Marriage Reg. #1902,002210.). He died on 4 Oct 1915 LaBroquerie, Manitoba, at age 36 (Ibid., Death Reg. #1915,210216.).

Napoleon Hebert was born Joliette, Quebec (MM, page 582.).

67. **Marie Louise Eva Vandal** was born on 19 Mar 1892 R.M. of Montcalm, Manitoba (MB Vital Statistics, Birth Reg. #1892,005369.). She married **Alfred Nault,** son of **Andre Nault** and **Marie Harrison,** on 10 Jan 1910 Woodridge, Manitoba (MM, page 913.).

Alfred Nault was born on 1 Jan 1891 R.M. of La Broquerie, Manitoba (LFAN *La Famille Amable Nault* C.SsR. compiled by Charles Eugene Voyer, (Ste.Anne des Chenes, Manitoba, 15 Mar 1978).) (MB Vital Statistics, Birth Reg. #1891,004038.).

68. **Josephine Vandal** was born on 18 May 1860 Pembina, Pembina County, Dakota Territory (AP, page 231-232, B-159.). She was baptized on 19 May 1860 Assumption, Pembina, Pembina County, Dakota Territory (Ibid.). She married **Emile Wendt** before 1878. She died on 7 Jul 1947 Walhalla, Pembina County, North Dakota, at age 87 (Rod Mac Quarrie, 28 Dec 2011.) (ND Death Index.).

Emile Wendt was born circa 1847 Germany (SJL-D, page 20.). He died on 23 Mar 1910 Walhalla, Pembina County, North Dakota (Ibid.). He was buried on 25 Mar 1910 St.Boniface, Walhalla, Pembina County, North Dakota (Ibid.).

69. **Marie Octavie Vandal** was born on 5 Apr 1863 Dakota Territory (Rod Mac Quarrie, 28 Dec 2011.). She married **Francois Gervais,** son of **Francois Gervais** and **Josephte Bruyere,** circa 1878 Pembina County, Dakota Territory (1880 U. S. Census, Dakota Territory, National Archives of the United States, Washington D.C., page 14.). She died circa 18 Feb 1903 Walhalla, Pembina County, North Dakota (SJL-2, page 14.). She was buried on 18 Feb 1903 St.Boniface, Walhalla, Pembina County, North Dakota (SJL-D, page 14.).

Francois Gervais was born in Jan 1841 St.Francois Xavier, (Manitoba) (MBS, C-14928.). He married **Madeleine Gagnon,** daughter of **Joseph Gagnon** and **Marie Pelletier,** before 1867 (Ibid.). He married **Cecile Desmarais,** daughter of **Michel Desmarais** and **Josephte Rochon,** after 1903.

70. **Hormidas Vandal** was born circa 1868 Dakota Territory (Ancestry.com, 1880 Census.). He married **Marie Anne Catherine Houle,** daughter of **Louis Houle** and **Caroline Berthelet,** on 19 Jan 1892 St.Joseph, Leroy, Pembina County, North Dakota (SJL-2, M-1.).

Marie Anne Catherine Houle was baptized on 4 Apr 1875 Ste.Agathe, Manitoba (IBMS.).

Children of **Hormidas Vandal** and **Marie Anne Catherine Houle** were:

    i.   Joseph Vandal was born circa Jun 1894 (SJL-D, page 5.). He died on 26 Jul 1894 Leroy, Pembina County, North Dakota (Ibid.). He was buried on 28 Jul 1894 St.Joseph, Leroy, Pembina County, North Dakota (Ibid.).

71. **Clemence Vandal** was born on 16 Jun 1869 Dakota Territory (Rod Mac Quarrie, 28 Dec 2011.). She married **William Petit dit Thomas,** son of **Joseph Petit dit Thomas** and **Catherine Vivier,** in 1891 (1900C-ND, 214-214.). She died circa 26 Apr 1917 Walhalla, Pembina County, North Dakota (SJL-2.). She was buried on 26 Apr 1917 St.Boniface, Walhalla, Pembina County, Dakota Territory (Ibid.).

William Petit dit Thomas was born on 9 Apr 1870 Dakota Territory (Al Yerbury, Al Yerbury; 23 Dec 1995.) (1915-TMC 1915 Census of the Turtle Mountain Chippewa, North Dakota, National Archives of the United States, Washington D.C.). He married **Mary Jane Fournier,** daughter of **Norbert Fournier** and **Mary (--?--),** on 19 Mar 1917 (1936-TMC, page 119.) (1916-TMC 1916 Census of the Turtle Mountain Chippewa, North Dakota, National Archives of the United States, Washington D.C.). He married **Marie Anne Patenaude,** daughter of **Charles Patenaude** and **Marguerite Swain,** before 1926 (1930C ND, District 40-29, page 14A, line 27.).

72. **Joseph Vandal** was born on 8 Sep 1879 Pembina County, Dakota Territory (SJL-1, page 95, B-66.). He was baptized on 12 Oct 1879 St.Joseph, Leroy, Pembina County, Dakota Territory (Ibid.). He married **Mary (--?--)** in 1907 (1910C ND, District 60, page 28A, line 9.).

Mary (--?--) was born in 1890 (Ibid.). She died before 1920 (1920C-ND 1920 Federal Census North Dakota, National Archives of the United States, Washington D.C., District 40, page 7A, line 15.).

Children of **Joseph Vandal** and **Mary (--?--)** were as follows:

    i.   Herbert Joseph Vondal was born on 19 Oct 1907 (1910C ND, District 60, page 28A, line 9.) (Rod Mac Quarrie, 28 Dec 2011.). He married Mary Violet Dussiaume or Duciaume, daughter of Charles Dussiaume and Rosine White, circa 1929 (Ibid.). He died on 12 May 1980 Grand Forks County, North Dakota, at age 72 (SSDI.) (ND Death Index.).

         Mary Violet Dussiaume or Duciaume was born on 7 Feb 1915 (SSDI.) (ND Death Index.). She died on 21 Jan 1987 at age 71 (Ibid.) (SSDI.).

    ii. Elizabeth "Lizzie" Vandal was born circa Apr 1910 (1910C ND, District 60, page 28A, line 9.).

    iii. Edna Vondal was born on 26 Jul 1911 North Dakota (1920C-MTl, District 40, page 7A, line 15.) (Rod Mac Quarrie, 28 Dec 2011.). She married David Edward Goulet, son of David Goulet and Marie Pauline Lafferty, on 9 Oct 1928 Walhalla, Pembina County, North Dakota (Ibid.). She died on 4 Aug 1984 Grand Forks County, North Dakota, at age 73 (Ibid.).

         David Edward Goulet was born on 4 Feb 1909 Leyden, Pembina County, North Dakota (ND Death Index.). He died on 29 May 1972 Grand Forks, Grand Forks County, North Dakota, at age 63 (Ibid.) (SSDI.). He was buried on 1 Jun 1972 Walhalla, Pembina County, North Dakota (Rod Mac Quarrie, 28 Dec 2011.).

    iv. Mary J. Vandal was born circa 1913 (1920C-MTl, District 40, page 7A, line 15.).

    v.   Stella Vandal was born circa 1915 (Ibid.).

73. **Marie Rose Vandal** was born on 7 Aug 1872 North Dakota (1900C-ND, 238-238.) (Rod Mac Quarrie, 28 Dec 2011.). She married **Patrice Gourneau,** son of **Joseph Gourneau** and **Judith Delorme,** circa 1892. She married **William Laverdure,** son of **Joseph Laverdure** and **Marie Martel,** circa 1934 (Ibid.). She died on 2 Feb 1946 Rolette County, North Dakota, at age 73 (ND Death Index.).

Patrice Gourneau was born on 17 Jul 1857 Red Lake, Minnesota (AP, page 176, B-520.). He was baptized on 1 Sep 1857 Assumption, Pembina, Pembina County, Dakota Territory (Ibid.). He died on 29 Jan 1927 Belcourt, Rolette County, North Dakota, at age 69 (Rod Mac Quarrie, 28 Dec 2011.) (1927-TMC-ND 1927 Census of the Chippewa Indians of Turtle Mountain Agency, North Dakota, United States Indian Service Department of the Interior, Belcourt, North Dakota, superintendent James H. Hyde, 30 June 1927.).

William Laverdure was born on 12 Feb 1862 Dakota Territory (BIA-TM-BMD.). He was born circa Oct 1867 (NWHBSI, page 111.). He was born on 21 Jan 1868 North Dakota (1922 Turtle Mountain Chippewa Indian Census Roll, United States Indian Service Department of the Interior, Turtle Mountain Indian Agency, North Dakota, 30 June 1922 , Census No. 2388-2390.). He married **Mathilde Wilkie**, daughter of **Jean Baptiste Wilkie** and **Isabelle Patenaude**, in 1891 (1900C-ND, House 221, page 296B.). He died on 26 Apr 1948 Belcourt, Rolette County, North Dakota, at age 86 (BIA-TM-BMD.) (ND Death Index.).

74. Francois Joseph "Frank" Vandal was born on 11 Oct 1875 Walhalla, North Dakota (1900C-ND, 137-137.) (1914-TMC 1914 Census of the Turtle Mountain Chippewa, North Dakota, National Archives of the United States, Washington D.C.). He married **Marie McLeod**, daughter of **Pierre McLeod** and **Sara Emond,** in 1895 (1900C-ND, 137-137.). He and **Georgianna Houle** obtained a marriage license on 30 Dec 1930 (TM Star, 1 January 1931.). He died on 15 Oct 1962 Mercy Hospital, Williston, Williams County, North Dakota, at age 87 (Rod Mac Quarrie, 28 Dec 2011.) (ND Death Index.). He was buried on 19 Oct 1962 Trenton, Williams County, North Dakota (Rod Mac Quarrie, 28 Dec 2011.).

Marie McLeod was born on 6 Jan 1878 St.Francois Xavier, Manitoba (MB Vital Statistics, Birth Reg. #1884,002270.). She was baptized on 10 Jan 1878 St.Francois Xavier, Manitoba (SFXI-Kipling, B-1.). She died on 25 May 1930 Rolette County, North Dakota, at age 52 (ND Death Index.) (1930-TMC-ND 1930 Census of the Chippewa Indians of Turtle Mountain Agency, North Dakota, United States Indian Service Department of the Interior, Belcourt, North Dakota, 1 April 1930 , TMC Deaths.).

Children of **Francois Joseph "Frank" Vandal** and **Marie McLeod** were as follows:

    i.   Mary Louise Vandal was born on 22 May 1898 North Dakota (1900C-ND, 137-137.) (ND Death Index.) (1914-TMC.). She married Joseph Theodore Morin, son of Isidore Morin and Mathilde Zace, before 1917. She married Alphonse "Alfred" Falcon, son of Job Falcon and Marie Larocque, on 1 Nov 1919 Williston, Williams County, North Dakota (Rod Mac Quarrie, 27 Mar 2013.). She died on 20 Aug 1933 Trenton, Williams County, North Dakota, at age 35 (ND Death Index.) (1934-TMC Census of the Turtle Mountain Chippewa Indians, United States Indian Service Department of the Interior, Turtle Mountain Agency, North Dakota, 1 Apr 1934 , Census No. 1939-1950, page 164.). She was buried on 23 Aug 1933 Trenton, Williams County, North Dakota (Rod Mac Quarrie, 28 Dec 2011.).

        Joseph Theodore Morin was born on 7 Mar 1896 Belcourt, Rolette County, North Dakota (BIA-TM-BMD.). He died on 3 Apr 1919 North Dakota at age 23 (Ibid.). He was buried in Apr 1919 Catholic Cemetery, Belcourt, Rolette County, North Dakota (Ibid.).

        Alphonse "Alfred" Falcon was born on 27 Aug 1888 St.John, North Dakota (1889-TMC 1889 Census of Half Breed Chippewas residing in the vicinity of, but not on the Turtle Mountain Reservation, Dakota Territory, National Archives of the United States, Washington D.C., #181.) (ND Death Index.). He was baptized on 5 Sep 1888 St.John, Rolette County, North Dakota (Rod Mac Quarrie, 27 Mar 2013.). He and **Louise 'Elise' Levay** met before 1914. He married **Sarah Anne Leduc**, daughter of **Louis Leduc** and **Marie Celina Morin,** on 15 Nov 1915 Williston, Williams County, North Dakota (Ibid.). He married **Elvina Lillian Morin**, daughter of **Isidore Morin** and **Mathilde Zace**, circa 1936. He died on 8 Jul 1957 Trenton, Williams County, North Dakota, at age 68 (ND Death Index.). He was buried on 11 Jul 1957 Williston, Williams County, North Dakota (Rod Mac Quarrie, 27 Mar 2013.).

    ii. William Vandal was born on 6 Sep 1900 (1936-TMC, page 123.) (1914-TMC.). He married Josephine Morin, daughter of Isidore Morin and Mathilde Zace, circa 1929 (BIA-TM Bureau of Indian Affairs, Turtle Mountain Enrollment and Probate Papers, Belcourt, North Dakota, Frank (Francois) Laducer Probate.). He died on 4 Jul 1930 Rolette County, North Dakota, at age 29 (Rod Mac Quarrie, 28 Dec 2011.) (*1930-TMC-ND*, TMC Deaths.).

        Josephine Morin was born on 5 Apr 1911 Belcourt, Rolette County, North Dakota (BIA-TM-BMD, page 46.). She married **Francois 'Frank' Ladouceur**, son of **Joseph Alfred Ladouceur** and **Adele Brien,** on 1 Jun 1931 (BIA-TM, Frank (Francois) Laducer Probate.). She died on 13 Mar 1933 at age 21 (Ibid.).

    iii. Andrew Vandal was born circa 1902 (1906-TMC 1906 Census of the Turtle Mountain Chippewa, United States Indian Service Department of the Interior, Belcourt, North Dakota, 30 June 1906.). He died before 1908 (1936-TMC, page 123.).

    iv. Edmond "Edwin" Vandal was born on 6 Feb 1902 (*1906-TMC.*) (1914-TMC.). He married Ernestine Laroque, daughter of Olivier Larocque and Marie Rose St.Germain, on 17 Jan 1928 Williston, Williams County, North Dakota (Rod Mac Quarrie, 28 Dec 2011.). He died on 12 Nov 1986 Wolf Point, Roosevelt County, Montana, at age 84 (SSDI.) (MT Death.). He was buried on 15 Nov 1986 Greenwood Cemetery, Wolf Point, Roosevelt County, Montana (Rod Mac Quarrie, 28 Dec 2011.).

        Ernestine Laroque was born on 23 May 1902 (MT Death.) (SSDI.). She died on 3 Oct 1992 Wolf Point, Roosevelt County, Montana, at age 90 (MT Death.) (SSDI.).

    v. Daniel Vandal was born on 16 Oct 1905 (*1906-TMC.*). He died before 1909 (1936-TMC, page 123.).

    vi. Alfred Vandal was born on 25 Jul 1908 (Ibid.) (1909-TMC 1909 Census of the Turtle Mountain Chippewa, United States Indian Service Department of the Interior, Devils Lake, North Dakota, 30 June 1909.) (1914-TMC.). He married Palma Althea Kringen before 1932 (Rod Mac Quarrie, 28 Dec 2011.). He died on 23 Jul 1990 Trenton, Williams County, North Dakota, at age 81 (SSDI.) (ND Death Index.).

        Palma Althea Kringen was born on 10 Mar 1903 Marshall, South Dakota (Rod Mac Quarrie, 28 Dec 2011.). She died on 22 Mar 1983 San Diego, California, at age 80 (Ibid.).

    vii. Rosina Vandal was born on 29 Nov 1909 North Dakota (BIA-TM-BMD, page 31.) (1914-TMC.). She married Albert Theodore Falcon, son of Job Falcon and Marie Larocque, on 28 Apr 1925 St.John's Church, Trenton,

Williams County, North Dakota (Rod Mac Quarrie, 28 Dec 2011.). She died on 3 Apr 1992 Bismarck, North Dakota, at age 82 (ND Death Index.). She was buried on 7 Apr 1992 Trenton, Williams County, North Dakota (Rod Mac Quarrie, 28 Dec 2011.).

Albert Theodore Falcon was born on 17 Nov 1900 North Dakota (1910C ND, page 13B, family 53.) (ND Death Index.). He died on 31 May 1977 Trenton, Williams County, North Dakota, at age 76 (Ibid.). He was buried on 31 May 1977 Williston, Williams County, North Dakota (Rod Mac Quarrie, 28 Dec 2011.).

viii.   Ernest Vandal was born on 22 Aug 1911 (1936-TMC, page 123.) (BIA-TM-BMD, page 49.) (1914-TMC.). He married Agnes Philomene Lavallee, daughter of Antoine Lavallee and Marie Louise Morin, before 1934. He died on 9 Oct 1981 Williams County, North Dakota, at age 70 (ND Death Index.) (SSDI.).

Agnes Philomene Lavallee was born on 1 Oct 1906 (1936-TMC, page 148.) (*1937-TMC*.). She married **Kenneth Olson** before 1928. She married **Phillip Baker** before 1933.

ix.   Mary Catherine Vandal was born on 8 Jul 1914 (1936-TMC, page 123.) (*1937-TMC*, page 202, Census No. 2416.) (1914-TMC.). She married Charles Grady before 1933 (*1937-TMC*, page 202, Census No. 2416.). She died on 29 Apr 1970 Ward County, North Dakota, at age 55 (ND Death Index.).

Charles Grady was born on 16 Aug 1895. He died on 22 Apr 1973 Mountrail County, North Dakota, at age 77 (Ibid.) (SSDI.).

x.   Veronica Vandal was born on 12 Jul 1916 (1936-TMC, page 123.) (*1921 TMC*.). She and Alder Olson met before 1933 (*1937-TMC*, page 506, Census No. 5922-5930.). She married Robert Andrew Granbois, son of Michael Grandbois and Mary Ann Brien, before 1936. She died on 3 Oct 1975 Williston, Williams County, North Dakota, at age 59 (ND Death Index.).

Robert Andrew Granbois was born on 17 May 1911 Poplar, Roosevelt County, Montana (Mary McClammy.) (BIA-TM-BMD, page 52.). He died on 29 Aug 1980 Yellowstone County, Montana, at age 69 (MT Death.) (SSDI.). He was buried circa Aug 1980 Poplar, Roosevelt County, Montana (MT Death.).

xi.   Madeline Vandal was born on 5 May 1921 (*1937-TMC*, page 506, Census No. 5922-5930.).

Georgianna Houle was born on 17 Sep 1911 (1936-TMC, page 118.) (BIA-TM-BMD, page 50.).

Children of **Francois Joseph "Frank" Vandal** and **Georgianna Houle** are as follows:

i.   Rose Vandal was born on 25 Mar 1932 (*1937-TMC*, page 506, Census No. 5922-5930.).
ii.   Albert Vandal was born on 6 Aug 1933 (Ibid.).
iii.   Leonard J. Vandal was born on 2 Apr 1935 (Ibid.).
iv.   Victoria Mary Vandal was born on 17 Mar 1937 Rolette County, North Dakota (*1937-TMC*.).
v.   Phillip Vandal was born on 20 Dec 1938 Rolette County, North Dakota (Ibid.).

75. Angelique Vandal was born on 15 Apr 1878 North Dakota (1900C-ND, 260-260.) (Rod Mac Quarrie, 28 Dec 2011.). She and **Edward Norman Petit dit Thomas** met in 1904. She married **Pierre Herman**, son of **Edouard Herman** and **Marguerite Dauphinais**, before 1906 (1936-TMC, page 115.). She died on 25 May 1923 Belcourt, Rolette County, North Dakota, at age 45 (*1924-TMC-ND*, Census No. 1837-1844.).

Edward Norman Petit dit Thomas was born on 7 Oct 1882 Olga, Cavalier County, North Dakota (Olga, page 4, B-5.). He was baptized on 8 Oct 1882 Olga, Cavalier County, North Dakota (Ibid.). He married **Helene Nicholas**, daughter of **Antoine Nicholas** and **Eliza Villeneuve**, before 1912 (*St.Ann's Centennial, 100 Years of Faith - 1885-1985*; Belcourt, North Dakota: St.Ann Parish, 1985), page 479.). He died on 29 Mar 1965 Rolette County, North Dakota, at age 82 (BIA-TM-BMD.) (ND Death Index.). He was buried on 29 Mar 1965 St.Ann's Cemetery, Belcourt, Rolette County, North Dakota (TM Star, page 6.).

Pierre Herman was born between 1859 and 1860 (1936-TMC, page 115.). He married **Nancy Lattergrass**, daughter of **Jean Baptiste Lattergrass** and **Nancy Daniel,** on 5 May 1885 St.Claude Mission, St.John, Rolette County, North Daktoa (Dominique Ritchot Research,, 26 Jan 2006.). He married **Sarah Morin** before 30 Jun 1924 (*1924-TMC-ND*, Census No. 1837-1844.). He died on 18 Apr 1932 Belcourt, Rolette County, North Dakota (TM Star, 21 Apr 1932, page 1.).

76. Celina Vandal was born on 30 Nov 1880 North Dakota (1900C-ND, 363-363.) (1916-TMC.) (1918-TMC.). She married **Albert Wilkie**, son of **Jean Baptiste Wilkie** and **Sarah Gourneau**, in 1899 (1900C-ND, 363-363.). She died between 1918 and 1919.

Albert Wilkie was born on 23 Mar 1879 (SJL-1, page 93, B-51.). He was baptized on 9 Apr 1879 St.Joseph, Leroy, Pembina County, Dakota Territory (Ibid.). He married **Elizabeth "Betsy" Allard**, daughter of **Elzear Allard** and **Julia Morin**, circa 1920 (TM Star, 5 Oct 1933.). He died on 23 Feb 1936 Rolette County, North Dakota, at age 56 (ND Death Index.) (1936-TMC Census of the Turtle Mountain Chippewa Indians, United States Indian Service Department of the Interior, Turtle Mountain Agency, North Dakota, 1 Apr 1936.).

77. Marie Henriette Vandal was born on 6 Jun 1883 Leroy, Pembina County, Dakota Territory (SJL-1, page 126, B-278.). She was baptized on 22 Jun 1883 St.Joseph, Leroy, Pembina County, Dakota Territory (Ibid.). She married **Joseph Robert Azure**, son of **Jean Baptiste Azure** and **Rosalie Plante,** on 17 Nov 1902 Belcourt, Rolette County, North Dakota (Rod Mac Quarrie, 28 Dec 2011.). She died on 8 Sep 1953 Wolf Point, Montana, at age 70 (Brenda Snider Research, 11 Dec 2011.) (Rod Mac Quarrie, 28 Dec 2011.).

Joseph Robert Azure was born on 18 Feb 1884 Leroy, Pembina County, Dakota Territory (SJL-1, page 132, B-327.). He was baptized on 19 Feb 1884 St.Joseph, Leroy, Pembina County, Dakota Territory (Ibid.). He died on 3 Aug 1966 Roosevelt County, Montana, at age 82 (MT Death.) (SSDI.).

78. John Baptiste Vandal was born on 11 Sep 1885 (1884-TMC 1884-1886 Census of Half Breed Chippewas of Turtle Mountain, Dakota Territory, National Archives of the United States, Washington D.C.) (*1919 Turtle Mountain*, Census No. 3153-3155.). He married **Eliza Jane Gourneau**, daughter of **Joseph Gourneau Jr.** and **Elise McLeod**, before 1913 St.Ann's, Belcourt, Rolette County, North Dakota (1936-TMC, page 123.) (*St.Ann's Centennial*, page 544.). He died on 22 Feb 1976 Belcourt, Rolette County, North Dakota, at age 90 (Ibid.) (ND Death Index.).

Eliza Jane Gourneau was born on 3 Jun 1892 Rolette County, North Dakota (*St.Ann's Centennial*, page 544.) (ND Death Index.) (*1919 Turtle Mountain*, Census No. 3153-3155.). She died on 9 Aug 1949 Rolette County, North Dakota, at age 57 (ND Death Index.).

Children of **John Baptiste Vandal** and **Eliza Jane Gourneau** were as follows:

    i.   Joseph Michael Vandal was born on 30 Dec 1913 (1936-TMC, page 123.) (*St.Ann's Centennial*, page 544.) (*1937-TMC*, page 508, Census No. 5952-5954.) (*1919 Turtle Mountain*, Census No. 3153-3155.). He married Florence Martin, daughter of Frederick Raphael Martin and Mary Ernestine Wilkie, before 1936 (*St.Ann's Centennial*, page 544.). He married Joyce Grisqra before 1950 (Ibid.). He died on 16 Dec 1985 Crosby, Crow Wing County, Minnesota, at age 71 (Rod Mac Quarrie, 28 Dec 2011.) (MN Death Index.).

         Florence Martin was born on 27 Feb 1916 Rolette County, North Dakota (1936-TMC, page 168.) (*St.Ann's Centennial*, page 544.) (1932-TMC Census of the Turtle Mountain Chippewa Indians, United States Indian Service Department of the Interior, Turtle Mountain Agency, North Dakota, 1 Apr 1932 , page 309, Census No. 3424-3429.).

    ii.   Rita Frances Vandal was born on 17 May 1916 (1936-TMC, page 124.) (*St.Ann's Centennial*, page 544.) (*1937-TMC*, page 507, Census No. 5931-5936.). She married Edward Ferris (*St.Ann's Centennial*, page 544.). She died on 16 Dec 2002 West Hills, Los Angeles County, California, at age 86 (SSDI.) (TM Star, 23 Dec 2002, page 2.). She was buried on 19 Dec 2002 San Fernando Mission Cemetery, Mission Hills, California (Ibid.).

         Edward Ferris was born on 30 Dec 1913 (SSDI.). He died in Dec 1981 West Hills, Los Angeles County, California (Ibid.).

    iii.   Marie Cecelia Vandal was born on 29 Sep 1919 (*St.Ann's Centennial*, page 544.) (SSDI.) (*1937-TMC*, page 507, Census No. 5931-5936.). She married Leroy Martin, son of Patrice Martin and Josephine Ouellette, on 15 Mar 1944 Salem, Oregon (*St.Ann's Centennial*, page 544.) (Rod Mac Quarrie, 28 Dec 2011.). She died on 24 Dec 2007 Belcourt, Rolette County, North Dakota, at age 88 (SSDI.) (ND Death Index.).

         Leroy Martin was born on 9 Sep 1917 (*St.Ann's Centennial*, page 544.) (SSDI.). He died on 24 Oct 2006 Belcourt, Rolette County, North Dakota, at age 89 (Ibid.).

    iv.   Esther Beulah Vandal was born on 27 Oct 1927 (1936-TMC, page 124.) (*St.Ann's Centennial*, page 544.) (*1937-TMC*, page 507, Census No. 5931-5936.). She married Roy Allard, son of Joseph R. Allard and Justine Wilkie (*St.Ann's Centennial*, page 544.).

         Roy Allard was born in 1925 North Dakota (*1937-TMC*, page 6, Census No. 60-66.).

    v.   Marie Gertrude Vandal was born on 3 Jun 1933 (1936-TMC, page 124.) (*St.Ann's Centennial*, page 544.) (*1937-TMC*, page 507, Census No. 5931-5936.). She married Cliff Trombley (*St.Ann's Centennial*, page 544.). She married George Marengo (Rod Mac Quarrie, 28 Dec 2011.).

79. Patrice Vandal was born on 3 Aug 1887 North Dakota (ND Death Index.). He married **Marie Clara Monette**, daughter of **Napoleon Gregoire Monet dit Belhumeur** and **Philomene Wilkie**, in 1909 (Rod Mac Quarrie, 28 Dec 2011.). He died on 27 Nov 1920 Belcourt, Rolette, North Dakota, at age 33 (*St.Ann's Centennial*, page 545.) (ND Death Index.).

Marie Clara Monette was born on 22 Aug 1887 Olga, Cavalier County, North Dakota (Olga, page 127, B-34.). She was baptized on 22 Aug 1887 Olga, Cavalier County, North Dakota (Ibid.). She married **John Baptist Landry**, son of **Maxime Landry** and **Marguerite Pelletier,** before 1922 (1936-TMC, page 142.). She died on 13 Feb 1972 Rolette County, North Dakota, at age 84 (ND Death Index.).

Children of **Patrice Vandal** and **Marie Clara Monette** were as follows:

    i.   Margaret Vandal was born on 11 Jun 1913 (1936-TMC, page 123.) (1915-TMC.). She married Fred Martin Martell, son of Francois Martel and Rosalie Lizotte, on 10 May 1932 St.John, Rolette County, North Dakota (TM Star, 12 May 1932, page 5.).

         Fred Martin Martell was born on 7 Apr 1910 (1936-TMC, page 166.) (BIA-TM-BMD, page 35.).

    ii.   Josephine Vandal was born on 17 Mar 1915 (1936-TMC, page 123.) (*1937-TMC*, page 182, Census No. 2167.). She married Raymond Foster before 1937 (Ibid.).

    iii.   Marie Louise Vandal was born on 13 Feb 1918 (1936-TMC, page 123.) (1923-TMC-ND 1923 Census of the Chippewa Indians of Turtle Mountain Agency, North Dakota, United States Indian Service Department of the Interior, Belcourt, North Dakota, superintendent H. J. McQuigg, 30 June 1923.).

    iv.   Mary Petroline Vandal was born on 3 Jun 1920 (1936-TMC, page 123.) (*1923-TMC-ND.*) (*1937-TMC.*). She married Patrick Laverdure, son of Louis Grant and Mary Jane Delorme, on 31 Jan 1941 Belcourt, Rolette County, North Dakota (Rod Mac Quarrie, 28 Dec 2011.). She died on 21 May 1996 Trinity Medical Center, Minot, Ward County, North Dakota, at age 75 (ND Death Index.).

         Patrick Laverdure was born on 29 Apr 1918 Rolette County, North Dakota (1936-TMC, page 107.) (ND Death Index.) (*1934-TMC.*). He died on 23 Jan 1964 Rolette County, North Dakota, at age 45 (ND Death Index.).

80. Joseph Vandal was born on 13 Mar 1891 (Ibid.) (1914-TMC.). He married **Agatha Rose Lafontaine**, daughter of **Octave Lafontaine** and **Marie Josephine Wilkie,** on 21 Jul 1914 (1936-TMC, page 123.) (1914-TMC.) (1915-TMC.). He died on 18 May 1952 Ward County, North Dakota, at age 61 (ND Death Index.).

Agatha Rose Lafontaine was born on 8 Jan 1896 North Dakota (1900C-ND, 93-93.) (1914-TMC.). She died on 14 Nov 1955 Belcourt, Rolette County, North Dakota, at age 59 (*St.Ann's Centennial*, page 544.) (Turtle Mountain Reservation Probate Record, #1585, Branch of Trust & Natural Resources.) (ND Death Index.).

Children of **Joseph Vandal** and **Agatha Rose Lafontaine** were as follows:

    i.   Louis Patrick Vandal was born on 19 May 1917 North Dakota (1918-TMC.) (ND Death Index.). He and Agnes May Olson met before 1935. He married Mary Celina Azure, daughter of John Baptiste Azure No. 3 and Mary Jane Dauphinais, before 1941. He died on 27 Oct 1986 Belcourt, Rolette County, North Dakota, at age 69 (Ibid.) (SSDI.).

         Agnes May Olson was born on 16 Apr 1917 (1933-TMC Census of the Turtle Mountain Chippewa Indians, United States Indian Service Department of the Interior, Turtle Mountain Agency, North Dakota, 1 Apr 1933 , Census No. 4202-4206.).

Mary Celina Azure was born on 14 Nov 1914 Rolette County, North Dakota (1936-TMC, page 27.) (1916-TMC, Census No. 354-357.). She died on 19 May 1999 Dunseith, Rolette County, North Dakota, at age 84 (SSDI.) (ND Death Index.).

ii. Mary May Vandal was born on 9 Oct 1920 (1928-TMC-ND 1928 Census of the Chippewa Indians of Turtle Mountain Agency, North Dakota, United States Indian Service Department of the Interior, Belcourt, North Dakota, superintendent H. J. McQuigg, 30 June 1928.) (*1937-TMC*, page 507, Census No. 5938-5943.).

iii. Raymond Joseph Vandal was born on 10 Jun 1922 (*1928-TMC-ND.*) (*1937-TMC*, page 507, Census No. 5938-5943.) (ND Death Index.). He died on 5 Aug 1981 Rolette County, North Dakota, at age 59 (Ibid.).

iv. John Ernest Vandal was born on 5 Oct 1924 (1936-TMC, page 123.) (1924-25-TMC Birth-Deaths of the Turtle Mountain Chippewa Indians, United States Indian Service Department of the Interior, Turtle Mountain Agency, North Dakota, F. J. Scott Superintendent, 1 July 1924-30 June 1925.).

v. Lorene Vandal was born on 29 Apr 1929 (*1937-TMC*, page 507, Census No. 5938-5943.). She married Kenneth Reichenberger on 14 Feb 1945 Roosevelt County, Montana (Rod Mac Quarrie, 28 Dec 2011.).

Kenneth Reichenberger was born in 1923 (Ibid.).

81. St.Ann Vandal was born on 7 Sep 1893 North Dakota (1900C-ND, 260-260.) (1914-TMC.) (1915-TMC.) (Rod Mac Quarrie, 28 Dec 2011.). She married Alcide Nicolas St.Arnaud, son of Jean Baptiste St.Arnaud and Marguerite Laderoute, on 3 Dec 1912 (1936-TMC, page 113.) (1913-TMC 1913 Census of the Turtle Mountain Chippewa, North Dakota, National Archives of the United States, Washington D.C.). She died on 9 Feb 1923 Rolette County, North Dakota, at age 29 (ND Death Index.).

Alcide Nicolas St.Arnaud was born on 24 Aug 1874 St.Boniface, Manitoba (SB-Rozyk, page 27, B-55.). He was baptized on 24 Aug 1874 St.Boniface, Manitoba (Ibid.). He married Mary Jane Belgarde, daughter of Louis Belgarde and Louise Delorme, before 1930. He died on 22 Apr 1959 Rolette County, North Dakota, at age 84 (ND Death Index.).

82. Mary Jane Vandal was born on 27 Jun 1897 North Dakota (1900C-ND, 260-260.) (ND Death Index.). She married John Baptiste Decouteau, son of Daniel Decouteau and Judith Smith, on 16 Nov 1914 Belcourt, Rolette County, North Dakota (1936-TMC, page 66.) (Rod Mac Quarrie, 28 Dec 2011.). She died on 8 Nov 1974 McLean County, North Dakota, at age 77 (ND Death Index.).

John Baptiste Decouteau was born on 19 Apr 1893 North Dakota (1900C-ND, House 280, page 305A.) (1893-TMC 1893 Census of Half Breed Chippewas of Turtle Mountain, Dakota Territory, National Archives of the United States, Washington D.C., page 12, Census No. 306-309.) (SSDI.). He died on 7 May 1965 Belcourt, Rolette County, North Dakota, at age 72 (Ibid.) (ND Death Index.). He was buried on 11 May 1965 St.Ann's Cemetery, Belcourt, Rolette County, North Dakota (TM Star, May 13, 1965, page 5.).

83. Ernestine Vandal was born circa 1881. She married Joseph Frederick Ouellette, son of Pierre Ouellette and Marguerite Grandbois, on 11 Aug 1901 Walhalla, North Dakota (Rod Mac Quarrie, 28 Dec 2011.).

Joseph Frederick Ouellette was born on 6 Oct 1875 Ste.Agathe, Manitoba (INB, page 137.). He was baptized on 8 Oct 1875 Ste.Agathe, Manitoba (Ibid.).

84. Sara Vandal was born on 3 Apr 1884 Walhalla, North Dakota (Olga, page 42, B-12.). She was baptized on 4 May 1884 (Walhalla), Olga, Cavalier County, North Dakota (Ibid.). She married Daniel Dauphinais, son of Pierre Dauphinais and Isabel Petit dit Thomas, on 8 Jan 1899 St.Joseph, Leroy, Pembina County, North Dakota (SJL-2, M-1.). She was buried on 10 Nov 1918 St.Boniface, Walhalla, Pembina County, North Dakota (W-D.).

Daniel Dauphinais was born on 30 Apr 1876 (SJL-1, page 71, B-15.). He was baptized on 1 May 1876 St.Joseph, Leroy, Pembina County, Dakota Territory (Ibid.).

85. Alexandre Vandal was born on 30 Mar 1887 North Dakota (1900C ND, District 45, page 15A, family 1, line 1-4.) (Ancestry.com, WWI Draft Registration.). He married Angelique Langer, daughter of Francois Xavier Langer and Angelique Dauphinais, circa 1906 (1910C ND, District 65, page 6A, line 52.). He married Delia Laferte, daughter of Jean Laferte and Marie Mathilde Morin, before 1917. He died on 7 Dec 1971 Pembina County, North Dakota, at age 84 (ND Death Index.).

Angelique Langer was born in Jan 1890 (1900C ND, District 45, page 2B, line 77.). She died on 17 Jun 1915 Olga, Cavalier County, North Dakota, at age 25 (Olga, S-429, page 13.). She was buried on 19 Jun 1915 Olga, Cavalier County, North Dakota (Ibid.).

Children of Alexandre Vandal and Angelique Langer were as follows:

i. Mary E. Vandal was born on 28 Jan 1911 North Dakota (1920C-MTI, District 101, page 2A, line 6.) (1940C ND 1940 North Dakota, Sixteenth Census of the United States, National Archives of the United States, Washington, D.C., page 4B, house 69.) (SSDI.). She married Paul Arthur Goulet, son of David Goulet and Marie Pauline Lafferty, before 1930. She died on 13 Dec 1997 Walhalla, Pembina County, North Dakota, at age 86 (Ibid.).

Paul Arthur Goulet was born on 2 Feb 1906 (Ibid.). He died on 5 Jan 1972 Walhalla, Pembina County, North Dakota, at age 65 (ND Death Index.) (SSDI.).

ii. Patrice Vandal was born on 21 Mar 1913 Olga, Cavalier County, North Dakota (Olga, page 55, B-_.). He was baptized on 3 Apr 1913 Olga, Cavalier County, North Dakota (Ibid.). He died on 3 Oct 1990 Pembina County, North Dakota, at age 77 (ND Death Index.).

iii. Charles August Vandal was born on 12 Jun 1915 Olga, Cavalier County, North Dakota (Olga, page 13, S-428.). He died on 14 Jun 1915 Olga, Cavalier County, North Dakota (Ibid.). He was buried on 15 Jun 1915 Olga, Cavalier County, North Dakota (Ibid.).

Delia Laferte was born on 21 Oct 1896 (SJL-2, page 95, B-30.) (ND Death Index.). She was baptized on 22 Nov 1896 St.Joseph, Leroy, Pembina County, North Dakota (SJL-2, page 95, B-30.). She died on 29 Jul 1964 Pembina County, North Dakota, at age 67 (ND Death Index.).

Children of Alexandre Vandal and Delia Laferte are as follows:

i. Amelia Rose Vandal was born circa 1917 (1920C-MTI, District 101, page 2A, line 6.).

ii. Gilbert Vandal was born circa Sep 1918 (W-D.). He was buried on 17 Jan 1920 St.Boniface, Walhalla, Pembina County, North Dakota (Ibid.).

iii. Mable Vondal was born circa 1922 (1930C ND, District 34-34, page 1B, line 51.).

iv. Ulysius Vondal was born circa 1924 (Ibid.).

    v.   Leo Vondal was born circa 1926 (Ibid.).

    vi.   Leone or Helen Vondal was born circa Dec 1929 (Ibid.).

    vii.   Loretta Vondal was born circa 1932 (1940C ND, District 34-35, page 1A.).

    viii.   Alex Vondal was born circa 1936 (Ibid.).

86. Peter Vandal was born on 27 Sep 1890 Walhalla, North Dakota (1920C-MTl, District 101, page 1A-B, family 9, line 49-54.) (Ancestry.com, WWI Draft Registration Card.). He married **Delia Houle,** daughter of **Damase Houle** and **Marie Virginie Charette,** before 1913. He died on 18 Dec 1957 Pembina County, North Dakota, at age 67 (ND Death Index.).

  Delia Houle was born on 12 Oct 1894 Olga, Cavalier County, North Dakota (Ibid.). She was born on 12 Oct 1894 St.Joseph, Walhalla, North Dakota (1917 RB Tentative Roll of Rocky Boy Indians, 30 May 1917, Copied by Verne Dusenbery, 15 Apr 1953, Rocky Boy Agency, Montana, #77.) (Olga, page 237, B-_.). She was baptized on 23 Oct 1894 Olga, Cavalier County, North Dakota (Ibid.). She died on 6 Feb 1963 Pembina County, North Dakota, at age 68 (ND Death Index.).

Children of **Peter Vandal** and **Delia Houle** were as follows:

    i.   Joseph Alphonse Vondal was born on 8 Sep 1913 Walhalla, Pembina County, North Dakota (1920C-MTl, District 101, page 1A-B, family 9, line 49-54.) (ND Death Index.). He died on 12 Jul 1991 Walhalla, Pembina County, North Dakota, at age 77 (Ibid.).

    ii.   Marie Clara "Irene" Vandal was born on 20 Jul 1914 Olga, Cavalier County, North Dakota (Olga, page 69, B-_.). She was baptized on 1 Aug 1914 Olga, Cavalier County, North Dakota (Ibid.). She was born on 15 Jul 1915 Olga, Calavier County, North Dakota (Rod Mac Quarrie, 28 Dec 2011.). She married George Leon Goodrie on 12 Nov 1934 Walhalla, Pembina County, North Dakota (Ibid.). She died on 14 Mar 1975 Sidney, Richland County, Montana, at age 60 (Ibid.).

    iii.   Peter Albert Vandal was born on 15 Oct 1916 Olga, Cavalier County, North Dakota (1920C-MTl, District 101, page 1A-B, family 9, line 49-54.) (ND Death Index.). He died on 28 Apr 1994 Grand Forks County, North Dakota, at age 77 (Ibid.).

    iv.   Lawrence Vandal was born circa Oct 1918 North Dakota (1920C-MTl, District 101, page 1A-B, family 9, line 49-54.).

    v.   Wilfred Vondal was born circa 1921 (1940C ND, District 10-38, page 4B.).

    vi.   Agnes Mae Vondal was born on 20 May 1924 Walhalla, Pembina County, North Dakota (Ibid.) (ND Death Index.). She married Harvey Martin Skaro in 1950 Inkster, North Dakota (Rod Mac Quarrie, 28 Dec 2011.). She died on 4 Feb 1998 Sheldon, Ransom County, North Dakota, at age 73 (ND Death Index.).

      Harvey Martin Skaro was born on 6 Jan 1923 North Dakota (Ibid.). He died on 9 Feb 1963 Cass County, North Dakota, at age 40 (Ibid.).

    vii.   Leonard J. Vondal was born on 1 Feb 1928 Olga, Cavalier County, North Dakota (1940C ND, District 10-38, page 4B.) (ND Death Index.). He died on 1 Nov 2004 Mercer County, North Dakota, at age 76 (SSDI.) (ND Death Index.).

    viii.   Charles Vondal was born circa 1931 (1940C ND, District 10-38, page 4B.).

    ix.   Robert Vandal was born circa 1935 (Ibid.).

87. Veronique Vandal was born in Jul 1874 Edmonton, (Alberta) (HBSI.) (ArchiviaNet.). She was baptized on 25 Aug 1874 St.Albert, (Alberta) (Rod Mac Quarrie, 28 Dec 2011.). She married **Emilien Dumas or Dumais,** son of **Charles Dumas or Dumais** and **Marie St.Arnaud,** on 1 Oct 1895 Batoche, (Saskatchewan) (HBSI.) (BSAP, page 128, M-6.).

  Emilien Dumas or Dumais was born in 1874 Edmonton, (Alberta) (HBSI.) (ArchiviaNet.).

88. Maggie Vandal was born on 10 Mar 1882 (1901 Canada, #202, g, page 1-2, family 11, line 46-49, 1-9.). She married **Raoul Leontz Moser** before 1908 (Rod Mac Quarrie, 28 Dec 2011.). She died on 28 Aug 1968 Leduc, Alberta, at age 86 (Ibid.).

  Raoul Leontz Moser was born on 28 Jan 1872 Magny En Vixen, France (Ibid.). He died on 6 Aug 1963 Leduc, Alberta, at age 91 (Ibid.).

89. Marie Rose Vandal was born on 24 Sep 1877 Batoche, (Saskatchewan) (SL-SK, page 4, B-45.). She was baptized on 7 Oct 1877 St.Laurent-de-Grandin, (Saskatchewan) (Ibid.). She married **Clovis Nogier,** son of **Joseph Nogier** and **Celine Dumais,** on 24 Apr 1899 Batoche, (Saskatchewan) (Denney.).

  Clovis Nogier was born on 8 Aug 1876 (1901 Canada, Fish Creek, page 1, Family 4, Line 10-12.).

90. Rose Germaine Vandal was born on 8 Feb 1881 Batoche, (Saskatchewan) (HBSI.) (SL-SK, page 48, B-3.) (ArchiviaNet.). She was baptized on 10 Feb 1881 St.Laurent-de-Grandin, (Saskatchewan) (SL-SK, page 48, B-3.). She married **Alexandre Lavallee,** son of **Charles Martin Lavallee** and **Marguerite Courchene,** on 27 Sep 1897 St.Vital, Battleford, (Saskatchewan) (SV, M-3.).

  Alexandre Lavallee was born on 15 Mar 1874 St.Francois Xavier, Manitoba (SFXI-Kipling, B-14.). He was baptized on 15 Mar 1874 St.Francois Xavier, Manitoba (Ibid.) (INB, page 103.).

91. Marie Emelie Vandal was born on 27 May 1877 St.Norbert, Manitoba (SN2, B-19.). She was baptized on 28 May 1877 St.Norbert, Manitoba (Ibid.). She married **Joseph Ross,** son of **William Ross** and **Marie Lefort,** circa 1903.

  Joseph Ross was born on 22 Dec 1872 St.Francois Xavier, Manitoba (SFXI-Kipling, B-81.) (INB, page 159.). He was baptized on 24 Dec 1872 St.Francois Xavier, Manitoba (SFXI-Kipling, B-81.) (INB, page 159.). He married **Melanie Deschamps,** daughter of **Jean Baptiste Deschamps** and **Catherine Vandal,** on 26 Jan 1897 Batoche, (Saskatchewan) (BSAP, page 141, M-2.).

92. Frederick Vandal was born on 17 Jun 1879 (SN2, B-35.). He was baptized on 18 Jun 1879 St.Norbert, Manitoba (Ibid.). He was born on 27 Jun 1879 west of Fort Ellice, (Manitoba) (Denney.). He married **Sophia Mary Fiddler,** daughter of **John William Fidler** and **Julienne Delorme,** on 30 Jan 1905 (Louis Verhagen Research.). He died on 26 Sep 1964 Prince Albert, Saskatchewan, at age 85 (Ibid.). He was buried on 30 Sep 1964 South Hill, Prince Albert, Saskatchewan (Ibid.).

Children of **Frederick Vandal** and **Sophia Mary Fiddler** were as follows:

    i.   Alice Vandale.

    ii.   Marcelline Vandale.

    iii.   Leo Vandale.

    iv.   Jack Vandale.

    v.   Norman Vandale.

    vi.   Dorothy Vandale.

    vii.   Irene Vandale.

    viii.   Olivier Vandale.

    ix.   Ida Beatrice Vandal was born on 3 Nov 1905 Fish Creek, (Saskatchewan) (SK Vital Statistics, Birth Reg. #5001.). She married William Ross, son of Joseph Ross and Melanie Deschamps, before 1926. She died before 1985 (Rod Mac Quarrie, 28 Dec 2011.).

        William Ross was born on 4 Jul 1899 Fish Creek, (Saskatchewan) (SK Vital Statistics, #1506.). He died on 18 Jan 1985 Prince Albert, Saskatchewan, at age 85 (Rod Mac Quarrie, 28 Dec 2011.). He was buried on 22 Jan 1985 South Hill Cemetery, Prince Albert, Saskatchewan (Ibid.).

93. **Mathilde Vandal** was born on 27 Jan 1881 Montagne la Bosse (SN2, B-4.) (ArchiviaNet, C-15008.). She was baptized on 29 Jan 1881 St.Norbert, Manitoba (SN2, B-4.). She married **John Fidler**, son of **John William Fidler** and **Julienne Delorme,** before 1904. She married **Louis Grassick** before 1921 (1921 Census of Canada from the National Archives of Canada (Transcription by ancestry.com), Ottawa, Canada, District 216-59, page 4.). She died on 22 Jan 1958 Cudworth, Saskatchewan, at age 76 (Louis Verhagen.).

    John Fidler was born on 26 May 1883 Fish Creek, (Saskatchewan) (BSAP, page 15, B-13.) (HBSI.). He was baptized on 4 Jun 1883 Batoche, (Saskatchewan) (BSAP, page 15, B-13.). He died before 1921.

    Louis Grassick was born in 1876 (1921 Canada, District 216-59, page 4.).

94. **Francois Vandal** was born on 2 Jan 1883 Batoche, (Saskatchewan) (BSAP, [page 12a], B-1.). He was baptized on 2 Jan 1883 Batoche, (Saskatchewan) (Ibid.). He married **Anna (Skierra) Skarra,** daughter of **Jacob (Skierra) Skarra** and **Anna Bzotokoski,** on 20 Sep 1910 Howell, Saskatchewan (Denney.). He died on 1 Nov 1918 Cudworth, Saskatchewan, at age 35 (Ibid.).

    Anna (Skierra) Skarra was born on 17 Sep 1890 Marble, Minnesota (Ibid.). She died on 30 Nov 1970 Agassiz, British Columbia, at age 80 (Ibid.).

Children of **Francois Vandal** and **Anna (Skierra) Skarra** were:

    i.   Lawrence Edward Vandal was born on 19 Apr 1911 Fish Creek, Saskatchewan (Ibid.). He died on 16 Oct 1956 Oakland, California, at age 45 (Ibid.).

95. **Marie Virginie Vandal** was born on 13 May 1879 St.Norbert, Manitoba (SN2, B-27.). She was baptized on 15 May 1879 St.Norbert, Manitoba (Ibid.). She married **William Sauve**, son of **Joseph Sauve** and **Eulalie Carriere,** on 20 Jan 1902 St.Malo, DeSalaberry, Manitoba (MM.) (MB Vital Statistics, Marriage Reg. #1902,002210.). She died on 12 Apr 1904 RM DeSalaberry, Manitoba, at age 24 (Ibid., Death Reg. #1904,003016.).

    William Sauve was born on 16 Feb 1879 (Saskatchewan) (1901 Canada, #10, a-3, page 13, family 101, line 12-13.) (SL-SK, page 27, B-2.). He was baptized on 16 Feb 1879 St.Laurent-de-Grandin, (Saskatchewan) (Ibid.). He married **Marie Olivine Vandal,** daughter of **Louis Vandal** and **Reine Victoria Ducharme,** on 25 Sep 1905 Woodridge, Manitoba (MM.). He died on 4 Oct 1915 LaBroquerie, Manitoba, at age 36 (MB Vital Statistics, Death Reg. #1915,210216.).

96. **Elise Vandal** was born on 8 Jun 1882 Batoche, (Saskatchewan) (BSAP, page 8, B-11.) (1901 Canada, page 4, Family 30, #45-47.). She was baptized on 8 Jun 1882 Batoche, (Saskatchewan) (BSAP, page 8, B-11.). She married **Chrysostome Boyer**, son of **William Boyer** and **Julienne Bousquet,** on 6 Mar 1905 Batoche, (Saskatchewan) (Ibid., page 232, M-2.).

    Chrysostome Boyer was born on 8 Oct 1878 St.Francois Xavier, Manitoba (SFXI-Kipling, B-31.). He was baptized 9 Oct 1878 St.Francois Xavier, Manitoba (Ibid.) (Rosemary Rozyk.).

Ahnentafel between Joseph Vandal and Etienne Vandal

--- 1st Generation ---

1. JOSEPH VANDAL was born on 9 Jul 1797 at Sorel, Richelieu, Quebec (PRDH online index, http://www.genealogic.umontreal.ca, No. 696346.). He was baptized on 9 Jul 1797 at Sorel, Richelieu, Quebec (Ibid.). He married **MARIE LACHEVRETIERE**, daughter of **JOSEPH LACHEVRATIERE** and **INDIAN WOMAN**, before 1825. He married **ADELAIDE CHARBONNEAU**, daughter of **JEAN BAPTISTE CHARBONNEAU** and **LOUISE BOUCHER**, on 8 Oct 1850 at St.Andrews, (Manitoba) (Denney Papers, Charles D. Denney, Glenbow Archives, Calgary, Alberta.) (Rod MacQuarrie Research, 28 Jan 2012.) (ArchiviaNet 1886-1901, 1906 Half-Breed Scrip Applications Index, RG15-21, Volume 1333 through 1371, Microfilm Reel Number C-14944 through C-15010, National Archives of Canada, Ottawa, Ontario, http://www.collectionscanada.gc.ca.). He died on 20 Nov 1877 at St.Boniface, (Manitoba), at age 80 (Ibid.) (Rod Mac Quarrie, 28 Jan 2012.). He was buried on 21 Nov 1877 at St.Boniface, (Manitoba) (Ibid.) (ArchiviaNet.).

--- 2nd Generation ---

2. AUGUSTIN VANDAL was born on 9 Apr 1754 at Neuville, Quebec (PRDH online, No. 241022.). He was baptized on 9 Apr 1754 at Neuville, Quebec (Ibid.). He married **CATHERINE LECLERC**, daughter of **NICOLAS LECLERC** and **MARIE-JOSEPHE PELOQUIN DIT FELIX**, on 12 Apr 1779 at St.Pierre, Sorel, Richelieu, Quebec (*SPS Saint-Pierre de Sorel*, Roland J. Auger, page 251.) (PRDH online, No. 226245.). He died on 15 Aug 1835 at Sorel, Richelieu, Quebec, at age 81 (Ibid., No. 795166.). He was buried on 16 Aug 1835 at Sorel, Richelieu, Quebec (Ibid.).

--- 3rd Generation ---

4. JEAN-BAPTISTE-MATHIEU VANDAL (DGFQ Jette, Rene, *Dictionnaire Genealogique des Familles du Quebec des Origines a 1730* (Montreal, Quebec, Canada: University of Montreal Press, 1983), page 1112.) (Ibid.) was baptized on 21 Sep 1718 at Neuville, Quebec (Ibid.). He was born on 21 Sep 1718 at Neuville, Quebec (Ibid.). He married **MARIE-JOSEPHTE FOURNEL**, daughter of **JACQUES FOURNEL** and **MARIE-MARGUERITE RICHARD**, on 5 Oct 1744 at Pointe-aux-Trembles, Quebec (DNCF *Dictionnaire National des Canadiens-Francais Tome I & II* Gabriel Drouin, editor (revised 1985; Siege Social, 4184, rue St-Denis, Montreal, Canada: l'Institut Genealogique Drouin, 1979), page 1325.) (PRDH online.). He married **MARIE-ANGELIQUE AUGER**, daughter of **LOUIS-JOSEPH AUGER**

and GENEVIEVE GODIN, on 9 Jun 1749 at Neuville, Quebec (DNCF, page 1325.) (PRDH online, #27164.) (Ibid., No. 156368.). He married MARIE LOUISE GUEGUIN DIT LATERREUR, daughter of FRANCOIS GUEGUIN DIT LATERREUR and MARIE MADELEINE BEAUDIN DIT DESJARDINS, on 10 Feb 1766 at St-Charles-sur-Richelieu, Quebec (Ibid., #43342.). He died on 20 May 1773 at Sorel, Richelieu, Quebec, at age 54 (Ibid., No. 377519.). He was buried on 21 May 1773 at Sorel, Richelieu, Quebec (Ibid.).

--- 4th Generation ---

8. FRANCOIS VANDAL was born on 3 Feb 1682 at Neuville, Quebec (DGFQ, page 1112.) (PRDH online, No. 53621.). He was baptized on 8 Feb 1682 at Neuville, Quebec (DGFQ, page 1112.) (PRDH online, No. 53621.). He married MARIE-ANTOINETTE RIPAULT, daughter of ROCH RIPAULT DIT ROLET OR ROLLET and MARIE-ANNE AUBERT, on 10 Feb 1716 at Grondines, Quebec (DNCF, page 1325.) (DGFQ, page 1112.) (PRDH online, No. 56137.). A contract for the marriage to MARIE-ANTOINETTE RIPAULT, daughter of ROCH RIPAULT DIT ROLET OR ROLLET and MARIE-ANNE AUBERT, was signed on 16 Feb 1716 (DGFQ, page 1112.). He was buried on 22 Feb 1742 at Neuville, Quebec (PRDH online, No. 156598.).

--- 5th Generation ---

16. FRANCOIS VANDAL lived at at Verantes, Saumur, Angers, Anjou (Maine-et-Loire) (DNCF, page 1325.) (DGFQ, page 1112.). He was also known as FRANCOIS VANDALE (DNCF, page 1239.). He was born between 1645 and 1651 (DGFQ, page 1112.). He married MARIE-MADELEINE PINEL, daughter of GILLES PINEL and ANNE LEDET, on 19 Mar 1680 at Neuville, Quebec (Ibid.). He was buried on 6 Dec 1697 at Neuville, Quebec (Ibid.).

--- 6th Generation ---

32. ETIENNE VANDAL married JULIENNE GROLE.

Descendants of Joseph Vandal

Generation One

1. **Joseph Vandal** was born on 9 Jul 1797 Sorel, Richelieu, Quebec (PRDH online index, http://www.genealogic.umontreal.ca, No. 696346.). He was baptized on 9 Jul 1797 Sorel, Richelieu, Quebec (Ibid.). He married **Marie Lachevretiere**, daughter of **Joseph Lachevratiere** and **Indian woman**, before 1825. He married **Adelaide Charbonneau**, daughter of **Jean Baptiste Charbonneau** and **Louise Boucher**, on 8 Oct 1850 St.Andrews, (Manitoba) (Denney Papers, Charles D. Denney, Glenbow Archives, Calgary, Alberta.) (Rod MacQuarrie Research, 28 Jan 2012.) (ArchiviaNet 1886-1901, 1906 Half-Breed Scrip Applications Index, RG15-21, Volume 1333 through 1371, Microfilm Reel Number C-14944 through C-15010, National Archives of Canada, Ottawa, Ontario, http://www.collectionscanada.gc.ca.). He died on 20 Nov 1877 St.Boniface, (Manitoba), at age 80 (Ibid.) (Rod Mac Quarrie, 28 Jan 2012.). He was buried on 21 Nov 1877 St.Boniface, (Manitoba) (Ibid.) (ArchiviaNet.).

Question: *Probable son of Augustin Vandal and Marie Catherine Lecerc.*

Marie Lachevretiere was born circa 1805.

Children of **Joseph Vandal** and **Marie Lachevretiere** were as follows:

    2   i. Josephte Vandal, b. 18 Jul 1825 St.Boniface, (Manitoba); m. Louis Lacerte; d. 23 Dec 1878 St.Norbert, Manitoba; bur. 24 Dec 1878 St.Norbert, Manitoba.

    3   ii. Marie Vandal, b. 12 Jul 1826 St.Andrews, (Manitoba); m. Jean Baptiste Desrosiers.

         iii. Pierre Vandal was born on 14 Jul 1829 St.Boniface, (Manitoba) (SB 1825-1834 St.Boniface Roman Catholic Registre des Baptemes, Mariages & Sepultures, 1825-1834, page 29, B-567. Hereinafter cited as SB 1825-1834.). He was baptized on 2 Aug 1829 St.Boniface, (Manitoba) (Ibid.). He was buried on 1 Mar 1833 St.Boniface, (Manitoba) (Ibid., page 93, S-41.).

    4   iv. Antoine Vandal, b. 10 Dec 1831 St.Boniface, (Manitoba); m. Emelie Morin.

    5   v. Louis Vandal, b. 10 Feb 1834 St.Andrews, (Manitoba); m. Marie Hamelin.

    6   vi. Victoire Vandal, b. before 1838; m. Baptiste Charbonneau.

    7   vii. John Vandal, b. 10 Aug 1839 St.Andrews, (Manitoba); m. Eliza Lambert.

Adelaide Charbonneau was born on 26 Sep 1834 St.Boniface, (Manitoba) (Ibid., page 147, B-864.). She was baptized on 26 Sep 1834 St.Boniface, (Manitoba) (Ibid.).

Children of **Joseph Vandal** and **Adelaide Charbonneau** were as follows:

    8   i. Joseph Vandal, b. 28 Oct 1851 St.Andrews, (Manitoba); m. Isabelle Sayer; m. Monique Desjardins; m. Marguerite Henault; m. Therese Wells.

    9   ii. Catherine Vandal, b. 30 Jul 1853 St.Andrews, (Manitoba); m. Samuel Sinclair; m. Toussaint Chagnon; d. 24 May 1927 Winnipeg, Manitoba.

    10   iii. Veronique Vandal, b. 11 Apr 1859; m. Jean-Baptiste Perreault dit Morin.

         iv. Olivier Vandal was born on 21 Jul 1861 St.Boniface, (Manitoba) (SB-Rozyk St. Boniface Roman Catholic Church, Manitoba, Canada, Baptisms, Marriages and Burials 1860-1875 Extractions, Compiled by Rosemary Rozyk, page 24, B-99.). He was baptized on 23 Jul 1861 St.Boniface, (Manitoba) (Ibid.). He died on 29 Jun 1879 St.Boniface, Manitoba, at age 17 (MBS Scrip Applications, Original White Settlers & Halfbreeds residing in Manitoba on 15 July 1870, RG15-19, C-14934.). He was buried on 1 Jul 1879 St.Boniface, Manitoba (Ibid.).

         v. Louise Vandal was born on 21 Sep 1863 St.Boniface, (Manitoba) (SB-Rozyk, page 128, B-141.). She was baptized on 22 Sep 1863 St.Boniface, (Manitoba) (MBS, C-14934.) (SB-Rozyk, page 128, B-141.). She died on 6 Sep 1872 St.Boniface, Manitoba, at age 8 (MBS, C-14934.) (SB-Rozyk, page 250, S-34.). She was buried on 8 Sep 1872 St.Boniface, Manitoba (MBS, C-14934.) (SB-Rozyk, page 250, S-34.).

    11   vi. Augustin 'Gustave' Vandal, b. 19 Mar 1866 St.Boniface, Manitoba; m. Marie Adele Pelagie Nolin.

         vii. Marguerite Vandal was born on 16 Nov 1868 (Ibid., page 137, B-148.). She was baptized on 19 Nov 1868 St.Boniface, (Manitoba) (Ibid.). She married Pierre Falcon, son of Pierre Falcon and Marie Leveille, on 18 Jul 1887 Ste.Anne, Manitoba (MM *Manitoba Marriages* in *Publication 45*, Volumes 1-3, compiled and edited by:

Paul J. Lareau, Fr. Julien Hamelin, (240 Avenue Daly, Ottawa, Ontario K1N 6G2: Le Centre de Genealogie S.C., 1984).).

Pierre Falcon was born on 13 Jul 1867 St.Francois Xavier, (Manitoba) (SFXI-Kipling St.Francois Xavier Register Index, 1834-1900; compiled by Clarence Kipling , B-77.). He was baptized on 13 Jul 1867 St.Francois Xavier, (Manitoba) (Ibid.). He married **Cecile Marie Belgarde**, daughter of **Gilbert Belgarde** and **Sophia Descoteaux**, on 21 Sep 1926 Sidney, Richland County, Montana (RLCM Richland County Courthouse, Montana; Marriage Record Licenses and Certificates; 1865-1950, familysearch.org, Hereinafter cited as RLCM.). He died on 24 Oct 1938 Montana at age 71 (MT Death Montana State Genealogical Society Death Index.).

12 viii. Adele Vandal, b. 3 Jan 1871; m. Alfred Berard; d. before 1898.

  ix. Pierre Vandal was born on 31 Jul 1874 St.Boniface, Manitoba (MBS, C-14934.). He was baptized on 2 Aug 1874 St.Boniface, Manitoba (Ibid.). He died on 10 Dec 1877 St.Boniface, Manitoba, at age 3 (Ibid.). He was buried on 11 Dec 1877 St.Boniface, Manitoba (Ibid.).

Generation Two

2. Josephte Vandal was born on 18 Jul 1825 St.Boniface, (Manitoba) (Ibid., C-14929.). She married **Louis Lacerte**, son of **Louis Lacerte** and **Marie Martin**, before 1844. She died on 23 Dec 1878 St.Norbert, Manitoba, at age 53 (SN2 Catholic Parish Register of St.Norbert, S-30. Hereinafter cited as SN2.). She was buried on 24 Dec 1878 St.Norbert, Manitoba (Ibid.).

Louis Lacerte was born circa 1814 Red River, (Manitoba) (1850Ci-MN *Minnesota Territorial Census, 1850*, Harpole, Patricia C. and Mary D. Nagle, ed., (St.Paul, Minnesota: Minnesota Historical Society, 1972), page 18, Dwelling 6, Family 6.). He was born on 15 Jan 1821 North West Territories (MBS, C-14929.). He married **Charlotte Lesperance**, daughter of **Alexis Bonami Lesperance** and **Marguerite Grenon**, on 24 Nov 1879 St.Francois Xavier, Manitoba (SFXI-Kipling, M-14.).

3. Marie Vandal was born on 12 Jul 1826 St.Andrews, (Manitoba) (MBS, C-14927.). She married **Jean Baptiste Desrosiers**, son of **Jean Baptiste Desrosiers** and **Marie Suzanne Gerbeau dit Bellegarde or Gibeau**, before 1845.

Jean Baptiste Desrosiers was born on 18 Oct 1797 (Louiseville), Riviere-du-Loup, Quebec (PRDH online, No. 488705.). He was baptized on 19 Oct 1797 (Louiseville), Riviere-du-Loup, Quebec (Ibid.).

4. Antoine Vandal was born on 10 Dec 1831 St.Boniface, (Manitoba). He married **Emelie Morin**, daughter of **Jean-Baptiste Perreault** and **Marie Charon dit Ducharme**, circa 1852.

Emelie Morin was born on 28 Sep 1832 St.Boniface, (Manitoba) (SB 1825-1834, page 77, B-481.). She was baptized on 29 Sep 1832 St.Boniface, (Manitoba) (Ibid.).

Children of **Antoine Vandal** and **Emelie Morin** were as follows:

13 i. Helena Vandal, m. Augustin Amedee Bernier.

14 ii. Marie Rose Vandal, b. 24 Oct 1852 St.Boniface, (Manitoba); m. Hermenegilde Payette; d. 6 Mar 1887 Ste.Anne, Manitoba.

15 iii. Euchariste Vandal, b. 23 Feb 1854 St.Boniface, (Manitoba); m. Sarah Parenteau; m. Josephine Agnes Huppe.

16 iv. Melanie Vandal, b. 30 Mar 1857 St.Boniface, (Manitoba); m. Francis Xavier Gagnier; m. William Alfred Plouffe.

  v. Remi Vandal was born circa 1859 (SB-Rozyk, page 178, S-10.). He died on 26 Feb 1865 St.Boniface, (Manitoba) (Ibid.). He was buried on 28 Feb 1865 St.Boniface, (Manitoba) (Ibid.).

17 vi. Antoine Vandal, b. 24 Dec 1861 St.Boniface, (Manitoba); m. Melanie Berard.

  vii. Marie Eulalie Vandal was born on 4 Jul 1864 St.Boniface, (Manitoba) (MBS, C-14934.) (SB-Rozyk, page 157, B-76.). She was baptized on 9 Jul 1864 St.Boniface, (Manitoba) (MBS, C-14934.) (SB-Rozyk, page 157, B-76.). She married Onesime Duhamel on 30 Jan 1882 Ste.Anne, Manitoba (MM.). She married Jean Baptiste Bonin on 27 Apr 1913 Ste.Anne, Manitoba (Ibid.).

    Onesime Duhamel died before 1882.

18 viii. Marie Vandal, b. 3 May 1867; m. Jeremie Berard; m. Avila Nolette.

  ix. Justine Vandal was born on 15 Jan 1870 (MBS, C-14934.) (SB-Rozyk, page 171, B-7.). She was baptized on 23 Jan 1870 St.Boniface, (Manitoba) (MBS, C-14934.) (SB-Rozyk, page 171, B-7.).

  x. Marie Melina Vandal was baptized on 22 Apr 1872 Ste.Anne, Manitoba (IBMS *Index des Baptemes, Mariages et Sepultures* (La Societe Historique de Saint-Boniface).).

19 xi. Clemence Vandal, b. 23 Mar 1875 Ste.Anne, Manitoba; m. Alfred Berard; d. before 1901.

5. Louis Vandal was baptized on 9 Feb 1834 St.Boniface, (Manitoba) (Rosemary Helga (Morrissette) Rozyk Research, 16 Sep 1998 extraction, page 2, M-1 [note] but no entry found for baptism.). He was born on 10 Feb 1834 St.Andrews, (Manitoba) (MBS, C-14934.). He married **Marie Hamelin**, daughter of **Jean Baptiste Hamelin** and **Francoise Ducharme**, on 8 Jan 1861 St.Boniface, (Manitoba) (SB-Rozyk, page 2, M-1.).

Marie Hamelin was born on 10 Oct 1839 St.Boniface, (Manitoba) (MBS, C-14934.).

Children of **Louis Vandal** and **Marie Hamelin** were as follows:

  i. Marie Vandal was born on 2 May 1862 St.Boniface, (Manitoba) (SB-Rozyk, page 62, B-65.). She was baptized on 2 May 1862 St.Boniface, (Manitoba) (Ibid.). She died on 30 Oct 1875 St.Boniface, Manitoba, at age 13 (Ibid., page 69, S-47.). She was buried on 1 Nov 1875 St.Boniface, (Manitoba) (Ibid.).

20 ii. Louis Vandal, b. 19 Nov 1863; m. Marie Delphine Lariviere; d. 1936; bur. 1936 St.Peters, Manitoba.

  iii. Firmin Vandal was born on 2 Aug 1865 (Ibid., page 10, B-69.). He was baptized on 4 Aug 1865 St.Boniface, (Manitoba) (Ibid.). He died in 1936 (Denney.). He was buried in 1936 St.Peters, Manitoba (Ibid.).

  iv. Antoine Vandal was born on 12 Feb 1867 St.Boniface, (Manitoba) (SB-Rozyk, page 78, B-16.). He was baptized on 13 Feb 1867 St.Boniface, (Manitoba) (Ibid.). He married Rosanna Gauthier on 31 Jan 1910 Lorette, Manitoba (Ibid., page 78, B-16 (note).). He died in 1941 (Denney.). He was buried in 1941 St.Peters, Manitoba (Ibid.).

  v. Elisabeth Vandal was born on 8 Aug 1868 (SB-Rozyk, page 130, B-121.). She was baptized on 9 Aug 1868 St.Boniface, (Manitoba) (Ibid.). She married Francois Gauthier, son of Pierre Gauthier and Christine Hudon, on 19 Apr 1898 St.Boniface, Manitoba (RMSB.).

vi. Adele Vandal was born on 25 Jan 1870 (SB-Rozyk, page 172, B-8.). She was baptized on 28 Jan 1870 St.Boniface, (Manitoba) (Ibid.).

vii. Victoire Vandal was born on 25 Aug 1871 St.Boniface, Manitoba (Ibid., page 218, B-53.). She was baptized on 26 Aug 1871 St.Boniface, Manitoba (Ibid.). She died on 10 Nov 1883 St.Boniface, Manitoba, at age 12 (MB Vital Statistics, Death Reg. #1883,002246.).

viii. Joseph Vandal was born on 22 Apr 1873 (SB-Rozyk, page 276, B-45.). He was baptized on 14 May 1873 St.Boniface, Manitoba (Ibid.). He married Marguerite Lariviere, daughter of Francois Lariviere and Arsene Nault, on 28 Jun 1897 Ste.Agathe, Manitoba (MM.).

Marguerite Lariviere was born circa 1879 Ste.Agathe, Manitoba (1881 Canada, C-13282, District 184-D-1, page 2, household 10.).

ix. Jean Baptiste Vandal was born on 2 Feb 1875 (SB-Rozyk, page 46, B-9.). He was baptized on 6 Feb 1875 St.Boniface, Manitoba (Ibid.).

6. Victoire Vandal was born before 1838 (1838C RRS HBCA E5/9 1838 Census of the Red River Settlement, HBCA E5/9, Hudson's Bay Company Archives, Provincial Archives, 200 Vaughan Street, Winnipeg, MB R3C 1T5, Canada., page 31.). She married **Baptiste Charbonneau** before 1862.

Baptiste Charbonneau was born circa 1833 (SJL-1, page 8, S-3.). He died on 7 May 1869 Fort Totten, Dakota Territory (Ibid.). He was buried on 5 May 1871 St.Joseph, Leroy, Dakota Territory (Ibid.).

7. John Vandal was born on 10 Aug 1839 St.Andrews, (Manitoba) (MBS, C-14934.). He married **Eliza Lambert**, daughter of **Michel Lambert** and **Margaret 'Peggy' Favel**, on 11 Feb 1861 St.Boniface, (Manitoba) (RMSB, page 479.).

Eliza Lambert was born in Aug 1841 St.Andrews, (Manitoba) (MBS, C-14934.). She was baptized on 10 Feb 1861 St.Boniface, (Manitoba) (SB-Rozyk, page 7, B-20.).

Children of **John Vandal** and **Eliza Lambert** were as follows:

i. John William Vandal was born on 5 Dec 1861 St.Andrews, (Manitoba) (Ibid., page 39, B-150.). He was baptized on 7 Dec 1861 St.Boniface, (Manitoba) (MBS, C-14934.) (SB-Rozyk, page 39, B-150.). He married Marguerite Slater, daughter of Jeremie Slater and Mary Sinclair, on 22 Jan 1879 St.Boniface, Manitoba (RMSB.).

ii. Marguerite Vandal was born on 11 Jul 1863 St.Andrews, (Manitoba) (MBS, C-14934.). She was baptized on 11 Jul 1863 St.Boniface, (Manitoba) (Ibid.) (SB-Rozyk, page 121, B-104.). She died on 12 Apr 1872 at age 8 (Ibid., page 236, S-11.). She was buried on 14 Apr 1872 St.Boniface, Manitoba (MBS, C-14934.) (SB-Rozyk, page 236, S-11.).

iii. Louis Vandal was born on 28 Jul 1865 St.Andrews, (Manitoba) (MBS, C-14934.) (SB-Rozyk, page 10, B-68.). He was baptized on 30 Jul 1865 St.Boniface, (Manitoba) (MBS, C-14934.) (SB-Rozyk, page 10, B-68.).

iv. Marie Anne Vandal was born on 16 Apr 1868 St.Andrews, (Manitoba) (MBS, C-14934.) (SB-Rozyk, page 114, B-39.). She was baptized on 18 Apr 1868 St.Boniface, (Manitoba) (MBS, C-14934.) (SB-Rozyk, page 114, B-39.).

v. Julie Vandal was born on 25 Apr 1870 St.Andrews, (Manitoba) (MBS, C-14934.) (SB-Rozyk, page 179, B-33.). She was baptized on 26 Apr 1870 St.Boniface, (Manitoba) (MBS, C-14934.) (SB-Rozyk, page 179, B-33.). She died on 22 Mar 1887 St.Boniface, Manitoba, at age 16 (MB Vital Statistics, Death Reg. #1887,001275.).

21 vi. Alexandre Vandal, b. 7 Aug 1872 St.Boniface, Manitoba; m. Delima Huppe.

vii. Joseph Vandal was born on 20 Jan 1875 (SB-Rozyk, page 50, B-10.). He was baptized on 20 Feb 1875 St.Boniface, Manitoba (Ibid.). He died on 3 May 1875 (Ibid., page 56, S-25.). He was buried on 6 May 1875 St.Boniface, Manitoba (IBMS.) (SB-Rozyk, page 56, S-25.).

8. Joseph Vandal was born on 28 Oct 1851 St.Andrews, (Manitoba) (MBS, C-14934.). He married **Isabelle Sayer**, daughter of **George Sayer** and **Marie Caplette**, on 1 Jun 1870 St.Boniface, (Manitoba) (SB-Rozyk, page 184, M-15.). He married **Monique Desjardins**, daughter of **Jean Baptiste Desjardins** and **Marguerite Hamelin**, on 16 Oct 1876 Ste.Anne, Manitoba (MM.). He married **Marguerite Henault**, daughter of **Pierre Henault** and **Marguerite Larocque**, on 27 Sep 1880 Ste.Anne, Manitoba (Ibid.). He married **Therese Wells**, daughter of **Jean Baptiste Wells** and **Angelique Chalifoux**, circa 1885 (Rod Mac Quarrie, 28 Jan 2012.).

Isabelle Sayer was born in 1853 (MBS, C-14934.). She died on 10 Jul 1874 Baie St.Paul, Manitoba (Ibid.). She was buried on 12 Jul 1874 St.Eustache, Manitoba (Denney.).

Children of **Joseph Vandal** and **Isabelle Sayer** were as follows:

i. Marie Vandal was born on 18 Mar 1871 St.Boniface, Manitoba (SB-Rozyk, page 209, B-21.). She was baptized on 18 Mar 1871 St.Boniface, Manitoba (Ibid.). She died on 13 May 1872 at age 1 (Ibid., page 238, S-15.). She was buried on 15 May 1872 St.Boniface, Manitoba (Ibid.).

ii. Alexandre Vandal was born circa 1872 (1881 Canada, District 184-E-1, page 41, house 197.).

iii. Isabelle Vandal was born circa 1874 (IBMS.). She died on 16 Mar 1875 Ste.Anne, Manitoba (Ibid.).

Monique Desjardins was born on 6 Feb 1854 St.Vital, (Manitoba) (MBS, C-14927.). She married **Godfroi Nault**, son of **Jean Baptiste Nault** and **Catherine Ducharme**, on 30 Jan 1872 St.Boniface, Manitoba (SB-Rozyk, page 227, M-6.).

Children of **Joseph Vandal** and **Monique Desjardins** were as follows:

i. Marguerite Vandal was born circa 1879 (1881 Canada, District 184-E-1, page 41, house 197.).

ii. Joseph Olivier Vandal was born in Apr 1880 (Ibid.). He married Marie Rose Anna Nault, daughter of Alfred Nault and Appoline Zace, on 5 May 1903 La Broquerie, Manitoba (MM.) (MB Vital Statistics, Mar. Reg. #1903,003054.).

Marie Rose Anna Nault was born on 25 Jan 1883 St.Pierre Jolys, Manitoba (LFAN *La Famille Amable Nault* C.SsR. compiled by Charles Eugene Voyer, (Ste.Anne des Chenes, Manitoba, 15 Mar 1978).).

Marguerite Henault was born circa 31 May 1859 (INB, page 29.). She was baptized on 16 Jun 1859 Montagne du Tondre (Ibid.).

Children of **Joseph Vandal** and **Marguerite Henault** were as follows:

i. Claudtide V. Vandal was born in Mar 1881 (1881 Canada, District 184-E-1, page 41, house 197.).

    ii.   Charles Vandale was born on 19 Apr 1882 Ste.Anne, Manitoba (MB Vital Statistics, Birth Reg. #1882,002023.). He died on 27 Apr 1883 Ste.Anne, Manitoba, at age 1 (Ibid., Death Reg. #1883,001643.).

    iii.   Marguerite Victoria Vandale was born on 2 Jan 1884 RM Ste.Anne, Manitoba (Ibid., Birth Reg. #1884,003161.).

    iv.   Pierre Arthur Vandal was born on 22 Jul 1885 Ste.Anne, Manitoba (Ibid., Birth Reg. #1885,001558.).

Therese Wells was born on 14 Apr 1854 (SFXI-Kipling, B-159.) (SFXI 1851-1868 St.Francois Xavier 1852-1861 Register Index, B-159. Hereinafter cited as SFXI 1851-1868.). She was baptized on 29 Apr 1854 St.Francois Xavier, (Manitoba) (SFXI-Kipling, B-159.) (SFXI 1851-1868, B-159.). She married **Alexandre Nolin** on 13 Jan 1873 Ste.Anne, Manitoba (MM, page 930 and 1304.).

    9.   **Catherine Vandal** was born on 30 Jul 1853 St.Andrews, (Manitoba) (Denney.). She married **Samuel Sinclair**, son of **William Sinclair** and **Elizabeth Anderson**, on 11 Jan 1871 St.Boniface, Manitoba (SB-Rozyk, page 204, M-1.). She married **Toussaint Chagnon** in 1889 Selkirk, Manitoba (Rod Mac Quarrie, 28 Jan 2012.). She died on 24 May 1927 Winnipeg, Manitoba, at age 73 (MB Vital Statistics, Death Reg. #1927,024153.).

    Samuel Sinclair was born on 18 Jun 1849 St.Andrews, (Manitoba) (MBS, C-14934.) (Rod Mac Quarrie, 28 Jan 2012.). He was baptized on 19 Jun 1849 St.Andrews, (Manitoba) (Ibid.). He was baptized on 11 Jan 1871 St.Boniface, Manitoba (SB-Rozyk, page 203, Abj.).

    Toussaint Chagnon was born in Mar 1848 Quebec (Ibid., Death Reg. No. 1918,048062.). He married **Emilie Lamy** before 1870 (1881 Canada, District 184-E-1, page 79, house 370.). He died on 9 Aug 1918 Brokenhead, Manitoba, at age 70 (MB Vital Statistics, Death Reg. No. 1918,048062.).

    10.   **Veronique Vandal** was born on 11 Apr 1859. She married **Jean-Baptiste Perreault dit Morin**, son of **Baptiste Perreault dit Morin Jr.** and **Catherine Grouette**, on 17 Feb 1874 Ste.Anne, Manitoba (MM.).

    Jean-Baptiste Perreault dit Morin was born on 12 Mar 1849 St.Boniface, (Manitoba) (MBS, C-14932.).

    11.   **Augustin 'Gustave' Vandal** was born on 19 Mar 1866 St.Boniface, Manitoba (INB.). He was baptized on 21 Mar 1866 St.Boniface, Manitoba (Ibid.). He married **Marie Adele Pelagie Nolin**, daughter of **Augustin Nolin** and **Marie Domitilde Perreault dit Morin**, on 31 Jan 1887 Ste.Anne, Manitoba (MM.).

    Marie Adele Pelagie Nolin was born on 10 Sep 1868 (SB-Rozyk, page 132, B-129.). She was baptized on 11 Sep 1868 St.Boniface, (Manitoba) (Ibid.).

Children of **Augustin 'Gustave' Vandal** and **Marie Adele Pelagie Nolin** were as follows:

    i.   Cyrille Vandal was born on 11 Dec 1887 Ste.Anne, Manitoba (MB Vital Statistics, Birth Reg. #1887,001884.). He married Marie Rose Champagne on 3 Jan 1923 Richer, Manitoba (MM.).

    ii.   Alfred Vandale was born on 18 Jul 1889 Ste.Anne, Manitoba (MB Vital Statistics, Birth Reg. #1889,002762.).

    iii.   Joseph Edmond Vandale was born on 14 Nov 1890 R.M. of Ste.Anne, Manitoba (Ibid., Birth Reg. #1890,003513.).

    iv.   Joseph Vandale was born on 27 Aug 1892 R.M. of La Broquerie, Manitoba (Ibid., Birth Reg. #1892,002488.).

22   v.   Justine Vandal, b. 25 Mar 1894 R.M. of La Broquerie, Manitoba; m. Joseph Perreault.

    vi.   Joseph Adelard Vandal was born on 2 Sep 1896 R.M. of La Broquerie, Manitoba (Ibid., Birth Reg. #1896,001738.).

    vii.   Rosa Vandal was born on 27 Feb 1898 (1901 Canada, #10 (e-3), page 2, family 10, line 2-7.). She married Joseph Therrien on 19 Jun 1927 Richer, Manitoba (MM.).

    viii.   Alphonse Marius Vandal was born on 19 Jul 1901 RM of LaBroquerie, Manitoba (MB Vital Statistics, Birth Reg. #1901,001346.).

    12.   **Adele Vandal** was born on 3 Jan 1871 (SB-Rozyk, page 203, B-2.). She was baptized on 9 Jan 1871 St.Boniface, Manitoba (Ibid.). She married **Alfred Berard**, son of **Jeremie Berard** and **Philomene Huppe,** on 7 Feb 1887 Ste.Anne, Manitoba (MM.) (MB Vital Statistics, Marriage Reg. #1887,001391.). She died before 1898.

    Alfred Berard was born on 6 Aug 1863 (SB-Rozyk, page 124, B-118.). He was baptized on 9 Aug 1863 (Pointe-des-Chenes), St.Boniface, (Manitoba) (Ibid.). He married **Clemence Vandal**, daughter of **Antoine Vandal** and **Emelie Morin**, on 18 Apr 1898 La Broquerie, Manitoba (MM.) (MB Vital Statistics, Marriage Reg. #1898,002210.). He married **Elizabeth Huppe**, daughter of **Julien Huppe** and **Veronique Nault**, on 16 Oct 1906 RM La Broquerie, Manitoba (MM.) (MB Vital Statistics, Marriage Reg. #1906,002990.). He died on 21 Dec 1917 Ste.Anne, Manitoba, at age 54 (Ibid., Death Reg. #1917,072236.).

Generation Three

    13.   **Helena Vandal** married **Augustin Amedee Bernier**, son of **Cyrille Bernier** and **Desanges Chouinard**, on 24 Nov 1890 Ste.Anne, Manitoba (MM.).

    Augustin Amedee Bernier was born circa 1861 St-Eugene, Rimouski, Quebec (Ibid., page 102.).

    14.   **Marie Rose Vandal** was born on 24 Oct 1852 St.Boniface, (Manitoba) (MBS, C-14932.). She married **Hermenegilde Payette**, son of **Jean Baptiste Payette** and **Marguerite Isabella Lafournaise**, on 16 Feb 1874 Ste.Anne, Manitoba (MM.). She died on 6 Mar 1887 Ste.Anne, Manitoba, at age 34 (MB Vital Statistics, Death Reg. #1887,001808.).

    Hermenegilde Payette was born in 1853 Isle-a-la-Crosse, (Saskatchewan) (MBS, C-14932.). He died on 18 Nov 1920 Sprague, Manitoba (MB Vital Statistics, Death Reg. #1920,064087.).

    15.   **Euchariste Vandal** was born on 23 Feb 1854 St.Boniface, (Manitoba) (MBS, C-14934.). He married **Sarah Parenteau**, daughter of **Pierre Parenteau** and **Marie Anne Caron**, on 14 Jan 1878 St.Norbert, Manitoba (SN2, M-2.). He married **Josephine Agnes Huppe**, daughter of **Joseph Huppe** and **Josephte Cyr**, on 10 Jun 1895 Tache, Manitoba (MB Vital Statistics, Marriage Reg. #1895,001460.).

    Sarah Parenteau was born on 28 Feb 1855 St.Norbert, (Manitoba) (MBS, C-14931.).

Children of **Euchariste Vandal** and **Sarah Parenteau** were as follows:

    i.   Lelie Vandal was born circa 1879 Manitoba (1881 Canada, Film #C-13283, District 184, Sub-District E, page 9, household 43.).

23   ii.   Pierre Vandal, b. Apr 1881 Manitoba; m. Aurelie Berard.

24   iii.   Georgiana Vandal, b. 5 Aug 1883 RM Ste.Anne, Manitoba; m. Alphonse Joseph Berard.

    iv.   Joseph Vandal was born in 1885 Manitoba (1901 Canada, #10, E-1, page 9, family 78, line 21-26.).

    v.   Marie Marcelline Vandale was born on 6 Apr 1886 Ste.Anne, Manitoba (MB Vital Statistics, Birth Reg. #1886,003877.).

    vi.   Joseph Isaac Vandale was born on 17 Jun 1887 RM Ste.Anne, Manitoba (Ibid., Birth Reg. #1887,004155.).

    vii. Alphonse Vandal was born in Apr 1888 Manitoba (1901 Canada, #10, E-1, page 9, family 78, line 21-28.).

25 viii. Vitaline Vandal, b. 13 Feb 1889 R.M. of Montcalm, Manitoba; m. Jean Baptiste Huppe.

    ix. Marie Eugenie Vandale was born on 16 Sep 1890 R.M. of Ste.Anne, Manitoba (MB Vital Statistics, Birth Reg. #1890,003506.).

    x. Felix William Vandale was born on 29 Oct 1891 R.M. of La Broquerie, Manitoba (Ibid., Birth Reg. #1891,004119.).

    xi. Marie Christine Justine Vandale was born on 9 Feb 1893 R.M. of La Broquerie, Manitoba (Ibid., Birth Reg. #1893,004105.).

Josephine Agnes Huppe was born in 1850 St.Boniface, (Manitoba) (MBS, C-14925.). She was born on 2 Apr 1850 (Marie Beaupre Extractions.). She was born on 25 Dec 1850 (Manitoba) (1901 Canada, #10, E-1, page 9, family 78, line 21-28.). She was baptized on 27 Jun 1852 Fort Resolution, (Northwest Territory) (Marie Beaupre.). She married **Simon Berard**, son of **Pierre Berard** and **Marie Fortin**, on 23 Jan 1866 St.Boniface, (Manitoba) (SB-Rozyk, page 40, M-3.).

16. **Melanie Vandal** was born on 30 Mar 1857 St.Boniface, (Manitoba) (MBS, C-14928.). She married **Francis Xavier Gagnier**, son of **Pierre Gagnier** and **Marie Beaudoin**, on 13 Jan 1874 Ste.Anne, Manitoba (MM.). She married **William Alfred Plouffe**, son of **Jean Baptiste Plouffe** and **Josephte Hamelin**, on 26 Jun 1906 (La Broquerie), Ste.Anne, Manitoba (Ibid., page 1026.) (MB Vital Statistics, Marriage Reg. #1906,004759.).

Francis Xavier Gagnier was born on 4 May 1837 Quebec (1870C-MB, page 227, #27.) (1901 Canada, District 10-e-1, page 3, family 23, line 8-17.). He died before 1906.

William Alfred Plouffe was born on 4 Oct 1869 (MBS, C-14932.) (SB-Rozyk, page 164, B-123.). He was baptized on 5 Oct 1869 St.Boniface, (Manitoba) (MBS, C-14932.) (SB-Rozyk, page 164, B-123.). He married **Marie Marguerite Grouette**, daughter of **Jean Baptiste Grouette** and **Julie Perreault dit Morin**, on 28 Oct 1890 Ste.Anne, Manitoba (MM, page 1026.) (MB Vital Statistics, Marriage Reg. #1890,001562.). He died on 9 Sep 1918 St.Boniface, Manitoba, at age 48 (Ibid., Death Reg. #1918,053026.).

17. **Antoine Vandal** was born on 24 Dec 1861 St.Boniface, (Manitoba) (MBS, C-14934.) (SB-Rozyk, page 41, B-156.). He was baptized on 25 Dec 1861 St.Boniface, (Manitoba) (MBS, C-14934.) (SB-Rozyk, page 41, B-156.). He married **Melanie Berard**, daughter of **Simon Berard** and **Josephine Agnes Huppe**, on 20 Jan 1885 Ste.Anne, Manitoba (MM.) (Rosemary Rozyk, 9 Jun 2009.).

Melanie Berard was born on 15 Jun 1869 Ste.Anne, (Manitoba) (MBS, C-14925.) (SB-Rozyk, page 155, B-61.). She was baptized on 11 Jul 1869 (Pointe-des-Chenes), St.Boniface, (Manitoba) (MBS, C-14925.) (SB-Rozyk, page 155, B-61.).

Children of **Antoine Vandal** and **Melanie Berard** were as follows:

26 i. Octave Vandal, b. 14 Nov 1885 Ste.Anne, Manitoba; m. Marie Rose Anna Desjarlais.

27 ii. Justine Vandal, b. 6 Jun 1888 Ste.Anne, Manitoba; m. Hermenegilde Huppe.

    iii. Arthur Raoul Vandale was born on 9 Oct 1889 Ste.Anne, Manitoba (MB Vital Statistics, Birth Reg. #1889,002773.).

28 iv. Josephine Vandal, b. 14 Oct 1891 R.M. of Tache, Manitoba; m. Jeremie Huppe; m. Leon Belisle.

    v. Joseph Albert Raymond Vandal was born on 9 Mar 1894 R.M. of Tache, Manitoba (Ibid., Birth Reg. #1894,001984.).

29 vi. Maurice Vandal, b. circa 1895; m. Julie Huppe.

30 vii. Louis Vandal, b. 2 Apr 1895 R.M. of Tache, Manitoba; m. Marie Anne Ducharme.

    viii. Doralis Vandal was born on 13 Apr 1897 R.M. of La Broquerie, Manitoba (Ibid., Birth Reg. #1897,005911.). She married Jean Baptiste Huppe, son of Julien Huppe and Veronique Nault, on 15 Aug 1928 Richer, Manitoba (MM.).

        Jean Baptiste Huppe was born on 5 Apr 1876 Manitoba (1901 Canada, #10, e-3, page 1, family 7, line 32-39.). He married **Marie Victoria Desjarlais**, daughter of **Jean Baptiste Desjarlais** and **Catherine Gladu**, on 8 Jan 1917 Richer, Manitoba (MM.). He married **Marie Louise Cadotte**, daughter of **Joseph Cadotte** and **Louise Bousquet**, on 6 Aug 1955 Richer, Manitoba (Ibid.).

    ix. William Vandal was born on 25 Nov 1899 Ste.Anne, Manitoba (MB Vital Statistics, Birth Reg. #1899,006894.). He was born on 26 Nov 1899 R.M. of La Broquerie, Manitoba (Ibid., Birth Reg. #1899,002170.). He married Rose Alma Ducharme, daughter of Jean Baptiste Ducharme and Clara Lefort, on 26 Feb 1922 St.Boniface, Manitoba (RMSB.).

    x. Joseph Amedee Vandal was born on 27 Dec 1902 R.M. of La Broquerie, Manitoba (MB Vital Statistics, Birth Reg. #1902,006643.). He married Celestine Plouffe, daughter of Georges Plouffe dit Gervais and Josephine Huppe, on 9 Nov 1923 St.Boniface, Manitoba (Ibid., Marriage Reg. #1923,043031.).

        Celestine Plouffe was born on 6 Apr 1904 St.Vital, Manitoba (Ibid., Birth Reg. #1904,23121404.).

31 xi. Maria Vandal, b. 6 Sep 1905 R.M. of La Broquerie, Manitoba; m. Alexandre Nault.

    xii. Bruno Vandal was born in Aug 1907 Manitoba (1911 Canada, #12, page 7, family 58, line 27-34.). He married Virginie Vandal, daughter of Maurice Vandal and Julie Huppe, on 21 Aug 1952 Richer, Manitoba (MM.).

18. **Marie Vandal** was born on 3 May 1867 (MBS, C-14934.) (SB-Rozyk, page 87, B-50.). She was baptized on 8 Jun 1867 St.Boniface, (Manitoba) (MBS, C-14934.) (SB-Rozyk, page 87, B-50.). She married **Jeremie Berard**, son of **Jeremie Berard** and **Philomene Huppe**, on 8 Feb 1886 Ste.Anne, Manitoba (MM.) (MB Vital Statistics, Marriage Reg. #1886,001250.). She married **Avila Nolette**, son of **Hilaire Nolette** and **Marie Chouinard**, on 21 Apr 1903 Ste.Anne, Manitoba (MM.).

Jeremie Berard was born on 8 Jan 1862 St.Boniface, (Manitoba) (SB-Rozyk, page 44, B-3.). He was baptized on 9 Jan 1862 St.Boniface, (Manitoba) (Ibid.). He died on 24 Jan 1900 La Broquerie, Manitoba, at age 38 (MB Vital Statistics, Death Reg. #1900,004029.).

Avila Nolette was born circa 1863 Longueuil, Quebec (MM, page 929.).

19. **Clemence Vandal** was born on 23 Mar 1875 Ste.Anne, Manitoba (INB.). She was baptized on 23 Mar 1875 Ste.Anne, Manitoba (Ibid.). She married **Alfred Berard**, son of **Jeremie Berard** and **Philomene Huppe**, on 18 Apr 1898 La Broquerie, Manitoba (MM.) (MB Vital Statistics, Marriage Reg. #1898,002210.). She died before 1901.

Alfred Berard was born on 6 Aug 1863 (SB-Rozyk, page 124, B-118.). He was baptized on 9 Aug 1863 (Pointe-des-Chenes), St.Boniface, (Manitoba) (Ibid.). He married **Adele Vandal**, daughter of **Joseph Vandal** and **Adelaide Charbonneau**, on 7 Feb 1887 Ste.Anne, Manitoba (MM.) (MB Vital Statistics, Marriage Reg. #1887,001391.). He married **Elizabeth Huppe**, daughter of **Julien Huppe** and **Veronique Nault**, on 16 Oct 1906 RM La Broquerie, Manitoba (MM.) (MB Vital Statistics, Marriage Reg. #1906,002990.). He died on 21 Dec 1917 Ste.Anne, Manitoba, at age 54 (Ibid., Death Reg. #1917,072236.).

20. Louis Vandal was born on 19 Nov 1863 (SB-Rozyk, page 132, B-163.). He was baptized on 21 Nov 1863 St.Boniface, (Manitoba) (Ibid.). He married **Marie Delphine Lariviere**, daughter of **Francois Lariviere** and **Arsene Nault,** on 19 Nov 1888 Ste.Agathe, Manitoba (MM.). He died in 1936 (Denney.). He was buried in 1936 St.Peters, Manitoba (Ibid.).

Marie Delphine Lariviere was born on 20 Oct 1865 Ste.Agathe, (Manitoba) (MBS, C-14929.). She was born on 24 Nov 1865 (SB-Rozyk, page 32, B-129.). She was baptized on 25 Nov 1865 St.Boniface, (Manitoba) (Ibid.).

Children of **Louis Vandal** and **Marie Delphine Lariviere** are as follows:

 i. Joseph Alfred Vandal was born on 16 Apr 1898 R.M. of St.Clements, Manitoba (MB Vital Statistics, Birth Reg. #1898,001481.).
 ii. Marie Emma Vandal was born on 10 Oct 1899 R.M. of St.Clements, Manitoba (Ibid., Birth Reg. #1900,002121.) (Ibid., Birth Reg. #1899,001190.).
 iii. Marie Rosalie Vandal was born on 3 Nov 1901 R.M. of Morris, Manitoba (Ibid., Birth Reg. #1902,003210.).
 iv. Marie Philomene Vandal was born on 29 Jan 1902 R.M. of St.Clements, Manitoba (Ibid., Birth Reg. #1902,004282.).
 v. William Vandal was born on 25 Feb 1904 R.M. of St.Clements, Manitoba (Ibid., Birth Reg. #1904,005317.).
 vi. Mary Josephine Vandal was born on 13 Feb 1905 R.M. of St.Clements, Manitoba (Ibid., Birth Reg. #1905,004149.).

21. Alexandre Vandal was born on 7 Aug 1872 St.Boniface, Manitoba (SB-Rozyk, page 248, B-57.). He was baptized on 8 Aug 1872 St.Boniface, Manitoba (Ibid.). He married **Delima Huppe**, daughter of **John Huppe** and **Catherine Perreault**, on 9 Jan 1900 (Ste.Anne), La Broquerie, Manitoba (MM.) (MB Vital Statistics, Marriage Reg. #1900,001947.).

Delima Huppe was born on 15 Mar 1881 Manitoba (1901 Canada, #10, e-2, page 3, family 19, line 6-14.).

Children of **Alexandre Vandal** and **Delima Huppe** are as follows:

 32 i. Edmond Vandal, m. Marie Louise Prairie.
  ii. Wilfrid Vandal married Louisa Fillion on 24 May 1933 Ste.Anne, Manitoba (MM.).
 33 iii. Rosario Vandal, b. 4 Oct 1900 La Broquerie, Manitoba; m. Josephine Prairie; m. Marie Cecile Normand.

22. Justine Vandal was born on 25 Mar 1894 R.M. of La Broquerie, Manitoba (MB Vital Statistics, Birth Reg. #1894,006659.). She married **Joseph Perreault**, son of **Damase Perreault dit Morin** and **Anne St.Germain**, on 4 Aug 1914 Richer, Manitoba (MM.).

Joseph Perreault was baptized on 5 Jul 1874 Ste.Anne, Manitoba (IBMS.).

Generation Four

23. Pierre Vandal was born in Apr 1881 Manitoba (1881 Canada, Film #C-13283, District 184, Sub-District E, page 9, household 43.). He married **Aurelie Berard**, daughter of **Simon Berard** and **Josephine Agnes Huppe**, on 13 Oct 1900 La Broquerie, Manitoba (MM.) (MB Vital Statistics, Marriage Reg. #1900,001051.).

Aurelie Berard was born circa 1878 (Denney.).

Children of **Pierre Vandal** and **Aurelie Berard** are as follows:

 i. Vital Vandal married Clarisse Berard, daughter of Alfred Berard and Elizabeth Huppe, on 15 May 1935 Richer, Manitoba (MM.).
 ii. Aurele Vandal married Lucie Belisle on 25 Nov 1942 Ste.Anne, Manitoba (Ibid.).
 34 iii. Joseph Vandal, m. Eleonore Vandal.
 35 iv. Majoric Vandal, b. 3 Aug 1905 R.M. of La Broquerie, Manitoba; m. Solange Proulx.
 36 v. Albert Vandal, b. circa 1909; m. Doria Florida Harrison.
  vi. Leona Vandal was born circa 1913. She married Louis Vincent on 29 Sep 1937 Ste.Anne, Manitoba (Ibid.).

24. Georgiana Vandal was born on 5 Aug 1883 RM Ste.Anne, Manitoba (MB Vital Statistics, Birth Reg. #1883,004364.). She married **Alphonse Joseph Berard**, son of **Simon Berard** and **Josephine Agnes Huppe,** on 22 Jul 1907 RM La Broquerie, Manitoba (MM.) (MB Vital Statistics, Marriage Reg. #1907,002235.).

Alphonse Joseph Berard was born on 14 Apr 1887 RM St.Anne, Manitoba (Ibid., Birth Reg. #1887,004147.). He married **Rosalie Desjarlais**, daughter of **Jean Baptiste Desjarlais** and **Catherine Gladu**, on 3 Nov 1917 Richer, Manitoba (MM.).

25. Vitaline Vandal was born on 13 Feb 1889 R.M. of Montcalm, Manitoba (Ibid., Birth Reg. #1889,005344.). She married **Jean Baptiste Huppe**, son of **John Huppe** and **Catherine Perreault**, on 30 Aug 1910 Ste.Anne, Manitoba (MM.).

Jean Baptiste Huppe was born on 31 Mar 1883 Ste.Anne, Manitoba (MB Vital Statistics, Birth Reg. #1883,002473.). He married **Marie Adeline Virginie Nolin**, daughter of **Joseph Augustin Nolin** and **Adelaide Larence**, on 25 Jul 1905 (Ste.Anne), La Broquerie, Manitoba (MM.) (MB Vital Statistics, Marriage Reg. #1905,001253.). He married **Marie Yolande (Helelolande) Nault**, daughter of **Andre Nault** and **Caroline Cyr,** on 6 Aug 1906 RM La Broquerie, Manitoba (LFAN.) (MB Vital Statistics, Marriage Reg. #1906,002988.).

26. Octave Vandal was born on 14 Nov 1885 Ste.Anne, Manitoba (MB Vital Statistics, Birth Reg. #1885,001572.). He married **Marie Rose Anna Desjarlais**, daughter of **Antoine Desjarlais** and **Marie Falcon**, on 20 Nov 1906 (Ste-Anne), RM La Broquerie, Manitoba (MM, page 1264 & 536.) (MB Vital Statistics, Marriage Reg. #1906,002975.).

Marie Rose Anna Desjarlais was baptized on 10 Mar 1888 St.Claude Mission, St.John, Rolette County, North Dakota (St.Claude BMD, Dominique Ritchot, B-363, page 73.).

Children of **Octave Vandal** and **Marie Rose Anna Desjarlais** are as follows:

 37 i. Alexandrine Vandal, m. Elie Godefrie Nault.
 38 ii. Laura (Dora) Vandal, m. Charles Nault.
 39 iii. Rose Vandal, m. Leopold Sabot.

iv.   Bernadette Vandal married Arthur Boivin on 29 Dec 1934 Richer, Manitoba (MM.).

27. Justine Vandal was born on 6 Jun 1888 Ste.Anne, Manitoba (MB Vital Statistics, Birth Reg. #1888,004736.). She married **Hermenegilde Huppe**, son of **Julien Huppe** and **Veronique Nault,** on 16 Oct 1906 RM La Broquerie, Manitoba (MM.) (MB Vital Statistics, Marriage Reg. #1906,002989.).

Hermenegilde Huppe was born on 15 Mar 1879 Manitoba (1901 Canada, #10, e-3, page 1, family 7, line 32-39.).

28. Josephine Vandal was born on 14 Oct 1891 R.M. of Tache, Manitoba (Ibid., Birth Reg. #1891,001142.). She married **Jeremie Huppe**, son of **Julien Huppe** and **Veronique Nault,** on 24 Oct 1907 RM La Broquerie, Manitoba (MM.) (MB Vital Statistics, Marriage Reg. #1907,002244.). She married **Leon Belisle** on 9 Aug 1949 Richer, Manitoba (MM.).

Jeremie Huppe was born on 25 Mar 1875 Manitoba (1901 Canada, #10, e-3, page 1, family 7, line 32-39.). He was born circa 1878 (1881 Canada, District 184-E-1, page 16, house 76.).

29. Maurice Vandal was born circa 1895. He married **Julie Huppe**, daughter of **Julien Huppe** and **Veronique Nault,** on 25 Oct 1922 Ste.Anne, Richer, Manitoba (MM.) (MB Vital Statistics, Marriage Reg. #1922,041630.).

Julie Huppe was born on 12 Apr 1896 R.M. of La Broquerie, Manitoba (1901 Canada, #10, e-3, page 1, family 7, line 32-39.) (MB Vital Statistics, Birth Reg. #1896,004703.).

Children of **Maurice Vandal** and **Julie Huppe** are as follows:

        i.   Marie Anne Vandal married Alfred Chartier on 26 Jun 1951 Richer, Manitoba (MM.).

40   ii.   Louise Vandal, m. Aurele Vandal.

      iii.   Virginie Vandal married Bruno Vandal, son of Antoine Vandal and Melanie Berard, on 21 Aug 1952 Richer, Manitoba (Ibid.).

         Bruno Vandal was born in Aug 1907 Manitoba (1911 Canada, #12, page 7, family 58, line 27-34.).

30. Louis Vandal was born on 2 Apr 1895 R.M. of Tache, Manitoba (MB Vital Statistics, Birth Reg. #1895,004043.). He married **Marie Anne Ducharme**, daughter of **Pierre Ducharme** and **Virginie Huppe,** on 3 Jun 1919 Richer, Manitoba (MM.).

Marie Anne Ducharme was born on 26 Jul 1899 R.M. of LaBroquerie, Manitoba (1901 Canada, #10, E-3, page 304, family 31, line 46-50, 1.) (MB Vital Statistics, Birth Reg. #1899,002153.).

Children of **Louis Vandal** and **Marie Anne Ducharme** are:

41   i.   Aurele Vandal, m. Louise Vandal.

31. Maria Vandal was born on 6 Sep 1905 R.M. of La Broquerie, Manitoba (Ibid., Birth Reg. #1905,007381.). She married **Alexandre Nault**, son of **Andre Nault** and **Marie Harrison,** on 28 Jan 1929 St.Boniface, Manitoba (RMSB.).

Alexandre Nault was born on 31 Mar 1895 Ste.Anne, Manitoba (MB Vital Statistics, Birth Reg. #1896,11313492 (Reg 04/10/1928).). He died in 1975 (LFAN.).

32. Edmond Vandal married **Marie Louise Prairie**, daughter of **Alphonse Prairie** and **Marie Gauthier,** on 14 Oct 1925 Ste.Anne, Manitoba (Ibid.).

Children of **Edmond Vandal** and **Marie Louise Prairie** are as follows:

        i.   Aime Vandal married Therese Paquet on 17 Jun 1950 Transcona, Manitoba (Ibid.).

      ii.   Albert Vandal married Anita Mondor on 23 Feb 1963 Ile des Chenes, Manitoba (Ibid.).

33. Rosario Vandal was born on 4 Oct 1900 La Broquerie, Manitoba (1901 Canada, #10, e-2, page 3, family 19, line 6-14.). He married **Josephine Prairie** on 3 Oct 1923 Ste.Anne, Manitoba (MM.). He married **Marie Cecile Normand**, daughter of **Alfred Joseph Albert Normand** and **Helene Claire Lamirande,** on 16 Oct 1929 St.Norbert, Manitoba (Ibid.).

Josephine Prairie died before 1929.

Marie Cecile Normand was born on 17 Mar 1911 Woodridge, Manitoba (MB Vital Statistics, Birth Reg. #1911,27630800, Reg Date: 23/03/1989.). She died on 19 Mar 1993 Ste.Anne des Chenes, Manitoba, at age 82 (Rod Mac Quarrie, 17 Jan 2013.).

Children of **Rosario Vandal** and **Marie Cecile Normand** were as follows:

        i.   Rita Vandal married Reginald Cayer on 1 Oct 1949 Ste.Anne, Manitoba (MM.).

      ii.   Anita Vandal married Vianney Perreault on 23 May 1953 Ste.Anne, Manitoba (Ibid.).

     iii.   Diana Vandal married Robert Allard on 23 May 1953 Ste.Anne, Manitoba (Ibid.).

42   iv.   Eleonore Vandal, m. Joseph Vandal.

      v.   Rene Vandal was born circa 1936 (Ibid.). He married Jeannette Vandal, daughter of Alphonse Vandal and Agnes Gauthier, on 10 May 1958 Ste.Anne, Manitoba (Ibid.).

         Jeannette Vandal was born circa 1940.

      vi.   Irene Vandal was born circa 1937 (Ibid.). She married Oscar Levesque on 6 Sep 1958 Ste.Anne, Manitoba (Ibid.).

    vii.   Noella Vandal was born circa 1938 (Ibid.). She married Henry Kehler on 8 Apr 1961 Ste.Anne, Manitoba (Ibid.).

   viii.   Real Vandal was born circa 1941 (Ibid.). He married Gratia Vandal, daughter of Alphonse Vandal and Agnes Gauthier, on 31 Dec 1960 Ste.Anne, Manitoba (Ibid.).

         Gratia Vandal was born circa 1941.

     ix.   Dorothee Vandal was born circa 1945 (Ibid.). She married Cecil Main on 1 Jun 1963 Ste.Anne, Manitoba (Ibid.).

      x.   Lucille Vandal was born circa 1947 (Ibid.). She married Charles Sansregret on 13 Jun 1964 Ste.Anne, Manitoba (Ibid.).

Generation Five

34. Joseph Vandal married **Eleonore Vandal**, daughter of **Rosario Vandal** and **Marie Cecile Normand,** on 25 Apr 1942 Ste.Anne, Manitoba (Ibid.).

Children of **Joseph Vandal** and **Eleonore Vandal** are as follows:

        i.   Maurice Vandal married Lise Saindon on 18 Sep 1976 Richer, Manitoba (Ibid.).

      ii.   Aurise Vandal was born circa 1944 (Ibid.). She married Roger Andre on 21 Oct 1961 Ste.Anne, Manitoba (Ibid.).

     iii.   Rolande Vandal was born circa 1946 (Ibid.). She married Rene St.Laurent on 12 Oct 1963 Ste.Anne, Manitoba (Ibid.).

     iv.   Andre Vandal was born circa 1949 (Ibid.). He married Olive Ross on 31 Jul 1971 Ste.Anne, Manitoba (Ibid.).

v. Marie Paule Vandal was born circa 1957 (Ibid.). She married Michel Nault, son of Joseph Charles Leo Nault and Alice Lavigne, on 15 Mar 1975 Ste.Anne, Manitoba (Ibid.).

Michel Nault was born circa 1953 St.Pierre Jolys, Manitoba (Ibid.).

35. **Majoric Vandal** was born on 3 Aug 1905 R.M. of La Broquerie, Manitoba (MB Vital Statistics, Birth Reg. #1905,007375.). He married **Solange Proulx** on 19 Jan 1929 Ste.Anne, Manitoba (MM.).

Children of **Majoric Vandal** and **Solange Proulx** are:

i. Juliette Vandal married Gerard Nault, son of Andre Nault and Christine Beriault, on 31 Dec 1955 Ste.Anne, Manitoba (Ibid.).

Gerard Nault was born of, Thibaultville, Manitoba (Ibid.).

36. **Albert Vandal** was born circa 1909. He married **Doria Florida Harrison** on 15 Nov 1933 Ste.Anne, Manitoba (Ibid.).

Children of **Albert Vandal** and **Doria Florida Harrison** are:

i. Roger Vandal was born circa 1938. He married Anne Marie Jolicoeur on 16 Jun 1962 Ste.Anne, Manitoba (Ibid.).

37. **Alexandrine Vandal** married **Elie Godefrie Nault**, son of **Andre Nault** and **Marie Harrison**, on 8 Feb 1929 St.Boniface, Manitoba (RMSB.).

Elie Godefrie Nault was born on 6 Aug 1889 Ste.Anne, Manitoba (MB Vital Statistics, Birth Reg. #1889,005349.).

38. **Laura (Dora) Vandal** married **Charles Nault**, son of **Andre Nault** and **Marie Harrison**, on 3 Nov 1925 Winnipeg, Manitoba (MB Vital Statistics, Marriage Reg. #1925,047088 (Winnipeg).).

Charles Nault was born circa 1904.

39. **Rose Vandal** married **Leopold Sabot**, son of **Pierre Sabot** and **Nathalie Cuzuel**, on 3 Jun 1925 Richer, Manitoba (Ibid.).

Children of **Rose Vandal** and **Leopold Sabot** are as follows:

i. Jeannette Sabot married Lionel Rivard on 13 Sep 1958 Richer, Manitoba (Ibid., page 1121.). She married Marcel Nault, son of Joseph Alphonse Napoleon Neault and Bernadette Larocque, on 14 Jun 1975 Richer, Manitoba (Ibid.).

ii. Donat Sabot married Lina Phaneuf on 1 Aug 1951 Richer, Manitoba (Ibid.).

iii. Eveline Sabot married Eugene Saindon on 29 Apr 1946 Richer, Manitoba (Ibid.).

iv. George Sabot married Eveline Saindon on 22 Aug 1953 Richer, Manitoba (Ibid.).

40. **Louise Vandal** married **Aurele Vandal**, son of **Louis Vandal** and **Marie Anne Ducharme**, on 20 Jan 1920 St.Jean Baptiste, Manitoba (MM.).

Children of **Louise Vandal** and **Aurele Vandal** are:

i. Cecile Vandal married Ronald Kohut on 19 Sep 1964 Richer, Manitoba (Ibid.).

41. **Aurele Vandal** married **Louise Vandal**, daughter of **Maurice Vandal** and **Julie Huppe**, on 20 Jan 1920 St.Jean Baptiste, Manitoba (Ibid.).

Children of **Aurele Vandal** and **Louise Vandal** are:

i. Cecile Vandal married Ronald Kohut on 19 Sep 1964 Richer, Manitoba (Ibid.).

42. **Eleonore Vandal** married **Joseph Vandal**, son of **Pierre Vandal** and **Aurelie Berard**, on 25 Apr 1942 Ste.Anne, Manitoba (Ibid.).

Ahnentafel between Pierre Vandal and Etienne Vandal

--- 1st Generation ---

1. **PIERRE VANDAL** was born on 29 Jun 1787 at Sorel, Quebec (PRDH online index, http://www.genealogic.umontreal.ca, No. 695687.). He was baptized on 29 Jun 1787 at Sorel, Quebec (Ibid.). He married **CHARLOTTE HUGHES**, daughter of **JAMES HUGHES** and **NANTOUCHE CORBEAU**, before 1818.

--- 2nd Generation ---

2. **ANTOINE VANDAL** was born on 26 Oct 1752 at Sorel, Richelieu, Quebec (Ibid., #120717.). He was baptized on 27 Oct 1752 at Sorel, Richelieu, Quebec (Ibid.). He married **MARIE CHARLOTTE MANDEVILLE**, daughter of **ALEXIS MANDEVILLE** and **FRANCOISE HUS**, on 11 Feb 1771 at Sorel, Quebec (Ibid., No. 226165.). He died on 30 Apr 1824 at Sorel, Richelieu, Quebec, at age 71 (Ibid., #120717.). He was buried on 1 May 1824 at Sorel, Richelieu, Quebec (Ibid.).

--- 3rd Generation ---

4. **JACQUES VANDAL** (DGFQ Jette, Rene, *Dictionnaire Genealogique des Familles du Quebec des Origines a 1730* (Montreal, Quebec, Canada: University of Montreal Press, 1983), page 1112.) (Ibid.) (Ibid.) was baptized on 8 Oct 1725 at Neuville, Quebec (Ibid.). He married **MARIE ANTOINETTE BEAUGRAND DIT CHAMPAGNE**, daughter of **ANTOINE BEAUGRAND DIT CHAMPAGNE** and **MARIE JOSEPHE COUTU**, on 15 Jan 1748 at Lanoraie, Quebec (PRDH online.). He married **MARIE THERESE VENNE**, daughter of **LOUIS VENNE** and **LOUISE MARIE THERESE DESAUTELS DIT LAPOINTE**, on 14 Feb 1757 at Sorel, Quebec (Ibid., No. 321957.). He died on 20 Jan 1779 at Sorel, Quebec, at age 53 (Ibid., No. 377577.). He was buried on 21 Jan 1779 at Sorel, Quebec (Ibid.).

--- 4th Generation ---

8. **FRANCOIS VANDAL** was born on 3 Feb 1682 at Neuville, Quebec (DGFQ, page 1112.) (PRDH online, No. 53621.). He was baptized on 8 Feb 1682 at Neuville, Quebec (DGFQ, page 1112.) (PRDH online, No. 53621.). He married **MARIE-ANTOINETTE RIPAULT**, daughter of **ROCH RIPAULT DIT ROLET OR ROLLET** and **MARIE-ANNE AUBERT**, on 10 Feb 1716 at Grondines, Quebec (DNCF *Dictionnaire National des Canadiens-Francais Tome I & II* Gabriel Drouin, editor (revised 1985; Siege Social, 4184, rue St-Denis, Montreal, Canada: l'Institut Genealogique Drouin, 1979), page 1325.) (DGFQ, page 1112.) (PRDH online, No. 56137.). A contract for the marriage to **MARIE-ANTOINETTE RIPAULT**, daughter of **ROCH RIPAULT DIT ROLET OR ROLLET** and **MARIE-ANNE AUBERT**, was signed on 16 Feb 1716 (DGFQ, page 1112.). He was buried on 22 Feb 1742 at Neuville, Quebec (PRDH online, No. 156598.).

--- 5th Generation ---

16. FRANCOIS VANDAL lived at at Verantes, Saumur, Angers, Anjou (Maine-et-Loire) (DNCF, page 1325.) (DGFQ, page 1112.). He was also known as FRANCOIS VANDALE (DNCF, page 1239.). He was born between 1645 and 1651 (DGFQ, page 1112.). He married MARIE-MADELEINE PINEL, daughter of GILLES PINEL and ANNE LEDET, on 19 Mar 1680 at Neuville, Quebec (Ibid.). He was buried on 6 Dec 1697 at Neuville, Quebec (Ibid.).

--- 6th Generation ---

32. ETIENNE VANDAL married JULIENNE GROLE.

Descendants of Pierre Vandal

Generation One

1. **Pierre Vandal** was born on 29 Jun 1787 Sorel, Quebec (PRDH online index, http://www.genealogic.umontreal.ca, No. 695687.). He was baptized on 29 Jun 1787 Sorel, Quebec (Ibid.). He married **Charlotte Hughes**, daughter of **James Hughes** and **Nan-touche Corbeau,** before 1818.

Question: *Probable son of Antoine Vandal and Marie Charlotte Mandeville.*

Charlotte Hughes was born in 1796 (SB 1825-1834 St.Boniface Roman Catholic Registre des Baptemes, Mariages & Sepultures, 1825-1834, page 149-150, B-876. Hereinafter cited as SB 1825-1834.). She was baptized on 30 Sep 1834 St.Boniface, (Manitoba) (Ibid.). She died on 15 Feb 1872 St.Norbert, Manitoba (MBS   Scrip Applications, Original White Settlers & Halfbreeds residing in Manitoba on 15 July 1870, RG15-19, C-14934.) (SN1 Catholic Parish Register of St.Norbert 1857-1873, S-12. Hereinafter cited as SN1.). She was buried on 17 Feb 1872 St.Norbert, Manitoba (MBS, C-14934.) (SN1, S-12.).

Children of **Pierre Vandal** and **Charlotte Hughes** were as follows:

   2   i.   Antoine Vandal, b. circa 1819 North West; m. Isabelle Beauchemin.

       ii.   Joseph Vandal was born circa 1824 (1870C-MB 1870 Manitoba Census, National Archives of Canada, Ottawa, Ontario, Microfilm Reel Number C-2170., #628, page 21.). He died on 1 Nov 1873 St.Norbert, Manitoba (MBS, Extraction; C-14934.) (SN1, S-35.). He was buried on 2 Nov 1873 St.Norbert, Manitoba (MBS, Extraction; C-14934.) (SN1, S-35.).

   3   iii.   Augustin Vandal, b. circa 1826 Red River, (Manitoba); m. Marie Dupuis; d. 6 Jan 1862 St.Norbert, (Manitoba); bur. 8 Jan 1862 St.Norbert, (Manitoba), England.

       iv.   Pierre Vandal was born circa 1828 (SB 1825-1834, page 130, B-797.). He was baptized on 8 Jul 1834 St.Boniface, (Manitoba) (Ibid.). He died on 22 Aug 1834 St.Boniface, (Manitoba) (Ibid., page 140, S-69.). He was buried on 22 Aug 1834 St.Boniface, (Manitoba) (Ibid.).

       v.   Marguerite Vandal was born in 1822 Red River (1870C-MB, #627, page 21.). She was born circa 1829 (SB 1825-1834, page 130-131, B-798.). She was baptized on 8 Jul 1834 St.Boniface, (Manitoba) (Ibid.).

   4   vi.   Jean Baptiste Vandal, b. circa 1832; m. Marie Primeau; d. 22 Feb 1888 Batoche, (Saskatchewan); bur. 24 Feb 1888 Batoche, (Saskatchewan).

Generation Two

2. **Antoine Vandal** was born circa 1819 North West (MBS, C-14934.). He was born on 10 Dec 1822 (Automated Genealogy 1901 Census Transcription Project and Census Images from the National Archives of Canada, http://www.automatedgenealogy.com, microfilm, T-6553, Bellevue, page 8, Family 74, line 9-17.). He married **Isabelle Beauchemin**, daughter of **Benjamin Beauchemin** and **Marie Parenteau,** before 1848.

Isabelle Beauchemin was born circa Jun 1828 St.Boniface, (Manitoba) (MBS, C-14934.). She died on 26 Aug 1878 St.Norbert, Manitoba (St-N Cem *St.Norbert Parish Cemetery 1859-1906, We Remember*; Winnipeg, Manitoba, Canada: St.Norbert Parish-La Barriere Metis Council of the Metis Federation of Manitoba, 29 May 2010).) (SN2 Catholic Parish Register of St.Norbert, S-36. Hereinafter cited as SN2.). She was buried on 27 Aug 1878 St.Norbert, Manitoba (St-N Cem.) (SN2, S-36.).

Children of **Antoine Vandal** and **Isabelle Beauchemin** were as follows:

   5   i.   Pierre Vandal, b. 15 Jan 1848; m. Louise Poitras.

   6   ii.   Antoine Vandal, b. 10 Jul 1849; m. Alphosine Henry.

       iii.   Anonyme Vandal was born on 1 Aug 1850 (AP Records of the Assumption Roman Catholic Church, Pembina, North Dakota: Baptisms, Marriages, Sepultures, 1848-1896; compiled by Reverend Father J. M. Belleau, 2 October 1944, page 43, S-13. Hereinafter cited as AP.). She died on 7 Aug 1850 (Ibid.). She was buried on 11 Aug 1850 Assumption, Pembina, Pembina County, Dakota Territory (Ibid.).

   7   iv.   Isabelle Vandal, b. 25 Dec 1852 St.Norbert, (Manitoba); m. Maurice Henry; bur. 15 Jul 1882 Lebret, (Saskatchewan).

   8   v.   Joseph Vandal, b. 29 Oct 1856 St.Norbert, (Manitoba); m. Rosalie Rocheleau; d. 19 Jan 1879 St.Norbert, Manitoba; bur. 21 Jan 1879 St.Norbert, Manitoba.

   9   vi.   Melanie Vandal, b. 11 Apr 1859 St.Norbert, (Manitoba); m. Jean Baptiste Rocheleau; d. 3 Jun 1885 Batoche, (Saskatchewan); bur. 5 Jun 1885 Batoche, (Saskatchewan).

       vii.   Marie Vandal was born on 29 Oct 1861 St.Norbert, (Manitoba) (SN1, page 48, B-36.). She was baptized on 30 Oct 1861 St.Norbert, (Manitoba) (Ibid.). She died on 13 Mar 1880 St.Norbert, Manitoba, at age 18 (SN2, S-6.). She was buried on 15 Mar 1880 St.Norbert, Manitoba (Ibid.).

       viii.   Francois Vandal was born on 29 Oct 1861 St.Norbert, (Manitoba) (SN1, page 48, B-35.). He was baptized on 30 Oct 1861 St.Norbert, (Manitoba) (Ibid.). He died on 23 Feb 1862 St.Norbert, (Manitoba) (Ibid., page 55, S-3.). He was buried on 24 Feb 1862 St.Norbert, (Manitoba) (Ibid.).

       ix.   Jean Baptiste Vandal was born on 8 May 1864 St.Norbert, (Manitoba) (MBS, C-14934.) (SN1, page 104, B-29.). He was baptized on 5 Sep 1864 St.Norbert, (Manitoba) (Ibid.). He died on 25 Dec 1872 St.Norbert, Manitoba, at age 8 (MBS, C-14934.) (SN1, S-20.). He was buried on 27 Dec 1872 St.Norbert, Manitoba (MBS, C-14934.) (SN1, S-20.).

    x.   Sara Vandal was born on 6 Nov 1866 (Ibid., page 88, B-62.). She was baptized on 25 Nov 1866 St.Norbert, (Manitoba) (Ibid.). She died on 6 Jun 1867 (Ibid., S-11.). She was buried on 8 Jun 1867 St.Norbert, (Manitoba) (Ibid.).

    xi.   Philomene Vandal was born on 16 Jul 1868 St.Norbert, (Manitoba) (Ibid., B-27.). She was baptized on 19 Jul 1868 St.Norbert, (Manitoba) (Ibid.). She died on 24 Jan 1885 Batoche, (Saskatchewan), at age 16 (BSAP Records of the Parish of Batoche, St.Antoine de Pudoue Roman Catholic Church: Register for Baptisms, Marriages, Deaths, Volume One, 1881-1909., page 29, S-2. Hereinafter cited as BSAP.). She was buried on 26 Jan 1885 Batoche, (Saskatchewan) (Ibid.).

    xii.   Alexandre Vandal was born on 25 Aug 1871 St.Norbert, Manitoba (SN1, page 150, B-44.). He was baptized on 26 Aug 1871 St.Norbert, Manitoba (Ibid.). He died on 24 Dec 1889 Fish Creek, (Saskatchewan), at age 18 (Denney Papers, Charles D. Denney, Glenbow Archives, Calgary, Alberta.) (BSAP, page 78, S-11.). He was buried on 25 Dec 1889 Batoche, (Saskatchewan) (Ibid.).

    xiii.   Marie Therese Vandal was born on 6 May 1874 St.Norbert, Manitoba (SN2, B-21.). She was baptized on 7 May 1874 St.Norbert, Manitoba (Ibid.). She died on 11 Sep 1874 St.Norbert, Manitoba (Ibid., S-25.). She was buried on 12 Sep 1874 St.Norbert, Manitoba (Ibid.).

3. Augustin Vandal was born circa 1826 Red River, (Manitoba) (1850Ci-MN *Minnesota Territorial Census, 1850*, Harpole, Patricia C. and Mary D. Nagle, ed., (St.Paul, Minnesota: Minnesota Historical Society, 1972), page 30, Dwelling 118, Family 118.). He married **Marie Dupuis**, daughter of **Jean Baptiste Dupuis** and **Marie Corbeau dit Hughes**, before 1857. He died on 6 Jan 1862 St.Norbert, (Manitoba) (SN1, S-1.). He was buried on 8 Jan 1862 St.Norbert, (Manitoba), England (Ibid.).

Marie Dupuis was born in 1831 St.Boniface, (Manitoba) (MBS, C-14930.). She and **John Logan** met before 15 Jul 1870.

Children of **Augustin Vandal** and **Marie Dupuis** were as follows:

  10 i.   Augustin Vandal, b. Jul 1857 St.Norbert, (Manitoba); m. Sophie Parisien; d. before 1895.

      ii.   Marie Vandal was born circa 1858 (SN1, page 63, S-11.). She died on 6 Oct 1862 (Ibid.). She was buried on 8 Oct 1862 St.Norbert, (Manitoba) (Ibid.).

      iii.   Isabelle Vandal was born circa 1858 (Ibid., page 61, S-10.). She died on 11 Sep 1862 (Ibid.). She was buried on 13 Sep 1862 St.Norbert, (Manitoba) (Ibid.).

  11 iv.   Melanie Vandal, b. 25 Dec 1858; m. John Henry.

      v.   Marie Jane Vandal was born on 29 Mar 1862 St.Norbert, (Manitoba) (Ibid., page 56, B-8.). She was baptized on 30 Mar 1862 St.Norbert, (Manitoba) (Ibid.).

4. Jean Baptiste Vandal was born in Jul 1830 Edmonton, (Alberta) (MBS, C-14934.). He was born circa 1832 (SB 1825-1834, page 131, B-799.). He was baptized on 8 Jul 1834 St.Boniface, (Manitoba) (Ibid.). He married **Marie Primeau**, daughter of **Joseph Primeau** and **Marguerite Stevenson**, circa 1857. He died on 22 Feb 1888 Batoche, (Saskatchewan) (BSAP, page 65, S-1.). He was buried on 24 Feb 1888 Batoche, (Saskatchewan) (Ibid.).

Marie Primeau was born in 1839 Fort Alexandre (MBS, C-14934.). She was born in 1840 (Manitoba) (1901 Canada, page 5, Family 37, #32.).

Children of **Jean Baptiste Vandal** and **Marie Primeau** were as follows:

  12 i.   Joseph Vandal, b. circa 1857 (Manitoba); m. Elizabeth Champagne; d. 20 Dec 1885 Batoche, (Saskatchewan); bur. 22 Dec 1885 Batoche, (Saskatchewan).

  13 ii.   Rosalie Vandal, b. 22 Aug 1859 St.Norbert, (Manitoba); m. Charles Pruden; d. before 1901.

  14 iii.   William Vandal, b. 15 Aug 1861; m. Virginie Boyer.

      iv.   Anne Vandal was born on 26 Sep 1863 St.Norbert, (Manitoba) (SN1, page 87, B-32.). She was baptized on 27 Sep 1863 St.Norbert, (Manitoba) (Ibid.). She died on 30 Dec 1885 Batoche, (Saskatchewan), at age 22 (BSAP, page 42, S-28.). She was buried on 31 Dec 1885 Batoche, (Saskatchewan) (Ibid.).

  15 v.   Pierre Modeste Vandal, b. 1 Feb 1866 St.Norbert, (Manitoba); m. Adelaide Parenteau.

  16 vi.   Norbert Vandal, b. circa Dec 1868; m. Virginie Carriere.

  17 vii.   Marie Louise Vandal, b. 2 Mar 1873 Batoche, (Saskatchewan); m. Joseph Fisher.

  18 viii.   Eulalie Vandal, b. 8 Nov 1878 Batoche, (Saskatchewan); m. Louis Gervais.

Generation Three

5. Pierre Vandal was born on 15 Jan 1848 (1901 Canada, Fish Creek, page 1, Family 5, Line 13-24.). He married **Louise Poitras**, daughter of **Ignace Poitras** and **Helene McGillis**, on 9 Jun 1874 St.Francois Xavier, Manitoba (SFXI-Kipling St.Francois Xavier Register Index, 1834-1900; compiled by Clarence Kipling , M-11.).

Louise Poitras was born on 1 Jul 1857 (Ibid., B-217.). She was baptized on 6 Sep 1857 St.Francois Xavier, (Manitoba) (Ibid.) (INB *Index des Naissances and Baptemes* (St.Boniface, Manitoba: La Societe Historique de Saint-Boniface., c1995), page 152.).

Children of **Pierre Vandal** and **Louise Poitras** were as follows:

      i.   Marie Philomene Vandal was born on 24 Apr 1875 (Denney.) (INB.) (SL-SK St.Laurent-de-Grandin Roman Catholic Registre des Baptemes, Mariages & Sepltures, St.Laurent, Saskatchewan, 1872-1896, page 37, B-9. Hereinafter cited as SL-SK.). She was baptized on 26 Apr 1875 St.Laurent-de-Grandin, (Saskatchewan) (Ibid.). She died on 15 Jan 1893 Fish Creek, (Saskatchewan), at age 17 (Denney.) (BSAP, page 103, S-1.). She was buried on 16 Jan 1893 Batoche, (Saskatchewan) (Ibid.).

      ii.   Pierre Louis Vandal was born on 16 Oct 1876 Batoche, (Saskatchewan) (ArchiviaNet 1886-1901, 1906 Half-Breed Scrip Applications Index, RG15-21, Volume 1333 through 1371, Microfilm Reel Number C-14944 through C-15010, National Archives of Canada, Ottawa, Ontario, http://www.collectionscanada.gc.ca, C-15008.). He died circa 16 Nov 1878 (SL-SK, page 23, S-21.). He was buried on 16 Nov 1878 St.Laurent-de-Grandin, (Saskatchewan) (Ibid.).

19   iii.   Marie Rose Vandal, b. 24 Sep 1877 Batoche, (Saskatchewan); m. Clovis Nogier.

iv.   Marie Emelie Vandal was born on 24 Dec 1878 (Ibid., page 24, B-57.). She was baptized on 24 Dec 1878 St.Laurent-de-Grandin, (Saskatchewan) (Ibid.). She died on 14 Jun 1900 Fish Creek, (Saskatchewan), at age 21 (Saskatchewan Vital Statistics online, http://vsgs.health.gov.sk.ca, Death Reg. #235.) (ArchiviaNet, C-15008.).

v.   Etienne Vandal was born on 17 Jan 1880 Duck Lake, (Saskatchewan) (DL Register of Sacre Coeur Roman Catholic Church, Duck Lake, Saskatchewan, 1870-1893, page 30, B-1. Hereinafter cited as DL.). He was baptized on 19 Jan 1880 Duck Lake, (Saskatchewan) (Ibid.).

20   vi.   Rose Germaine Vandal, b. 8 Feb 1881 Batoche, (Saskatchewan); m. Alexandre Lavallee.

vii.   William Vandal was born on 11 Oct 1882 Fish Creek, (Saskatchewan) (BSAP, page 10, B-24.) (ArchiviaNet, C-15008.). He was baptized on 12 Oct 1882 Batoche, (Saskatchewan) (BSAP, page 10, B-24.). He married Alvina Parenteau, daughter of Louis Parenteau and Rosalie Letendre, on 21 Feb 1911 Batoche, Saskatchewan (Denney.).
   Alvina Parenteau was born on 30 Mar 1891 Batoche, (Saskatchewan) (BSAP, page 88, B-6.) (SK Vital Statistics, Birth Reg. #7600.). She was baptized on 30 Mar 1891 Batoche, (Saskatchewan) (BSAP, page 88, B-6.).

viii.   Eulalie Vandal was born on 25 Mar 1884 Fish Creek, (Saskatchewan) (Ibid., page 20, B-6.). She was baptized on 26 Mar 1884 Batoche, (Saskatchewan) (Ibid.).

ix.   Simon Vandal was born on 4 Dec 1886 Fish Creek, (Saskatchewan) (ArchiviaNet, C-15008.). He was baptized on 5 Dec 1886 Batoche, (Saskatchewan) (Denney.).

x.   Josephine Vandal was born on 4 Mar 1888 Batoche, (Saskatchewan) (BSAP, page 65, B-6.). She was baptized on 5 Mar 1888 Batoche, (Saskatchewan) (Ibid.).

xi.   Florentine Vandal was born on 9 Nov 1889 Fish Creek, (Saskatchewan) (1901 Canada, Fish Creek, page 1, Family 5, Line 13-24.).

xii.   Virginie Vandal was born on 16 Nov 1891 Fish Creek, (Saskatchewan) (BSAP, page 91, B-18.). She was baptized on 23 Nov 1891 Batoche, (Saskatchewan) (Ibid.). She married Pierre Lavallee on 29 Jul 1913 Batoche, Saskatchewan (Denney.).

xiii.   Louis David Vandal was born on 18 Dec 1893 Fish Creek, (Saskatchewan) (BSAP, page 112, B-32.). He was baptized on 19 Dec 1893 Batoche, (Saskatchewan) (Ibid.). He died on 28 Oct 1894 Fish Creek, (Saskatchewan) (Ibid., page 119, S-12.). He was buried on 30 Oct 1894 Batoche, (Saskatchewan) (Ibid.).

xiv.   Napoleon Norbert Vandal was born on 1 Jun 1895 Fish Creek, (Saskatchewan) (Ibid., page 124, B-15.). He was baptized on 2 Jun 1895 Batoche, (Saskatchewan) (Ibid.).

xv.   Joseph Albert Vandal was born on 18 Dec 1897 Fish Creek, (Saskatchewan) (1901 Canada, Fish Creek, page 8, Family 5, Line 13-24.).

xvi.   Elmira Vandal was born on 9 Mar 1899 Fish Creek, (Saskatchewan) (Ibid.).

6. Antoine Vandal was born on 10 Jul 1849 (Ibid., microfilm, T-6553, Bellevue, page 8, Family 74, line 9-17.). He was born circa 1850 Red River, (Manitoba). He married **Alphosine Henry**, daughter of **Alexis Henry** and **Marie Daunais dit Lyonnaise,** on 16 Jan 1872 St.Norbert, Manitoba (SN1, M-3.).

Alphosine Henry was born on 10 Aug 1851 St.Vital, (Manitoba) (MBS, C-14934.) (1901 Canada, microfilm, T-6553, Bellevue, page 8, Family 74, line 9-17.).

Children of **Antoine Vandal** and **Alphosine Henry** were as follows:

i.   Emelie Cecile Vendale was born on 23 May 1873 St.Norbert, Manitoba (SN1, B-31.). She was baptized on 24 May 1873 St.Norbert, Manitoba (Ibid.). She died on 4 May 1874 St.Norbert, Manitoba (SN2, S-9.). She was buried on 6 May 1874 St.Norbert, Manitoba (Ibid.).

ii.   Joseph Elzear Vendal was born on 10 Mar 1874 St.Norbert, Manitoba (Ibid., B-13.). He was baptized on 11 Mar 1874 St.Norbert, Manitoba (Ibid.). He died on 3 Dec 1876 St.Norbert, Manitoba, at age 2 (Ibid., S-13.). He was buried on 4 Dec 1876 St.Norbert, Manitoba (Ibid.).

iii.   Pierre Maxime Vandal was born on 28 Jun 1875 St.Norbert, Manitoba (Ibid., B-22.). He was baptized on 28 Jun 1875 St.Norbert, Manitoba (Ibid.). He died on 28 Jun 1875 St.Norbert, Manitoba (Ibid., S-16.). He was buried on 29 Jun 1875 St.Norbert, Manitoba (Ibid.).

iv.   Virginie Vandal was born circa Apr 1876 (Ibid., S-7.). She died on 18 May 1876 St.Norbert, Manitoba (Ibid.). She was buried on 19 May 1876 St.Norbert, Manitoba (Ibid.).

21   v.   Marie Emelie Vandal, b. 27 May 1877 St.Norbert, Manitoba; m. Joseph Ross.

22   vi.   Frederick Vandal, b. 17 Jun 1879; m. Sophia Mary Fiddler; d. 26 Sep 1964 Prince Albert, Saskatchewan; bur. 30 Sep 1964 South Hill, Prince Albert, Saskatchewan.

23   vii.   Mathilde Vandal, b. 27 Jan 1881 Montagne la Bosse; m. John Fidler; m. Louis Grassick; d. 22 Jan 1958 Cudworth, Saskatchewan.

24   viii.   Francois Vandal, b. 2 Jan 1883 Batoche, (Saskatchewan); m. Anna (Skierra) Skarra; d. 1 Nov 1918 Cudworth, Saskatchewan.

ix.   Leon Salomon Vandal was born on 9 Feb 1885 Batoche, (Saskatchewan) (BSAP, page 29, B-2.). He was baptized on 16 Feb 1885 Batoche, (Saskatchewan) (Ibid.).

x.   Theodore Vandal was born on 27 Jan 1886 Batoche, (Saskatchewan) (Ibid., page 43, B-2.). He was baptized on 28 Jan 1886 Batoche, (Saskatchewan) (Ibid.).

xi.   Helene Vandal was born on 11 Feb 1888 Batoche, (Saskatchewan) (Ibid., page 65, B-5.). She was baptized on 13 Feb 1888 Batoche, (Saskatchewan) (Ibid.).

xii.   Patrice Vandal was born on 4 May 1891 Batoche, (Saskatchewan) (Ibid., page 89, B-11.). He was baptized on 5 May 1891 Batoche, (Saskatchewan) (Ibid.). He died on 8 Jun 1891 Batoche, (Saskatchewan) (Ibid., page 90, S-8.). He was buried on 9 Jun 1891 Batoche, (Saskatchewan) (Ibid.).

7. Isabelle Vandal was born on 25 Dec 1852 St.Norbert, (Manitoba) (MBS, C-14929.). She married **Maurice Henry**, son of **Alexis Henry** and **Marie Daunais dit Lyonnaise**, on 16 Jan 1872 St.Norbert, Manitoba (SN1, M-4.). She was buried on 15 Jul 1882 Lebret, (Saskatchewan) (L2 Lebret, Mission de St.Florent, Roman Catholic Registre des Baptemes, Mariages & Seplutures, Qu'Appelle, Saskatchewan, Book Two: 1881-1887, FHC microfilm 1032949., page 38, S-14. Hereinafter cited as L2.).

Maurice Henry was born on 8 Jan 1847 St.Norbert, (Manitoba) (MBS, C-14929.). He married **Blandine Ross**, daughter of **Donald Ross** and **Catherine Delorme**, on 18 Feb 1884 Batoche, (Saskatchewan) (BSAP, page 19, M-1.). He died on 1 Apr 1934 at age 87.

8. Joseph Vandal was born on 29 Oct 1856 St.Norbert, (Manitoba) (MBS, C-14934.). He married **Rosalie Rocheleau**, daughter of **Jean Baptiste Rocheleau** and **Marie Anne Carriere**, on 10 Oct 1876 St.Norbert, Manitoba (SN2, M-6.). He died on 19 Jan 1879 St.Norbert, Manitoba, at age 22 (Ibid., S-3.). He was buried on 21 Jan 1879 St.Norbert, Manitoba (Ibid.).

Rosalie Rocheleau was born circa 1855 Fort Ellice, Manitoba (Denney.). She married **Joseph Nault**, son of **Andre Nault** and **Anastasie Landry**, on 16 Feb 1874 St.Norbert, Manitoba (SN2, M-3.). She married **Napoleon Carriere**, son of **Elie Carriere** and **Elmire Landry**, on 27 May 1883 Batoche, (Saskatchewan) (BSAP, page 15, M-2.).

Children of **Joseph Vandal** and **Rosalie Rocheleau** all born St.Norbert, Manitoba, were as follows:

  i. Patrice Vandal was born on 31 Jul 1877 (SN2, B-28.). He was baptized on 31 Jul 1877 St.Norbert, Manitoba (Ibid.). He died on 29 Apr 1878 St.Norbert, Manitoba (Ibid., S-21.). He was buried on 5 May 1878 St.Norbert, Manitoba (Ibid.).

  ii. Marie Alvina Vandal was born on 31 Jul 1877 (Ibid., B-29.). She was baptized on 31 Jul 1877 St.Norbert, Manitoba (Ibid.). She died on 31 Jan 1878 St.Norbert, Manitoba (Ibid., S-6.). She was buried on 2 Feb 1878 St.Norbert, Manitoba (Ibid.).

25 iii. Marie Virginie Vandal, b. 13 May 1879; m. William Sauve; d. 12 Apr 1904.

9. Melanie Vandal was born on 11 Apr 1859 St.Norbert, (Manitoba) (SN1, page 9-10, B-9.). She was baptized on 12 Apr 1859 St.Norbert, (Manitoba) (Ibid.). She married **Jean Baptiste Rocheleau**, son of **Jean Baptiste Rocheleau** and **Marie Anne Carriere**, on 10 Oct 1876 St.Norbert, Manitoba (SN2, M-5.). She died on 3 Jun 1885 Batoche, (Saskatchewan), at age 26 (BSAP, page 35, S-29.). She was buried on 5 Jun 1885 Batoche, (Saskatchewan) (Ibid.).

Jean Baptiste Rocheleau was born on 8 Jan 1851 St.Norbert, (Manitoba) (1870C-MB, #1959, page 64.) (1901 Canada, Fish Creek, page 1, Family 10, Line 42-46.) (MBS, Reel T-12030.).

10. Augustin Vandal was born in Jul 1857 St.Norbert, (Manitoba) (MBS, C-14934.). He married **Sophie Parisien**, daughter of **Andre Parisien** and **Julie Zace**, on 8 Jan 1885 St.Norbert, Manitoba (SN2, M-3.). He died before 1895.

Sophie Parisien was born on 18 Nov 1862 St.Norbert, (Manitoba) (SN1, page 65, B-34.). She was baptized on 18 Nov 1862 St.Norbert, (Manitoba) (Ibid.). She married **Andre Morisseau**, son of **Andre Morisseau** and **Cecile Monet dit Belhumeur**, on 29 Jul 1895 Ste.Rose, Manitoba (MM *Manitoba Marriages* in *Publication 45*, Volumes 1-3, compiled and edited by: Paul J. Lareau, Fr. Julien Hamelin, (240 Avenue Daly, Ottawa, Ontario K1N 6G2: Le Centre de Genealogie S.C., 1984).).

Children of **Augustin Vandal** and **Sophie Parisien** were as follows:

  i. Toussaint Vandal was born on 1 Nov 1885 St.Norbert, Manitoba (SN2, B-53.) (Manitoba Vital Statistics online, http://web2.gov.mb.ca, Birth Reg. #1885,0016391.). He was baptized on 2 Nov 1885 St.Norbert, Manitoba (SN2, B-53.). He died on 30 Mar 1887 St.Norbert, Manitoba, at age 1 (Ibid., S-6.) (MB Vital Statistics, Death Reg. #1887,001827.). He was buried on 1 Apr 1887 St.Norbert, Manitoba (SN2, S-6.).

  ii. Joseph Jeremie Vandal was born on 22 Jan 1887 RM of St.Nobert, Manitoba (MB Vital Statistics, Birth Reg. #1887,004181.) (SN2, B-8.). He was baptized on 25 Jan 1887 St.Norbert, Manitoba (Ibid.).

  iii. Ursule Vandal was born on 8 Apr 1889 St.Nobert, Manitoba (MB Vital Statistics, Birth Reg. #1889,005395.) (SN2, B-20.). She was baptized on 9 Apr 1889 St.Norbert, Manitoba (Ibid.).

  iv. Joseph Philias Vandal was born on 10 May 1891 R.M. of Turtle Mountain, Manitoba (MB Vital Statistics, Birth Reg. #1891,001670.). He married Ema Pelter on 15 Feb 1926 RM of Lawrence, Manitoba (Ibid., Marriage Reg. #1926,007266.).

  v. Adolphus Vandal was born on 29 Jun 1893 (1901 Canada, District 9-1-1, page 11, family 88, line 2-9.) (Rod MacQuarrie Research, 28 Dec 2011.).

11. Melanie Vandal was born on 25 Dec 1858 (SN1, page 9, B-5.). She was baptized on 5 Mar 1859 St.Norbert, (Manitoba) (Ibid.). She married **John Henry**, son of **John Henry** and **Josephte Parisien**, on 9 Feb 1880 St.Norbert, Manitoba (SN2, M-2.).

John Henry was born on 7 Apr 1851 St.Norbert, (Manitoba) (MBS, C-14928.).

12. Joseph Vandal was born circa 1857 (Manitoba) (1881 Canada, C-13285, District 192-1, page 24, household 109.). He married **Elizabeth Champagne**, daughter of **Emmanuel Champagne** and **Marie Letendre**, on 14 Jul 1879 St.Boniface, Manitoba (RMSB.). He died on 20 Dec 1885 Batoche, (Saskatchewan) (BSAP, page 41, S-37.). He was buried on 22 Dec 1885 Batoche, (Saskatchewan) (Ibid.).

Elizabeth Champagne was born on 30 Aug 1853 Pine Creek, (Manitoba) (MBS, C-14925.). She married **Joseph Azure**, son of **Joseph Azure** and **Angelique Martel**, on 29 Dec 1873 Lebret, (Saskatchewan) (L1 Lebret Mission de St.Florent Roman Catholic Registre des Baptemes, Mariages & Seplutures, Qu'Appelle, Saskatchewan, 1868-1881., page 127, M-9. Hereinafter cited as L1.). She married **Thomas Petit**, son of **Thomas Petit** and **Josephte Ouellette**, on 24 Jan 1888 Batoche, (Saskatchewan) (BSAP, page 64, M-1.).

Children of **Joseph Vandal** and **Elizabeth Champagne** were as follows:

  i. Joseph Vandal was born on 4 Jun 1880 Batoche, (Saskatchewan) (ArchiviaNet, C-15008.). He was baptized on 5 Jun 1880 Duck Lake, (Saskatchewan) (DL, page 31, B-8.).

26 ii. Elise Vandal, b. 8 Jun 1882 Batoche, (Saskatchewan); m. Chrysostome Boyer.

  iii. Marie Adelaide Vandal was born on 3 Nov 1884 Battleford, (Saskatchewan) (SV St.Vital Roman Catholic Registre des Baptemes, Mariages & Seplutures, Battleford, Saskatchewan, 1878-1896, B-29. Hereinafter cited as SV.). She was baptized on 4 Nov 1884 St.Vital, Battleford, (Saskatchewan) (Ibid.). She married Francois Villeneuve on 24 Nov 1903 Fish Creek, (Saskatchewan) (Heather Hallett Research, 22 Jan 2002.).

13. **Rosalie Vandal** was born on 22 Aug 1859 St.Norbert, (Manitoba) (SN1, B-27, page 18.). She was baptized on 23 Aug 1859 St.Norbert, (Manitoba) (Ibid.). She married **Charles Pruden**, son of **James Pruden** and **Genevieve Desjarlais,** on 7 Jan 1880 Duck Lake, (Saskatchewan) (DL, page 31, M-1.). She died before 1901 (1901 Canada, District 205-u(1), pare 11, line 33.).

Charles Pruden was born on 7 Feb 1856 McKenzie River (Denney.). He died on 14 Jan 1917 Prince Albert, Saskatchewan, at age 60 (Ibid.).

14. **William Vandal** was born on 15 Aug 1861 (SB-Rozyk St. Boniface Roman Catholic Church, Manitoba, Canada, Baptisms, Marriages and Burials 1860-1875 Extractions, Compiled by Rosemary Rozyk, page 27, B-105.). He was baptized on 17 Aug 1861 St.Boniface, (Manitoba) (Ibid.). He married **Virginie Boyer**, daughter of **Jean Baptiste Boyer** and **Elizabeth Bousquet,** on 7 Feb 1882 St-Laurent-de-Grandin, (Saskatchewan) (SL-SK, page 56-57, M-2.).

Virginie Boyer was born on 24 Jan 1865 St.Boniface, (Manitoba) (SB-Rozyk, page 175, B-8.). She was baptized on 24 Jan 1865 St.Boniface, (Manitoba) (Ibid.).

Children of **William Vandal** and **Virginie Boyer** were as follows:

- i. William Vandal was born on 3 Dec 1882 St.Laurent, (Saskatchewan) (SL-SK, page 62, B-22.). He was baptized on 4 Dec 1882 St.Laurent, (Saskatchewan) (Ibid.). He died on 5 Jan 1905 Batoche, (Saskatchewan), at age 22 (BSAP, page 231, S-1.). He was buried on 17 Jan 1905 Batoche, (Saskatchewan) (Ibid.).
- ii. Virginie Vandal was born on 11 May 1884 St.Laurent, (Saskatchewan) (ArchiviaNet, C-15008.). She was baptized on 12 May 1884 St.Laurent, (Saskatchewan) (Denney.). She died on 5 Feb 1885 Batoche, (Saskatchewan) (ArchiviaNet, C-15008.).
- iii. Jean Baptiste Vandal was born on 27 Feb 1886 Batoche, (Saskatchewan) (BSAP, page 44, B-6.). He was baptized on 28 Feb 1886 Batoche, (Saskatchewan) (Ibid.).
- iv. Marie Vandal was born on 17 Jan 1888 Batoche, (Saskatchewan) (Ibid., page 64, B-3.). She was baptized on 18 Jan 1888 Batoche, (Saskatchewan) (Ibid.). She died on 16 Mar 1890 Batoche, (Saskatchewan), at age 2 (Ibid., page 81, S-7.). She was buried on 17 Mar 1890 Batoche, (Saskatchewan) (Ibid.).
- v. Joseph Aimie Vandal was born on 6 May 1890 Batoche, (Saskatchewan) (Ibid., page 82, B-12.). He was baptized on 7 May 1890 Batoche, (Saskatchewan) (Ibid.).
- vi. George Alfred Vandal was born on 19 Jan 1892 St.Laurent, (Saskatchewan) (Denney.). He was baptized on 20 Jan 1892 St.Laurent, (Saskatchewan) (Ibid.).
- vii. Norbert Vandal was born on 28 May 1894 (BSAP, page 115, B-10.). He was baptized on 2 Jun 1894 Batoche, (Saskatchewan) (Ibid.).
- viii. Alcide Vandal was born in Jul 1896 (Denney.). He was baptized on 8 Oct 1896 Batoche, (Saskatchewan) (Ibid.).
- ix. Marguerite Eudore Vandal was born on 6 Nov 1898 (Ibid.). She was baptized on 18 Dec 1898 Batoche, (Saskatchewan) (Ibid.). She married M. Birmingham on 27 Aug 1920 Saskatoon, Saskatchewan (Ibid.).
     M. Birmingham was born of, Saskatoon, (Saskatchewan).
- x. Henri Vandal was baptized Batoche, (Saskatchewan) (Ibid.). He was born on 29 Jul 1900 (Ibid.).

15. **Pierre Modeste Vandal** was born on 1 Feb 1866 St.Norbert, (Manitoba) (SN1, page 78-79, B-7.). He was baptized on 3 Feb 1866 St.Norbert, (Manitoba) (Ibid.). He married **Adelaide Parenteau**, daughter of **Pierre Parenteau** and **Marie Anne Caron,** on 26 Apr 1887 Batoche, (Saskatchewan) (BSAP, page 57, M-4.).

Adelaide Parenteau was born on 3 Nov 1868 St.Norbert, (Manitoba) (SN1, B-51.). She was baptized on 3 Nov 1868 St.Norbert, (Manitoba) (Ibid.).

Children of **Pierre Modeste Vandal** and **Adelaide Parenteau** were as follows:

- i. Anne Vandal was born on 29 Jul 1888 Batoche, (Saskatchewan) (BSAP, page 69, B-12.). She was baptized on 29 Jul 1888 Batoche, (Saskatchewan) (Ibid.).
- ii. Modeste Vandal was born on 7 May 1891 Batoche, (Saskatchewan) (Ibid., page 89, B-12.). He was baptized on 10 May 1891 Batoche, (Saskatchewan) (Ibid.).
- iii. Joseph Norbert Vandal was born on 2 Jun 1893 Batoche, (Saskatchewan) (Ibid., page 107, B-14.). He was baptized on 3 Jun 1893 Batoche, (Saskatchewan) (Ibid.). He died on 25 Mar 1894 Batoche, (Saskatchewan) (Ibid., page 114, S-5.). He was buried Batoche, (Saskatchewan). He was buried on 26 Mar 1894 Batoche, (Saskatchewan) (Ibid.).
- iv. Marie Louise Vandal was born in Jun 1895. She died on 7 Aug 1896 Batoche, (Saskatchewan), at age 1.
- v. Marie Ernestine Emelie Vandal was born in 1897. She died on 21 Aug 1897 Prince Albert, (Saskatchewan). She was buried Batoche, (Saskatchewan).

16. **Norbert Vandal** was born circa Dec 1868 (SB-Rozyk, page 155, B-59.). He was baptized on 2 Jul 1869 St.Boniface, (Manitoba) (Ibid.). He married **Virginie Carriere**, daughter of **Charles Toussaint Carriere** and **Cecile Beauchemin,** on 24 Sep 1895 Batoche, (Saskatchewan) (BSAP, page 127, M-5.).

Virginie Carriere was born on 11 Sep 1875 St.Norbert, Manitoba (SN2, B-38.). She was baptized on 12 Sep 1875 St.Norbert, Manitoba (Ibid.).

Children of **Norbert Vandal** and **Virginie Carriere** were as follows:

- i. Marie Louise Vandal was born on 21 May 1897 Batoche, (Saskatchewan) (SK Vital Statistics, Birth Reg. #7915.). She died on 6 Jul 1897 Batoche, (Saskatchewan) (Ibid., Death Reg. #1281.).
- ii. Emma Vandal was born on 2 Aug 1897 Batoche, (Saskatchewan) (1901 Canada, Fish Creek, page 16, Family 169, Line 28-31.) (SK Vital Statistics, Birth Reg. #1521.).
- iii. Alice Vandal was born on 9 Dec 1898 Fish Creek, (Saskatchewan) (1901 Canada, Fish Creek, page 16, Family 169, Line 28-31.) (SK Vital Statistics, Birth Reg. #2119.).
- iv. Georgine Vandal was born in Aug 1908 (Automated Genealogy 1911 Census Transcription Project and Census Images from the National Archives of Canada, http://www.automatedgenealogy.com, District 10, page 6, family 80, line 23-28.).

v. William Vandal was born in Feb 1911 (Ibid.).

17. Marie Louise Vandal was born on 2 Mar 1873 Batoche, (Saskatchewan) (HBSI.) (SL-SK, page 18, B-8.). She was baptized on 21 Mar 1873 St.Laurent-de-Grandin, (Saskatchewan) (Ibid.). She married **Joseph Fisher**, son of **George Fisher** and **Emelie Boyer**, on 10 May 1892 Lebret, (Saskatchewan) (Art Fisher Research, From Joyce Black Genealogy, 1981.).

Joseph Fisher was born on 16 Sep 1870 St.Boniface, Manitoba (SB-Rozyk, page 194, B-80.). He was baptized on 16 Sep 1870 St.Boniface, Manitoba (Ibid.). He died on 8 Aug 1922 Saskatoon, Saskatchewan, at age 51 (Joyce Black Research.).

18. Eulalie Vandal was born on 8 Nov 1878 Batoche, (Saskatchewan) (HBSI.) (ArchiviaNet.) (SL-SK, page 23, B-55.). She was baptized on 12 Nov 1878 St.Laurent-de-Grandin, (Saskatchewan) (Ibid.). She married **Louis Gervais**, son of **Alexis Gervais** and **Madeleine Fagnant**, on 17 May 1899 Batoche, (Saskatchewan) (Denney.).

Louis Gervais was born on 1 Jun 1875 Fish Creek, (Saskatchewan) (HBSI.) (ArchiviaNet.).

Generation Four

19. Marie Rose Vandal was born on 24 Sep 1877 Batoche, (Saskatchewan) (SL-SK, page 4, B-45.). She was baptized on 7 Oct 1877 St.Laurent-de-Grandin, (Saskatchewan) (Ibid.). She married **Clovis Nogier**, son of **Joseph Nogier** and **Celine Dumais**, on 24 Apr 1899 Batoche, (Saskatchewan) (Denney.).

Clovis Nogier was born on 8 Aug 1876 (1901 Canada, Fish Creek, page 1, Family 4, Line 10-12.).

20. Rose Germaine Vandal was born on 8 Feb 1881 Batoche, (Saskatchewan) (HBSI.) (SL-SK, page 48, B-3.) (ArchiviaNet.). She was baptized on 10 Feb 1881 St.Laurent-de-Grandin, (Saskatchewan) (SL-SK, page 48, B-3.). She married **Alexandre Lavallee**, son of **Charles Martin Lavallee** and **Marguerite Courchene**, on 27 Sep 1897 St.Vital, Battleford, (Saskatchewan) (SV, M-3.).

Alexandre Lavallee was born on 15 Mar 1874 St.Francois Xavier, Manitoba (SFXI-Kipling, B-14.). He was baptized on 15 Mar 1874 St.Francois Xavier, Manitoba (Ibid.) (INB, page 103.).

21. Marie Emelie Vandal was born on 27 May 1877 St.Norbert, Manitoba (SN2, B-19.). She was baptized on 28 May 1877 St.Norbert, Manitoba (Ibid.). She married **Joseph Ross**, son of **William Ross** and **Marie Lefort**, circa 1903.

Joseph Ross was born on 22 Dec 1872 St.Francois Xavier, Manitoba (SFXI-Kipling, B-81.) (INB, page 159.). He was baptized on 24 Dec 1872 St.Francois Xavier, Manitoba (SFXI-Kipling, B-81.) (INB, page 159.). He married **Melanie Deschamps**, daughter of **Jean Baptiste Deschamps** and **Catherine Vandal**, on 26 Jan 1897 Batoche, (Saskatchewan) (BSAP, page 141, M-2.).

22. Frederick Vandal was born on 17 Jun 1879 (SN2, B-35.). He was baptized on 18 Jun 1879 St.Norbert, Manitoba (Ibid.). He was born on 27 Jun 1879 west of Fort Ellice, (Manitoba) (Denney.). He married **Sophia Mary Fiddler**, daughter of **John William Fidler** and **Julienne Delorme**, on 30 Jan 1905 (Louis Verhagen Research.). He died on 26 Sep 1964 Prince Albert, Saskatchewan, at age 85 (Ibid.). He was buried on 30 Sep 1964 South Hill, Prince Albert, Saskatchewan (Ibid.).

Children of **Frederick Vandal** and **Sophia Mary Fiddler** were as follows:

 i. Alice Vandale.
 ii. Marcelline Vandale.
 iii. Leo Vandale.
 iv. Jack Vandale.
 v. Norman Vandale.
 vi. Dorothy Vandale.
 vii. Irene Vandale.
 viii. Olivier Vandale.
27 ix. Ida Beatrice Vandal, b. 3 Nov 1905 Fish Creek, (Saskatchewan); m. William Ross; d. before 1985.

23. Mathilde Vandal was born on 27 Jan 1881 Montagne la Bosse (SN2, B-4.) (ArchiviaNet, C-15008.). She was baptized on 29 Jan 1881 St.Norbert, Manitoba (SN2, B-4.). She married **John Fidler**, son of **John William Fidler** and **Julienne Delorme**, before 1904. She married **Louis Grassick** before 1921 (1921 Census of Canada from the National Archives of Canada (Transcription by ancestry.com), Ottawa, Canada, District 216-59, page 4.). She died on 22 Jan 1958 Cudworth, Saskatchewan, at age 76 (Louis Verhagen.).

John Fidler was born on 26 May 1883 Fish Creek, (Saskatchewan) (BSAP, page 15, B-13.) (HBSI.). He was baptized on 4 Jun 1883 Batoche, (Saskatchewan) (BSAP, page 15, B-13.). He died before 1921.

Louis Grassick was born in 1876 (1921 Canada, District 216-59, page 4.).

24. Francois Vandal was born on 2 Jan 1883 Batoche, (Saskatchewan) (BSAP, [page 12a], B-1.). He was baptized on 2 Jan 1883 Batoche, (Saskatchewan) (Ibid.). He married **Anna (Skierra) Skarra**, daughter of **Jacob (Skierra) Skarra** and **Anna Bzotokoski**, on 20 Sep 1910 Howell, Saskatchewan (Denney.). He died on 1 Nov 1918 Cudworth, Saskatchewan, at age 35 (Ibid.).

Anna (Skierra) Skarra was born on 17 Sep 1890 Marble, Minnesota (Ibid.). She died on 30 Nov 1970 Agassiz, British Columbia, at age 80 (Ibid.).

Children of **Francois Vandal** and **Anna (Skierra) Skarra** were:

 i. Lawrence Edward Vandal was born on 19 Apr 1911 Fish Creek, Saskatchewan (Ibid.). He died on 16 Oct 1956 Oakland, California, at age 45 (Ibid.).

25. Marie Virginie Vandal was born on 13 May 1879 St.Norbert, Manitoba (SN2, B-27.). She was baptized on 15 May 1879 St.Norbert, Manitoba (Ibid.). She married **William Sauve**, son of **Joseph Sauve** and **Eulalie Carriere**, on 20 Jan 1902 St.Malo, DeSalaberry, Manitoba (MM.) (MB Vital Statistics, Marriage Reg. #1902,002210.). She died on 12 Apr 1904 RM DeSalaberry, Manitoba, at age 24 (Ibid., Death Reg. #1904,003016.).

William Sauve was born on 16 Feb 1879 (Saskatchewan) (1901 Canada, #10, a-3, page 13, family 101, line 12-13.) (SL-SK, page 27, B-2.). He was baptized on 16 Feb 1879 St.Laurent-de-Grandin, (Saskatchewan) (Ibid.). He married **Marie Olivine Vandal**, daughter of **Louis Vandal** and **Reine Victoria Ducharme**, on 25 Sep 1905 Woodridge, Manitoba (MM.). He died on 4 Oct 1915 LaBroquerie, Manitoba, at age 36 (MB Vital Statistics, Death Reg. #1915,210216.).

26. Elise Vandal was born on 8 Jun 1882 Batoche, (Saskatchewan) (BSAP, page 8, B-11.) (1901 Canada, page 4, Family 30, #45-47.). She was baptized on 8 Jun 1882 Batoche, (Saskatchewan) (BSAP, page 8, B-11.). She married **Chrysostome Boyer**, son of **William Boyer** and **Julienne Bousquet**, on 6 Mar 1905 Batoche, (Saskatchewan) (Ibid., page 232, M-2.).

Chrysostome Boyer was born on 8 Oct 1878 St.Francois Xavier, Manitoba (SFXI-Kipling, B-31.). He was born in 1879 (Manitoba) (1901 Canada, page 4, Family 24, #8-14.). He was born on 7 Jun 1881 Batoche, (Saskatchewan) (HBS 1886-1901, 1906 Half-Breed Scrip Applications, RG15-21, Volume 1337, C-14952.).

Generation Five

27. **Ida Beatrice Vandal** was born on 3 Nov 1905 Fish Creek, (Saskatchewan) (SK Vital Statistics, Birth Reg. #5001.). She married **William Ross**, son of **Joseph Ross** and **Melanie Deschamps**, before 1926. She died before 1985 (Rod Mac Quarrie, 28 Dec 2011.).

William Ross was born on 4 Jul 1899 Fish Creek, (Saskatchewan) (SK Vital Statistics, #1506.). He died on 18 Jan 1985 Prince Albert, Saskatchewan, at age 85 (Rod Mac Quarrie, 28 Dec 2011.). He was buried on 22 Jan 1985 South Hill Cemetery, Prince Albert, Saskatchewan (Ibid.).

Ahnentafel between Toussaint Vaudry and Adrien Vaudry

--- 1st Generation ---

1. **Toussaint Vaudry.** Question: *Probable son of Toussaint Vaudry.* He was born circa 1799 at Ruperts Land (1829C RRS HBCA E5/3 1829 Census of the Red River Settlement, HBCA E5/3, Hudson's Bay Company Archives, Provincial Archives, 200 Vaughan Street, Winnipeg, MB R3C 1T5, Canada., page 2.). He married **Marie Anne Crebassa**, daughter of **John Crebassa** and **Suzanne Saulteaux**, before 1819.

--- 2nd Generation ---

2. **Toussaint Vaudry** (PRDH online index, http://www.genealogic.umontreal.ca, #677606.) (Ibid.) married according to the custom of the country **Native Woman (--?--).** He was baptized on 13 Nov 1767 at Lachenaie, Quebec (Ibid., #83720.). *Vaudry, Toussaint [1]. A French-Canadian who was in the service of the North West Company. In 1803, he was in charge of the post on the Rivière aux Morts (see Dubord, J.), and the following year he was a guide on the Red River. In 1812, he was director of the fort on the Turtle River. Six years later, he was one of the witnesses in the trial that his company underwent for the part that it played in the Battle of Seven Oaks (see Bourassa, Michel). At that time, Vaudry declared that he had lived at the Red River for over thirty years and had seen the ruin of the former French forts in the region* (Peter J. Gagne, *FCW-Gagne French-Canadians of the West, A Biographical Dictionary of French-Canadians and French Metis of the Western United States and Canada;*Pawtucket, Rhode Island: Quintin Publications, c1999), page 241.).

--- 3rd Generation ---

4. **Toussaint Vaudry** (PRDH online, #677606.) (Ibid., #73351.) (Ibid.) was baptized on 6 Jul 1707 at St-Francois-de-Sales (Ile-Jesus), Quebec (Ibid.). He married **Marie Anne Bombardier dit Labombarde**, daughter of **Andre Bombardier** and **Marie Josephe Anne Poudret dit Lavigne**, on 5 Nov 1753 at Chambly, Quebec (Ibid., #83720.).

--- 4th Generation ---

8. **Jacques Vaudry** (Ibid., #73345.) (Ibid.) (Ibid.) was born circa 1670 (Ibid.). He married **Marie Francoise Joly**, daughter of **Nicolas Joly** and **Francoise Hunault**, on 13 Jan 1699 at Pointe-aux-Trembles, Quebec (Ibid., #85891.). He died on 22 Jun 1743 at Lachenaie, Quebec (Ibid., #73345.). He was buried on 23 Jun 1743 at Lachenaie, Quebec (Ibid.).

--- 5th Generation ---

16. **Jacques Vaudry** lived at at Notre-Dame de Lamberville, Dieppe, Rouen, Normandie (Seine-Maritime) (DGFQ Jette, Rene, *Dictionnaire Genealogique des Familles du Quebec des Origines a 1730* (Montreal, Quebec, Canada: University of Montreal Press, 1983), page 1114.). He was born between 1627 and 1634 (Ibid.). A contract for the marriage to **Jeanne Renaud**, daughter of **Vincent Renaud** and **Marie Martin,** was signed on 29 Jan 1661 (Ibid., page 1115.). He married **Jeanne Renaud**, daughter of **Vincent Renaud** and **Marie Martin**, on 14 Feb 1661 at Trois-Rivieres, Quebec (Ibid.). He died between 1 Nov 1687 and 8 Nov 1688 at Louiseville, Quebec (Ibid., page 1114.).

--- 6th Generation ---

32. **Adrien Vaudry** married **Marthe Deschamps.**

Descendants of Toussaint Vaudry

Generation One

1. **Toussaint Vaudry** was born circa 1799 Ruperts Land (1829C RRS HBCA E5/3 1829 Census of the Red River Settlement, HBCA E5/3, Hudson's Bay Company Archives, Provincial Archives, 200 Vaughan Street, Winnipeg, MB R3C 1T5, Canada., page 2.). He married **Marie Anne Crebassa**, daughter of **John Crebassa** and **Suzanne Saulteaux**, before 1819.

Marie Anne Crebassa was born circa 1805 (SJL-1 Register of Baptisms, Marriages, and Burials, St.Joseph, Leroy, North Dakota, Diocese of Saint Paul, Minnesota, 1870-1888, Book 1, page 141, S-143. Hereinafter cited as SJL-1.). She was born in Jul 1807 Fort Alexandre (MBS Scrip Applications, Original White Settlers & Halfbreeds residing in Manitoba on 15 July 1870, RG15-19, C-14926.). She died on 7 Mar 1885 Leroy, Pembina County, Dakota Territory, at age 77 (SJL-1, page 141, S-143.). She was buried on 9 Mar 1885 St.Joseph, Leroy, Pembina County, Dakota Territory (Ibid.).

Children of **Toussaint Vaudry** and **Marie Anne Crebassa** were as follows:

2   i.   Marie Vaudry, b. circa 1819; m. Romain Lagimoniere; d. 16 Feb 1875 St.Boniface, Manitoba; bur. 19 Feb 1875 St.Boniface, Manitoba.

3   ii.   Toussaint Vaudry, b. 28 Dec 1826 Pembina; m. Louise McDougall; d. 24 Apr 1880 St.Boniface, Manitoba.

     iii.   Louise Vaudry was born circa 1830 (SB 1825-1834 St.Boniface Roman Catholic Registre des Baptemes, Mariages & Sepultures, 1825-1834, page 156, S-79. Hereinafter cited as SB 1825-1834.). She died on 23 Nov 1834 St.Boniface, (Manitoba) (Ibid.). She was buried on 24 Nov 1834 St.Boniface, (Manitoba) (Ibid.).

iv. Joseph Vaudry was born on 20 Dec 1832 (Ibid., page 86, B-509.). He was baptized on 25 Dec 1832 St.Boniface, (Manitoba) (Ibid.).

4 v. Suzanne Vaudry, b. 7 Mar 1839 St.Boniface, (Manitoba); m. Charles Emile Bouvette; d. 4 Apr 1919 St.Boniface, Provencher, Manitoba; bur. 5 Aug 1919 Cathedral Cemetery, St.Boniface, Provencher, Manitoba.

5 vi. Rosalie Vaudry, b. 7 Apr 1839 St.Boniface, (Manitoba); m. Pierre Ritchot.

6 vii. Maxime Vaudry, b. 26 Jul 1852 St.Boniface, (Manitoba); m. Clementine Beaudry.

Generation Two

2. Marie Vaudry was born circa 1819 (MBS, C-14929.). She married **Romain Lagimoniere**, son of **Jean Baptiste Lagimoniere** and **Marie Anne Gaboury**, in 1841. She died on 16 Feb 1875 St.Boniface, Manitoba (Ibid.) (SB-Rozyk St. Boniface Roman Catholic Church, Manitoba, Canada, Baptisms, Marriages and Burials 1860-1875 Extractions, Compiled by Rosemary Rozyk, page 49, S-6.). She was buried on 19 Feb 1875 St.Boniface, Manitoba (MBS, C-14929.) (SB-Rozyk, page 49, S-6.).

Romain Lagimoniere was born on 11 Jan 1819 St.Boniface, (Manitoba) (MBS, C-14929.). He died on 14 Mar 1905 St.Laurent, Manitoba, at age 86 (CWLR *The Collected Writings Of Louis Riel*, 5 (University of Alberta Press, 1985), page 283.).

3. Toussaint Vaudry was born on 28 Dec 1826 Pembina (MBS, C-14934.). He married **Louise McDougall**, daughter of **Duncan McDougall** and **Marguerite McDonell**, on 4 Jul 1866 St.Boniface, (Manitoba) (SB-Rozyk, page 57, M-18.). He died on 24 Apr 1880 St.Boniface, Manitoba, at age 53 (MBS, C-14934.).

Louise McDougall was born on 12 Mar 1838 St.Boniface, (Manitoba) (Ibid.).

Children of **Toussaint Vaudry** and **Louise McDougall** were as follows:

i. Alexander Angus Vaudry.

ii. Duncan John Vaudry married Leontine Beriault, daughter of Louis Beriault and Marguerite Nolin, on 23 Nov 1903 St.Boniface, Manitoba (RMSB.).

    Leontine Beriault was born in Oct 1880 Manitoba (1881 Church of Latter Day Saints Census Transcription Project of Census Images from the National Archives of Canada, Ottawa, Canada, http://www.familysearch.org, Film #C-13283, District 184, Sub-district E, page 25, household 119.).

iii. Toussaint Modeste Vaudry was born on 6 Jun 1867 St.Boniface, (Manitoba) (SB-Rozyk, page 87, B-48.). He was baptized on 6 Jun 1867 St.Boniface, (Manitoba) (Ibid.).

iv. Alfred Vaudry was baptized on 10 Feb 1869 St.Boniface, (Manitoba) (Ibid., page 145, B-9.). He was born on 10 Feb 1869 St.Boniface, (Manitoba) (Ibid.). He married Emelie Harrison, daughter of Auguste Harrison and Lucie Champagne, on 15 Apr 1901 Ste.Anne, Manitoba (MM.).

    Emelie Harrison was born on 8 Jan 1874 (INB *Index des Naissances and Baptemes* (St.Boniface, Manitoba: La Societe Historique de Saint-Boniface., c1995), page 79.). She was baptized on 10 Jan 1874 Ste.Anne, Manitoba (IBMS *Index des Baptemes, Mariages et Sepultures* (La Societe Historique de Saint-Boniface).) (INB, page 79.).

v. Marie Anne Vaudry was baptized on 29 Oct 1870 St.Boniface, Manitoba (SB-Rozyk, page 197, B-90.). She was born on 29 Oct 1870 St.Boniface, Manitoba (Ibid.).

vi. James William Vaudry was born on 2 Dec 1870 Lorette, Manitoba (MBS, C-14934.). She died on 15 Mar 1876 at age 5 (Ibid.).

7 vii. Marie Louise Vaudry, b. 10 Feb 1873; m. Treffle Bonneau.

4. Suzanne Vaudry was born on 7 Mar 1839 St.Boniface, (Manitoba) (Ibid., C-14925.). She married **Charles Emile Bouvette**, son of **Francois Bouvette** and **Marguerite Marchand**, on 8 Feb 1860 St.Boniface, (Manitoba) (Rod MacQuarrie Research, 12 Sep 2006.). She died on 4 Apr 1919 St.Boniface, Provencher, Manitoba, at age 80 (MB Vital Statistics, Death Reg. #1919,047031.). She was buried on 5 Aug 1919 Cathedral Cemetery, St.Boniface, Provencher, Manitoba (Rod Mac Quarrie, 12 Sep 2006.).

Charles Emile Bouvette was born on 10 Feb 1838 St.Johns, (Manitoba) (MBS, C-14925.).

5. Rosalie Vaudry was born on 7 Apr 1839 St.Boniface, (Manitoba) (MBS, C-14932.). She married **Pierre Ritchot**, son of **Joseph-Michel Ritchot** and **Josephte Maillou**, before 1857.

Pierre Ritchot was born circa 1834 (SJL-1, page 168, S-4.). He died on 17 Jul 1888 Leroy, Pembina County, Dakota Territory (Ibid.). He was buried on 18 Jul 1888 St.Joseph, Leroy, Pembina County, Dakota Territory (Ibid.).

6. Maxime Vaudry was born on 15 Jul 1849 (1901 Canada, (#10), N-1, page 1, Family 2, Line 8-16.). He was born on 26 Jul 1852 St.Boniface, (Manitoba) (MBS, C-14934.). He married **Clementine Beaudry**, daughter of **Louis Gaudry dit Beaudry** and **Charlotte Brabant**, on 11 Jan 1870 St.Boniface, (Manitoba) (SB-Rozyk, page 170, M-2.).

Clementine Beaudry was born on 7 Oct 1845 (1901 Canada, (#10), N-1, page 1, Family 2, Line 8-16.). She was born on 15 Oct 1848 St.Boniface, (Manitoba) (MBS, C-14934.).

Children of **Maxime Vaudry** and **Clementine Beaudry** were as follows:

i. Marie Vaudry was born on 3 Dec 1870 St.Boniface, Manitoba (Ibid.) (SB-Rozyk, page 199, B-96.). She was baptized on 3 Dec 1870 St.Boniface, Manitoba (MBS, C-14934.) (SB-Rozyk, page 199, B-96.). She died on 15 May 1873 St.Boniface, Manitoba, at age 2 (MBS, C-14934.). She was buried on 16 May 1873 St.Boniface, Manitoba (Ibid.) (SB-Rozyk, page 276, S-31.).

ii. Lucie Vaudry was born on 5 Aug 1872 St.Boniface, Manitoba (Ibid., page 247, B-55.). She was baptized on 6 Aug 1872 St.Boniface, Manitoba (Ibid.). She died on 20 Apr 1873 (Ibid., page 273, S-25.). She was buried on 22 Apr 1873 St.Boniface, Manitoba (Ibid.).

iii. Louise Marguerite Vaudry was born on 13 Feb 1874 (Ibid., page 9, B-14.). She was baptized on 17 Feb 1874 St.Boniface, Manitoba (Ibid.).

iv. Michel Vaudry was born on 17 Jan 1877 St.Boniface, Manitoba (1901 Canada, (#10), N-1, page 1, Family 2, Line 8-16.).

v. Melanie Vaudry was born on 7 Nov 1879 St.Boniface, Manitoba (Ibid.).

vi. Alexandre Vaudry was born in Nov 1880 (1881 Canada, District 184-E-1, page 54, house 252.).

   vii.   Elise Vaudry was born on 4 Jul 1885 St.Boniface, Manitoba (1901 Canada, (#10), N-1, page 1, Family 2, Line 8-16.).

  viii.   Henri Vaudry was born on 7 Feb 1888 St.Boniface, Manitoba (Ibid.).

   ix.   Remi Vaudry was born on 18 Jul 1890 St.Boniface, Manitoba (Ibid.).

    x.   Malvina Vaudry was born on 16 Jul 1893 St.Boniface, Manitoba (Ibid.).

Generation Three

7. **Marie Louise Vaudry** was born on 10 Feb 1873 (SB-Rozyk, page 271, B-33.). She was baptized on 16 Mar 1873 St.Boniface, Manitoba (Ibid.). She married **Treffle Bonneau** before 1892.

   Treffle Bonneau was born on 15 Jul 1863 Quebec (1901 Canada, Willowbunch, page 4, Family 31, Line 1-8.).

Ahnentafel between Pierre Venne and Jean Venne or Voyne

--- 1st Generation ---

1. **PIERRE VENNE** (MBS Scrip Applications, Original White Settlers & Halfbreeds residing in Manitoba on 15 July 1870, RG15-19, C-14934.) (Ibid.) was also known as **PIERRE JEANVENNE**. He was born on 4 Oct 1788 at L'Assomption, L'Assomption, Quebec (Ibid.). He married **MARIE ANN CHARETTE**, daughter of **JEAN BAPTISTE CHARETTE** and **CHARLOTTE SANSREGRET**, circa 1825 at Red River, (Manitoba). He died on 25 Nov 1887 at Olga, Cavalier County, North Dakota, at age 99 (Olga Our Lady of the Sacred Heart, Olga, North Dakota 1882-1900, page 134, S-12. Hereinafter cited as Olga.). He was buried on 26 Nov 1887 at Olga, Cavalier County, North Dakota (Ibid.).

--- 2nd Generation ---

2. **JOSEPH ALEXIS VENNE** (Roger W. Lawrence Research, 11 Oct 1999 e-mail, source: PRDH.) (Ibid., 11 Oct 1999 e-mail, source: Jette page 1118.) (DGFQ Jette, Rene, *Dictionnaire Genealogique des Familles du Quebec des Origines a 1730* (Montreal, Quebec, Canada: University of Montreal Press, 1983), page 1118.) was born on 30 Jul 1755 at L'Assomption, L'Assomption, Quebec (Roger W. Lawrence, 11 Oct 1999 e-mail, source: PRDH.) (PRDH online index, http://www.genealogic.umontreal.ca, #53876.). He was baptized on 1 Aug 1755 at L'Assompton, L'Assompton, Quebec (Ibid.). He married **MARIE MARGUERITE GELINAS DIT LACOURSE**, daughter of **JEAN-BAPTISTE GELINAS DIT LACOURSE** and **MARIE-JOSEPHE VACHER DIT LACERTE**, on 10 Sep 1777 at Yamachiche, Quebec (Roger W. Lawrence, 11 Oct 1999 e-mail, source: PRDH.) (PRDH online, No. 227307.). He died on 10 Nov 1827 at L'Assomption, L'Assomption, Quebec, at age 72 (Ibid., #53876.). He was buried on 12 Nov 1827 at L'Assompton, L'Assompton, Quebec (Ibid.).

--- 3rd Generation ---

4. **JEAN-BAPTISTE VENNE** (Roger W. Lawrence, 11 Oct 1999 e-mail, source: Jette page 1118.) (DGFQ, page 1118.) was born on 23 Nov 1724 at Pointe-aux-Trembles, Quebec (Roger W. Lawrence, 11 Oct 1999 e-mail, source: Jette page 1118.) (DGFQ, page 1118.) (PRDH online, No. 11276.). He was baptized on 25 Nov 1724 at Pointe-aux-Trembles, Quebec (Ibid.). He married **MARIE-ANGELIQUE CHEVAUDIER DIT LEPINE**, daughter of **JACQUES CHEVAUDIER DIT LEPINE** and **MARIE-MADELEINE LANTHIER**, on 24 Feb 1751 at L'Assomption, L'Assomption, Quebec (Roger W. Lawrence, 11 Oct 1999 e-mail, source: PRDH.) (PRDH online, No. 286448.). He married **MARIE THEOTISTE POLIQUIN**, daughter of **JEAN-BAPTISTE POLIQUIN** and **MARIE ANGELIQUE FILTEAU**, on 7 Sep 1790 at L'Assompton, L'Assompton, Quebec (Ibid., #146376.). He died on 26 Nov 1792 at L'Assomption, L'Assomption, Quebec, at age 68 (Ibid.). He was buried on 27 Nov 1792 at L'Assomption, L'Assomption, Quebec (Ibid.).

--- 4th Generation ---

8. **JOSEPH VENNE** (DGFQ, page 1118.) was born on 14 Sep 1697 at Pointe-aux-Trembles, Quebec (Ibid., page 1117.). He was baptized on 15 Sep 1697 at Pointe-aux-Trembles, Quebec (Ibid.). He married **SUZANNE SENET DIT LALIBERTE**, daughter of **NICOLAS SENET DIT LALIBERTE** and **MARIE-GERTRUDE DAUNAY**, on 23 Nov 1722 at Pointe-aux-Trembles, Quebec (DNCF *Dictionnaire National des Canadiens-Francais Tome I & II* Gabriel Drouin, editor (revised 1985; Siege Social, 4184, rue St-Denis, Montreal, Canada: l'Institut Genealogique Drouin, 1979), page 1349.) (DGFQ, page 1118.) (PRDH online, #69047.). He was buried on 1 Nov 1767 at L'Assompton, L'Assompton, Quebec (Ibid.).

--- 5th Generation ---

16. **JEAN VENNE** was also known as **JEAN VOYNE**. He was born circa 1657 at St-Antoine, Gradour, Germeville, Angiykenem Angiynius *Angiykenem Charente) (DGFQ, page 1117.) (PRDH online, #74071.). He married **MARGUERITE BEAUJEAN**, daughter of **ELIE BEAUJEAN** and **SUZANNE COIGNON**, on 15 Nov 1677 at Montreal, Montreal, Quebec (DGFQ, page 1117.). He married **FRANCOISE BEAUCHAMP**, daughter of **JACQUES BEAUCHAMP** and **MARIE DARDENNE**, on 25 Jun 1685 at Pointe-aux-Trembles, Quebec (DNCF, page 1349.) (DGFQ, page 1117.). He died on 10 Apr 1736 at L'Assompton, L'Assompton, Quebec (PRDH online, #74071.). He was buried on 12 Apr 1736 at L'Assompton, L'Assompton, Quebec (Ibid.).

--- 6th Generation ---

32. **JEAN VENNE OR VOYNE** (DGFQ, page 1117.) was born circa 1626 (Ibid.). He married **FRANCOISE MANSEAU** circa 1645 (Ibid.). He was buried on 2 Nov 1687 at Pointe-aux-Trembles, Quebec (Ibid.).

Descendants of Pierre Venne

Generation One

1. **Pierre Venne** was born on 4 Oct 1788 L'Assomption, L'Assomption, Quebec (MBS Scrip Applications, Original White Settlers & Halfbreeds residing in Manitoba on 15 July 1870, RG15-19, C-14934.). He married **Marie Ann Charette**, daughter of **Jean Baptiste Charette** and **Charlotte Sansregret**, circa 1825 Red River, (Manitoba). He died on 25 Nov 1887 Olga, Cavalier County, North Dakota, at age 99 (Olga Our Lady of the Sacred Heart, Olga, North Dakota 1882-1900, page 134, S-12. Hereinafter cited as Olga.). He was buried on 26 Nov 1887 Olga, Cavalier County, North Dakota (Ibid.).

   Marie Ann Charette was born circa Jul 1804 Lac Qu'Apelle, North West (MBS, C-14934.). She died on 14 Aug 1886 Olga, Cavalier County, North Dakota (Olga, page 105, S-12.).

Children of **Pierre Venne** and **Marie Ann Charette** were as follows:

2   i.   Marie Venne, b. 1825 North West Territories; m. Jean Baptiste Moreau.

3   ii.   Jean Baptiste Venne, b. Nov 1832 St.Norbert, (Manitoba); m. Isabelle Houle; d. 16 Jul 1884 Leroy, Pembina County, Dakota Territory; bur. 18 Jul 1884 St.Joseph, Leroy, Pembina County, Dakota Territory.

   iii.   Joseph Venne was baptized on 21 Nov 1832 St.Boniface, (Manitoba) (SB 1825-1834 St.Boniface Roman Catholic Registre des Baptemes, Mariages & Sepultures, 1825-1834, page 81, B-498. Hereinafter cited as SB 1825-1834.). He was born on 21 Nov 1832 St.Boniface, (Manitoba) (Ibid.).

4   iv.   Salomon Venne, b. 12 Aug 1837 St.Norbert, (Manitoba); m. Josephte St.Arnaud; d. 1922 Batoche, Saskatchewan.

5   v.   Pierre Venne, b. circa 1840; m. Marie Belgarde; m. Rosalie Lesperance dit Bonami.

6   vi.   David Venne, b. 17 Dec 1843 St.Norbert, (Manitoba); m. Josephte Beauchamp.

7   vii.   Ursule Venne, b. circa 1845; m. Marcel Roy.

8   viii.   Michel Venne, b. 10 May 1848 St.Norbert, (Manitoba); m. Cecile Larence; d. between 1900 and 1910.

9   ix.   Charlotte Venne, b. 14 Dec 1850 St.Norbert, (Manitoba); m. Cyrille Dumas.

10   x.   William Venne, b. circa 1853; m. Rosalie Jolibois.

11   xi.   Alexandre Venne, b. circa 1856; m. Marie Desjarlais.

Generation Two

2. Marie Venne was born in 1825 North West Territories. She was born circa 1830 Pembina County (1850Ci-MN *Minnesota Territorial Census, 1850*, Harpole, Patricia C. and Mary D. Nagle, ed., (St.Paul, Minnesota: Minnesota Historical Society, 1972), page 22, Dwelling 41, Family 41.). She married **Jean Baptiste Moreau**, son of **Jean Baptiste Moreau** and **Charlotte Lafeuille or Gariepy or Vallee**, before 1848.

Jean Baptiste Moreau was born circa 1820 Pembina County (Ibid.). He was born in Nov 1824 North West Territory (MBS, C-14931.).

3. Jean Baptiste Venne was born in Nov 1832 St.Norbert, (Manitoba) (MBS, C-14934.). He married **Isabelle Houle**, daughter of **Charles Houle** and **Madeleine Breland**, on 21 Apr 1863 St.Norbert, (Manitoba) (SN1, page 77, M-4.). He died on 16 Jul 1884 Leroy, Pembina County, Dakota Territory, at age 51 (SJL-1, page 136, S-139.). He was buried on 18 Jul 1884 St.Joseph, Leroy, Pembina County, Dakota Territory (Ibid.).

Isabelle Houle was born in 1812 (Manitoba) (SJL-D, page 21.). She was born between 1821 and 1822 North West (MBS, C-14934.) (1850Ci-MN, page 21; Dwelling 30; Family 30.). She married **Antoine Lambert**, son of **Antoine Lambert** and **Marie Sauteuse**, circa 1846. She died on 10 Apr 1911 Pembina County, North Dakota (North Dakota Department of Health Public Death Index.). She was buried on 12 Apr 1911 St.Joseph, Leroy, Pembina County, North Dakota (SJL-D, page 21.).

Children of **Jean Baptiste Venne** and **Isabelle Houle** were:

12   i.   Jean Baptiste Venne, b. 12 Feb 1864 St.Norbert, (Manitoba); m. Elise Berthelet; d. 15 Oct 1936 Pembina County, North Dakota.

4. Salomon Venne was born on 12 Aug 1837 St.Norbert, (Manitoba) (MBS, C-14934.). He married **Josephte St.Arnaud**, daughter of **Bonaventure St.Arnaud dit Tourond** and **Genevieve Contre**, before 1857. He died in 1922 Batoche, Saskatchewan (CWLR *The Collected Writings Of Louis Riel*, 5 (University of Alberta Press, 1985), page 355.).

Josephte St.Arnaud was born on 4 Mar 1834 North West Territories (MBS, C-14934.).

Children of **Salomon Venne** and **Josephte St.Arnaud** were as follows:

13   i.   Salomon Venne, b. 21 Aug 1857 St.Norbert, (Manitoba); m. Marie Rose Marion.

14   ii.   Josephte Venne, b. 12 Jan 1859 St.Norbert, (Manitoba); m. Roger Goulet.

   iii.   David Venne was born on 17 Nov 1860 St.Norbert, (Manitoba) (SN1, page 35, B-42.). He was baptized on 18 Nov 1860 St.Norbert, (Manitoba) (Ibid.).

   iv.   Marie Celina Venne was born on 31 Oct 1862 St.Norbert, (Manitoba) (Ibid., page 64, B-28.). She was baptized on 31 Oct 1862 St.Norbert, (Manitoba) (Ibid.). She died on 7 Jan 1864 St.Norbert, (Manitoba), at age 1 (Ibid., page 95, S-1.). She was buried on 8 Jan 1864 St.Norbert, (Manitoba) (Ibid.).

15   v.   Joseph Napoleon Venne, b. 17 Oct 1864 St.Norbert, (Manitoba); m. Marie Therese Tourond; m. Marie Louise Parenteau.

   vi.   William Venne was born circa 1867 Manitoba (1881 Church of Latter Day Saints Census Transcription Project of Census Images from the National Archives of Canada, Ottawa, Canada, http://www.familysearch.org, NA Film #C-13283, District 184, Sub-district F, page 41, house 191.).

   vii.   Marie Alexandre Venne was born on 19 Jul 1868 St.Norbert, (Manitoba) (SN1, B-28.). He was baptized on 19 Jul 1868 St.Norbert, (Manitoba) (Ibid.).

16   viii.   Louis Bruno Venne, b. 23 Nov 1870 St.Norbert, Manitoba; m. Florestine Letendre; d. 11 Nov 1900 Batoche, (Saskatchewan).

   ix.   Marie Elmire Venne was born on 7 Nov 1872 St.Norbert, Manitoba (Ibid., B-45.). She was baptized on 8 Nov 1872 St.Norbert, Manitoba (Ibid.).

   x.   Zenaide Venne was born on 4 Mar 1875 St.Laurent, (Saskatchewan) (INB *Index des Naissances and Baptemes* (St.Boniface, Manitoba: La Societe Historique de Saint-Boniface., c1995.)) (SL-SK St.Laurent-de-Grandin Roman Catholic Registre des Baptemes, Mariages & Sepltures, St.Laurent, Saskatchewan, 1872-1896, page 36, B-6. Hereinafter cited as SL-SK.) (ArchiviaNet 1886-1901, 1906 Half-Breed Scrip Applications Index, RG15-21, Volume 1333 through 1371, Microfilm Reel Number C-14944 through C-15010, National Archives of Canada, Ottawa, Ontario, http://www.collectionscanada.gc.ca, C-15008.). She was baptized on 8 Mar 1875 St.Laurent-de-Grandin, (Saskatchewan) (SL-SK, page 36, B-6.). She died on 1 Dec 1882 Cartier, Manitoba, at age 7 (Manitoba Vital Statistics online, http://web2.gov.mb.ca, Death Reg. #1882,001383.) (SN2 Catholic Parish Register of St.Norbert, S-35. Hereinafter cited as SN2.). She was buried on 2 Dec 1882 St.Norbert, Manitoba (Ibid.).

xi.   Marie Rose Venne was born on 10 Jul 1877 St.Norbert, Manitoba (Ibid., B-24.). She was baptized on 12 Jul 1877 St.Norbert, Manitoba (Ibid.). She died on 18 Apr 1878 St.Norbert, Manitoba (Ibid., S-20.). She was buried on 19 Apr 1878 St.Norbert, Manitoba (Ibid.).

5. Pierre Venne was born circa 1840. He married **Marie Belgarde**, daughter of **Alexis Belgarde** and **Nancy Gingras**, on 16 Jun 1862 Assumption, Pembina, Pembina County, Dakota Territory (AP, page 259, M-10.). He married **Rosalie Lesperance dit Bonami**, daughter of **Alexis Bonami Lesperance** and **Marguerite Grenon**, on 28 Jan 1892 St.Joseph, Leroy, Pembina County, North Dakota (SJL-2 Register of Baptisms, Marriages, and Burials, St.Joseph, Leroy, North Dakota, Diocese of Saint Paul, Minnesota, 1888-1900, Book 2, M-2. Hereinafter cited as SJL-2.).

Marie Belgarde was born circa 1847 (1850Ci-MN, page 22, Dwelling 46, Family 46.).

Children of **Pierre Venne** and **Marie Belgarde** were as follows:

    i.   Jerome Jeanvenne was born on 7 Jul 1874 (AP, page 91, B-47.). He was baptized on 2 Aug 1874 Assumption, Pembina, Pembina County, Dakota Territory (Ibid.).

    ii.   Pierre Jeanvenne was born on 28 Aug 1876 (L1 Lebret Mission de St.Florent Roman Catholic Registre des Baptemes, Mariages & Seplutures, Qu'Appelle, Saskatchewan, 1868-1881., page 201, B-50. Hereinafter cited as L1.). He was baptized on 8 Jan 1877 Lebret, (Saskatchewan) (Ibid.).

Rosalie Lesperance dit Bonami was born on 13 Aug 1838 St.Boniface, (Manitoba) (MBS, C-14930.). She married **Duncan McDougall**, son of **Duncan McDougall** and **Marguerite McDonell**, before 1858. She died on 27 Jan 1910 Tache, Manitoba, at age 71 (MB Vital Statistics, Death Reg. #1910,001815.).

6. David Venne was born on 17 Dec 1843 St.Norbert, (Manitoba) (MBS, C-14934.). He married **Josephte Beauchamp**, daughter of **Pierre Beauchamp** and **Marie Comtois dit Morin**, on 21 Apr 1863 St.Norbert, (Manitoba) (MM, page 56.) (SN1, page 78, M-5.).

Josephte Beauchamp was born in 1843 St.Boniface, (Manitoba) (MBS, C-14929.). She died on 17 Oct 1888 Olga, Cavalier County, North Dakota (Olga, page 152, S-17.). She was buried on 19 Oct 1888 Olga, Cavalier County, North Dakota (Ibid.).

Children of **David Venne** and **Josephte Beauchamp** were as follows:

17   i.   Marie Agathe Venne, b. 7 Feb 1864 St.Norbert, (Manitoba); m. Onesime Wilkie; d. 15 Oct 1885 Olga, Cavalier County, North Dakota; bur. 16 Oct 1885 Olga, Cavalier County, North Dakota.

18   ii.   Julienne Venne, b. 1 Apr 1866 Ste.Agathe, (Manitoba); m. William Jerome.

    iii.   Justine Venne was born on 11 May 1868 Ste.Agathe, (Manitoba) (MBS, C-14934.) (SN1, B-21.). She was baptized on 7 Jun 1868 St.Norbert, (Manitoba) (Ibid.). She married Francois Pepin, son of Narcisse Pepin and Marie Beaulieu, on 22 Nov 1887 Olga, Cavalier County, North Dakota (Olga, page 133, M-7.).

        Francois Pepin was born on 13 Mar 1854 Athabaska Lake (MBS, C-14932.).

19   iv.   Josephte Venne, b. 25 Oct 1870 Ste.Agathe, Manitoba; m. Joseph Gariepy; d. 15 May 1892 Olga, Cavalier County, North Dakota; bur. 17 May 1892 Olga, Cavalier County, North Dakota.

    v.   Marie Rose Venne was born on 2 Jan 1873 St.Norbert, Manitoba (SN1, B-1.). She was baptized on 3 Jan 1873 St.Norbert, Manitoba (Ibid.).

    vi.   Elmire Venne was born on 17 Jan 1876 (SJL-1, page 69, B-9.). She was baptized on 27 Feb 1876 St.Joseph, Leroy, Pembina County, Dakota Territory (Ibid.). She was buried on 7 Sep 1892 Olga, Cavalier County, North Dakota (Olga, page 214, S-11.).

20   vii.   Delphine Venne, b. 22 May 1878; m. Napoleon Larence; d. 28 Jan 1900 Leroy, North Dakota; bur. 30 Jan 1900 St.Joseph, Leroy, North Dakota.

21   viii.   Marguerite Florestine Venne, b. 20 Nov 1880; m. Michel Alfred Laframboise.

    ix.   Clara Venne was born on 18 Mar 1885 Olga, Cavalier County, North Dakota (Ibid., page 65, B-11.). She was baptized on 19 Mar 1885 Olga, Cavalier County, North Dakota (Ibid.). She died on 13 Dec 1885 Olga, Cavalier County, North Dakota (Ibid., page 83, S-20.). She was buried on 14 Dec 1885 Olga, Cavalier County, North Dakota (Ibid.).

7. Ursule Venne was born circa 1845. She married **Marcel Roy**, son of **Francois Roy** and **Isabelle Lafreniere**, on 10 Jan 1860 St.Norbert, (Manitoba) (SN1, M-4, page 24.).

Marcel Roy was born on 15 Aug 1838 St.Norbert, (Manitoba) (MBS, C-14932.).

8. Michel Venne was born on 10 May 1848 St.Norbert, (Manitoba) (MBS, C-14934.). He married **Cecile Larence**, daughter of **Norbert Larence** and **Josephte Parenteau**, on 6 Jan 1871 St.Norbert, (Manitoba) (SN1, page 138, M-1.). He died between 1900 and 1910 (Eugene E. Venne Research, Letter, 4 Dec 1997.).

Cecile Larence was born on 1 Apr 1853 Pembina, Pembina County, Dakota Territory (AP, page 84, B-56.). She was baptized on 1 Apr 1853 Assumption, Pembina, Pembina County, Dakota Territory (Ibid.).

Children of **Michel Venne** and **Cecile Larence** were as follows:

22   i.   Joseph Zephirin Venne, b. Jan 1872 Dakota Territory; m. Rosie V. (--?--).

    ii.   James Venne was born circa 1874 Dakota Territory (Eugene Venney, Letter, 4 Dec 1997.).

    iii.   Didyme Venne was born on 5 Sep 1874 St.Laurent, (Saskatchewan) (SL-SK, page 32, B-28.) (ArchiviaNet.). He was baptized on 5 Sep 1874 St.Laurent-de-Grandin, (Saskatchewan) (SL-SK, page 32, B-28.). He died on 14 Mar 1898 St.Joe, Pembina County, North Dakota, at age 23 (ArchiviaNet.).

    iv.   Veronique Venne was born on 5 Sep 1874 Batoche, (Saskatchewan) (HBSI Index 1886-1901, 1906 Halfbreed Scrip Applications, RG15-21.). She died on 14 Mar 1898 St.Joe, Pembina County, North Dakota, at age 23 (Ibid.).

    v.   Alexander Arthur Venne was born on 4 Apr 1877 Duck Lake, (Saskatchewan) (SL-SK, page 72, B-17.). He was baptized on 7 Jul 1877 St.Laurent-de-Grandin, (Saskatchewan) (Ibid.).

23   vi.   Michael Alfred Venne, b. 24 Aug 1879 Leroy, Pembina County, Dakota Territory; m. Sara Williams; d. Jan 1971 Sebastopol, Sonoma, California.

24   vii.   Patrick Hector Venne, b. 19 Dec 1881 Dakota Territory; m. Eva Mary Caisse; m. Bernice Marie Brill; d. 1 May 1967 Dunedin, Florida.

> viii. Marie Cecile Venne was born on 17 Jan 1884 Olga, Cavalier County, North Dakota (Olga, page 34, B-2.). She was baptized on 18 Jan 1884 Olga, Cavalier County, North Dakota (Ibid.). She died on 21 Jan 1887 Olga, Cavalier County, North Dakota, at age 3 (Ibid., page 114, S-1.). She was buried on 22 Jan 1887 Olga, Cavalier County, North Dakota (Ibid.).
>
> ix. Marie Venne was born on 3 Nov 1886 Olga, Cavalier County, North Dakota (Ibid., page 110, B-54.). She was baptized on 6 Nov 1886 Olga, Cavalier County, North Dakota (Ibid.).
>
> x. Marie Celestia Venne was born on 12 Nov 1888 Leroy, Pembina County, Dakota Territory (SJL-2, B-16.). She was baptized on 15 Nov 1888 St.Joseph, Leroy, Pembina County, Dakota Territory (Ibid.). She died on 6 Apr 1905 Leroy, Pembina County, North Dakota, at age 16 (SJL-D, page 16.). She was buried on 8 Apr 1905 St.Joseph, Leroy, Pembina County, North Dakota (Ibid.).
>
> 25 xi. Ernestine Venne, b. 9 Jun 1892 Neche, Pemina, North Dakota; m. E. Ray White.
>
> xii. Edmond Venne was born on 4 Jan 1896 Leroy, Pembina County, North Dakota (SJL-2, page 88, B-1.). He was baptized on 6 Jan 1896 St.Joseph, Leroy, Pembina County, North Dakota (Ibid.). He died in Aug 1941 at age 45 (Eugene Venney, Letter, 4 Dec 1997.).

9. Charlotte Venne was born on 14 Dec 1850 St.Norbert, (Manitoba) (MBS, C-14927.). She married **Cyrille Dumas**, son of **Michel Dumas** and **Henriette Landry**, on 21 Jan 1862 St.Norbert, (Manitoba) (SN1, page 52, M-3.).

Cyrille Dumas was born on 7 Sep 1841 St.Vital, (Manitoba) (MBS, C-14927.). He died on 13 Jun 1928 Fort Garry, Manitoba, at age 86 (MB Vital Statistics, Death Reg. #1928,0030093.).

10. William Venne was born circa 1853 (BIA-TM Bureau of Indian Affairs, Turtle Mountain Enrollment and Probate Papers, Belcourt, North Dakota.). He married **Rosalie Jolibois**, daughter of **Jean Baptiste Jolibois** and **Marguerite Robillard**, on 17 Jan 1874 St.Norbert, Manitoba (SN2, M-4.).

Rosalie Jolibois was born on 15 Feb 1857 St.Norbert, (Manitoba) (MBS, C-14934.).

Children of **William Venne** and **Rosalie Jolibois** were as follows:

> i. Marie Adeline Venne was born on 8 Dec 1874 St.Norbert, Manitoba (SN2, B-52.). She was baptized on 10 Dec 1874 St.Norbert, Manitoba (Ibid.). She died on 18 Apr 1875 St.Norbert, Manitoba (Ibid., S-12.). She was buried on 19 Apr 1875 St.Norbert, Manitoba (Ibid.).
>
> ii. Guillaume Venne was born on 29 Apr 1876 St.Norbert, Manitoba (Ibid., B-15.). He was baptized on 30 Apr 1876 St.Norbert, Manitoba (Ibid.). He died on 10 Apr 1877 St.Norbert, Manitoba (Ibid., S-5.). He was buried on 12 Apr 1877 St.Norbert, Manitoba (Ibid.).
>
> iii. Patrice Calixte Venne was born on 14 Jan 1878 St.Norbert, Manitoba (Ibid., B-4.). He was baptized on 15 Jan 1878 St.Norbert, Manitoba (Ibid.). He died on 5 Jun 1934 Havre, Hill County, Montana, at age 56 (BIA-TM-BMD Bureau of Indian Affairs, Turtle Mountain Death certificates: 1916-1952, extracted by Mary M. McClammy; Birth, Marriage, Death Records 1904-1950; Family record cards 1908; Family History Center; FHC Film #1249904.). He was buried in Jun 1934 Calvary Cemetery, Havre, Montana (Ibid.).
>
> iv. Isidore Venne was born on 3 Sep 1879 St.Norbert, Manitoba (SN2, B-49.). He was baptized on 5 Sep 1879 St.Norbert, Manitoba (Ibid.). He died on 1 May 1880 St.Norbert, Manitoba (Ibid., S-18.). He was buried on 3 May 1880 St.Norbert, Manitoba (Ibid.).
>
> v. Roger Jay Venne was born on 10 May 1882 Devils Lake, Ramsey, North Dakota. He died on 11 Mar 1968 Ogden, Utah, at age 85. He was buried Crow Agency.
>
> vi. Joseph Pierre Venne was born on 23 Jul 1882 Leroy, Pembina County, Dakota Territory (SJL-1, page 119, B-229.). He was baptized on 23 Jul 1882 St.Joseph, Leroy, Pembina County, Dakota Territory (Ibid.).
>
> vii. Joseph Roger Venne was born on 10 May 1884 Leroy, Pembina County, Dakota Territory (Ibid., page 134, B-341.). He was baptized on 11 May 1884 St.Joseph, Leroy, Pembina County, Dakota Territory (Ibid.).
>
> viii. Moise Frederic Onesime Venne was born on 14 Oct 1885 Leroy, Pembina County, Dakota Territory (Ibid., page 145, B-435.). He was baptized on 15 Oct 1885 St.Joseph, Leroy, Pembina County, Dakota Territory (Ibid.).
>
> ix. Marie Marguerite Exilda Venne was born on 29 Dec 1886 Leroy, Pembina County, Dakota Territory (Ibid., page 154-155, B-516.). She was baptized on 1 Jan 1887 St.Joseph, Leroy, Pembina County, Dakota Territory (Ibid.). She died on 18 Mar 1889 Leroy, Pembina County, North Dakota, at age 2 (SJL-D, page 1.). She was buried on 19 Mar 1889 St.Joseph, Leroy, Pembina County, North Dakota (Ibid.).
>
> x. Adrien Venne was born on 2 Sep 1888 Leroy, Pembina County, Dakota Territory (SJL-2, B-6.). He was baptized on 16 Sep 1888 St.Joseph, Leroy, Pembina County, Dakota Territory (Ibid.).
>
> xi. Julius Arthur Venne was born on 8 Mar 1892 Leroy, Pembina County, North Dakota (Ibid., page 45, B-14.). He was baptized on 22 Mar 1892 St.Joseph, Leroy, Pembina County, North Dakota (Ibid.).

11. Alexandre Venne was born circa 1856. He married **Marie Desjarlais**, daughter of **Charles Desjarlais** and **Marguerite Montour**, on 21 Feb 1876 Assumption, Pembina, Pembina County, Dakota Territory (AP, M-3.).

Marie Desjarlais was born on 12 Nov 1854 Pembina, Pembina County, Dakota Territory (Ibid., page 117, B-319.). She was baptized on 13 Nov 1854 Assumption, Pembina, Pembina County, Dakota Territory (Ibid.).

Children of **Alexandre Venne** and **Marie Desjarlais** were as follows:

> i. Alexandre Venne was born on 21 Dec 1876 Dakota Territory (Ibid., B-2.). He was baptized on 17 Jan 1877 Assumption, Pembina, Pembina County, Dakota Territory (Ibid.).
>
> ii. Patrick Venne was born in 1882 Maple Creek, (Saskatchewan) (ArchiviaNet, C-15008.).

Generation Three

12. Jean Baptiste Venne was born on 12 Feb 1864 St.Norbert, (Manitoba) (SN1, page 99, B-17.). He was baptized on 13 Feb 1864 St.Norbert, (Manitoba) (Ibid.). He married **Elise Berthelet**, daughter of **Joseph Berthelet** and **Angelique Laferte**, on 29 Jan 1883 St.Joseph, Leroy, Pembina County, Dakota Territory (SJL-1, page 123, M-44.). He died on 15 Oct 1936 Pembina County, North Dakota, at age 72 (ND Death Index.).

Elise Berthelet was born on 23 Jul 1869 Ste.Agathe, (Manitoba) (MBS, C-14925.) (SN1, B-32.). She was baptized on 22 Aug 1869 St.Norbert, (Manitoba) (Ibid.).

Children of **Jean Baptiste Venne** and **Elise Berthelet** were as follows:

    i.   Joseph Venne was born on 20 Feb 1884 Leroy, Pembina County, Dakota Territory (SJL-1, page 132, B-329.). He was baptized on 24 Feb 1884 St.Joseph, Leroy, Pembina County, Dakota Territory (Ibid.).

26   ii.   Jean Baptiste Venne, b. 18 Mar 1885 Leroy, Pembina County, Dakota Territory; m. Vitaline (--?--); d. 13 Sep 1941 Pembina County, North Dakota.

27   iii.   Marie Emma Venne, b. 3 Oct 1886 Leroy, Pembina County, Dakota Territory.

    iv.   Noel Romain Venne was born on 7 Apr 1888 Leroy, Pembina County, Dakota Territory (Ibid., page 167, B-13.). He was baptized on 22 Apr 1888 St.Joseph, Leroy, Pembina County, Dakota Territory (Ibid.).

    v.   William Venne was born on 8 Apr 1889 (ND Death Index.). He died on 23 May 1949 Rolette County, North Dakota, at age 60 (Ibid.).

    vi.   Jean Baptiste Venne was born on 9 Jul 1890 Leroy, Pembina County, North Dakota (SJL-2, page 28, B-18.). He was baptized on 9 Jul 1890 St.Joseph, Leroy, Pembina County, North Dakota (Ibid.).

    vii.   Marie Rose Venne was born on 2 Apr 1892 Leroy, Pembina County, North Dakota (Ibid., page 46, B-15.). She was baptized on 17 Apr 1892 St.Joseph, Leroy, Pembina County, North Dakota (Ibid.).

28   viii. Joseph Patrice Venne, b. 31 Mar 1894 Leroy, Pembina County, North Dakota; d. 17 Apr 1944 Belcourt, Rolette County, North Dakota.

13. Salomon Venne was born on 21 Aug 1857 St.Norbert, (Manitoba) (MBS, C-14934.). He married **Marie Rose Marion**, daughter of **Edouard Marion** and **Eliza McDougall**, on 5 Jul 1879 St.Joseph, Leroy, Pembina County, Dakota Territory (SJL-1, page 94, M-7.).

Marie Rose Marion was born on 19 Nov 1858 Pembina, Pembina County, Dakota Territory (AP, page 201, B-605.). She was baptized on 21 Nov 1858 Assumption, Pembina, Pembina County, Dakota Territory (Ibid.).

Children of **Salomon Venne** and **Marie Rose Marion** were as follows:

    i.   Salomon Edouard Venne was born on 12 Aug 1880 Leroy, Pembina County, Dakota Territory (SJL-1, page 103, B-115.). He was baptized on 12 Aug 1880 St.Joseph, Leroy, Pembina County, Dakota Territory (Ibid.).

    ii.   Rose Anne Venne was born on 28 Mar 1882 Leroy, Pembina County, Dakota Territory (Ibid., page 117, B-208.). She was baptized on 28 Mar 1882 St.Joseph, Leroy, Pembina County, Dakota Territory (Ibid.).

    iii.   Marie Elmire Venne was born on 29 Sep 1883 Leroy, Pembina County, Dakota Territory (Ibid., page 129, B-303.). She was baptized on 7 Oct 1883 St.Joseph, Leroy, Pembina County, Dakota Territory (Ibid.).

    iv.   Jean Cullen Venne was born on 8 Mar 1885 Leroy, Pembina County, Dakota Territory (Ibid., page 141, B-395.). He was baptized on 17 Mar 1885 St.Joseph, Leroy, Pembina County, Dakota Territory (Ibid.). He died on 7 Apr 1885 Leroy, Pembina County, Dakota Territory (Ibid., page 141, S-146.). He was buried on 8 Apr 1885 St.Joseph, Leroy, Pembina County, Dakota Territory (Ibid.).

    v.   Florestine Elizabeth Alphonsine Venne was born on 30 Jan 1886 Leroy, Pembina County, Dakota Territory (Ibid., page 147, B-452.). She was baptized on 7 Feb 1886 St.Joseph, Leroy, Pembina County, Dakota Territory (Ibid.).

    vi.   Marie Jeanne Venne was born on 30 Dec 1887 Leroy, Pembina County, Dakota Territory (Ibid., page 165, B-1.). She was baptized on 1 Jan 1888 St.Joseph, Leroy, Pembina County, Dakota Territory (Ibid.).

    vii.   Julius Josue Venne was born on 20 Sep 1889 Leroy, Pembina County, North Dakota (SJL-2, page 15, B-33.). He was baptized on 20 Sep 1889 St.Joseph, Leroy, Pembina County, North Dakota (Ibid.).

    viii. Marie Josephine Venne was born on 12 Aug 1891 Leroy, Pembina County, North Dakota (Ibid., page 38, B-25.). She was baptized on 12 Aug 1891 St.Joseph, Leroy, Pembina County, North Dakota (Ibid.).

    ix.   Alexander Venne was born on 11 Dec 1892 Leroy, Pembina County, North Dakota (Ibid., page 54, B-50.). He was baptized on 11 Dec 1892 St.Joseph, Leroy, Pembina County, North Dakota (Ibid.). He died on 13 Dec 1892 Leroy, Pembina County, North Dakota (SJL-D, page 4.). He was buried on 14 Dec 1892 St.Joseph, Leroy, Pembina County, North Dakota (Ibid.).

    x.   Aldina Venne was born on 12 Nov 1893 Leroy, Pembina County, North Dakota (SJL-2, page 64, B-31.). She was baptized on 14 Nov 1893 St.Joseph, Leroy, Pembina County, North Dakota (Ibid.).

    xi.   Joseph Albert Venne was born on 18 Aug 1895 Leroy, Pembina County, North Dakota (Ibid., page 83, B-29.). He was baptized on 18 Aug 1895 St.Joseph, Leroy, Pembina County, North Dakota (Ibid.).

    xii.   Marie Rose Venne was born on 27 Aug 1897 Leroy, Pembina County, North Dakota (Ibid., page 107, B-47.). She was baptized on 5 Sep 1897 St.Joseph, Leroy, Pembina County, North Dakota (Ibid.).

14. Josephte Venne was born on 12 Jan 1859 St.Norbert, (Manitoba) (SN1, page 9, B-3.). She was baptized on 12 Jan 1859 St.Norbert, (Manitoba) (Ibid., B-3.). She married **Roger Goulet**, son of **Moise Goulet** and **Marie Beauchamp**, on 4 Mar 1878 St.Norbert, Manitoba (SN2, M-6.).

Roger Goulet was born in Oct 1857 St.Norbert, (Manitoba) (MBS, C-14928.).

15. Joseph Napoleon Venne was born on 17 Oct 1864 St.Norbert, (Manitoba) (SN1, page 110, B-38.). He was baptized on 17 Oct 1864 St.Norbert, (Manitoba) (Ibid.). He married **Marie Therese Tourond**, daughter of **Joseph Tourond** and **Josephte Paul**, on 30 Jun 1887 Batoche, (Saskatchewan) (BSAP, page 59, M-6.). He married **Marie Louise Parenteau**, daughter of **Joseph Daudais Parenteau** and **Julie Houle**, on 16 Nov 1895 St.Vital, Battleford, (Saskatchewan) (SV, M-5.).

Marie Therese Tourond was born on 18 Jan 1866 St.Francois Xavier, (Manitoba) (SFXI-Kipling, B-10.). She was baptized on 19 Jan 1866 St.Francois Xavier, (Manitoba) (Ibid.). She died on 18 Aug 1891 Batoche, (Saskatchewan), at age 25 (BSAP, page 9, S-7.). She was buried on 20 Aug 1891 Batoche, (Saskatchewan) (Ibid.).

Children of **Joseph Napoleon Venne** and **Marie Therese Tourond** were as follows:

    i.   Albert Venne was born on 2 May 1888 (Ibid., page 67, B-12.). He was baptized on 16 May 1888 Batoche, (Saskatchewan) (Ibid.).

ii. Marie Helene Venne was born on 27 Dec 1889 Batoche, (Saskatchewan) (Ibid., page 79, S-1.). She died on 4 Jan 1890 Batoche, (Saskatchewan) (Ibid.). She was buried on 5 Jan 1890 Batoche, (Saskatchewan) (Ibid.).

Marie Louise Parenteau was born on 20 Feb 1871 Duck Lake, (Saskatchewan) (ArchiviaNet, C-15008.) (SL-SK, page 4, B-15.). She was baptized on 20 Feb 1871 St.Laurent, (Saskatchewan) (Ibid.).

Children of **Joseph Napoleon Venne** and **Marie Louise Parenteau** were as follows:

i. Robert Venne was born on 22 Sep 1896 (Saskatchewan) (1901 Canada, microfilm, T-6553, Duck Lake, page 12, Family 108, line 8-14.) (Saskatchewan Vital Statistics online, http://vsgs.health.gov.sk.ca, Birth Reg. #6764.) (SV, B-28.). He was baptized on 23 Sep 1896 St.Vital, Battleford, (Saskatchewan) (Ibid.).

ii. Georgine Venne was born on 29 Jul 1898 Duck Lake, (Saskatchewan) (1901 Canada, microfilm, T-6553, Duck Lake, page 12, Family 108, line 8-14.).

16. Louis Bruno Venne was born on 23 Nov 1870 St.Norbert, Manitoba (SN1, page 135, B-48.). He was baptized on 24 Nov 1870 St.Norbert, (Manitoba) (Ibid.). He married **Florestine Letendre**, daughter of **Francois Xavier Letendre** and **Marguerite Parenteau**, on 4 Sep 1894 Batoche, (Saskatchewan) (BSAP, page 117, M-3.). He died on 11 Nov 1900 Batoche, (Saskatchewan), at age 29 (Denney Papers, Charles D. Denney, Glenbow Archives, Calgary, Alberta.).

Florestine Letendre was born on 23 Dec 1877 St.Laurent, (Saskatchewan) (SL-SK, page 8, B-61.). She was baptized on 24 Dec 1877 St.Laurent-de-Grandin, (Saskatchewan) (Ibid.). She died on 30 Jun 1901 Batoche, (Saskatchewan), at age 23 (Denney.).

Children of **Louis Bruno Venne** and **Florestine Letendre** were as follows:

i. Louis Bruno Venne was born on 14 Oct 1895 Batoche, (Saskatchewan) (BSAP, page 128, B-25.) (SK Vital Statistics, #7837.). He was baptized on 14 Oct 1895 Batoche, (Saskatchewan) (BSAP, page 128, B-25.).

ii. Horace Stanley Venne was born on 11 Dec 1896 (Saskatchewan) (SK Vital Statistics, #7889.). He died in 1899 (Denney.). He was buried in 1899 Batoche, (Saskatchewan) (Ibid.).

iii. Eva Venne was born on 16 Dec 1897 Bellevue, (Saskatchewan) (1901 Canada, microfilm, T-6553, Bellevue, page 7, Family 64, line 7-10.) (SK Vital Statistics, #7928.).

iv. Marie Augustine Venne was born on 15 Jun 1899 Batoche, (Saskatchewan) (Ibid., Birth Reg. #1782.).

v. Alice Venne was born on 14 Dec 1899 Bellevue, (Saskatchewan) (1901 Canada, microfilm, T-6553, Bellevue, page 7, Family 64, line 7-10.).

vi. Armand Hector Venne was born on 16 Aug 1900 Batoche, (Saskatchewan) (Denney.) (SK Vital Statistics, Birth Reg. #2122.). He died in 1901 Batoche, (Saskatchewan) (Denney.).

17. Marie Agathe Venne was born on 7 Feb 1864 St.Norbert, (Manitoba) (MBS, C-14934.) (SN1, page 99, B-15.). She was baptized on 8 Feb 1864 St.Norbert, (Manitoba) (Ibid.). She married **Onesime Wilkie**, son of **Jean Baptiste Wilkie** and **Marie Laframboise,** on 27 Nov 1883 Olga, Cavalier County, North Dakota (Olga, page 27, M-9.). She died on 15 Oct 1885 Olga, Cavalier County, North Dakota, at age 21 (Ibid., page 83, S-19.). She was buried on 16 Oct 1885 Olga, Cavalier County, North Dakota (Ibid.).

Onesime Wilkie was born on 20 Mar 1856 (AP, page 147, B-410.). He was born on 12 Apr 1856 (ND Death Index.). He was baptized on 11 May 1856 Assumption, Pembina, Pembina County, Dakota Territory (AP, page 147, B-410.). He died on 16 May 1936 Rolette County, North Dakota, at age 80 (ND Death Index.).

18. Julienne Venne was born on 1 Apr 1866 Ste.Agathe, (Manitoba) (MBS, C-14934.) (SN1, page 80, B-18.). She was baptized on 2 Apr 1866 St.Norbert, (Manitoba) (Ibid.). She married **William Jerome**, son of **Louis Jerome** and **Angelique Boyer,** on 28 Nov 1882 Olga, Cavalier County, North Dakota (Olga, page 6, M-3.).

William Jerome was born on 14 Nov 1860 Pembina, Pembina County, Dakota Territory (AP, page 228, B-42.). He was baptized on 18 Nov 1860 Assumption, Pembina, Pembina County, Dakota Territory (Ibid.). He died on 21 Mar 1912 Pembina County, North Dakota, at age 51 (ND Death Index.). He was buried on 26 Mar 1912 St.Joseph, Leroy, Pembina County, North Dakota (SJL-D, page 22.).

19. Josephte Venne was born on 25 Oct 1870 Ste.Agathe, Manitoba (MBS, C-14934.) (SN1, page 135, B-45.). She was baptized on 29 Oct 1870 St.Norbert, Manitoba (Ibid.). She married **Joseph Gariepy**, son of **Joseph Gariepy** and **Cecilia Wilkie,** before 1890. She died on 15 May 1892 Olga, Cavalier County, North Dakota, at age 21 (Olga, page 210, S-4.). She was buried on 17 May 1892 Olga, Cavalier County, North Dakota (Ibid.).

Joseph Gariepy was born in 1862.

20. Delphine Venne was born on 22 May 1878 (SJL-1, page 88, B-15.). She was baptized on 13 Jun 1878 St.Joseph, Leroy, Pembina County, Dakota Territory (Ibid.). She married **Napoleon Larence**, son of **Charles Larence** and **Madeleine Ritchot,** on 2 Mar 1897 St.Joseph, Leroy, Pembina County, North Dakota (SJL-2, M-2.). She died on 28 Jan 1900 Leroy, North Dakota, at age 21 (SJL-D, page 10.). She was buried on 30 Jan 1900 St.Joseph, Leroy, North Dakota (Ibid.).

Napoleon Larence was born on 14 Sep 1871 (SJL-1, page 16, B-20.). He was baptized on 17 Sep 1871 St.Joseph, Leroy, Dakota Territory (Ibid.).

21. Marguerite Florestine Venne was born on 20 Nov 1880 (SJL-1, page 107, B-135.). She was baptized on 8 Jan 1881 St.Joseph, Leroy, Pembina County, Dakota Territory (Ibid.). She married **Michel Alfred Laframboise**, son of **Louis Laframboise** and **Josephine Allard,** before 1898.

Michel Alfred Laframboise was born on 26 Aug 1874 (Ibid., page 50, B-21.). He was baptized on 10 Sep 1874 St.Joseph, Leroy, Pembina County, Dakota Territory (Ibid.). He married **Elizabeth Mary Norris**, daughter of **John Norris** and **Ann Sutherland,** in 1898 (ArchiviaNet.). He married **Marie Ange Cardinal** in 1902 (Automated Genealogy 1911 Census Transcription Project and Census Images from the National Archives of Canada, http://www.automatedgenealogy.com, page 2, family 198, line 14-16.) (Rod Mac Quarrie, 22 Dec 2009.). He died on 1 Aug 1947 at age 72 (Ibid.).

22. Joseph Zephirin Venne was born in Jan 1872 Dakota Territory (Eugene Venney, Letter, 4 Dec 1997.). He married **Rosie V. (--?--)** circa 1899 (Ibid.).

Rosie V. (--?--) was born circa Sep 1879 Minnesota (Ibid.).

Children of **Joseph Zephirin Venne** and **Rosie V. (--?--)** are:

29   i. James S. Venne, b. 1903; m. Laura Blacknik.

23. Michael Alfred Venne was born on 24 Aug 1879 Leroy, Pembina County, Dakota Territory (Ibid.) (SJL-1, page 95, B-62.). He was baptized on 26 Aug 1879 St.Joseph, Leroy, Pembina County, Dakota Territory (Ibid.). He married **Sara Williams** in 1906 Carlisle, Pennsylvania (Eugene Venney, Letter, 4 Dec 1997.). He died in Jan 1971 Sebastopol, Sonoma, California, at age 91 (Ibid.).

Sara Williams died in Jan 1971 Sebastopol, Sonoma, California (Ibid.).

Children of **Michael Alfred Venne** and **Sara Williams** were as follows:

    i.   Viola Venne was born on 22 May 1907 (Ibid.).

    ii. Alfred Michael Venne Jr was born circa 1910 Lawrence, Kansas (Ibid.).

    iii. Victoria Haskell Venne was born circa 1913 Lawrence, Kansas (Ibid.). She married William G. Stone on 19 Mar 1950 San Francisco, California (Ibid.). She died on 17 May 1990 Martinez, California (Ibid.).

         William G. Stone was born circa 1908 Springfield, Illinois (Ibid.). He died in Dec 1989 (Ibid.).

    iv. Sarah Ruth Venne was born circa 1916 Chilocco (Ibid.).

24. Patrick Hector Venne was born on 18 Nov 1881 Neche, Pembina County, North Dakota (Ibid.). He was born on 19 Dec 1881 Dakota Territory (AP, page 200, B-2.). He was baptized on 8 Jan 1882 Assumption, Pembina, Pembina, Dakota Territory (Ibid.). He married **Eva Mary Caisse** on 23 Dec 1905 Lawrence, Douglas, Kansas (Eugene Venney, Letter, 4 Dec 1997.). He married **Bernice Marie Brill**, daughter of **Charles Wesley Brill** and **Lydia Margaret Sackett,** on 1 Jul 1922 Los Angeles, Los Angeles, California (Ibid.). He died on 1 May 1967 Dunedin, Florida, at age 85 (Ibid.).

Eva Mary Caisse was born in Aug 1884 Minnesota (Ibid.).

Bernice Marie Brill was born on 24 Dec 1891 Harmony, Clay, Indiana (Ibid.). She died on 24 Jul 1967 Dunedin, Florida, at age 75 (Ibid.).

Children of **Patrick Hector Venne** and **Bernice Marie Brill** were as follows:

  30   i.   Palmer Allen Venne, b. 17 Jan 1924; m. Ursula Kaiser; d. 22 Feb 1971 Dunedin, Florida.

  31   ii. Cecile Marie Venne, b. 17 Dec 1925 Chilocco, Kay, Oklahoma; m. Casey Eugene Westell Jr.

  32   iii. Eugene Edmond Venne, b. 5 Sep 1928 Chilocco, Kay, Oklahoma; m. Ruth Jean Dow.

25. Ernestine Venne was born on 9 Jun 1892 Neche, Pemina, North Dakota (Ibid.). She married **E. Ray White.**

Generation Four

26. Jean Baptiste Venne was born on 18 Mar 1885 Leroy, Pembina County, Dakota Territory (SJL-1, page 141, B-397.). He was baptized on 22 Mar 1885 St.Joseph, Leroy, Pembina County, Dakota Territory (Ibid.). He married **Vitaline (--?--)** before 1910 (1930C ND Fifteenth Census of the United States: 1930; North Dakota, National Archives of the United States, Washington, D.C., page 1B.). He died on 13 Sep 1941 Pembina County, North Dakota, at age 56 (ND Death Index.).

Vitaline (--?--) was born on 9 Oct 1890 (1930C ND, page 1B.) (ND Death Index.). She died on 4 Dec 1953 Walsh County, North Dakota, at age 63 (Ibid.).

Children of **Jean Baptiste Venne** and **Vitaline (--?--)** were as follows:

    i.   Maggie Venne was born circa 1910 (1930C ND, page 1B.).

    ii. John Venne was born on 4 Oct 1911 (Ibid.) (ND Death Index.). He died on 1 Apr 1984 Pembina County, North Dakota, at age 72 (Ibid.).

    iii. Mary Venne was born circa 1914 (1930C ND, page 1B.).

    iv. Clarence Edward Venne was born on 23 Feb 1916 (Ibid.) (ND Death Index.). He died on 6 Oct 1984 Pembina County, North Dakota, at age 68 (Ibid.).

    v. Wilbert Louis Venne was born on 29 Mar 1918 (1930C ND, page 1B.) (ND Death Index.). He died on 3 Oct 1986 Grand Forks County, North Dakota, at age 68 (Ibid.).

    vi. Thelma Venne was born circa Feb 1921 (1930C ND, page 1B.).

    vii. Irene Venne was born circa Dec 1923 (Ibid.).

    viii. Katherine Venne was born circa Aug 1926 (Ibid.).

    ix. Josephine Venne was born circa 1929 (Ibid.).

    x. Elsie Venne was born circa 1933 (1940C ND 1940 North Dakota, Sixteenth Census of the United States, National Archives of the United States, Washington, D.C., page 5A.).

    xi. Laura Venne was born circa 1936 (Ibid.).

27. Marie Emma Venne was born on 3 Oct 1886 Leroy, Pembina County, Dakota Territory (SJL-1, page 152, B-502.). She was baptized on 6 Oct 1886 St.Joseph, Leroy, Pembina County, Dakota Territory (Ibid.). She married **Robert Lillico (Sillico)** before 1904.

28. Joseph Patrice Venne was born on 31 Mar 1894 Leroy, Pembina County, North Dakota (SJL-2, page 69, B-14.). He was baptized on 3 Apr 1894 St.Joseph, Leroy, Pembina County, North Dakota (Ibid.). He married **Philomene Davis**, daughter of **Michel Davis** and **Flavie Henry,** before 1924 Froid, Sheridan County, Montana (*St.Ann's Centennial, 100 Years of Faith - 1885-1985*; Belcourt, North Dakota: St.Ann Parish, 1985), page 541.). He died on 17 Apr 1944 Belcourt, Rolette County, North Dakota, at age 50 (Ibid.) (ND Death Index.).

Philomene Davis was born on 24 Mar 1892 (Ibid.). She died on 2 Sep 1957 Rolette County, North Dakota, at age 65 (*St.Ann's Centennial*, page 541.) (ND Death Index.).

Children of **Joseph Patrice Venne** and **Philomene Davis** were as follows:

  33   i.   Elmer John Venne, b. 8 Jun 1924 St-Amalie, Manitoba; m. Malvina Thomas; d. 17 Aug 2004 Dunseith, Rolette County, North Dakota.

       ii. Laura Sibyl Venne was born on 30 Aug 1927 (1937-TMC Indian Census Roll of the Turtle Mountain Reservation, United States Indian Service Department of the Interior, Belcourt, North Dakota, J. E. Balmer, 1 January 1937, page 509, Census No. 5958-5960.) (Social Security Death Index, . Hereinafter cited as SSDI.). She married (--?--) St.Germaine. She died on 21 Jul 2009 North Dakota at age 81 (Ibid.).

29. James S. Venne was born in 1903. He married **Laura Blacknik** before 1938 (1987LS 1987-92 Little Shell Band of Chippewa Roll.).

Laura Blacknik was born in 1914 (Ibid.).

Children of **James S. Venne** and **Laura Blacknik** are:

      i.   Montana C. Venne was born on 24 Oct 1938 Missoula, Missoula County, Montana (Ibid.).

30. **Palmer Allen Venne** was born on 17 Jan 1924 (Eugene Venney, Letter, 4 Dec 1997.). He married **Ursula Kaiser** (Ibid.). He died on 22 Feb 1971 Dunedin, Florida, at age 47 (Ibid.).

Ursula Kaiser was born on 30 May 1928 Ratibor, Germany (Ibid.).

Children of **Palmer Allen Venne** and **Ursula Kaiser** are as follows:

      i.   Charmaine M. Venne was born on 17 Oct 1954 Houston, Texas (Ibid.).

     ii.   Sharon Lynn Venne was born on 8 Jun 1960 Tyndall Air Force Base, Florida (Ibid.).

31. **Cecile Marie Venne** was born on 17 Dec 1925 Chilocco, Kay, Oklahoma (Ibid.). She married **Casey Eugene Westell Jr** (Ibid.).

Casey Eugene Westell Jr was born on 29 Oct 1926 (Ibid.).

32. **Eugene Edmond Venne** was born on 5 Sep 1928 Chilocco, Kay, Oklahoma (Ibid.). He married **Ruth Jean Dow**, daughter of **Fred Harrison Dow** and **Edna Opal Wheeler**, on 15 Jul 1950 Indianapolis, Indiana (Ibid.).

Ruth Jean Dow was born on 8 Feb 1931 Paragon, Morgan, Indiana (Ibid.).

Generation Five

33. **Elmer John Venne** was born on 8 Jun 1924 St-Amalie, Manitoba (*St.Ann's Centennial*, page 541.) (SSDI.). He was baptized on 21 Jun 1924 St-Amalie, Manitoba (*St.Ann's Centennial*, page 541.). He married **Malvina Thomas**, daughter of **Clement Petit dit Thomas** and **Mary Cecelia Poitras**, on 26 Jan 1962 Nevada (Ibid.). He died on 17 Aug 2004 Dunseith, Rolette County, North Dakota, at age 80 (SSDI.) (ND Death Index.).

Malvina Thomas was born on 12 Mar 1920 Rolette, Rolette County, Manitoba (*St.Ann's Centennial*, page 541.) (SSDI.). She was baptized on 19 Mar 1920 St-Michael's, Thorne, Rolette County, North Dakota (*St.Ann's Centennial*, page 541.). She died on 25 Dec 2004 Rolla, Rolette County, North Dakota, at age 84 (SSDI.) (ND Death Index.).

Descendants of Joseph Vermette

Generation One

1. **Joseph Vermette** married according to the custom of the country **Josephte Plouf dit Villebrun** before 1806 (Denney Papers, Charles D. Denney, Glenbow Archives, Calgary, Alberta.). He died before 10 Jan 1830.

Josephte Plouf dit Villebrun was born circa 1790. She married according to the custom of the country **Allan McDonald** before 1807 (Ibid.). She died before 1825.

Children of **Joseph Vermette** and **Josephte Plouf dit Villebrun** were:

   2   i.   Joseph Vermette, b. circa 1806 Ruperts Land; m. Angelique Laliberte; d. 31 Jan 1900 RM Ritchot, Manitoba; bur. 2 Feb 1900 St.Norbert, Manitoba.

Generation Two

2. **Joseph Vermette** was born circa 1806 Ruperts Land (1831C RRS HBCA E5/5 1831 Census of the Red River Settlement, HBCA E5/5, Hudson's Bay Company Archives, Provincial Archives, 200 Vaughan Street, Winnipeg, MB R3C 1T5, Canada., page 16.). He was born in 1810 St.Norbert, (Manitoba) (MBS Scrip Applications, Original White Settlers & Halfbreeds residing in Manitoba on 15 July 1870, RG15-19, C-14934.). He was baptized on 10 Jan 1830 St.Boniface, (Manitoba) (SB 1825-1834 St.Boniface Roman Catholic Registre des Baptemes, Mariages & Sepultures, 1825-1834, page 36, B-596. Hereinafter cited as SB 1825-1834.). He married **Angelique Laliberte**, daughter of **Pierre Cyril Chippewan Laliberte** and **Josephte Baudry**, on 11 Jan 1830 St.Boniface, (Manitoba) (Ibid., page 36, M-93.). He died on 31 Jan 1900 RM Ritchot, Manitoba (Manitoba Vital Statistics online, http://web2.gov.mb.ca, Death Reg. No. 1900,001108.) (St-N Cem *St.Norbert Parish Cemetery 1859-1906, We Remember*; Winnipeg, Manitoba, Canada: St.Norbert Parish-La Barriere Metis Council of the Metis Federation of Manitoba, 29 May 2010).). He was buried on 2 Feb 1900 St.Norbert, Manitoba (Ibid.).

Angelique Laliberte was born circa 1810 (SB 1825-1834, page 12, B-118.). She was born in 1815 Swan Lake, North West Territories (MBS, C-14934.). She was baptized on 25 Sep 1825 St.Boniface, (Manitoba) (SB 1825-1834, page 12, B-118.). She died on 9 Oct 1905 Ritchot, Manitoba (MB Vital Statistics, Death Reg. #1905,002486.). She was buried on 12 Oct 1905 St.Norbert, Manitoba (St-N Cem.).

Children of **Joseph Vermette** and **Angelique Laliberte** were as follows:

   3   i.   Joseph Vermette, b. 8 Feb 1832 St.Boniface, (Manitoba); m. Marguerite Sayer; d. 24 Apr 1885 Fish Creek, (Saskatchewan); bur. 27 Apr 1885 Batoche, (Saskatchewan).

   4   ii.   Antoine Vermette, b. 27 Apr 1833 St.Boniface, (Manitoba); m. Cecile Rocque; m. Marguerite Nolin; m. Clarisse Josephine Nolin; d. 6 Apr 1924 St.Vital, Manitoba.

   5   iii.   Louis Vermette, b. circa 1837 Red River; m. Julie Cadotte; d. 9 Nov 1902 RM Montcalm, Manitoba.

   6   iv.   Alexis Vermette, b. circa 1837 St.Norbert, (Manitoba); m. Philomene Beauchemin; d. 29 Oct 1924 St.Vital, Manitoba.

   7   v.   Pierre Vermette, b. 1838 St.Norbert, (Manitoba); m. Caroline St.Denis; d. 10 Nov 1918 St.Laurent, Manitoba.

   8   vi.   Norbert Vermette, b. circa 1841; m. Genevieve Rocheleau; d. 29 Sep 1874 St.Norbert, Manitoba; bur. 1 Oct 1874 St.Norbert, Manitoba.

   9   vii.   Maxime Vermette, b. Jun 1847 St.Norbert, (Manitoba); m. Sophie McCarthy dit Mercredi; d. 28 Feb 1906 DeSalaberry, Manitoba.

  10 viii.   Augustin Vermette, b. circa 1848; m. Melanie Frobisher; d. 16 Jun 1935 Ritchot, Manitoba.

  11   ix.   Toussaint Vermette, b. 15 Jan 1849 St.Norbert, (Manitoba); m. Elise Tourond; d. 8 Aug 1930 DeSalaberry, Manitoba.

        x.   Francois Vermette was born circa 1850.

      xi.   William Vermette was born circa 1854 (SN1 Catholic Parish Register of St.Norbert 1857-1873, page 77, S-1. Hereinafter cited as SN1.). He died on 31 Dec 1865 St.Norbert, (Manitoba) (Ibid.). He was buried on 1 Jan 1866 St.Norbert, (Manitoba) (Ibid.).

12   xii.   Anne Vermette, b. 1857 St.Norbert, (Manitoba); m. Isidore Tourond; d. 8 Dec 1922 St.Boniface, Manitoba.

Generation Three

3. Joseph Vermette was born on 8 Feb 1832 St.Boniface, (Manitoba) (SB 1825-1834, page 52, B-401.). He was baptized on 19 Feb 1832 St.Boniface, (Manitoba) (Ibid.). He married **Marguerite Sayer**, daughter of **Pierre Guillaume Sayer** and **Josephte Frobisher,** before 1855. He died on 24 Apr 1885 Fish Creek, (Saskatchewan), at age 53 (Denney.) (BSAP Records of the Parish of Batoche, St.Antoine de Pudoue Roman Catholic Church: Register for Baptisms, Marriages, Deaths, Volume One, 1881-1909., page 32, S-11. Hereinafter cited as BSAP.). He was buried on 27 Apr 1885 Batoche, (Saskatchewan) (Ibid.).

Marguerite Sayer was born circa 1837.

Children of **Joseph Vermette** and **Marguerite Sayer** were as follows:

13   i.   Alexandre Vermette, b. 25 Jan 1855 St.Norbert, (Manitoba); m. Angelique Larence; d. 31 Oct 1924 Ellice, Manitoba.

ii.   Louis Vermette was born on 25 Nov 1857 St.Francois Xavier, (Manitoba) (SFXI-Kipling St.Francois Xavier Register Index, 1834-1900; compiled by Clarence Kipling , B-215.). He was baptized on 27 Nov 1857 St.Francois Xavier, (Manitoba) (Ibid.) (SFXI 1851-1868 St.Francois Xavier 1852-1861 Register Index, B-215. Hereinafter cited as SFXI 1851-1868.).

iii.   Rose Vermette was born on 24 Oct 1859 St.Norbert, (Manitoba) (SFXI-Kipling, B-390.) (MBS, C-14934.). She was baptized on 26 Oct 1859 St.Francois Xavier, (Manitoba) (SFXI-Kipling, B-390.). She died on 3 Sep 1874 St.Norbert, Manitoba, at age 14 (SN2 Catholic Parish Register of St.Norbert, S-23. Hereinafter cited as SN2.). She was buried on 4 Sep 1874 St.Norbert, Manitoba (MBS, C-14934.) (SN2, S-23.).

iv.   William Vermette was born on 3 Sep 1861 St.Francois Xavier, (Manitoba) (SFXI-Kipling, B-97.). He was baptized on 8 Sep 1861 St.Francois Xavier, (Manitoba) (Ibid.). He died on 1 Feb 1863 St.Francois Xavier, (Manitoba), at age 1 (Ibid., S-6.) (SFXI 1851-1868, S-6.). He was buried on 3 Feb 1863 St.Francois Xavier, (Manitoba) (SFXI-Kipling, S-6.) (SFXI: 1851-1869 St.Francois Xavier 1851-69 Register Index.) (SFXI 1851-1868, S-6.).

14   v.   Roger Vermette, b. 28 Sep 1863; m. Madeleine Fisher.

15   vi.   Marie Vermette, b. 7 Oct 1865 St.Norbert, (Manitoba); m. Jerome Henry.

16   vii.   Anne Vermette, b. 4 Oct 1867 St.Norbert, (Manitoba); m. Antoine Parisien; m. Joseph Primeau.

viii.   Josephte Vermette was born on 5 Aug 1870 North West Territories (MBS, C-14934.). She was born on 20 Sep 1870 Dakota Territory (AP Records of the Assumption Roman Catholic Church, Pembina, North Dakota: Baptisms, Marriages, Sepultures, 1848-1896; compiled by Reverend Father J. M. Belleau, 2 October 1944, page 44, B-17. Hereinafter cited as AP.). She was baptized on 25 Sep 1870 Assumption, Pembina, Pembina County, Dakota Territory (Ibid.).

17   ix.   Joseph Albert Vermette, b. 1 Jun 1873 St.Norbert, Manitoba; m. Sarah Jane Delorme.

x.   Anonyme Vermette was born on 6 Apr 1875 St.Norbert, Manitoba (SN2, B-16 and S-11.). He/she was baptized on 6 Apr 1875 St.Norbert, Manitoba (Ibid.). He/she died on 6 Apr 1875 St.Norbert, Manitoba (Ibid.). He/she was buried on 6 Apr 1875 St.Norbert, Manitoba (Ibid.).

18   xi.   John Vermette, b. 2 Oct 1876 St.Norbert, Manitoba; m. Helene Racette.

19   xii.   Marie Adele Vermette, b. 14 Apr 1878 St.Norbert, Manitoba; m. Joseph Schmidt; d. 19 Jan 1907 Prince Albert, (Saskatchewan).

xiii.   Louis Robert Vermette was born on 23 Apr 1884 Batoche, (Saskatchewan) (BSAP, page 21, B-10.). He was baptized on 27 Apr 1884 Batoche, (Saskatchewan) (Ibid.).

4. Antoine Vermette was born on 27 Apr 1833 St.Boniface, (Manitoba) (SB 1825-1834, page 99, B-582.). He was baptized on 29 Apr 1833 St.Boniface, (Manitoba) (Ibid.). He married **Cecile Rocque,** daughter of **Joseph Rocque** and **Francoise Paul,** before 1859. He married **Marguerite Nolin,** daughter of **Augustin Nolin** and **Marie Domitilde Perreault dit Morin,** on 6 Oct 1910 St.Norbert, Manitoba (MM *Manitoba Marriages* in *Publication 45*, Volumes 1-3, compiled and edited by: Paul J. Lareau, Fr. Julien Hamelin, (240 Avenue Daly, Ottawa, Ontario K1N 6G2: Le Centre de Genealogie S.C., 1984).). He married **Clarisse Josephine Nolin,** daughter of **Joseph Augustin Nolin** and **Adelaide Larence,** on 26 Oct 1914 St.Norbert, Manitoba (Ibid.). He died on 6 Apr 1924 St.Vital, Manitoba, at age 90 (MB Vital Statistics, Death Reg. #1924,016514.).

Cecile Rocque was born in Aug 1838 St.Boniface, (Manitoba) (MBS, C-14934.).

Children of **Antoine Vermette** and **Cecile Rocque** were as follows:

i.   Jean Vermette was born on 18 Apr 1859 St.Norbert, (Manitoba) (SN1, B-13, page 15.). He was baptized on 19 Apr 1859 St.Norbert, (Manitoba) (Ibid.). He married Marie Louise Rosalie Morand, daughter of Louis Morand and Catherine Eneau dit Delorme, on 15 Feb 1904 (St.Norbert), Ritchot, Manitoba (MM.) (MB Vital Statistics, Marriage Reg. #1904,002538.).

   Marie Louise Rosalie Morand was born on 5 Aug 1862 St.Norbert, (Manitoba) (SN1, pabe 59, B-19.). She was baptized on 6 Aug 1862 St.Norbert, (Manitoba) (MBS, C-14931.) (SN1, pabe 59, B-19.).

20   ii.   William Vermette, b. 25 Jan 1861 St.Norbert, (Manitoba); m. Nancy Vandal; m. Nancy Frobisher; d. 20 Dec 1925 St.Vital, Manitoba.

21   iii.   Louis Jean Joseph Vermette, b. 18 Sep 1862 St.Boniface, (Manitoba); d. 16 Feb 1936 RM Ste.Anne, Manitoba.

22   iv.   Angelique Vermette, b. 16 Dec 1864 St.Norbert, (Manitoba); m. Joseph Campeau; d. 9 Nov 1885 St.Norbert, Manitoba; bur. 11 Nov 1885 St.Norbert, Manitoba.

23   v.   Alexandre Vermette, b. 20 May 1867 St.Norbert, (Manitoba); m. Julienne Frobisher; d. 16 Sep 1898 (Ritchot), St.Boniface, Manitoba.

vi.   Marie Rose Anna Vermette was born on 28 Jan 1869 St.Norbert, (Manitoba) (Ibid., B-3.). She was baptized on 29 Jan 1869 St.Norbert, (Manitoba) (Ibid.). She married Alexandre Trottier, son of Elie Trottier and Emelie

Dauost, on 4 Feb 1890 St.Norbert, Manitoba (MB Vital Statistics, Marriage Reg. #1890,002028.) (SN2, M-3.). She married Joseph Pelland on 29 Apr 1908 St.Norbert, Manitoba (MM.).

Alexandre Trottier was born circa 1852. He married **Melina Menard** before 1879. He died on 13 Feb 1901 RM Ritchot, Manitoba (MB Vital Statistics, Death Reg. #1901,003382.) (SN2, S-4.). He was buried on 15 Feb 1901 St.Norbert, Manitoba (St-N Cem.) (SN2, S-4.).

- vii. Marie Philomene Vermette was born on 12 Apr 1871 St.Norbert, Manitoba (SN1, page 144, B-22.). She was baptized on 13 Apr 1871 St.Norbert, Manitoba (Ibid.). She died on 26 May 1871 St.Norbert, Manitoba (Ibid., page 146, S-9.). She was buried on 27 May 1871 St.Norbert, Manitoba (Ibid.).
- viii. Joseph Alfred Vermette was born on 5 Apr 1872 St.Norbert, Manitoba (Ibid., B-17.). He was baptized on 6 Apr 1872 St.Norbert, Manitoba (Ibid.). He married Annie Clara Genthon, daughter of Elie Genthon and Genevieve Larence, on 27 Feb 1900 St.Boniface, Manitoba (RMSB *Repertoire des Mariages de Saint-Boniface (Manitoba) 1825-1983* compiled by Julien Hamelin S.C., (240, avenue Daly; Ottawa, Ontario K1N 6G2: Le Centre de Genealogie S. C., Publication #67, 1985), page 484.) (MB Vital Statistics, Marriage Reg. #1900,001790.).

   Annie Clara Genthon was born on 4 Sep 1866 St.Boniface, (Manitoba) (MBS, C-14928.) (SB-Rozyk St. Boniface Roman Catholic Church, Manitoba, Canada, Baptisms, Marriages and Burials 1860-1875 Extractions, Compiled by Rosemary Rozyk, page 63, B-106.). She was baptized on 5 Sep 1866 St.Boniface, (Manitoba) (MBS, C-14928.) (SB-Rozyk, page 63, B-106.).

- 24 ix. Philomene Vermette, b. 31 Mar 1874 St.Norbert, Manitoba; m. John Rowan.
- x. Patrice Vermette was born on 18 May 1876 St.Norbert, Manitoba (SN2, B-17.). He was baptized on 20 May 1876 St.Norbert, Manitoba (Ibid.). He died on 8 Sep 1898 Ritchot, Manitoba, at age 22 (MB Vital Statistics, Death Reg. No. 1898,002898.). He was buried on 10 Sep 1898 St.Norbert, Manitoba (St-N Cem.).
- xi. Frederic Vermette was born on 8 Apr 1879 (SN2, B-19.). He was baptized on 12 Apr 1879 St.Norbert, Manitoba (Ibid.). He married Delphine Charette, daughter of Jean Baptiste Charette and Isabelle Dease, on 12 Jan 1904 (St.Malo), DeSalaberry, Manitoba (MM.) (MB Vital Statistics, Marriage Reg. #1904,003599.). He died on 11 Dec 1904 (Ritchot), St.Boniface, Manitoba, at age 25 (Ibid., Death Reg. No. 1904,001390.) (Ibid., Death Reg. No. 1904,001830.). He was buried on 13 Dec 1904 St.Norbert, Manitoba (St-N Cem.).

   Delphine Charette was born on 9 Jan 1881 (SJL-1 Register of Baptisms, Marriages, and Burials, St.Joseph, Leroy, North Dakota, Diocese of Saint Paul, Minnesota, 1870-1888, Book 1, page 107, B-137. Hereinafter cited as SJL-1.). She was baptized on 19 Jan 1881 St.Joseph, Leroy, Pembina County, Dakota Territory (Ibid.). She married **Adolphe St.Jean** on 7 Feb 1912 St.Norbert, Manitoba (MM.) (MB Vital Statistics, Marriage Reg. #1912,005572.).

Marguerite Nolin was born on 14 Jan 1853 St.Boniface, (Manitoba) (MBS, C-14925.). She married **Pierre Berard**, son of **Louis Berard** and **Catherine Hughes**, on 16 Aug 1874 Ste.Anne, Manitoba (MM.). She died on 18 Feb 1914 Ritchot, Manitoba, at age 61 (MB Vital Statistics, Death Reg. #1914,0079402.).

Clarisse Josephine Nolin was born on 9 Oct 1892 Manitoba (Automated Genealogy 1901 Census Transcription Project and Census Images from the National Archives of Canada, http://www.automatedgenealogy.com, District #10, Subdistrict e-1, page 6, family 32, line 32-37.) (MB Vital Statistics, Birth Reg. #1892,002493.). She married **Francois Emery dit Henry**, son of **Francois Emery** and **Jeanne Mocoer**, on 22 Jan 1927 St.Norbert, Manitoba (MM.).

Children of **Antoine Vermette** and **Clarisse Josephine Nolin** are:
- i. Rene Antonio Vermette was born circa 30 May 1916 St.Norbert, Manitoba (1916 Census of Canada from the National Archives of Canada (Transcription by ancestry.com), Ottawa, Canada, District 12-7, page 28, line 10.).

5. **Louis Vermette** was born circa 1837 Red River (1870C-MB 1870 Manitoba Census, National Archives of Canada, Ottawa, Ontario, Microfilm Reel Number C-2170., #664, page 22.). He married **Julie Cadotte**, daughter of **Laurent Cadotte** and **Elisabeth Thomas**, on 2 Feb 1858 St.Norbert, (Manitoba) (SN1, page 4, M-6.). He died on 9 Nov 1902 RM Montcalm, Manitoba (MB Vital Statistics, Death Reg. No. 1902,001243.).

Julie Cadotte was born in 1845 St.Norbert, (Manitoba) (MBS, C-14934.).

Children of **Louis Vermette** and **Julie Cadotte** were as follows:
- 25 i. Louis Vermette, b. 4 Jan 1859 St.Norbert, (Manitoba); m. Adele Delorme.
- ii. Roger Vermette was born on 18 Nov 1860 St.Norbert, (Manitoba) (SN1, page 35, B-43.). He was baptized on 19 Nov 1860 St.Norbert, (Manitoba) (Ibid.). He died on 22 Nov 1888 RM Montcalm, Manitoba, at age 28 (MB Vital Statistics, Death Reg. No. 1888,002459.).
- iii. Patrice Vermette was born on 28 Mar 1862 St.Norbert, (Manitoba) (SN1, page 56, B-7.). He was baptized on 28 Mar 1862 St.Norbert, (Manitoba) (Ibid.). He died on 19 Aug 1864 St.Norbert, (Manitoba), at age 2 (Ibid., page 107, S-7.). He was buried on 20 Aug 1864 St.Norbert, (Manitoba) (Ibid.).
- iv. Frederic Vermette was born on 25 Sep 1864 St.Norbert, (Manitoba) (Ibid., page 108, B-33.). He was baptized on 25 Sep 1864 St.Norbert, (Manitoba) (Ibid.). He died on 5 Oct 1865 St.Norbert, (Manitoba), at age 1 (Ibid., page 135, S-16.). He was buried on 6 Oct 1865 St.Norbert, (Manitoba) (Ibid.).
- 26 v. Marie Virginie Vermette, b. 25 Feb 1866 St.Norbert, (Manitoba); m. Frederic Vandal; d. after 9 Jan 1893.
- vi. Marie Eliza Vermette was born on 28 Jul 1868 St.Norbert, (Manitoba) (Ibid., B-29.). She was baptized on 29 Jul 1868 St.Norbert, (Manitoba) (Ibid.). She died on 10 Jan 1885 Montcalm, Manitoba, at age 16 (MB Vital Statistics, Death Reg. #1885,002323.).
- vii. Anne Vermette was born on 1 Feb 1870 St.Norbert, (Manitoba) (SN1, B-6.). She was baptized on 1 Feb 1870 St.Norbert, (Manitoba) (Ibid., page 126, B-6.). She married Basile Lesperance, son of Louis Lesperance and Genevieve Turcotte, on 28 Oct 1890 St.Jean Baptiste, Manitoba (MM.).

   Basile Lesperance was born on 14 Jun 1864 St.Boniface, (Manitoba) (MBS, C-14930.) (SB-Rozyk, page 154, B-62.). He was baptized on 14 Jun 1864 St.Boniface, (Manitoba) (MBS, C-14930.) (SB-Rozyk, page 154, B-62.).

viii. Elzear Vermette was born on 27 May 1871 St.Norbert, Manitoba (SN1, page 146, B-28.). He was baptized on 28 May 1871 St.Norbert, Manitoba (Ibid.). He died on 27 Nov 1872 St.Norbert, Manitoba, at age 1 (Ibid., S-16.). He was buried on 28 Nov 1872 St.Norbert, Manitoba (Ibid.).

27 ix. Marie Eustasie Vermette, b. 13 May 1873 St.Norbert, Manitoba; m. Albert Gariepy; d. 6 Jul 1909 R.M. of Montcalm, Manitoba.

x. Henry Vermette was born on 13 Sep 1874 St.Norbert, Manitoba (SN2, B-41.). He was baptized on 14 Sep 1874 St.Norbert, Manitoba (Ibid.).

xi. Joseph Vermette was born on 16 Mar 1876 St.Norbert, Manitoba (Ibid., B-7.). He was baptized on 17 Mar 1876 St.Norbert, Manitoba (Ibid.).

xii. Marie Rosalida Vermette was born on 13 Aug 1882 R.M. of Montcalm, Manitoba (MB Vital Statistics, Birth Reg. No. 1882,001721.). She died on 11 Nov 1883 RM Montcalm, Manitoba, at age 1 (Ibid., Death Reg. #1883,002396.).

6. **Alexis Vermette** was born circa 1837 St.Norbert, (Manitoba). He married **Philomene Beauchemin**, daughter of **Benjamin Beauchemin** and **Marie Parenteau,** on 8 Jan 1866 St.Norbert, (Manitoba) (SN1, page 147-148, M-1.). He died on 29 Oct 1924 St.Vital, Manitoba (MB Vital Statistics, Death Reg. #1924,040389.).

Philomene Beauchemin was born on 15 Apr 1848 St.Norbert, (Manitoba) (MBS, C-14934.). She died on 12 Dec 1936 St.Vital, Manitoba, at age 88 (MB Vital Statistics, Death Reg. No. 1937,048510.).

Children of **Alexis Vermette** and **Philomene Beauchemin** were as follows:

i. Alexandre Vermette was born on 11 Jan 1867 St.Norbert, (Manitoba) (SN1, B-5.). He was baptized on 13 Jan 1867 St.Norbert, (Manitoba) (Ibid.).

ii. Toussaint Joseph Vermette was baptized on 12 Oct 1868 St.Norbert, (Manitoba) (Ibid., B-47.). He was born on 12 Oct 1868 St.Norbert, (Manitoba) (Ibid.).

iii. Marie Virginie Vermette was born on 28 Aug 1870 St.Norbert, Manitoba (Ibid., page 133, B-36.). She was baptized on 29 Aug 1870 St.Norbert, Manitoba (Ibid.). She was buried on 14 Mar 1873 St.Norbert, Manitoba (IBMS *Index des Baptemes, Mariages et Sepultures* (La Societe Historique de Saint-Boniface).).

iv. Joseph Alfred Vermette was born on 20 Aug 1872 St.Norbert, Manitoba (SN1, B-36.). He was baptized on 22 Aug 1872 St.Norbert, Manitoba (Ibid.). He died on 15 Mar 1873 St.Nobert, Manitoba (Ibid., S-7.). He was buried on 16 Mar 1873 St.Norbert, Manitoba (Ibid.).

28 v. Melanie Vermette, b. 4 Feb 1874 St.Norbert, Manitoba; m. Joseph Jean Baptiste Cyr.

29 vi. Patrice Vermette, b. 26 Apr 1876 St.Norbert, Manitoba; m. Catherine Rowand.

30 vii. William Vermette, b. 22 May 1877 Manitoba; m. Domitilde Marchand; d. 5 Dec 1936 St.Boniface, Manitoba.

viii. Joseph Vermette was born on 13 Jun 1878 St.Norbert, Manitoba (SN2, B-28.). He was baptized on 14 Jun 1878 St.Norbert, Manitoba (Ibid.). He died on 26 Apr 1879 St.Norbert, Manitoba (Ibid., S-12.). He was buried on 27 Apr 1879 St.Norbert, Manitoba (Ibid.).

ix. William Vermette was born on 18 May 1880 St.Norbert, Manitoba (Ibid., B-24.). He was baptized on 20 May 1880 St.Norbert, Manitoba (Ibid.).

31 x. Marie Anne Vermette, b. 23 Jul 1882 St.Norbert, Manitoba; m. Alexandre Normand.

xi. Frederic Vermette was born on 19 Sep 1884 St.Norbert, Manitoba (MB Vital Statistics, Birth Reg. No. 1884,001269.) (SN2, B-51.). He was baptized on 21 Sep 1884 St.Norbert, Manitoba (Ibid., B-51 [Note].). He married Cecilia Larence, daughter of Joseph Larence and Marie Cleophie Lepine, on 20 Apr 1920 Winnipeg, Manitoba (Ibid.).

Cecilia Larence was born on 25 Apr 1888 Manitoba (1901 Canada, #10, J-1, page 1, family 12, line 38-43.).

xii. Josephte Eugenie Vermette was born on 8 Oct 1886 RM St.Norbert, Manitoba (MB Vital Statistics, Birth Reg. No. 1886,001584.) (SN2, B-52.). She was baptized on 10 Oct 1886 St.Norbert, Manitoba (Ibid.). She died on 23 Oct 1886 St.Norbert, Manitoba (Ibid., S-29.) (MB Vital Statistics, Death Reg. #1886,001355.). She was buried on 24 Oct 1886 St.Norbert, Manitoba (SN2, S-29.).

xiii. Marie Emma Vermette was born on 24 Apr 1888 St.Norbert, Manitoba (MB Vital Statistics, Birth Reg. No. 1888,004793.) (SN2, B-24.). She was baptized on 27 Apr 1888 St.Norbert, Manitoba (Ibid.).

xiv. Ernest Vermette was born on 4 Jan 1891 Manitoba (1901 Canada, #10, (h-1), page 3, family 20, line 5-10.).

xv. Joseph Alphonse Vermette was born on 20 Jan 1894 R.M. of Ritchot, Manitoba (MB Vital Statistics, Birth Reg. No. 1898,006172.).

7. **Pierre Vermette** was born in 1838 St.Norbert, (Manitoba) (MBS, C-14934.). He married **Caroline St.Denis**, daughter of **Jacques St.Denis** and **Genevieve Durant,** on 10 Jan 1860 St.Norbert, (Manitoba) (SN1, M-1, page 23.). He died on 10 Nov 1918 St.Laurent, Manitoba (MB Vital Statistics, Death Reg. No. 1918,066405.).

Caroline St.Denis was born in 1840 St.Norbert, (Manitoba) (MBS, C-14934.).

Children of **Pierre Vermette** and **Caroline St.Denis** were as follows:

32 i. Goodwin Vermette, b. 23 Nov 1860 St.Norbert, (Manitoba); m. Isabelle Rivard; m. Adeline Rocheleau.

33 ii. Joseph Vermette, b. 5 Jan 1864 St.Norbert, (Manitoba); m. Justine Lambert; m. Josephine Rivard; d. 10 Sep 1923 Brandon, Manitoba.

iii. Norbert Vermette was born on 7 Sep 1865 St.Norbert, (Manitoba) (SN1, page 132, B-34.). He was baptized on 10 Sep 1865 St.Norbert, (Manitoba) (Ibid.).

34 iv. Rosalie Vermette, b. 18 Feb 1867 St.Norbert, (Manitoba); m. Joseph Elzear Rocheleau; d. 3 Jun 1918 St.Norbert, Manitoba.

35 v. Marie Vermette, b. 9 Oct 1869 St.Norbert, (Manitoba); m. Norbert Spirilion Charette; m. Joseph Tourond.

vi. Patrice Francois Vermette was born on 28 Jan 1871 St.Norbert, Manitoba (Ibid., page 140, B-4.). He was baptized on 29 Jan 1871 St.Norbert, Manitoba (Ibid.). He died on 3 Feb 1878 St.Norbert, Manitoba, at age 7 (SN2, S-8.). He was buried on 5 Feb 1878 St.Norbert, Manitoba (Ibid.).

vii. Victor Nazaire Vermette was baptized on 28 Jul 1872 St.Norbert, Manitoba (SN1, B-32.). He was born on 28 Jul 1872 St.Norbert, Manitoba (Ibid.).

36 viii. Hermenegilde Vermette, b. 3 Dec 1873 St.Norbert, Manitoba; m. Emma Rocheleau.

37 ix. Marie Alvina Vermette, b. 29 Nov 1875 St.Norbert, Manitoba; m. Marie Alpha Cyr; d. 16 Jul 1898 Ritchot, Manitoba; bur. 18 Jul 1898 St.Norbert, Manitoba.

x. Marguerite Vermette was born on 13 Mar 1877 St.Norbert, Manitoba (SN2, B-6.). She was baptized on 15 Mar 1877 St.Norbert, Manitoba (Ibid.).

xi. Anonyme Vermette was born on 23 Mar 1879 St.Norbert, Manitoba (Ibid., B-15 and S-9.). He/she was christened on 23 Mar 1879 St.Norbert, Manitoba (Ibid.). He/she died on 23 Mar 1879 St.Norbert, Manitoba (Ibid.). He/she was buried on 24 Mar 1879 St.Norbert, Manitoba (Ibid.).

xii. Cyrille William Vermette was born on 20 May 1880 St.Norbert, Manitoba (Ibid., B-25.). He was baptized on 21 May 1880 St.Norbert, Manitoba (Ibid.).

xiii. Joseph Avila Vermette was born on 20 Feb 1882 Cartier, Manitoba (MB Vital Statistics, Birth Reg. No. 1882,001374.) (SN2, B-8 and B-9.). He was baptized on 21 Feb 1882 St.Norbert, Manitoba (Ibid.).

xiv. Alexandre Bruno Vermette was born on 20 Feb 1882 Cartier, Manitoba (MB Vital Statistics, Birth Reg. No. 1882,001375.) (SN2, B-8 and B-9.). He was baptized on 21 Feb 1882 St.Norbert, Manitoba (Ibid.).

8. Norbert Vermette was born circa 1841 (1870C-MB, #726, page 24.). He was born circa 1844 (SN2, S-29.). He married **Genevieve Rocheleau**, daughter of **Guillaume Rocheleau** and **Marie Adam,** on 22 Jan 1867 St.Norbert, (Manitoba) (SN1, M-6.). He died on 29 Sep 1874 St.Norbert, Manitoba (MBS, C-14934.) (SN2, S-29.). He was buried on 1 Oct 1874 St.Norbert, Manitoba (MBS, C-14934.) (SN2, S-29.).

Genevieve Rocheleau was born in Oct 1840 St.Norbert, (Manitoba) (MBS, C-14934.). She married **Joseph Lambert**, son of **Antoine Lambert** and **Marie Sauteuse,** on 13 Oct 1876 St.Norbert, Manitoba (SN2, M-7.). She died on 28 Jun 1906 Ritchot, Manitoba, at age 65 (MB Vital Statistics, Death Reg. #1906,005321.). She was buried on 30 Jun 1906 St.Norbert, Manitoba (St-N Cem.).

Children of **Norbert Vermette** and **Genevieve Rocheleau** were:

i. Marguerite Vermette was born circa 1863 St.Norbert, Manitoba (MBS, C-14934.). She died in Feb 1873 St.Norbert, Manitoba (Ibid.).

9. Maxime Vermette was born on 29 Jun 1846 (1901 Canada, #10, (a-2), page 7, family 55, line 7-18.). He was born in Jun 1847 St.Norbert, (Manitoba) (MBS, C-14934.). He married **Sophie McCarthy dit Mercredi**, daughter of **Francois Mercredi** and **Genevieve Lamirande,** on 11 Jun 1871 Duck Lake, (Saskatchewan) (DL Register of Sacre Coeur Roman Catholic Church, Duck Lake, Saskatchewan, 1870-1893, page 10, M-5. Hereinafter cited as DL.). He died on 28 Feb 1906 DeSalaberry, Manitoba, at age 58 (MB Vital Statistics, Death Reg. No. 1906,004916.).

Sophie McCarthy dit Mercredi was born circa 1855. She was born on 19 Feb 1856 (1901 Canada, #10, (a-2), page 7, family 55, line 7-18.).

Children of **Maxime Vermette** and **Sophie McCarthy dit Mercredi** were as follows:

i. Maxime Vermette was born circa Jun 1872 (DL, page 14, B-49.). He was baptized on 7 Jul 1872 Duck Lake, (Saskatchewan) (Ibid.).

ii. Virginie Vermette was born circa Feb 1874 Cumberland House, (Saskatchewan) (SN2, S-17.) (ArchiviaNet 1886-1901, 1906 Half-Breed Scrip Applications Index, RG15-21, Volume 1333 through 1371, Microfilm Reel Number C-14944 through C-15010, National Archives of Canada, Ottawa, Ontario, http://www.collectionscanada.gc.ca, C-15008.). She died on 11 Aug 1874 St.Norbert, Manitoba (SN2, S-17.). She was buried on 12 Aug 1874 St.Norbert, Manitoba (Ibid.).

38 iii. Henry Vermette, b. 5 Apr 1875 St.Norbert, Manitoba; m. Marie Celina Sutherland; m. Marie Lea Beaugrand dit Champage.

iv. Adeline Vermette was born on 1 Apr 1877 Ste.Agathe, Manitoba (Ibid., B-26.). She was baptized on 22 Jul 1877 St.Norbert, Manitoba (Ibid.). She married Joseph Gobeil on 7 Jan 1896 St.Pierre Jolys, Manitoba (MM.).

v. Placide Vermette was born on 15 Feb 1879 Manitoba (1901 Canada, #10, (a-2), page 7, family 55, line 7-18.). He married Maria Hardy, daughter of Francois Hardy and Alphonsine Nolin, on 18 Jun 1901 St.Boniface, Manitoba (RMSB, page 484.).

Maria Hardy was born on 5 Nov 1884 (1901 Canada, District #10 (i-3), page 3, family 23, line 20-23.).

vi. Bernadette Vermette was born circa Apr 1881 Ste.Agathe, Manitoba (1881 Church of Latter Day Saints Census Transcription Project of Census Images from the National Archives of Canada, Ottawa, Canada, http://www.familysearch.org, District 184-D-1, page 10, household 46.). She married David Beaulieu on 31 Jul 1900 St.Pierre Jolys, Manitoba (MM.).

vii. Marie Rose Vermette was born on 5 May 1883 R.M. of De Salaberry, Manitoba (Ibid., page 1278.) (MB Vital Statistics, Birth Reg. No. 1883,001777.). She married Alphonse Albert Sutherland, son of Pierre Sutherland and Marie Eulalie Galarneau, on 6 Feb 1902 St.Pierre Jolys, Manitoba (MM.).

Alphonse Albert Sutherland was born on 15 Jul 1873 St.Boniface, Manitoba (SB-Rozyk, page 284, B-61.). He was baptized on 15 Jul 1873 St.Boniface, Manitoba (Ibid.).

viii. Joseph Vermette was born on 23 Apr 1885 Salaberry, Manitoba (MB Vital Statistics, Birth Reg. No. 1885,003059.). He married Marie-Anna Vermette, daughter of Henri Vermette and Marguerite Gladu, on 9 Jul 1932 St.Boniface, Manitoba (RMSB, page 485.).

ix. Celina Vermette was born on 6 Apr 1887 R.M. of De Salaberry, Manitoba (MB Vital Statistics, Birth Reg. No. 1887,003270.). She died on 28 Jun 1896 De Salaberry, Manitoba, at age 9 (Ibid., Death Reg. #1896,001481.).

x. Arthur Vermette was born on 28 Jul 1889 R.M. of De Salaberry, Manitoba (Ibid., Birth Reg. No. 1889,001869.). He married Honorine Carriere, daughter of Joseph Albert Andre Carriere and Marie Elizabeth Sauve, on 15 Nov 1933 St.Pierre Jolys, Manitoba (MM.).

Honorine Carriere was born circa 1907 St.Pierre Jolys, Manitoba (Automated Genealogy 1911 Census Transcription Project and Census Images from the National Archives of Canada, http://www.automatedgenealogy.com, District 17, page 10, line 49.). She died on 7 Dec 1953 Misericordia Hospital, Winnipeg, Manitoba (*Winnipeg Free Press*, Winnipeg, Manitoba, Dec 8, 1953.).

xi. Rose Anne Vermette was born on 22 May 1892 R.M. of De Salaberry, Manitoba (MB Vital Statistics, Birth Reg. No. 1892,004903.). She married Amedee Lagace on 25 Oct 1910 St.Pierre Jolys, Manitoba (MM.).

xii. Joseph Adelard Alfred Vermette was born on 27 Apr 1895 R.M. of De Salaberry, Manitoba (MB Vital Statistics, Birth Reg. No. 1895,002372.). He married Lillian Lussier, daughter of John Lussier and Amanda Rheault, on 29 Sep 1935 St.Boniface, Manitoba (RMSB, page 484.).

xiii. Philibert Vermette was born on 11 Jul 1897 Manitoba (1901 Canada, #10, (a-2), page 7, family 55, line 7-18.). He married Lucille Carriere, daughter of Joseph Albert Andre Carriere and Marie Elizabeth Sauve, on 16 Aug 1933 St.Pierre Jolys, Manitoba (MM.).

Lucille Carriere was born circa 1913 (1916 Canada, District 4-15, page 26, line 46.).

10. Augustin Vermette was born circa 1848. He married **Melanie Frobisher,** daughter of **Thomas Frobisher** and **Scholastique Pilon,** on 27 Jan 1874 St.Norbert, Manitoba (SN2, M-2.). He died on 16 Jun 1935 Ritchot, Manitoba (MB Vital Statistics, Death Reg. No. 1935,024425.).

Melanie Frobisher was born in 1855 St.Norbert, (Manitoba) (MBS, C-14934.). She died on 22 Mar 1890 St.Norbert, Manitoba (St-N Cem.) (SN2, S-8.). She was buried on 24 Mar 1890 St.Norbert, Manitoba (St-N Cem.) (SN2, S-8.).

Children of **Augustin Vermette** and **Melanie Frobisher** were as follows:

i. Marie Rose Vermette was born on 26 Nov 1874 St.Norbert, Manitoba (Ibid., B-49.). She was baptized on 27 Nov 1874 St.Norbert, Manitoba (Ibid.). She died on 17 Aug 1875 St.Norbert, Manitoba (Ibid., S-18.). She was buried on 18 Aug 1875 St.Norbert, Manitoba (Ibid.).

ii. Marie Pauline Vermette was born on 26 Nov 1874 St.Norbert, Manitoba (Ibid., B-50.). She was baptized on 27 Nov 1874 St.Norbert, Manitoba (Ibid.).

iii. Marie Rose Emma Vermette was born on 24 Jul 1876 St.Norbert, Manitoba (Ibid., B-23.). She was baptized on 25 Jul 1876 St.Norbert, Manitoba (Ibid.).

iv. Isidore William Remi Vermette was born on 14 May 1878 St.Norbert, Manitoba (Ibid., B-22.). He was baptized on 15 May 1878 St.Norbert, Manitoba (Ibid.).

v. Nancy Eugenie Vermette was born on 29 Feb 1880 St.Norbert, Manitoba (Ibid., B-10.). She was baptized on 2 Mar 1880 St.Norbert, Manitoba (Ibid.). She died on 5 Mar 1880 St.Norbert, Manitoba (Ibid., S-4.). She was buried on 6 Mar 1880 St.Norbert, Manitoba (Ibid.).

vi. Pierre Robert Vermette was born on 28 Jun 1881 St.Norbert, Manitoba (Ibid., B-26.). He was baptized on 29 Jun 1881 St.Norbert, Manitoba (Ibid.).

vii. Joseph Arthur Vermette was born on 16 Jul 1883 RM St.Norbert, Manitoba (MB Vital Statistics, Birth Reg. No. 1883,004383.) (SN2, B-22.). He was baptized on 19 Jul 1883 St.Norbert, Manitoba (Ibid.).

viii. Jacques Vermette was born on 1 Aug 1884 St.Norbert, Manitoba (MB Vital Statistics, Birth Reg. No. 1884,001258.) (SN2, B-43.). He was baptized on 3 Aug 1884 St.Norbert, Manitoba (Ibid.). He died on 17 Dec 1884 St.Norbert, Manitoba (Ibid., S-31.) (MB Vital Statistics, Death Reg. #1884,001574.). He was buried on 19 Dec 1884 St.Norbert, Manitoba (SN2, S-31.).

ix. Joseph Georges Alexandre Vermette was born on 14 Nov 1885 St.Norbert, Manitoba (Ibid., B-56.) (MB Vital Statistics, Birth Reg. No. 1885,001638.). He was baptized on 16 Nov 1885 St.Norbert, Manitoba (SN2, B-56.). He died on 9 May 1937 Portage la Prairie, Manitoba, at age 51 (MB Vital Statistics, Death Reg. No. 1937,020038.).

x. James Leopold Vermette was born on 10 Apr 1888 St.Norbert, Manitoba (Ibid., Birth Reg. No. 1888,004795.) (SN2, B-22.). He was baptized on 13 Apr 1888 St.Norbert, Manitoba (Ibid.).

xi. Marie Anne Josephine Vermette was born on 15 Mar 1890 St.Norbert, Manitoba (MB Vital Statistics, Birth Reg. No. 1890,006186.) (SN2, B-13.). She was baptized on 16 Mar 1890 St.Norbert, Manitoba (Ibid.). She died on 11 Jun 1890 St.Norbert, Manitoba (St-N Cem.) (MB Vital Statistics, Death Reg. #1890,002601.). She was buried on 12 Jun 1890 St.Norbert, Manitoba (Ibid.) (SN2, S-21.).

11. Toussaint Vermette was born on 25 Dec 1848 (1901 Canada, District 10, (A-2), page 5, family 41, line 6-16.). He was born on 15 Jan 1849 St.Norbert, (Manitoba) (MBS, C-14934.). He married **Elise Tourond,** daughter of **Joseph Tourond** and **Rosalie Laderoute,** on 12 Jan 1872 St.Norbert, Manitoba (SN1, M-2.). He died on 8 Aug 1930 DeSalaberry, Manitoba, at age 81 (MB Vital Statistics, Death Reg. No. 1930,045101.).

Elise Tourond was born on 15 Aug 1850 (1901 Canada, District 10, (A-2), page 5, family 41, line 6-16.). She died on 26 Jan 1932 DeSalaberry, Manitoba, at age 81 (MB Vital Statistics, Death Reg. No. 1932,004235.).

Children of **Toussaint Vermette** and **Elise Tourond** were as follows:

39 i. Marie Josephine Elmire Vermette, b. 9 Mar 1873 St.Nobert, Manitoba; m. Alfred Adrien Carriere; d. 4 Aug 1956 Tache Hospital, St.Boniface, Manitoba.

ii. Joseph Vermette was born on 2 Jan 1875 St.Norbert, Manitoba (SN2, S-1 and S-2.). He was baptized on 2 Jan 1875 St.Norbert, Manitoba (Ibid.). He died on 7 Jan 1875 St.Norbert, Manitoba (Ibid.). He was buried on 8 Jan 1875 St.Norbert, Manitoba (Ibid.).

iii. Marie Rosalie Vermette was baptized on 2 Jan 1875 St.Norbert, Manitoba (Ibid.). She was born on 2 Jan 1875 St.Norbert, Manitoba (Ibid.). She died on 7 Jan 1875 St.Norbert, Manitoba (Ibid.). She was buried on 8 Jan 1875 St.Norbert, Manitoba (Ibid.).

40   iv.   Rosalie Vermette, b. 9 Apr 1878 Manitoba; m. Victor Charette.

41   v.   Isidore Vermette, b. 22 Jun 1880 Manitoba; m. Anna Laplante.

42   vi.   Henri Vermette, b. 25 Mar 1882 Youville, Manitoba; m. Marguerite Gladu; d. 5 Mar 1927 RM De Salaberry, Manitoba.

      vii.   Anastasie Cecile Vermette was born on 9 Apr 1884 R.M. of De Salaberry, Manitoba (1901 Canada, District 10, (A-2), page 5, family 41, line 6-16.) (MB Vital Statistics, Birth Reg. No. 1884,002210.).

      viii.   Marie Vermette was born on 20 Jun 1885 Manitoba (1901 Canada, District 10, (A-2), page 5, family 41, line 6-16.).

      ix.   Marie Josephine Vermette was born on 20 Jun 1886 R.M. of De Salaberry, Manitoba (MB Vital Statistics, Birth Reg. No. 1886,003030.).

43   x.   Marie Angeline Evangeline Vermette, b. 7 Dec 1888 R.M. of De Salaberry, Manitoba; m. Joseph Alexander Beaugrand dit Champagne.

44   xi.   Joseph Augustin Vermette, b. 9 Feb 1891 R.M. of De Salaberry, Manitoba; m. Marie Blanche Desjardins; m. Agnes Philomene Gladu.

      xii.   Joseph Vermette was born circa 1895 (MM, page 1276.). He married Marie Emma Goulet, daughter of Moise Goulet and Marguerite Charette, on 11 Feb 1919 St.Pierre Jolys, Manitoba (Ibid.).

          Marie Emma Goulet was born on 3 Jun 1894 St.Boniface, Manitoba (MB Vital Statistics, Birth Reg. #1894,006049.).

12. **Anne Vermette** was born in 1857 St.Norbert, (Manitoba) (MBS, C-14934.). She married **Isidore Tourond**, son of **Joseph Tourond** and **Rosalie Laderoute**, on 5 Jan 1870 St.Norbert, (Manitoba) (SN1, M-3.). She died on 8 Dec 1922 St.Boniface, Manitoba (MB Vital Statistics, Death Reg. #1922,046051.).

Isidore Tourond was born in 1847 St.Norbert, (Manitoba) (MBS, C-14934.). He died on 11 Feb 1923 LaBroquerie, Manitoba (MB Vital Statistics, Death Reg. #1923-008405.).

Generation Four

13. **Alexandre Vermette** was born on 25 Jan 1855 St.Norbert, (Manitoba) (MBS, C-14934.) (1901 Canada, #9, T-2, page 6, family 53, line 31-35.). He married **Angelique Larence**, daughter of **Norbert Larence** and **Josephte Parenteau**, on 26 Jan 1875 St.Norbert, (Manitoba) (SN2, M-4.). He died on 31 Oct 1924 Ellice, Manitoba, at age 69 (MB Vital Statistics, Death Reg. #1924,048330.).

Angelique Larence was born on 26 Nov 1855 Assumption, Pembina, Pembina County, Dakota Territory (AP, page 138, B-391.). She was baptized on 26 Nov 1855 Assumption, Pembina, Pembina County, Dakota Territory (Ibid.).

Children of **Alexandre Vermette** and **Angelique Larence** were as follows:

      i.   Marie Mathilde Alexandrine Vermette was born on 28 Nov 1875 St.Norbert, Manitoba (SN2, B-47.). She was baptized on 29 Nov 1875 St.Norbert, Manitoba (Ibid.). She died on 16 Apr 1886 Batoche, (Saskatchewan), at age 10 (BSAP, page 46, S-7.). She was buried on 17 Apr 1886 Batoche, (Saskatchewan) (Ibid.).

      ii.   Joseph Alexander Vermette was born on 23 Oct 1877 St.Laurent, (Saskatchewan) (SL-SK St.Laurent-de-Grandin Roman Catholic Registre des Baptemes, Mariages & Sepltures, St.Laurent, Saskatchewan, 1872-1896, page 5, B-45. Hereinafter cited as SL-SK.). He was baptized on 23 Oct 1877 St.Laurent-de-Grandin, (Saskatchewan) (Ibid.). He died in Aug 1878 St.Norbert, Manitoba (ArchiviaNet, C-15008.).

      iii.   Octave Alfred Vermette was born on 9 Sep 1879 Leroy, Pembina County, Dakota Territory (SJL-1, page 95, B-63.). He was baptized on 10 Sep 1879 St.Joseph, Leroy, Pembina County, Dakota Territory (Ibid.). He married Annie Virginie Pritchard, daughter of Edward Pritchard and Marie Desjarlais, before 1906.

          Annie Virginie Pritchard was born on 16 Oct 1887 (Denney.).

      iv.   Wilfred Vermette was born circa 1880 Cartier, Provencher, Manitoba (1881 Canada, NA Film #C-13283, District 184, Sub-district F, page 37, house 176.). He married Virginie Pritchard on 15 Feb 1904 Ellice, Manitoba (MB Vital Statistics, Marriage Reg. #1904,003639.).

      v.   Marie Rosina Vermette was born on 11 Jan 1882 St.Norbert, Manitoba (ArchiviaNet.) (MB Vital Statistics, Birth Reg. No. 1882,001370.) (SN2, B-2.). She was baptized on 13 Jan 1882 St.Norbert, Manitoba (Ibid.). She married John Fleury, son of Edouard Fleury and Melanie Morand, between 1898 and 1899 (HBSI Index 1886-1901, 1906 Halfbreed Scrip Applications, RG15-21.) (ArchiviaNet.). She died on 12 Nov 1906 Ellice, Manitoba, at age 24 (MB Vital Statistics, Death Reg. #1906,002909.).

          John Fleury was born in Jul 1878 Duck Lake, (Saskatchewan) (ArchiviaNet.).

      vi.   Napoleon Vermette was born on 12 Jun 1890 (1901 Canada, #9, T-2, page 6, family 53, line 31-35.). He married Catherine Pritchard, daughter of William Pritchard and Marie Malaterre, on 27 Feb 1911 Ellice, Manitoba (MB Vital Statistics, Marriage Reg. #1911,006065.).

          Catherine Pritchard was born on 11 Dec 1891 R.M. of Ellice, Manitoba (Ibid., Birth Reg. #1892,002317.). She died on 27 May 1924 at age 32 (Denney.).

      vii.   Desire Vermette was born circa 1892. He married Philomene Ducharme, daughter of Cleophas Ducharme and Victoria Ledoux, on 23 Nov 1915 Ellice, Manitoba (MB Vital Statistics, Marriage Reg. #1915,211108.).

          Philomene Ducharme was born on 13 Dec 1895 (SPMT St.Peter's Mission; Volume I; Marriage Register 1859-1895; Translated & Transcribed by Reverend Dale McFarlane, Archivist, Diocese of Great Falls-Billings, Montana; Spring 1981.). She was baptized on 15 Dec 1895 St.Peter's Mission, Cascade County, Montana (Ibid.).

14. **Roger Vermette** was born on 28 Sep 1863 (SFXI-Kipling, B-96.). He was baptized on 16 Oct 1863 St.Francois Xavier, (Manitoba) (Ibid.). He married **Madeleine Fisher**, daughter of **Ambroise Fisher** and **Rosalie Chalifoux,** on 7 May 1895 Duck Lake, (Saskatchewan) (Denney.).

Madeleine Fisher was born on 12 Apr 1873 St.Laurent, (Saskatchewan) (SL-SK, page 21, B-17.). She was baptized on 12 Apr 1873 St.Laurent-de-Grandin, (Saskatchewan) (Ibid.).

Children of **Roger Vermette** and **Madeleine Fisher** were as follows:

   i. Michel Vermette.

  ii. Russel Vermette.

 iii. Marie Elise Vermette was born on 5 Apr 1896 Duck Lake, (Saskatchewan) (1901 Canada, microfilm, T-6553, Duck Lake, page 7, Family 63, line 25-32.). She married Gordon Ireland (Joyce Black Research.).

 iv. Elmire V. Vermette was born on 7 Nov 1897 Duck Lake, (Saskatchewan) (1901 Canada, microfilm, T-6553, Duck Lake, page 7, Family 63, line 25-32.).

  v. Georges Alfred Vermette was born on 16 Jun 1899 Duck Lake, (Saskatchewan) (Ibid.) (Saskatchewan Vital Statistics online, http://vsgs.health.gov.sk.ca, Birth Reg. #1783.). He died on 7 May 1901 at age 1 (Joyce Black.).

 vi. Charlotte Marie Alexandrine Vermette was born on 1 Dec 1901 Duck Lake, (Saskatchewan) (SK Vital Statistics, Birth Reg. #2342.).

        Question: *Seven months between Charlotte and George.*

 vii. Marie Alexandrine Vermette was born on 10 May 1904 Duck Lake, (Saskatchewan) (Ibid., Birth Reg. #3972.).

viii. Marie Eva Vermette was born on 10 May 1904 Duck Lake, (Saskatchewan) (Ibid., Birth Reg. #3973.).

 ix. Joseph Alexandre Vermette was born on 9 Apr 1906 Duck Lake, (Saskatchewan) (Ibid., Birth Reg. #6336.). He married Lena Smith (Joyce Black.). He died in 1965 (Ibid.).

      Lena Smith died in 1965 (Ibid.).

15. Marie Vermette was born on 7 Oct 1865 St.Norbert, (Manitoba) (MBS, C-14934.) (SFXI-Kipling, B-97.). She was baptized on 17 Oct 1865 St.Francois Xavier, (Manitoba) (Ibid.). She married **Jerome Henry**, son of **Alexis Henry** and **Marie Daunais dit Lyonnaise,** on 14 Sep 1880 St.Norbert, Manitoba (MBS, C-14928.) (MM.) (SN2, M-8.).

Jerome Henry was born on 25 Oct 1856 St.Norbert, (Manitoba) (MBS, C-14928.).

Children of **Marie Vermette** and **Jerome Henry** were as follows:

   i. Pierre Henry was born on 1 Jul 1881 St.Norbert, Manitoba (ArchiviaNet.) (SN2, B-27.). He was baptized on 1 Jul 1881 St.Norbert, Manitoba (Ibid.).

  ii. Marie Florestine Henry was born on 9 Jul 1883 Fish Creek, (Saskatchewan) (BSAP, page 16, B-14.) (ArchiviaNet.). She was baptized on 12 Jul 1883 Batoche, (Saskatchewan) (BSAP, page 16, B-14.).

 iii. Catherine Henry was born on 20 Jun 1884 Fort Pitt, (Saskatchewan) (ArchiviaNet.).

 iv. Rose Henry was born on 18 Jun 1885 Vermillion Lake, (Saskatchewan) (L2 Lebret, Mission de St.Florent, Roman Catholic Registre des Baptemes, Mariages & Seplutures, Qu'Appelle, Saskatchewan, Book Two: 1881-1887, FHC microfilm 1032949., page 116, B-71. Hereinafter cited as L2.). She was baptized on 28 Jun 1885 Lebret, (Saskatchewan) (Ibid.). She died on 23 Mar 1886 Fish Creek, (Saskatchewan) (Denney.) (BSAP, page 44, S-3.). She was buried on 24 Mar 1886 Batoche, (Saskatchewan) (Ibid.).

  v. William Henry was born on 26 Jan 1890 (Ibid., page 79,B-3.). He was baptized on 24 Nov 1890 Batoche, (Saskatchewan) (Ibid.).

 vi. Marie M. Henry was born on 9 May 1893 (1901 Canada, Fish Creek, page 1, Family 7, Line 30-38.).

 vii. Joseph Henry was born on 22 Nov 1895 Batoche, (Saskatchewan) (BSAP, page 129, B-27.). He was baptized on 24 Nov 1895 Batoche, (Saskatchewan) (Ibid.).

viii. Maria Victoria Henry was born on 30 May 1899 Batoche, (Saskatchewan) (SK Vital Statistics, Birth Reg. #730.).

16. Anne Vermette was born on 4 Oct 1867 St.Norbert, (Manitoba) (SFXI-Kipling, B-101.). She was baptized on 14 Oct 1867 St.Francois Xavier, (Manitoba) (Ibid.). She and **Antoine Parisien** met before 1884. She married **Joseph Primeau** between 1886 and 1906.

17. Joseph Albert Vermette was born on 1 Jun 1873 St.Norbert, Manitoba (SN1, B-32.). He was baptized on 2 Jun 1873 St.Norbert, Manitoba (Ibid.). He married **Sarah Jane Delorme**, daughter of **Jean Baptiste Delorme** and **Marguerite Pepin,** before 1900.

Sarah Jane Delorme was born on 19 Feb 1881 Carlton, (Saskatchewan) (ArchiviaNet, C-15008.).

Children of **Joseph Albert Vermette** and **Sarah Jane Delorme** both born Prince Albert, (Saskatchewan), are as follows:

  i. Irene Victoria Vermette was born on 17 Apr 1904 (SK Vital Statistics, Birth Reg. #3968.).

 ii. Maxime Vermette was born on 3 Dec 1905 (Ibid., Birth Reg. #5015.).

18. John Vermette was born on 2 Oct 1876 St.Norbert, Manitoba (SN2, B-31.). He was baptized on 8 Oct 1876 St.Norbert, Manitoba (Ibid.). He married **Helene Racette**, daughter of **Charles Racette** and **Helene Boyer,** before 1900 (ArchiviaNet, C-15008.).

Helene Racette was born on 17 May 1875 St.Laurent, (Saskatchewan) (SL-SK, page 38-39, B-17.). She was baptized on 18 May 1875 St.Laurent-de-Grandin, (Saskatchewan) (Ibid.).

Children of **John Vermette** and **Helene Racette** are:

  i. Mark Alfred Vermette was born on 10 Oct 1904 Prince Albert, (Saskatchewan) (SK Vital Statistics, Birth Reg. #3976.).

19. Marie Adele Vermette was born on 14 Apr 1878 St.Norbert, Manitoba (ArchiviaNet, C-15002.). She married **Joseph Schmidt**, son of **Louis Schmidt dit Laferte** and **Justine Laviolette,** before 1900. She died on 19 Jan 1907 Prince Albert, (Saskatchewan), at age 28 (Denney.).

Joseph Schmidt was born on 21 Mar 1872 St.Boniface, Manitoba (SB-Rozyk, page 234, B-26.). He was baptized on 21 Mar 1872 St.Boniface, Manitoba (Ibid.).

20. William Vermette was born on 25 Jan 1861 St.Norbert, (Manitoba) (SN1, page 40, B-3.). He was baptized on 25 Jan 1861 St.Norbert, (Manitoba) (Ibid., B-3.). He married **Nancy Vandal**, daughter of **Antoine Vandal** and **Scholastique Frobisher,** on 11 Nov 1879 St.Jean Baptiste, Manitoba (MM.). He married **Nancy Frobisher**, daughter of **Thomas Frobisher** and **Scholastique Pilon,** on 30 Nov 1900 (Ritchot), St.Norbert, Manitoba (MB Vital Statistics, Marriage Reg. #1900,001265.). He died on 20 Dec 1925 St.Vital, Manitoba, at age 64 (Ibid., Death Reg. No. 1925,052409.).

Nancy Vandal was born on 21 Feb 1861 (SN1, page 41, B-6.). She was baptized on 22 Feb 1861 St.Norbert, (Manitoba) (Ibid.). She died on 14 Dec 1899 Ritchot, Manitoba, at age 38 (St-N Cem.) (MB Vital Statistics, Death Reg. #1899,002690.). She was buried on 16 Dec 1899 St.Norbert, Manitoba (St-N Cem.).

Children of **William Vermette** and **Nancy Vandal** were as follows:

i. Albert Robert Vermette was born on 21 Nov 1880 St.Norbert, Manitoba (SN2, B-56.). He was baptized on 22 Nov 1880 St.Norbert, Manitoba (Ibid.).

ii. William Vermette was born on 1 Apr 1882 St.Norbert, Manitoba (MB Vital Statistics, Birth Reg. No. 1882,002066.) (SN2, B-12.). He was baptized on 1 Apr 1882 St.Norbert, Manitoba (Ibid.). He married Josephine Frobisher, daughter of Francois Frobisher and Colombe Parenteau, on 27 Nov 1906 (Ritchot), St.Norbert, Manitoba (MM.) (MB Vital Statistics, Marriage Reg. #1906,003215.).

   Josephine Frobisher was born on 22 Oct 1887 St.Norbert, Manitoba (Ibid., Reg. #1887,001909.) (SN2, B-44.). She was baptized on 30 Oct 1887 St.Norbert, Manitoba (Ibid.).

iii. Nancy Vermette was born on 23 Jun 1883 RM St.Norbert, Manitoba (MB Vital Statistics, Birth Reg. No. 1883,002509.) (SN2, B-18.). She was baptized on 24 Jun 1883 St.Norbert, Manitoba (Ibid.).

iv. Josephine Vermette was born on 2 Jun 1884 Ritchot, Manitoba (1901 Canada, #10, h-1, page 7, family 56, line 28-36.).

v. Marie Agnes Vermette was born on 1 Feb 1885 St.Norbert, Manitoba (MB Vital Statistics, Birth Reg. No. 1885,003968.) (SN2, B-6.). She was baptized on 3 Feb 1885 St.Norbert, Manitoba (Ibid.). She married Louis Alphie Deslauriers, son of Norbert Deslauriers dit Legault and Marie Frobisher, on 10 Feb 1902 St.Norbert, Manitoba (MM.). She died in 1956 (Denney.).

   Louis Alphie Deslauriers was born on 22 Aug 1880 St.Francois Xavier, Manitoba (SFXI-Kipling, B-46.). He was baptized 23 Aug 1880 St.Francois Xavier, Manitoba (Ibid.) (Rosemary Rozyk). He died in 1956 (Denney.).

vi. Marie Ernestine Vermette was born on 12 Dec 1885 St.Norbert, Manitoba (SN2, B-59.) (MB Vital Statistics, Birth Reg. #1885,001641.). She was baptized on 12 Dec 1885 St.Norbert, Manitoba (SN2, B-59.). She died on 20 Dec 1885 St.Norbert, Manitoba (Ibid., S-28.). She was buried on 21 Dec 1885 St.Norbert, Manitoba (Ibid.).

vii. Anonyme Vermette was born on 15 Sep 1886 RM St.Norbert, Manitoba (MB Vital Statistics, Birth Reg. #1886,001582.) (SN2, S-21.). She died on 15 Sep 1886 St.Norbert, Manitoba (Ibid.) (MB Vital Statistics, Death Reg. #1886,001351.). She was buried on 16 Sep 1886 St.Norbert, Manitoba (SN2, S-21.).

viii. Anonyme Vermette was born on 17 Sep 1887 St.Norbert, Manitoba (MB Vital Statistics, Birth Reg. #1887,001903.) (SN2, S-21 & 22, B-35 & 36.). He died on 17 Sep 1887 St.Norbert, Manitoba (Ibid.). He was buried on 18 Sep 1887 St.Norbert, Manitoba (Ibid.).

ix. Anonyme Vermette was born on 17 Sep 1887 St.Norbert, Manitoba (MB Vital Statistics, Birth Reg. #1887,001904.) (SN2, S-21 & 22, B-35 & 36.). She died on 17 Sep 1887 St.Norbert, Manitoba (Ibid.). She was buried on 18 Sep 1887 St.Norbert, Manitoba (Ibid.).

x. Joseph Arthur Vermette was born on 18 Nov 1888 St.Norbert, Manitoba (MB Vital Statistics, Birth Reg. #1888,002408.) (SN2, B-51.). He was baptized on 18 Nov 1888 St.Norbert, Manitoba (Ibid.). He died on 11 May 1893 Ritchot, Manitoba, at age 4 (MB Vital Statistics, Death Reg. #1893,002407.).

xi. Joseph Julien Vermette was born on 13 Aug 1891 St.Norbert, Manitoba (Ibid., Birth Reg. #1891,005218.) (SN2, B-54.). He was baptized on 16 Aug 1891 St.Norbert, Manitoba (Ibid.). He married Agnes Amanda Celina Riel, daughter of Joseph Riel and Julienne Amanda Perreault, on 4 Jan 1921 St.Boniface, Manitoba (MB Vital Statistics, Marriage Reg. #1921,002022.) (SN2, B-54 (note).). He died on 16 Apr 1959 St.Boniface Hospital, St.Boniface, Manitoba, at age 67 (Rod MacQuarrie Research, 28 Dec 2011.).

   Agnes Amanda Celina Riel was born on 14 Aug 1901 St.Boniface, Manitoba (MB Vital Statistics, Birth Reg. #1901,002636.).

xii. Anne Vermette was born on 24 Jul 1893 (1901 Canada, #10, h-1, page 7, family 56, line 28-36.) (Rod Mac Quarrie, 28 Dec 2011.). She married Louis David Riel, son of Joseph Riel and Eleanor Poitras, on 11 Nov 1913 St.Boniface, Manitoba (RMSB.) (MB Vital Statistics, Marriage Reg. #1913,064061.). She married Louis Riel, son of Alexandre Riel and Marie Louise Elise Poitras, on 22 Feb 1923 St.Boniface, Manitoba (RMSB.). She died on 19 Feb 1993 St.Boniface Hospital, St.Boniface, Manitoba, at age 99 (Rod Mac Quarrie, 28 Dec 2011.).

   Louis David Riel was born on 28 Jan 1888 (Cartier), St.Norbert, Manitoba (1901 Canada, (#10), N-1, page 1, Family 1, Line 3-7.) (MB Vital Statistics, Birth Reg. #1888,003555.) (Ibid., Birth Reg. #1888,004786.). He died on 8 Jan 1921 St.Vital, Manitoba, at age 32 (Ibid., Death Reg. #1921,003422.).

   Louis Riel was born on 1 Apr 1884 (R.M. of Cartier), RM St.Norbert, Manitoba (Ibid., Birth Reg. #1884,003198.) (Ibid., Birth Reg. #1884,001802.) (1901 Canada, (#10), N-1, page 1, Family 7, Line 37-47.). He married **Alexandrine Amanda Dufault**, daughter of **Simeon Dufault** and **Marie Louise Gagnon**, on 26 Apr 1910 St.Boniface, Manitoba (MB Vital Statistics, Marriage Reg. #1910,004560.).

xiii. Marie Alice Adrienne Vermette was born on 24 Aug 1896 R.M. of Ritchot, Manitoba (Ibid., Birth Reg. #1896,006355.). She was baptized on 26 Aug 1896 St.Norbert, Manitoba (Rod Mac Quarrie, 28 Dec 2011.). She died on 19 Feb 1900 RM Ritchot, Manitoba, at age 3 (St-N Cem.) (MB Vital Statistics, Death Reg. #1900,001110.). She was buried on 20 Feb 1900 St.Norbert, Manitoba (St-N Cem.).

xiv. Anonyme Vermette was born on 5 Apr 1898 Ritchot, Manitoba (Ibid.). He died on 7 Apr 1898 Ritchot, Manitoba (Ibid.) (MB Vital Statistics, Death Reg. #1898,002885.). He was buried on 9 Apr 1898 St.Norbert, Manitoba (St-N Cem.).

xv. Marie Anne Vermette was born on 13 Dec 1899 R.M. of Ritchot, Manitoba (MB Vital Statistics, Birth Reg. #1899,002740.). She was baptized on 15 Dec 1899 St.Norbert, Manitoba (Rod Mac Quarrie, 28 Dec 2011.). She died on 15 Dec 1899 Ritchot, Manitoba (St-N Cem.) (MB Vital Statistics, Death Reg. #1899,002680.). She was buried on 16 Dec 1899 St.Norbert, Manitoba (Rod Mac Quarrie, 28 Dec 2011.).

Nancy Frobisher was born on 21 Oct 1858 St.Norbert, (Manitoba) (SN1, page 6, B-28.). She was baptized on 22 Oct 1858 St.Norbert, (Manitoba) (MBS, C-14928.) (SN1, page 6, B-28.). She married **Antoine Brabant**, son of **Zephirin Brabant** and **Celina Beaudry**, on

1 Mar 1897 St.Norbert, Manitoba (MB Vital Statistics, Marriage Reg. #1898,001551.). She died on 14 Sep 1935 St.Vital, Manitoba, at age 76 (Ibid., Death Reg. No. 1935,036408.).

21. **Louis Jean Joseph Vermette** was born on 18 Sep 1862 St.Boniface, (Manitoba) (SB-Rozyk, page 85, B-154.). He was baptized on 19 Sep 1862 St.Boniface, (Manitoba) (Ibid.). He married **Christine Villebrun**, daughter of **Louis Villebrun** and **Isabelle Berard,** on 18 Nov 1884 St.Norbert, Manitoba (MM.) (SN2, M-14.). He died on 16 Feb 1936 RM Ste.Anne, Manitoba, at age 73 (MB Vital Statistics, Death Reg. No. 1936,008523.).

Christine Villebrun was born on 19 Dec 1866 St.Norbert, (Manitoba) (SN1, page 89, B-68.). She was baptized on 20 Dec 1866 St.Norbert, (Manitoba) (Ibid.).

Children of **Louis Jean Joseph Vermette** and **Christine Villebrun** were as follows:

i. Marie Elmyre Vermette was born on 28 Sep 1885 St.Norbert, Manitoba (SN2, B-42.) (MB Vital Statistics, Birth Reg. #1885,001632.). She was baptized on 1 Oct 1885 St.Norbert, Manitoba (SN2, B-42.). She died on 14 Sep 1886 St.Norbert, Manitoba (Ibid., S-20.). She was buried on 16 Sep 1886 St.Norbert, Manitoba (Ibid.).

ii. Jean Louis Joachim Vermette was born on 30 Dec 1886 RM St.Norbert, Manitoba (MB Vital Statistics, Birth Reg. #1887,004177.) (SN2, B-1.). He was baptized on 1 Jan 1887 St.Norbert, Manitoba (Ibid.). He married Marie Eleonore Frobisher, daughter of Francois Frobisher and Colombe Parenteau, on 19 Feb 1912 (Ritchot), St.Norbert, Manitoba (MM.) (MB Vital Statistics, Marriage Reg. #1912,005573.) (SN2, B-1 (note).).

Marie Eleonore Frobisher was born on 27 Sep 1885 St.Norbert, Manitoba (Ibid., B-41.) (MB Vital Statistics, Birth Reg. #1885,001628.). She was baptized on 29 Sep 1885 St.Norbert, Manitoba (SN2, B-41.).

iii. James Antoine Vermette was born on 3 Sep 1888 St.Norbert, Manitoba (MB Vital Statistics, Birth Reg. No. 1888,002397.) (SN2, B-40.). He was baptized on 4 Sep 1888 St.Norbert, Manitoba (Ibid.).

iv. Marie Josephine Vermette was born on 26 Jan 1891 R.M. of Ritchot, Manitoba (MB Vital Statistics, Birth Reg. #1891,005169.) (SN2, B-5.). She was baptized on 28 Jan 1891 St.Norbert, Manitoba (Ibid.). She married Joseph Leopold Breton, son of Adelard Breton and Marie Rose Vandal, on 15 Aug 1916 (St.Norbert), Fort Garry, Manitoba (MM, page 1277.) (MB Vital Statistics, Marriage Reg. #1916,046016.).

Joseph Leopold Breton was born on 18 Oct 1885 RM of Montcalm, Manitoba (1891 Census of Canada from the National Archives of Canada, Ottawa, Canada, District 8h, page 31, line 14.).

v. Marie Elise Zenaide Vermette was born on 23 May 1893 R.M. of Ritchot, Manitoba (MB Vital Statistics, Birth Reg. #1893,004964.). She married Leonide Neault, son of Andre Nault and Rosalie Flamand, on 25 Nov 1925 Richer, Manitoba (MM.).

Leonide Neault was born on 30 Nov 1901 R.M. of La Broquerie, Manitoba (MB Vital Statistics, Birth Reg. #1901,001369.) (Ibid., Birth Reg. #1902,001931.).

vi. Alfred Vermette was born on 22 Jan 1896 R.M. of Ritchot, Manitoba (Ibid., Birth Reg. #1898,006312.). He married Clarisse Richard, daughter of Napoleon Richard and Emma Godard, on 22 May 1937 Richer, Manitoba (MM.). He died before 1959.

Clarisse Richard married **Romeo Proulx** on 1 Aug 1959 Ste.Anne, (Manitoba).

vii. Amable Vermette was born on 22 Jan 1897 Manitoba (1901 Canada, #10, (h-1), page 3, family 22, line 16-22.).

viii. Louis Vermette was born on 27 Mar 1898 R.M. of Ritchot, Manitoba (MB Vital Statistics, Birth Reg. #1898,006437.).

ix. Marie Olivine Vermette was born on 22 Jan 1900 R.M. of Ritchot, Manitoba (Ibid., Birth Reg. #1900,001771.). She died on 6 May 1900 RM Ritchot, Manitoba (St-N Cem.) (MB Vital Statistics, Death Reg. #1900,001098.). She was buried on 7 May 1900 St.Norbert, Manitoba (St-N Cem.).

x. Joseph Jean Alfred Vermette was born on 18 Mar 1901 Ritchot, Manitoba (MB Vital Statistics, Birth Reg. #1901,006029.) (SN2, B-12.). He was baptized on 18 Mar 1901 St.Norbert, Manitoba (Ibid.).

xi. Marie Vermette was born on 24 Aug 1903 Ritchot, Manitoba (MB Vital Statistics, Birth Reg. #1903,003394.).

xii. Valentine Vermette was born circa 1905 Manitoba (1916 Canada, page 27-28, family 186, line 45-50, 1-4.). She married Paul Morin on 16 Jun 1926 Richer, Manitoba (MM.). She married William Robert on 26 Aug 1967 Ste.Genevieve, Manitoba (Ibid.).

Paul Morin died before 1967.

xiii. Marie Alma Vermette was born on 22 Mar 1906 Ritchot, Manitoba (MB Vital Statistics, Birth Reg. #1906,004491.). She married Gregoire Emond on 16 May 1936 Richer, Manitoba (MM.).

xiv. Marie Eva Vermette was born on 25 Jun 1910 R.M. of Ritchot, Manitoba (MB Vital Statistics, Birth Reg. #1910,007996.). She married Madore Guillaume Neault, son of Andre Nault and Rosalie Flamand, on 28 Nov 1934 Richer, Manitoba (MM.).

Madore Guillaume Neault was born on 2 Feb 1909 R.M. of Ste.Anne, Manitoba (MB Vital Statistics, Birth Reg. #1909,004962.).

22. **Angelique Vermette** was born on 16 Dec 1864 St.Norbert, (Manitoba) (SN1, page 115, B-50.). She was baptized on 16 Dec 1864 St.Norbert, (Manitoba) (Ibid.). She married **Joseph Campeau**, son of **Pierre Campeau** and **Julie Legault,** on 14 Apr 1884 St.Norbert, Manitoba (SN2, M-7.). She died on 9 Nov 1885 St.Norbert, Manitoba, at age 20 (Ibid., S-25.). She was buried on 11 Nov 1885 St.Norbert, Manitoba (Ibid.).

Joseph Campeau married **Emeline Tourigny**, daughter of **Luc Tourigny** and **Agnes Morand,** on 19 Jan 1887 St.Norbert, Manitoba (Ibid., M-4.).

23. **Alexandre Vermette** was born on 20 May 1867 St.Norbert, (Manitoba) (SN1, B-17.). He was baptized on 20 May 1867 St.Norbert, (Manitoba) (Ibid.). He married **Julienne Frobisher**, daughter of **Thomas Frobisher** and **Scholastique Pilon,** on 4 Feb 1891 St.Norbert, Manitoba (SN2, M-4.). He died on 16 Sep 1898 (Ritchot), St.Boniface, Manitoba, at age 31 (MB Vital Statistics, Death Reg. No. 1898,002456.) (Ibid., Death Reg. No. 1898,002899.).

Julienne Frobisher was born on 25 Aug 1862 St.Norbert, (Manitoba) (SN1, pabe 60, B-20.). She was baptized on 27 Aug 1862 St.Norbert, (Manitoba) (MBS, C-14928.) (SN1, pabe 60, B-20.). She died on 16 Apr 1905 Ritchot, Manitoba, at age 42 (MB Vital Statistics, Death Reg. #1905,004187.). She was buried on 19 Apr 1905 St.Norbert, Manitoba (St-N Cem.).

Children of **Alexandre Vermette** and **Julienne Frobisher** were as follows:

    i.   Marie Louise Antoinette Vermette was born on 29 Nov 1891 R.M. of Ritchot, Manitoba (MB Vital Statistics, Birth Reg. #1891,005211.) (SN2, B-78.). She was baptized on 29 Nov 1891 St.Norbert, Manitoba (Ibid.).

    ii.   Lucie Antoinette Vermette was born on 15 Jan 1893 R.M. of Ritchot, Manitoba (MB Vital Statistics, Birth Reg. #1893,004997.).

    iii.   Eugenie Yvonne Vermette was born on 16 Jun 1897 R.M. of Ritchot, Manitoba (Ibid., Birth Reg. #1898,006397.) (Ibid., Birth Reg. #1897,19414168.). She married Albert Honore Riel, son of Joseph Riel and Julienne Amanda Perreault, on 28 Jan 1920 (St.Norbert), Fort Garry, Manitoba (MM.) (MB Vital Statistics, Marriage Reg. #1920,009311.).

        Albert Honore Riel was born on 26 Jul 1898 St.Boniface, Manitoba (1901 Canada, (#10), N-1, page 1, Family 1, Line 3-7.) (MB Vital Statistics, Birth Reg. #1898,001468.).

    iv.   Marie Alice Patricia Vermette was born on 3 Feb 1899 Ritchot, Manitoba (Ibid., Birth Reg. No. 1899,006566.). She married Alexandre Ferdinand Alberic Nault, son of Alexander Nault and Mathilde Carriere, on 16 Apr 1923 Winnipeg, Manitoba (Ibid., Marriage Reg. #1923,015163.).

        Alexandre Ferdinand Alberic Nault was born on 2 Aug 1905 St.Boniface, Manitoba (Ibid., Birth Reg. #1905,006299.).

24. Philomene Vermette was born on 31 Mar 1874 St.Norbert, Manitoba (SN2, B-17.). She was baptized on 1 Apr 1874 St.Norbert, Manitoba (Ibid.). She married **John Rowan**, son of **John Rowan** and **Marianne Harrison,** on 11 Sep 1894 St.Norbert, Manitoba (MM, page 1109.).

John Rowan was born on 8 Feb 1869 (1901 Canada, District 10-j-1, page 2-3, family 22, line 48-50, 1-5.).

25. Louis Vermette was born on 4 Jan 1859 St.Norbert, (Manitoba) (MBS, C-14934.) (SN1, page 8, B-1.). He was baptized on 5 Jan 1859 St.Norbert, (Manitoba) (Ibid.). He married **Adele Delorme**, daughter of **Joseph Delorme** and **Angele Courchene,** on 9 Sep 1879 St.Jean Baptiste, Manitoba (MM.).

Adele Delorme was born on 5 Mar 1861 St.Norbert, (Manitoba) (SN1, page 42, B-9.). She was baptized on 6 Mar 1861 St.Norbert, (Manitoba) (Ibid.).

Children of **Louis Vermette** and **Adele Delorme** were as follows:

    i.   Joseph Louis Vermette was born on 20 Jun 1880 St. Jean-Baptiste, Manitoba (Rod Mac Quarrie, 16 April 2005.). He died on 16 Nov 1881 St. Jean-Baptiste, Manitoba, at age 1 (Ibid.).

    ii.   Joseph Vermette was born on 4 Apr 1881 Manitoba (Ibid.). He died on 12 Apr 1881 St. Jean-Baptiste, Manitoba (Ibid.).

    iii.   Joseph Aime Vermette was born on 19 May 1882 R.M. of Montcalm, Manitoba (MB Vital Statistics, Birth Reg. No. 1882,001696.).

    iv.   Joseph Jean Baptiste Georges Homere Vermette was born on 19 Apr 1884 R.M. of Montcalm, Manitoba (Ibid., Birth Reg. No. 1884,002601.). He died on 4 Apr 1885 Montcalm, Manitoba (Ibid., Death Reg. #1885,002324.).

    v.   Remi Vermette was born on 17 Mar 1886 MacDonald, Manitoba (SN2, S-8.) (MB Vital Statistics, Birth Reg. No. 1886,003343.). He died on 15 Jul 1886 St.Norbert, Manitoba (SN2, S-8.). He was buried on 17 Jul 1886 St.Norbert, Manitoba (Ibid.) (St-N Cem.).

    vi.   Georgianna Vermette was born on 17 Mar 1886 R.M. of Montcalm, Manitoba (MB Vital Statistics, Birth Reg. No. 1886,003311.). She married Edouard Lacombe on 24 Nov 1903 Lasalle, Manitoba (MM.).

    vii.   Joseph Napoleon Gregoire Vermette was born on 13 Jan 1888 R.M. of Montcalm, Manitoba (MB Vital Statistics, Birth Reg. No. 1888,004170.).

    viii.   Charles Roger Vermette was born on 19 Oct 1889 Cartier, Manitoba (Ibid., Birth Reg. No. 1889,001524.) (SN2, B-62.). He was baptized on 21 Oct 1889 St.Norbert, Manitoba (Ibid.). He married Marie E. Masse on 5 Jan 1928 Ste.Agathe, Manitoba (Ibid., B-62 (note).).

    ix.   Marie Vermette was born on 17 Sep 1891 Montcalm, Manitoba (Rod Mac Quarrie, 16 April 2005.).

    x.   Louis Philippe Vermette was born on 8 Nov 1893 MacDonald, Manitoba (MB Vital Statistics, Birth Reg. No. 1893,002425.).

    xi.   Joseph Adrian Vermette was born on 4 Dec 1895 MacDonald, Manitoba (Ibid., Birth Reg. No. 1895,005833.).

    xii.   Joseph Elie Onesime Vermette was born on 20 Sep 1897 MacDonald, Manitoba (Ibid., Birth Reg. No. 1897,003060.).

    xiii.   Joseph Urbain Albert Vermette was born on 23 Jul 1899 MacDonald, Manitoba (Ibid., Birth Reg. No. 1899,002311.).

    xiv.   Marie Ange Bernadette Vermette was born on 31 May 1901 MacDonald, Manitoba (Ibid., Birth Reg. #1901,005222.).

    xv.   George Joseph Vermette was born on 3 Oct 1903 MacDonald, Manitoba (Ibid., Birth Reg. #1903,002658.).

    xvi.   Marie Blanche Bertha Vermette was born on 9 Nov 1906 R.M. of MacDonald, Manitoba (Ibid., Birth Reg. #1906,001460.).

26. Marie Virginie Vermette was born on 25 Feb 1866 St.Norbert, (Manitoba) (INB *Index des Naissances and Baptemes* (St.Boniface, Manitoba: La Societe Historique de Saint-Boniface., c1995).). She was baptized on 25 Feb 1866 St.Norbert, (Manitoba) (Ibid.). She married **Frederic Vandal**, son of **Antoine Vandal** and **Scholastique Frobisher,** on 19 Jan 1886 St.Jean Baptiste, RM of Montcalm, Manitoba (MB Vital Statistics, Marriage Reg. #1886,001195.). She died after 9 Jan 1893.

Frederic Vandal was born on 22 Dec 1864 St.Norbert, (Manitoba) (SN1, page 115, B-51.). He was baptized on 22 Dec 1864 St.Norbert, (Manitoba) (Ibid.).

27. Marie Eustasie Vermette was born on 13 May 1873 St.Norbert, Manitoba (SN1, B-28.). She was baptized on 14 May 1873 St.Norbert, Manitoba (Ibid.). She married **Albert Gariepy**, son of **Urgel Gariepy** and **Angelique Soucy**, on 6 Nov 1893 St.Jean Baptiste, Manitoba (MM.) (MB Vital Statistics, Marriage Reg. No. 1893,001149.). She died on 6 Jul 1909 R.M. of Montcalm, Manitoba, at age 36 (Ibid., Death Reg. No. 1909,002384.).

Albert Gariepy was born on 6 Nov 1872 (1901 Canada, District 7-c-1, page 8, family 64, line 10-15.). He married **Emelie Henriette Deslauriers**, daughter of **Norbert Deslauriers dit Legault** and **Marie Frobisher**, on 29 May 1912 St.Francois Xavier, Manitoba (MM.).

28. Melanie Vermette was born on 4 Feb 1874 St.Norbert, Manitoba (SN2, B-7.). She was baptized on 4 Feb 1874 St.Norbert, Manitoba (Ibid.). She married **Joseph Jean Baptiste Cyr**, son of **Jean Cyr** and **Madeleine Perreault**, on 21 Jun 1892 St.Boniface, Manitoba (RMSB.) (MB Vital Statistics, Marriage Reg. #1892,001950.).

Joseph Jean Baptiste Cyr was born on 23 Oct 1871 Ste.Anne, Manitoba (Rosemary Helga (Morrissette) Rozyk Research, 9 Jun 2009.). He was baptized on 24 Oct 1871 Ste.Anne, Manitoba (IBMS.) (Rosemary Rozyk, 9 Jun 2009.) (INB, page 40.).

29. Patrice Vermette was born on 26 Apr 1876 St.Norbert, Manitoba (SN2, B-13.). He was baptized on 28 Apr 1876 St.Norbert, Manitoba (Ibid.). He married **Catherine Rowand**, daughter of **John Rowand** and **Elise McKarn**, on 7 Apr 1905 St.Boniface, Manitoba (RMSB.).

Catherine Rowand was born on 4 Sep 1873 Ontario (1901 Canada, #10, J-1, page 1, family 5, line 19-21.) (1881 Canada, District 183-D, page 35, house 142.). She married **Patrice Cadotte**, son of **Jean Baptiste Cadotte** and **Elise Pilon**, on 3 May 1900 St.Norbert, Manitoba (MM, page 1109.).

Children of **Patrice Vermette** and **Catherine Rowand** are as follows:
- i. Adelard Vermette married Valentine Campeau on 14 Jul 1908 St.Jean Baptiste, Manitoba (MM.).
- ii. Marie Elise Vermette was born on 16 Nov 1908 R.M. of Tache, Manitoba (MB Vital Statistics, Birth Reg. #1908,009813.).
- iii. Joseph Jean Vermette was born on 26 Feb 1911 R.M. of Ritchot, Manitoba (Ibid., Birth Reg. #1911,005011.).
- iv. Marie Rita Patricia Vermette was born on 21 Oct 1912 R.M. of Ritchot, Manitoba (Ibid., Birth Reg. #1912,005430.).

30. William Vermette was born on 22 May 1877 Manitoba (1901 Canada, page 3, line 5-10, family 20.). He married **Domitilde Marchand**, daughter of **Joseph Marchand** and **Elise Sayis**, on 2 Jun 1906 St.Boniface, Manitoba (RMSB, page 485.) (MB Vital Statistics, Marriage Reg. #1906,0045.). He died on 5 Dec 1936 St.Boniface, Manitoba, at age 59 (Ibid., Death Reg. #1936,048046.).

Domitilde Marchand was born on 20 Dec 1882 St.Norbert, Manitoba (1901 Canada, #10, (i-2), page 9-10, family 71, line 50, 1-5.) (SN2, B-50.) (MB Vital Statistics, Birth Reg. #1882,002093.). She was baptized on 22 Dec 1882 St.Norbert, Manitoba (SN2, B-50.). She died on 14 Aug 1965 Tache Hospital, Winnipeg, Manitoba, at age 82 (Rod Mac Quarrie, 18 Sep 2010.).

Children of **William Vermette** and **Domitilde Marchand** are as follows:
- i. Marie Ernestine Elise Vermette was born on 7 Jan 1908 Ritchot, Manitoba (MB Vital Statistics, Birth Reg. #1908,003666.).
- ii. William Alexandre Vermette was born on 11 Mar 1912 R.M. of Ritchot, Manitoba (Ibid., Birth Reg. #1912,015303.).

31. Marie Anne Vermette was born on 23 Jul 1882 St.Norbert, Manitoba (Ibid., Birth Reg. No. 1882,002076.) (SN2, B-27.). She was baptized on 30 Jul 1882 St.Norbert, Manitoba (Ibid.). She married **Alexandre Normand**, son of **Joseph Normand** and **Angelique Pilon**, on 24 Jul 1900 St.Norbert, Manitoba (MM.) (MB Vital Statistics, Marriage Reg. #1900,001267.).

Alexandre Normand was born on 3 Nov 1880 St.Norbert, Manitoba (SN2, B-54.). He was baptized on 4 Nov 1880 St.Norbert, Manitoba (Ibid.). He died on 23 Jun 1962 St.Boniface, Manitoba, at age 81 (Rod Mac Quarrie, 17 Jan 2013.).

32. Goodwin Vermette was born on 23 Nov 1860 St.Norbert, (Manitoba) (SN1, page 35, B-44.). He was baptized on 23 Nov 1860 St.Norbert, (Manitoba) (Ibid.). He married **Isabelle Rivard**, daughter of **Pierre Rivard** and **Marie Rocheleau**, on 17 May 1887 St.Norbert, Manitoba (MM, page 1275 and 1017.) (SN2, M-9.). He married **Adeline Rocheleau**, daughter of **Guillaume Rocheleau** and **Pauline Gaudry**, on 10 Jul 1897 (Ritchot), St.Norbert, Manitoba (MM, page 1095.) (MB Vital Statistics, Marriage Reg. #1898,001554.).

Isabelle Rivard was baptized on 14 Aug 1868 St.Norbert, (Manitoba) (SN1, B-36.). She was born on 14 Aug 1868 St.Norbert, (Manitoba) (Ibid.). She died on 2 Apr 1896 Ritchot, Manitoba, at age 27 (MB Vital Statistics, Death Reg. #1898,002844.). She was buried on 4 Apr 1896 St.Norbert, Manitoba (St-N Cem.).

Children of **Goodwin Vermette** and **Isabelle Rivard** were as follows:
- i. Marie Rose Claire Vermette was born on 18 Feb 1888 Cartier, Manitoba (MB Vital Statistics, Birth Reg. #1888,003557.) (SN2, B-13.). She was baptized on 18 Feb 1888 St.Norbert, Manitoba (Ibid.). She died on 7 Feb 1892 Ritchot, Manitoba, at age 3 (St-N Cem.) (MB Vital Statistics, Death Reg. #1892,002048.). She was buried on 9 Feb 1892 St.Norbert, Manitoba (St-N Cem.).
- ii. Joseph Michel George Vermette was born on 28 Sep 1889 Cartier, Manitoba (MB Vital Statistics, Birth Reg. No. 1889,001522.) (SN2, B-57.). He was baptized on 29 Sep 1889 St.Norbert, Manitoba (Ibid.). He died on 16 Feb 1892 Ritchot, Manitoba, at age 2 (St-N Cem.) (MB Vital Statistics, Death Reg. #1892,002057.). He was buried on 18 Feb 1892 St.Norbert, Manitoba (St-N Cem.).
- iii. Louis Albert Vermette was born on 15 Jun 1891 R.M. of Ritchot, Manitoba (MB Vital Statistics, Birth Reg. #1891,005223.) (SN2, B-48.). He was baptized on 16 Jul 1891 St.Norbert, Manitoba (Ibid.). He married Marie Cleophee Berthelet, daughter of Francois Berthelet dit Savoyard and Melanie Ducharme, on 22 Jul 1913 LaBroquerie, Manitoba (MM.) (MB Vital Statistics, Marriage Reg. #1913,040086.).

   Marie Cleophee Berthelet was born on 25 Apr 1896 R.M. of Montcalm, Manitoba (Ibid., Birth Reg. #1896,004893.).
- iv. Marie Louise Eleonore Vermette was born on 25 Feb 1893 St.Norbert, Manitoba (Ibid., Birth Reg. No. 1893,004991.) (Rod Mac Quarrie, 13 Jul 2009.). She was baptized on 25 Feb 1893 St.Norbert, Manitoba (Ibid.). She died on 7 Mar 1893 St.Norbert, Manitoba (St-N Cem.). She was buried on 9 Mar 1893 St.Norbert, Manitoba (Ibid.).

v. Marie Anne Vermette was born on 2 Mar 1894 R.M. of Ritchot, Manitoba (MB Vital Statistics, Birth Reg. #1898,006187.). She married Philippe Martin Parisien, son of Elzear Parisien and Marie Azilda Carriere, on 26 Jan 1911 Winnipeg, Manitoba (Ibid., Marriage Reg. #1911,004531.).

Philippe Martin Parisien was born on 17 Apr 1889 R.M. of La Broquerie, Manitoba (Ibid., Birth Reg. #1889,004655.).

vi. Marie Yvonne Emma Vermette was born on 12 Mar 1896 R.M. of Ritchot, Manitoba (Ibid., Birth Reg. #1898,006318.). She was baptized on 13 Mar 1896 St.Norbert, Manitoba (Rod Mac Quarrie, 13 Jul 2009.). She died on 28 Jul 1896 Ritchot, Manitoba (MB Vital Statistics, Death Reg. #1898,002850.). She was buried on 30 Jul 1896 St.Norbert, Manitoba (St-N Cem.).

Adeline Rocheleau was baptized on 20 Dec 1875 Ste.Agathe, Manitoba (IBMS.). She died on 24 Mar 1902 Ritchot, Manitoba, at age 26 (MB Vital Statistics, Death Reg. #1902,002756.). She was buried on 26 Mar 1902 St.Norbert, Manitoba (St-N Cem.).

Children of **Goodwin Vermette** and **Adeline Rocheleau** were:

i. Joseph Avila Vermette was born on 10 May 1898 R.M. of Ritchot, Manitoba (MB Vital Statistics, Birth Reg. #1898,006442.). He died on 19 Mar 1899 Ritchot, Manitoba (St-N Cem.) (MB Vital Statistics, Death Reg. #1899,001423.). He was buried on 20 Mar 1899 St.Norbert, Manitoba (St-N Cem.).

33. Joseph Vermette was born on 5 Jan 1864 St.Norbert, (Manitoba) (SN1, page 94, B-3.). He was baptized on 6 Jan 1864 St.Norbert, (Manitoba) (Ibid.). He married **Justine Lambert**, daughter of **Guillaume Lambert** and **Marguerite Dupuis**, on 26 Feb 1900 St.Norbert, Manitoba (MM.). He married **Josephine Rivard**, daughter of **Pierre Rivard** and **Marie Rocheleau**, on 23 May 1904 St.Norbert, Manitoba (Ibid.). He died on 10 Sep 1923 Brandon, Manitoba, at age 59 (MB Vital Statistics, Death Reg. No. 1923,036009.).

Justine Lambert was born on 15 Jul 1881 (1901 Canada, #10, (h-2), page 12, family 108, line 35-36.). She died on 11 Jun 1901 RM Ritchot, Manitoba, at age 19 (St-N Cem.) (MB Vital Statistics, Death Reg. #1901,003372.) (SN2, S-14.). She was buried on 13 Jun 1901 St.Norbert, Manitoba (St-N Cem.) (SN2, S-14.).

Children of **Joseph Vermette** and **Justine Lambert** were:

i. Marie Victorine Vermette was born on 20 Apr 1901 Ritchot, Manitoba (MB Vital Statistics, Birth Reg. #1901,006029.) (SN2, B-18.). She was baptized on 20 Apr 1901 St.Norbert, Manitoba (Ibid.). She died on 15 Aug 1901 Ritchot, Manitoba (St-N Cem.) (MB Vital Statistics, Death Reg. #1901,002087.) (SN2, S-20.). She was buried on 17 Aug 1901 St.Norbert, Manitoba (St-N Cem.) (SN2, S-20.).

Josephine Rivard was born on 6 Nov 1877 St.Norbert, Manitoba (Ibid., B-43.). She was baptized on 7 Nov 1877 St.Norbert, Manitoba (Ibid.). She died on 28 Feb 1914 Fort Garry, Manitoba, at age 36 (MB Vital Statistics, Death Reg. No. 1914,087216.).

Children of **Joseph Vermette** and **Josephine Rivard** are as follows:

i. Adelard Ernest Vermette was born on 15 Jan 1905 Ritchot, Manitoba (Ibid., Birth Reg. #1905,003417.).
ii. Marie Olvina Eugenie Vermette was born on 17 Jul 1906 R.M. of Ritchot, Manitoba (Ibid., Birth Reg. #1906,002190.).
iii. Marie Delia Clara Vermette was born on 16 Nov 1907 R.M. of Ritchot, Manitoba (Ibid., Birth Reg. #1907,003039.).
iv. Joseph Alexander Vermette was born on 8 Sep 1909 Ritchot, Manitoba (Ibid., Birth Reg. #1909,002443.).

34. Rosalie Vermette was born on 18 Feb 1867 St.Norbert, (Manitoba) (SN1, B-12.). She was baptized on 18 Feb 1867 St.Norbert, (Manitoba) (Ibid.). She married **Joseph Elzear Rocheleau**, son of **Guillaume Rocheleau** and **Pauline Gaudry**, on 3 Feb 1902 St.Norbert, Manitoba (MM.) (MB Vital Statistics, Marriage Reg. #1902,002515.). She died on 3 Jun 1918 St.Norbert, Manitoba, at age 51 (Ibid., Death Reg. #1918,036143.).

Joseph Elzear Rocheleau was born on 16 Aug 1873 Pembina, Pembina County, Dakota Territory (AP, page 75, B-23.). He was baptized on 18 Aug 1873 Assumption, Pembina, Pembina County, Dakota Territory (Ibid.). He married **Madeleine Rose Delima Gaudry**, daughter of **Isidore Gaudry** and **Elise Bousquet,** on 12 Nov 1924 St.Boniface, Manitoba (MB Vital Statistics, Marriage Reg. #1924,043030.) (RMSB, page 413.).

35. Marie Vermette was baptized on 9 Oct 1869 St.Norbert, (Manitoba) (SN1, B-37.). She was born on 9 Oct 1869 St.Norbert, (Manitoba) (Ibid.). She married **Norbert Spirilion Charette**, son of **Joseph Charette** and **Marie Gosselin**, on 5 Apr 1890 St.Norbert, Manitoba (SN2, M-4.). She married **Joseph Tourond**, son of **Jacques Tourond** and **Marie Courchene,** on 28 Jul 1903 St.Norbert, Manitoba (MM, page 1233.).

Norbert Spirilion Charette was born on 21 Mar 1869 St.Norbert, (Manitoba) (MBS, C-14926.) (SN1, B-13.). He was baptized on 21 Mar 1869 St.Norbert, (Manitoba) (Ibid.). He died on 9 May 1894 St.Norbert, Manitoba, at age 25 (St-N Cem.). He was buried on 11 May 1894 St.Norbert, Manitoba (Ibid.).

Joseph Tourond was born on 14 Apr 1860 St.Norbert, (Manitoba) (SN1, page 28, B-14.). He was baptized on 16 Apr 1860 St.Norbert, (Manitoba) (Ibid.). He married **Rosalie Laberge**, daughter of **Francois Laberge** and **Marguerite Gladu**, on 17 Nov 1885 De Salaberry, Manitoba (MM, page 1233.) (MB Vital Statistics, Marriage Reg. #1885,001433.).

36. Hermenegilde Vermette was born on 3 Dec 1873 St.Norbert, Manitoba (SN1, B-70.). He was baptized on 5 Dec 1873 St.Norbert, Manitoba (Ibid.). He married **Emma Rocheleau**, daughter of **Guillaume Rocheleau** and **Pauline Gaudry**, on 26 Feb 1900 (Ritchot), St.Norbert, Manitoba (MB Vital Statistics, Marriage Reg. #1900,002089.).

Emma Rocheleau was born on 19 Jan 1877 Manitoba (1901 Canada, #10, (h-2), page 12, family 111, line 46-47.).

Children of **Hermenegilde Vermette** and **Emma Rocheleau** were as follows:

i. Joseph Onisime Hermenegilde Vermette was born on 9 Dec 1901 Ritchot, Manitoba (MB Vital Statistics, Birth Reg. #1901,002312.) (SN2, B-49.). He was baptized on 19 Dec 1901 St.Norbert, Manitoba (Ibid.). He died on 1 Nov 1902 RM Ritchot, Manitoba (St-N Cem.) (MB Vital Statistics, Death Reg. #1902,001429.). He was buried on 3 Nov 1902 St.Norbert, Manitoba (St-N Cem.).
ii. Marie Oliva Victorina Vermette was born on 31 May 1903 R.M. of Ritchot, Manitoba (MB Vital Statistics, Birth Reg. #1903,007630.). She married Cyrille Bernier on 21 Sep 1921 St.Norbert, Manitoba (MM.).

iii. Pierre Tobie Vermette was born on 7 Mar 1905 Ritchot, Manitoba (MB Vital Statistics, Birth Reg. #1905,003420.). He died on 1 Feb 1906 Ritchot, Manitoba (St-N Cem.) (MB Vital Statistics, Death Reg. #1906,005308.). He was buried on 3 Feb 1906 St.Norbert, Manitoba (St-N Cem.).

iv. Marie Elizabeth Vermette was born on 8 Feb 1907 Ritchot, Manitoba (MB Vital Statistics, Birth Reg. #1907,005908.).

v. Evangeline Vermette was born on 19 Jul 1908 R.M. of Ritchot, Manitoba (Ibid., Birth Reg. #1908,012744.).

vi. Marie Cecile Elise Vermette was born on 25 Nov 1910 R.M. of Ritchot, Manitoba (Ibid., Birth Reg. #1910,004318.). She died on 23 Dec 1910 RM of Ritchot, Manitoba (Ibid., Death Reg. #1910,004556.).

vii. Joseph Edmond Avila Vermette was born on 22 Apr 1912 R.M. of Ritchot, Manitoba (Ibid., Birth Reg. #1912,015315.).

37. Marie Alvina Vermette was born on 29 Nov 1875 St.Norbert, Manitoba (SN2, B-48.). She was baptized on 30 Nov 1875 St.Norbert, Manitoba (Ibid.). She married **Marie Alpha Cyr**, son of **Jean Cyr** and **Madeleine Perreault**, on 15 Oct 1895 (Ritchot), St.Norbert, Manitoba (MM, page 283.) (MB Vital Statistics, Marriage Reg. #1898,001535 (at Ritchot).). She died on 16 Jul 1898 Ritchot, Manitoba, at age 22 (Ibid., Death Reg. No. 1898,002891.). She was buried on 18 Jul 1898 St.Norbert, Manitoba (St-N Cem.).

Marie Alpha Cyr was baptized on 27 Nov 1874 Ste.Anne, Manitoba (IBMS.) (Rosemary Rozyk, 9 Jun 2009.) (INB, page 41.). He was born on 27 Nov 1874 Ste.Anne, Manitoba (Rosemary Rozyk, 9 Jun 2009.).

38. Henry Vermette was born on 5 Apr 1875 St.Norbert, Manitoba (SN2, B-15.). He was baptized on 6 Apr 1875 St.Norbert, Manitoba (Ibid.). He married **Marie Celina Sutherland**, daughter of **Pierre Sutherland** and **Marie Eulalie Galarneau**, on 29 Dec 1899 St.Pierre Jolys, Manitoba (MM.). He married **Marie Lea Beaugrand dit Champage**, daughter of **David Beuagrand dit Champagne** and **Melanie Carriere**, on 7 Oct 1919 St.Boniface, Manitoba (RMSB.).

Marie Celina Sutherland was born on 8 Sep 1880 St.Norbert, Manitoba (SN2, B-47.). She was baptized on 12 Sep 1880 St.Norbert, Manitoba (Ibid.). She died on 30 May 1907 DeSalaberry, Manitoba, at age 26 (MB Vital Statistics, Death Reg. #1907,005308.).

Children of **Henry Vermette** and **Marie Celina Sutherland** are:

i. Aldina Vermette was born circa 1904 (1906 Canada, District 7-09, page 12, family 73, line 1-3.).

Marie Lea Beaugrand dit Champage was born on 21 Apr 1880 (1881 Canada, District 183A, page 41, house 170.) (1901 Canada, #10, a-2, page 7, family 59, line 31-40.).

39. Marie Josephine Elmire Vermette was born on 9 Mar 1873 St.Nobert, Manitoba (SN1, B-16.). She was baptized on 10 Mar 1873 St.Norbert, Manitoba (Ibid.). She married **Alfred Adrien Carriere**, son of **Adrien Carriere** and **Philomene Beauchemin**, on 12 Jan 1897 St.Pierre, De Salaberry, Manitoba (MB Vital Statistics, Marriage Reg. #1897,002180.). She died on 4 Aug 1956 Tache Hospital, St.Boniface, Manitoba, at age 83 (Rod Mac Quarrie, 17 Jan 2013.).

Alfred Adrien Carriere was born on 17 Feb 1870 St.Norbert, (Manitoba) (SN1, B-9.). He was baptized on 20 Feb 1870 St.Norbert, (Manitoba) (Ibid.). He died on 22 May 1940 DeSalaberry, Manitoba, at age 70 (MB Vital Statistics, Death Reg. #1940,020381.).

40. Rosalie Vermette was born on 9 Apr 1878 Manitoba (1901 Canada, District 10, (A-2), page 5, family 41, line 6-16.). She married **Victor Charette**, son of **Jean Baptiste Charette** and **Isabelle Dease**, on 11 Jan 1904 (St.Pierre), DeSalaberry, Manitoba (MM.) (MB Vital Statistics, Marriage Reg. #1905,001123.).

Victor Charette was born on 18 Feb 1876 St.Norbert, Manitoba (SN2, B-5.). He was baptized on 20 Feb 1876 St.Norbert, Manitoba (Ibid.).

41. Isidore Vermette was born on 22 Jun 1880 Manitoba (1901 Canada, District 10, (A-2), page 5, family 41, line 6-16.). He married **Anna Laplante**, daughter of **Boniface Laplante** and **Caroline Laferte,** on 24 Nov 1903 (Ste.Agathe), DeSalaberry, Manitoba (MM.) (MB Vital Statistics, Marriage Reg. #1904,003600.).

Anna Laplante was born on 10 Oct 1884 (1901 Canada, District 10-a-1, page 1, family 10, line 44-50.).

Children of **Isidore Vermette** and **Anna Laplante** were as follows:

i. Therese Vermette married Joseph Lafrance, son of Nazaire Lafrance and Agnes Desjardins, on 22 Sep 1938 St-Pierre, Manitoba (MM, page 674.) (Ibid., page 1280.).

Joseph Lafrance was born circa 1916 Broquerie, Manitoba (Ibid., page 674.).

ii. Marie Agnes Vermette was born on 2 Oct 1905 R.M. of De Salaberry, Manitoba (MB Vital Statistics, Birth Reg. #1905,006742.).

iii. Joseph Victor Vermette was born on 17 Feb 1907 R.M. of De Salaberry, Manitoba (Ibid., Birth Reg. #1907,21818951, Reg. Date: 11/07/1961.). He married Henriette Zaste, daughter of Joseph Zace and Celina Laramee, on 12 Nov 1927 St.Boniface, Manitoba (RMSB, page 486.) (MB Vital Statistics, Marriage Reg. #1927,053044.).

iv. Joseph Ernest Vermette was born on 26 Jan 1910 St.Boniface, Manitoba (Ibid., Birth Reg. #1910,008690.). He married Marie Champagne, daughter of Joseph Alexander Beaugrand dit Champagne and Marie Angeline Evangeline Vermette, on 25 May 1938 St.Pierre Jolys, Manitoba (Rod Mac Quarrie, 17 Jan 2013.). He died on 4 May 2002 Winnipeg, Manitoba, at age 92 (*Free Press*, 8 May 2002.).

Marie Champagne was born on 13 Jun 1916 St.Pierre Jolys, Manitoba (Rod Mac Quarrie, 17 Jan 2013.). She died on 22 Mar 2003 Winnipeg, Manitoba, at age 86 (*Free Press*, 27 Mar 2003.).

42. Henri Vermette was born on 25 Mar 1882 Youville, Manitoba (1901 Canada, District 10, (A-2), page 5, family 41, line 6-16.) (MB Vital Statistics, Birth Reg. No. 1882,002463.). He married **Marguerite Gladu**, daughter of **William Gladu** and **Eulalie Riel,** on 24 Oct 1905 St.Pierre, De Salaberry, Manitoba (MM.) (MB Vital Statistics, Mar. Reg. #1905,001130 (De Salaberry).). He died on 5 Mar 1927 RM De Salaberry, Manitoba, at age 44 (Ibid., Death Reg. No. 1927,015104.).

Marguerite Gladu was born on 25 Aug 1885 (1901 Canada, #10, A-3, page 11-12, family 90, line 50, 1-9.).

Children of **Henri Vermette** and **Marguerite Gladu** are as follows:

i. Jeanne Vermette married Arthur Audette on 7 Nov 1928 St.Pierre Jolys, Manitoba (MM.).

ii. Marie-Anna Vermette married Joseph Vermette, son of Maxime Vermette and Sophie McCarthy dit Mercredi, on 9 Jul 1932 St.Boniface, Manitoba (RMSB, page 485.).

Joseph Vermette was born on 23 Apr 1885 Salaberry, Manitoba (MB Vital Statistics, Birth Reg. No. 1885,003059.).

    iii.   Emme Vermette was born circa 1911 (MM.). She married Edouard Gobeil on 8 Nov 1933 St.Pierre Jolys, Manitoba (Ibid.).

43. Marie Angeline Evangeline Vermette was born on 7 Dec 1888 R.M. of De Salaberry, Manitoba (1901 Canada, District 10, (A-2), page 5, family 41, line 6-16.) (MB Vital Statistics, Birth Reg. No. 1888,001497.). She married **Joseph Alexander Beaugrand dit Champagne**, son of **David Beuagrand dit Champagne** and **Melanie Carriere,** on 17 Jan 1911 DeSalaberry, Manitoba (Ibid., Marriage Reg. #1911,006048.).

Joseph Alexander Beaugrand dit Champagne was born on 21 Jun 1882 Youville, Manitoba (1901 Canada, #10, a-2, page 7, family 59, line 31-40.) (MB Vital Statistics, Birth Reg. #1882,002473.).

44. Joseph Augustin Vermette was born on 9 Feb 1891 R.M. of De Salaberry, Manitoba (1901 Canada, District 10, (A-2), page 5, family 41, line 6-16.) (MB Vital Statistics, Birth Reg. No. 1891,003491.). He married **Marie Blanche Desjardins**, daughter of **Francois Desjardins** and **Marguerite Leclerc dit Leclair,** on 17 Jun 1913 Broquerie, Manitoba (MM.). He married **Agnes Philomene Gladu**, daughter of **William Gladu** and **Eulalie Riel,** on 14 Jan 1918 St.Pierre Jolys, Manitoba (Ibid.).

Marie Blanche Desjardins died in 1916.

Agnes Philomene Gladu was born on 17 Jul 1891 R.M. of De Salaberry, Manitoba (MB Vital Statistics, Birth Reg. #1891,003508.). She died in 1963 (Denney.).

Children of **Joseph Augustin Vermette** and **Agnes Philomene Gladu** are as follows:

    i.   Augustine Vermette was born circa 1919 (MM.). She married Emile Abraham, son of Charles Abraham and Annie Berrett, on 17 Jun 1936 St.Pierre Jolys, Manitoba (Ibid., page 11.).

       Emile Abraham was born circa 1914 Winnipeg, Manitoba (Ibid.).

    ii.   Elise Vermette was born circa 1921 (MM.). She married Aurel Tellier on 20 Jun 1944 St.Pierre Jolys, Manitoba (Ibid.).

    iii.   Estelle Vermette was born circa 1930 (Ibid.). She married Paul Tellier on 17 Sep 1949 St.Pierre Jolys, Manitoba (Ibid.).

Ahnentafel between Louis Versailles and Ignace Bourquin

--- 1st Generation ---

1. Louis Versailles (PRDH online index, http://www.genealogic.umontreal.ca, #117279.) (Ibid.). Question: *Probable son of Louis Bourquin dit Versailles and Louise Garigou.* He was baptized on 20 Oct 1743 at Montreal, Montreal, Quebec (Ibid., No. 148128.). He was born on 20 Oct 1743 at Montreal, Montreal, Quebec (Ibid.). As of 20 Oct 1743, he was also known as **Louis Bourquin dit Versailles** (Ibid.). He married according to the custom of the country **Magdeleine Montagnaise** before 1793.

--- 2nd Generation ---

2. Louis Bourquin dit Versailles (Ibid., #117279.) (Ibid., #117278.) (Ibid.) was born on 3 Oct 1717 at Notre-Dame de Versailles, Paris (Ibid.). He was baptized on 5 Oct 1717 at Notre-Dame de Versailles, Paris (Ibid.). He married **Louise Garigou or Gariou**, daughter of **Martial Garigou or Gariou** and **Marie-Madeleine Charbonneau,** on 29 Jan 1748 at Montreal, Montreal, Quebec (Ibid., #117279.) (Ibid., No. 150365.).

--- 3rd Generation ---

4. Ignace Bourquin (Ibid., #117278.) married **Marie Chaume**.

Descendants of Louis Versailles

Generation One

1. Louis Versailles was born on 20 Oct 1743 Montreal, Montreal, Quebec (PRDH online index, http://www.genealogic.umontreal.ca, No. 148128.). He was baptized on 20 Oct 1743 Montreal, Montreal, Quebec (Ibid.). He married according to the custom of the country **Magdeleine Montagnaise** before 1793.

Question: *Probable son of Louis Bourquin dit Versailles and Louise Garigou.* He was contracted as a voyageur between 1799 and 1804 *1799: NWCo clerk, Lower Red River Dept., wages 800 livres (Masson, Les Bourgeois, p. 62)*
1804: NWCo interpreter at English River, after fusion of 1804 (Masson, Les Bourgeois, p. 399) (Rod MacQuarrie Research, 3 June 2010.).

Magdeleine Montagnaise was born circa 1773 (SB 1825-1834 St.Boniface Roman Catholic Registre des Baptemes, Mariages & Sepultures, 1825-1834, page 96, B-564. Hereinafter cited as SB 1825-1834.). She was baptized on 6 Apr 1833 St.Boniface, (Manitoba) (Ibid.).

Children of **Louis Versailles** and **Magdeleine Montagnaise** were as follows:

    i.   Louis Versailles was born circa 1793 Ruperts Land (1843C RRS HBCA E5/11 1843 Census of the Red River Settlement, HBCA E5/11, Hudson's Bay Company Archives, Provincial Archives, 200 Vaughan Street, Winnipeg, MB R3C 1T5, Canada., page 23.) (SB 1825-1834, page 96, B-564.). He married Louise Assiniboine before 1863. He was buried on 15 Mar 1869 St.Boniface, (Manitoba) (SB-Rozyk St. Boniface Roman Catholic Church, Manitoba, Canada, Baptisms, Marriages and Burials 1860-1875 Extractions, Compiled by Rosemary Rozyk, page 147, S-5.).

       Louise Assiniboine was born circa 1793 (Ibid., page 108, S-5.). She died on 29 Mar 1863 (Ibid.). She was buried on 30 Mar 1863 St.Boniface, (Manitoba) (Ibid.).

  2 ii.   Pierre Versailles, b. circa 1801; m. Josephte Letendre; d. before 1849.

3   iii.   Jean Baptiste Versailles, b. circa 1802 Ruperts Land; m. Genevieve Short.

4   iv.   Louise Versailles, b. circa 1802; m. Jean Baptiste Jolibois; m. Jacques Goulet; d. 8 Feb 1857 Pembina County, Dakota Territory; bur. 10 Feb 1857 Assumption, Pembina, Pembina County, Dakota Territory.

Generation Two

2. Pierre Versailles was born circa 1801 (Denney Papers, Charles D. Denney, Glenbow Archives, Calgary, Alberta.). He married **Josephte Letendre**, daughter of **Jean Baptiste "Okimawaskawikinam" Letendre** and **Josephte Indian**, on 6 Jun 1825 St.Boniface, (Manitoba) (SB 1825-1834, page 1-2, M-13.). He died before 1849.

Josephte Letendre was born circa 1798 (SN1 Catholic Parish Register of St.Norbert 1857-1873, page 89, S-24. Hereinafter cited as SN1.). She died on 9 Dec 1866 St.Norbert, (Manitoba) (Ibid.). She was buried on 11 Dec 1866 St.Norbert, (Manitoba) (Ibid.).

Children of **Pierre Versailles** and **Josephte Letendre** were as follows:

5   i.   Marie Anne Versailles, b. Apr 1821 North West Territory; m. Abraham Belanger.

6   ii.   Scholastique Versailles, b. 15 Jun 1825 St.Boniface, (Manitoba); m. William McKay; m. Pierre Beauchamp.

7   iii.   Marie Versailles, b. 22 Feb 1830 St.Boniface, (Manitoba); m. Francois Xavier Perreault dit Morin.

8   iv.   Susanne Versailles, b. 1832 St.Norbert, (Manitoba); m. William McKay.

     v.   Marguerite Versaille was born on 19 Sep 1833 St.Boniface, (Manitoba) (SB 1825-1834, page 108, B-666.). She was baptized on 20 Sep 1833 St.Boniface, (Manitoba) (Ibid.).

9   vi.   Euphrosine Versailles, b. circa 1834 (Manitoba); m. Jean Baptiste Racette dit Dos Croche.

3. Jean Baptiste Versailles was born circa 1802 Ruperts Land (1827C RRS HBCA E5/1 1827 Census of the Red River Settlement, HBCA E5/1, Hudson's Bay Company Archives, Provincial Archives, 200 Vaughan Street, Winnipeg, MB R3C 1T5, Canada., page 9.). He was born circa 1810 (1870C-MB 1870 Manitoba Census, National Archives of Canada, Ottawa, Ontario, Microfilm Reel Number C-2170., #780, page 26.). He was baptized on 18 Feb 1833 St.Boniface, (Manitoba) (SB 1825-1834, page 90, B-541.). He married according to the custom of the country **Genevieve Short**, daughter of **James Short** and **Betsy Sauteuse**, before 1829. He married **Genevieve Short**, daughter of **James Short** and **Betsy Sauteuse**, on 18 Feb 1833 St.Boniface, (Manitoba) (Ibid., page 92, M-103.).

Genevieve Short was born in 1803 North West (MBS Scrip Applications, Original White Settlers & Halfbreeds residing in Manitoba on 15 July 1870, RG15-19, C-14934.). She was born circa 1808 (SB 1825-1834, page 90, B-539.). She was baptized on 29 Jan 1821 St.Johns, Beaver Creek, (Manitoba) (HBCR Hudson Bay Company Register of Anglican Church Baptisms, Marriages, and Burials for the Red River Settlement, 1821-1841; Hudson's Bay Company Archives, Winnipeg, Manitoba, E.4/1a, folio 31d. Hereinafter cited as HBCR.). She was baptized on 17 Feb 1833 St.Boniface, (Manitoba) (SB 1825-1834, page 90, B-539.). She married **Joseph White** on 29 Jan 1821 (St.Johns), Beaver Creek, (Manitoba) (HBCR, M-14.). She died on 3 Nov 1883 St.Norbert, Manitoba (SN2 Catholic Parish Register of St.Norbert, S-31. Hereinafter cited as SN2.). She was buried on 5 Nov 1883 St.Norbert, Manitoba (Ibid.).

Children of **Jean Baptiste Versailles** and **Genevieve Short** were as follows:

10   i.   Marie Versailles, b. circa 1829 St.Boniface, (Manitoba); m. Pierre Matrigane Chartrand; m. Jeremie Cardinal; d. 7 Nov 1893 St.Boniface, Manitoba; bur. 9 Nov 1893 St.Boniface, Manitoba.

     ii.   Pierre Versailles was born on 24 Jun 1829 (SB 1825-1834, page 26, B-556.). He was baptized on 28 Jun 1829 St.Boniface, (Manitoba) (Ibid.).

11   iii.   Genevieve Versailles, b. Jul 1833 St.Norbert, (Manitoba); m. Francois Sayis; d. 2 Mar 1883 St.Norbert, Manitoba; bur. 4 Mar 1883 St.Norbert, Manitoba.

     iv.   Jean Baptiste Versaille was born on 21 Jul 1833 (Ibid., page 105, B-633.). He was baptized on 5 Aug 1833 St.Boniface, (Manitoba) (Ibid.). He died on 7 Dec 1893 St.Boniface, Manitoba, at age 60 (Rod Mac Quarrie, 3 June 2010.). He was buried on 9 Dec 1893 St.Boniface, Manitoba (Ibid.).

12   v.   Marie Anne Versailles, b. 3 Jul 1838 St.Francois Xavier, (Manitoba); m. Antoine McLeod; m. Francois Parisien; d. 29 Sep 1898 Winnipeg, Manitoba; bur. 1 Oct 1898 St.Boniface, Manitoba.

     vi.   Antoine Versailles was born circa 1842 (SFXI-Kipling St.Francois Xavier Register Index, 1834-1900; compiled by Clarence Kipling , S-21.). He died on 26 Jun 1868 St.Francois Xavier, (Manitoba) (Ibid.). He was buried on 27 Jun 1868 St.Francois Xavier, (Manitoba) (Ibid.).

13   vii.   David Versailles, b. 1845 St.Norbert, (Manitoba); m. Scholastique Boyer; d. 14 Jun 1906 (Ritchot), St.Boniface, Manitoba.

4. Louise Versailles was born circa 1802 (SB 1825-1834, page 33, B-586.). She was baptized on 2 Nov 1829 St.Boniface, (Manitoba) (Ibid.). She married **Jean Baptiste Jolibois**, son of **Jean-Baptiste Bincette dit Jolibois** and **Marie Anne Thierry dit Quessy**, before 1822. She married **Jacques Goulet**, son of **Jacques Goulet** and **Marie Genevieve Desmarais**, on 3 Nov 1829 St.Boniface, (Manitoba) (Ibid., page 33-34, M-91.). She died on 8 Feb 1857 Pembina County, Dakota Territory (AP Records of the Assumption Roman Catholic Church, Pembina, North Dakota: Baptisms, Marriages, Sepultures, 1848-1896; compiled by Reverend Father J. M. Belleau, 2 October 1944, page 165, S-67. Hereinafter cited as AP.). She was buried on 10 Feb 1857 Assumption, Pembina, Pembina County, Dakota Territory (Ibid.).

Jean Baptiste Jolibois was born on 6 Nov 1795 Laprairie, Quebec (BSHSB Bulletin de la Société historique de Saint-Boniface, #1, 1993, page 30-31.) (PRDH online, No. 568064.). He was baptized on 6 Nov 1795 LaPrairie, Quebec (BSHSB , #1, 1993, page 30-31.) (PRDH online, No. 568064.).

Jacques Goulet was born on 1 Dec 1779 St-Denis-sur-Richelieu, Quebec (PRDH online, No. 704623.). He was baptized on 1 Dec 1779 St-Denis-sur-Richelieu, Quebec (Ibid.). He married **Genevieve Begnet** before 1811.

Generation Three

5. Marie Anne Versailles was born in Apr 1821 North West Territory (MBS, C-14925.). She was born circa 1823 Red River, (Manitoba) (1850Ci-MN *Minnesota Territorial Census, 1850*, Harpole, Patricia C. and Mary D. Nagle, ed., (St.Paul, Minnesota: Minnesota Historical Society, 1972), page 29, Dwelling 112, Family 112.). She married **Abraham Belanger**, son of **Louis Belanger** and **Josephte Daze**, before 1841.

Abraham Belanger was born in Jun 1818 Pembina County (MBS, C-14925.). He was born circa 1820 Red River, (Manitoba) (1850Ci-MN, page 29, Dwelling 112, Family 112.).

6. Scholastique Versailles was born on 15 Jun 1825 St.Boniface, (Manitoba) (SB 1825-1834, page 3, B- _.). She was baptized on 16 Jun 1825 St.Boniface, (Manitoba) (Ibid.). She and **William McKay** met circa 1847. She married **Pierre Beauchamp**, son of **Jean Baptiste Beauchamp** and **Josephte Daze**, on 27 Apr 1863 St.Norbert, (Manitoba) (MM, page 56.) (SN1, page 78-79, M-6.).

William McKay was born in Mar 1823 Swan River, (Manitoba) (Denney.) (Ron Schell Collection, July 1999.). He married **Susanne Versailles**, daughter of **Pierre Versailles** and **Josephte Letendre**, before 1845. He died on 19 Apr 1889 Loon Creek area, (Saskatchewan), at age 66 (T. R. "Pat" McCloy, McKay Descendancy, 19 Jan 1994.).

Pierre Beauchamp was born circa 1810 (1831C RRS HBCA E5/5 1831 Census of the Red River Settlement, HBCA E5/5, Hudson's Bay Company Archives, Provincial Archives, 200 Vaughan Street, Winnipeg, MB R3C 1T5, Canada., page 3.). He married **Marie Comtois dit Morin**, daughter of **Etienne Morin dit Comtois** and **Marguerite Sarcie**, circa 1831. He died on 30 Mar 1865 St.Norbert, (Manitoba) (SN1, page 125, S-7.) (St-N Cem.). He was buried on 1 Apr 1865 St.Norbert, (Manitoba) (SN1, page 125, S-7.) (St-N Cem.).

7. Marie Versailles was born on 22 Feb 1830 St.Boniface, (Manitoba) (SB 1825-1834, page 44, B-617.). She was baptized on 24 Feb 1830 St.Boniface, (Manitoba) (Ibid.). She married **Francois Xavier Perreault dit Morin**, son of **Francois Perreault dit Morin** and **Marguerite (--?--)**, on 16 Feb 1849 Assumption, Pembina, Pembina County, Minnesota Territory (AP, page 14, M-6.).

Francois Xavier Perreault dit Morin was born circa Jun 1829 (SB 1825-1834, page 32, B-582.). He was baptized on 18 Oct 1829 St.Boniface, (Manitoba) (Ibid.). He died before 8 May 1876 (SN2, S-5 (father).).

8. Susanne Versailles was born in 1832 St.Norbert, (Manitoba). She married **William McKay**, son of **John Richards McKay** and **Lareine Trottier**, before 1845.

William McKay was born in Mar 1823 Swan River, (Manitoba) (Denney.) (Ron Schell.). He and **Scholastique Versailles** met circa 1847. He died on 19 Apr 1889 Loon Creek area, (Saskatchewan), at age 66 (T. R. McCloy, 19 Jan 1994.).

9. Euphrosine Versailles was born circa 1834 (Manitoba) (1870C-MB, page 315, #2296.). She married **Jean Baptiste Racette dit Dos Croche**, son of **George Racette** and **Francoise Guilbeau**, before 1853.

Jean Baptiste Racette dit Dos Croche was born circa 1832 (Manitoba) (Ibid., page 315, #2295.).

10. Marie Versailles was born circa 1829 St.Boniface, (Manitoba) (MBS, C-14926.). She married **Pierre Matrigane Chartrand**, son of **Pierre Chartrand** and **Indian Woman (--?--)**, on 20 Sep 1859 St.Francois Xavier, (Manitoba) (MM, page 1287.). She married **Jeremie Cardinal**, son of **Jeremie Cardinal** and **Marie Louise Adam**, on 18 Nov 1890 St.Norbert, Manitoba (MB Vital Statistics, Marriage Reg. #1890,001569.). She died on 7 Nov 1893 St.Boniface, Manitoba (Ibid., Death Reg. #1893,003255.). She was buried on 9 Nov 1893 St.Boniface, Manitoba (Rod Mac Quarrie, 3 June 2010.).

Pierre Matrigane Chartrand was born in 1825 North West (MBS, C-14926.). He died on 14 Mar 1886 St.Norbert, Manitoba (St-N Cem.) (SN2, S-3.). He was buried on 16 Mar 1886 St.Norbert, Manitoba (St-N Cem.) (SN2, S-3.).

Jeremie Cardinal was born circa 1837 Red River, (Manitoba) (1870C-MB, #1687, page 55.). He was born on 3 Jan 1842 St.Norbert, (Manitoba) (MBS, C-14926.). He married **Francoise Sayis**, daughter of **Francois Sayis or Sahys** and **Marguerite Sauteux**, on 30 Sep 1862 St.Norbert, (Manitoba) (SN1, page 62, M-11.). He died on 6 Feb 1901 RM of Ritchot, Manitoba (MB Vital Statistics, Death Reg. #1901,003381.) (SN2, S-5.). He was buried on 18 Feb 1901 St.Norbert, Manitoba (St-N Cem.) (SN2, S-5.).

11. Genevieve Versailles was born in Jul 1833 St.Norbert, (Manitoba) (MBS, C-14933.). She married **Francois Sayis**, son of **Francois Sayis or Sahys** and **Marguerite Sauteux**, before 1852. She died on 2 Mar 1883 St.Norbert, Manitoba, at age 49 (SN2, S-10.). She was buried on 4 Mar 1883 St.Norbert, Manitoba (Ibid.).

Francois Sayis was born in Nov 1821 (Rod Mac Quarrie, 18 Sep 2010.). He was born in Nov 1826 North West Territories (MBS, C-14933.). He died on 9 Feb 1879 St.Norbert, Manitoba, at age 57 (SN2, S-4.). He was buried on 11 Feb 1879 St.Norbert, Manitoba (Ibid.).

12. Marie Anne Versailles was born on 3 Jul 1838 St.Francois Xavier, (Manitoba) (MBS, C-14931.). She married **Antoine McLeod**, son of **Joseph McLeod** and **Angelique Lacerte**, on 24 Apr 1854 St.Francois Xavier, (Manitoba) (Rod Mac Quarrie, 3 June 2010.). She married **Francois Parisien**, son of **Francois Parisien** and **Genevieve Lavallee dit Plante**, on 31 Jan 1881 St.Francois Xavier, Manitoba (SFXI-Kipling, M-3.). She died on 29 Sep 1898 Winnipeg, Manitoba, at age 60 (Rod Mac Quarrie, 3 June 2010.). She was buried on 1 Oct 1898 St.Boniface, Manitoba (Ibid.).

Antoine McLeod was born circa 1822 North West Territory (1870C-MB, page 286, #1381.). He was born on 1 Nov 1824 North West (MBS, C-14931.). He was baptized on 1 Aug 1825 Drummond Island (Rod Mac Quarrie, 3 June 2010.). He died on 31 Jan 1876 St.Francois Xavier, Manitoba, at age 51 (SFXI-Kipling, S-2.).

Francois Parisien was born circa 1856 of, St.Norbert, (Manitoba). He died on 31 Aug 1898 St.Boniface, Manitoba (MB Vital Statistics, Death Reg. #1893,002446.).

13. David Versailles was born circa 1842 (1870C-MB, 1779, page 58.). He was born in 1845 St.Norbert, (Manitoba) (MBS, C-14934.). He married **Scholastique Boyer**, daughter of **Jean Baptiste Boyer** and **Elise Allard**, on 4 Feb 1862 St.Norbert, (Manitoba) (SN1, page 53, M-6.). He died on 14 Jun 1906 (Ritchot), St.Boniface, Manitoba (MB Vital Statistics, Death Reg. #1906,005319.) (Ibid., Death Reg. #1906,004800.) (St-N Cem.).

Scholastique Boyer was born in 1845 North West Territories (MBS, C-14934.).

Children of **David Versailles** and **Scholastique Boyer** were as follows:

    i. Marie Versailles was born on 23 Nov 1862 St.Norbert, (Manitoba) (SN1, page 66, B-35.). She was born on 23 Nov 1862 St.Norbert, (Manitoba) (Ibid.). She died on 14 May 1876 St.Norbert, Manitoba, at age 13 (SN2, S-6.). She was buried on 16 May 1876 St.Norbert, Manitoba (Ibid.).

14 ii. Joseph Edwin Versailles, b. 30 Dec 1864 St.Norbert, (Manitoba); m. Marie Agathe Henry; d. 7 Oct 1890 St.Norbert, Manitoba; bur. 9 Oct 1890 St.Norbert, Manitoba.

    iii. Rosalie Versailles was born on 13 Sep 1866 St.Norbert, (Manitoba) (SN1, page 84-85, B-42.). She was baptized on 14 Sep 1866 St.Norbert, (Manitoba) (Ibid.). She died on 31 Mar 1881 St.Norbert, Manitoba, at age 14 (SN2, S-6.). She was buried on 2 Apr 1881 St.Norbert, Manitoba (Ibid.).

    iv. Elise Versailles was born on 11 May 1868 St.Norbert, (Manitoba) (SN1, B-19.). She was baptized on 12 May 1868 St.Norbert, (Manitoba) (Ibid.). She died on 14 Apr 1887 St.Norbert, Manitoba, at age 18 (SN2, S-8.) (MB Vital Statistics, Death Reg. #1887,001828.). She was buried on 16 Apr 1887 St.Norbert, Manitoba (SN2, S-8.).

v.   Marie Clemence Versailles was born on 11 Aug 1870 St.Norbert, Manitoba (SN1, page 132, B-32.). She was baptized on 11 Aug 1870 St.Norbert, Manitoba (Ibid.). She died on 10 Jun 1888 St.Norbert, Manitoba, at age 17 (SN2, S-11.) (MB Vital Statistics, Death Reg. #1888,001815.). She was buried on 12 Jun 1888 St.Norbert, Manitoba (SN2, S-11.).

vi.   Marguerite Versailles was born on 5 Aug 1872 St.Norbert, Manitoba (SN1, B-34.). She was baptized on 6 Aug 1872 St.Norbert, Manitoba (Ibid.). She died on 4 May 1889 St.Norbert, Manitoba, at age 16 (St-N Cem.) (SN2, S-15.). She was buried on 6 May 1889 St.Norbert, Manitoba (St-N Cem.) (SN2, S-15.).

vii.   Louis Marie Versailles was born on 2 Aug 1874 St.Norbert, Manitoba (Ibid., B-38.). He was baptized on 3 Aug 1874 St.Norbert, Manitoba (Ibid.).

viii.   Albert Versaille was born on 19 Feb 1877 St.Norbert, Manitoba (Ibid., B-5.). He was baptized on 19 Feb 1877 St.Norbert, Manitoba (Ibid.). He died on 23 Feb 1877 St.Norbert, Manitoba (Ibid., S-2.). He was buried on 24 Feb 1877 St.Norbert, Manitoba (Ibid.).

ix.   Joseph Jean Baptiste Versailles was born on 18 May 1878 St.Norbert, Manitoba (Ibid., B-23.). He was baptized on 19 May 1878 St.Norbert, Manitoba (Ibid.). He died on 15 Jun 1882 St.Norbert, Manitoba, at age 4 (Ibid., S-15.). He was buried on 16 Jun 1882 St.Norbert, Manitoba (Ibid.).

x.   David Versailles was born on 31 May 1880 St.Norbert, Manitoba (Ibid., B-28.). He was baptized on 31 May 1880 St.Norbert, Manitoba (Ibid.). He died on 2 Apr 1881 St.Norbert, Manitoba (Ibid., S-7.). He was buried on 3 Apr 1881 St.Norbert, Manitoba (Ibid.).

Generation Four

14. Joseph Edwin Versailles was born on 30 Dec 1864 St.Norbert, (Manitoba) (SN1, page 116, B-53.). He was baptized on 30 Dec 1864 St.Norbert, (Manitoba) (Ibid.). He married **Marie Agathe Henry**, daughter of **John Henry** and **Josephte Parisien,** on 27 Nov 1888 St.Norbert, Manitoba (MB Vital Statistics, Marriage Reg. #1888,002481.) (SN2, M-11.). He died on 7 Oct 1890 St.Norbert, Manitoba, at age 25 (MB Vital Statistics, Death Reg. #1890,001701.) (SN2, S-31.). He was buried on 9 Oct 1890 St.Norbert, Manitoba (St-N Cem.) (SN2, S-31.).

Marie Agathe Henry was born on 17 Sep 1867 St.Norbert, (Manitoba) (SN1, B-32.). She was baptized on 18 Sep 1867 St.Norbert, (Manitoba) (Ibid.). She died on 27 Aug 1893 St.Norbert, Manitoba, at age 25 (St-N Cem.). She was buried on 29 Aug 1893 St.Norbert, Manitoba (Ibid.).

Children of **Joseph Edwin Versailles** and **Marie Agathe Henry** were:

i.   Louis Versailles was born on 18 Apr 1890 St.Norbert, Manitoba (SN2, B-18.) (MB Vital Statistics, Birth Reg. #1890,006181.). He was baptized on 18 Apr 1890 St.Norbert, Manitoba (SN2, B-18.). He died on 28 Jul 1890 RM St.Norbert, Manitoba (St-N Cem.) (MB Vital Statistics, Death Reg. #1890,001696.) (SN2, S-25.). He was buried on 30 Jul 1890 St.Norbert, Manitoba (St-N Cem.) (SN2, S-25.).

Descendants of Louis Villebrun dit Plouf

Generation One

1. Louis Villebrun dit Plouf was born circa 1775 Ruperts Land (1827C RRS HBCA E5/1 1827 Census of the Red River Settlement, HBCA E5/1, Hudson's Bay Company Archives, Provincial Archives, 200 Vaughan Street, Winnipeg, MB R3C 1T5, Canada., page 4.). He married according to the custom of the country **Marie Anne Nation of Collets** before 1801.

Children of **Louis Villebrun dit Plouf** and **Marie Anne Nation of Collets** were as follows:

2   i.   Louis Villebrun, b. circa 1801; m. Louise Collin; d. 3 Feb 1873 St.Boniface, Manitoba; bur. 5 Feb 1873 St.Boniface, Manitoba.

3   ii.   Brigitte Villebrun dit Plouf, b. 1805 North West Territories; m. Joseph Delorme; d. 9 Jun 1888 Cartier, Manitoba; bur. 11 Jun 1888 St.Norbert, Manitoba.

4   iii.   Antoine Villebrun, b. circa 1809 Ruperts Land; m. Archange Marcellais.

5   iv.   Marguerite Villebrun dit Plouf, b. circa 1810; m. Thomas Kipling dit Pishk; m. Francois Desmarais.

Generation Two

2. Louis Villebrun was born circa 1801 (SB 1825-1834 St.Boniface Roman Catholic Registre des Baptemes, Mariages & Sepultures, 1825-1834, page 20, B-143. Hereinafter cited as SB 1825-1834.). He was born circa 1805 Ruperts Land (1831C RRS HBCA E5/5 1831 Census of the Red River Settlement, HBCA E5/5, Hudson's Bay Company Archives, Provincial Archives, 200 Vaughan Street, Winnipeg, MB R3C 1T5, Canada., page 12.). He was baptized on 20 Nov 1825 St.Boniface, (Manitoba) (SB 1825-1834, page 20, B-143.). He married **Louise Collin**, daughter of **Joseph Collin** and **Josephte Sauteuse,** on 21 Nov 1825 St.Boniface, (Manitoba) (Ibid., page 20, M-30.). He died on 3 Feb 1873 St.Boniface, Manitoba (SB-Rozyk St. Boniface Roman Catholic Church, Manitoba, Canada, Baptisms, Marriages and Burials 1860-1875 Extractions, Compiled by Rosemary Rozyk, page 264-265, S-4.). He was buried on 5 Feb 1873 St.Boniface, Manitoba (Ibid.).

Louise Collin was born in 1807 North West (MBS Scrip Applications, Original White Settlers & Halfbreeds residing in Manitoba on 15 July 1870, RG15-19, C-14926.). She was baptized on 20 Nov 1825 St.Boniface, (Manitoba) (SB 1825-1834, page 20, B-144.).

Children of **Louis Villebrun** and **Louise Collin** were as follows:

6   i.   Louise Plouff dit Villebrun, b. circa 1827; m. Joseph Lambert; d. 17 Jan 1867 St.Norbert, (Manitoba); bur. 19 Jan 1867 St.Norbert, (Manitoba).

7   ii.   Louis Villebrun, b. 11 Jun 1829; m. Isabelle Berard; d. 23 Jun 1867 St.Norbert, (Manitoba); bur. 25 Jun 1867 St.Norbert, (Manitoba).

8   iii.   Julie Villebrun, b. Aug 1831 St.Charles, (Manitoba); m. Jean Baptiste Branconnier; d. 13 Aug 1915 Charleswood, Manitoba.

9   iv.   Marie Villebrun, b. 22 May 1832 St.Boniface, (Manitoba); m. Jean Baptiste Flamand; m. Joseph Vallee.

    10   v.   Guillaume Villebrun dit Ploufe, b. 1835 St.Boniface, (Manitoba); m. Flora Hope.

    11   vi.   Joseph Villebrun, b. 1838 St.Boniface, (Manitoba); m. Marie Robillard.

    12   vii.   Francois Villebrun Sr, b. circa 1839 (Manitoba); m. Genevieve Adam; m. Marie St.Cyr.

          viii.   Leon Villebrun was born in Nov 1846 St.Boniface, (Manitoba) (MBS, C-14934.).

    13   ix.   Maxime Villebrun, b. circa 1847 (Manitoba); m. Annabella Spence; d. 15 Feb 1891 St.Boniface, Manitoba.

    14   x.   Daniel Villebrun, b. 1849; m. Catherine Attak-a-koup Chatelain; m. Marie Louise Chastelain; d. 24 May 1921 Green Lake, Saskatchewan.

    15   xi.   Philomene Villebrun, b. 8 Sep 1850; m. John Bell; m. John Bagley.

    3. Brigitte Villebrun dit Plouf was born in 1805 North West Territories (Ibid., C-14926.). She married **Joseph Delorme**, son of **Jean Baptiste Henault** and **Marie Elisabeth Page,** before 1821. She died on 9 Jun 1888 Cartier, Manitoba (SN2 Catholic Parish Register of St.Norbert, S-10. Hereinafter cited as SN2.) (Manitoba Vital Statistics online, http://web2.gov.mb.ca, Death Reg. #1888,001374.). She was buried on 11 Jun 1888 St.Norbert, Manitoba (SN2, S-10.).

    Joseph Delorme was born on 7 Jul 1797 Berthierville, Quebec (PRDH online index, http://www.genealogic.umontreal.ca, No. 439884.). He was baptized on 8 Jul 1797 Berthier-en-Haut, Quebec (Ibid.). He was born circa 1799 Quebec (1828C RRS HBCA E5/2 1828 Census of the Red River Settlement, HBCA E5/2, Hudson's Bay Company Archives, Provincial Archives, 200 Vaughan Street, Winnipeg, MB R3C 1T5, Canada., page 7.). He married **Josephte McLean** before 1817. He died on 16 Aug 1869 St.Norbert, (Manitoba), at age 72 (SN1 Catholic Parish Register of St.Norbert 1857-1873, S-6. Hereinafter cited as SN1.). He was buried on 17 Aug 1869 St.Norbert, (Manitoba) (Ibid.).

    4. Antoine Villebrun was born circa 1806 Red River, (Manitoba) (1850Ci-MN, page 27, Dwelling 88, Family 88.). He was born circa 1809 Ruperts Land (1831C RRS HBCA E5/5, page 12.). He married **Archange Marcellais**, daughter of **Jean Baptiste Marcellais** and **Angelique Assiniboine**, on 5 Mar 1832 St.Boniface, (Manitoba) (SB 1825-1834, page 57, M-66.).

    Archange Marcellais was born circa 1815 Pembina (1850Ci-MN, page 27, Dwelling 88, Family 88.).

Children of **Antoine Villebrun** and **Archange Marcellais** were as follows:

    16   i.   Catherine Villebrun dit Plouffe, b. circa 1834 Red River, (Manitoba); m. Charles Sayis or Saice.

          ii.   Gabriel Plouffe was born circa 1837 Red River, (Manitoba) (Ibid.). He died on 21 Sep 1861 (SB-Rozyk, page 33, S-22.). He was buried on 23 Sep 1861 St.Boniface, (Manitoba) (Ibid.).

    17   iii.   Madeleine Villebrun dit Plouffe, b. circa 1839 Pembina County; m. Joseph E. Perreault.

          iv.   Baptiste Plouffe was born circa 1844 Pembina County (1850Ci-MN, page 27, Dwelling 88, Family 88.).

    18   v.   Pierre Villebrun dit Plouffe, b. circa 1846 Pembina County; m. Charlotte (--?--).

          vi.   Michel Plouffe dit Villebrun was born circa 1848.

          vii.   Francois Xavier Plouffe was born on 1 Mar 1850 Pembina County, Minnesota Territory (AP, page 27, B-69.). He was baptized on 1 Mar 1850 Assumption, Pembina, Pembina County, Minnesota Territory (Ibid.). He died on 21 Dec 1850 Pembina, Pembina County, Minnesota Territory (Ibid., page 47, S-3.). He was buried on 22 Dec 1850 Assumption, Pembina, Pembina County, Minnesota Territory (Ibid.).

          viii.   Anonyme Plouffe was born on 1 Mar 1850 Pembina County, Minnesota Territory (Ibid., page 27-28, S-7.). He/she died on 1 Mar 1850 Pembina County, Minnesota Territory (Ibid.). He/she was buried on 1 Mar 1850 Assumption, Pembina, Pembina County, Minnesota Territory (Ibid.).

          ix.   Antoine Plouffe was born on 17 Jan 1852 Pembina, Pembina County, Dakota Territory (Ibid., page 68, B-3.). He was baptized on 28 Jan 1852 Assumption, Pembina, Pembina County, Dakota Territory (Ibid.).

    19   x.   Paul Plouffe dit Villebrun, b. 22 Sep 1854 Pembina, Pembina County, Dakota Territory; m. Angelique Roy; m. Anastasia Saice; d. 23 May 1942 Mahnomen, Mahnomen County, Minnesota.

          xi.   Cuthbert Plouffe dit Villebrun was born circa 1857.

    5. Marguerite Villebrun dit Plouf was born circa 1810 (1860-DT-Inx, page 7.). She married **Thomas Kipling dit Pishk**, son of **John James Kipling** and **Marguerite Okkanens Saulteaux**, circa 1822. She married **Francois Desmarais**, son of **Jean Baptiste Desmarais** and **Josephte Sauteuse,** on 5 Feb 1833 St.Boniface, (Manitoba) (SB 1825-1834, page 87-88, M-94.).

Question: *Marguerite was alone in 1832. Did she marry for the second time?*

    Thomas Kipling dit Pishk was born circa 1792 Ruperts Land (1827C RRS HBCA E5/1, page 4.). He was born circa 1800 (Manitoba) (1870C-MB, page 159, #68.). He married **Elizabeth (--?--)** before 1843. He married **Nancy Indian** before 1870 (Ibid., page 159, #69.).

    Francois Desmarais was born circa 18 Aug 1804 Ruperts Land (1833C RRS HBCA E5/7 1833 Census of the Red River Settlement, HBCA E5/7, Hudson's Bay Company Archives, Provincial Archives, 200 Vaughan Street, Winnipeg, MB R3C 1T5, Canada., page 6.) (SB 1825-1834, page 3, B-_.). He was baptized on 26 Jun 1825 St.Boniface, (Manitoba) (Ibid.). He married **Rosalie Collin**, daughter of **Antoine Collin** and **Josephte Paul**, on 27 Jun 1825 St.Boniface (Ibid., page 4, M-17.).

Generation Three

    6. Louise Plouff dit Villebrun was born circa 1827. She married **Joseph Lambert**, son of **Antoine Lambert** and **Marie Sauteuse**, before 1845. She died on 17 Jan 1867 St.Norbert, (Manitoba) (SN1, S-2.). She was buried on 19 Jan 1867 St.Norbert, (Manitoba) (Ibid.).

Question: *Probable parents.*

    Joseph Lambert was born on 23 Dec 1826 St.Norbert, (Manitoba) (MBS, C-14929.). He married **Genevieve Rocheleau**, daughter of **Guillaume Rocheleau** and **Marie Adam**, on 13 Oct 1876 St.Norbert, Manitoba (SN2, M-7.). He died on 17 Sep 1903 at age 76 (St-N Cem.). He was buried on 19 Sep 1903 St.Norbert, Manitoba (Ibid.).

    7. Louis Villebrun was born on 11 Jun 1829 (SB 1825-1834, page 24, B-551.). He was baptized on 14 Jun 1829 St.Boniface, (Manitoba) (Ibid.). He married **Isabelle Berard**, daughter of **Louis Berard** and **Catherine Hughes,** before 1855. He died on 23 Jun 1867 St.Norbert, (Manitoba), at age 38 (SN1, S-12.). He was buried on 25 Jun 1867 St.Norbert, (Manitoba) (Ibid.).

    Isabelle Berard was born circa 1831 (SB 1825-1834, page 131, B-803.). She was born in 1832 Saskatchewan Valley (MBS, C-14934.). She was baptized on 8 Jul 1834 St.Boniface, (Manitoba) (SB 1825-1834, B-803.).

Children of **Louis Villebrun** and **Isabelle Berard** were as follows:

    20   i.   Pierre Villebrun, b. 10 Aug 1855 St.Norbert, (Manitoba); m. Jeannette Ritchot; d. 10 May 1910 Tache, Manitoba.

21   ii.   Louis Villebrun, b. 25 Oct 1856 St.Norbert, (Manitoba); m. Marie Rose Esther Pilon; m. Sarah Sutherland; d. 18 May 1920 St.Boniface, Manitoba.

22   iii.   Marie Villebrun, b. 10 Jun 1859 St.Norbert, (Manitoba); m. Roger Roy; m. Louis Wenceslas Lamirande.

     iv.   Joseph Villebrun was born on 9 Feb 1860 St.Norbert, (Manitoba) (SN1, B-8, page 28.). He was baptized on 10 Feb 1860 St.Norbert, (Manitoba) (Ibid.). He was buried on 20 Mar 1864 St.Norbert, (Manitoba) (IBMS.).

     v.   Anonyme Villebrun dit Plouff was born circa 1862 (SN1, page 101, S-3.). He/she died on 19 Mar 1864 St.Norbert, (Manitoba) (Ibid.). He/she was buried on 20 Mar 1864 St.Norbert, (Manitoba) (Ibid.).

     vi.   Rosalie Plouff dit Villebrun was born on 10 Nov 1864 St.Norbert, (Manitoba) (Ibid., page 111, B-41.). She was baptized on 11 Nov 1864 St.Norbert, (Manitoba) (Ibid.). She died on 24 Oct 1865 St.Norbert, (Manitoba) (Ibid., page 137, S-25.). She was buried on 26 Oct 1865 St.Norbert, (Manitoba) (Ibid.).

23   vii.   Christine Villebrun, b. 19 Dec 1866 St.Norbert, (Manitoba); m. Louis Jean Joseph Vermette.

8.   **Julie Villebrun** was born in Aug 1831 St.Charles, (Manitoba) (MBS, C-14926.). She married **Jean Baptiste Branconnier**, son of **Jean Baptiste Branconnier** and **Louise Beauchemin**, before 1853. She died on 13 Aug 1915 Charleswood, Manitoba (MB Vital Statistics, Death Reg. #1915,190166.).

   Jean Baptiste Branconnier was born on 20 Jul 1828 St.James, (Manitoba) (MBS, C-14926.). He died on 15 Apr 1901 St.Charles, Manitoba, at age 72 (Rosemary Helga (Morrissette) Rozyk Research, 28 Jan 1999 report.). He was buried on 18 Apr 1901 St.Charles, Manitoba (Ibid.).

9.   **Marie Villebrun** was born on 22 May 1832 St.Boniface, (Manitoba) (MBS, C-14934.). She was baptized on 25 May 1832 St.Boniface, (Manitoba) (SB 1825-1834, page 65, B-437.). She and **Jean Baptiste Flamand** met before 1854. She married **Joseph Vallee**, son of **Louis Vallee** and **Louise Martel**, on 10 Feb 1863 St.Boniface, (Manitoba) (SB-Rozyk, page 103, M-13.).

   Jean Baptiste Flamand married **Marie Azure** before 1857.

   Joseph Vallee was born in Mar 1846 Assiniboia Settlement (MBS, C-14934.). He died on 29 Apr 1892 St.Boniface, Manitoba, at age 46 (MB Vital Statistics, Death Reg. #1892,002662.).

10.   **Guillaume Villebrun dit Ploufe** was born in 1835 St.Boniface, (Manitoba). He married **Flora Hope**, daughter of **James Hope** and **Judith Desjarlais**, on 21 Jul 1867 Lac la Biche, (Alberta) (LLBR1 Notre Dame des Tidoren, St.Paul Diocese, Lac La Biche, Registre des Baptemes, Mariages & Sepltures, Volume 1, 1853-1898., page 83, M-58. Hereinafter cited as LLBR1.).

   Flora Hope was born in 1848 Slave Lake, (Alberta) (HBSI Index 1886-1901, 1906 Halfbreed Scrip Applications, RG15-21.) (ArchiviaNet 1886-1901, 1906 Half-Breed Scrip Applications Index, RG15-21, Volume 1333 through 1371, Microfilm Reel Number C-14944 through C-15010, National Archives of Canada, Ottawa, Ontario, http://www.collectionscanada.gc.ca.).

Children of **Guillaume Villebrun dit Ploufe** and **Flora Hope** were as follows:

     i.   Joseph Villebrun was born in 1868 (NWHBS, C-14942.). He was born circa Oct 1871 Lac la Biche, (Alberta) (ArchiviaNet, C-15008.). He died in 1868 (NWHBS, C-14942.). He died circa Oct 1871 Lac la Biche, (Alberta) (ArchiviaNet, C-15008.).

     ii.   Louis Villebrun was born on 20 Jul 1868 Dunvegan, (Alberta) (Ibid.).

     iii.   Elise Villebrun was born on 15 Jan 1872 Lac la Biche, (Alberta) (LLBR1, page 127, B-4.). She was baptized on 28 Jan 1872 Lac la Biche, (Alberta) (Ibid.).

     iv.   Emma Villebrun was born on 19 Jun 1874 Lac la Biche, (Alberta) (Ibid., page 143, B-10.). She was baptized on 21 Jun 1874 Lac la Biche, (Alberta) (Ibid.). She married Francois Trottier, son of Antoine Trottier and Angelique Laframboise, before 1900 (ArchiviaNet, C-15008.). She died between 1891 and 1894 Fort Benton, Montana (Ibid.).

        Francois Trottier was born on 1 Jan 1867 (SFXI: 1835-1852, B-40.). He was baptized on 18 May 1867 St.Francois Xavier, (Manitoba) (Ibid.). Question: *Is Francois the widower of Emma Villebrun?* (ArchiviaNet, C-15008.).

24   v.   Flora Villebrun, b. 23 Jan 1877 Lac la Biche, (Alberta).

     vi.   Gilbert Villebrun was born on 10 Apr 1880 Lac la Biche, (Alberta) (LLBR1, page 196, B-17.). He was baptized on 14 Apr 1880 Lac la Biche, (Alberta) (Ibid.). He died in 1892 Havre, Montana (ArchiviaNet, C-15008.).

     vii.   Francois Villebrun was born on 10 Oct 1882 Lac la Biche, (Alberta) (LLBR1, page 222, B-29.). He was baptized on 14 Oct 1882 Lac la Biche, (Alberta) (Ibid.).

     viii.   Maxime Villebrun was born in 1885 Battleford, (Saskatchewan) (ArchiviaNet, C-15008.). He died in May 1886 (Ibid.).

11.   **Joseph Villebrun** was born in 1838 St.Boniface, (Manitoba) (MBS, C-14934.). He married **Marie Robillard**, daughter of **Jean Baptiste Robillard** and **Catherine Ducharme**, on 10 May 1864 St.Boniface, (Manitoba) (SB-Rozyk, page 150, M-10.).

   Marie Robillard was born on 25 May 1847 St.Boniface, (Manitoba).

Children of **Joseph Villebrun** and **Marie Robillard** were as follows:

     i.   Louise Villebrun was born circa 1864 (Ibid., page 196, S-33.). She died on 23 Oct 1870 St.Boniface, Manitoba (Ibid.). She was buried on 24 Oct 1870 St.Boniface, Manitoba (Ibid.).

25   ii.   Marie Philomene Villebrun, b. 10 Oct 1868; m. Samuel Bellerose.

     iii.   Joseph Villebrun was baptized on 30 Apr 1871 St.Laurent, Manitoba (IBMS.). He died on 30 Apr 1873 at age 2 (SB-Rozyk, page 275, S-27.). He was buried on 2 May 1873 St.Boniface, Manitoba (Ibid.).

     iv.   Marie Desanges Villebrun was born on 3 May 1873 St.Boniface, Manitoba (Ibid., page 278, B-48.). She was baptized on 4 May 1873 St.Boniface, Manitoba (Ibid.). She died on 13 Apr 1875 St.Boniface, Manitoba, at age 1 (Ibid., page 53, S-17.). She was buried on 14 Apr 1875 St.Boniface, Manitoba (Ibid.).

     v.   William Villebrun was born in 1879 Wood Mountain, (Saskatchewan) (1881 Church of Latter Day Saints Census Transcription Project of Census Images from the National Archives of Canada, Ottawa, Canada, http://www.familysearch.org, Film C-13285, District 192, page 7, Household 18.) (ArchiviaNet, C-15008.).

vi.   Marie Adeline Villebrun was born on 7 Sep 1880 (L2 Lebret, Mission de St.Florent, Roman Catholic Registre des Baptemes, Mariages & Seplutures, Qu'Appelle, Saskatchewan, Book Two: 1881-1887, FHC microfilm 1032949., page 38, B-78. Hereinafter cited as L2.). She was baptized on 16 Jul 1882 Lebret, (Saskatchewan) (Ibid.).

26   vii.   Marie Olive Villebrun, b. 11 Feb 1886 Lebret, (Saskatchewan); m. Julien Lalande; m. Alfred Brown.

12. Francois Villebrun Sr was born circa 1839 (Manitoba) (1881 Census of Canada from the National Archives of Canada, Ottawa, Canada, District 192-T, page 2, family 11.). He married **Genevieve Adam**, daughter of **Joseph Adam** and **Angelique Racette**, circa 1858. He married **Marie St.Cyr**, daughter of **Jean Baptiste St.Cyr** and **Julie Mercredi**, in 1866 Fort Chipewyan (ArchiviaNet, C-15008.).

Genevieve Adam was born on 2 Aug 1832 (SB 1825-1834, page 71, B-471.). She was baptized on 3 Aug 1832 St.Boniface, (Manitoba) (Ibid.). She married **Isidore Arcand** before 1852. She married **Andre Trottier** before 1854. She married **Joseph Stanley** before 15 Jul 1870 (1870C-MB, #51-52, St.Boniface, page 2.).

Children of **Francois Villebrun Sr.** and **Genevieve Adam** were:

27   i.   Sarah Villebrun, b. 16 Nov 1858; m. Isidore Fisher; d. before 1896.

Marie St.Cyr was born on 1 Nov 1846 Fort Chipewyan, Northwest Territories (ArchiviaNet, C-15008.).

Children of **Francois Villebrun Sr.** and **Marie St.Cyr** were as follows:

28   i.   Onesime Villebrun, b. circa 1869; m. Belle Lepine.

29   ii.   Francois Villebrun Jr, b. circa 1869 Fond du Lac, Athabasca, (Alberta); m. Rosalie Tourangeau.

iii.   Lillian Mary Villebrun was born circa 1872 (1881 Canada, District 192-T, page 2, family 11.).

iv.   Frederick Villebrun was born circa 1874 (Ibid.).

v.   Maxime Villebrun was born circa 1879 (Ibid.).

vi.   Isidore Villebrun was born circa Mar 1881 (Ibid.).

vii.   John Noel Villebrun was born circa 1883 (1901 Canada, District 206-a-6, page 4, family 20, line 17-21.).

viii.   Victoire Villebrun was born circa 1886 (Ibid.).

13. Maxime Villebrun was born circa 1847 (Manitoba) (1870C-MB, page 105, #157.). He married **Annabella Spence**, daughter of **Samuel Spence** and **Sally Sarah Sanderson**, on 14 Feb 1871 St.Boniface, Manitoba (SB-Rozyk, page 206, M-2.). He died on 15 Feb 1891 St.Boniface, Manitoba (MB Vital Statistics, Death Reg. #1891,001574.).

Annabella Spence was born on 23 Apr 1853 North West (MBS, C-14934.). She was baptized on 10 Dec 1871 St.Boniface, Manitoba (SB-Rozyk, page 222, B-76.).

Children of **Maxime Villebrun** and **Annabella Spence** were as follows:

i.   Maxime Villebrun was born on 9 Dec 1871 St.Boniface, Manitoba (Ibid., page 222, B-75.). He was baptized on 9 Dec 1871 St.Boniface, Manitoba (Ibid.). He died on 2 Feb 1889 RM St.Clements, Manitoba, at age 17 (MB Vital Statistics, Death Reg. #1889,001032.).

ii.   Sara Bella Villebrun was born on 1 Aug 1873 St.Boniface, Manitoba (SB-Rozyk, page 287, B-66.). She was baptized on 1 Aug 1873 St.Boniface, Manitoba (Ibid.).

iii.   Christie Villebrun was born on 31 May 1885 Archibald, Manitoba (MB Vital Statistics, Birth Reg. #1885,004220.).

iv.   Margaret Victoria Villebrun was born on 25 Jan 1887 Winnipeg, Manitoba (Ibid., Birth Reg. #1887,002609.).

14. Daniel Villebrun was born in 1849 (Denney.). He married **Catherine Attak-a-koup Chatelain**, daughter of **David Chastelain** and **Marie Grant dit La Manche**, on 22 May 1870 St.Joachim, Fort Edmonton, (Alberta) (MSJ-FA-E Register des Baptemes, Mariages & Sepultures 1858-1861 Mission St.Joachim, Fort Auguste, Fort des Prairies, Edmonton, No. 1, page 69, M-1. Hereinafter cited as MSJ-FA-E.). He married **Marie Louise Chastelain**, daughter of **David Chastelain** and **Marie Grant dit La Manche**, in 1871 Carlton, (Saskatchewan) (ArchiviaNet, C-14959.). He died on 24 May 1921 Green Lake, Saskatchewan (Denney.).

Question: *Son of Louis Villebrun and Louise Collin????*

Catherine Attak-a-koup Chatelain was born circa 1850 Carlton, (Saskatchewan). She was born in 1854 near Battleford, (Saskatchewan) (ArchiviaNet.). She died in Aug 1870 Carlton, (Saskatchewan).

Children of **Daniel Villebrun** and **Catherine Attak-a-koup Chatelain** were:

i.   Maria Villebrun was born in Apr 1869 Carlton, (Saskatchewan).

Marie Louise Chastelain was born in Jan 1854 Battleford, (Saskatchewan) (Ibid., C-14959.).

Children of **Daniel Villebrun** and **Marie Louise Chastelain** were as follows:

i.   Pierre Villebrun was born on 20 Feb 1875 betwee Battleford and Fort Pitt, (Saskatchewan) (Ibid., C-15008.). He was baptized on 8 May 1875 St.Laurent-de-Grandin, (Saskatchewan) (SL-SK St.Laurent-de-Grandin Roman Catholic Registre des Baptemes, Mariages & Seplutures, St.Laurent, Saskatchewan, 1872-1896, page 39, B-21. Hereinafter cited as SL-SK.).

ii.   Marguerite Villebrun was born on 20 Aug 1876 Carlton, (Saskatchewan) (ArchiviaNet, C-15008.). She died on 21 Oct 1894 Jackfish Lake, (Saskatchewan), at age 18 (Ibid.).

iii.   Joseph Villebrun was born on 12 Aug 1877 Fort Pitt, (Saskatchewan) (Ibid.).

iv.   Elise Villebrun was born on 12 Nov 1879 (1901 Canada, microfilm, T-6553, North Battleford, page 5, Family 41, line #2-3.). She was born on 25 Nov 1879 Fort Pitt, (Saskatchewan) (HBS 1886-1901, 1906 Half-Breed Scrip Applications, RG15-21, Volume 1335; C-14948.). She married Joseph Alexandre Belanger, son of Abraham Belanger and Philomene Delorme, before 7 Aug 1900.

    Joseph Alexandre Belanger was born on 26 May 1871 St.Norbert, Manitoba (SN1, page 146, B-27.). He was baptized on 27 May 1871 St.Norbert, Manitoba (Ibid.).

v.   Caroline Villebrun was born on 14 Mar 1883 Fort Pitt, (Saskatchewan) (ArchiviaNet, C-15008.). She died on 9 Sep 1897 Jackfish Lake, (Saskatchewan), at age 14 (Ibid.).

vi.   Marie Emma Villebrun was born on 1 Apr 1884 Battleford, (Saskatchewan) (Ibid.).

vii.   Sophie Magdeleine Villebrun was born on 16 Nov 1886 Battleford, (Saskatchewan) (SV St.Vital Roman Catholic Registre des Baptemes, Mariages & Seplutures, Battleford, Saskatchewan, 1878-1896, B-39. Hereinafter cited as

SV.). She was baptized on 17 Nov 1886 St.Vital, Battleford, (Saskatchewan) (Ibid.). She was buried on 25 Jan 1887 St.Vital, Battleford, (Saskatchewan) (Denney.).

viii. Guillaume Villebrun was born on 1 Jul 1888 Battleford, (Saskatchewan) (SV, B-23.). He was baptized on 2 Jul 1888 St.Vital, Battleford, (Saskatchewan) (Ibid.).

ix. George Villebrun was born on 12 Jan 1890 Battleford, (Saskatchewan) (1901 Canada, microfilm, T-6553, North Battleford, page 4, Family 45, line #45-50.).

x. Jean Baptiste Villebrun was born on 7 Feb 1892 Battleford, (Saskatchewan) (SV, S-1.). He died on 7 Feb 1892 Battleford, (Saskatchewan) (Ibid.). He was buried on 9 Feb 1892 St.Vital, Battleford, (Saskatchewan) (Ibid.).

xi. Anonyme Villebrun was born on 15 Nov 1895 Battleford, (Saskatchewan) (Ibid., S-11.). She died on 15 Nov 1895 Battleford, (Saskatchewan) (Ibid.). She was buried on 16 Nov 1895 St.Vital, Battleford, (Saskatchewan) (Ibid.).

15. Philomene Villebrun was born on 8 Sep 1850 (MBS, C-14925.). She and **John Bell** met circa 1873. She married **John Bagley** before 28 Jul 1875 (Ibid.).

Children of **Philomene Villebrun** include:

    30   i.   Adelaide Villebrun, b. 2 Oct 1865 St.Boniface, (Manitoba); m. Napoleon St.Germain; d. before 1901.

16. Catherine Villebrun dit Plouffe was born circa 1834 Red River, (Manitoba) (1850Ci-MN, page 27, Dwelling 88, Family 88.). She married **Charles Sayis or Saice**, son of **Francois Sayis or Sahys** and **Marguerite Sauteux**, circa 1864 (Rod Mac Quarrie, 18 Sep 2010.).

Charles Sayis or Saice was born circa 1839 Minnesota Territory (1880 Minnesota Census, National Archives of the United States, Washington D.C., page 152B.). He married **Cecile Grandbois**, daughter of **Michel Grandbois** and **Marguerite Landry**, on 15 Jan 1861 St.Norbert, (Manitoba) (SN1, page 38-39, M-4.).

17. Madeleine Villebrun dit Plouffe was born circa 1839 Pembina County (1850Ci-MN, page 27, Dwelling 88, Family 88.). She married **Joseph E. Perreault** before 1864.

Joseph E. Perreault was born circa 1842 (1895-WE 1895 Census of Pembina Chippewa of White Earth, Minnesota, National Archives of the United States, Washington D.C., #26-27.). He died on 9 Jul 1931 Becker County, Minnesota (Minnesota Department of Health Public Death Index.).

18. Pierre Villebrun dit Plouffe was born circa 1846 Pembina County (1850Ci-MN, page 27, Dwelling 88, Family 88.). He married **Charlotte (--?--)** before 1870 Minnesota Territory (1880C Minn, page 153C, family 8.).

Charlotte (--?--) was born in 1850 (Ibid.).

Children of **Pierre Villebrun dit Plouffe** and **Charlotte (--?--)** were as follows:

        i.   Sophia Villebrun was born circa 1870 Minnesota (Ibid.).

        ii.   Ellen Villebrun was born circa 1872 Minnesota (Ibid.).

    31   iii.   Antoine Villebrun, b. circa 1876 Minnesota; m. Mary White.

        iv.   Angeline Villebrun was born circa 1879 Minnesota (Ibid.).

    32   v.   Romain Villebrun, b. circa 1893; m. Rosetta A. Saice.

19. Paul Plouffe dit Villebrun was born on 22 Sep 1854 Pembina, Pembina County, Dakota Territory (AP, page 114, B-316.). He was baptized on 23 Sep 1854 Assumption, Pembina, Pembina County, Dakota Territory (Ibid.). He married **Angelique Roy**, daughter of **Francois Roy** and **Marguerite (--?--)**, before 1880 (1880C Minn, page 153C, family 9.). He married **Anastasia Saice**, daughter of **Joseph Sayis or Saice** and **Louise Picard**, circa 1920 (Rod Mac Quarrie, 18 Sep 2010.). He died on 23 May 1942 Mahnomen, Mahnomen County, Minnesota, at age 87 (MN Death Index.).

Angelique Roy was born in Mar 1851 Minnesota Territory (1900C Minn Twelfth Census of the United States: 1900; Minnesota, District 340a, page 17, line 21.). She died on 11 Mar 1908 Mahnomen, Mahnomen County, Minnesota (MN Death Index.).

Children of **Paul Plouffe dit Villebrun** and **Angelique Roy** were:

        i.   Antoine Villebrun was born on 26 Jun 1886 White Earth Agency, Minnesota (Ancestry.com Website, WWI Draft Registration.) (Social Security Death Index, . Hereinafter cited as SSDI.). He died on 4 Oct 1967 Mahnomen, Mahnomen County, Minnesota, at age 81 (Ibid.) (MN Death Index.).

Anastasia Saice was born in May 1854 North Dakota (1900C-ND, House 299, page 307B.). She was born in 1855 (Rod Mac Quarrie, 18 Sep 2010.). She married **George Gardner** in 1872 (1900C-ND, House 299, page 307B.). She married **Joseph Rolette**, son of **Joseph Rolette** and **Angelique Jerome**, in 1897 (Ibid.). She died on 28 Nov 1945 North Dakota at age 91 (North Dakota Department of Health Public Death Index.).

Generation Four

20. Pierre Villebrun was born on 10 Aug 1855 St.Norbert, (Manitoba) (MBS, C-14934.). He married **Jeannette Ritchot**, daughter of **Andre Ritchot** and **Marguerite Ladouceur**, on 11 Jan 1876 St.Boniface, Manitoba (RMSB.). He died on 10 May 1910 Tache, Manitoba, at age 54 (MB Vital Statistics, Death Reg. #1910,001821.).

Jeannette Ritchot was born on 9 Aug 1859 Grande-Pointe, (Manitoba) (1870C-MB, #348, page 12.) (Dominique Ritchot Research,, 2 Jun 2009.). She married **Alfred Theriault**, son of **Alfred Theriault** and **Julienne Cyr**, on 5 Jul 1915 Winnipeg, Manitoba (Ibid.) (MB Vital Statistics, Marriage Reg. #1915,186088.). She married **Albert Robillard**, son of **Joseph Robillard**, on 30 Aug 1925 St.Boniface, Manitoba (Dominique Ritchot, 2 Jun 2009.) (RMSB, page 411.). She died on 21 Oct 1941 Winnipeg, Manitoba, at age 82 (Dominique Ritchot, 2 Jun 2009.). She was buried on 23 Oct 1941 St.Mary's, Winnipeg, Manitoba (Ibid.).

Children of **Pierre Villebrun** and **Jeannette Ritchot** were as follows:

        i.   Marie Josephine Villebrun was born on 6 May 1877 St.Norbert, Manitoba (SN2, B-13.). She was baptized on 6 May 1877 St.Norbert, Manitoba (Ibid.). She died on 30 Mar 1881 St.Norbert, Manitoba, at age 3 (Ibid., S-5.). She was buried on 1 Apr 1881 St.Norbert, Manitoba (Ibid.).

        ii.   Joseph Edmond Villebrun was born on 8 Mar 1880 St.Norbert, Manitoba (Ibid., B-13.). He was baptized on 8 Mar 1880 St.Norbert, Manitoba (Ibid.). He married Justine Morin, daughter of Charles Perreault dit Morin and Marie Dauphinais, on 8 Oct 1904 Winnipeg, Manitoba (MB Vital Statistics, Marriage Reg. #1904,001792.).

Justine Morin was born on 7 Oct 1882 Wood Mountain, (Saskatchewan) (SIWB, B-1, page 1.). She was baptized on 22 Oct 1882 St.Ignace, Willow Bunch, (Saskatchewan) (Ibid.).

iii. Virginie Villebrun was born on 22 Jul 1882 Manitoba (1901 Canada, #10, J-1, page 1, family 3, line 8-14.). She married Pierre Ethier on 7 Jan 1902 St.Norbert, Manitoba (MM.).

iv. Andre Pierre Villebrun was born on 6 Jul 1884 St.Boniface, Manitoba (MB Vital Statistics, Birth Reg. #1884,004161.) (Ibid.).

v. Alfred Villebrun was born on 29 Oct 1886 RM St.Norbert, Manitoba (Ibid., Birth Reg. #1886,001587.) (SN2, B-57.). He was baptized on 30 Oct 1886 St.Norbert, Manitoba (Ibid.). He married Marie Sansregret, daughter of Mathias Sansregret and Marie Eugenie Desjarlais, on 24 Jul 1905 Tache, Manitoba (MB Vital Statistics, Marriage Reg. #1905,001667.). He died on 3 Feb 1935 Winnipeg, Manitoba, at age 48 (Ibid., Death Reg. #1935,008075.).

   Marie Sansregret was born on 28 May 1883 Lebret, (Saskatchewan) (L2, page 65, B-36.). She was baptized on 29 May 1883 Lebret, (Saskatchewan) (Ibid.).

vi. Joseph Frederic Villebrun was born on 31 Dec 1888 St.Norbert, Manitoba (MB Vital Statistics, Birth Reg. #1889,005388.) (Ibid., Birth Reg. #1889,004036.). He died on 5 Feb 1893 Ritchot, Manitoba, at age 4 (Ibid., Death Reg. #1893,002384.). He was buried on 7 Feb 1893 St.Norbert, Manitoba (St-N Cem.).

vii. Marie Alex Villebrun was born on 2 May 1891 (Ibid.) (SN2, B-31.). He was baptized on 4 May 1891 St.Norbert, Manitoba (Ibid.). He died on 24 Jan 1892 Ritchot, Manitoba (St-N Cem.) (MB Vital Statistics, Death Reg. #1892,002049.).

viii. Marie Elise Villebrun was born on 10 Mar 1893 R.M. of Ritchot, Manitoba (Ibid., Birth Reg. #1893,004989.). She died on 10 Jan 1903 at age 9 (St-N Cem.). She was buried on 12 Jan 1903 St.Norbert, Manitoba (Ibid.).

21. Louis Villebrun was born on 25 Oct 1856 St.Norbert, (Manitoba) (MBS, C-14934.). He married **Marie Rose Esther Pilon**, daughter of **Pierre Pilon** and **Helene Sauve**, before 1877. He married **Sarah Sutherland**, daughter of **Pierre Sutherland** and **Suzanne McMillan**, on 21 Feb 1882 St.Norbert, Manitoba (SN2, M-4.). He died on 18 May 1920 St.Boniface, Manitoba, at age 63 (MB Vital Statistics, Death Reg. #1920,027055.).

Marie Rose Esther Pilon was born on 6 Sep 1861 St.Boniface, (Manitoba) (SB-Rozyk, page 30, B-120.). She was baptized on 7 Sep 1861 St.Boniface, (Manitoba) (Ibid.). She died on 25 Sep 1880 St.Norbert, Manitoba, at age 19 (SN2, S-27.). She was buried on 27 Sep 1880 St.Norbert, Manitoba (Ibid.).

Children of **Louis Villebrun** and **Marie Rose Esther Pilon** both born St.Norbert, Manitoba, were as follows:

i. Marie Emma Villebrun was born on 24 Nov 1878 (Ibid., B-44.). She was baptized on 24 Nov 1878 St.Norbert, Manitoba (Ibid.). She married Maxime Dumas or Dumais, son of Maxime Dumas or Dumais and Marguerite Lagimoniere, on 4 Sep 1900 St.Norbert, Manitoba (MM.). She married Alexander Nault, son of Andre Nault and Anastasie Landry, on 12 Jan 1954 St.Boniface, Manitoba (RMSB.).

   Maxime Dumas or Dumais was born on 18 Aug 1869 (SB-Rozyk, page 160, B-107.). He was baptized on 20 Aug 1869 St.Boniface, (Manitoba) (Ibid.). He married **Eleonore Bouvette**, daughter of **Charles Emile Bouvette** and **Suzanne Vaudry**, on 15 Nov 1887 Winnipeg, Manitoba (Rod Mac Quarrie, 12 Sep 2006.). He died before 1954.

   Alexander Nault was born on 1 Mar 1874 St.Vital, Manitoba (MBS, C-14931.) (SB-Rozyk, page 10, B-20.). He was baptized on 2 Mar 1874 St.Boniface, Manitoba (MBS, C-14931.) (SB-Rozyk, page 10, B-20.). He married **Mathilde Carriere**, daughter of **Damase Carriere** and **Marie Pelagie Parenteau,** on 28 Nov 1893 St.Pierre, De Salaberry, Manitoba (MB Vital Statistics, Mar. Reg. #1893,001049.). He died on 21 Dec 1965 at age 91 (Fort Garry St.Vital Roman Catholic Cemetery; Cemetery Transcription #42; Betty Atkinson, Lorne Harris Kathy Stokes, Unit E, 1045 St.James Street, Winnipeg, Manitoba, Canada %3H 1B1: Manitoba Genealogical Society, Inc., 1980-1981; update 1995, page 5.).

ii. Marie Eugenie Villebrun was born on 30 Aug 1880 (SN2, B-44.). She was baptized on 1 Sep 1880 St.Norbert, Manitoba (Ibid.). She died on 13 Feb 1881 St.Norbert, Manitoba (Ibid., S-3.). She was buried on 14 Feb 1881 St.Norbert, Manitoba (Ibid.).

Sarah Sutherland was born circa 1852. She married **Felix Cadotte**, son of **Laurent Cadotte** and **Elisabeth Thomas,** on 28 Jan 1873 St.Norbert, Manitoba (SN1, M-2.).

Children of **Louis Villebrun** and **Sarah Sutherland** were as follows:

i. Marie Olive Josephine Villebrun was born on 24 Nov 1882 St.Norbert, Manitoba (SN2, B-44.). She was baptized on 25 Nov 1882 St.Norbert, Manitoba (Ibid.).

ii. Joseph Adelard Villebrun was born on 14 Mar 1884 St.Norbert, Manitoba (1901 Canada, #10, h-1, page 7, family 54, line 9-22.) (SN2, B-12.). He was baptized on 16 Mar 1884 St.Norbert, Manitoba (Ibid.). He married Marie Rosalie Julie St.Germain, daughter of Augustin St.Germain and Eulalie Perreault, on 1 Aug 1910 (St.Norbert), Ritchot, Manitoba (MM.) (MB Vital Statistics, Mar. Reg. #1910,001204 (Ritchot).) (SN2, B-12 (note).).

   Marie Rosalie Julie St.Germain was born on 25 Apr 1890 Manitoba (1901 Canada, page 3-4, line 48-50, 1-6, family 27.).

iii. Olive Villebrun was born on 25 Nov 1885 Manitoba (Ibid., #10, h-1, page 7, family 54, line 9-22.).

iv. Georges Villebrun was born on 14 Dec 1886 Manitoba (Ibid.).

v. Albert Villebrun was born on 5 Aug 1887 Manitoba (Ibid.).

vi. Eugene Villebrun was born on 13 Oct 1887 St.Norbert, Manitoba (MB Vital Statistics, Birth Reg. #1887,001906.). He married Eva Malo on 29 Oct 1912 St.Malo, (Manitoba).

vii. Marie Catherine Villebrun was born on 10 Sep 1889 St.Norbert, Manitoba (Ibid., Birth Reg. #1889,002786.). She married Charles Stewart on 24 Nov 1915 St.Norbert, Manitoba (MM.).

viii. Jean Baptiste Anaclet Villebrun was born on 6 Jul 1891 (SN2, B-45.). He was baptized on 7 Jul 1891 St.Norbert, Manitoba (Ibid.).

ix. Sara Villebrun was born on 6 Mar 1895 R.M. of Ritchot, Manitoba (1901 Canada, #10, h-1, page 7, family 54, line 9-22.) (MB Vital Statistics, Birth Reg. #1898,006242.). She married **Pierre Auguste Berard** on 21 Nov 1916 St.Norbert, Manitoba (MM.).

x. Edward Villebrun was born on 8 Dec 1897 R.M. of Ritchot, Manitoba (MB Vital Statistics, Birth Reg. #1898,006418.).

xi. Agnes Villebrun was born on 4 Nov 1900 R.M. of Ritchot, Manitoba (Ibid., Birth Reg. #1900,005307.). She married **Louis Lavallee**, son of **Louis Lavallee** and **Octavie Riel**, on 26 Nov 1918 St.Norbert, Manitoba (MM.).

    Louis Lavallee was born on 30 Apr 1889 St.Francois Xavier, Manitoba (SFXI-Kipling, B-17.). He married **Josephine Riel**, daughter of **Alexandre Riel** and **Marie Louise Elise Poitras**, on 28 Jan 1913 St.Boniface, Manitoba (MB Vital Statistics, Marriage Reg. #1913,014202.).

22. Marie Villebrun was born on 10 Jun 1859 St.Norbert, (Manitoba) (MBS, C-14934.). She married **Roger Roy**, son of **Francois Roy** and **Isabelle Lafreniere**, on 21 Jan 1879 St.Norbert, Manitoba (Ibid.) (SN2, M-2.). She married **Louis Wenceslas Lamirande**, son of **Alexis Lamirande** and **Marie Pilon**, on 2 May 1882 St.Norbert, Manitoba (MM.) (SN2, M-5.).

    Roger Roy was born on 16 Feb 1860 St.Norbert, (Manitoba) (SN1, page 28, B-11.). He was baptized on 18 Feb 1860 St.Norbert, (Manitoba) (Ibid.). He died on 26 Feb 1880 St.Norbert, Manitoba, at age 20 (SN2, S-3.). He was buried on 27 Feb 1880 St.Norbert, Manitoba (Ibid.).

    Louis Wenceslas Lamirande was born on 17 Feb 1861 St.Norbert, (Manitoba) (SN1, page 41, B-5.). He was baptized on 18 Feb 1861 St.Norbert, (Manitoba) (Ibid.). He died on 20 Mar 1917 Grande Pointe, Manitoba, at age 56 (MB Vital Statistics, Birth Reg. #1917,018198.).

23. Christine Villebrun was born on 19 Dec 1866 St.Norbert, (Manitoba) (SN1, page 89, B-68.). She was baptized on 20 Dec 1866 St.Norbert, (Manitoba) (Ibid.). She married **Louis Jean Joseph Vermette**, son of **Antoine Vermette** and **Cecile Rocque**, on 18 Nov 1884 St.Norbert, Manitoba (MM.) (SN2, M-14.).

    Louis Jean Joseph Vermette was born on 18 Sep 1862 St.Boniface, (Manitoba) (SB-Rozyk, page 85, B-154.). He was baptized on 19 Sep 1862 St.Boniface, (Manitoba) (Ibid.). He died on 16 Feb 1936 RM Ste.Anne, Manitoba, at age 73 (MB Vital Statistics, Death Reg. No. 1936,008523.).

24. Flora Villebrun was born on 23 Jan 1877 Lac la Biche, (Alberta) (LLBR1, page 166, B-4.). She was baptized on 25 Jan 1877 Lac la Biche, (Alberta) (Ibid.). She married **Alexandre Swain**, son of **William Swain** and **Marie Laviolette**, on 10 Jun 1890 St.Peter's Mission, Cascade County, Montana (SPMT St.Peter's Mission; Volume I; Marriage Register 1859-1895; Translated & Transcribed by Reverend Dale McFarlane, Archivist, Diocese of Great Falls-Billings, Montana; Spring 1981, page 51, #310.).

    Alexandre Swain was born on 16 Nov 1868 Milk River, Montana (NWHBS, C-14941.).

25. Marie Philomene Villebrun was born on 10 Oct 1868 (SB-Rozyk, page 135, B-141.). She was baptized on 11 Oct 1868 St.Boniface, (Manitoba) (Ibid.). She married **Samuel Bellerose**, son of **Olivier Bellerose** and **Catherine Surprenant**, on 21 Sep 1886 Lebret, (Saskatchewan) (L2, page 157, M-8.).

    Samuel Bellerose was born on 1 Nov 1864 (1901 Canada, #203, u(1), page 1, family 12, line 34-42.).

26. Marie Olive Villebrun was born on 11 Feb 1886 Lebret, (Saskatchewan) (L2, page 136, B-11.). She was baptized on 12 Feb 1886 Lebret, (Saskatchewan) (Ibid.). She married **Julien Lalande** on 26 Sep 1903 St.Norbert, Manitoba (MM.). She married **Alfred Brown**, son of **Peter Brown** and **Mary Jane Strannigan**, on 23 Jan 1912 Lestock, Saskatchewan (L2, page 136, B-11.).

    Alfred Brown was born on 15 Aug 1885 Touchwood Hills, (Saskatchewan) (HBS 1886-1901, 1906 Half-Breed Scrip Applications, RG15-21, Volume 1338, C-14953.).

27. Sarah Villebrun was born on 16 Nov 1858 (SN1, page 7, B-33.). She was baptized on 21 Nov 1858 St.Norbert, (Manitoba) (Ibid.). She married **Isidore Fisher**, son of **John Fisher** and **Elizabeth Brabant**, on 21 Jul 1874 St.Boniface, Manitoba (SB-Rozyk, page 24-25, M-15.). She died before 1896.

    Isidore Fisher was born in 1848 (NWHBSI, page 43.). He married **Marie Adeline Arcand**, daughter of **Isidore Arcand** and **Marie Chartrand**, on 13 Apr 1896 St.Boniface, Manitoba (RMSB.).

28. Onesime Villebrun was born circa 1869 (1901 Canada, Athabaska A-6, page 3, Family 17, line 28-31.) (ArchiviaNet, C-15008.). He married **Belle Lepine**, daughter of **Baptiste Lepine** and **Madeleine Houle**, on 9 Sep 1896 (Ibid.).

Belle Lepine was born on 15 Aug 1875 Fort Simpson (Ibid.).

Children of **Onesime Villebrun** and **Belle Lepine** are as follows:

i. Marie Dora Villebrun was born circa 1897 (1901 Canada, Athabaska A-6, page 3, Family 17, line 28-31.).

ii. Augustine Villebrun was born circa 1899 (Ibid.).

29. Francois Villebrun Jr was born circa 1869 Fond du Lac, Athabasca, (Alberta) (ArchiviaNet, C-15008.) (1881 Canada, District 192-T, page 2, family 11.). He married **Rosalie Tourangeau** before 1897 (ArchiviaNet, C-15007.).

Rosalie Tourangeau was born in Jun 1870 Athabasca District, (Alberta) (Ibid.). She died before 1906 Smith's Landing, Athabasca, (Alberta) (Automated Genealogy 1906 Census Transcription Project and Census Images from the National Archives of Canada, http://www.automatedgenealogy.com, family 46.).

Children of **Francois Villebrun Jr.** and **Rosalie Tourangeau** were as follows:

i. Francis Villebrun was born on 1 Feb 1897 (ArchiviaNet, C-15008.).

ii. Louis Napoleon Villebrun was born on 4 Feb 1899 (1901 Canada, District 206-a(1), page 3, family 5, line 6-10.) (ArchiviaNet, C-15008.).

iii. Albert Villebrun was born circa 1900 (1901 Canada, District 206-a(1), page 3, family 5, line 6-10.).

iv. Philip Villebrun was born circa 1902 Smith's Landing, Athabasca, (Alberta) (1906 Canada, family 46.).

30. Adelaide Villebrun was born on 2 Oct 1865 St.Boniface, (Manitoba) (MBS, C-14934.) (SB-Rozyk, page 18, B-93.). She was baptized on 2 Oct 1865 St.Boniface, (Manitoba) (MBS, C-14934.) (SB-Rozyk, page 18, B-93.). She married **Napoleon St.Germain**, son of **Joseph St.Germain** and **Anne McGillivray**, on 19 Feb 1884 St.Norbert, Manitoba (MB Vital Statistics, Mar. Reg. #1884,001712.) (SN2, M-2.). She died before 1901.

Napoleon St.Germain was born circa 1855 (1870C-MB, #1922-1930, page 62-63.). He was born on 6 May 1859 (1901 Canada, page 1, Family 9, Line 45.). He died on 19 Aug 1934 St.Boniface, Manitoba (MB Vital Statistics, Death Reg. #1934,036036.).

31. Antoine Villebrun was born circa 1876 Minnesota (1880C Minn, page 153C, family 8.). He married **Mary White** before 1903 (Rod Mac Quarrie, 15 May 2012.).

Children of **Antoine Villebrun** and **Mary White** are:

      i.   Lawrence Peter Villebrun was born on 27 Oct 1916 (Ibid.). He married Dawn Amelia Perrault, daughter of Romain E. Perrault and Leonora "Nora" Saice, before 1945 (Ibid.).

          Dawn Amelia Perrault was born on 17 Aug 1925 Mahnomen County, Minnesota (Ibid.). She died on 5 Oct 1998 St.Louis County, Minnesota, at age 73 (Ibid.).

32. Romain Villebrun was born circa 1893. He married **Rosetta A. Saice**, daughter of **Francois "Frank" Sayis or Saice** and **Mary Brunell**, before 1916 (Ibid.).

Rosetta A. Saice was born on 2 Oct 1897 Minnesota (Ibid., 18 Sep 2010.). She died on 11 Aug 1991 St.Louis County, Minnesota, at age 93 (Ibid.).

Children of **Romain Villebrun** and **Rosetta A. Saice** were:

      i.   Earl Romaine Villebrun was born on 12 Sep 1916 Minnesota (Ibid., 15 May 2012.). He married Alvina Christine Saice, daughter of Gabriel Sayis or Saice and Elizabeth Beauchamp, before 1950. He died on 6 Dec 1999 Minneapolis, Hennepin County, Minnesota, at age 83 (Ibid.) (MN Death Index.). He was buried on 10 Dec 1999 Fort Snelling National Cemetery, Minneapolis, Hennepin County, Minnesota (Rod Mac Quarrie, 15 May 2012.).

          Alvina Christine Saice was born on 29 Nov 1912 Minnesota (1913-WE 1913 Census of Pembina Chippewa of White Earth, Minnesota, National Archives of the United States, Washington D.C., Census No. 77-86.) (Rod Mac Quarrie, 8 May 2012.). She died on 2 Oct 1988 Hennepin County, Minnesota, at age 75 (Ibid.) (MN Death Index.). She was buried on 5 Oct 1988 Fort Snelling National Cemetery, Minneapolis, Hennepin County, Minnesota (Rod Mac Quarrie, 15 May 2012.).

Ahnentafel between Francois Villeneuve dit la Fourche and Augustin Amiot dit Villeneuve

--- 1st Generation ---

1. FRANCOIS VILLENEUVE DIT LA FOURCHE was baptized on 28 Sep 1811 at St.Eustache, Quebec (Rod MacQuarrie Research, 16 Oct 2009, Source: Drouin.). He was born on 28 Sep 1811 at St.Eustache, Quebec (Ibid.). He married according to the custom of the country **HELENE VALLEE**, daughter of **ANTOINE VALLEE** and **SUZANNE LEFEBVRE OR FAVEL**, before 1836. He married **HELENE VALLEE**, daughter of **ANTOINE VALLEE** and **SUZANNE LEFEBVRE OR FAVEL**, on 12 Sep 1842 at Fort-des-Prairies, (Alberta) (FDP Baptisms & Marriages Fort des Prairie, Saskatchewan District, C Kipling, M-10. Hereinafter cited as FDP.). He married **ANGELIQUE HOULE**, daughter of **CHARLES HOULE** and **MADELEINE BRELAND,** before 1858.

--- 2nd Generation ---

2. AUGUSTIN AMIOT DIT VILLENEUVE (PRDH online index, http://www.genealogic.umontreal.ca, #68385.) was born on 25 May 1764 at Montreal, Montreal, Quebec (Ibid., #223616.). He was baptized on 25 May 1764 at Montreal, Montreal, Quebec (Ibid.). He married **MARGUERITE PROULX DIT CLEMENT**, daughter of **JOSEPH PROULX DIT CLEMENT** and **MARIE AMABLE DEVOYAUX DIT LAFRAMBOISE,** on 12 Oct 1790 at St.Eustache, Quebec (Ibid., #68385.) (Rod Mac Quarrie, 17 Oct 2009, Source: Drouin.).

--- 3rd Generation ---

4. AUGUSTIN AMIOT DIT VILLENEUVE (PRDH online, #68385.) (Ibid., #159585.) (Ibid.) was born on 24 Jul 1734 at St-Augustin, Quebec (Ibid.). He was baptized on 25 Jul 1734 at St-Augustin, Quebec (Ibid.). He married **MARGUERITE BRAZEAU**, daughter of **ETIENNE BRAZEAU** and **LOUISE PICARD**, on 27 Oct 1769 (DGFC Tanguay, Cyprien, *Dictionnaire Genealogique des Familles Canadiennes* (28 Felsmere Avenue, Pawtucket, Rhode Island 02861-2903: Quintin Publications, 1996 reprint), Volume 2, page 457.). He died on 6 May 1794 at St-Eustache, Quebec, at age 59 (PRDH online, #159585.). He was buried on 7 May 1794 at St-Eustache, Quebec (Ibid.).

Descendants of Francois Villeneuve dit la Fourche

Generation One

1. Francois Villeneuve dit la Fourche was baptized on 28 Sep 1811 St.Eustache, Quebec (Rod MacQuarrie Research, 16 Oct 2009, Source: Drouin.). He was born on 28 Sep 1811 St.Eustache, Quebec (Ibid.). He married according to the custom of the country **Helene Vallee**, daughter of **Antoine Vallee** and **Suzanne Lefebvre or Favel**, before 1836. He married **Helene Vallee**, daughter of **Antoine Vallee** and **Suzanne Lefebvre or Favel,** on 12 Sep 1842 Fort-des-Prairies, (Alberta) (FDP Baptisms & Marriages Fort des Prairie, Saskatchewan District, C Kipling, M-10. Hereinafter cited as FDP.). He married **Angelique Houle**, daughter of **Charles Houle** and **Madeleine Breland,** before 1858.

Helene Vallee was born in 1818. She died before 21 Feb 1870 (SN1 Catholic Parish Register of St.Norbert 1857-1873, M-6. Hereinafter cited as SN1.).

Children of **Francois Villeneuve dit la Fourche** and **Helene Vallee** were as follows:

   2   i.   Helene Villeneuve, b. circa 1836; m. Francois Xavier Bonin.

   3   ii.   Francois Villeneuve, b. circa 1837; m. Justine Robillard.

   4 iii.   Theophile Joseph Villeneuve, b. 1843 Peace River, (Alberta); m. Eliza McGillis.

   5 iv.   Isidore Villeneuve, b. 23 Sep 1845 Fort Edmonton, (Alberta); m. Mathilde Henry.

   6   v.   David Villeneuve, b. 24 Sep 1846; m. Louise Boghiu or McKay; bur. 5 Nov 1901 Fort Providence, (Northwest Territory).

   7 vi.   Hyacinthe Villeneuve, b. 10 Nov 1847 Grande Prairie, (Alberta); m. Josephte Appoline Larence; d. 12 Dec 1933 Langdon, Cavalier County, North Dakota.

8 vii. Cuthbert Villeneuve, b. 25 Jan 1851; m. Genevieve Frederick dit Langis; d. 10 Nov 1908 Neche, Pembina County, North Dakota.

9 viii. Severe Villeneuve, b. circa 19 Feb 1854 Edmonton, (Alberta); m. Nancy Courteoreille; m. Julie Boucher.

Angelique Houle was born on 20 Oct 1825 St.Boniface, (Manitoba) (SB 1825-1834 St.Boniface Roman Catholic Registre des Baptemes, Mariages & Sepultures, 1825-1834, page 17, B-137. Hereinafter cited as SB 1825-1834.). She was baptized on 23 Oct 1825 St.Boniface, (Manitoba) (Ibid.). She married **Joseph Dauphinais**, son of **Michel Genthon dit Dauphinais or Dauphine** and **Victoire Ouellette**, before 1843.

Children of **Francois Villeneuve dit la Fourche** and **Angelique Houle** were as follows:

10 i. Eliza Villeneuve, b. 9 Apr 1858 North Dakota; m. Antoine Nicholas; d. 4 Apr 1927 Devils Lake, Ramsey County, North Dakota.

11 ii. Alexandre Villeneuve, b. 17 Jan 1860 Pembina County, Dakota Territory; m. Marie McDonald; m. Marie Bottineau.

iii. Caroline Villeneuve was born on 4 Feb 1862 (SN1, page 54, B-2.). She was baptized on 6 Feb 1862 St.Norbert, (Manitoba) (Ibid.). She married Benjamin Rondeau in Feb 1876 Moorhead, Minnesota.

iv. Napoleon Villeneuve was born on 3 Jun 1864 (SB-Rozyk St. Boniface Roman Catholic Church, Manitoba, Canada, Baptisms, Marriages and Burials 1860-1875 Extractions, Compiled by Rosemary Rozyk, page 153, B-57.). He was baptized on 4 Jun 1864 St.Boniface, (Manitoba) (Ibid.).

v. Patrice Villeneuve was born circa 1866.

Generation Two

2. **Helene Villeneuve** was born circa 1836 (CCRPNW-V *Catholic Church Records of the Pacific Northwest, Vancouver, Volumes I and II and Stellamaris Mission* Translated by: Mikell de Lores Wormell Warner and Annotated by: Harriet Duncan Munnick, (St.Paul, Oregon: French Prairie Press, 1972), page 8, B-78.). She was baptized on 6 Sep 1838 Fort Edmonton (Ibid.). She married **Francois Xavier Bonin** on 1 Jul 1851 Fort-des-Prairies, (Alberta) (FDP, M-29.).

3. **Francois Villeneuve** was born circa 1837 (CCRPNW-V, page 8, B-77.). He was baptized on 6 Sep 1838 Fort Edmonton (Ibid.). He married **Justine Robillard**, daughter of **Jean Baptiste Robillard** and **Marie-Rose Antoinette Lagimoniere**, before 1859.

Justine Robillard was born before 1840. Question: *Is Justine the daughter of J. B. Robillard?*

Children of **Francois Villeneuve** and **Justine Robillard** were as follows:

i. Esther Villeneuve was born on 7 Aug 1859 (SB-Rozyk, page 13, B-43.). She was baptized on 19 Feb 1861 Lake Manitoba, St.Boniface, (Manitoba) (Ibid.).

ii. Justine Marie Villeneuve was born on 7 Jun 1861 (Ibid., page 22, B-90.). She was baptized on 27 Jun 1861 St.Boniface, (Manitoba) (Ibid.).

12 iii. Pascal Villeneuve, b. Aug 1873 North Dakota; m. Marie Celina Gariepy; m. Elise Parisien; d. 5 Nov 1934 Rolette County, North Dakota.

4. **Theophile Joseph Villeneuve** was born in 1843 Peace River, (Alberta) (NWHBS 1885 Scrip Applications, North-West Halfbreeds residing outside Manitoba on 15 July 1870, RG15-20, C-14942.). He was baptized on 24 Sep 1843 (Denney Papers, Charles D. Denney, Glenbow Archives, Calgary, Alberta.). He married **Eliza McGillis**, daughter of **Alexandre McGillis** and **Marguerite Bottineau,** in 1864 St.Francois Xavier, (Manitoba) (NWHBS, C-14942.).

Eliza McGillis was born on 13 Jun 1844 St.Francois Xavier, (Manitoba) (SFX: 1834-1850 St.Francois Xavier 1834-1851 Register, B-526. Hereinafter cited as SFX: 1834-1850.). She was baptized on 15 Jun 1844 St.Francois Xavier, (Manitoba) (Ibid.).

Children of **Theophile Joseph Villeneuve** and **Eliza McGillis** were as follows:

i. Marie Rose Villeneuve was born circa Jan 1867 Carlton, (Saskatchewan) (SFXI-Kipling St.Francois Xavier Register Index, 1834-1900; compiled by Clarence Kipling , B-56.) (Denney.). She was baptized on 26 May 1867 St.Francois Xavier, (Manitoba) (SFXI-Kipling, B-56.).

13 ii. Daniel Villeneuve, b. 10 Apr 1868 Touchwood Hills, (Saskatchewan); m. Marie Rose Ouellette.

iii. Rosalie Villeneuve was born on 5 Oct 1869 Saddle Lake, (Alberta) (ArchiviaNet 1886-1901, 1906 Half-Breed Scrip Applications Index, RG15-21, Volume 1333 through 1371, Microfilm Reel Number C-14944 through C-15010, National Archives of Canada, Ottawa, Ontario, http://www.collectionscanada.gc.ca, C-15008.). She died on 17 Nov 1879 Saddle Lake, (Alberta), at age 10 (Ibid.).

14 iv. Marie Villeneuve, b. 11 Nov 1871; m. Joseph Nolin.

v. Pierre Villeneuve was born on 10 May 1872 Carlton, (Saskatchewan) (Ibid.).

vi. Marie Marguerite Villeneuve was born on 13 Oct 1874 St.Paul, Saskatchewan River (HBSI Index 1886-1901, 1906 Halfbreed Scrip Applications, RG15-21.) (SL-SK St.Laurent-de-Grandin Roman Catholic Registre des Baptemes, Mariages & Sepltures, St.Laurent, Saskatchewan, 1872-1896, page 40, B-23. Hereinafter cited as SL-SK.). She was baptized on 10 Jun 1875 St.Laurent-de-Grandin, (Saskatchewan) (Ibid.). She married (--?--) Paradis before 1901.

vii. David Villeneuve was born in Dec 1876 Buffalo Lake (ArchiviaNet, C-15008.). He married Justine McKay, daughter of Guillaume McKay and Marie St.Denis, before 1901 (Automated Genealogy 1901 Census Transcription Project and Census Images from the National Archives of Canada, http://www.automatedgenealogy.com, District 205-h(1), page 2, family 20, line 47-48.).

Justine McKay was born on 2 Mar 1883 (Ibid.).

15 viii. Marguerite Villeneuve, b. 1878 Maple Creek, (Saskatchewan); m. Patrice Dumont.

ix. Severe Villeneuve was born on 2 Jan 1878 (SL-SK, page 10, B-8.). He was baptized on 31 Jan 1878 St.Laurent-de-Grandin, (Saskatchewan) (Ibid.). He died on 6 Mar 1894 Battleford, (Saskatchewan), at age 16 (ArchiviaNet, C-15008.).

16 x. Isabelle Villeneuve, b. 4 Jul 1878 Maple Creek, (Saskatchewan); m. Adelard Lafournaise.

xi. Alexander Villeneuve was born on 15 May 1881 Maple Creek, (Saskatchewan) (HBSI.) (1901 Canada, microfilm, T-6553, Egg Lake, page 4, Family 25, line 30-34.).

5. Isidore Villeneuve was born on 23 Sep 1845 Fort Edmonton, (Alberta). He married **Mathilde Henry**, daughter of **Alexis Henry** and **Marie Daunais dit Lyonnaise,** before 1871.

Mathilde Henry was born circa 1845 Red River, (Manitoba) (1850C-MNT 1850 Minnesota Territory Census, Nation Archives of the United States, Washington D.C., 146, 146, called Michel.). She was born in Jul 1847 St.Boniface, (Manitoba) (MBS Scrip Applications, Original White Settlers & Halfbreeds residing in Manitoba on 15 July 1870, RG15-19, C-14934.).

Children of **Isidore Villeneuve** and **Mathilde Henry** were as follows:

17   i.   Isidore Villeneuve Jr, b. 12 Apr 1871 Dunvegan, (Alberta); m. Rosalie Champagne.

     ii.   Joseph Albert Villeneuve was born on 28 Jan 1873 (SB-Rozyk, page 263, B-18.). He was baptized on 29 Jan 1873 St.Boniface, Manitoba (Ibid.). He died on 6 Jul 1875 St.Charles, Manitoba, at age 2 (ArchiviaNet, C-15008.).

     iii.   Mathilde Villeneuve was born on 31 Jul 1874 St.Boniface, Manitoba (SB-Rozyk, page 26, B-49.). She was baptized on 31 Jul 1874 St.Boniface, Manitoba (Ibid.). She died in Apr 1877 St.Charles, Manitoba, at age 2 (ArchiviaNet, C-15008.).

18   iv.   Joseph Villeneuve, b. 12 Dec 1876 St.Charles, Manitoba; m. Julienne Parenteau.

     v.   John Villeneuve was born on 3 Feb 1879 Fort Ellice, Manitoba (Ibid.).

     vi.   Francois Villeneuve was born on 29 Apr 1881 Fort Ellice, Manitoba (Ibid.).

     vii.   Virginie Villeneuve was born on 16 Sep 1883 Fish Creek, (Saskatchewan) (BSAP Records of the Parish of Batoche, St.Antoine de Pudoue Roman Catholic Church: Register for Baptisms, Marriages, Deaths, Volume One, 1881-1909., page 17, B-22. Hereinafter cited as BSAP.). She was baptized on 16 Sep 1883 Batoche, (Saskatchewan) (Ibid.). She died on 18 May 1885 Batoche, (Saskatchewan), at age 1 (Ibid., page 34, S-23.). She was buried on 19 May 1885 Batoche, (Saskatchewan) (Ibid.).

     viii.   Francois Xavier Villeneuve was born on 3 Oct 1887 Batoche, (Saskatchewan) (Ibid., page 61, B-11.). He was baptized on 5 Oct 1887 Batoche, (Saskatchewan) (Ibid.). He died on 23 Oct 1887 Batoche, (Saskatchewan) (Ibid., page 62, S-13.). He was buried on 24 Oct 1887 Batoche, (Saskatchewan) (Ibid.).

     ix.   Alfred Villeneuve was born on 29 Sep 1888 Batoche, (Saskatchewan) (Ibid., page 70, B-25.). He was baptized on 1 Oct 1888 Batoche, (Saskatchewan) (Ibid.). He died on 9 Jun 1889 Batoche, (Saskatchewan) (Ibid., page 75, S-8.). He was buried on 11 Jun 1889 Batoche, (Saskatchewan) (Ibid.).

6. David Villeneuve was born on 24 Sep 1846. He married **Louise Boghiu or McKay** before 1867. He was buried on 5 Nov 1901 Fort Providence, (Northwest Territory) (Marie Beaupre Extractions.).

Louise Boghiu or McKay was born circa 1841 (1881 Census of Canada from the National Archives of Canada, Ottawa, Canada, District 192-U, page 3, family 10.).

Children of **David Villeneuve** and **Louise Boghiu or McKay** were as follows:

19   i.   Joseph Villeneuve, b. circa 1867; m. Marie Augustine Bouvier.

     ii.   Eliza Villeneuve was born on 2 Jul 1873 Fort Resolution, (Northwest Territory) (Marie Beaupre.). She was baptized on 4 Jul 1873 Fort Resolution, (Northwest Territory) (Ibid.).

7. Hyacinthe Villeneuve was born on 10 Nov 1847 Grande Prairie, (Alberta) (Nellie Nault Research, 27 Aug 1993.). He married **Josephte Appoline Larence**, daughter of **Norbert Larence** and **Josephte Parenteau**, on 21 Feb 1870 St.Norbert, (Manitoba) (SN1, M-6.). He died on 12 Dec 1933 Langdon, Cavalier County, North Dakota, at age 86 (Nellie Nault, 27 Aug 1993.) (North Dakota Department of Health Public Death Index.).

Josephte Appoline Larence was born on 2 Apr 1853 Pembina, Pembina County, Dakota Territory (AP Records of the Assumption Roman Catholic Church, Pembina, North Dakota: Baptisms, Marriages, Sepultures, 1848-1896; compiled by Reverend Father J. M. Belleau, 2 October 1944, page 85, B-58. Hereinafter cited as AP.). She was baptized on 2 Apr 1853 Assumption, Pembina, Pembina County, Dakota Territory (Ibid.). She died on 28 Jul 1911 Olga, Cavalier County, North Dakota, at age 58 (Olga Our Lady of the Sacred Heart, Olga, North Dakota 1882-1900, page 8, S-403. Hereinafter cited as Olga.). She was buried on 31 Jul 1911 Olga, Cavalier County, North Dakota (Ibid.).

Children of **Hyacinthe Villeneuve** and **Josephte Appoline Larence** were as follows:

     i.   Alfred Villeneuve was born on 15 Feb 1871 (SJL-1 Register of Baptisms, Marriages, and Burials, St.Joseph, Leroy, North Dakota, Diocese of Saint Paul, Minnesota, 1870-1888, Book 1, page 8, B-5. Hereinafter cited as SJL-1.). He was baptized on 26 Feb 1871 St.Joseph, Leroy, Dakota Territory (Ibid.). He married Delphine Laplante, daughter of Antoine Laplante and Marie Rose Lucier, before 1907. He died on 8 Apr 1907 Olga, Cavalier County, North Dakota, at age 36 (Olga, page 353, S-_.). He was buried on 10 Apr 1907 Olga, Cavalier County, North Dakota (Ibid.).

        Delphine Laplante was born on 18 Jun 1885 (Ibid., page 74, B-33.). She was baptized on 26 Jun 1885 Olga, Cavalier County, North Dakota (Ibid.). She married **Antoine Larocque** before 1912.

     ii.   Pauline Villeneuve was born on 25 Aug 1872 (SJL-1, page 29, B-24.). She was baptized on 29 Aug 1872 St.Joseph, Leroy, Pembina County, Dakota Territory (Ibid.). She died on 4 Aug 1873 Leroy, Pembina County, Dakota Territory (Ibid., page 37, S-9.). She was buried on 5 Aug 1873 St.Joseph, Leroy, Pembina County, Dakota Territory (Ibid.).

20   iii.   Josephte Melanie Villeneuve, b. 19 Feb 1874; m. Albert Belisle; bur. 13 Oct 1908 St.Joseph, Leroy, Pembina County, North Dakota.

21   iv.   Norbert Villeneuve, b. 22 Apr 1876; m. Rose Laplante; d. 9 Feb 1960 Grand Forks County, North Dakota.

22   v.   Marie Genevieve Villeneuve, b. 8 Sep 1877 Willow Bunch, (Saskatchewan); m. Charles Nault; d. 13 May 1949 Victoria, British Columbia.

23   vi.   Agnes Villeneuve, b. circa 1878; m. Antoine Lariviere.

vii. Eleonore Villeneuve was born on 12 Oct 1879 Leroy, Pembina County, Dakota Territory (Ibid., page 96, B-67.). She was baptized on 12 Oct 1879 St.Joseph, Leroy, Pembina County, Dakota Territory (Ibid.).

viii. Francois D. Villeneuve was born on 12 Jul 1881 Leroy, Pembina County, Dakota Territory (Ibid., page 111, B-167.). He was baptized on 17 Jul 1881 St.Joseph, Leroy, Pembina County, Dakota Territory (Ibid.).

ix. Pierre George Villeneuve was born on 21 Jun 1883 (Ibid., page 127, B-284.). He was baptized on 8 Jul 1883 St.Joseph, Leroy, Pembina County, Dakota Territory (Ibid.).

x. Eugene Villeneuve was born on 28 Oct 1884 Neche, Dakota Territory (Ibid., page 139, B-380.). He was baptized on 21 Dec 1884 St.Joseph, Leroy, Pembina County, Dakota Territory (Ibid.).

xi. Marie Emma Valida Villeneuve was born on 8 May 1886 Leroy, Pembina County, Dakota Territory (Ibid., page 149, B-479.). She was baptized on 13 May 1886 St.Joseph, Leroy, Pembina County, Dakota Territory (Ibid.).

xii. Benedict Villeneuve was born on 26 Jul 1887 Leroy, Pembina County, Dakota Territory (Ibid., page 161, B-569.). He was baptized on 1 Aug 1887 St.Joseph, Leroy, Pembina County, Dakota Territory (Ibid.). He died on 22 Aug 1887 Leroy, Pembina County, Dakota Territory (Ibid., page 161, S-97.). He was buried on 23 Aug 1887 St.Joseph, Leroy, Pembina County, Dakota Territory (Ibid.).

xiii. Eva Villeneuve was born circa 1890. She married Wiliam McDowell on 5 Oct 1915 Olga, Cavalier County, North Dakota (Olga, page 21, M-_.).

Wiliam McDowell was born Concord, Kansas (Ibid.).

8. Cuthbert Villeneuve was born on 25 Jan 1851. He married **Genevieve Frederick dit Langis**, daughter of **Joseph Frederick dit Langis or Langer** and **Marie Anne Keplin**, before 2 Sep 1879 (SJL-1, page 95, M-9.). He married **Alphonsine Laframboise**, daughter of **Louis Laframboise** and **Marie Louise Martel**, on 2 Sep 1879 St.Joseph, Leroy, Pembina County, Dakota Territory (Ibid.). He died on 10 Nov 1908 Neche, Pembina County, North Dakota, at age 57 (Rod Mac Quarrie, 22 Dec 2009.).

Genevieve Frederick dit Langis was born circa Nov 1852 (AP, page 84, B-55.). She was baptized on 20 Feb 1853 Assumption, Pembina, Pembina County, Dakota Territory (Ibid.). She died before Sep 1879 (SJL-1, page 95, M-9.).

Alphonsine Laframboise was born on 16 Oct 1863 Walhalla, Pembina County, Dakota Territory (Ibid.) (Rod Mac Quarrie, 22 Dec 2009.). She died on 28 Feb 1941 Neche, Pembina County, North Dakota, at age 77 (ND Death Index.).

Children of **Cuthbert Villeneuve** and **Alphonsine Laframboise** were as follows:

i. Marie Virginie Villeneuve was born on 25 May 1880 (SJL-1, page 101, B-100.). She was baptized on 30 May 1880 St.Joseph, Leroy, Pembina County, Dakota Territory (Ibid.).

ii. Marie Eleanore Villeneuve was born on 7 Jul 1883 Olga, Cavalier County, North Dakota (Olga, page 12, B-3.). She was baptized on 9 Jul 1883 Olga, Cavalier County, North Dakota (Ibid.). She died on 12 Mar 1891 Neche, Pembina County, North Dakota, at age 7 (Rod Mac Quarrie, 22 Dec 2009.).

iii. Joseph Francois Albert Villeneuve was born on 27 Feb 1884 (Olga, page 40, B-11.). He was baptized on 25 Mar 1884 Olga, Cavalier County, North Dakota (Ibid.). He died on 10 Dec 1963 Grand Forks County, North Dakota, at age 79 (ND Death Index.).

iv. Joseph Marie Villeneuve was born on 9 Aug 1886 (Olga, page 106, B-42.). He was baptized on 15 Aug 1886 Olga, Cavalier County, North Dakota (Ibid.). He married Zepherine Bartlett on 28 Nov 1914 (Rod Mac Quarrie, 22 Dec 2009.). He died on 21 Nov 1958 Portland, Oregon, at age 72 (Ibid.).

v. Marie Lina Villeneuve was born on 4 Nov 1888 Neche, Pembina County, North Dakota (SJL-2 Register of Baptisms, Marriages, and Burials, St.Joseph, Leroy, North Dakota, Diocese of Saint Paul, Minnesota, 1888-1900, Book 2, page 21, B-21. Hereinafter cited as SJL-2.). She was baptized on 4 Nov 1888 St.Joseph, Leroy, Pembina County, North Dakota (Ibid.). She married George Allard on 4 Oct 1908 (Rod Mac Quarrie, 22 Dec 2009.).

vi. Henry Edward Villeneuve was born on 4 Nov 1890 Neche, Pembina County, North Dakota (1900CI-ND-Rolette *1900 Turtle Mountain Indian Reservation Census Index, Rolette County, North Dakota* compiled by Mary Ann Quiring and Lily B. Zwolle, (n.p.: Mary Ann Quiring and Lily B. Zwolle, 1984), #107-06b-93.) (Rod Mac Quarrie, 22 Dec 2009.). He married Marie Louise Cecelia Ruest, daughter of Epiphane Ruest and Marguerite Laderoute, circa 1910. He died on 13 Apr 1950 at age 59 (Ibid.).

Marie Louise Cecelia Ruest was baptized on 4 Oct 1889 Olga, North Dakota (Olga, page 171, B-39.). She died on 18 Jun 1986 at age 96 (Rod Mac Quarrie, 22 Dec 2009.). She was buried after 18 Jun 1986 St.Augustine's Roman Catholic Cemetery, Humboldt, Saskatchewan (Ibid.).

vii. Alphonse Morris Villeneuve was born on 22 Jul 1898 Neche, Pembina County, North Dakota (1900CI-ND-Rolette, #107-06b-93.) (Rod Mac Quarrie, 22 Dec 2009.). He died on 26 Jun 1923 Neche, Pembina County, North Dakota, at age 24 (Ibid.).

viii. Ellen Villeneuve was born on 8 Nov 1904 North Dakota (Ibid.). She married William Raymond Buck on 11 Nov 1926 Neche, Pembina County, North Dakota (Ibid.). She died on 10 Feb 1977 Lincoln, Nebraska, at age 72 (Ibid.).

William Raymond Buck was born on 14 Jul 1892 Chillicothe, Missouri (Ibid.). He died on 31 Oct 1972 Lincoln, Nebraska, at age 80 (Ibid.).

9. Severe Villeneuve was born circa 19 Feb 1854 Edmonton, (Alberta) (NWHBS, C-14942.). He was baptized on 19 Mar 1854 St.Albert, (Alberta) (Ibid.). He married **Nancy Courteoreille**, daughter of **Jacques Courteoreille** and **Marie Hamelin**, between 1872 and 1873 Peace River, (Alberta) (Ibid.). He married **Julie Boucher**, daughter of **Thomas Boucher** and **Catherine Gladu**, on 12 Jan 1891 St.Albert, (Alberta) (Denney.).

Nancy Courteoreille was born in 1857 St.Albert, (Alberta) (NWHBS, C-14942.).

Children of **Severe Villeneuve** and **Nancy Courteoreille** were as follows:

i. Eliza Villeneuve was born in 1875 Peace River, (Alberta) (ArchiviaNet.). She married (--?--) Paquette before 1900 (Ibid.).

ii. Alfred Villeneuve was born in May 1877 Dunvegan, (Alberta) (Ibid., C-15008.).

24 iii. Marie Pauline Villeneuve, b. 27 May 1877 Peace River, Dunvegan, (Alberta).

    iv. Francois Villeneuve was born in 1880 Vermillion, (Alberta) (HBSI.) (ArchiviaNet.). He died in Jun 1898 (HBSI.) (ArchiviaNet.).

    v. Severe Louis Villeneuve was born on 19 May 1883 St.Albert, (Alberta) (Denney.).

    vi. Jean Severe Villeneuve was born in 1885 St.Albert, (Alberta) (HBSI.) (ArchiviaNet.). He died in Jun 1892 (HBSI.) (ArchiviaNet.).

Julie Boucher was born in 1865 Lac Ste.Anne, (Alberta) (NWHBS, C-14936.).

Children of **Severe Villeneuve** and **Julie Boucher** were as follows:

    i. Paul Michel Villeneuve was baptized on 23 Jul 1893 St.Albert, (Alberta) (Denney.). He married Maggie St.Denis in 1917 Calgary, Alberta (Ibid.). He died on 21 Jan 1961 Calgary, Alberta, at age 67 (Ibid.).

    ii. Henry Villeneuve was born in 1898 Dawson, North West Territories. He died on 22 Sep 1972 Edmonton, (Alberta).

10. Eliza Villeneuve was born on 9 Apr 1858 North Dakota (1900C-ND 1900 United States Census, North Dakota, National Archives of the United States, Washington, D. C., 234-235.) (ND Death Index.). She married **Antoine Nicholas** in 1876 (1900C-ND, 234-235.). She died on 4 Apr 1927 Devils Lake, Ramsey County, North Dakota, at age 68 (ND Death Index.).

    Antoine Nicholas was born on 28 Mar 1848 Prescott County, Ontario (1900C-ND, House 235, page 298B.) (ND Death Index.). He died on 9 Jan 1928 Devils Lake, Ramsey County, North Dakota, at age 79 (Ibid.).

11. Alexandre Villeneuve was born on 17 Jan 1860 Pembina County, Dakota Territory (AP, page 223, B-146.). He was baptized on 2 Feb 1860 Assumption, Pembina, Pembina County, Dakota Territory (Ibid.). He married **Marie McDonald** before 1878. He married **Marie Bottineau** before 1880.

Children of **Alexandre Villeneuve** and **Marie McDonald** were:

    i. Charles William Augustin Henri Villeneuve was born on 20 Feb 1878 (SJL-1, page 86, B-4.). He was baptized on 2 Mar 1878 St.Joseph, Leroy, Pembina County, Dakota Territory (Ibid.).

Children of **Alexandre Villeneuve** and **Marie Bottineau** were:

    i. Marie Anne Villeneuve was born on 23 Mar 1880 (Ibid., page 99, B-86.). She was baptized on 28 Mar 1880 St.Joseph, Leroy, Pembina County, Dakota Territory (Ibid.).

Generation Three

12. Pascal Villeneuve was born in Aug 1873 North Dakota (1900C-ND, 448-448.). He married **Marie Celina Gariepy**, daughter of **Norbert Gariepy** and **Marie des Anges Desjarlais**, in 1898 (Ibid.). He married **Elise Parisien**, daughter of **Edouard Parisien** and **Blandine Poitras**, circa 1911. He died on 5 Nov 1934 Rolette County, North Dakota, at age 61 (1934-TMC Census of the Turtle Mountain Chippewa Indians, United States Indian Service Department of the Interior, Turtle Mountain Agency, North Dakota, 1 Apr 1934.) (ND Death Index.).

Marie Celina Gariepy was born on 18 Jan 1877 Big Bend - Milk River, Montana Territory (SPMT St.Peter's Mission; Volume I; Marriage Register 1859-1895; Translated & Transcribed by Reverend Dale McFarlane, Archivist, Diocese of Great Falls-Billings, Montana; Spring 1981, page 104, #2271.). She was baptized on 1 Feb 1877 (St.Peter's Mission), Big Bend - Milk River, Montana Territory (Ibid.). She died on 25 Jun 1908 Belcourt, Rolette County, North Dakota, at age 31.

Children of **Pascal Villeneuve** and **Marie Celina Gariepy** were as follows:

    25 i. Marie Agnes Villeneuve, b. 26 Jan 1899 North Dakota; m. Louis St.Claire.

    26 ii. Josephine Christine Villeneuve, b. 9 Aug 1900; m. Gideon Nicholas.

    27 iii. Edward Villeneuve, b. 25 Aug 1902; m. Florence Amyotte; d. 7 Mar 1923 Rolette County, North Dakota.

    28 iv. Mary Alice Villeneuve, b. 7 Sep 1904; m. Emery St.Claire.

    29 v. Joseph Alfred Villeneuve, b. 14 Jul 1906; m. Rachel St.Claire.

Elise Parisien was born on 6 Oct 1888 Rolette County, North Dakota (Rod Mac Quarrie, 17 Jan 2013.) (ND Death Index.). She died on 19 Jul 1968 Rolette County, North Dakota, at age 79 (Ibid.).

Children of **Pascal Villeneuve** and **Elise Parisien** were as follows:

    30 i. Herman P. Villeneuve, b. 10 Oct 1911; m. Ernestine Lafontaine; d. 29 Oct 1985.

    ii. Joseph Alphonse Villeneuve was born on 6 Nov 1912 (1936-TMC, page 124.) (BIA-TM-BMD, page 60.). He died before 1936 (1936-TMC, page 124.).

    iii. Alfred Louis Villeneuve was born on 11 Jun 1914 (Ibid.) (1916-TMC 1916 Census of the Turtle Mountain Chippewa, North Dakota, National Archives of the United States, Washington D.C.). He died on 1 Feb 1926 Rolette County, North Dakota, at age 11 (ND Death Index.) (1926-27-TMC Deaths of the Turtle Mountain Chippewa Indians, United States Indian Service Department of the Interior, Turtle Mountain Agency, North Dakota, F. J. Scott Superintendent, 1 July 1926-30 June 1927.).

    iv. Henry Villeneuve was born on 6 Mar 1916 (*1937-TMC.*).

    v. Martin Villeneuve was born on 15 Oct 1918 (Ibid.). He died on 8 May 2002 Dunseith, North Dakota, at age 83 (SSDI.) (ND Death Index.).

    vi. Eugene Albert Villeneuve was born on 2 Apr 1921 (*1937-TMC.*). He died on 7 Feb 1988 Mountrail County, North Dakota, at age 66 (ND Death Index.).

    vii. Nora Rosalie Villeneuve was born on 29 Apr 1924 (*1937-TMC.*).

    viii. Emelia Villeneuve was born on 5 Jul 1926 (Ibid.). She died on 21 Nov 1980 Rolette County, North Dakota, at age 54 (ND Death Index.).

    ix. Evangeline Orel Villeneuve was born on 26 Sep 1928 (1928-32-TMC Birth-Deaths of the Turtle Mountain Chippewa Indians, United States Indian Service Department of the Interior, Turtle Mountain Agency, North Dakota, F. J. Scott Superintendent, 1 July 1928-30 June 1932.). She died in 1929 (Ibid.).

13. Daniel Villeneuve was born on 10 Apr 1868 Touchwood Hills, (Saskatchewan) (SFXI-Kipling, B-36.). He was baptized on 3 May 1868 St.Francois Xavier, (Manitoba) (Ibid.). He married **Marie Rose Ouellette**, daughter of **Jean Baptiste Ouellette** and **Cecile**

Courchene, on 25 Feb 1895 St.Vital, Battleford, (Saskatchewan) (SV St.Vital Roman Catholic Registre des Baptemes, Mariages & Sepltures, Battleford, Saskatchewan, 1878-1896, M-2. Hereinafter cited as SV.).

Marie Rose Ouellette was born on 23 Dec 1873 Buffalo Lake, Edmonton District, (Alberta) (1901 Canada, #205, J(2), page 2, family 11, line 9-18.) (ArchiviaNet, C-15008.).

Children of Daniel Villeneuve and Marie Rose Ouellette all born (Saskatchewan) were as follows:

    i.   Marie Villeneuve was born on 10 Feb 1896 (1901 Canada, #205, J(2), page 2, family 11, line line 9-18.).

    ii.   Marie A. Villeneuve was born on 15 Dec 1897 (Ibid.).

    iii.   George Villeneuve was born on 10 Dec 1900 (Ibid.).

14. Marie Villeneuve was born on 31 Oct 1869 Victoria (HBSI.). She was born on 11 Nov 1871 (1901 Canada, #205, H(1), page 1, family 1, line 1-8.). She married Joseph Nolin, son of Joseph Nolin and Marie Anne Gaudry, on 2 Feb 1891 St.Vital, Battleford, (Saskatchewan) (SV, page 89, M-1.).

Joseph Nolin was born on 17 May 1867 St.Boniface, (Manitoba) (SB-Rozyk, page 85, B-39.). He was baptized on 17 May 1867 St.Boniface, (Manitoba) (Ibid.).

15. Marguerite Villeneuve was born in 1878 Maple Creek, (Saskatchewan) (ArchiviaNet, C-14967.). She married Patrice Dumont, son of St.Pierre Dumont and Betsy Breland, before 1898 (1901 Canada, microfilm, T-6553, Egg Lake, page 1, Family 3, line 11-16.).

Patrice Dumont was born in Feb 1868 (NWHBS, C-14936.). He was baptized on 25 Mar 1868 St.Albert, (Alberta) (Ibid.).

16. Isabelle Villeneuve was born on 4 Jul 1878 Maple Creek, (Saskatchewan) (Ibid., Birth Reg. #12172.). She married Adelard Lafournaise, son of Elzear Lafournaise dit Laboucane and Agathe Gariepy, before 1905.

Adelard Lafournaise was born in 1876 Buffalo Lake, (Alberta) (ArchiviaNet.).

17. Isidore Villeneuve Jr was born on 12 Apr 1871 Dunvegan, (Alberta) (1901 Canada, Fish Creek, page 1, Family 1, Line 1-3.) (ArchiviaNet, C-15008.). He married Rosalie Champagne, daughter of Ambroise Champagne and Judith Frederick or Langer, before 1899 (Ibid.).

Rosalie Champagne was born on 4 Jan 1876 (L1 Lebret Mission de St.Florent Roman Catholic Registre des Baptemes, Mariages & Sepltures, Qu'Appelle, Saskatchewan, 1868-1881., page 175, B-45. Hereinafter cited as L1.). She was baptized on 8 Jan 1876 Lebret, (Saskatchewan) (Ibid.). She died on 6 Apr 1941 Batoche, Saskatchewan, at age 65 (Denney.).

Children of Isidore Villeneuve Jr. and Rosalie Champagne are as follows:

    i.   Isidore Villeneuve was born on 14 Sep 1899 Batoche, (Saskatchewan) (SK Vital Statistics, Birth Reg. #1790.).

    ii.   Elise Villeneuve was born on 5 Nov 1907 Batoche, Saskatchewan (BSAP, page 248, B-12.). She was baptized on 11 Nov 1907 Batoche, Saskatchewan (Ibid.).

18. Joseph Villeneuve was born on 12 Dec 1876 St.Charles, Manitoba (1901 Canada, Fish Creek, page 8, Family 6, Line 25-29.) (Rod Mac Quarrie, 17 Jan 2013.). He was baptized on 12 Dec 1876 St.Charles, Manitoba (Ibid.). He married Julienne Parenteau, daughter of Pierre Parenteau and Helene Normand, on 12 Aug 1902 Batoche, (Saskatchewan) (BSAP, page 217, M-3.).

Julienne Parenteau was born on 15 Mar 1872 St.Norbert, Manitoba (SN1, B-13.). She was baptized on 15 Mar 1872 St.Norbert, Manitoba (Ibid.).

Children of Joseph Villeneuve and Julienne Parenteau were as follows:

    i.   Julienne Villeneuve was born on 20 Dec 1903 Batoche, (Saskatchewan) (BSAP, page 224, B-17.) (SK Vital Statistics, Birth Reg. #3295.). She was baptized on 22 Dec 1903 Batoche, (Saskatchewan) (BSAP, page 224, B-17.).

    ii.   Laurent Villeneuve was born on 21 Jul 1905 St.Julien, (Saskatchewan) (Ibid., page 237, S-4.) (SK Vital Statistics, Birth Reg. #5026.). He died on 25 Mar 1906 Batoche, (Saskatchewan) (BSAP, page 237, S-4.). He was buried on 27 Mar 1906 Batoche, (Saskatchewan) (Ibid.).

    iii.   Jules Villeneuve was born on 12 Jul 1907 Batoche, Saskatchewan (Ibid., page 246, B-7.) (SK Vital Statistics, Birth Reg. #7921.). He was baptized on 19 Jul 1907 Batoche, Saskatchewan (BSAP, page 246, B-7.). He died on 13 Jan 1908 Batoche, Saskatchewan (Ibid., page 250, S-1.) (SK Vital Statistics, Death Reg. #1881.). He was buried on 15 Jan 1908 Batoche, Saskatchewan (BSAP, page 250, S-1.).

    iv.   Marie Lucie Villeneuve was born on 16 Jul 1909 (Ibid., page 258, B-12.). She was baptized on 8 Aug 1909 Batoche, Saskatchewan (Ibid.). She married Octave Fiddler, son of John William Fidler and Julienne Delorme, on 17 Dec 1925 (Louis Verhagen Research.). She died on 9 Dec 1992 Batoche, Saskatchewan, at age 83 (Ibid.).

        Octave Fiddler was born on 24 Oct 1894 Batoche, (Saskatchewan) (BSAP, page 119, B-19.) (SK Vital Statistics, #7792.). He was baptized on 28 Oct 1894 Batoche, (Saskatchewan) (BSAP, page 119, B-19.). He died on 17 Aug 1975 Batoche, Saskatchewan, at age 80 (Louis Verhagen.).

    v.   Leonie Villeneuve was born in Jul 1910 (Automated Genealogy 1911 Census Transcription Project and Census Images from the National Archives of Canada, http://www.automatedgenealogy.com, District 2, page 15, line 15.).

    vi.   George Villeneuve was born circa 1913 (1916 Census of Canada from the National Archives of Canada (Transcription by ancestry.com), Ottawa, Canada, District 25-8, page 19, line 10.).

19. Joseph Villeneuve was born circa 1867 (1881 Canada, District 192-U, page 3, family 10.). He married Marie Augustine Bouvier, daughter of Joseph Bouvier and Marguerite Laferte, on 30 Jul 1896 Fort Providence, (Northwest Territory) (Marie Beaupre.).

Marie Augustine Bouvier was born on 28 Jun 1879 Fort Providence, (Northwest Territory) (Ibid.). She was baptized on 28 Jun 1879 Fort Providence, (Northwest Territory) (Ibid.).

Children of Joseph Villeneuve and Marie Augustine Bouvier all born Fort Providence, (Northwest Territory), were as follows:

    i.   Joseph Villeneuve was born on 20 May 1898 (Ibid.). He was baptized on 20 May 1898 Fort Providence, (Northwest Territory) (Ibid.).

    ii.   Xavier Villeneuve was born on 25 Apr 1900 (Ibid.). He was baptized on 26 Apr 1900 Fort Providence, (Northwest Territory) (Ibid.). He was buried on 5 Nov 1901 Fort Providence, (Northwest Territory) (Ibid.).

    iii.   Isidore Villeneuve was born on 6 Sep 1902 (Ibid.). He was baptized on 6 Sep 1902 Fort Providence, (Northwest Territory) (Ibid.).

     iv.   Jeanne Villeneuve was born on 23 Mar 1905 (Ibid.). She was baptized on 23 Mar 1905 Fort Providence, (Northwest Territory) (Ibid.).

     v.   Marguerite Villeneuve was baptized on 24 Sep 1907 (Ibid.).

     vi.   Rosalie Villeneuve was born on 19 Sep 1910 (Ibid.). She was baptized on 20 Sep 1910 Fort Providence, (Northwest Territory) (Ibid.).

20. Josephte Melanie Villeneuve was born on 19 Feb 1874 (SJL-1, page 44-45, B-8.). She was baptized on 21 Feb 1874 St.Joseph, Leroy, Pembina County, Dakota Territory (Ibid.). She married **Albert Belisle**, son of **Jean Belisle** and **Delia Lamoureux**, on 16 Oct 1897 St.Joseph, Leroy, Pembina County, North Dakota (SJL-2, M-_.). She was buried on 13 Oct 1908 St.Joseph, Leroy, Pembina County, North Dakota (SJL-D St.Joseph Leroy, North Dakota, Record of Interments 1888-1932, page 19.).

21. Norbert Villeneuve was born on 22 Apr 1876 (SJL-1, page 70, B-13.) (ND Death Index.). He was baptized on 23 Apr 1876 St.Joseph, Leroy, Pembina County, Dakota Territory (SJL-1, page 70, B-13.). He married **Rose Laplante**, daughter of **Guillaume Laplante** and **Marguerite Sansregret**, before 1902. He died on 9 Feb 1960 Grand Forks County, North Dakota, at age 83 (ND Death Index.).

    Rose Laplante was born on 30 Oct 1884 Batoche, (Saskatchewan) (BSAP, page 26, B-29.). She was baptized on 3 Nov 1884 Batoche, (Saskatchewan) (Ibid.).

    Children of **Norbert Villeneuve** and **Rose Laplante** are as follows:

     i.   Alfred Victor Theodore Villeneuve was baptized on 9 Nov 1902 Olga, Cavalier County, North Dakota (Olga, page 321, B-_.).

     ii.   Antoine Maurice Laurence Villeneuve was born on 22 Apr 1904 Olga, Cavalier County, North Dakota (Ibid., page 335, B-_.). He was baptized on 24 May 1904 Olga, Cavalier County, North Dakota (Ibid.).

     iii.   Ida Villeneuve was born circa 1914 North Dakota (1930C ND Fifteenth Census of the United States: 1930; North Dakota, National Archives of the United States, Washington, D.C., Sheet 2A, family 25, line 11-16.).

     iv.   Viola Villeneuve was born circa 1915 North Dakota (Ibid.).

     v.   Louis Villeneuve was born circa 1918 North Dakota (Ibid.).

     vi.   Lorraine Villeneuve was born circa 1922 North Dakota (Ibid.).

22. Marie Genevieve Villeneuve was born on 8 Sep 1877 Willow Bunch, (Saskatchewan) (Nellie Nault, 27 Aug 1993.). She married **Charles Nault**, son of **Charles Nault** and **Marie Louise Morin**, between 24 Aug 1899 and 10 Sep 1899 Olga, Cavalier County, North Dakota (Olga, page 289, M-_.). She died on 13 May 1949 Victoria, British Columbia, at age 71 (Nellie Nault, 27 Aug 1993.).

    Charles Nault was born on 5 Jul 1870 St.Boniface, (Manitoba) (SB-Rozyk, page 187, B-58.). He was baptized on 6 Jul 1870 St.Boniface, (Manitoba) (Ibid.). He died on 21 Jun 1953 Victoria, British Columbia, at age 82 (Nellie Nault, 27 Aug 1993.).

23. Agnes Villeneuve was born circa 1878. She married **Antoine Lariviere**, son of **Antoine Lariviere** and **Therese Laliberte**, in 1896 Olga, Cavalier County, North Dakota (Denney.).

    Antoine Lariviere was born on 8 Aug 1875 St.Boniface, (Manitoba) (Ibid.). He died on 29 Nov 1957 at age 82 (Ibid.).

24. Marie Pauline Villeneuve was born on 27 May 1877 Peace River, Dunvegan, (Alberta) (HBS 1886-1901, 1906 Half-Breed Scrip Applications, RG15-21, Volume 1336; C-14949.) (1901 Canada, #202, D-4, page 4, family 30, line 20-22.). She married **Jeremie Belcourt**, son of **Edwin Belcourt** and **Louise Paul**, before 1900 St.Albert, (Alberta) (1901 Alberta Census Index, Alberta Genealogical Society, Edmonton, Alberta, www.agsedm.edmonton.ab.ca, page 4, line 20-22, St.Albert.).

    Jeremie Belcourt was born on 10 Jan 1877 St.Albert, (Alberta) (HBS, Volume 1335; C-14948.) (1901 Canada, #202, D-4, page 4, family 30, line 20-22.). He was baptized on 19 Nov 1877 Ste.Anne, (Alberta) (HBS, Volume 1335; C-14948.).

Generation Four

25. Marie Agnes Villeneuve was born on 26 Jan 1899 North Dakota (1900C-ND, 448-448.) (1916-TMC.). She married **Louis St.Claire**, son of **Alexander Sinclair** and **Adeline Amyotte**, on 2 Aug 1915 Belcourt, Rolette County, North Dakota.

    Louis St.Claire was born in Feb 1894 North Dakota (1900C-ND, 452-452.). He died on 16 Dec 1972 Fort Totten, North Dakota, at age 78.

26. Josephine Christine Villeneuve was born on 9 Aug 1900 (1936-TMC, page 182.) (1918-TMC, Census No. 2521-2524.). She married **Gideon Nicholas**, son of **Antoine Nicholas** and **Eliza Villeneuve**, before 1915 (1936-TMC, page 182.).

    Gideon Nicholas was born on 28 Dec 1897 (Ibid.) (1918-TMC, Census No. 2521-2524.). He died in Mar 1965 at age 67 (SSDI.).

27. Edward Villeneuve was born on 25 Aug 1902 (1936-TMC, page 124.) (1916-TMC.). He married **Florence Amyotte**, daughter of **Louis Amyotte** and **Marie Philomene Lafontaine**, before 1923 (*1937-TMC*, page 195, Census No. 2324-2331.). He died on 7 Mar 1923 Rolette County, North Dakota, at age 20 (ND Death Index.).

    Florence Amyotte was born on 30 Dec 1905 (1936-TMC, page 22.) (1922 Turtle Mountain Chippewa Indian Census Roll, United States Indian Service Department of the Interior, Turtle Mountain Indian Agency, North Dakota, 30 June 1922, Census No. 264-275.). She married **William Godon** circa 1924 (*1937-TMC*, page 195, Census No. 2324-2331.).

    Children of **Edward Villeneuve** and **Florence Amyotte** are:

     i.   Sarah Villeneuve was born on 20 Mar 1923 (Ibid.).

28. Mary Alice Villeneuve was born on 7 Sep 1904 (1936-TMC, page 124.) (1916-TMC.). She married **Emery St.Claire**, son of **Alexander Sinclair** and **Adeline Amyotte**, before 1921 (*1937-TMC*, page 473, Census No. 5518-5523.).

    Emery St.Claire was born in Jul 1897 North Dakota (1900C-ND, 452-452.).

29. Joseph Alfred Villeneuve was born on 14 Jul 1906 (1936-TMC, page 124.) (1916-TMC.). He married **Rachel St.Claire** before 1929 (*1937-TMC*, page 510, Census No. 5967-5973.).

    Rachel St.Claire was born circa 1911 (Ibid.).

    Children of **Joseph Alfred Villeneuve** and **Rachel St.Claire** were as follows:

     i.   Louise Villeneuve was born on 7 Apr 1929 (Ibid.).

     ii.   Leona Villeneuve was born on 27 Aug 1930 (Ibid.).

iii. Grace Telephine Villeneuve was born on 7 Jan 1933 (Ibid.). She married William F. Decoteau on 5 Jul 1955 Dunseith, Rolette County, North Dakota. She died on 20 Jul 2014 Belcourt, Rolette County, North Dakota, at age 81.

    William F. Decoteau was born on 22 Jul 1930 (SSDI.). He died on 28 Feb 1998 Dunseith, Rolette County, North Dakota, at age 67 (Ibid.).

iv. Lorraine M. Villeneuve was born on 2 Aug 1935 (*1937-TMC*, page 510, Census No. 5967-5973.).

30. Herman P. Villeneuve was born on 10 Oct 1911 (1936-TMC, page 124.) (BIA-TM-BMD, page 51.) (1919 Turtle Mountain Indian Census Roll, United States Indian Service Department of the Interior, Turtle Mountain Indian Agency, North Dakota, 30 June 1919 , Census No. 3157-3163.). He married **Ernestine Lafontaine**, daughter of **Pierre Frederic Lafontaine** and **Isabelle Delaunay**, before 1934 (*1937-TMC*, page 509, Census No. 5962-5966.). He died on 29 Oct 1985 Saint Paul, Ramsey County, Minnesota, at age 74 (SSDI.) (Minnesota Department of Health Public Death Index.).

Ernestine Lafontaine was born on 26 Mar 1917 (1936-TMC, page 134.) (*1937-TMC*, page 509, Census No. 5962-5966.) (SSDI.). She died on 1 Oct 2002 Saint Paul, Ramsey County, Minnesota, at age 85 (Ibid.).

Children of **Herman P. Villeneuve** and **Ernestine Lafontaine** were as follows:

i. Rose Marie Villeneuve was born on 2 Sep 1934 (*1937-TMC*, page 509, Census No. 5962-5966.).

ii. Michael Joseph Villeneuve was born on 7 Oct 1935 (Ibid.). He died on 1 Oct 2010 Forest Lake, Washington County, Minnesota, at age 74 (SSDI.).

iii. Martha Villeneuve was born on 18 Oct 1936 (*1937-TMC*, page 509, Census No. 5962-5966.).

Descendants of Thomas Vincent

Generation One

1. Thomas Vincent was born in 1776 England (Denney Papers, Charles D. Denney, Glenbow Archives, Calgary, Alberta.). He married according to the custom of the country **Jane Renton**, daughter of **William Renton** and **Bay Wife (--?--)**, before 1797. He married **Jane Sutherland**, daughter of **James Sutherland,** circa 1817 (HBCA-B Hudson's Bay Company Archives - biographical sketches, Hudson's Bay Company Archives; Winnipeg, Manitoba.). He died on 30 Mar 1832 Hartlepool, Durham, England (Ibid.) (Rod MacQuarrie Research, 4 June 2010.).

Jane Renton was born circa 1778 Moose Factory (HBCA-B.). She died on 17 Sep 1858 Moose Factory (Rod Mac Quarrie, 4 June 2010.).

Children of **Thomas Vincent** and **Jane Renton** were as follows:

2 i. John Vincent, b. 15 Jul 1797 North West; m. Charlotte Thomas; m. Charlotte Thomas; d. 27 Jan 1874 St.Paul, Manitoba.

3 ii. Harriet Vincent, b. circa 1798; m. David Ramsey Stewart; m. George Gladman Jr; d. 31 Oct 1877 Port Hope, Hope Township, Durham County, Ontario.

4 iii. Elizabeth Vincent, b. 1802; m. Jacob Truthwaite; d. 6 Jul 1875 St.Andrews, Manitoba; bur. 8 Jul 1875 St.Andrews, Manitoba.

    iv. James Vincent was born circa 1803 (HBCA-B, A.36/14; A.44/2, p. 57.).

    v. Jane Vincent was born in 1806 (Ibid., MS311 #2, MS 161, Ontario Archives; A.36/14; A.44/2, p. 57.). She was baptized on 17 Sep 1809 Albany (Ibid.). She married Edward Chambers in 1832 (Ibid.).

    vi. Thomas Vincent was born on 18 Jan 1810 (Ibid., MS311 #2, MS 161, Ontario Archives.). He was baptized on 10 Feb 1810 Moose Factory (Ibid.). He was baptized on 1 Nov 1820 Stromness, Orkney, Scotland (Rod Mac Quarrie, 4 June 2010.). He died in 1851 London, England (HBCA-B, MS311 #2, MS 161, Ontario Archives.).

Generation Two

2. John Vincent was born on 15 Jul 1797 North West (Denney.). He married according to the custom of the country **Charlotte Thomas**, daughter of **William Thomas**, before 1824. He married **Charlotte Thomas**, daughter of **William Thomas,** on 21 Dec 1843 (St.Johns), Upper Church, Red River Settlement, Rupertsland (HBCR Hudson Bay Company Register of Anglican Church Baptisms, Marriages, and Burials for the Red River Settlement, 1821-1841; Hudson's Bay Company Archives, Winnipeg, Manitoba, No. _. Hereinafter cited as HBCR.). He died on 27 Jan 1874 St.Paul, Manitoba, at age 76 (Denney.).

Charlotte Thomas was born on 27 Aug 1806 North West (Ibid.). She died on 8 Dec 1894 St.Paul, Manitoba, at age 88 (Manitoba Vital Statistics online, http://web2.gov.mb.ca, Death Reg. #1894,002830.).

Children of **John Vincent** and **Charlotte Thomas** were as follows:

5 i. Elisabeth Vincent, b. 9 Oct 1824 North West; m. Alexander Dahl.

6 ii. Mary Vincent, b. circa 1826; m. William Peebles; d. 19 Nov 1846 Upper Church District, Red River, Rupertsland.

7 iii. John Vincent, b. 5 Feb 1830; m. Mary Thomas; m. Elizabeth Slater; d. 9 May 1904.

    iv. Eleanor Vincent was born circa 1833 (Denney.). She was baptized on 22 Sep 1840 St.Johns, Red River Settlement, (Manitoba) (HBCR, E.4/1a, folio 171.). She died on 27 Dec 1843 Upper Church District, Red River, Rupertsland (Rod Mac Quarrie, 4 June 2010.). She was buried on 27 Dec 1843 Upper Church District, Red River, Rupertsland (Ibid.).

8 v. Archdeacon Thomas Vincent, b. 1 Mar 1835 Osnaburg House, Keewatin; m. Eliza Ann Gladman; d. 16 Jan 1907 Albany; bur. Jan 1907 Moose Factory.

9 vi. William Thomas Vincent, b. 14 Oct 1837 St.Paul, (Manitoba); m. Catherine Ross; d. 12 Jan 1915 Rockwood, Manitoba.

    vii. Harriet Vincent was born circa 1838 (Denney.). She was baptized on 22 Sep 1840 St.Johns, Red River Settlement, (Manitoba) (HBCR, E.4/1a, folio 171d.). She died on 23 Dec 1843 St.Johns, (Manitoba) (Denney.). She was buried in Dec 1843 St.Johns, (Manitoba) (Ibid.).

10 viii. Sarah Jane Vincent, b. between 1841 and 1847; m. John Fraser; d. 11 Apr 1929.

11 ix. James Vincent, b. 20 Jan 1842 Red River, (Manitoba); m. Clara Caroline Gladman; m. Ann Agnes Linklater; d. 30 Oct 1909 Stonewall, Manitoba.

x. Albert Thomas Vincent was baptized on 5 Jan 1845 St.Johns, (Manitoba) (Ibid.). He died on 2 Mar 1850 St.Johns, (Manitoba), at age 5 (Ibid.).

12 xi. Charlotte Vincent, b. 25 Nov 1849 St.Paul, (Manitoba); m. Charles Richard Thomas; d. 9 Apr 1902 Winnipeg, Manitoba.

xii. Henry Vincent was born in 1851 (Manitoba) (Ibid.).

13 xiii. George Gladman Vincent, b. 28 Feb 1852 St.Paul, (Manitoba); m. Harriet Mary Work; d. 27 Apr 1921 Winnipeg, Manitoba.

3. Harriet Vincent was born circa 1798 (HBCA-B, B.3/a/112; MS311 #2, MS 161, Ontario Archives; A.36/14; A.44/2.). She was baptized on 17 Sep 1809 Albany (HBCA-B.). She married **David Ramsey Stewart** before 1818. She married **George Gladman Jr.**, son of **George Gladman Sr.** and **Mary Indian**, circa 1827 (Ibid., B.3/a/112; MS311 #2, MS 161, Ontario Archives; A.36/14; A.44/2.) (Ibid., A.36/14, Will 15 Feb 1841; DCB IX.). She died on 31 Oct 1877 Port Hope, Hope Township, Durham County, Ontario (Rod Mac Quarrie, 4 June 2010.).

David Ramsey Stewart was born on 26 Sep 1787 Glenmuick, Aberdeen, Scotland (Ibid.).

George Gladman Jr was born on 23 Jun 1800 Brunswick Lake, (Ontario) (*DCB-V9 Dictionary of Canadian Biography - Volume Nine*;Toronto, Ontario: University of Toronto Press, 2000).). He died on 24 Sep 1863 Port Hope, Durham County, Ontario, at age 63 (Ibid.).

4. Elizabeth Vincent was born in 1802 (MBS Scrip Applications, Original White Settlers & Halfbreeds residing in Manitoba on 15 July 1870, RG15-19, C-14934.). She was baptized on 17 Sep 1809 Albany (HBCA-B, B.3/a/112; MS311 #2, MS 161, Ontario Archives; A.36/14; A.44/2, p. 57.). She was baptized on 12 Mar 1830 St.Johns, Red River Settlement, (Manitoba) (HBCR, E.4/1a, folio 75d.). She married according to the custom of the country **Jacob Truthwaite**, son of **Mathew Truthwaite** and **Elizabeth Indian,** before 1816. She married **Jacob Truthwaite**, son of **Mathew Truthwaite** and **Elizabeth Indian**, on 12 Mar 1830 Red River Settlement, (Manitoba) (Ibid., M-196.) (HBCA-B, E.4/1a fo. 75d; E.4/1b, fo. 227.). She died on 6 Jul 1875 St.Andrews, Manitoba (MBS, C-14934.). She was buried on 8 Jul 1875 St.Andrews, Manitoba (Denney.).

Jacob Truthwaite was born circa 1786 (HBCA-B.). He was born circa 1790 Ruperts Land (1830C RRS HBCA E5/4 1830 Census of the Red River Settlement, HBCA E5/4, Hudson's Bay Company Archives, Provincial Archives, 200 Vaughan Street, Winnipeg, MB R3C 1T5, Canada., page 14.) (1870C-MB 1870 Manitoba Census, National Archives of Canada, Ottawa, Ontario, Microfilm Reel Number C-2170., page 194, #543.). He was baptized on 12 Mar 1830 St.Johns, Red River Settlement, (Manitoba) (HBCR, E.4/1a, folio 75d.). He died on 8 Jan 1873 St.Andrews, Manitoba (MBS, C-14934.). He was buried on 11 Jan 1873 St.Andrews, Manitoba (Ibid.).

Generation Three

5. Elisabeth Vincent was born on 9 Oct 1824 North West (MBS, C-14934.). She was baptized on 28 Sep 1840 St.Johns, Red River Settlement, (Manitoba) (HBCR, E.4/1a, folio 171d.). She married **Alexander Dahl**, son of **Peter Dahl** and **Catherine Murray**, on 18 Apr 1844 (St.Johns), Upper Church, Red River Settlement, (Manitoba) (Ibid., No. __.).

Alexander Dahl was born on 26 May 1822 St.Paul, (Manitoba) (MBS, C-14926.) (HBCR, E.4/1a, folio 37.). He was baptized on 9 Jun 1822 St.Johns, Red River Colony, (Manitoba) (Ibid.). He married according to the custom of the country **Jane Folster**, daughter of **James Folster** and **Jane Cree**, before 1848. He died on 11 Dec 1879 St.Paul, Manitoba, at age 57 (Denney.).

6. Mary Vincent was born circa 1826 (Rod Mac Quarrie, 4 June 2010.). She married **William Peebles**, son of **James Peebles** and **Mary Indian**, on 5 Jun 1842 Albany (HBCA-B.). She died on 19 Nov 1846 Upper Church District, Red River, Rupertsland (Rod Mac Quarrie, 4 June 2010.).

William Peebles was born on 12 May 1812 Albany House, North West (MBS, C-14932.). He was baptized on 5 Jun 1842 (HBCA-B, B.3/a/147.). He married **Catherine Harcus**, daughter of **David Harcus** and **Margaret Richards**, on 1 Mar 1849 (St.Andrews), The Rapids, Red River Settlement, (Manitoba) (HBCA-B.) (HBCR, No. 180.). He died on 13 Dec 1883 St.Andrews, Manitoba, at age 71 (MB Vital Statistics, Death Reg. #1883,002557.).

7. John Vincent was born on 5 Feb 1830 (Denney.). He was baptized on 22 Sep 1840 St.Johns, Red River Settlement, (Manitoba) (HBCR, E.4/1a, folio 171d.). He married **Mary Thomas** before 1852. He married **Elizabeth Slater**, daughter of **John Slater** and **Elizabeth Dennett**, on 26 Mar 1863 St.Andrews, (Manitoba) (Denney.). He died on 9 May 1904 at age 74 (Ibid.).

Mary Thomas died before 1863.

Children of **John Vincent** and **Mary Thomas** all born St.Paul, (Manitoba), were as follows:

i. Catherine Vincent was baptized on 13 Apr 1852 (Ibid.).

14 ii. Thomas Vincent, b. 28 Apr 1853; m. Mary Tait; d. 12 Feb 1934.

iii. Pheobe Sophie 'Sarah' Vincent was born on 3 Apr 1855 (Ibid.). She was baptized on 29 Apr 1855 St.Paul, (Manitoba) (Ibid.).

iv. William Charles Vincent was baptized in Jul 1857 (Ibid.).

v. Frances Jane Vincent was born on 3 Sep 1859 (MBS, C-14934.). She was baptized on 25 Oct 1859 St.Paul, (Manitoba) (Denney.).

vi. Mary Vincent was born in 1860 (Ibid.). She died on 17 May 1861 St.Paul, (Manitoba) (Ibid.).

Elizabeth Slater was born on 12 May 1836 St.Andrews, (Manitoba) (MBS, Supplementary Returns, C-14934.). She was baptized on 24 May 1836 St.Johns, Red River Settlement, (Manitoba) (HBCR, E.4/1a, folio 128d.). She died on 1 Sep 1917 Rockwood, Manitoba, at age 81 (MB Vital Statistics, Death Reg. #1917,054208.).

Children of **John Vincent** and **Elizabeth Slater** were as follows:

15 i. John George Vincent, b. 12 Sep 1865 St.Paul, (Manitoba); m. Elizabeth Jane McDonald; m. Eliza Frances Irvine.

ii. Clara Isabella Vincent was baptized on 6 Jun 1867 St.Paul, (Manitoba) (Denney.). She was buried in 1867 St.Paul, (Manitoba) (Ibid.).

16 iii. Laura Vincent, b. 19 Sep 1870 St.Pauls, Manitoba; m. Charles Stuart Vincent; d. 13 Jun 1947 Stonewall, Manitoba.

iv.   Alice Vincent was baptized on 12 Dec 1875 St.Johns, Manitoba (Ibid.). She married James Henry Airth, son of James Airth and Caroline Appleyard, on 31 May 1905 Winnipeg, Manitoba (Automated Genealogy 1906 Census Transcription Project and Census Images from the National Archives of Canada, http://www.automatedgenealogy.com, District 8-17, page 10, family 69, line 34-40.) (MB Vital Statistics, Marriage Reg. #1905,001736.).

James Henry Airth was born on 18 Jul 1883 R.M. of Woodlands, Manitoba (1906 Canada, District 8-17, page 10, family 69, line 34-40.) (MB Vital Statistics, Birth Reg. #1883,004593.).

8. Archdeacon Thomas Vincent was born on 1 Mar 1835 Osnaburg House, Keewatin (Denney.). He was baptized on 22 Sep 1840 St.Johns, Red River Settlement, (Manitoba) (HBCR, E.4/1a, folio 171d.). He married **Eliza Ann Gladman**, daughter of **Joseph Gladman** and **Margaret Auld**, on 11 Sep 1861 (Denney.). He died on 16 Jan 1907 Albany at age 71 (Ibid.). He was buried in Jan 1907 Moose Factory (Ibid.).

Eliza Ann Gladman was born on 26 Feb 1828 Albany (Ibid.). She died on 12 Nov 1891 Moose Factory at age 63 (Ibid.).

Children of **Archdeacon Thomas Vincent** and **Eliza Ann Gladman** were as follows:

17   i.   John Horden Vincent, b. 1862.

ii.   George Thomas Vincent was born in 1863.

iii.   Clara Caroline Vincent was born in 1865.

iv.   Mary Minnie Vincent was born in 1867.

18   v.   Charles Stuart Vincent, b. 2 Feb 1873 Manitoba; m. Laura Vincent; d. 8 Dec 1934 Selkirk, Manitoba.

9. William Thomas Vincent was born on 14 Oct 1837 St.Paul, (Manitoba) (Ibid.) (1901 Canada, #11, H-5, page 3, family 26, line 21-28.). He was baptized on 22 Sep 1840 St.Johns, Red River Settlement, (Manitoba) (HBCR, E.4/1a, folio 171d.). He married **Catherine Ross**, daughter of **George Ross** and **Catherine Berland**, on 22 Jan 1863 St.Andrews, (Manitoba) (Denney.). He died on 12 Jan 1915 Rockwood, Manitoba, at age 77 (MB Vital Statistics, Death Reg. #1915,148360.).

Catherine Ross was baptized on 8 May 1841 St.Johns, Red River Settlement, (Manitoba) (HBCR, E.4/1a, folio 173.). She died on 12 Oct 1912 Victoria at age 71 (Denney.). She was buried in Oct 1912 All Saints, Victoria (Ibid.).

Children of **William Thomas Vincent** and **Catherine Ross** were as follows:

i.   Donald R. Vincent was born on 18 Jun 1863 St.Paul, (Manitoba) (MBS, C-14934.). He died on 1 May 1873 St.Paul, Manitoba, at age 9 (Ibid.).

19   ii.   John Albert Vincent, b. 24 Jan 1868 St.Paul, (Manitoba); m. Alice Henrietta Helen Scott; d. 19 Feb 1937 Rockwood, Manitoba.

20   iii.   William Thomas Vincent, b. 15 Dec 1869 St.Paul, (Manitoba); m. Mabel Stokes; d. 16 Dec 1923 Stonewall, Manitoba.

iv.   James Vincent was born on 8 Mar 1873 (Denney.). He married Marjorie Martin Fall on 12 Oct 1914 Rockwood, Manitoba (MB Vital Statistics, Marriage Reg. #1914,138191.). He died on 9 Dec 1916 Rockwood, Manitoba, at age 43 (Ibid., Death Reg. #1916,072212.).

   Marjorie Martin Fall was born circa 1876 (Ibid., Death Reg. #1916,072211.). She died on 9 Dec 1916 Rockwood, Manitoba (Ibid.).

21   v.   Elizabeth H. Vincent, b. circa 1876; m. George Gladman Vincent.

22   vi.   Samuel L. Vincent, b. 15 May 1881; m. Catherine Ann Truthwaite; d. 31 Jan 1944 Winnipeg, Manitoba.

vii.   Laura Ida Cecelia Vincent was born on 12 Oct 1883 R.M. of Rockwood, Manitoba (Ibid., Birth Reg. #1883,004279.). She married Ernest Marshall on 26 Apr 1916 Winnipeg, Manitoba (Ibid., Marriage Reg. #1916,021243.). She died on 14 Apr 1931 Rockwood, Manitoba, at age 47 (Ibid., Death Reg. #1931,032406.).

10. Sarah Jane Vincent was born between 1841 and 1847. She was baptized on 5 Nov 1847 St.Johns, (Manitoba) (Denney.). She married **John Fraser**, son of **Colin Fraser** and **Nancy Gaudry**, on 30 Jul 1866 St.Paul, (Manitoba) (Ibid.). She died on 11 Apr 1929 (Ibid.).

John Fraser was born in 1841 Jaspar House, (Alberta) (NWHBS 1885 Scrip Applications, North-West Halfbreeds residing outside Manitoba on 15 July 1870, RG15-20, C-14938.). He was baptized on 16 Apr 1846 Fort-des-Prairies (INB *Index des Naissances and Baptemes* (St.Boniface, Manitoba: La Societe Historique de Saint-Boniface., c1995), page 65.). He died on 29 Jan 1919 (Denney.).

11. James Vincent was born on 20 Jan 1842 Red River, (Manitoba) (Denney.). He was baptized on 23 Jan 1842 St.Johns, (Manitoba) (Ibid.). He married **Clara Caroline Gladman**, daughter of **Joseph Gladman** and **Margaret Auld**, on 10 Jul 1867 St.Paul, (Manitoba) (Ibid.). He married **Ann Agnes Linklater** before 1892 (MB Vital Statistics, Death Reg. #1899,002759.) (HBCA-B.). He died on 30 Oct 1909 Stonewall, Manitoba, at age 67 (MB Vital Statistics, Death Reg. #1909,002054.).

Clara Caroline Gladman was born on 16 Jan 1846 (Denney.). She died on 30 Jul 1884 at age 38 (Ibid.).

Children of **James Vincent** and **Clara Caroline Gladman** were as follows:

i.   Joseph Gladman Vincent was born on 21 Jan 1868 probably, Fort Hope, Ontario (Ibid.). He died on 10 Aug 1896 Moose Factory at age 28 (Ibid.).

23   ii.   Erland Erlandson Vincent, b. 8 Apr 1870 Montreal River, Nipissing North, Ontario; m. Jane Taylor; m. Susanne Harriet Graham; d. 4 Sep 1940 Stonewall, Manitoba.

iii.   Harriet M. Caroline Vincent was born on 11 Apr 1872. She died in Aug 1935 at age 63. She was buried in Aug 1935 Denver, Denver, Colorado.

iv.   James William Vincent was born on 26 May 1874. He died on 28 Nov 1910 at age 36.

v.   Annie S. J. Vincent was born in Apr 1878 (Ibid.). She died on 16 Nov 1882 at age 4 (Ibid.).

vi.   Josephine Clara Stuart Vincent was born on 28 Apr 1882 (Ibid.). She died in Jan 1939 Stonewall, Manitoba, at age 56 (Ibid.).

Ann Agnes Linklater was born circa 1871 (MB Vital Statistics, Death Reg. #1899,002759.). She died on 17 Sep 1899 Rockwood, Manitoba (Ibid.).

Children of **James Vincent** and **Ann Agnes Linklater** are:

     i.   Stanley Vincent was born circa 1892 (1906 Canada, District 8-18, page 9, family 65, line 1-7.).

12. Charlotte Vincent was born on 25 Nov 1849 St.Paul, (Manitoba) (MBS, C-14934.). She was baptized on 5 Dec 1849 St.Johns, (Manitoba) (Denney.). She married **Charles Richard Thomas**, son of **William Thomas** and **Eleanor Bunn,** on 22 Jul 1869 St.Paul, (Manitoba) (Ibid.). She died on 9 Apr 1902 Winnipeg, Manitoba, at age 52 (MB Vital Statistics, Death Reg. #1902,002081.).

Charles Richard Thomas was born on 28 Apr 1839 St.Paul, (Manitoba) (MBS, C-14934.). He was baptized on 26 May 1839 St.Johns, Red River Settlement, (Manitoba) (HBCR, E.4/1a, folio 160d.). He died on 25 Jan 1911 Winnipeg, Manitoba, at age 71 (MB Vital Statistics, Death Reg. #1911,002841.).

13. George Gladman Vincent was born on 28 Feb 1852 St.Paul, (Manitoba) (Denney.). He was baptized on 7 Mar 1852 St.Paul, (Manitoba) (Ibid.). He married **Harriet Mary Work**, daughter of **William Work** and **Barbara Halcrow**, on 14 Apr 1870 St.Paul, Stonewall, Manitoba (Ibid.). He died on 27 Apr 1921 Winnipeg, Manitoba, at age 69 (MB Vital Statistics, Death Reg. #1921,015255.).

Harriet Mary Work was born on 22 May 1852 (Denney.). She died on 5 Aug 1921 Winnipeg, Manitoba, at age 69 (MB Vital Statistics, Death Reg. #1921,031100.).

Children of **George Gladman Vincent** and **Harriet Mary Work** were as follows:

     i.   William John Vincent was baptized on 23 Mar 1871 St.Paul, Manitoba (Denney.). He died circa 1941 (Ibid.).

24   ii.   George Gladman Vincent, b. 29 Sep 1872 St.Paul, Manitoba; m. Elizabeth H. Vincent; d. 12 Feb 1930 Rockwood, Manitoba.

    iii.   Joseph Alexander Vincent was baptized on 24 May 1874 St.Paul, Manitoba (Ibid.).

    iv.   Catherine Jane Vincent was baptized on 25 Nov 1875 St.Johns, Manitoba (Ibid.).

25   v.   Barbara Elizabeth Vincent, b. 25 May 1879 St.Paul, Manitoba; m. Henry Olinthus Beddome; d. 30 Jan 1917 Winnipeg, Manitoba.

    vi.   Thomas James Vincent was born on 5 Aug 1880 RM St.Paul, Manitoba (MB Vital Statistics, Birth Reg. #1883,002594.).

    vii.   Lillie Annabelle Vincent was born circa May 1882 (Ibid., Death Reg. #1883,001725.). She died on 26 Jun 1883 St.Paul, Manitoba (Ibid.).

    viii.   Maida May Vincent was born on 4 May 1884 RM St.Paul, Manitoba (Ibid., Birth Reg. #1884,003246.). She died on 10 Aug 1900 Winnipeg, Manitoba, at age 16 (Ibid., Death Reg. #1900,001562.).

    ix.   Sarah Ann Vincent was born on 22 Jul 1885 St.Paul, Manitoba (Ibid., Birth Reg. #1885,001583.). She died on 6 Apr 1887 St.Paul, Manitoba, at age 1 (Ibid., Death Reg. #1887,001838.).

    x.   Demill Wallace Vincent was born on 30 Jan 1891 R.M. of Rockwood, Manitoba (Ibid., Birth Reg. #1891,005078.).

    xi.   Roderick Lionel Vincent was born on 30 Jan 1891 R.M. of Rockwood, Manitoba (Ibid., Birth Reg. #1891,005079.).

Generation Four

14. Thomas Vincent was born on 28 Apr 1853 St.Paul, (Manitoba) (1901 Canada, #11, H-2, page 7, family 35, line 13-23.). He was baptized on 30 Apr 1853 St.Paul, (Manitoba) (Denney.). He married **Mary Tait**, daughter of **Joseph Tait** and **Madeleine Corrigal**, before 1877. He died on 12 Feb 1934 Winnipeg, Manitoba, at age 80 (MB Vital Statistics, Death Reg. #1934,008138.).

Mary Tait was born on 11 Sep 1857 St.Andrews, (Manitoba) (MBS, C-14933.). She was baptized on 27 Sep 1857 St.Andrews, (Manitoba) (Ibid.). She died on 16 Mar 1926 Rockwood, Manitoba, at age 68 (MB Vital Statistics, Death Reg. #1926,013220.).

Children of **Thomas Vincent** and **Mary Tait** were as follows:

     i.   John Edward Vincent was born on 29 Mar 1877 Prince Albert, (Saskatchewan) (1901 Canada, #11, H-2, page 7, family 35, line 13-23.) (ArchiviaNet, C-15008.).

    ii.   Flora Mary Vincent was born on 13 Dec 1879 Prince Albert, (Saskatchewan) (Ibid.).

    iii.   Frances Jane Vincent was born on 9 Jan 1881 Prince Albert, (Saskatchewan) (1901 Canada, #11, H-2, page 7, family 35, line 13-23.) (ArchiviaNet, C-15008.).

    iv.   Alfred William Vincent was born on 29 Jul 1883 Prince Albert, (Saskatchewan) (Denney.) (1901 Canada, #11, H-2, page 7, family 35, line 13-23.). He died in 1952 (Denney.).

    v.   Ethel Alice Vincent was born on 4 Jun 1885 R.M. of Rockwood, Manitoba (MB Vital Statistics, Birth Reg. #1885,001285.). She married William John Batchelor, son of James Batchelor and Louisa Bond, on 24 Mar 1904 Rockwood, Manitoba (Ibid., Marriage Reg. #1903,003208.).

         William John Batchelor was born on 24 Sep 1874 R.M. of Montcalm, Manitoba (Ibid., Birth Reg. #1885,003400.).

    vi.   Myra Maud Vincent was born on 14 Nov 1887 R.M. of Rockwood, Manitoba (Ibid., Birth Reg. #1888,004444.).

    vii.   Norah Ann Vincent was born on 9 Apr 1889 R.M. of Rockwood, Manitoba (Ibid., Birth Reg. #1889,11313295, registration date: 03/21/1928.).

    viii.   Caroline Vincent was born on 10 Sep 1895 Manitoba (1901 Canada, #11, H-2, page 7, family 35, line 13-23.).

    ix.   Edith Vincent was born on 11 Jul 1896 Manitoba (Ibid.).

    x.   Horace Alexander Vincent was born on 12 Sep 1900 R.M. of Rockwood, Manitoba (MB Vital Statistics, Birth Reg. #1900,005055.).

    xi.   Wilfred James Vincent was born on 12 Oct 1901 R.M. of Rockwood, Manitoba (Ibid., Birth Reg. #1901,002018.). He died on 7 Oct 1979 at age 77.

15. John George Vincent was born on 12 Sep 1865 St.Paul, (Manitoba) (MBS, C-14934.). He was baptized on 14 Sep 1865 St.Paul, (Manitoba) (Denney.). He married **Elizabeth Jane McDonald**, daughter of **Duncan McDonald** and **Elizabeth Tait**, on 7 Jan 1892 Winnipeg, Manitoba (MB Vital Statistics, Marriage Reg. #1892,002203.). He married **Eliza Frances Irvine**, daughter of **Cornelius Irvine** and **Catherine Lambert**, on 24 Sep 1906 Selkirk, Manitoba (Ibid., Marriage Reg. #1906,002691.).

Elizabeth Jane McDonald was born on 11 Sep 1866 St.Andrews, (Manitoba) (Denney.). She was baptized on 11 Sep 1866 St.Andrews, (Manitoba) (Ibid.).

Children of **John George Vincent** and **Elizabeth Jane McDonald** were as follows:

     i.   Frank Arthur Vincent was born on 29 Dec 1892 R.M. of Rockwood, Manitoba (1901 Canada, #11, L-2, page 4, family 32 line 11-17.) (MB Vital Statistics, Birth Reg. #1893,005028.).

    ii.   Vernon Vincent was born on 22 Sep 1894 R.M. of Rockwood, Manitoba (Ibid., Birth Reg. #1894,004493.).

    iii.   Donald Vincent was born on 19 Jun 1896 R.M. of Rockwood, Manitoba (Ibid., Birth Reg. #1896,002574.).

    iv.   Norman Vincent was born on 23 Aug 1898 R.M. of Rockwood, Manitoba (Ibid., Birth Reg. #1898,001125.).

    v.   Hector Earl Vincent was born on 10 Jan 1901 R.M. of St.Andrews, Manitoba (1901 Canada, #11, L-2, page 4, family 32 line 11-17.) (MB Vital Statistics, Birth Reg. #1901,006332.).

    vi.   Elizabeth "Bessie" Vincent was born on 25 Aug 1902 R.M. of St.Andrews, Manitoba (Ibid., Birth Reg. #1902,007957.).

Eliza Frances Irvine was born on 5 Sep 1878 (1891 Census of Canada from the National Archives of Canada, Ottawa, Canada, Dictrict 6, family 53.) (1901 Canada, District 11-l-6, page 7, family 62, line 41-44.).

Children of **John George Vincent** and **Eliza Frances Irvine** are as follows:

    i.   Herbert Glen Vincent was born on 29 Jan 1905 R.M. of St.Andrews, Manitoba (MB Vital Statistics, Birth Reg. #1905,004123.).

    ii.   George Vincent was born in Jul 1909 (Automated Genealogy 1911 Census Transcription Project and Census Images from the National Archives of Canada, http://www.automatedgenealogy.com, District 37, page 10, family 21, line 7-18.).

    iii.   Walter Vincent was born on 30 Oct 1910 R.M. of Rockwood, Manitoba (MB Vital Statistics, Birth Reg. #1910,004436.).

16. Laura Vincent was born on 19 Sep 1870 St.Pauls, Manitoba (ArchiviaNet, C-15008.). She married **Charles Stuart Vincent**, son of **Archdeacon Thomas Vincent** and **Eliza Ann Gladman**, on 6 Jul 1894 Rockwood, Manitoba (MB Vital Statistics, Marriage Reg. #1894,002345.). She died on 13 Jun 1947 Stonewall, Manitoba, at age 76 (Denney.).

Charles Stuart Vincent was born on 2 Feb 1873 Manitoba (1901 Canada, #11, H-5, page 3, family 25, line 18-20.) (ArchiviaNet, C-15008.). He died on 8 Dec 1934 Selkirk, Manitoba, at age 61 (MB Vital Statistics, Death Reg. #1934,048282.).

Children of **Laura Vincent** and **Charles Stuart Vincent** were as follows:

    i.   Cyril Stewart Vincent was born on 24 May 1897 R.M. of Rockwood, Manitoba (Ibid., Birth Reg. #1897,006781.). He married Gertrude Sarah Stethem on 9 Feb 1925 Stonewall, Manitoba (Ibid., Marriage Reg. #1925,007217.).

    ii.   Stanley Edgar Vincent was born on 18 Sep 1899 Selkirk, Manitoba (Ibid., Birth Reg. #1899,001142.).

    iii.   Frederick Herbert Vincent was born on 19 Mar 1904 R.M. of Rockwood, Manitoba (Ibid., Birth Reg. #1904,004845.).

    iv.   Josephine Clara Vincent was born on 27 Dec 1906 R.M. of Rockwood, Manitoba (Ibid., Birth Reg. #1907,005969.).

17. John Horden Vincent was born in 1862 (1901 Canada, District C-7, page 1, family 6, line 27-29.) (ArchiviaNet.). He married **Ann Elizabeth McIvor**, daughter of **Murdoch McIvor** and **Mary Bearman,** in 1897 (Ibid., C-15008.).

Ann Elizabeth McIvor was born on 2 Apr 1871 Trout Lake (Ibid.).

Children of **John Horden Vincent** and **Ann Elizabeth McIvor** are:

    i.   Lester James Horden Vincent was born circa 1899 (1901 Canada, District C-7, page 1, family 6, line 27-29.).

18. Charles Stuart Vincent was born on 2 Feb 1873 Manitoba (Ibid., #11, H-5, page 3, family 25, line 18-20.) (ArchiviaNet, C-15008.). He married **Laura Vincent**, daughter of **John Vincent** and **Elizabeth Slater**, on 6 Jul 1894 Rockwood, Manitoba (MB Vital Statistics, Marriage Reg. #1894,002345.). He died on 8 Dec 1934 Selkirk, Manitoba, at age 61 (Ibid., Death Reg. #1934,048282.).

Laura Vincent was born on 19 Sep 1870 St.Pauls, Manitoba (ArchiviaNet, C-15008.). She died on 13 Jun 1947 Stonewall, Manitoba, at age 76 (Denney.).

Children of **Charles Stuart Vincent** and **Laura Vincent** were as follows:

    i.   Cyril Stewart Vincent was born on 24 May 1897 R.M. of Rockwood, Manitoba (MB Vital Statistics, Birth Reg. #1897,006781.). He married Gertrude Sarah Stethem on 9 Feb 1925 Stonewall, Manitoba (Ibid., Marriage Reg. #1925,007217.).

    ii.   Stanley Edgar Vincent was born on 18 Sep 1899 Selkirk, Manitoba (Ibid., Birth Reg. #1899,001142.).

    iii.   Frederick Herbert Vincent was born on 19 Mar 1904 R.M. of Rockwood, Manitoba (Ibid., Birth Reg. #1904,004845.).

    iv.   Josephine Clara Vincent was born on 27 Dec 1906 R.M. of Rockwood, Manitoba (Ibid., Birth Reg. #1907,005969.).

19. John Albert Vincent was born on 24 Jan 1868 St.Paul, (Manitoba) (MBS, C-14934.). He was baptized on 14 Mar 1868 St.Paul, (Manitoba) (Ibid.). He married **Alice Henrietta Helen Scott**, daughter of **William Scott** and **Ann Setter,** on 16 Nov 1892 St.Andrews, Manitoba (MB Vital Statistics, Marriage Reg. #1892,001791.). He died on 19 Feb 1937 Rockwood, Manitoba, at age 69 (Ibid., Death Reg. #1937,008505.).

Alice Henrietta Helen Scott was born on 11 Mar 1869 St.Andrews, (Manitoba) (MBS, C-14933.). She was baptized on 4 Apr 1869 St.Andrews, (Manitoba) (Denney.). She died on 17 Nov 1941 Stonewall, Manitoba, at age 72 (MB Vital Statistics, Death Reg. #1941,044420.).

Children of **John Albert Vincent** and **Alice Henrietta Helen Scott** all born R.M. of Rockwood, Manitoba, were as follows:

    i.   Reginald William Vincent was born on 7 Jun 1894 (Ibid., Birth Reg. #1894,001543.). He died on 24 Feb 1959 Biggar, Saskatchewan, at age 64 (Denney.).

    ii.   Henrietta Mary Vincent was born on 7 Apr 1897 (MB Vital Statistics, Birth Reg. #1897,006776.).

    iii.   Unnamed Vincent was born on 14 Oct 1909 (Ibid., Birth Reg. #1909,002564.).

20. William Thomas Vincent was born on 15 Dec 1869 St.Paul, (Manitoba) (MBS, C-14934.). He was baptized on 23 Jan 1870 St.Paul, (Manitoba) (Ibid.). He married **Mabel Stokes**, daughter of **George Stokes** and **Emily Pinchan,** on 3 Aug 1904 Rockwood,

Manitoba (MB Vital Statistics, Marriage Reg. #1904,002554.). He died on 16 Dec 1923 Stonewall, Manitoba, at age 54 (Ibid., Death Reg. #1923,075025.).

Mabel Stokes was born on 17 Dec 1877 (1901 Canada, District 11-h-3, page 10, family 93, line 34-41.).

Children of **William Thomas Vincent** and **Mabel Stokes** were as follows:

    i. Arthur William Vincent was born on 12 Oct 1906 Stonewall, Manitoba (MB Vital Statistics, Birth Reg. #1906,007731.).

    ii. Frank James Vincent was born on 21 Apr 1917 (Denney.). He died on 17 Jun 1917 (Ibid.). He was buried All Saints, Victoria (Ibid.).

    iii. John K. Vincent was born circa 1919 (1921 Census of Canada from the National Archives of Canada (Transcription by ancestry.com), Ottawa, Canada, District 35-54, page 14.).

21. Elizabeth H. Vincent was born circa 1876 (1881 Canada, District D-2, page 11, family 50.). She married **George Gladman Vincent**, son of **George Gladman Vincent** and **Harriet Mary Work**, on 23 Oct 1900 Winnipeg, Manitoba (MB Vital Statistics, Marriage Reg. #1900,002436.).

George Gladman Vincent was baptized on 29 Sep 1872 St.Paul, Manitoba (Denney.). He died on 12 Feb 1930 Rockwood, Manitoba, at age 57 (MB Vital Statistics, Death Reg. #1930,015178.).

Children of **Elizabeth H. Vincent** and **George Gladman Vincent** are as follows:

    i. Myrtle Vincent was born circa 1901 (1921 Canada, District 35-10, page 15.).

    ii. Clarence William Vincent was born circa 1908 (Ibid.). He married Ada Kathleen Ryan on 22 Jun 1933 Stonewall, Manitoba (MB Vital Statistics, Marriage Reg. #1933,022291.).

       Ada Kathleen Ryan was born on 18 May 1913 R.M. of Morton, Manitoba (Ibid., Birth Reg. #1913,037412.).

    iii. Laura Vincent was born circa 1920 (1921 Canada, District 35-10, page 15.).

22. Samuel L. Vincent was born on 15 May 1881 (Denney.). He married **Catherine Ann Truthwaite**, daughter of **Jacob Truthwaite** and **Jane (--?--)**, on 10 Jul 1907 St.Andrews, Manitoba (MB Vital Statistics, Marriage Reg. #1907,002585.). He died on 31 Jan 1944 Winnipeg, Manitoba, at age 62 (Ibid., Death Reg. #1944,008090.).

Catherine Ann Truthwaite was born on 7 May 1877 (1901 Canada, Family 35, Line 15-22, page 4.). She died on 6 May 1943 at age 65 (Denney.).

Children of **Samuel L. Vincent** and **Catherine Ann Truthwaite** are as follows:

    i. Florence Catherine Vincent was born on 3 Jun 1908 Stonewall, Manitoba (MB Vital Statistics, Birth Reg. #1908,001541.).

    ii. Elizabeth Evelyn Jean Vincent was born on 23 Jan 1910 Stonewall, Manitoba (Ibid., Birth Reg. #1910,005893; Reg. Date: 24/02/1910.).

    iii. Mary Margaret Vincent was born on 13 Apr 1913 Stonewall, Manitoba (Ibid., Birth Reg. #1913,023087.).

    iv. Lillian Vincent was born on 12 Oct 1914 R.M. of Stonewall, Manitoba (Ibid., Birth Reg. #1914,000100.).

    v. Irene Vincent was born circa 1917 (1921 Canada, District 35-10, page 14.).

    vi. Harriet Vincent was born circa 1919 (Ibid.).

23. Erland Erlandson Vincent was born on 8 Apr 1870 Montreal River, Nipissing North, Ontario (1901 Canada, District 44-a(3), page 4, family 23, line 13-14.) (1871 Census of Canada from the National Archives of Canada, Ottawa, Canada, District 84-01, page 1, family 5.). He married **Jane Taylor** before 1891. He married **Susanne Harriet Graham**, daughter of **James Graham** and **Harriet Sophia Thomas**, on 10 Jul 1916 Winnipeg, Manitoba (MB Vital Statistics, Marriage Reg. #1916,039104.). He died on 4 Sep 1940 Stonewall, Manitoba, at age 70 (Ibid., Death Reg. #1940,036280.).

Jane Taylor was born on 18 Dec 1876 (1901 Canada, District 44-a(3), page 4, family 23, line 13-14.).

Children of **Erland Erlandson Vincent** and **Jane Taylor** are:

    i. Clara Caroline Vincent was baptized on 2 Aug 1891 St.Thomas (Denney.).

Susanne Harriet Graham was born on 29 Apr 1886 Victoria (Ibid.).

Children of **Erland Erlandson Vincent** and **Susanne Harriet Graham** are as follows:

    i. Edwin James H. Vincent was born on 8 Oct 1914 R.M. of Coldwell, Manitoba (MB Vital Statistics, Birth Reg. #1914,11917200; Reg. Date: 03/06/1930.).

    ii. Edith Vincent was born circa 1917 (1921 Canada, District 35-54, page 9.).

    iii. Muriel Vincent was born circa Jan 1921 (Ibid.).

24. George Gladman Vincent was baptized on 29 Sep 1872 St.Paul, Manitoba (Denney.). He married **Elizabeth H. Vincent**, daughter of **William Thomas Vincent** and **Catherine Ross**, on 23 Oct 1900 Winnipeg, Manitoba (MB Vital Statistics, Marriage Reg. #1900,002436.). He died on 12 Feb 1930 Rockwood, Manitoba, at age 57 (Ibid., Death Reg. #1930,015178.).

Elizabeth H. Vincent was born circa 1876 (1881 Canada, District D-2, page 11, family 50.).

Children of **George Gladman Vincent** and **Elizabeth H. Vincent** are as follows:

    i. Myrtle Vincent was born circa 1901 (1921 Canada, District 35-10, page 15.).

    ii. Clarence William Vincent was born circa 1908 (Ibid.). He married Ada Kathleen Ryan on 22 Jun 1933 Stonewall, Manitoba (MB Vital Statistics, Marriage Reg. #1933,022291.).

       Ada Kathleen Ryan was born on 18 May 1913 R.M. of Morton, Manitoba (Ibid., Birth Reg. #1913,037412.).

    iii. Laura Vincent was born circa 1920 (1921 Canada, District 35-10, page 15.).

25. Barbara Elizabeth Vincent was born on 25 May 1879 St.Paul, Manitoba (Denney.). She married **Henry Olinthus Beddome**, son of **Henry Septimus Beddome M. D.** and **Frances Omand**, on 25 Jun 1902 Winnipeg, Manitoba (MB Vital Statistics, Marriage Reg. #1902,001981.). She died on 30 Jan 1917 Winnipeg, Manitoba, at age 37 (Ibid., Death Reg. #1917,005273.).

Henry Olinthus Beddome was born on 29 Mar 1874 (1901 Canada, District 12-E-2, page 4, family 30, line 4.). He died in 1946 (Denney.).

Ahnentafel between Moise Visignault or Vezina and Jacques Vezina

--- 1st Generation ---

1. MOISE VISIGNAULT OR VEZINA (AP Records of the Assumption Roman Catholic Church, Pembina, North Dakota: Baptisms, Marriages, Sepultures, 1848-1896; compiled by Reverend Father J. M. Belleau, 2 October 1944, page 244, B-215. Hereinafter cited as AP.) was born on 8 Apr 1830 at St.Benoit, Quebec (Rod MacQuarrie Research, 29 Mar 2012.). He was baptized on 8 Apr 1830 at St.Benoit, Quebec (Ibid., 3 Apr 2012.). He married JULIE PEPIN, daughter of PIERRE PEPIN and JOSEPHTE PATENAUDE, on 19 Sep 1859 at Assumption, Pembina, Pembina County, Dakota Territory (AP, page 219, M-81.).

--- 2nd Generation ---

2. SIMON VEZINA was baptized on 5 Nov 1806 at St.Benoit, Quebec (Rod Mac Quarrie, 3 Apr 2012.). He was born on 4 Dec 1806 at St.Benoit, Quebec (Ibid.). He married MARGUERITE PALLEN DIT LAFLEUR, daughter of PIERRE PALLEN DIT LAFLEUR and MARGUERITE LANGEVIN DITE LACROIX, on 24 Jan 1825 at St.Benoit, Quebec (Ibid.).

--- 3rd Generation ---

4. FRANCOIS VEZINA (Ibid.) (Ibid.) was born on 10 Sep 1779 at Montreal, Quebec (Ibid.) (PRDH online index, http://www.genealogic.umontreal.ca, #467851.). He was baptized on 10 Sep 1779 at Montreal, Quebec (Rod Mac Quarrie, 3 Apr 2012.) (PRDH online, #467851.). He married SUZANNE COUSINEAU, daughter of JEAN NOEL COUSINEAU and MARIE JOSEPHE SABOURIN, on 3 Nov 1801 at St.Laurent, Quebec (Rod Mac Quarrie, 3 Apr 2012.).

--- 4th Generation ---

8. JEAN BAPTISTE VEZINA (Ibid.) (PRDH online, #54843.) (Ibid.) was baptized on 14 Jul 1746 at Ste-Genevieve-de-Batiscan, Quebec (Ibid., #127493.) (Rod Mac Quarrie, 3 Apr 2012.). He was born on 14 Jul 1746 at Ste-Genevieve-de-Batiscan, Quebec (PRDH online, #127493.). He married MARIE MARGUERITE LAURENT, daughter of JEAN BAPTISTE LAURENT and MARIE ANNE ETHIER, on 2 Mar 1767 at Ste-Anne-de-Bellevue, Quebec (Ibid.). He married MARIE JOSEPHE NIOF DITE LAFRANCE, daughter of FRANCOIS-MICHEL NIOF DIT LAFRANCE and MARIE JOSEPHE ROSEAU, on 16 Nov 1778 at St.Laurent, Quebec (Ibid., No. 216496.) (Rod Mac Quarrie, 3 Apr 2012.).

--- 5th Generation ---

16. FRANCOIS VEZINA (PRDH online, #54843.) (DGFQ Jette, Rene, *Dictionnaire Genealogique des Familles du Quebec des Origines a 1730* (Montreal, Quebec, Canada: University of Montreal Press, 1983), page 1123.) (Ibid.) was born on 25 Dec 1710 at L'Ange-Gardien, Quebec (Ibid.). He was baptized on 26 Dec 1710 at L'Ange-Gardien, Quebec (Ibid.). He married MARIE-ANNE ROUILLARD DIT FONDVILLE, daughter of JOSEPH ROUILLARD DIT FONDVILLE and MARIE-CHARLOTTE TROTTAIN DIT ST.SURIN, on 9 Jan 1736 at Batiscan, Quebec (Rod Mac Quarrie, 3 Apr 2012.) (PRDH online, No. 108870.). He married MARIE JOSEPHE BERTRAND DIT ST.ARNAU, daughter of PAUL BERTRAND and MARIE JOSEPHE JUNEAU DIT LATULIPPE, on 19 Feb 1753 at Ste-Genevieve-de-Batiscan, Quebec (Ibid., #92896.). He married MARIE ANNE ROUILLARD DIT PRONOVOST, daughter of MATHIEU ROUILLARD DIT PRONOVOST and MARIE ANNE LEMAY, on 30 May 1757 at Ste-Genevieve-de-Batiscan, Quebec (Ibid.).

--- 6th Generation ---

32. CHARLES VEZINA (DGFQ, page 1123.) (Ibid.) (Ibid.) was born on 25 Jan 1685 at L'Ange-Gardien, Quebec (Ibid.). He was baptized on 26 Jan 1685 at L'Ange-Gardien, Quebec (Ibid.). He married LOUISE GODIN, daughter of CHARLES GODIN OR GAUDIN and MARIE BOUCHER, on 27 Jul 1705 at L'Ange-Gardien, Quebec (Ibid.). A contract for the marriage to LOUISE GODIN, daughter of CHARLES GODIN OR GAUDIN and MARIE BOUCHER, was signed on 27 Jul 1705 (Ibid.).

--- 7th Generation ---

64. FRANCOIS VEZINA OR VOISINAT (Ibid.) (Ibid., page 1122.) (Ibid.) was born on 28 Aug 1657 (Ibid.). He was baptized on 2 Sep 1657 at St-Nicolas, LaRochelle, Aunis (Charente-Maritime) (Ibid.). A contract for the marriage to MARIE CLEMENT, daughter of JEAN CLEMENT DIT LAPOINTE and MADELEINE SURGET, was signed on 31 Jan 1679 (Ibid., page 1123.). He married MARIE CLEMENT, daughter of JEAN CLEMENT DIT LAPOINTE and MADELEINE SURGET, on 10 Apr 1679 at L'Ancienne Lorette, Quebec (Ibid.). He was buried on 20 Jan 1703 at L'Ange-Gardien, Quebec (Ibid.).

--- 8th Generation ---

128. JACQUES VEZINA was born between 1609 and 1611 (Ibid., page 1122.). He married MARIE BOISDON, daughter of JEAN BOISDON and MARIE BARDIN, circa 1641 at Puyravault, Rochefort, La Rochelle, Normandie (Charente-Maritime) (Ibid.). He died on 28 Jun 1687 at L'Ange-Gardien, Quebec (Ibid.) (PRDH online, No. 34502.). He was buried on 29 Jun 1687 at L'Ange-Gardien, Quebec (DGFQ, page 1122.) (PRDH online, No. 34502.).

Descendants of Moise Visignault or Vezina

Generation One

1. Moise Visignault or Vezina was born on 8 Apr 1830 St.Benoit, Quebec (Rod MacQuarrie Research, 29 Mar 2012.). He was baptized on 8 Apr 1830 St.Benoit, Quebec (Ibid., 3 Apr 2012.). He married Julie Pepin, daughter of Pierre Pepin and Josephte Patenaude, on 19 Sep 1859 Assumption, Pembina, Pembina County, Dakota Territory (AP Records of the Assumption Roman Catholic Church, Pembina, North Dakota: Baptisms, Marriages, Sepultures, 1848-1896; compiled by Reverend Father J. M. Belleau, 2 October 1944, page 219, M-81. Hereinafter cited as AP.).

Julie Pepin was born in Mar 1839 North West (MBS Scrip Applications, Original White Settlers & Halfbreeds residing in Manitoba on 15 July 1870, RG15-19, C-14934.). She was baptized on 12 Jun 1842 Fort-des-Prairies, (Alberta) (INB *Index des Naissances and Baptemes* (St.Boniface, Manitoba: La Societe Historique de Saint-Boniface., c1995), page 146.).

Children of **Moise Visignault or Vezina** and **Julie Pepin** were as follows:

     i.   Marie Louise Visignault was born on 18 Sep 1858 (Rod Mac Quarrie, 29 Mar 2012.).

  2 ii.   Elizabeth Visignault, b. 12 Jul 1861; m. William Donald; d. 1 Sep 1898 St.Andrews, Manitoba.

  3 iii. Joseph Visignault, b. 15 Sep 1864; m. Mary Todd; m. Ellen Linklater; d. 21 Sep 1932 Selkirk, Manitoba; bur. 23 Sep 1932 Little Britain Cemetery, St.Andrews, Manitoba.

4   iv.   Jane Visignault, b. 1866 (Manitoba); m. Robert John Donald; m. James McCorrister; d. 27 Mar 1894 St.Clements, Manitoba.

        v.   Domithilde Visignault was born on 12 Sep 1866 (Ibid.).

5   vi.   Louis Moise Visignault, b. 12 Jul 1868; m. Emma Hester Alice Mowat; d. 1945.

       vii.   Ellen Harriet Visnaugh was born in 1872 (Ibid.). She married James Clarke, son of William Clarke and Mary McKay, on 24 Jan 1894 Selkirk, Manitoba (Manitoba Vital Statistics online, http://web2.gov.mb.ca, Mar. Reg. #1894,001416.). She died on 11 Feb 1900 St.Andrews, Manitoba (Ibid., Death Reg. #1900,001200.).

          James Clarke was born on 9 Nov 1855 St.Andrews, (Manitoba) (MBS, C-14926.).

     viii.   Salomon Visignault was born in 1873 (Rod Mac Quarrie, 29 Mar 2012.).

       ix.   William Vezina was born on 12 May 1874 Poplar Point, Manitoba (Ibid.). He married Margaret Jane Fidler, daughter of Peter Fidler and Therese Swain, on 12 May 1897 Prince Albert, (Saskatchewan). He died on 2 May 1961 St.Louis, Saskatchewan, at age 86 (Edsel Bourque Research.).

          Margaret Jane Fidler was born on 14 Apr 1878 Regina, (Saskatchewan) (L1 Lebret Mission de St.Florent Roman Catholic Registre des Baptemes, Mariages & Seplutures, Qu'Appelle, Saskatchewan, 1868-1881., page 222, B-5. Hereinafter cited as L1.) (Louis Verhagen Research.). She was baptized on 29 Apr 1878 Lebret, (Saskatchewan) (L1, page 222, B-5.). She died on 16 Sep 1970 St.Louis, Saskatchewan, at age 92 (Louis Verhagen.).

        x.   Pierre Visignault was born in 1876 (Rod Mac Quarrie, 29 Mar 2012.).

       xi.   Edouard Visignault was born on 11 Mar 1877 (Ibid.). He died on 3 Sep 1878 St.Eustache, Manitoba, at age 1 (Ibid.). He was buried on 4 Sep 1878 St.Eustache, Manitoba (Ibid.).

Generation Two

2. Elizabeth Visignault was born on 12 Jul 1861 (Ibid.). She married **William Donald**, son of **William Donald** and **Jane Firth**, on 25 Nov 1886 Portage la Prairie, Manitoba (MB Vital Statistics, Marriage Reg. #1886,001011.). She died on 1 Sep 1898 St.Andrews, Manitoba, at age 37 (Ibid., Death Reg. #1898,003048.).

   William Donald was born on 2 Aug 1864 St.Andrews, (Manitoba) (HBC-PN Public Notice of land claims of Half-Breed Children, Address: Provincial Archives of Manitoba, Winnipeg, Manitoba, File Reference: MG4D13 Box 1, St.Andrews, #149.). He was baptized on 6 Aug 1864 St.Andrews, (Manitoba) (Denney Papers, Charles D. Denney, Glenbow Archives, Calgary, Alberta.). He married **Catherine Janet Smith**, daughter of **John Smith** and **Mary Taylor**, on 10 Dec 1903 St.Andrews, Manitoba (MB Vital Statistics, Marriage Reg. #1903,002110.).

3. Joseph Visignault was born on 15 Sep 1864 (Rod Mac Quarrie, 29 Mar 2012.). He married **Mary Todd**, daughter of **William Todd** and **Elizabeth (--?--)**, on 15 Mar 1883 Portage la Prairie, Manitoba (MB Vital Statistics, Marriage Reg. #1883,001210.). He married **Mary Todd**, daughter of **William Todd** and **Elizabeth (--?--)**, on 30 May 1883 St.Marys, Portage-la-Prairie, Manitoba (SMACPLP St.Marys Anglican Church, Portage La Prairie, Manitoba, Baptisms, Marriages, Burials, 1855-1883, transcribed by Clarence Kipling , M-104.). He married **Ellen Linklater**, daughter of **James Stuart Linklater** and **Nancy Donald**, on 31 Jul 1890 St.Andrews, Manitoba (MB Vital Statistics, Marriage Reg. #1890,001554.). He died on 21 Sep 1932 Selkirk, Manitoba, at age 68 (Ibid., Death Reg. #1932,036266.). He was buried on 23 Sep 1932 Little Britain Cemetery, St.Andrews, Manitoba (*Free Press*, 24 Sep 1932.).

Mary Todd was born circa 1868 (SMACPLP, M-104.). She died before 1890.

Children of **Joseph Visignault** and **Mary Todd** were as follows:

       i.   Joseph Visignault was born circa 1885 (MB Vital Statistics, Death Reg. #1886,001171.). He died on 7 Jul 1886 Portage la Prairie, Manitoba (Ibid.).

      ii.   Alice Visignault was born on 1 Jul 1886 (1901 Canada, District #8 (k-9), page 5, line 19.). She married Howard A. McGowan, son of John McGowan and Mary McFarland, on 16 Jun 1908 Portage la Prairie, Manitoba (MB Vital Statistics, Marriage Reg. #1908,004240.).

          Howard A. McGowan was born on 2 Nov 1875 Ontario (1901 Canada, District 8-n-1, page 4, family 31, line 22-26.). He died on 29 Nov 1940 Westbourne, Manitoba, at age 65 (MB Vital Statistics, Death Reg. #1940,048541.).

Ellen Linklater was born on 2 May 1873 Grand Marais, Manitoba (Rod Mac Quarrie, 29 Mar 2012.). She died on 5 Nov 1946 Selkirk, Manitoba, at age 73 (*Free Press*, 9 Nov 1946, Saturday, page 30.). She was buried on 8 Nov 1946 Little Britain Cemetery, St.Andrews, Manitoba (Ibid.).

Children of **Joseph Visignault** and **Ellen Linklater** were as follows:

       i.   Mary Ann Visignault was born in Mar 1891 (1891 Canada, District 7W, page 135, line 23.). She died on 17 Feb 1893 St.Andrews, Manitoba, at age 1 (MB Vital Statistics, Death Reg. #1893,002445.).

      ii.   Archibald James Visignault was born on 3 Jan 1893 R.M. of St.Andrews, Manitoba (Ibid., Birth Reg. #1893,005101.). He died on 15 Sep 1916 France at age 23 (Rod Mac Quarrie, 29 Mar 2012.).

     iii.   Mabel Visignault was born on 7 Dec 1894 (1901 Canada, District #8 (k-9), page 5, line 19.).

     iv.   Dinah Visignault was born on 4 Feb 1896 (Ibid.). She married Malcolm Andrew Downey on 9 Jul 1919 Portage la Prairie, Manitoba (MB Vital Statistics, Marriage Reg. #1919,039026.).

          Malcolm Andrew Downey was born on 17 Sep 1892 Gladstone, RM of Westbourne, Manitoba (Ibid., Birth Reg. #1892,1749860.).

       v.   William Visignault was born on 12 Jun 1898 Portage la Prairie, Manitoba (1901 Canada, District #8 (k-9), page 5, line 19.) (WWI Canada Canadian Soldiers of the First World War (1914-1918) National Archives of Canada, Ottawa, Ontario, http://www.collectionscanada.gc.ca.). He died on 15 Sep 1916 France at age 18 (Rod Mac Quarrie, 29 Mar 2012.).

      vi.   Ruth Lucy Visignault was born on 14 Dec 1901 Portage la Prairie, Manitoba (Automated Genealogy 1906 Census Transcription Project and Census Images from the National Archives of Canada, http://www.automatedgenealogy.com, District #6-19-B, page 37, line 19.) (Rod Mac Quarrie, 29 Mar 2012.).

vii. Edith Visignault was born on 9 Oct 1904 (1906 Canada, District #6-19-B, page 37, line 19.) (MB Vital Statistics, Birth Reg. #1904,007110.). She married Russel Thompson Gillespie on 23 Nov 1922 Mayfield, R.M. of Westbourne, Manitoba (Ibid., Marriage Reg. #1922,045015.).

Russel Thompson Gillespie was born on 29 Mar 1900 Portage la Prairie, Manitoba (Ibid., Birth Reg. #1900,19113578.).

viii. Ethel Visignault was born in Jun 1907 (Ibid., Death Reg. #1913,010309.). She died on 17 Feb 1913 RM of Portage la Prairie, Manitoba, at age 5 (Ibid.).

ix. Myrtle May Visignault was born in Oct 1910 (Automated Genealogy 1911 Census Transcription Project and Census Images from the National Archives of Canada, http://www.automatedgenealogy.com, District 36, page 4, line 45.). She died on 6 Jun 1959 St.Boniface, Manitoba, at age 48 (Rod Mac Quarrie, 29 Mar 2012.).

4. Jane Visignault was born in 1866 (Manitoba) (Denney.). She married **Robert John Donald**, son of **William Donald** and **Jane Firth,** on 5 Mar 1885 Little Britain, Manitoba (Ibid.). She married **James McCorrister**, son of **Henry McCorrister** and **Marie Tait,** circa 1892 (MB Vital Statistics, Birth Reg. #1893,003163.). She died on 27 Mar 1894 St.Clements, Manitoba (Ibid., Birth Reg. #1894,001863.).

Robert John Donald was born on 14 Nov 1860 St.Andrews, (Manitoba) (HBC-PN , St.Andrews, #148.). He was baptized on 25 Nov 1860 St.Andrews, (Manitoba) (Denney.). He died on 10 Jan 1890 St.Andrews, Manitoba, at age 29 (MB Vital Statistics, Death Reg. #1890,002492.).

James McCorrister was born on 13 Nov 1850 St.Andrews, (Manitoba) (MBS, C-14930.). He was baptized on 11 Dec 1850 St.Andrews, (Manitoba) (Denney.). He married **Elizabeth Corrigal**, daughter of **John Corrigal** and **Eliza Firth,** before 1875 (MBS, C-14930.). He died on 8 Apr 1912 Portage la Prairie, Manitoba, at age 61 (MB Vital Statistics, Death Reg. #1912,002014.).

5. Louis Moise Visignault was born on 12 Jul 1868 (Rod Mac Quarrie, 29 Mar 2012.). He married **Emma Hester Alice Mowat**, daughter of **Robert Mowat** and **Charlotte Firth,** on 27 Aug 1890 Selkirk, Manitoba (MB Vital Statistics, Marriage Reg. #1890,001258.). He died in 1945 (Rod Mac Quarrie, 29 Mar 2012.).

Emma Hester Alice Mowat was born on 19 Sep 1870 St.Andrews, Manitoba (Ibid.). She was baptized on 5 Mar 1871 St.Andrews, Manitoba (Denney.). She died on 11 May 1945 Selkirk, Manitoba, at age 74 (*Free Press*, 12 May 1945, page 4, 20.).

Children of **Louis Moise Visignault** and **Emma Hester Alice Mowat** were as follows:

i. Mary Ellen Viznaugh was born on 6 May 1892 (Rod Mac Quarrie, 29 Mar 2012.). She married Joseph Smith, son of Joseph Smith and Jane Pruden, on 2 Sep 1908 R.M. of St.Andrews, Manitoba (MB Vital Statistics, Marriage Reg. #1908,001661.). She died on 14 May 1961 Beausejour, Manitoba, at age 69 (*Free Press*, May 15, 1961, page 26.).

Joseph Smith was born on 30 Jul 1883 R.M. of St.Andrews, Manitoba (MB Vital Statistics, Birth Reg. #1883,004415.). He was baptized on 26 Aug 1883 St.Andrews, Manitoba (Rod Mac Quarrie, 29 May 2013.). He died on 17 Sep 1945 at age 62 (*Free Press*, May 15, 1961, page 26.).

ii. Walter Edward Viznaugh was born on 6 Feb 1894 RM of St.Andrews, Manitoba (MB Vital Statistics, Birth Reg. #1894,001824.). He died on 23 Nov 1901 RM of St.Andrews, Manitoba, at age 7 (Ibid., Death Reg. #1901,002154.).

iii. William Hector Vizena was born on 22 Jan 1896 St.Andrews, Manitoba (Rod Mac Quarrie, 29 Mar 2012.). He died on 30 Aug 1918 France at age 22 (Ibid.).

iv. Louis Vizena was born on 20 Dec 1897 Lockport, RM of St.Andrews, Manitoba (Ibid.). He died on 22 Oct 1918 France at age 20 (Ibid.).

v. Peter Viznaugh was born on 12 May 1900 RM of St.Andrews, Manitoba (MB Vital Statistics, Birth Reg. #1900,002104.). He died on 16 Apr 1901 RM of St.Andrews, Manitoba (Ibid., Death Reg. #1901,003462.).

vi. Charlotte Ann Viznaugh was born on 17 Feb 1902 RM of St.Andrews, Manitoba (Ibid., Birth Reg. #1902,004235.).

vii. Joseph Viznaugh was born on 2 Mar 1904 RM of St.Andrews, Manitoba (Ibid., Birth Reg. #1904,005296.). He died on 15 Jun 1907 RM of St.Andrews, Manitoba, at age 3 (Ibid., Death Reg. #1907,001506.).

viii. Edna Margaret Viznaugh was born on 9 Mar 1907 RM of St.Andrews, Manitoba (Ibid., Birth Reg. #1907,006549.). She married James Stewart Linklater, son of William Linklater and Annie Swain, on 30 Apr 1927 St.Clements, Manitoba (Ibid., Marriage Reg. #1927,023259.).

James Stewart Linklater was born on 5 Dec 1904 Portage la Prairie, Manitoba (Ibid., Birth Reg. #1904,001624.).

ix. Orton Irwin Viznaugh was born on 9 Mar 1907 Little Britain, RM of St.Andrews, Manitoba (Rod Mac Quarrie, 29 Mar 2012.) (MB Vital Statistics, Birth Reg. #1907,006548.). He married Elizabeth Jean Hill before 1956 (Rod Mac Quarrie, 29 Mar 2012.). He died on 2 Oct 1956 General Hospital, Winnipeg, Manitoba, at age 49 (Ibid.).

Elizabeth Jean Hill died on 6 Jun 1990 Dryden, Ontario (Ibid.).

x. Norman Viznaugh was born on 20 May 1909 RM of St.Andrews, Manitoba (Ibid.). He married Florence May Hourie, daughter of William Hourie and Mary Alice Folster, on 8 Nov 1929 Brokenhead Reserve, Manitoba (Ibid., 29 May 2013.). He died on 6 Mar 1962 Selkirk, Manitoba, at age 52 (Ibid., 29 Mar 2012.).

Florence May Hourie was born on 12 Jun 1913 Poplar Park, R.M. of St.Clements, Manitoba (MB Vital Statistics, Birth Reg. #1913,031696; Reg. Date: 20/06/1913.). She died on 29 Mar 1999 Concordia Hospital, Winnipeg, Manitoba, at age 85 (*Free Press*, 1999.).

xi. Philip Viznaugh was born on 6 Jul 1911 RM of St.Andrews, Manitoba (MB Vital Statistics, Birth Reg. #1911,004030.). He died in 1977 (Rod Mac Quarrie, 29 Mar 2012.). He was buried in 1977 Balsam Bay, Manitoba (Ibid.).

xii. John R. Viznaugh was born in 1913 (Ibid.). He died in 1974 (Ibid.). He was buried in 1974 Balsam Bay, Manitoba (Ibid.).

xiii. Benjamin Viznaugh was born in 1922 St.Louis, Saskatchewan (Ibid.). He died on 3 Mar 1984 (Ibid.).

Ahnentafel between Alexis Vivier and Gregoire Vivier

--- 1st Generation ---

1. ALEXIS VIVIER was born on 24 Mar 1768 at Cap-de-la-Madeleine, Quebec (PRDH online index, http://www.genealogic.umontreal.ca, No. 569208.). He was baptized on 25 Mar 1768 at Cap-de-la-Madeleine, Quebec (Ibid.). He was born circa 1769 at Cap-de-Magdelaine, Champlain, Quebec (Denney Papers, Charles D. Denney, Glenbow Archives, Calgary, Alberta.). He married **MARIE ANNE ASSINIBOINE** before 1796. He married **MARIE ANNE ASSINIBOINE** on 21 Jan 1834 at St.Francois Xavier, (Manitoba) (SFXI: 1834-1852 St.Francois Xavier 1834-1852 Register Index, M-5. Hereinafter cited as SFXI: 1835-1852.) (MM *Manitoba Marriages* in *Publication 45*, Volumes 1-3, compiled and edited by: Paul J. Lareau, Fr. Julien Hamelin, (240 Avenue Daly, Ottawa, Ontario K1N 6G2: Le Centre de Genealogie S.C., 1984), page 9.). He died on 11 Sep 1862 at St.Francois Xavier, (Manitoba), at age 94 (SFXI-Kipling St.Francois Xavier Register Index, 1834-1900; compiled by Clarence Kipling , S-12.). He was buried on 12 Sep 1862 at St.Francois Xavier, (Manitoba) (Ibid.) (SFXI: 1851-1869 St.Francois Xavier 1851-69 Register Index.) (SFXI 1851-1868 St.Francois Xavier 1852-1861 Register Index, S-12. Hereinafter cited as SFXI 1851-1868.).

--- 2nd Generation ---

2. JOSEPH VIVIER was born on 23 Jan 1733 at Quebec, Quebec, Quebec (PRDH online, No. 159671.). He was baptized on 24 Jan 1733 at Quebec, Quebec, Quebec (Ibid.). As of 24 Jan 1733, he was also known as **LOUIS JOSEPH VIVIER** (Ibid.). He married **MARIE JOSEPHE GAUTHIER**, daughter of **JEAN-BAPTISTE GAUTHIER** and **CATHERINE LEMAY**, on 21 Feb 1757 at Cap-de-la-Madeleine, Champlain, Quebec (DNCF *Dictionnaire National des Canadiens-Francais Tome I & II* Gabriel Drouin, editor (revised 1985; Siege Social, 4184, rue St-Denis, Montreal, Canada: l'Institut Genealogique Drouin, 1979), page 1346.). He married **LOUISE LABADIE**, daughter of **PIERRE LABADIE** and **MARIE JOSEPHE GILBERT DIT GUEBERT**, on 10 Jan 1763 at Cap-de-la-Madeleine, Champlain, Quebec (Ibid.) (PRDH online, No. 267193.). He died on 6 May 1811 at Cap-de-la-Madeleine, Quebec, at age 78 (Ibid., No. 1143068.). He was buried on 8 May 1811 at Cap-de-la-Madeleine, Champlain, Quebec (Ibid.).

--- 3rd Generation ---

4. PIERRE VIVIER (Ibid., #74639.) (Ibid.) was born on 30 Sep 1679 at Charlesbourg, Quebec (DGFQ Jette, Rene, *Dictionnaire Genealogique des Familles du Quebec des Origines a 1730* (Montreal, Quebec, Canada: University of Montreal Press, 1983), page 1130.) (DGFC Tanguay, Cyprien, *Dictionnaire Genealogique des Familles Canadiennes* (28 Felsmere Avenue, Pawtucket, Rhode Island 02861-2903: Quintin Publications, 1996 reprint), Volume 7, page 478.). He was baptized on 30 Sep 1679 at Charlesbourg, Quebec (DGFQ, page 1130.). He married **MARIE-CATHERINE DAUPHIN**, daughter of **RENE DAUPHIN** and **SUZANNE GIGNARD**, on 30 May 1718 at Beauport, Quebec (DNCF, page 1346.) (DGFQ, page 1131.). He died on 20 Apr 1742 at Hotel-Dieu, Quebec, Quebec, Quebec, at age 62 (PRDH online, #74639.). He was buried on 21 Apr 1742 at Hotel-Dieu, Quebec, Quebec, Quebec (Ibid.).

--- 4th Generation ---

8. PIERRE VIVIER lived at at Thire, Lucon, Poitou (DNCF, page 1346.). He was born in 1638 (DGFC, Volume 7, page 477.). A contract for the marriage to **MARGUERITE ROY**, daughter of **MATHURIN ROY** and **MARGUERITE BIRE**, was signed on 4 Feb 1665 (DGFQ, page 1130.). He married **MARGUERITE ROY**, daughter of **MATHURIN ROY** and **MARGUERITE BIRE**, on 16 Feb 1665 at Quebec, Quebec, Quebec (Ibid.) (DNCF, page 1346.) (PRDH online.). He died on 17 Apr 1702 at Charlesbourg, Quebec, Quebec (DGFQ, page 1131.). He was buried on 18 Apr 1702 at Charlesbourg, Quebec, Quebec (Ibid.).

--- 5th Generation ---

16. GREGOIRE VIVIER married **CLEMENCE ADJOURNE**.

Descendants of Alexis Vivier

Generation One

1. Alexis Vivier was born on 24 Mar 1768 Cap-de-la-Madeleine, Quebec (PRDH online index, http://www.genealogic.umontreal.ca, No. 569208.). He was baptized on 25 Mar 1768 Cap-de-la-Madeleine, Quebec (Ibid.). He was born circa 1769 Cap-de-Magdeleine, Champlain, Quebec (Denney Papers, Charles D. Denney, Glenbow Archives, Calgary, Alberta.). He married **Marie Anne Assiniboine** before 1796. He married **Marie Anne Assiniboine** on 21 Jan 1834 St.Francois Xavier, (Manitoba) (SFXI: 1834-1852 St.Francois Xavier 1834-1852 Register Index, M-5. Hereinafter cited as SFXI: 1835-1852.) (MM *Manitoba Marriages* in *Publication 45*, Volumes 1-3, compiled and edited by: Paul J. Lareau, Fr. Julien Hamelin, (240 Avenue Daly, Ottawa, Ontario K1N 6G2: Le Centre de Genealogie S.C., 1984), page 9.). He died on 11 Sep 1862 St.Francois Xavier, (Manitoba), at age 94 (SFXI-Kipling St.Francois Xavier Register Index, 1834-1900; compiled by Clarence Kipling , S-12.). He was buried on 12 Sep 1862 St.Francois Xavier, (Manitoba) (Ibid.) (SFXI: 1851-1869 St.Francois Xavier 1851-69 Register Index.) (SFXI 1851-1868 St.Francois Xavier 1852-1861 Register Index, S-12. Hereinafter cited as SFXI 1851-1868.).

Marie Anne Assiniboine was born circa 1784 (SFXI-Kipling, S-9.). She was born circa 1789 (SFXI: 1835-1852, B-9.). She was baptized on 20 Jan 1834 St.Francois Xavier, (Manitoba) (SFXI-Kipling, B-9.) (SFXI: 1835-1852, B-9.). She died on 18 Apr 1874 St.Francois Xavier, Manitoba (SFXI-Kipling, S-9.). She was buried on 20 Apr 1874 St.Francois Xavier, Manitoba (Ibid.).

Children of **Alexis Vivier** and **Marie Anne Assiniboine** were as follows:

> 2   i.   Alexis Vivier, b. circa 1796; m. Isabelle Short; d. 19 Apr 1876 Baie St.Paul, Manitoba; bur. 20 Apr 1876 Baie St.Paul, Manitoba.
>
> 3   ii.   Madeleine Vivier, b. circa 1811; m. Urbain Delorme; d. 6 Mar 1875 St.Francois Xavier, Manitoba; bur. 8 Mar 1875 St.Francois Xavier, Manitoba.
>
> 4   iii.   Marguerite Vivier, b. circa 1812; m. Michel Desmarais; d. 28 Aug 1832; bur. 30 Aug 1832 St.Boniface, (Manitoba).
>
> 5   iv.   Joseph Vivier, b. circa 1813 Ruperts Land; m. Marguerite Martineau; m. Marguerite Hamelin; d. 1 Dec 1890 St.Daniel, Manitoba.
>
> 6   v.   Marie Vivier, b. 1 Jan 1817 North West; m. Joseph Malaterre.
>
> 7   vi.   Josette Vivier, b. circa 1818; m. Francois Larocque.
>
> 8   vii.   Michel Vivier, b. 1 Jan 1820 Red River, (Manitoba); m. Madeleine Fournier.
>
> 9   viii.   Olivier "Carlouche" Vivier, b. circa 1821; m. Louise Vallee.
>
> 10   ix.   Louise Vivier, b. circa 1825; m. Joseph Nault; d. 17 Apr 1865 St.Francois Xavier, (Manitoba); bur. 19 Apr 1865 St.Francois Xavier, (Manitoba).

Generation Two

2. Alexis Vivier was born circa 1796 (MBS Scrip Applications, Original White Settlers & Halfbreeds residing in Manitoba on 15 July 1870, RG15-19, C-14934.). He was born circa 1808 Moose District (1870C-MB 1870 Manitoba Census, National Archives of Canada, Ottawa, Ontario, Microfilm Reel Number C-2170., page 369, #1355.). He married **Isabelle Short**, daughter of **James Short** and **Betsy Sauteuse**, on 27 Jan 1834 St.Francois Xavier, (Manitoba) (SFXI: 1835-1852, M-6.). He married **Angelique Chalifoux**, daughter of **Michel Chalifoux dit Richard** and **Isabelle Collin,** before 1861. He died on 19 Apr 1876 Baie St.Paul, Manitoba (MBS, C-14934.). He was buried on 20 Apr 1876 Baie St.Paul, Manitoba (Ibid.).

Isabelle Short was born circa 1804 Ruperts Land (SFXI-Kipling, B-10, page 2.). She was baptized on 27 Jan 1834 St.Francois Xavier, (Manitoba) (Ibid.) (SFXI: 1835-1852, B-10.). She married according to the custom of the country **John James Favel**, son of **Thomas Favel** and **Sally Cree Pa-sa Trout,** before 1822.

Children of **Alexis Vivier** and **Isabelle Short** were as follows:

> 11   i.   Alexis Vivier, b. circa 1825; m. Elise Bousquet; m. Isabelle (--?--); d. 15 Aug 1924 Portage la Prairie, Manitoba.
>
> 12   ii.   Joseph Vivier, b. 1825 St.Francois Xavier, (Manitoba).
>
> 13   iii.   Marie Vivier, b. 5 Oct 1832 White Horse Plains, (Manitoba); m. Michel Lecuyer.
>
> 14   iv.   Marie Madelaine Vivier, b. 26 Jun 1836 St.Francois Xavier, (Manitoba); m. Pierre Descoteaux.
>
> 15   v.   Josephte Vivier, b. 3 Sep 1838 St.Francois Xavier, (Manitoba); m. Francois Xavier Lecuyer.
>
> 16   vi.   Bernard Vivier, b. 9 Jul 1840 St.Francois Xavier, (Manitoba); m. Angelique Sauteuse; m. Isabelle Ducharme; d. 14 Jan 1929 Portage la Prairie, Manitoba.
>
> 17   vii.   Alexis Vivier, b. 20 Oct 1842; m. Julie Wells.
>
> 18   viii.   Caroline Vivier, b. 8 Apr 1845 St.Francois Xavier, (Manitoba); m. Joseph Gouin.
>
> 19   ix.   Charles Vivier, b. 15 Mar 1847; m. Marguerite Parenteau.

Angelique Chalifoux was born in 1805 North West (MBS, C-14934.). She was born before 1822 (SFX: 1834-1850 St.Francois Xavier 1834-1851 Register, M-48. Hereinafter cited as SFX: 1834-1850.). She married **Jean Baptiste Wells**, son of **Jean Baptiste Wells** and **Marie Crise,** on 13 Jan 1840 St.Francois Xavier, (Manitoba) (Ibid.).

Children of **Alexis Vivier** and **Angelique Chalifoux** were:

> 20   i.   Marie Anne Vivier, b. 20 Sep 1861 Baie St.Paul, (Manitoba); m. Thomas Favel.

3. Madeleine Vivier was born circa 1811 (SFXI-Kipling, S-7.). She married **Urbain Delorme**, son of **Francois Delorme** and **Madeleine Saulteaux,** before 1824. She died on 6 Mar 1875 St.Francois Xavier, Manitoba (Ibid.). She was buried on 8 Mar 1875 St.Francois Xavier, Manitoba (Ibid.).

Urbain Delorme was born circa 1797 (Manitoba) (1870C-MB, page 273, #978.). He was born circa 1798 Ruperts Land (1835C RRS HBCA E5/8 1835 Census of the Red River Settlement, HBCA E5/8, Hudson's Bay Company Archives, Provincial Archives, 200 Vaughan Street, Winnipeg, MB R3C 1T5, Canada., page 25.). He was born in 1800 Headingley, (Manitoba) (MBS, C-14927.) (1838C RRS HBCA E5/9 1838 Census of the Red River Settlement, HBCA E5/9, Hudson's Bay Company Archives, Provincial Archives, 200

Vaughan Street, Winnipeg, MB R3C 1T5, Canada., page 34.). He died on 18 Aug 1886 St.Daniel, Carman, Manitoba (SFXI-Kipling.) (Manitoba Vital Statistics online, http://web2.gov.mb.ca, Death Reg. #1886,001319.). He was buried on 20 Aug 1886 St.Daniel, Carman, Manitoba (SFXI-Kipling.).

4. Marguerite Vivier was born circa 1812. She married **Michel Desmarais**, son of **Jean Baptiste Desmarais** and **Louise Saulteaux**, on 11 Jan 1830 St.Boniface, (Manitoba) (SB 1825-1834 St.Boniface Roman Catholic Registre des Baptemes, Mariages & Sepultures, 1825-1834, page 37, M-96. Hereinafter cited as SB 1825-1834.). She died on 28 Aug 1832 (Ibid., page 73, S-_.). She was buried on 30 Aug 1832 St.Boniface, (Manitoba) (Ibid.).

Michel Desmarais was born circa 1810 Ruperts Land (1833C RRS HBCA E5/7 1833 Census of the Red River Settlement, HBCA E5/7, Hudson's Bay Company Archives, Provincial Archives, 200 Vaughan Street, Winnipeg, MB R3C 1T5, Canada., page 20.). He was baptized on 10 Jan 1830 St.Boniface, (Manitoba) (SB 1825-1834, page 38, B-598.). He married **Josephte Rochon**, daughter of **Joseph Rochon** and **Josephte Ducharme**, on 8 Sep 1835 St.Francois Xavier, (Manitoba) (SFX: 1834-1850, M-17.). He died on 15 May 1880 Lebret, (Saskatchewan) (L1, page 262, S-16.). He was buried on 17 May 1880 Lebret, (Saskatchewan) (Ibid.).

5. Joseph Vivier was born in 1811 Pembina County (MBS, C-14934.). He was born circa 1813 Ruperts Land (1843C RRS HBCA E5/11 1843 Census of the Red River Settlement, HBCA E5/11, Hudson's Bay Company Archives, Provincial Archives, 200 Vaughan Street, Winnipeg, MB R3C 1T5, Canada., page 29.). He married **Marguerite Martineau**, daughter of **Ambroise Martineau** and **Josephte Indian**, on 20 May 1839 St.Francois Xavier, (Manitoba) (SFX: 1834-1850, M-41.). He married **Marguerite Hamelin**, daughter of **Joseph Hamelin** and **Therese Ducharme**, before 1862. He died on 1 Dec 1890 St.Daniel, Manitoba (SFXI-Kipling, S-26.).

Marguerite Martineau was born circa 1799 (SFX: 1834-1850, B-251.). She was born in Feb 1805 Sault Ste.Marie, (Ontario) (MBS, C-14934.). She was baptized on 19 May 1839 St.Francois Xavier, (Manitoba) (SFX: 1834-1850, B-251.). She married according to the custom of the country **Francois Gourneau** before 1825.

Marguerite Hamelin was born in 1836 St.Vital, (Manitoba) (MBS, C-14929.). She was born circa 1839 (1892 Oct 1 McCumber Census of the Turtle Mountain band of Chippewa Indians, Belcourt, North Dakota, National Archives of the United States, Washington D.C., Document No. 229, Family 131, #561.). She married **John Kipling**, son of **John James Kipling** and **Marguerite Okkanens Saulteaux**, before 1854.

Children of **Joseph Vivier** and **Marguerite Hamelin** were as follows:

    i.   Joseph Vivier was born on 19 Mar 1863 St.Charles, (Manitoba) (SB-Rozyk St. Boniface Roman Catholic Church, Manitoba, Canada, Baptisms, Marriages and Burials 1860-1875 Extractions, Compiled by Rosemary Rozyk, page 113, B-70.). He was baptized on 20 Mar 1863 St.Boniface, (Manitoba) (Ibid.).

    ii.   Modeste Vivier was born on 26 Oct 1864 (Ibid., page 166, B-107.). He was baptized on 1 Nov 1864 St.Boniface, (Manitoba) (Ibid.).

    iii.   Catherine Vivier was born on 18 May 1866 St.Charles, (Manitoba) (MBS, C-14934.). She was baptized on 20 May 1866 St.Boniface, (Manitoba) (Ibid.). She died on 3 May 1872 St.Charles, (Manitoba), at age 5 (Ibid.). She was buried on 6 May 1872 St.Boniface, (Manitoba) (Ibid.).

    iv.   Marguerite Catherine Hamelin was born on 18 May 1866 (SB-Rozyk, page 50, B-59.). She was baptized on 20 May 1866 St.Boniface, (Manitoba) (Ibid.). She married John Burns on 25 Jun 1891 St.Francois Xavier, Manitoba (SFXI-Kipling, M-6.). She died on 19 Nov 1896 St.Daniel, Manitoba, at age 30 (Ibid., S-17.).

        John Burns was born circa 1860 Fort Benton, Choteau County, Montana (Ibid., M-6 (note).). He married **Elise Ouellette**, daughter of **Pierre Ouellette** and **Marguerite Grandbois**, circa 1881. He married **Rosalie Desjardins**, daughter of **Joseph Desjardins** and **Genevieve Guiboche**, on 10 Jan 1883 St.Francois Xavier, Manitoba (SFXI-Kipling.). He married **Ellen Burke** circa 1885. He married **Mary Crosby** before 1895.

    v.   Sophie Vivier was born circa 1867 (Manitoba) (1870C-MB, page 238, #372.). She was born in May 1870 (SFXI-Kipling, S-4.). She died on 25 Mar 1885 Elm River, Manitoba (Ibid.) (MB Vital Statistics, Death Reg. #1885,002255.).

    vi.   Patrice Vivier was born on 18 Mar 1876 RM of Elm River, Manitoba (Ibid., Birth Reg. #1884,004663.).

21 vii.   Adelaide Vivier, b. 18 Aug 1878 RM of Elm River, Manitoba; m. Pierre Isidore Ouellette; d. 13 Oct 1912 Ste.Rose, Manitoba.

    viii. Francois Vivier was born on 3 Apr 1880 RM of Elm River, Manitoba (SFXI-Kipling, S-8.) (MB Vital Statistics, Birth Reg. #1884,004670.). He died on 10 Jun 1896 St.Daniel, Manitoba, at age 16 (SFXI-Kipling, S-8.).

6. Marie Vivier was born on 1 Jan 1817 North West (MBS, C-14930.). She married **Joseph Malaterre**, son of **Jean Baptiste Malaterre** and **Angelique Adam**, on 11 Jan 1842 St.Francois Xavier, (Manitoba) (SFX: 1834-1850, M-65.).

Joseph Malaterre was born circa 1818 (SFXI-Kipling, S-23.). He was born circa 1823 Ruperts Land (1843C RRS HBCA E5/11, page 27.). He died on 3 Sep 1863 St.Francois Xavier, (Manitoba) (SFXI-Kipling, S-23.) (SFXI 1851-1868, S-23.). He was buried on 5 Sep 1863 St.Francois Xavier, (Manitoba) (SFXI-Kipling, S-23.) (SFXI-1834-54.) (SFXI 1851-1868, S-23.).

7. Josette Vivier was born circa 1818. She married **Francois Larocque** before 1836. Question: *Is Josette the daughter of Alexis Vivier?*

8. Michel Vivier was born on 1 Jan 1820 Red River, (Manitoba) (NWHBS 1885 Scrip Applications, North-West Halfbreeds residing outside Manitoba on 15 July 1870, RG15-20, C-14942.). He married **Madeleine Fournier**, daughter of **Francois Fournier** and **Angelique Methote**, on 11 Jan 1842 St.Francois Xavier, (Manitoba) (SFX: 1834-1850, M-67.).

Madeleine Fournier was born in Sep 1823 Pembina (MBS, C-14934.). She was born on 13 Sep 1825 St.Boniface, (Manitoba) (SB 1825-1834, page 17, B-138.). She was baptized on 23 Oct 1825 St.Boniface, (Manitoba) (Ibid.). She died on 30 Aug 1902 St.Boniface, Manitoba, at age 76 (MB Vital Statistics, Death Reg. #1902,003804.).

Children of **Michel Vivier** and **Madeleine Fournier** were as follows:

    i.   Madeline Vivier was born on 14 Mar 1843 St.Francois Xavier, (Manitoba) (SFX: 1834-1850, B-452.). She was baptized on 14 Mar 1843 St.Francois Xavier, (Manitoba) (Ibid.). She died on 7 Dec 1843 (Ibid., S-93.). She was buried on 9 Dec 1843 St.Francois Xavier, (Manitoba) (Ibid.).

22 ii.   Marie Vivier, b. 30 Oct 1844; m. Michel Matwewinind.

23   iii.   Michel Vivier, b. 15 Apr 1847; m. Elise Deschamps.
        iv.   Iphigenie Vivier was born on 10 Feb 1851 St.Francois Xavier, (Manitoba) (Ibid., B-890.). She was baptized on 10 Feb 1851 St.Francois Xavier, (Manitoba) (Ibid.). She died on 26 Jul 1861 St.Francois Xavier, (Manitoba), at age 10 (SFXI-Kipling, S-15.). She was buried on 27 Jul 1861 St.Francois Xavier, (Manitoba) (Ibid.) (SFXI-1834-54.).
        v.   Sophie Vivier was born on 27 Jan 1853 St.Francois Xavier, (Manitoba) (SFXI-Kipling, B-58.) (SFXI 1851-1868, B-58.). She was baptized on 29 Jan 1853 St.Francois Xavier, (Manitoba) (SFXI-Kipling, B-58.) (SFXI 1851-1868, B-58.). She died on 28 Jan 1855 St.Francois Xavier, (Manitoba), at age 2 (SFXI-Kipling, S-9.) (SFXI 1851-1868, S-9.). She was buried on 29 Jan 1855 St.Francois Xavier, (Manitoba) (SFXI-Kipling, S-9.) (SFXI 1851-1868, S-9.).
        vi.   Angelique Vivier was born on 3 Feb 1855 St.Francois Xavier, (Manitoba) (SFXI-Kipling, B-16.) (SFXI 1851-1868, B-16.). She was baptized on 3 Feb 1855 St.Francois Xavier, (Manitoba) (SFXI-Kipling, B-16.) (SFXI 1851-1868, B-16.). She died on 24 May 1870 St.Francois Xavier, (Manitoba), at age 15 (SFXI-Kipling, S-15.). She was buried on 25 May 1870 St.Francois Xavier, (Manitoba) (Ibid.).
        vii.   Norbert Vivier was born on 19 Nov 1857 St.Francois Xavier, (Manitoba) (Ibid., B-216.). He was baptized on 25 Nov 1857 St.Francois Xavier, (Manitoba) (Ibid.) (INB *Index des Naissances and Baptemes* (St.Boniface, Manitoba: La Societe Historique de Saint-Boniface., c1995), page 184.). He died on 6 Nov 1865 St.Francois Xavier, (Manitoba), at age 7 (SFXI-Kipling, S-41.). He was buried on 7 Nov 1865 St.Francois Xavier, (Manitoba) (Ibid.) (SFXI-1834-54.).
        viii.   Maxime Vivier was born circa 1859 (SFXI-Kipling, S-26.). He died on 6 Oct 1863 St.Francois Xavier, (Manitoba) (Ibid.). He was buried on 7 Oct 1863 St.Francois Xavier, (Manitoba) (Ibid.).
        ix.   Emile Vivier was born on 24 Apr 1860 St.Francois Xavier, (Manitoba) (Ibid., B-20.). He was baptized on 25 Apr 1860 St.Francois Xavier, (Manitoba) (Ibid.).
        x.   Bernard Vivier was born on 7 Aug 1862 St.Francois Xavier, (Manitoba) (Ibid., B-68.). He was baptized on 8 Aug 1862 St.Francois Xavier, (Manitoba) (Ibid.). He died on 28 May 1878 St.Francois Xavier, Manitoba, at age 15 (Ibid., S-31.).
24   xi.   Jean Baptiste Vivier, b. 29 Aug 1864 St.Francois Xavier, (Manitoba); m. Caroline Lucier; d. 24 Dec 1909 St.Francois Xavier, Manitoba.
        xii.   Marie Vivier was born circa 1865 (Manitoba) (1870C-MB, page 275, #1021.).
25   xiii.   Elzear Vivier, b. 18 Mar 1867 St.Francois Xavier, (Manitoba); m. Rosalie Rolette.

9. Olivier "Carlouche" Vivier was born circa 1821. He married **Louise Vallee**, daughter of **Antoine Vallee** and **Suzanne Lefebvre or Favel,** on 27 Sep 1842 Fort-des-Prairies, (Alberta) (FDP Baptisms & Marriages Fort des Prairie, Saskatchewan District, C Kipling, M-24. Hereinafter cited as FDP.). He married **Louise Vallee**, daughter of **Antoine Vallee** and **Suzanne Lefebvre or Favel,** before 1853. **Louise Vallee** was born in 1817.
Children of **Olivier "Carlouche" Vivier** and **Louise Vallee** were as follows:
        i.   Elizabeth Vivier was born before 1842 (Ibid.).
        ii.   Alexandre Vivier was born in 1844 Fort Pitt, (Saskatchewan) (ArchiviaNet, C-15009.). He died in 1872 Fort Pitt, (Saskatchewan) (Ibid.).
        iii.   Marie Vivier was born circa 1846. She married Wates-eo-wen [?] (--?--) (Ibid.).
        iv.   Scholastique Vivier was born circa 1848. She married William Assakang [?] (Ibid.).
26   v.   Christianne Vivier, b. circa 1851; m. Theodore Decoine; m. Henri Eric Lapoudre dit Decoine; d. circa Jul 1885 Lac la Biche, (Alberta).
27   vi.   Emelie Vivier, b. 1853 Fort Pitt, (Saskatchewan); m. Alfred 'Rabasca' Schmidt.
        vii.   Dolphus Augustin Vivier was born circa Aug 1853 (LLBR1, B-3.). He was baptized on 5 Sep 1853 Lac la Biche, (Alberta) (Ibid.).
        viii.   Jonas Vivier was born circa Oct 1855 (Ibid., page 19, B-102.). He was baptized on 6 Sep 1856 Lac la Biche, (Alberta) (Ibid.).
        ix.   Isidore Vivier was born circa Dec 1857 (Ibid., page 30, B-164.). He was baptized on 26 Oct 1858 Lac la Biche, (Alberta) (Ibid.).

10. Louise Vivier was born circa 1825 (SFXI-Kipling, S-17.). She married **Joseph Nault** on 30 Jan 1847 St.Francois Xavier, (Manitoba) (SFX: 1834-1850, M-99.). She died on 17 Apr 1865 St.Francois Xavier, (Manitoba) (SFXI-Kipling, S-17.). She was buried on 19 Apr 1865 St.Francois Xavier, (Manitoba) (Ibid.).
Joseph Nault was born circa 1782. He was born circa 1789 Quebec (1835C RRS HBCA E5/8, page 27.). He married **Josephte (--?--)** before 1827 (1827C RRS HBCA E5/1 1827 Census of the Red River Settlement, HBCA E5/1, Hudson's Bay Company Archives, Provincial Archives, 200 Vaughan Street, Winnipeg, MB R3C 1T5, Canada., page 9.). He died on 12 Apr 1865 St.Francois Xavier, (Manitoba) (SFXI-Kipling, S-16.). He was buried on 14 Apr 1865 St.Francois Xavier, (Manitoba) (Ibid.) (SFXI-1834-54.).

Generation Three

11. Alexis Vivier was born circa 1815 (Manitoba) (1870C-MB, page 240, #426.). He was born on 7 Mar 1817 bank of the Assiniboine River, St.Francois Xavier, (Manitoba) (*Winnipeg Free Press*, Winnipeg, Manitoba, 8 Mar 1919.). He was born circa 1825 (1870C-MB, page 240, #426.). He was born in 1829 St.Francois Xavier, (Manitoba) (MBS, C-14934.). He married **Elise Bousquet**, daughter of **Michel Bousquet** and **Louise Vendette,** before 1861. He married **Isabelle (--?--)** before 1881 (1881 Church of Latter Day Saints Census Transcription Project of Census Images from the National Archives of Canada, Ottawa, Canada, http://www.familysearch.org, District 183A, page 58, house 233.). He died on 15 Aug 1924 Portage la Prairie, Manitoba (MB Vital Statistics, Death Reg. #1924,032023.).
Elise Bousquet was born circa 1844 (INB, page 21.). She was born circa 1845 (MBS, C-14934.). She was baptized on 25 Jun 1845 Fort-des-Prairies (INB, page 21.). She was born circa 1847 North West Territory (1870C-MB, page 240, #427.). She died on 14 Jun 1875 St.Charles, Manitoba (MBS, C-14934.). She was buried on 15 Jun 1875 St.Boniface, Manitoba (Ibid.).

Children of **Alexis Vivier** and **Elise Bousquet** were as follows:

> 28   i.   Alexis Vivier, b. 23 Aug 1861 St.Charles, (Manitoba); m. Marie McKay.
>
>   ii.   Guillaume Vivier was born on 12 Jan 1863 (SB-Rozyk, page 112, B-65.). He was baptized on 14 Jan 1863 St.Boniface, (Manitoba) (Ibid.). He died on 14 Mar 1865 at age 2 (Ibid., page 180, S-13.). He was buried on 15 Mar 1865 St.Boniface, (Manitoba) (Ibid.).
>
> 29   iii.   Marie Vivier, b. 9 Oct 1865 St.Charles, (Manitoba); m. William Branconnier; d. 5 Jan 1954 37 McLean Street, Winnipeg, Manitoba; bur. 9 Jan 1954 St.Charles, Winnipeg, Manitoba.
>
>   iv.   Marie Madeleine Vivier was born on 20 Nov 1867 St.Charles, (Manitoba) (MBS, C-14934.) (SB-Rozyk, page 98, B-99.). She was baptized on 24 Nov 1867 St.Boniface, (Manitoba) (MBS, C-14934.) (SB-Rozyk, page 98, B-99.). She died on 22 Mar 1875 St.Charles, Manitoba, at age 7 (MBS, C-14934.). She was buried on 24 Mar 1875 St.Boniface, Manitoba (Ibid.).
>
> 30   v.   Guillaume Vivier, b. 31 May 1870 St.Charles, (Manitoba); m. Marie Rose Fidler.
>
>   vi.   William Vivier was born on 16 Apr 1874 St.Eustache, Manitoba (INB, page 184.). He was baptized on 16 Apr 1874 St.Eustache, Manitoba (IBMS.) (INB, page 184.).
>
>   vii.   Patrice Vivier was baptized on 18 Apr 1874 St.Eustache, Manitoba (IBMS.). He married Louise Lapointe, daughter of Francois Lapointe and Julie Bousquet, in 1897 (ArchiviaNet, C-15009.).
>
>   **Louise Lapointe** was born in 1877 Carlton, (Saskatchewan) (Ibid.).

Isabelle (--?--) was born circa 1839 (1881 Canada, District 183A, page 58, house 233.).

12. Joseph Vivier was born in 1825 St.Francois Xavier, (Manitoba) (MBS, C-14934.). He married **Caroline Swain**, daughter of **Thomas Swain** and **Elizabeth Sabiston,** before 1856.

Caroline Swain was born in Feb 1833 (Ibid.). She was baptized on 12 Mar 1837 St.Johns, Red River Settlement, (Manitoba) (HBCR, E.4/1a, folio 139.). She died on 4 Aug 1885 Portage la Prairie, Manitoba, at age 52 (MB Vital Statistics, Death Reg. #1885,001725.).

Children of **Joseph Vivier** and **Caroline Swain** were as follows:

> 31   i.   Isabelle Vivier, b. circa 1856 (Manitoba); m. Joseph Allary; d. 8 Aug 1894 St.Eustache, Manitoba; bur. 10 Aug 1894 St.Eustache, Manitoba.
>
>   ii.   Isabelle Vivier was born circa Dec 1859 (SFXI-Kipling, S-8.). She died on 4 Apr 1860 St.Francois Xavier, (Manitoba) (Ibid.). She was buried on 6 Apr 1860 St.Francois Xavier, (Manitoba) (Ibid.) (SFXI-1834-54.).
>
>   iii.   Joseph Vivier was born on 20 Feb 1861 (SB-Rozyk, page 11, B-32.). He was baptized on 10 Mar 1861 St.Boniface, (Manitoba) (Ibid.).
>
> 32   iv.   John Alexandre Vivier, b. circa 1863 Red River, (Manitoba); m. Virginie Hogue; d. 13 Nov 1890 RM Belcourt, Manitoba.
>
> 33   v.   Thomas Vivier, b. circa 1864 Long Lake, (Manitoba); m. Catherine Hogue; d. 5 Dec 1894 St.Francois Xavier, Manitoba.
>
>   vi.   Caroline Victoria Vivier was born on 30 Dec 1869 Baie St.Paul, (Manitoba) (MBS, C-14934.). She died on 15 May 1872 Poplar Point, Manitoba, at age 2 (Ibid.). She was buried on 16 May 1872 St.Ann, Poplar Point, Manitoba (Ibid.).
>
>   vii.   Mary Vivier was born circa 1876 Manitoba (1881 Canada, C-13283, District 186, Sub-district L, page 25, Household 114.).
>
>   viii.   James Vivier was born circa 1879 Manitoba (Ibid.).

13. Marie Vivier was born on 5 Oct 1832 White Horse Plains, (Manitoba) (SB 1825-1834, page 80, B-492.). She was baptized on 21 Oct 1832 St.Boniface, (Manitoba) (Ibid.). She married **Michel Lecuyer**, son of **Amable Lecuyer** and **Marie Saulteaux**, on 16 May 1853 St.Francois Xavier, (Manitoba) (SFXI-Kipling, M-14.) (SFXI 1851-1868, M-14.).

Michel Lecuyer was born circa 1837 Ste.Agathe, (Manitoba) (MBS, C-14930.).

14. Marie Madelaine Vivier was born on 26 Jun 1836 St.Francois Xavier, (Manitoba) (SFX: 1834-1850, B-127.). She was baptized on 26 Jun 1836 St.Francois Xavier, (Manitoba) (Ibid.). She married **Pierre Descoteaux**, son of **Pierre Descoteaux** and **Josephte Belgarde,** before 1861.

Pierre Descoteaux was born circa 1839 Red River, (Manitoba) (1850Ci-MN *Minnesota Territorial Census, 1850*, Harpole, Patricia C. and Mary D. Nagle, ed., (St.Paul, Minnesota: Minnesota Historical Society, 1972), page 20; Dwelling 17, Family 17.). He was born circa 1841 (SV St.Vital Roman Catholic Registre des Baptemes, Mariages & Septlures, Battleford, Saskatchewan, 1878-1896, page 89, S-1. Hereinafter cited as SV.). He married **Marie Watanny**, daughter of **Wa-ta-nee (--?--)** and **Ka-ma-yio-wawisk (--?--),** in 1878 Battleford, (Saskatchewan) (HBSI Index 1886-1901, 1906 Halfbreed Scrip Applications, RG15-21.) (ArchiviaNet.). He died on 3 Feb 1891 about 13 miles from, Battleford, (Saskatchewan) (SV, page 89, S-1.). He was buried on 6 Feb 1891 St.Vital, Battleford, (Saskatchewan) (Ibid.).

15. Josephte Vivier was born on 3 Sep 1838 St.Francois Xavier, (Manitoba) (SFX: 1834-1850, B-203.). She was baptized on 3 Sep 1838 St.Francois Xavier, (Manitoba) (Ibid.). She married **Francois Xavier Lecuyer**, son of **Amable Lecuyer** and **Marie Saulteaux,** before 1858.

Francois Xavier Lecuyer was born circa 1820 (Olga Our Lady of the Sacred Heart, Olga, North Dakota 1882-1900, page 263, S-_. Hereinafter cited as Olga.). He married **Clemence Laframboise**, daughter of **Louis Laframboise** and **Marie Louise Martel**, on 1 Nov 1880 Assumption, Pembina, Pembina County, Dakota Territory (AP, page 177, M-2.). He was buried on 18 Mar 1897 Olga, Cavalier County, North Dakota (Olga, page 263, S-_.).

16. Bernard Vivier was born on 9 Jul 1840 St.Francois Xavier, (Manitoba) (SFX: 1834-1850, B-311.). He was baptized on 12 Jul 1840 St.Francois Xavier, (Manitoba) (Ibid.). He married **Angelique Sauteuse** on 23 May 1866 St.Francois Xavier, (Manitoba) (SFXI-Kipling, M-5.) (MM, page 10.). He married **Isabelle Ducharme**, daughter of **Pierre or Francois Ducharme** and **Marie Louise Caplette,** on 24 Jun 1877 St.Eustache, Manitoba (MM.) (ST-BSP St.Eustache (Baie St.Paul) 1877-1900 Register, M-9. Hereinafter cited as ST-BSP.). He died on 14 Jan 1929 Portage la Prairie, Manitoba, at age 88 (MB Vital Statistics, Death Reg. #1929,004053.).

Angelique Sauteuse died before 1877.

Children of **Bernard Vivier** and **Angelique Sauteuse** were as follows:

     i.   Charles Vivier was born on 2 Apr 1867 (SFXI-Kipling, B-46.). He was baptized on 20 May 1867 St.Francois Xavier, (Manitoba) (Ibid.).

     ii.   Bernard Vivier was born on 15 Jan 1870 (Ibid., B-35.). He was baptized on 17 May 1870 St.Francois Xavier, (Manitoba) (Ibid.).

     iii.   Melanie Vivier was born on 5 Mar 1872 (Ibid., B-24.) (INB, page 184.). She was baptized on 2 Apr 1872 St.Francois Xavier, Manitoba (Ibid.) (SFXI-Kipling, B-24.).

Isabelle Ducharme was born on 10 Sep 1863 St.Boniface, (Manitoba) (MBS, C-14927.).

Children of **Bernard Vivier** and **Isabelle Ducharme** were as follows:

  34   i.   Marie Rose Vivier, b. circa 1879 Marquette, Manitoba; m. Joseph Allary.

     ii.   Patrice Vivier was born in Jan 1881 Marquette, Manitoba (1881 Canada, Film No. C-13283, District 186, Sub-district K, page 2, Household No. 7.).

     iii.   William Thomas Vivier was born on 20 Feb 1884 Winnipeg, Manitoba (MB Vital Statistics, Birth Reg. #1884,005541.).

     iv.   Annable Vivier was born on 1 Nov 1885 R.M. of Woodlands, Manitoba (Ibid., Birth Reg. #1885,001784.).

     v.   Joseph Vivier was born on 25 Mar 1888 (1901 Canada, #11, N-3, page 8-9, Family 68, Line 49-50, 1-4.).

     vi.   Modeste Vivier was born on 5 May 1890 (Ibid.).

     vii.   Marie Louise Vivier was born on 2 Apr 1892 St.Francois Xavier, Manitoba (MB Vital Statistics, Birth Reg. #1892,006237.). She died on 12 Apr 1893 St.Francois Xavier, Manitoba, at age 1 (Ibid., Death Reg. #1893,002556.).

     viii.   Celestin Vivier was born on 8 Feb 1894 St.Francois Xavier, Manitoba (Ibid., Birth Reg. #1894,001926.). He died on 31 Mar 1895 St.Francois Xavier, Manitoba, at age 1 (Ibid., Death Reg. #1895,001713.).

     ix.   Jean Vivier was born on 23 Mar 1896 R.M. of St.Francois Xavier, Manitoba (Ibid., Birth Reg. #1896,006056.).

     x.   Alexandre Vivier was born on 12 Mar 1898 R.M. of St.Francois Xavier, Manitoba (Ibid., Birth Reg. #1898,003627.).

     xi.   Jean Alfred Vivier was born on 25 Apr 1900 R.M. of St.Francois Xavier, Manitoba (Ibid., Birth Reg. #1900,002212.).

     xii.   Christie Vivier was born in 1905 (Automated Genealogy 1906 Census Transcription Project and Census Images from the National Archives of Canada, http://www.automatedgenealogy.com, #4, 15, page 5, family 32, line 3-7.).

17. Alexis Vivier was born on 20 Oct 1842 (SFX: 1834-1850, B-429.). He was baptized on 4 Nov 1842 St.Francois Xavier, (Manitoba) (Ibid.). He married **Julie Wells**, daughter of **Jean Baptiste Wells** and **Angelique Chalifoux**, on 7 May 1865 St.Francois Xavier, (Manitoba) (SFXI-Kipling, M-4.).

Julie Wells was born on 3 May 1847 (SFX: 1834-1850, B-679.). She was baptized on 11 May 1847 St.Francois Xavier, (Manitoba) (Ibid.).

Children of **Alexis Vivier** and **Julie Wells** were as follows:

  35   i.   Alexandre Vivier, b. circa Oct 1865; m. Caroline Victoria Morissette.

  36   ii.   Guillaume Jean Vivier, b. 18 Apr 1869; m. Philomene Gladu.

  37   iii.   Ambroise Vivier, b. 18 Nov 1870 St.Francois Xavier, Manitoba; m. Marie Madeleine Favel; m. Philomene May White.

  38   iv.   Nathaline Vivier, b. 5 Oct 1872; m. Charles Gladu; d. 31 Jul 1894 Baie St. Paul, Manitoba; bur. 2 Aug 1894 St.Eustache, Manitoba.

  39   v.   Marie Vivier, b. between 1873 and 1876 Manitoba; m. Baptiste Lavallee; d. 25 Jan 1896 R.M. of St.Laurent, Manitoba.

     vi.   Jean Baptiste Vivier was born circa 1877. He married Marguerite Gladu, daughter of Louis Gladu and Philomene Morissette, on 2 Aug 1898 St.Eustache, Manitoba (MM.). He died on 1 Feb 1901 St.Francois Xavier, Manitoba (MB Vital Statistics, Death Reg. #1901,003500.).

             Marguerite Gladu was born on 12 Sep 1880 St.Eustache, Manitoba (Denney.).

     vii.   Victoria Vivier was born circa 1880 Manitoba (1881 Canada, Film No. C-13283, District 186, Sub-district K, page 28, Household No. 132.).

     viii.   Joseph Vivier was born on 1 Mar 1883 RM Belcourt, Manitoba (MB Vital Statistics, Birth Reg. #1883,001470.).

18. Caroline Vivier was born on 8 Apr 1845 St.Francois Xavier, (Manitoba) (SFX: 1834-1850, B-563.). She was baptized on 9 Apr 1845 St.Francois Xavier, (Manitoba) (Ibid.). She married **Joseph Gouin**, son of **Antoine Gouin** and **Francoise Boucher,** on 15 Sep 1873 St.Francois Xavier, Manitoba (SFXI-Kipling, M-13.).

Children of **Caroline Vivier** include:

     i.   Alexandre Vivier was born in Feb 1872 (INB, page 183.). He was baptized on 25 Mar 1872 St.Francois Xavier, Manitoba (IBMS.) (INB, page 183.). He was buried on 4 Mar 1873 St.Francois Xavier, Manitoba (IBMS.).

Joseph Gouin was born circa Aug 1848. He was baptized on 21 May 1849 Fort-des-Prairies (INB, page 74.).

19. Charles Vivier was born on 15 Mar 1847 (SFX: 1834-1850, B-672.). He was baptized on 21 Mar 1847 St.Francois Xavier, (Manitoba) (Ibid.). He married **Marguerite Parenteau**, daughter of **Joseph Parenteau** and **Suzanne Daigneault,** on 23 Jun 1872 St.Francois Xavier, Manitoba (SFXI-Kipling, M-8.).

Marguerite Parenteau was born on 27 Apr 1842 Winnipeg, (Manitoba) (MBS, C-14934.). She and **Henry Munro Fisher** met before 1860. She married **William Racette**, son of **Augustin Racette** and **Suzanne Groulx,** on 9 Feb 1864 St.Boniface, (Manitoba) (SB-Rozyk, page 144, M-5.). She married **Joseph McLeod**, son of **Joseph McLeod** and **Angelique Lacerte,** on 18 Oct 1884 St.Francois Xavier, Manitoba (SFXI-Kipling, M-8.).

Children of **Charles Vivier** and **Marguerite Parenteau** were as follows:

  40   i.   Rosalie Vivier, b. 24 Nov 1870 St.Francois Xavier, Manitoba; m. Norbert Houle.

41   ii.   Elie Vivier, b. 13 Jan 1873 Dakota Territory; m. Virginie Azure; d. 25 Aug 1952.

42   iii.   Louise Vivier, b. 9 Mar 1875; m. Pierre Roger McLeod.

43   iv.   Joseph Vivier, b. 30 Jun 1879 Manitoba; m. Rosine Trottier; d. 1 Jun 1940 Belcourt, Rolette County, North Dakota.

      v.   Alexander Vivier was born circa 1880 Manitoba (1881 Canada, C-13283, District 186, Sub-district L, page 25, Household 114.).

      vi.   Christiana Vivier was born circa 1880 Manitoba (Ibid.).

20. Marie Anne Vivier was born on 20 Sep 1861 Baie St.Paul, (Manitoba) (SFXI-Kipling, B-118.) (MBS, C-14934.). She was baptized on 14 Nov 1861 St.Francois Xavier, (Manitoba) (Ibid.) (SFXI-Kipling, B-118.). She married **Thomas Favel**, son of **John Favel** and **Margaret Swain**, on 8 Jul 1877 St.Eustache, Manitoba (ST-BSP, M-10.).

Thomas Favel was born on 5 Jan 1857 St.Francois Xavier, (Manitoba) (MBS, C-14927.). He married **Marguerite Lecuyer**, daughter of **Michel Lecuyer dit Curier** and **Marguerite Morissette**, on 13 May 1901 St.Francois Xavier, Manitoba (MB Vital Statistics, Marriage Reg. No. 1901,002277.).

21. Adelaide Vivier was born on 18 Aug 1878 RM of Elm River, Manitoba (MB Vital Statistics, Birth Reg. #1884,004649.). She married **Pierre Isidore Ouellette**, son of **Pierre Ouellette** and **Marguerite Grandbois**, on 17 Feb 1892 St.Francois Xavier, Manitoba (SFXI-Kipling, M-5.). She died on 13 Oct 1912 Ste.Rose, Manitoba, at age 34 (MB Vital Statistics, Death Reg. #1912,001133.).

Pierre Isidore Ouellette was born on 9 May 1869 St.Norbert, (Manitoba) (SN1 Catholic Parish Register of St.Norbert 1857-1873, B-19. Hereinafter cited as SN1.). He was baptized on 11 May 1869 St.Norbert, (Manitoba) (IBMS.) (SN1, B-19.).

22. Marie Vivier was born on 30 Oct 1844 (SFX: 1834-1850, B-549.). She was baptized on 10 Nov 1844 St.Francois Xavier, (Manitoba) (Ibid.). She married **Michel Matwewinind**, son of **Joseph Matwewinind** and **Marguerite Nohequa or Nabiquet or Nakekway**, on 22 Aug 1864 St.Francois Xavier, (Manitoba) (SFXI-Kipling, M-3.).

Michel Matwewinind was born circa 1842 Red River, (Manitoba) (1850Ci-MN, page 18, Dwelling 3, Family 3.). He married **Mary Spence** after 1873 (Rarihokwats Research, 10 July 2006.).

23. Michel Vivier was born on 15 Apr 1847 (SFX: 1834-1850, B-675.). He was baptized on 27 Apr 1847 St.Francois Xavier, (Manitoba) (Ibid.). He married **Elise Deschamps**, daughter of **Joseph Deschamps** and **Marie Sauteuse**, on 16 Sep 1867 St.Francois Xavier, (Manitoba) (SFXI-Kipling, M-25.).

Elise Deschamps was born circa 1845 (Ibid., B-73.). She was baptized on 20 Aug 1865 St.Francois Xavier, (Manitoba) (Ibid.).

Children of **Michel Vivier** and **Elise Deschamps** were as follows:

      i.   Elise Vivier was born on 24 Jul 1868 (SPMT St.Peter's Mission; Volume I; Marriage Register 1859-1895; Translated & Transcribed by Reverend Dale McFarlane, Archivist, Diocese of Great Falls-Billings, Montana; Spring 1981.). She was baptized on 1 Apr 1870 (St.Peter's Mission), Teton River, Montana (Ibid., page 64, #1539.). She married Norbert Boyer, son of Joseph Boyer and Felicite Patenaude, on 16 Jan 1921 St.Lazare, Fort Ellice, Manitoba (Denney.). Question: *Is she the wife of Norbert Boyer?*

         Norbert Boyer was born on 31 Jan 1862 Indian Head (NWHBS, C-14936.). He was baptized on 22 May 1862 St.Francois Xavier, (Manitoba) (SFXI-Kipling, B-52.). He married **Julie Swain**, daughter of **William Swain** and **Angelique Bruyere**, on 13 Apr 1884 Strathclair, Manitoba (MB Vital Statistics, Marriage Reg. #1884,001879.). He died on 17 Nov 1932 Ellice, Manitoba, at age 70 (Ibid., Death Reg. #1932,044296.).

      ii.   Isabelle Vivier was born on 24 Oct 1870 Cypress Hills, (Saskatchewan) (L1, page 44, B-77.) (HBS, Volume 1337, C-14952.). She was baptized on 3 Jun 1871 Lebret, (Saskatchewan) (Ibid.) (L1, page 44, B-77.). She married John Boyer, son of Joseph Boyer and Felicite Patenaude, on 12 Feb 1895 Elice, Manitoba (HBS, Volume 1337, C-14952.) (MB Vital Statistics, Marriage Reg. #1896,001023.). She died on 20 Jun 1898 (Ellice), Moosowin, Manitoba, at age 27 (HBS, Volume 1337, C-14952.). She was buried on 13 Nov 1898 St.Andrews, North West Territories (Ibid.).

         John Boyer was born on 20 Aug 1870 St.Francois Xavier, Manitoba (SFXI-Kipling, B-69.) (HBS, Volume 1337, C-14952.). He was baptized on 21 Aug 1870 St.Francois Xavier, Manitoba (SFXI-Kipling, B-69.) (HBS, Volume 1337, C-14952.). He married **Florestine Morisseau** before 1907. He died on 18 Feb 1916 RM Ellice, Manitoba, at age 45 (MB Vital Statistics, Death Reg. #1916,012109.).

      iii.   Florestine Vivier was born on 6 May 1873 near, Swift Current, (Saskatchewan) (L1, page 121, B-44.) (ArchiviaNet.). She was baptized on 5 Sep 1873 Lebret, (Saskatchewan) (L1, page 121, B-44.). She married Louis Gonneville before 1898. She died on 22 Sep 1898 Moosomin at age 25 (ArchiviaNet.).

      iv.   Suzanne Vivier was born on 1 Mar 1876 Cypress Hills, (Saskatchewan) (Ibid., C-15009.). She was baptized on 28 Mar 1876 Lebret, (Saskatchewan) (Denney.). She died on 2 Apr 1891 Qu'Appelle Mission, (Saskatchewan), at age 15 (ArchiviaNet, C-15009.).

      v.   Helene Vivier was born on 11 Jan 1879 Lebret, (Saskatchewan) (L1, page 285, B-_.) (ArchiviaNet, C-15009.). She was baptized on 12 Jan 1879 Lebret, (Saskatchewan) (L1, page 285, B-_.). She died in Oct 1897 Wood Mountain, (Saskatchewan), at age 18 (ArchiviaNet, C-15009.).

      vi.   Rebecca Vivier was born in May 1881 Judith Basin, Montana (Ibid.). She died in Jun 1881 Judith Basin, Montana (Ibid.).

      vii.   Marie Vivier was born in Aug 1881 Cypress Hills, (Saskatchewan) (Ibid.). She died on 17 Apr 1890 Qu'Appelle Mission, (Saskatchewan), at age 8 (Ibid.).

      viii.   Sara Vivier was born on 28 Jul 1884 (L2 Lebret, Mission de St.Florent, Roman Catholic Registre des Baptemes, Mariages & Seplutures, Qu'Appelle, Saskatchewan, Book Two: 1881-1887, FHC microfilm 1032949., page 88, B-51. Hereinafter cited as L2.). She was baptized on 4 Aug 1884 Lebret, (Saskatchewan) (Ibid.). She died on 24 May 1893 Qu'Appelle Mission, (Saskatchewan), at age 8 (ArchiviaNet, C-15009.).

24. Jean Baptiste Vivier was born on 29 Aug 1864 St.Francois Xavier, (Manitoba) (SFXI-Kipling, B-43.). He was baptized on 31 Aug 1864 St.Francois Xavier, (Manitoba) (Ibid.). He married **Caroline Lucier**, daughter of **Joseph Lucier** and **Josephte Farquarhson**

dit Ferguson, on 26 Nov 1889 St.Eustache, Manitoba (MM.). He died on 24 Dec 1909 St.Francois Xavier, Manitoba, at age 45 (MB Vital Statistics, Death Reg. #1909,002895.).

Caroline Lucier was born on 17 Nov 1874 St.Eustache, Manitoba (Denney.). She was baptized on 19 Nov 1874 St.Eustache, Manitoba (INB, page 113.). She married **William Ledoux,** son of **Isaac Ledoux** and **Marie Lingan,** on 23 Nov 1910 St.Francois Xavier, Manitoba (MB Vital Statistics, Marriage Regn #1910,001371.).

Children of **Jean Baptiste Vivier** and **Caroline Lucier** were as follows:

    i.   Jean Baptiste Vivier was born on 21 Jun 1892 St.Francois Xavier, Manitoba (SFXI-Kipling, page 91, B-29.) (MB Vital Statistics, Birth Reg. #1892,006237.). He married Vitaline Allary, daughter of Elzear Allary and Mary Ann Magdelaine Bremner, on 17 Aug 1920 St.Eustache, Manitoba (MM, page 18.) (MB Vital Statistics, Marriage Reg. #1920,042332.).

           Vitaline Allary was born on 13 Jan 1904 R.M. of St.Francois Xavier, Manitoba (Ibid., Birth Reg. #1904,002642.).

    ii. Marie Mathilde Vivier was born on 21 May 1894 St.Francois Xavier, Manitoba (SFXI-Kipling, page 37, B-14.) (MB Vital Statistics, Birth Reg. #1894,001916.).

    iii. Joseph Archie Vivier was born on 31 May 1896 R.M. of St.Francois Xavier, Manitoba (SFXI-Kipling, page 164, B-20.) (MB Vital Statistics, Birth Reg. #1896,006048.). He died on 7 Jun 1896 St.Francois Xavier, Manitoba (SFXI-Kipling, page 84, S-6.) (MB Vital Statistics, Death Reg. #1896,002721.).

    iv. Marie Mabel Vivier was born on 6 Jul 1897 St.Francois Xavier, Manitoba (1901 Canada, #11, N-3, page 4, Family 31, Line 44-49.).

    v. Florence Magdelene Vivier was born in Aug 1899 R.M. of St.Francois Xavier, Manitoba (MB Vital Statistics, Birth Reg. #1899,003439.).

  44 vi. Marie Melanie Vivier, b. 10 Jun 1900 R.M. of St.Francois Xavier, Manitoba; m. Alfred Ledoux.

    vii. Joseph Adelard Vivier was born on 14 Nov 1902 R.M. of St.Francois Xavier, Manitoba (Ibid., Birth Reg. #1902,008060.). He married Marie Jeanne Fitzpatrick on 11 May 1925 St.Francois Xavier, Manitoba (MM.).

    viii. Joseph Albert Vivier was born on 18 Jun 1905 R.M. of St.Francois Xavier, Manitoba (MB Vital Statistics, Birth Reg. #1905,004218.).

25. Elzear Vivier was born on 18 Mar 1867 St.Francois Xavier, (Manitoba) (SFXI-Kipling, B-19.). He was baptized on 19 Mar 1867 St.Francois Xavier, (Manitoba) (Ibid.). He married **Rosalie Rolette** on 6 Jul 1889 Westbourne, Manitoba (MB Vital Statistics, Mar. Reg. #1888,002059.).

Children of **Elzear Vivier** and **Rosalie Rolette** were:

    i.   Jean Baptiste Vivier was born on 29 Oct 1895 Gladstone, Manitoba (Ibid., Birth Reg. #1896,003882.).

26. Christianne Vivier was born circa 1851. She married **Theodore Decoine,** son of **Pierre Francois Decoine** and **Josephte Desjarlais,** on 29 Sep 1868 Lac la Biche, (Alberta) (LLBR1, page 95-96, M-70.). She married **Henri Eric Lapoudre dit Decoine,** son of **Pierre Decoine dit Lapoudre** and **Therese Cardinal,** on 5 Dec 1871 Lac la Biche, (Alberta) (Ibid., page 125, M-9.). She died circa Jul 1885 Lac la Biche, (Alberta) (ArchiviaNet.).

Theodore Decoine was born circa 1845 (LLBR1, page 114-115, S-1.). He died in Sep 1870 Lac la Biche, (Alberta). He was buried on 1 Oct 1870 Lac la Biche, (Alberta) (Ibid.).

Henri Eric Lapoudre dit Decoine was born on 2 Jan 1850 (1901 Canada, microfilm T-6550, Athabaska Landing, page 3, family 27, line 29-38.). He married **Pelagie Mustatip Cardinal,** daughter of **Antoine Cardinal** and **Marie Cardinal,** circa Apr 1886 Lac la Biche, (Alberta) (HBS, Volume 1340, C-14956.).

27. Emelie Vivier was born in 1853 Fort Pitt, (Saskatchewan) (Ibid., C-15002.). She married **Alfred 'Rabasca' Schmidt,** son of **Peter Schmidt** and **Marie Anne Genereux,** on 5 Apr 1867 Fort Pitt, (Saskatchewan) (Ibid.).

Alfred 'Rabasca' Schmidt was born on 20 Dec 1820 (1901 Canada, microfilm, T-6553, South Battleford, page 1, Family 4, line 20-22.). He was born in 1825 Slave Lake (NWHBS, C-14941.). He married **Marguerite Lesperance,** daughter of **Alexis Bonami Lesperance** and **Marguerite Grenon,** in 1847 St.Boniface, (Manitoba) (Ibid.). He and **Josephte Cree** met circa 1861. He and **Maggie "Kasa-wa-asso" Carlow** met before 1864. He died in 1901.

Generation Four

28. Alexis Vivier was born on 23 Aug 1861 St.Charles, (Manitoba) (SFXI-Kipling, B-76.). He was baptized on 25 Aug 1861 St.Francois Xavier, (Manitoba) (Ibid.). He married **Marie McKay** on 7 Jan 1877 St.Eustache, Manitoba (ST-BSP, M-1.) (MM, page 865 and 1295.).

Marie McKay was born on 29 May 1860 (1901 Canada, #8, k-13, page 4, family 36, line 28-33.).

Children of **Alexis Vivier** and **Marie McKay** were as follows:

    i.   Madeleine Vivier was born on 6 Apr 1878 Manitoba (Ibid.). She married Paul Richard, son of Isaie Richard and Julie Boucher, on 9 Jan 1897 St.Laurent, Manitoba (MB Vital Statistics, Marriage Reg. #1897,002416.).

           Paul Richard was born on 1 Jan 1876 St.Laurent, Manitoba (Denney.). He died on 2 May 1900 St.Laurent, Manitoba, at age 24 (MB Vital Statistics, Death Reg. #1900,001299.) (ArchiviaNet, C-14999.).

    ii. Louis Vivier was born before 22 May 1878. He died on 22 May 1878 St.Eustache, Manitoba (Denney.). He was buried on 23 May 1878 St.Eustache, Manitoba (Ibid.).

    iii. Pierre Vivier was born on 30 Jun 1878 Manitoba (1901 Canada, #8, k-13, page 4, family 36, line 28-33.).

    iv. Alexander W. J. Vivier was born on 17 Mar 1883 Manitoba (Ibid.).

    v. Rosine Vivier was born on 2 Mar 1888 Manitoba (Ibid.).

29. Marie Vivier was born on 9 Oct 1865 St.Charles, (Manitoba) (MBS, C-14934.) (SB-Rozyk, page 19, B-96.). She was baptized on 9 Oct 1865 St.Boniface, (Manitoba) (MBS, C-14934.) (SB-Rozyk, page 19, B-96.). She married **William Branconnier,** son of **Jean Baptiste Branconnier** and **Julie Villebrun,** on 29 Dec 1882 Assiniboia, Manitoba (MB Vital Statistics, Mar. Reg. #1882,001652.). She died on 5 Jan 1954 37 McLean Street, Winnipeg, Manitoba, at age 88 (Rosemary Rozyk, 28 Jan 1999 report.). She was buried on 9 Jan 1954 St.Charles, Winnipeg, Manitoba (Ibid.).

William Branconnier was born on 12 Oct 1858 St.Charles, Manitoba (Ibid.) (1901 Canada, page 8-9, Family 66, Line 50, 1-5.). He died on 19 Aug 1941 Lot 78, St.Charles, Manitoba, at age 82 (Rosemary Rozyk, 28 Jan 1999 report.). He was buried in Aug 1941 St.Charles, Winnipeg, Manitoba (Ibid.).

30. Guillaume Vivier was born on 31 May 1870 St.Charles, (Manitoba) (MBS, C-14934.). He was baptized on 2 Jun 1870 St.Boniface, (Manitoba) (Ibid.). He married **Marie Rose Fidler**, daughter of **George Fidler** and **Marie Laplante,** on 10 Aug 1886 St.Eustache, Manitoba (MM.).

Marie Rose Fidler was born on 8 Jun 1864 (SFXI-Kipling, B-24.). She was baptized on 10 Jun 1864 St.Francois Xavier, (Manitoba) (Ibid.).

Children of **Guillaume Vivier** and **Marie Rose Fidler** were as follows:

    i.   Anonyme Vivier was born on 6 Apr 1887 RM Belcourt, Manitoba (MB Vital Statistics, Birth Reg. #1887,002865.).

    ii.   Anonyme Vivier was born on 6 Apr 1887 RM Belcourt, Manitoba (Ibid., Birth Reg. #1887,002864.).

    iii.   Isabelle Vivier was born on 20 Mar 1889 St.Eustache, Manitoba (Denney.).

    iv.   Marie Rose Vivier was born on 11 Dec 1892 R.M. of St.Francois Xavier, Manitoba (MB Vital Statistics, Birth Reg. #1892,003452.).

    v.   Marie Rose Vivier was born on 12 Dec 1899 St.Francois Xavier, Manitoba (1901 Canada, #11, N-3, page 6, Family 47, Line 22-24.).

31. Isabelle Vivier was born circa 1856 (Manitoba) (1870C-MB, page 368, #1324-1329.). She married **Joseph Allary**, son of **Louis Allary** and **Marguerite Cyr,** on 16 Jun 1888 (St.Eustache), Belcourt, Manitoba (MM, page 16.) (MB Vital Statistics, Marriage Reg. #1888,001365 (Belcourt).) (Ibid., Marriage Reg. #1888,002303 (Belcourt).). She died on 8 Aug 1894 St.Eustache, Manitoba (Rosemary Rozyk, 28 Nov 2006.). She was buried on 10 Aug 1894 St.Eustache, Manitoba (Ibid.).

Joseph Allary was born on 12 Jun 1870 St.Francois Xavier, (Manitoba) (SFXI-Kipling, B-54.). He was baptized on 14 Jun 1870 St.Francois Xavier, (Manitoba) (Ibid.). He married **Marie Rose Vivier**, daughter of **Bernard Vivier** and **Isabelle Ducharme,** on 6 Aug 1900 (St.Eustache), St.Francois Xavier, Manitoba (MM, page 16 (St.Eustache).) (MB Vital Statistics, Marriage Reg. #1900,001338 (SFX).). He married **Eva Gladu**, daughter of **Charles Gladu** and **Isola Lacroix,** on 22 Sep 1914 (Cartier), St.Eustache, Manitoba (MM, page 16 & 512.) (MB Vital Statistics, Marriage Reg. #1914,145120 (Cartier).).

32. John Alexandre Vivier was born circa 1863 Red River, (Manitoba) (1870C-MB, page 368, #1327.). He married **Virginie Hogue**, daughter of **Amable Hogue** and **Betsy Morissette,** on 25 Jan 1881 St.Eustache, Manitoba (MM.) (ST-BSP, M-3.) (MB Vital Statistics, Mar. Reg. #1891,002016 (SFX).). He died on 13 Nov 1890 RM Belcourt, Manitoba (Ibid., Death Reg. #1890,001299.).

Virginie Hogue was born on 15 Jan 1867 St.Boniface, (Manitoba) (SB-Rozyk, page 75, B-7.). She was baptized on 20 Jan 1867 St.Boniface, (Manitoba) (Ibid.). She married **Patrice Gladu**, son of **Francois Gladu** and **Marguerite Wells,** on 20 Dec 1891 (St.Francois Xavier), St.Eustache, Manitoba (MM.) (MB Vital Statistics, Mar. Reg. #1891,002016 (St.Francois Xavier).). She died on 29 Jul 1935 St.Francois Xavier, Manitoba, at age 68 (Ibid., Death Reg. #1935,048525.).

Children of **John Alexandre Vivier** and **Virginie Hogue** were as follows:

    i.   Marguerite Vivier was born on 19 Jan 1882 Belcourt, Manitoba (Ibid., Birth Reg. #1882,001265.).

    ii.   John Alexander Vivier was born on 2 Dec 1883 RM Belcourt, Manitoba (Ibid., Birth Reg. #1884,001729.).

    iii.   Marie Vivier was born on 1 Nov 1887 (1901 Canada, #11, N-3, page 8, family 63, line 16-23.).

33. Thomas Vivier was born circa 1861 (MB Vital Statistics, Death Reg. #1894,002971.). He was born circa 1864 Long Lake, (Manitoba) (1870C-MB, page 368, #1328.). He was born in 1867 St.Boniface, Manitoba (MB Vital Statistics, Birth Reg. #1890,004595 (1867).). He married **Catherine Hogue**, daughter of **Amable Hogue** and **Betsy Morissette,** on 4 Feb 1890 St.Boniface, Manitoba (Ibid., Mar. Reg. #1890,001822.). He died on 5 Dec 1894 St.Francois Xavier, Manitoba (Ibid., Death Reg. #1894,002971.).

Catherine Hogue was born circa 1869 (Manitoba) (1870C-MB, page 239, #387.). She was born on 1 Oct 1870 St.Charles, Manitoba (Rosemary Rozyk, 26 Nov 2006.). She died on 1 May 1894 St.Francois Xavier, Manitoba, at age 23 (MB Vital Statistics, Death Reg. #1894,001887.). She was buried on 2 May 1894 St.Eustache, Manitoba (Rosemary Rozyk, 26 Nov 2006.).

Children of **Thomas Vivier** and **Catherine Hogue** were:

    i.   Philomene Vivier was born on 4 Jul 1891 (1901 Canada, District 10-i-2, page 1, family 3, line 13-16.).

34. Marie Rose Vivier was born circa 1879 Marquette, Manitoba (1881 Canada, Film No. C-13283, District 186, Sub-district K, page 2, Household No. 7.). She was born on 29 Dec 1882 Belcourt, Manitoba (MB Vital Statistics, Birth Reg. #1883,001468.). She married **Joseph Allary**, son of **Louis Allary** and **Marguerite Cyr,** on 6 Aug 1900 (St.Eustache), St.Francois Xavier, Manitoba (MM, page 16 (St.Eustache).) (MB Vital Statistics, Marriage Reg. #1900,001338 (SFX).).

Joseph Allary was born on 12 Jun 1870 St.Francois Xavier, (Manitoba) (SFXI-Kipling, B-54.). He was baptized on 14 Jun 1870 St.Francois Xavier, (Manitoba) (Ibid.). He married **Isabelle Vivier**, daughter of **Joseph Vivier** and **Caroline Swain,** on 16 Jun 1888 (St.Eustache), Belcourt, Manitoba (MM, page 16.) (MB Vital Statistics, Marriage Reg. #1888,001365 (Belcourt).) (Ibid., Marriage Reg. #1888,002303 (Belcourt).). He married **Eva Gladu**, daughter of **Charles Gladu** and **Isola Lacroix,** on 22 Sep 1914 (Cartier), St.Eustache, Manitoba (MM, page 16 & 512.) (MB Vital Statistics, Marriage Reg. #1914,145120 (Cartier).).

35. Alexandre Vivier was born circa Oct 1865 (SFXI-Kipling, B-63.). He was baptized on 27 May 1866 St.Francois Xavier, (Manitoba) (Ibid.). He married **Caroline Victoria Morissette**, daughter of **Francois Morissette** and **Louise Lebrun,** on 15 Feb 1887 (Belcourt), St.Eustache, Manitoba (MM.) (MB Vital Statistics, Mar. Reg. #1887,001217 (Belcourt).).

Caroline Victoria Morissette was born on 11 Feb 1872 Baie St.Paul, Manitoba (SFXI-Kipling, B-15.) (INB, page 129.). She was baptized on 18 Feb 1872 St.Francois Xavier, Manitoba (SFXI-Kipling, B-15.). She married **James Alexander Bourke**, son of **Andrew Bourke** and **Madeleine Lallemont dit Welsh,** on 19 May 1908 St.Francois Xavier, Manitoba (MM.). She died on 23 Jun 1924 at age 52 (Denney.). She was buried in Jun 1924 Portage la Prairie, Manitoba (Ibid.).

Children of **Alexandre Vivier** and **Caroline Victoria Morissette** were as follows:

    i.   William Vivier was born on 15 Nov 1888 Belcourt, Manitoba (MB Vital Statistics, Birth Reg. #1888,001075.).

    ii.   Adele Vivier was born on 5 Aug 1892 R.M. of St.Francois Xavier, Manitoba (Ibid., Birth Reg. #1892,003430.). She died on 14 May 1894 St.Francois Xavier, Manitoba, at age 1 (Ibid., Death Reg. #1894,001890.).

36. **Guillaume Jean Vivier** was born on 18 Apr 1869 (SFXI-Kipling, B-59.). He was baptized on 11 Jul 1869 St.Francois Xavier, (Manitoba) (Ibid.). He married **Philomene Gladu**, daughter of **Louis Gladu** and **Philomene Morissette,** on 19 Feb 1889 (Belcourt), St.Eustache, Manitoba (MM.) (MB Vital Statistics, Mar. Reg. #1889,001105 (Belcourt).).

Philomene Gladu was born on 26 Mar 1874 (INB, page 71.). She was baptized on 7 Apr 1874 St.Eustache, Manitoba (Ibid.).

Children of **Guillaume Jean Vivier** and **Philomene Gladu** all born R.M. of St.Francois Xavier, Manitoba, were as follows:

    i.   Jean Alexandre Vivier was born on 4 Jan 1891 (MB Vital Statistics, Birth Reg. #1891,006077.).

    ii.   Marie Bella Vivier was born on 28 Dec 1892 (Ibid., Birth Reg. #1892,005237.). She died on 22 Apr 1894 St.Francois Xavier, Manitoba, at age 1 (Ibid., Death Reg. #1894,001885.).

    iii.   Alma Victoria Vivier was born on 16 Jan 1900 (Ibid., Birth Reg. #1900,002192.).

    iv.   James Alexander Vivier was born on 28 May 1901 (Ibid., Birth Reg. #1901,002701.).

37. **Ambroise Vivier** was born on 18 Nov 1870 St.Francois Xavier, Manitoba (SFXI-Kipling, B-92.). He was baptized on 4 Dec 1870 St.Francois Xavier, Manitoba (Ibid.). He married **Marie Madeleine Favel**, daughter of **Alexander Favel** and **Madeleine Gladu,** on 1 Mar 1892 (St.Eustache), St.Francois Xavier, Manitoba (MM, (St.Eustache).) (MB Vital Statistics, Marriage Reg. #1892,001027 (SFX).). He married **Philomene May White**, daughter of **Charles White** and **Marie Josephte Lecuyer,** on 3 Apr 1899 St.Eustache, Manitoba (MM, page 1307.).

Marie Madeleine Favel was born on 3 May 1877 Duck Lake, (Saskatchewan) (Denney.). She was baptized on 26 May 1877 Duck Lake, (Saskatchewan) (ArchiviaNet, C-15009.). She died circa 1895 Oakville (Denney.).

Children of **Ambroise Vivier** and **Marie Madeleine Favel** were:

    i.   Marie Vivier was born on 12 Apr 1894 St.Francois Xavier, Manitoba (MB Vital Statistics, Birth Reg. #1894,001934.).

Philomene May White was born on 15 Aug 1881 Duck Lake, (Saskatchewan) (ArchiviaNet, C-15009.).

38. **Nathaline Vivier** was born on 5 Oct 1872 (L1, page 80, B-23.). She was baptized on 3 Nov 1872 Lebret, (Saskatchewan) (Ibid.). She married **Charles Gladu**, son of **Louis Gladu** and **Philomene Morissette,** on 15 Oct 1889 (Belcourt), St.Eustache, Manitoba (MM, page 512.) (MB Vital Statistics, Mar. Reg. #1889,001511 (Belcourt).) (Rosemary Rozyk, 22 Mar 2008.). She died on 31 Jul 1894 Baie St. Paul, Manitoba, at age 21 (MM.) (Rosemary Rozyk, 22 Mar 2008.). She was buried on 2 Aug 1894 St.Eustache, Manitoba (Ibid.).

Charles Gladu was born circa 1869 Red River, (Manitoba) (1870C-MB, page 369, #1346.). He married **Isola Lacroix**, daughter of **Louis Lacroix** and **Cesarie Beauregard,** on 16 Jul 1895 (St.Francois Xavier), St.Eustache, Manitoba (MM, page 512.) (MB Vital Statistics, Mar. Reg. #1895,002166 (St.Francois Xavier).). He died on 10 Jun 1909 Winnipeg, Manitoba (Ibid., Death Reg. #1909,004714.).

39. **Marie Vivier** was born between 1873 and 1876 Manitoba (1881 Canada, Film No. C-13283, District 186, Sub-district K, page 28, Household No. 132.) (MB Vital Statistics, Death Reg. #1896,002722.). She married **Baptiste Lavallee**, son of **Andre Lavallee** and **Eliza Chaboyer,** on 12 Feb 1893 St.Laurent, Manitoba (Ibid., Marriage Reg. #1895,001454.). She died on 25 Jan 1896 R.M. of St.Laurent, Manitoba (Ibid., Death Reg. #1896,002722.).

Baptiste Lavallee was born on 10 Mar 1870 St.Laurent, Manitoba (1901 Canada, #11, o, page 11, family 78, line 16-17.). He was baptized on 17 Mar 1870 St.Laurent, (Manitoba) (IBMS.).

40. **Rosalie Vivier** was born on 24 Nov 1870 St.Francois Xavier, Manitoba (SFXI-Kipling, B-91.). She was baptized on 4 Dec 1870 St.Francois Xavier, Manitoba (Ibid.). She married **Norbert Houle**, son of **Joseph Houle** and **Catherine Lapierre,** on 10 Nov 1889 St.Francois Xavier, Manitoba (Ibid., M-12.) (MB Vital Statistics, Mar. Reg. #1889,001798.).

Norbert Houle was born on 6 Oct 1859 St.Joseph, Walhalla, Pembina County, North Dakota (Denney.) (SFXI-Kipling, page 477, B-30.). He was baptized on 13 May 1860 St.Francois Xavier, (Manitoba) (Denney.) (SFXI-Kipling, B-30.). He married **Caroline McLeod**, daughter of **Antoine McLeod** and **Marie Anne Versailles,** on 13 Jan 1884 St.Francois Xavier, Manitoba (Ibid., M-1.).

41. **Elie Vivier** was born on 13 Jan 1873 Dakota Territory (AP, page 71, B-5.). He was baptized on 21 Jan 1873 Assumption, Pembina, Pembina County, Dakota Territory (Ibid.). He married **Virginie Azure**, daughter of **Charles Azure** and **Josephte Gladu,** on 27 Feb 1893 (BIA-TM Bureau of Indian Affairs, Turtle Mountain Enrollment and Probate Papers, Belcourt, North Dakota, Virginia Azure Vivier Family History Card.). He died on 25 Aug 1952 at age 79 (Turtle Mountain Reservation Probate Record, Elie Vivier Probate 3705-54, Branch of Trust & Natural Resources.).

Virginie Azure was born on 1 Jul 1866 Walhalla, Pembina County, North Dakota (BIA-TM.). She died on 13 Feb 1948 Belcourt, Rolette County, North Dakota, at age 81 (BIA-TM-BMD.) (ND Death Index.). She was buried in Feb 1948 St.Anthonys, Rolette County, North Dakota (BIA-TM-BMD.).

Children of **Elie Vivier** and **Virginie Azure** were as follows:

    i.   Charles Vivier was born on 21 Jul 1894 (BIA-TM, Virginia Azure Vivier Family History Card.) (1919 Turtle Mountain Indian Census Roll, United States Indian Service Department of the Interior, Turtle Mountain Indian Agency, North Dakota, 30 June 1919 , Census No. 3188-3190.). He married Rosine Cecilia Elizabeth McCloud, daughter of Pierre McLeod and Marie Madeleine Vallee, in Jan 1919 Thorne, North Dakota (*St.Ann's Centennial, 100 Years of Faith - 1885-1985*; Belcourt, North Dakota: St.Ann Parish, 1985), page 542.). He died on 17 Apr 1966 Rolette County, North Dakota, at age 71 (Ibid.) (SSDI.).

         Rosine Cecilia Elizabeth McCloud was born on 22 Jan 1900 (*St.Ann's Centennial*, page 542.) (ND Death Index.). She died on 21 Jul 1979 Belcourt, Rolette County, North Dakota, at age 79 (*St.Ann's Centennial*, page 542.) (ND Death Index.).

    ii.   Joseph Vivier was born on 29 May 1896 (BIA-TM, Virginia Azure Vivier Family History Card.). He died on 29 Sep 1897 at age 1 (Ibid.).

    iii.   Alexander Vivier was born on 22 Mar 1898 (Ibid.). He died on 20 Dec 1952 Cass County, North Dakota, at age 54 (Probate, Elie Vivier Probate 3705-54.) (ND Death Index.).

    iv.   Philip Vivier was born on 29 Oct 1900 (Ibid.). He was born on 23 Nov 1900 (BIA-TM, Virginia Azure Vivier Family History Card.) (*1919 Turtle Mountain*, Census No. 3181-3186.). He married Margaret Nadeau, daughter of Joseph Nadeau and Suzanne Pitwewekijik dit Lerat, circa 1925 (Eileen Horan Research, 4 Jan 2006.). He died on 29 Sep 1967 Rolette County, California, at age 66 (ND Death Index.).

    Margaret Nadeau was born on 8 Dec 1902 (Ibid.). She died on 4 Jan 1966 Rolette County, California, at age 63 (Ibid.).

    v.   Francois Vivier was born on 2 Sep 1902 (BIA-TM, Virginia Azure Vivier Family History Card.) (*1919 Turtle Mountain*, Census No. 3181-3186.). He died on 7 Jul 1934 Rolette County, North Dakota, at age 31 (Probate, Elie Vivier Probate 3705-54.) (ND Death Index.).

    vi.   Mary St.Ann Vivier was born on 10 Apr 1905 Estevan, (Saskatchewan) (BIA-TM, Virginia Azure Vivier Family History Card.). She married Moses Azure, son of James Azure and Marie Elise Delorme, on 11 Oct 1937 Rolla, Rolette County, North Dakota (BIA-TM.). She died on 19 Jun 1977 North Dakota at age 72 (Ibid.).

    Moses Azure was born on 26 Jan 1896 North Dakota (Ibid.) (1916-TMC 1916 Census of the Turtle Mountain Chippewa, North Dakota, National Archives of the United States, Washington D.C., Census No. 322.). He died on 28 Oct 1983 North Dakota at age 87 (BIA-TM.).

    vii.   Flora Vivier was born on 4 Apr 1907 (Ibid., Virginia Azure Vivier Family History Card.) (SSDI.) (*1919 Turtle Mountain*, Census No. 3181-3186.). She married Ambroise Nadeau, son of Joseph Nadeau and Suzanne Pitwewekijik dit Lerat, before 1927. She died on 15 Nov 1987 Belcourt, Rolette, North Dakota, at age 80 (SSDI.) (ND Death Index.).

    Ambroise Nadeau was born on 8 Jun 1900 (Cindy Charlebois Research.). He died on 9 May 1963 Belcourt, Rolette County, North Dakota, at age 62 (ND Death Index.).

    viii.   Robert Vivier was born on 10 Jan 1909 (BIA-TM, Virginia Azure Vivier Family History Card.) (BIA-TM-BMD, page 19.) (*1919 Turtle Mountain*, Census No. 3181-3186.).

42. **Louise Vivier** was born on 9 Mar 1875 (INB, page 184.). She was baptized on 20 Mar 1875 St.Eustache, Manitoba (IBMS.) (INB, page 184.). She married **Pierre Roger McLeod**, son of **Joseph McLeod** and **Isabelle Delorme**, in 1893 (HBSI.) (ArchiviaNet.).

    Pierre Roger McLeod was born on 26 Jun 1871 St.Francois Xavier, Manitoba (SFXI-Kipling, B-51.). He was baptized on 26 Jun 1871 St.Francois Xavier, Manitoba (Ibid.).

43. **Joseph Vivier** was born on 30 Jun 1879 Manitoba (1881 Canada, C-13283, District 186, Sub-district L, page 25, Household 114.) (ND Death Index.). He married **Rosine Trottier**, daughter of **Vital Trottier** and **Veronique Lingan,** before 1898. He died on 1 Jun 1940 Belcourt, Rolette County, North Dakota, at age 60 (Ibid.).

Rosine Trottier was born on 20 Nov 1879 St.Francois Xavier, Manitoba (SFXI-Kipling, B-68.).

Children of **Joseph Vivier** and **Rosine Trottier** were as follows:

    i.   Joseph Norman Vivier was born in 1898.

    ii.   Ellen Alice Vivier was born on 26 Nov 1899 Belcourt, Rolette County, North Dakota (1936-TMC, page 81.) (ND Death Index.). She married Alfred Demontigny, son of Maxime Demontigny and Theresa Vivier, before 1919 (1936-TMC, page 81.). She died on 15 Jun 1960 Belcourt, Rolette County, North Dakota, at age 60 (ND Death Index.).

    Alfred Demontigny was born on 23 Dec 1898 Rolette County, North Dakota (1936-TMC, page 81.) (ND Death Index.). He died on 2 Jan 1976 Rolette County, North Dakota, at age 77 (Ibid.).

    iii.   Rosine Vivier was born on 15 Jun 1901 (1936-TMC, page 126.) (*1919 Turtle Mountain*, Census No. 3191-3197.) (ND Death Index.) (SSDI.). She married Frederick Wilkie, son of Antoine Alexander Wilkie and Magdeleine Bercier, on 18 Oct 1918 St.Ann's, Belcourt, Rolette County, North Dakota (*St.Ann's Centennial*, page 546.). She died on 15 Dec 1968 Belcourt, Rolette County, North Dakota, at age 67 (Ibid.) (ND Death Index.) (SSDI.).

    Frederick Wilkie was born on 2 Oct 1897 Rolette County, North Dakota (*St.Ann's Centennial*, page 546.) (ND Death Index.). He was born on 2 Feb 1898 (1916-TMC.). He married **Elise Zaste**, daughter of **Elzear Zaste** and **Adele Blackbird,** on 8 Oct 1971 Belcourt, Rolette County, North Dakota (*St.Ann's Centennial*, page 548.). He died on 21 Aug 1989 Rolette County, North Dakota, at age 91 (ND Death Index.).

    iv.   Alfred Vivier was born on 18 Jul 1906 (1936-TMC, page 126.) (*1919 Turtle Mountain*, Census No. 3191-3197.). He died on 12 Nov 1981 Belcourt, Rolette County, North Dakota, at age 75 (SSDI.) (ND Death Index.).

    v.   William Vivier was born on 14 Mar 1908 (*1919 Turtle Mountain*, Census No. 3191-3197.). He married Margaret Demontigny, daughter of Maxime Demontigny and Theresa Vivier, before 1937 (*1937-TMC*, page 514, Census No. 6026-6027.). He died on 23 Apr 1972 Rolla, Rolette County, North Dakota, at age 64 (ND Death Index.) (SSDI.).

    Margaret Demontigny was born on 18 Apr 1909 (1936-TMC, page 81.) (BIA-TM-BMD, page 22.). She married **Alex Trester** before 1930 (*1937-TMC*, page 496, Census No. 5800.). She died on 15 May 1989 Bridgeport, Harrison, West Virginia, at age 80 (SSDI.).

    vi.   Martin Vivier was born on 31 Dec 1909 (1936-TMC, page 126.) (BIA-TM-BMD, page 32.). He died on 9 Dec 1974 Rolla, Rolette County, North Dakota, at age 64 (SSDI.) (ND Death Index.).

    vii.   Ernestine Vivier was born on 1 Feb 1912 (1936-TMC, page 126.) (BIA-TM-BMD, page 54.). She married James Lafournaise, son of Joseph Lafournaise and Marguerite Bercier, on 23 Jun 1931 Belcourt, Rolette County, North Dakota (*1937-TMC*, page 271, Census No. 3281-3284.) (Turtle Mountain Star, Rolla, North Dakota, Thursday, June 25, 1931, page 5.). She died on 20 Jun 2000 Belcourt, Rolette County, North Dakota, at age 88 (ND Death Index.).

    James Lafournaise was born on 9 Apr 1903 (1936-TMC, page 135.) (ND Death Index.). He died on 5 Aug 1979 Pierce County, North Dakota, at age 76 (Ibid.).

    viii.   Eugene Vivier was born on 27 Mar 1914 (*1937-TMC*, page 512, Census No. 5996-5999.). He married Delima Wallett, daughter of Joseph Ouellette and Mary Caroline Martin, in 1942 St.Ann's Catholic Church, Belcourt,

Rolette County, North Dakota. He died on 13 Mar 1988 Rolette County, North Dakota, at age 73 (ND Death Index.).

Delima Wallett was born on 15 Jun 1924 Belcourt, Rolette County, North Dakota (1936-TMC, page 127.) (1926-TMC-ND 1926 Census of the Chippewa Indians of Turtle Mountain Agency, North Dakota, United States Indian Service Department of the Interior, Belcourt, North Dakota, superintendent H. J. McQuigg, 30 June 1926 , Census No. 4056-4062.). She died on 7 May 2014 Belcourt, Rolette County, North Dakota, at age 89 (Ancestry.com Website, Find a Grave, obituary.).

44. **Marie Melanie Vivier** was born on 10 Jun 1900 R.M. of St.Francois Xavier, Manitoba (MB Vital Statistics, Birth Reg. #1900,002187.). She married **Alfred Ledoux**, son of **Isaac Ledoux** and **Marie Lingan**, on 22 Jan 1920 St.Francois Xavier, Manitoba (MM.) (MB Vital Statistics, Mar. Reg. #1920,004080.).

Alfred Ledoux was born on 31 Jul 1882 St.Francois Xavier, Manitoba (SFXI-Kipling, B-44.) (MB Vital Statistics, Birth Regn #1882,001990.). He married **Marie Albina Zace**, daughter of **Edouard Alfred Zastre** and **Justine Lafreniere**, on 17 May 1931 St.Francois Xavier, Manitoba (MM.).

Descendants of James Voller

Generation One

1. **James Voller** was born circa 1800 Guildford, Surrey, England (MBS Scrip Applications, Original White Settlers & Halfbreeds residing in Manitoba on 15 July 1870, RG15-19, C-14934.). He married **Nancy Birston**, daughter of **Alexander Birston** and **Metis or Native**, on 18 Mar 1830 St.Johns, Red River Settlement, (Manitoba) (HBCR Hudson Bay Company Register of Anglican Church Baptisms, Marriages, and Burials for the Red River Settlement, 1821-1841; Hudson's Bay Company Archives, Winnipeg, Manitoba, M-198. Hereinafter cited as HBCR.).

Nancy Birston was born in 1812 North West (MBS, C-14934.). She was baptized on 12 Aug 1821 Norway House (HBCR, E.4/1a, folio 35.). She died in 1887 (HBCA-B Hudson's Bay Company Archives - biographical sketches, Hudson's Bay Company Archives; Winnipeg, Manitoba.).

Children of **James Voller** and **Nancy Birston** were as follows:

2   i.   Mary Voller, b. 25 Sep 1832 St.Andrews, (Manitoba); m. Edward Kipling.

     ii.   William Voller was born circa 1834 (Denney Papers, Charles D. Denney, Glenbow Archives, Calgary, Alberta.). He married Margaret Moody on 3 Jan 1856 St.Andrews, (Manitoba) (Ibid.).

3   iii.   Nancy Voller, b. 2 Jul 1835 St.Johns, Red River Settlement, (Manitoba); m. Thomas Folster; d. 23 Jan 1873 St.Clements, (Manitoba); bur. 25 Jan 1873 St.Clements, (Manitoba).

4   iv.   Elizabeth Voller, b. 25 Apr 1837 St.Johns, Red River Settlement, (Manitoba); m. George Daniel; m. William Donald.

     v.   Catherine Voller was baptized on 11 Sep 1839 St.Johns, Red River Settlement, (Manitoba) (HBCR, E.4/1a, folio 163.). She died on 17 Mar 1840 St.Andrews, (Manitoba) (Denney.).

5   vi.   Sarah Voller, b. 4 May 1841 St.Johns, Red River Settlement, (Manitoba); m. William Sinclair.

     vii.   Angus Voller was baptized on 21 Oct 1842 St.Johns, (Manitoba) (Ibid.). He died on 29 Mar 1843 St.Andrews, (Manitoba) (Ibid.).

     viii.   Charles Voller was christened on 18 Apr 1844 St.Johns, (Manitoba). He died on 6 Jun 1845 at age 1. He was buried St.Andrews, (Manitoba).

6   ix.   Eliza Voller, b. 23 Jan 1849 St.Andrews, (Manitoba); m. Robert Alexander Taylor; d. 19 Feb 1921 R. M. of St.Clements, Manitoba.

7   x.   Caroline Voller, b. 25 Jun 1851 St.Andrews, (Manitoba); m. Edward Richard McKay; d. 9 Dec 1917 Lockport, Manitoba.

8   xi.   Maria Voller, b. 25 Apr 1855 St.Andrews, (Manitoba); m. James Sinclair; d. before 1911.

Generation Two

2. **Mary Voller** was born on 25 Sep 1832 St.Andrews, (Manitoba) (MBS, C-14929.). She was baptized on 30 Oct 1832 St.Johns, Red River Settlement, (Manitoba) (HBCR, E.4/1a, folio 92d.). She married **Edward Kipling**, son of **George Kipling** and **Isabella Landry**, on 29 Nov 1852 St.Andrews, (Manitoba) (Denney.).

Edward Kipling was born in Nov 1831 St.Clements, (Manitoba) (MBS, C-14929.).

3. **Nancy Voller** was born St.Andrews, (Manitoba). She was baptized on 2 Jul 1835 St.Johns, Red River Settlement, (Manitoba) (HBCR, E.4/1a, folio 122.). She married **Thomas Folster**, son of **James Folster** and **Jane Cree**, on 3 Dec 1854 St.Andrews, (Manitoba) (Denney.). She died on 23 Jan 1873 St.Clements, (Manitoba), at age 37. She was buried on 25 Jan 1873 St.Clements, (Manitoba).

Thomas Folster was born in 1828 St.Paul, (Manitoba) (MBS, C-14927.). He was baptized on 14 Oct 1828 St.Johns, (Manitoba) (Denney.). He married **Fanny Daniel**, daughter of **Griffith Daniel** and **Marguerite Indian**, on 30 Jan 1851 St.Andrews, (Manitoba) (*FJD The Family of Jenkin Daniel 1750 - 1900 Comprising Over a Century of Service with the Hudson's Bay Company*, Lynne C. (Begg) Charles & Mabel A. (Quirk) Hykaway, #1203 - 1327 E. Keith Rd., North Vancouver, B.C. V7J 3T5: Lynne Charles, November 1996), page 24.) (HBCA-B.) (HBCR, No. 203.). He married **Charlotte Moore**, daughter of **John Moar** and **Nancy Harcus**, before 1880.

4. **Elizabeth Voller** was baptized on 25 Apr 1837 St.Johns, Red River Settlement, (Manitoba) (HBCR, E.4/1a, folio 141.). She was born on 17 Mar 1838 St.Andrews, (Manitoba) (MBS, C-14926.). She married **George Daniel**, son of **Jacob Daniel** and **Margaret "Peggy" Goodwin**, on 31 Dec 1857 St.Andrews, (Manitoba) (*The Family of Jenkin Daniel*, page 79.). She married **William Donald**, son of **William Donald** and **Elizabeth Laviolette**, before 1881 (1881 Canada, District 185-C-1, page 27, house 129.).

George Daniel was baptized on 23 Sep 1840 St.Johns, (Manitoba) (Denney.). He died circa 1867 Edmonton, (Alberta) (Ibid.).

William Donald was baptized on 6 Apr 1841 St.Johns, Red River Settlement, (Manitoba) (HBCR, E.4/1a, folio 172d.). He married **Jane Firth**, daughter of **Thomas Firth** and **Eliza Boucher**, on 15 Aug 1860 St.Andrews, (Manitoba) (Denney.).

5. **Sarah Voller** was baptized on 4 May 1841 St.Johns, Red River Settlement, (Manitoba) (HBCR, E.4/1a, folio 173.). She was born on 27 Mar 1843 St.Andrews, (Manitoba) (MBS, C-14933.). She married **William Sinclair**, son of **Bakie Sinclair** and **Elizabeth Swain**, in Dec 1857 St.Andrews, (Manitoba) (Denney.).

   William Sinclair was born in 1838 Oxford House (MBS, C-14933.).

6. **Eliza Voller** was born on 23 Jan 1849 St.Andrews, (Manitoba) (Denney.). She was baptized on 27 Mar 1849 St.Andrews, (Manitoba) (Ibid.). She married **Robert Alexander Taylor**, son of **George Taylor II** and **Jane Prince**, on 27 Jun 1867 St.Andrews, (Manitoba) (HBCA-B.). She died on 19 Feb 1921 R. M. of St.Clements, Manitoba, at age 72 (MB Vital Statistics, Death Reg. #1921,070502.).

   Robert Alexander Taylor was born in 1836 Fort of the Rockies (MBS, C-14933.) (Denney.). He was baptized on 9 Mar 1836 St.Johns, Red River Settlement, (Manitoba) (HBCA-B.) (HBCR, E.4/1a, folio 127d.). He died on 26 Mar 1919 St.Clements, Manitoba, at age 83 (MB Vital Statistics, Death Reg. #1919,018439.).

7. **Caroline Voller** was born on 25 Jun 1851 St.Andrews, (Manitoba) (MBS, C-14931.). She married **Edward Richard McKay**, son of **John McKay** and **Mary England**, on 26 Dec 1867 St.Andrews, (Manitoba) (Denney.). She died on 9 Dec 1917 Lockport, Manitoba, at age 66 (MB Vital Statistics, Death Reg. #1917,072234.).

   Edward Richard McKay was born on 14 Nov 1847 North West (MBS, C-14931.). He died on 8 Apr 1927 St.Andrews, Manitoba, at age 79 (MB Vital Statistics, Death Reg. #1927,020239.).

8. **Maria Voller** was born on 25 Apr 1855 St.Andrews, (Manitoba) (MBS, C-14934.). She was baptized on 20 May 1855 St.Andrews, (Manitoba) (Denney.). She married **James Sinclair**, son of **Bakie Sinclair** and **Elizabeth Swain**, on 31 Jan 1870 Fort Garry, (Manitoba) (Ibid.). She died before 1911.

   James Sinclair was born on 10 Apr 1848 St.Andrews, (Manitoba) (MBS, Supplementary Returns: C-14934.). He was baptized on 14 Nov 1848 St.Andrews, (Manitoba) (Denney.).

Descendants of John Ward

Generation One

1. **John Ward** was born circa 1777 London, England (Denney Papers, Charles D. Denney, Glenbow Archives, Calgary, Alberta.).

Children of **John Ward** include:

2	i.	Nancy "Anne" Ward, b. 1800 Saskatchewan District; m. George Spence; d. 15 Apr 1878; bur. Apr 1878 St.Margarets, High Bluff, Manitoba.
3	ii.	George Ward, b. 1801; m. Elizabeth 'Betsy' Turcotte.
4	iii.	John Ward, b. circa 1806 St.Albert, (Alberta); m. Angelique Bruyere.

Generation Two

2. **Nancy "Anne" Ward** was born in 1800 Saskatchewan District. She was baptized on 6 May 1821 (Fort Douglas), St.Johns, (Manitoba) (Ibid.) (HBCA-B Hudson's Bay Company Archives - biographical sketches, Hudson's Bay Company Archives; Winnipeg, Manitoba.). She married **George Spence**, son of **James Spence** and **Margaret Nestichio Batt**, on 6 May 1821 (Fort Douglas), St.Johns, (Manitoba) (HBCR Hudson Bay Company Register of Anglican Church Baptisms, Marriages, and Burials for the Red River Settlement, 1821-1841; Hudson's Bay Company Archives, Winnipeg, Manitoba, M-21. Hereinafter cited as HBCR.). She died on 15 Apr 1878 (Denney.). She was buried in Apr 1878 St.Margarets, High Bluff, Manitoba (Ibid.).

   George Spence was born circa 1792 Ruperts Land (1827C RRS HBCA E5/1 1827 Census of the Red River Settlement, HBCA E5/1, Hudson's Bay Company Archives, Provincial Archives, 200 Vaughan Street, Winnipeg, MB R3C 1T5, Canada., #85, page 3.). He was baptized on 6 May 1821 (Fort Douglas), St.Johns, (Manitoba) (HBCA-B.) (HBCR, E.4/1a, folio 32d.). He was buried on 31 Dec 1845 St.Andrews, (Manitoba) (Denney.).

3. **George Ward** was born in 1801 (FDP Baptisms & Marriages Fort des Prairie, Saskatchewan District, C Kipling, M-27. Hereinafter cited as FDP.) (NWHBSI Index 1885 Scrip Applications, North-West Halfbreeds residing outside Manitoba on 15 July 1870, RG15-20, page 86.). He was baptized on 29 Jan 1843 Edmonton House (RTR Rundle, Reverend R. T., Journal of Baptisms & Marriages in Saskatchewan District,1840 - 1848, B-275. Hereinafter cited as RTR.). He married according to the custom of the country **Elizabeth 'Betsy' Turcotte**, daughter of **(--?--) Turcotte** and **(--?--) Kaganawab**, in 1828 (NWHBSI, page 86.). He married **Elizabeth 'Betsy' Turcotte**, daughter of **(--?--) Turcotte** and **(--?--) Kaganawab**, on 29 Jan 1843 Edmonton House, Saskatchewan District (RTR, M-39.). He married **Elizabeth 'Betsy' Turcotte**, daughter of **(--?--) Turcotte** and **(--?--) Kaganawab**, on 23 Feb 1852 Fort-des-Prairies, (Alberta) (FDP, M-27.).

   Elizabeth 'Betsy' Turcotte was born in 1812 (NWHBSI, page 79.). She was baptized on 29 Jan 1843 Edmonton House (RTR, B-276.).

Children of **George Ward** and **Elizabeth 'Betsy' Turcotte** were as follows:

	i.	Isabelle Ward.
5	ii.	James Ward, b. circa 1831; m. Catherine Bruneau.
6	iii.	George Ward, b. circa 1832; m. Rosalie Ma-Ne-Wis-Ta-quan Indian; d. Oct 1870.
7	iv.	William Ward, b. circa 1834; m. Jeanne Morin dit Lapatate.
8	v.	Peter Ward, b. circa 1837; m. Rosalie Bisson.
9	vi.	John Ward, b. circa 1838; m. Jane Courteoreille.
10	vii.	Catherine Ward, b. circa 1840; m. St.Pierre Dumont; d. before 1885.
	viii.	Kitty Ward was baptized on 5 Feb 1843 Edmonton House, Saskatchewan District (Ibid., B-280.).
11	ix.	Nancy Ward, b. Jun 1844; m. Pierre Beauchamp.
	x.	Alexis Ward was born circa Jan 1847 (INB *Index des Naissances and Baptemes* (St.Boniface, Manitoba: La Societe Historique de Saint-Boniface., c1995).). He was baptized on 3 Apr 1847 Fort des Prairie, Edmonton, (Alberta) (Denney.) (INB, page 184.).

xi. Antoine Ward was born on 27 Oct 1848 Fort-des-Prairies, (Alberta) (Ibid.). He was baptized on 29 Oct 1848 Fort-des-Prairies, (Alberta) (Ibid.).

xii. Alexander Ward was born in 1849 St.Albert, (Alberta) (ArchiviaNet 1886-1901, 1906 Half-Breed Scrip Applications Index, RG15-21, Volume 1333 through 1371, Microfilm Reel Number C-14944 through C-15010, National Archives of Canada, Ottawa, Ontario, http://www.collectionscanada.gc.ca, C-15009.).

xiii. Marguerite Ward was born circa Mar 1858 (INB, page 184.). She was baptized on 18 May 1858 Fort-des-Prairies, (Alberta) (Ibid.).

xiv. Margaret Ward was born circa Mar 1858 (Denney.) (INB.). She was baptized on 18 May 1858 Fort des Prairie, Edmonton, (Alberta) (Denney.) (INB.). She died before 1885.

4. **John Ward** was born circa 1806 St.Albert, (Alberta) (Denney.). He married according to the custom of the country **Angelique Bruyere**, daughter of **Jean Baptiste Bruyere** and **Francoise Serpente,** before 1826.

Angelique Bruyere was born in 1801 North West (MBS, C-14932.). She was born circa 1804 (SFX: 1834-1850 St.Francois Xavier 1834-1851 Register, B-502. Hereinafter cited as SFX: 1834-1850.). She was baptized on 7 Apr 1844 St.Francois Xavier, (Manitoba) (Ibid.). She married **Francois Galipeau dit Wabicier Robertson or Robinson**, son of **Colin Robertson** and **Marguerite Grant,** on 1 Jun 1848 St.Francois Xavier, (Manitoba) (Ibid., M-112.). She died on 9 Jul 1891 St.Francois Xavier, Manitoba (SFXI-Kipling St.Francois Xavier Register Index, 1834-1900; compiled by Clarence Kipling , S-11.).

Children of **John Ward** and **Angelique Bruyere** were as follows:

12   i. Nancy Ward, b. 6 May 1821 St.Johns, Red River Settlement, (Manitoba); m. John Norquay; m. Archibald Flett; d. 26 May 1912 St.Clements, Manitoba.

13   ii. Marie Anne Ward, b. circa 1829; m. Jean Baptiste Caplette.

14   iii. John Ward, b. circa 1831; m. Marguerite Ducharme; d. circa Sep 1872 Buffalo Lake, (Alberta).

15   iv. Marguerite Ward, b. circa 1832; m. Alexis Malaterre.

16   v. Joseph Ward, b. circa 1836; m. Angelique Welsh; d. 15 Mar 1861 St.Francois Xavier, (Manitoba); bur. 16 Mar 1861 St.Francois Xavier, (Manitoba).

      vi. Henry Ward was born circa 1839 (RTR, B-126.). He was baptized on 23 Aug 1841 Edmonton House, Saskatchewan District (Ibid.). He was baptized on 29 May 1842 (Fort Carlton), Fort-des-Prairies, (Saskatchewan) (FDP, B-9.). He died on 4 May 1843 (SFX: 1834-1850, S-84.). He was buried on 5 May 1843 St.Francois Xavier, (Manitoba) (Ibid.).

17   vii. Angelique Ward, b. 24 Aug 1842 St.Francois Xavier, (Manitoba); m. Jean Baptiste Fagnant; d. 19 Jan 1902 Willow Bunch, (Saskatchewan); bur. 21 Jan 1902 St.Ignace, Willow Bunch, (Saskatchewan).

Generation Three

5. **James Ward** was born circa 1831. He was baptized on 5 Feb 1843 Edmonton House, Saskatchewan District (RTR, B-279.). He was baptized on 22 Aug 1847 Fort des Prairie, Edmonton, (Alberta) (INB, page 184.). He married **Catherine Bruneau**, daughter of **Isidore Bruneau** and **Piakwesekutew Wetzewick Indian,** on 10 Oct 1850 (Edmonton), Fort-des-Prairies, (Alberta) (FDP, M-131.).

Catherine Bruneau was born circa 1834.

Children of **James Ward** and **Catherine Bruneau** were as follows:

18   i. Isabelle Ward, b. circa Jul 1851; m. Louis Boucher.

19   ii. James Gervais Ward, b. 9 Dec 1855; m. Eve Boucher.

      iii. John Ward was born circa Jun 1858 (MSJ-FA-E Register des Baptemes, Mariages & Sepultures 1858-1861 Mission St.Joachim, Fort Auguste, Fort des Prairies, Edmonton, No. 1, page 5, B-36. Hereinafter cited as MSJ-FA-E.). He was baptized on 25 Jul 1858 St.Joachim, Fort Edmonton, (Alberta) (Ibid.).

      iv. Patrick Ward was born on 25 May 1861 Fort Edmonton, (Alberta) (Ibid., page 34, B-79.). He was baptized on 26 May 1861 St.Joachim, Fort Edmonton, (Alberta) (Ibid., page 34-35, B-79.).

      v. Felix Ward was born in 1864 Edmonton, (Alberta) (NWHBS 1885 Scrip Applications, North-West Halfbreeds residing outside Manitoba on 15 July 1870, RG15-20, C-14942.).

      vi. Vitaline Ward was born in 1867 Edmonton, (Alberta) (ArchiviaNet, C-14981.). She was born in 1872 Edmonton, (Alberta) (Ibid., C-15009.). She married Pierre Landry, son of Louis Landry and Isabelle Chalifoux, circa Apr 1886 Fort Assiniboine (HBSI Index 1886-1901, 1906 Halfbreed Scrip Applications, RG15-21.). She died between 1888 and 1891 Fort Carrol, Montana (Ibid.) (ArchiviaNet, C-14981.).

        Pierre Landry was born on 11 Jun 1856 St.Francois Xavier, (Manitoba) (SFXI-Kipling, B-126.). He was baptized on 11 Jun 1856 St.Francois Xavier, (Manitoba) (Ibid.). He married **Therese Lapierre**, daughter of **Francois Xavier Lapierre** and **Marie Rose Swain,** on 13 May 1895 Augusta, Lewis & Clark County, Montana (L&CCM Lewis & Clark County, Montana; Marriage Record Licenses and Certificates; 1865-1950; familysearch.org, Hereinafter cited as L&CCM.). He married **Therese Lapierre**, daughter of **Francois Xavier Lapierre** and **Marie Rose Swain,** on 30 Oct 1896 St.Peter's Mission, Montana (SPMT St.Peter's Mission; Volume I; Marriage Register 1859-1895; Translated & Transcribed by Reverend Dale McFarlane, Archivist, Diocese of Great Falls-Billings, Montana; Spring 1981, page 3, #12.).

      vii. Norman Ward was born in 1875 Buffalo Lake (ArchiviaNet, C-15009.). He died in 1907 Montana.

6. **George Ward** was born circa 1832 (CCRPNW-V *Catholic Church Records of the Pacific Northwest, Vancouver, Volumes I and II and Stellamaris Mission* Translated by: Mikell de Lores Wormell Warner and Annotated by: Harriet Duncan Munnick, (St.Paul, Oregon: French Prairie Press, 1972), page 13, B-126.). He was baptized on 3 Oct 1838 Jaspar House, (Alberta) (Ibid.). He married **Rosalie Ma-Ne-Wis-Ta-quan Indian** before 1863. He died in Oct 1870 (ArchiviaNet, C-15009.).

Rosalie Ma-Ne-Wis-Ta-quan Indian died before 1900.

Children of **George Ward** and **Rosalie Ma-Ne-Wis-Ta-quan Indian** all born St.Albert, (Alberta), were as follows:

      i. Jean Baptiste Ward was born in 1864 (Ibid.). He died in 1870 (Ibid.).

      ii. Marie Ward was born in 1867 (Ibid.). She died in Sep 1870 (Ibid.).

iii.   John Ward was born circa Apr 1870 (Ibid.). He died in Oct 1870 (Ibid.).

7. William Ward was born circa 1834 (CCRPNW-V, page 12, B-125.). He was baptized on 3 Oct 1838 Jaspar House, (Alberta) (Ibid.). He married **Jeanne Morin dit Lapatate** on 1 Feb 1856 Fort-des-Prairies, (Alberta) (FDP, M-75.).

Jeanne Morin dit Lapatate was born circa 1839 (INB, page 98.). She was baptized on 10 Feb 1856 Fort-des-Prairies (Ibid.).

Children of **William Ward** and **Jeanne Morin dit Lapatate** were as follows:

    i.   William Ward was born in Jan 1856 (Ibid., page 185.). He was baptized on 9 Feb 1856 Fort-des-Prairies, (Alberta) (Ibid.).

    ii.   Madeleine Ward was born circa Jul 1857 (INB.). She was baptized on 24 Sep 1857 Fort des Prairie, Edmonton, (Alberta) (Ibid.).

20   iii.   Adelaide Ward, b. Jul 1857 Edmonton, (Alberta); m. John Horace Nelson Brazeau; d. 1 Jul 1880 Edmonton, (Alberta).

    iv.   Marie Anne Ward was born in 1859 Edmonton, (Alberta) (NWHBS, C-14942.). She died circa Oct 1870 St.Albert, (Alberta) (Ibid.).

21   v.   George Ward, b. circa Nov 1859; m. Veronique Gladu.

    vi.   Jane Ward was born in 1861 St.Albert, (Alberta) (Ibid.). She died circa Oct 1870 St.Albert, (Alberta) (Ibid.).

    vii.   Samuel Ward was born in 1863 Edmonton, (Alberta) (Ibid.). He died circa Oct 1870 St.Albert, (Alberta) (Ibid.).

    viii.   Samuel Ward was born on 30 Jun 1878 Edmonton, (Alberta). He died in Oct 1878.

8. Peter Ward was born circa 1837 (CCRPNW-V, page 13, B-127.). He was baptized on 3 Oct 1838 Jaspar House, (Alberta) (Ibid.). He was born in 1840 Edmonton, (Alberta) (NWHBS, C-14942.). He married **Rosalie Bisson**, daughter of **Jean Baptiste Bisson** and **Rosalie Waneyande Simon Bruneau**, on 26 Jul 1858 St.Albert, (Alberta) (Ibid.) (Ibid., C-14936.).

Rosalie Bisson was born in 1843 Slave Lake, (Alberta) (Ibid.). She was baptized on 19 Oct 1845 Fort des Prairie (Denney.).

Children of **Peter Ward** and **Rosalie Bisson** were as follows:

    i.   Louise Ward was born circa Apr 1860 (MSJ-FA-E, page 24, B-29.). She was baptized on 8 May 1860 St.Joachim, Fort Edmonton, (Alberta) (Ibid.). She married John Shikak in 1883 St.Albert, (Alberta) (NWHBS, C-14942.).
        John Shikak died in 1884.

22   ii.   Jonas Ward, b. 16 Sep 1862 St.Albert, (Alberta); m. Madeleine Charland.

    iii.   Emelien Ward was born in 1865 St.Albert, (Alberta) (Ibid.). He was baptized circa Oct 1865 St.Albert, (Alberta) (Ibid.).

    iv.   Joseph Ward was born in Mar 1869 St.Albert, (Alberta) (Ibid.). He was baptized on 19 Apr 1869 St.Albert, (Alberta) (Ibid.). He died on 9 Jan 1875 St.Albert, (Alberta), at age 5 (Ibid.). He was buried on 9 Jan 1875 St.Albert, (Alberta) (Ibid.).

    v.   Anonyme Ward was born after 1870 (Ibid., C-14936.). She died after 1870 (Ibid.).

    vi.   Amelia Ward was born after 1870 (Ibid.). She died after 1870 (Ibid.).

    vii.   John Ward was born in 1871 St.Albert, (Alberta) (ArchiviaNet, C-15009.). He died in 1876 near Hand Hills (Ibid.).

    viii.   Emilie Ward was born in 1875 St.Albert, (Alberta) (Ibid.). She died in 1879 (Ibid.).

    ix.   Lucie Ward was born in 1877 St.Albert, (Alberta) (Ibid.). She died in Mar 1878 (Ibid.).

    x.   Julien Ward was born on 21 Apr 1879 St.Albert, (Alberta) (Ibid.). He was baptized on 21 Apr 1879 St.Albert, (Alberta) (Ibid.).

    xi.   Laurent Ward was born on 16 Feb 1883 St.Albert, (Alberta) (Denney.). He died on 22 Jan 1959 Ponoka, Alberta, at age 75 (Ibid.).

9. John Ward was born circa 1838 (Ibid.). He was baptized on 29 Jan 1843 Edmonton House, Saskatchewan District (RTR, B-278.). He was baptized on 29 Jul 1846 Fort-des-Prairies, (Alberta) (INB, page 129.). He married **Jane Courteoreille**, daughter of **Michel Courteoreille** and **Okimaiskwon (--?--)**, on 6 Sep 1860 Fort des Prairie (Denney.).

Jane Courteoreille was born circa 1842 (INB, page 39.). She was baptized on 2 May 1846 Lesser Slave Lake (Ibid.).

Children of **John Ward** and **Jane Courteoreille** were:

    i.   Jean Baptiste Ward was born in 1868 Lesser Slave Lake, (Alberta) (NWHBS, C-14942.).

10. Catherine Ward was born circa 1840. She was baptized on 29 Jan 1843 Edmonton House, Saskatchewan District (RTR, B-277.). She was baptized on 23 May 1846 Fort-des-Prairies, (Alberta) (INB, page 129.). She married **Joseph Bruneau**, son of **Pierre Bruneau** and **Marie Misaronne or Mistatem**, before 1857. She married **St.Pierre Dumont**, son of **Gabriel Dumont** and **Suzanne Lussier**, before 1865. She died before 1885.

Joseph Bruneau was born in 1834 (MBS.). He was baptized on 4 Sep 1842 Fort-des-Prairies (Ibid.) (INB, page 26.). He died before 1870.

St.Pierre Dumont was born in Jan 1842 Morleyville, Bow River, (Alberta) (INB, page 56.) (NWHBS, C-14938.). He was baptized on 26 Jun 1842 Fort-des-Prairies (INB, page 56.). He married **Betsy Breland**, daughter of **Francois Berland** and **Therese Karakonti L'Iroquois**, in 1866 (NWHBS, C-14938.). He married **Anne Callihoo**, daughter of **Chief Michel Callihoo** and **Marie Savard**, on 18 Dec 1871 Lac Ste.Anne, (Alberta) (Denney.).

11. Nancy Ward was born in Jun 1844 (RTR, B-433.). She was baptized on 20 Feb 1845 Edmonton House, Saskatchewan District (Ibid.). She was baptized on 26 Jun 1846 Fort-des-Prairies, (Alberta) (INB, page 129.). She married **Pierre Beauchamp**, son of **Pierre Beauchamp** and **Marie Comtois dit Morin**, on 21 Dec 1858 St.Joachim, Fort Edmonton, (Alberta) (MSJ-FA-E, page 8, M-3.).

Pierre Beauchamp was born before 1837.

12. Nancy Ward was baptized on 6 May 1821 St.Johns, Red River Settlement, (Manitoba) (HBCR, E.4/1a, folio 12d.). She was born in 1826 North West (MBS, C-14928.). She was baptized on 29 May 1842 (Fort Carlton), Fort-des-Prairies, (Saskatchewan) (FDP, B-16 and B-17.). She married **John Norquay**, son of **Oman Norquay** and **Jane Morwick**, on 9 Oct 1845 (St.Andrews), Rapids Church, (Manitoba) (HBCA-B.) (HBCR, No. 142.). She married **Archibald Flett**, son of **William Flett** and **Elisabeth "Betsy" (--?--)**, circa 1853 St.Andrews, (Manitoba). She died on 26 May 1912 St.Clements, Manitoba, at age 91 (Manitoba Vital Statistics online, http://web2.gov.mb.ca, Death Reg. #1912,003913.).

John Norquay was born circa 1810 Ruperts Land (1832C RRS HBCA E5/6 1832 Census of the Red River Settlement, HBCA E5/6, Hudson's Bay Company Archives, Provincial Archives, 200 Vaughan Street, Winnipeg, MB R3C 1T5, Canada., page 14.). He was baptized on 17 Jun 1822 St.Johns, Red River Colony, (Manitoba) (HBCR, E.4/1a, folio 28.) (HBCA-B.). He married **Isabella Truthwaite**, daughter of **Jacob Truthwaite** and **Elizabeth Vincent**, on 21 Feb 1832 St.Johns, Red River Settlement, (Manitoba) (HBCR, M-235.) (HBCA-B, E.4/1b fo. 234.). He died in Jun 1849 St.Johns, (Manitoba) (Denney.) (HBCA-B.). He was buried on 10 Jun 1849 St.Johns, (Manitoba) (Ibid., E.4/2 fo. 158.).

Archibald Flett was born in 1827 North West (MBS, C-14927.). He was baptized on 9 Sep 1834 (St.Andrews), Rapids of Red River, (Manitoba) (HBCA-B, E.4/1a fo. 112.). He died on 5 Sep 1908 St.Clements, Manitoba (MB Vital Statistics, Death Reg. #1908,001335.).

13. Marie Anne Ward was born circa 1829 (Ibid.). She was baptized on 29 May 1842 (Fort Carlton), Fort-des-Prairies, (Alberta) (FDP, B-16 and B-17.) (INB, page 184.). She married **Jean Baptiste Caplette**, son of **Joseph Caplette** and **Angelique Guiboche**, on 29 Aug 1847 St.Francois Xavier, (Manitoba) (SFX: 1834-1850, M-103.).

Jean Baptiste Caplette was born circa 1821 (1863-T Chippewas of the Red Lake and Pembina bands - Treaty of 1863-1864, , page 227.). He married **Madeleine Parisien**, daughter of **Bonaventure Parisien** and **Marguerite Sauteuse**, on 16 Feb 1858 St.Norbert, (Manitoba) (SN1 Catholic Parish Register of St.Norbert 1857-1873, M-13, page 5. Hereinafter cited as SN1.). He died in 1875 Pembina, Dakota Territory (McIntyre Report - Determination of validity of scrip issued for Half-breed Chippewas of the Pembina band, Red Lake band, White Earth band, 1880, #187.).

14. John Ward was born circa 1831 (CCRPNW-V, page 6, B-57.). He was born circa 1837 near, Edmonton, (Alberta) (NWHBS, C-14942.). He was baptized on 6 Sep 1838 Fort Edmonton (CCRPNW-V, page 6, B-57.). He married **Marguerite Ducharme**, daughter of **Antoine Ducharme** and **Jane Lambert**, circa 1857 Lac Manitoba, (Manitoba) (NWHBS, C-14942.) (Ibid., C-14938.). He died circa Sep 1872 Buffalo Lake, (Alberta) (Ibid., C-14942.).

Marguerite Ducharme was born circa 1841 near Fort Garry, (Manitoba) (Ibid., C-14938.). She was born circa 1845 (Manitoba) (1870C-MB, page 282, #1265.). She married **Paul Fagnant**, son of **Francois Fagnant** and **Madeleine Lemire**, in Oct 1871 (NWHBS, C-14938.).

Children of **John Ward** and **Marguerite Ducharme** were as follows:

23   i.   Marguerite Ward, b. 3 May 1860 St.Boniface, (Manitoba); m. William Scullen or Scollen.
24   ii.   John Ward, b. circa Jan 1862; m. Julie Minnetooch; d. before 1901.
      iii.   Marie Anne Ward was born on 1 Aug 1864 St.Francois Xavier, (Manitoba) (SFXI-Kipling, B-33.) (MBS, C-14934.). She was baptized on 3 Aug 1864 St.Francois Xavier, (Manitoba) (SFXI-Kipling, B-33.) (MBS, C-14934.).
25   iv.   James Ward, b. 2 Mar 1867 St.Francois Xavier, (Manitoba); m. Marguerite Jeanne Dumont; m. Isabelle Dumont.
26   v.   Peter Ward, b. circa Dec 1869 St.Albert, (Alberta); m. Marie Dumont.
      vi.   Jane Ward was born circa 1870 North West Territory (1870C-MB, page 282, #1270.).
          Question: *Was Jane actually Peter?*
      vii.   George Charles Ward was born on 18 Apr 1875 St.Eustache, Manitoba (INB, page 184.). He was baptized on 19 Apr 1875 St.Eustache, Manitoba (Ibid.).

15. Marguerite Ward was born circa Apr 1830 Edmonton, (Alberta) (MBS, C-14930.). She was born circa 1832 (CCRPNW-V, page 9, B-86.). She was baptized on 10 Sep 1838 Fort Edmonton (Ibid.). She married **Alexis Malaterre**, son of **Jean Baptiste Malaterre** and **Angelique Adam,** on 14 Jan 1850 St.Francois Xavier, (Manitoba) (SFX: 1834-1850, M-123.).

Alexis Malaterre was born in Jul 1825 St.Francois Xavier, (Manitoba) (MBS, C-14930.). He was buried on 15 Mar 1885 St.Claude Mission, St.John, Rolette County, North Dakota (St. Claude Mission, St. John, North Dakota, Baptisms, Marriages, Burials 1882-1888, 2006, Dominique Ritchot, S-32, p. 41.).

16. Joseph Ward was born circa 1836 (CCRPNW-V, page 9, B-87.). He was born circa 1837 (SFXI-Kipling, S-3.). He was baptized on 10 Sep 1838 Fort Edmonton (CCRPNW-V, page 9, B-87.). He married **Angelique Welsh**, daughter of **Francois Xavier Welsh** and **Charlotte Sauve,** before 1859. He died on 15 Mar 1861 St.Francois Xavier, (Manitoba) (SFXI-Kipling, S-3.). He was buried on 16 Mar 1861 St.Francois Xavier, (Manitoba) (Ibid.).

Angelique Welsh was born on 27 May 1841 St.Boniface, (Manitoba) (MBS, C-14927.) (1870C-MB, page 237, #324-329.). She and **John Francis Grant** met circa 1864. She married **Pierre Desjardins**, son of **Jean Baptiste Desjardins** and **Marguerite Hamelin,** before 1874 (MBS, C-14927.). She died on 12 Nov 1927 St.Boniface, Manitoba, at age 86 (MB Vital Statistics, Death Reg. #1927,054041.).

Children of **Joseph Ward** and **Angelique Welsh** were:

      i.   Guillaume Ward was born circa 1859. He married Catherine Thorne, daughter of George Thorne Sr. and Marie Lemire, on 10 Jan 1882 St.Francois Xavier, Manitoba (SFXI-Kipling, M-1.).
          Catherine Thorne was born on 3 Aug 1855 St.Francois Xavier, (Manitoba) (Ibid., B-53.). She was baptized on 4 Aug 1855 St.Francois Xavier, (Manitoba) (Ibid.). Question: *The groom was called William Bourke.*

17. Angelique Ward was born on 24 Aug 1842 St.Francois Xavier, (Manitoba) (SFX: 1834-1850, B-415.). She was baptized on 25 Aug 1842 St.Francois Xavier, (Manitoba) (Ibid.). She married **Jean Baptiste Fagnant**, son of **Jean Baptiste Fagnant** and **Josephte Monet dit Belhumeur,** on 29 Aug 1860 St.Francois Xavier, (Manitoba) (SFXI-Kipling, M-18.). She died on 19 Jan 1902 Willow Bunch, (Saskatchewan), at age 59 (SIWB St.Ignace Roman Catholic Registre des Baptemes, Mariages & Sepltures, Willow Bunch, Saskatchewan, 1882-1917, FHC #1290091., page 139. Hereinafter cited as SIWB.). She was buried on 21 Jan 1902 St.Ignace, Willow Bunch, (Saskatchewan) (Ibid.).

Jean Baptiste Fagnant was born on 30 Jan 1836 St.Francois Xavier, (Manitoba) (MBS, C-14927.) (SFX: 1834-1850, B-113.). He was baptized on 30 Jan 1836 St.Francois Xavier, (Manitoba) (Ibid.). He was buried on 3 Mar 1915 St.Ignace, Willow Bunch, Saskatchewan (SIWB, page 141.).

Generation Four

18. Isabelle Ward was born circa Jul 1851 (INB, page 184.). She was baptized on 2 Oct 1851 Fort-des-Prairies, (Alberta) (Ibid.). She married **Louis Boucher**, son of **Pierre Boucher** and **Marie Amable Bruneau,** before 1872.

Louis Boucher was born circa Oct 1846 (Ibid., page 19.). He was baptized on 5 Nov 1846 Fort-des-Prairies (Ibid.).

19. James Gervais Ward was born on 9 Dec 1855 (Denney.) (INB.). He was baptized on 19 Dec 1855 Fort des Prairie, Edmonton, (Alberta) (Denney.) (INB.). He married **Eve Boucher**, daughter of **Pierre Boucher** and **Marie Amable Bruneau**, in 1876 High River, North West Territories (HBS, Volume 1337, C-14951.).

Eve Boucher was born in 1861 St.Albert, (Alberta) (Ibid.).

Children of **James Gervais Ward** and **Eve Boucher** were as follows:
  i.   Anonyme Ward was born in 1878 (Ibid.). He/she died in 1878 (Ibid.).
  ii.   Vitaline Victorine Ward was born in 1880 Macleod, (Alberta) (ArchiviaNet, C-14997.). She married Frederick Piche before 1901 (Ibid.). She died in 1901 Flathead Agency, Montana (Ibid.).
  iii. John James Ward was born before 1886.

20. Adelaide Ward was born in Jul 1857 Edmonton, (Alberta) (NWHBS, C-14942.). She was baptized on 24 Sep 1857 Fort des Prairie (Denney.). She married **John Horace Nelson Brazeau**, son of **Joseph Edward Brazeau** and **Marguerite Brabant**, on 9 Sep 1878 Fort Saskatchewan, (Saskatchewan). She died on 1 Jul 1880 Edmonton, (Alberta) (Ibid.).

John Horace Nelson Brazeau was born on 17 Mar 1850 Fort Assiniboine (Clarence Kipling Research.). He was born circa Feb 1851 (INB, page 23.). He was baptized on 17 Apr 1851 Fort-des-Prairies (Ibid.). He married **Louise Belcourt**, daughter of **Alexis Belcourt** and **Nancy Rowand**, on 12 Dec 1881 Lac Ste.Anne, (Alberta) (Denney.).

21. George Ward was born circa Nov 1859 (MSJ-FA-E, page 17, B-48.). He was baptized on 18 Dec 1859 St.Joachim, Fort Edmonton, (Alberta) (Ibid.). He married **Veronique Gladu**, daughter of **Charles Quinn or Gladu** and **Jane Thomas**, on 4 Oct 1883 St.Joachim, Edmonton, (Alberta) (Ibid., page 93, M-3.).

Veronique Gladu was born in Apr 1869 Edmonton, (Alberta) (HBSI.) (ArchiviaNet.).

Children of **George Ward** and **Veronique Gladu** were as follows:
  i.   Jane Ward was born on 2 Aug 1893 (1901 Canada, District 202-p(3), page 2, family 14, line 10-14.).
  ii.   John Ward was born on 4 Jan 1899 (Ibid.).
  iii. Sarah Ward was born on 4 Dec 1900 (Ibid.).

22. Jonas Ward was born on 16 Sep 1862 St.Albert, (Alberta) (NWHBS, C-14942.). He was baptized on 26 Sep 1862 St.Albert, (Alberta) (Ibid.). He married **Madeleine Charland**, daughter of **Louis Charland** and **Julie Daigneault**, before 1888.

Madeleine Charland was born on 18 Jul 1868 Lac la Biche, (Alberta) (LLBR1 Notre Dame des Tidoren, St.Paul Diocese, Lac La Biche, Registre des Baptemes, Mariages & Sepltures, Volume 1, 1853-1898., page 93, B-441. Hereinafter cited as LLBR1.). She was baptized on 19 Jul 1868 Lac la Biche, (Alberta) (Ibid.).

Children of **Jonas Ward** and **Madeleine Charland** were as follows:
  i.   Eleanor Ward was born on 18 May 1888 (Denney.).
  ii.   Eloisa Ward was born on 12 Oct 1890 (Ibid.).
  iii. Olivine Ward was born on 15 Feb 1892 (Ibid.).

23. Marguerite Ward was born on 3 May 1860 St.Boniface, (Manitoba) (NWHBS, C-14941.) (1901 Canada, #202, v, page 17, family 152-153, line 41-50.). She married **William Scullen or Scollen** in 1878 Calgary, (Alberta) (NWHBS, C-14941.).

William Scullen or Scollen was born circa 1854 England (1881 Church of Latter Day Saints Census Transcription Project of Census Images from the National Archives of Canada, Ottawa, Canada, http://www.familysearch.org, District 192-2, page 19, house 120.). He died before 1901.

24. John Ward was born circa Jan 1862 (SB-Rozyk St. Boniface Roman Catholic Church, Manitoba, Canada, Baptisms, Marriages and Burials 1860-1875 Extractions, Compiled by Rosemary Rozyk, page 75, B-118.). He was baptized on 18 May 1862 St.Andrews, (Manitoba) (Denney.). He was baptized on 20 Jul 1862 St.Boniface, (Manitoba) (SB-Rozyk, page 75, B-118.). He married **Julie Minnetooch**, daughter of **Louis Minnetooch alias Icenowooskum (Indian)** and **Marie Esqwoo (Indian)**, in 1883 Lesser Slave Lake, (Alberta) (ArchiviaNet, C-15009.). He died before 1901 (1901 Canada, District 206-A-4, page 31, family 3, line 5-7.).

Julie Minnetooch was born in 1866 Waypiscack, (Alberta) (ArchiviaNet, C-15009.). She married **Louis Seeweeassoo** in 1879 Dunvegan, (Alberta) (Ibid.).

Children of **John Ward** and **Julie Minnetooch** were as follows:
  i.   Ellen Ward was born in 1892 (Ibid.). She died in 1895 (Ibid.).
  ii.   Mary Jane Ward was born in 1897 Lesser Slave Lake, (Alberta) (Denney.).
  iii. Edward Ward was born circa Sep 1900 Athabaska, (Alberta) (1901 Canada, District 206-A-4, page 31, family 3, line 5-7.).

25. James Ward was born on 2 Mar 1867 St.Francois Xavier, (Manitoba) (SFXI-Kipling, B-13.). He was baptized on 3 Mar 1867 St.Francois Xavier, (Manitoba) (Ibid.). He married **Marguerite Jeanne Dumont**, daughter of **Isidore Dumont** and **Angelique Landry**, on 9 Jul 1888 St.Laurent, (Saskatchewan) (Denney.). He married **Isabelle Dumont**, daughter of **Isidore Dumont** and **Judith Parenteau**, on 20 Jun 1890 St.Laurent, (Saskatchewan) (Ibid.).

Marguerite Jeanne Dumont was born on 5 Mar 1868 (SB-Rozyk, page 116, B-45.). She was baptized on 3 May 1868 (St.Charles), St.Boniface, (Manitoba) (Ibid.). She was buried on 4 May 1890 St.Laurent, (Saskatchewan) (Denney.).

Children of **James Ward** and **Marguerite Jeanne Dumont** were:
  i.   Antoine Ward was born on 3 Nov 1889 St.Laurent, (Saskatchewan) (SK Vital Statistics, Birth Reg. #7549.). He died on 22 Jan 1890 St.Laurent, (Saskatchewan) (Denney.).

Isabelle Dumont was born in Mar 1858 (NWHBSI, page 40.). She married **Francois Page**, son of **Henry Page** and **Eliza Grant**, on 9 Apr 1877 (Denney.).

Children of **James Ward** and **Isabelle Dumont** were as follows:
  i.   Flora Ward was born on 18 Jun 1891 (Saskatchewan) (SK Vital Statistics, Birth Reg. #8239.). She was baptized on 19 Jun 1891 St.Laurent, (Saskatchewan) (Denney.).
  ii.   William Jules Ward was born on 8 Oct 1892 Duck Lake, (Saskatchewan) (DL Register of Sacre Coeur Roman Catholic Church, Duck Lake, Saskatchewan, 1870-1893, page 112, B-28. Hereinafter cited as DL.) (SK Vital

Statistics, Birth Reg. #8231.). He was baptized on 8 Oct 1892 Duck Lake, (Saskatchewan) (DL, page 112, B-28.). He died on 7 Jun 1893 Duck Lake, (Saskatchewan) (Ibid., page 118, S-14.). He was buried on 8 Jun 1893 Duck Lake, (Saskatchewan) (Ibid.).

26. **Peter Ward** was born circa Dec 1869 St.Albert, (Alberta) (NWHBS, C-14942.). He married **Marie Dumont**, daughter of **Gabriel Dumont** and **Madeleine Wilkie,** before 1881.

Marie Dumont was born circa 1863 (SL-SK St.Laurent-de-Grandin Roman Catholic Registre des Baptemes, Mariages & Sepltures, St.Laurent, Saskatchewan, 1872-1896, page 15, B-29. Hereinafter cited as SL-SK.). She was baptized on 20 Apr 1878 St.Laurent-de-Grandin, (Saskatchewan) (Ibid.).

Children of **Peter Ward** and **Marie Dumont** were:

    i. Simon Ward was born in 1881 (NWHBS, C-14942.). He was buried on 19 Jan 1882 St-Laurent-de-Grandin, (Saskatchewan) (SL-SK, page 55, S-2.).

Ahnentafel between Jean Baptiste Wells and Christophe Wells

--- 1st Generation ---

1. **JEAN BAPTISTE WELLS.** Tribal Affiliation: *Quebec Metis.* He was born on 28 Oct 1785 at Berthier, Quebec (Denis Garand Research,7 Feb 2002, Source: BMD Berthier 1727-1900.) (PRDH online index, http://www.genealogic.umontreal.ca, No. 438270.). He was baptized on 30 Oct 1785 at Ste-Genevieve, Berthier, Quebec (Denis Garand, 7 Feb 2002, Source: BMD Berthier 1727-1900.) (PRDH online, No. 438270.). He was contracted as a voyageur on 27 Dec 1802 at Berthier, Quebec, *Welles, Jean-Bapt., Berthier, milieu-hiv., postes du nord, 2 ans, McTavish Frob.&Co., 700ff-1, 27-12-1802, DeGlandon, exempt du Nipigon et Rabaska* (Denis Garand, 7 Feb 2002.). He married **MARIE CRISE** before 1820. As of 1830, he was also known as **JEAN BAPTISTE WILLS** (1830C RRS HBCA E5/4 1830 Census of the Red River Settlement, HBCA E5/4, Hudson's Bay Company Archives, Provincial Archives, 200 Vaughan Street, Winnipeg, MB R3C 1T5, Canada., page 14.). As of 13 Jan 1840, he was also known as **JEAN BAPTISTE WELLS DIT LALLEMONT** (SFX: 1834-1850 St.Francois Xavier 1834-1851 Register, M-48 (father). Hereinafter cited as SFX: 1834-1850.).

--- 2nd Generation ---

2. **JOSEPH WELLS** was born circa 1748 at Alsace, France (PRDH online, #220356.). He married **MARGUERITE MARION**, daughter of **LOUIS-NICOLAS "FRANCOIS" MARION** and **MARIE ANGELIQUE COLIN DIT LALIBERTE**, on 3 May 1784 at Ste-Genevieve, Berthier, Quebec (Denis Garand, 7 Feb 2002, Source: BMD Berthier 1727-1900.) (PRDH online, No. 214993.). He died on 7 Dec 1835 at Sorel, Richelieu, Quebec (Ibid., #220356.).

--- 3rd Generation ---

4. **CHRISTOPHE WELLS** married **MARIE TIMS OR TINS.**

Descendants of Jean Baptiste Wells

Generation One

1. **Jean Baptiste Wells** was born on 28 Oct 1785 Berthier, Quebec (Denis Garand Research,7 Feb 2002, Source: BMD Berthier 1727-1900.) (PRDH online index, http://www.genealogic.umontreal.ca, No. 438270.). He was baptized on 30 Oct 1785 Ste-Genevieve, Berthier, Quebec (Denis Garand, 7 Feb 2002, Source: BMD Berthier 1727-1900.) (PRDH online, No. 438270.). He married **Marie Crise** before 1820.

He was contracted as a voyageur on 27 Dec 1802 Berthier, Quebec, *Welles, Jean-Bapt., Berthier, milieu-hiv., postes du nord, 2 ans, McTavish Frob.&Co., 700ff-1, 27-12-1802, DeGlandon, exempt du Nipigon et Rabaska* (Denis Garand, 7 Feb 2002.).

Marie Crise was born circa 1791 (SFX: 1834-1850 St.Francois Xavier 1834-1851 Register, S-63. Hereinafter cited as SFX: 1834-1850.). She died on 3 Jul 1841 (Ibid.). She was buried on 4 Jul 1841 St.Francois Xavier, (Manitoba) (Ibid.).

Children of **Jean Baptiste Wells** and **Marie Crise** were as follows:

  2 i. Jean Baptiste Wells, b. circa 1820 Ruperts Land; m. Angelique Chalifoux.

  3 ii. Marie Wells, b. circa 1829; m. Antoine Lafreniere; d. 21 Jul 1848 St.Francois Xavier, (Manitoba); bur. 23 Jul 1848 St.Francois Xavier, (Manitoba).

Generation Two

2. **Jean Baptiste Wells** was born circa 1820 Ruperts Land. He married **Angelique Chalifoux**, daughter of **Michel Chalifoux dit Richard** and **Isabelle Collin,** on 13 Jan 1840 St.Francois Xavier, (Manitoba) (Ibid., M-48.).

Angelique Chalifoux was born in 1805 North West (MBS Scrip Applications, Original White Settlers & Halfbreeds residing in Manitoba on 15 July 1870, RG15-19, C-14934.). She was born before 1822 (SFX: 1834-1850, M-48.). She married **Alexis Vivier**, son of **Alexis Vivier** and **Marie Anne Assiniboine**, before 1861.

Children of **Jean Baptiste Wells** and **Angelique Chalifoux** were as follows:

  4 i. Angelique Wells, b. 3 May 1842 St.Francois Xavier, (Manitoba); m. Joseph Espervier.

    ii. Cecile Lallemand was born on 27 May 1844 St.Francois Xavier, (Manitoba) (Ibid., B-520.). She was baptized on 28 May 1844 St.Francois Xavier, (Manitoba) (Ibid.).

  5 iii. Julie Wells, b. 3 May 1847; m. Alexis Vivier.

  6 iv. Marguerite Wells, b. 5 Jul 1849; m. Francois Gladu; d. 29 Aug 1896 St.Francois Xavier, Manitoba.

    v. Joseph Wells dit Lallemont was born on 4 May 1851 St.Francois Xavier, (Manitoba) (Ibid., B-902.). He was baptized on 5 May 1851 St.Francois Xavier, (Manitoba) (Ibid.).

  7 vi. Therese Wells, b. 14 Apr 1854; m. Alexandre Nolin; m. Joseph Vandal.

3. **Marie Wells** was born circa 1829. She married **Antoine Lafreniere**, son of **Antoine Lafreniere** and **Marie Versaille**, on 16 Jan 1848 St.Francois Xavier, (Manitoba) (Ibid., M-106.). She died on 21 Jul 1848 St.Francois Xavier, (Manitoba) (Ibid., S-210.). She was buried on 23 Jul 1848 St.Francois Xavier, (Manitoba) (Ibid.).

Antoine Lafreniere was born circa 1806 (SFXI-Kipling St.Francois Xavier Register Index, 1834-1900; compiled by Clarence Kipling , S-24.). He was born circa 1810. He married **Marguerite Gonneville**, daughter of **Antoine Gonneville** and **Marguerite Labine dit Lacouture**, on 18 Jan 1837 St.Francois Xavier, (Manitoba) (SFXI: 1834-1852 St.Francois Xavier 1834-1852 Register Index, M-25. Hereinafter cited as SFXI: 1835-1852.). He married **Marie Bouvier**, daughter of **Jean Baptiste Bouvier** and **Marguerite Paul**, on 17 Nov 1851 St.Francois Xavier, (Manitoba) (SFXI-Kipling, M-143.). He married **Ursule Moran**, daughter of **Jean Baptiste Morand** and **Marie Dubois**, on 19 Sep 1854 St.Francois Xavier, (Manitoba) (Ibid., M-1.). He died on 14 Oct 1874 St.Francois Xavier, Manitoba (Ibid., S-24.). He was buried on 16 Oct 1874 St.Francois Xavier, Manitoba (MBS, C-14929.) (SFXI-Kipling, S-24.).

Children of **Marie Wells** and **Antoine Lafreniere** were:

      i.   Anonyme Lafreniere was born on 21 Jul 1848 St.Francois Xavier, (Manitoba) (SFX: 1834-1850, S-210.). He/she died on 21 Jul 1848 St.Francois Xavier, (Manitoba) (Ibid.). He/she was buried on 23 Jul 1848 St.Francois Xavier, (Manitoba) (Ibid.).

Generation Three

4. Angelique Wells was born on 3 May 1842 St.Francois Xavier, (Manitoba) (Ibid., B-404.). She was baptized on 4 May 1842 St.Francois Xavier, (Manitoba) (Ibid.). She married **Joseph Espervier**, son of **(--?--) Espervier**, on 4 Mar 1862 St.Francois Xavier, (Manitoba) (SFXI-Kipling, M-3.).

Joseph Espervier was born circa 1840 (Manitoba) (1870C-MB 1870 Manitoba Census, National Archives of Canada, Ottawa, Ontario, Microfilm Reel Number C-2170., page 317, #2363.).

5. Julie Wells was born on 3 May 1847 (SFX: 1834-1850, B-679.). She was baptized on 11 May 1847 St.Francois Xavier, (Manitoba) (Ibid.). She married **Alexis Vivier**, son of **Alexis Vivier** and **Isabelle Short**, on 7 May 1865 St.Francois Xavier, (Manitoba) (SFXI-Kipling, M-4.).

Alexis Vivier was born on 20 Oct 1842 (SFX: 1834-1850, B-429.). He was baptized on 4 Nov 1842 St.Francois Xavier, (Manitoba) (Ibid.).

6. Marguerite Wells was born on 5 Jul 1849 (SFX: 1834-1850, B-792.). She was baptized on 15 Jul 1849 St.Francois Xavier, (Manitoba) (Ibid.). She married **Francois Gladu**, son of **Louis Gladu** and **Suzanne Desjarlais**, on 10 Jan 1871 St.Francois Xavier, Manitoba (SFXI-Kipling, M-2.). She died on 29 Aug 1896 St.Francois Xavier, Manitoba, at age 47 (MB Vital Statistics, Death Reg. #1896,001872.).

Francois Gladu was born in Mar 1846 Baie St.Paul, (Manitoba) (MBS, C-14928.). He died on 20 Apr 1904 RM of St.Francois Xavier, Manitoba, at age 58 (MB Vital Statistics, Death Reg. #1904,003611.).

7. Therese Wells was born on 14 Apr 1854 (SFXI-Kipling, B-159.) (SFXI 1851-1868, B-159.). She was baptized on 29 Apr 1854 St.Francois Xavier, (Manitoba) (SFXI-Kipling, B-159.) (SFXI 1851-1868, B-159.). She married **Alexandre Nolin** on 13 Jan 1873 Ste.Anne, Manitoba (MM, page 930 and 1304.). She married **Joseph Vandal**, son of **Joseph Vandal** and **Adelaide Charbonneau**, circa 1885 (Rod MacQuarrie Research, 28 Jan 2012.).

Joseph Vandal was born on 28 Oct 1851 St.Andrews, (Manitoba) (MBS, C-14934.). He married **Isabelle Sayer**, daughter of **George Sayer** and **Marie Caplette**, on 1 Jun 1870 St.Boniface, (Manitoba) (SB-Rozyk, page 184, M-15.). He married **Monique Desjardins**, daughter of **Jean Baptiste Desjardins** and **Marguerite Hamelin**, on 16 Oct 1876 Ste.Anne, Manitoba (MM.). He married **Marguerite Henault**, daughter of **Pierre Henault** and **Marguerite Larocque**, on 27 Sep 1880 Ste.Anne, Manitoba (Ibid.).

Ahnentafel between Francois Xavier Welsh and Christophe Wells

--- 1st Generation ---

1. FRANCOIS XAVIER WELSH was also known as XAVIER WELLS (1838C RRS HBCA E5/9 1838 Census of the Red River Settlement, HBCA E5/9, Hudson's Bay Company Archives, Provincial Archives, 200 Vaughan Street, Winnipeg, MB R3C 1T5, Canada., page 32.). Tribal Affiliation: *Quebec Metis.* He was born on 30 Nov 1796 at Berthier, Quebec (Denis Garand Research,7 Feb 2002, Source: BMD Berthier 1727-1900.) (PRDH online index, http://www.genealogic.umontreal.ca, #490908.). He was baptized on 10 Dec 1796 at Ste-Genevieve, Berthier, Quebec (Denis Garand, 7 Feb 2002, Source: BMD Berthier 1727-1900.) (PRDH online, #490908.). As of 10 Dec 1796, he was also known as FRANCOIS WELLS (Denis Garand, 7 Feb 2002, Source: BMD Berthier 1727-1900.). He was born circa 1797 at Quebec (1838C RRS HBCA E5/9, page 32.). He was contracted as a voyageur on 22 Dec 1816 at Berthier, Quebec, *Welles, François, Berthier, milieu-hiv., Nord-Ouest, 6 ans, McTavish McG.&Co., 600ff-1, 22-12-1814, Beek J.G., de Ste-Elizabeth de Berthier* (Denis Garand, 7 Feb 2002.). He was contracted as a voyageur on 20 May 1818 at Montreal, Montreal, Quebec, *Welles, François, Montréal, milieu-hiv., terres H.B.C., 2 ans, cie Baie d'Hudson, 800ff-1, 20-05-1818, Desautels Jh* (Ibid.). He married CHARLOTTE SAUVE, daughter of JEAN BAPTISTE SAUVE and MARGUERITE MASKEGONE OR SAULTEAUX, before 1837. He died before 1867.

--- 2nd Generation ---

2. JOSEPH WELLS was born circa 1748 at Alsace, France (PRDH online, #220356.). He married MARGUERITE MARION, daughter of LOUIS-NICOLAS "FRANCOIS" MARION and MARIE ANGELIQUE COLIN DIT LALIBERTE, on 3 May 1784 at Ste-Genevieve, Berthier, Quebec (Denis Garand, 7 Feb 2002, Source: BMD Berthier 1727-1900.) (PRDH online, No. 214993.). He died on 7 Dec 1835 at Sorel, Richelieu, Quebec (Ibid., #220356.).

--- 3rd Generation ---

4. CHRISTOPHE WELLS married MARIE TIMS OR TINS.

Descendants of Francois Xavier Welsh

Generation One

1. **Francois Xavier Welsh** was born on 30 Nov 1796 Berthier, Quebec (Denis Garand Research,7 Feb 2002, Source: BMD Berthier 1727-1900.) (PRDH online index, http://www.genealogic.umontreal.ca, #490908.). He was baptized on 10 Dec 1796 Ste-Genevieve, Berthier, Quebec (Denis Garand, 7 Feb 2002, Source: BMD Berthier 1727-1900.) (PRDH online, #490908.). He was born circa 1797

Quebec (1838C RRS HBCA E5/9 1838 Census of the Red River Settlement, HBCA E5/9, Hudson's Bay Company Archives, Provincial Archives, 200 Vaughan Street, Winnipeg, MB R3C 1T5, Canada., page 32.). He married **Charlotte Sauve**, daughter of **Jean Baptiste Sauve** and **Marguerite Maskegone or Saulteaux,** before 1837. He died before 1867.

He was contracted as a voyageur on 22 Dec 1816 Berthier, Quebec, *Welles, François, Berthier, milieu-hiv., Nord-Ouest, 6 ans, McTavish McG.&Co., 600ff-1, 22-12-1814, Beek J.G., de Ste-Elizabeth de Berthier* (Denis Garand, 7 Feb 2002.). He was contracted as a voyageur on 20 May 1818 Montreal, Montreal, Quebec, *Welles, François, Montréal, milieu-hiv., terres H.B.C., 2 ans, cie Baie d'Hudson, 800ff-1, 20-05-1818, Desautels Jh* (Ibid.).

Charlotte Sauve was born on 12 Nov 1808 Polar Sea. She died on 14 Oct 1888 St.Francois Xavier, Manitoba, at age 79 (SFXI-Kipling St.Francois Xavier Register Index, 1834-1900; compiled by Clarence Kipling , S-18.).

Children of **Francois Xavier Welsh** and **Charlotte Sauve** were as follows:

2   i.   Madeleine Lallemont dit Welsh, b. 21 Jan 1837 St.Boniface, (Manitoba); m. Andrew Bourke; d. 3 Nov 1903 St.Francois Xavier, Manitoba.

3   ii.   Angelique Welsh, b. 27 May 1841 St.Boniface, (Manitoba); m. Joseph Ward; m. John Francis Grant; m. Pierre Desjardins; d. 12 Nov 1927 St.Boniface, Manitoba.

4   iii.   Francois Welsh, b. Dec 1842 St.Boniface, (Manitoba); m. Esther Lariviere; m. Mary Anne Hogue; m. Ernestine Page.

5   iv.   Norbert Welsh, b. 15 Aug 1844 St.Boniface, (Manitoba); m. Cecile Boyer; m. Marguerite Hogue.

6   v.   Antoine Welsh, b. Nov 1844 St.Boniface, (Manitoba); m. Mary Ann Good; m. Elizabeth 'Betsy' Brown; d. 23 Mar 1904 Assiniboia, Manitoba.

   vi.   Louis Lafontaine was born circa 1843. He was born in Jun 1845 (1900C-ND 1900 United States Census, North Dakota, National Archives of the United States, Washington, D. C., House 314, page 309A.). He was born in 1848 (Manitoba) (Automated Genealogy 1901 Census Transcription Project and Census Images from the National Archives of Canada, http://www.automatedgenealogy.com, page 5, Family 33, #9-12.). He married Marie Madeleine Pelletier, daughter of Pierre Pelletier and Angelique Comtois, before 1864. He married Emelie Desjarlais before 1890. He died on 11 Apr 1939 Belcourt, Rolette County, North Dakota, at age 93 (North Dakota Department of Health Public Death Index.).

      Marie Madeleine Pelletier was born on 24 Jun 1845 Pembina, Pembina County, Minnesota Territory. She was baptized on 10 Jul 1845 St.Francois Xavier, (Manitoba) (SFX: 1834-1850 St.Francois Xavier 1834-1851 Register, B-578. Hereinafter cited as SFX: 1834-1850.).

      Emelie Desjarlais was born on 4 Jul 1844 (ND Death Index.). She was born in Oct 1855 North Dakota (1900C-ND, House 314, page 309A.). She married **Francois Pitwewekijik dit Lerat** before 1872. She died on 13 Jun 1943 Belcourt, Rolette County, North Dakota, at age 87 (ND Death Index.).

   vii.   Marguerite Welsh was born circa 1852 (Manitoba) (1870C-MB 1870 Manitoba Census, National Archives of Canada, Ottawa, Ontario, Microfilm Reel Number C-2170., page 237, #326.).

Generation Two

2. **Madeleine Lallemont dit Welsh** was born on 21 Jan 1837 St.Boniface, (Manitoba) (MBS Scrip Applications, Original White Settlers & Halfbreeds residing in Manitoba on 15 July 1870, RG15-19, C-14925.). She married **Andrew Bourke**, son of **John Palmer Bourke** and **Nancy Campbell,** on 3 Feb 1861 St.Boniface, (Manitoba) (RMSB *Repertoire des Mariages de Saint-Boniface (Manitoba) 1825-1983* compiled by Julien Hamelin S.C., (240, avenue Daly; Ottawa, Ontario K1N 6G2: Le Centre de Genealogie S. C., Publication #67, 1985).) (SB-Rozyk St. Boniface Roman Catholic Church, Manitoba, Canada, Baptisms, Marriages and Burials 1860-1875 Extractions, Compiled by Rosemary Rozyk, page 5, M-6.). She died on 3 Nov 1903 St.Francois Xavier, Manitoba, at age 66 (Manitoba Vital Statistics online, http://web2.gov.mb.ca, Death Reg. #1903,001737.).

Andrew Bourke was born on 10 Aug 1832 (SB 1825-1834 St.Boniface Roman Catholic Registre des Baptemes, Mariages & Sepultures, 1825-1834, page 74, B-488. Hereinafter cited as SB 1825-1834.). He was baptized on 2 Sep 1832 St.Boniface, (Manitoba) (Ibid.). He married **Angelique Chalifoux** before 1881 (HBS 1886-1901, 1906 Half-Breed Scrip Applications, RG15-21, Volume 1339, C-14954.). He died on 8 Sep 1899 St.Eustache, Manitoba, at age 67 (SFXI-Kipling, S-7.). He was buried on 17 Sep 1899 St.Francois Xavier, Manitoba (SFXI-Kipling, S-7.) (Rosemary Rozyk.).

3. **Angelique Welsh** was born on 27 May 1841 St.Boniface, (Manitoba) (MBS, C-14927.) (1870C-MB, page 237, #324-329.). She married **Joseph Ward**, son of **John Ward** and **Angelique Bruyere,** before 1859. She and **John Francis Grant** met circa 1864. She married **Pierre Desjardins**, son of **Jean Baptiste Desjardins** and **Marguerite Hamelin,** before 1874 (MBS, C-14927.). She died on 12 Nov 1927 St.Boniface, Manitoba, at age 86 (MB Vital Statistics, Death Reg. #1927,054041.).

Children of **Angelique Welsh** include:

   i.   Henry John Welsh was born circa 1863 (Manitoba) (1870C-MB, page 237, #328.).

Joseph Ward was born circa 1836 (CCRPNW-V *Catholic Church Records of the Pacific Northwest, Vancouver, Volumes I and II and Stellamaris Mission* Translated by: Mikell de Lores Wormell Warner and Annotated by: Harriet Duncan Munnick, (St.Paul, Oregon: French Prairie Press, 1972), page 9, B-87.). He was born circa 1837 (SFXI-Kipling, S-3.). He was baptized on 10 Sep 1838 Fort Edmonton (CCRPNW-V, page 9, B-87.). He died on 15 Mar 1861 St.Francois Xavier, (Manitoba) (SFXI-Kipling, S-3.). He was buried on 16 Mar 1861 St.Francois Xavier, (Manitoba) (Ibid.).

Children of **Angelique Welsh** and **Joseph Ward** were:

   i.   Guillaume Ward was born circa 1859. He married Catherine Thorne, daughter of George Thorne Sr. and Marie Lemire, on 10 Jan 1882 St.Francois Xavier, Manitoba (Ibid., M-1.).

      Catherine Thorne was born on 3 Aug 1855 St.Francois Xavier, (Manitoba) (Ibid., B-53.). She was baptized on 4 Aug 1855 St.Francois Xavier, (Manitoba) (Ibid.). Question: *The groom was called William Bourke.*

John Francis Grant was born on 7 Jan 1831 Fort Assiniboine (MBS, C-14928.). He was baptized on 16 Nov 1836 Trois-Rivieres, Quebec (Anita Steele Research, e-mail 20 May 1998.). He married **Louise Serpent** before 1851. He married **Quarra 'Cora' Bannock**

before 1856. He married **Isabelle Lussier** before 1862. He married **Clotilde Bruneau**, daughter of **Francois Bruneau** and **Marguerite Harrison**, on 7 May 1868 St.Boniface, (Manitoba) (SB-Rozyk, page 117, M-14.). He died on 16 May 1907 at age 76.

Pierre Desjardins was born in 1849 St.Vital, (Manitoba) (MBS, C-14927.). He died on 21 Mar 1889 Assiniboia, Manitoba (MB Vital Statistics, Death Reg. #1889,001618.).

4. **Francois Welsh** was born in Dec 1842 St.Boniface, (Manitoba). He and **Esther Lariviere** met circa 1866. He married **Mary Anne Hogue**, daughter of **Louis Amable Hogue** and **Marguerite Taylor**, circa 1869. He married **Ernestine Page**, daughter of **Alexandre Page** and **Adelaide Lepine**, on 19 Nov 1883 St.Francois Xavier, Manitoba (SFXI-Kipling, M-6.).

Esther Lariviere was born circa 1842 Red River, (Manitoba) (1870C-MB, #316-318, page 11.). She married **Antoine Vallee**, son of **Jean Baptiste Vallee** and **Marie Kipling**, on 20 Jun 1877 St.Boniface, (Manitoba). She married **Roger Henault**, son of **Pierre Henault** and **Marguerite Larocque**, on 7 Sep 1885 St.Boniface, Manitoba (RMSB.).

Children of **Francois Welsh** and **Esther Lariviere** were:

    i. Eliza Lariviere dit Vallee was born on 14 Sep 1866 St.Boniface, (Manitoba) (MBS, C-14929.) (SB-Rozyk, page 65, B-115.). She was baptized on 16 Sep 1866 St.Boniface, (Manitoba) (Ibid.). She married Alexis Parisien, son of Alexis Parisien and Marguerite Comtois, on 5 Feb 1884 Winnipeg, Manitoba (MB Vital Statistics, Marriage Reg. #1884,001603.).

        Alexis Parisien was born on 4 Aug 1859 St.Norbert, (Manitoba) (SN1, B-24, page 18.). He was baptized on 7 Aug 1859 St.Norbert, (Manitoba) (Ibid.). He married **Cecile Lund**, daughter of **Thomas Lund** and **Sara Flamand**, before 1901 (1901 Canada, District 10-H-1, page 13, family 117, line 47-50.). He died on 17 Dec 1923 St.Boniface, Manitoba, at age 64 (MB Vital Statistics, Death Reg. #1923,048054.).

Mary Anne Hogue was born in Oct 1850 St.James, (Manitoba) (MBS, C-14934.). She died on 20 Feb 1883 Assiniboia, Manitoba, at age 32 (MB Vital Statistics, Death Reg. #1883,001218.).

Children of **Francois Welsh** and **Mary Anne Hogue** were:

    i. Sarah Jane Welsh was born on 24 Apr 1870 St.Charles, (Manitoba) (MBS, C-14934.). She was baptized on 25 Apr 1870 St.Charles, (Manitoba) (Ibid.) (Rosemary Rozyk, 27 Sep 2009.). She married Wilfred Page, son of Alexandre Page and Adelaide Lepine, on 17 Feb 1890 St.Francois Xavier, Manitoba (SFXI-Kipling, M-5.).

        Wilfred Page was born on 28 Feb 1868 (SB-Rozyk, page 109, B-20.). He was baptized on 1 Mar 1868 St.Boniface, (Manitoba) (Ibid.). He died on 5 Dec 1898 St.Francois Xavier, Manitoba, at age 30 (SFXI-Kipling, S-20.).

    ii. Marie Welsh was born 30 Aug 1872 St.Charles, Manitoba (SFXI-Kipling, M-1.). She married Frederic Shirtliff, son of George Shirtliff and Marie Walker, on 13 Jul 1893 St.Francois Xavier, Manitoba (Ibid., M-1.).

        Frederic Shirtliff was born circa 1866 England (Ibid.).

    iii. Helene Welsh was born circa 1875. She married George Shirtliff on 6 Nov 1900 St.Francois Xavier, Manitoba (SFXI-Kipling.).

Ernestine Page was born circa 1857 (Manitoba) (1870C-MB, page 248, #88.). She married **Eusebe Perras** on 9 Feb 1880 St.Francois Xavier, Manitoba (SFXI-Kipling, M-2.).

Children of **Francois Welsh** and **Ernestine Page** all born St.Francois Xavier, Manitoba, were as follows:

    i. John William Welsh was born on 30 Oct 1884 (Ibid., B-48.).

    ii. Francois Alexander Welsh was born on 18 Jan 1886 (Ibid., B-4.).

    iii. Joseph Jean Baptiste Welsh was born on 24 Jun 1887 (Ibid., B-32.).

    iv. Gilbert Henry Welsh was born on 30 Jul 1890 (Ibid., B-35.). He died on 19 Feb 1891 St.Francois Xavier, (Manitoba).

    v. Henri Albert Ernest Welsh was born on 5 Dec 1891 (Ibid., B-54.). He died on 20 Jan 1892 St.Francois Xavier, Manitoba (Ibid., S-3.).

    vi. Catherine Welsh was born on 3 Aug 1893 (Ibid., B-15.). She married Albert Gagnier on 7 Mar 1916 (Ibid., B-15 (note).).

    vii. Joseph Albert Welsh was born on 24 Aug 1895 (Ibid., B-26.). He was buried on 31 Oct 1895 St.Francois Xavier, Manitoba (Ibid., S-15.).

5. **Norbert Welsh** was born on 15 Aug 1844 St.Boniface, (Manitoba) (MBS, C-14934.). He married **Cecile Boyer**, daughter of **Louis Boyer** and **Madeleine Trottier**, on 27 May 1867 St.Francois Xavier, (Manitoba) (SFXI-Kipling, M-14.). He married **Marguerite Hogue**, daughter of **Joseph Hogue** and **Pelagie Turcotte**, before 1903.

Cecile Boyer was born in Apr 1846 (SFX: 1834-1850, B-608.). She was baptized on 17 May 1846 St.Francois Xavier, (Manitoba) (Ibid.). She was buried on 15 Feb 1902 Lebret, (Saskatchewan) (Denney.).

Children of **Norbert Welsh** and **Cecile Boyer** were as follows:

    i. William Welsh was born on 25 Feb 1868 North West Territories (MBS, C-14934.) (SFXI-Kipling, B-32.) (Ibid., B-51.). He was baptized on 1 May 1868 St.Francois Xavier, (Manitoba) (MBS, C-14934.) (SFXI-Kipling, B-32.). He was baptized on 13 May 1868 St.Francois Xavier, (Manitoba) (Ibid., B-51.). He was buried on 18 Feb 1880 Lebret, (Saskatchewan) (L1 Lebret Mission de St.Florent Roman Catholic Registre des Baptemes, Mariages & Seplutures, Qu'Appelle, Saskatchewan, 1868-1881., page 256, S-4. Hereinafter cited as L1.).

    ii. Marie Cecile Welsh was born on 2 Dec 1869 North West Territories (MBS, C-14934.) (SFXI-Kipling, B-37.). She was baptized on 19 May 1870 St.Francois Xavier, (Manitoba) (MBS, C-14934.) (SFXI-Kipling, B-37.). She died on 31 May 1879 Lebret, (Saskatchewan), at age 9 (L1, page 248, S-20.). She was buried on 2 Jun 1879 Lebret, (Saskatchewan) (Ibid.).

  7 iii. Albert Robert Welsh, b. 1 Dec 1871 (Saskatchewan); m. Isabelle Racette.

    iv. Emelie Welsh was born on 4 Mar 1874 Duck Lake, (Saskatchewan) (DL Register of Sacre Coeur Roman Catholic Church, Duck Lake, Saskatchewan, 1870-1893, page 20, B-77. Hereinafter cited as DL.) (ArchiviaNet 1886-1901, 1906 Half-Breed Scrip Applications Index, RG15-21, Volume 1333 through 1371, Microfilm Reel Number C-

14944 through C-15010, National Archives of Canada, Ottawa, Ontario, http://www.collectionscanada.gc.ca, C-15009.). She was baptized on 4 Mar 1874 Duck Lake, (Saskatchewan) (DL, page 20, B-77.). She married St. Pierre Blondeau, son of Simon Blondeau and Francoise Desjarlais, before 1900 (1901 Canada, #203, h(1), page 2, family 17, line 25-26.).

    St. Pierre Blondeau was born on 28 Feb 1867 Lac Qu'Appelle, (Saskatchewan) (NWHBS 1885 Scrip Applications, North-West Halfbreeds residing outside Manitoba on 15 July 1870, RG15-20, C-14936.) (SN1, B-10.). He was baptized on 3 Apr 1867 (Fort Qu'Appelle), St.Norbert, (Manitoba) (Ibid.).

8   v.   Francois Xavier Welsh, b. 25 Jan 1876 Cypress Hills, (Saskatchewan); m. Veronique Beaulieu dit Sinclair.

    vi.   Marie Philomene Welsh was born on 1 Sep 1878 Fort Qu'Appelle, (Saskatchewan) (HBSI Index 1886-1901, 1906 Halfbreed Scrip Applications, RG15-21.) (L1, page 234, B-58.). She was baptized on 2 Sep 1878 Lebret, (Saskatchewan) (Ibid.). She died on 28 Nov 1880 Lebret, (Saskatchewan), at age 2 (Ibid., page 289, S-_.) (ArchiviaNet, C-15009.). She was buried on 29 Nov 1880 Lebret, (Saskatchewan) (L1, page 289, S-_.).

   vii.   Philomene Welsh was born on 8 Aug 1881 Lebret, (Saskatchewan) (L2 Lebret, Mission de St.Florent, Roman Catholic Registre des Baptemes, Mariages & Seplutures, Qu'Appelle, Saskatchewan, Book Two: 1881-1887, FHC microfilm 1032949., page 10, B-44. Hereinafter cited as L2.). She was baptized on 8 Aug 1881 Lebret, (Saskatchewan) (Ibid.). She died on 18 Sep 1889 Fort Qu'Appelle, (Saskatchewan), at age 8 (ArchiviaNet, C-15009.).

  viii.   Victoire Welsh was born on 11 May 1883 Fort Qu'Appelle, (Saskatchewan) (L2, page 64, B-31.). She was baptized on 12 May 1883 Lebret, (Saskatchewan) (Ibid.). She died on 23 May 1890 Fort Qu'Appelle, (Saskatchewan), at age 7 (ArchiviaNet, C-15009.).

    ix.   Jean Welsh was born on 4 Jun 1885 Fort Qu'Appelle, (Saskatchewan) (L2, page 115, B-67.) (ArchiviaNet, C-15009.). He was baptized on 5 Jun 1885 Lebret, (Saskatchewan) (L2, page 115, B-67.). He died on 3 Jun 1886 Fort Qu'Appelle, (Saskatchewan) (Ibid., page 151, S-38.) (ArchiviaNet, C-15009.). He was buried on 4 Jun 1886 Lebret, (Saskatchewan) (L2, page 151, S-38.).

    x.   Marie Virginie Elise Welsh was born on 5 Apr 1887 (Ibid., page 176, B-32.). She was baptized on 5 Apr 1887 Lebret, (Saskatchewan) (Ibid.). She died on 14 Dec 1887 (Ibid., page 193, S-26.). She was buried on 15 Dec 1887 Lebret, (Saskatchewan) (Ibid.).

    xi.   William John Welsh was born on 4 Oct 1889 (Saskatchewan) (Saskatchewan Vital Statistics online, http://vsgs.health.gov.sk.ca, #8903.).

Marguerite Hogue was born on 20 Mar 1876 St.Charles, Manitoba (Denney.). She married **Jean Joseph McDougall**, son of **John Peter McDougall** and **Elise Delorme,** on 26 Nov 1895 St.Francois Xavier, Manitoba (SFXI-Kipling, M-3.) (MB Vital Statistics, Mar. Reg. #1895,002165.).

Children of **Norbert Welsh** and **Marguerite Hogue** are as follows:

    i.   Norbert Jean Baptiste Welsh was born on 12 Dec 1903 File Hills, (Saskatchewan) (SK Vital Statistics, #3400.).

    ii.   Cecelia Welsh was born circa 1905 (Saskatchewan) (Automated Genealogy 1906 Census Transcription Project and Census Images from the National Archives of Canada, http://www.automatedgenealogy.com, #15, (41), page 33-34, family 275, line 37-40, 1-3.).

   iii.   Marie Jean Baptiste Edmond Welsh was born on 26 Jul 1907 Lebret, (Saskatchewan) (SK Vital Statistics, #8149.).

    iv.   Edmund Welsh was born circa 1908 (1916 Census of Canada from the National Archives of Canada (Transcription by ancestry.com), Ottawa, Canada, District 28-10, page 6, line 41.).

    v.   Joseph Welsh was born circa 1910 (Ibid.).

    vi.   Jeanne Welsh was born circa 1913 (Ibid.).

6. Antoine Welsh was born in Nov 1844 St.Boniface, (Manitoba) (MBS, C-14934.). He and **Mary Ann Good** met before 1864. He married **Elizabeth 'Betsy' Brown**, daughter of **Peter Brown** and **Sarah Bremner,** before 1870. He died on 23 Mar 1904 Assiniboia, Manitoba, at age 59 (MB Vital Statistics, Death Reg.#1904,002943.).

    Mary Ann Good was born England. She and **Joseph Armstrong** met before 1859. She and **William Fidler** met before 1862.

Children of **Antoine Welsh** and **Mary Ann Good** were:

9   i.   Delilah Talmann or Welsh, b. 24 May 1864 St.James, (Manitoba); m. Charles Alexander Fidler.

    Elizabeth 'Betsy' Brown was born in Apr 1844 St.Charles, (Manitoba) (MBS, C-14934.). She was baptized on 7 Jun 1844 St.Johns, (Manitoba) (Denney.). She married **Thomas Bird**, son of **(--?--) Bird,** before 1861. She died on 2 Apr 1928 East St.Paul, Manitoba (MB Vital Statistics, Death Reg.#1928,020243.).

Children of **Antoine Welsh** and **Elizabeth 'Betsy' Brown** were as follows:

    i.   Jacques Albert "James" Welsh was born on 29 Dec 1870 St.Charles, Manitoba (ArchiviaNet, C-15009.).

    ii.   Ellen Welsh was born circa 1874 Manitoba (1881 Church of Latter Day Saints Census Transcription Project of Census Images from the National Archives of Canada, Ottawa, Canada, http://www.familysearch.org, Film No. C-13283, District 186, Sub-district K, page 25, Household No. 118.).

   iii.   Elisabeth Welsh was born on 2 Sep 1877 (SFXI-Kipling, S-11.). She died on 7 May 1893 St.Francois Xavier, Manitoba, at age 15 (Ibid.).

    iv.   Maria Daloris Welsh was born circa 1879 (Ibid., S-6.). She died on 9 May 1894 St.Francois Xavier, Manitoba (Ibid.).

    v.   Rosine Welsh was born circa 1881 (Ibid., S-7.). She died on 7 May 1894 St.Francois Xavier, Manitoba (Ibid.).

    vi.   Joseph Antoine Wilfred Welsh was born on 13 Jan 1883 St.Francois Xavier, Manitoba (Ibid., B-4.). He married Marie Louise Auger on 20 Oct 1917 Winnipeg, Manitoba (Ibid., B-4 (note).).

   vii.   Francois Xavier Welsh was born on 13 Oct 1885 St.Francois Xavier, Manitoba (Ibid., B-48.). He married Lizzie Land on 5 Dec 1917 St.Marys, Winnipeg, Manitoba (Ibid., B-48 (note).).

  viii.   Francois Xavier Alexandre Welsh was born on 7 Jun 1888 St.Francois Xavier, Manitoba (Ibid., B-22.).

Generation Three

7. Albert Robert Welsh was born on 1 Dec 1871 (Saskatchewan) (1901 Canada, #203, h(1), page 3, family 24-26, line 6-11.). He married **Isabelle Racette**, daughter of **Charles Racette** and **Helene Boyer,** before 1892.

Isabelle Racette was born on 9 Feb 1872 Fish Creek, (Saskatchewan) (Denney.) (SL-SK St.Laurent-de-Grandin Roman Catholic Registre des Baptemes, Mariages & Sepltures, St.Laurent, Saskatchewan, 1872-1896, page 3, B-_. Hereinafter cited as SL-SK.). She was baptized on 10 Feb 1872 St.Laurent-de-Grandin, (Saskatchewan) (Ibid.).

Children of **Albert Robert Welsh** and **Isabelle Racette** were as follows:

    i.   Helen Philomene Welsh was born on 6 Nov 1892 (Saskatchewan) (SK Vital Statistics, #9190.).

    ii.   Henri Albert Welsh was born on 3 Apr 1895 (Saskatchewan) (Ibid., #9353.).

    iii.   Emilie Victoria Welsh was born on 7 Jul 1897 Ituna, (Saskatchewan) (Ibid., #13112.).

    iv.   Edward Welsh was born on 10 Nov 1899 File Hills, (Saskatchewan) (Ibid., #1846.).

    v.   Marie Marguerite Welsh was born on 21 Mar 1905 File Hills, (Saskatchewan) (Ibid., #5150.).

8. Francois Xavier Welsh was born on 18 Jan 1876 Cypress Hills, (Saskatchewan) (ArchiviaNet, C-15009.). He was born on 25 Jan 1876 Cypress Hills, (Saskatchewan) (L1, page 184, B-113.). He was baptized on 2 Apr 1876 Lebret, (Saskatchewan) (Ibid.). He married **Veronique Beaulieu dit Sinclair**, daughter of **Thomas Beaulieu dit Sinclair** and **Marguerite Fisher,** on 14 Nov 1898 Lebret, (Saskatchewan) (Eileen Horan Research, 4 Jun 2012.).

Veronique Beaulieu dit Sinclair was born on 25 May 1871 Qu'Appelle, (Saskatchewan) (L1, page 47, B-91.). She was baptized on 27 Nov 1871 Lebret, (Saskatchewan) (Ibid.).

Children of **Francois Xavier Welsh** and **Veronique Beaulieu dit Sinclair** all born File Hills, (Saskatchewan), are as follows:

    i.   William Thomas Welsh was born on 10 Sep 1899 (SK Vital Statistics, #2843.).

    ii.   Joseph Edward Welsh was born on 10 Jan 1901 (Ibid., #2395.).

    iii.   Marie Emilie Welsh was born on 27 Oct 1902 (Ibid., #2825.).

    iv.   Cecile Elizabeth Welsh was born on 5 Mar 1905 (Ibid., #5146.).

9. Delilah Talmann or Welsh was born on 24 May 1864 St.James, (Manitoba) (MBS, C-14934.). She was baptized on 29 May 1864 St.James, (Manitoba) (SJAC St.James Anglican Church Extractions, Manitoba Genealogy Society, Winnipeg, Manitoba, B-152.). She married **Charles Alexander Fidler**, son of **Cornelius Fidler** and **Jane Birston,** on 13 Dec 1879 St.James, Manitoba (SJAC.).

Charles Alexander Fidler was born on 15 Oct 1856 St.James, (Manitoba) (MBS, C-14927.). He died on 31 Aug 1900 RM Portage la Prairie, Manitoba, at age 43 (MB Vital Statistics, Death Reg. #1900,002669.). He was buried on 1 Sep 1900 St.Ann, Poplar Point, Manitoba (Louis Verhagen Research.).

Descendants of Willard Ferdinand Wensell

Generation One

1. Willard Ferdinand Wensell was born Norway. He married according to the custom of the country **Magdelaine Montagnais** before 1806. He married according to the custom of the country **Agathe Letendre**, daughter of **Jean Baptiste "Okimawaskawikinam" Letendre** and **Josephte Indian,** before 1808. He died before 1850.

Children of **Willard Ferdinand Wensell** and **Magdelaine Montagnais** were:

  2   i.   Alexander Wensell, b. circa 1806 Ruperts Land; m. Marie Anne Laferte; d. 26 Jan 1866 St.Norbert, (Manitoba); bur. 28 Jan 1866 St.Norbert, (Manitoba).

Agathe Letendre was born circa 1790. She married according to the custom of the country **William Henry**, son of **Alexander Henry the Elder** and **Julia (–?–),** before 1813. She married **Joseph Page**, son of **Joseph Page dit Quercy** and **Madeleine Casaubon,** before 1829.

Children of **Willard Ferdinand Wensell** and **Agathe Letendre** were:

  3   i.   Helene Wensell, b. circa 1808; m. Duncan McDougall; m. Louis Goulet.

Children of **Willard Ferdinand Wensell** and **Francoise Snake** were:

    i.   Guillaume Wensell was born before 1829. He married Marie Emilie Molelis on 6 May 1850 Vancouver, Oregon Territory (CCRPNW-V *Catholic Church Records of the Pacific Northwest, Vancouver, Volumes I and II and Stellamaris Mission* Translated by: Mikell de Lores Wormell Warner and Annotated by: Harriet Duncan Munnick, (St.Paul, Oregon: French Prairie Press, 1972), page 109, M-2.).

        Marie Emilie Molelis was born in 1836 Oregon Territory (Ibid., page 109, B-7.). She was baptized on 5 May 1850 Vancouver, Oregon Territory (Ibid.).

Generation Two

2. Alexander Wensell was born circa 1801 (SN1 Catholic Parish Register of St.Norbert 1857-1873, page 78, S-4. Hereinafter cited as SN1.). He was born circa 1806 Ruperts Land (1833C RRS HBCA E5/7 1833 Census of the Red River Settlement, HBCA E5/7, Hudson's Bay Company Archives, Provincial Archives, 200 Vaughan Street, Winnipeg, MB R3C 1T5, Canada., page 18.) (SB 1825-1834 St.Boniface Roman Catholic Registre des Baptemes, Mariages & Sepultures, 1825-1834, page 97, B-570. Hereinafter cited as SB 1825-1834.). He was baptized on 6 Apr 1833 St.Boniface, (Manitoba) (Ibid.). He married **Marie Anne Laferte**, daughter of **Pierre-Michel Laferte** and **Marie Anne Genereux,** before 1851. He died on 26 Jan 1866 St.Norbert, (Manitoba) (SN1, page 78, S-4.). He was buried on 28 Jan 1866 St.Norbert, (Manitoba) (Ibid.).

Marie Anne Laferte was born in 1833 St.Boniface, (Manitoba) (MBS Scrip Applications, Original White Settlers & Halfbreeds residing in Manitoba on 15 July 1870, RG15-19, C-14934.). She married **James White**, son of **Joseph White** and **Genevieve Short,** on 5 Feb 1879 Ste.Agathe, Manitoba (MM *Manitoba Marriages* in *Publication 45*, Volumes 1-3, compiled and edited by: Paul J. Lareau, Fr. Julien Hamelin, (240 Avenue Daly, Ottawa, Ontario K1N 6G2: Le Centre de Genealogie S.C., 1984).).

Children of **Alexander Wensell** and **Marie Anne Laferte** were as follows:

  4   i.   Alexander Wensell, b. 17 Sep 1851 St.Boniface, (Manitoba); m. Rosalie Morin; d. before 1893.

    ii.   Joseph Wensell was born on 12 Jan 1858 Ste.Agathe, (Manitoba) (MBS, C-14934.). He was buried on 26 Mar 1888 Ste.Agathe, Manitoba (Ste.Agathe Roman Catholic Cemetery; Cemetery Transcription #485; E. Bjornson and K. Stokes F. Cox, Rm. 420 - 167 Lombard Ave., Winnipeg, Manitoba, Canada R3B 0T6: Manitoba Genealogical Society, Inc., June 1988, page 10.).

    iii.   Boniface Wensell was born on 25 May 1861 Ste.Agathe, (Manitoba) (MBS, C-14934.) (SN1, page 45, B-21.). He was baptized on 19 Jun 1861 St.Norbert, (Manitoba) (Ibid.).

    iv.   Julien Wensell was born on 19 Sep 1863 (Ibid., page 88, B-34.). He was baptized on 10 Oct 1863 St.Norbert, (Manitoba) (Ibid.). He died on 27 Nov 1865 St.Norbert, (Manitoba), at age 2 (Ibid., page 142, S-17.). He was buried on 29 Nov 1865 St.Norbert, (Manitoba) (Ibid.).

    v.   Olivier Wensell was born on 4 Jun 1866 Ste.Agathe, (Manitoba) (MBS, C-14934.) (SN1, page 83, B-29.). He was baptized on 6 Jul 1866 St.Norbert, (Manitoba) (Ibid.). He was buried on 14 May 1887 Ste.Agathe, Manitoba (MGS: St.Agathe Cemetery, page 10.).

3. Helene Wensell was born circa 1808 (SB 1825-1834, page 117, B-701.). She was baptized on 16 Nov 1833 St.Boniface, (Manitoba) (Ibid., B-701.). She married according to the custom of the country **Duncan McDougall** before 1828. She married according to the custom of the country **Francois Lariviere**, son of **Bonaventure Lariviere** and **Marie Forest,** before 1830. She married **Louis Goulet** before 1832.

    Francois Lariviere was born on 29 Jan 1796 St.Jacques l'Achigan, Quebec (Pat Turenne Research, e-mail 27 Mar 1999, source: RAB du PRDH #550010.). He was baptized on 29 Jan 1796 St.Jacques l'Achigan, Quebec (Ibid.). He married **Marguerite St.Germain** before 1838. He married **Catherine Landry** before 1842. He married **Louise Lambert**, daughter of **Louis Lambert** and **Angelique Belleau,** before 15 Jul 1870. He died on 16 Oct 1873 St.Vital, Manitoba, at age 77 (CWLR *The Collected Writings Of Louis Riel*, 5 (University of Alberta Press, 1985).) (SB-Rozyk St. Boniface Roman Catholic Church, Manitoba, Canada, Baptisms, Marriages and Burials 1860-1875 Extractions, Compiled by Rosemary Rozyk, page 293, S-61.). He was buried on 18 Oct 1873 St.Boniface, Manitoba (Ibid.).

    Louis Goulet was born circa 1804 Quebec (1835C RRS HBCA E5/8 1835 Census of the Red River Settlement, HBCA E5/8, Hudson's Bay Company Archives, Provincial Archives, 200 Vaughan Street, Winnipeg, MB R3C 1T5, Canada., page 9.). He died before 1861.

Generation Three

4. Alexander Wensell was born on 17 Sep 1851 St.Boniface, (Manitoba) (Ibid., C-14934.). He married **Rosalie Morin**, daughter of **Louis Morin** and **Marie Anne Beauchemin,** on 15 Oct 1872 St.Norbert, Manitoba (SN1, M-16.). He died before 1893.

    Rosalie Morin was born on 27 Oct 1847 Ste.Agathe, (Manitoba) (MBS, C-14934.). She married **Napoleon White**, son of **James White** and **Julie Frederic,** on 3 Oct 1893 Ste.Agathe, Manitoba (MM.).

Children of **Alexander Wensell** and **Rosalie Morin** were as follows:

    i.   Leonore Wensell was born on 30 Aug 1873 (INB *Index des Naissances and Baptemes* (St.Boniface, Manitoba: La Societe Historique de Saint-Boniface., c1995), page 186.). She was baptized on 6 Oct 1873 Ste.Agathe, Manitoba (IBMS *Index des Baptemes, Mariages et Sepultures* (La Societe Historique de Saint-Boniface.)) (INB, page 186.) (Rosemary Helga (Morrissette) Rozyk Research, 9 Feb 2010.). She died on 18 Nov 1877 Ste.Agathe, Manitoba, at age 4 (MGS: St.Agathe Cemetery, page 10.).

    ii.   Marie Rosalie Wensell was born on 31 Dec 1874 (Rosemary Rozyk, 9 Feb 2010.). She was baptized on 3 Jan 1875 Ste.Agathe, Manitoba (IBMS.) (Rosemary Rozyk, 9 Feb 2010.). She married Jean Baptiste Napoleon Laferte, son of Olivier Laferte and Madeleine Faille, on 22 Feb 1897 St.Boniface, Manitoba (RMSB *Repertoire des Mariages de Saint-Boniface (Manitoba) 1825-1983* compiled by Julien Hamelin S.C., (240, avenue Daly; Ottawa, Ontario K1N 6G2: Le Centre de Genealogie S. C., Publication #67, 1985).). She died on 30 Nov 1898 St.Boniface, Manitoba, at age 23 (MB Vital Statistics, Death Reg. #1898,002486.).

        Jean Baptiste Napoleon Laferte was born on 28 May 1871 (SN1, page 146, B-31.). He was baptized on 25 Jun 1871 St.Norbert, Manitoba (Ibid.). He married **Pauline Laplante**, daughter of **Boniface Laplante** and **Angelique Larocque,** on 11 Feb 1902 Ste.Agathe, Manitoba (MM, page 667 & 716.) (MB Vital Statistics, Marriage Reg. #1902,002521.). He married **Rosalie Mainville**, daughter of **Augustin Mainville** and **Magdeleine Sauteuse,** on 28 Nov 1907 Whitemouth, Manitoba (Ibid., Marriage Reg. #1907,002665.). He married **Marie Agnes Ladouceur** on 13 Nov 1915 Manitoba (Ibid., Marriage Reg. #1915,208048.). He died on 9 Jul 1925 St.Boniface, Manitoba, at age 54 (Ibid., Death Reg. #1925,031055.).

    iii.   Alexandre Wensell was born circa 1877 Manitoba (1881 Church of Latter Day Saints Census Transcription Project of Census Images from the National Archives of Canada, Ottawa, Canada, http://www.familysearch.org, NA Film No. C-13283, District 184, Sub-district F, page 12, household 59.).

    iv.   Marie Wensell was born circa 1879 Manitoba (Ibid.).

Descendants of George White

Generation One

1. George White married **Rosalie (--?--)** before 1836.

Children of **George White** and **Rosalie (--?--)** were:

    2   i.   Charles White, b. circa 1836; m. Marie Josephte Lecuyer; bur. 5 Sep 1921 St.Boniface, Walhalla, Pembina County, North Dakota.

Generation Two

2. Charles White was born circa 1836 (W-D St.Boniface, Walhalla, North Dakota, Death Register 1913-1931.). He married **Marie Josephte Lecuyer**, daughter of **Francois Xavier Lecuyer** and **Josephte Vivier**, on 7 Jan 1874 Assumption, Pembina, Pembina County, Dakota Territory (AP Records of the Assumption Roman Catholic Church, Pembina, North Dakota: Baptisms, Marriages, Sepultures,

1848-1896; compiled by Reverend Father J. M. Belleau, 2 October 1944, page 98, M-3. Hereinafter cited as AP.). He was buried on 5 Sep 1921 St.Boniface, Walhalla, Pembina County, North Dakota (W-D.).

Marie Josephte Lecuyer was born on 13 Jul 1858 St.Francois Xavier, (Manitoba) (SFXI-Kipling St.Francois Xavier Register Index, 1834-1900; compiled by Clarence Kipling , B-274.). She was baptized on 13 Jul 1858 St.Francois Xavier, (Manitoba) (Ibid.). She died on 22 Aug 1925 Walhalla, Pembina County, North Dakota, at age 67 (W-D.). She was buried on 25 Aug 1925 St.Boniface, Walhalla, Pembina County, North Dakota (Ibid.).

Children of **Charles White** and **Marie Josephte Lecuyer** were as follows:

     i. Samuel White was born on 1 Mar 1872 Duck Lake, (Saskatchewan) (ArchiviaNet 1886-1901, 1906 Half-Breed Scrip Applications Index, RG15-21, Volume 1333 through 1371, Microfilm Reel Number C-14944 through C-15010, National Archives of Canada, Ottawa, Ontario, http://www.collectionscanada.gc.ca, C-15009.). He died in Jun 1872 Duck Lake, (Saskatchewan) (Ibid.).

3   ii. Elzear White, b. 15 Nov 1874 Pembina, Pembina County, Dakota Territory; m. Pauline Dubois.

    iii. William White was born on 5 Aug 1876 Pembina County, Dakota Territory (AP, B-41.). He was baptized on 27 Aug 1876 Assumption, Pembina, Pembina County, Dakota Territory (Ibid.). He married Eliza Dubois, daughter of Francois Dubois and Elise Desjardins, in 1898 Langdon, North Dakota (ArchiviaNet, C-15009.).

        Eliza Dubois was born in Aug 1881 Wood Mountain, (Saskatchewan) (Ibid.).

    iv. John White was born in 1878 Duck Lake, (Saskatchewan) (Ibid.).

    v. Philomene Veronique White was born on 15 Aug 1878 Dakota Territory (AP, B-25.). She was baptized on 2 Sep 1878 Assumption, Pembina, Pembina County, Dakota Territory (Ibid.).

    vi. Philomene May White was born on 15 Aug 1881 Duck Lake, (Saskatchewan) (ArchiviaNet, C-15009.). She married Ambroise Vivier, son of Alexis Vivier and Julie Wells, on 3 Apr 1899 St.Eustache, Manitoba (MM *Manitoba Marriages* in *Publication 45*, Volumes 1-3, compiled and edited by: Paul J. Lareau, Fr. Julien Hamelin, (240 Avenue Daly, Ottawa, Ontario K1N 6G2: Le Centre de Genealogie S.C., 1984), page 1307.).

        Ambroise Vivier was born on 18 Nov 1870 St.Francois Xavier, Manitoba (SFXI-Kipling, B-92.). He was baptized on 4 Dec 1870 St.Francois Xavier, Manitoba (Ibid.). He married **Marie Madeleine Favel**, daughter of **Alexander Favel** and **Madeleine Gladu**, on 1 Mar 1892 (St.Eustache), St.Francois Xavier, Manitoba (MM, (St.Eustache).) (Manitoba Vital Statistics online, http://web2.gov.mb.ca, Marriage Reg. #1892,001027 (SFX).).

    vii. Amos White was born on 9 Aug 1882 Duck Lake, (Saskatchewan) (ArchiviaNet, C-15009.).

    viii. Marie Genevieve White was born on 6 Oct 1883 Duck Lake, (Saskatchewan) (HBSI Index 1886-1901, 1906 Halfbreed Scrip Applications, RG15-21.) (ArchiviaNet.). She was born on 6 Oct 1884 Neche, Dakota Territory (SJL-1 Register of Baptisms, Marriages, and Burials, St.Joseph, Leroy, North Dakota, Diocese of Saint Paul, Minnesota, 1870-1888, Book 1, page 138, B-473. Hereinafter cited as SJL-1.). She was baptized on 12 Oct 1884 St.Joseph, Leroy, Pembina County, Dakota Territory (Ibid., page 138, B-273.). She married Robert Henderson circa Oct 1901 Morden, Manitoba (HBSI.).

    ix. Francois Alexandre White was born on 5 Dec 1886 Neche, Pembina County, Dakota Territory (SJL-1, page 155, B-521.). He was baptized on 16 Jan 1887 St.Joseph, Leroy, Pembina County, Dakota Territory (Ibid.).

    x. Elisabeth White was born on 28 Dec 1895 (Olga Our Lady of the Sacred Heart, Olga, North Dakota 1882-1900, page 252, B-_. Hereinafter cited as Olga.). She was baptized on 4 Apr 1896 Olga, Cavalier County, North Dakota (Ibid.).

    xi. Rosine Sara White was born on 29 May 1898 (Ibid., page 278, B-_.). She was baptized on 26 Jul 1898 Olga, Cavalier County, North Dakota (Ibid.).

Generation Three

3. Elzear White was born on 15 Nov 1874 Pembina, Pembina County, Dakota Territory (AP, page 95, B-61.). He was baptized on 22 Nov 1874 Assumption, Pembina, Pembina County, Dakota Territory (Ibid.). He married **Pauline Dubois**, daughter of **Eugene Dubois** and **Betsy George**, in 1894 Duck Lake, (Saskatchewan) (ArchiviaNet, C-15009.).

Pauline Dubois was born on 1 Feb 1876 St.Boniface, Manitoba (Ibid.). She married **Daniel Lepine**, son of **Athanase Lepine** and **Marie Belanger**, on 13 Jul 1892 St.Francois Xavier, Manitoba (SFXI-Kipling, M-9.).

Children of **Elzear White** and **Pauline Dubois** are as follows:

    i. Maggie Rose White was born on 29 Dec 1895 (Olga, page 252, B-_.). She was baptized on 4 Apr 1896 Olga, Cavalier County, North Dakota (Ibid.).

    ii. Elzear Charles White was born on 13 Jul 1898 (Ibid., page 278, B-_.). He was baptized on 26 Jul 1898 Olga, Cavalier County, North Dakota (Ibid.).

Descendants of Joseph White

Generation One

1. Joseph White was born circa 1800. He married **Genevieve Short**, daughter of **James Short** and **Betsy Sauteuse**, on 29 Jan 1821 (St.Johns), Beaver Creek, (Manitoba) (HBCR Hudson Bay Company Register of Anglican Church Baptisms, Marriages, and Burials for the Red River Settlement, 1821-1841; Hudson's Bay Company Archives, Winnipeg, Manitoba, M-14. Hereinafter cited as HBCR.).

Genevieve Short was born in 1803 North West (MBS Scrip Applications, Original White Settlers & Halfbreeds residing in Manitoba on 15 July 1870, RG15-19, C-14934.). She was born circa 1808 (SB 1825-1834 St.Boniface Roman Catholic Registre des Baptemes, Mariages & Sepultures, 1825-1834, page 90, B-539. Hereinafter cited as SB 1825-1834.). She was baptized on 29 Jan 1821 St.Johns, Beaver Creek, (Manitoba) (HBCR, E.4/1a, folio 31d.). She was baptized on 17 Feb 1833 St.Boniface, (Manitoba) (SB 1825-1834, page 90, B-539.). She married according to the custom of the country **Jean Baptiste Versailles**, son of **Louis Versailles** and **Magdeleine Montagnaise**, before 1829. She married **Jean Baptiste Versailles**, son of **Louis Versailles** and **Magdeleine Montagnaise**, on 18 Feb

1833 St.Boniface, (Manitoba) (Ibid., page 92, M-103.). She died on 3 Nov 1883 St.Norbert, Manitoba (SN2 Catholic Parish Register of St.Norbert, S-31. Hereinafter cited as SN2.). She was buried on 5 Nov 1883 St.Norbert, Manitoba (Ibid.).

Children of **Joseph White** and **Genevieve Short** were:

> 2   i.   James White, b. 1 Jan 1823 North West Territories; m. Julie Frederic; m. Marie Anne Laferte; d. 5 Apr 1903 St.Boniface, Manitoba.

Generation Two

2. James White was born on 1 Jan 1823 North West Territories (MBS, C-14934.). He was baptized on 27 Jun 1824 St.Johns, Red River Settlement, (Manitoba) (HBCR, E.4/1a, folio 49.). He married **Julie Frederic**, daughter of **Jean Baptiste Paul Frederic** and **Josephte 'Chipmunk' Bourre**, before 1850. He married **Marie Anne Laferte**, daughter of **Pierre-Michel Laferte** and **Marie Anne Genereux**, on 5 Feb 1879 Ste.Agathe, Manitoba (MM *Manitoba Marriages* in *Publication 45*, Volumes 1-3, compiled and edited by: Paul J. Lareau, Fr. Julien Hamelin, (240 Avenue Daly, Ottawa, Ontario K1N 6G2: Le Centre de Genealogie S.C., 1984).). He died on 5 Apr 1903 St.Boniface, Manitoba, at age 80 (Manitoba Vital Statistics online, http://web2.gov.mb.ca, Death Reg. #1903,002752.).

Julie Frederic was born in 1830 St.Boniface, (Manitoba) (MBS, C-14934.). She died on 7 Feb 1877 Ste.Agathe, Manitoba (Ste.Agathe Roman Catholic Cemetery; Cemetery Transcription #485; E. Bjornson and K. Stokes F. Cox, Rm. 420 - 167 Lombard Ave., Winnipeg, Manitoba, Canada R3B 0T6: Manitoba Genealogical Society, Inc., June 1988, page 4.).

Children of **James White** and **Julie Frederic** were as follows:

> 3   i.   Elise White, b. 1850 St.Norbert, (Manitoba); m. Pierre Comtois.
>
> 4   ii.   Genevieve White, b. 21 Jul 1850 St.Boniface, (Manitoba); m. Octave Allard; d. 1905 St.Adelard, Manitoba.
>
>   iii.   Frederic White was born circa 1855 (SN1 Catholic Parish Register of St.Norbert 1857-1873, page 135, S-17. Hereinafter cited as SN1.). He died on 6 Oct 1865 St.Norbert, (Manitoba) (Ibid.). He was buried on 7 Oct 1865 St.Norbert, (Manitoba) (Ibid.).
>
> 5   iv.   Roger White, b. 2 Dec 1857 St.Norbert, (Manitoba); m. Elise Laferte; m. Rosalie Henry; m. Margaret (--?--); d. 1 Mar 1937 St.Boniface, Manitoba.
>
> 6   v.   Julie White, b. 13 Sep 1859 St.Norbert, (Manitoba); m. Stuart Johnson; m. Henry Parisien; d. before 1900.
>
>   vi.   Napoleon White was born on 19 Nov 1861 (Ibid., page 49, B-43.). He was baptized on 21 Nov 1861 St.Norbert, (Manitoba) (Ibid.). He married Marguerite Dupuis, daughter of Jean Baptiste Dupuis and Euphrosine Rocheleau, on 6 May 1889 Ste.Agathe, Manitoba (MM.). He married Rosalie Morin, daughter of Louis Morin and Marie Anne Beauchemin, on 3 Oct 1893 Ste.Agathe, Manitoba (Ibid.).
>
>   **Marguerite Dupuis** was born on 11 Oct 1856 St.Norbert, (Manitoba) (GI General Index to Manitoba and North-West Territories Half-Breeds and Original White Settlers who have preferred claims - April 1885, Microfilm Reel Number C-11878, National Archives of Canada, Ottawa, Ontario, page 37.). She married **Guillaume Lambert**, son of **Joseph Lambert** and **Louise Plouff dit Villebrun**, on 28 Aug 1877 St.Norbert, Manitoba (SN2, M-6.) (MB Vital Statistics, Marriage Reg. #1889,001792.) (Ibid., Marriage Reg. #1889,002123.). She died on 20 May 1890 St.Norbert, Manitoba, at age 33 (Ibid., Death Reg. #1890,002587.). She was buried on 22 May 1890 Ste.Agathe, Manitoba (MGS: St.Agathe Cemetery, page 4.).
>
>   **Rosalie Morin** was born on 27 Oct 1847 Ste.Agathe, (Manitoba) (MBS, C-14934.). She married **Alexander Wensell**, son of **Alexander Wensell** and **Marie Anne Laferte**, on 15 Oct 1872 St.Norbert, Manitoba (SN1, M-16.).
>
>   vii.   Marie White was born on 28 Jul 1864 St.Norbert, (Manitoba) (Ibid., page 106, B-36.). She was baptized on 31 Jul 1864 St.Norbert, (Manitoba) (Ibid.).
>
>   viii.   Judith White was born before 7 Oct 1865. She was buried on 7 Oct 1865 St.Norbert, (Manitoba) (IBMS *Index des Baptemes, Mariages et Sepultures* (La Societe Historique de Saint-Boniface).).
>
> 7   ix.   Joseph White, b. 1 Mar 1867; m. Isabelle Gladu.
>
> 8   x.   Justine White, b. 29 Jun 1870 St.Norbert, (Manitoba); m. Modeste Delorme; m. Patrick Beauchene.
>
>   xi.   Adele White was born circa 1873. She married Lucien Charbonneau, son of Jean Baptiste Charbonneau and Louise Boucher, on 28 Jul 1891 St.Boniface, Manitoba (RMSB *Repertoire des Mariages de Saint-Boniface (Manitoba) 1825-1983* compiled by Julien Hamelin S.C., (240, avenue Daly; Ottawa, Ontario K1N 6G2: Le Centre de Genealogie S. C., Publication #67, 1985).).
>
>   **Lucien Charbonneau** was born on 28 Jul 1848 St.Boniface, (Manitoba) (MBS, C-14926.). He married **Eulalie Nolin**, daughter of **Norbert Jean Baptiste Nolin** and **Marie Anne Ducharme**, on 24 Jul 1871 Ste.Anne, Manitoba (MM.). He died on 11 Sep 1895 St.Boniface, Manitoba, at age 47 (MB Vital Statistics, Death Reg. #1895,002123.).
>
> 9   xii.   Marie Christine White, b. 12 Feb 1875 Ste.Agathe, Manitoba; m. Pierre Laferte; d. 17 Apr 1945 RM Alexander, Manitoba.

Marie Anne Laferte was born in 1833 St.Boniface, (Manitoba) (MBS, C-14934.). She married **Alexander Wensell**, son of **Willard Ferdinand Wensell** and **Magdelaine Montagnais**, before 1851.

Generation Three

3. Elise White was born in 1850 St.Norbert, (Manitoba) (Ibid., C-14926.). She married **Pierre Comtois**, son of **Etienne Comtois** and **Marguerite Martin**, on 27 Nov 1866 St.Norbert, (Manitoba) (SN1, page 88-89, M-6.). Question: *Father Samuel Eccles on 1870 census.*

Pierre Comtois was born circa 1845 St.Norbert, (Manitoba) (MBS, C-14926.).

4. Genevieve White was born on 21 Jul 1850 St.Boniface, (Manitoba) (MBS, C-14934.) (Automated Genealogy 1901 Census Transcription Project and Census Images from the National Archives of Canada, http://www.automatedgenealogy.com, Family 21, Line 28-38, page 3.). She married **Octave Allard**, son of **Antoine Allard** and **Theotiste Baillargeon**, on 7 Apr 1874 St.Norbert, Manitoba (SN2, M-5.) (MM, page 21.). She died in 1905 St.Adelard, Manitoba (Al Yerbury Research.).

Octave Allard was born on 9 Jun 1833 St-Denis-sur-Richelieu, Quebec (Rosemary Helga (Morrissette) Rozyk Research, 22 Oct 2006.). He was baptized on 9 Jun 1833 St-Denis-sur-Richelieu, Quebec (Ibid.). He married **Celeste Lagimoniere**, daughter of **Benjamin Lagimoniere** and **Angelique Carriere**, circa 1860. He married **Marie Rose Gaudry**, daughter of **Amable Gaudry** and **Helene Charron**

dit Ducharme, on 3 Jul 1866 St.Boniface, (Manitoba) (SB-Rozyk, page 55, M-15.). He died on 18 Feb 1906 St.Boniface, Manitoba, at age 72 (Rosemary Rozyk, 22 Oct 2006.) (MB Vital Statistics, Death Reg. #1906,004722.). He was buried on 8 Feb 1906 St.Boniface, Manitoba (Rosemary Rozyk, 22 Oct 2006.).

   5.   **Roger White** was born on 2 Dec 1857 St.Norbert, (Manitoba) (SN1, page 3, B-1.). He was baptized on 4 Dec 1857 St.Norbert, (Manitoba) (Ibid.). He married **Elise Laferte**, daughter of **Olivier Laferte** and **Madeleine Faille,** on 18 Nov 1879 Ste.Agathe, Manitoba (MM.). He married **Rosalie Henry**, daughter of **John Henry** and **Josephte Parisien**, on 9 Sep 1890 St.Norbert, Manitoba (Ibid.) (MB Vital Statistics, Marriage Reg. #1890,001572.) (SN2, M-7.). He married **Margaret (--?--)** circa 1900 (1901 Canada, District 203-t, page 1, line 21.). He died on 1 Mar 1937 St.Boniface, Manitoba, at age 79 (MB Vital Statistics, Death Reg. #1937,016026.).

   Elise Laferte was born on 15 Jun 1860 Ste.Agathe, (Manitoba) (MBS, C-14929.). She died on 24 Jun 1882 Cartier, Manitoba, at age 22 (MB Vital Statistics, Death Reg. #1882,001370.).

   Children of **Roger White** and **Elise Laferte** were:

   i.   Agathe White was born in Oct 1880 Cartier, Provencher, Manitoba (1881 Canada, NA Film No. C-13283, District 184, Sub-district F, page 12, household 58.).

   Rosalie Henry was born on 4 Apr 1863 St.Norbert, (Manitoba) (SN1, page 76, B-9.). She was baptized on 5 Apr 1863 St.Norbert, (Manitoba) (Ibid.). She died on 18 Feb 1895 St.Norbert, Manitoba, at age 31 (St-N Cem.). She was buried on 20 Feb 1895 St.Norbert, Manitoba (Ibid.).

   Children of **Roger White** and **Rosalie Henry** both born R.M. of Ritchot, Manitoba, were as follows:

   i.   Phileas White was born on 4 Jul 1892 (MB Vital Statistics, Birth Reg. #1892,003194.). He died on 7 Mar 1893 Ritchot, Manitoba (Ibid., Birth Reg. #1893,002389.). He was buried on 9 Mar 1893 St.Norbert, Manitoba (St-N Cem.).

   ii. Marie Louise White was born on 11 Nov 1894 (MB Vital Statistics, Birth Reg. #1898,006220.). She died on 15 Aug 1895 Ritchot, Manitoba (Ibid., Birth Reg. #1898,002822.). She was buried on 17 Aug 1895 St.Norbert, Manitoba (St-N Cem.).

   Margaret (--?--) was born on 8 Apr 1879 (1901 Canada, District 203-t, page 1, line 21.). She died before 1916.

   Children of **Roger White** and **Margaret (--?--)** were as follows:

   i.   Mary White was born on 14 Jan 1900 (Ibid.).

   ii. Maria White was born in Mar 1902 (Automated Genealogy 1911 Census Transcription Project and Census Images from the National Archives of Canada, http://www.automatedgenealogy.com, District 5, page 26, line 20.).

   iii. Alexander White was born in 1904 (Automated Genealogy 1906 Census Transcription Project and Census Images from the National Archives of Canada, http://www.automatedgenealogy.com, District 11-38, page 1, line 11.).

   iv. Clementine White was born in Aug 1910 (1911 Canada, District 5, page 26, line 20.).

   6.   **Julie White** was born on 13 Sep 1859 St.Norbert, (Manitoba) (SN1, B-34, page 20.). She was baptized on 14 Sep 1859 St.Norbert, (Manitoba) (Ibid.). She married **Stuart Johnson** before 1876. She married **Henry Parisien**, son of **Alexis Parisien** and **Marguerite Comtois**, on 30 Dec 1893 St.Norbert, Manitoba (MM, page 968.). She died before 1900.

   Stuart Johnson died before 1893.

   Henry Parisien was born on 8 Sep 1865 St.Norbert, (Manitoba) (SN1, page 132, B-33.). He was baptized on 10 Sep 1865 St.Norbert, Manitoba (Ibid.). He married **Marie Jeanne St.Denis**, daughter of **Jacques St.Denis** and **Charlotte Rocheleau**, on 30 Apr 1900 (St.Norbert), Ritchot, Manitoba (MB Vital Statistics, Marriage Reg. #1900,002084.) (MM, page 969.). He married **Catherine Parisien**, daughter of **Pascal Parisien** and **Catherine Courchene**, on 19 Jul 1906 St.Boniface, Manitoba (RMSB, page 366.) (MB Vital Statistics, Marriage Reg. #1906,002717.). He died on 10 Jan 1934 Winnipeg, Manitoba, at age 68 (Ibid., Death Reg. #1934,8004113.).

   7.   **Joseph White** was born on 1 Mar 1867 (SN1, B-24.). He was baptized on 14 Jul 1867 St.Norbert, (Manitoba) (Ibid.). He married **Julia Ritchot**, daughter of **Michel Ritchot** and **Marguerite Petit dit Thomas,** before 1902. He married **Isabelle Gladu**, daughter of **Michel Gladu** and **Catherine Wilkie,** before 1910.

   Julia Ritchot was born circa 1878 Leroy, Pembina County, North Dakota (SJL-D St.Joseph Leroy, North Dakota, Record of Interments 1888-1932, page 15.). She was buried on 12 Apr 1904 St.Joseph, Leroy, Pembina County, North Dakota (Ibid.).

   Children of **Joseph White** and **Julia Ritchot** are:

   i.   M. Michel Leblanc was born circa Dec 1902 (Ibid., page 14.). He was buried on 27 Jan 1903 St.Joseph, Leroy, Pembina County, North Dakota (Ibid.).

   Isabelle Gladu was born before 1858 (SJL-1 Register of Baptisms, Marriages, and Burials, St.Joseph, Leroy, North Dakota, Diocese of Saint Paul, Minnesota, 1870-1888, Book 1, page 66, M-1. Hereinafter cited as SJL-1.). She married **Raphael Ritchot**, son of **Joseph Ritchot** and **Marguerite Martel**, on 25 Jan 1876 St.Joseph, Leroy, Pembina County, Dakota Territory (Ibid.).

   8.   **Justine White** was born on 29 Jun 1870 St.Norbert, (Manitoba) (SN1, page 131, B-27.). She was baptized on 3 Jul 1870 St.Norbert, (Manitoba) (Ibid.). She married **Modeste Delorme**, son of **Boniface Delorme** and **Marguerite Laferte**, on 31 Jan 1899 (Ritchot), Ste.Agathe, Manitoba (MM.) (MB Vital Statistics, #1899,001385.). She married **Patrick Beauchene**, son of **Joseph Beauchene** and **Josephte Flett**, on 3 Feb 1923 St.Boniface, Manitoba (Ibid., Marriage Reg. #1923,007017.) (RMSB, page 20.).

   Modeste Delorme was born on 18 Nov 1867 St.Boniface, (Manitoba) (SB-Rozyk, page 98, B-98.). He was baptized on 19 Nov 1867 St.Boniface, (Manitoba) (Ibid.). He married **Zoe Cote**, daughter of **Magloire Cote** and **Marie Pelletier**, on 27 Nov 1894 (Ritchot), St.Norbert, Manitoba (MM, page 270 & 309.) (MB Vital Statistics, #1898,001524.). He died on 14 Aug 1922 St.Boniface, Manitoba, at age 54 (Ibid., Death Reg. #1922,030052.).

   Patrick Beauchene was born circa 1877 Manitoba (1881 Canada, Film #C-13282, District 183, Sub-district A, page 1, household 5.).

   9.   **Marie Christine White** was born on 12 Feb 1875 Ste.Agathe, Manitoba (INB.). She was baptized on 14 Feb 1875 Ste.Agathe, Manitoba (IBMS.) (INB.). She married **Pierre Laferte**, son of **Olivier Laferte** and **Madeleine Faille**, on 26 Nov 1894 Ste.Agathe, Manitoba (MM.). She died on 17 Apr 1945 RM Alexander, Manitoba, at age 70 (MB Vital Statistics, Death Reg. #1945,016345.).

   Pierre Laferte was born on 1 Jan 1858 Ste.Agathe, (Manitoba) (MBS, C-14929.). He married **Emelie Boyer**, daughter of **Jean Baptiste Boyer** and **Marie Boudreau**, on 5 May 1879 Ste.Agathe, Manitoba (MM.). He died on 11 Jun 1945 Pine Falls, Manitoba, at age 87 (MB Vital Statistics, Death Reg. #1945,024372.).

Descendants of Thomas White

Generation One

1. **Thomas White**, son of David White, was born on 12 Feb 1807 Ireland (MBS   Scrip Applications, Original White Settlers & Halfbreeds residing in Manitoba on 15 July 1870, RG15-19, C-14934.).   He married **Mary Cunningham**, daughter of **Patrick Cunningham** and **Nancy Bruce,** on 3 Jul 1846 Upper Church, St.Johns, MacDonald, (Manitoba) (HBCR   Hudson Bay Company Register of Anglican Church Baptisms, Marriages, and Burials for the Red River Settlement, 1821-1841; Hudson's Bay Company Archives, Winnipeg, Manitoba, No. _. Hereinafter cited as HBCR.).   He died on 20 Apr 1888 St.John, Manitoba, at age 81 (Denney Papers, Charles D. Denney, Glenbow Archives, Calgary, Alberta.).

Mary Cunningham was born in Mar 1824 St.Johns, (Manitoba) (MBS, C-14934.).   She was baptized on 27 Aug 1826 St.Johns, (Manitoba) (HBCR, E.4/1a, folio 61d, #586.).   She died on 23 Apr 1907 St.Johns, Manitoba, at age 83 (Denney.).

Children of **Thomas White** and **Mary Cunningham** were as follows:

    i.   David White was baptized on 23 Sep 1849 St.Johns, (Manitoba) (Ibid.).

    ii.   Ann White was born in 1851 (1870C-MB 1870 Manitoba Census, National Archives of Canada, Ottawa, Ontario, Microfilm Reel Number C-2170., page 98, 1725.).   She married Donald Bruce, son of James Bruce and Mary McNab, on 27 Apr 1871 St.Johns, Manitoba (Denney.).

        Donald Bruce was born on 2 Apr 1848 St.Johns, (Manitoba) (MBS, C-14925.).   He married **Charlotte Taylor**, daughter of **James Taylor** and **Amelia Bird,** on 11 Jan 1877 St.Ann's, Poplar Point, Manitoba (Rod MacQuarrie Research, 18 Oct 2010.).   He died on 17 Jun 1926 Woodlands, Manitoba, at age 78 (Manitoba Vital Statistics online, http://web2.gov.mb.ca, Death Reg. #1926,028225.).

    iii.   Isabella White was baptized on 8 Jan 1854 St.Johns, (Manitoba) (Denney.).

    iv.   Mary White was baptized on 10 Feb 1856 St.Johns, (Manitoba) (MBS, C-14934.).   She married Henry Cook, son of William Cook and Mary Anne Beardy, on 21 Dec 1873 St.Johns, Manitoba (Denney.).

        Henry Cook was born in 1853 (Ibid.).

    v.   James White was born on 15 Jun 1858 St.Johns, (Manitoba) (MBS, C-14934.).   He was baptized on 4 Jul 1858 St.Johns, (Manitoba) (Ibid.).

    vi.   Sarah White was born on 2 Jul 1860 St.Johns, (Manitoba) (Ibid.).   She was baptized on 22 Jul 1860 St.Johns, (Manitoba) (Ibid.).

2   vii.   Jane Maria White, b. 28 Oct 1862 St.Johns, (Manitoba); m. Daniel Gagnon.

    viii.   Elizabeth 'Eliza' White was born on 21 Dec 1865 St.Johns, (Manitoba) (Ibid.).   She was baptized on 30 Dec 1865 St.Johns, (Manitoba) (Ibid.).

    ix.   Letitia White was baptized on 11 Aug 1872 St.Johns, Manitoba (Denney.).

Generation Two

2. **Jane Maria White** was born on 28 Oct 1862 St.Johns, (Manitoba) (MBS, C-14934.).   She was baptized on 28 Dec 1862 St.Johns, (Manitoba) (Ibid.).   She married **Daniel Gagnon**, son of **Louis Gagnon** and **Mary McKenzie,** on 28 Jun 1884 St.Francois Xavier, Manitoba (SFXI-Kipling St.Francois Xavier Register Index, 1834-1900; compiled by Clarence Kipling , M-7.).

Daniel Gagnon was born on 8 Mar 1863 (Ibid., B-14.).   He was baptized on 17 Mar 1863 St.Francois Xavier, (Manitoba) (Ibid.).

Descendants of James Whiteway

Generation One

1. **James Whiteway** was born circa 1778 (1827C RRS HBCA E5/1 1827 Census of the Red River Settlement, HBCA E5/1, Hudson's Bay Company Archives, Provincial Archives, 200 Vaughan Street, Winnipeg, MB R3C 1T5, Canada., page 4.).   He married **Mary Park** before 1823 (HBCA-B   Hudson's Bay Company Archives - biographical sketches, Hudson's Bay Company Archives; Winnipeg, Manitoba, E.4/1a fo. 43.).   He married **Anne "Nancy" Monkman**, daughter of **James Monkman** and **Mary Swampy Cree,** on 20 Feb 1826 St.Johns, Red River Settlement, (Manitoba) (HBCR   Hudson Bay Company Register of Anglican Church Baptisms, Marriages, and Burials for the Red River Settlement, 1821-1841; Hudson's Bay Company Archives, Winnipeg, Manitoba, M-113. Hereinafter cited as HBCR.).   He was buried on 2 Jan 1838 St.Johns, Red River Settlement, (Manitoba) (Ibid., Burial No. 234.).

Mary Park died before 1823 (HBCA-B, E.4/1a fo. 43.).

Children of **James Whiteway** and **Mary Park** were:

    i.   John Whiteway was baptized on 5 Jun 1823 St.Johns, Red River Settlement, Manitoba (Ibid.) (HBCR, E.4/1a, folio 43.).

Anne "Nancy" Monkman was born circa 1807 (Denney Papers, Charles D. Denney, Glenbow Archives, Calgary, Alberta.).   She was baptized on 22 Feb 1825 St.Johns, Red River Colony, (Manitoba) (HBCR, E.4/1a, folio 53d.).   She married **James Spence** on 22 Apr 1839 (St.Andrews), Grand Rapids, Red River Settlement, (Manitoba) (Ibid., No. 414.).   She was buried on 13 Oct 1839 St.Johns, Red River Settlement, (Manitoba) (Ibid., Burial No. 177.).

Children of **James Whiteway** and **Anne "Nancy" Monkman** were as follows:

2   i.   James Whiteway, b. 26 Dec 1826 St.Johns, Red River Settlement, (Manitoba); m. Chloe Spence; d. 9 May 1912 St.Andrews, Manitoba.

    ii.   Mary Ann Whiteway was baptized in Aug 1828 St.Johns, (Manitoba) (Denney.).   She was buried on 23 Oct 1839 St.Johns, Red River Settlement, (Manitoba) (HBCR, Burial No. 178.).

    iii.   Catherine Whiteway was baptized on 26 Jan 1830 St.Johns, (Manitoba) (Ibid., E.4/1a, folio 74, #131.).   She was buried on 14 Nov 1839 St.Johns, Red River Settlement, (Manitoba) (Ibid., Burial No. 179.).

3   iv.   William Whiteway, b. 2 Oct 1831 St.Johns, Red River Settlement, (Manitoba); m. Jane (--?--); d. 18 Nov 1905.

     v.   Margaret Whiteway was baptized on 26 Oct 1833 St.Johns, Red River Settlement, (Manitoba) (HBCA-B, HBCA, PAM, E.4/1a fo. 105.) (HBCR, E.4/1a, folio 105.). She died on 6 Mar 1835 St.Johns, (Manitoba), at age 1 (Denney.).

4   vi.   Joseph Whiteway, b. 25 May 1835 St.Johns, Red River Settlement, (Manitoba); m. Elisabeth Hamelin; d. 25 Apr 1910 Winnipeg, Manitoba.

    vii.   Mary Whiteway was baptized on 6 Nov 1837 St.Johns, Red River Settlement, (Manitoba) (HBCA-B, HBCA, PAM, E.4/1a fo. 146d.) (HBCR, E.4/1a, folio 146d.). She was buried on 7 Oct 1839 St.Johns, Red River Settlement, (Manitoba) (Ibid., Burial No. 176.).

Generation Two

2. James Whiteway was born in 1826 St.Johns, (Manitoba) (MBS Scrip Applications, Original White Settlers & Halfbreeds residing in Manitoba on 15 July 1870, RG15-19, C-14934.). He was baptized on 26 Dec 1826 St.Johns, Red River Settlement, (Manitoba) (HBCA-B, HBCA, PAM, E.4/11 fo.63; A.16/48 fo. 636, 640; A.6/25 p. 318.) (HBCR, E.4/1a, folio 63.). He married **Chloe Spence**, daughter of **Andrew Spence** and **Margaret Cree Indian Woman**, on 3 Feb 1847 (St.Andrews), Rapids Church, (Manitoba) (Ibid., No. 161.). He died on 9 May 1912 St.Andrews, Manitoba, at age 85 (HBCA-B, PAM, St.Clements #597.) (Manitoba Vital Statistics online, http://web2.gov.mb.ca, Death Reg. #1912,003838.).

Chloe Spence was baptized on 7 Jul 1829 St.Johns, (Manitoba) (Denney.). She died on 12 Feb 1912 St.Andrews, Manitoba, at age 82 (MB Vital Statistics, Death Reg. #1912,003822.).

Children of **James Whiteway** and **Chloe Spence** were:

5   i.   Mary Ann Whiteway, b. 25 Jun 1848 St.Andrews, (Manitoba); m. Charles McDonald; d. 12 Jan 1919 St.Andrews, Manitoba.

3. William Whiteway was baptized on 2 Oct 1831 St.Johns, Red River Settlement, (Manitoba) (HBCA-B, HBCA, PAM, E.4/1a fo. 85, d. 18 Nov 1905; A.16/48 fo. 637, 647; A.6/25 p. 318.) (HBCR, E.4/1a, folio 85d.). He married **Jane (--?--)** before 1852. He died on 18 Nov 1905 at age 74 (HBCA-B, HBCA, PAM, E.4/1a fo. 85, d. 18 Nov 1905; A.16/48 fo. 637, 647; A.6/25 p. 318.).

Children of **William Whiteway** and **Jane (--?--)** were as follows:

6   i.   Eliza Whiteway, b. 9 Jan 1852 St.Johns, (Manitoba); m. Henri Deschambault.

7   ii.   James Whiteway, b. 21 Aug 1853 St.Andrews, (Manitoba).

   iii.   Robert William Whiteway was baptized on 13 Jan 1856 St.Paul, (Manitoba) (Denney.). He married Eliza Monkman, daughter of George Monkman and Harriet Sinclair, on 7 Nov 1906 St.Andrews, Manitoba (MB Vital Statistics, Marriage Reg. #1906,003340.). He died on 26 Apr 1928 RM Fisher Branch, Manitoba, at age 72 (Ibid., Death Reg. #1928,040107.).

       Eliza Monkman was born on 18 Dec 1885 Swan Creek, (Manitoba) (HBSI Index 1886-1901, 1906 Halfbreed Scrip Applications, RG15-21.) (ArchiviaNet 1886-1901, 1906 Half-Breed Scrip Applications Index, RG15-21, Volume 1333 through 1371, Microfilm Reel Number C-14944 through C-15010, National Archives of Canada, Ottawa, Ontario, http://www.collectionscanada.gc.ca.) (MB Vital Statistics, Birth Reg. #1886,001270.). She married **John Chartrand**, son of **Pierre Chartrand** and **Julie Desjarlais**, on 30 Jan 1905 Posen, Manitoba (Ibid., Marriage Reg. #1905,002668.).

   iv.   Joseph Whiteway was baptized on 22 Aug 1858 St.Peters, (Manitoba) (Denney.).

   v.   Mary Jane Whiteway was baptized on 19 May 1861 St.Peters, (Manitoba) (Ibid.).

   vi.   Donald Whiteway was baptized on 14 Nov 1865 St.Peters, (Manitoba) (Ibid.).

   vii.   Catherine Whiteway was born in 1868 Deer Lake, North West Territories (Ibid.). She died on 16 Sep 1903 Selkirk, Manitoba (MB Vital Statistics, Death Reg. #1903,001051.).

4. Joseph Whiteway was born in 1830 St.Andrews, (Manitoba) (MBS, C-14934.). He was baptized on 25 May 1835 St.Johns, Red River Settlement, (Manitoba) (HBCR, E.4/1a, folio 120d.). He married **Elisabeth Hamelin** before 1864 (1870C-MB 1870 Manitoba Census, National Archives of Canada, Ottawa, Ontario, Microfilm Reel Number C-2170., page 161, #143-146.). He died on 25 Apr 1910 Winnipeg, Manitoba, at age 74 (HBCA-B, St.Clements #514; A.16/48 fo. 638, 648; A.6/25 p. 318.) (MB Vital Statistics, Death Reg. #1910,005176.) (Ibid., Death Reg. #1910,005788.).

Elisabeth Hamelin was born circa 1842.

Children of **Joseph Whiteway** and **Elisabeth Hamelin** were as follows:

   i.   James Francis Whiteway was baptized on 27 Nov 1864 St.Peters, (Manitoba) (Denney.).

8   ii.   Joseph William Whiteway, b. 1 Mar 1867; m. Marie Alice Genthon; d. 28 Nov 1926 St.Boniface, Manitoba.

   iii.   Edward Whiteway was born in Dec 1868 (Automated Genealogy 1911 Census Transcription Project and Census Images from the National Archives of Canada, http://www.automatedgenealogy.com, page 8, family 66, line 18.). He married Lucie Belle McCorrister, daughter of William McCorrister and Louisa Rachel Young, on 22 Jul 1903 Selkirk, Manitoba (MB Vital Statistics, Marriage Reg. #1903,001477.). He died on 10 Jun 1928 St.Clements, Manitoba, at age 59 (Ibid., Death Reg. #1928,030203.).

       Lucie Belle McCorrister was born on 5 Dec 1885 R.M. of St.Clements, Manitoba (Ibid., Birth Reg. #1885,001545.). She died on 25 May 1904 RM of St.Clements, Manitoba, at age 18 (Ibid., Death Reg. #1904,003586.).

9   iv.   Charles Whiteway, b. Apr 1870; m. Jane Marguerite Adelaide McKay.

Generation Three

5. Mary Ann Whiteway was born on 25 Jun 1848 St.Andrews, (Manitoba) (MBS, C-14930.). She married **Charles McDonald**, son of **Donald 'Little' McDonald** and **Nancy Ferguson**, on 23 Jul 1868 St.Andrews, (Manitoba) (Denney.). She died on 12 Jan 1919 St.Andrews, Manitoba, at age 70 (MB Vital Statistics, Death Reg. #1919,006356.).

Charles McDonald was born in 1841 St.Andrews, (Manitoba) (MBS, C-14930.). He was baptized on 7 Mar 1841 St.Johns, (Manitoba) (Denney.). He died on 4 Mar 1915 St.Andrews, Manitoba (MB Vital Statistics, Death Reg. #1915,163588.).

6. **Eliza Whiteway** was born circa 1850 (SB-Rozyk St. Boniface Roman Catholic Church, Manitoba, Canada, Baptisms, Marriages and Burials 1860-1875 Extractions, Compiled by Rosemary Rozyk, page 60, B-25.). She was baptized on 9 Jan 1852 St.Johns, (Manitoba) (Denney.). She was baptized on 11 Jul 1875 St.Boniface, Manitoba (SB-Rozyk, page 60, B-25.). She married **Henri Deschambault**, son of **George Fleury Deschambault** and **Marguerite Loyer or McKenzie**, before 1872.

Henri Deschambault was born circa 1852.

7. **James Whiteway** was baptized on 21 Aug 1853 St.Andrews, (Manitoba) (Denney.).

Children of **James Whiteway** include:

      i.   James Whiteway.

8. **Joseph William Whiteway** was born on 1 Mar 1867 (Ibid.). He was baptized on 8 Mar 1867 St.Peters, (Manitoba) (Ibid.). He married **Marie Alice Genthon**, daughter of **Elie Genthon** and **Genevieve Larence**, before 1905. He died on 28 Nov 1926 St.Boniface, Manitoba, at age 59 (MB Vital Statistics, Death Reg. #1926,052080.).

Marie Alice Genthon was baptized on 12 Feb 1873 St.Norbert, Manitoba (SN1 Catholic Parish Register of St.Norbert 1857-1873, B-8. Hereinafter cited as SN1.). She was born on 12 Feb 1873 St.Norbert, Manitoba (Ibid.).

Children of **Joseph William Whiteway** and **Marie Alice Genthon** are as follows:

      i.   Joseph Alexandre Whiteway was born on 17 Sep 1905 St.Boniface, Manitoba (MB Vital Statistics, Birth Reg. #1905,006323.).

     ii.   William Whiteway was born in Feb 1906 (1911 Canada, page 4, family 9, line 20-24.).

    iii.   Mary Whiteway was born in Sep 1907 (Ibid.).

    iv.   Soulange Whiteway was born in Sep 1910 (Ibid.).

9. **Charles Whiteway** was born in Apr 1870 (Ibid., page 8, family 66, line 17.). He married **Jane Marguerite Adelaide McKay**, daughter of **Angus McKay** and **Virginie Rolette**, circa 1893.

Jane Marguerite Adelaide McKay was born on 28 Jan 1877 St.Francois Xavier, Manitoba (SFXI-Kipling St.Francois Xavier Register Index, 1834-1900; compiled by Clarence Kipling , B-3.).

Children of **Charles Whiteway** and **Jane Marguerite Adelaide McKay** were as follows:

      i.   Charles Angus Whiteway was born on 2 Nov 1894 Selkirk, Manitoba (MB Vital Statistics, Birth Reg. #1894,003017.).

     ii.   Frederick William Whiteway was born on 22 Nov 1896 R.M. of St.Andrews, Manitoba (Ibid., Birth Reg. #1896,002895.).

    iii.   May Hilda Whiteway was born on 11 Feb 1898 Selkirk, Manitoba (Ibid., Birth Reg. #1898,004847.). She married Osbery McGiffin on 28 Jun 1920 Winnipeg, Manitoba (Ibid., Marriage Reg. #1920,037057.).

    iv.   Violet Virginia Whiteway was born on 19 Mar 1901 Selkirk, Manitoba (Ibid., Birth Reg. #1901,007691.). She married Jack Kesten on 17 Feb 1921 Winnipeg, Manitoba (Ibid., Marriage Reg. #1921,006147.).

     v.   Joseph James Whiteway was born on 14 Jul 1905 Berens River, Manitoba (Ibid., Birth Reg. #1905,22219692, registration date: 27/06/1962.).

Descendants of James Peter Whitford

Generation One

1. **James Peter Whitford** was born on 26 Mar 1766 St.Pauls Parish, London, England (HBCA-B Hudson's Bay Company Archives - biographical sketches, Hudson's Bay Company Archives; Winnipeg, Manitoba, A.16/34, fo 41d.). He married according to the custom of the country **Sarah Indian** before 1792. He died on 5 May 1818 Red River Settlement, (Manitoba), at age 52 (HBCA-B.).

Sarah Indian was born circa 1775 (Ibid., E.4/2, fo. 146.). She was buried on 27 Apr 1845 Upper Church, (Manitoba) (Ibid.).

Children of **James Peter Whitford** and **Sarah Indian** were as follows:

  2   i.   James Whitford, b. circa 1792 Ruperts Land; m. Mary Nancy Spence; d. 1872.

  3   ii.   George Whitford, b. circa 1795 Ruperts Land; m. Mary Catherine Joke; d. 18 May 1860.

  4 iii.   Peter Whitford, b. 1795 Ruperts Land; m. Christiana Spence; d. before 1885.

  5 iv.   Margaret "Peggy" Whitford, b. 1796 Swan River, North West; m. George Flett; d. 27 Mar 1877 St.Ann, Poplar Point, Manitoba.

  6   v.   Nancy Ann Whitford, b. circa 1801; m. James Sanderson; d. 1842.

  7 vi.   Joseph Whitford, b. circa 1806; m. Ellen Kennedy; d. 1846.

  8 vii.   Francois Whitford, b. circa 1807 Ruperts Land; m. Marie Gladu; d. 7 Jul 1860 St.Francois Xavier, (Manitoba); bur. 9 Jul 1860 St.Francois Xavier, (Manitoba).

  9 viii.   Sally Whitford, b. circa 1811; m. Michel Saulteaux.

      ix.   Thomas Whitford was born circa 1815 (Denney Papers, Charles D. Denney, Glenbow Archives, Calgary, Alberta.). He was baptized on 5 May 1833 St.Johns, Red River Settlement, (Manitoba) (HBCR Hudson Bay Company Register of Anglican Church Baptisms, Marriages, and Burials for the Red River Settlement, 1821-1841; Hudson's Bay Company Archives, Winnipeg, Manitoba, E.4/1a, folio 100. Hereinafter cited as HBCR.). He died on 19 Mar 1835 (Denney.).

Generation Two

2. **James Whitford** was born circa 1792 Ruperts Land (1827C RRS HBCA E5/1 1827 Census of the Red River Settlement, HBCA E5/1, Hudson's Bay Company Archives, Provincial Archives, 200 Vaughan Street, Winnipeg, MB R3C 1T5, Canada., page 6.). He was baptized on 26 Nov 1820 St.Johns, Red River Settlement, (Manitoba) (HBCA-B, A.30/14, fo 9d; E.4/1a, fo. 28.) (HBCR, E.4/1a, folio 28.). He married **Mary Nancy Spence**, daughter of **Magnus Spence** and **Christiana Cree**, on 27 Nov 1820 (Fort Douglas), St.Johns, (Manitoba) (Ibid., M-5.) (HBCA-B, E.4/1b, fo. 254d.). He died in 1872 (Denney.).

Mary Nancy Spence was born circa 1802 (Ibid.). She was baptized on 26 Nov 1820 St.Johns, Red River Colony, (Manitoba) (HBCR, E.4/1a, folio 28.). She died in 1877 (Denney.).

Children of **James Whitford** and **Mary Nancy Spence** were as follows:

    10   i.   Jane Whitford, b. 10 Nov 1821 St.Johns, Red River Colony, (Manitoba); m. Samuel Spence.

    11   ii.   John Whitford, b. 1824 St.Andrews, (Manitoba); m. Margaret Indian; m. Mary Hudson.

    12   iii.   Mary Whitford, b. between 1826 and 1827 St.Andrews, (Manitoba); m. George Sanderson.

         iv.   Mary Whitford was baptized on 22 Jan 1826 St.Johns, (Manitoba) (HBCA-B, E.4/1a, fo. 59.). She was buried on 10 May 1833 (Ibid., E.4/1b, fo. 297d.).

    13   v.   Philip Whitford, b. circa 1828 Swan River; m. Mary Morisseau; m. Rachel Bangs.

         vi.   Eliza Whitford was baptized on 6 Oct 1828 St.Johns, (Manitoba) (Denney.).

    14   vii.   James Whitford, b. 1829 St.Andrews, (Manitoba); m. Mary Robillard; d. 16 Apr 1872 White Mud, Manitoba; bur. 17 Apr 1872 White Mud, Manitoba.

    15   viii.   Peter Whitford, b. 22 May 1832 St.Johns, Red River Settlement, (Manitoba); m. Louise Chaboillez dit Chaboyer; m. Nancy Indian.

    16   ix.   Sarah Whitford, b. 17 Jun 1833 St.Johns, Red River Settlement, (Manitoba); m. William Norn.

    17   x.   Francis Whitford, b. 1835; m. Jane Anderson; d. before 1885.

    18   xi.   Andrew Whitford, b. 1839 St.Andrews, (Manitoba); m. Eliza Gill or Gilles; d. 16 Apr 1902.

    19   xii.   Margaret Whitford, b. 1840 St.Andrews, (Manitoba); m. David Magnus Cusitor.

    20   xiii.   Donald Whitford, b. 10 Jun 1843 Portage la Prairie, (Manitoba); m. Margaret 'Peggy' Cayen; d. 1927.

    21   xiv.   Nancy Whitford, b. 3 Oct 1848 St.Johns, (Manitoba); m. Andrew Spence.

3. George Whitford was born circa 1795 Ruperts Land (1835C RRS HBCA E5/8 1835 Census of the Red River Settlement, HBCA E5/8, Hudson's Bay Company Archives, Provincial Archives, 200 Vaughan Street, Winnipeg, MB R3C 1T5, Canada., page 23.). He was baptized on 23 Jun 1833 St.Johns, Red River Settlement, (Manitoba) (HBCR, E.4/1a, folio 101d.). He was baptized on 11 Sep 1834 (St.Peters), Indian Settlement, (Manitoba) (Ibid., E.4/1a, folio 113.). He married **Mary Catherine Joke** before 1813. He died on 18 May 1860.

    Question: *George Whitford - Indian and Mary - an Indian were m. at SJ 27 Oct 1834* (Denney.).

Mary Catherine Joke was born circa 1805 (Ibid.). She was baptized on 23 Jun 1833 St.Johns, Red River Settlement, (Manitoba) (HBCR, E.4/1a, folio 101d.).

Children of **George Whitford** and **Mary Catherine Joke** were as follows:

    22   i.   James Whitford, b. circa 1813; m. Charlotte (--?--).

    23   ii.   George Whitford, b. 1822 Cumberland House, (Saskatchewan); m. Sarah Sanderson.

         iii.   Mary Whitford was baptized on 23 Jun 1833 St.Johns, Red River Settlement, (Manitoba) (Ibid.).

4. Peter Whitford was born in 1795 Ruperts Land (1827C RRS HBCA E5/1, page 6.). He was baptized on 26 Nov 1820 St.Johns, Red River Colony, (Manitoba) (HBCA-B, E.4/1a, fo. 28.) (HBCR, E.4/1a, folio 28.). He married **Christiana Spence**, daughter of **Magnus Spence** and **Christiana Cree,** on 27 Nov 1820 Fort Douglas, (Manitoba) (Ibid., M-6.). He died before 1885.

Christiana Spence was born in 1804 (Denney.). She was baptized on 26 Nov 1820 St.Johns, Red River Colony, (Manitoba) (HBCR, E.4/1a, folio 28.).

Children of **Peter Whitford** and **Christiana Spence** were as follows:

    24   i.   Samuel Whitford, b. Apr 1821 St.Francois Xavier, (Manitoba); m. Mary Henderson.

         ii.   Emma Whitford was baptized on 21 Nov 1823 St.Johns, Red River Colony, (Manitoba) (*DCB-V12 Dictionary of Canadian Biography - Volume Twelve*;Toronto, Ontario: University of Toronto Press, 2000), E.4/1a, fo. 46d.) (HBCR, E.4/1a, folio 46d.).

    25   iii.   Eleanor 'Ellen' Whitford, b. 1825 St.Andrews, (Manitoba); m. Peter Henderson; d. Sep 1902 Portage la Prairie, Manitoba.

    26   iv.   Simon Whitford, b. 10 Mar 1826 Red River, (Manitoba); m. Maria Spence; m. Frances Hope.

         v.   Margaret Whitford was baptized on 24 Apr 1829 St.Johns, (Manitoba) (Denney.).

    27   vi.   Magnus Whitford, b. 19 Jul 1831 St.Johns, Red River Settlement, (Manitoba); m. Sarah Spence; m. Mary Beads.

    28   vii.   Christiana Whitford, b. circa 1833 St.Andrews, (Manitoba); m. John Anderson; d. 3 Jan 1878 Prince Albert, (Saskatchewan).

         viii.   Peter Whitford was baptized on 27 Sep 1836 St.Johns, Red River Settlement, (Manitoba) (HBCA-B, E.4/1a, fo. 131.) (HBCR, E.4/1a, folio 131.). He died on 26 Feb 1837 St.Andrews, (Manitoba) (Denney.). He was buried on 28 Feb 1837 St.Johns, (Manitoba) (HBCA-B, E.4/1b, fo. 304.).

    29   ix.   Charles Whitford, b. circa 1838 St.Andrews, (Alberta); m. Nancy "Ann" Anderson.

    30   x.   Nancy Whitford, b. 6 Jul 1841 St.Johns, Red River Settlement, (Manitoba); m. James Spence; m. Henry Monkman.

    31   xi.   Alexander Whitford, b. 4 Sep 1843 St.Johns, (Manitoba); m. Elizabeth Jane Cook; m. Harriet Pocha or Paquin.

    32   xii.   John Whitford, b. 1846 St.Andrews, (Manitoba); m. Jane Mary Tait.

    33   xiii.   Isabella Whitford, b. 9 Oct 1849 St.Johns, (Manitoba); m. William Morris.

         xiv.   Catherine Whitford was baptized on 16 Dec 1854 St.Johns, (Manitoba) (Denney.). She died on 18 Dec 1854 (Ibid.).

5. Margaret "Peggy" Whitford was born in 1796 Swan River, North West (MBS Scrip Applications, Original White Settlers & Halfbreeds residing in Manitoba on 15 July 1870, RG15-19, C-14928.) (Denney.). She was baptized on 7 Dec 1823 St.Johns, Red River Settlement, (Manitoba) (HBCA-B, E.4/1a, fo. 47.) (HBCR, E.4/1a, folio 47.). She married **George Flett** on 7 Dec 1823 St.Johns, (Manitoba) (Ibid., M-69.). She died on 27 Mar 1877 St.Ann, Poplar Point, Manitoba (Denney.).

George Flett was born in 1775 Firth, Orkney, Scotland (Ibid.) (HBCA-B.). He died on 10 Jun 1850 Red River, (Manitoba) (Denney.) (HBCA-B, HBRS II p. 213, A.36/1b, fo 85-87.).

6. **Nancy Ann Whitford** was born circa 1801 (Denney.). She was baptized on 6 May 1832 St.Johns, Red River Settlement, (Manitoba) (HBCR, E.4/1a, folio 89.). She married **James Sanderson**, son of **James Sanderson or Sandison** and **Nelly Cree Indian Woman,** on 9 Feb 1832 St.Johns, (Manitoba) (Ibid., M-229.). She died in 1842 (Denney.).

James Sanderson was born circa 1793 Ruperts Land (1827C RRS HBCA E5/1, page 1.). He was baptized on 30 Mar 1821 St.Johns, (Manitoba) (Denney.). He married **Sarah "Sally" Cree** on 31 Oct 1823 Red River Colony, (Manitoba) (HBCR, M-66.). He married **Margaret Louis**, daughter of **Joseph Louis**, on 20 Nov 1827 St.Johns, (Manitoba) (Ibid., M-138.). He married **Mary Favel**, daughter of **Thomas Favel** and **Sally Cree Pa-sa Trout**, on 23 Nov 1843 (St.Andrews), Grand Rapids, Red River Settlement, Manitoba (Ibid., No. 112.). He died on 26 Nov 1873 St.Andrews, Manitoba (Denney.). He was buried on 29 Nov 1873 St.Andrews, Manitoba (Ibid.).

7. **Joseph Whitford** was born circa 1806 (Denney.). He was baptized on 5 May 1833 St.Johns, Red River Settlement, (Manitoba) (HBCR, E.4/1a, folio 100.). He married **Ellen Kennedy** on 14 Nov 1833 St.Johns, (Manitoba) (Denney.). He died in 1846 (Ibid.).

Question: *Marriage entry not found in the HBCA marriage register.*

Ellen Kennedy was born circa 1821 Northwest Territories (1881 Church of Latter Day Saints Census Transcription Project of Census Images from the National Archives of Canada, Ottawa, Canada, http://www.familysearch.org, District 185-C-2, pagae 15, house 86.). She married **George Sutherland** before 1860.

Children of **Joseph Whitford** and **Ellen Kennedy** were as follows:

    34   i.   Elizabeth Whitford, b. 1840 St.Peters, (Manitoba); m. Thomas Sinclair (Metis).

           ii.   Sarah Whitford was baptized on 16 Mar 1841 (St.Peters), Muscaigo, (Manitoba) (HBCR, E.4/1a, folio 174d.).

          iii.   Helen Whitford was born circa 1845 (Manitoba) (1870C-MB 1870 Manitoba Census, National Archives of Canada, Ottawa, Ontario, Microfilm Reel Number C-2170., page 166, #339.).

8. **Francois Whitford** was born circa 1805 (SFXI: 1851-1869 St.Francois Xavier 1851-69 Register Index.) (SFXI 1851-1868 St.Francois Xavier 1852-1861 Register Index, S-14. Hereinafter cited as SFXI 1851-1868.). He was born circa 1807 Ruperts Land (1830C RRS HBCA E5/4 1830 Census of the Red River Settlement, HBCA E5/4, Hudson's Bay Company Archives, Provincial Archives, 200 Vaughan Street, Winnipeg, MB R3C 1T5, Canada., page 14.). He was baptized on 27 Aug 1824 St.Johns, Red River Settlement, (Manitoba) (HBCA-B, E.4/1a, fo. 51.) (HBCR, E.4/1a, folio 51.). He married **Marie Gladu**, daughter of **Charles Gladu** and **Marguerite Ross**, on 29 Nov 1825 Red River Settlement, (Manitoba) (Ibid., M-103.) (HBCA-B, E.4/1b, fo. 209.). He died on 7 Jul 1860 St.Francois Xavier, (Manitoba) (SFXI-Kipling St.Francois Xavier Register Index, 1834-1900; compiled by Clarence Kipling , S-14.). He was buried on 9 Jul 1860 St.Francois Xavier, (Manitoba) (Ibid.) (SFXI-1834-54.).

Marie Gladu was born in 1805 North West (1870C-MB, #582.). She was baptized on 27 Aug 1824 St.Johns, (Manitoba) (Denney.). She died on 27 Mar 1877 St.Francois Xavier, Manitoba (SFXI-Kipling, S-4.).

Children of **Francois Whitford** and **Marie Gladu** were as follows:

    35   i.   James Francois 'Jimmy' Whitford, b. 10 Jan 1827 North West; m. Marguerite Fagnant; d. 19 Nov 1908 Willow Bunch, Saskatchewan; bur. 21 Nov 1908 St.Ignace, Willow Bunch, Saskatchewan.

           ii.   Marguerite Whitford was born circa 1828 (SFX: 1834-1850 St.Francois Xavier 1834-1851 Register, S-177. Hereinafter cited as SFX: 1834-1850.). She died on 4 Jul 1846 St.Francois Xavier, (Manitoba) (Ibid.). She was buried on 4 Jul 1846 St.Francois Xavier, (Manitoba) (Ibid.).

    36   iii.   William Francis Whitford, b. 1830 St.Boniface, (Manitoba); m. Louise Desjarlais.

    37   iv.   Genevieve Whitford, b. 12 May 1833; m. Ambroise Chartrand; m. Joseph Langer; m. St.Pierre Morin.

    38   v.   Sarah Whitford, b. circa 1834 Red River, (Manitoba); m. Peter Hourie; d. 1910 Indian Head.

           vi.   Alexis Whitford was born on 7 Jan 1836 St.Francois Xavier, (Manitoba) (SFXI: 1834-1852 St.Francois Xavier 1834-1852 Register Index, B-110. Hereinafter cited as SFXI: 1835-1852.). He was baptized on 7 Jan 1836 St.Francois Xavier, (Manitoba) (Ibid.).

          vii.   Marie Whiteford was born on 9 Mar 1838 St.Francois Xavier, (Manitoba) (SFX: 1834-1850, B-193.). She was baptized on 10 Mar 1838 St.Francois Xavier, (Manitoba) (Ibid.).

        viii.   Angelique Whiteford was born circa 1840. She married Baptiste Ferland Ettawekipik before 1858.

              Question: *Probable sister of Genevieve Whitford.*

              Baptiste Ferland Ettawekipik married **Harriet Cook** before 1876.

9. **Sally Whitford** was born circa 1811. She married **Michel Saulteaux** before 1829.

Children of **Sally Whitford** and **Michel Saulteaux** were:

           i.   Angelique Michel was born on 7 Jan 1829 North West Territories (MBS, C-14928.). She married Francois Indian before 1855.

Generation Three

10. **Jane Whitford** was baptized on 10 Nov 1821 St.Johns, Red River Colony, (Manitoba) (HBCA-B, E.4/1a, fo. 36.) (HBCR, E.4/1a, folio 36.). She married **Samuel Spence** on 17 May 1838 Red River Settlement, (Manitoba) (HBCA-B, E.4/1b, fo. 254d.) (HBCR, No. 389.).

Children of **Jane Whitford** and **Samuel Spence** were:

           i.   Charles Thomas Spence was baptized on 4 Feb 1840 St.Johns, Red River Settlement, (Manitoba) (Ibid., E.4/1a, folio 164d.).

11. **John Whitford** was born in 1824 St.Andrews, (Manitoba) (Denney.). He was baptized on 23 May 1824 St.Johns, Red River Settlement, (Manitoba) (HBCA-B, E.4/1a, fo. 48.) (HBCR, E.4/1a, folio 48.). He married **Margaret Indian** in 1868 Fort Victoria (Denney.). He married **Mary Hudson**, daughter of **George Hudson** and **Mary Thomas**, circa 1874 (NWHBS 1885 Scrip Applications, North-West Halfbreeds residing outside Manitoba on 15 July 1870, RG15-20, C-14939.).

Children of **John Whitford** and **Margaret Indian** were:

    39   i.   David Whitford, b. 15 Jul 1875 High River, (Alberta); m. Genevieve Berard.

Children of **John Whitford** include:

           i.   Mary Whitford (adopted) was born on 15 Apr 1870 (ArchiviaNet, C-15010.).

Mary Hudson was born in 1845 Carlton, (Saskatchewan) (NWHBS, C-14939.). She married **Louis Ketanakeenew Sutherland** in 1868 (Ibid.).

Children of **John Whitford** and **Mary Hudson** were as follows:

  - i. Nancy Whitford was born on 1 Aug 1874 Whitford Lake, (Alberta) (Denney.) (Automated Genealogy 1901 Census Transcription Project and Census Images from the National Archives of Canada, http://www.automatedgenealogy.com, #202, i, page 1, family 8, line 28-39.).
  - ii. Ellen Whitford was born on 16 May 1880 Beaver Lake, (Alberta) (Denney.) (1901 Canada, #202, i, page 1, family 8, line 28-39.).
  - iii. James Whitford was born on 15 May 1882 Beaver Lake, (Alberta) (ArchiviaNet, C-15010.).

12. Mary Whitford was born between 1826 and 1827 St.Andrews, (Manitoba) (NWHBS, C-14942.) (1891C SK District of Saskatchewan Index to the Census of Canada 1891, Inc - Regina Branch Saskatchewan Genealogical Society, 67 Marquis Crescent, Regina, SK S4S 6J8, page 71.). She was baptized on 22 Jan 1826 St.Johns, Red River Settlement, (Manitoba) (HBCR, E.4/1a, folio 59.). She married **George Sanderson**, son of **George Sanderson** and **Elizabeth Lagimoniere,** on 12 Dec 1843 (St.Andrews), Grand Rapids, Red River Settlement, (Manitoba) (Ibid., No. 117.).

George Sanderson was born in 1823 St.Paul, (Manitoba) (Denney.). He was baptized on 1 Jun 1823 St.Johns, Red River Colony, (Manitoba) (HBCR, E.4/1a, folio 42d.).

13. Philip Whitford was born circa 1828 Swan River (NWHBS, C-14942.). He was baptized in Oct 1828 St.Johns, (Manitoba) (Denney.). He married **Mary Morisseau** in 1855 Fairford, (Manitoba) (NWHBS, C-14942.). He married **Rachel Bangs**, daughter of **Arthur Bangs** and **Jessie Kepestah Cardinal,** in 1868 White Fish Lake, (Alberta) (Ibid.).

Children of **Philip Whitford** and **Mary Morisseau** were as follows:

  40 i. Gilbert Whitford, b. 1857 Partridge Crop; m. Marcelline Blandion.
  41 ii. Alfred Whitford, b. 25 Aug 1861 St.Mary's Anglican Church, Portage la Prairie, (Manitoba); m. Annie Fraser; m. Adele Lafournaise.
  42 iii. Mary Julia Whitford, b. 11 Oct 1863 Portage la Prairie, (Manitoba); m. Godfrey McNeil Steele.
      iv. Philip Whitford was born on 20 Feb 1867 Portage la Prairie, (Manitoba) (Ibid.). He was baptized on 17 Mar 1867 St.Mary's Anglican Church, Portage la Prairie, (Manitoba) (SMACPLP, page 36, B-284.). He married Connie Blayon on 29 Sep 1891 Choteau, Montana (SPMT St.Peter's Mission; Volume I; Marriage Register 1859-1895; Translated & Transcribed by Reverend Dale McFarlane, Archivist, Diocese of Great Falls-Billings, Montana; Spring 1981, page 52, #313.).

Rachel Bangs was born in 1853 Fort Pitt, (Saskatchewan) (NWHBS, C-14942.).

Children of **Philip Whitford** and **Rachel Bangs** were as follows:

  - i. Eliza Whitford was born in Jul 1869 Black Mud, (Alberta) (Ibid.). She married Cleophas Norn, son of William Norn and Sarah Whitford, before 1901.
      Cleophas Norn was born on 31 Aug 1867 Victoria, (Alberta) (Ibid., C-14940.).
  - ii. Robert Whitford was born in 1872 Whitford, (Alberta) (Ibid., C-14942.) (ArchiviaNet, C-15010.). He died in Sep 1872 Whitford, (Alberta) (NWHBS, C-14942.) (ArchiviaNet, C-15010.).
  43 iii. Jessie Whitford, b. Jan 1874 Whitford Lake, (Alberta); m. Robert John Littlechild; d. 1948.
      iv. Frederick Whitford was born in 1876 Pakan, (Alberta) (NWHBS, C-14942.) (ArchiviaNet, C-15010.). He died in 1882 (NWHBS, C-14942.) (ArchiviaNet, C-15010.).
      v. Rachel Ann Whitford was born in Jan 1880 Saddle Lake, (Alberta) (NWHBS, C-14942.) (1881 Canada, Film No. C-13285, District 192, page 7, Household No. 28.) (ArchiviaNet, C-15010.). She died circa Oct 1883 (NWHBS, C-14942.) (ArchiviaNet, C-15010.).
      vi. Edith Whitford was born on 1 Jul 1889 (1901 Canada, #202-y(4), page 2, family 25, line 47-49.).

14. James Whitford was born circa 1822 Red River, (Manitoba) (1870C-MB, page 336, #133.). He was born in 1829 St.Andrews, (Manitoba) (MBS, C-14934.). He was baptized on 10 Aug 1830 St.Johns, Red River Settlement, (Manitoba) (HBCA-B, E.4/1a, fo. 79d.) (HBCR, E.4/1a, folio 79d.). He married **Mary Robillard**, daughter of **Peter Robillard** and **Margaret Indian**, on 9 Dec 1851 St.Andrews, (Manitoba) (Denney.). He died on 16 Apr 1872 White Mud, Manitoba (MBS, C-14934.). He was buried on 17 Apr 1872 White Mud, Manitoba (Ibid.).

Mary Robillard was born circa 1824 Lake Sale (1870C-MB, page 336, #134.). She was born in 1829 North West (MBS, C-14934.).

Children of **James Whitford** and **Mary Robillard** were as follows:

  44 i. Mary Ann Whitford, b. 15 Nov 1852 Poplar Point, (Manitoba); m. Henry Charles Desmarais.
  45 ii. Euphemia Whitford, b. 4 Jan 1855 Portage la Prairie, (Manitoba); m. George William Sanderson; d. 8 Jan 1914 Saskatchewan.
  46 iii. James William Rupert Whitford, b. 8 Feb 1857 Fairford, (Manitoba); m. Marie Hebert or Lebret.
  47 iv. William Rupert Whitford, b. 9 Aug 1859 Fairford, (Manitoba); m. Elizabeth McIver.
  48 v. Andrew Whitford, b. 10 Sep 1861 Portage la Prairie, (Manitoba); m. Christine Anderson Isbister.
      vi. Simon Whitford was baptized on 7 Jan 1864 St.Mary's Anglican Church, Portage la Prairie, (Manitoba) (SMACPLP, page 26, B-202.). He was buried on 12 Mar 1864 St.Mary's Anglican Church, Portage la Prairie, (Manitoba) (Ibid., page 5, S-33.).
      vii. Peter Charles Whitford was born on 16 Apr 1864 Portage la Prairie, (Manitoba) (Denney.). He was baptized on 7 May 1865 St.Mary's Anglican Church, Portage la Prairie, (Manitoba) (SMACPLP, page 31, B-241.).
      viii. Catherine Whitford was baptized on 17 Mar 1867 St.Mary's Anglican Church, Portage la Prairie, (Manitoba) (Ibid., page 36, B-285.). She was buried on 28 Jan 1868 St.Mary's Anglican Church, Portage la Prairie, (Manitoba) (Ibid., page 8, S-63.).
  49 ix. John Joseph Whitford, b. 24 Dec 1868 Big Point; m. Catherine Lacouette; m. Esther Lacouette.
  50 x. Margaret Whitford, b. circa 1870.

xi. Edwin Whitford was born on 17 Mar 1879. He married Christina Ermit Tanner, daughter of James Tanner and Ann Elisabeth Sanderson, on 5 Jan 1904 Westbourne, Manitoba (MB Vital Statistics, Marriage Reg. #1904,001207.).

  Christina Ermit Tanner was born on 4 Mar 1887 R.M. of Westbourne, Manitoba (Ibid., Birth Reg. #1887,004405.).

15. Peter Whitford was baptized on 22 May 1832 St.Johns, Red River Settlement, (Manitoba) (HBCA-B, E.4/1a, fo. 89d.) (HBCR, E.4/1a, folio 89d.). He married **Louise Chaboillez dit Chaboyer**, daughter of **Louis Chaboillez or Chaboyer** and **Louise Chartrand**, on 14 Mar 1853 St.Peters, (Manitoba) (Denney.). He married **Nancy Indian** before 1863.

Louise Chaboillez dit Chaboyer was born in 1840 Lac Manitoba, (Manitoba) (NWHBS, C-14939.). She and **Francois Laframboise** met circa 1860. She married **Francois Laframboise**, son of **Jean Baptiste Laframboise** and **Suzanne Beaudry or Gaudry**, on 17 Jun 1867 St.Francois Xavier, (Manitoba) (SFXI-Kipling, M-16.). She died circa Jul 1871 North West Territories (NWHBS, C-14939.).

Children of **Peter Whitford** and **Louise Chaboillez dit Chaboyer** were as follows:

51 i. Philip Whitford, b. 1855 Oak Point, Manitoba Lake, Manitoba; m. Rosalie Dumont.

52 ii. John Whitford, b. 22 May 1855; m. Maria Bremner.

Children of **Peter Whitford** and **Nancy Indian** were:

53 i. Benjamin Whitford, b. 1 Sep 1863 between Whitefish Lake and Victoria, (Alberta); m. Elsie Anehay.

16. Sarah Whitford was baptized on 17 Jun 1833 St.Johns, Red River Settlement, (Manitoba) (HBCA-B, E.4/1a, fo. 109d.) (HBCR, E.4/1a, folio 109.). She married **William Norn** on 5 Dec 1850 St.Andrews, (Manitoba) (NWHBS, C-14940.) (HBCR, No. 200.).

William Norn was born in 1823 (Dorothy J. Chartrand Research.).

17. Francis Whitford was born in 1835 (NWHBSI, page 85.) (SMACPLP, page 6, M-11.). He was baptized on 22 Dec 1836 St.Johns, Red River Settlement, (Manitoba) (HBCA-B, E.4/1a, fo. 135d.) (HBCR, E.4/1a, folio 135d.). He married **Jane Anderson**, daughter of **Thomas Anderson** and **Catherine Landry**, on 29 Sep 1859 St.Mary's Anglican Church, Portage la Prairie, (Manitoba) (SMACPLP, page 6, M-11.). He died before 1885.

Jane Anderson was born in 1843 Winnipeg, (Manitoba) (Denney.). She was baptized on 1 Feb 1843 St.Johns, (Manitoba) (Ibid.). She was born in 1845 Winnipeg, (Manitoba) (NWHBS, C-14942.).

Children of **Francis Whitford** and **Jane Anderson** were as follows:

54 i. Anne Whitford, b. 15 Feb 1862 Portage la Prairie, (Manitoba); m. Felix Blandion.

  ii. Lilly Whitford was baptized on 27 Dec 1863 St.Marys, Portage-la-Prairie, Manitoba (SMACPLP, B-196.).

55 iii. Lottie Whitford, b. 1865; m. Frank Greenwood.

56 iv. Margaret Whitford, b. 29 Oct 1866 Victoria, North West Territory; m. Alexander James McCorrister.

57 v. Catherine Whitford, b. 1 Jul 1870; m. Baptiste Larocque; d. 22 Mar 1944 Penticton, British Columbia.

  vi. John Whitford was born in 1871 Victoria, (Alberta) (ArchiviaNet, C-15010.). He died in 1873 Victoria, (Alberta) (Ibid.).

  vii. James Thomas Whitford was born on 26 Sep 1872 Victoria, (Alberta) (Ibid.). He died in 1879 Pigeon Lake, (Alberta) (Ibid.).

  viii. Ellen Whitford was born in 1873 near, Battle River, (Alberta) (Ibid.). She died in 1873 Battle River, (Alberta) (Ibid.).

58 ix. Archibald Whitford, b. 16 Mar 1874 Buffalo Lake, (Alberta); m. Harriet Todd.

  x. Francis 'Frank' Whitford was born on 17 Feb 1877 Morley, (Alberta) (Ibid.).

  xi. Mary Whitford was born on 7 Jan 1879 Buffalo Lake, (Alberta) (1881 Canada, Film No. C-13285, District 192, page 35, Household No. 175.) (ArchiviaNet, C-15010.).

  xii. Lucy Whitford was born circa 1880 Battleford, (Saskatchewan) (1881 Canada, Film No. C-13285, District 192, page 35, Household No. 175.).

  xiii. Elizabeth Julia Whitford was born on 14 Feb 1881 Pigeon Lake, (Alberta) (ArchiviaNet, C-15010.). She married Thomas Kerr before 1901 (1901 Canada, District 202-v(4), page 36, family 373, line 36-38.). She died on 10 Oct 1970 Edmonton, (Alberta), at age 89.

  xiv. Andrew Whitford was born on 9 May 1883 Edmonton, (Alberta) (ArchiviaNet, C-15009.). He died on 10 Oct 1970 Edmonton, Alberta, at age 87 (Denney.).

18. Andrew Whitford was born in 1839 St.Andrews, (Manitoba) (NWHBS, C-14942.). He was baptized on 19 Mar 1839 St.Johns, Red River Settlement, (Manitoba) (HBCA-B, E.4/1a, fo. 159d.) (HBCR, E.4/1a, folio 159d.). He married **Eliza Gill or Gilles**, daughter of **Robert Gill** and **Sophia Harper**, on 9 Jan 1861 St.Mary's Anglican Church, Portage la Prairie, (Manitoba) (SMACPLP, page 7, M-14.). He died on 16 Apr 1902 (Denney.).

Eliza Gill or Gilles was born in 1845 York Factory (NWHBS, C-14942.).

Children of **Andrew Whitford** and **Eliza Gill or Gilles** were as follows:

  i. Margaret Whitford was born on 16 Jan 1861 Portage la Prairie, Manitoba (Ibid.) (Rod MacQuarrie Research, 11 Nov 2007.) (1901 Canada, #202, m(1), page 22-23, line 49-50, 1-2.). She was baptized on 5 Jan 1863 St.Mary's Anglican Church, Portage la Prairie, (Manitoba) (SMACPLP, page 16, B-122.).

  ii. Thomas William Whitford was baptized on 4 Oct 1863 St.Mary's Anglican Church, Portage la Prairie, (Manitoba) (Ibid., page 23, B-184.).

  iii. John Whitford was baptized on 14 Nov 1865 Fort Victoria, (Alberta) (Denney.).

  iv. Ellen 'Nellie' Whitford was born on 3 Apr 1866 Victoria, (Alberta) (NWHBS, C-14942.). She was baptized on 6 May 1867 Victoria, (Alberta) (Denney.).

59 v. Harriet Whitford, b. 19 Aug 1867 Victoria, (Alberta); m. Simon McGillivray; d. 1950.

  vi. Benjamin Whitford was born on 7 Oct 1868 Fort Victoria, (Alberta) (ArchiviaNet, C-15009.). He died in Jan 1869 Victoria, (Alberta) (Ibid.).

  vii. Annie Whitford was born on 3 Mar 1872 Victoria, (Alberta) (Ibid.). She died in 1879 Victoria, (Alberta) (Ibid.).

viii. Andrew Whitford was born on 1 Jun 1874 Victoria, (Alberta) (Ibid.). He died in 1877 Victoria, (Alberta) (Ibid.).

ix. Mary Whitford was born in 1876 Buffalo Lake, (Alberta). She married (--?--) McGillivray before 1900.

x. Edward Whitford was born on 3 Apr 1879 Fort Victoria, (Alberta) (Ibid., C-15010.).

xi. John Whitford was born in 1881 (1901 Canada, District 202-y(4), page 33, family 381, line 16-21.).

xii. Flora Whitford was born on 27 Jan 1884 Fort Victoria, (Alberta) (Denney.).

xiii. Sophia Whitford was born in 1886 (1901 Canada, District 202-y(4), page 33, family 381, line 16-21.).

19. Margaret Whitford was born in 1840 St.Andrews, (Manitoba) (MBS, C-14934.). She was baptized on 1 Aug 1841 St.Johns, (Manitoba) (HBCA-B, E.4/2, fo. 4d.). She married **David Magnus Cusitor**, son of **John Cusitor,** before 1857.

David Magnus Cusitor was born on 17 Mar 1822. He died on 18 Nov 1887 Portage la Prairie, Manitoba, at age 65 (Denney.). He was buried on 18 Nov 1887 St.Mary's Anglican Church, Portage la Prairie, Manitoba (SMACPLP, page 24, S-188.). Question: *Notes from C. Kipling David Cusitar and his family lived at Portage in the 1870s. He had 8 children.*

David Cusitor may have been born in 1827, but on the tombstone in St.Mary's Anglican church yard at Portage la Prairie it says he was born Feb 17th, 1822 (Denney.).

20. Donald Whitford was born on 10 Jun 1843 Portage la Prairie, (Manitoba) (NWHBS, C-14942.) (1901 Canada, District 202-r(4), page 4, family 41, line 40-50.). He was baptized on 3 Jun 1844 St.Johns, (Manitoba) (Denney.) (HBCA-B, E.4/2, fo. 14d.). He married **Margaret 'Peggy' Cayen**, daughter of **Paul Cayen** and **Marie**, circa Apr 1870 Victoria, (Alberta) (NWHBS, C-14942.) (Ibid., C-14937.). He died in 1927 (Denney.) (HBCA-B.).

Margaret 'Peggy' Cayen was born on 5 Jul 1853 near, Calgary, (Alberta) (NWHBS, C-14937.) (1901 Canada, District 202-r(4), page 4, family 41, line 40-50.).

Children of **Donald Whitford** and **Margaret 'Peggy' Cayen** were as follows:

i. Colin James Whitford was born on 5 May 1871 Fort Victoria, (Alberta) (Denney.). He was baptized on 8 May 1871 Fort Victoria, (Alberta) (Ibid.). He died in 1889 Bears Hills (ArchiviaNet, C-15010.).

ii. Charles Whitford was born in May 1873 Pigeon Lake, (Alberta) (Ibid.). He died in 1873 Morley, (Alberta) (Ibid.).

iii. John Whitford was born in Feb 1875 Pigeon Lake, (Alberta) (Ibid.). He died in 1975 Hand Hills, (Alberta) (Ibid.).

iv. Flora Whitford was born in 1876 Buffalo Lake, (Alberta) (HBSI.) (ArchiviaNet.). She married (--?--) Chalmerson before 1900. She died in 1963 (Denney.).

v. Anne Whitford was born circa 4 Jun 1878 Battle River, (Alberta) (HBSI.) (1901 Canada, District 202-r(4), page 4, family 41, line 40-50.). She married (--?--) Foureyes before 1900.

vi. William Whitford was born in Oct 1881 Pigeon Lake, (Alberta) (ArchiviaNet, C-15010.). He died in 1889 Bears Hills, (Alberta) (Ibid.).

vii. Eliza Whitford was born on 14 Jul 1883 Bears Hills, (Alberta) (NWHBS, C-14942.) (ArchiviaNet.) (1901 Canada, District 202-r(4), page 4, family 41, line 40-50.). She married (--?--) Little Voice in May 1900 Hobbema Reserve (ArchiviaNet.).

viii. Catherine E. Whitford was born on 12 Jun 1885 (1901 Canada, District 202-r(4), page 4, family 41, line 40-50.).

ix. George Whitford was born on 10 Nov 1888 (Ibid.).

x. Samuel Whitford was born on 6 Dec 1890 (Ibid.).

21. Nancy Whitford was baptized on 3 Oct 1848 St.Johns, (Manitoba) (HBCA-B, E.4/2, fo. 65d.). She married **Andrew Spence**, son of **Magnus Spence** and **Sarah 'Sally' Favel,** on 26 Jan 1865 St.Mary's Anglican Church, Portage la Prairie, (Manitoba) (SMACPLP, page 17, M-33.).

Andrew Spence was baptized on 18 Aug 1842 St.Johns, (Manitoba) (Denney.). He died in 1880 (Ibid.).

22. James Whitford was born circa 1813. He was baptized on 2 Jul 1833 St.Johns, Red River Settlement, (Manitoba) (HBCR, E.4/1a, folio 101d.). He was baptized on 22 Jul 1833 St.Johns, Red River Settlement, (Manitoba) (Ibid., E.4/1a, folio 103.). He married **Charlotte (--?--)** on 5 Feb 1834 St.Johns, Red River Settlement, (Manitoba) (Ibid., No. 269.).

Charlotte (--?--) was born circa 1822 (Manitoba). She was baptized on 23 Jun 1833 St.Johns, Red River Settlement, (Manitoba) (Ibid., E.4/1a, folio 103.). She was baptized on 2 Jul 1833 St.Johns, Red River Settlement, (Manitoba) (Ibid., E.4/1a, folio 102.).

Children of **James Whitford** and **Charlotte (--?--)** were as follows:

i. James Whitford was baptized on 30 Jun 1833 St.Johns, Red River Settlement, (Manitoba) (Ibid., E.4/1a, folio 101d.). He was baptized on 22 Jul 1833 St.Johns, Red River Settlement, (Manitoba) (Ibid., E.4/1a, folio 103.).

ii. Maria Whitford was baptized on 23 Jun 1836 St.Johns, Red River Settlement, (Manitoba) (Ibid., E.4/1a, folio 129.).

iii. Nancy Whitford was baptized on 5 Aug 1838 St.Johns, Red River Settlement, (Manitoba) (Ibid., E.4/1a, folio 154d.).

iv. Magnus Whitford was baptized on 12 Apr 1841 St.Johns, Red River Settlement, (Manitoba) (Ibid., E.4/1a, folio 174d.).

v. Harriet Whitford was baptized on 12 Nov 1843 St.Peters, (Manitoba) (Denney.).

vi. William Whitford was baptized on 31 May 1846 St.Peters, (Manitoba) (Ibid.).

23. George Whitford was born in 1822 Cumberland House, (Saskatchewan) (MBS, C-14934.). He was born on 5 Oct 1822 (1901 Canada, microfilm, T-6553, Brancepeth, page 1, Family 3, line 18-21.). He was born circa 1830 (Manitoba) (1870C-MB, page 161, #149.). He married **Sarah Sanderson**, daughter of **George Sandison** and **Nancy Indian,** before 1848.

Sarah Sanderson was born in 1825 North West (MBS, C-14934.). She was baptized on 25 Mar 1830 St.Johns, Red River Settlement, (Manitoba) (HBCR, E.4/1a, folio 76d.).

Children of **George Whitford** and **Sarah Sanderson** all born St.Peters, (Manitoba), were as follows:

i. Mary Whitford was baptized on 1 Dec 1848 (Denney.).

ii. Theresa Whitford was baptized on 15 Feb 1850 (Ibid.).

iii. Harriet Whitford was baptized on 22 Sep 1851 (Ibid.).

60 iv. Jacob Whitford, b. 22 May 1853; m. Rachel Kennedy.

  v. Jane Whitford was baptized on 19 Nov 1854 (Ibid.).

61 vi. Sarah Whitford, b. 11 Jan 1856; m. John George Kennedy.

62 vii. George Francis Whitford, b. 15 May 1862; m. Isabel Johnston.

  viii. William James Whitford was baptized on 8 Sep 1866 (Ibid.).

  ix. Jeremiah Whitford was baptized on 29 Mar 1868 (Ibid.).

24. Samuel Whitford was born in Apr 1821 St.Francois Xavier, (Manitoba) (Ibid.). He was baptized on 13 May 1821 St.Johns, Red River Colony, (Manitoba) (HBCR, E.4/1a, fo. 33.). He married **Mary Henderson**, daughter of **Peter Henderson** and **Charlotte Garston Yorkstone (Cree Indian),** on 16 Dec 1844 (St.Andrews), Grand Rapids, (Manitoba) (Ibid., No. 134.).

 Mary Henderson was born in Jul 1826 St.Andrews, (Manitoba) (MBS, C-14928.). She was baptized on 23 Jul 1826 St.Johns, Red River Settlement, (Manitoba) (HBCR, E.4/1a, folio 61.).

 Children of **Samuel Whitford** and **Mary Henderson** were as follows:

63 i. Jane Whitford, b. 18 Nov 1845 (Manitoba); m. Joseph Alexander Turner; d. 15 Dec 1928 Fort Saskatchewan, Alberta.

  ii. James Peter Whitford was baptized on 12 Dec 1847 St.Andrews, (Manitoba) (Denney.).

64 iii. Simon Peter Whitford, b. 17 Feb 1848 St.Andrews, (Manitoba); m. Elizabeth Anderson.

65 iv. William Whitford, b. Jul 1850 St.Andrews, (Manitoba); m. Charlotte Henderson.

  v. Mary Ann Whitford was baptized on 9 Jan 1853 St.Andrews, (Manitoba) (Ibid.). She died on 16 Jan 1855 St.Andrews, (Manitoba), at age 2 (Ibid.).

66 vi. Samuel Whitford, b. 27 Feb 1856 Portage la Prairie, (Manitoba); m. Mary Jane Pruden; d. 4 Jun 1933 Waskatenau, Alberta.

  vii. Mary Matilda Whitford was baptized on 2 Aug 1857 St.Mary's Anglican Church, Portage la Prairie, (Manitoba) (SMACPLP, page 4, B-32.). She died on 20 Sep 1858 St.Andrews, (Manitoba), at age 1 (Denney.).

67 viii. Annabella Whitford, b. 25 Sep 1859 St.Mary's Anglican Church, Portage la Prairie, (Manitoba); m. Edward Anderson.

68 ix. Caroline Whitford, b. 12 Jan 1862 St.Mary's Anglican Church, Portage la Prairie, (Manitoba); m. John Alexander Mitchell; d. 1933 Pakan, Alberta.

  x. Elizabeth Margaret Whitford was born in 1865 Portage la Prairie, (Manitoba) (ArchiviaNet, C-15010.). She died in 1867 Fort Victoria, (Alberta) (Ibid.).

  xi. Jane Whitford was born circa 1868 (Saskatchewan) (1881 Canada, Film No. C-13285, District 192, page 1, Household No. 2.).

  xii. Maria Whitford was born in 1868 Fort Victoria, (Alberta) (ArchiviaNet, C-15010.). She died in 1874 Fort Victoria, (Alberta) (Ibid.).

25. Eleanor 'Ellen' Whitford was born in 1825 St.Andrews, (Manitoba) (MBS, C-14934.). She married **Peter Henderson**, son of **Peter Henderson** and **Charlotte Garston Yorkstone (Cree Indian),** on 21 Dec 1843 (St.Andrews), Grand Rapids, Red River Settlement, (Manitoba) (HBCR, No. 120.). She died in Sep 1902 Portage la Prairie, Manitoba (*Winnipeg Tribune*, Winnipeg, Manitoba, Wednesday, 17 Sep 1902, page 10.).

 Peter Henderson was born in 1824 North West (MBS, C-14934.). He was baptized on 26 Oct 1824 St.Johns, Red River Colony, (Manitoba) (HBCR, E.4/1a, folio 52d.). He died on 14 Jan 1906 Portage la Prairie, Manitoba (Denney.) (*Free Press*, Manitoba Morning Free Press, Monday, 22 Jan 1906, page 5.).

26. Simon Whitford was born on 10 Mar 1826 Red River, (Manitoba) (NWHBSI, page 85.) (1901 Canada, District 202-j(3), page 3, family 24, line 4-7.). He was baptized on 25 Mar 1826 St.Johns, Red River Settlement, (Manitoba) (HBCR, E.4/1a, fo. 59d, #557.) (HBCA-B, E.4/1a, fo. 59d.). He married **Maria Spence**, daughter of **Magnus Spence** and **Sarah 'Sally' Favel,** on 12 Dec 1850 St.Andrews, (Manitoba) (NWHBSI, page 85.) (HBCR, No. 201.). He married **Frances Hope**, daughter of **James Hope** and **Judith Desjarlais,** before 1874 Lac la Biche, (Alberta).

 Maria Spence was baptized on 9 Aug 1836 St.Johns, Red River Settlement, (Manitoba) (Ibid., E.4/1a, folio 130.).

 Children of **Simon Whitford** and **Maria Spence** were as follows:

  i. Annabelle Whitford was baptized on 19 Aug 1853 St.Johns, (Manitoba) (Denney.). She was buried on 23 Jun 1857 St.Mary's Anglican Church, Portage la Prairie, (Manitoba) (SMACPLP, page 1, S-5.).

69 ii. Charles Thomas Whitford, b. 20 Jan 1856 St.Mary's Anglican Church, Portage la Prairie, (Manitoba); m. Mary Jane Sanderson; m. Catherine Paquin.

  iii. Sarah Ellen Whitford was baptized on 27 Nov 1859 St.Mary's Anglican Church, Portage la Prairie, (Manitoba) (Ibid., page 8, B-64.).

  iv. Angus Whitford was baptized on 25 Aug 1861 St.Mary's Anglican Church, Portage la Prairie, (Manitoba) (Ibid., page 14, B-107.). He was buried on 3 Feb 1864 St.Mary's Anglican Church, Portage la Prairie, (Manitoba) (Ibid., page 4, S-30.).

 Frances Hope was born on 17 Feb 1855 Lac la Biche, (Alberta) (LLBR1 Notre Dame des Tidoren, St.Paul Diocese, Lac La Biche, Registre des Baptemes, Mariages & Sepltures, Volume 1, 1853-1898., page 12, B-63. Hereinafter cited as LLBR1.). She was baptized on 18 Feb 1855 Lac la Biche, (Alberta) (Ibid.). She married **Jean Baptiste Cardinal**, son of **Laurent Cardinal** and **Marie Mondion,** on 21 Apr 1869 Lac la Biche, (Alberta) (Ibid., page 100, M-4.).

 Children of **Simon Whitford** and **Frances Hope** were as follows:

  i. Simon Whitford was born in May 1873 Victoria, (Alberta) (ArchiviaNet, C-15010.). He died circa May 1873 Victoria, (Alberta) (Ibid.).

  ii. Cornelius Whitford was born on 28 Apr 1874 Pipe Stone Creek, (Alberta) (Ibid.).

70 iii. Frederick Whitford, b. 22 Jun 1876 Prince Albert, (Saskatchewan).

  iv. Georgiana Whitford was born circa 1878 Battleford, (Saskatchewan) (1881 Canada, Film No. C-13285, District 192, page 5, Household No. 22.).

     v. Sarah Whitford was born on 23 Oct 1882 Edmonton, (Alberta) (ArchiviaNet, C-15010.). She married William James Gullion, son of James Ingram Gullion and Flora Fraser, in 1908 Fort Saskatchewan (Denney.).

          William James Gullion was born on 19 Apr 1882 Edmonton, (Alberta) (NWHBSI.) (ArchiviaNet.). He died on 23 Nov 1969 Edmonton, Alberta, at age 87 (Denney.).

     vi. Nancy Sophia Whitford was born on 7 Apr 1885 Calgary, (Alberta) (ArchiviaNet, C-15010.). She died in 1888 Blind Man River (Ibid.).

     vii. Ray E. Whitford was born on 25 Mar 1897 (1901 Canada, District 202-j(3), page 3, family 24, line 4-7.).

27. Magnus Whitford was baptized on 19 Jul 1831 St.Johns, Red River Settlement, (Manitoba) (HBCA-B, E.4/1a, fo. 84d.) (HBCR, E.4/1a, folio 84d.). He married **Sarah Spence** on 11 Feb 1854 St.Andrews, (Manitoba) (Denney.). He married **Mary Beads**, daughter of **John Beads** and **Margaret (--?--)**, on 3 Aug 1862 St.Mary's Anglican Church, Portage la Prairie, (Manitoba) (SMACPLP, page 11, M-21.).

  Sarah Spence was buried on 24 Dec 1861 St.Mary's Anglican Church, Portage la Prairie, (Manitoba) (Denney.) (SMACPLP, page 3, S-19.).

  Children of **Magnus Whitford** and **Sarah Spence** were as follows:

     i. Magnus Whitford was baptized on 16 Feb 1855 St.Andrews, (Manitoba) (Denney.).

     ii. George Whitford was baptized on 25 May 1856 St.Mary's Anglican Church, Portage la Prairie, (Manitoba) (SMACPLP, page 2, B-9.). He was buried on 22 Jan 1864 St.Mary's Anglican Church, Portage la Prairie, (Manitoba) (Ibid., page 4, S-29.).

     iii. William Whitford was baptized on 23 May 1858 St.Mary's Anglican Church, Portage la Prairie, (Manitoba) (Ibid., page 6, B-41.). He was buried on 28 May 1859 St.Mary's Anglican Church, Portage la Prairie, (Manitoba) (Ibid., page 2, S-13.).

  71 iv. Margaret Whitford, b. 25 May 1860.

     v. George Whitford was born in 1861 Portage la Prairie, (Manitoba) (NWHBS, C-14942.).

  Mary Beads was born in 1837 Winnipeg, (Manitoba) (Ibid., C-14936.). She was baptized on 23 Nov 1838 Red River Settlement, (Manitoba) (HBCA-B.) (HBCR, E.4/1a folio 157d.).

  Children of **Magnus Whitford** and **Mary Beads** were as follows:

     i. John Charles Whitford was born on 11 Apr 1863 Portage la Prairie, (Manitoba) (Denney.). He was baptized on 10 May 1863 St.Mary's Anglican Church, Portage la Prairie, (Manitoba) (SMACPLP, page 22, B-173.).

  72 ii. Elizabeth Ann Whitford, b. 13 Aug 1865 Fort MacLeod, (Alberta); m. Joseph Munroe.

     iii. Charlotte Whitford was born on 16 Jul 1867 Fort Victoria, (Alberta) (NWHBS, C-14942.).

     iv. Isabella Whitford was born on 9 Mar 1869 (NWHBSI, page 85.). She died on 9 May 1883 at age 14 (Ibid.).

     v. James Whitford was born in 1874 Fort Victoria (HBSI.) (ArchiviaNet.). He died in 1879 Prince Albert, (Saskatchewan) (HBSI.) (ArchiviaNet.).

     vi. Sara Ellen Whitford was born in 1876 Fort Victoria (HBSI.) (ArchiviaNet.). She died in 1889 Browning, Glacier County, Montana (HBSI.) (ArchiviaNet.).

28. Christiana Whitford was born circa 1833 St.Andrews, (Manitoba) (MBS, C-14925.). She was baptized on 24 Feb 1834 St.Johns, Red River Settlement, (Manitoba) (HBCA-B, E.4/1a, fo. 107d.) (HBCR, E.4/1a, folio 107.). She married **John Anderson**, son of **John Anderson** and **Mary Anne Desmarais**, on 20 May 1854 St.Mary's Anglican Church, Portage la Prairie, (Manitoba) (SMACPLP, M-1.). She died on 3 Jan 1878 Prince Albert, (Saskatchewan) (Denney.).

  John Anderson was born in 1827 St.Andrews, (Manitoba) (MBS, C-14925.). He was baptized on 12 Jul 1831 Red River Settlement, (Manitoba) (HBCR, E.4/1a folio 84d.).

29. Charles Whitford was born circa 1838 St.Andrews, (Alberta) (Denney.). He was baptized on 8 May 1838 St.Johns, Red River Settlement, (Manitoba) (HBCA-B, E.4/1a, fo. 151.) (HBCR, E.4/1a, folio 151.). He married **Nancy "Ann" Anderson**, daughter of **Thomas Anderson** and **Catherine Landry**, on 4 Dec 1858 St.Mary's Anglican Church, Portage la Prairie, (Manitoba) (SMACPLP, page 2, M-4.).

  Nancy "Ann" Anderson was born in 1840 St.Andrews, (Manitoba) (NWHBS, C-14942.). She was baptized on 27 Nov 1840 Red River Settlement, (Manitoba) (HBCR, E.4/1a folio 172.).

  Children of **Charles Whitford** and **Nancy "Ann" Anderson** were as follows:

  73 i. Flora Whitford, b. 1 Sep 1860 Portage la Prairie, (Manitoba); m. William Charles Anderson.

  74 ii. Colin Alexander Whitford, b. 11 Jan 1862 Portage la Prairie, (Manitoba); m. Angelique Lemire.

  75 iii. John Edmund Whitford, b. 13 Mar 1863 Portage la Prairie, (Manitoba); m. Nancy "Annie" Anderson; d. 1945 Alberta.

  76 iv. Henry Charles Whitford, b. 27 Dec 1864 Portage la Prairie, (Manitoba); m. Catherine Collin; d. 18 Jul 1951 Blaine County, Montana.

  77 v. Isabella Ann Whitford, b. 16 Apr 1867 Portage la Prairie, (Manitoba); m. Alexander Scott Kruger.

  78 vi. Jeremiah Whitford, b. 18 Sep 1868 Victoria, (Alberta); m. Isabelle Desjarlais.

  79 vii. Thomas Whitford, b. 20 May 1870 Victoria, (Alberta); m. Marguerite Sauve.

     viii. Elizabeth Dinah Whitford was born on 2 Jan 1872 Victoria, (Alberta) (Denney.). She was baptized on 10 Feb 1872 Victoria, (Alberta) (Ibid.). She married Alexander Spence before 1900 (ArchiviaNet, C-15004.).

     ix. Adam Ira Whitford was born on 1 Nov 1873 Whitford, (Alberta) (Ibid., C-15010.). He died in 1875 Battle River, (Alberta) (Ibid.).

     x. Simon Peter Whitford was born on 15 Mar 1874 Battle River, (Alberta) (Ibid.). He died in Feb 1884 Fort MacLeod, (Alberta), at age 9 (Ibid.).

     xi. James Whitford was born on 19 Nov 1876 Prince Albert, (Saskatchewan) (Ibid.).

     xii. Edward George Whitford was born on 15 Feb 1878 Prince Albert, (Saskatchewan) (Ibid.). He married Vitaline Fortier, daughter of Andre Henri Fortier and Pelagie Decoine, before 1900 (Ibid.).

Vitaline Fortier was born on 17 Nov 1879 Lac la Biche, (Alberta) (LLBR1, B-33.). She was baptized on 17 Nov 1879 Lac la Biche, (Alberta) (Ibid.).

80   xiii.   Walter Scott Whitford, b. 4 Feb 1882 Battleford, (Saskatchewan); m. Isabelle Desjarlais; d. 23 Jul 1968 Columbus, Stillwater, Montana.

     xiv.   Cornelius Whitford was born on 21 Jun 1884 Macleod, (Alberta) (ArchiviaNet, C-15010.). He died on 24 Jun 1884 Macleod, (Alberta) (Ibid.).

30. Nancy Whitford was baptized on 6 Jul 1841 St.Johns, Red River Settlement, (Manitoba) (HBCA-B, E.4/1a, fo. 173d.) (HBCR, E.4/1a, folio 173d.). She married **James Spence**, son of **Magnus Spence** and **Sarah 'Sally' Favel**, on 6 Sep 1859 St.Mary's Anglican Church, Portage la Prairie, (Manitoba) (SMACPLP, page 5, M-9.). She married **Henry Monkman**, son of **James Monkman** and **Nancy Chaboyer**, on 27 Feb 1868 St.Mary's Anglican Church, Portage la Prairie, (Manitoba) (Ibid., page 24, M-48.).

James Spence was baptized on 21 May 1839 St.Johns, Beaver Creek, (Manitoba) (HBCR, E.4/1a, folio 160d.). He was buried on 9 Dec 1864 St.Mary's Anglican Church, Portage la Prairie, (Manitoba) (SMACPLP, page 6, S-44.).

Henry Monkman was born on 1 Jun 1834 (Denney.). He was baptized on 22 Mar 1837 St.Johns, Red River Settlement, (Manitoba) (HBCR, E.4/1a, folio 139.). He married **Louise McLeod** before 1861. He died in Aug 1926 Good Fish Lake, Vegreville, Alberta, at age 92 (Denney.). He was buried on 31 Aug 1926 Whitford, Alberta (Ibid.).

31. Alexander Whitford was born circa Jul 1843 St.Andrews, (Manitoba) (Ibid., District 202-y(4), page 2, family 21, line 30-37.). He was baptized on 4 Sep 1843 St.Johns, (Manitoba) (HBCA-B, E.4/2, fo. 12.). He married **Elizabeth Jane Cook**, daughter of **Charles Cook** and **Margaret Spence**, on 19 Mar 1868 St.Mary's Anglican Church, Portage la Prairie, (Manitoba) (SMACPLP, page 25, M-49.). He married **Harriet Pocha or Paquin**, daughter of **John Paquin dit Pocha** and **Harriet Spence**, before 1888 (Valencia T. R. Miller Research, 11 Jul 1998 pedigree chart.).

Elizabeth Jane Cook was born on 31 Jan 1851 St.Andrews, (Manitoba) (MBS, C-14934.). She died before 1888 (ArchiviaNet, C-15009.).

Children of **Alexander Whitford** and **Elizabeth Jane Cook** were as follows:

81   i.   Archibald Whitford, b. circa 1868 Portage la Prairie, (Manitoba); m. Mary Pocha; m. Nellie Spence.

     ii.   Elizabeth Jane Whitford was born on 13 Jun 1870 Portage la Prairie, Manitoba (MBS, C-14928.). She was baptized on 9 Jun 1871 St.Mary's Anglican Church, Portage la Prairie, Manitoba (Ibid.) (SMACPLP, page 46, B-364.). She died on 15 Oct 1871 Victoria Mission, Manitoba, at age 1 (MBS, C-14928.).

     iii.   Ann Harriet Whitford was born on 11 Apr 1873 Victoria, (Alberta) (HBS 1886-1901, 1906 Half-Breed Scrip Applications, RG15-21, Volume 1338, C-14953.). She married James Brown before 4 Sep 1894 (Ibid.).

     iv.   Louise Whitford was born on 11 May 1875 Prince Albert, (Saskatchewan) (HBSI.) (ArchiviaNet.). She married Charles Richard Monkman, son of Henry Monkman and Nancy Whitford, before 1900.

       Charles Richard Monkman was born in Jan 1872 Fort Victoria (HBSI.) (ArchiviaNet.). He was baptized on 10 Feb 1872 (Denney.).

82   v.   Edwin Whitford, b. 24 May 1877 Prince Albert, (Saskatchewan); m. Mary Margaret (--?--).

     vi.   John James Whitford was born on 29 Feb 1880 Prince Albert, (Saskatchewan) (ArchiviaNet, C-15010.). He married Margaret Atkinson, daughter of William George Atkinson and Ellen McNab, circa 1900 (1901 Canada, #202-y(4), page 2, family 22, line 38-39.) (ArchiviaNet, C-15010.).

       Margaret Atkinson was born on 17 Aug 1875 Fort Pelly, (Saskatchewan) (Ibid.).

     vii.   Florence Whitford was born on 31 May 1883 Prince Albert, (Saskatchewan) (HBSI.) (ArchiviaNet.). She married (--?--) Henderson before 1901.

     viii.   Margaret Edith Whitford was born in May 1884 Prince Albert, (Saskatchewan) (Ibid., C-15009.). She died in Sep 1884 Prince Albert, (Saskatchewan) (Ibid.).

     ix.   Alexander Whitford was born on 5 Aug 1885 Prince Albert, (Saskatchewan) (Ibid.). He died in 1887 Prince Albert, (Saskatchewan) (Ibid.).

Harriet Pocha or Paquin was born on 30 Nov 1857 (HBC-PN , Poplar Point and High Bluff, #194.). She was baptized on 14 Dec 1857 St.Andrews, (Manitoba) (Denney.). She married **Charles Alexander Fidler**, son of **Edward Fidler** and **Ann Bremner**, on 23 Jan 1877 Holy Trinity, Headingley, Manitoba (Ibid.).

Children of **Alexander Whitford** and **Harriet Pocha or Paquin** were as follows:

     i.   Alice Robina Whitford was born on 6 Sep 1888 (1901 Canada, District 202-y(4), page 2, family 21, line 30-37.).

     ii.   Clara Mary Whitford was born on 17 Sep 1890 (Valencia Miller, 11 Jul 1998 pedigree chart.) (1901 Canada, District 202-y(4), page 2, family 21, line 30-37.).

     iii.   Edward Thomas Whitford was born on 1 Jan 1893 (Ibid.).

     iv.   Christina Whitford was born on 11 Mar 1895 (Ibid.).

     v.   Ethel May Whitford was born on 17 Apr 1900 (Ibid.).

32. John Whitford was born in 1846 St.Andrews, (Manitoba) (NWHBS, C-14942.). He was baptized on 23 Aug 1846 St.Johns, (Manitoba) (HBCA-B, E.4/2, fo. 45.). He married **Jane Mary Tait**, daughter of **William Tait** and **Mary Bear (Cree)**, in 1867 Fort Victoria, (Alberta) (NWHBS, C-14942.).

Jane Mary Tait was born on 8 Jan 1843 Point Douglas, (Manitoba) (Denney.). She was baptized on 21 Apr 1844 St.Johns, (Manitoba) (Ibid.).

Children of **John Whitford** and **Jane Mary Tait** were as follows:

     i.   Philip Whitford was born on 5 Sep 1868 Victoria, (Alberta) (NWHBS, C-14942.). He died on 10 May 1885 Prince Albert, (Saskatchewan), at age 16 (Ibid.). He was buried on 10 May 1885 St.Catherines, Prince Albert District, (Saskatchewan) (Ibid.).

    ii.   William Richard Whitford was born on 23 Mar 1870 Victoria, (Alberta) (Ibid.). He died on 3 Feb 1881 Prince Albert, (Saskatchewan), at age 10 (Ibid.). He was buried on 3 Feb 1881 St.Catherines, Prince Albert District, (Saskatchewan) (Ibid.).

    iii.   Peter James Whitford was born on 2 Feb 1872 Victoria, (Alberta) (Ibid.) (ArchiviaNet, C-15010.). He died on 25 Oct 1882 Prince Albert, (Saskatchewan), at age 10 (NWHBS, C-14942.) (ArchiviaNet, C-15010.).

    iv.   Joseph Alexander Whitford was born on 10 Nov 1873 Victoria, (Alberta) (NWHBS, C-14942.) (ArchiviaNet, C-15010.). He died on 3 Jul 1884 Prince Albert, (Saskatchewan), at age 10 (NWHBS, C-14942.).

    v.   Robert Whitford was born on 25 Oct 1875 Prince Albert, (Saskatchewan) (Ibid.) (ArchiviaNet, C-15010.). He died on 10 Jul 1878 Prince Albert, (Saskatchewan), at age 2 (NWHBS, C-14942.) (ArchiviaNet, C-15010.).

    vi.   Mathilda Ann Whitford was born on 17 Sep 1877 Prince Albert, (Saskatchewan) (NWHBS, C-14942.) (ArchiviaNet, C-15010.). She died on 6 Feb 1882 Prince Albert, (Saskatchewan), at age 4 (NWHBS, C-14942.) (ArchiviaNet, C-15010.).

    vii.   John Hector Whitford was born on 25 Mar 1879 Prince Albert, (Saskatchewan) (NWHBS, C-14942.) (ArchiviaNet, C-15010.). He died on 1 May 1885 Prince Albert, (Saskatchewan), at age 6 (NWHBS, C-14942.) (ArchiviaNet, C-15010.).

    viii.   Archibald Whitford was born on 23 Sep 1880 Prince Albert, (Saskatchewan) (NWHBS, C-14942.) (ArchiviaNet, C-15010.). He died on 14 Apr 1885 Prince Albert, (Saskatchewan), at age 4 (NWHBS, C-14942.) (ArchiviaNet, C-15010.).

    ix.   Mary Margaret Whitford was born on 5 Feb 1883 Prince Albert, (Saskatchewan) (NWHBS, C-14942.) (ArchiviaNet, C-15010.).

    x.   Edward Whitford was born on 17 Apr 1885 Prince Albert, (Saskatchewan) (HBSI.) (ArchiviaNet, C-15010.). He died on 14 Apr 1887 Prince Albert, (Saskatchewan), at age 1 (HBSI.) (ArchiviaNet, C-15010.).

33. Isabella Whitford was baptized on 9 Oct 1849 St.Johns, (Manitoba) (HBCA-B, E.4/2, fo. 72.). She married **William Morris** before 1877.

    William Morris married **Sarah Anne McNab**, daughter of **Andrew McNab** and **Annie Pratt,** in 1881 Touchwood Hills, (Saskatchewan) (HBSI.) (ArchiviaNet.).

34. Elizabeth Whitford was born in 1840 St.Peters, (Manitoba) (MBS, C-14934.) (ArchiviaNet, C-15010.). She married **Thomas Sinclair (Metis)** on 18 Dec 1858 St.Peters, (Manitoba) (Denney.).

    Thomas Sinclair (Metis) was born circa 1841 (1891 Census of Canada from the National Archives of Canada, Ottawa, Canada.).

35. James Francois 'Jimmy' Whitford was born on 10 Jan 1827 North West (MBS, C-14934.). He was baptized on 23 Mar 1828 St.Johns, Red River Settlement, (Manitoba) (HBCA-B, E.4/2, fo. 69.) (HBCR, E.4/1a, folio 69.). He married **Marguerite Fagnant**, daughter of **Jean Baptiste Fagnant** and **Josephte Monet dit Belhumeur,** on 10 Feb 1852 St.Francois Xavier, (Manitoba) (SFXI-Kipling, M-3.) (SFXI 1851-1868, M-3.). He died on 19 Nov 1908 Willow Bunch, Saskatchewan, at age 81 (SIWB St.Ignace Roman Catholic Registre des Baptemes, Mariages & Sepltures, Willow Bunch, Saskatchewan, 1882-1917, FHC #1290091., page 139. Hereinafter cited as SIWB.). He was buried on 21 Nov 1908 St.Ignace, Willow Bunch, Saskatchewan (Ibid.).

    Marguerite Fagnant was born in May 1826 St.Francois Xavier, (Manitoba) (MBS, C-14934.).

    Children of **James Francois 'Jimmy' Whitford** and **Marguerite Fagnant** were as follows:

    83   i.   Marie Whitford, b. 6 Nov 1852; m. Jean Baptiste Desjarlais.

    84   ii.   James Whitford, b. 14 Sep 1854 Pembina, Pembina County, Dakota Territory; m. Sarah Gladu.

    85   iii.   Maxime Whitford, b. 16 Nov 1856 Portage la Prairie, (Manitoba); m. Adelaide Campbell.

    iv.   Elzear Whitford was born on 6 Feb 1859 St.Francois Xavier, (Manitoba) (SFXI-Kipling, B-307.). He was baptized on 7 Feb 1859 St.Francois Xavier, (Manitoba) (Ibid.).

    86   v.   Louis Napoleon Whitford, b. 8 Sep 1861 St.Francois Xavier, (Manitoba); m. Marie Rose Lingan; d. 29 May 1923 Deer Lodge County, Montana.

    vi.   William Whitford was born on 7 Oct 1863 (Ibid., B-98.). He was baptized on 24 Oct 1863 St.Francois Xavier, (Manitoba) (Ibid.). He was buried on 27 Nov 1865 St.Francois Xavier, (Manitoba) (Ibid., S-50.) (SFXI-1834-54.).

    87   vii.   Athalie Rose Whitford, b. 23 Mar 1866 St.Francois Xavier, (Manitoba); m. Patrice Trottier; d. 1933.

    viii.   Genevieve Marguerite Whitford was born on 4 Apr 1870 North West Territory (SFXI-Kipling, B-33.) (1870C-MB, page 284, #1307.). She was baptized on 16 May 1870 St.Francois Xavier, (Manitoba) (SFXI-Kipling, B-33.).

    ix.   William Whitford was born in Oct 1872 Moose Mountain (ArchiviaNet, C-15010.). He died in 1874 St.Francois Xavier, Manitoba (Ibid.).

    88   x.   Jean Marie Whitford, b. 3 Oct 1874 Saskatoon, (Saskatchewan); m. Marguerite McGillis; d. Dec 1948 North Battleford, Saskatchewan.

    xi.   Isabelle Whitford was born in Jul 1877 between Oxboro and Estevan (Ibid.). She died in Jul 1877 between Oxboro and Estevan (Ibid.).

36. William Francis Whitford was born in 1830 St.Boniface, (Manitoba) (Ibid.). He married **Louise Desjarlais**, daughter of **Jean Baptiste Desjarlais** and **Charlotte Cardinal,** on 19 Sep 1853 St.Francois Xavier, (Manitoba) (SFXI-Kipling, M-19.) (SFXI 1851-1868, M-19.).

    Louise Desjarlais was born in 1839 St.Boniface, (Manitoba) (HBSI.).

    Children of **William Francis Whitford** and **Louise Desjarlais** were as follows:

    i.   Marie Whitford was born on 19 Aug 1854 (SFXI-Kipling, B-188.) (SFXI 1851-1868, B-188.). She was baptized on 25 Aug 1854 St.Francois Xavier, (Manitoba) (SFXI-Kipling, B-188.) (SFXI 1851-1868, B-188.).

    ii.   William Francis Whitford was born on 20 Sep 1856 (SFXI-Kipling, B-189.). He was baptized on 29 May 1857 St.Francois Xavier, (Manitoba) (Ibid.). He married Marguerite Arcand, daughter of Isidore Arcand and Marguerite (--?--), on 15 Jul 1878 St-Laurent-de-Grandin, (Saskatchewan) (SL-SK St.Laurent-de-Grandin Roman Catholic

Registre des Baptemes, Mariages & Sepltures, St.Laurent, Saskatchewan, 1872-1896, page 19, M-3. Hereinafter cited as SL-SK.).

    Marguerite Arcand was born circa 1858 (Ibid.).

  iii. Louis Whitford was born on 15 Jan 1858 (SFXI-Kipling, B-232.). He was baptized on 23 Apr 1858 St.Francois Xavier, (Manitoba) (Ibid.).

89 iv. Francois Whitford, b. 15 Mar 1860; m. Marguerite Desjarlais.

90 v. Elie Joseph Whitford, b. 5 Feb 1862; m. Mary Blackbird (Indian).

91 vi. Genevieve Whitford, b. 1 May 1864; m. John Cabe.

  vii. Marie Caroline Whitford was born on 18 Oct 1866 near Lac Qu'Appelle, (Saskatchewan) (SN1, page 103, B-1.). She was baptized on 26 Mar 1867 (Fort Qu'Appelle), St.Norbert, (Saskatchewan) (Ibid.). She died in Mar 1873 near, Saskatoon, (Saskatchewan), at age 6 (ArchiviaNet, C-15010.). She was buried on 25 Apr 1873 Lebret, (Saskatchewan) (L1, page 76, S-4.).

  viii. Leon Whitford was born on 4 Nov 1869 (Ibid., page 12, B-39.). He was baptized on 10 Dec 1869 Lebret, (Saskatchewan) (Ibid.). He died in 1886 Stoney Mountain Penitentiary (ArchiviaNet, C-15010.).

92 ix. Madeleine Whitford, b. 26 Jun 1872 Qu'Appelle, (Saskatchewan); m. Johnny Andowes.

  x. Jean Whitford was born on 17 Dec 1874 Duck Lake, (Saskatchewan) (Denney.) (SL-SK, page 34, B-2.). He was baptized on 14 Jan 1875 St.Laurent-de-Grandin, (Saskatchewan) (Ibid.).

  xi. Rosalie Whitford was born on 25 Dec 1877 Blackfoot Crossing (HBSI.) (ArchiviaNet.). She married Alfred McKay, son of Alexander McKay and Virginie Larocque, before 1900 (HBSI.).

    Alfred McKay was born on 20 Nov 1868 Fort Qu'Appelle, (Saskatchewan) (Ibid.). He married **Jane Fitzpatrick** on 1 Feb 1889 Medicine Hat, (Alberta) (T. R. McCloy, McKay Descendancy.).

  xii. Joseph Whitford was born on 8 Jun 1879 Battle River, (Saskatchewan) (SV St.Vital Roman Catholic Registre des Baptemes, Mariages & Sepltures, Battleford, Saskatchewan, 1878-1896, B-13. Hereinafter cited as SV.). He was baptized on 8 Jun 1879 St.Vital, Battleford, (Saskatchewan) (Ibid.). He died between 1883 and 1884 Battleford, (Saskatchewan) (ArchiviaNet, C-15010.).

37. Genevieve Whitford was born on 12 May 1833 (SB 1825-1834 St.Boniface Roman Catholic Registre des Baptemes, Mariages & Sepultures, 1825-1834, page 101, B-588. Hereinafter cited as SB 1825-1834.). She was baptized between 17 May 1833 and 22 May 1833 St.Boniface, (Manitoba) (Ibid.). She married **Ambroise Chartrand**, son of **Paul Chartrand** and **Josephte Cadotte**, on 12 Sep 1854 St.Francois Xavier, (Manitoba) (SFXI-Kipling, M-30.) (SFXI 1851-1868, M-30.). She married **Joseph Langer**, son of **Edouard Langer** and **Marguerite Coulombe**, on 30 Nov 1870 Lebret, (Saskatchewan) (L1, page 39, M-5.). She married **St.Pierre Morin**, son of **Antoine Morin** and **Therese Rocque**, circa 1905 (BIA-TM Bureau of Indian Affairs, Turtle Mountain Enrollment and Probate Papers, Belcourt, North Dakota.).

  Ambroise Chartrand was born in Aug 1837 St.Laurent, (Manitoba) (MBS, C-14926.). He died before 13 Nov 1870 (L1, page 39, M-5.).

  Joseph Langer was born circa 1847 Red River, (Manitoba) (1850Ci-MN *Minnesota Territorial Census, 1850*, Harpole, Patricia C. and Mary D. Nagle, ed., (St.Paul, Minnesota: Minnesota Historical Society, 1972), page 34, Dwelling 166, Family 166.).

  St.Pierre Morin was born circa 1845 Red River, (Manitoba) (1870C-MB, #194, page 7.). He was born in Aug 1846 North Dakota (1900C-ND 1900 United States Census, North Dakota, National Archives of the United States, Washington, D. C., House 158, page 289A.). He was born circa 1849 (Ancestry.com, 1920 Census Index.). He married **Elisabeth Gonneville**, daughter of **Alexis Gonneville** and **Josephte Trottier**, on 27 Feb 1871 Duck Lake, (Saskatchewan) (DL Register of Sacre Coeur Roman Catholic Church, Duck Lake, Saskatchewan, 1870-1893, page 7, M-2. Hereinafter cited as DL.). He died on 28 Oct 1937 Rolette County, North Dakota (ND Death Index.).

38. Sarah Whitford was born circa 1834 Red River, (Manitoba). She was baptized on 2 Jun 1834 St.Johns, (Manitoba) (Denney.). She married **Peter Hourie**, son of **John Hourie** and **Margaret Cree**, before 1856. She died in 1910 Indian Head (Ibid.).

  Peter Hourie was born circa 1825 Red River, (Manitoba) (NWHBSI, page 110.). He was baptized on 30 Nov 1830 St.Johns, (Manitoba) (HBCR, E.4/1a, folio 80, #219.) (HBCA-B, E.4/1a, fo.80.). He died on 17 Sep 1910 Regina, Saskatchewan, at age 79 (Denney.) (SK Vital Statistics, Death Reg. #1359.).

Generation Four

39. David Whitford was born on 15 Jul 1875 High River, (Alberta) (ArchiviaNet, C-15010.) (1901 Canada, District 205-s(1), page 24, family 263, line 42.). He married **Genevieve Berard**, daughter of **John Roger Berard** and **Rosa Archange Belcourt**, circa 1893 Beaver Lake, (Alberta) (HBS, C-14949.).

  Genevieve Berard was born in Jun 1874 St.Albert, (Alberta) (Ibid.). She died circa Apr 1896.

  Children of **David Whitford** and **Genevieve Berard** were:

  i. Clara Whitford was born on 13 Apr 1895 Beaver Lake, (Alberta) (1901 Canada, #202, i, page 1, family 8, line 28-39.).

  Children of **David Whitford** include:

  i. Lloyd Whitford was born on 4 Nov 1898 (Ibid.).

  ii. Flora Whitford was born on 7 Dec 1899 (Ibid.).

40. Gilbert Whitford was born in 1857 Partridge Crop (NWHBS, C-14942.). He married **Marcelline Blandion**, daughter of **Antoine Blandion or Dion** and **Marie Desjarlais**, on 1 Aug 1882 St.Thomas, Duhamel, (Alberta) (DA Register of the Duhamel, Alberta Roman Catholic Church: 1881-1921, M-3. Hereinafter cited as DA.).

  Marcelline Blandion was born in 1864 St.Albert, (Alberta) (NWHBS, C-14938.).

  Children of **Gilbert Whitford** and **Marcelline Blandion** were as follows:

  i. Andrew Whitford was born in Sep 1883 Peace Hills, (Alberta) (Ibid., C-14942.) (ArchiviaNet, C-15010.). He was baptized on 25 Sep 1883 St.Thomas, Duhamel, (Alberta) (DA, B-28.).

ii. Dolphus Whitford was baptized on 10 Sep 1885 St.Thomas, Duhamel, (Alberta) (Ibid., B-13.). He died on 4 Mar 1887 at age 1 (Ibid., S-2.). He was buried on 11 Mar 1887 St.Thomas, Duhamel, (Alberta) (Ibid.).

41. **Alfred Whitford** was baptized on 25 Aug 1861 St.Mary's Anglican Church, Portage la Prairie, (Manitoba) (SMACPLP, page 14, B-108.). He was baptized on 23 May 1889 St.Thomas, Duhamel, (Alberta) (DA, B-3.). He married **Annie Fraser**, daughter of **John Fraser** and **Sarah Jane Vincent**, in Jun 1885 Edmonton, (Alberta) (NWHBS, C-14942.). He married **Adele Lafournaise**, daughter of **Gabriel Lafournaise dit Laboucane** and **Elizabeth Landry**, on 24 Jun 1889 St.Thomas, Duhamel, (Alberta) (DA, M-3.).

Annie Fraser was born circa 1868.

Children of **Alfred Whitford** and **Annie Fraser** were:

i. Philip Whitford was born on 1 Dec 1885 Wetaskiwin, (Alberta) (ArchiviaNet, C-15009.). He died on 15 Aug 1886 Peace Hills, (Alberta) (Ibid.).

Adele Lafournaise was born on 18 Apr 1865 (SFXI-Kipling, B-30.). She was baptized on 10 May 1865 St.Francois Xavier, (Manitoba) (Ibid.).

Children of **Alfred Whitford** and **Adele Lafournaise** were as follows:

i. Adelaide ? Whitford was baptized on 5 Feb 1891 St.Thomas, Duhamel, (Alberta) (DA, B-3.).

ii. Alexandre Whitford was born in Feb 1895 (Ibid., B-6.). He was baptized on 16 Apr 1895 Beaver Lake, (Alberta) (Ibid.).

42. **Mary Julia Whitford** was born on 11 Oct 1863 Portage la Prairie, (Manitoba) (NWHBS, C-14942.). She was baptized on 11 Oct 1863 St.Mary's Anglican Church, Portage la Prairie, (Manitoba) (SMACPLP, page 24, B-188.). She married **Godfrey McNeil Steele** on 21 Jan 1881 Edmonton, (Alberta) (Denney.).

Godfrey McNeil Steele was born on 2 Mar 1855 (1901 Canada, #202, q(1)-1, page 2, family 22, line 30-35.).

43. **Jessie Whitford** was born in Jan 1874 Whitford Lake, (Alberta) (HBSI.) (ArchiviaNet.). She was born on 10 Dec 1876 (1901 Canada, Whitford Y(4), page 1, line 40-43, family 10.). She married **Robert John Littlechild**, son of **John Robert Littlechild** and **Margaret Ann Bell**, on 11 Jan 1895 Fort Saskatchewan, (Saskatchewan) (HBSI.). She died in 1948 (Denney.).

Robert John Littlechild was born in 1873 England (Ibid.). He was born on 7 Jan 1876 (1901 Canada, Whitford Y(4), page 1, line 40-43, family 10.). He died in 1949.

44. **Mary Ann Whitford** was born on 15 Nov 1852 Poplar Point, (Manitoba) (MBS, C-14927.). She was baptized on 20 Dec 1852 St.Andrews, (Manitoba) (Denney.). She married **Henry Charles Desmarais**, son of **Jean Baptiste Desmarais** and **Sophia Erasmus**, on 12 Sep 1867 St.Mary's Anglican Church, Portage la Prairie, (Manitoba) (SMACPLP, page 23, M-45.).

Henry Charles Desmarais was born on 29 Oct 1846 St.Andrews, (Manitoba) (MBS, C-14927.).

45. **Euphemia Whitford** was born on 4 Jan 1855 Portage la Prairie, (Manitoba) (1870C-MB, page 336, #135.) (Rod Mac Quarrie, 31 Mar 2011.). She was baptized on 14 Jan 1855 Portage la Prairie, (Manitoba) (Ibid.). She married **George William Sanderson**, son of **James Sanderson** and **Elizabeth Anderson**, in 1873 Westbourne, Manitoba (Ibid.) (ArchiviaNet.). She died on 8 Jan 1914 Saskatchewan at age 59 (SK Vital Statistics, Death Reg. #146.).

George William Sanderson was born on 29 Sep 1844 Lesser Slave Lake (1870C-MB, page 348, #690.) (Rod Mac Quarrie, 16 Dec 2010.). He married **Elizabeth Barbara Adams**, daughter of **George Adams** and **Ann Haywood**, in 1867 High Bluff, Manitoba (Ibid.). He died on 9 Aug 1936 Prince Albert, Saskatchewan, at age 91 (Ibid.).

46. **James William Rupert Whitford** was born on 8 Feb 1857 Fairford, (Manitoba) (Denney.). He was born on 23 Dec 1858 (1901 Canada, #202-b(3), page 2, family 13, line 4-8.). He married **Marie Hebert or Lebret**, daughter of **Basile Hebert** and **Isabelle Piche**, before 1891.

Marie Hebert or Lebret was born on 4 Jan 1874 Buffalo Lake (ArchiviaNet, C-15010.).

Children of **James William Rupert Whitford** and **Marie Hebert or Lebret** were as follows:

i. Donald Whitford was born on 10 May 1891 (1901 Canada, #202-b(3), page 2, family 13, line 4-8.).

ii. William Whitford was born on 30 Sep 1892 (Ibid.).

iii. Gilbert Whitford was born on 15 Aug 1894 (Ibid.).

47. **William Rupert Whitford** was born on 9 Aug 1859 Fairford, (Manitoba) (Denney.). He married **Elizabeth McIver**, daughter of **Allen McIver** and **Elizabeth Beads**, before 1881.

Elizabeth McIver was baptized on 12 Jan 1861 St.Mary's Anglican Church, Portage la Prairie, (Manitoba) (SMACPLP, page 12, B-90.). She married **Alfred Clee** before 1885.

Children of **William Rupert Whitford** and **Elizabeth McIver** both born Russell, Manitoba, were as follows:

i. Ellen Whitford was born in 1881 (ArchiviaNet, C-15010.). She married John Lorus Meikle in Nov 1899 (Ibid.).

ii. William James Whitford was born in Oct 1882 (Ibid.). He was baptized on 20 Oct 1882 Russell, Manitoba (Ibid.).

48. **Andrew Whitford** was born on 10 Sep 1861 Portage la Prairie, (Manitoba) (SMACPLP, B-104.). He was baptized on 6 Oct 1862 St.Mary's Anglican Church, Portage la Prairie, (Manitoba) (Ibid., page 15, B-114.). He married **Christine Anderson Isbister**, daughter of **James Isbister** and **Margaret Bear**, circa 1884 (Denney.).

Christine Anderson Isbister was born on 2 Aug 1867 (NWHBSI, page 39.) (1901 Canada, #205, Y-1, page 3-4, family 26, line 43-50, 1.).

Children of **Andrew Whitford** and **Christine Anderson Isbister** were as follows:

i. Mary Ann Whitford was born on 20 Dec 1885 St.Catherines, Prince Albert District, (Saskatchewan) (Ibid.) (ArchiviaNet, C-15010.).

ii. George Whitford was born on 2 Feb 1889 St.Catherines, Prince Albert District, (Saskatchewan) (1901 Canada, #205, Y-1, page 3-4, family 26, line 43-50, 1.).

iii. Edward Whitford was born on 8 May 1893 St.Catherines, Prince Albert District, (Saskatchewan) (Ibid.).

iv. Andrew Whitford was born on 22 Sep 1895 (Saskatchewan) (Automated Genealogy 1906 Census Transcription Project and Census Images from the National Archives of Canada, http://www.automatedgenealogy.com, #16, 21, page 7, family 37, line 4-13.) (SK Vital Statistics, Birth Reg. #7052.).

- v. Joseph Whitford was born on 15 Sep 1898 St.Catherines, Prince Albert District, (Saskatchewan) (1901 Canada, #205, Y-1, page 3-4, family 26, line 43-50, 1.).
- vi. Alexander Whitford was born on 31 Dec 1900 St.Catherines, Prince Albert District, (Saskatchewan) (1906 Canada, #16, 21, page 7, family 37, line 4-13.) (1901 Canada, #205, Y-1, page 3-4, family 26, line 43-50, 1.).
- vii. Stanley Whitford was born on 18 Apr 1903 Lily Plain, (Saskatchewan) (1906 Canada, #16, 21, page 7, family 37, line 4-13.) (SK Vital Statistics, Birth Reg. #3423.).
- viii. Duncan Whitford was born circa Dec 1905 (Saskatchewan) (1906 Canada, #16, 21, page 7, family 37, line 4-13.).
- ix. Margaret Effie May Whitford was born on 30 Sep 1906 St.Catherines, Prince Albert District, (Saskatchewan) (SK Vital Statistics, Birth Reg. #7580.). She married Owen S. Sanderson, son of George William Sanderson and Euphemia Whitford, on 12 Nov 1946 (Rod Mac Quarrie, 31 Mar 2011.).

Owen S. Sanderson was born on 23 May 1894 St.Catherines, (Saskatchewan) (Ibid.).

49. John Joseph Whitford was born on 24 Dec 1868 Big Point (Denney.). He married **Catherine Lacouette**, daughter of **Jean Baptiste Lacouette** and **Madeleine Belhumeur**, before 1889. He married **Esther Lacouette**, daughter of **Augustin Lacouette** and **Marie Bone or Oskinigig,** on 4 Aug 1902 R.M. of Ochre River, Manitoba (MB Vital Statistics, Marriage Reg. #1902,001309.).

Catherine Lacouette was born on 28 Sep 1871 (1901 Canada, District 8-j-1, page 14, family 149, line 37-43.). She died on 5 Nov 1900 R.M. of Dauphin, Manitoba, at age 29 (MB Vital Statistics, Death Reg. #1900,002345.). Question: *Is Catherine the daughter of Jean Baptiste Lacouette and Madeleine Belhumeur?*

Children of **John Joseph Whitford** and **Catherine Lacouette** were as follows:

- i. Lizzie Whitford was born on 18 May 1889 (1901 Canada, District 8-j-1, page 14, family 149, line 37-43.).
- ii. Norman Whitford was born on 5 Dec 1891 (Ibid.).
- iii. Louisa Whitford was born on 30 Jul 1894 (Ibid.).
- iv. Mary Antoinette Whiteford was born on 8 Aug 1897 R.M. of Dauphin, Manitoba (Ibid.) (MB Vital Statistics, Birth Reg. #1899,001602.).
- v. Joseph Napoleon Whiteford was born on 5 Nov 1900 R.M. of Dauphin, Manitoba (1901 Canada, District 8-j-1, page 14, family 149, line 37-43.) (MB Vital Statistics, Birth Reg. #1900,004069.).

Esther Lacouette was born on 17 Apr 1879 Sandy Bay, (Manitoba) (ArchiviaNet.).

Children of **John Joseph Whitford** and **Esther Lacouette** were as follows:

- i. Sarah Whitford was born in Feb 1903 (Automated Genealogy 1911 Census Transcription Project and Census Images from the National Archives of Canada, http://www.automatedgenealogy.com, District 31, page 2, family 13, line 31-37.).
- ii. John Robert Whitford was born in Feb 1906 (Ibid.).

50. Margaret Whitford was born circa 1870.

Children of **Margaret Whitford** include:

- i. Michel Whitford was born on 20 Jan 1885 St.Laurent, Manitoba (MB Vital Statistics, Birth Reg.#1885,004284.).

51. Philip Whitford was born in 1855 Oak Point, Manitoba Lake, Manitoba (NWHBS, C-14942.). He married **Rosalie Dumont,** daughter of **Gabriel Dumont** and **Suzanne Lussier,** in 1875 Red Deer River, (Alberta) (Ibid.).

Rosalie Dumont was born circa Sep 1844 (INB, page 56.). She was baptized on 27 Mar 1845 Fort-des-Prairies (Ibid.). She married **Edouard Beaudry**, son of **Joseph Beaudry** and **Louise Ladouceur,** on 24 Nov 1862 St.Albert, (Alberta) (Denney.). She married **Francois Berland**, son of **Francois Berland** and **Therese Karakonti L'Iroquois,** on 26 Aug 1867 (Ibid.). She married according to the custom of the country **Abraham 'Abe' Salois**, son of **Joseph Abraham Salois** and **Suzanne Bouvette,** before 1874 (ArchiviaNet, C-15001.). She died in 1886 St.Albert, (Alberta) (Denney.).

Children of **Philip Whitford** and **Rosalie Dumont** were as follows:

- i. Philip Whitford.
- ii. Rosalie Whitford.
- iii. Isabelle Whitford was born in 1877 Red Deer River, (Alberta) (HBSI.) (ArchiviaNet.). She married (--?--) Graham before 1900.
- iv. Francis Whitford was born in 1877 Red Deer River, (Alberta) (NWHBS, C-14942.) (ArchiviaNet, C-15010.).
- v. Mary Whitford was born on 17 Mar 1881 Lee's Creek (Ibid.). She died in Apr 1881 Montana (Ibid.).
- vi. Eliza Whitford was born in 1882 Lee's Creek (Ibid.). She died in Jun 1885 (Ibid.).
- vii. Anonyme Whitford was born in 1885 Big Lake (Ibid.). She died in Jul 1885 (Ibid.).

52. John Whitford was born on 22 May 1855 (1901 Canada, District 202-i(2), page 2, family 22, line 49-50, 1-8.). He married **Maria Bremner,** daughter of **William Bremner** and **Marie Allary,** circa 1876 (Ibid.) (1911 Canada, District 42, page 1, family 4, line 34-40.).

Maria Bremner was born on 25 Nov 1865 (1901 Canada, District 202-i(2), page 2, family 22, line 49-50, 1-8.).

Children of **John Whitford** and **Maria Bremner** were as follows:

- i. James Whitford was born in 1876 Battleford, (Saskatchewan) (1891 Canada, District 197, family 119.) (ArchiviaNet, C-15010.). He married Maria (--?--) before 1906 (1911 Canada, District 42, page 1, family 5, line 41-45.).

  Maria (--?--) was born in Feb 1888 (Ibid.).
- ii. William Whitford was born in 1878 Fort Walsh, (Saskatchewan) (ArchiviaNet, C-15010.). He died on 5 Nov 1880 Cypress Hills, (Saskatchewan) (Ibid.).
- iii. William George Whitford was born on 5 Apr 1881 (1901 Canada, District 202-i(2), page 2, family 22, line 49-50, 1-8.).
- iv. Andrew C. Whitford was born in Jul 1883 Macleod, (Alberta) (1891 Canada, District 197, family 119.) (ArchiviaNet, C-15010.). He died in Jul 1891 Baqttle River, Hobema, (Alberta) (Ibid.).
- v. Cleophas Whitford was born on 26 Oct 1886 (1901 Canada, District 202-i(2), page 2, family 22, line 49-50, 1-8.).

    vi.   Mary James Whitford was born on 19 Mar 1889 (Ibid.).

    vii.   Archie Whitford was born on 20 Jun 1892 (Ibid.).

    viii.   Louise Whitford was born on 10 Mar 1895 (Ibid.).

    ix.   Richard Whitford was born on 13 Dec 1900 (Ibid.).

    x.   Cornelius Whitford was born in Jul 1905 (1911 Canada, District 42, page 1, family 4, line 34-40.).

53. Benjamin Whitford was born on 1 Sep 1863 between Whitefish Lake and Victoria, (Alberta) (ArchiviaNet, C-15009.). He married **Elsie Anehay**, daughter of **(--?--) Anehay (Indian)** and **Marie Sanawayenctum**, on 6 Sep 1881 Dunvegan, (Alberta) (Ibid.). **Elsie Anehay** was born in Mar 1863 Grand Prairie (Denney.).

Children of **Benjamin Whitford** and **Elsie Anehay** were as follows:

    i.   Albert Whitford was born in 1882 Dunvegan, (Alberta) (ArchiviaNet, C-15009.).

    ii.   Albertine Whitford was born in 1884 Dunvegan, (Alberta) (Ibid.).

    iii.   Francis Whitford was born in 1886 Dunvegan, (Alberta) (Ibid.).

    iv.   John Whitford was born circa 1887 (1906 Canada, Distric 22-02, page 15, family 177, line 26-33.).

    v.   Charlotte Whitford was born circa 1888 (1891 Canada, District 201, family 3.).

    vi.   Eliza Whitford was born circa 1889 (1906 Canada, Distric 22-02, page 15, family 177, line 26-33.).

    vii.   Minnie Whitford was born in 1891 Lesser Slave Lake, (Alberta) (ArchiviaNet, C-15009.).

    viii.   George Robert Whitford was born circa 1893 (1906 Canada, Distric 22-02, page 15, family 177, line 26-33.).

    ix.   Charles Henry Whitford was born circa 1898 (Ibid.).

    x.   William John Whitford was born circa 1902 (Ibid.).

54. Anne Whitford was born on 15 Feb 1862 Portage la Prairie, (Manitoba) (SMACPLP, page 17, B-130.) (ArchiviaNet, C-15009.). She was baptized on 2 Mar 1862 St.Mary's Anglican Church, Portage la Prairie, (Manitoba) (SMACPLP, page 17, B-130.). She married **Felix Blandion**, son of **Antoine Blandion or Dion** and **Marie Desjarlais**, on 16 Nov 1879 Edmonton, (Alberta) (NWHBS, C-14936.) (HBS, Volume 1336; C-14950.).

Felix Blandion was born on 1 Mar 1859 Fish Lake (Ibid.). He was baptized on 12 Apr 1859 St.Albert, (Alberta) (NWHBS, C-14936.).

55. Lottie Whitford was born in 1865 (NWHBS, C-14938.). She married **Frank Greenwood** on 15 Mar 1884 Edmonton, (Alberta) (Ibid.).

56. Margaret Whitford was born on 29 Oct 1866 Victoria, North West Territory (NWHBS, C-14942.). She was baptized on 14 Nov 1866 (Denney.). She married **Alexander James McCorrister**, son of **James McCorrister** and **Sarah Atkinson,** on 22 Apr 1884 Edmonton, (Alberta) (NWHBS, C-14942.).

Alexander James McCorrister was born circa 1862 Minnesota (1870C-MB, page 342, #322.). He was baptized on 5 Jun 1864 St.Mary's Anglican Church, Portage la Prairie, (Manitoba) (SMACPLP, page 29, B-226.).

57. Catherine Whitford was born on 1 Jul 1870 (NWHBSI, page 85.). She married **Baptiste Larocque**, son of **Francois Larocque** and **Angelique Sayis**, before 1891 (ArchiviaNet, C-15010.). She died on 22 Mar 1944 Penticton, British Columbia, at age 73.

Baptiste Larocque was born in 1861 Winnipeg, (Manitoba) (NWHBS, C-14939.). He was born in Feb 1861 (Manitoba) (1911 Canada, District 47, page 6, family 55, line 12-20.).

58. Archibald Whitford was born on 16 Mar 1874 Buffalo Lake, (Alberta) (1901 Canada, District 202-v(4), page 36, family 370, line 20-23.) (ArchiviaNet, C-15009.). He married **Harriet Todd**, daughter of **Donald Todd** and **Susanne Durand or Dumont**, before 1897 (1901 Canada, District 202-v(4), page 36, family 370, line 20-23.).

Harriet Todd was born on 15 Feb 1876 Tail Creek, (Alberta) (Ibid.) (ArchiviaNet, C-15010.).

Children of **Archibald Whitford** and **Harriet Todd** were as follows:

    i.   Elizabeth Whitford was born on 25 Oct 1897 (1901 Canada, District 202-v(4), page 36, family 370, line 20-23.).

    ii.   James W. Whitford was born on 10 Mar 1899 (Ibid.).

59. Harriet Whitford was born on 19 Aug 1867 Victoria, (Alberta) (NWHBS, C-14942.). She married **Simon McGillivray**, son of **Edward McGillivray** and **Isabelle Fraser,** before 1890. She died in 1950 (Denney.).

Simon McGillivray was born in 1865 Lesser Slave Lake, (Alberta) (NWHBS, C-14940.). He died circa 1927.

60. Jacob Whitford was baptized on 22 May 1853 St.Peters, (Manitoba) (Denney.). He married **Rachel Kennedy**, daughter of **James Kennedy** and **Eliza Sinclair**, in 1873 St.Peters, Manitoba (ArchiviaNet.).

Rachel Kennedy was born in 1857 St.Peters, (Manitoba) (HBSI.) (ArchiviaNet.).

Children of **Jacob Whitford** and **Rachel Kennedy** were as follows:

    i.   Alice Margaret Whitford was born on 15 Feb 1878 South Branch, (Saskatchewan) (HBSI.) (ArchiviaNet.). She married John Peter Hourie, son of Thomas Hourie and Agnes Bird, before 1900 (Denney.).

         John Peter Hourie was born in Jun 1872 Qu'Appelle, (Saskatchewan) (ArchiviaNet.). He died on 26 Apr 1900 Prince Albert, (Saskatchewan), at age 27 (Ibid.).

    ii.   Agnes Matilda Whitford was born on 24 Jul 1879 South Branch, (Saskatchewan) (Ibid., C-15009.).

    iii.   Abraham Whitford was born on 1 Jan 1881 South Branch, (Saskatchewan) (HBSI.) (ArchiviaNet, C-15010.). He died on 3 Oct 1886 South Branch, (Saskatchewan), at age 5 (HBSI.) (ArchiviaNet, C-15010.).

    iv.   Sarah Catherine Whitford was born on 3 Oct 1883 South Branch, (Saskatchewan) (Ibid.). She died on 16 May 1884 South Branch, (Saskatchewan) (Ibid.).

    v.   George Whitford was born circa 1884.

    vi.   Walter Whitford was born on 25 May 1885 South Branch, (Saskatchewan) (Ibid.).

    vii.   James Abraham Whitford was born on 31 Oct 1888 (1901 Canada, microfilm, T-6553, Brancepeth, page 1, Family 3, line 18-21.).

    viii.   Pembridge Augustus Whitford was born on 22 Jul 1889 (Saskatchewan) (SK Vital Statistics, Birth Reg. #7952.).

    ix.   Cora Whitford was born on 26 Sep 1891 (Saskatchewan) (Ibid., Birth Reg. #8018.).

    x.   Blanche Whitford was born on 2 Mar 1892 (1901 Canada, microfilm, T-6553, Brancepeth, page 1, Family 3, line 18-21.).

      xi.   Hector Whitford was born on 9 Jul 1894 (Saskatchewan) (SK Vital Statistics, Birth Reg. #7273.).

     xii.   Clara Whitford was born on 19 Sep 1897 (Saskatchewan) (Ibid., Birth Reg. #9591.).

61. **Sarah Whitford** was baptized on 11 Jan 1856 St.Peters, (Manitoba) (Denney.). She married **John George Kennedy** before 1877.

62. **George Francis Whitford** was baptized on 15 May 1862 St.Peters, (Manitoba) (Denney.). He married **Isabel Johnston**, daughter of **Thomas James Johnston** and **Margaret Peebles,** before 1888.

Isabel Johnston was born on 3 Oct 1869 (1901 Canada, District 205-g, page 3, family 23, line 7-14.).

Children of **George Francis Whitford** and **Isabel Johnston** were as follows:

      i.   Sarah T. Whitford was born on 13 Oct 1888 (Ibid.).

     ii.   David W. Whitford was born on 18 Sep 1891 (Ibid.).

    iii.   Ann Bella Whitford was born on 21 Sep 1892 (Ibid.).

    iv.   John Pider Whitford was born on 3 Oct 1894 (Saskatchewan) (SK Vital Statistics, Birth Reg. #7282.).

     v.   Alford T. Whitford was born on 18 Oct 1896 (1901 Canada, District 205-g, page 3, family 23, line 7-14.).

    vi.   Wilford Whitford was born on 13 Feb 1899 (Ibid.).

63. **Jane Whitford** was born on 18 Nov 1845 (Manitoba) (Denney.). She was baptized on 4 Dec 1845 St.Andrews, (Manitoba) (Ibid.). She married **Joseph Alexander Turner**, son of **Philip Turner** and **Jane Chisholm Boland**, on 9 Jan 1862 St.Mary's Anglican Church, Portage la Prairie, (Manitoba) (SMACPLP, page 10, M-19.). She died on 15 Dec 1928 Fort Saskatchewan, Alberta, at age 83 (Denney.).

Joseph Alexander Turner was born on 5 Dec 1838 Moose Factory (Ibid.) (ArchiviaNet, C-15007.). He died on 14 Nov 1912 Fort Saskatchewan, Alberta, at age 73 (Denney.).

64. **Simon Peter Whitford** was born on 17 Feb 1848 St.Andrews, (Manitoba) (NWHBS, C-14942.) (1901 Canada, 202, j(3), page 1, family 5, line 18-26.). He married **Elizabeth Anderson**, daughter of **John Anderson** and **Christiana Whitford,** on 20 May 1873 Victoria, (Alberta) (NWHBS.).

Elizabeth Anderson was born on 2 Jun 1858 Portage la Prairie, (Manitoba) (Denney.). She was baptized on 6 Jun 1858 St.Mary's Anglican Church, Portage la Prairie, (Manitoba) (SMACPLP, page 6, B-42.).

Children of **Simon Peter Whitford** and **Elizabeth Anderson** were as follows:

      i.   Roderick Whitford was born on 27 Mar 1874 Victoria, (Alberta) (NWHBS, C-14942.) (ArchiviaNet, C-15010.). He married Isabella (--?--) before 1894 (1901 Canada, 202, j(3), page 1, family 3, line 9-13.).

         Isabella (--?--) was born on 1 Mar 1873 (Ibid.).

     ii.   Mary Ann Whitford was born on 3 Dec 1876 Buffalo Lake, (Alberta) (NWHBS, C-14942.) (1901 Canada, 202, j(3), page 1, family 5, line 18-26.) (ArchiviaNet, C-15010.).

    iii.   William Whitford was born on 14 Apr 1878 Victoria, (Alberta) (NWHBS, C-14942.) (ArchiviaNet, C-15010.). He married Lillian 'Lilly' Erasmus, daughter of Peter Erasmus and Marguerite 'Peggy' Stanley, before 1904 Pakan, (Alberta) (Denney.) (1906 Canada, District 20-10, page 3, family 34, line 28-30.). He died in Apr 1954 (Denney.).

         Lillian 'Lilly' Erasmus was born on 31 May 1884 Whitefish Lake, (Alberta) (HBSI.).

    iv.   Edwin James Whitford was born on 21 Nov 1880 Victoria, (Alberta) (NWHBS, C-14942.) (ArchiviaNet, C-15010.). He died in 1954 Lac la Biche, Alberta (Denney.).

     v.   John Charles Whitford was born on 14 Jul 1882 Pakan, (Alberta) (NWHBS, C-14942.) (1901 Canada, 202, j(3), page 1, family 5, line 18-26.) (ArchiviaNet, C-15010.). He died in May 1962 Lac la Biche, Alberta, at age 79 (Denney.).

    vi.   Ellen Whitford was born on 19 Jun 1885 Victoria, (Alberta) (ArchiviaNet, C-15010.). She died on 25 Feb 1889 Victoria, (Alberta), at age 3 (Ibid.).

    vii.   Gordon Arthur Whitford was born on 10 Feb 1887 Pakan, (Alberta) (1901 Canada, 202, j(3), page 1, family 5, line 18-26.). He married Ida Belle Anderson Pakan, Alberta (Denney.).

   viii.   Herbert Francis Whitford was born on 23 Jun 1890 Pakan, (Alberta) (1901 Canada, 202, j(3), page 1, family 5, line 18-26.). He married Isabella Cromarty, daughter of Magnus Cromarty and Ann Frances Henderson, Pakan, Alberta (Denney.). He died in 1929 (Ibid.). He was buried in 1929 Riverside Cemetery (Ibid.).

         Isabella Cromarty was born on 25 Mar 1894 (1906 Canada, District 20-10, page 4, family 45, line 25-32.) (1901 Canada, District 202, j(3), page 1, family 6, line 27-36.).

    ix.   Rosabelle Whitford was born on 19 Apr 1897 Pakan, (Alberta) (Ibid., 202, j(3), page 1, family 5, line 18-26.). She married Cleophas Thompson, son of Louis Thompson and Adeline Norn, Pakan, Alberta (Denney.).

         Cleophas Thompson was born on 30 Mar 1891 Pakan, (Alberta) (1901 Canada, District 202-j(3), page 1, family 7, line 37-45.).

65. **William Whitford** was born in Jul 1850 St.Andrews, (Manitoba) (MBS, C-14934.). He was baptized on 21 Jul 1850 St.Andrews, (Manitoba) (Denney.). He married **Charlotte Henderson**, daughter of **Charles Henderson** and **Mary Johnstone**, circa 1877 Victoria, (Alberta) (Ibid.).

Charlotte Henderson was born on 12 Mar 1859 St.Andrews, (Manitoba) (MBS, C-14928.). She was baptized on 3 Apr 1859 St.Andrews, (Manitoba) (Ibid.).

Children of **William Whitford** and **Charlotte Henderson** were as follows:

      i.   Charles Whitford was born on 9 Oct 1878 Victoria, (Alberta) (1901 Canada, Whitford Y(4), page 1, line 8-17, family 3.) (ArchiviaNet, C-15010.).

     ii.   Maria Jane Whitford was born on 20 Jun 1880 Victoria, (Alberta) (1901 Canada, Whitford Y(4), page 1, line 8-17, family 3.) (ArchiviaNet, C-15010.).

    iii.   Richard Whitford was born on 15 Aug 1882 Victoria, (Alberta) (1901 Canada, Whitford Y(4), page 1, line 8-17, family 3.) (ArchiviaNet, C-15010.).

    iv.   Edward Whitford was born on 7 Aug 1884 Victoria, (Alberta) (Ibid.). He died in Feb 1887 Victoria, (Alberta), at age 2 (Ibid.).

     v.   John Whitford was born on 21 Sep 1886 (1901 Canada, Whitford Y(4), page 1, line 8-17, family 3.).

vi. Clara Whitford was born on 23 Sep 1889 (Ibid.).

vii. Nellie Whitford was born on 22 Aug 1892 (Ibid.).

viii. George Whitford was born on 9 Sep 1894 (Ibid.).

ix. Frank Whitford was born on 6 Aug 1899 (Ibid.).

x. Lilian B. Whitford was born circa 1902 (1906 Canada, District 20-10, page 3-4, family 38, line 40, 1-9.).

xi. Mabel Whitford was born circa 1904 (Ibid.).

66. Samuel Whitford was born on 27 Feb 1856 Portage la Prairie, (Manitoba) (MBS, C-14934.). He married **Mary Jane Pruden**, daughter of **Patrick Pruden** and **Isabelle Bruneau**, on 21 Dec 1884 Lac la Biche, (Alberta) (LLBR1, M-7.). He died on 4 Jun 1933 Waskatenau, Alberta, at age 77.

Mary Jane Pruden was born on 16 Aug 1865 Lac la Biche, (Alberta) (Ibid., page 68, B-352.). She was baptized on 18 Aug 1865 Lac la Biche, (Alberta) (Ibid.). She died on 25 Nov 1923 Abilene, Alberta, at age 58.

Children of **Samuel Whitford** and **Mary Jane Pruden** were as follows:

i. Ellen Whitford was born on 25 Oct 1885 Lac la Biche, (Alberta). She married Peter Henderson, son of Charles Henderson and Mary Johnstone, on 17 Aug 1903 Bruderheim, (Alberta). She died on 10 Dec 1932 at age 47 (Rod Mac Quarrie, 29 May 2013.).

Peter Henderson was born on 6 Jun 1873 St.Andrews, Manitoba (HBSI.) (ArchiviaNet.).

ii. Mary Margaret Whitford was born on 1 Mar 1887 (Alberta) (1901 Canada, District 202-g(4), page 1, family 12, line 14-28.). She married Axel York. She died on 9 Sep 1943 at age 56 (Rod Mac Quarrie, 29 May 2013.).

Axel York was born Goteborg, Sweden. He died in 1960 Edmonton, Alberta.

iii. Annie Whitford was born on 1 May 1889 (Alberta) (1901 Canada, District 202-g(4), page 1, family 12, line 14-28.). She married Robert John "Jack" Hawke on 10 Dec 1910. She died on 28 Jan 1928 at age 38 (Rod Mac Quarrie, 29 May 2013.).

Robert John "Jack" Hawke was born on 22 May 1884 Mylor, Cornwall, England. He died on 1 Feb 1968 St.Paul, Alberta, at age 83.

iv. Elizabeth Whitford was born on 17 May 1891 (Alberta) (1901 Canada, District 202-g(4), page 1, family 12, line 14-28.). She married Jeremie Coulson on 21 Sep 1921 (Rod Mac Quarrie, 29 May 2013.). She died on 6 Sep 1924 at age 33 (Ibid.).

Jeremie Coulson married **Maude Lillian Whitford**, daughter of **Samuel Whitford** and **Mary Jane Pruden**, on 16 Feb 1927 (Ibid.).

v. Percy Whitford was born on 15 Feb 1894 (Alberta) (1901 Canada, District 202-g(4), page 1, family 12, line 14-28.). He married Lily Mae Williams on 27 Nov 1923 (Rod Mac Quarrie, 29 May 2013.). He died in Jun 1949 at age 55.

vi. Homer Scott Whitford was born on 5 Dec 1897 (Alberta) (1901 Canada, District 202-g(4), page 1, family 12, line 14-28.). He married Laura Burkholder after 1921.

vii. Maude Lillian Whitford was born on 17 Apr 1900 Saddle Lake, (Alberta) (Ibid.). She married Jeremie Coulson on 16 Feb 1927 (Rod Mac Quarrie, 29 May 2013.). She died on 21 Jan 1976 at age 75 (Ibid.).

Jeremie Coulson married **Elizabeth Whitford**, daughter of **Samuel Whitford** and **Mary Jane Pruden**, on 21 Sep 1921 (Ibid.).

viii. Peter Joseph Clifford Whitford was born on 10 Nov 1905 (1906 Canada, District 20-08, page 21, line 10.).

ix. Rena Edith Edna Whitford was born on 18 Jul 1907 (1911 Canada, District 64, page 24, line 1.). She married Frederick Burrell.

67. Annabella Whitford was baptized on 25 Sep 1859 St.Mary's Anglican Church, Portage la Prairie, (Manitoba) (SMACPLP, page 8, B-61.). She married **Edward Anderson**, son of **John Anderson** and **Christiana Whitford**, circa 1882 (Denney.).

Edward Anderson was baptized on 7 Jun 1860 St.Mary's Anglican Church, Portage la Prairie, (Manitoba) (SMACPLP, page 10, B-76.).

68. Caroline Whitford was baptized on 12 Jan 1862 St.Mary's Anglican Church, Portage la Prairie, (Manitoba) (SMACPLP, page 16, B-123.). She married **John Alexander Mitchell** on 22 May 1883 Fort Victoria (Denney.). She died in 1933 Pakan, Alberta (Ibid.).

John Alexander Mitchell was born in 1860 Portage la Prairie, (Manitoba) (Ibid.). He married **Marie Anne Piche**, daughter of **Unknown Piche**, before 1883. He died in 1947 (Ibid.). He was buried in 1947 Pakan, Alberta (Ibid.).

69. Charles Thomas Whitford was baptized on 20 Jan 1856 St.Mary's Anglican Church, Portage la Prairie, (Manitoba) (SMACPLP, page 1, B-4.). He and **Mary Jane Sanderson** met before 1876. He married **Catherine Paquin**, daughter of **Joseph Paquin** and **Marie Lapointe**, on 6 Feb 1879 St.Catherines, Prince Albert District, (Saskatchewan) (Denney.).

Mary Jane Sanderson was baptized on 24 Oct 1848 St.Andrews, (Manitoba) (Ibid.). She and **William Anderson** met circa 1878. She married **John Hourie** in Jan 1884 Prince Albert, (Saskatchewan) (NWHBS, C-14941.).

Children of **Charles Thomas Whitford** and **Mary Jane Sanderson** were:

i. Abraham Whitford or Hourie was born on 24 Apr 1876 Victoria, (Alberta) (ArchiviaNet, C-15009.). He married Hermeline Linklater, daughter of Archibald Linklater and Eleonore Morris, before 1901 (Saskatchewan) (1901 Canada, #205, Y-1, page 2, family 11, line 6-9.).

Hermeline Linklater was born on 18 Jan 1883 Ile-a-la-Crosse, (Saskatchewan) (ArchiviaNet, C-15010.).

Catherine Paquin was born in 1856 St.Andrews, (Manitoba) (MBS, C-14934.). She was baptized on 8 Jun 1856 St.Andrews, (Manitoba) (Denney.).

70. Frederick Whitford was born on 22 Jun 1876 Prince Albert, (Saskatchewan) (ArchiviaNet, C-15010.). He married **Catherine Anderson**, daughter of **John Michael Anderson** and **Hannah Harriet Halcrow**, circa 1900 (Ibid.).

Catherine Anderson was born on 2 Sep 1884 Prince Albert, (Saskatchewan).

Children of **Frederick Whitford** and **Catherine Anderson** were as follows:

i. Ray W. Whitford was born on 12 Nov 1900 (1901 Canada, District 202-j(3), page 3, family 23, line 1-3.).

ii. Alan C. Whitford was born circa 1903 (1906 Canada, District 20-10, page 1, family 8, line 32-35.).

iii. Sarah J. Whitford was born circa 1905 (Ibid.).

71. Margaret Whitford was born on 25 May 1860 (1901 Canada, District 202-j(3), page 2, family 18, line 23-31.). She was baptized on 10 Jun 1860 St.Mary's Anglican Church, Portage la Prairie, (Manitoba) (SMACPLP, page 10, B-77.). She married **Henry Anderson**, son of **Thomas Anderson** and **Elizabeth Desmarais,** before 1887 (1901 Canada, District 202-j(3), page 2, family 18, line 23-31.).

Henry Anderson was baptized on 27 Sep 1857 St.Mary's Anglican Church, Portage la Prairie, (Manitoba) (SMACPLP, page 5, B-36.).

72. Elizabeth Ann Whitford was born on 13 Aug 1865 Fort MacLeod, (Alberta) (NWHBS, C-14940.). She was baptized on 5 Sep 1865 Fort Victoria, (Alberta) (Denney.). She married **Joseph Munroe**, son of **John William 'Piscon' Munroe** and **Isabelle Lussier,** circa Feb 1884 Fort MacLeod, (Alberta) (NWHBS, C-14940.).

Joseph Munroe was born in 1862 Lac Ste.Anne, (Alberta) (Ibid.). He was baptized on 21 Aug 1862 Fort des Prairie (Denney.).

73. Flora Whitford was born on 1 Sep 1860 Portage la Prairie, (Manitoba) (NWHBS, C-14936.). She was baptized on 5 Sep 1860 St.Mary's Anglican Church, Portage la Prairie, (Manitoba) (SMACPLP, page 10, B-80.). She married **William Charles Anderson**, son of **James Francis Anderson** and **Fanny Gill,** in 1877 Prince Albert, (Saskatchewan) (Denney.).

William Charles Anderson was born circa 1854 Portage la Prairie, (Manitoba) (1870C-MB, page 334, #120.). He died on 26 Dec 1926 (Denney.). He was buried in Dec 1926 Logan Cemetery, Tofield, Alberta (Ibid.). Question: *Charles Denney says he rec'd scrip in MB.*

74. Colin Alexander Whitford was born on 11 Jan 1862 Portage la Prairie, (Manitoba) (NWHBS, C-14942.). He was baptized on 26 Jan 1862 St.Mary's Anglican Church, Portage la Prairie, (Manitoba) (SMACPLP, B-127.). He and **Angelique Lemire** met before 1884.

Angelique Lemire was born in 1861 St.Albert, (Alberta) (HBSI.). She and **Alexander James Folster** met before 1880 (HBS, Volume 1334; C-14946.). She married **Adam Ballendine**, son of **John "A" Ballendine** and **Mary Jebb (Cree),** circa Oct 1885 Battleford, (Saskatchewan) (Ibid.).

Children of **Colin Alexander Whitford** and **Angelique Lemire** were:

i. Julienne Lemire was born circa Apr 1884 Battleford, (Saskatchewan) (HBSI.) (ArchiviaNet.). She died in 1885 Battleford, (Saskatchewan) (HBSI.) (ArchiviaNet.).

75. John Edmund Whitford was born on 13 Mar 1863 Portage la Prairie, (Manitoba) (Ibid., C-15010.). He was baptized on 5 Apr 1863 St.Mary's Anglican Church, Portage la Prairie, (Manitoba) (SMACPLP, page 21, B-167.). He married **Nancy "Annie" Anderson**, daughter of **Thomas Anderson** and **Fanny Pocha,** on 11 May 1889 Great Falls, Cascade County, Montana (CaCM Cascade County, Montana; Marriage Record Licenses and Certificates; 1865-1950; familysearch.org, Hereinafter cited as CaCM.). He died in 1945 Alberta.

Nancy "Annie" Anderson was baptized on 23 Jun 1872 St.Mary's Anglican Church, Portage la Prairie, Manitoba (SMACPLP, page 49, B-389.). She married **Norbert Gray**, son of **Michel Gray** and **Caroline Campion,** on 24 Nov 1886 St.Peter's Mission, Montana Territory (SPMT , page 47, #285.). She died on 16 Sep 1939 Elko, British Columbia, at age 67 (BC Vital Statistics.).

Children of **John Edmund Whitford** and **Nancy "Annie" Anderson** were as follows:

i. Robert Whitford was born circa 1891 Montana (1900C MT Twelfth Census of the United States: 1900; Montana, District 196, page 1A, family 11, line 25.).

ii. Mary Whitford was born circa 1892 Montana (Ibid.).

iii. Nancy Whitford was born circa 1893 Montana (Ibid.).

iv. Harriet Whitford was born on 22 May 1895 Big Timber, Montana (Ibid.) (BC Vital Statistics.). She married Alexander Thomas Brown (Ibid.). She died on 24 Sep 1983 Esquimalt, British Columbia, at age 88 (Ibid.).

v. Florence Whitford was born circa 1896 Montana (1900 MT, District 196, page 1A, family 11, line 25.).

vi. Samuel Whitford was born circa 1897 Montana (Ibid.).

vii. Pearl Whitford was born circa 1899 Montana (Ibid.).

viii. William Whitford was born circa 1902 (1916 Canada, District 11, page 9, family 107.).

ix. John Whitford was born circa 1905 (Ibid.).

x. Charles Richard Whitford was born on 8 Jan 1910 Montana (BC Vital Statistics.). He died on 16 Sep 1939 Elko, British Columbia, at age 29 (Ibid.).

xi. Albert Whitford was born circa 1913 (1916 Canada, District 11, page 9, family 107.).

xii. Hanlin Whitford was born circa 1915 (Ibid.).

xiii. Evelyn Whitford was born circa 1916 (1921 Census of Canada from the National Archives of Canada (Transcription by ancestry.com), Ottawa, Canada, District 12-16, page 15.).

xiv. Arthur Whitford was born circa 1919 (Ibid.).

76. Henry Charles Whitford was born on 27 Dec 1864 Portage la Prairie, (Manitoba) (NWHBS, C-14942.). He was baptized on 22 Jan 1865 St.Mary's Anglican Church, Portage la Prairie, (Manitoba) (SMACPLP, page 30, B-237.). He married **Catherine Collin**, daughter of **Joseph Collin** and **Sophie Loyer,** on 19 Dec 1884 Calgary, (Alberta) (ArchiviaNet, C-15010.). He died on 18 Jul 1951 Blaine County, Montana, at age 86 (MT Death Montana State Genealogical Society Death Index.).

Catherine Collin was born in 1864 St.Albert, (Alberta) (ArchiviaNet, C-15010.). She married **Alexander Dawell** before 1883 (Ibid.).

Children of **Henry Charles Whitford** and **Catherine Collin** were as follows:

i. George Charles Whitford was born on 4 Nov 1885 Blind Man River, (Alberta) (Ibid.). He married Margaret Pepin, daughter of Henri Pepin and Mary (--?--), on 4 Dec 1914 Toole County, Montana (1917 RB Tentative Roll of Rocky Boy Indians, 30 May 1917, Copied by Verne Dusenbery, 15 Apr 1953, Rocky Boy Agency, Montana, #626.) (ToCM Toole County, Montana; Marriage Record Licenses and Certificates; 1865-1950; familysearch.org, Hereinafter cited as ToCM.). He married Margaret Pepin, daughter of Henri Pepin and Mary (--?--), before 1922 (1930C MT 1930 Montana, Fifteenth Census of the United States, National Archives of the United States, Washington, D.C., District 4, page 1B, family 17, line 71.). He died on 8 Nov 1946 Montana at age 61 (MT Death.).

Margaret Pepin was born on 3 May 1897 Butte, Silver Bow County, Montana (1917 RB, #626.) (MT Death.) (Social Security Death Index, . Hereinafter cited as SSDI.). She died on 17 Jan 1987 Cascade County, Montana, at age 89 (MT Death.) (SSDI.).

ii. Lillie Whitford was born circa 1896 Whitford Lake, (Alberta) (1917 RB, #624.). She married (--?--) Favel before 1933. She married Peter Lewis, son of William Lewis, on 30 Oct 1933 Browning, Glacier, Montana (GCM Glacier County, Montana; Marriage Record Licenses and Certificates; 1865-1950; familysearch.org, Hereinafter cited as GCM.).

iii. Caroline Whitford was born on 15 May 1899 near Birch Creek, Montana (1917 RB, #365.) (SSDI.). She married Malcolm Mitchell (Yellowbird), son of Elzear Nepissing and Marie Josephine Bruneau, on 4 Jan 1915 Havre, Hill County, Montana (1917 RB, #364.) (HCM Hill County, Montana; Marriage Record Licenses and Certificates; 1865-1950; familysearch.org, Hereinafter cited as HCM.). She died on 25 Dec 1973 Hill County, Montana, at age 74 (MT Death.) (SSDI.).

Malcolm Mitchell (Yellowbird) was born on 6 Jan 1889 Blackfeet Reservation, Montana (1917 RB, #364.) (SSDI.). He married **Rose Denny** before 1911. He died on 21 Jan 1976 Hill County, Montana, at age 87 (MT Death.) (SSDI.).

iv. Rebecca Whitford was born on 12 Sep 1905 Tofield, (Alberta) (GCM.). She married George S. Salois, son of Salomon 'Sam' Salois and Caroline Dumais, on 25 Aug 1921 Browning, Glacier, Montana (Ibid.).

George S. Salois was born on 16 Dec 1896 Dupuyer, Montana (SSDI.) (GCM.). He died on 29 Jun 1977 Cascade County, Montana, at age 80 (SSDI.) (MT Death.).

v. William Whitford was born circa 1908 Viking, Alberta (1917 RB, #623.). He married Justine Flammond, daughter of St.Pierre Flamand and Eliza Lafond, on 31 Mar 1933 Browning, Glacier County, Montana (GCM.). He married Theda Rose Hagerty, daughter of Hiram Woodward and Rosa Paul, on 7 Mar 1936 Cut Bank, Glacier, Montana (Ibid.).

Justine Flammond was born on 20 Jun 1915 Dupuyer, Ponderas County, Montana (1937-1987-LS Basic Roll Basic Membership Roll of the Landless Indians of Montana; 1937 Census Taken by Dr. Henry Roe Cloud; Edited c1987 to include official correspondence regarding 1937 membership; ** in Present Roll Number column indicates 1940s information added., #421.). She married **George Peterson**, son of **Peter Peterson** and **Sarah Mcassey,** on 12 Jun 1935 Cut Bank, Glacier County, Montana (1987LS 1987-92 Little Shell Band of Chippewa Roll.) (GCM.).

Theda Rose Hagerty was born circa 1918 (1923-BF 1923 Census of Pikuni (Blackfoot), National Archives of the United States, Washington D.C., Census No. 1159-1164.) (GCM.).

77. Isabella Ann Whitford was born on 16 Apr 1867 Portage la Prairie, (Manitoba) (NWHBS, C-14942.). She was baptized on 12 May 1867 St.Mary's Anglican Church, Portage la Prairie, (Manitoba) (SMACPLP, page 36, B-286.). She married **Alexander Scott Kruger** circa 1884.

78. Jeremiah Whitford was born on 18 Sep 1868 Victoria, (Alberta) (NWHBS, C-14942.). He married **Isabelle Desjarlais**, daughter of **Louis Desjarlais** and **Angelique Mistaskanik,** before 1899 (1900 MT, District 134, page 1B, family 4, line 31.).

Isabelle Desjarlais was born on 2 May 1874 (L1, page 113, B-18.). She was baptized on 8 May 1874 Lebret, (Saskatchewan) (Ibid.). She married **Milo Collins** before 1892 (1910C MT Thirteenth Census of the United States: 1910; Montana, National Archives of the United States, Washington D.C., District 223, page 12A, family 1.). She married **Walter Scott Whitford**, son of **Charles Whitford** and **Nancy "Ann" Anderson,** before 1903. She died in 1938 Reedpoint, Montana (BIA-LS Bureau of Indian Affairs, Little Shell Enrollment Papers.). She was buried in 1938 Mountain View Cemetery, Columbus, Stillwater County, Montana. Question: *Isabelle Desjarlais, wife of Walter Scott Whitford, is the probable daughter of Louis Desjarlais and Angelqiue Mistaskanik.*

Children of **Jeremiah Whitford** and **Isabelle Desjarlais** were as follows:

i. Charles Nathan Whitford was born on 18 Sep 1899 Whitford, (Alberta) (1910C MT, District 223, page 12A, family 1.). He died on 8 May 1983 Yellowstone County, Montana, at age 83.

ii. Jerry Whitford was born circa 1902 (MT Death.). He died on 3 Oct 1909 Montana (Ibid.).

79. Thomas Whitford was born on 20 May 1870 Victoria, (Alberta) (NWHBS, C-14942.). He married **Marguerite Sauve**, daughter of **Baptiste Sauve** and **Helene Cardinal,** before 1896 (1901 Canada, #202, u(2), page 1, family 4, line 18-21.).

Marguerite Sauve was born on 1 Sep 1880 Fort Saskatchewan, (Saskatchewan) (ArchiviaNet, C-15010.).

Children of **Thomas Whitford** and **Marguerite Sauve** were as follows:

i. Jeremiah Whitford was born on 10 Nov 1896 (1901 Canada, #202, u(2), page 1, family 4, line 18-21.).

ii. Herbert James Whitford was born on 28 Jan 1900 (Ibid.).

80. Walter Scott Whitford was born on 4 Feb 1882 Battleford, (Saskatchewan) (ArchiviaNet, C-15010.). He married **Isabelle Desjarlais**, daughter of **Louis Desjarlais** and **Angelique Mistaskanik,** before 1903. He died on 23 Jul 1968 Columbus, Stillwater, Montana, at age 86.

Isabelle Desjarlais was born on 2 May 1874 (L1, page 113, B-18.). She was baptized on 8 May 1874 Lebret, (Saskatchewan) (Ibid.). She married **Milo Collins** before 1892 (1910C MT, District 223, page 12A, family 1.). She married **Jeremiah Whitford**, son of **Charles Whitford** and **Nancy "Ann" Anderson,** before 1899 (1900 MT, District 134, page 1B, family 4, line 31.). She died in 1938 Reedpoint, Montana (BIA-LS.). She was buried in 1938 Mountain View Cemetery, Columbus, Stillwater County, Montana. Question: *Isabelle Desjarlais, wife of Walter Scott Whitford, is the probable daughter of Louis Desjarlais and Angelqiue Mistaskanik.*

Children of **Walter Scott Whitford** and **Isabelle Desjarlais** were as follows:

i. Jesse J. Whitford was born circa 1903 (1910C MT, District 223, page 12A, family 1.).

ii. Frank Scott Whitford was born on 23 Dec 1905 Reed Point, Stillwater County, Montana (Ibid.). He married Evelyn Thompson before 1936 (1987-92LS.). He died on 23 Jul 1968 Ephrata, Grant County, Washington, at age 62.

Evelyn Thompson was born before 1916.

iii. Pheobe Whitford was born on 28 Dec 1908 Reed Point, Montana (1996-00LS 1996-2000 Little Shell Band of Chippewa Roll.) (Birth Certificate.). She married Sheldon Lewis before 1932 (1996-00LS.).

Sheldon Lewis was born on 17 Sep 1899 (Ibid.).

    iv.   Ruby Whitford was born circa 1911 Reed Point, Montana (JCM Jefferson County Courthouse, Montana; Marriage Record Licenses and Certificates; 1865-1950, familysearch.org, Hereinafter cited as JCM.). She married Mayleon Berry on 26 Feb 1934 Boulder, Jefferson County, Montana (Ibid.).

        Mayleon Berry was born circa 1899 Plummer, Idaho (Ibid.).

    v.   Edward G. Whitford was born on 25 Oct 1912 Reed Point, Stillwater, Montana (CCM Carbon County, Montana; Marriage Record Licenses and Certificates; 1865-1950; familysearch.org, Hereinafter cited as CCM.) (MT Death.). He married Pricilla Cotter, daughter of Louis Cotter and Marie V. Lefebre, on 30 Aug 1947 Carbon County, Montana (CCM.). He died on 2 May 1995 Reed Point, Stillwater, Montana, at age 82 (MT Death.).

        Pricilla Cotter was born in 1911 Somerset, Wisconsin (CCM.). She died in 1995.

    vi.   Nancy Whitford was born circa 1914 Montana (1920C-MT 1920 Federal Census Montana, National Archives of the United States, Washington D.C., District 126, page 4A, family 89, line 50.).

81. Archibald Whitford was born circa 1868 Portage la Prairie, (Manitoba) (1870C-MB, page 346, #472.). He married **Mary Pocha** before 1890 (SK Vital Statistics, Birth Reg. #7966.). He married **Nellie Spence**, daughter of **Andrew Spence** and **Nancy Whitford**, before 1894.

Children of **Archibald Whitford** and **Mary Pocha** were:

    i.   Mary Whitford was born on 21 Jan 1890 (Saskatchewan) (Ibid., Birth Reg. #7966.).

Nellie Spence was born on 18 Jan 1878 Victoria, (Alberta) (ArchiviaNet, C-15010.).

Children of **Archibald Whitford** and **Nellie Spence** were as follows:

    i.   Lena Whitford was born on 16 Oct 1894 (1901 Canada, #202-y(4), page 2, family 19, line 19-22.).

    ii.   Ida Whitford was born on 16 Nov 1896 (Ibid.).

82. Edwin Whitford was born on 24 May 1877 Prince Albert, (Saskatchewan) (ArchiviaNet, C-15010.). He married **Mary Margaret (--?--)** before 1905.

Mary Margaret (--?--) was born circa 1889 (1921 Canada, District 5-15, page 11.).

Children of **Edwin Whitford** and **Mary Margaret (--?--)** were as follows:

    i.   Adalbert Whitford was born circa 1905 (Ibid.).

    ii.   Alberson Whitford was born on 19 May 1907 (Denney.). He died on 16 Oct 1977 at age 70 (Ibid.).

    iii.   Charles Clifford Whitford was born circa 1909 (1921 Canada, District 5-15, page 11.).

    iv.   John Tomlin Whitford was born circa 1911 (Ibid.).

    v.   Wilfred Alexander Whitford was born circa 1913 (Ibid.).

    vi.   Roy Oliver Whitford was born circa 1915 (Ibid.).

    vii.   Elmer Ray Whitford was born circa 1917 (Ibid.).

    viii.   Viola Alice Louise Whitford was born circa 1919 (Ibid.). She died on 29 Dec 1969 Edmonton, Alberta (Denney.).

    ix.   Clarence 'Sidney' Whitford was born in 1921.

    x.   Elsie Whitford was born in 1927.

83. Marie Whitford was born on 6 Nov 1852 (SFXI-Kipling, B-44.). She was baptized on 29 Nov 1852 St.Francois Xavier, (Manitoba) (Ibid.) (SFXI 1851-1868, B-44.). She married **Jean Baptiste Desjarlais**, son of **Antoine Desjarlais** and **Louise Richard**, on 29 Jun 1874 St.Francois Xavier, Manitoba (SFXI-Kipling, M-14.).

Jean Baptiste Desjarlais was born on 26 Aug 1853 (Ibid., B-131.) (SFXI 1851-1868, B-131.). He was baptized on 3 Oct 1853 St.Francois Xavier, (Manitoba) (SFXI-Kipling, B-131.) (SFXI 1851-1868, B-131.).

84. James Whitford was born on 14 Sep 1854 Pembina, Pembina County, Dakota Territory (AP, page 113, B-312.). He was baptized on 14 Sep 1854 Assumption, Pembina, Pembina County, Dakota Territory (Ibid.). He married **Sarah Gladu**, daughter of **Antoine Gladu** and **Catherine Fagnant**, on 13 Jun 1878 St.Francois Xavier, Manitoba (SFXI-Kipling, M-11.).

Sarah Gladu was born on 23 Jun 1860 Pembina, Pembina County, Dakota Territory (AP, page 233, B-161.). She was baptized on 23 Jun 1860 Assumption, Pembina, Pembina County, Dakota Territory (Ibid.). She married **Louis Joseph Eugene Lafontaine**, son of **Antoine Lafontaine** and **Philomene Jeannotte or Jannot**, on 30 Oct 1890 Brenda, Manitoba (MB Vital Statistics, Mar. Reg. #1890,001291.).

Children of **James Whitford** and **Sarah Gladu** were as follows:

    i.   Marie Philomene Whitford was born on 11 May 1879 St.Eustache, Manitoba (Rosemary Helga (Morrissette) Rozyk Research, 19 Sep 2009.). She was baptized on 28 May 1879 St.Eustache, Manitoba (Ibid.).

    ii.   James Whiteford was born on 10 Jan 1881 Oak Lake (HBSI.) (ArchiviaNet, C-15010.). He married Marie Celina Langer, daughter of Edouard Langer and Marie Page, on 14 Oct 1907 St.Ignace, Willow Bunch, Saskatchewan (SIWB, M-3, page 115.).

        Marie Celina Langer was born on 11 May 1885 (L2, page 117, B-72.). She was baptized on 21 Jun 1885 Lebret, (Saskatchewan) (Ibid.). She was buried on 3 Jul 1915 St.Ignace, Willow Bunch, Saskatchewan (SIWB, page 141.).

    iii.   Elzear Whitford was born on 11 Jan 1883 Oak Lake (ArchiviaNet.).

    iv.   Joseph Whitford was born on 8 Jan 1884 Oak Lake (Ibid., C-15010.). He died in 1891 (Ibid.).

85. Maxime Whitford was born on 16 Nov 1856 Portage la Prairie, (Manitoba) (MBS, C-14934.) (SFXI-Kipling, B-149.). He was baptized on 22 Nov 1856 St.Francois Xavier, (Manitoba) (Ibid.). He married **Adelaide Campbell**, daughter of **Louis Campbell** and **Marie Thomas**, on 8 Jun 1894 Dunvegan, (Alberta) (ArchiviaNet, C-15009.).

Adelaide Campbell was born on 15 Jan 1871 Grande Prairie, Athabasca, (Alberta) (Ibid.).

Children of **Maxime Whitford** and **Adelaide Campbell** were as follows:

    i.   Alexander James Whitford was born on 30 Oct 1894 Dunvegan, (Alberta) (Ibid.).

    ii.   Caroline Whitford was born on 1 Jul 1896 Sturgeon Lake, Athabasca, (Alberta) (Ibid.).

    iii.   Mary Jane Whitford was born on 18 Oct 1898 Dunvegan, (Alberta) (1916 Canada, District 29, page 36, family 447.) (ArchiviaNet, C-15009.).

iv. Alice Whitford was born circa 1905 (1916 Canada, District 29, page 36, family 447.).

v. Emma Whitford was born circa 1907 (Ibid.).

vi. Flora Whitford was born circa 1909 (Ibid.).

86. Louis Napoleon Whitford was born on 8 Sep 1861 St.Francois Xavier, (Manitoba) (SFXI-Kipling, B-96.). He was baptized on 8 Sep 1861 St.Francois Xavier, (Manitoba) (Ibid.). He married **Marie Rose Lingan**, daughter of **Jean Baptiste Lingan** and **Angelique St.Germain**, on 17 Jul 1883 St.Claude Mission, St.John, Rolette County, North Daktoa (Dominique Ritchot Research,, 26 Jan 2006.) (St. Claude Mission, St. John, North Dakota, Baptisms, Marriages, Burials 1882-1888, 2006, Dominique Ritchot, page 13, M-11.). He died on 29 May 1923 Deer Lodge County, Montana, at age 61 (MT Death.).

Marie Rose Lingan was born on 17 Jan 1867 St.Francois Xavier, (Manitoba) (SFXI-Kipling, B-3.). She was baptized on 19 Jan 1867 St.Francois Xavier, (Manitoba) (Ibid.). She died after 1934 Dodson, Phillips County, Montana.

Children of **Louis Napoleon Whitford** and **Marie Rose Lingan** were as follows:

i. Marie Rose Whiteford was born on 10 Oct 1884 Moose Mountain (St.Claude BMD, Dominique Ritchot, page 39, B-167.) (ArchiviaNet, C-15010.). She was baptized on 19 Oct 1884 St.Claude, St.John, Rolette County, North Dakota (St.Claude BMD, Dominique Ritchot, page 39, B-167.). She married Pierre Tobie McGillis, son of Angus McGillis and Isabelle Fagnant, on 28 Oct 1901 St.Ignace, Willow Bunch, (Saskatchewan) (SIWB, M-5, page 114.). She died on 11 Jan 1915 at age 30 (Rod Mac Quarrie, 27 Mar 2013.).

> **Pierre Tobie McGillis** was born on 15 Feb 1868 St.Francois Xavier, (Manitoba) (SFXI-Kipling, B-13.). He was baptized on 16 Feb 1868 St.Francois Xavier, (Manitoba) (Ibid.). He died in 1951 St.Victor, Saskatchewan (Denney.) (Bonnie Lingle-Harrington Research, e-mail 31 Mar 1999.). He was buried in 1951 St.Victor, Saskatchewan (Ibid.).

ii. Elzear Whitford was baptized on 15 May 1886 St.Claude Mission, St.John, Rolette County, North Dakota (St.Claude BMD, Dominique Ritchot, B-257, page 54.). He married Liza (--?--) before 1911 (1911 Canada, District 12, page 2, family 21, line 8-9.).

> **Liza (--?--)** was born in Mar 1891 (Ibid.).

iii. Alfred Whitford was born on 1 May 1887 (1901 Canada, #204, y(2), page 1, family 9, line 32-42.). He married Marie Eliza Simpson, daughter of John Simpson and Catherine Robillard, circa 1915 (Rod Mac Quarrie, 27 Mar 2013.).

> **Marie Eliza Simpson** was born on 9 May 1883 Fort Qu'Appelle, (Saskatchewan) (HBSI.) (L2, page 64, B-32.) (ArchiviaNet.). She was baptized on 15 May 1883 Lebret, (Saskatchewan) (L2, page 64, B-32.). She married **Jean Marie McGillis**, son of **Angus McGillis** and **Isabelle Fagnant,** before 1901. She died on 8 Jul 1918 at age 35 (Rod Mac Quarrie, 27 Mar 2013.).

iv. Daniel Whitford was born on 20 May 1889 (1901 Canada, #204, y(2), page 1, family 9, line 32-42.).

v. Justine Whitford was born on 23 Jan 1891 (Ibid.). She married Amable Gaudry, son of Andre Gaudry and Marie Beauchamp, circa 1906.

> **Amable Gaudry** was born on 18 Feb 1884 Willow Bunch, (Saskatchewan) (SIWB, B-3, page 6.). He was baptized on 20 Feb 1884 St.Ignace, Willow Bunch, (Saskatchewan) (Ibid.).

vi. Ambrose Whitford was born on 26 Jan 1894 Glasgow, Valley County, Montana (1937-1987-LS Basic Roll, #547.). He and Rose Parenteau obtained a marriage license on 30 Dec 1922 Phillips County, Montana (PhCM Phillips County Courthouse, Montana; Marriage Record Licenses and Certificates; 1865-1950, familysearch.org, Hereinafter cited as PhCM.). He married Rose Parenteau, daughter of Leon Parenteau and Ursule Trottier, on 30 Dec 1922 Corpus Christi Catholic Church, Malta, Valley County, Montana (Ibid.). He died on 10 May 1945 Montana at age 51 (MT Death.).

> **Rose Parenteau** was born on 12 Aug 1898 Sweet Grass, Toole County, Montana (SPMT , page 27, #105.) (1937-1987-LS Basic Roll, #549.). She was baptized on 29 Aug 1898 St.Peter's Mission, Montana (SPMT , page 27, #105.). She died on 12 Mar 1979 Chinook, Blaine County, Montana, at age 80 (MT Death.).

vii. Frederic Whitford was born on 22 Jun 1895 (1901 Canada, #204, y(2), page 1, family 9, line 32-42.). He married Marie Josephine Martin, daughter of Gilbert Martin and Marie Clemence Simpson, before 1916.

> **Marie Josephine Martin** was born on 5 Feb 1899 Long Lake, (Saskatchewan) (SK Vital Statistics, Birth Reg. #1051.).

viii. Eliza Whiteford was born on 12 Jan 1898 (1901 Canada, #204, y(2), page 1, family 9, line 32-42.). She married Joseph M. Simpson before 1916. She died before 1934.

> **Joseph M. Simpson** was born before 1896. He died after 1937.

ix. Louis Ovila Whiteford was born on 31 Mar 1901 Willow Bunch, (Saskatchewan) (SIWB, B-6, page 38.). He was baptized on 1 Apr 1901 St.Ignace, Willow Bunch, (Saskatchewan) (Ibid.).

x. Louis Pierre "Peter" Whiteford was born on 19 Sep 1902 (Ibid., B-11, page 43.). He was baptized on 21 Apr 1903 St.Ignace, Willow Bunch, (Saskatchewan) (Ibid.). He married Irene Monroe, daughter of Carl Leroy Monroe and Mary Rose Swan, on 29 Jun 1927 Phillips County, Montana (PhCM.). He died on 15 Nov 1986 Dilon, Beaverhead County, Montana, at age 84 (MT Death.) (SSDI.).

> **Irene Monroe** was born on 2 Nov 1910 (Ibid.). She died on 15 Aug 1998 Dilon, Beaverhead County, Montana, at age 87 (Ibid.) (MT Death.).

xi. Joseph Maxime Whiteford was born on 23 Nov 1903 (SIWB, B-5, page 47.). He was baptized on 15 Apr 1905 St.Ignace, Willow Bunch, Saskatchewan (Ibid.).

xii. Jean Napoleon "John Paul" Whiteford was born on 14 Jun 1909 Willow Bunch, Saskatchewan (Ibid., B-14, page 58.). He was baptized on 15 Jun 1909 St.Ignace, Willow Bunch, Saskatchewan (Ibid.). He married Elsie Bishop, daughter of Harry W. Bishop and Madeleine Emily, on 10 Jul 1939 Malta, Phillips County, Montana (PhCM.). He married Elizabeth Falcon, daughter of Alfred Alexandre Falcon and Emma Emily, circa 18 Sep 1950 Our Lady of Lourdes, Great Falls, Cascade County, Montana (SIWB, B-14, page 58.). He died on 6 Feb 1970 Cascade County, Montana, at age 60 (MT Death.).

Elsie Bishop was born circa 1921 Montana (PhCM.). She died on 2 Nov 1940 Phillips County, Montana (MT Death.).

Elizabeth Falcon was born on 2 Aug 1914 Dodson, Phillips County, Montana (*HDN Havre Daily News*, Havre, Montana, Thursday, 3 Mar 1988, page 2. Hereinafter cited as HDN.). She married **Joseph Parenteau**, son of **Gabriel Parenteau** and **Isabelle Amiotte**, before 1931. She married **Gerald Brown** in Nov 1972 (Ibid.). She died on 2 Mar 1988 Great Falls, Cascade County, Montana, at age 73 (SSDI.) (MT Death.) (*HDN*, Thursday, 3 Mar 1988, page 2.).

87. **Athalie Rose Whitford** was born on 23 Mar 1866 St.Francois Xavier, (Manitoba) (SFXI-Kipling, B-20.). She was baptized on 25 Mar 1866 St.Francois Xavier, (Manitoba) (Ibid.). She married **Patrice Trottier**, son of **Jean Baptiste Trottier** and **Rose McGillis**, before 1894. She died in 1933.

Patrice Trottier was born on 1 Nov 1868 Lake Pelchie, (Saskatchewan) (Ibid., B-75.). He was baptized on 22 Aug 1869 St.Francois Xavier, (Manitoba) (Ibid.) (INB, page 178.). He died after 1936 Val Marie, Saskatchewan (BIA-LS.).

88. **Jean Marie Whitford** was born on 3 Oct 1874 Saskatoon, (Saskatchewan) (ArchiviaNet, C-15010.). He married **Marguerite McGillis**, daughter of **Modeste McGillis** and **Isabelle Poitras**, on 29 Dec 1903 St.Ignace, Willow Bunch, (Saskatchewan) (SIWB, M-2, page 114.). He died in Dec 1948 North Battleford, Saskatchewan, at age 74 (Lesa (Trotchie) Zimmerman Research, 19 Jun 2001.).

Marguerite McGillis was born on 23 Jan 1883 near, Willow Bunch, (Saskatchewan) (HBSI.) (BSAP Records of the Parish of Batoche, St.Antoine de Pudoue Roman Catholic Church: Register for Baptisms, Marriages, Deaths, Volume One, 1881-1909., page 14, B-11. Hereinafter cited as BSAP.) (ArchiviaNet.). She was baptized on 13 May 1883 Batoche, (Saskatchewan) (BSAP, page 14, B-11.).

Children of **Jean Marie Whitford** and **Marguerite McGillis** were as follows:

    i.   Marie Flora Whiteford was born on 7 Oct 1904 Willow Bunch, (Saskatchewan) (SIWB, B-17, page 46.). She was baptized on 9 Oct 1904 St.Ignace, Willow Bunch, (Saskatchewan) (Ibid.).

    ii.   Jean Jacques Whiteford was born on 24 Mar 1906 Willow Bunch, Saskatchewan (Ibid., B-7, page 49.) (SK Vital Statistics, Birth Reg. #6599.). He was baptized on 26 Mar 1906 St.Ignace, Willow Bunch, Saskatchewan (SIWB, B-7, page 49.).

    iii.   Joseph Marie Whiteford was born on 23 Nov 1907 Willow Bunch, Saskatchewan (Ibid., B-18, page 53.). He was baptized on 1 Dec 1907 St.Ignace, Willow Bunch, Saskatchewan (Ibid.).

    iv.   Marie Pruscielle Whiteford was born on 7 Mar 1909 Willow Bunch, Saskatchewan (Ibid., B-3, page 57.). She was baptized on 8 Mar 1909 St.Ignace, Willow Bunch, Saskatchewan (Ibid.). She married George Pritchard, son of Salomon 'Sam' Pritchard and Rosalie Trottier, on 20 Jan 1926 St.Ignace, Willow Bunch, Saskatchewan (Ibid., B-3, page 57 (note).).

        George Pritchard was born in 1901.

    v.   Marie Jeanne Whitford was born on 26 Sep 1910 Willow Bunch, Saskatchewan (Lesa Zimmerman, 19 Jun 2001.). She married Edward Trottier, son of Andre Trottier and Rosalie Trottier, on 20 Jan 1926 Red Pheasant, Saskatchewan (Ibid.). She died on 28 Jun 1972 Saskatoon, Saskatchewan, at age 61 (Ibid.).

        Edward Trottier was born on 20 Apr 1906 Swift Current, Saskatchewan (Ibid.). He died on 10 Oct 1961 North Battleford, Saskatchewan, at age 55 (Ibid.).

    vi.   Emma Whitford was born circa 1914 (Ibid.).

    vii.   Andre Whitford was born circa 1916 (Ibid.).

    viii.   Louis Whitford was born on 27 Oct 1918 (Ibid.).

    ix.   Joseph Napoleon Whitford was born on 3 Mar 1922 (Ibid.).

89. **Francois Whitford** was born on 15 Mar 1860 (SFXI-Kipling, B-31.). He was baptized on 13 May 1860 St.Francois Xavier, (Manitoba) (Ibid.). He married **Marguerite Desjarlais**, daughter of **Joseph Friday** and **Marguerite Hamelin**, in 1877 St.Laurent, (Saskatchewan) (HBS, Volume 1337, C-14951.).

Marguerite Desjarlais was born in 1858 near Battle River, Lac la Biche, (Alberta) (Ibid.). She married **Pierre Boudreau**, son of **Francois Xavier Boudreau dit Graveline** and **Emelie Aubuchon**, in 1880 Frog Lake, (Saskatchewan) (Ibid.).

Children of **Francois Whitford** and **Marguerite Desjarlais** were as follows:

    i.   Elise Whitford was born on 29 Apr 1879 Battleford, (Saskatchewan) (SV, B-7, page 3.). She was baptized on 6 May 1879 St.Vital, Battleford, (Saskatchewan) (Ibid.).

    ii.   William Whitford was born in 1880 Onion Lake, (Saskatchewan) (ArchiviaNet, C-15010.). He was baptized on 2 Feb 1881 Lac la Biche, (Alberta) (Ibid.).

90. **Elie Joseph Whitford** was born on 5 Feb 1862 (SFXI-Kipling, B-45.). He was baptized on 25 May 1862 St.Francois Xavier, (Manitoba) (Ibid.). He married **Mary Blackbird (Indian)** before 1895.

Children of **Elie Joseph Whitford** and **Mary Blackbird (Indian)** were as follows:

    i.   Marie Delima Whiteford was born on 5 Aug 1895 (SIWB, B-11, page 29.). She was baptized on 16 Aug 1896 St.Ignace, Willow Bunch, (Saskatchewan) (Ibid.).

    ii.   Elizabeth Whitford was born on 20 Apr 1898 (Saskatchewan) (SK Vital Statistics, Birth Reg. #1591.).

91. **Genevieve Whitford** was born on 1 May 1864 (SFXI-Kipling, B-15.). She was baptized on 10 May 1864 St.Francois Xavier, (Manitoba) (Ibid.). She married **John Cabe** before 1882 (ArchiviaNet, C-15003.).

92. **Madeleine Whitford** was born on 26 Jun 1872 Qu'Appelle, (Saskatchewan) (L1, page 57, B-31.). She was baptized on 30 Jun 1872 Lebret, (Saskatchewan) (Ibid.). She married **Johnny Andowes** before 1896 (SV, B-30.).

Descendants of Alexander Wilkie

Generation One

1. Alexander Wilkie was born Scotland. He married **Me-ha-ka-may-ki-ji-kok** (--?--) before 1803.

Me-ha-ka-may-ki-ji-kok (--?--) was born before 1783.

Children of **Alexander Wilkie** and **Me-ha-ka-may-ki-ji-kok** (--?--) were as follows:

    2   i.   Jean Baptiste Wilkie, b. circa 1803 Pembina County; m. Amable Azure; d. 5 Nov 1884 Olga, Cavalier County, North Dakota; bur. 6 Nov 1884 Olga, Cavalier County, North Dakota.

    3   ii.   Elizabeth Wilkie, b. circa 1809 Pembina County, Minnesota Territory; m. Martin Jerome.

    4   iii.   Marie Wilkie, b. 1810 St.Laurent, (Manitoba); m. Jean Baptiste Marcellais; m. John Ferguson or Farquarson; m. Toussaint Faille.

Generation Two

2. Jean Baptiste Wilkie was born circa 1803 Pembina County (1850Ci-MN *Minnesota Territorial Census, 1850*, Harpole, Patricia C. and Mary D. Nagle, ed., (St.Paul, Minnesota: Minnesota Historical Society, 1972), page 27, Dwelling 94; Family 94.). He married **Amable Azure**, daughter of **Pierre Azure** and **Marguerite Assinibwan,** before 1824. He died on 5 Nov 1884 Olga, Cavalier County, North Dakota (Olga Our Lady of the Sacred Heart, Olga, North Dakota 1882-1900, page 56, S-21. Hereinafter cited as Olga.). He was buried on 6 Nov 1884 Olga, Cavalier County, North Dakota (Ibid.).

Amable Azure was born in 1808 Pembina County (1850Ci-MN, page 27, Dwelling 94; Family 94.). She was buried on 10 Dec 1888 Olga, Cavalier County, North Dakota (Olga, page 155, S-20.).

Children of **Jean Baptiste Wilkie** and **Amable Azure** were as follows:

    5   i.   Jean Baptiste Wilkie, b. Aug 1824 North Dakota; m. Marie Laframboise; m. Isabelle Patenaude; m. Marie Masson.

    6   ii.   Judith Wilkie, b. circa 1825; m. Pierre Berger.

    7   iii.   Augustin Wilkie, b. circa 1829 Pembina County; m. Marie Wissakickam Paquin.

    8   iv.   Alexander Wilkie, b. Sep 1831 Dakota Territory; m. Louise Gariepy.

    9   v.   Catherine Wilkie, b. 24 Nov 1834 St.Boniface, (Manitoba); m. Michel Gladu; d. 17 Nov 1884 Leroy, Pembina County, Dakota Territory; bur. 19 Nov 1884 St.Joseph, Leroy, Pembina County, Dakota Territory.

    10   vi.   Madeleine Wilkie, b. circa 1837 Pembina, Pembina County, Dakota Territory; m. Gabriel Dumont; d. circa Oct 1885 Fort Benton, Choteau County, Montana.

    11   vii.   Elizabeth Wilkie, b. circa 1839 Pembina County, Minnesota Territory; d. 1912 Lewistown, Fergus County, Montana.

    12   viii.   Cecilia Wilkie, b. circa 1843 Pembina; m. Joseph Gariepy; d. before 17 Aug 1890.

    13   ix.   Agathe Wilkie, b. Nov 1844; m. Patrice Joseph Fleury; d. 20 Sep 1941 St.Laurent, Saskatchewan.

    14   x.   Marie Marguerite Wilkie, b. circa 1845 Pembina; m. Henri Bousquet; m. Joseph Lagimoniere.

    15   xi.   Antoine Wilkie, b. 3 Sep 1848 Pembina, Pembina County, Minnesota Territory; m. Esther Gladu; d. 5 Oct 1923 Rolette County, North Dakota.

         xii.   Mary Wilkie was born circa 1849 Pembina County (1850Ci-MN, page 27, Dwelling 94; Family 94.).

         xiii.   David Wilkie was born on 7 Sep 1853 Pembina, Pembina County, Dakota Territory (AP Records of the Assumption Roman Catholic Church, Pembina, North Dakota: Baptisms, Marriages, Sepultures, 1848-1896; compiled by Reverend Father J. M. Belleau, 2 October 1944, page 96, B-98. Hereinafter cited as AP.). He was baptized on 9 Sep 1853 Assumption, Pembina, Pembina County, Dakota Territory (Ibid.). He died on 15 Jan 1854 Pembina, Pembina County, Dakota Territory (Ibid., page 101, S-38.). He was buried on 16 Jan 1854 Assumption, Pembina, Pembina County, North Dakota (Ibid.).

3. Elizabeth Wilkie was born circa 1809 Pembina County, Minnesota Territory. She married **Martin Jerome**, son of **Martin Jerome** and **Louise Indian Amerindienne,** circa 1831.

Martin Jerome was born circa 1800 Red River, (Manitoba) (1850Ci-MN, page 24, Dwelling 62, Family 62.) (1828C RRS HBCA E5/2 1828 Census of the Red River Settlement, HBCA E5/2, Hudson's Bay Company Archives, Provincial Archives, 200 Vaughan Street, Winnipeg, MB R3C 1T5, Canada., page 9.). He married **Angelique Letendre**, daughter of **Jean Baptiste "Okimawaskawikinam"** **Letendre** and **Josephte Indian,** on 6 Jun 1825 St.Boniface, (Manitoba) (SB 1825-1834 St.Boniface Roman Catholic Registre des Baptemes, Mariages & Sepultures, 1825-1834, page 2, M-14. Hereinafter cited as SB 1825-1834.). He died on 29 Jul 1879 Leroy, Pembina County, Dakota Territory (SJL-1 Register of Baptisms, Marriages, and Burials, St.Joseph, Leroy, North Dakota, Diocese of Saint Paul, Minnesota, 1870-1888, Book 1, page 94, S-22. Hereinafter cited as SJL-1.). He was buried on 31 Jul 1879 St.Joseph, Leroy, Pembina County, Dakota Territory (Ibid.).

4. Marie Wilkie was born in 1810 St.Laurent, (Manitoba) (MBS, C-14927.). She married **Jean Baptiste Marcellais**, son of **Jean Baptiste Marcellais** and **Angelique Assiniboine,** before 1825. She married according to the custom of the country **John Ferguson or Farquarson** circa 1841 (Rod Mac Quarrie, 14 Sep 2006.). She married **Toussaint Faille**, son of **Joseph Faille** and **Francoise Brossard,** before 1846.

Jean Baptiste Marcellais was born circa 1796 Ruperts Land (1831C RRS HBCA E5/5 1831 Census of the Red River Settlement, HBCA E5/5, Hudson's Bay Company Archives, Provincial Archives, 200 Vaughan Street, Winnipeg, MB R3C 1T5, Canada., page 10.). Question: *Son of Jean Baptiste Marcellais and Angelique Assiniboine?*

John Ferguson or Farquarson was born circa 1809 Indian Territory (HBCA-B Hudson's Bay Company Archives - biographical sketches, Hudson's Bay Company Archives; Winnipeg, Manitoba.). He married **Monique Hamelin**, daughter of **Jacques Hamelin** and **Angelique Tourangeau,** before 1838 (SB-Rozyk St. Boniface Roman Catholic Church, Manitoba, Canada, Baptisms, Marriages and Burials 1860-1875 Extractions, Compiled by Rosemary Rozyk, page 71, S-70.). He married according to the custom of the country **Josephte Morissette**, daughter of **Unconnected Morissette,** before 1840 (Rod Mac Quarrie, 14 Sep 2006.). He married according to the custom of the country **Sophie Montour**, daughter of **Robert Bonhomme Montour** and **Josette Spence,** circa 1849 (Ibid.). He died on 26 Dec 1866 (SB-Rozyk, page 71, S-70.). He was buried on 28 Dec 1866 St.Boniface, (Manitoba) (Ibid.).

Toussaint Faille was born circa 1791 Montreal, Montreal, Quebec (MBS, C-14927.) (1870C-MB, #1587, page 52.). He was born on 15 Sep 1795 St-Constant, Quebec (PRDH online index, http://www.genealogic.umontreal.ca, No. 666819.). He was baptized on 15 Sep 1795 St-Constant, Quebec (Ibid.). He was born circa 1797 Quebec (1835C RRS HBCA E5/8 1835 Census of the Red River Settlement, HBCA E5/8, Hudson's Bay Company Archives, Provincial Archives, 200 Vaughan Street, Winnipeg, MB R3C 1T5, Canada., page 8.). He married **Angelique Contree**, daughter of **Jean Baptiste Contre** and **Louise Montagnaise,** before 1827. He died on 9 May 1875 Baie St.Paul, Manitoba, at age 79 (MBS, C-14927.). He was buried on 11 May 1875 Ste.Agathe, Manitoba (Ibid.) (Ste.Agathe Roman Catholic Cemetery; Cemetery Transcription #485; E. Bjornson and K. Stokes F. Cox, Rm. 420 - 167 Lombard Ave., Winnipeg, Manitoba, Canada R3B 0T6: Manitoba Genealogical Society, Inc., June 1988, page 4.).

Generation Three

5.   Jean Baptiste Wilkie was born in Aug 1824 North Dakota (1900C-ND, 241-241.). He was born circa 1826 Pembina County (1850Ci-MN, page 30, Dwelling 123, Family 123.). He married **Marie Laframboise**, daughter of **Francois Laframboise** and **Betsy Maskegonne**, on 24 Jun 1850 Assumption, Pembina, Pembina County, Minnesota Territory (AP, page 39, M-16.). He married **Isabelle Patenaude**, daughter of **Michel Patenaude** and **Josephte Bourassa**, on 7 Sep 1857 Assumption, Pembina, Pembina County, Dakota Territory (Ibid., page 178-179, M-57.). He married **Marie Masson**, daughter of **Francois Masson** and **Therese Charron dit Ducharme**, on 4 Jan 1876 Assumption, Pembina, Pembina County, Dakota Territory (Ibid., M-1.).

**   Marie Laframboise** was born in Jun 1831 North Dakota (1900C-ND, 241-241.). She was born circa 1833 (AP, page 146, S-52.). She died circa 20 Mar 1856 on the plains near Pembina, Dakota Territory (Ibid.). She was buried on 1 Apr 1856 Assumption, Pembina, Pembina County, Minnesota Territory (Ibid.).

Children of **Jean Baptiste Wilkie** and **Marie Laframboise** were as follows:

      i.   Jean Baptiste Wilkie was born on 19 Oct 1851 (Ibid., page 59-60, B-56.). He was baptized on 13 Nov 1851 Assumption, Pembina, Pembina County, Dakota Territory (Ibid.).

      ii.   Victoire Wilkie was born on 29 Jul 1853 (Ibid., page 94, B-90.). She was baptized on 4 Sep 1853 Assumption, Pembina, Pembina County, Dakota Territory (Ibid.). She died on 15 May 1856 Pembina County, Dakota Territory, at age 2 (Ibid., page 148, S-59.). She was buried on 17 May 1856 Assumption, Pembina, Pembina County, Dakota Territory (Ibid.).

      iii.   Anonyme Wilkie was born circa 13 Apr 1855 Pembina County, Dakota Territory (Ibid., page 127, S-56.). He was buried on 21 Apr 1855 Assumption, Pembina, Pembina County, Dakota Territory (Ibid.).

16   iv.   Onesime Wilkie, b. 20 Mar 1856; m. Marie Agathe Venne; d. 16 May 1936 Rolette County, North Dakota.

Isabelle Patenaude was born in 1840. She was baptized on 28 Mar 1841 Rocky Mountain House, Saskatchewan District (RTR Rundle, Reverend R. T., Journal of Baptisms & Marriages in Saskatchewan District,1840 - 1848, B-17. Hereinafter cited as RTR.). She died on 19 Mar 1875 Pembina County, Dakota Territory (SJL-1, page 60, S-11.). She was buried on 16 Oct 1875 St.Joseph, Leroy, Pembina County, Dakota Territory (Ibid.).

Children of **Jean Baptiste Wilkie** and **Isabelle Patenaude** were as follows:

17   i.   Albert Wilkie, b. 4 May 1859; m. Marie Josephine Laverdure; d. 17 Jun 1941 Belcourt, Rolette County, North Dakota.

18   ii.   Eliza Wilkie, b. circa 1861 Dakota Territory; m. Jean Baptiste Ducept; d. before Jun 1893.

19   iii.   Philomene Wilkie, b. 1863 St.Joseph, Pembina County, Dakota Territory; m. Napoleon Gregoire Monet dit Belhumeur; d. 1926.

20   iv.   Gabriel "Kabi-ush" Wilkie, b. 22 Jul 1866 North Dakota; m. Marie Charette; d. 30 Sep 1939 Rolette County, North Dakota.

21   v.   Mathilde Wilkie, b. circa 1868; m. William Laverdure; d. 3 Aug 1929 Rolette County, North Dakota.

      vi.   Jerome Wilkie was born in May 1870 Saint Joseph, Pembina County, Dakota Territory (1870 Dakota Territory Census, National Archives of the United States, Washington D.C., family 26, line 35-40, 1-2.).

22   vii.   Marie Celina Wilkie, b. 6 Mar 1873 Lebret, (Saskatchewan); m. Pierre Ducept; d. 27 Apr 1948 Belcourt, Rolette County, North Dakota.

Marie Masson was born in 1831 Minnesota. She was born circa 1833 Pembina (1850Ci-MN, page 19, Dwelling 10, Family 10.). She married **Paul Laronde**, son of **Paul Laronde,** before 1850. She married **Paul Laronde**, son of **Paul Laronde,** before 1870 (MBS, C-14929.).

6.   Judith Wilkie was born circa 1813 Pembina (1850Ci-MN, page 24, Dwelling 59, Family 59.). She was born circa 1825. She married **Pierre Berger**, son of **Jacques Berger** and **Cecile Dumont,** before 1841.

**   Pierre Berger** was born circa 1816 Red River, (Manitoba) (Ibid.). He died on 12 Apr 1907. Question: *1850 Census: Narcisse Berger age 20 with Pierre's family.*

7.   Augustin Wilkie was born circa 1829 Pembina County (1850Ci-MN, page 27, Dwelling 94; Family 94.). He was baptized on 15 Nov 1829 St.Boniface, (Manitoba) (SB 1825-1834, page 34, B-589.). He married **Marie Wissakickam Paquin**, daughter of **Jean Baptiste Paquin** and **Gevevieve Laterregrasse**, on 14 Jun 1852 Assumption, Pembina, Pembina County, Dakota Territory (AP-Reg Assumption Parish Register, Pembina, North Dakota, page 90-91, M-32. Hereinafter cited as Assumption Register.).

Question: *Married 9 Sep 1852 Leroy, ND?*

**   Marie Wissakickam Paquin** was born circa 1832 Red River, (Manitoba) (1850Ci-MN, page 22, Dwelling 39, Family 39.). She was born circa 1833 (Olga, page 8, S-3.). She died on 2 Jul 1882 (Ibid., page 7, S-3.). She was buried on 4 Jul 1882 Olga, Cavalier County, North Dakota (Ibid.). Question: *Is Marie the daughter of Jean Baptiste Paquin and Genevieve Laterregrasse?*

Children of **Augustin Wilkie** and **Marie Wissakickam Paquin** were as follows:

23   i.   Augustin Wilkie, b. 1853 Lac Qu'Appelle, (Saskatchewan); m. Rose Octavie Herman; d. 2 Aug 1938 Rolette County, North Dakota.

24   ii.   Jean Baptiste Wilkie, b. 4 Mar 1855 Pembina, Pembina County, Dakota Territory; m. Sarah Gourneau; d. 2 Mar 1920 Belcourt, Rolette County, North Dakota; bur. 4 Mar 1920 Belcourt, Rolette County, North Dakota.

iii. Marie Wilkie was baptized on 11 Aug 1856 Assumption, Pembina, Pembina County, Dakota Territory (AP, page 155, B-333.).

iv. Agathe Wilkie was born in Jul 1857 (Ibid., page 174, B-514.). She was baptized on 31 Aug 1857 Assumption, Pembina, Pembina County, Dakota Territory (Ibid.).

v. Angelique Wilkie was born on 8 Dec 1858 Pembina, Pembina County, Dakota Territory (Ibid., page 202, B-609.). She was baptized on 9 Dec 1858 Assumption, Pembina, Pembina County, Dakota Territory (Ibid.). She was born in 1861 (1936-TMC 1936 Tribal Roll, Turtle Mountain Indian Reservation, Office of Indian Affairs, received 28 Jan 1938, National Archives of the United States, Washington D.C., page 101.). She married Joseph Gourneau, son of Gaspard Louis Gourneau and Genevieve Allard, circa 1888 (Ibid.).

Joseph Gourneau was born on 17 Jan 1851 Pembina, Pembina County, Dakota Territory (AP, page 51, B-8.). He was baptized on 18 Jan 1851 Assumption, Pembina, Pembina County, Dakota Territory (Ibid.). He married **Virginie Chunuwachi** before 1880. He died on 29 Jan 1938 Rolette County, North Dakota, at age 87.

vi. Alexandre Wilkie was born in 1860 (NWHBSI Index 1885 Scrip Applications, North-West Halfbreeds residing outside Manitoba on 15 July 1870, RG15-20, page 88.). He died on 21 Jul 1873 Leroy, Pembina County, Dakota Territory (SJL-1, page 37, S-8.). He was buried on 22 Jul 1873 St.Joseph, Leroy, Pembina County, Dakota Territory (Ibid.).

vii. Augustin Wilkie was born on 22 Apr 1862 Pembina, Pembina County, Dakota Territory (AP, page 253, B-15.). He was baptized on 22 Apr 1862 Assumption, Pembina, Pembina County, Dakota Territory (Ibid.).

viii. Jeremie Wilkie was born circa 1865 Dakota Territory (1870 DT, family 27, line 3-11.).

ix. Justine Wilkie was born circa 1867 (SJL-1, page 112, S-66.). She died on 2 Sep 1881 (Ibid.). She was buried on 4 Sep 1881 St.Joseph, Leroy, Pembina County, Dakota Territory (Ibid.).

25 x. Madeleine Wilkie, b. circa 1869 Dakota Territory; m. James Decouteau.

26 xi. Joseph Wilkie, b. 15 Sep 1870; m. Alphonsine "Jennie" Bruce; d. 6 Jun 1961 Rolette County, North Dakota.

xii. Agnes Wilkie was born on 27 Jan 1874 Leroy, Pembina County, Dakota Territory (Ibid., page 43, B-4.). She was baptized on 28 Jan 1874 St.Joseph, Leroy, Pembina County, Dakota Territory (Ibid.). She died on 28 Feb 1880 Leroy, Pembina County, Dakota Territory, at age 6 (Ibid., page 99, S-39.). She was buried on 29 Feb 1880 St.Joseph, Leroy, Pembina County, Dakota Territory (Ibid.).

xiii. Josephine Wilkie was born on 23 Jul 1876 (L1, page 200, B-43.). She was baptized on 7 Jan 1877 Lebret, (Saskatchewan) (Ibid.). She died on 24 Feb 1880 Leroy, Pembina County, Dakota Territory, at age 3 (SJL-1, page 98, S-37.). She was buried on 25 Feb 1880 St.Joseph, Leroy, Pembina County, Dakota Territory (Ibid.).

xiv. Justine Wilkie was born circa 1877 Dakota Territory (1885-TMC, #418-422.).

8. **Alexander Wilkie** was born in Sep 1831 Dakota Territory (1850Ci-MN, page 27, Dwelling 94; Family 94.) (1900C-ND, House 74, page 278A.). He married **Louise Gariepy**, daughter of **Francois Gariepy** and **Louise Gladu**, on 14 Jun 1852 Assumption, Pembina, Pembina County, Dakota Territory (Assumption Register, page 90, M-31.).

Louise Gariepy was born in Apr 1829 Dakota Territory (1900C-ND, House 74, page 278A.). She was born circa 1836. She was born circa 1839 Pembina County.

Children of **Alexander Wilkie** and **Louise Gariepy** were as follows:

i. Alexandre Wilkie was born on 8 May 1853 Pembina County, Dakota Territory (AP, page 89, B-76.). He was baptized on 8 May 1853 Assumption, Pembina, Pembina County, Dakota Territory (Ibid.). He was buried on 30 Jan 1855 Assumption, Pembina, Pembina County, Dakota Territory (Ibid., page 123, S-41.).

27 ii. Marie Josephine Wilkie, b. 1 Sep 1854 Pembina County, Dakota Territory; m. Octave Lafontaine; d. 19 Mar 1937 Rolla, Rolette County, North Dakota; bur. 23 Mar 1937 St.Ann, Belcourt, Rolette County, North Dakota.

iii. Joseph Ephrem Wilkie was born on 14 Sep 1856 (Ibid., page 159, B-345.). He was baptized on 19 Nov 1856 Assumption, Pembina, Pembina County, Dakota Territory (Ibid.). He was buried on 23 May 1874 Lebret, (Saskatchewan) (L1, page 135, S-_.).

28 iv. Julienne Wilkie, b. 24 Feb 1859 Pembina, Pembina County, Dakota Territory; m. Bernard Lafontaine; m. Joseph Wells; d. 14 Jun 1885 Batoche, (Saskatchewan); bur. 16 Jun 1885 Batoche, (Saskatchewan).

v. Baptiste Jerome Wilkie was born on 17 Jul 1861 (AP, page 245, B-221.). He was baptized on 2 Sep 1861 Assumption, Pembina, Pembina County, Dakota Territory (Ibid.). He died on 16 Jul 1869 at age 7 (SJL-1, page 4, S-6.). He was buried on 14 Dec 1870 St.Joseph, Leroy, Dakota Territory (Ibid.).

vi. Louise Wilkie was born circa 1865. She married John Thomas Welsh, son of Edouard Wills and Isabelle McGillis, on 14 Mar 1883 (St.Peter's Mission), Judith Basin, Montana Territory (SPMT , page 40, #241.) (MeaCM Meagher County, Montana; Marriage Record Licenses and Certificates; 1865-1950; familysearch.org: District 86, page 2B, family 47, line 82. Hereinafter cited as MeaCCM.).

John Thomas Welsh was born in 1834.

vii. Marie Wilkie was born circa 1872 (1886-TMC 1886 Census of Half Breed Chippewas of Turtle Mountain, Dakota Territory, National Archives of the United States, Washington D.C., #939.).

viii. Marguerite Wilkie was born on 5 Oct 1875 (L1, page 177, B-64.). She was baptized on 31 Jan 1876 Lebret, (Saskatchewan) (Ibid.).

9. **Catherine Wilkie** was born on 24 Nov 1834 St.Boniface, (Manitoba) (SB 1825-1834, page 156, B-895.). She was baptized on 25 Nov 1834 St.Boniface, (Manitoba) (Ibid.). She married **Michel Gladu**, son of **Charles Gladu** and **Marguerite Ross**, on 12 Jan 1852 Assumption, Pembina, Pembina County, Dakota Territory (AP, page 67, M-1.). She died on 17 Nov 1884 Leroy, Pembina County, Dakota Territory, at age 49 (SJL-1, page 138, S-145.). She was buried on 19 Nov 1884 St.Joseph, Leroy, Pembina County, Dakota Territory (Ibid.).

Michel Gladu was born circa 1822 (SJL-D, page 10.). He was born on 10 May 1830 St.Francois Xavier, (Manitoba) (MBS, C-14928.). He married **Camille Ritchot**, daughter of **Joseph Ritchot** and **Marguerite Martel**, on 22 Jul 1888 St.Joseph, Leroy, Pembina County,

Dakota Territory (SJL-1, page 168, M-2.). He was buried on 15 Jul 1900 St.Joseph, Leroy, Pembina County, North Dakota (SJL-D, page 10.).

10. **Madeleine Wilkie** was born circa 1837 Pembina, Pembina County, Dakota Territory (1850Ci-MN, page 27, Dwelling 94; Family 94.). She married **Gabriel Dumont**, son of **Isidore Dumont** and **Louise Laframboise**, on 7 Sep 1857 Assumption, Pembina, Pembina County, Dakota Territory (AP, page 179, M-58.). She died circa Oct 1885 Fort Benton, Choteau County, Montana (Denney.).

Gabriel Dumont was born in Dec 1837 St.Boniface, (Manitoba) (CWLR, page 251.) (*DCB-V13 Dictionary of Canadian Biography - Volume Thirteen*;Toronto, Ontario: University of Toronto Press, 2000).). He died on 19 May 1906 Batoche, (Saskatchewan), at age 68 (CWLR, page 251.) (*DCB-V13.*) (BSAP Records of the Parish of Batoche, St.Antoine de Pudoue Roman Catholic Church: Register for Baptisms, Marriages, Deaths, Volume One, 1881-1909., page 239, S-7. Hereinafter cited as BSAP.) (Saskatchewan Vital Statistics online, http://vsgs.health.gov.sk.ca, Death Reg. #541.). He was buried on 21 May 1906 Batoche, (Saskatchewan) (BSAP, page 239, S-7.).

11. **Elizabeth Wilkie** was born in Aug 1836 (1900C Fergus Co, MT Twelfth Census of the United States: 1900; Montana; Fergus County.). She was born circa 1839 Pembina County, Minnesota Territory (1850Ci-MN, page 27, Dwelling 94; Family 94.). She married **Antoine Fleury**, son of **Louis Fleury** and **Josephte Belly**, on 14 Sep 1857 Assumption, Pembina, Pembina County, Dakota Territory (AP, page 179-180, M-59.). She died in 1912 Lewistown, Fergus County, Montana (1936-LS Henry Roe Cloud Roll 1936-1937, Pembina Band of Chippewa Indians Who Were Under the Leadership of Chief Thomas Little Shell, J. H. Dussome, Zortman, Montana and Vice-President: George SinClaire, Chinook, Montana, #27.).

Antoine Fleury was born in Nov 1829 (1900 MT, Fergus Co.). He died on 11 Jul 1908 Lewistown, Fergus County, Montana, at age 78 (1936-LS, #27.) (MT Death, 1-0086.).

12. **Cecilia Wilkie** was born circa 1843 Pembina (1850Ci-MN, page 27, Dwelling 94; Family 94.) (NWHBSI, page 88.). She married **Joseph Gariepy**, son of **Francois Gariepy** and **Helene Poitras**, before 1862. She died before 17 Aug 1890 (Olga, page 183, S-30.).

Joseph Gariepy was born on 22 Jan 1842 St.Francois Xavier, (Manitoba) (SFX: 1834-1850, B-392.). He was baptized on 22 Jan 1842 St.Francois Xavier, (Manitoba) (Ibid.). He was buried on 8 May 1889 Olga, Cavalier County, North Dakota (Olga, page 164, S-8.).

13. **Agathe Wilkie** was born on 14 Oct 1841 St.Norbert, (Manitoba) (Terry Larocque Research, 17 May 1994.). She was born in Nov 1844 (MBS, C-14928.). She married **Patrice Joseph Fleury**, son of **Louis Fleury** and **Josephte Belly**, on 14 Dec 1862 Assumption, Pembina, Pembina County, Dakota Territory (AP, page 265, M-_.). She died on 20 Sep 1941 St.Laurent, Saskatchewan, at age 96 (Terry Larocque, 17 May 1994.).

Patrice Joseph Fleury was born on 14 Oct 1848 St.Francois Xavier, (Manitoba) (MBS, C-14928.). He died on 18 Sep 1943 St.Laurent, Saskatchewan, at age 94 (Denney.).

14. **Marie Marguerite Wilkie** was born circa 1845 Pembina (1850Ci-MN, page 27, Dwelling 94; Family 94.). She was born circa 1846 North West Territory (MBS, C-14925.). She married **Henri Bousquet**, son of **Louis Bousquet** and **Elizabeth Fisher**, on 3 Sep 1866 Leroy, Pembina County, North Dakota. She married **Joseph Lagimoniere**, son of **Joseph Lagimoniere** and **Josephte Lussier**, on 21 Sep 1880 St.Boniface, Manitoba (RMSB *Repertoire des Mariages de Saint-Boniface (Manitoba) 1825-1983* compiled by Julien Hamelin S.C., (240, avenue Daly; Ottawa, Ontario K1N 6G2: Le Centre de Genealogie S. C., Publication #67, 1985).).

Henri Bousquet was born circa 1845 Red River, (Manitoba) (1870C-MB, page 72, #2228.). He died on 30 Jun 1873 Lake Qu'Appelle, (Saskatchewan) (MBS, C-14925.) (L1, page 96, S-13.). He was buried on 1 Jul 1873 Lebret, (Saskatchewan) (Ibid.).

Joseph Lagimoniere was born on 20 Jan 1849 St.Boniface, (Manitoba) (MBS, C-14929.). He married **Marie Blondeau**, daughter of **Louis Blondeau** and **Josephte Desfonds**, on 28 Jan 1868 St.Boniface, (Manitoba) (SB-Rozyk, page 105, M-3.).

15. **Antoine Wilkie** was born on 3 Sep 1848 Pembina, Pembina County, Minnesota Territory (AP, page 6, B-7.). He was baptized on 4 Sep 1848 Assumption, Pembina, Pembina County, Minnesota Territory (Ibid.). He married **Esther Gladu**, daughter of **Charles Gladu** and **Genevieve Parisien**, on 28 Feb 1876 Lebret, (Saskatchewan) (L1, page 180-181, M-13.). He died on 5 Oct 1923 Rolette County, North Dakota, at age 75 (ND Death Index.).

Esther Gladu was born on 15 Dec 1858 Pembina, Pembina County, Dakota Territory (AP, page 202, B-610.). She was baptized on 16 Dec 1858 Assumption, Pembina, Pembina County, Dakota Territory (Ibid.). She died in 1917 (Jackie Gladue Jordan Research, Family group sheet 13 Jun 1998.).

Children of **Antoine Wilkie** and **Esther Gladu** were as follows:

29   i.   Antoine Alexander Wilkie, b. 9 Jul 1877 St.Peter's Mission, Cascade County, Montana; m. Magdeleine Bercier; d. 6 Jan 1914 Rolette County, North Dakota.

     ii.   Joseph Albert Wilkie was born on 16 Mar 1879 Leroy, Pembina County, Dakota Territory (SJL-1, page 93, B-50.). He was baptized on 18 Mar 1879 St.Joseph, Leroy, Pembina County, Dakota Territory (Ibid.). He died on 2 Oct 1881 Leroy, Pembina County, Dakota Territory, at age 2 (Ibid., page 114, S-70.).

     iii.   Marie Clemence Wilkie was born on 4 Nov 1881 Leroy, Pembina County, Dakota Territory (Ibid., page 114, B-185.). She was baptized on 9 Nov 1881 St.Joseph, Leroy, Pembina County, Dakota Territory (Ibid.).

30   iv.   Mary Ernestine Wilkie, b. 4 Nov 1881; m. Frederick Raphael Martin.

31   v.   Napoleon Elzear Wilkie, b. 21 Aug 1883 Olga, Cavalier County, North Dakota; m. Clemence Laviolette; d. 15 Oct 1947 Rolette County, North Dakota.

     vi.   Frederick Wilkie was born on 23 May 1885 Olga, Cavalier County, North Dakota (Olga, page 70, B-22.). He was baptized on 24 May 1885 Olga, Cavalier County, North Dakota (Ibid.). He died on 4 Jul 1933 Cavalier County, North Dakota, at age 48 (ND Death Index.).

32   vii.   Moise Wilkie, b. 22 May 1887 Olga, Cavalier County, North Dakota; m. Isabella Demarais; d. 2 Nov 1965 Sioux County, North Dakota.

33   viii.   John Baptiste Joseph Wilkie, b. 9 Feb 1889 Olga, Cavalier County, North Dakota; m. Mary Jane Belgarde; d. 1 Jan 1950 Rolette County, North Dakota.

34   ix.   Mary Jane Wilkie, b. circa Mar 1891; m. Ambroise Demontigny; d. 27 May 1926 Rolette County, North Dakota.

35   x.   Marie Delia Wilkie, b. Mar 1894; d. 9 Mar 1928 Rolette County, North Dakota.

36   xi.   Louis O. Wilkie, b. 6 May 1895 Rolette County, North Dakota; m. Eliza Decouteau; d. 17 Aug 1964 Rolette County, North Dakota.

37   xii.   Marie Clara 'Laura' Wilkie, b. 31 Oct 1899 Rolette County, North Dakota; m. John Louis Demontigny; d. 7 Feb 1987 Grand Forks County, North Dakota.

Generation Four

16.   Onesime Wilkie was born on 20 Mar 1856 (AP, page 147, B-410.). He was born on 12 Apr 1856 (ND Death Index.). He was baptized on 11 May 1856 Assumption, Pembina, Pembina County, Dakota Territory (AP, page 147, B-410.). He married **Marie Agathe Venne**, daughter of **David Venne** and **Josephte Beauchamp**, on 27 Nov 1883 Olga, Cavalier County, North Dakota (Olga, page 27, M-9.). He died on 16 May 1936 Rolette County, North Dakota, at age 80 (ND Death Index.).

Marie Agathe Venne was born on 7 Feb 1864 St.Norbert, (Manitoba) (MBS, C-14934.) (SN1, page 99, B-15.). She was baptized on 8 Feb 1864 St.Norbert, (Manitoba) (Ibid.). She died on 15 Oct 1885 Olga, Cavalier County, North Dakota, at age 21 (Olga, page 83, S-19.). She was buried on 16 Oct 1885 Olga, Cavalier County, North Dakota (Ibid.).

Children of **Onesime Wilkie** and **Marie Agathe Venne** were:

    i.   Gabriel Frederick Wilkie was born on 26 Nov 1884 Olga, Cavalier County, North Dakota (Ibid., page 58, B-38.). He was baptized on 27 Nov 1884 Olga, Cavalier County, North Dakota (Ibid.).

17.   Albert Wilkie was born on 4 May 1859 (SFXI-Kipling, B-345.). He was baptized on 29 May 1859 St.Francois Xavier, (Manitoba) (Ibid.). He married **Marie Josephine Laverdure**, daughter of **Joseph Laverdure** and **Marie Martel**, in 1891 (1900C-ND, 200-200.). He died on 17 Jun 1941 Belcourt, Rolette County, North Dakota, at age 82 (*St.Ann's Centennial, 100 Years of Faith - 1885-1985*; Belcourt, North Dakota: St.Ann Parish, 1985), page 546.).

Marie Josephine Laverdure was born on 1 Jul 1873 (L1, page 120, B-42.) (ND Death Index.) (ArchiviaNet, C-15010.). She was baptized on 5 Sep 1873 Lebret, (Saskatchewan) (L1, page 120, B-42.). She died on 22 May 1951 Belcourt, Rolette County, North Dakota, at age 77 (*St.Ann's Centennial*, page 546.) (ND Death Index.).

Children of **Albert Wilkie** and **Marie Josephine Laverdure** were as follows:

    i.   Mary Wilkie was born on 24 Apr 1891 (1922 Turtle Mountain Chippewa Indian Census Roll, United States Indian Service Department of the Interior, Turtle Mountain Indian Agency, North Dakota, 30 June 1922 , Census No. 2424-2428.). She married Robert Lucier, son of Alexandre Lucier and Rosalie Laviolette, before 1910 (1936-TMC, page 160.). She died on 20 Jun 1937 Rolette County, North Dakota, at age 46 (1937-TMC Indian Census Roll of the Turtle Mountain Reservation, United States Indian Service Department of the Interior, Belcourt, North Dakota, J. E. Balmer, 1 January 1937 , page 332, Census No. 4018-4022.) (ND Death Index.).

        Robert Lucier was born on 16 May 1879 St.Francois Xavier, Manitoba (SFXI-Kipling, page 192, B-27.). He died on 17 Aug 1960 Rolette County, North Dakota, at age 81 (ND Death Index.).

    ii.   Clara Wilkie was born on 2 Jan 1895 North Dakota (1900C-ND, 200-200.) (Social Security Death Index, . Hereinafter cited as SSDI.). She married William Barrett before 1937 (*1937-TMC*, page 38, Census No. 431.). She died on 17 Apr 1977 Garrison, McLean County, North Dakota, at age 82 (ND Death Index.) (SSDI.). She was buried circa 20 Apr 1977 Sunset Memorial Gardens, Minot, Ward County, North Dakota.

    iii.   Louis G. Wilkie was born on 10 Aug 1896 North Dakota (1900C-ND, 200-200.) (ND Death Index.). He married St.Ann Dauphinais, daughter of David Dauphinais and Marie Angelique Martin, circa 1921. He died on 27 May 1945 Rolette County, North Dakota, at age 48 (Ibid.).

        St.Ann Dauphinais was born on 23 Jul 1902 (Ibid.) (*1937-TMC*, page 530, Census No. 6327-6329.). She married **Daniel Louis Houle**, son of **Baptiste Houle** and **Virginie Lafontaine**, on 24 Dec 1949 Crookston, Minnesota (Rod Mac Quarrie, 9 Aug 2012.). She died on 10 Oct 1988 Rolette County, Minnesota, at age 86 (ND Death Index.).

    iv.   Alfred Wilkie was born in Mar 1899 North Dakota (1900C-ND, 200-200.).

    v.   Jerome Wilkie was born on 14 Sep 1905 (*1937-TMC*, page 527, Census No. 6165-6167.). He married Mary E. Dubois, daughter of Alexander Dubois and Mary Georgianna Pelletier, before 1936 (Ibid.). He died on 14 Aug 1967 Minot, Ward County, North Dakota, at age 61 (SSDI.) (ND Death Index.).

        Mary E. Dubois was born on 30 Nov 1916 (*1937-TMC*, page 527, Census No. 6165-6167.). She was born on 6 Nov 1919 (1924-TMC-ND 1924 Census of the Chippewa Indians of Turtle Mountain Agency, North Dakota, United States Indian Service Department of the Interior, Belcourt, North Dakota, superintendent H. J. McQuigg, 30 June 1924 , Census No. 1356-1360.).

    vi.   Mary Margaret Wilkie was born on 12 Aug 1908 (1936-TMC, page 129.) (BIA-TM-BMD, page 16.). She married Clement Philip Poitras, son of Henri Poitras and Marie Grant, before 1925.

        Clement Philip Poitras was born on 17 Oct 1903 North Dakota (1936-TMC, page 198.) (1919 Turtle Mountain Indian Census Roll, United States Indian Service Department of the Interior, Turtle Mountain Indian Agency, North Dakota, 30 June 1919 , Census No. 2749-2752.).

    vii.   Emil Wilkie was born on 20 Oct 1910 Rolette County, North Dakota (BIA-TM-BMD, page 41.) (Turtle Mountain Star, Rolla, North Dakota.) (ND Death Index.). He died on 17 Aug 1930 Rolette County, North Dakota, at age 19 (TM Star.) (ND Death Index.).

    viii.   Robert Wilkie was born on 5 Mar 1913 Rolette County, North Dakota (1936-TMC, page 129.) (ND Death Index.). He died on 26 Mar 1958 Rolette County, North Dakota, at age 45 (Ibid.).

    ix.   Mary Dorothy Wilkie was born on 23 Apr 1917 (*1937-TMC*, page 524, Census No. 6132-6135.). She died on 23 Dec 1937 Rolette County, North Dakota, at age 20 (Ibid.) (ND Death Index.).

18.   Eliza Wilkie was born circa 1861 Dakota Territory (SJL-1, page 111, M-29.). She married **Jean Baptiste Ducept**, son of **Pierre Ducept** and **Madeleine Lafontaine**, on 26 Jul 1881 St.Joseph, Leroy, Pembina County, Dakota Territory (Ibid.). She died before Jun 1893 (1900C-ND, 233-233.) (1896-TMC, page 16, #405-408.) (1893-TMC 1893 Census of Half Breed Chippewas of Turtle Mountain, Dakota Territory, National Archives of the United States, Washington D.C., page 11, Census No. 272-275.).

Jean Baptiste Ducept was born in Nov 1860 North Dakota (1900C-ND, House 234, page 298B.). He died before 1938 (1936-TMC, page 85.).

19. Philomene Wilkie was born in 1863 St.Joseph, Pembina County, Dakota Territory (BIA-TM Bureau of Indian Affairs, Turtle Mountain Enrollment and Probate Papers, Belcourt, North Dakota.). She married **Napoleon Gregoire Monet dit Belhumeur**, son of **Michel Monet dit Belhumeur** and **Josephte Bruyere**, on 2 Mar 1878 St.Joseph, Leroy, Pembina County, Dakota Territory (SJL-1, page 86, M-2.). She died in 1926 (BIA-TM.).

Napoleon Gregoire Monet dit Belhumeur was born on 16 Dec 1854 Pembina, Pembina County, Dakota Territory (AP, page 118, B-328.). He was baptized on 17 Dec 1854 Assumption, Pembina, Pembina County, Dakota Territory (Ibid.). He died on 24 Jun 1931 Rolette County, North Dakota, at age 76 (ND Death Index.).

20. Gabriel "Kabi-ush" Wilkie was born on 22 Jul 1866 North Dakota (1900C-ND, House 149, page 287B.) (ND Death Index.). He married **Marie Charette**, daughter of **Jean Baptiste Charette** and **Marie Anne Laverdure**, on 3 May 1886 St.Claude Mission, St.John, Rolette County, North Daktoa (BIA-TM, Married by priest.) (Dominique Ritchot Research,, 26 Jan 2006.). He died on 30 Sep 1939 Rolette County, North Dakota, at age 73 (BIA-TM.) (ND Death Index.).

Marie Charette was born in Sep 1869 Fargo, North Dakota (1900C-ND, House 149, page 287B.) (TM Star, 24 Jul 1930.). She died on 15 Jul 1930 Rolette County, North Dakota, at age 60 (ND Death Index.) (TM Star, 24 Jul 1930.).

Children of **Gabriel "Kabi-ush" Wilkie** and **Marie Charette** were as follows:

  i. John R. Wilkie was born on 25 Jun 1887 (Al Yerbury.). He married Eva St.Arnaud, daughter of Jean Baptiste St.Arnaud and Julie St.Arnaud, before 1915. He died on 27 Dec 1928 Pheonix, Maricopa, Arizona, at age 41 (Ibid.) (TM Star, 24 Jul 1930.) (1929-TMC-ND 1929 Census of the Chippewa Indians of Turtle Mountain Agency, North Dakota, United States Indian Service Department of the Interior, Belcourt, North Dakota, 30 June 1929 , Census No. 4612-4613.).

  Eva St.Arnaud was born in 1890 (1936-TMC, page 131.).

  ii. Raphael Cyprian Wilkie was born on 26 Jan 1890 (WIS Birth Wisconsin Birth/Christening Index.). He died on 24 Jan 1974 Los Angeles County, California, at age 83 (Ibid.).

  iii. Pierre Alfred 'Peter' Wilkie was born on 12 Jul 1892 (Minnesota Department of Health Public Death Index.). He died on 23 Aug 1959 Stearns County, Minnesota, at age 67 (Ibid.).

  iv. Michael Wilkie was born on 3 Oct 1895 (Ancestry.com, WWI Draft Registration.). He married Lula B. Goodreau before 1920 (1920C-ND 1920 Federal Census North Dakota, National Archives of the United States, Washington D.C., page 7A.). He died on 5 Dec 1949 St.Paul, Ramsey County, Minnesota, at age 54 (Al Yerbury.) (Ancestry.com, Find a Grave.).

  Lula B. Goodreau was born on 17 Jul 1898 (1920C-MTl, page 7A.). She died on 7 Jul 1997 Alameda County, California, at age 98 (WIS Birth.) (SSDI.).

  v. Rose Victoria Wilkie was born on 28 Feb 1897 (Al Yerbury.). She married Frank Wendell Livermont on 21 Aug 1919 (Ibid.). She married Royal C. Renno on 25 May 1950 Riverside, California. She married Francis T. Gray on 28 Feb 1957 Los Angeles, Los Angeles, California. She died circa 6 Jul 1970 (Ibid.).

  Frank Wendell Livermont was born on 12 Aug 1898 South Dakota (SSDI.). He died on 22 Nov 1960 Los Angeles, Los Angeles, California, at age 62 (Ibid.).

  vi. Virginia Wilkie was born on 28 Jul 1900 (Al Yerbury.). She married Joseph Welsh before 1926 (*St.Ann's Centennial*, page 550.) (*1937-TMC*, page 521, Census No. 6103-6104.). She died on 19 Sep 1970 Gresham, Multnomah County, Oregon, at age 70 (SSDI.).

  Joseph Welsh was born on 3 Apr 1901 (Ibid.). He died on 9 Sep 1975 Multnomah County, Oregon, at age 74 (Ibid.).

  vii. Agnes Wilkie was born on 22 Aug 1902 (Al Yerbury.). She married James Henry Reardon, son of James H. Reardon and Janet Cameron or Cole, on 29 Sep 1922 (*St.Ann's Centennial*, page 550.). She died on 13 Nov 1962 at age 60 (Al Yerbury.).

  James Henry Reardon was born on 7 Feb 1902 San Francisco, San Francisco, California (1937-1987-LS Basic Roll, #436.) (PonCM Pondera County Courthouse, Montana; Marriage Record Licenses and Certificates; 1865-1950, familysearch.org, Hereinafter cited as PonCM.). He married **Myrtle May Bushman**, daughter of **Adolphe Beauchman** and **Helene Salois**, on 24 Feb 1931 Conrad, Pondera County, Montana (Ibid.). He died on 25 Mar 1981 Choteau, Teton County, Montana, at age 79 (SSDI.) (MT Death.).

  viii. Ernestine Wilkie was born on 24 Jun 1906 (Al Yerbury.). She married Russell Milligan before 1937 (*1937-TMC*, page 358, Census No. 6208.).

  ix. Angeline Wilkie was born on 28 Dec 1912 (BIA-TM-BMD, page 62.). She married Emil Belgarde, son of Thomas Petit and Marguerite Herman, before 1934.

  Emil Belgarde was born in 1904 (1936-TMC, page 38.).

21. Mathilde Wilkie was born circa 1868 (1885-TMC, #381.). She was born in Aug 1868 North Dakota. She married **William Laverdure**, son of **Joseph Laverdure** and **Marie Martel**, in 1891 (1900C-ND, House 221, page 296B.). She died on 3 Aug 1929 Rolette County, North Dakota (ND Death Index.).

William Laverdure was born on 12 Feb 1862 Dakota Territory (BIA-TM-BMD.). He was born circa Oct 1867 (NWHBSI, page 111.). He was born on 21 Jan 1868 North Dakota (*1922 TMC*, Census No. 2388-2390.). He married **Marie Rose Vandal**, daughter of **John Baptiste Vandal** and **Marguerite Vivier**, circa 1934 (Rod Mac Quarrie, 28 Dec 2011.). He died on 26 Apr 1948 Belcourt, Rolette County, North Dakota, at age 86 (BIA-TM-BMD.) (ND Death Index.).

22. Marie Celina Wilkie was baptized on 6 Mar 1873 Lebret, (Saskatchewan) (L1, page 87, B-61.). She was born on 6 Mar 1873 Lebret, (Saskatchewan) (Ibid.). She married **Pierre Ducept**, son of **Pierre Ducept** and **Madeleine Lafontaine**, in 1888 (1900C-ND, House 118, page 283A.). She died on 27 Apr 1948 Belcourt, Rolette County, North Dakota, at age 75 (BIA-TM-BMD.) (ND Death Index.).

Pierre Ducept was born on 5 Sep 1859 St.Norbert, (Manitoba) (SN1, B-32, page 19.). He was baptized on 5 Sep 1859 St.Norbert, (Manitoba) (Ibid.). He married **Louise Gosselin**, daughter of **Joseph Gosselin** and **Marie Vallee**, on 26 Jul 1881 St.Joseph, Leroy, Pembina County, Dakota Territory (NWHBS, C-14938.) (SJL-1, page 112, M-30.).

23. **Augustin Wilkie** was born in 1853 Lac Qu'Appelle, (Saskatchewan) (NWHBS, C-14942.). He was baptized on 4 Sep 1853 Assumption, Pembina, Pembina County, Dakota Territory (AP, page 94, B-89.). He married **Rose Octavie Herman**, daughter of **Edouard Herman** and **Marguerite Dauphinais**, on 30 Jan 1882 Olga, Cavalier County, North Dakota (Olga, page 10, M-3.). He died on 2 Aug 1938 Rolette County, North Dakota (ND Death Index.) (*1937-TMC*, page 525, Census No. 6142.).

Rose Octavie Herman was born on 5 Oct 1861 Pembina County, Dakota Territory (AP, page 248, B-131.). She was baptized on 10 Nov 1861 Assumption, Pembina, Pembina County, Dakota Territory (Ibid.). She was born in 1863 on the plains. She died before 1 Jun 1900 (1900C-ND, House 255, page 301B.).

Children of **Augustin Wilkie** and **Rose Octavie Herman** were as follows:

    i. Rosalie Wilkie was baptized on 11 Dec 1883 Olga, Cavalier County, North Dakota (Olga, page 29, B-35.). She was born on 11 Dec 1883 Olga, Cavalier County, North Dakota (Ibid.). She married John James Lillie, son of Daniel Napoleon Lillie and Marie Esther McLeod, before 1917 (1936-TMC, page 158.). She died on 23 Aug 1932 Rolette County, North Dakota, at age 48 (ND Death Index.).

        John James Lillie was born on 10 Nov 1883 Rock Lake, (Manitoba) (HBSI.) (ArchiviaNet.). He was born on 29 Feb 1884 (SFXI-Kipling, B-21.). He was baptized 4 May 1884 St.Francois Xavier, Manitoba (Ibid.) (Rosemary Rozyk.). He died on 4 May 1966 Walsh County, North Dakota, at age 82 (ND Death Index.).

    ii. Madeleine Wilkie was born circa 1886. She died before 1936.

    iii. Virginie Wilkie was born on 4 Apr 1886 Rolette County, North Dakota (St. Claude Mission, St. John, North Dakota, Baptisms, Marriages, Burials 1882-1888, 2006, Dominique Ritchot, B-247, page 53.). She was baptized on 11 Apr 1886 St.Claude Mission, St.John, Rolette County, North Dakota (Ibid.).

    iv. Mary Cecile Wilkie was born in May 1890 (1936-TMC, page 36.) (1890-TMC, #1165-1170.). She married Pierre Belgarde, son of Louis Belgarde and Louise Delorme, before 1912 (1936-TMC, page 36.).

        Pierre Belgarde was born on 1 Dec 1883 Olga, Cavalier County, North Dakota (Olga, page 29, B-34.). He was baptized on 2 Dec 1883 Olga, Cavalier County, North Dakota (Ibid.). He died on 6 Jul 1946 Rolette County, North Dakota, at age 62 (ND Death Index.).

    v. John Augustine Wilkie was born circa Apr 1892.

    vi. Joseph N. Wilkie was born on 23 May 1896 Rolette County, North Dakota (*St.Ann's Centennial*, page 550.). He married Georgiana Dionne, daughter of Moses Dionne and Marie Petit, on 24 Oct 1916 St.Ann's, Belcourt, Rolette County, North Dakota (TM Star, 28 Jun 1934.). He married Agnes Belgarde, daughter of Firmin Belgarde and Pauline Langer, on 18 Apr 1938 St.Ann's, Belcourt, Rolette County, North Dakota (*St.Ann's Centennial*, page 550.). He died on 16 Jun 1969 Cass County, North Dakota, at age 73 (Ibid.) (ND Death Index.).

        Georgiana Dionne was born on 2 Jul 1900 Belcourt, Rolette County, North Dakota (1936-TMC, page 130.) (TM Star, 28 Jun 1934.). She died on 21 Jun 1934 Belcourt, Rolette County, North Dakota, at age 33 (Ibid.). She was buried on 23 Jun 1934 St.Ann's, Belcourt, Rolette County, North Dakota (Ibid.).

        Agnes Belgarde was born on 6 Aug 1916 Rolette County, North Dakota (1936-TMC, page 37.) (*1919 Turtle Mountain*, Census No. 517-524.). She died on 7 Mar 1987 Rolette County, North Dakota, at age 70 (ND Death Index.).

24. **Jean Baptiste Wilkie** was born on 4 Mar 1855 Pembina, Pembina County, Dakota Territory (AP, page 126, B-344.). He was baptized on 4 Mar 1855 Assumption, Pembina, Pembina County, Dakota Territory (Ibid.). He married **Sarah Gourneau**, daughter of **Joseph Gourneau** and **Judith Delorme**, on 4 Feb 1873 St.Joseph, Leroy, Pembina County, Dakota Territory (SJL-1, page 33, M-1.). He died on 2 Mar 1920 Belcourt, Rolette County, North Dakota, at age 64 (BIA-TM-BMD.). He was buried on 4 Mar 1920 Belcourt, Rolette County, North Dakota (Ibid.).

Sarah Gourneau was born on 7 Mar 1853 (AP, page 89, B-73.). She was baptized on 1 May 1853 Assumption, Pembina, Pembina County, Dakota Territory (Ibid.). She died on 12 Mar 1939 Rolette County, North Dakota, at age 86 (ND Death Index.).

Children of **Jean Baptiste Wilkie** and **Sarah Gourneau** were as follows:

    i. Sarah Wilkie was born on 5 Jan 1874 (SJL-1, page 43, B-2.). She was baptized on 11 Jan 1874 St.Joseph, Leroy, Pembina County, Dakota Territory (Ibid.). She married Ferdinand Bourbonnais, son of Henri Bourbonnais and Adeline Forain, on 31 Oct 1889 Olga, Cavalier County, North Dakota (Olga, page 173, M-9.). She died on 23 Mar 1891 Olga, Cavalier County, North Dakota, at age 17 (Ibid., page 196, S-13.). She was buried on 25 Mar 1891 Olga, Cavalier County, North Dakota (Ibid.).

    ii. Marguerite Wilkie was born on 5 Feb 1875 (SJL-1, page 56, B-4.). She was baptized on 7 Feb 1875 St.Joseph, Leroy, Pembina County, Dakota Territory (Ibid.). She died on 14 Feb 1875 (Ibid., page 56, S-4.). She was buried on 15 Feb 1875 St.Joseph, Leroy, Pembina County, Dakota Territory (Ibid.).

    iii. Jean Baptiste Wilkie was born on 16 Mar 1876 (L1, page 199-200, B-42.). He was baptized on 7 Jan 1877 Lebret, (Saskatchewan) (Ibid.). He married Josephine Aiken, daughter of Archibald Aiken and Marie Poitras, in 1899 (1900C-ND, 380-380.) (1936-TMC, page 132.). He died on 22 Dec 1950 Rolette County, North Dakota, at age 74 (ND Death Index.).

        Josephine Aiken was born on 19 Mar 1877 (SPMT, page 112, #2373.). She was baptized on 11 Jun 1877 St.Peter's Mission, Montana Territory (Ibid.). She was born in Dec 1877 North Dakota (1900C-ND, House 256, page 301B.). She died on 1 Sep 1930 Bottineau County, North Dakota, at age 53 (ND Death Index.).

    iv. Augustin Wilkie was born on 14 Dec 1877 (SJL-1, page 84, B-14.). He was baptized on 26 Dec 1877 St.Joseph, Leroy, Pembina County, Dakota Territory (Ibid.).

    v. Albert Wilkie was born on 23 Mar 1879 (Ibid., page 93, B-51.). He was baptized on 9 Apr 1879 St.Joseph, Leroy, Pembina County, Dakota Territory (Ibid.). He married Celina Vandal, daughter of John Baptiste Vandal and

Marguerite Vivier, in 1899 (1900C-ND, 363-363.). He married Elizabeth "Betsy" Allard, daughter of Elzear Allard and Julia Morin, circa 1920 (TM Star, 5 Oct 1933.). He died on 23 Feb 1936 Rolette County, North Dakota, at age 56 (ND Death Index.) (1936-TMC Census of the Turtle Mountain Chippewa Indians, United States Indian Service Department of the Interior, Turtle Mountain Agency, North Dakota, 1 Apr 1936.).

Celina Vandal was born on 30 Nov 1880 North Dakota (1900C-ND, 363-363.) (1916-TMC 1916 Census of the Turtle Mountain Chippewa, North Dakota, National Archives of the United States, Washington D.C.) (1918-TMC.). She died between 1918 and 1919.

Elizabeth "Betsy" Allard was born circa 1900 (1910C ND Thirteenth Census of the United States: 1910; North Dakota, National Archives of the United States, Washington D.C., District 153, page 19B.). She married **Jean Baptiste Davis**, son of **Jean Baptiste Davis** and **Emerise Lavallee**, on 15 Feb 1939 Belcourt, Rolette County, North Dakota (*St.Ann's Centennial*, page 301.).

vi. Marie Wilkie was born on 29 Oct 1881 Leroy, Pembina County, Dakota Territory (SJL-1, page 114, B-181.). She was baptized on 2 Nov 1881 St.Joseph, Leroy, Pembina County, Dakota Territory (Ibid.). She died on 29 Mar 1886 Olga, Cavalier County, North Dakota, at age 4 (Olga, page 93, S-4.). She was buried on 30 Mar 1886 Olga, Cavalier County, North Dakota (Ibid.).

vii. Marie Virginie Wilkie was born on 6 Jul 1884 Olga, Cavalier County, North Dakota (Ibid., page 48, B-23.). She was baptized on 7 Jul 1884 Olga, Cavalier County, North Dakota (Ibid.). She married Pierre Azure, son of Francois Azure and Julie Pelletier, circa 1906. She married William Kingen before 1937 (*1937-TMC*, page 255, Census No. 3064.). She died on 23 Nov 1963 Devils Lake, Ramsey County, North Dakota, at age 79 (ND Death Index.).

Pierre Azure was born on 1 Jan 1882 North Dakota (BIA-TM, Francois Azure Family History Card.) (ND Death Index.). He married **Mary Rose Vanasse** in 1943 (BIA-TM, Pierre Azure Family History Card.). He died on 23 Jul 1948 Sioux County, North Dakota, at age 66 (ND Death Index.).

William Kingen was born on 22 Oct 1889 (Ibid.). He died on 28 Sep 1978 Towner County, North Dakota, at age 88 (Ibid.).

viii. Jean Marie Wilkie was born on 9 Jun 1886 Olga, Cavalier County, North Dakota (Olga, page 101, B-34.). He was baptized on 9 Jun 1886 Olga, Cavalier County, North Dakota (Ibid.). He was buried on 23 May 1887 Olga, Cavalier County, North Dakota (Ibid., page 121, S-_.).

ix. Joseph F. Wilkie was born on 22 Apr 1888 Olga, Cavalier County, North Dakota (Ibid., page 142, B-11.). He was baptized on 22 Apr 1888 Olga, Cavalier County, North Dakota (Ibid.). He married Eliza Grandbois, daughter of Isidore Grandbois and Sarah Morin, before 1911. He married Mary Lafountain on 18 Oct 1952 St.Ann, Belcourt, North Dakota (Ibid., page 142, B-11 (note).). He died on 16 Jun 1968 Rolette County, North Dakota, at age 80 (ND Death Index.).

Eliza Grandbois was born circa 1886 (1892 Oct 1 McCumber Census of the Turtle Mountain band of Chippewa Indians, Belcourt, North Dakota, National Archives of the United States, Washington D.C., Document No. 229, Family 111, #474-481.). She was born circa 1888 (1936-TMC, page 132.) (*1937-TMC*, page 529-530, Census No. 6307-6319.). She was born on 12 Aug 1893 (1892C-TMC , Family 111, #474-481.). She died on 4 Jan 1940 Rolette County, North Dakota (ND Death Index.).

x. William Wilkie was baptized on 31 Aug 1890 Olga, Cavalier County, North Dakota (Olga, page 184, B-64.). He was born on 31 Aug 1890 Olga, Cavalier County, North Dakota (Ibid.). He was born in Oct 1891 North Dakota (1900C-ND, 110-110.). He married Marie Virginia Plante, daughter of John B. Plante and Virginie Rosalie Godon, before 1913. He married Pauline Allard, daughter of William Allard and Marie St.Germain, before 1922. He died on 8 Jan 1941 Rolette County, North Dakota, at age 50 (ND Death Index.).

Marie Virginia Plante was born on 14 Nov 1892 Leroy, Pembina County, North Dakota (SJL-2, page 53, B-45.). She was baptized on 15 Nov 1892 St.Joseph, Leroy, Pembina County, North Dakota (Ibid.). She died on 29 Nov 1918 Belcourt, Rolette County, North Dakota, at age 26 (BIA-TM-BMD.).

Pauline Allard was born on 16 Jun 1898 North Dakota (ND Death Index.). She died on 23 Jan 1954 Belcourt, Rolette County, North Dakota, at age 55 (Ibid.).

xi. Justine Wilkie was born in Aug 1893 North Dakota (1900C-ND, 110-110.). She was born in 1894 (1936-TMC, page 17.). She married Joseph R. Allard, son of William Allard and Marie St.Germain, in 1912. She died on 20 Apr 1928 Rolette County (ND Death Index.).

Joseph R. Allard was born on 13 Oct 1892. He married **Adele Laverdure**, daughter of **Pierre Laverdure** and **Agnes Parenteau**, on 18 Oct 1934 (David Courchane, Courchane/Courchene Family Research.). He died on 5 Sep 1971 Belcourt, Rolette County, North Dakota, at age 78 (ND Death Index.).

25. Madeleine Wilkie was born circa 1869 Dakota Territory (1870 DT, family 27, line 3-11.). She married **James Decouteau**, son of **Francois Decouteau**, before 1892.

James Decouteau was born on 4 Jul 1868 North Dakota (ND Death Index.). He was born in 1871 (BIA-TM, Lucille Scholastica Poitra DOB chart.) (1936-TMC, page 68.). He was born in Jun 1876 North Dakota (1900C-ND, House 115, page 282B.). He married **Anna Emilia Pelletier**, daughter of **Jean Baptiste Pelletier** and **Caroline Sanderson**, in 1898 (Ibid.). He died on 5 Jun 1937 Rolette County, North Dakota, at age 68 (ND Death Index.).

26. Joseph Wilkie was born on 15 Sep 1870 (SJL-1, page 3, B-41.). He was baptized on 12 Oct 1870 St.Joseph, Leroy, Dakota Territory (Ibid.). He married **Alphonsine "Jennie" Bruce**, daughter of **Joseph Bruce** and **Isabelle Ladouceur**, in 1895 (1900C-ND, House 330, page 310B.). He died on 6 Jun 1961 Rolette County, North Dakota, at age 90 (ND Death Index.).

Alphonsine "Jennie" Bruce was born on 2 Dec 1881 (SN2, B-51.). She was baptized on 7 Dec 1881 St.Norbert, Manitoba (Ibid.). She died on 17 Sep 1957 Rolette County, North Dakota, at age 75 (ND Death Index.).

Children of **Joseph Wilkie** and **Alphonsine "Jennie" Bruce** were as follows:

i. Elizabeth Wilkie was born on 16 Dec 1899 North Dakota (1923-TMC-ND 1923 Census of the Chippewa Indians of Turtle Mountain Agency, North Dakota, United States Indian Service Department of the Interior, Belcourt, North Dakota, superintendent H. J. McQuigg, 30 June 1923 , Census No. 2133-2134.). She married Daniel Lafontaine, son of Louis Lafontaine and Emelie Desjarlais, before 1915. She died on 8 Jul 1932 Belcourt, Rolette County, North Dakota, at age 32 (ND Death Index.).

Daniel Lafontaine was born on 10 Mar 1894 North Dakota (*1923-TMC-ND*, Census No. 2133-2134.). He married **Philomene Azure**, daughter of **Benjamin Azure** and **Marie Therese Boyer**, before 1937 (1936-TMC, page 69.). He died on 5 Jan 1977 Rolette County, North Dakota, at age 82 (ND Death Index.).

ii. Joseph Wilkie was born on 9 Dec 1902 Rolette County, North Dakota (Ibid.). He married Eliza Peltier, daughter of Joseph Pelletier and Adeline Dauphinais, before 1922 (1930C ND Fifteenth Census of the United States: 1930; North Dakota, National Archives of the United States, Washington, D.C., page 1A-1B, family 11, line 48-50, 1-2.). He died on 6 Sep 1974 William County, North Dakota, at age 71 (ND Death Index.).

Eliza Peltier was born on 25 Mar 1904 (SSDI.). She died on 28 Jul 1968 Burke County, North Dakota, at age 64 (Ibid.) (ND Death Index.).

iii. Marie St.Ann Wilkie was born on 2 Jun 1907 (BIA-TM-BMD, page 2.). She married John Norwood before 1928 (*1937-TMC*, page 386, Census No. 4552-4555.).

iv. Margaret Zilda Wilkie was born on 10 May 1909 Rolette County, North Dakota (1936-TMC, page 132.) (BIA-TM-BMD, page 24.). She married Joseph Decouteau, son of Norbert Decouteau and Rose Belgarde, before 30 Jun 1924 Rolette County, North Dakota (1936-TMC, page 70.) (1925-TMC-ND 1925 Census of the Chippewa Indians of Turtle Mountain Agency, North Dakota, United States Indian Service Department of the Interior, Belcourt, North Dakota, superintendent H. J. McQuigg, 30 June 1925 , Census No. 1115-1116.) (*1924-TMC-ND*, Census No. 1104-1105.).

Joseph Decouteau was born on 24 Jan 1895 Rolette County, North Dakota (1916-TMC, Census No. 984.).

v. Marie Rachel Wilkie was born on 21 Jan 1912 (1936-TMC, page 132.) (BIA-TM-BMD, page 53.). She and Joseph Lawrence Thomas met circa 1935 (*1937-TMC*, page 529, Census No. 6303-6306.).

Joseph Lawrence Thomas was born on 18 Dec 1913 (*St.Ann's Centennial*, page 528.) (SSDI.) (ND Death Index.). He married **Rita Marie Azure**, daughter of **John Louis Azure** and **Catherine Laverdure**, on 14 Oct 1946 Rolla, Rolette County, North Dakota (*St.Ann's Centennial*, page 528.). He died on 12 Jun 1985 Rolla, Rolette County, North Dakota, at age 71 (ND Death Index.) (SSDI.).

vi. Clemence V. Wilkie was born on 19 Dec 1914 Rolette County, North Dakota (1936-TMC, page 133.) (*1937-TMC*, page 30, Census No. 329-331.). She married Maxim Michael Azure, son of Andre Azure and Clara Gerle or Gerlly or Gerally, before 1935 (Ibid.).

Maxim Michael Azure was born on 27 Aug 1912 Rolette County, North Dakota (BIA-TM, Individual history card of Andre Azure.) (BIA-TM-BMD, page 60.). He died before 1936 (Ibid.).

vii. Pierre Wilkie was born before 1915 (1936-TMC, page 132.).

viii. Fabian S. Wilkie was born on 2 Feb 1917 Rolette County, North Dakota (ND Death Index.) (*1937-TMC*, page 525, Census No. 6151-6152.). He married Delia Josie Peltier, daughter of Julius Peltier and Ida Jane Fagnant, before 1937 (Ibid.). He died on 2 Feb 1976 Rolette County, North Dakota, at age 59 (ND Death Index.).

Delia Josie Peltier was born on 6 Apr 1919 (*1919 Turtle Mountain*, Census No. 2685-2686.).

ix. Edna Wilkie was born on 25 Jul 1919 Rolette County, North Dakota (1936-TMC, page 133.) (ND Death Index.). She died on 21 Sep 1934 Rolette County, North Dakota, at age 15 (Ibid.).

x. Blanche Wilkie was born on 18 Dec 1921 North Dakota (1936-TMC, page 133.) (*1924-TMC-ND*, Census No. 3942-3948.). She married Eli Morin, son of Peter Morin and Julia (--?--), on 24 May 1939 St.Ann's, Belcourt, Rolette County, North Dakota (TM Star, 21 Dec 2009.). She died on 11 Dec 2009 Belcourt, Rolette County, North Dakota, at age 87 (Ibid.).

Eli Morin was born on 11 Dec 1917 (SSDI.). He married **Melina Edna Charette**, daughter of **Pierre Charette** and **Catherine Desjarlais**, on 30 Jun 1936 (*1937-TMC*, page 369, Census No. 4347.) (TM Star, 21 Oct 1937.). He died on 12 Apr 1999 Belcourt, Rolette, North Dakota, at age 81 (SSDI.).

27. Marie Josephine Wilkie was born on 1 Sep 1854 Pembina County, Dakota Territory (AP, page 113, B-310.). She was baptized on 2 Sep 1854 Assumption, Pembina, Pembina County, Dakota Territory (Ibid.). She married **Octave Lafontaine**, son of **Calixte Lafontaine** and **Charlotte Adam**, on 9 Feb 1875 Lebret, (Saskatchewan) (L1, page 148, M-5.). She died on 19 Mar 1937 Rolla, Rolette County, North Dakota, at age 82 (TM Star, 25 Mar 1937.) (ND Death Index.) (*1937-TMC*, page 267, Census No. 3229.). She was buried on 23 Mar 1937 St.Ann, Belcourt, Rolette County, North Dakota (TM Star, 25 Mar 1937.).

Octave Lafontaine was born on 20 Dec 1853 (AP, page 106, B-286.). He was baptized on 26 Apr 1854 Assumption, Pembina, Pembina County, Dakota Territory (Ibid.). He died on 28 Sep 1916 Rolette County, North Dakota, at age 62 (ND Death Index.).

28. Julienne Wilkie was born on 24 Feb 1859 Pembina, Pembina County, Dakota Territory (AP, page 204, B-615.). She was baptized on 25 Feb 1859 Assumption, Pembina, Pembina County, Dakota Territory (Ibid.). She married **Bernard Lafontaine**, son of **Calixte Lafontaine** and **Charlotte Adam,** on 27 Dec 1877 (St.Peter's Mission), Milk River, Montana Territory (SPMT , page 19, M-93.). She married **Joseph Wells**, son of **Daniel Wells** and **Louise Collin**, on 30 Apr 1883 (St.Peter's Mission), Judith Basin, Meagher County, Montana Territory (Ibid., page 40, M-243.). She died on 14 Jun 1885 Batoche, (Saskatchewan), at age 26 (BSAP, page 36, S-30.). She was buried on 16 Jun 1885 Batoche, (Saskatchewan) (Ibid.).

Bernard Lafontaine was born on 13 Aug 1858 St.Francois Xavier, (Manitoba) (SFXI-Kipling, B-281.). He was baptized on 13 Aug 1858 St.Francois Xavier, (Manitoba) (Ibid.). He died circa Jul 1879.

Joseph Wells was born on 18 Nov 1863 Devils Lake, Dakota Territory (Al Yerbury.). He married **Catherine Fleury**, daughter of **Antoine Fleury** and **Elizabeth Wilkie**, on 29 Oct 1888 Lewistown, Fergus County, Montana (Ibid., Fergus County Marriages.) (FerCM.). He married **Marie Adele Laverdure**, daughter of **Francois Xavier Laverdure** and **Marguerite Pelletier**, on 21 Nov 1892

Lewistown, Fergus County, Montana (Al Yerbury, Fergus County Marriages.) (FerCM.). He married **Maria Celina Laverdure**, daughter of **Francois Xavier Laverdure** and **Marguerite Pelletier**, before 1912. He died on 15 Jan 1942 Lewistown, Fergus County, Montana, at age 78.

29. **Antoine Alexander Wilkie** was born on 9 Jul 1877 St.Peter's Mission, Cascade County, Montana (SPMT.). He was baptized on 9 Jul 1877 St.Peter's Mission, Montana (Ibid., page 112, #2378.). He married **Magdeleine Bercier**, daughter of **Jean Baptiste Bercier** and **Marguerite Thibert**, before 1895 (*St.Ann's Centennial*, page 319.). He died on 6 Jan 1914 Rolette County, North Dakota, at age 36 (ND Death Index.).

Magdeleine Bercier was born on 17 Mar 1877 St.Francois Xavier, Manitoba (SFXI-Kipling, B-13.). She was baptized on 18 Mar 1877 St.Francois Xavier, Manitoba (Ibid.) (Rosemary Rozyk.). She married **Jean Baptiste Langer**, son of **Antoine Langer** and **Louise Collin**, before 1920 North Dakota (1920 Turtle Mountain Chippewa Indian Census Roll, United States Indian Service Department of the Interior, Turtle Mountain Indian Agency, North Dakota, 30 June 1920 , Census No. 2077.) (1930C ND, page 1A, family 7, line 35-36 & 40.).

Children of **Antoine Alexander Wilkie** and **Magdeleine Bercier** were as follows:

    i.   Frederick Wilkie was born on 2 Oct 1897 Rolette County, North Dakota (*St.Ann's Centennial*, page 546.) (ND Death Index.). He was born on 2 Feb 1898 (1916-TMC.). He married Rosine Vivier, daughter of Joseph Vivier and Rosine Trottier, on 18 Oct 1918 St.Ann's, Belcourt, Rolette County, North Dakota (*St.Ann's Centennial*, page 546.). He married Elise Zaste, daughter of Elzear Zaste and Adele Blackbird, on 8 Oct 1971 Belcourt, Rolette County, North Dakota (Ibid., page 548.). He died on 21 Aug 1989 Rolette County, North Dakota, at age 91 (ND Death Index.).

        Rosine Vivier was born on 15 Jun 1901 (1936-TMC, page 126.) (*1919 Turtle Mountain*, Census No. 3191-3197.) (ND Death Index.) (SSDI.). She died on 15 Dec 1968 Belcourt, Rolette County, North Dakota, at age 67 (*St.Ann's Centennial*, page 546.) (ND Death Index.) (SSDI.).

        Elise Zaste was born on 16 Aug 1902 Belcourt, Rolette County, North Dakota (1936-TMC, page 121.) (*St.Ann's Centennial*, page 548.). She married **Pierre 'Peter' Turcotte**, son of **Jean Baptiste Turcotte** and **Marguerite Descoteaux**, in Jun 1918 Belcourt, Rolette County, North Dakota (Ibid.). She died on 22 Oct 1982 Belcourt, Rolette County, North Dakota, at age 80 (Ibid.) (ND Death Index.).

    ii.   David Wilkie was born in 1901 (1936-TMC, page 130.).

    iii. Marie Rose Louise Wilkie was born on 9 Mar 1899 (ND Death Index.). She was born on 9 Mar 1901 Rolette County, North Dakota (1936-TMC, page 119.) (1934-TMC Census of the Turtle Mountain Chippewa Indians, United States Indian Service Department of the Interior, Turtle Mountain Agency, North Dakota, 1 Apr 1934 , page 215-216, Census No. 2593-2600.). She married Hyacinthe Houle, son of Cuthbert Houle and Nancy Pelletier, before 1917 (1936-TMC, page 119.). She died on 29 Dec 1936 Rolette County, North Dakota, at age 35 (ND Death Index.).

        Hyacinthe Houle was born in May 1897 North Dakota (1900C-ND, House 102, page 281A.).

    iv. Adele Wilkie was born on 21 Feb 1906 North Dakota (*St.Ann's Centennial*, page 320.) (SSDI.). She married Wilfred Decouteau, son of Alexander Decoutcau and Marie Anne Lafontaine, before 1928 (*St.Ann's Centennial*, page 320.). She died on 5 Aug 1976 Rolla, Rolette County, North Dakota, at age 70 (SSDI.) (ND Death Index.).

        Wilfred Decouteau was born on 18 Dec 1905 North Dakota (1936-TMC, page 65.) (SSDI.). He died on 11 Mar 1970 Belcourt, Rolette County, North Dakota, at age 64 (Ibid.) (ND Death Index.).

    v.   Nora Wilkie was born on 26 May 1908 North Dakota (*St.Ann's Centennial*, page 320.) (SSDI.). She married Alexander Decouteau, son of Alexander Decouteau and Marie Anne Lafontaine, before 1928 (*St.Ann's Centennial*, page 320.). She died in Jun 1977 Devils Lake, Ramsey County, North Dakota, at age 69 (SSDI.).

        Alexander Decouteau was born on 4 Oct 1903 North Dakota (1936-TMC, page 65.) (SSDI.). He died in Sep 1996 Rolla, Rolette County, North Dakota, at age 92 (Ibid.).

    vi. Eva Wilkie was born on 18 Jun 1910 (*St.Ann's Centennial*, page 320.) (BIA-TM-BMD, page 36.). She married Patrice Decouteau, son of Alexander Decouteau and Marie Anne Lafontaine, on 12 Dec 1928 St.Ann's, Belcourt, Rolette County, North Dakota (*St.Ann's Centennial*, page 320.) (TM Star, 15 Dec 1928.).

        Patrice Decouteau was born on 8 Jan 1910 North Dakota (1936-TMC, page 65.) (BIA-TM-BMD, page 32.) (SSDI.). He died on 11 Sep 1988 Rolla, Rolette County, North Dakota, at age 78 (Ibid.) (ND Death Index.).

    vii. George Joseph Wilkie was born on 22 Feb 1912 Rolette County, North Dakota (Ibid.) (BIA-TM-BMD, page 53.). He died on 25 Nov 1913 Rolette County, North Dakota, at age 1 (ND Death Index.).

30. **Mary Ernestine Wilkie** was born on 4 Nov 1881 (Ibid.). She married **Frederick Raphael Martin**, son of **Theophile Martin dit Barnabe** and **Elise St.Denis**, on 20 Feb 1900 Turtle Mountain, Rolette County, North Dakota. She died on 26 Oct 1967 Rolette County, North Dakota, at age 85 (Ibid.).

Frederick Raphael Martin was born on 11 Sep 1881 St.Francois Xavier, Manitoba (*St.Ann's Centennial*, page 519-520; 458-459.) (BIA-TM-BMD.) (SFXI-Kipling, B-46.). He died on 29 Dec 1925 Couture, Rolette County, North Dakota, at age 44 (BIA-TM-BMD.) (*St.Ann's Centennial*, page 519-520; 458-459.) (ND Death Index.). He was buried on 1 Jan 1926 Belcourt, Rolette County, North Dakota (BIA-TM-BMD.).

31. **Napoleon Elzear Wilkie** was born on 21 Aug 1883 Olga, Cavalier County, North Dakota (Olga, page 18, B-17.) (ND Death Index.). He was baptized on 21 Aug 1883 Olga, Cavalier County, North Dakota (Olga, page 18, B-17.). He married **Clemence Laviolette**, daughter of **Albert Laviolette** and **Florestine Richard**, circa 1910 (Genie Graves Research, 11 Jan 2006, source: "St.John - The City at the End of the Rainbow."). He died on 15 Oct 1947 Rolette County, North Dakota, at age 64 (ND Death Index.).

Clemence Laviolette was born circa 1895 North Dakota (1910C ND, page 5B, family 11, line 27-33.) (1940C ND 1940 North Dakota, Sixteenth Census of the United States, National Archives of the United States, Washington, D.C., page 1A.). She died on 27 Nov 1988 Chicago, Cook County, Illinois (Ancestry.com, Cook County Genealogy Records (Deaths).).

Children of **Napoleon Elzear Wilkie** and **Clemence Laviolette** were as follows:

i. Stephen Wilkie was born on 1 Feb 1920 (*1937-TMC*, page 532, Census No. 6349-6355.). He died on 26 Aug 2003 Dunseith, Rolette County, North Dakota, at age 83 (SSDI.).

ii. Leo D. Wilkie was born on 19 Feb 1921 Olga, Cavalier County, North Dakota (*1937-TMC*, page 532, Census No. 6349-6355.). He married Mary Eva Lenoir, daughter of Louis Lenoir and Marie Emilie Pelletier, in 1961 (Ancestry.com, Find a Grave, obituary.). He died on 4 Sep 1986 Belcourt, Rolette County, North Dakota, at age 65 (Ibid.).

   Mary Eva Lenoir was born on 18 May 1916 North Dakota (1936-TMC, page 157.) (*1937-TMC*, page 132, Census No. 1570-1571.). She married **Eugene Norbert Delonais**, son of **Francois Delauney dit Delonais** and **Mary Rose Belgarde**, before 1937 (*St.Ann's Centennial*, page 324.). She died on 29 Sep 2010 Belcourt, Rolette County, North Dakota, at age 94 (ND Death Index.).

iii. Leona Wilkie was born on 6 Dec 1923 (*1937-TMC*, page 532, Census No. 6349-6355.). She married Robert Tucknott. She died on 17 Feb 2005 Chicago, Cook County, Illinois, at age 81 (SSDI.).

iv. Mary Ann Wilkie was born on 12 Feb 1926 (ND Death Index.) (*1937-TMC*, page 532, Census No. 6349-6355.). She married Louis Riel Boyer, son of Joseph Boyer and Josephine Baker, on 5 Jun 1945 (TM Star, 12 Apr 2010.). She died on 11 Jun 2002 St.John, Rolette County, North Dakota, at age 76 (Ibid.) (ND Death Index.).

   Louis Riel Boyer was born on 3 Oct 1917 Rolette County, North Dakota (1936-TMC, page 43.) (*1924-TMC-ND*, Census No. 703-708.). He married **Emily M. Nadeau**, daughter of **Pierre Nadeau** and **Josephine Lafontaine**, on 25 Apr 1936 Belcourt, Rolette County, North Dakota (TM Star, 12 Apr 2010.). He died on 3 Apr 2010 Belcourt Hospital, Belcourt, Rolette County, North Dakota, at age 92 (Ibid.).

v. Amelia Wilkie was born on 26 Apr 1931 (*1937-TMC*, page 532, Census No. 6349-6355.). She married Lenwood Wendlick on 17 Dec 1951 North Dakota. She died on 11 May 2014 Finley, North Dakota, at age 83.

vi. Napoleon Wilkie was born on 15 Apr 1935 (Ibid.).

32. Moise Wilkie was born on 22 May 1887 Olga, Cavalier County, North Dakota (Olga, page 121, B-15.) (ND Death Index.). He was baptized on 22 May 1887 Olga, Cavalier County, North Dakota (Olga, page 121, B-15.). He married **Isabella Demarais** before 1910. He died on 2 Nov 1965 Sioux County, North Dakota, at age 78 (ND Death Index.).

Isabella Demarais was born on 14 Sep 1890 Canada (1920C-MTl, page 5A.) (SSDI.). She died on 15 Apr 1975 Cowlitz County, Washington, at age 84 (Ibid.) (Washington State Digital Archives, Secretary of State, State Archives, http://www.digitalcarchives.wa./gov, 960 Washington Street, Cheney, WA 99004.).

Children of **Moise Wilkie** and **Isabella Demarais** were as follows:

i. Rose Anne Wilkie was born on 2 Oct 1910 (1936-TMC, page 130.) (BIA-TM-BMD, page 41.).

ii. Moses Edward Wilkie was born on 20 Feb 1913 (1936-TMC, page 130.) (BIA-TM-BMD, page 63.). He died on 26 Dec 1982 Vancouver, Clark County, Washington, at age 69 (SSDI.) (WA Vital Statistics.).

iii. Annabelle Wilkie was born on 26 Jul 1917 (*1937-TMC*, page 531-532, Census No. 6341-6348.).
   Question: *Annabelle is the adopted niece of Moses and Bella Wilkie. Parents unknown.*

iv. Esther Wilkie was born on 16 Apr 1920 (Ibid.).

v. Charles Anthony Wilkie was born on 23 May 1922 (Ibid.). He died on 16 Mar 1994 San Bernardino County, California, at age 71 (SSDI.) (WIS Birth.).

vi. Lucille Wilkie was born on 17 May 1924 (*1937-TMC*, page 531-532, Census No. 6341-6348.).

vii. Eugene David Wilkie was born on 9 Mar 1927 (Ibid.). He died on 6 Mar 2008 Sacramento, Sacramento County, California, at age 80 (SSDI.).

33. John Baptiste Joseph Wilkie was born on 9 Feb 1889 Olga, Cavalier County, North Dakota (Olga, page 159, B-11.) (ND Death Index.). He was baptized on 9 Feb 1889 Olga, Cavalier County, North Dakota (Olga, page 159, B-11.). He married **Mary Jane Belgarde**, daughter of **Theodore Belgarde** and **Louise Desjarlais**, before 1909. He died on 1 Jan 1950 Rolette County, North Dakota, at age 60 (ND Death Index.).

Mary Jane Belgarde was born on 3 Aug 1890 Rolette County, North Dakota (Ibid.). She died on 9 Sep 1987 Rolette County, North Dakota, at age 97 (Ibid.).

Children of **John Baptiste Joseph Wilkie** and **Mary Jane Belgarde** were as follows:

i. Mary Agnes Wilkie was born on 20 May 1909 (1936-TMC, page 130.) (BIA-TM-BMD, page 25.). She married James Russell Turcotte, son of Daniel Turcotte and Marie Rosine Delaunay, before 1934. She married James Trottier, son of Napoleon "Paul" Trottier and Bibiane Eulalie Slater, before 1934 (*1937-TMC*, Census No. 5839-5841.).

   James Russell Turcotte was born on 9 Feb 1913 North Dakota (Ibid., page 501, Census No. 5864-5866.).

   James Trottier was born on 12 Sep 1910 (1920C-MTl, page 5B, family 64, line 66-74.) (ND Death Index.). He died on 4 Feb 1985 Rolette, North Dakota, at age 74 (Ibid.).

ii. Ernest Wilkie was born on 2 Sep 1912 Rolette County, North Dakota (1936-TMC, page 130.) (ND Death Index.) (BIA-TM-BMD, page 61.). He died on 19 Dec 1972 Rolette County, North Dakota, at age 60 (ND Death Index.).

iii. Mabel Bebian Wilkie was born on 24 Aug 1914 (*1924-TMC-ND*, Census No. 3881-3889.).

iv. Mary Edna Wilkie was born on 5 Jul 1916 (ND Death Index.). She died on 13 Jul 1925 Rolette County, North Dakota, at age 9 (Ibid.).

v. Alice Wilkie was born on 22 Feb 1918 (*1937-TMC*, page 527-528, Census No. 6172-6181.).

vi. Cecile Wilkie was born on 26 Jun 1921 (Ibid.).

vii. Wilbur E. Wilkie was born on 13 Aug 1923 (Ibid.). He died on 6 Dec 1995 Rolla, Rolette County, North Dakota, at age 72 (SSDI.).

viii. John Wilkie was born on 9 Aug 1925 (*1937-TMC*, page 527-528, Census No. 6172-6181.).

ix. Martha Wilkie was born on 1 Aug 1928 (Ibid.).

x. Florestine Wilkie was born on 2 Jun 1930 (Ibid.).

xi. Helen A. Wilkie was born on 25 May 1932 (Ibid.).

34. Mary Jane Wilkie was born circa Mar 1891. She was born on 2 Mar 1891 Olga, Cavalier County, North Dakota (Olga, page 195, B-5.). She married **Ambroise Demontigny**, son of **Hermas Demontigny** and **Leocadie Sansregret,** before 1910 (1936-TMC, page 80-81.). She died on 27 May 1926 Rolette County, North Dakota (ND Death Index.).

Ambroise Demontigny was born on 3 Jul 1881 near Boissevan (ArchiviaNet.).

35. Marie Delia Wilkie was born in Mar 1894 (1900C-ND, 95-95.). She married **Joseph Napoleon Vivier**, son of **Ambroise Vivier** and **Genevieve Azure,** in 1922 (Probate, Napoleon Vivier Probate.). She died on 9 Mar 1928 Rolette County, North Dakota (Ibid.) (ND Death Index.).

Joseph Napoleon Vivier was born on 21 Jul 1882 R.M. of Montcalm, Manitoba (BIA-TM, Family history of Ambrose Vivier.) (MB Vital Statistics, Birth Reg. #1882,001717.) (*1919 Turtle Mountain,* Census No. 3173-3180.). He married **Virginie Houle**, daughter of **Abraham Houle** and **Marguerite Desjarlais,** circa 1900 (Probate, Napoleon Vivier Probate.). He died on 22 Sep 1956 at age 74 (Ibid.).

Children of **Marie Delia Wilkie** and **Joseph Napoleon Vivier** were as follows:

    i. Mary Clara Vivier was born on 10 Nov 1909 (BIA-TM-BMD, page 30.) (1910-TMC 1910 Census of the Turtle Mountain Chippewa, United States Indian Service Department of the Interior, Turtle Mountain Agency, North Dakota, 30 June 1910 , Census No. 2590-2595.). She died before 1912 (1936-TMC, page 125.).

    ii. Elizabeth Vivier was born in 1919 (Ibid.) (*1920 TMC*, Census No. 3268-3275.). She died on 25 Jan 1920 (Ibid.).

    iii. Ernest Vivier was born on 8 Jul 1923 (Probate, Napoleon Vivier Probate.) (*1937-TMC*, page 513, Census No. 6005-6012.).

    iv. Napoleon "Johnny" Vivier was born on 8 Apr 1926 (Probate, Napoleon Vivier Probate.).

    v. Esther Vivier was born on 28 Jan 1928 (Ibid.). She married (--?--) Laducer (Ibid.).

36. Louis O. Wilkie was born on 6 May 1895 Rolette County, North Dakota (1936-TMC, page 129.) (ND Death Index.). He married **Eliza Decouteau**, daughter of **Alexander Decouteau** and **Marie Anne Lafontaine,** before 1918. He died on 17 Aug 1964 Rolette County, North Dakota, at age 69 (Ibid.).

Eliza Decouteau was born on 12 Apr 1898 (SSDI.). She died on 15 Feb 1968 Rolla, Rolette County, North Dakota, at age 69 (Ibid.).

Children of **Louis O. Wilkie** and **Eliza Decouteau** were as follows:

    i. Louis Napoleon Wilkie was born on 4 Jul 1918 (*1937-TMC*, page 530-531, Census No. 6330-6339.). He died on 11 Apr 1981 Rolla, Rolette County, North Dakota, at age 62 (SSDI.) (ND Death Index.).

    ii. Marie Ann Wilkie was born on 30 Jan 1920 (*1937-TMC*, page 530-531, Census No. 6330-6339.).

    iii. Elmer Wilkie was born on 17 Feb 1922 (Ibid.).

    iv. Raymond M. Wilkie was born on 12 Jun 1924 (Ibid.). He married Albina Slater, daughter of John Slater and Marie Hannah McGillis, before 1947. He died on 23 Aug 2002 Dunseith, Rolette County, North Dakota, at age 78 (SSDI.).

        Albina Slater was born on 17 Oct 1928 North Dakota (*1937-TMC*, page 462, Census No. 5485-5490.).

    v. Veronica G. Wilkie was born on 30 Aug 1925 (Ibid., page 530-531, Census No. 6330-6339.). She married Peter Azure in 1947 Belcourt, Rolette County, North Dakota (Ancestry.com, Find a Grave, obituary.). She died on 2 Feb 2012 Belcourt, Rolette County, North Dakota, at age 86 (Ibid.).

    vi. Patrick Earl Wilkie was born on 26 Feb 1930 (*1937-TMC*, page 530-531, Census No. 6330-6339.). He married Mary Houle on 30 Nov 1957 St.Ann's, Belcourt, Rolette County, North Dakota (TM Star, 25 Feb 2013, page 2.). He died on 15 Feb 2013 Belcourt, Rolette County, North Dakota, at age 82 (ND Death Index.).

    vii. Pamela Lucille Wilkie was born on 29 Apr 1931 (*1937-TMC*, page 530-531, Census No. 6330-6339.).

    viii. Lois Ann Wilkie was born on 28 Jun 1934 (Ibid.).

37. Marie Clara 'Laura' Wilkie was born on 31 Oct 1899 Rolette County, North Dakota (ND Death Index.). She married **John Louis Demontigny,** son of **Hermas Demontigny** and **Julia Azure,** on 24 Jun 1922 (BIA-TM, Jean Louis Demontigny Probate.). She died on 7 Feb 1987 Grand Forks County, North Dakota, at age 87 (ND Death Index.).

John Louis Demontigny was born on 4 Jun 1897 Belcourt, Rolette County, North Dakota (BIA-TM, Family history card of Julia Azure Demontigny.). He died on 12 May 1954 Grand Forks, North Dakota, at age 56 (Ibid., Jean Louis Demontigny Probate.) (ND Death Index.).

Descendants of John Wills

Generation One

1. John Wills was born circa 1770 England. He married according to the custom of the country **Josephte Grant**, daughter of **Cuthbert Grant** and **Metisse or Cree (--?--),** before 1799. He died on 1 Jun 1815 Fort Gibralter.

Josephte Grant was born circa 1785. She married **Pierre Latour or Montour** before 1819.

Children of **John Wills** and **Josephte Grant** were as follows:

  2 i. John Wills, b. 1799; m. Marie McKay; d. 13 Jan 1890 Carlton, (Saskatchewan).

  3 ii. Emelie Wills, b. 1810 North West; m. Alexandre Duboishue Breland; d. 28 Jan 1894 St.Francois Xavier, Manitoba.

  4 iii. Edouard Wills, b. circa 1812 Red River, (Manitoba); m. Isabelle McGillis.

    iv. Josette Wills was born before 1815.

Generation Two

2. John Wills was born in 1799 (T. R. "Pat" McCloy, McKay Descendancy, McKay Descendancy.). He married **Marie McKay**, daughter of **John Richards McKay** and **Harriett Ballenden,** on 6 Sep 1842 St.Francois Xavier, (Manitoba) (SFX: 1834-1850 St.Francois Xavier 1834-1851 Register, M-71. Hereinafter cited as SFX: 1834-1850.). He died on 13 Jan 1890 Carlton, (Saskatchewan).

Marie McKay was born in Jul 1820 Brandon House (T. R. McCloy, 19 Jan 1994.). She was born on 21 Dec 1820 (Denney Papers, Charles D. Denney, Glenbow Archives, Calgary, Alberta.). She was baptized on 14 Jul 1822 St.Johns, Brandon House (HBCR Hudson

Bay Company Register of Anglican Church Baptisms, Marriages, and Burials for the Red River Settlement, 1821-1841; Hudson's Bay Company Archives, Winnipeg, Manitoba, E.4/1a, folio 38. Hereinafter cited as HBCR.). She was baptized on 6 Sep 1842 St.Francois Xavier, (Manitoba) (SFX: 1834-1850, B-419.).

Children of **John Wills** and **Marie McKay** were as follows:

   i. Rosia Wills married George Hammond (T. R. McCloy, McKay Descendancy.).
5 ii. Emelie Wills, b. circa Dec 1843 North West; m. Charles Bremner; d. 1918 Bresaylor, Saskatchewan.
6 iii. Henriette Wills, b. 29 Apr 1846; m. Thomas Beads; d. 1881 Prince Albert, (Saskatchewan); bur. 6 Jan 1881 Prince Albert, (Saskatchewan).
7 iv. John Wills, b. 27 Dec 1848 St.Francois Xavier, (Manitoba); m. Julie Tanner; d. 19 Jan 1910 Eagle Hills, Saskatchewan.
   v. Heloisa Wells was born circa Dec 1851 (SFXI 1851-1868 St.Francois Xavier 1852-1861 Register Index, B-21. Hereinafter cited as SFXI 1851-1868.). She was baptized on 6 Jun 1852 St.Francois Xavier, (Manitoba) (Ibid.).
   vi. Unnamed Wells was born on 6 Dec 1853 (AP Records of the Assumption Roman Catholic Church, Pembina, North Dakota: Baptisms, Marriages, Sepultures, 1848-1896; compiled by Reverend Father J. M. Belleau, 2 October 1944, page 106, B-288. Hereinafter cited as AP.). He/she was baptized on 27 Apr 1854 Assumption, Pembina, Pembina County, Dakota Territory (Ibid.).
   vii. Mary Wills was born on 4 Apr 1855 (T. R. McCloy, McKay Descendancy.).
8 viii. Elise Mary Wills, b. Nov 1856; m. Daniel Ledoux; d. 1922 Crow Reservation, Montana.
   ix. Marie Wills was born on 5 Apr 1857 (SFXI-Kipling St.Francois Xavier Register Index, 1834-1900; compiled by Clarence Kipling , B-184.). She was baptized on 24 May 1857 St.Francois Xavier, (Manitoba) (Ibid.).
   x. Sidonia Wills was born in 1861 Fort Ellice, Manitoba (T. R. McCloy, McKay Descendancy.). She was baptized on 16 Aug 1861 (Manitoba) (Ibid.). She married James Duffy (Ibid.).
   xi. Moses Welsh was born in Jun 1863 (SB-Rozyk St. Boniface Roman Catholic Church, Manitoba, Canada, Baptisms, Marriages and Burials 1860-1875 Extractions, Compiled by Rosemary Rozyk, page 128, B-143.). He was baptized on 21 Jul 1863 St.Boniface, (Manitoba) (Ibid.). He married Elizabeth J (T. R. McCloy, McKay Descendancy.).
   Elizabeth J was born circa 1874.
   xii. Rebecca Wells was born circa Oct 1865 Moose Mountain, Assiniboine (HBSI Index 1886-1901, 1906 Halfbreed Scrip Applications, RG15-21.) (SFXI-Kipling, B-64.) (ArchiviaNet 1886-1901, 1906 Half-Breed Scrip Applications Index, RG15-21, Volume 1333 through 1371, Microfilm Reel Number C-14944 through C-15010, National Archives of Canada, Ottawa, Ontario, http://www.collectionscanada.gc.ca.). She was baptized on 27 May 1866 St.Francois Xavier, (Manitoba) (SFXI-Kipling, B-64.). She married George Henry Parker before 1887 (T. R. McCloy, McKay Descendancy.).
   xiii. Alexander Wills was born in Mar 1877 Cypress Hills, (Saskatchewan) (Ibid.) (ArchiviaNet, C-15009.).

3. Emelie Wills was born in 1810 North West (MBS Scrip Applications, Original White Settlers & Halfbreeds residing in Manitoba on 15 July 1870, RG15-19, C-14926.). She married **Alexandre Duboishue Breland**, son of **Pierre Breland** and **Louise Belly,** before 1828. She died on 28 Jan 1894 St.Francois Xavier, Manitoba (SFXI-Kipling, S-1.).

Alexandre Duboishue Breland was born circa 1805 (1828C RRS HBCA E5/2 1828 Census of the Red River Settlement, HBCA E5/2, Hudson's Bay Company Archives, Provincial Archives, 200 Vaughan Street, Winnipeg, MB R3C 1T5, Canada., page 10.). He died in Mar 1858 Mississippi River (SFXI-Kipling, S-87.) (SFXI: 1851-1869 St.Francois Xavier 1851-69 Register Index.). He was buried on 15 Jan 1859 St.Francois Xavier, (Manitoba) (SFXI-Kipling, S-87.) (SFXI-1834-54.).

4. Edouard Wills was born circa 1812 Red River, (Manitoba) (1850Ci-MN *Minnesota Territorial Census, 1850*, Harpole, Patricia C. and Mary D. Nagle, ed., (St.Paul, Minnesota: Minnesota Historical Society, 1972), page 25, Dwelling 73, Family 73.). He married **Isabelle McGillis**, daughter of **Angus McGillis** and **Marguerite Sauteuse,** on 10 Oct 1836 St.Francois Xavier, (Manitoba) (SFX: 1834-1850, M-22.).

Isabelle McGillis was born in 1817 Minnesota. She was born circa 1819 Red River (1850C-MNT 1850 Minnesota Territory Census, Nation Archives of the United States, Washington D.C., page 25, Dwelling 73, Family 73.).

Children of **Edouard Wills** and **Isabelle McGillis** were as follows:

   i. John Thomas Welsh was born in 1834. He married Louise Wilkie, daughter of Alexander Wilkie and Louise Gariepy, on 14 Mar 1883 (St.Peter's Mission), Judith Basin, Montana Territory (SPMT St.Peter's Mission; Volume I; Marriage Register 1859-1895; Translated & Transcribed by Reverend Dale McFarlane, Archivist, Diocese of Great Falls-Billings, Montana; Spring 1981, page 40, #241.) (MeaCM Meagher County, Montana; Marriage Record Licenses and Certificates; 1865-1950; familysearch.org: District 86, page 2B, family 47, line 82. Hereinafter cited as MeaCCM.).
   Louise Wilkie was born circa 1865.
9 ii. Daniel Wills or Wells or Welsh, b. 1835; m. Louise Collin; d. 14 Dec 1911 Tyler, Fergus County, Montana.
10 iii. Edouard Wills or Wells or Welsh, b. 11 Aug 1837 St.Francois Xavier, (Manitoba); m. Marie Demontigny; d. 7 Jan 1911 Lewistown, Fergus County, Montana.
   iv. Jean Wills was born circa Nov 1838 (SFX: 1834-1850, B-253.). He was baptized on 1 Jun 1839 St.Francois Xavier, (Manitoba) (Ibid.). He died on 30 Oct 1840 (Ibid., S-56.). He was buried on 2 Nov 1840 St.Francois Xavier, (Manitoba) (Ibid.).
   v. Donald Wills was baptized on 27 May 1840 St.Francois Xavier, (Manitoba) (Ibid., B-307.).
11 vi. Marie Wills, b. 28 Dec 1841; m. George Muller.
   vii. Allan Alkmund Wells was born on 18 Jan 1844 St.Francois Xavier, (Manitoba) (Ibid., B-490.). He was baptized on 19 Jan 1844 St.Francois Xavier, (Manitoba) (Ibid.).
12 viii. Priscille Wills, b. 15 May 1847; m. Jerome Lafournaise dit Laboucane.

13   ix. John Wills or Wells, b. 20 Dec 1848; m. Marie Philomene Ouellette.

       x. Marie Virginie Wells was born on 24 May 1851 Pembina, Pembina County, Dakota Territory (AP, page 55, B-29.). She was baptized on 24 May 1851 Assumption, Pembina, Pembina County, Dakota Territory (Ibid.). She married Michael Langevin, son of Michael Langevin and Flavie Lontant, on 1 May 1874 Lebret, (Saskatchewan) (L1, page 132, M-12.). She died on 6 Aug 1905 Lewistown, Fergus County, Montana, at age 54.

             Michael Langevin was born circa 1849 St.Jacques, Montreal, Montreal, Quebec (BIA-LS Bureau of Indian Affairs, Little Shell Enrollment Papers.) (L1, page 132, M-12.). He died on 14 Dec 1898 Lewistown, Fergus County, Montana.

14   xi. Gregoire Alphonse Wills, b. 28 Apr 1853 Assumption, Pembina, Pembina County, Dakota Territory; m. Rose Ross; d. 1880 on the plains, near Wood Mountain, (Saskatchewan).

      xii. Magdeleine Wells was born on 15 May 1856 Pembina, Pembina County, Dakota Territory (AP, page 147, B-409.). She was baptized on 15 May 1856 Assumption, Pembina, Pembina County, Dakota Territory (Ibid.).

15 xiii. Jean James Wills, b. 6 Oct 1858 Pembina County, Dakota Territory; m. Celina Ouellette; m. Marguerite Berger; d. 25 Jan 1909 Lewiston, Fergus County, Montana.

     xiv. Marie Rose Wells was born on 7 Feb 1861 Pembina, Pembina County, Dakota Territory (Ibid., page 229, B-148.). She was baptized on 8 Feb 1861 Assumption, Pembina, Pembina County, Dakota Territory (Ibid.). She married William Laframboise, son of Francois Laframboise and Marie Trottier, circa 1877. She died in Mar 1878 at age 17 (L1, page 220, B-19 [S-19].). She was buried on 16 Apr 1878 Lebret, (Saskatchewan) (Ibid.).

             William Laframboise was born in Mar 1853 (SFXI-Kipling, B-69.) (SFXI 1851-1868, B-69.). He was baptized on 3 May 1853 St.Francois Xavier, (Manitoba) (SFXI-Kipling, B-69.) (SFXI 1851-1868, B-69.). He married **Catherine Berger**, daughter of **Pierre Berger** and **Judith Wilkie**, on 10 May 1880 (St.Peter's Mission), Judith Basin, Montana Territory (SPMT, page 26, #136.).

Generation Three

5. Emelie Wills was born circa Dec 1843 North West (SFX: 1834-1850, B-503.). She was baptized on 21 Apr 1844 St.Francois Xavier, (Manitoba) (Ibid.). She married **Charles Bremner**, son of **Alexander Bremner** and **Elizabeth Twat**, on 28 Aug 1860 Headingley, (Manitoba) (Denney.). She died in 1918 Bresaylor, Saskatchewan (T. R. McCloy, McKay Descendancy.).

Charles Bremner was born in 1840 St.Charles, (Manitoba) (MBS, C-14926.). He was baptized on 24 Apr 1853 St.James, (Manitoba) (SJAC St.James Anglican Church Extractions, Manitoba Genealogy Society, Winnipeg, Manitoba, B-6.). He died on 16 May 1919 Battenberg, Gibbons, Alberta (Denney.).

6. Henriette Wills was born on 29 Apr 1846 (SFX: 1834-1850, B-601.). She was baptized on 3 May 1846 St.Francois Xavier, (Manitoba) (Ibid.). She married **Thomas Beads**, son of **John Beads** and **Margaret (--?--)**, before 1864 (T. R. McCloy, McKay Descendancy.). She died in 1881 Prince Albert, (Saskatchewan). She was buried on 6 Jan 1881 Prince Albert, (Saskatchewan).

Thomas Beads was born circa 1831 (Ibid.). He was baptized on 31 Mar 1840 Red River Settlement, Manitoba (HBCR, E.4/1a folio 165d.). He died circa 1892 Prince Albert, (Saskatchewan) (T. R. McCloy, McKay Descendancy.).

7. John Wills was born on 27 Dec 1848 St.Francois Xavier, (Manitoba) (SFX: 1834-1850, B-758.). He was baptized on 31 Dec 1848 St.Francois Xavier, (Manitoba) (Ibid.). He married **Julie Tanner**, daughter of **Joseph Tanner** and **sister of Chief Yellow Quill**, on 15 Oct 1869 St.Francois Xavier, (Manitoba) (SFXI-Kipling, M-13.). He died on 19 Jan 1910 Eagle Hills, Saskatchewan, at age 61 (T. R. McCloy, McKay Descendancy.).

Julie Tanner was born in 1849 Portage la Prairie, (Manitoba) (Denney.).

Children of **John Wills** and **Julie Tanner** were as follows:

16   i. Solomon Wills, b. 2 Jan 1870.

      ii. Marius Welsh was born in 1871 Regina, (Saskatchewan) (ArchiviaNet, C-15009.). He died on 2 Jan 1871 (L1, page 30, S-1.). He was buried on 6 Feb 1871 Lebret, (Saskatchewan) (Ibid.).

17   iii. Jean Baptiste Wills or Wells or Welsh, b. 2 Jan 1872 Saskatoon, (Saskatchewan); m. Mary Jane Hodgson; d. 14 Apr 1946 LeGoff, Alberta; bur. Apr 1946 St.Raphael, Le Goff, Alberta.

18   iv. Alexandre Wills or Wells or Welsh, b. 28 Jan 1874 Duck Lake, (Saskatchewan); m. Eleonore Ouellette.

      v. Abraham John Welsh was born on 28 May 1876 Fort Walsh, (Saskatchewan) (SL-SK St.Laurent-de-Grandin Roman Catholic Registre des Baptemes, Mariages & Sepltures, St.Laurent, Saskatchewan, 1872-1896, page 61, B-32. Hereinafter cited as SL-SK.) (ArchiviaNet, C-15009.). He was baptized on 17 Aug 1876 St.Laurent-de-Grandin, (Saskatchewan) (SL-SK, page 61, B-32.). He died on 8 Mar 1877 Bow River (Rarihokwats Research, 26 Apr 1997.) (L1, page 194, S-4.). He was buried on 14 May 1877 Lebret, (Saskatchewan) (Ibid.).

     vi. Marie Athalie Wells was born on 10 Jul 1878 between Fort Assiniboine and the boundary, (Saskatchewan) (ArchiviaNet, C-15009.). She died in 1883 Bresaylor, (Saskatchewan) (Ibid.).

   vii. Joseph Isaac Wells was born in Apr 1883 Red Deer River, (Saskatchewan) (Rarihokwats, 26 Apr 1997.) (ArchiviaNet, C-15009.). He died on 14 Jul 1889 Bresaylor, (Saskatchewan), at age 6 (Ibid.).

  viii. Charles Jacob Wells was born on 27 Apr 1887 (1901 Canada, microfilm, T-6553, North Battleford, page 6, Family 59, line #44-50.) (SV St.Vital Roman Catholic Registre des Baptemes, Mariages & Sepltures, Battleford, Saskatchewan, 1878-1896, B-14. Hereinafter cited as SV.). He was baptized on 8 May 1887 St.Vital, Battleford, (Saskatchewan) (Ibid.).

8. Elise Mary Wills was born in Nov 1856 (T. R. McCloy, McKay Descendancy.). She married **Daniel Ledoux**, son of **Eusebe Ledoux** and **Louise Desjarlais**, on 20 Jul 1869 St.Francois Xavier, (Manitoba) (SFXI-Kipling, M-8.). She died in 1922 Crow Reservation, Montana.

Daniel Ledoux was born in May 1848 (T. R. McCloy, McKay Descendancy.). He died in 1919 Crow Reservation.

9. Daniel Wills or Wells or Welsh was born in 1835. He married **Louise Collin**, daughter of **Jean Baptiste Collin** and **Betsy Honore dit Henry,** before 1859. He died on 14 Dec 1911 Tyler, Fergus County, Montana.

Louise Collin was born circa 1833 Red River, (Manitoba) (1850Ci-MN, page 23; Dwelling 58; Family 58.). She was baptized on 27 Sep 1834 St.Boniface, (Manitoba) (SB 1825-1834.). She married **Antoine Langer**, son of **Francois Langer** and **Marguerite George**, on 16 Jan 1854 Assumption, Pembina, Pembina County, Dakota Territory (AP, page 101-102, M-41.). She died on 8 Oct 1902 Lewistown, Fergus County, Montana.

Children of **Daniel Wills or Wells or Welsh** and **Louise Collin** were as follows:

    i.   Betsy Wells was born on 3 May 1859 Pembina, Pembina County, Dakota Territory (Ibid., page 216, B-127.). She was baptized on 16 May 1859 Assumption, Pembina, Pembina County, Dakota Territory (Ibid.). She married Pierre Ross, son of Roderick Ross and Marie Delorme, before 1881.

            Pierre Ross was born on 29 Jun 1859 (SFXI-Kipling, B-368.). He was baptized on 21 Aug 1859 St.Francois Xavier, (Manitoba) (Ibid.) (INB, page 159.).

    ii.   Mary Daisy Wells was born circa 1863 Montana (Al Yerbury Research, Fergus County Marriages.). She married Pascal Turcotte, son of Vital Turcotte and Madeleine Caplette, before 1879. She married Norbert Laverdure, son of Francois Xavier Laverdure and Marguerite Pelletier, on 5 Nov 1888 Fergus County, Montana (Ibid., Metis Marriages of Fergus Co., MT; p.8; Norbert Laverdure (Ganaza & Marguerite LaFountain) age 24; b.p. Montana to Mary Wells (David & Louis ?) age 25; b.p. Montana married 5 Nov 1888.) (FerCM Fergus County Courthouse, Montana; Marriage Record Licenses and Certificates, 1865-1950, familysearch.org., Hereinafter cited as FerCM.). She died on 15 Apr 1923 Lewistown, Fergus County, Montana (Al Yerbury, From Creel Funeral Home Records: Mary Daisy Laverdure, age 63, b. 1860, d. 15 Apr 1923, parents: Dan Wells & Louise Collins.).

            Pascal Turcotte was born on 23 Aug 1857 St.Boniface, (Manitoba) (MBS, C-14934.). He was born circa 1876 Dakota Territory (AYM Documentation of Metis Families of Red River and the Northwest Territories; Census, Biographical, and Historical: 1881 Census Qu'Appelle, Wood Mountain, Lac la Biche; History of the Turtle Mountain Band of Chippewas; Census for the Turtle Mountain Reservation 1884-1886; Pembina, Dakota Territory 1850 Census; Various Metis Census Records for Pembina County, ND 1910; compiled by Al Yerbery, 1996, Fergus County Marriages.).

            Norbert Laverdure was born circa 1864 Montana (Al Yerbury, Fergus County Marriages.). He was born circa 1866 Dakota Territory (1880 Montana Census, National Archives of the United States, Washington D.C., page 429A, 56-57.). He died on 25 Jun 1931 Lewistown, Fergus County, Montana (Al Yerbury, From Creel Funeral Home Records: Norbert Laverdure, age 61, b. 1870 Dakota, d. 25 June 1931; parents: Xavier Laverdure, Margaret LaFontain.) (Ancestry.com Website, Death Index.).

19   iii.   Joseph Wills or Wells, b. 18 Nov 1863 Devils Lake, Dakota Territory; m. Julienne Wilkie; m. Catherine Fleury; m. Marie Adele Laverdure; m. Maria Celina Laverdure; d. 15 Jan 1942 Lewistown, Fergus County, Montana.

20   iv.   Thomas Wills or Wells, b. circa 1866; m. Zilda Daniels; d. 1913 Lewistown, Fergus County, Montana.

    v.   Alfred Welsh was born in Jan 1870 (L1, page 19, B-17.). He was baptized on 28 Apr 1870 Lebret, (Saskatchewan) (Ibid.). He died circa May 1870 (ArchiviaNet, C-15009.).

    vi.   St.Pierre "Peter" Wells was born on 28 Jun 1871 Lebret, (Saskatchewan) (L1, page 44, B-79.). He was baptized on 29 Jun 1871 Lebret, (Saskatchewan) (Ibid.). He married Philomene Berger, daughter of Isidore Berger and Domitilde Laframboise, on 26 Dec 1894 Lewistown, Fergus County, Montana (FerCM.). He married Mary Ouellette, daughter of Antoine Ratte Ouellette and Angelique Bottineau, in 1899 Fergus County, Montana (Ibid.). He died circa Jan 1910 Grass Range, Montana (*Missoulian Newspaper*, Missoula, Montana, 9 Jul 1911.).

            Philomene Berger was born circa 1874 (FerCM.).

            Mary Ouellette was born on 19 Mar 1880 Lewistown, Fergus County, Montana (HBSI.) (ArchiviaNet.). She married **Joseph Dominique Ducharme**, son of **Francois Ducharme** and **Josephte Carriere**, on 2 Feb 1903 Lewistown, Fergus County, Montana (Al Yerbury, Metis Marriages of Fergus Co. MT.) (FerCM.).

    vii.   Louise Anne Welsh was born on 9 Sep 1876 (L1, page 198, B-35.). She was baptized on 6 Dec 1876 Lebret, (Saskatchewan) (Ibid.).

    viii.   Francois "Frank" Wells was born on 17 Oct 1876 Wood Mountain, (Saskatchewan) (ArchiviaNet, C-15009.).

    ix.   Rose Wells was born on 4 Sep 1877 Maple Creek, (Saskatchewan) (Ibid.). She married Frank Laverdure, son of Francois Xavier Laverdure and Marguerite Pelletier, on 3 Sep 1903 Fergus County, Montana (Al Yerbury, Fergus County Marriages.) (FerCM.). She died on 7 Nov 1961 at age 84.

            Frank Laverdure was born on 10 Jul 1878 Milk River, Montana (SPMT , page 118, #2500.). He was baptized on 27 Nov 1878 St.Peter's Mission, Cascade County, Montana (Ibid.). He died on 7 Mar 1947 Montana at age 68 (Ancestry.com, Death Index.).

    x.   Clement Welsh was born on 20 Mar 1879 (SPMT , page 127, #2663.). He was baptized on 21 Sep 1879 (St.Peter's Mission), Judith Basin, Montana (Ibid.).

10. Edouard Wills or Wells or Welsh was born on 11 Aug 1837 St.Francois Xavier, (Manitoba) (SFX: 1834-1850, B-172.). He was baptized on 12 Aug 1837 St.Francois Xavier, (Manitoba) (Ibid.). He married **Marie Demontigny**, daughter of **Charles Demontigny** and **Marie Desjarlais**, on 1 Jun 1863 St.Francois Xavier, (Manitoba) (SFXI-Kipling, M-12.) (SFXI 1851-1868, M-12.). He died on 7 Jan 1911 Lewistown, Fergus County, Montana, at age 73.

Marie Demontigny was born on 22 Jun 1841 (SFX: 1834-1850, B-363.). She was baptized on 22 Aug 1841 St.Francois Xavier, (Manitoba) (Ibid.). She died on 13 Oct 1921 Tyler, Fergus County, Montana, at age 80.

Children of **Edouard Wills or Wells or Welsh** and **Marie Demontigny** were as follows:

21   i.   Marie Ernestine Wills, b. 8 Apr 1864; m. Antoine Fleury; d. 1 Jan 1952 Montana.

    ii.   Mary Natalie Wells was born on 24 Dec 1865 Broken Bow, North Dakota (1936-LS Henry Roe Cloud Roll 1936-1937, Pembina Band of Chippewa Indians Who Were Under the Leadership of Chief Thomas Little Shell, J. H. Dussome, Zortman, Montana and Vice-President: George SinClaire, Chinook, Montana, #340.) (1937-1987-LS Basic Roll, #340.). She married Daniel Laverdure, son of Pierre Laverdure and Catherine Charette, on 10 Apr

1883 (St.Peter's Mission), Judith Basin, Montana Territory (SPMT , page 40, #245.). Question: *From Creel Funeral Home Records: Natalie Belanger, b. 1847, d. 1948 Could this be her? (Al Yerbury.).*

Daniel Laverdure was born on 16 Dec 1859 Devils Lake, Dakota Territory (David Courchane, Courchane/Courchene Family Research.). He died on 2 Sep 1939 Lewistown, Fergus County, Montana, at age 79 (MT Death.).

iii. Sarah Ann Wells was born circa 1867 White Horse Plains, (Manitoba) (1870C-MB, page 388, #568.). She was born on 25 Sep 1869 (1937-1987-LS Basic Roll, #502.). She married George Tivies before 1888. She died on 22 Aug 1949 Lewistown, Fergus County, Montana.

George Tivies was born before 1870 (1902-1930 Fergus County, Montana School Census; Courthouse, Lewistown, Montana: Superintendent of Schools, Fergus County.).

iv. Samuel Welsh dit Wells was born on 18 Nov 1870 (L1, page 40, B-55.). He was baptized on 16 Dec 1870 Lebret, (Saskatchewan) (Ibid.). He married Virginie Paul, daughter of Elzear Paul and Rose Laplante, on 28 Nov 1923 Lewistown, Fergus County, Montana (FerCM.).

Virginie Paul was born on 7 Dec 1878 St.Francois Xavier, Manitoba (SFXI-Kipling, B-44.). She married **Odelin Janeaux**, son of **Francois Avila Janeaux** and **Virginie Laverdure**, on 3 Nov 1894 Lewistown, Fergus County, Montana (Al Yerbury, Fergus County Marriages.) (FerCM.). She died on 9 Feb 1952 Lewistown, Fergus County, Montana, at age 73 (Al Yerbury.).

v. Florestine Welsh dit Wells was born on 6 Dec 1871. She was baptized on 21 Jan 1872 Lebret, (Saskatchewan) (L1, page 62, B-53.). She married Charles Gardener, son of Edward Gardener and Martha Lovejoy, on 9 Dec 1889 Lewistown, Fergus County, Montana (FerCM.).

Charles Gardener was born in 1861 Ohio (Ibid.). He married **Rosalie Decoteau**, daughter of **Joseph Ducharme dit Decouteau** and **Helene Houle,** before 1895.

vi. Jean Marie Welsh was born on 3 Dec 1873. He was baptized on 5 Dec 1873 Lebret, (Saskatchewan) (L1, page 125, B-72.). He died in 1894 Lewistown, Montana (ArchiviaNet, C-15009.).

vii. Marie Alexina Wells was born on 6 Feb 1876 (L1, page 185, B-123.). She was baptized on 5 Apr 1876 Lebret, (Saskatchewan) (Ibid.). She married Joseph Laverdure, son of Pierre Laverdure and Catherine Charette, on 10 Apr 1883 (St.Peter's Mission), Judith Basin, Montana (SPMT , page 40, #244.). She married Francois 'Frank' Ouellette, son of Antoine Ratte Ouellette and Angelique Bottineau, on 2 Mar 1893 Lewistown, Fergus County, Montana (Al Yerbury, Metis Marriages of Fergus Co. MT.). She died on 31 Aug 1918 Edam, Saskatchewan, at age 42.

Joseph Laverdure was born on 11 Mar 1853 (AP, page 85, B-59.). He was baptized on 18 Apr 1853 Assumption, Pembina, Pembina County, Dakota Territory (Ibid.). He died on 4 Aug 1913 Montana at age 60 (Ancestry.com, Death Index.).

Francois 'Frank' Ouellette was born on 14 Oct 1868 Devils Lake, Dakota Territory. He died on 28 Aug 1965 Lewistown, Fergus County, Montana, at age 96.

viii. Edouard Welsh was baptized on 12 Dec 1877 Lebret, (Saskatchewan) (L1, page 219, B-7.) (ArchiviaNet, C-15009.). He died on 15 Dec 1877 (L1, page 219, S-12.). He was buried on 12 Apr 1878 Lebret, (Saskatchewan) (Ibid.).

ix. Antoine Welsh dit Wells was born on 20 Nov 1878 (SPMT , page 127, #2665.). He was baptized on 21 Sep 1879 (St.Peter's Mission), Judith Basin, Montana (Ibid.). He died on 1 Jun 1949 Lewistown, Fergus County, Montana, at age 70 (Al Yerbury.).

x. Domitille Wills was born circa 1882 (1902-1930 Fergus Co, MT.).

xi. Edward Wells was born on 27 Jan 1885 (1937-1987-LS Basic Roll, #535.). He died on 11 Dec 1948 Lewistown, Fergus County, Montana, at age 63 (Al Yerbury.).

11. Marie Wills was born on 28 Dec 1841 (SFX: 1834-1850, B-386.). She was baptized on 30 Dec 1841 St.Francois Xavier, (Manitoba) (Ibid.). She married **George Muller** before 1865.

Children of **Marie Wills** and **George Muller** were:

i. Marguerite Muller was born circa Apr 1865 (SB-Rozyk, page 62, B-103.). She was baptized on 15 Aug 1865 (Lac Winnipeg), St.Boniface, (Manitoba) (Ibid.).

12. Priscille Wills was born on 15 May 1847 (SFX: 1834-1850, B-688.). She was baptized on 23 May 1847 St.Francois Xavier, (Manitoba) (Ibid.). She married **Jerome Lafournaise dit Laboucane**, son of **Jean Baptiste Lafournaise** and **Marguerite Gosselin,** before 1870 St.Joe, Pembina County, North Dakota (Denney.).

Jerome Lafournaise dit Laboucane was born circa 1837 (1863-T Chippewas of the Red Lake and Pembina bands - Treaty of 1863-1864.). He was born in 1846 Salle River (ArchiviaNet.). He died on 16 Sep 1903 Duhamel, (Alberta) (Denney.).

13. John Wills or Wells was born on 20 Dec 1848 (SFX: 1834-1850, B-760.). He was baptized on 27 Dec 1848 St.Francois Xavier, (Manitoba) (Ibid.). He married **Marie Philomene Ouellette**, daughter of **Antoine Ratte Ouellette** and **Angelique Bottineau,** on 27 Aug 1887 Fergus County, Montana (Al Yerbury, Metis Marriages of Fergus Co. MT.) (FerCM.).

Marie Philomene Ouellette was born on 25 Feb 1872 Wood Mountain, (Saskatchewan) (HBSI.) (L1, page 64, B-62.). She was baptized on 25 Feb 1872 Lebret, (Saskatchewan) (Ibid.).

Children of **John Wills or Wells** and **Marie Philomene Ouellette** were as follows:

i. John Wells was born circa 1888 (1902-1930 Fergus Co, MT.).

ii. Frank Wells was born on 10 Oct 1890 Lewistown, Fergus County, Montana (1936-LS, #539.) (1937-1987-LS Basic Roll, #539.). He married Annie Gladu, daughter of Modeste Gladu and Melanie Azure, on 29 Jul 1919 Zortman, Phillips County, Montana (PhCM Phillips County Courthouse, Montana; Marriage Record Licenses and Certificates; 1865-1950, familysearch.org: #440, Hereinafter cited as PhCM.).

Annie Gladu was born on 12 Mar 1893 Dodson, Phillips County, Montana (1937-1987-LS Basic Roll, #260.) (Ibid., #538.).

iii. James Wells was born circa 1891 (1902-1930 Fergus Co, MT.).

iv. Frederick Wells was born circa 1893 (Ibid.) (St.Leo's Roman Catholic Church: Baptisms and Marriages, Lewistown, Montana.). He was baptized on 1 Aug 1893 St.Leo's, Lewistown, Fergus County, Montana (Ibid.).

v. Marie Elisa Wells was born on 22 Dec 1894 Lewistown, Fergus County, Montana (1902-1930 Fergus Co, MT.) (St.Leo's.). She was baptized on 24 Dec 1894 St.Leo's, Lewistown, Fergus County, Montana (Ibid.).

vi. Eveline Wells was born circa 1896 (1902-1930 Fergus Co, MT.).

vii. Maxime Wells was born on 28 Sep 1898 Lewistown, Fergus County, Montana (Ibid.) (St.Leo's.). He was baptized on 10 Oct 1898 St.Leo's, Lewistown, Fergus County, Montana (Ibid.).

viii. Josephine Wells was born on 18 Jul 1900 Lewistown, Fergus County, Montana (1902-1930 Fergus Co, MT.) (St.Leo's.). She was baptized on 24 Jul 1900 St.Leo's, Lewistown, Fergus County, Montana (Ibid.).

14. Gregoire Alphonse Wills was baptized on 28 Apr 1853 Assumption, Pembina, Pembina County, Dakota Territory (AP, page 88, B-68.). He married **Rose Ross**, daughter of **Roderick Ross** and **Marie Delorme**, on 18 Apr 1876 Lebret, (Saskatchewan) (L1, page 187, M-16.). He died in 1880 on the plains, near Wood Mountain, (Saskatchewan) (NWHBS 1885 Scrip Applications, North-West Halfbreeds residing outside Manitoba on 15 July 1870, RG15-20, C-14942.).

Rose Ross was born on 24 Jun 1857 (SFXI-Kipling, B-206.). She was baptized on 27 Jun 1857 St.Francois Xavier, (Manitoba) (Ibid.). She married **Alexandre Pelletier**, son of **Joseph Pelletier** and **Louise St.Denis**, on 6 Aug 1882 Lebret, (Saskatchewan) (L2 Lebret, Mission de St.Florent, Roman Catholic Registre des Baptemes, Mariages & Seplutures, Qu'Appelle, Saskatchewan, Book Two: 1881-1887, FHC microfilm 1032949., page 40, M-11. Hereinafter cited as L2.).

Children of **Gregoire Alphonse Wills** and **Rose Ross** were as follows:

i. Marie Euphrosine Walsh was born in 1876 Cypress Hills, (Saskatchewan) (HBSI.) (ArchiviaNet.). She died in 1879 Cypress Hills, (Saskatchewan) (HBSI.) (ArchiviaNet.).

ii. Alexander Wells was born on 28 Apr 1879 (SPMT , page 127, #2660.). He was baptized on 20 Sep 1879 (St.Peter's Mission), Judith Basin, Montana (Ibid.). He married Marie Plante, daughter of Francois Xavier Plante and Madeleine Fisher, on 27 Aug 1906 Lewistown, Fergus County, Montana (FerCM.). He married Virginia J. Kline, daughter of William Klyne and Emerise Poitras, before 1925.

Marie Plante was born in 1883 Wood Mountain, (Saskatchewan) (ArchiviaNet.). She married (--?--) **Winsborough** before 1900 (Ibid.).

Virginia J. Kline was born on 15 Apr 1888. She married **Mathew Hanley** before 1920.

15. Jean James Wills was born on 6 Oct 1858 Pembina County, Dakota Territory (AP, page 198, B-596.). He was baptized on 6 Oct 1858 Assumption, Pembina, Pembina County, Dakota Territory (Ibid.). He married **Celina Ouellette**, daughter of **Antoine Ratte Ouellette** and **Angelique Bottineau**, on 10 Feb 1885 Lewistown, Meagher County, Montana (Rod Mac Quarrie, 28 Oct 2012, Montana marriage certificate.). He married **Marguerite Berger**, daughter of **Isaie Berger** and **Clemence Gourneau**, on 7 Apr 1896 Lewistown, Fergus County, Montana (Al Yerbury, Fergus County Marriages.) (FerCM.). He died on 25 Jan 1909 Lewiston, Fergus County, Montana, at age 50 (Ancestry.com, Rupertslander's Family.).

Celina Ouellette was born circa 1865. She died on 20 Jan 1891 Lewistown, Fergus County, Montana (Rod Mac Quarrie, 28 Oct 2012.).

Children of **Jean James Wills** and **Celina Ouellette** both born Lewistown, Montana, were as follows:

i. Rosa Wells was born on 14 Apr 1884 (ArchiviaNet, C-15009.).

ii. Marie Agnes Wells was born in Apr 1887 (1900C MT Twelfth Census of the United States: 1900; Montana, District 27, page 21A, line 2.). She married George Christopher Barrett, son of Robert A. Barrett and Elizabeth Mockel, on 23 Mar 1917 Helena, Lewis & Clark, Montana (L&CCM Lewis & Clark County, Montana; Marriage Record Licenses and Certificates; 1865-1950; familysearch.org, Hereinafter cited as L&CCM.). She died on 14 Mar 1949 Helena, Lewis & Clark, Montana, at age 61 (MT Death.). She was buried circa 18 Mar 1949 Forestvale Cemetery, Helena, Lewis & Clark, Montana (Rod Mac Quarrie, 28 Oct 2012.).

George Christopher Barrett was born on 23 Oct 1891 Helena, Lewis & Clark, Montana (Ibid.). He died on 29 Sep 1959 Helena, Lewis & Clark, Montana, at age 67 (MT Death.). He was buried on 1 Oct 1959 Forestvale Cemetery, Helena, Lewis & Clark, Montana (Rod Mac Quarrie, 28 Oct 2012.).

Marguerite Berger was born on 2 Feb 1875 (L1, page 148, B-35.). She was baptized on 8 Feb 1875 Lebret, (Saskatchewan) (Ibid.). She married **Joseph Turcotte**, son of **Pascal Turcotte** and **Mary Daisy Wells**, on 17 Oct 1910 Lewistown, Fergus County, Montana (Al Yerbury, Fergus County Marriages.) (FerCM.). She died on 7 May 1936 Lewistown, Fergus County, Montana, at age 61 (Al Yerbury.) (Rod Mac Quarrie, 28 Oct 2012.) (MT Death.).

Children of **Jean James Wills** and **Marguerite Berger** were as follows:

i. Clara Ruth Wells was born on 10 Feb 1897 Lewistown, Fergus County, Montana (St.Leo's.). She was baptized on 14 Feb 1897 St.Leo's, Lewistown, Fergus County, Montana (Ibid.). She married William Hugh Owens, son of William Richard Owens and Mary T. Williams, on 16 Apr 1917 Lewistown, Fergus County, Montana (FerCM.). She died on 16 May 1981 Calgary, Alberta, at age 84 (Rod Mac Quarrie, 22 Dec 2009.).

William Hugh Owens was born on 4 Jul 1883 Adda Lane, Llanddusant, Anglessey, Wales (Ancestry.com, G. Holman's Family.). He died on 29 Dec 1948 Hanna, Alberta, at age 65 (Ibid.) (Ibid., Rupertslander's Family.).

ii. James Anthony Wells was born on 9 Oct 1902 Lewistown, Fergus County, Montana (St.Leo's.) (Social Security Death Index, . Hereinafter cited as SSDI.) (MT Death.). He was baptized on 19 Oct 1902 St.Leo's, Lewistown, Fergus County, Montana (St.Leo's.). He married Marie Anna Lang before 1939 (1987LS 1987-92 Little Shell Band of Chippewa Roll.). He married Marie Anna Long on 4 Jan 1960 White Sulphur Springs, Meagher County, Montana (MeaCCM.). He died on 13 Apr 1980 Great Falls, Cascade County, Montana, at age 77 (MT Death.) (SSDI.).

Marie Anna Long was born in 1909 Tacoma, Pierce County, Washington (Rod Mac Quarrie, 28 Oct 2012.).

iii. Alice Wells was born circa 1907 Fergus County, Montana (1910C MT Thirteenth Census of the United States: 1910; Montana, National Archives of the United States, Washington D.C., District 107, page 22A.).

16. **Solomon Wills** was born on 2 Jan 1870 (1901 Canada, microfilm, T-6553, North Battleford, page 11, Family 97, line 8-14.). He was born on 20 Jan 1870 Dirt Hills, (Saskatchewan) (L1, page 22, B-24.) (ArchiviaNet, C-15009.). He was baptized on 26 Jun 1870 Lebret, (Saskatchewan) (L1, page 22, B-25.). He married **Florestine Poitras**, daughter of **Tobie David Poitras** and **Madeleine Gesson dit St.Denis**, on 28 Jul 1890 St.Vital, Battleford, (Saskatchewan) (SV, page 85-86, M-7.).

Florestine Poitras was born on 19 Mar 1871 Qu'Appelle, (Saskatchewan) (ArchiviaNet, C-15009.). She was baptized on 25 Mar 1871 Lebret, (Saskatchewan) (L1, page 31, B-9.).

Children of **Solomon Wills** and **Florestine Poitras** were as follows:

     i.   Joseph Solomon Welsh was born on 24 Aug 1891 (Saskatchewan) (Saskatchewan Vital Statistics online, http://vsgs.health.gov.sk.ca, #6448.).

     ii. John George Welsh was born on 7 Feb 1893 (Saskatchewan) (Ibid., #6724.).

     iii. Heli Henoch Welsh was born on 17 Mar 1895 (Saskatchewan) (Ibid., #6734.).

     iv. Francois Wells was born on 27 Apr 1896 (Saskatchewan) (1901 Canada, #205, d, page 11, family 97, line 8-14.).

     v.   Marie Athalia Wells was born on 5 Jun 1899 (Saskatchewan) (SK Vital Statistics, #1838.).

     vi. Marie Virginie Malerna Wells was born on 4 Nov 1902 Battleford, (Saskatchewan) (Ibid., #2826.).

     vii. Moise Arthur Wills was born on 20 Oct 1904 Battleford, (Saskatchewan) (Ibid., #4117.).

17. **Jean Baptiste Wills or Wells or Welsh** was born on 2 Jan 1872 Saskatoon, (Saskatchewan) (ArchiviaNet, C-15009.). He married **Mary Jane Hodgson**, daughter of **Thomas Hodgson** and **Marie Capisiset**, on 29 Jun 1897 Battleford, (Saskatchewan) (Rarihokwats, 26 Apr 1997.). He died on 14 Apr 1946 LeGoff, Alberta, at age 74 (Ibid.). He was buried in Apr 1946 St.Raphael, Le Goff, Alberta (Ibid.).

Mary Jane Hodgson was born on 31 Jan 1880 Battleford, (Saskatchewan) (SV, B-2.). She was baptized on 1 Feb 1880 St.Vital, Battleford, (Saskatchewan) (Ibid.). She died on 6 Aug 1961 Elk Point, Alberta, at age 81 (Rarihokwats, 26 Apr 1997.). She was buried in Aug 1961 St.Raphael, Le Goff, Alberta (Ibid.).

Children of **Jean Baptiste Wills or Wells or Welsh** and **Mary Jane Hodgson** all born Battleford, (Saskatchewan), were as follows:

     i.   John Thomas Wells was born on 30 May 1898 (1901 Canada, microfilm, T-6553, South Battleford, page 4, Family 35, line 22-26.).

     ii. Alexander Salomon Wells was born on 7 Oct 1900 (Ibid.) (SK Vital Statistics, #2176.).

     iii. Isabelle Victoria Wells was born on 9 Dec 1902 (Automated Genealogy 1906 Census Transcription Project and Census Images from the National Archives of Canada, http://www.automatedgenealogy.com, District 16, page 13, family 89, lin 1-4.) (SK Vital Statistics, Birth Reg. #2831.).

     iv. George Wells was born on 11 Mar 1905 (Ibid., #5147.).

18. **Alexandre Wills or Wells or Welsh** was born on 28 Jan 1874 Duck Lake, (Saskatchewan) (DL, B-73.). He was baptized on 31 Jan 1874 Duck Lake, (Saskatchewan) (Ibid.). He married **Eleonore Ouellette**, daughter of **Jean Baptiste Ouellette** and **Cecile Courchene,** on 20 Jul 1896 St.Vital, Battleford, (Saskatchewan) (SV, M-5.).

Eleonore Ouellette was born on 8 Mar 1879 St.Laurent, (Saskatchewan) (1901 Canada, microfilm, T-6553, North Battleford, page 6, Family 59, line #44-50.) (SL-SK, page 30, B-11.). She was baptized on 8 Mar 1879 St.Laurent-de-Grandin, (Saskatchewan) (Ibid.).

Children of **Alexandre Wills or Wells or Welsh** and **Eleonore Ouellette** all born Battleford, (Saskatchewan), are as follows:

     i.   Mary Wells was born on 26 Aug 1897 (1901 Canada, microfilm, T-6553, North Battleford, page 6, Family 59, line #44-50.).

     ii. Angele Wells was born on 6 Jul 1900 (Ibid.) (SK Vital Statistics, #2171.).

     iii. Marie Rose Alexandrine Wells was born on 17 Apr 1902 (Ibid., #2812.).

     iv. Marie Adile Alexandrine Wells was born on 5 May 1903 (Ibid., #3376.).

19. **Joseph Wills or Wells** was born on 18 Nov 1863 Devils Lake, Dakota Territory (Al Yerbury.). He married **Julienne Wilkie**, daughter of **Alexander Wilkie** and **Louise Gariepy**, on 30 Apr 1883 (St.Peter's Mission), Judith Basin, Meagher County, Montana Territory (SPMT , page 40, M-243.). He married **Catherine Fleury**, daughter of **Antoine Fleury** and **Elizabeth Wilkie**, on 29 Oct 1888 Lewistown, Fergus County, Montana (Al Yerbury, Fergus County Marriages.) (FerCM.). He married **Marie Adele Laverdure**, daughter of **Francois Xavier Laverdure** and **Marguerite Pelletier**, on 21 Nov 1892 Lewistown, Fergus County, Montana (Al Yerbury, Fergus County Marriages.) (FerCM.). He married **Maria Celina Laverdure**, daughter of **Francois Xavier Laverdure** and **Marguerite Pelletier,** before 1912. He died on 15 Jan 1942 Lewistown, Fergus County, Montana, at age 78.

Julienne Wilkie was born on 24 Feb 1859 Pembina, Pembina County, Dakota Territory (AP, page 204, B-615.). She was baptized on 25 Feb 1859 Assumption, Pembina, Pembina County, Dakota Territory (Ibid.). She married **Bernard Lafontaine**, son of **Calixte Lafontaine** and **Charlotte Adam**, on 27 Dec 1877 (St.Peter's Mission), Milk River, Montana Territory (SPMT , page 19, M-93.). She died on 14 Jun 1885 Batoche, (Saskatchewan), at age 26 (BSAP Records of the Parish of Batoche, St.Antoine de Pudoue Roman Catholic Church: Register for Baptisms, Marriages, Deaths, Volume One, 1881-1909., page 36, S-30. Hereinafter cited as BSAP.). She was buried on 16 Jun 1885 Batoche, (Saskatchewan) (Ibid.).

There were no children of **Joseph Wills or Wells** and **Julienne Wilkie**.

Catherine Fleury was born on 27 Dec 1868 Devils Lake, Dakota Territory (ArchiviaNet.).

Children of **Joseph Wills or Wells** and **Catherine Fleury** are:

     i.   Thomas Wells was born in Apr 1890 (1900C Fergus Co, MT Twelfth Census of the United States: 1900; Montana; Fergus County.). He was born on 5 Apr 1891 Lewistown, Fergus County, Montana (1937-1987-LS Basic Roll, #542.). He married Adeline Beauchamp, daughter of Roger Beauchamp and Rose Seamans, on 9 Feb 1911 Lewistown, Fergus County, Montana (FerCM.).

         Adeline Beauchamp was born in 1894 Lewistown, Fergus County, Montana (1937-1987-LS Basic Roll, #542.) (FerCM.). She died on 18 Jul 1926 Lewistown, Fergus County, Montana (Al Yerbury.).

Marie Adele Laverdure was born on 12 Dec 1876 Devils Lake, Dakota Territory (L1, page 201-202, B-56.). She was baptized on 9 Jan 1877 Lebret, (Saskatchewan) (Ibid., page 201-201, B-56.).

Children of **Joseph Wills or Wells** and **Marie Adele Laverdure** were as follows:

   i.   Emma Wells was born circa 1892 (Al Yerbury, Fergus County Marriages.). She married Thomas Joseph Laverdure, son of Daniel Laverdure and Mary Natalie Wells, on 26 Jun 1911 Lewistown, Fergus County, Montana (Ibid.) (FerCM.).

        Thomas Joseph Laverdure was born in Oct 1882 (Al Yerbury.). He was born circa 1887 Lewistown, Fergus County, Montana (1902-1930 Fergus Co, MT.) (Al Yerbury, Fergus County Marriages.). He died on 5 Mar 1951 Lewistown, Fergus County, Montana (Ibid., Creel Funeral Home Records.) (MT Death.).

   ii.   Lena Wells was born circa 1895. She died on 23 Jul 1901 (Patty Severns Papers on Wells family.).

   iii.   Albert Wells was born on 26 Jul 1899 Lewistown, Fergus County, Montana (1902-1930 Fergus Co, MT.) (St.Leo's.). He was baptized on 3 Sep 1899 St.Leo's, Lewistown, Fergus County, Montana (Ibid.). He married Mary R. Charette, daughter of Jean Baptiste Charette and Marie Beauchamp, on 7 Jun 1918 Lewistown, Fergus County, Montana (FerCM.).

        Mary R. Charette was born on 14 Jun 1884 Lewistown, Fergus County, Montana (BIA-LS.). She married **Sam Lavallee** before 1914.

   iv.   Celina Wells was born circa 1902 (1902-1930 Fergus Co, MT.).

   v.   Raymond Wells Sr was born on 10 May 1905 Lewistown, Fergus County, Montana (SSDI.). He married Helen Grace Beauchamp, daughter of Simon Beauchamp and Virginia Swan, on 1 Mar 1935 Fergus County, Montana (FerCM.). He died on 4 Aug 1975 Cascade County, Montana, at age 70 (SSDI.) (MT Death.).

        Helen Grace Beauchamp was born on 9 Jun 1914 Lewistown, Fergus County, Montana (1937-1987-LS Basic Roll, #536.) (Ibid.). She married **Louis Fayant**, son of **Joseph Jean Marie Fagnant** and **Helene Gariepy**, on 12 Nov 1930 Lewistown, Fergus County, Montana (FerCM.). She died on 30 Dec 1974 at age 60.

   vi.   Clarence Andrew Wells was born on 26 Aug 1909 Lewistown, Fergus County, Montana (1902-1930 Fergus Co, MT.) (St.Leo's.). He was baptized on 26 Aug 1909 St.Leo's, Lewistown, Fergus County, Montana (Ibid.). He married Lena McCarty, daughter of Arthur McCarty and Frances M. Berger, on 11 Feb 1929 Lewistown, Fergus County, Montana (FerCM.). He married Mathilda Maria Corth, daughter of Frank Corth and Minnie Johnke, on 2 Mar 1943 Yellowstone County, Montana (YCM Yellowstone County, Montana; Marriage Record Licenses and Certificates; 1865-1950; familysearch.org, Hereinafter cited as YCM.).

        Lena McCarty was born in 1907 Lewistown, Fergus County, Montana (FerCM.) (1920C-MT 1920 Federal Census Montana, National Archives of the United States, Washington D.C., 9A.). She married **Ben Lafountaine** before 1925. She married **John Koloff**, son of **Kalo Koloff or Evanhoff** and **Evana (--?--)**, on 6 Feb 1931 Lewistown, Fergus County, Montana (FerCM.). She died in 1958.

        Mathilda Maria Corth was born in 1910 (YCM.).

   vii.   Wilbur Wells was born circa 1910 Montana (1920C-MT, Sheet No. 1A, family 7, line 30-38.). He married Orpha Rose Allison, daughter of George Allison and Emma Parker, on 24 Aug 1934 Fergus County, Montana (FerCM.).

        Orpha Rose Allison was born in 1909 (Ibid.).

Maria Celina Laverdure was born on 5 Jan 1880 Lewistown, Fergus County, Montana (1937-1987-LS Basic Roll, #534.). She died on 5 Oct 1949 Lewistown, Fergus County, Montana, at age 69.

Children of **Joseph Wills or Wells** and **Maria Celina Laverdure** all born Tyler, Fergus County, Montana, were as follows:

   i.   Victor Nelson Wells was born on 10 Jun 1920 (1936-LS, #534.) (1937-1987-LS Basic Roll, #534.) (SSDI.). He married Rita Charette, daughter of John Charette and Margaret Dess, on 21 May 1940 Lewistown, Fergus County, Montana (FerCM.). He married Mary Agnes Paul, daughter of Joseph Paul and Caroline Berger, on 24 Jun 1947 Great Falls, Cascade County, Montana (CaCM Cascade County, Montana; Marriage Record Licenses and Certificates; 1865-1950; familysearch.org, Hereinafter cited as CaCM.). He married Helen Kathryn Gray, daughter of Gabriel Gray and Elizabeth Delorme, before 1952 (1987-92LS.). He died on 2 Jan 2008 Helena, Lewis & Clark County, Montana, at age 87 (SSDI.).

        Rita Charette was born in 1921 (FerCM.).

        Mary Agnes Paul was born on 29 Oct 1917 Grass Range, Fergus County, Montana (St.Leo's.). She was baptized on 18 Dec 1917 St.Leo's, Lewistown, Fergus County, Montana (Ibid.). She married **James Scott** before 1943. She married **Alexander Bernard Malatare**, son of **Charles Malaterre** and **Mary Sophie Swan**, on 6 Aug 1945 Great Falls, Cascade County, Montana (CaCM.). She married **Earl Valentine**, son of **John R. Valentine** and **Laura Wilcut**, on 6 Oct 1949 Roundup, Musselshell County, Montana (MSCM Musselshell County, Montana; Marriage Record Licenses and Certificates; 1865-1950; familysearch.org, Hereinafter cited as MSCM.). She died on 8 Apr 1997 Tacoma, Pierce County, Washington, at age 79 (SSDI.).

        Helen Kathryn Gray was born on 18 Feb 1925 Helena, Lewis and Clark County, Montana (1987-92LS.) (1937-1987-LS Basic Roll, #86.). She married **Lawrence George Wells**, son of **Joseph Wills or Wells** and **Maria Celina Laverdure**, on 20 Feb 1943 Helena, Lewis & Clark County, Montana (L&CCM.). She died on 6 May 1998 Billings, Yellowstone County, Montana, at age 73 (SSDI.) (*BG Billings Gazette*, Billings, Montana, Friday, 8 May 198, 2M. Hereinafter cited as BG.).

   ii.   Lawrence George Wells was born on 18 Mar 1913 (1987-92LS.) (SSDI.). He married Edna Lewis, daughter of W. H. Lewis and Mary Ann Sanderson, on 9 Sep 1934 Fergus County, Montana (FerCM.). He married Helen Kathryn Gray, daughter of Gabriel Gray and Elizabeth Delorme, on 20 Feb 1943 Helena, Lewis & Clark County, Montana (L&CCM.). He married Agnes Kucera before 1955 (1996-00LS 1996-2000 Little Shell Band of Chippewa Roll.). He died on 24 Jan 1989 Yellowstone County, Montana, at age 75 (SSDI.).

        Edna Lewis was born in 1909 (FerCM.).

        Helen Kathryn Gray was born on 18 Feb 1925 Helena, Lewis and Clark County, Montana (1987-92LS.) (1937-1987-LS Basic Roll, #86.). She married **Victor Nelson Wells**, son of **Joseph Wills or Wells** and **Maria Celina**

Laverdure, before 1952 (1987-92LS.). She died on 6 May 1998 Billings, Yellowstone County, Montana, at age 73 (SSDI.) (*BG*, Friday, 8 May 198, 2M.).

Agnes Kucera was born on 18 Oct 1918 (1996-00LS.).

iii. Doris Fay Wells was born on 4 Jan 1915 (1987-92LS.). She married Martin James Tafolla, son of Jose Onofre Tafolla and Rosalie Ferguson, on 3 Dec 1932 Fergus County, Montana (FerCM.). She married Chesley N. Lewis before 1935 (1987-92LS.). She died on 10 Oct 1993 Billings, Yellowstone County, Montana, at age 78 (SSDI.) (MT Death.).

Martin James Tafolla was born on 10 Nov 1904 Lewistown, Fergus County, Montana (1940C MT 1940 Montana, Sixteenth Census of the United States, National Archives of the United States, Washington, D.C., District 14-6, page 2A, line 14.) (SSDI.). He was baptized on 25 Dec 1904 St.Leo's, Lewistown, Fergus County, Montana (Ancestry.com, Rosemary Pierce.). He married **Ada O. Wells**, daughter of **Thomas Joseph Laverdure** and **Emma Wells**, on 31 Jan 1935 Lewistown, Fergus County, Montana (FerCM.). He married **Helen Alberta Carlile**, daughter of **Harry Carlile** and **Mabel M. Barrow**, on 10 Oct 1942 Lewistown, Fergus County, Montana (Ibid.). He died on 20 Feb 1981 Malta, Phillips County, Montana, at age 76 (MT Death.) (Brenda Snider Research, 20 Oct 2014.) (SSDI.).

Chesley N. Lewis was born on 9 Feb 1903.

iv. Earl James Wells was born on 1 Oct 1924 (1987-92LS.) (1937-1987-LS Basic Roll, #534.). He married Doris May Vanderpool, daughter of Fred Milo Vanderpool and Edna M. Miller, on 16 Mar 1946 Bozeman, Gallatin County, Montana (GalCM Gallatin County Courthouse, Montana; Marriage Record Licenses and Certificates; 1865-1950, familysearch.org, Hereinafter cited as GalCM.). He died on 4 Feb 1999 Bellevue, King County, Washington, at age 74 (SSDI.) (Ancestry.com, Veterans Gravesites.). He was buried on 11 Feb 1999 Tahoma National Cemetery, Kent, Washington (Ibid.).

Doris May Vanderpool was born in 1924 (GalCM.).

20. **Thomas Wills or Wells** was born circa 1866. He was born in 1871 (1936-LS, #108.). He married **Zilda Daniels**, daughter of **Francois Dagneau** and **Eliza Laverdure**, on 8 Jan 1891 Lewistown, Fergus County, Montana (FerCM.). He died in 1913 Lewistown, Fergus County, Montana (1936-LS, #108.).

Zilda Daniels was born on 8 Jan 1872. She married **George Strohm**, son of **George R. Strohm** and **Pada B. Baca,** on 19 Feb 1908 Harlowton, Meagher County, Montana (familysearch.org Website, Meagher County Marriages.). She died on 9 Jul 1953 Great Falls, Cascade County, Montana, at age 81.

Children of **Thomas Wills or Wells** and **Zilda Daniels** are as follows:

i. Agnes Wells was born circa 1892 (1902-1930 Fergus Co, MT.).

ii. Florence Wells was born on 3 Aug 1893 Lewistown, Fergus County, Montana (St.Leo's.). She was baptized on 20 Aug 1893 St.Leo's, Lewistown, Fergus County, Montana (Ibid.). She married Caryl York, son of Frank York and Isabel Eddy, on 25 Jan 1913 Fergus County, Montana (FerCM.).

Caryl York was born in 1888 Chicago, Illinois (Ibid.).

iii. Eugene Godefried Wells was born on 7 Jun 1897 Lewistown, Fergus County, Montana (St.Leo's.). He was baptized on 8 Jun 1897 St.Leo's, Lewistown, Fergus County, Montana (Ibid.).

iv. Alice Matilda Wells was born on 22 Aug 1898 Lewistown, Fergus County, Montana (Ibid.) (1902-1930 Fergus Co, MT.). She was born on 26 Oct 1900 Lewistown, Fergus County, Montana (1937-1987-LS Basic Roll, #108.). She married Harvie Boyer before 1936.

v. Albert William Wells was born on 17 Jun 1900 Lewistown, Fergus County, Montana (St.Leo's.). He was baptized on 15 Jul 1900 St.Leo's, Lewistown, Fergus County, Montana (Ibid.). He married Ida G. Gardipee, daughter of Zacharie Gariepy and Cecelia Fagnant, on 3 Aug 1926 Fort Benton, Chouteau County, Montana (1930C MT 1930 Montana, Fifteenth Census of the United States, National Archives of the United States, Washington, D.C.) (ChCM Chouteau County, Montana; Marriage Record Licenses and Certificates; 1865-1950; familysearch.org, Hereinafter cited as ChCM.).

Ida G. Gardipee was born on 23 Sep 1907 Fergus County, Montana (1936-LS, #945.). She married **Joseph Morissette**, son of **Jean Morissette** and **Philomene St.Denis**, before 1930. She died on 1 Jun 1996 Havre, Hill County, Montana, at age 88 (MT Death.) (SSDI.).

vi. Kate Wells was born in 1903 (SBCM Silver Bow County, Montana; Marriage Record Licenses and Certificates; 1865-1950; familysearch.org, Hereinafter cited as SBCM.). She married Thomas Holmes, son of James Holmes and Rebecca Pool, on 12 Nov 1927 Silver Bow County, Montana (Ibid.).

Thomas Holmes was born in 1901 (Ibid.).

vii. Adolph Wells was born on 25 Jun 1904 Lewistown, Fergus County, Montana (St.Leo's.). He was baptized on 22 Jul 1904 St.Leo's, Lewistown, Fergus County, Montana (Ibid.).

21. **Marie Ernestine Wills** was born on 8 Apr 1864 (SFXI-Kipling, B-8.). She was baptized on 24 Apr 1864 St.Francois Xavier, (Manitoba) (Ibid.). She married **Antoine Fleury**, son of **Antoine Fleury** and **Elizabeth Wilkie**, on 4 May 1880 (St.Peter's Mission), Judith Basin, Meagher County, Montana Territory (SPMT , page 25, #135.). She died on 1 Jan 1952 Montana at age 87 (MT Death, Fer 1972.).

Antoine Fleury was born on 9 Aug 1858 (SFXI-Kipling, B-283.). He was baptized on 15 Aug 1858 St.Francois Xavier, (Manitoba) (Ibid.).

Descendants of Thomas Wishart

Generation One

1. **Thomas Wishart** was born circa 1795 Scotland (1827C RRS HBCA E5/1 1827 Census of the Red River Settlement, HBCA E5/1, Hudson's Bay Company Archives, Provincial Archives, 200 Vaughan Street, Winnipeg, MB R3C 1T5, Canada., page one.). He was born circa 1797 probably, Orkney, Scotland (Shirley Wishart Research, 11 Dec 1992, Newsletter.). He married **Barbara Spence**, daughter of **James Spence** and **Mary Stone Indian,** in 1823.

Barbara Spence was born circa 1800 Ruperts Land (Denney Papers, Charles D. Denney, Glenbow Archives, Calgary, Alberta.). She was baptized on 1 Apr 1824 St.Johns, Red River Colony, (Manitoba) (HBCR Hudson Bay Company Register of Anglican Church Baptisms, Marriages, and Burials for the Red River Settlement, 1821-1841; Hudson's Bay Company Archives, Winnipeg, Manitoba, E.4/1a, folio 47. Hereinafter cited as HBCR.).

Children of **Thomas Wishart** and **Barbara Spence** were as follows:

        i.   Jane Wishart was born in 1821 (HBCA-B Hudson's Bay Company Archives - biographical sketches, Hudson's Bay Company Archives; Winnipeg, Manitoba.). She was baptized on 27 May 1823 St.Johns, Red River Settlement, (Manitoba) (HBCR, E.4/1a, folio 42d.). She was buried on 28 May 1823 St.Johns, Red River Colony, (Manitoba) (Ibid., No. 14.).

        ii.   Elizabeth Wishart was baptized on 26 Sep 1824 (St.Peters), Red River Colony, (Manitoba) (HBCA-B.) (HBCR, E.4/1a, folio 51d.).

        iii.   Solomon Wishart was baptized on 15 Apr 1827 St.Johns, Red River Settlement, (Manitoba) (Ibid., E.4/1a, folio 63d, #633.).

  2   iv.   Jane Wishart, b. 8 Nov 1829 St.Johns, Red River Settlement, (Manitoba); m. Leverette Hooler Alvond; m. Evrington Van Warner; d. 25 Jan 1879 Wisconsin.

  3   v.   James Wishart, b. 5 Aug 1831 Winnipeg, (Manitoba); m. Elizabeth Flett; d. 4 Jul 1906 Calgary, Alberta.

  4   vi.   Mary Wishart, b. 1835 St.Johns, (Manitoba); m. John McNab.

        vii.   Elijah Wishart was baptized on 21 Nov 1837 St.Johns, (Manitoba) (Denney.) (HBCA-B.).

Generation Two

2. **Jane Wishart** was baptized on 8 Nov 1829 St.Johns, Red River Settlement, (Manitoba) (HBCR, E.4/1a, folio 72d.). She married **Leverette Hooler Alvond** circa 1850. She married **Evrington Van Warner** before 1867. She died on 25 Jan 1879 Wisconsin at age 49 (Denney.).

Leverette Hooler Alvond was born in 1824 Vermont (Ibid.). He died on 26 Aug 1896 Blue Jacket, Indian Territory (Ibid.).

3. **James Wishart** was born on 5 Aug 1831 Winnipeg, (Manitoba) (MBS Scrip Applications, Original White Settlers & Halfbreeds residing in Manitoba on 15 July 1870, RG15-19, C-14934.) (Denney.). He was baptized on 18 Sep 1831 St.Johns, Red River Settlement, (Manitoba) (HBCR, E.4/1a, folio 85d.). He married **Elizabeth Flett**, daughter of **Peter Flett** and **Euphemia Halcrow,** on 23 Sep 1853 St.Paul, (Manitoba) (Denney.) (HBCA-B.). He died on 4 Jul 1906 Calgary, Alberta, at age 74 (Denney.).

Elizabeth Flett was born on 1 Nov 1835 St.Paul, (Manitoba) (MBS, C-14934.) (Denney.). She was baptized on 22 Nov 1835 St.Johns, Red River Settlement, (Manitoba) (HBCA-B, E.4/1a, folio 124d.). She died on 15 Feb 1900 Rosebud, Alberta, at age 64 (Denney.).

4. **Mary Wishart** was born in 1835 St.Johns, (Manitoba) (MBS, Supplementary Returns, C-14934.). She was baptized on 21 Nov 1837 St.Johns, Red River Settlement, (Manitoba) (HBCR, E.4/1a, folio 147.). She married **John McNab**, son of **John McNab** and **Jane Margaret Sanderson,** on 7 Aug 1856 St.Johns, (Manitoba) (Denney.).

John McNab was born in 1835 St.Johns, (Manitoba) (MBS, Supplementary Returns, C-14934.). He was baptized on 10 Sep 1837 St.Johns, Red River Settlement, (Manitoba) (HBCR, E.4/1a, folio 145.).

Generation Three

5. **Barbara Wishart** was born on 4 Jul 1856 Poplar Point, (Manitoba) (MBS, C-14933.). She was baptized on 27 Jul 1856 St.Paul, (Manitoba) (Denney.). She married **James Slater**, son of **William Slater** and **Maria Rowland,** before 1873. She died before 1881 Poplar Point, Manitoba (1881 Canada, District 186-F, page 14, house 59.).

James Slater was born on 19 Jun 1847 St.Paul, (Manitoba) (MBS, C-14934.). He was baptized on 4 Jul 1847 St.Johns, (Manitoba) (Denney.).

6. **Joseph James Wishart** was born on 3 Feb 1858 St.Paul, (Manitoba) (MBS, C-14934.) (1901 Canada, District 9-q-5, page 7, family 76, line 18-29.). He was baptized on 14 Mar 1858 St.Paul, (Manitoba) (Denney.). He married **Margaret Mary Ann Gowler**, daughter of **William Gowler** and **Ann Miller,** on 12 Mar 1879 (Ibid.). He died on 21 Aug 1934 Russell, Manitoba, at age 76 (MB Vital Statistics, Death Reg. #1934,032240.).

Margaret Mary Ann Gowler was born on 25 Jan 1863 Poplar Point, (Manitoba) (HBC-PN Public Notice of land claims of Half-Breed Children, Address: Provincial Archives of Manitoba, Winnipeg, Manitoba, File Reference: MG4D13 Box 1, Poplar Point and High Bluff, #92.).

Children of **Joseph James Wishart** and **Margaret Mary Ann Gowler** were as follows:

        i.   Elizabeth Ann Wishart was born on 14 Apr 1880 (1901 Canada, District 9-q-5, page 7, family 76, line 18-29.). She married William Auld Pettigrew on 15 Dec 1911 Winnipeg, Manitoba (MB Vital Statistics, Marriage Reg. #1911,003821.).

  14   ii.   Laura Amelia Wishart, b. 26 Jul 1881; m. Robert Alexander Thomson; d. 7 Sep 1979 Winnipeg, Manitoba; bur. Sep 1979 Elmwood Cemetery, Winnipeg, Manitoba.

  15   iii.   Lindy Ethel Wishart, b. 1 Jul 1883 Poplar Point, Manitoba; m. Neil Kenneth Wilkie.

        iv.   Joseph Allen Wishart was born on 9 Feb 1885 R.M. of Silver Creek, Manitoba (Ibid., Birth Reg. #1885,004110.) (ArchiviaNet, C-15010.). He was baptized on 8 Aug 1894 (Ibid.).

        v.   Walter Henry Wishart was born on 9 Sep 1886 R.M. of Silver Creek, Manitoba (MB Vital Statistics, Birth Reg. #1886,001756.) (ArchiviaNet, C-15010.). He was baptized on 8 Aug 1894 (Ibid.).

        vi.   Charles James Wishart was born on 23 Jun 1888 R.M. of Silver Creek, Manitoba (MB Vital Statistics, Birth Reg. #1888,002503.).

        vii.   Sidney Clifton Wishart was born on 14 Jan 1891 R.M. of Silver Creek, Manitoba (Ibid., Birth Reg. #1891,001063; Reg. Date: 13/02/1891.).

viii. Mabel Jane Wishart was born on 21 Jun 1893 R.M. of Silver Creek, Manitoba (Ibid., Birth Reg. #1893,005343.). She married William Allen Merrett on 22 Jun 1915 Russell, Manitoba (Ibid., Marriage Reg. #1915,177107.).

ix. Mary Edith Wishart was born on 19 May 1895 R.M. of Silver Creek, Manitoba (Ibid., Birth Reg. #1895,1007786; Reg. Date: 21/09/1922.). She married Andrew Herman on 15 Jul 1922 Brandon, Manitoba (Ibid., Marriage Reg. #1922,025008.).

x. Herbert Braebro Wishart was born on 27 Nov 1896 R.M. of Silver Creek, Manitoba (Ibid., Birth Reg. #1896,10911376; Reg. Date: 29/10/1926.). He married Helen Josephine Margaret Berglove on 3 Feb 1922 Winnipeg, Manitoba (Ibid., Marriage Reg. #1922,006059.).

xi. Albert Victor Wishart was born on 20 Apr 1901 R.M. of Silver Creek, Manitoba (Ibid., Birth Reg. #1901,1007788; Reg. Date: 21/09/1922.). He married Mary Amy Cromwell on 19 Jan 1926 Russell, Manitoba (Ibid., Marriage Reg. #1926,003227.). He died Russell, Manitoba (Denney.).

7. George Robert Wishart was born on 3 May 1859 (HBC-PN , Poplar Point and High Bluff, #353.). He married **Caroline Forbister**, daughter of **James Forbister** and **Catherine Foulds,** before 1879 Poplar Point, Manitoba (Denney.). He married **Minnie Anderson** on 5 Oct 1911 Winnipeg, Manitoba (MB Vital Statistics, Marriage Reg. #1911,003110.). He died on 24 Sep 1943 Russell, Manitoba, at age 84 (Ibid., Death Reg. #1943,040328.).

Caroline Forbister was born on 21 Jul 1859 (HBC-PN , Poplar Point and High Bluff, #85.). She died on 16 Mar 1900 RM Russell, Manitoba, at age 40 (MB Vital Statistics, Death Reg. #1900,001136.).

Children of **George Robert Wishart** and **Caroline Forbister** were as follows:

16   i.   Robert James Wishart, b. 17 Feb 1879 Prince Albert, (Saskatchewan); m. Dora Lopthein; d. 18 Jan 1963 Vancouver, British Columbia; bur. Jan 1963 Mountainview, Vancouver, British Columbia.

17   ii. Andrew Murray Wishart, b. 29 Jun 1880 Portage la Prairie, Manitoba; m. Beatrice Winnifred McNichol; d. 20 Nov 1982 Winnipeg, Manitoba; bur. 1982 Russell, Manitoba.

iii. Peter Henry Wishart was born on 30 Oct 1881 Portage la Prairie, Manitoba (1901 Canada, District 9-h-1[x], page 7, family 97, line 18-27.) (ArchiviaNet, C-15010.).

iv. Flora Ann Wishart was born on 12 Apr 1883 Silver Creek, Manitoba (MB Vital Statistics, Birth Reg. #1884,001390.). She married William Brownridge (Denney.).

v. Emma Jane Wishart was born on 15 May 1885 Portage la Prairie, Manitoba (ArchiviaNet, C-15010.). She died on 10 Jun 1897 Gilbert Plains, Manitoba, at age 12 (Ibid.).

vi. Herbert Scott Wishart was born on 29 May 1887 R.M. of Silver Creek, Manitoba (MB Vital Statistics, Birth Reg. #1887,004293.). He married Anna Augustine Hoefer on 30 Nov 1921 Shellmouth, Manitoba (Ibid., Marriage Reg. #1921,042515.). He died Russell, Manitoba (Denney.).

vii. Lilly Wishart was born on 26 Apr 1890 Russell, Manitoba (MB Vital Statistics, Birth Reg. #1890,006073.).

viii. Walter William Wishart was born on 14 Mar 1894 Russell, Manitoba (Ibid., Birth Reg. #1894,001584.).

ix. George William Wishart was born on 8 Oct 1896 R.M. of Strathclair, Manitoba (Ibid., Birth Reg. #1896,002833.).

x. Caroline Wishart was born on 16 Mar 1900 R.M. of Russell, Manitoba (Ibid., Birth Reg. #1900,001847.).

xi. Mary Wishart was born on 16 Mar 1900 R.M. of Russell, Manitoba (Ibid., Birth Reg. #1900,001848.). She died on 10 May 1901 RM Russell, Manitoba, at age 1 (Ibid., Death Reg. #1901,003398.).

Minnie Anderson was born in 1868 Ontario.

Children of **George Robert Wishart** and **Minnie Anderson** are as follows:

i. Cecil Clifford Wishart was born on 9 Aug 1912 Russell, Manitoba (Ibid., Birth Reg. #1912,009772.). He married Marion (Denney.).

ii. Mabel Ellen Irene Wishart was born circa 1917 (1921 Census of Canada from the National Archives of Canada (Transcription by ancestry.com), Ottawa, Canada, Distric 3-47, page 9.). She married William Funk (Denney.).

iii. Wilma Anita Wishart was born circa 1920 (1921 Canada, Distric 3-47, page 9.). She married Jan Miciah (Denney.).

8. Peter Henry Wishart was born on 13 Mar 1862 Baie St.Paul, (Manitoba) (HBC-PN , Poplar Point and High Bluff, #354.). He was baptized on 6 Apr 1862 St.Paul, (Manitoba) (Denney.). He married **Harriet Spence**, daughter of **David Spence** and **Catherine Hallett,** on 3 Mar 1887 Portage la Prairie, Manitoba (MB Vital Statistics, Marriage Reg. #1887,001353.). He died on 22 Jan 1936 RM Ochre River, Manitoba, at age 73 (Ibid., Death Reg. #1936,004403.).

Harriet Spence was born on 17 Jun 1863 Poplar Point, (Manitoba) (MBS, C-14933.). She was baptized on 6 Mar 1864 St.Mary's Anglican Church, Portage la Prairie, (Manitoba) (Ibid.) (SMACPLP, page 27, B-214.). She died on 27 May 1927 RM Ochre River, Manitoba, at age 63 (MB Vital Statistics, Death Reg. #1927,025166.).

Children of **Peter Henry Wishart** and **Harriet Spence** were as follows:

i. Florence Wishart was born on 9 Apr 1887 Elm River, Portage la Prairie, Manitoba (Denney.). She married Gus Langford (Ibid.). She died on 9 Jan 1953 at age 65 (Ibid.).

ii. Harry Allan Wishart was born on 11 May 1889 Elm River, Portage la Prairie, Manitoba (Ibid.). He married Kathleen Maggie Payne on 1 Jun 1920 Lawrence, Manitoba (MB Vital Statistics, Marriage Reg. #1920,032121.). He died on 23 Jul 1976 Winnipeg, Manitoba, at age 87 (Denney.).

iii. Edgar Franklin Wolsely Wishart was born on 4 Feb 1891 Elm River, Portage la Prairie, Manitoba (Ibid.). He married Mary Ethel Neilson on 24 Dec 1925 St.Boniface, Manitoba (MB Vital Statistics, Marriage Reg. #1925,051044.). He died on 23 Oct 1957 at age 66 (Denney.).

iv. Edna Wishart was born on 29 Mar 1896 Elm River, Portage la Prairie, Manitoba (Ibid.).

v. Ruby Emma Eliza Wishart was born on 4 Dec 1897 Oakville, Manitoba (MB Vital Statistics, Birth Reg. #1897,22820890, Reg. Date: 12/03/1964.).

vi. Edith Wishart was born on 6 Jan 1900 Elm River, Portage la Prairie, Manitoba (Denney.). She married Thomas Hoy (Ibid.). She died on 10 Jun 1971 at age 71 (Ibid.).

vii. Herbert Wishart was born on 5 Aug 1901 Elm River, Portage la Prairie, Manitoba (Ibid.).

9. **Margaret Jane Wishart** was born on 3 Mar 1864 Poplar Point, (Manitoba) (HBC-PN , Poplar Point and High Bluff, #355.). She was baptized on 7 Mar 1864 St.Mary's Anglican Church, Portage la Prairie, (Manitoba) (SMACPLP, page 27, B-216.). She married **Clarence Wilson** in 1885 (Denney.). She married **James John Cumming**, son of **Samuel Cumming** and **Margaret (--?--)**, in 1898 Rosebud, (Alberta) (Ibid.). She died on 24 Feb 1928 Drumheller, Alberta, at age 63 (Ibid.).

James John Cumming was born on 3 Oct 1867 Scotland (1901 Canada, District 202-a(5), page 1, family 10, line 28-34.).

10. **David Charles Wishart** was born on 9 Aug 1866 Poplar Point, (Manitoba) (HBC-PN , Poplar Point and High Bluff, #356.). He married **Maude Eva Mary Vigar** before 1898 Rosebud Creek (Denney.). He died in May 1956 Lethbridge, Alberta, at age 89 (Shirley Wishart, Apr 1997.).

Maude Eva Mary Vigar was born on 16 Jul 1876 Croyden, Surrey, England (Ibid.). She died on 11 Jul 1960 at age 83 (Ibid.).

Children of **David Charles Wishart** and **Maude Eva Mary Vigar** both born Rosebud Creek, (Alberta), were as follows:

    i. Florence Frances Wishart was born on 16 Apr 1898 (Denney.). She died on 11 Dec 1945 at age 47 (Ibid.).

    ii. Roy David Wishart was born on 17 Sep 1904 (Ibid.). He died on 9 Jan 1959 Calgary, Alberta, at age 54 (Ibid.).

11. **Mary Elizabeth Wishart** was born on 2 May 1869 Poplar Point, (Manitoba) (HBC-PN , Poplar Point and High Bluff, #357.). She was born on 22 May 1870 (1901 Canada, District 202-i(2), page 1, family 7, line 30-35.). She married **William David Cook**, son of **Matthew Cook** and **Matilda McKenzie**, circa 1 Oct 1890 (Alberta) (Denney.). She died on 17 Mar 1944 at age 74 (Ibid.).

William David Cook was born on 26 Jun 1864 (HBC-PN , Poplar Point and High Bluff, #66.). He was born on 29 Jun 1865 (1901 Canada, District 202-i(2), page 1, family 7, line 30-35.). He died on 3 Aug 1938 at age 74 (Denney.).

12. **Benjamin Wishart** was born on 15 Dec 1873 (1901 Canada, District 202-a(5), page 2, family 22, line 26-30.). He married **Mary Martin** on 15 May 1895 (Denney.). He died in 1931 (Ibid.).

Mary Martin was born on 6 Nov 1874 Ontario (1901 Canada, District 202-a(5), page 2, family 22, line 26-30.). She died in 1933 (Denney.).

Children of **Benjamin Wishart** and **Mary Martin** were as follows:

    i. Esther Wishart was born on 1 Feb 1896 (Automated Genealogy 1911 Census Transcription Project and Census Images from the National Archives of Canada, http://www.automatedgenealogy.com, District 50, page 9, family 73, line 37-40.) (1901 Canada, District 202-a(5), page 2, family 22, line 26-30.).

    ii. Margaret Wishart was born on 11 Aug 1897 (1911 Canada, District 50, page 9, family 73, line 37-40.) (1901 Canada, District 202-a(5), page 2, family 22, line 26-30.).

13. **Herbert Allen Wishart** was born on 12 May 1879 (familysearch.org Website, WWI Draft Registration.). He married **Florence Ledoux**, daughter of **George Ledoux** and **Adelaide Gingras**, on 6 Aug 1905 (David Courchane, Courchane/Courchene Family Research.). He died on 15 Oct 1946 Polson, Lake County, Montana, at age 67 (MT Death Montana State Genealogical Society Death Index.) (familysearch.org, Montana Death Index.).

Florence Ledoux was born on 5 Jun 1886 Flathead Reservation, Montana (1937-FB 1937 Census of the Flathead, Montana, United States Indian Service Department of the Interior, Washington D.C., 31 Dec 1937 , Census No. 3065-3070.). She died on 2 Aug 1953 Polson, Lake County, Montana, at age 67 (familysearch.org, Montana Death Index.).

Children of **Herbert Allen Wishart** and **Florence Ledoux** were as follows:

    i. Amy Allan Wishart was born on 5 Apr 1909 Vernon, British Columbia (D. Courchane.). She died on 1 Oct 1913 at age 4 (Ibid.).

    ii. John Allen "Jack" Wishart was born on 5 Aug 1911 Big Arm, Montana (*1937-FH*, Census No. 3065-3070.). He died on 24 Aug 1986 Tulare County, California, at age 75 (familysearch.org, California Death Index.).

    iii. Charles Allen Wishart was born on 16 Jun 1913 Big Arm, Montana (D. Courchane.) (1920 Flathead Indian Census Roll of the Flathead Reservation, United States Indian Service Department of the Interior, Flathead Indian Agency, Montana, 30 June 1920 , Census No. 2508-2512.) (*1937-FH*, Census No. 3065-3070.). He married Floretta June Carlson, daughter of Carl Elvick Carlson and Ruth McNickle, on 23 Mar 1938 Lake County, Montana (LakeCM Lake County, Montana; Marriage Record Licenses and Certificates; 1865-1950; familysearch.org, Hereinafter cited as LakeCM.).

        Floretta June Carlson was born circa 1922 (Ibid.).

    iv. Patricia Allen Wishart was born on 31 Jul 1918 Big Arm, Montana (D. Courchane.) (*1920 Flathead*, Census No. 2508-2512.) (*1937-FH*, Census No. 3065-3070.) (Social Security Death Index, . Hereinafter cited as SSDI.). She married Robert Earl Mullen, son of Harve Mullen and Elsie Hatfield, on 19 Mar 1940 Lake County, Montana (LakeCM.). She died on 19 Jun 1993 Sanders County, Montana, at age 74 (SSDI.).

        Robert Earl Mullen was born circa 1917 (LakeCM.). He died on 24 Mar 1973 Lake County, Montana (familysearch.org, Montana Death Index.).

    v. Florence Effie Allen Wishart was born on 14 Dec 1919 Big Arm, Montana (D. Courchane.) (*1920 Flathead*, Census No. 2508-2512.) (*1937-FH*, Census No. 3065-3070.). She married Walter Kenneth Jackson, son of Andrew Jackson and Eleanor Sophia Lounberg, on 15 Apr 1940 Lake County, Montana (LakeCM.).

        Walter Kenneth Jackson was born circa 1913 (Ibid.).

    vi. Josephine Allen Wishart was born on 23 Mar 1922 Polson, Lake County, Montana (Denney.) (*1937-FH*, Census No. 3065-3070.).

Generation Four

14. **Laura Amelia Wishart** was born on 26 Jul 1881 (1901 Canada, District 9-q-5, page 7, family 76, line 18-29.). She married **Robert Alexander Thomson** on 12 Mar 1902 Silver Creek, Manitoba (MB Vital Statistics, Marriage Reg. #1902,002557.). She died on 7 Sep 1979 Winnipeg, Manitoba, at age 98 (Denney.). She was buried in Sep 1979 Elmwood Cemetery, Winnipeg, Manitoba (Ibid.).

Robert Alexander Thomson was born circa 1875 Ontario (1921 Canada, District 226-23, page 8.). He died in 1945 (Denney.).

15. Lindy Ethel Wishart was born on 1 Jul 1883 Poplar Point, Manitoba (1901 Canada, District 9-q-5, page 7, family 76, line 18-29.) (ArchiviaNet, C-15010.). She was baptized on 30 Aug 1884 (Ibid.). She married **Neil Kenneth Wilkie,** son of **Donald Wilkie** and **Annie McLeod,** on 31 Aug 1904 Russell, Manitoba (MB Vital Statistics, Marriage Reg. #1904,002586.).

Neil Kenneth Wilkie was born on 5 Apr 1874 Bruce, Ontario (Ontario, Canada Births 1869-1913, ancestry.com, Hereinafter cited as ON Births.).

16. Robert James Wishart was born on 17 Feb 1879 Prince Albert, (Saskatchewan) (1901 Canada, District 9-h-1[x], page 7, family 97, line 18-27.) (ArchiviaNet, C-15010.). He married **Dora Lopthein** on 22 Jan 1905 Silver Creek, Manitoba (MB Vital Statistics, Marriage Reg. #1905,001579.). He died on 18 Jan 1963 Vancouver, British Columbia, at age 83 (Denney.). He was buried in Jan 1963 Mountainview, Vancouver, British Columbia (Ibid.).

Dora Lopthein was born on 3 Jan 1887 England (Ibid.). She died in Jul 1947 Vancouver, British Columbia, at age 60 (Ibid.). She was buried in Jul 1947 Mountainview, Vancouver, British Columbia (Ibid.).

Children of **Robert James Wishart** and **Dora Lopthein** are as follows:

    i.   Lawrence Robert Henry Wishart was born on 27 Oct 1906 R.M. of Russell, Manitoba (MB Vital Statistics, Birth Reg. #1906,002454.).

    ii.   Roderick George Wishart was born on 28 Oct 1907 R.M. of Russell, Manitoba (Ibid., Birth Reg. #1907,003237.).

    iii.   William Wishart was born in Oct 1908 (1911 Canada, District 87, page 6, family 69, line 5-9.).

    iv.   Edward Thomas Robert Wishart was born on 7 Dec 1909 R.M. of Grandview, Manitoba (MB Vital Statistics, Birth Reg. #1910,006744.).

17. Andrew Murray Wishart was born on 29 Jun 1880 Portage la Prairie, Manitoba (Denney.). He married **Beatrice Winnifred McNichol,** daughter of **Henry McNichol** and **Minnie Poppe,** on 31 Dec 1909 Grandview, Manitoba (MB Vital Statistics, Marriage Reg. #1910,004345.). He died on 20 Nov 1982 Winnipeg, Manitoba, at age 102 (Denney.). He was buried in 1982 Russell, Manitoba (Ibid.).

Beatrice Winnifred McNichol was born on 15 Mar 1890 Ontario. She died on 23 Sep 1965 at age 75 (Ibid.).

Children of **Andrew Murray Wishart** and **Beatrice Winnifred McNichol** were as follows:

    i.   George Andrew Wishart was born on 21 Apr 1910 R.M. of Grandview, Manitoba (MB Vital Statistics, Birth Reg. #1910,006770.). He died on 14 May 1942 Brandon, Manitoba, at age 32 (Ibid., Death Reg. #1942,020012.).

    ii.   Sarah Jane Kathleen Wishart was born on 30 Nov 1911 R.M. of Grandview, Manitoba (Ibid., Birth Reg. #1912,013952.).

    iii.   Henry Murray Wishart was born on 7 Apr 1913 Russell, Manitoba (Ibid., Birth Reg. #1913,023073.).

    iv.   Chester Warnock Wishart was born circa 1915 (Ibid., Death Reg. #1936,024409.). He died on 14 Jun 1936 RM Russell, Manitoba (Ibid.).

    v.   Charles Wishart was born circa 1917 (1921 Canada, Distric 3-43, page 9.).

    vi.   Arthur Wishart was born circa 1919 (Ibid.).

    vii.   Doreen Wishart was born circa 1921 (Ibid.).

Descendants of Alexander Work

Generation One

1. Alexander Work was born circa 1785 Rousay, Orkney, Scotland (HBCA-B Hudson's Bay Company Archives - biographical sketches, Hudson's Bay Company Archives; Winnipeg, Manitoba.). He was born circa 1787 (1827C RRS HBCA E5/1 1827 Census of the Red River Settlement, HBCA E5/1, Hudson's Bay Company Archives, Provincial Archives, 200 Vaughan Street, Winnipeg, MB R3C 1T5, Canada., page 3.). He married **Isabella Elizabeth Indian** on 30 Jul 1824 Red River Settlement, (Manitoba) (HBCR Hudson Bay Company Register of Anglican Church Baptisms, Marriages, and Burials for the Red River Settlement, 1821-1841; Hudson's Bay Company Archives, Winnipeg, Manitoba, M-78. Hereinafter cited as HBCR.). He died on 7 May 1850 St.Johns, (Manitoba) (Denney Papers, Charles D. Denney, Glenbow Archives, Calgary, Alberta.). He was buried on 7 May 1850 Middlechurch, (Manitoba) (HBCA-B, recorded in St. John's Register PAM, Anglican Registers Card Index.).

Isabella Elizabeth Indian was born circa 1786. She was baptized on 29 Sep 1830 St.Johns, (Manitoba) (HBCR, #200.). She was baptized on 29 Sep 1830 St.Johns, Red River Settlement, (Manitoba) (Ibid., E.4/1a, folio 78d.). She died in 1846.

Children of **Alexander Work** and **Isabella Elizabeth Indian** were as follows:

  2   i.   William Work, b. 18 Jul 1822 North West; m. Barbara Halcrow.

  3   ii.   Jane Work, b. 30 Jul 1824 St.Johns, Red River Colony, (Manitoba); m. John Cunningham.

Generation Two

2. William Work was born on 18 Jul 1822 North West (MBS Scrip Applications, Original White Settlers & Halfbreeds residing in Manitoba on 15 July 1870, RG15-19, Supplementary Returns, C-14934.). He was baptized on 30 Jul 1824 St.Johns, Red River Colony, (Manitoba) (HBCA-B.) (HBCR, E.4/1a, folio 50.). He married **Barbara Halcrow,** daughter of **Thomas Halcrow** and **Mary Southward Indian Woman,** on 8 Dec 1842 St.Johns, (Manitoba) (Denney.).

Barbara Halcrow was baptized on 31 Oct 1824 St.Johns, Red River Colony, (Manitoba) (HBCA-B.) (HBCR, E.4/1a, folio 52d.).

Children of **William Work** and **Barbara Halcrow** were as follows:

  4   i.   Jane Work, b. 1843 St.Paul, (Manitoba); m. James Colin Inkster; d. 7 Mar 1914 RM Dauphin, Manitoba.

    ii.   Alexander Thomas Work was baptized on 10 Aug 1845 St.Johns, (Manitoba) (Denney.).

  5   iii.   Joseph Work, b. 18 Jul 1847; m. Mary Helen 'Ellen' Miller; d. 12 Oct 1890 RM St.Paul, (Manitoba).

  6   iv.   Peter Garriock Work, b. 12 Dec 1848; m. Margaret J. Saunders.

  7   v.   Harriet Mary Work, b. 22 May 1852; m. George Gladman Vincent; d. 5 Aug 1921 Winnipeg, Manitoba.

    vi.   Madeline Work was born in Aug 1854 St.Paul, (Manitoba) (Ibid.). She was baptized on 17 Sep 1854 St.Paul, (Manitoba) (Ibid.). She died on 3 Apr 1862 St.Paul, (Manitoba), at age 7 (Ibid.).

8   vii.   Elizabeth Ann Work, b. 10 Jan 1856 St.Paul, (Manitoba); m. George Paquin or Pocha; d. 7 Jul 1894 St.Paul, Lindsay, (Saskatchewan).

9   viii.   Catherine Work, b. 7 Dec 1858 Middlechurch, (Manitoba); m. Thomas James Slater; d. 17 Apr 1925 Onion Lake, Saskatchewan.

10   ix.   William James Work, b. 2 Apr 1861; m. Sarah Jane Harcus; d. 5 Oct 1938 Winnipeg, Manitoba.

   x.   Colin Campbell Work was born in 1864 St.Paul, (Manitoba) (Ibid.). He died on 6 Nov 1865 St.Paul, (Manitoba) (Ibid.).

   xi.   James Curtis Work was born in 1866 (Ibid.). He died on 25 Dec 1866 St.Paul, (Manitoba) (Ibid.).

   xii.   Anabella Work was born on 22 Jan 1868 (Ibid.). She was baptized on 25 Feb 1868 St.Paul, (Manitoba) (Ibid.). She married Alfred Grove Sutherland on 29 Oct 1885 Winnipeg, Manitoba (Manitoba Vital Statistics online, http://web2.gov.mb.ca, Marriage Reg. #1885,001239.).

   xiii.   Barbara Work was born in Nov 1870 (Denney.). She was baptized on 6 Dec 1870 St.Paul, (Manitoba) (Ibid.). She died on 9 Dec 1870 St.Paul, (Manitoba) (Ibid.).

3. Jane Work was baptized on 30 Jul 1824 St.Johns, Red River Colony, (Manitoba) (HBCA-B.) (HBCR, E.4/1a, folio 50.). She married **John Cunningham**, son of **Patrick Cunningham** and **Nancy Bruce**, on 26 Jan 1837 Red River Settlement, (Manitoba) (HBCA-B.) (HBCR, No. 333.).

John Cunningham was born on 16 Feb 1818 (HBCA-B.). He was baptized on 27 Aug 1826 St.Johns, (Manitoba) (HBCR, E.4/1a, folio 61d, #583.). He was baptized on 12 Sep 1846 Lac Ste.Anne, (Alberta) (INB *Index des Naissances and Baptemes* (St.Boniface, Manitoba: La Societe Historique de Saint-Boniface., c1995), page 40.). He married **Margaret Mondion** on 28 Feb 1841 Rocky Mountain House, Saskatchewan District (RTR Rundle, Reverend R. T., Journal of Baptisms & Marriages in Saskatchewan District, 1840 - 1848, M-1. Hereinafter cited as RTR.). He married **Rosalie L'Hirondelle**, daughter of **Jacques L'Hirondelle** and **Josephte Pilon**, on 15 Sep 1846 Fort-des-Prairies, (Alberta) (FDP Baptisms & Marriages Fort des Prairie, Saskatchewan District, C Kipling, M-110. Hereinafter cited as FDP.). He died in 1870 Tail Creek, (Alberta) (Denney.).

Generation Three

4. Jane Work was born in 1843 St.Paul, (Manitoba) (MBS, C-14929.). She married **James Colin Inkster**, son of **James Inkster** and **Elizabeth Sutherland**, on 4 Mar 1861 St.Paul, (Manitoba) (Denney.). She died on 7 Mar 1914 RM Dauphin, Manitoba (MB Vital Statistics, Death Reg. #1914,087194.).

James Colin Inkster was born on 24 Sep 1831 St.Paul, (Manitoba) (MBS, C-14929.). He was baptized on 9 Oct 1831 St.Johns, Red River Settlement, (Manitoba) (HBCA-B, E.4/1a, fo. 85d.) (HBCR, E.4/1a, folio 85d.). He died before 1901 (MB Vital Statistics, Death Reg. #1914,087194.).

5. Joseph Work was born on 18 Jul 1847 (Denney.). He married **Mary Helen 'Ellen' Miller**, daughter of **Robert Miller or Millar** and **Elizabeth Setter**, on 12 Jul 1877 Kildonan, Manitoba (Ibid.). He died on 12 Oct 1890 RM St.Paul, (Manitoba), at age 43 (MB Vital Statistics, Death Reg. #1890,001661.).

Mary Helen 'Ellen' Miller was born on 10 Apr 1863 (Denney.). She was baptized on 17 May 1863 St.Andrews, Manitoba (Ibid.). She married **George Knight**, son of **John Knight** and **Sophia Bird**, on 21 Sep 1892 Selkirk, Manitoba (MB Vital Statistics, Marriage Reg. #1892,001486.).

Children of **Joseph Work** and **Mary Helen 'Ellen' Miller** were as follows:

   i.   William James Curtis Work was born circa 1880 St.Paul, Manitoba (1881 Canada, C-13283, District 185-A, page 15, house 61.).

   ii.   Joseph Work was born circa 1882 Manitoba (1891 Census of Canada from the National Archives of Canada, Ottawa, Canada.).

   iii.   Thomas Havelin Work was born on 2 May 1884 RM St.Paul, Manitoba (MB Vital Statistics, Birth Reg. #1884,003245.). He died on 3 Mar 1885 St.Paul, Manitoba (Ibid., Death Reg. #1885,001201.).

   iv.   William James Curtis Work was born circa Oct 1884 St.Paul, Manitoba (Ibid., Death Reg. #1885,001200.).

   v.   Peter Garrioch Work was born on 14 Jul 1886 RM St.Paul, Manitoba (Ibid., Birth Reg. #1886,001597.).

   vi.   Annabella Work was born on 15 Nov 1888 St.Paul, Manitoba (Ibid., Birth Reg. #1889,005424.).

6. Peter Garriock Work was born on 12 Dec 1848 (Denney.). He was baptized on 6 Jan 1850 St.Paul, (Manitoba) (Ibid.). He married **Margaret J. Saunders**, daughter of **Palm Saunders** and **Jane Forbes**, before 1872 (1881 Canada, C-13283, District 192-2, page 47, house 257.).

Margaret J. Saunders was born circa 1854 (1870C-MB 1870 Manitoba Census, National Archives of Canada, Ottawa, Ontario, Microfilm Reel Number C-2170., page 89, #1434.).

Children of **Peter Garriock Work** and **Margaret J. Saunders** were as follows:

11   i.   Peter Allan Work, b. circa 1872 Manitoba; m. Margaret Ann Isbister.

12   ii.   Catherine Jane Work, b. 8 Mar 1878 South Branch, (Saskatchewan); m. Charles Stevens; d. 24 May 1896 South Branch, (Saskatchewan).

   iii.   John Work was born circa 1880 (ArchiviaNet 1886-1901, 1906 Half-Breed Scrip Applications Index, RG15-21, Volume 1333 through 1371, Microfilm Reel Number C-14944 through C-15010, National Archives of Canada, Ottawa, Ontario, http://www.collectionscanada.gc.ca, C-15010.).

   iv.   Joseph Work was born on 8 Mar 1880 Halcro, (Saskatchewan) (Ibid.). He died on 27 Mar 1880 Halcro, (Saskatchewan) (Ibid.). He was buried on 29 Mar 1880 Halcrow Mission, South Branch, (Saskatchewan) (Ibid.).

   v.   Alexander Work was born on 30 Apr 1881 Halcro, (Saskatchewan) (1881 Canada, C-13283, District 192-2, page 47, house 257.) (ArchiviaNet, C-15010.) (Automated Genealogy 1901 Census Transcription Project and Census Images from the National Archives of Canada, http://www.automatedgenealogy.com, District 205-g, page 2, family 18, line 17-26.).

   vi.   Margaret Work was born on 8 Apr 1883 South Branch, (Saskatchewan) (Ibid.) (ArchiviaNet, C-15010.).

   vii.   William Arnold Work was born on 3 Jun 1885 Prince Albert, (Saskatchewan) (Ibid.).

viii. Anabella Work was born on 26 Aug 1888 (1901 Canada, District 205-g, page 2, family 18, line 17-26.).
ix. Elisabeth Work was born on 12 Dec 1890 (Ibid.).
x. Elizabeth Margaret Work was born on 16 Dec 1891 (Saskatchewan) (Saskatchewan Vital Statistics online, http://vsgs.health.gov.sk.ca, Birth Reg. #8035.).
xi. Sarah Work was born on 24 Dec 1896 (1901 Canada, District 205-g, page 2, family 18, line 17-26.).
xii. George Work was born on 23 Nov 1898 (Saskatchewan) (SK Vital Statistics, Birth Reg. #1611.).
xiii. George Work was born on 25 Nov 1898 (1901 Canada, District 205-g, page 2, family 18, line 17-26.).

7. Harriet Mary Work was born on 22 May 1852 (Denney.). She married **George Gladman Vincent**, son of **John Vincent** and **Charlotte Thomas**, on 14 Apr 1870 St.Paul, Stonewall, Manitoba (Ibid.). She died on 5 Aug 1921 Winnipeg, Manitoba, at age 69 (MB Vital Statistics, Death Reg. #1921,031100.).

George Gladman Vincent was born on 28 Feb 1852 St.Paul, (Manitoba) (Denney.). He was baptized on 7 Mar 1852 St.Paul, (Manitoba) (Ibid.). He died on 27 Apr 1921 Winnipeg, Manitoba, at age 69 (MB Vital Statistics, Death Reg. #1921,015255.).

8. Elizabeth Ann Work was born on 10 Jan 1856 St.Paul, (Manitoba) (MBS, C-14931.). She married **George Paquin or Pocha**, son of **Joseph Paquin** and **Marie Lapointe**, before 1875 St.James, Manitoba (Denney.). She died on 7 Jul 1894 St.Paul, Lindsay, (Saskatchewan), at age 38 (Ibid.).

George Paquin or Pocha was baptized on 19 Oct 1851 St.Andrews, (Manitoba) (Ibid.). He was born in Jan 1852 (MBS, C-14934.). He died circa 1931 (Denney.).

9. Catherine Work was born on 7 Dec 1858 Middlechurch, (Manitoba) (Ibid.). She was baptized on 2 Jan 1859 St.Paul, (Manitoba) (Ibid.). She married **Thomas James Slater**, son of **Thomas James Slater** and **Elizabeth "Betsy" Taylor**, on 6 Apr 1882 St.Pauls, Manitoba (MB Vital Statistics, Marriage Reg. #1882,001446.). She died on 17 Apr 1925 Onion Lake, Saskatchewan, at age 66 (Denney.).
Question: *Heather says b. 6 Dec 1860.*

Thomas James Slater was born on 6 Oct 1857 St.Paul, (Manitoba) (MBS, C-14933.). He was baptized on 1 Nov 1857 St.Paul, (Manitoba) (Denney.). He died on 7 Jul 1948 at age 90 (Ibid.).

10. William James Work was born on 2 Apr 1861 (Denney.). He was baptized in Jun 1861 St.Paul, (Manitoba) (Ibid.). He married **Sarah Jane Harcus**, daughter of **George Harcus** and **Nancy Ann Lillie**, before 1881 (1881 Canada, NA Film #C-13283, District 185, Sub-district A, page 10, house 36.). He died on 5 Oct 1938 Winnipeg, Manitoba, at age 77 (MB Vital Statistics, Death Reg. #1938,040164.).

Sarah Jane Harcus was born on 3 May 1861 St.Andrews, (Manitoba) (HBC-PN , St.Andrews, #256.). She was baptized on 30 Jun 1861 St.Andrews, (Manitoba) (Denney.). She died on 1 Nov 1896 St.Paul, Manitoba, at age 35 (MB Vital Statistics, Death Reg. #1896,001901.).

Children of **William James Work** and **Sarah Jane Harcus** were as follows:
i. Thomas A. L. Work was born on 7 Jan 1882 Manitoba (1901 Canada, #11, R-1, page 5, family 126, line 18-21.).
ii. William J. Curtis Work was born on 17 Nov 1883 Manitoba (Ibid.).
iii. Colin Hugh Work was born on 3 Aug 1886 RM St.Paul, Manitoba (MB Vital Statistics, Birth Reg. #1886,001595.). He died on 11 Aug 1887 St.Paul, Manitoba, at age 1 (Ibid., Death Reg. #1887,002858.).
iv. Lilly Ann May Work was born on 26 Apr 1888 St.Paul, Manitoba (Ibid., Birth Reg. #1888,004760.). She died on 1 Mar 1889 St.Paul, Manitoba (Ibid., Death Reg. #1889,001069.).
v. Annabella Work was born on 21 Dec 1889 St.Paul, Manitoba (Ibid., Birth Reg. #1889,002817.). She died on 14 May 1890 St.Paul, Manitoba (Ibid., Death Reg. #1890,002618.).
vi. Thornhall Stewart Work was born on 23 May 1892 St.Paul, Manitoba (Ibid., Birth Reg. #1892,006192.).

Generation Four

11. Peter Allan Work was born circa 1872 Manitoba (1881 Canada, C-13283, District 192-2, page 47, house 257.). He married **Margaret Ann Isbister** before 1898 (SK Vital Statistics, Birth Reg. #1612.).
Children of **Peter Allan Work** and **Margaret Ann Isbister** are:
i. Edith May Work was born on 8 Oct 1898 (Saskatchewan) (Ibid.).

12. Catherine Jane Work was born on 8 Mar 1878 South Branch, (Saskatchewan) (1881 Canada, C-13283, District 192-2, page 47, house 257.) (ArchiviaNet, C-15004.). She married **Charles Stevens** before 1895 (Ibid.). She died on 24 May 1896 South Branch, (Saskatchewan), at age 18 (Ibid.).

Ahnentafel between Louis Gonzague Isaac Zace and Christian Zasse

--- 1st Generation ---

1. Louis Gonzague Isaac Zace was also known as **Gonzacque Zastre** (1833C RRS HBCA E5/7 1833 Census of the Red River Settlement, HBCA E5/7, Hudson's Bay Company Archives, Provincial Archives, 200 Vaughan Street, Winnipeg, MB R3C 1T5, Canada., page 18.). He was born on 5 Apr 1802 at Berthierville, Quebec (MBS Scrip Applications, Original White Settlers & Halfbreeds residing in Manitoba on 15 July 1870, RG15-19, C-14934.) (HBCA-B Hudson's Bay Company Archives - biographical sketches, Hudson's Bay Company Archives; Winnipeg, Manitoba.) (PRDH online index, http://www.genealogic.umontreal.ca, #2371764.). He was baptized on 5 Apr 1802 at Berthierville, Quebec (Ibid.). He married **Angelique Parisien**, daughter of **Jean Baptiste Parisien** and **Louise Forcier**, on 28 May 1833 at St.Boniface, (Manitoba) (SB 1825-1834 St.Boniface Roman Catholic Registre des Baptemes, Mariages & Sepultures, 1825-1834, page 104, M-106. Hereinafter cited as SB 1825-1834.). He died on 10 Sep 1888 at St.Francois Xavier, Manitoba, at age 86 (SFXI-Kipling St.Francois Xavier Register Index, 1834-1900; compiled by Clarence Kipling , S-14.) (Manitoba Vital Statistics online, http://web2.gov.mb.ca, Death Reg. #1888,002663.). As of 10 Sep 1888, he was also known as **Gonzague Zastre** (Ibid.).

--- 2nd Generation ---

2. Jean Andre Zasse (Fred Zastre Research, e-mail 30 May 1998.) (PRDH online, #222777.) (Ibid.) was also known as **Sase** (Fred Zastre, e-mail 30 May 1998.). He was also known as **Jean-Andre Zass** (HBCA-B.). He was born circa 1757 at Calvin, Magdebourg,

Germainy (PRDH online, #222777.). He married MARIE REINE CONTRE DIT SANSOUCY, daughter of FRANCOIS CONTRE DIT SANSOUCY and MARIE MARGUERITE TESSIER DIT LAVIGNE, on 3 Feb 1785 at Berthierville, Quebec (Fred Zastre, e-mail 30 May 1998.) (PRDH online, #99998.). He died on 13 Oct 1810 at Berthierville, Quebec (Ibid., #222777.). He was buried on 14 Oct 1810 at Berthierville, Quebec (Ibid.).

--- 3rd Generation ---

4. CHRISTIAN ZASSE (Ibid.) was born at Madebourg, Germany (Fred Zastre, e-mail 30 May 1998.). He married CATHERINE SPOLERDER.

Descendants of Louis Gonzague Isaac Zace

Generation One

1. Louis Gonzague Isaac Zace was born on 5 Apr 1802 Berthierville, Quebec (MBS Scrip Applications, Original White Settlers & Halfbreeds residing in Manitoba on 15 July 1870, RG15-19, C-14934.) (HBCA-B Hudson's Bay Company Archives - biographical sketches, Hudson's Bay Company Archives; Winnipeg, Manitoba.) (PRDH online index, http://www.genealogic.umontreal.ca, #2371764.). He was baptized on 5 Apr 1802 Berthierville, Quebec (Ibid.). He married **Angelique Parisien**, daughter of **Jean Baptiste Parisien** and **Louise Forcier**, on 28 May 1833 St.Boniface, (Manitoba) (SB 1825-1834 St.Boniface Roman Catholic Registre des Baptemes, Mariages & Sepultures, 1825-1834, page 104, M-106. Hereinafter cited as SB 1825-1834.). He died on 10 Sep 1888 St.Francois Xavier, Manitoba, at age 86 (SFXI-Kipling St.Francois Xavier Register Index, 1834-1900; compiled by Clarence Kipling , S-14.) (Manitoba Vital Statistics online, http://web2.gov.mb.ca, Death Reg. #1888,002663.).

Angelique Parisien was born circa 1811 (SB 1825-1834, page 103, B-596.). She was born in 1812 North West (MBS, C-14934.). She was baptized on 6 Jun 1833 St.Boniface, (Manitoba) (SB 1825-1834, page 103, B-596.). She died on 5 Nov 1904 St.Francois Xavier, Manitoba (MB Vital Statistics, Death Reg. #1904,001978.).

Children of **Louis Gonzague Isaac Zace** and **Angelique Parisien** were as follows:

- 2   i.   Angelique Zace, b. 1 Jun 1832 St.Boniface, (Manitoba); m. Augustin Gosselin.
- 3   ii.   Jean Baptiste Zace, b. 4 Dec 1832 North West Territory; m. Marguerite Riel; m. Brigitte Courchene; d. 12 Jan 1903 Ritchot, Manitoba; bur. 14 Jan 1903 St.Norbert, Manitoba.
- 4   iii.   Genevieve Zace, b. 31 May 1834 St.Boniface, (Manitoba); m. Pierre Allary; d. 22 Dec 1912 St.Francois Xavier, Manitoba.
- 5   iv.   Gonzague Zace, b. 1836 St.Vital, (Manitoba); m. Marie Parisien.
- 6   v.   Julie Zace, b. 1837 St.Norbert, (Manitoba); m. Andre Parisien; d. 29 Aug 1933 Ritchot, Manitoba.
- 7   vi.   Alexis Zace, b. 10 Jul 1843 North West; m. Angelique Ross.
-      vii.   Lucie Zace was born circa 1844 (SFXI-Kipling, S-45.). She died on 26 Sep 1866 (Ibid.). She was buried on 28 Sep 1866 St.Francois Xavier, (Manitoba) (Ibid.) (SFXI 1851-1868 St.Francois Xavier 1852-1861 Register Index, S-45. Hereinafter cited as SFXI 1851-1868.).
- 8   viii.   Louise Zace, b. 8 May 1847 St.Boniface, (Manitoba); m. Paul Paul; d. 8 Dec 1909.
- 9   ix.   Andre Zace, b. 15 Mar 1849 Pembina County, Minnesota Territory; m. Mathilde Ross.
- 10   x.   Elise Zace, b. 26 Nov 1850 Pembina, Pembina County, Minnesota Territory; m. Elzear Thibert; d. 10 Feb 1948.
- 11   xi.   Marie Zace, b. Jun 1852 Winnipeg, (Manitoba); m. James Slater; d. 2 Jun 1938 Rolette County, North Dakota.
- 12   xii.   Isidore Zace, b. 10 Jun 1855 St.Francois Xavier, (Manitoba); m. Domitilde Bousquet; d. 11 Nov 1931 Winnipeg, Manitoba.
- 13   xiii.   Guillemine Zace, b. circa 1856 (Manitoba); m. Charles Laviolette.

Generation Two

2. Angelique Zace was born on 1 Jun 1832 St.Boniface, (Manitoba) (SB 1825-1834, page 67, B-444.). She was baptized on 10 Jun 1832 St.Boniface, (Manitoba) (Ibid.). She married **Augustin Gosselin**, son of **Augustin Gosselin**, on 4 Jun 1849 Assumption, Pembina, Pembina County, Minnesota Territory (AP Records of the Assumption Roman Catholic Church, Pembina, North Dakota: Baptisms, Marriages, Sepultures, 1848-1896; compiled by Reverend Father J. M. Belleau, 2 October 1944, page 16, M-7. Hereinafter cited as AP.).

Augustin Gosselin was born before 1828.

3. Jean Baptiste Zace was born on 4 Dec 1832 North West Territory (MBS, C-14934.). He married **Marguerite Riel**, daughter of **Louis Riel** and **Swampy Creek Indian**, before 1861. He married **Brigitte Courchene**, daughter of **Antoine Courchene** and **Helene Delorme**, on 21 Aug 1877 St.Norbert, Manitoba (SN2 Catholic Parish Register of St.Norbert, M-5. Hereinafter cited as SN2.). He died on 12 Jan 1903 Ritchot, Manitoba, at age 70 (Rod MacQuarrie Research, 16 April 2005.). He was buried on 14 Jan 1903 St.Norbert, Manitoba (St-N Cem St.Norbert Parish Cemetery 1859-1906, We Remember; Winnipeg, Manitoba, Canada: St.Norbert Parish-La Barriere Metis Council of the Metis Federation of Manitoba, 29 May 2010.).

Marguerite Riel was born circa 1840 Rainy Lake, Ruperts Land (SN2, B-21.). She died on 7 May 1874 St.Norbert, Manitoba (Ibid., S-10.). She was buried on 9 May 1874 St.Norbert, Manitoba (Ibid.).

Children of **Jean Baptiste Zace** and **Marguerite Riel** were as follows:

- 14   i.   Jane Amelia Zace, b. 22 Aug 1861 St.Boniface, (Manitoba); m. Urbain Delorme.
- 15   ii.   Appoline Zace, b. 9 Sep 1863; m. Alfred Nault.
- 16   iii.   Joseph Zace, b. Mar 1866; m. Celina Laramee.
- 17   iv.   Louis Zace, b. 2 Jun 1868; m. Marie Josephine Courchene; d. 26 Oct 1904 Ritchot, Manitoba; bur. 28 Oct 1904 St.Norbert, Manitoba.
-      v.   Marie Elise Zace was born on 4 Mar 1871 St.Norbert, Manitoba (SN1, page 142, B-12.). She was baptized on 5 Mar 1871 St.Norbert, Manitoba (Ibid.).
-      vi.   Jules Arthur Zace was born on 22 Jul 1873 (Ibid., B-41.). He was baptized on 27 Jul 1873 St.Norbert, Manitoba (Ibid.). He died on 8 Feb 1874 St.Norbert, Manitoba (SN2, S-1.). He was buried on 9 Feb 1874 St.Norbert, Manitoba (Ibid.). He was buried on 5 Mar 1874 St.Norbert, Manitoba (Ibid., S-4.).

Brigitte Courchene was born on 25 Dec 1857 Red River, (Manitoba) (Rod Mac Quarrie, 16 April 2005.).

Children of **Jean Baptiste Zace** and **Brigitte Courchene** were as follows:

  i. Marie Rosina Zasse was born on 15 Jul 1878 St.Norbert, Manitoba (SN2, B-33.). She was baptized on 16 Jul 1878 St.Norbert, Manitoba (Ibid.).

  ii. Marie Josephine Octavie Zace was born on 20 Nov 1879 St.Norbert, Manitoba (Ibid., B-58.). She was baptized on 23 Nov 1879 St.Norbert, Manitoba (Ibid.). She married Aime Hubert Dambly, son of Jean-Baptiste Dambly and Sophie Dossogne, on 5 Aug 1913 (St.Norbert), Fort Garry, Manitoba (MM *Manitoba Marriages* in *Publication 45*, Volumes 1-3, compiled and edited by: Paul J. Lareau, Fr. Julien Hamelin, (240 Avenue Daly, Ottawa, Ontario K1N 6G2: Le Centre de Genealogie S.C., 1984).) (MB Vital Statistics, Marriage Reg. #1913,048054.).

   Aime Hubert Dambly was born Belgium (MM, page 290.).

  iii. Marie Florestine Zaida Zastre was born on 28 Aug 1881 St.Norbert, Manitoba (SN2, B-33.). She was baptized on 29 Aug 1881 St.Norbert, Manitoba (Ibid.).

  iv. Marie Evangeline Zasse was born on 8 Aug 1884 R.M. of Cartier, Manitoba (MB Vital Statistics, Birth Reg. #1884,004324.) (SN2, B-44.). She was baptized on 10 Aug 1884 St.Norbert, Manitoba (Ibid.). She married Jean Baptiste Lavallee, son of Noe Lavallee and Esther Laplante, on 21 Jul 1903 St.Norbert, Manitoba (MM, page 1314.) (Rosemary Helga (Morrissette) Rozyk Research, 2 Nov 2006.) (MB Vital Statistics, Marriage Reg. #1903,001963.). She died on 3 Jul 1920 St.Norbert, Manitoba, at age 35 (Rosemary Rozyk, 2 Nov 2006.) (MB Vital Statistics, Death Reg. #1920,039150.). She was buried on 4 Jul 1920 St.Norbert, Manitoba (Rosemary Rozyk, 2 Nov 2006.).

   Jean Baptiste Lavallee was born circa 1882 St-Michel, Napierville (MM.).

  v. Marie Agnes Zace was born on 7 Jun 1886 St.Norbert, Manitoba (SN2, B-25.). She was baptized on 8 Jun 1886 St.Norbert, Manitoba (Ibid.). She died on 14 Sep 1886 St.Norbert, Manitoba (Ibid., S-19.). She was buried on 15 Sep 1886 St.Norbert, Manitoba (Ibid.).

18 vi. Marie Zaida Zace, b. 28 Dec 1887 R.M. of Cartier, Manitoba; m. Wilfred Joseph Lemay.

4. Genevieve Zace was born on 31 May 1834 St.Boniface, (Manitoba) (SB 1825-1834, page 129, B-792.). She was baptized on 1 Jun 1834 St.Boniface, (Manitoba) (Ibid.). She married **Pierre Allary**, son of **Michel Allary** and **Marguerite Saulteux,** before 1857. She died on 22 Dec 1912 St.Francois Xavier, Manitoba, at age 78 (MB Vital Statistics, Death Reg. #1912,001103.).

Pierre Allary was born circa 1832 (SB 1825-1834, page 155, B-893.). He was baptized on 23 Nov 1834 St.Boniface, (Manitoba) (Ibid.). He died on 12 May 1924 Elie, Manitoba (MB Vital Statistics, Death Reg. #1924,020348.).

5. Gonzague Zace was born on 3 Nov 1835 (Manitoba) (Diane Stigen Research, 19 Mar 2003, Source: 1901 Manitoba census.). He was born in 1836 St.Vital, (Manitoba) (MBS, C-14934.). He married **Marie Parisien**, daughter of **Bonaventure Parisien** and **Marguerite Sauteuse,** on 21 Nov 1859 St.Norbert, (Manitoba) (SN1, M-7, page 21-22.).

Marie Parisien was born on 7 May 1840 (Manitoba) (Diane Stigen, 19 Mar 2003, Source: 1901 Manitoba census.). She was born on 15 Sep 1842 St.Norbert, (Manitoba) (MBS, C-14934.).

Children of **Gonzague Zace** and **Marie Parisien** were as follows:

  i. Elise Zace was born on 15 Dec 1860 (SN1, page 36, B-47.). She was baptized on 19 Dec 1860 St.Norbert, (Manitoba) (Ibid.). She died on 29 Jan 1861 St.Norbert, (Manitoba) (Ibid., page 40, S-1.). She was buried on 30 Jan 1861 St.Norbert, (Manitoba) (Ibid.).

19 ii. Napoleon Zace, b. 10 Dec 1861 St.Norbert, (Manitoba); m. Pauline St.Denis.

  iii. Norbert Zaste was born on 27 Jul 1864 St.Norbert, (Manitoba) (Ibid., page 105, B-34.). He was baptized on 28 Jul 1864 St.Norbert, (Manitoba) (Ibid.). He died on 19 Nov 1865 St.Norbert, (Manitoba), at age 1 (Ibid., page 140, S-34.). He was buried on 20 Nov 1865 St.Norbert, (Manitoba) (Ibid.).

  iv. Marie Mathilde Zace was born on 25 Aug 1866 St.Norbert, (Manitoba) (Ibid., page 84, B-38.). She was baptized on 26 Aug 1866 St.Norbert, (Manitoba) (Ibid.).

20 v. Rosalie Angelique Zace, b. 1 Oct 1868 St.Norbert, (Manitoba); m. Joseph Roy.

  vi. Christine Zace was born on 27 Nov 1870 St.Norbert, Manitoba (Ibid., page 136, B-49.). She was baptized on 27 Nov 1870 St.Norbert, Manitoba (Ibid.). She married Emile Abraham on 21 Apr 1897 Ste.Rose, Dauphin, Manitoba (MM, page 11.) (MB Vital Statistics, Mar. Reg. #1899,001152 (Dauphin).).

21 vii. Joseph Albert Zace, b. 4 Jun 1873 St.Norbert, Manitoba; m. Cecile Constance Lacouette.

  viii. Joseph Thelesphore Zasse was born on 18 Aug 1875 St.Norbert, Manitoba (SN2, B-33.). He was baptized on 18 Aug 1875 St.Norbert, Manitoba (Ibid.). He died on 29 Aug 1875 St.Norbert, Manitoba (Ibid., S-22.). He was buried on 30 Aug 1875 St.Norbert, Manitoba (Ibid.).

22 ix. Octavie Zace, b. 10 Jul 1876 St.Norbert, Manitoba; m. Louis Schmidt.

23 x. Elzear Zace, b. 24 Apr 1880 Cartier, Provencher, Manitoba; m. Victoire Rose Ritchot.

  xi. Marie Nathalie Pelagie Zasse was born on 10 Dec 1882 Cartier, Manitoba (MB Vital Statistics, Birth Reg. #1882,001392.) (SN2, B-47.). She was baptized on 11 Dec 1882 St.Norbert, Manitoba (Ibid.). She died on 29 Apr 1884 St.Norbert, Manitoba, at age 1 (Ibid., S-15.). She was buried on 1 May 1884 St.Norbert, Manitoba (Ibid.).

6. Julie Zace was born in 1837 St.Norbert, (Manitoba) (MBS, C-14932.). She married **Andre Parisien**, son of **Hyacinthe Parisien** and **Josephte Carriere,** on 9 Feb 1858 St.Norbert, (Manitoba) (SN1, page 4, M-10.). She died on 29 Aug 1933 Ritchot, Manitoba (MB Vital Statistics, Death Reg. #1933,031357.).

Andre Parisien was born in 1827 St.Norbert, (Manitoba) (MBS, C-14932.). He died on 4 Jun 1899 Ritchot, Manitoba (MB Vital Statistics, Death Reg. #1899,001430.).

7. Alexis Zace was born on 10 Jul 1843 North West (MBS, C-14934.). He married **Angelique Ross**, daughter of **Hugh Ross** and **Sarah Short,** on 10 Jan 1865 St.Francois Xavier, (Manitoba) (SFXI-Kipling, M-1.).

Angelique Ross was born on 7 May 1844 St.Francois Xavier, (Manitoba) (SFX: 1834-1850 St.Francois Xavier 1834-1851 Register, B-517. Hereinafter cited as SFX: 1834-1850.). She was baptized on 11 May 1844 St.Francois Xavier, (Manitoba) (Ibid.).

Children of **Alexis Zace** and **Angelique Ross** were as follows:

24   i.   Marie Zace, b. 22 Nov 1865 St.Francois Xavier, (Manitoba); m. James Phillips.

25   ii.   Elise Zace, b. 23 Jan 1873; m. Francois Allary.

26   iii.   Mathilde Zace, b. 24 Jul 1875 St.Francois Xavier, Manitoba; m. Isidore Morin; d. 28 Apr 1963 Belcourt, Rolette County, North Dakota.

     iv.   Elzear Zaste was born on 14 Jul 1882 St.John, Rolette County, North Dakota (St. Claude Mission, St. John, North Dakota, Baptisms, Marriages, Burials 1882-1888, 2006, Dominique Ritchot, page 4, B-21.). He was baptized on 15 Jul 1882 St.Claude, St.John, Rolette County, North Dakota (Ibid.). He married Adele Blackbird, daughter of Jean Letourneau dit Blackbird and Marguerite Langer, in 1900 Belcourt, Rolette County, North Dakota (*St.Ann's Centennial, 100 Years of Faith - 1885-1985*; Belcourt, North Dakota: St.Ann Parish, 1985), page 553-554.). He died on 29 Aug 1959 Belcourt, Rolette County, North Dakota, at age 77 (Ibid.) (ND Death Index.).

        Adele Blackbird was born in 1881 (1936-TMC 1936 Tribal Roll, Turtle Mountain Indian Reservation, Office of Indian Affairs, received 28 Jan 1938, National Archives of the United States, Washington D.C., page 121.) (BIA-TM-BMD, page 28.). She was born circa 1885. She died on 8 Mar 1929 Belcourt, Rolette County, North Dakota (*St.Ann's Centennial*, page 553-554.) (ND Death Index.).

27   v.   John Baptiste Zace, b. 12 Aug 1883; m. Josephine (--?--); d. 28 Nov 1976 Williams County, North Dakota.

8. Louise Zace was born on 8 May 1847 St.Boniface, (Manitoba) (MBS, C-14932.). She married **Paul Paul**, son of **Olivier Paul** and **Madeleine Gervais**, on 21 Apr 1863 St.Francois Xavier, (Manitoba) (SFXI-Kipling, M-6.) (SFXI 1851-1868, M-6.). She died on 8 Dec 1909 at age 62 (Denney.).

Paul Paul was born on 3 Dec 1842 St.Francois Xavier, (Manitoba) (SFX: 1834-1850, B-437.). He was baptized on 3 Dec 1842 St.Francois Xavier, (Manitoba) (Ibid.). He died on 31 Oct 1931 San Clara, Manitoba, at age 88 (Denney.).

9. Andre Zace was born on 15 Mar 1849 Pembina County, Minnesota Territory (AP, page 15, B-28.). He was baptized on 16 Mar 1849 Assumption, Pembina, Pembina County, Minnesota Territory (Ibid.). He married **Mathilde Ross**, daughter of **Hugh Ross** and **Sarah Short**, on 28 Feb 1870 St.Francois Xavier, (Manitoba) (SFXI-Kipling, M-9.).

Mathilde Ross was born on 11 Dec 1852 St.Francois Xavier, (Manitoba) (Ibid., B-49.) (SFXI 1851-1868, B-49.). She was baptized on 20 Dec 1852 St.Francois Xavier, (Manitoba) (SFXI-Kipling, B-49.) (SFXI 1851-1868, B-49.). She died on 6 Apr 1943 RM Ste.Rose du Lac, Manitoba, at age 90 (MB Vital Statistics, Death Reg. #1943,016382.).

Children of **Andre Zace** and **Mathilde Ross** were as follows:

28   i.   Marie Mathilde Zace, b. 11 Dec 1870 St.Francois Xavier, Manitoba; m. Pierre Thibert.

     ii.   Marie Emerise Zace was born on 18 Sep 1872 St.Francois Xavier, Manitoba (SFXI-Kipling, B-53.). She was baptized on 21 Sep 1872 St.Francois Xavier, Manitoba (Ibid.) (INB, page 187.). She died on 10 Mar 1884 St.Francois Xavier, Manitoba, at age 11 (SFXI-Kipling, S-5.).

29   iii.   Louise Zace, b. 3 Oct 1874 St.Francois Xavier, Manitoba; m. Joseph Josue Allary; d. Apr 1913 St.Eustache, Manitoba.

30   iv.   Jean Zace, b. 12 Oct 1876 St.Francois Xavier, Manitoba; m. Marguerite Lepine; d. 28 Nov 1976 Trenton, North Dakota.

31   v.   Virginie Zace, b. 24 Oct 1878 St.Francois Xavier, Manitoba; m. Joseph Morand.

32   vi.   Agnes Zace, b. 16 Nov 1880 St.Francois Xavier, Manitoba; m. Napoleon Barron; d. 1950.

     vii.   Alex Zace was born on 16 Jan 1882 (1901 Canada, MB, Selkirk, (#11), SFX, N-1, page 7-8, family 62, Line 48-50, 1-8.). He was born on 17 Jan 1883 St.John, Rolette County, North Dakota (St.Claude BMD, Dominique Ritchot, page 7, B-36.). He was baptized on 17 Jan 1883 St.Claude, St.John, Rolette County, North Dakota (Ibid.).

     viii.   Marie Thadee Zastre was born on 6 Jun 1885 St.Francois Xavier, Manitoba (MB Vital Statistics, Birth Reg. #1885,004020.). She was baptized on 7 Jun 1885 St.Francois Xavier, Manitoba (SFXI-Kipling, B-24.).

     ix.   Edouard Alfred Zastre was born on 6 Jun 1885 St.Francois Xavier, Manitoba (MB Vital Statistics, Birth Reg. #1885,004019.). He was baptized on 7 Jun 1885 St.Francois Xavier, Manitoba (SFXI-Kipling, B-22.). He married Justine Lafreniere, daughter of Ambroise Lafreniere and Emerise Houle, on 8 Jan 1907 St.Francois Xavier, Manitoba (MM.) (MB Vital Statistics, Marriage Reg. #1907,004547.).

        Justine Lafreniere was born on 26 Dec 1887 St.Francois Xavier, Manitoba (SFXI-Kipling, B-59.).

     x.   Anatalie Rose Zastre was born on 5 Jun 1887 St.Francois Xavier, Manitoba (Ibid., B-30.) (MB Vital Statistics, Birth Reg. #1887,004213.). She was baptized on 7 Jun 1887 St.Francois Xavier, Manitoba (SFXI-Kipling, B-30.) (Rosemary Rozyk, 28 Jan 1999 report.). She married Joseph Aime Barron, son of Charles Barron and Marie Comtois, on 24 Nov 1908 St.Francois Xavier, Manitoba (MM, page 52.) (MB Vital Statistics, Marriage Reg. #1908,001678.).

        Joseph Aime Barron was born on 1 Apr 1880 Fort Qu'Appelle, (Saskatchewan) (HBS 1886-1901, 1906 Half-Breed Scrip Applications, RG15-21, Volume 1334; C-14947.). He was baptized on 4 Apr 1880 Lebret, (Saskatchewan) (L1, page 257, B-10.). He married **Elizabeth Lepine**, daughter of **Daniel Lepine** and **Rose Lingan,** on 25 Nov 1902 St.Francois Xavier, Manitoba (MM, page 52.).

     xi.   Marie Victoire Exerine Zastre was born on 28 Jul 1890 St.Francois Xavier, Manitoba (SFXI-Kipling, B-34.) (MB Vital Statistics, Birth Reg. #1890,003600.). She married Didyine Breland, son of Moise Breland and Philomene Page, on 22 Oct 1907 St.Francois Xavier, Manitoba (Ibid., Marriage Reg. #1907,002602.).

        Didyine Breland was born on 27 Mar 1867 (1901 Canada, MB, Selkirk, (#11), SFX, N-1, page 2, family 22, Line 20-30.).

xii. Edmond Zastre was born on 28 Jul 1890 St.Francois Xavier, Manitoba (SFXI-Kipling, B-33.) (MB Vital Statistics, Birth Reg. #1890,003599.). He married Rose Patenaude on 15 Apr 1918 Lawrence, Manitoba (SFXI-Kipling, B-33 (note).) (MB Vital Statistics, Mar. Reg. #1918,022087.).

xiii. Melanie Zastre was born on 4 Mar 1895 St.Francois Xavier, Manitoba (SFXI-Kipling, B-5.) (MB Vital Statistics, Birth Reg. #1895,003989.). She married Frank Fitzpatrick on 10 Nov 1919 Lawrence, Manitoba (SFXI-Kipling, B-5 (note).) (MB Vital Statistics, Mar. Reg. #1919,064088.).

10. **Elise Zace** was born on 26 Nov 1850 Pembina, Pembina County, Minnesota Territory (AP, page 46, B-117.). She was baptized on 27 Nov 1850 Assumption, Pembina, Pembina County, Minnesota Territory (Ibid.). She married **Elzear Thibert**, son of **Pierre Thibert** and **Julie Belcourt**, on 28 Feb 1870 St.Francois Xavier, (Manitoba) (SFXI-Kipling, M-10.). She died on 10 Feb 1948 at age 97 (MBS.).
Elzear Thibert was born on 12 Jun 1849 North West (Ibid., C-14934.). He died on 18 Apr 1917 RM Cartier, Manitoba, at age 67 (MB Vital Statistics, Death Reg. #1917,024077.).

11. **Marie Zace** was born in Jun 1852 Winnipeg, (Manitoba) (MBS, C-14933.). She married **James Slater**, son of **James Slater** and **Josephte Morissette**, on 28 Nov 1871 St.Francois Xavier, Manitoba (SFXI-Kipling, M-11.). She died on 2 Jun 1938 Rolette County, North Dakota (ND Death Index.).
James Slater was born circa 1847 (Manitoba) (1870C-MB, page 252, #220.).

12. **Isidore Zace** was born on 10 Jun 1855 St.Francois Xavier, (Manitoba) (MBS, C-14934.). He married **Domitilde Bousquet**, daughter of **Louis Bousquet** and **Elizabeth Fisher**, on 5 Jun 1877 St.Boniface, Manitoba (RMSB *Repertoire des Mariages de Saint-Boniface (Manitoba) 1825-1983* compiled by Julien Hamelin S.C., (240, avenue Daly; Ottawa, Ontario K1N 6G2: Le Centre de Genealogie S. C., Publication #67, 1985).). He died on 11 Nov 1931 Winnipeg, Manitoba, at age 76 (MB Vital Statistics, Death Reg. #1931,048141.).
Domitilde Bousquet was born on 9 May 1858 St.Boniface, (Manitoba) (MBS, C-14925.).
Children of **Isidore Zace** and **Domitilde Bousquet** were as follows:

33   i. Domitilde Zace, b. 25 Jun 1878 St.Francois Xavier, Manitoba; m. Alexandre Lafreniere.

ii. Marie Elisabeth Zace was born circa 1880 (SFXI-Kipling, S-6.). She died on 13 Apr 1889 St.Francois Xavier, Manitoba (Ibid.).

iii. Marie Madeleine Zastre was born on 29 May 1882 St.Francois Xavier, Manitoba (Ibid., B-35.) (MB Vital Statistics, Birth Reg. #1882,001981.). She married Alfred Napoleon McDougall, son of John Peter McDougall and Elise Delorme, on 6 Feb 1905 St.Francois Xavier, Manitoba (MM, page 1317.).
   Alfred Napoleon McDougall was born on 31 Oct 1877 St.Francois Xavier, Manitoba (SFXI-Kipling, B-50.). He was baptized on 1 Nov 1877 St.Francois Xavier, Manitoba (Ibid.) (Rosemary Rozyk.).

34   iv. Marie Lucie Zace, b. 15 Dec 1883 St.Francois Xavier, Manitoba; m. Napoleon Brazeau.

v. Jean Joseph Arthur Zastre was born on 10 Jun 1885 St.Francois Xavier, Manitoba (1901 Canada, #11, N-3, page 4-5, Family 32, Line 50, 1-10.) (MB Vital Statistics, Birth Reg. #1885,004021.). He married Regina Marie Albert on 10 Jul 1934 St.Eustache, Manitoba (MM.).

vi. Marie Rose Melanie Zastre was born on 25 Mar 1887 St.Francois Xavier, Manitoba (SFXI-Kipling, B-10.) (MB Vital Statistics, Birth Reg. #1887,004201.). She married Harry Pont on 22 Oct 1917 St.Francois Xavier, Manitoba (MM.).

vii. Louis Gonzaque Zastre was born on 11 Jan 1889 St.Francois Xavier, Manitoba (SFXI-Kipling, B-1.) (MB Vital Statistics, Birth Reg. #1889,005467.). He married Aurelia St.Godard on 9 Oct 1918 St.Francois Xavier, Manitoba (MM.).

viii. Eleonore Octavie Zastre was born on 4 Jul 1890 St.Francois Xavier, Manitoba (SFXI-Kipling, B-29.) (MB Vital Statistics, Birth Reg. #1890,003596.).

ix. Marie Josephina Zastre was born on 18 Mar 1892 St.Francois Xavier, Manitoba (SFXI-Kipling, B-12.) (MB Vital Statistics, Birth Reg. #1892,006217.). She died on 18 Aug 1892 St.Francois Xavier, Manitoba (SFXI-Kipling, S-24.).

x. Asilda Malvina Zace was born on 8 Jul 1894 St.Francois Xavier, Manitoba (Ibid., B-19.). She died on 26 Aug 1894 St.Francois Xavier, Manitoba (Ibid., S-12.).

xi. Henri Albert Zastre was born on 17 Apr 1896 St.Francois Xavier, Manitoba (Ibid., B-17.) (MB Vital Statistics, Birth Reg. #1896,006044.). He married Lilanne Goulet on 6 Apr 1920 St.Boniface, Manitoba (RMSB.) (MB Vital Statistics, Mar. Reg. #1920,019028.).

xii. Alphonse Eugene Isidore Zastre was born on 12 Apr 1898 St.Francois Xavier, Manitoba (SFXI-Kipling, B-20.) (MB Vital Statistics, Birth Reg. #1898,003634.).

xiii. Julien Zastre was born on 10 Jan 1901 R.M. of St.Francois Xavier, Manitoba (Ibid., Birth Reg. #1901,006414.).

xiv. Ernest Zastre was born on 31 Mar 1905 R.M. of St.Francois Xavier, Manitoba (Ibid., Birth Reg. #1905,004210.).

13. **Guillemine Zace** was born circa 1856 (Manitoba) (1870C-MB, page 255, #300.) (1889-TMC-off, #353.). She married **Charles Laviolette**, son of **Jean Baptiste Laviolette** and **Nancy Paul**, on 24 Sep 1872 St.Francois Xavier, (Manitoba) (SFXI-Kipling, M-15.).
Charles Laviolette was born on 2 Dec 1851 St.Francois Xavier, (Manitoba) (SFX: 1834-1850, B-909.). He was baptized on 3 Dec 1851 St.Francois Xavier, (Manitoba) (Ibid.).
Children of **Guillemine Zace** and **Charles Laviolette** were as follows:

i. Marie Laviolette was born on 25 Nov 1873 St.Francois Xavier, Manitoba (SFXI-Kipling, B-75.). She was baptized on 26 Nov 1873 St.Francois Xavier, Manitoba (Ibid.) (INB, page 105.). She was buried on 27 Jun 1875 St.Francois Xavier, Manitoba (IBMS.) (SFXI-Kipling, S-29.).

ii. Josue Noe Laviolette was born on 8 Jun 1875 St.Francois Xavier, Manitoba (Ibid., B-21.). He was baptized on 8 Jun 1875 St.Francois Xavier, Manitoba (Ibid.) (INB, page 105.). He died circa 20 Jun 1875 St.Francois Xavier, Manitoba (SFXI-Kipling, S-27.). He was buried on 22 Jun 1875 St.Francois Xavier, Manitoba (IBMS.) (SFXI-Kipling, S-28.).

iii. Mili Laviolette was born circa 1876 (1889-TMC-off, #354.).

iv. Napoleon Laviolette was born on 17 May 1878 Batoche, (Saskatchewan) (HBSI.) (ArchiviaNet.). He married Melanie Bouvier in 1899 St.John, Rolette County, North Dakota (HBSI.) (ArchiviaNet.). He died on 20 Aug 1943 Ward County, North Dakota, at age 65 (ND Death Index.).

v. Tobie Laviolette was born on 13 May 1880 Batoche, (Saskatchewan) (HBSI.) (ArchiviaNet.). He married Placidie Jeannotte or Jannot, daughter of Jean Baptiste Jeannotte and Agnes Madona Breland, in 1899 St.John, Rolette County, North Dakota (HBSI.) (ArchiviaNet.).

Placidie Jeannotte or Jannot was born on 12 Apr 1881 St.Francois Xavier, Manitoba (SFXI-Kipling, B-27.).

vi. Emerise Laviolette was born on 25 Feb 1882 Rolette County, North Dakota (St.Claude BMD, Dominique Ritchot, page 1, B-4.). She was baptized on 13 May 1882 St.Claude, St.John, Rolette County, North Dakota (Ibid.).

vii. Hyacinthe Laviolette was born on 17 Feb 1884 St.John, Rolette County, North Dakota (Ibid., page 23, B-95.). He was baptized on 19 Feb 1884 St.Claude, St.John, Rolette County, North Dakota (Ibid.).

viii. Mary Jane Laviolette was baptized on 27 May 1887 St.Claude Mission, St.John, Rolette County, North Dakota (Ibid., B-329, page 65.).

ix. Joseph Jacob Laviolette was born circa Apr 1889 (1889-TMC-off, #359.).

x. Anna Laviolette was born circa 1891 North Dakota (1930C ND Fifteenth Census of the United States: 1930; North Dakota, National Archives of the United States, Washington, D.C., District 1, page 3A, family 49, line 14.). She married Paschal Warren, son of John Warren and Elisabeth Montour, before 1910 (TM Star, 18 Jan 2010.).

Paschal Warren was born on 25 Feb 1873 (L1, page 87, B-59.). He was baptized on 5 Mar 1873 Lebret, (Saskatchewan) (Ibid.). He died on 14 Jun 1936 Rolette County, North Dakota, at age 63 (ND Death Index.).

xi. Elvina Laviolette was born circa 1893 (1900C ND Twelfth Census of the United States: 1900, North Dakota, District 153, page 14A, family 272, line 17.).

xii. William Laviolette was born circa 1897 (Ibid.).

xiii. Fred Laviolette was born circa 1904 Manitoba (1916 Census of Canada from the National Archives of Canada (Transcription by ancestry.com), Ottawa, Canada, Distirict 18, page 8, family 78.).

Generation Three

14. **Jane Amelia Zace** was born on 22 Aug 1861 St.Boniface, (Manitoba) (SB-Rozyk, page 28, B-110.). She was baptized on 22 Aug 1861 St.Boniface, (Manitoba) (Ibid.). She married **Urbain Delorme**, son of **Alexis Delorme** and **Helene Frederic dit Paul**, on 9 Jan 1883 (Cartier), St.Norbert, Manitoba (SN2, M-3.) (MB Vital Statistics, #1883,001257.).

Urbain Delorme was born on 9 Dec 1857 St.Norbert, (Manitoba) (SN1, page 3, B-2.). He was baptized on 9 Dec 1857 St.Norbert, (Manitoba) (Ibid.).

15. **Appoline Zace** was born on 9 Sep 1863 (SB-Rozyk, page 127, B-135.). She was baptized on 10 Sep 1863 St.Boniface, (Manitoba) (Ibid.). She married **Alfred Nault**, son of **Amable Nault** and **Josephte Lagimoniere**, on 25 Aug 1879 St.Norbert, Manitoba (SN2, M-10.).

Alfred Nault was born on 31 Jan 1854 St.Boniface, (Manitoba) (MBS, C-14931.). He married **Cecile Lafournaise**, daughter of **Gabriel Lafournaise** and **Susanne Collin**, on 21 Oct 1873 St.Norbert, Manitoba (SN1, M-10.). He died on 8 Aug 1922 Springfield, Manitoba, at age 68 (MB Vital Statistics, Death Reg. #1922,030458.).

16. **Joseph Zace** was born in Mar 1866 (SB-Rozyk, page 50, B-60.). He was baptized on 20 May 1866 St.Boniface, (Manitoba) (Ibid.). He married **Celina Laramee**, daughter of **Pierre Laramee** and **Marie Hamel,** on 18 Sep 1894 (St.Norbert), Ritchot, Manitoba (MM, page 723.) (MB Vital Statistics, Marriage Reg. #1898,001522.).

Celina Laramee was born circa 1876 (MM, page 723.).

Children of **Joseph Zace** and **Celina Laramee** were as follows:

i. Jean Baptiste Zastre married Victoire Normand, daughter of William Edmond Normand and Marie Anne Daunais, on 9 Feb 1932 St.Norbert, Manitoba (MM.).

Victoire Normand was born in May 1911 St.Norbert, Manitoba (Automated Genealogy 1911 Census Transcription Project and Census Images from the National Archives of Canada, http://www.automatedgenealogy.com, page 1, Family 6, Line 24-28.).

ii. Henriette Zaste married Joseph Victor Vermette, son of Isidore Vermette and Anna Laplante, on 12 Nov 1927 St.Boniface, Manitoba (RMSB, page 486.) (MB Vital Statistics, Marriage Reg. #1927,053044.).

Joseph Victor Vermette was born on 17 Feb 1907 R.M. of De Salaberry, Manitoba (Ibid., Birth Reg. #1907,21818951, Reg. Date: 11/07/1961.).

iii. Marie Alphonsine Zaste was born on 10 May 1896 R.M. of Ritchot, Manitoba (Ibid., Birth Reg. #1898,006327.). She married Joseph Louis Tobie Carriere, son of Louis Elie Carriere and Rose Perreault, on 17 Jul 1917 RM of Ritchot, Manitoba (Ibid., Marriage Reg. #1917,040079.). She died in 1998 St.Boniface, Manitoba (Rod Mac Quarrie, 17 Jan 2013.).

Joseph Louis Tobie Carriere was born on 8 Jun 1885 Salaberry, Manitoba (MB Vital Statistics, Birth Reg. #1885,003066.). He died in 1953 (Rod Mac Quarrie, 17 Jan 2013.).

iv. Joseph Arthur Zaste was born on 7 Oct 1897 R.M. of Ritchot, Manitoba (MB Vital Statistics, Birth Reg. #1898,006412.). He married Marie Victorine Roy, daughter of Jean Baptiste Roy and Marie Rocheleau, on 22 Jun 1920 (St.Norbert), Fort Garry, Manitoba (Ibid., Marriage Reg. #1920,032096.) (MM, page 1316 and 1118.).

Marie Victorine Roy was born circa 1903.

v. Joseph Noel Octave Zaste was born on 13 Jun 1899 Ritchot, Manitoba (MB Vital Statistics, Birth Reg. #1899,006564.). He married Catherine Kroker on 19 Feb 1925 Winnipeg, Manitoba (Ibid., Marriage Reg. #1925,007164.).

vi. Marie Alexandrine Zaste was born on 7 Aug 1900 R.M. of Ritchot, Manitoba (Ibid., Birth Reg. #1900,005314.).

vii. Marie Emilienne Zaste was born on 6 Sep 1902 St.Boniface, Manitoba (Ibid., Birth Reg. #1902,22921050, date 1-6-1964.) (Ibid., Birth Reg. #1902,005739.).

viii. Marie Rose Alexandrine Zaste was born on 16 May 1904 R.M. of Ritchot, Manitoba (Ibid., Birth Reg. #1904,004697.).

ix. Margaret Florida Zaste was born on 4 May 1906 R.M. of Ritchot, Manitoba (Ibid., Birth Reg. #1906,11213009, date 31-12-1927.).

x. Elie Zace was born circa 1912 (MM.). He married Henriette Grouette on 29 Aug 1936 St.Norbert, Manitoba (Ibid.).

17. Louis Zace was born on 2 Jun 1868 (SB-Rozyk, page 132, B-130.). He was baptized on 14 Sep 1868 St.Boniface, (Manitoba) (Ibid.). He married **Marie Josephine Courchene**, daughter of **Antoine Courchene** and **Helene Delorme**, on 16 Jun 1891 (St.Norbert), Ritchot, Manitoba (SN2, M-7.) (MB Vital Statistics, Marriage Reg. #1891,001871.). He died on 26 Oct 1904 Ritchot, Manitoba, at age 36 (Ibid., Death Reg. #1904,001839.). He was buried on 28 Oct 1904 St.Norbert, Manitoba (St-N Cem.).

Marie Josephine Courchene was born on 4 Sep 1872 St.Norbert, Manitoba (SN1, B-42.). She was baptized on 5 Sep 1872 St.Norbert, Manitoba (Ibid.). She died on 18 Jun 1902 Ritchot, Manitoba, at age 29 (St-N Cem.) (MB Vital Statistics, Death Reg. #1902,002754.). She was buried on 20 Jun 1902 St.Norbert, Manitoba (St-N Cem.).

Children of **Louis Zace** and **Marie Josephine Courchene** were as follows:

i. Marie Louise Zaste was born on 12 Dec 1892 R.M. of Ritchot, Manitoba (MB Vital Statistics, Birth Reg. #1892,003216.). She died on 28 Nov 1896 Ritchot, Manitoba, at age 3 (Ibid., Death Reg. #1898,002858.). She was buried on 30 Nov 1896 St.Norbert, Manitoba (St-N Cem.).

ii. Marie Celina Zaste was born on 9 Nov 1894 Ritchot, Manitoba (MB Vital Statistics, Birth Reg. #1898,006218.). She died on 28 Feb 1895 Ritchot, Manitoba (Ibid., Death Reg. #1898,002813.). She was buried on 1 Mar 1895 St.Norbert, Manitoba (St-N Cem.).

iii. Marie Delima Zaste was born on 13 Mar 1896 R.M. of Ritchot, Manitoba (MB Vital Statistics, Birth Reg. #1898,006319.). She died on 23 Mar 1897 Ritchot, Manitoba, at age 1 (Ibid., Death Reg. #1898,002869.). She was buried on 24 Mar 1897 St.Norbert, Manitoba (St-N Cem.).

iv. Joseph Louis Zaste was born on 8 Apr 1898 R.M. of Ritchot, Manitoba (MB Vital Statistics, Birth Reg. #1898,006439.). He died on 16 Apr 1900 RM Ritchot, Manitoba, at age 2 (Ibid., Birth Reg. #1900,001118.). He was buried on 17 Apr 1900 St.Norbert, Manitoba (St-N Cem.).

v. Marie Florida Zaste was born on 27 Aug 1900 R.M. of Ritchot, Manitoba (MB Vital Statistics, Birth Reg. #1900,005317.). She died on 3 Nov 1922 Springfield, Manitoba, at age 22 (Ibid., Birth Reg. #1922,042420.).

18. Marie Zaida Zace was born on 28 Dec 1887 R.M. of Cartier, Manitoba (Ibid., Birth Reg. #1887,005315.) (SN2, B-62.). She was baptized on 28 Dec 1887 St.Norbert, Manitoba (Ibid.). She married **Wilfred Joseph Lemay**, son of **Joseph Octave Lemay** and **Marie Camille Auger,** on 6 Sep 1908 (St.Norbert), RM Ritchot, Manitoba (MM, page 778.) (MB Vital Statistics, Marriage Reg. #1908,001540.).

Wilfred Joseph Lemay was born on 27 Dec 1867 Dakota Territory (AP, page 34, B-19.). He was baptized on 29 Dec 1867 Assumption, Pembina, Pembina County, Dakota Territory (Ibid., page 28, B-13.). He was baptized on 12 Sep 1868 Assumption, Pembina, Pembina County, Dakota Territory (Ibid., page 34, B-19.). He married **Marie Dubord**, daughter of **Joseph Dubord** and **Marie Louise Hedwige Hamelin,** on 27 Jun 1888 St.Norbert, Manitoba (SN2, M-8.).

19. Napoleon Zace was born on 10 Dec 1861 St.Norbert, (Manitoba) (SN1, page 50, B-46.). He was baptized on 11 Dec 1861 St.Norbert, (Manitoba) (Ibid.). He married **Pauline St.Denis**, daughter of **Jacques St.Denis** and **Charlotte Rocheleau,** on 25 Feb 1884 St.Norbert, Manitoba (SN2, M-4.).

Pauline St.Denis was born on 6 Nov 1866 St.Norbert, (Manitoba) (SN1, page 87, B-58.). She was baptized on 7 Nov 1866 St.Norbert, (Manitoba) (Ibid.).

Children of **Napoleon Zace** and **Pauline St.Denis** were as follows:

i. Joseph Napoleon Zace was born on 2 Mar 1885 Cartier, Manitoba (SN2, B-12.) (MB Vital Statistics, Birth Reg. #1885,002709.). He was baptized on 3 Mar 1885 St.Norbert, Manitoba (SN2, B-12.).

ii. Joseph Phileas Zace was born on 12 May 1887 R.M. of Cartier, Manitoba (MB Vital Statistics, Birth Reg. #1887,002927.) (SN2, B-18.). He was baptized on 14 May 1887 St.Norbert, Manitoba (Ibid.).

iii. Marie Louise Zace was born circa Jan 1889 (Ibid., S-8.). She died on 7 Feb 1889 (Ibid.). She was buried on 9 Feb 1889 St.Norbert, Manitoba (Ibid.).

iv. Alfred Zastre was born on 19 May 1892 Ste.Rose, Manitoba (MB Vital Statistics, Birth Reg. #1892,21518349, date 14-9-1960.). He married Louisa Whitford on 14 Apr 1913 Ste.Rose, Manitoba (Ibid., Marriage Reg. #1913,019134.). He married Marie Monica Roussin, daughter of Pierre Roussin and Marie Rose Klyne, on 17 Nov 1914 RM St.Rose, Manitoba (Ibid., Marriage Reg. #1914,138259.).

   Marie Monica Roussin was born on 21 Jan 1898 Leroy, Pembina County, North Dakota (SJL-2 Register of Baptisms, Marriages, and Burials, St.Joseph, Leroy, North Dakota, Diocese of Saint Paul, Minnesota, 1888-1900, Book 2, page 97, B-5. Hereinafter cited as SJL-2.). She was baptized on 27 Jan 1898 St.Joseph, Leroy, Pembina County, North Dakota (Ibid.).

v. Georges Zaste was born circa 16 Dec 1893 Manitoba (Diane Stigen, 23 Mar 2003, Source: 1901 Manitoba census.). He married Josephine Ross on 7 Aug 1917 St.Clements, Manitoba (MB Vital Statistics, Marriage Reg. #1917,046057.).

vi. Joseph Zastre was born on 25 Dec 1897 R.M. of Dauphin, Manitoba (Ibid., Birth Reg. #1899,001593.).

vii. Louis Zastre was born on 25 Dec 1897 R.M. of Dauphin, Manitoba (Ibid., Birth Reg. #1899,001594.).

20. Rosalie Angelique Zace was born on 1 Oct 1868 St.Norbert, (Manitoba) (SN1, B-46.). She was baptized on 2 Oct 1868 St.Norbert, (Manitoba) (Ibid.). She married **Joseph Roy**, son of **Jean Baptiste Roy** and **Catherine Morand,** on 3 Feb 1891 (St.Norbert), Ritchot, Manitoba (SN2, M-3.) (MB Vital Statistics, Marriage Reg. #1891,001875.).

Joseph Roy was born on 17 Apr 1869 St.Norbert, (Manitoba) (MBS, C-14932.) (SN2, B-15.). He was baptized on 18 Apr 1869 St.Norbert, (Manitoba) (MBS, C-14932.) (SN2, B-15.).

21. **Joseph Albert Zace** was born on 4 Jun 1873 St.Norbert, Manitoba (SN1, B-34.). He was baptized on 5 Jun 1873 St.Norbert, Manitoba (Ibid.). He married **Cecile Constance Lacouette**, daughter of **Augustin Lacouette** and **Marie Bone or Oskinigig**, on 11 Jul 1901 Ste.Rose, Dauphin, Manitoba (MB Vital Statistics, Marriage Reg. #1901,003043 (Dauphin).).

Cecile Constance Lacouette was born on 3 Jun 1873 Sandy Bay, (Manitoba) (ArchiviaNet.) (INB, page 91.). She was baptized on 23 Jun 1873 St.Laurent, Manitoba (Ibid.).

Children of **Joseph Albert Zace** and **Cecile Constance Lacouette** were:
  i.   Joseph Albert Zastre was born on 23 Jun 1902 R.M. of Ochre River, Manitoba (MB Vital Statistics, Birth Reg. #1902,007167.).

22. **Octavie Zace** was born on 10 Jul 1876 St.Norbert, Manitoba (SN2, B-22.). She was baptized on 11 Jul 1876 St.Norbert, Manitoba (Ibid.). She married **Louis Schmidt**, son of **Alfred 'Rabasca' Schmidt** and **Maggie "Kasa-wa-asso" Carlow**, on 4 Jan 1897 Ste.Rose du Lac, Dauphin, Manitoba (MM.) (MB Vital Statistics, Marriage Reg. #1899,001151 (Dauphin).).

Louis Schmidt was born on 12 May 1864 Fort Pitt, (Saskatchewan) (Diane Stigen, 19 Mar 2003, Source: 1901 Manitoba census.) (ArchiviaNet, C-15002.).

23. **Elzear Zace** was born on 24 Apr 1880 Cartier, Provencher, Manitoba (Ibid., 19 Mar 2003.) (SN2, B-21.). He was baptized on 25 Apr 1880 St.Norbert, Manitoba (Ibid.). He married **Victoire Rose Ritchot**, daughter of **Louis Ritchot** and **Isabelle Nault,** on 29 Jun 1901 Ste.Rose, Dauphin, Manitoba (MM, page 1078.) (MB Vital Statistics, Mar. Reg. #1901,003041 (Dauphin).).

Victoire Rose Ritchot was born on 18 Jul 1879 Manitoba (1901 Canada, page 9, line 42-50, family 99.).

Children of **Elzear Zace** and **Victoire Rose Ritchot** are as follows:
  i.   Marie Antoinette Zastre was born on 17 Aug 1901 Dauphin, Manitoba (MB Vital Statistics, Birth Reg. #1901,008192.). She married William Henry Sutherland on 20 Apr 1918 Swan River, Manitoba (Ibid., Marriage Reg. #1918,022031.).
  ii. Marie Rose Celina Zaste was born on 4 Apr 1903 R.M. of Ste.Rose, Manitoba (Ibid., Birth Reg. #1903,008206.).
  iii. Louis Alfred Joseph Zaste was born on 11 Dec 1904 Ste.Rose, Manitoba (Ibid., Birth Reg. #1904,002767.).
  iv. Joseph Zaste was born on 24 Nov 1907 Ste.Rose, Manitoba (Ibid., Birth Reg. #1906,003020.).

24. **Marie Zace** was born on 22 Nov 1865 St.Francois Xavier, (Manitoba) (SFXI-Kipling, B-104.) (MBS, C-14934.). She was baptized on 24 Nov 1865 St.Francois Xavier, (Manitoba) (SFXI-Kipling, B-104.) (MBS, C-14934.). She married **James Phillips**, son of **Henry Phillips** and **Catherine Williams**, on 10 Jun 1884 St.Claude Mission, St.John, Rolette County, North Daktoa (Dominique Ritchot, 26 Jan 2006.).

James Phillips was born circa 1851 Tavistock, Tevonshire, England (Rod Mac Quarrie, 8 Aug 2012.). He married **Melanie Sutherland**, daughter of **Antoine Sutherland** and **Elise Ritchot**, on 7 Mar 1902 Winnipeg, Manitoba (Ibid.). He married **Louise Victoire Ouellette**, daughter of **Francois Ouellette** and **Marguerite Dupuis**, on 17 Aug 1917 Pentecostal Church, 133 Wolsley Avenue, Winnipeg, Manitoba (Ibid.). He died on 28 May 1935 Deer Lodge Hospital, Winnipeg, Manitoba (Ibid.).

25. **Elise Zace** was born on 23 Jan 1873 (HBS, Volume 1333; C-14944.). She was baptized on 24 Jan 1873 St.Francois Xavier, Manitoba (SFXI-Kipling, B-4.) (INB, page 187.). She married **Francois Allary**, son of **Antoine Allary** and **Julie Larocque dit Rocbrune**, in 1890 (HBS, Volume 1333; C-14944.).

Francois Allary was born on 5 Oct 1862 (SFXI-Kipling, B-94.). He was baptized on 21 Nov 1862 St.Francois Xavier, (Manitoba) (Ibid.). He married **Eliza Patenaude**, daughter of **Charles Patenaude** and **Rosalie Pritchard,** on 7 Aug 1883 St.Claude Mission, St.John, Rolette County, North Daktoa (Dominique Ritchot, 26 Jan 2006.) (St.Claude BMD, Dominique Ritchot, page 13, M-13.).

26. **Mathilde Zace** was born on 24 Jul 1875 St.Francois Xavier, Manitoba (SFXI-Kipling, B-32.) (INB, page 187.). She was baptized on 25 Jul 1875 St.Francois Xavier, Manitoba (SFXI-Kipling, B-32.) (INB, page 187.). She married **Isidore Morin**, son of **Andre Morin** and **Adelaide Grandbois**, on 8 Jul 1890 (BIA-TM Bureau of Indian Affairs, Turtle Mountain Enrollment and Probate Papers, Belcourt, North Dakota.). She died on 28 Apr 1963 Belcourt, Rolette County, North Dakota, at age 87 (Ibid.) (ND Death Index.).

Isidore Morin was born on 6 Mar 1870 North Dakota (SN1, page 129, B-14.) (Ibid., page 130, B-19.). He was baptized on 31 Mar 1870 St.Norbert, (Manitoba) (Ibid., B-14.) (Ibid., B-19.). He died on 16 Dec 1943 Belcourt, Rolette County, North Dakota, at age 73 (BIA-TM.) (ND Death Index.).

27. **John Baptiste Zace** was born on 12 Aug 1883 (ND Death Index.). He was born circa 1886 (1890-TMC, #588-592.). He married **Josephine (--?--)** before 1915 (1930C ND, District 30, page 10B.). He died on 28 Nov 1976 Williams County, North Dakota, at age 93 (ND Death Index.).

Josephine (--?--) was born on 22 Feb 1898 Williams County, North Dakota (Ibid.). She died on 1 Jan 1983 Williams County, North Dakota, at age 84 (Ibid.).

Children of **John Baptiste Zace** and **Josephine (--?--)** were as follows:
  i.   Julius Jaste was born circa 1917 (1930C ND, District 30, page 10B.).
  ii.   Rosella Jaste was born circa 1918 (Ibid.). She married Edward Laducer, son of Francois 'Frank' Ladouceur and Angelique Poitras, before 1936 (*1937-TMC*, page 258, Census No. 3100-3101.).
        Edward Laducer was born on 19 May 1914 (BIA-TM, Frank (Francois) Laducer Probate.). He died on 6 Nov 1975 Grand Forks County, North Dakota, at age 61 (ND Death Index.).
  iii. Isabell Jaste was born circa 1920 (1930C ND, District 30, page 10B.).
  iv.   Albert Jaste was born circa 1921 (Ibid.).
  v.   Victoria Jaste was born circa 1922 (Ibid.).
  vi.   Agnes Jaste was born circa 1923 (Ibid.).
  vii. Evelyn Jaste was born circa 1925 (Ibid.).
  viii. George J. Zaste was born on 29 Jun 1926 Williams County, North Dakota (Ibid.) (ND Death Index.). He died on 21 Jul 1994 Williams County, North Dakota, at age 68 (Ibid.).

ix. John Francis Zaste was born on 1 Dec 1928 Williams County, North Dakota (Ibid.). He married Marian Jeannette Falcon, daughter of Job Peter Joseph Falcon and Mary Josephine Turcotte, on 19 Jun 1940 Belcourt, Rolette County, North Dakota (Rod Mac Quarrie, 27 Mar 2013.). He died on 13 Jul 1979 Williams County, North Dakota, at age 50 (ND Death Index.).

    Marian Jeannette Falcon was born on 20 Apr 1927 Trenton, Williams County, North Dakota (*1937-TMC*, page 176-177, Census No. 2105-2113.). She died on 27 May 1997 Williston, Williams County, North Dakota, at age 70 (ND Death Index.).

x. Lorraine Jaste was born circa 1930 (1940C ND 1940 North Dakota, Sixteenth Census of the United States, National Archives of the United States, Washington, D.C.).

xi. Sylvia M. Jaste was born circa 1939 (Ibid.).

28. Marie Mathilde Zace was born on 11 Dec 1870 St.Francois Xavier, Manitoba (MBS, C-14934.) (SFXI-Kipling, B-93.). She was baptized on 12 Dec 1870 St.Francois Xavier, Manitoba (MBS, C-14934.) (SFXI-Kipling, B-93.). She married **Pierre Thibert**, son of **Pierre Thibert** and **Louise Racette,** on 22 Nov 1887 St.Francois Xavier, Manitoba (Ibid., M-11.) (MB Vital Statistics, Mar. Reg. #1888,001100.) (Ibid., Mar. Reg. #1888,001591.).

Pierre Thibert was born on 1 May 1868 St.Francois Xavier, (Manitoba) (SFXI-Kipling, B-31.). He was baptized on 1 May 1868 St.Francois Xavier, (Manitoba) (Ibid.).

29. Louise Zace was born on 3 Oct 1874 St.Francois Xavier, Manitoba (Ibid., B-54.) (INB, page 187.). She was baptized on 4 Oct 1874 St.Francois Xavier, Manitoba (Ibid.) (SFXI-Kipling, B-54.). She married **Joseph Josue Allary**, son of **Pierre Allary** and **Genevieve Zace**, on 10 May 1899 Winnipeg, Manitoba (MB Vital Statistics, Mar. Reg. #1899,001797 (Winnipeg).). She married **Joseph Josue Allary**, son of **Pierre Allary** and **Genevieve Zace**, on 21 Jan 1900 St.Eustache, Manitoba (MM, page 16 (St.Eustache).). She died in Apr 1913 St.Eustache, Manitoba, at age 38 (Treasure of Time, page 281.).

Joseph Josue Allary was born on 25 Oct 1875 St.Eustache, Manitoba (Denney.). He was baptized on 26 Oct 1875 St.Eustache, Manitoba (Ibid.). He married **Adeline Laferte** on 30 Jun 1926 St.Boniface, Manitoba (MB Vital Statistics, Marriage Reg. #1926,026035.).

30. Jean Zace was born on 12 Oct 1876 St.Francois Xavier, Manitoba (SFXI-Kipling, B-37.). He married **Marguerite Lepine**, daughter of **Daniel Lepine** and **Rose Lingan,** on 17 Nov 1903 St.Francois Xavier, Manitoba (MM.) (MB Vital Statistics, Marriage Reg. #1903,002114.). He married **Josephine Allary**, daughter of **Hyacinthe Allary** and **Marie Melanie Rose Gonneville,** before 1927. He died on 28 Nov 1976 Trenton, North Dakota, at age 100 (*St.Ann's Centennial*, page 555.).

Marguerite Lepine was born on 2 Sep 1887 R.M. of St.Francois Xavier, Manitoba (MB Vital Statistics, Birth Reg. #1887,001945.). She was baptized on 3 Sep 1887 St.Francois Xavier, Manitoba (SFXI-Kipling, B-38.).

Children of **Jean Zace** and **Marguerite Lepine** were as follows:

i. Eleonore Zastre was born on 9 Apr 1905 R.M. of St.Francois Xavier, Manitoba (MB Vital Statistics, Birth Reg. #1905,004212.). She died on 19 Mar 1906 St.Francois Xavier, Manitoba (Ibid., Death Reg. #1906,005463.).

ii. Marie Rose Zastre was born on 20 Feb 1907 R.M. of St.Francois Xavier, Manitoba (Ibid., Birth Reg. #1907,006597.).

iii. Jean Joseph Zastre was born on 2 Oct 1908 R.M. of St.Francois Xavier, Manitoba (Ibid., Birth Reg. #1908,013622.).

iv. Marie Elisabeth Victoria Zastre was born on 3 Jul 1910 R.M. of St.Francois Xavier, Manitoba (Ibid., Birth Reg. #1910,005018.). She married Ernest Albert Aime Breland, son of Albert Breland and Rose Victoria Anne Thibert (Rod Mac Quarrie, 27 Mar 2013.). She died on 28 Feb 1973 at age 62 (Ibid.).

    Ernest Albert Aime Breland was born on 6 Feb 1910 R.M. of St.Francois Xavier, Manitoba (MB Vital Statistics, Birth Reg. #1910,010938.). He died on 8 Aug 1974 Quesnel, British Columbia, at age 64 (Rod Mac Quarrie, 27 Mar 2013.).

v. Aime Honore Israel Zastre was born on 8 Jun 1912 St.Francois Xavier, Manitoba (MB Vital Statistics, Birth Reg. #1912,26728787.).

vi. Maria Louise Ernestine Zace was born on 9 Apr 1914 R.M. of St.Francois Xavier, Manitoba (Ibid., Birth Reg. #1914,091869.).

vii. Marie Celina Zace was born on 29 Feb 1916 (1916 Canada, District 2-1 page 11, line 32.) (Rod Mac Quarrie, 27 Mar 2013.). She married Lucien Precourt circa 1940 (*Winnipeg Free Press*, Winnipeg, Manitoba, 16 Mar 2006.). She died on 10 Mar 2006 Seven Oaks Hospital, Winnipeg, Manitoba, at age 90 (Ibid.).

Josephine Allary was born on 25 Dec 1889 (1901 Canada, #11, N-3, page 7, Family 54, Line 25-32.).

Children of **Jean Zace** and **Josephine Allary** were as follows:

i. Isabel Zaste married John Phillip Lavallee, son of John B. Lavallee and Louise Ann Morin, before 1936.

    John Phillip Lavallee was born on 26 Jan 1916 North Dakota (1936-TMC, page 150.) (1932-TMC Census of the Turtle Mountain Chippewa Indians, United States Indian Service Department of the Interior, Turtle Mountain Agency, North Dakota, 1 Apr 1932 , page 270, Census No. 3153-3162.) (ND Death Index.). He was born on 12 Nov 1916 (*1937-TMC*, page 307-308, Census No. 3728-3729, 6188-6194.). He died on 17 Sep 1966 Rolette County, North Dakota, at age 50 (ND Death Index.).

ii. George Zaste.

iii. John Zaste died before 1983 (*St.Ann's Centennial*, page 554.).

iv. Evelyn Zaste.

v. Rose Ann Zaste.

vi. Agnes Zaste.

vii. Sylvia Zaste.

viii. Lorraine Zaste was born on 6 Oct 1930 Belcourt, Rolette County, North Dakota (ND Death Index.). She married Lee William Falcon, son of Alexander Falcon and Adele Boyer, on 16 Mar 1950 Williston, Williams County,

North Dakota. She died on 4 Dec 1984 Trenton, Williams County, North Dakota, at age 54 (*St.Ann's Centennial*, page 554.) (ND Death Index.).

Lee William Falcon was born on 20 Mar 1928 Trenton, Williams County, North Dakota (*1937-TMC*, page 174-175, Census No. 2078-2082.). He died on 19 Jan 1952 Trenton, Williams County, North Dakota, at age 23 (ND Death Index.).

31. **Virginie Zace** was born on 24 Oct 1878 St.Francois Xavier, Manitoba (SFXI-Kipling, B-35.). She married **Joseph Morand**, son of **Joseph Morand** and **Caroline Lepine,** on 22 Apr 1902 (St.Norbert), Ritchot, Manitoba (MM.) (MB Vital Statistics, Marriage Reg. #1902,002518.).

Joseph Morand was born on 26 Jan 1877 R.M. of Ritchot, Manitoba (Ibid., Birth Reg. #1877,1007306.).

32. **Agnes Zace** was born on 16 Nov 1880 St.Francois Xavier, Manitoba (SFXI-Kipling, B-65.). She was baptized on 19 Nov 1880 St.Francois Xavier, Manitoba (Ibid.). She married **Napoleon Barron**, son of **Napoleon Barron** and **Josephte Lepine,** on 8 Jul 1902 St.Francois Xavier, Manitoba (MM, page 52.) (MB Vital Statistics, Mar. Reg. #1902,001558.). She died in 1950.

Napoleon Barron was born on 14 Nov 1880 St.Francois Xavier, Manitoba (SFXI-Kipling, B-63.). He was baptized on 15 Nov 1880 St.Francois Xavier, Manitoba (Ibid.) (Rosemary Rozyk, 28 Jan 1999 report.). He died in 1952.

33. **Domitilde Zace** was born on 25 Jun 1878 St.Francois Xavier, Manitoba (SFXI-Kipling.). She was born on 25 Jun 1878 St.Francois Xavier, (Manitoba). She married **Alexandre Lafreniere**, son of **Jean Baptiste Lafreniere** and **Ursule St.Germain,** on 18 Oct 1898 St.Francois Xavier, Manitoba (Ibid., M-11.) (MB Vital Statistics, Marriage Reg. #1898,001713.).

Alexandre Lafreniere was born on 17 May 1868 St.Francois Xavier, (Manitoba) (SFXI-Kipling, B-56.). He was baptized on 19 May 1868 St.Francois Xavier, (Manitoba) (Ibid.).

34. **Marie Lucie Zace** was born on 15 Dec 1883 St.Francois Xavier, Manitoba (SFXI-Kipling, B-57.) (MB Vital Statistics, Birth Reg. #1883,004357.). She married **Napoleon Brazeau**, son of **Joseph Brazeau** and **Cecile Morisseau,** on 30 Aug 1907 RM Grey, Manitoba (Ibid., Mar. Reg. #1907,002198.).

Napoleon Brazeau was born in May 1888 (1911 Canada, #64, Twp 29, page 3, Family 25, Line 2-4.). He was baptized on 29 May 1888 St.Claude Mission, St.John, Rolette County, North Dakota (St.Claude BMD, Dominique Ritchot, B-382, page 76.).

Bibliography

100SCM Copy of the First 100 Marriage Records in Stevens County, Territory of Washington, secured by Esther Reed Chapter, D. A. R. of Spokane, Washington, 1922.

1666C Quebec 1666 Census, Hugh L. Armstrong Transcription.

1671C 1671 Acadian Census, translation by Lucie LeBlanc Consentino, from the extracted study from Les origines françaises des premières familles acadiennes by Nicole T. Bujold and Maurice Caillebeau and edited by the Conseil Général of Vienna in 1979. The original manuscript, produced by Geneviève Massignon in her thesis Les Parlers Français d'Acadie is on file at the National Archives of Paris., Acadian Genealogy Homepage: http://www.acadian.org/census1671.

1827C RRS HBCA E5/1 1827 Census of the Red River Settlement, HBCA E5/1, Hudson's Bay Company Archives, Provincial Archives, 200 Vaughan Street, Winnipeg, MB R3C 1T5, Canada.

1828C RRS HBCA E5/2 1828 Census of the Red River Settlement, HBCA E5/2, Hudson's Bay Company Archives, Provincial Archives, 200 Vaughan Street, Winnipeg, MB R3C 1T5, Canada.

1829C RRS HBCA E5/3 1829 Census of the Red River Settlement, HBCA E5/3, Hudson's Bay Company Archives, Provincial Archives, 200 Vaughan Street, Winnipeg, MB R3C 1T5, Canada.

1830C RRS HBCA E5/4 1830 Census of the Red River Settlement, HBCA E5/4, Hudson's Bay Company Archives, Provincial Archives, 200 Vaughan Street, Winnipeg, MB R3C 1T5, Canada.

1831C RRS HBCA E5/5 1831 Census of the Red River Settlement, HBCA E5/5, Hudson's Bay Company Archives, Provincial Archives, 200 Vaughan Street, Winnipeg, MB R3C 1T5, Canada.

1832C RRS HBCA E5/6 1832 Census of the Red River Settlement, HBCA E5/6, Hudson's Bay Company Archives, Provincial Archives, 200 Vaughan Street, Winnipeg, MB R3C 1T5, Canada.

1833C RRS HBCA E5/7 1833 Census of the Red River Settlement, HBCA E5/7, Hudson's Bay Company Archives, Provincial Archives, 200 Vaughan Street, Winnipeg, MB R3C 1T5, Canada.

1835C RRS HBCA E5/8 1835 Census of the Red River Settlement, HBCA E5/8, Hudson's Bay Company Archives, Provincial Archives, 200 Vaughan Street, Winnipeg, MB R3C 1T5, Canada.

1838C RRS HBCA E5/9 1838 Census of the Red River Settlement, HBCA E5/9, Hudson's Bay Company Archives, Provincial Archives, 200 Vaughan Street, Winnipeg, MB R3C 1T5, Canada.

1840C RRS HBCA E5/10 1840 Census of the Red River Settlement, HBCA E5/10, Hudson's Bay Company Archives, Provincial Archives, 200 Vaughan Street, Winnipeg, MB R3C 1T5, Canada.

1843C RRS HBCA E5/11 1843 Census of the Red River Settlement, HBCA E5/11, Hudson's Bay Company Archives, Provincial Archives, 200 Vaughan Street, Winnipeg, MB R3C 1T5, Canada.

1845 Oregon Territorial Census, National Archives of the United States, Washington D.C.

1850 Oregon Territory Census, National Archives of the United States, Washington D.C., Film Number M432-742.

1850C-IA 1850 Iowa Census, National Archives of the United States, Washington D.C.

1850Ci-MN Minnesota Territorial Census, 1850, Harpole, Patricia C. and Mary D. Nagle, ed., (St.Paul, Minnesota: Minnesota Historical Society, 1972).

1850-Minn 1850 Minnesota Territory Census.

1854T Half-Breed Scrip: Chippewas of Lake Superior: The Correspondence and Action of the Treaty with the Chippewa Indians of Lake Superior and the Mississippi, Concluded at La Pointe, in the State of Wisconsin, September 30, 1854 (House Ex. Doc. 193, 42d Congress, 2d session, Government Printing Office, Washington, D. C., 1874).

1860 Dakota Territorial Census, National Archives of the United States, Washington, D.C.

1860C BRV Bitter Root Valley - (MT) 1860 Washington Territory Census, Margery H. Bell, Katherine Schaffer and Dennis Richards, n.p.: n.pub., n.d.

1860C-IA 1860 Iowa Census, National Archives of the United States, Washington D.C.

1860C-Minn 1860 Minnesota Census, National Archives of the United States, Washington D.C.

1860C-OR 1860 Oregon Census, National Archives of the United States, Washington D.C.

1860C-WA 1860 Washington Territorial Census, National Archives of the United States, Washington D.C.

1860-DT-Inx Index to 1860 Census of Dakota Territory, Rogers-Patton Researchers; P. O. Box 64, Hill City, S.D. 57701: Rogers-Patton Researchers.

1863-4T Chippewas of the Red Lake and Pembina bands - Treaty of 1863-1864, House Executive Document 193, 42d Congress, 2d session; Washington D.C.: Congress of the United States, 1865, 171-228, 244-259<, [CD]>.

1868-PBAL 1868 Pembina Band Annuity List, National Archives of the United States, Washington, D.C.

1870 Dakota Territory Census, National Archives of the United States, Washington D.C.

1870C-MB 1870 Manitoba Census, National Archives of Canada, Ottawa, Ontario, Microfilm Reel Number C-2170.

1871 Census of Canada from the National Archives of Canada, Ottawa, Canada.

1871 Washington Territory Census, National Archives of the United States, Washington D.C.

1875 Minnesota Census, National Archives of the United States, Washington D.C.

1880 Census, Spokane County, Washington Territory; Spokane, Washington: Eastern Washington Genealogical Society, 1973).

1880 Minnesota Census, National Archives of the United States, Washington D.C.

1880 Montana Census, National Archives of the United States, Washington D.C.

1880 Stevens County, Washington Census Index; Eastern Washington Genealogical Society, 1973.

1880 U. S. Census, Dakota Territory, National Archives of the United States, Washington D.C.

1880 U. S. Census, Washington Territory, National Archives of the United States, Washington D.C.

1880C-MT-LS 1880 Census, Montana Territory, Table 6, Little Shell (MT): Proposed Finding - Technical Report.

1881 Census of Canada from the National Archives of Canada, Ottawa, Canada.

1881 Church of Latter Day Saints Census Transcription Project of Census Images from the National Archives of Canada, Ottawa, Canada, http://www.familysearch.org.

1884-TMC 1884-1886 Census of Half Breed Chippewas of Turtle Mountain, Dakota Territory, National Archives of the United States, Washington D.C.

1885-TMC 1885 Census of Half Breed Chippewas of Turtle Mountain, Dakota Territory, National Archives of the United States, Washington D.C.

1886-TMC 1886 Census of Half Breed Chippewas of Turtle Mountain, Dakota Territory, National Archives of the United States, Washington D.C.

1887-TMC 1887 Census of Half Breed Chippewas of Turtle Mountain, Dakota Territory, National Archives of the United States, Washington D.C.

1888-TMC 1888 Census of Half Breed Chippewas of Turtle Mountain, Dakota Territory, National Archives of the United States, Washington D.C.

1888-WE 1888 Census of Pembina Chippewa of White Earth, Minnesota, National Archives of the United States, Washington D.C.

1889-TMC 1889 Census of Half Breed Chippewas of Turtle Mountain, Dakota Territory, National Archives of the United States, Washington D.C.

1889-TMC 1889 Census of Half Breed Chippewas residing in the vicinity of, but not on the Turtle Mountain Reservation, Dakota Territory, National Archives of the United States, Washington D.C.

1890-TMC 1890 Census of Half Breed Chippewas of Turtle Mountain, Dakota Territory, National Archives of the United States, Washington D.C.

1891 Census of Canada from the National Archives of Canada, Ottawa, Canada.

1891 Fort Belknap Indian Census Roll of the Fort Belknap Assiniboine & Gros Ventre Reservation, Department of the Interior, United States Indian Service, Fort Belknap Indian Agency, Montana, Aug 1891.

1891C SK District of Saskatchewan Index to the Census of Canada 1891, Saskatchewan Genealogical Society, Inc - Regina Branch, 67 Marquis Crescent, Regina, SK S4S 6J8.

1891-CdA-ID 1891 Census of the Coeur d'Alene Indians, Department of the Interior, United States Indian Service, Colville Agency, Washington, 30 June 1891.

1891-WE 1891 Census of Pembina Chippewa of White Earth, Minnesota, National Archives of the United States, Washington D.C.

1892 Oct 1 McCumber Census of the Turtle Mountain band of Chippewa Indians, Belcourt, North Dakota, National Archives of the United States, Washington D.C., Document No. 229.

1892-TMC 1892 Census of Half Breed Chippewas of Turtle Mountain, Dakota Territory, National Archives of the United States, Washington D.C.

1893 Fort Belknap Indian Census Roll of the Fort Belknap Assiniboine & Gros Ventre Reservation, Department of the Interior, United States Indian Service, Fort Belknap Indian Agency, Montana, 30 Jun 1893.

1893 Fort Belknap Indian Census Roll of the Fort Belknap Assiniboine & Gros Ventre Reservation, Department of the Interior, United States Indian Service, Fort Belknap Indian Agency, Montana, 30 Jun 1893.

1893-BF 1893 Census of Pikuni (Blackfoot), National Archives of the United States, Washington D.C.

1893-TMC 1893 Census of Half Breed Chippewas of Turtle Mountain, Dakota Territory, National Archives of the United States, Washington D.C.

1893-TMC 1893 Census of Half Breed Chippewas of Turtle Mountain, Dakota Territory, National Archives of the United States, Washington D.C.

1894 Fort Peck Indian Census Roll of the Fort Peck Yanktonai Sioux Reservation, Department of the Interior, United States Indian Service, Fort Peck Indian Agency, Montana, 30 Jun 1894.

1894-BF 1894 Census of Pikuni (Blackfoot), National Archives of the United States, Washington D.C.

1894-TMC 1894 Census of Half Breed Chippewas of Turtle Mountain, North Dakota, National Archives of the United States, Washington D.C.

1895 Fort Peck Indian Census Roll of the Fort Peck Yanktonai Sioux Reservation, Department of the Interior, United States Indian Service, Fort Peck Indian Agency, Montana, 30 Jun 1895.

1895C MN 1885 Minnesota State Census, National Archives of the United States, Washington D.C.

1895-TMC 1895 Census of Half Breed Chippewas of Turtle Mountain, Dakota Territory, National Archives of the United States, Washington D.C.

1895-WE 1895 Census of Pembina Chippewa of White Earth, Minnesota, National Archives of the United States, Washington D.C.

1896 Fort Belknap Indian Census Roll of the Fort Belknap Assiniboine & Gros Ventre Reservation, Department of the Interior, United States Indian Service, Fort Belknap Indian Agency, Montana, 30 Jun 1896.

1896 Fort Peck Indian Census Roll of the Fort Peck Yanktonai Sioux Reservation, Department of the Interior, United States Indian Service, Fort Peck Indian Agency, Montana, 30 Jun 1896.

1896-CCT-Okanogan Census of the Okanogan band of Colville Indians, Department of the Interior, United States Indian Service, Colville Indian Agency, Washington, 30 June 1896.

1896-TMC 1896 Census of Half Breed Chippewas of Turtle Mountain, Dakota Territory, National Archives of the United States, Washington D.C.

1897-TMC 1897 Census of Half Breed Chippewas of Turtle Mountain, Dakota Territory, National Archives of the United States, Washington D.C.

1897-WE 1897 Census of Pembina Chippewa of White Earth, Minnesota, National Archives of the United States, Washington D.C.

1898 Fort Belknap Indian Census Roll of the Fort Belknap Assiniboine & Gros Ventre Reservation, Department of the Interior, United States Indian Service, Fort Belknap Indian Agency, Montana, 30 Jun 1898.

1898 Louis & Clark County, Montana School Census; Courthouse, Helena, Montana: Superintendent of Schools.

1898-BF 1898 Census of Pikuni (Blackfoot), National Archives of the United States, Washington D.C.

1898-TMC 1898 Census of Half Breed Chippewas of Turtle Mountain, North Dakota, National Archives of the United States, Washington D.C.

1899-TMC 1899 Census of Half Breed Chippewas of Turtle Mountain, North Dakota, National Archives of the United States, Washington D.C.

1900-1960 Cascade County, Montana School Census; Courthouse, Great Falls, Montana: Superintendent of Schools, Cascade County.

1900C Fergus Co, MT Twelfth Census of the United States: 1900; Montana; Fergus County.

1900C Minn Twelfth Census of the United States: 1900; Minnesota.

1900C MT Twelfth Census of the United States: 1900; Montana.

1900C ND Twelfth Census of the United States: 1900, North Dakota.

1900C OR Twelfth Census of the United States: 1900; Oregon.

1900C WA Twelfth Census of the United States: 1900; Washington.

1900CI-ND-Rolette *1900 Turtle Mountain Indian Reservation Census Index, Rolette County, North Dakota* compiled by Mary Ann Quiring and Lily B. Zwolle, (n.p.: Mary Ann Quiring and Lily B. Zwolle, 1984).

1900CI-ND-Rolette *1900 Turtle Mountain Indian Reservation Census Index, Rolette County, North Dakota* compiled by Mary Ann Quiring and Lily B. Zwolle, (n.p.: Mary Ann Quiring and Lily B. Zwolle, 1984).

1900C-ND 1900 United States Census, North Dakota, National Archives of the United States, Washington, D. C.

1900-GR-OR 1900 Census of the Grand Ronde Reservation, Department of the Interior, United States Indian Service, Grand Ronde Agency, Oregon, 2 July 1900.

1900-Spokane Census of the Spokane Indians, Department of the Interior, United States Indian Service, Colville Indian Agency, Washington, 30 June 1900.

1900-TMC 1900 Census of Half Breed Chippewas of Turtle Mountain, North Dakota, National Archives of the United States, Washington D.C.

1901 Alberta Census Index, Alberta Genealogical Society, Edmonton, Alberta, www.agsedm.edmonton.ab.ca.

1901-LLB 1901 Census, Lac La Biche, North West Territories, Alberta, Canada, National Archives of Canada, Ottawa, Canada.

1901-Sioux 1901 Indian Census Roll of the Sioux Reservation, Department of the Interior, United States Indian Service, Devils Lake Agency, North Dakota, 30 Jun 1901.

1901-TMC 1901 Census of Half Breed Chippewas of Turtle Mountain, North Dakota, National Archives of the United States, Washington D.C.

1902 Fort Belknap Indian Census Roll of the Fort Belknap Assiniboine & Gros Ventre Reservation, Department of the Interior, United States Indian Service, Fort Belknap Indian Agency, Montana, 19 Jul 1902.

1902 L-MT Lewistown, Montana School District No. 1, 1902 Census.

1902-1930 Fergus County, Montana School Census; Courthouse, Lewistown, Montana: Superintendent of Schools, Fergus County.

1902-Sioux 1902 Indian Census Roll of the Sioux Reservation, Department of the Interior, United States Indian Service, Devils Lake Agency, North Dakota, 30 Jun 1902.

1903 Walla Walla Indian Census Roll of the Umatilla Reservation, Department of the Interior, United States Indian Service, Umatilla Indian Agency, Oregon, 30 June 1903.

1903-L-Spo 1903 Census of the Lower Spokane Indians, Department of the Interior, United States Indian Service, Colville, Washington, Albert M. Anderson, 30 June 1903.

1903-TMC Turtle Mountain Band of Chippewa Mixed Blood 1903 Census Roll, Department of the Interior, United States Indian Service, Turtle Mountain Agency, Rolette County, North Dakota, 1 July 1903.

1904 Fort Belknap Indian Census Roll of the Fort Belknap Assiniboine & Gros Ventre Reservation, Department of the Interior, United States Indian Service, Fort Belknap Indian Agency, Montana, 1 Jul 1904.

1904-TMC Turtle Mountain Band of Chippewa Mixed Blood 1904 Census Roll, Department of the Interior, United States Indian Service, Turtle Mountain Agency, Rolette County, North Dakota, July 1904.

1905C Minn 1905 Census of Minnesota, Population Schedule.

1905-CCT-Ok Census of the Colville Indians, Department of the Interior, United States Indian Service, Colville Indian Agency, Washington, 1905.

1905-TMC Turtle Mountain Band of Chippewa Mixed Blood 1905 Census Roll, Department of the Interior, United States Indian Service, Devils Lake, North Dakota, 30 June 1905.

1906-TMC 1906 Census of the Turtle Mountain Chippewa, Department of the Interior, United States Indian Service, Belcourt, North Dakota, 30 June 1906.

1907-Sioux 1907 Indian Census Roll of the Sioux Reservation, Department of the Interior, United States Indian Service, Devils Lake Agency, North Dakota, 30 Jun 1907.

1907-TMC 1907 Census of the Turtle Mountain Chippewa, Department of the Interior, United States Indian Service, Devils Lake, North Dakota, 30 June 1907.

1908-TMC 1908 Census of the Turtle Mountain Chippewa, Department of the Interior, United States Indian Service, Devils Lake, North Dakota, 30 June 1908.

1908-WE 1908 Census of Pembina Chippewa of White Earth, Minnesota, National Archives of the United States, Washington D.C.

1909 Fort Belknap Indian Census Roll of the Fort Belknap Assiniboine & Gros Ventre Reservation, Department of the Interior, United States Indian Service, Fort Belknap Indian Agency, Montana, 1 Jul 1909.

1909-Sioux 1909 Indian Census Roll of the Sioux Reservation, Department of the Interior, United States Indian Service, Devils Lake Agency, North Dakota, 1 Oct 1909.

1909-TMC 1909 Census of the Turtle Mountain Chippewa, Department of the Interior, United States Indian Service, Devils Lake, North Dakota, 30 June 1909.

1910 about- CCT Colville band of the Colville Indians, Department of the Interior, United States Indian Service, Colville Agency, Washington, c1910.

1910 Spokane Indians, Department of the Interior, United States Indian Service, Colville Agency, Washington, 30 Jun 1910.

1910c- CCT-Sanpoil Sanpoil band of the Colville Indians, Department of the Interior, United States Indian Service, Colville Agency, Washington, c1910.

1910C Fergus Co, MT Thirteenth Census of the United States: 1910; Montana; Fergus County, National Archives of the United States, Washington, D.C.

1910C Minn Thirteenth Census of the United States: 1910; Minnesota, National Archives of the United States, Washington D.C.

1910C MO Thirteenth Census of the United States: 1910; Missouri, National Archives of the United States, Washington D.C.

1910C MT Thirteenth Census of the United States: 1910; Montana, National Archives of the United States, Washington D.C.

1910C ND Thirteenth Census of the United States: 1910; North Dakota, National Archives of the United States, Washington D.C.

1910C OR Thirteenth Census of the United States: 1910; Oregon, National Archives of the United States, Washington D.C.

1910C WA Thirteenth Census of the United States: 1910; Washington, National Archives of the United States, Washington D.C.

1910C-IA 1910 Iowa Census, National Archives of the United States, Washington D.C.

1910-TMC 1910 Census of the Turtle Mountain Chippewa, Department of the Interior, United States Indian Service, Turtle Mountain Agency, North Dakota, 30 June 1910.

1910-WE 1910 Census of Pembina Chippewa of White Earth, Minnesota, National Archives of the United States, Washington D.C.

1911-CdA 1911 Coeur d'Alene Indian Census Roll, Department of the Interior, United States Indian Service, Coeur d'Alene Agency, Idaho, 30 Jun 1911.

1911-CdA 1911 Coeur d'Alene Indian Census Roll, Department of the Interior, United States Indian Service, Coeur d'Alene Agency, Idaho, 30 Jun 1911.

1911-Oj 1911 Census of Ojibwe of the Blackfeet Agency, Montana, National Archives of the United States, Washington D.C.

1911-TMC 1911 Census of the Turtle Mountain Chippewa, Department of the Interior, United States Indian Service, Turtle Mountain Agency, North Dakota, 30 June 1911.

1912 Flathead Indian Census Roll of the Flathead Reservation, Department of the Interior, United States Indian Service, Flathead Indian Agency, Montana, 1 July 1912.

1912-TMC 1912 Census of the Turtle Mountain Chippewa, Department of the Interior, United States Indian Service, Turtle Mountain Agency, North Dakota, 30 June 1912.

1913-Fort Peck 1913 Indian Census Roll of the Fort Peck Reservation, Department of the Interior, United States Indian Service, Fort Peck Agency, Poplar, Montana, 30 Jun 1913.

1913-TMC 1913 Census of the Turtle Mountain Chippewa, North Dakota, National Archives of the United States, Washington D.C.

1913-WE 1913 Census of Pembina Chippewa of White Earth, Minnesota, National Archives of the United States, Washington D.C.

1914-TMC 1914 Census of the Turtle Mountain Chippewa, North Dakota, National Archives of the United States, Washington D.C.

1915 Louis & Clark County, Montana School Census; Courthouse, Helena, MT: Superint. of Schools, Louis & Clark Co.

1915-CdA Census of the Couer d'Alene Indians, Department of the Interior, United States Indian Service, Coeur d'Alene Agency, Idaho, 30 Jun 1915.

1915C-ND 1915 Federal Census North Dakota, National Archives of the United States, Washington D.C.

1915-Fort Peck 1915 Indian Census Roll of the Fort Peck Reservation, Department of the Interior, United States Indian Service, Fort Peck Agency, Montana, 30 jun 1915.

1915-TMC 1915 Census of the Turtle Mountain Chippewa, North Dakota, National Archives of the United States, Washington D.C.

1916 Census of Canada from the National Archives of Canada (Transcription by ancestry.com), Ottawa, Canada.

1916 Fort Belknap Indian Census Roll of the Fort Belknap Assiniboine & Gros Ventre Reservation, Department of the Interior, United States Indian Service, Fort Belknap Indian Agency, Montana, 30 Jun 1916.

1916-TMC 1916 Census of the Turtle Mountain Chippewa, North Dakota, National Archives of the United States, Washington D.C.

1916-WE 1916 Census of Pembina Chippewa of White Earth, Minnesota, National Archives of the United States, Washington D.C.

1917 RB Tentative Roll of Rocky Boy Indians, 30 May 1917, Copied by Verne Dusenbery, 15 Apr 1953, Rocky Boy Agency, Montana.

1917-Fort Peck 1917 Indian Census Roll of the Fort Peck Reservation, Department of the Interior, United States Indian Service, Fort Peck Agency, Montana, 30 Jun 1917.

1917-TMC 1917 Census of the Turtle Mountain Chippewa, North Dakota, National Archives of the United States, Washington D.C.

1918-BF 1918 Census of the Blackfeet, National Archives of the United States, Washington D.C.

1918-TMC 1918 Census of the Turtle Mountain Chippewa, North Dakota, National Archives of the United States, Washington D.C.

1918-WE 1918 Census of Confederated Chippewa of White Earth, Minnesota, National Archives of the United States, Washington D.C.

1919 RB Rocky Boy Indians, 1 Jul 1919, Rocky Boy Agency, Box Elder, Montana, John B. Parker, Farmer in Charge.

1919 Turtle Mountain Indian Census Roll, Department of the Interior, United States Indian Service, Turtle Mountain Indian Agency, North Dakota, 30 June 1919.

1920 Flathead Indian Census Roll of the Flathead Reservation, Department of the Interior, United States Indian Service, Flathead Indian Agency, Montana, 30 June 1920.

1920 Fort Peck Indian Census Roll of the Fort Peck Sioux Reservation, Department of the Interior, United States Indian Service, Fort Peck Indian Agency, Montana, 30 Jun 1920.

1920 Turtle Mountain Chippewa Indian Census Roll, Department of the Interior, United States Indian Service, Turtle Mountain

1920 Umatilla 1920 Cayuse, Umatilla, and Wallaa Indian Census Roll of the Umatilla Reservation, Department of the Interior, United States Indian Service, Umatilla Indian Agency, Oregon, 30 June 1920.

1920C Minn Fourteenth Census of the United States: 1920; Minnesota, National Archives of the United States, Washington D.C.

1920C MO Fourteenth Census of the United States: 1910; Missouri, National Archives of the United States, Washington D.C.

1920C OR Fourteenth Census of the United States: 1920; Oregon, National Archives of the United States, Washington D.C.

1920C WA Fourteenth Census of the United States: 1920; Washington, National Archives of the United States, Washington D.C.

1920-CdA Census of the Couer d'Alene Indians, H. D. Lawsha, Department of the Interior, United States Indian Service, Coeur d'Alene Agency, Idaho, 30 Jun 1920.

1920C-MT 1920 Federal Census Montana, National Archives of the United States, Washington D.C.

1920C-ND 1920 Federal Census North Dakota, National Archives of the United States, Washington D.C.

1920C-SD 1920 Federal Census South Dakota, National Archives of the United States, Washington D.C.

1921 Census of Canada from the National Archives of Canada (Transcription by ancestry.com), Ottawa, Canada.

1921 Turtle Mountain Chippewa Indian Census Roll, Department of the Interior, United States Indian Service, Turtle Mountain Indian Agency, North Dakota, 30 June 1921.

1921-CdA Census of the Couer d'Alene Indians, H. D. Lawsha, Department of the Interior, United States Indian Service, Coeur d'Alene Agency, Idaho, 30 Jun 1921.

1921-Spo Census of the Spokane Indians, Department of the Interior, United States Indian Service, Colville Indian Agency, Washington, 30 Jun 1921.

1921-WE 1921 Census of Confederated Chippewa of White Earth, Minnesota, National Archives of the United States, Washington D.C.

1922 Turtle Mountain Chippewa Indian Census Roll, Department of the Interior, United States Indian Service, Turtle Mountain Indian Agency, North Dakota, 30 June 1922.

1922 Umatilla 1922 Cayuse, Umatilla, and Wallaa Indian Census Roll of the Umatilla Reservation, Department of the Interior, United States Indian Service, Umatilla Indian Agency, Oregon, 30 June 1922.

1922-RB Census of the Rocky Boy Indians, Department of the Interior, United States Indian Service, Rocky Boy Agency, Montana, 1 Jul 1922.

1923 CCT Census of the Colville Indians, Department of the Interior, United States Indian Service, Colville Indian Agency, Washington, 30 Jun 1923.

1923-BF 1923 Census of Pikuni (Blackfoot), National Archives of the United States, Washington D.C.

1923-Fort Belknap Census of the Assiniboine Indians of Fort Belknap, Montana, Department of the Interior, United States Indian Service, Fort Belknap Agency, Montana, J. T. Marshall, Superintendant, 30 Jun 1923.

1923-RB Census of the Rocky Boy Indians, Department of the Interior, United States Indian Service, Rocky Boy Agency, Montana, 30 Jun 1923.

1923-TMC-ND 1923 Census of the Chippewa Indians of Turtle Mountain Agency, North Dakota, Department of the Interior, United States Indian Service, Belcourt, North Dakota, H. J. McQuigg, superintendent, 30 June 1923.

1924 Flathead Indian Census Roll of the Flathead Reservation, Department of the Interior, United States Indian Service, Flathead Indian Agency, Montana, 30 June 1924.

1924-25-TMC Birth-Deaths of the Turtle Mountain Chippewa Indians, Department of the Interior, United States Indian Service, Turtle Mountain Agency, North Dakota, F. J. Scott Superintendent, 1 July 1924-30 June 1925.

1924-RB Census of the Rocky Boy Indians, Department of the Interior, United States Indian Service, Rocky Boy Agency, Montana, 30 Jun 1924.

1924-TMC-ND 1924 Census of the Chippewa Indians of Turtle Mountain Agency, North Dakota, Department of the Interior, United States Indian Service, Belcourt, North Dakota, H. J. McQuigg, superintendent, 30 June 1924.

1925-CdA 1925 Census of the Couer d'Alene Indians, Department of the Interior, United States Indian Service, Couer d'Alene Agency, Idaho, 30 June 1925.

1925C-ND 1925 State Census of North Dakota, National Archives of the United States, Washington D.C.

1925-Fort Belknap 1925 Indian Census Roll of the Fort Belknap Reservation, Department of the Interior, United States Indian Service, Fort Belknap Agency, Montana, 30 jun 1925.

1925-Fort Peck 1925 Indian Census Roll of the Fort Peck Reservation, Department of the Interior, United States Indian Service, Fort Peck Agency, Montana, 30 Jun 1925.

1925-Spokane 1925 Census of the Spokane Indians, Department of the Interior, United States Indian Service, Colville Agency, Washington, 30 June 1925.

1925-TMC-ND 1925 Census of the Chippewa Indians of Turtle Mountain Agency, North Dakota, Department of the Interior, United States Indian Service, Belcourt, North Dakota, H. J. McQuigg, superintendent, 30 June 1925.

1926 Flathead Indian Census Roll of the Flathead Reservation, Department of the Interior, United States Indian Service, Flathead Indian Agency, Montana, 30 June 1926.

1926-27-TMC Deaths of the Turtle Mountain Chippewa Indians, Department of the Interior, United States Indian Service, Turtle Mountain Agency, North Dakota, F. J. Scott Superintendent, 1 July 1926-30 June 1927.

1926-CdA 1926 Census of the Couer d'Alene Indians, Department of the Interior, United States Indian Service, Couer d'Alene Agency, Idaho, 30 June 1926.

1926-RB Census of the Rocky Boy Indians, Department of the Interior, United States Indian Service, Rocky Boy Agency, Montana, 30 Jun 1926.

1926-TMC-ND 1926 Census of the Chippewa Indians of Turtle Mountain Agency, North Dakota, Department of the Interior, United States Indian Service, Belcourt, North Dakota, H. J. McQuigg, superintendent, 30 June 1926.

1927 Flathead Indian Census Roll of the Flathead Reservation, Department of the Interior, United States Indian Service, Flathead Indian Agency, Montana, 30 June 1927.

1927-RB Census of the Rocky Boy Indians, Department of the Interior, United States Indian Service, Rocky Boy Agency, Montana, 30 Jun 1927.

1927-TMC-ND 1927 Census of the Chippewa Indians of Turtle Mountain Agency, North Dakota, Department of the Interior, United States Indian Service, Belcourt, North Dakota, James H. Hyde, superintendent, 30 June 1927.

1927-WE 1927 Census of Confederated Chippewa of White Earth, Minnesota, National Archives of the United States, Washington D.C.

1928-32-TMC Birth-Deaths of the Turtle Mountain Chippewa Indians, Department of the Interior, United States Indian Service, Turtle Mountain Agency, North Dakota, F. J. Scott Superintendent, 1 July 1928-30 June 1932.

1928-TMC-ND 1928 Census of the Chippewa Indians of Turtle Mountain Agency, North Dakota, Department of the Interior, United States Indian Service, Belcourt, North Dakota, H. J. McQuigg, superintendent, 30 June 1928.

1929-Fort Peck 1929 Indian Census Roll of the Fort Peck Reservation, Department of the Interior, United States Indian Service, Fort Peck Agency, Montana, 30 Jun 1929.

1929-RB Census of the Rocky Boy Indians, Department of the Interior, United States Indian Service, Rocky Boy Agency, Montana, 30 Jun 1929.

1929-TMC-ND 1929 Census of the Chippewa Indians of Turtle Mountain Agency, North Dakota, Department of the Interior, United States Indian Service, Belcourt, North Dakota, 30 June 1929.

1930C CA Fourteenth Census of the United States: 1930; California, National Archives of the United States, Washington D.C.

1930C Minn 1930 Minnesota, Fifteenth Census of the United States, National Archives of the United States, Washington, D.C.

1930C MT 1930 Montana, Fifteenth Census of the United States, National Archives of the United States, Washington, D.C.

1930C ND Fifteenth Census of the United States: 1930; North Dakota, National Archives of the United States, Washington, D.C.

1930C OR Fifteenth Census of the United States: 1930; Oregon, National Archives of the United States, Washington D.C.

1930C WA Fifteenth Census of the United States: 1930; Washington, National Archives of the United States, Washington D.C.

1930C WI Fifteenth Census of the United States: 1930; Wisconsin, National Archives of the United States, Washington D.C.

1930-TMC-ND 1930 Census of the Chippewa Indians of Turtle Mountain Agency, North Dakota, Department of the Interior, United States Indian Service, Belcourt, North Dakota, 1 April 1930.

1931-TMC Census of the Turtle Mountain Chippewa Indians, Department of the Interior, United States Indian Service, Turtle Mountain Agency, North Dakota, 1 Apr 1931.

1932-Fort Peck 1932 Indian Census Roll of the Fort Peck Reservation, taken by H. D. McCullough, Department of the Interior, United States Indian Service, Fort Peck Agency, Montana, 1 Apr 1932.

1932-RB Census of the Rocky Boy Indians, Department of the Interior, United States Indian Service, Rocky Boy Agency,

1932-Sioux 1932 Census of the Sioux Indians, Department of the Interior, United States Indian Service, Fort Totten Agency, North Dakota, O. C. Gray, 1 Apr 1932.

1932-TMC Census of the Turtle Mountain Chippewa Indians, Department of the Interior, United States Indian Service, Turtle Mountain Agency, North Dakota, 1 Apr 1932.

1933-BLFT 1933 Indian Census Roll of the Blackfeet Reservation, Department of the Interior, United States Indian Service, Blackfeet Indian Agency, Montana, Forrest E. Stens, 31 March 1933.

1933-CCT Census of the Colville Indians, Department of the Interior, United States Indian Service, Colville Indian Agency, Washington, 1 Apr 1933.

1933-RB Census of the Rocky Boy Indians, Department of the Interior, United States Indian Service, Rocky Boy Agency, Montana, 1 April 1933.

1933-TMC Census of the Turtle Mountain Chippewa Indians, Department of the Interior, United States Indian Service, Turtle Mountain Agency, North Dakota, 1 Apr 1933.

1934-FB 1934 Census of the Fort Belknap, Montana, Department of the Interior, United States Indian Service, Washington D.C., 1 Apr 1934.

1934-Fort Peck 1934 Indian Census Roll of the Fort Peck Reservation, taken by H. D. McCullough, Department of the Interior, United States Indian Service, Fort Peck Agency, Montana, 1 Apr 1934.

1934-RB Census of the Rocky Boy Indians, Department of the Interior, United States Indian Service, Rocky Boy Agency, Montana, 1 January 1934.

1934-TMC Census of the Turtle Mountain Chippewa Indians, Department of the Interior, United States Indian Service, Turtle Mountain Agency, North Dakota, 1 Apr 1934.

1934-Umatilla 1934 Census of Walla Walla & Umatilla Indians, National Archives of the United States, Washington D.C.

1935-BLFT 1935 Indian Census Roll of the Blackfeet Reservation, Department of the Interior, United States Indian Service, Blackfeet Indian Agency, Montana, 31 Dec 1935.

1935-TMC Census of the Turtle Mountain Chippewa Indians, Department of the Interior, United States Indian Service, Turtle Mountain Agency, North Dakota, F. T. Scott, Superintendant, 1 Apr 1935.

1936-BLFT 1936 Indian Census Roll of the Blackfeet Reservation, Department of the Interior, United States Indian Service, Blackfeet Indian Agency, Montana, C. L. Graves, 31 Dec 1936.

1936-Fort Peck 1936 Indian Census Roll of the Fort Peck Reservation, taken by John G. Hunter, Department of the Interior, United States Indian Service, Fort Peck Agency, Montana, 31 Dec 1936.

1936-LS Henry Roe Cloud Roll 1936-1937, Pembina Band of Chippewa Indians Who Were Under the Leadership of Chief Thomas Little Shell, J. H. Dussome, Zortman, Montana and Vice-President: George SinClaire, Chinook, Montana.

1936-TMC 1936 Tribal Roll, Turtle Mountain Indian Reservation, Office of Indian Affairs, received 28 Jan 1938, National Archives of the United States, Washington D.C.

1937-1987-LS Basic Roll Basic Membership Roll of the Landless Indians of Montana; 1937 Census Taken by Dr. Henry Roe Cloud; Edited c1987 to include official correspondence regarding 1937 membership; ** in Present Roll Number column indicates 1940s information added.

1937-CdA-ID 1937 Census of the Coeur d'Alene, Idaho Indians, Department of the Interior, United States Indian Service, Washington D.C., 1 Jan 1937.

1937-FB 1937 Census of the Flathead, Montana, Department of the Interior, United States Indian Service, Washington D.C., 31 Dec 1937.

1937-F-B 1937 Census of the Fort Berthold Grosventre, Montana, Department of the Interior, United States Indian Service, Washington D.C., 31 Dec 1937.

1937-Quinaielt Indian Census Roll of the Quinaielt Reservation, Department of the Interior, United States Indian Service, Taholah Indian Agency, Washington, 1 January 1937.

1937-RB Census of the Rocky Boy Indians, Department of the Interior, United States Indian Service, Rocky Boy Agency, Montana, 1 January 1937.

1937-Sioux Indian Census Roll of the Devils Lake Sioux Reservation, Department of the Interior, United States Indian Service, Fort Totten, North Dakota, O. C. Gray, 1 January 1937.

1937-Spokane Indian Census Roll of the Spokane Reservation, Department of the Interior, United States Indian Service, Colville Indian Agency, Washington, Harvey K. Meyer, United States Indian Agent, 1 January 1937.

1937-TMC Indian Census Roll of the Turtle Mountain Reservation, Department of the Interior, United States Indian Service, Belcourt, North Dakota, J. E. Balmer, 1 January 1937.

1937-TMC-deaths Births & Deaths occurring between the dates of December 31, 1936 to Jan 1, 1938, Department of the Interior, United States Indian Service, Belcourt, North Dakota, 1 January 1937.

1937-WE 1937 Census of Confederated Chippewa of White Earth, Minnesota, National Archives of the United States, Washington D.C.

1938-FB 1938 Census of the Fort Belknap, Montana, Department of the Interior, United States Indian Service, Washington D.C., 1 Jan 1938.

1938-Fort Peck 1938 Indian Census Roll of the Fort Peck Reservation, Live births taken in 1937, Department of the Interior, United States Indian Service, Fort Peck Agency, Montana, 1 Jan 1938.

1938-RL Census of the Red Lake Indians, Department of the Interior, United States Indian Service, Red Lake Agency, Minnesota, 1 January 1938.

1939 Fort Belknap Indian Census Roll of the Fort Belknap Chippewa Assiniboia Reservation, Department of the Interior, United States Indian Service, Fort Belknap Indian Agency, Montana, 1 Jan 1939.

1939-40 RB Adoptions to the Chippewa-Cree Tribe, Rocky Boy Agency, Montana, 1939-1940: Source 6 Feb 1968 letter to Mrs. Florence Standing Rock, Box Elder, Montana, from Jacob Ahtone, Tribal Operations Officer.

1939-Crow Indian Census Roll of the Crow Indian Reservation, Department of the Interior, United States Indian Service, Montana, 31 Dec 1939.

1939-F-B 1939 Census of the Fort Berthold Grosventre, Montana, Department of the Interior, United States Indian Service, Washington D.C., 1 Jan 1939.

1939-Flathead Indian Census Roll of the Flathead Reservation, Department of the Interior, United States Indian Service, Flathead Indian Agency, Montana, L. M. Shotwell, 31 Dec 1939.

1940C CA 1940 California, Sixteenth Census of the United States, National Archives of the United States, Washington, D.C.

1940C MN 1940 Minnesota, Sixteenth Census of the United States, National Archives of the United States, Washington, D.C.

1940C MT 1940 Montana, Sixteenth Census of the United States, National Archives of the United States, Washington, D.C.

1940C ND 1940 North Dakota, Sixteenth Census of the United States, National Archives of the United States, Washington, D.C.

1940C OR Sixteenth Census of the United States: 1940; Oregon, National Archives of the United States, Washington D.C.

1940C SD 1940 South Dakota, Sixteenth Census of the United States, National Archives of the United States, Washington, D.C.

1940C WI Fifteenth Census of the United States: 1930; Wisconsin, National Archives of the United States, Washington D.C.

1987LS 1987-92 Little Shell Band of Chippewa Roll.

1996-00LS 1996-2000 Little Shell Band of Chippewa Roll.

A History of Rolla North Dakota 1888-1988; n.pub., Rolla, North Dakota, c1989.

ACG American-Canadian Genealogist, unknown location.

Agathe Lafrance, letter. abt 1990, to Gail Morin.

Agathe Laroche, interview. July 1994, Minneapolis, Minnesota.

AI-Rozyk Anglican Index of Baptisms, Marriages and Burials Extractions, Hudson Bay Company Archives, Winnipeg, Manitoba, Canada, Selected and Compiled by Rosemary Rozyk.

Al Yerbury Research.

Alain Gariepy Research.

Alberta Family Histories Society: Birth, Marriage and Death Database, http://www.afhs.ab.ca/.

Alfred Stanislaus Lafleur Research.

Alice Belgarde Jackson Collection.

Ancestors of J. P. Bouchard and Monique Bastien, J. P. Bouchard, worldconnect.rootsweb.com.

Ancestors of James D. Campbell, compiled by Nora Gebhart, Suzy Campbell and James D. Campbell, September 28, 1998.

Ancestry.com Website.

Anita Roy Research.

Anita Steele Research.

Ann Vasconi Research.

Anne Marie St.Jean Research.

AP Records of the Assumption Roman Catholic Church, Pembina, North Dakota: Baptisms, Marriages, Sepultures, 1848-1896; compiled by Reverend Father J. M. Belleau, 2 October 1944.

AP-Reg Assumption Parish Register, Pembina, North Dakota.

April T. Mercredi Research.

ArchiviaNet 1886-1901, 1906 Half-Breed Scrip Applications Index, RG15-21, Volume 1333 through 1371, Microfilm Reel Number C-14944 through C-15010, National Archives of Canada, Ottawa, Ontario, http://www.collectionscanada.gc.ca.

Ardith "Ardi" Bryant Research.

Arlene Shannon Research.

ARSB Ancient Registers of Saint Boiniface: 1825-1834, compiled by P. Ant. Champagne, a.r.i.c., April-May 1970.

Art Fisher Research.

Automated Genealogy 1851 Census Transcription Project and Census Images from the National Archives of Canada, http://www.automatedgenealogy.com.

Automated Genealogy 1901 Census Transcription Project and Census Images from the National Archives of Canada, http://www.automatedgenealogy.com.

Automated Genealogy 1906 Census Transcription Project and Census Images from the National Archives of Canada, http://www.automatedgenealogy.com.

Automated Genealogy 1911 Census Transcription Project and Census Images from the National Archives of Canada, http://www.automatedgenealogy.com.

AYM Documentation of Metis Families of Red River and the Northwest Territories; Census, Biographical, and Historical: 1881 Census Qu'Appelle, Wood Mountain, Lac la Biche; History of the Turtle Mountain Band of Chippewas; Census for the Turtle Mountain Reservation 1884-1886; Pembina, Dakota Territory 1850 Census; Various Metis Census Records for Pembina County, ND 1910; compiled by Al Yerbery, 1996.

Barbara Baker Research.

BCM Blaine County, Montana; Marriage Record Licenses and Certificates; 1865-1950; familysearch.org.

Berna-Dean Holland (nee Gaudry) Research.

Berneice Lomond Research.

BG Billings Gazette, Billings, Montana.

BHCM Beaverhead County, Montana; Marriage Record Licenses and Certificates; 1865-1950; familysearch.org.

BHCM Big Horn County, Montana; Marriage Record Licenses and Certificates; 1865-1950; familysearch.org.

BIA -TM-BMD Bureau of Indian Affairs, Turtle Mountain Death certificates: 1916-1952, extracted by Mary M. McClammy; Birth, Marriage, Death Records 1904-1950; Family record cards 1908; Family History Center; FHC Film #1249904.

BIA-LS Bureau of Indian Affairs, Little Shell Enrollment Papers.

BIA-TM Bureau of Indian Affairs, Turtle Mountain Enrollment and Probate Papers, Belcourt, North Dakota.

Birth Certificate.

BM *Mariages de Boucherville, 1668-1900 Publication 23* compiled by Benoit Pontbriand, (2390 Marie-Victorin, Sillery, Quebec, Canada G1T 1K1: Benoit Pontbriand, 1964).

BMS-SS Collection Archange Godbout 1, *Bapteme, Mariages, Sepultures de la paroisse Saint-Sulpice (1706-1980)* (Montreal, Montreal, Quebec, Canada: Societe Genealogique Canadienne-Francaise, 1985).

Bonnie Lingle-Harrington Research.

Bonnie Robillard Research.

Bonny Cann Research.

Brenda Menard Research.

Brenda Page Bercier Research.

Brenda Snider Research.

British Columbia Archives: Vital Statistics, http://search.bcarchives.gov.bc.ca.

BSAP Records of the Parish of Batoche, St.Antoine de Pudoue Roman Catholic Church: Register for Baptisms, Marriages, Deaths, Volume One, 1881-1909.

BSHSB Bulletin de la Société historique de Saint-Boniface.

BwCM Broadwater County, Montana; Marriage Record Licenses and Certificates; 1865-1950; familysearch.org.

CA Company of Adventurers, Peter C. Newman; 2801 John Street, Markham, Ontario, Canada L3R 1B4: Viking, Penguin Books Canada Ltd., 1985.

CA Death California Death Index 1940-1997.

CA Marriage California Marriage Index 1960-1985.

CaCM Cascade County, Montana; Marriage Record Licenses and Certificates; 1865-1950; familysearch.org.

Canada Tree Newsletter: Keeping Families Together, edited by Margaret Clarke.

Carrie Stave Research.

Cathy Foley Research.

CCM Carbon County, Montana; Marriage Record Licenses and Certificates; 1865-1950; familysearch.org.

CCRPNW-GR Catholic Church Records of the PNW: Grand Ronde Register, Vol. I, (1860-1885), Vol. II (1886-1898), St.Michael the Archangel Parish, Grand Ronde Indian Reservation, Grand Ronde, Oregon, St. Patrick's Parish, Muddy Valley, Oregon, Harriet Duncan Munnick, Portland, Oregon: Binford & Mort, 1987).

CCRPNW-OC/S/J Catholic Church Records of the Pacific Northwest: Oregon City Register (1842-1890), Salem Register (1864-1885), Jacksonville Register (1854-1885); Portland, Oregon: Binford & Mort Publishing, 1984), Harriet Duncan Munnick.

CCRPNW-R&P *CCRPNW-R&P Catholic Church Records of the Pacific Northwest: Roseburg (1853-1911) Portland 1852-1871* , Compiled by Harriet Duncan Munnick, (2536 S.E. Eleventh, Portland, Oregon 97202: Binford & Mort, Thomas Binford, Publisher, 1986).

CCRPNW-SA/SR/WW *Catholic Church Records of the Pacific Northwest, Missions of St.Anne and St.Rose of the Cayouse 1847-1888, Walla Walla and Frenchtown 1859-1872, Frenchtown 1872-1888* , Harriet D. Munnick & Adrian R. Munnick (Portland Oregon: Binford & Mort, 1989).

CCRPNW-SA/SR/WW *Catholic Church Records of the Pacific Northwest, Missions of St.Anne and St.Rose of the Cayouse 1847-1888, Walla Walla and Frenchtown 1859-1872, Frenchtown 1872-1888* , Harriet D. Munnick & Adrian R. Munnick (Portland Oregon: Binford & Mort, 1989).

CCRPNW-SL Catholic Church Records of the Pacific North West St.Louis Register, Vol. I, (1845-1868), Volume II (1869-1900), Gervais Register (1875-1893), Brooks Register (1893-1909), Harriet Duncan Munnick, Portland, Oregon: Binford & Mort, 1982).

Gervais Register (1875-1893), Brooks Register (1893-1909), Harriet Duncan Munnick, Portland, Oregon: Binford & Mort, 1982).

CCRPNW-SP Compiled by Harriet Duncan Munnick and in collaboration Mikell de Lores Wormell Warner, *Catholic Church Records of the Pacific Northwest: St.Paul, Oregon 1839-1898, Volumes I, II and III* (2536 S.E. Eleventh, Portland, Oregon 97202: Binford & Mort, Thomas Binford, Publisher, 1979).

CCRPNW-V *Catholic Church Records of the Pacific Northwest, Vancouver, Volumes I and II and Stellamaris Mission* Translated by: Mikell de Lores Wormell Warner and Annotated by: Harriet Duncan Munnick, (St.Paul, Oregon: French Prairie Press, 1972).

CCRPNW-V *Catholic Church Records of the Pacific Northwest, Vancouver, Volumes I and II and Stellamaris Mission* Translated by: Mikell de Lores Wormell Warner and Annotated by: Harriet Duncan Munnick, (St.Paul, Oregon: French Prairie Press, 1972).

CCT - BIA Colville Confederated Tribe, Bureau of Indian Affairs, Realty Office, Family and Individual Histories.

CCT-R 24/6/1913 Report to Indian Office dated June 24, 1913, on the applications of 311 persons for enrollment with the Colville Indians, Council of November 26 to December 2, 1912.

Chane Salois Research.

Charlene Dorey Research.

ChCM Chouteau County, Montana; Marriage Record Licenses and Certificates; 1865-1950; familysearch.org.

Cheryl Whited Research.

Children of the Rivers Volume 1, June 1999, Heather Hallett.

Children of the Rivers Volume II, Oct 2002, Heather Hallet.

Church of Latter Day Saints - Ancestral File, 10 Feb 1993.

Cindy Charlebois Research.

Cindy Harcus Research.

Cindy K. Coffin Research.

Clara Rivera Research.

Clara Royer Research, 15 Mar 1997 Family Group Records.

Clarence Kipling Research.

Clyde King Research.

ColCM Columbus County Courthouse, Montana; Marriage Record Licenses and Certificates, 1865-1950, familysearch.org.

Courchane, David, Ancestors of Marie Catherine Forest-Marin, Jan 1999.

CuCM Custer County, Montana; Marriage Record Licenses and Certificates; 1865-1950; familysearch.org.

CWLR *The Collected Writings Of Louis Riel*, 5 (University of Alberta Press, 1985).

DA Register of the Duhamel, Alberta Roman Catholic Church: 1881-1921.

Dale Coombe Research.

Dan Diserlais Research.

DanCM Daniels County, Montana; Marriage Record Licenses and Certificates; 1865-1950; familysearch.org.

Daniel Lafrance Research.

David Pegg Research.

DawCM Dawson County, Montana; Marriage Record Licenses and Certificates; 1865-1950; familysearch.org.

DCB-V10 *Dictionary of Canadian Biography - Volume Ten* Toronto, Ontario: University of Toronto Press, 2000).

DCB-V11 *Dictionary of Canadian Biography - Volume Eleven* Toronto, Ontario: University of Toronto Press, 2000).

DCB-V12 *Dictionary of Canadian Biography - Volume Twelve* Toronto, Ontario: University of Toronto Press, 2000).

DCB-V13 *Dictionary of Canadian Biography - Volume Thirteen* Toronto, Ontario: University of Toronto Press, 2000).

DCB-V14 *Dictionary of Canadian Biography - Volume Fourteen* Toronto, Ontario: University of Toronto Press, 2000).

DCB-V4 *Dictionary of Canadian Biography: Volume Four*; Toronto, Ontario: University of Toronto Press, 2000).

DCB-V5 *Dictionary of Canadian Biography: Volume 5*; Toronto, Ontario: University of Toronto Press, 2000).

DCB-V6 *Dictionary of Canadian Biography: Volume Six*; Toronto, Ontario: University of Toronto Press, 2000).

DCB-V6 *Dictionary of Canadian Biography: Volume Six*; Toronto, Ontario: University of Toronto Press, 2000).

DCB-V7 *Dictionary of Canadian Biography: Volume Seven*; Toronto, Ontario: University of Toronto Press, 2000).

DCB-V8 *Dictionary of Canadian Biography - Volume Eight* Toronto, Ontario: University of Toronto Press, 2000).

DCB-V9 *Dictionary of Canadian Biography - Volume Nine* Toronto, Ontario: University of Toronto Press, 2000).

DCH *Daniels County History*; Daniels County Bicentennial Committee, 1977).

Death Certificate.

Debbie Eden Research.

Debbie Jackson Research.

Debbie Morin Ivers Research.

Debby Merriweather Research.

Delores Johnson Research.

Denis Garand Research.

Denney Papers, Charles D. Denney, Glenbow Archives, Calgary, Alberta.

Descendants of Jean Lemelin, Elmer Lehman, worldconnect.rootsweb.com.

Descendants of Louis Kwarakwante Kolliou Iroquois Callihoo.

DGFA Dictionnaire Genealogique des Families Acadiennes 1636-1714, Volume I A-G, Volume II H-Z, Stephan A. White; Universite de Moncton: Centre d'Etudes Acadiennes, 1999.

DGFC Tanguay, Cyprien, *Dictionnaire Genealogique des Familles Canadiennes* (28 Felsmere Avenue, Pawtucket, Rhode Island 02861-2903: Quintin Publications, 1996 reprint).

DGFQ Jette, Rene, *Dictionnaire Genealogique des Familles du Quebec des Origines a 1730* (Montreal, Quebec, Canada: University of Montreal Press, 1983).

Diane Stigen Research.

Dictionary of Oregon History, edited by Howard McKinley Corning, Portland, Oregon: Binford & Mort, 1989.

DL Register of Sacre Coeur Roman Catholic Church, Duck Lake, Saskatchewan, 1870-1893.

DLCM Deer Lodge County, Montana; Marriage Record Licenses and Certificates; 1865-1950; familysearch.org.

DNCF *Dictionnaire National des Canadiens-Francais Tome I & II* Gabriel Drouin, editor, (revised 1985; Siege Social, 4184, rue St-Denis, Montreal, Canada: l'Institut Genealogique Drouin, 1979).

Documents Relating to the North West Company: A Biographical Dictionary of the Nor'Westers, W. Stewart Wallace, M.A., Volume XXII;Toronto, Ontario, Canada: The Champlain Society, 1934.

Dominique Ritchot Research.

Donald John Inkster Research.

Donna Walraven Research.

Dorothy J. Chartrand Research.

Dr. Charles Durham, Bird Family Research.

E/C-M Repertoire des Mariages de la Paroisse Saint-Joachim Edmonton, Sainte-Famille, St.Mary's Calgary; J. Hamelin S. C. and H. Houle S. C.; 2244, Rue Fullum, Montreal, Qc H2K 3N9: Le Centre de Genealogie S. C., 1990, Publication Number 130.

Earl Belcourt Research.

Ed Jerome Research.

Ed Merck Research.

Edited by Pearl L. Weston. *Across the River: A History of the Turner, Thomson, Campbell Families*; 620-8th Ave. NE; Swift Current, SK S9H 2R3: n.pub., 1995).

Edsel Bourque Research.

Eileen Horan Research.

Eleanor C. Anderson Research.

Elize Huppe Hartley Research.

Eugene E. Venne Research.

familysearch.org Website.

Faye Morin Research.

FDP Baptisms & Marriages Fort des Prairie, Saskatchewan District, C Kipling.

FerCM Fergus County Courthouse, Montana; Marriage Record Licenses and Certificates, 1865-1950, familysearch.org.

Five Indian Tribes of the Upper Missouri - Sioux, Arickaras, Assiniboines, Crees, Crows, Edwin Thompson Denig, Publishing Division of the University: University of Oklahoma Press, 1961.

FJD The Family of Jenkin Daniel 1750 - 1900 Comprising Over a Century of Service with the Hudson's Bay Company, Lynne C. (Begg) Charles & Mabel A. (Quirk) Hykaway, #1203 - 1327 E. Keith Rd., North Vancouver, B.C. V7J 3T5: Lynne Charles, November 1996).

FlCM Flathead County, Montana; Marriage Record Licenses and Certificates; 1865-1950; familysearch.org.

Fort Garry St.Vital Roman Catholic Cemetery; Cemetery Transcription #42; Kathy Stokes, Betty Atkinson, Lorne Harris, Unit E, 1045 St.James Street, Winnipeg, Manitoba, Canada %3H 1B1: Manitoba Genealogical Society, Inc., 1980-1981; update 1995.

Franceene Watson Research.

Francis Fisher Research.

Frank Camp Research.

Fred Zastre Research.

Freda Stewart Research.

FTA Repertoire des Mariages du Fort Alexandre et Missions 1878-1955: Fort Alexandre (FTA), Manigotagan, Hole River; Agnes Labossiere, Compilation, Alfred Fortier, Verification; St.Boniface, Manitoba: La Cosiete Historique de Saint-Boniface, 1985.

Funeral Card.

Funeral or Death Card or Pamphlet.

GalCM Gallatin County Courthouse, Montana; Marriage Record Licenses and Certificates; 1865-1950, familysearch.org.

Garnet Parenteau Research.

GCM Glacier County, Montana; Marriage Record Licenses and Certificates; 1865-1950; familysearch.org.

Genie Graves Research.

Geoff Burtonshaw Research.

George and Joanne Ross Research.

GFFDRR Genealogy of the French Families of the Detroit River Region 1701-1936; 2 Volumes. (Rev. Fr. Christian Denissen and Editor: Harold Frederick Powell PhD, Detroit Public Library, Detroit, Michigan 48202: Detroit Society for Genealogical Research & the Burton Historical Collection, 1987 revision editior Robert L. Pilon, assistant editor Stephen F. Keller).

GI General Index to Manitoba and North-West Territoires Half-Breeds and Original White Settlers who have preferred claims - April 1885, Microfilm Reel Number C-11878, National Archives of Canada, Ottawa, Ontario.

Gilles Marion Research.

Ginger Landrie Research.

Gladys Frost Research.

Great Falls Tribune, Great Falls, Montana.

GVCM Golden Valley County Courthouse, Montana; Marriage Record Licenses and Certificates; 1865-1950, familysearch.org.

Half Breed Scrip issued on the 1864 Amendments to the Old Crossing between the Red Lake and Pembina Bands of Chippewa and the United States, http://www.maquash.net/Historical/Scrip/list.html#14.

Harriet McKay Research.

Harry Hansen Research.

HBCA-B Hudson's Bay Company Archives - biographical sketches, Hudson's Bay Company Archives; Winnipeg, Manitoba.

HBCE Hudson Bay Company employment records.

HBC-PN Public Notice of land claims of Half-Breed Children, Address: Provincial Archives of Manitoba, Winnipeg, Manitoba, File Reference: MG4D13 Box 1.

HBCR Hudson Bay Company Register of Anglican Church Baptisms, Marriages, and Burials for the Red River Settlement, 1821-1841.

HBS 1886-1901, 1906 Half-Breed Scrip Applications, RG15-21, Volume 1333 through 1371, Microfilm Reel Number C-14944 through C-15010, National Archives of Canada, Ottawa, Ontario.

HBSI Index 1886-1901, 1906 Halfbreed Scrip Applications, RG15-21, Microfilm Reel Number C-14943, National Archives of Canada, Ottawa, Ontario.

HCM Hill County, Montana; Marriage Record Licenses and Certificates; 1865-1950; familysearch.org.

HDN Havre Daily News, Havre, Montana.

Heather Devine Research.

Heather Gervais Research.

Heather Hallett Research.

Henriette Parenteau Research.

Historical Data Project, Bismarck, North Dakota.

History of North Washington, Western States Publishing, 1903.

Homestead Shacks Over Buffalo Tracks; http://www.rootsweb.com/~mtfergus/homestead/fer01.htm#doney159: rootsweb.com, 1990-1999.

IBMS *Index des Baptemes, Mariages et Sepultures* (La Societe Historique de Saint-Boniface).

ID Death Idaho Death Index 1911-1951.

In Early History: Some Early Marriage Licenses, (Colville, Washington: Examiner, January - February 1917).

INB *Index des Naissances and Baptemes* (St.Boniface, Manitoba: La Societe Historique de Saint-Boniface., c1995).

Index to St. Mary's Mission (Montana) Baptism Records 1864-1894 in *American Indian Family Lines*, David Courchane, E. 3308 29th Avenue, Spokane, Washington 99223: Am-Toola Publications.

International Genealogical Index (IGI).

Jackie Gladue Jordan Research.

Jackie Overstreet Research.

Jackie Trotchie Research.

James D. Hartman Research.

James Falcon Research.

James Falcon Research.

James Riel Research.

James W. Chesebro, PhD.

Jan Cavalier Research.

Jan Evans Research.

Jane Dubois Research.

Jane Tomkinson Research.

Jason Lepage Research.

JBCM Judith Basin County, Montana; Marriage Record Licenses and Certificates; 1865-1950; familysearch.org.

JCM Jefferson County Courthouse, Montana; Marriage Record Licenses and Certificates; 1865-1950, familysearch.org.

Jean-Marc Voisard Research.

John A. Coldwell Research.

John Laroche Research.

Joshua Dragon Research.

Joyce (Gunn) Anaka. *Donald Gunn Family History*, March 1996).

Joyce Anaka Research.

Joyce Black Research.

Judy Jacoby Research.

June Haybittle Research.

Justina McKay Research.

Karen MacKay Research.

Kathie MacGregor Donahue Research.

Kenneth G. Normand Research.

Kenneth J. Madson Research.

Kevin Veenstra.

Kimberly Tremlay Research.

L&CCM Lewis & Clark County, Montana; Marriage Record Licenses and Certificates; 1865-1950; familysearch.org.

L1 Lebret Mission de St.Florent Roman Catholic Registre des Baptemes, Mariages & Seplutures, Qu'Appelle, Saskatchewan, 1868-1881.

L2 Lebret, Mission de St.Florent, Roman Catholic Registre des Baptemes, Mariages & Seplutures, Qu'Appelle, Saskatchewan, Book Two: 1881-1887, FHC microfilm 1032949.

Laforest, Thomas. *OFCA Our French Canadian Ancestors* Palm Harbor, Florida: The LISI Press, 1997).

Lake Metigoshe Mirror, Bottineau, North Dakota.

LakeCM Lake County, Montana; Marriage Record Licenses and Certificates; 1865-1950; familysearch.org.

Larry Quinto Research.

Lauri Campbell Research.

Leah Tourond Research.

Leanne Laberge Research.

Lee Fraychineaud. *The Inkster Family of Lee Fraychineaud*, January 1999).

Len Dubois Research.

Len Last Research.

Len Mariner Research.

Len Solway Research.

Les familles francophone et metisse de l'Ouest canadien, Societe Historique de St. Boniface, shsb.mb.ca.

Lesa (Trotchie) Zimmerman Research.

Lesley Taylor Research.

LFAN *La Famille Amable Nault* C.SsR. compiled by Charles Eugene Voyer, (Ste.Anne des Chenes, Manitoba, 15 Mar 1978).

LHBCM List of Hudson Bay Company Marriages; 139 Cook Street; Victoria, B.C.; V8V 3W8: Edited by Joanne J. Hughes, 1977.

LibCM Liiberty County, Montana; Marriage Record Licenses and Certificates; 1865-1950; familysearch.org.

Linda Delorme Research.

Linda Turcotte Research.

LinkCM Lincoln County, Montana; Marriage Record Licenses and Certificates; 1865-1950; familysearch.org.

Lionel V. DeRagon Research.

Lisa Kisch Research.

LLBR1 Notre Dame des Tidoren, St.Paul Diocese, Lac La Biche, Registre des Baptemes, Mariages & Sepltures, Volume 1, 1853-1898.

LLBR2 Notre Dame des Tidoren, St.Paul Diocese, Lac La Biche, Registre des Baptemes, Mariages & Sepltures, Volume 1, 1881-1907.

Lloyd Good Research.

Lois Melville Research.

Lorne LaFleur.

Lorraine Freeman Research.

Lorretta Gammel Research.

Louis Verhagen Research.

Louise Vien Research.

Lynn Marion Research.

Lynn Roden Research.

Lynton Stewart Research.

Mabel Kelly Research.

MadCM Madison County, Montana; Marriage Record Licenses and Certificates; 1865-1950; familysearch.org.

Manitoba Vital Statistics online, http://web2.gov.mb.ca.

Margaret Doney Dills Research.

Margaret Nunn Research.

Margaret Sloan Research.

Maria Lepine Research.

Mariages de St.Ours, Immaculee Conception, Richelieu, unknown compiler, n.pub., n.d.

Marie Beaupre Extractions.

Marilyn Patricia Monkman Bean Research.

Marion Kotowich-Laval Research.

Marriage Certificate.

Marriages, Deaths, Volume One, 1881-1909.

Mary Conway Research.

Mary Delorme Research.

Mary McClammy Research.

Mathew Pulscher "Mathew Pulscher Research." E-mail message from matfranpulscher@sprint.ca at gmorin@televar.com.

Mavis Dumont Research.

May Grandbois Racine Research.

MBS Scrip Applications, Original White Settlers & Halfbreeds residing in Manitoba on 15 July 1870, RG15-19, Volume 1319 through 1324, 2128, Microfilm Reel Number C-14925 through C-14934, National Archives of Canada, Ottawa, Ontario.

MBSI Index Scrip Applications, Original White Settlers & Halfbreeds residing in Manitoba on 15 July 1870, RG15-19, Microfilm Reel Number C-14934, National Archives of Canada, Ottawa, Ontario.

McCCM McCone County, Montana; Marriage Record Licenses and Certificates; 1865-1950; familysearch.org.

McIntyre Report - Determination of validity of scrip issued for Half-breed Chippewas of the Pembina band, Red Lake band, White Earth band, 1880.

MCM Missoula County, Montana; Marriage Record Licenses and Certificates; 1865-1950; familysearch.org.

ME *The Mantle of Elias: The Story of Fathers Blanchet and Demers in Early Oregon* M. Leona Nichols (Portland, Oregon: Binfords & Mort, 1941).

MeaCM Meagher County, Montana; Marriage Record Licenses and Certificates; 1865-1950; familysearch.org.

Mel Barwin Research.

Melanie MacFarlane Research.

Melvin D. Beaudry Research.

Michael K. Keplin Research.

Michel Racicot Research.

Millie Lansing Research.

MineralCM Mineral County, Montana; Marriage Record Licenses and Certificates; 1865-1950; familysearch.org.

Minnesota Births and Christenings Index, 1840-1980 - Ancestry.com.

Minnesota Department of Health Public Death Index.

Minnesota Marriages Index, 1849-1950 - Ancestry.com.

Minot Daily News, Minot, North Dakota.

Missoulian Newspaper, Missoula, Montana.

MLC Meadow Lake, Saskatchewan Cemetery http://www.meadowlake.ca/2008-06/cemetery.php, before 2014.

MM *Manitoba Marriages* in *Publication 45*, Volumes 1-3, compiled and edited by: Paul J. Lareau, Fr. Julien Hamelin, (240 Avenue Daly, Ottawa, Ontario K1N 6G2: Le Centre de Genealogie S.C., 1984).

Mo Aschenbrenner Research.

Montour website, http://www.usinternet.com/users/dfnels/couc.htm.

Mose LaTray Family Papers compiled by Lily B. Zwolle and Mary Ann Quiring; Lewistown, MT: n.pub.

MSCM Musselshell County, Montana; Marriage Record Licenses and Certificates; 1865-1950; familysearch.org.

MSJ-FA-E Register des Baptemes, Mariages & Sepultures 1858-1861 Mission St.Joachim, Fort Auguste, Fort des Prairies, Edmonton, No. 1.

MT Death Montana State Genealogical Society Death Index.

Nancy Smith Research.

Nellie Nault Research.

Normand Chaunt Research.

North Dakota Department of Health Public Death Index.

Notre Dame des Tidoren, St.Paul Diocese, Lac La Biche, Registre des Baptemes, Mariages & Sepltures, Volume 1, 1853-1898.

NWC-L North West Company Ledger, Hudson's Bay Company Archives, Winnipeg, Manitoba.

NWHBS 1885 Scrip Applications, North-West Halfbreeds residing outside Manitoba on 15 July 1870, RG15-20, Volume 1325 through 1332, Microfilm Reel Number C-14936 through C-14942, National Archives of Canada, Ottawa, Ontario.

NWHBSI Index 1885 Scrip Applications, North-West Halfbreeds residing outside Manitoba on 15 July 1870, RG15-20, Microfilm Reel Number C-14942, National Archives of Canada, Ottawa, Ontario.

Oblate Cards: First Western Families.

Olga Our Lady of the Sacred Heart, Olga, North Dakota 1882-1900.

On Flatwillow Creek 1991 by Linda Grosskopf and Rick Newby Los Alamos NM: Exceptional Books, Ltd.

Ontario, Canada Births 1869-1913, ancestry.com.

Ontario, Canada Deaths 1869-1913 and Deaths Overseas 1939-1947, ancestry.com.

Ontario, Canada Marriages, 1801-1928, ancestry.com.

PaCM Park County, Montana; Marriage Record Licenses and Certificates; 1865-1950; familysearch.org.

Pat Neibergall Research.

Pat Turenne Research.

Patricia McCarthy Research.

Patty Severns Papers on Wells family.

Pauline Vaugeois Research.

Peter J. Gagne. *FCW-Gagne French-Canadians of the West, A Biographical Dictionary of French-Canadians and French Metis of the Western United States and Canada*; Pawtucket, Rhode Island: Quintin Publications, c1999).

PhCM Phillips County Courthouse, Montana; Marriage Record Licenses and Certificates; 1865-1950, familysearch.org.

Pierre Ducharme Association des Charron & Ducharme Inc.

PM Catholic Parish Register of Pembroke Mission, Ontario, Canada 1839-1842, 1856-1866, 1867-1878.

PonCM Pondera County Courthouse, Montana; Marriage Record Licenses and Certificates; 1865-1950, familysearch.org.

Poplar Standard Newspaper, Poplar, Montana.

Prairie Past and Mountain Memories: A History of Dunseith, North Dakota 1882-1982, n.pub., Dunseith, North Dakota, 1982.

PRDH online index, http://www.genealogic.umontreal.ca.

PRM *Mariages de la Paroisse de la Purifacation Repentigny (1669-1970) Publication No. 5* compiled by Lucien Rivest and Rosario Gauthier, (9247 - 24e Avenue, Montreal, Quebec H1Z 4A2: Editions Bergeron & Fils Enr'g, 1975).

Rarihokwats Research.

Raymond Morin Research.

RCM Ravalli County Courthouse, Montana; Marriage Record Licenses and Certificates; 1865-1950, familysearch.org.

Rene Brazeau Research.

Richard Garneau, Ganadian History a Distinct Viewpoint, 22 Nov 1999.

Richard Larson Research.

RLCM Richland County Courthouse, Montana; Marriage Record Licenses and Certificates; 1865-1950, familysearch.org.

RMSB *Repertoire des Mariages de Saint-Boniface (Manitoba) 1825-1983* compiled by Julien Hamelin S.C., (240, avenue Daly; Ottawa, Ontario K1N 6G2: Le Centre de Genealogie S. C., Publication #67, 1985).

Robby Vaudrin Research.

Robert J. Turcotte and Paul F. C. Mueller Research.

Robin Miotke Research.

Rod MacQuarrie Research.

Roger Nielsen Research.

Roger Ouimet Research.

Roger W. Lawrence Research.

Romy Lacerte Research.

Ron Hilde Research.

Ron Ohlfs Research.

Ron Schell Collection, July 1999.

Ronnie Burd Research.

RooCM Marriage Licenses and Certificates, Roosevelt County Courthouse, Wolf Point, Montana; FHC microfilm 1903324 and 1903325.

Rootsweb.com Website.

Rosemary Helga (Morrissette) Rozyk Research.

Roy Cemetery Transcription, GenWeb.

RTR Rundle, Reverend R. T., Journal of Baptisms & Marriages in Saskatchewan District,1840 - 1848.

SA Ste.Agathe Register.

SAC St.Ann Cemetery Records, Belcourt, North Dakota.

Sampson, Faye, Genealogy of Seagraves, Sampson and Kindred Lines, (Second edition; 1 Mar 1983)).

Sampson, Faye. *Genealogy of Seagraves, Sampson and Kindred Lines*. n.p.: n.pub., November 16, 1969.

SanCM Sanders County Courthouse, Montana; Marriage Record Licenses and Certificates; 1865-1950, familysearch.org.

Sandra Gertsch Research.

SAPC St.Albert Parish Cemetery - NW04-054-25 W4 Alberta Genealogical Society, about 1987.

Saskatchewan Vital Statistics online, http://vsgs.health.gov.sk.ca.

SB 1825-1834 St.Boniface Roman Catholic Registre des Baptemes, Mariages & Sepultures, 1825-1834.

SBCM Silver Bow County, Montana; Marriage Record Licenses and Certificates; 1865-1950; familysearch.org.

SB-Rozyk St. Boniface Roman Catholic Church, Manitoba, Canada, Baptisms, Marriages and Burials 1860-1875 Extractions, Compiled by Rosemary Rozyk.

SCW-M In Early History: Some Early Marriage Licenses, Stevens County Washington, edited by John Slater; Colville, Washington: Examiner, January - February 1917).

SD Sheridan County Historical Association, *Sheridan's Daybreak* (Great Falls, Montana: Blue Print & Letter Company, Printers, 1970).

SD-444 Senate Document No. 444; Washington, D.C.: United States Government.

SFDL St-Francois-Du-Lac, Yamaska, Province of Quebec Register Index: 1689-1872.

SFDLM *Mariages de St-Francois-du-Lac, 1687-1965 Publication 33* compiled by Benoit Pontbriand, (2390 Marie-Victorin, Sillery, Quebec, Canada G1T 1K1: Benoit Pontbriand, 1966).

SFX: 1834-1850 St.Francois Xavier 1834-1851 Register.

SFX-100 Yrs *SFX-100 Yrs Our First Hundred Years: History of St.Francois-Xavier Municipality*; St.Francois-Xavier, Manitoba, Canada: St.Francois-Xavier Municipality, July 1980).

SFXI 1851-1868 St.Francois Xavier 1852-1861 Register Index.

SFXI: 1834-1852 St.Francois Xavier 1834-1852 Register Index.

SFXI: 1851-1869 St.Francois Xavier 1851-69 Register Index.

SFXI-Kipling St.Francois Xavier Register Index, 1834-1900; compiled by Clarence Kipling.

SGCM Sweet Grass County, Montana; Marriage Record Licenses, 1865-1950, familysearch.org.

Shae Griffith Research.

Sharon Seal Research.

Sharron Gottbreht-Shen Research.

ShCM Sheridan County Courthouse, Plentywood, Montana; Marriage Record Licenses and Certificates; 1913-1952; FHC Film 1903321.

SHC-PA-SK Sacred Heart Cathedral, Prince Albert, Saskatchewan, baptisms, marriages and burials, 1874-1900.

Sheila McGivern Research.

Sherry Bernard Research.

Shirley Wishart Research.

SIWB St.Ignace Roman Catholic Registre des Baptemes, Mariages & Sepltures, Willow Bunch, Saskatchewan, 1882-1917, FHC #1290091.

SJAC St.James Anglican Church Extractions, Manitoba Genealogy Society, Winnipeg, Manitoba.

SJC Mission of St.Joseph, Cumberland; Registre de Baptemes, de Mariages, et de Sepultures.

SJCH Mission of St.Joseph, Cumberland House; Registre de Baptemes, de Mariages, et de Sepultures.

SJL-1 Register of Baptisms, Marriages, and Burials, St.Joseph, Leroy, North Dakota, Diocese of Saint Paul, Minnesota, 1870-1888, Book 1.

SJL-2 Register of Baptisms, Marriages, and Burials, St.Joseph, Leroy, North Dakota, Diocese of Saint Paul, Minnesota, 1888-1900, Book 2.

SJL-D St.Joseph Leroy, North Dakota, Record of Interments 1888-1932.

SLM Mariages de la Paroisse Saint-Laurent Montreal 1720-1974, Rosaria Gauthier and Marice Legault; 9247 - 24e Avenue, Montreal, PQ H1Z 4A2: Editions Bergeron & Fils Enrg, Publication No.: 32, 1976.

SL-SK St.Laurent-de-Grandin Roman Catholic Registre des Baptemes, Mariages & Sepltures, St.Laurent, Saskatchewan, 1872-1896.

SMACPLP St.Marys Anglican Church, Portage La Prairie, Manitoba, Baptisms, Marriages, Burials, 1855-1883, transcribed by Clarence Kipling.

SMYM *Mariages de St-Michel d'Yamaska, 1727-1965 Publication 34* compiled by Benoit Pontbriand, (2390 Marie-Victorin, Sillery, Quebec, Canada G1T 1K1: Benoit Pontbriand, 1966).

SN1 Catholic Parish Register of St.Norbert 1857-1873.

SN2 Catholic Parish Register of St.Norbert.

Social Security Death Index.

SPMT St.Peter's Mission; Volume I; Marriage Register 1859-1895; Translated & Transcribed by Reverend Dale McFarlane, Archivist, Diocese of Great Falls-Billings, Montana; Spring 1981.

SPS Saint-Pierre de Sorel, Roland J. Auger.

St. Claude Mission, St. John, North Dakota, Baptisms, Marriages, Burials 1882-1888, 2006, Dominique Ritchot.

St.Ann's Centennial, 100 Years of Faith - 1885-1985; Belcourt, North Dakota: St.Ann Parish, 1985).

St.James Anglican Cemetery; Cemetery Transcription #121; Mavis and Maureen Smith, Unit "E," 1045 St.James Street, Winnipeg, Manitoba, Canada R3H 1B1: Manitoba Genealogical Society, Inc., 1983.

St.Leo's Roman Catholic Church: Baptisms and Marriages, Lewistown, Montana.

St.Malo Roman Catholic Cemetery; Cemetery Transcription #485; F. Cox, E. Bjornson and K. Stokes, Rm. 420 - 167 Lombard Ave., Winnipeg, Manitoba, Canada R3B 0T6: Manitoba Genealogical Society, Inc., May 1990.

Stan Hulme Research.

ST-BSP St.Eustache (Baie St.Paul) 1877-1900 Register.

Ste.Agathe Roman Catholic Cemetery; Cemetery Transcription #485; F. Cox, E. Bjornson and K. Stokes, Rm. 420 - 167 Lombard Ave., Winnipeg, Manitoba, Canada R3B 0T6: Manitoba Genealogical Society, Inc., June 1988.

STMYI Index to St.Michel d'Yamaska, Quebec, 1727-1823 Baptisms, Marriages, and Burials.

St-N Cem *St.Norbert Parish Cemetery 1859-1906, We Remember*; Winnipeg, Manitoba, Canada: St.Norbert Parish-La Barriere Metis Council of the Metis Federation of Manitoba, 29 May 2010).

STRANGE EMPIRE: A Narrative of the Northwest; by Joseph Kinsey Howard; Greenwood Press; Westport, Connecticut; c. 1952.

Sue Stevenson Research.

SV St.Vital Roman Catholic Registre des Baptemes, Mariages & Sepltures, Battleford, Saskatchewan, 1878-1896.

T. R. "Pat" McCloy, McKay Descendancy.

TB-CCT Tardy's Book of Families, Colville Confederated Tribes, Enrollment Office, Nespelem, Washington.

TeCM Teton County, Montana; Marriage Record Licenses and Certificates; 1865-1950; familysearch.org.

Terrance McDougall Research.

Terry Hart Research.

Terry Larocque Research.

The Beaver Magazine, n.pub., n.p.

The New Nation - Christ's Chosen People, by Mary Madeleine Lee, 1987.

The Rivard Family by Mary Ann Mickey, worldconnect.rootsweb.com.

The Sidney Herald, Sidney, Montana.

The Star of Grand Coulee, Grand Coulee, Washington.

Thelma Soden Research.

Timothy Low Research.

TMC Alberta Murray, *These My Children* (Fairfied, Washington: Ye Galleon Press, 1976).

ToCM Toole County, Montana; Marriage Record Licenses and Certificates; 1865-1950; familysearch.org.

Tony Goodwin Research.

Treasure of Time: The Rural Municipality of Cartier: 1914-1984; n.p.: n.pub., 1984.

Trevor R. Teed Research.

Turtle Mountain Reservation Probate Record, Branch of Trust & Natural Resources.

Turtle Mountain Star, Rolla, North Dakota.

Valencia T. R. Miller Research.

VCM Valley County Courthouse, Glasgow, Montana; Marriage Record Licenses, 1865-1950, familysearch.org.

Voyager Index http://www.solutions.net/temp/jean-pierre/voyageur/index.cgi, 2000.

Wade Dimock Research.

Wanda Sinclair Research.

Washington State Digital Archives, Secretary of State, State Archives, http://www.digitalcarchives.wa./gov, 960 Washington Street, Cheney, WA 99004.

Wayne Paquin Research.

WCM Wheatland County Courthouse, Montana; Marriage Record Licenses, 1865-1950, familysearch.org.

W-D St.Boniface, Walhalla, North Dakota, Death Register 1913-1931.

Wendell Brave Research.

Weston, Pearl L., Edited. *Across the River: A History of the Turner, Thomson, Campbell Families*; 620-8th Ave. NE; Swift Current, SK S9H 2R3: n.pub., 1995).

WHQ Washington Historical Quarterly, n.pub., n.p.

Wilfred Gayleard Research.

Willow Bunch Catholic Cemetery http://willowbunch.ca/cemetery/cemetery_list.html?CemeteryID=17.

Wilma Klyne Research.

Wilmer Marcil Research.

Winnipeg Free Press, Winnipeg, Manitoba.

Winnipeg Tribune, Winnipeg, Manitoba.

WIS Birth Wisconsin Birth/Christening Index.

Wisconsin Historical Collections; Marriages, Vol. xviii; Baptisms, Vol. xix; edited by Reuben Gold Thwaites, LL.D., 1910.

WWI Canada Canadian Soldiers of the First World War (1914-1918) National Archives of Canada, Ottawa, Ontario, http://www.collectionscanada.gc.ca.

WWI United States Draft Registration Cards (1917-1919), familysearch.org.

YACT Olivier, Reginald L., *Your Ancient Canadian Ties* (P. O. Box 368, Logan, Utah 84321: The Everton Publishers, Inc., 1972).

YCM Yellowstone County, Montana; Marriage Record Licenses and Certificates; 1865-1950; familysearch.org.

Cooper: Charles Thomas (b. , d. 1846), 41, 71; Isabella (b. 1835,), 40, 41; Jeremiah (b. 1842, d. 1904), 70, 71; Louisa (b. 1837, d. 1908), 123

Corbeau: Nan-touche, 155, 186

Corrigal: Edward (bt. 1836, d. 1930), 96; Elizabeth (b. 1852,), 240; Jacob, 86; James (b. 1796, d. 1887), 31; John (b. 1816,), 240; John Henry (b. 1836,), 3; Joseph (b. 1839,), 84, 86; Louise (b. 1859,), 93, 96; Madeleine (b. 1832, d. 1915), 31, 32, 235; May Matilda (b. 1880,), 2, 3

Corth: Frank, 309; Mathilda Maria (b. 1910), 309

Costa: Frank (b. 1920), 134

Costello: Valentine DeLacy (b. 1889, d. 1973), 87

Cote: Magloire (b. 1831,), 267; Zoe (b. 1873, d. 1899), 267

Cotter: Louis, 288; Pricilla (b. 1911, d. 1995), 288

Coulombe: Marguerite (b. 1828,), 163, 280

Coulson: Jeremie, 285

Courchene: Adeline (b. 1875,), 72; Angele (b. 1827, d. 1883), 93, 211; Antoine (b. 1823, d. 1898), 95, 317, 322; Brigitte (b. 1857,), 317, 318; Catherine (b. 1837, d. 1871), 267; Cecelia (b. 1865, d. 1935), 23; Cecile (b. 1837, d. 1933), 230, 308; Elise (b. 1838,), 148; Francois (b. 1796, d. 1858), 94; Josephte (b. 1826, d. 1920), 38, 39; Marguerite (b. 1832,), 176, 191; Marie (b. 1810, d. 1908), 58; Marie (b. 1831, d. 1917), 93, 94, 103, 213; Marie Josephine (b. 1872, d. 1902), 317, 322; Maxime (b. 1852,), 72; Norbert (b. 1866,), 95; Sophie, 74

Courteoreille: Jacques (b. 1838,), 228; Jane (b. 1842,), 253, 255; Michel (b. 1824,), 255; Nancy (b. 1857,), 226, 228

Courtepatte: Dieudonne (b. 1855,), 18; Jean-Baptiste dit LePoteau (b. 1829, d. 1918), 18

Coutts: Mary Margaret (b. 1883,), 136, 139; Peter (b. 1849,), 139

Cowitz: Albert Frank, 54; Bertha Hazel, 48, 54

Cox: John, 40; John (b. 1795, d. 1872), 39, 40

Crebassa: John, 192; Marie Anne (b. 1807, d. 1885), 192

Cree: Chippewa Spokane Pend d'Oreille, 57, Christiana, 27, 270, 271; Genevieve, 140; Jane (b. 1783,), 233, 252; Josephte, 248; Lizette, 106; Margaret (b. 1787, d. 1847), 280; Marie "Okatshikew", 85; Mary, 4, 45; Rosalie (b. 1793, d. 1873), 58; Sarah "Sally" (b. 1787, d. 1827), 272; Sarah (b. 1786, d. 1846), 75

Cree Indian Woman: Margaret, 269; Nelly, 272

Crete: Adelaide, 30

Crin: Pash-ko-wagan, 85

Crise: Marie (b. 1791, d. 1841), 242, 258

Cromarty: Isabella (b. 1894,), 284; James (b. 1862, d. 1925), 59, 60; James Sr. (b. 1826, d. 1911), 60; Magnus (b. 1854,), 284

Cromwell: Mary Amy, 312

Crosby: Mary, 243

Crowden: Ivan Walter (b. 1904), 89, 90

Cumming: George William (, d. 1901), 34, 36; James John (b. 1867,), 313; Samuel (b. 1846,), 313

Cummings: Catherine (b. 1835,), 27, 28; Cuthbert (b. 1787, d. 1870), 1; Cuthbert (b. 1825, d. 1896), 1; Hannah (b. 1812, d. 1846), 123; Margaret (b. 1826, d. 1890), 30; Robert (b. 1795, d. 1863), 27

Cunningham: Catherine (b. 1832,), 4, 5; James (b. 1854, d. 1940), 118; John (b. 1818, d. 1870), 314, 315; Mary (b. 1824, d. 1907), 59, 268; Patrick (b. 1789, d. 1831), 5, 268, 315; William George (b. 1884,), 112, 118

Cusitor: David Magnus (b. 1822, d. 1887), 32, 271, 275; Jemima (b. 1862,), 53; John, 275; John (b. 1857,), 32

Cuzuel: Nathalie, 185

Cyr: Caroline (b. 1856, d. 1884), 183; Elise (b. 1850,), 10; Jean (b. 1848,), 212, 214; Joseph Jean Baptiste (b. 1871,), 204, 212; Josephte (b. 1822,), 181; Julienne, 222; Marguerite (b. 1834,), 249; Marie (b. 1855,), 101; Marie Alpha (b. 1874,), 205, 214; Victoire (b. 1843), 155, 157

Dagneau: Francois (b. 1830,), 310

Dahl: Alexander (b. 1822, d. 1879), 232, 233; Isabella (b. 1845, d. 1868), 76, 77; Peter (b. 1789, d. 1859), 233

Daignault: Helene (b. 1832,), 61

Daigneault: Joseph (b. 1795, d. 1867), 61; Joseph (b. 1825,), 61; Julie (b. 1846,), 257; Suzanne (b. 1817, d. 1890), 246

Dambly: Aime Hubert, 318; Jean-Baptiste, 318

Daniel: Fanny (bt. 1835,), 252; George (bt. 1840, d. 1867), 252; Griffith (b. 1790,), 252; Jacob (b. 1792, d. 1876), 252; Nancy (b. 1810,), 29; Nancy (b. 1818,), 173

Daniels: Zilda (b. 1872, d. 1953), 305, 310

Daoust: Marie Laure Delima, 10

Dardis: Patrick, 55; Patrick Francis "Frank" (b. 1883, d. 1964), 49, 55

Darning: Nancy, 151, 153

Daunais: Elzear (b. 1867,), 10, 11; Jean Baptiste (b. 1810, d. 1885), 10; Joseph (b. 1846,), 10, 11; Marie Anne (b. 1890, d. 1912), 321

Dauost: Emelie, 203

Dauphinais: Adeline (b. 1880,), 299; Angelique (b. 1869, d. 1949), 175; C. Pierre, 88; Charlotte Genthon dit (b. 1814,), 81; Daniel (b. 1876,), 163, 175; David (b. 1876, d. 1947), 295; Joseph (b. 1828,), 226; Marguerite (b. 1826,), 162, 173, 297; Marie (b. 1843,), 222; Marie Flavie (b. 1854, d. 1932), 25; Mary Jane (b. 1892, d. 1960), 174; Michel Genthon dit or Dauphine (b. 1781, d. 1858), 226; Pierre (b. 1846, d. 1913), 175; St.Ann (b. 1902, d. 1988), 295

Davis: Alice Mathilda (b. 1857,), 123; Francois (b. 1873, d. 1947), 125, 130; George (b. 1824, d. 1904), 123; Helene (b. 1838,), 144; Jean Baptiste (b. 1785,), 146; Jean Baptiste (b. 1822,), 143, 144; Jean Baptiste (b. 1849, d. 1912), 298; Jean Baptiste (b. 1882, d. 1968), 298; Marguerite (b. 1819), 164;

Michel (b. 1852, d. 1939), 200; Philomene (b. 1892, d. 1957), 200; Reine (b. 1847, d. 1918), 141, 143; William Sr. (b. 1824,), 130, 142, 146

Dawell: Alexander, 286

Day After Day: Margaret (b. 1874, d. 1932), 164

Daze: Josephte, 216, 217

Dease: Helene (b. 1841,), 97; Isabelle (b. 1852,), 203, 214; Margaret (b. 1818, d. 1903), 126, 158; Marguerite (b. 1853,), 68; Mary Anne (b. 1820, d. 1861), 78; Nancy (b. 1825,), 101

Debray: Gilbert William (b. 1926, d. 1997), 19; William Mark (b. 1881, obi. 1964), 19

Decoine: Pelagie (b. 1858,), 277; Pierre Francois (b. 1805, d. 1867), 248; Theodore (b. 1845, d. 1870), 244, 248

Decoteau: Rosalie (b. 1871), 306; William F. (b. 1930, d. 1998), 232

Decouteau: Alexander (b. 1874,), 300, 302; Alexander (b. 1903, d. 1996), 300; Daniel (b. 1872, d. 1961), 175; Eliza (b. 1898, d. 1968), 294, 302; Elzear (b. 1861, d. 1939), 149; Francois (b. 1855), 298; Francois (b. 1893, d. 1972), 146, 149; James (b. 1868, d. 1937), 293, 298; John Baptiste (b. 1893, d. 1965), 162, 175; Joseph (b. 1895), 299; Joseph Ducharme dit (b. 1829,), 306; Louis (b. 1840, d. 1907), 150; Louis Sr. (b. 1817,), 125, 145; Madeleine (b. 1889, d. 1966), 67, 68; Napoleon (b. 1899, d. 1922), 146, 149; Norbert (b. 1850, d. 1928), 68, 149, 299; Patrice (b. 1910, d. 1988), 300; St.Ann (b. 1894, d. 1983), 27; Wilfred (b. 1905, d. 1970), 300; William (b. 1884, d. 1957), 150

DeFlyer: George (b. 1878, d. 1953), 49, 55; John, 55

Delaronde: Francoise (b. 1840,), 37, 39; Henri (b. 1866,), 39

Delaunay: Isabelle (b. 1873, d. 1954), 149, 232; Marie Rosine (b. 1873, d. 1960), 117, 125, 129, 301

Delauney: Francois dit Daunais (b. 1848, d. 1880), 126, 129; Francois dit Delonais (b. 1876, d. 1937), 301; Francois Lionais dit or Delaunay (b. 1780, d. 1859), 67; Jean Baptiste or Donais or Doney (b. 1885, d. 1961), 116; John Marie dit Doney (b. 1858, obi. 1939), 133; Joseph (b. 1821, d. 1872), 126

Delonais: Eugene Norbert (b. 1911, d. 1946), 301

Delorme: Adele (b. 1861,), 203, 211; Alexis (b. 1829, d. 1888), 321; Angelique (b. 1845, d. 1889), 93, 94; Bernard (b. 1855, d. 1935), 144, 147; Betsy (b. 1893, d. 1988), 118; Boniface (b. 1845, d. 1925), 267; Catherine (b. 1825, d. 1895), 82, 96, 166, 189; Catherine Eneau dit (bt. 1825, d. 1890), 202; Charles Roger (b. 1865,), 93; Elise (b. 1849,), 160; Elise (b. 1850,), 89, 262, 320; Elise (b. 1888, d. 1922), 149; Eliza (b. 1856,), 151, 153; Elizabeth (b. 1891, d. 1972), 309; Francois (b. 1805, d. 1882), 67, 150; Francois (b. 1833, d. 1900), 93, 95; Francois (bt. 1767, d. 1847), 242; Helene (b. 1830, d. 1913), 95, 317, 322; Isabelle (b. 1834, d. 1876), 251; Isabelle

1832, d. 1886), 256; Marie (b. 1842,), 317, 318; Marie Adele (b. 1892,), 159; Marie Sara (b. 1871,), 145, 148; Pascal (b. 1820,), 267; Peter, 72; Philippe Martin (b. 1889,), 213; Pierre (b. 1839,), 101; Roger (b. 1859, d. 1943), 159; Sophie (b. 1862,), 157, 166, 187, 189; William (b. 1863, d. 1929), 95, 101

Park: Mary (, d. 1823), 268

Parker: Emma, 309; George Henry, 303; Thomas Exley, 135, 138

Parr: Ethel, 56

Partner: Frederick (, d. 1972), 87

Patenaude: Charles (b. 1838,), 13, 17, 171, 323; Eliza (b. 1864,), 20, 323; Felicite (b. 1830, d. 1885), 25, 247; Isabelle (b. 1840, d. 1875), 172, 291, 292; Josephte (b. 1812,), 238; Marie (b. 1866, d. 1931), 115; Marie Anne (bt. 1885,), 171; Mary Agnes (b. 1911), 117; Michel (b. 1773,), 8; Michel (b. 1781, d. 1863), 17; Michel (b. 1808, d. 1872), 8, 292; Rose, 320; Samson (b. 1870, d. 1947), 117

Paterson: (--?--), 8

Patrice: Francois, 36; Marguerite (b. 1830, d. 1914), 36

Paul: Bernard (b. 1848,), 108, 112; Elzear (b. 1857, d. 1941), 306; Francoise, 202; Jean Baptiste (b. 1788, d. 1877), 93, 112; Joseph (b. 1888, d. 1952), 309; Josephine (b. 1881,), 81; Josephte, 219; Josephte (b. 1831, d. 1928), 93, 198; Louise (b. 1857,), 231; Marguerite (b. 1798, d. 1868), 259; Marie Alice (b. 1885,), 64; Mary Agnes (b. 1917, d. 1997), 309; Michel dit Bonneau (b. 1840, d. 1914), 23; Nancy (b. 1829,), 320; Olivier (b. 1822, d. 1909), 319; Paul (b. 1842, d. 1931), 317, 319; Pierre (b. 1833,), 81; Rosa (b. 1887), 287; Virginie (b. 1878, d. 1952), 306; William (b. 1849, d. 1892), 64

Payette: Hermenegilde (b. 1853, d. 1920), 179, 181; Jean Baptiste, 159, 181; Martial (b. 1850, d. 1915), 159

Payne: Kathleen Maggie, 312

Pearson: Ina, 131

Pecheeto: Anonyme (b. 1872,), 38

Peebles: James (b. 1778, d. 1840), 73, 233; Margaret (bt. 1844, d. 1939), 60, 284; Robert (bt. 1836,), 71, 73; Thomas (b. 1838,), 28; William, 28; William (b. 1812, d. 1883), 232, 233

Pelland: Joseph, 203

Pelletier: Adolphe (b. 1868,), 145, 148; Alexandre (b. 1860,), 307; Alfred (b. 1887, d. 1950), 17, 20; Anna Emilia (b. 1882,), 298; Antoine (b. 1824, d. 1874), 127; Charles (b. 1796, d. 1853), 16, 81; Charlotte (b. 1833, d. 1922), 69, 147; Cuthbert (b. 1846,), 13, 16; Cuthbert (b. 1864,), 22, 25; Felicite (b. 1852,), 13, 16; Genevieve (b. 1820, d. 1907), 111; Helen "Ellen" (b. 1889, d. 1961), 149; Jean Baptiste (b. 1825, d. 1878), 25, 148; Jean Baptiste (b. 1846,), 298; Jean Baptiste (b. 1856,), 127; Joseph (b. 1825, d. 1913), 16, 307; Joseph (b. 1880, d. 1957), 299; Julie (b. 1855, d. 1941), 298; Marguerite (b. 1795,), 13;

Marguerite (b. 1845, d. 1925), 127, 299, 300, 305, 308; Marguerite (b. 1851,), 19; Marguerite (b. 1862, d. 1939), 174; Marie, 267; Marie (b. 1815, d. 1873), 171; Marie Emilie (b. 1882, d. 1969), 301; Marie Madeleine (b. 1845), 260; Mary Georgianna (b. 1895), 295; Nancy (b. 1875,), 300; Paul (bt. 1844, d. 1925), 20; Pierre (b. 1824, d. 1882), 260; Pierre (b. 1829, d. 1855), 80, 81; Therese (b. 1833, d. 1915), 19, 24, 114

Pelter: Ema, 166, 189

Peltier: Adele (b. 1888), 129, 133; Delia Josie (b. 1919), 299; Eliza (b. 1904, d. 1968), 299; Julius (b. 1926), 299

People: (--?--); Indian woman, 177; Native Woman, 192; Adjourne; Clemence, 241; Amiot; Augustin dit Villeneuve (24 Jul 1734-6 May 1794), 225; Augustin dit Villeneuve (25 May 1764-), 225; Assiniboine; Marie Anne (circa 1784-19 Mar 1874), 241; Aubert; Marie-Anne (circa 1671-29 Aug 1712), 154, 178, 185; Auger; Louis-Joseph (17 Nov 1694-), 177; Marie-Angelique (24 Jan 1726-22 Mar 1764), 177; Bardin; Marie, 238; Beauchamp; Francoise (20 Mar 1669-), 194; Jacques (8 Jul 1635-), 194; Beaudin; Marie Madeleine dit Desjardins, 178; Beaugrand; Antoine dit Champagne (6 Jun 1700-1 Feb 1781), 154, 185; Marie Antoinette dit Champagne (circa 1727-24 Nov 1755), 154, 185; Beaujean; Elie, 194; Marguerite (-15 Feb 1680), 194; Bedard; Catherine (26 Oct 1682-4 Mar 1726), 92; Bertrand; Marie Josephe dit St.Arnau, 238; Paul, 238; Berube; Marie Madeleine (15 Oct 1746-20 Nov 1834), 60; Bire; Marguerite (1616-27 Mar 1675-13 Nov 1675), 241; Blackfoot; Marie, 79; Boisdon; Jean, 238; Marie (between 1615 and 1617-28 Dec 1687), 238; Bombardier; Andre, 192; Marie Anne dit Labombarde (26 Feb 1739-18 Jan 1812), 192; Boucher; Louise (-1870), 177; Marie (11 Apr 1644-15 Jul 1730), 238; Bourquin; Ignace, 215; Louis dit Versailles (20 Oct 1743-), 215; Louis dit Versailles (3 Oct 1717-), 215; Brazeau; Etienne (14 Feb 1708-), 225; Marguerite (3 Apr 1742-18 Dec 1824), 225; Breland; Madeleine (circa 1800-), 225; Brunet; Louis dit Bourbonnais, 105; Marie-Josephe dit Bourbonnais (11 Dec 1721-17 Jun 1782), 105; Capel; Francoise (between 1626 and 1628-19 Apr 1699), 124; Julien, 124; Caplette; Joseph (1777-11 Feb 1862), 124; Madeleine (1818-21 Nov 1906), 124; Caron; Elisabeth, 61; Marie-Genevieve, 61; Charbonneau; Adelaide (26 Sep 1834-), 177; Jean Baptiste (15 Dec 1792-21 May 1882), 177; Marie-Madeleine (circa 1685-17 Jul 1731), 215; Charette; Jean Baptiste (9 Jan 1775-), 194; Marie Ann (circa Jul 1804-14 Aug 1886), 194; Charland; Catherine, 93; Chaume; Marie, 215; Chevalier; Josephe-Marguerite (18 Mar 1723-), 124; Chevaudier; Jacques dit Lepine (25 May 1704-), 194; Marie-Angelique dit Lepine (31 Dec

1729-), 194; Clement; Jean dit Lapointe (circa 1626-), 238; Marie (29 May 1662-11 Nov 1723), 238; Cloutier; Genevieve (19 May 1719-17 Sep 1770), 61; Jean-Baptitse (5 Feb 1681-5 Sep 1756), 61; Coignon; Suzanne, 194; Colin; Marie Angelique dit Laliberte (-5 May 1813), 258, 259; Contre; Francois dit Sansoucy (circa 1731-14 Dec 1796), 317; Marie Reine dit Sansoucy (26 Feb 1762-14 May 1804), 317; Corbeau; Nan-touche, 185; Couillaud; Francois dit Larocque or Larocquebrune (13 Oct 1731-30 Jun 1810), 79; Marie Charles dit Larocque or Rocbrune (8 Jan 1763-), 79; Cousineau; Jean Noel (22 Apr 1748-25 Apr 1824), 238; Suzanne (14 Jul 1777-), 238; Coutu; Marie Josephe (31 Dec 1706-), 154, 185; Crebassa; John, 192; Marie Anne (Jul 1807-7 Mar 1885), 192; Crise; Marie (circa 1791-3 Jul 1841), 258; Dardenne; Marie (between 1627 and 1639-7 Aug 1699), 194; Daunay; Marie-Gertrude (12 May 1670-25 May 1758), 194; Dauphin; Marie-Catherine (25 Jun 1699-30 May 1769), 241; Rene (14 Oct 1666-), 241; Desautels; Louise Marie Therese dit Lapointe, 154, 185; Deschamps; Marthe, 192; Desrosiers; Anne (12 Nov 1661-23 Feb 1731), 124; Antoine (between 1619 and 1620-8 Aug 1691), 124; Devoyaux; Marie Amable dit Laframboise (-9 Apr 1810), 225; Dubeau; Jacques (1 Apr 1681-3 Nov 1723), 92; Marie-Jeanne (10 Jan 1716-), 92; Dubey; Susanne (Metisse) (circa 1790-), 124; Dubois; Marie Therese (17 Oct 1737-5 Sep 1808), 92; Dubord; Julien or Guillian dit Lafontaine (between 1625 and 1641-), 124; Marie-Madeleine dit Fontaine (22 Mar 1692-), 124; Duclos; Marguerite (10 Oct 1679-), 124; Ducros; Marie-Louise (30 May 1730-7 Jul 1797), 124; Duteau; Jacques (circa 1674-), 124; Marie-Madeleine (30 Nov 1720-1 Sep 1795), 124; Ethier; Marie Anne (3 Mar 1707-), 238; Filteau; Marie Angelique, 194; Forcier; Louise, 316; Fortin; Julien, 61; Marie Marthe (2 Jan 1739-2 Nov 1820), 61; Fournel; Jacques, 177; Marie-Josephte, 177; Fournier; Jacquette (9 Apr 1659-), 61; Galarneau; Charles (26 May 1668-), 105; Jeanne, 105; Garigou; Louise or Gariou (13 Aug 1721-7 May 1773), 215; Martial or Gariou (circa 1680-), 215; Gauthier; Dorothee (26 Feb 1706-18 Aug 1772), 92; Jean-Baptiste, 241; Marie Josephe (circa 1726-), 241; Renee, 61; Gelinas; Jean-Baptiste dit Lacourse (22 Nov 1719-14 May 1781), 194; Marie Marguerite dit Lacourse (30 Oct 1758-27 Jan 1814), 194; Gerbert; Marie-Anne (circa 1687-), 61; Gignard; Suzanne (28 Feb 1667-), 241; Gilbert; Marie Josephe dit Guebert, 241; Girard; Marie-Madeleine, 105; Gladu; Charlotte (circa 1800-), 92; Godin; Charles or Gaudin (between 1629 and 1636-1 Dec 1706-18 Jan 1712), 238; Genevieve (22 Oct 1695-

270, 272; James (b. 1820, d. 1847), 281; James or Sandison (b. 1758, d. 1820), 272; Jane Margaret (b. 1810,   ), 311; Mary Ann, 309; Mary Jane (bt. 1848), 276, 285; Owen S. (b. 1894,   ), 282; Sally Sarah (bt. 1824, d. 1895), 221; Sarah (b. 1825,   ), 271, 275

Sandison: George (b. 1800,   ), 275

Sandovove: Angelique (, d. 1870), 91

Sansregret: Charles, 184; Charlotte (b. 1785,   ), 194; Hilaire (b. 1863,   ), 109, 114; Leocadie (bt. 1850, d. 1888), 302; Louis Pontbriand dit (b. 1820, d. 1884), 16; Marguerite (b. 1853,   ), 231; Marguerite Pontbriand dit (b. 1784,   ), 93; Marie (b. 1883,   ), 223; Mathias (b. 1852, d. 1918), 16, 223; Pierre dit Beaubrillant (b. 1840,   ), 24, 114; Pierre Pontbriand (b. 1867, d. 1932), 21, 24

Sarcie: Marguerite (b. 1787, d. 1868), 217

Saulteaux: Louise, 105, 243; Louise Kee-na-we-pinai-si, 111; Madeleine, 242; Marguerite Maskegone or, 260; Marguerite Okkanens (b. 1790,   ), 141, 219, 243; Marie, 245; Marie Suzette, 36; Mary (b. 1789, d. 1854), 121; Michel, 270, 272; Suzanne, 192

Saulteuse: Josephte (b. 1790,   ), 146

Saulteux: Marguerite (b. 1794), 13, 318

Saunders: Margaret J. (b. 1854,   ), 314, 315; Palm (b. 1822,   ), 315; William or Sanderson (b. 1832,   ), 73

Sauteaux Indian Woman: Mary (, d. 1838), 4

Sauteuse: Angelique (, d. 1877), 242, 245, 246; Angelique (b. 1780), 142, 154, 155; Betsy (b. 1783, d. 1863), 216, 242, 265; Josephte, 218, 219; Josephte "Cheoueninen" (, d. 1827), 12; Louise (b. 1791,   ), 67; Magdeleine, 264; Marguerite (b. 1776, d. 1866), 155; Marguerite (b. 1780, d. 1851), 303; Marguerite (b. 1801,   ), 140; Marguerite (b. 1810, d. 1867), 256, 318; Marie (b. 1790,   ), 36, 105; Marie (b. 1822,   ), 247; Marie (bt. 1832), 195, 205, 219

Sauteux: Marguerite (, d. 1875), 217, 222

Sauve: Alfred Augustin "Leo" (b. 1911), 170; Baptiste (b. 1858,   ), 287; Charlotte (b. 1808, d. 1888), 256, 260; Francois (b. 1864,   ), 21, 25; Helene (b. 1842, d. 1882), 11, 223; Jean Baptiste (b. 1767,   ), 260; Joseph (b. 1848,   ), 160, 169, 170, 177, 191; Joseph Alfred (b. 1882,   ), 159, 169, 170; Madeleine (b. 1860,   ), 114, 118; Marguerite (b. 1880,   ), 277, 287; Marie Elizabeth (b. 1879, d. 1928), 206; Marie Mathilde (b. 1894,   ), 160; Norbert (b. 1823,   ), 25; William (b. 1879, d. 1915), 160, 166, 170, 171, 177, 189, 191; William (b. 1913), 170

Savage: Etienne Felix Adolphe-Henri, 96, 102

Savard: Marie (b. 1828, d. 1869), 255

Savoie: Olive, 168

Sayer: Edouard (b. 1823, d. 1870), 112; George (b. 1806, d. 1882), 180, 259; Isabelle (b. 1853, d. 1874), 178, 180, 259; Marguerite (b. 1837,   ), 201, 202; Marie Marguerite (b. 1850, d. 1877), 20;

Pierre Guillaume (b. 1803,   ), 202; Rose (b. 1858,   ), 112

Sayis: Angelique (b. 1821, d. 1909), 283; Charles or Saice (b. 1839,   ), 219, 222; Elise (b. 1856, d. 1932), 212; Francois "Frank" or Saice (b. 1871, d. 1933), 225; Francois (b. 1821, d. 1879), 216, 217; Francois or Sahys (b. 1779, d. 1860), 217, 222; Francoise (b. 1848, d. 1881), 217; Gabriel or Saice (b. 1866,   ), 225; Joseph or Saice (b. 1821, d. 1912), 222

Scarbrough: Charlotte, 79

Schafer: Anton (b. 1862,   ), 23, 25, 26; George, 25

Schmidt: Alfred 'Rabasca' (b. 1825, d. 1901), 16, 244, 248, 323; Caroline (b. 1849,   ), 13, 16; Joseph (b. 1872,   ), 202, 208; Louis (b. 1864,   ), 318, 323; Louis dit Laferte (b. 1844, d. 1935), 208; Peter, 248

Schneider: Hannah, 70

Scott: Alice Henrietta Helen (b. 1869, d. 1941), 234, 236; James, 309; Jane (b. 1843, d. 1877), 2; William (b. 1815, d. 1894), 236

Scullen: William or Scollen (b. 1854, d. 1901), 256, 257

Seamans: Rose (b. 1873,   ), 308

Seely: Emma, 132

Seeweeassoo: Louis, 257

Serpent: Louise, 260

Serpente: Francoise (b. 1790, d. 1852), 254

Settee: James (Cree) (b. 1816, d. 1902), 5, 6, 86; James Jr. (bt. 1836,   ), 84, 86; Lydia Ann (b. 1856, d. 1935), 4, 6; Mary Ann (bt. 1842,   ), 4, 5, 6

Setter: Alexander 'Big Alex' (b. 1857, d. 1924), 1, 3; Alexander Hunter Murray (b. 1863, d. 1933), 47, 52; Ann (bt. 1824, d. 1914), 236; Duncan Richard (b. 1852, d. 1880), 5, 7; Elizabeth (b. 1822, d. 1891), 315; George (b. 1815, d. 1899), 7, 52; Isabella, 50; James (b. 1810,   ), 3; Sarah (bt. 1840,   ), 35

Severight: Colin, 39; Delbert, 39

Shanks: Guy Otis, 129, 134

Sharp: Justus (b. 1900, d. 1970), 128; William, 128

Sharpe: Judith Myrtle (b. 1929, d. 1997), 90

Shaw: Charlotte dit Ankenam or Akinam) (b. 1878), 46, 51; Felix dit Ankenam or Akinam, 51

Shibley: Alfred Myron Sr. (b. 1909, d. 1974), 148; Clarence Bertrom (b. 1886,   ), 148

Shikak: John (, d. 1884), 255

Ship: Charlotte, 52

Shirtliff: Frederic (b. 1866,   ), 261; George, 261; George (, d. 1893), 261

Short: Daniel (b. 1862, d. 1908), 117; Genevieve (b. 1808, d. 1883), 216, 263, 265, 266; Isabelle (b. 1804,   ), 14, 242, 259; James (b. 1767, d. 1840), 216, 242, 265; James (b. 1834, d. 1909), 54; Marie Marguerite (b. 1877,   ), 49, 54; Mathilde (b. 1865, d. 1940), 116; Michael (b. 1907, d. 1974), 117; Sarah (b. 1795,   ), 146, 147, 318, 319

Simpson: Frances Ramsey (b. 1812, d. 1853), 40; Geddes Mackenzie, 40; George, 40; George (b. 1786, d. 1860), 39, 40; John (b. 1833,   ), 289; Joseph M. (b. 1896, d. 1937), 289; Marie

Clemence (b. 1872,   ), 289; Marie Eliza (b. 1883, d. 1918), 289; Marjorie Florence, 94, 100, 103; Thomas, 8

Sinclair: Alexander (b. 1873, d. 1914), 231; Anne (b. 1796, d. 1861), 122; Bakie (b. 1802, d. 1887), 253; Benjamin (, d. 1885), 84; Catherine, 74; Catherine (b. 1801, d. 1851), 29; Donald, 72; Eliza, 283; Elizabeth "Betsy" (b. 1802, d. 1878), 40; Elizabeth Jane (b. 1874, d. 1940), 44; Francis "Fanny" (b. 1818, d. 1879), 7; Frederick (b. 1864,   ), 74; Harriet (b. 1861), 269; Howard Allen (b. 1924, d. 1984), 119; James (b. 1829, d. 1867), 36, 106, 107; James (b. 1848,   ), 252, 253; Jeremiah (b. 1876, d. 1952), 119; John Davis (b. 1908), 18; Margaret (b. 1900), 74; Marie (, d. 1889), 74; Mary, 180; Mary (b. 1805, d. 1892), 1, 34, 35, 86; Nancy (b. 1825, d. 1874), 77; Phoebe (b. 1792, d. 1848), 76; Samuel (b. 1849,   ), 178, 181; Thomas (b. 1809, d. 1870), 123; Thomas (b. 1841, d. 1888), 121, 123; Thomas (Metis) (b. 1841,   ), 272, 279; Toussaint Samuel (b. 1869, d. 1936), 18; William, 72; William (b. 1766, d. 1818), 40; William (b. 1791, d. 1862), 36, 107, 181; William (b. 1836,   ), 72; William (b. 1838,   ), 252, 253; William (b. 1850, d. 1875), 84; William dit McLeod (b. 1857,   ), 71, 72

Sioux: Marie (b. 1846,   ), 142, 146

Skaro: Harvey Martin (b. 1923, d. 1963), 176

Skarra: Anna (Skierra) (b. 1890, d. 1970), 166, 177, 188, 191; Jacob (Skierra), 177, 191

Slater: Albina (b. 1928), 302; Bibiane Eulalie (b. 1883), 111, 117, 130, 301; Catherine (b. 1854,   ), 58, 59; Charlotte (b. 1805,   ), 58; Elizabeth (b. 1836, d. 1917), 232, 233, 236; Elizabeth (b. 1846,   ), 62, 63; Emma Laura (b. 1910, d. 1996), 129, 134; Isabella (b. 1813,   ), 7; James (b. 1773, d. 1856), 47; James (b. 1811, d. 1875), 63, 320; James (b. 1847,   ), 117, 311, 317, 320; Jean Baptiste (b. 1881, d. 1963), 117, 134; Jeremie, 180; John (b. 1801, d. 1873), 233; John (b. 1906, d. 1965), 302; Marguerite, 180; Sophie (b. 1843,   ), 62, 63; Thomas James (b. 1857, d. 1948), 315, 316; Thomas James (bt. 1830, d. 1894), 45, 47, 316; William (b. 1820,   ), 59, 311

Smith: Alexander (b. 1861,   ), 29; Alexandre (b. 1864,   ), 9, 95; Angus (b. 1836, d. 1916), 29; Catherine Janet (b. 1865,   ), 239; Gordon Obadiah, 130, 134; Harriet (b. 1825, d. 1903), 121; Harriet Jane (b. 1877,   ), 42, 44; Israel (bt. 1861, d. 1924), 67, 69; Jacob (bt. 1851, d. 1883), 44; James Augustin, 6; John (b. 1821), 40, 41, 239; John James (b. 1791, d. 1850), 41, 72, 121; Joseph (b. 1833, d. 1895), 69, 147; Joseph (b. 1857, d. 1918), 147; Joseph (b. 1860, d. 1906), 240; Joseph (b. 1883, d. 1945), 240; Judith (b. 1857, d. 1945), 175; Leah Catherine (b. 1954), 103; Lena (, d. 1965), 208; Lillian, 57; Marguerite (b. 1839, d. 1900), 162; Marie Rosalie (b. 1887,   ), 9, 95; Miss

Swan: Adolph (b. 1905), 19; Albert (b. 1911), 19; Alexander (b. 1871, d. 1876), 22; Alfred P. (b. 1891), 19; Aloysius (b. 1921), 19; Anonyme (b. 1876, d. 1876), 16; Antoine Jordy (b. 1841,   ), 20; Arthur (b. 1921, d. 1995), 26; Caroline (b. 1884,   ), 25; Cecilia (b. 1897), 24; Charles (b. 1866, d. 1908), 22; Charles (b. 1885), 25; Daniel J. (b. 1900, d. 1943), 24; Domitilde (b. 1873,   ), 25; Earl Norman (b. 1925, d. 2007), 19; Edward (b. 1913), 19; Elisabeth (b. 1916), 19; Elizabeth (b. 1886,   ), 24; Florence (b. 1913), 26; Florestine (b. 1874, d. 1875), 16; Frances Charles (b. 1917, d. 1932), 26; Frank (b. 1909), 19; Gabriel (b. 1918), 19; James (b. 1925), 26; John (b. 1883,   ), 23; John (b. 1895), 19; John (b. 1924), 19; John Thomas (b. 1875,   ), 16; Joseph (b. 1860, d. 1924), 21; Joseph (b. 1878, d. 1884), 16; Josephine (b. 1879,   ), 16; Josephine (b. 1918, d. 1994), 26; Justine (b. 1883,   ), 16; Lucille Ursula (b. 1902), 24; Lucy (b. 1901), 18; Madeleine (b. 1874, d. 1944), 23; Margaret (b. 1922), 26; Marguerite (b. 1879, d. 1920), 19, 23; Marguerite (b. 1881,   ), 25; Marie (b. 1871, d. 1893), 16; Marie (b. 1875,   ), 16; Marie Julia (b. 1878, d. 1878), 23; Mary (b. 1898), 19; Mary Rose (b. 1888, d. 1944), 18, 289; Mary Sophie (b. 1894, d. 1976), 24, 309; Octavie (b. 1878, d. 1972), 23; Patrick (b. 1880,   ), 16; Patrick Joseph (b. 1882, d. 1968), 23; Pauline (b. 1872,   ), 16; Pierre (b. 1882,   ), 15; Rainie (b. 1895), 18; Romuald (b. 1854, d. 1855), 21; Rosa (b. 1899), 19; Rosalie (b. 1860, d. 1861), 15; Rose Mary (b. 1920, d. 1997), 26; Rosemary (b. 1920), 19; Sam (b. 1896), 24; Simeon (b. 1870,   ), 23; Thomas (b. 1904, d. 1975), 18; Victoria (b. 1891), 18; Virginia (b. 1890), 309; Virginie (b. 1875, d. 1884), 16; William (b. 1873,   ), 23

Tafolla: Jose Onofre (b. 1850, d. 1938), 310; Martin James (b. 1904, d. 1981), 310

Tait: Adelaide (b. 1872, d. 1901), 34; Albert or Tate (b. 1860,   ), 28, 30; Alexander (b. 1870,   ), 30; Alexander David (b. 1871,   ), 32; Alexander Thomas (b. 1867,   ), 33, 46; Alexander Thomas (bt. 1860,   ), 33; Andrew or Tate (bt. 1839,   ), 28, 30; Ann (b. 1851,   ), 28; Ann (b. 1852, d. 1925), 33, 35; Ann (b. 1856,   ), 33; Ann (bt. 1835,   ), 31, 32, 78; Anne (b. 1879,   ), 35; Annie (b. 1872, d. 1880), 30; Annie (b. 1890,   ), 35; Arabella Dunlop (b. 1892,   ), 34; Arthur (b. 1888,   ), 34; Aurora (b. 1888,   ), 35; Caroline Mary (b. 1882,   ), 34; Catherine (b. 1863,   ), 30; Cecil (b. 1897,   ), 35; Charles (b. 1841,   ), 32, 35; Charles (b. 1861, d. 1874), 30; Christie (b. 1897), 35; Clementine (b. 1879, d. 1879), 30; Colin (b. 1862, d. 1871), 34; Colin Charles (b. 1879, d. 1898), 34; Cyrille (b. 1895,   ), 35; David (b. 1837, d. 1873), 28, 30; David James (b. 1862, d. 1922), 33; David James McKenzie (b. 1868, d. 1871), 30; Edith (b. 1885,   ),

35; Eliza Margaret (b. 1867,   ), 32; Elizabeth (b. 1832,   ), 31, 32, 49, 122, 235; Elizabeth (b. 1846,   ), 28; Elizabeth (b. 1847, d. 1875), 33; Elizabeth Harriet (b. 1869,   ), 30; Ellen Harriet (b. 1865, d. 1920), 34, 36; Eugene (b. 1876, d. 1919), 30, 31; Florence Catherine (b. 1890,   ), 34, 36; Frances Jane (b. 1859,   ), 32; Frank (b. 1890,   ), 35; Fred (b. 1895,   ), 35; George (b. 1839,   ), 32, 34; George (b. 1869,   ), 33; Gwendoline (b. 1905), 35; Helen Jane (b. 1861, d. 1916), 33; Henry (b. 1874,   ), 33; Henry George (b. 1869, d. 1871), 30; Irene Maude Gertrude (b. 1893,   ), 35; Isabella (b. 1866, d. 1892), 34; James (b. 1758, d. 1834), 27; James (b. 1810,   ), 27; James (b. 1827, d. 1899), 32, 33; James (bt. 1834,   ), 31; James Charles (b. 1864,   ), 34; James or Tate (bt. 1831,   ), 28, 29; Jane (bt. 1845,   ), 32; Jane Mary (b. 1843,   ), 271, 278; Jemima Ellen (b. 1871,   ), 34; Johanah Eveline "Josie" (b. 1882,   ), 35; John (b. 1801,   ), 31; John (b. 1838,   ), 31; John (b. 1892,   ), 35; John (bt. 1832, d. 1916), 32, 34; John Gunn (b. 1860, d. 1907), 33; John McCallum (b. 1852, d. 1911), 33, 35; John or Tate (b. 1829, d. 1907), 28, 29; Joseph (b. 1856,   ), 33; Joseph (bt. 1830, d. 1893), 31, 32, 235; Joseph (bt. 1834,   ), 32; Mabel (b. 1883,   ), 35; Magnus (b. 1835,   ), 28; Margaret (b. 1824, d. 1901), 32, 33; Margaret (b. 1859, d. 1933), 33, 35; Margaret (bt. 1871, d. 1872), 34; Margaret Sarah (b. 1884,   ), 34; Maria (b. 1865,   ), 30, 31; Marie (b. 1820, d. 1905), 12, 27, 28, 240; Martha (b. 1865), 35; Mary (b. 1843,   ), 32; Mary (b. 1857, d. 1926), 32, 233, 235; Mary (b. 1867, d. 1873), 34; Mary (bt. 1840,   ), 31; Mary (bt. 1842,   ), 28; Mary (bt. 1858,   ), 29; Mary Agnes (b. 1880, d. 1880), 30; Mary Anabella (b. 1869,   ), 34; Mary Ann (b. 1855, d. 1901), 33; Mary Laura Evangaline (b. 1889,   ), 35; Matilda or Tate (b. 1829, d. 1861), 28, 29; Philip or Tate (b. 1827,   ), 28; Robert (b. 1830, d. 1912), 32, 34; Robert (b. 1863,   ), 32; Robert William "Bert" (b. 1899), 35; Robert William (b. 1857, d. 1922), 33, 35; Rubina (b. 1903,   ), 35; Sarah (b. 1851, d. 1931), 33, 35; Thomas Herbert (b. 1859, d. 1894), 34; Thomas William (b. 1867,   ), 30; Timoleon John (b. 1861,   ), 34; William (b. 1792, d. 1878), 27, 278; William (b. 1795,   ), 32; William (b. 1862,   ), 33; William (b. 1869,   ), 32; William Auld Sr. (b. 1826, d. 1900), 32, 33, 46; William Jr. (b. 1854,   ), 33; William McMurray (b. 1877,   ), 34

Tall: Joseph, 36

Tanner: Alexis (b. 1843,   ), 37, 38; Amelia (b. 1880, d. 1880), 38; Amelia Harriet (bt. 1867,   ), 38; Angelique (b. 1847,   ), 22, 37, 38; Anne (bt. 1857,   ), 37, 39; Anonyme, 36, 37; Basile (b. 1875,   ), 37; Basile Pitchito, 37; Bella (b. 1879,   ), 38, 39; Christina Ermit (b. 1887,   ), 274; Edward (b. 1832,   ), 36, 37;

Edward (b. 1862,   ), 37; Eliah, 36, 37; Emelie (b. 1876, d. 1881), 38; Henry Charles (bt. 1866,   ), 38; Isabella (bt. 1868,   ), 38; James (b. 1845, d. 1934), 274; James (Rev.) (b. 1805, d. 1870), 36, 107; John, 36, 37; John (b. 1837,   ), 36, 106, 107; John Baptiste (b. 1853,   ), 37, 38; John Falcon 'Shawshawwabanase' (b. 1781, d. 1846), 36; John II (b. 1851,   ), 37; John J., 36; Joseph (b. 1822), 37, 304; Joseph (b. 1841,   ), 37, 39; Joseph (b. 1869,   ), 38; Joseph (b. 1876,   ), 38; Joseph (b. 1877, d. 1877), 39; Julie (b. 1849,   ), 37, 39, 303, 304; Louise (b. 1832, d. 1895), 24, 37; Louise (b. 1874,   ), 38, 39; Lucy, 36; Marie (b. 1840,   ), 37, 39; Marie (b. 1854, d. 1924), 37, 38; Marie (b. 1875), 38; Marie Joseph Jeanne (b. 1862), 39; Marie Rose (b. 1845,   ), 37; Marie Rose (b. 1872,   ), 39; Martha Ann (b. 1830,   ), 36; Mary (b. 1809, d. 1820), 36; Mary Elizabeth (, d. 1883), 36; Patrick (b. 1865,   ), 38; Sadie, 37; Suzanne, 37; Therese (b. 1860,   ), 111; Thomas DeCorby dit Petitcho (, d. 1872), 36, 37; Thomas John, 111; Thomas John (b. 1842, d. 1936), 37; unnamed, 36

Tastawitch: Pelagie (b. 1853,   ), 92

Tate: Alexander (b. 1901), 31; Alfred H. (b. 1867,   ), 29; Alma Lena Roberta (b. 1901, d. 1923), 31; Andrew Tomlison (b. 1905, d. 1905), 31; Ann (b. 1867,   ), 30; Anne (b. 1885, d. 1885), 30; Anne Louisa (b. 1872, d. 1939), 29; Antoine (b. 1860,   ), 30; Barbara, 86; Benjamin (b. 1905), 31; Bertha May, 31; Caroline (b. 1858), 29; Caroline (b. 1874,   ), 30; Caroline (b. 1881, d. 1882), 30; Catherine (bt. 1859,   ), 30; Charles (b. 1841,   ), 28; Charles Richard (b. 1864, d. 1870), 28; Charlotte (b. 1856, d. 1875), 28; Christopher (b. 1874,   ), 29; Clara Emma (b. 1881,   ), 30; Colin (b. 1865,   ), 29; Colin Henry Fraser (b. 1897, d. 1933), 31; David (bt. 1837, d. 1873), 32; Elise Jane (b. 1884, d. 1885), 29; Eliza (b. 1858, d. 1877), 28; Eliza MacDonald (b. 1896,   ), 31; Ethel (b. 1903), 31; Eva Marie (b. 1910), 31; Frances Jessie Winnifred (b. 1884,   ), 35; Francis Phillip Hardisty (b. 1892,   ), 30; Fred (b. 1903), 31; Frederick (bt. 1841,   ), 28; George (b. 1876,   ), 29; George (bt. 1833,   ), 28; George Kenneth Maxwell (b. 1891,   ), 30; Gilbert (b. 1869,   ), 30; Harriet (bt. 1857, d. 1870), 29; Henry (b. 1880, d. 1885), 29; James (b. 1865,   ), 30; Jane (b. 1795,   ), 27; Jane (bt. 1830,   ), 31; Jane Mary (b. 1843,   ), 28; Jane Mary (b. 1854, d. 1870), 28; John (b. 1872,   ), 30; John (bt. 1827,   ), 31; Joseph (bt. 1837,   ), 28; Joseph William (b. 1861,   ), 30; Leslie James (b. 1913, d.   ), 31; Lilly Violet (b. 1904, d. 1923), 31; Louise Anne (b. 1894,   ), 30; Margaret (b. 1816,   ), 27; Margaret (b. 1869,   ), 29; Margaret (bt. 1863, d.   ), 30; Mary Ellen (b. 1914), 31; Mary Jane (bt. 1863, d. 1864), 29; Mary Matilda (b. 1864, d. 1875), 30; Nellie Elizabeth (b. 1907, d.

1923), 31; Olive Irene (b. 1909), 31; Peter (bt. 1835, d. 1843), 28; Philip (b. 1860,   ), 29; Phoebe (b. 1877,   ), 29; Robert (bt. 1830,   ), 28; Robert Edward (b. 1874, d. 1885), 29; Rubina Ellen (b. 1883, d. 1884), 30; Stuart Forest (b. 1912), 31; Thomas (bt. 1835,   ), 28; William (b. 1827, d. 1870), 27; William Collin (b. 1877, d. 1885), 29; Winnifred (b. 1919), 31

Taylor: Adeline Drusilla (b. 1893,   ), 43; Agnes Grace (b. 1902), 49; Agnes Schultz (b. 1894, d. 1958), 47, 52; Albert (b. 1844, d. 1844), 40; Albert (b. 1867,   ), 58, 60; Albert Scott (b. 1870,   ), 47, 52; Alexander (b. 1856,   ), 58; Alexander (b. 1860, d. 1862), 46; Alexander (bt. 1831,   ), 57; Alexander 'Sandy' (b. 1843, d. 1910), 45, 47, 48; Alexander Stanley (b. 1898,   ), 44; Alexander Thomas (b. 1875,   ), 42, 44; Alexandre (b. 1886,   ), 49; Alfred (b. 1862,   ), 58, 60; Alfred (b. 1875, d. 1905), 45; Alfred (b. 1900), 54, 57; Alfred Edward (b. 1890,   ), 60; Alfred Edward (b. 1905), 50; Alice (b. 1875,   ), 48, 53; Alice Ann (b. 1874, d. 1943), 46, 52; Alice Margaret (b. 1881,   ), 42; Alice Rose (b. 1904), 54; Allan (b. 1891), 50; Allan (b. 1935), 53; Allan Peterson (b. 1886, d. 1936), 48, 53; Amy Ruth (b. 1896,   ), 43; Andrew (b. 1894), 50; Andrew Stanley (b. 1891, d. 1982), 48, 54; Angus (b. 1876,   ), 59; Angus Chisholm (b. 1895, d. 1968), 49, 54; Ann (b. 1848, d. 1929), 45, 49; Ann Maria (b. 1884, d. 1951), 48, 53; Annabella (b. 1858,   ), 41, 43; Annie, 41; Annie (b. 1885,   ), 59; Annie (b. 1893), 50; Annie (b. 1919), 52; Anonyme (b. 1918, d. 1918), 52; Archibald (b. 1882,   ), 48; Archibald Bannerman (b. 1890, d. 1956), 47; Archibald Clarence (b. 1900), 60; Archie (b. 1915), 52; Arthur David (b. 1893, d. 1971), 48; Arthur Edmund (b. 1910), 50; Arthur Sydney (b. 1880,   ), 41; Belinda (b. 1890,   ), 43; Benjamin (b. 1864,   ), 58; Benjamin (b. 1875, d. 1962), 46; Bentley A. (b. 1897), 43; Bernice, 53; Beryl Jean (b. 1918), 54; Beverly D. (b. 1938), 57; Blanche Irene (b. 1892, d. 1977), 47; Caroline (b. 1871,   ), 42, 44; Caroline (b. 1897), 49; Caroline Emily (b. 1894,   ), 42; Caroline May Jessie (b. 1862,   ), 40, 42; Carrie Marie (b. 1917), 55; Catherine (b. 1875,   ), 42, 44; Catherine (b. 1905), 44; Catherine (bt. 1832,   ), 57; Catherine Ann (b. 1867,   ), 58; Catherine Ann (b. 1882,   ), 49, 55; Catherine Frances (b. 1915), 52; Catherine Jane (b. 1860,   ), 41, 43; Catherine Jane (b. 1900), 60; Catherine Jemima (b. 1877, d. 1943), 47, 52; Catherine 'Kate' (b. 1875, d. 1904), 2, 3; Cecil Charles (b. 1904), 50; Cecil Randolph (b. 1905), 43; Cecil William (b. 1917, d. 1974), 55; Charles (b. 1870, d. 1953), 48; Charles (b. 1895), 50; Charles Edward (b. 1879,   ), 59; Charles Lindsay (b. 1897, d. 1974), 49, 54; Charlie, 51; Charlotte (b. 1854, d. 1936), 58, 59, 268; Charlotte (bt. 1825,

), 57; Charlotte ELizabeth (b. 1899), 43; Clarence (b. 1878, d. 1961), 48, 53; Clarence Stanley (b. 1911), 53; Colin (b. 1882, d. 1950), 48; Colin Alexander (b. 1899), 52, 56; Collin (b. 1886,   ), 42; Curtis J. (b. 1892,   ), 60; Cuthbert 'Cubby' (b. 1876,   ), 47; Cuthbert Francis 'Cubby' (b. 1880, d. 1966), 48, 53; Dave, 51; Dave H. (b. 1952), 56; David (b. 1844, d. 1907), 45, 48; David (bt. 1835,   ), 57, 58; David Chalmers (b. 1920), 56; David Edwin (b. 1865, d. 1871), 58; David J. (b. 1874,   ), 59; David James (b. 1894,   ), 60; David Livingston (b. 1888, d. 1963), 48; David Oliver (b. 1897), 54; Donald Allan (b. 1922, d. 1944), 52; Donald Gunn (b. 1912, d. 1969), 51; Donald Herbert (b. 1868, d. 1953), 46, 51; Dora Jemima (b. 1887, d. 1977), 48, 54; Doris L. (b. 1914), 55; Doris Mary Spencer (b. 1899,   ), 51, 56; Dorothy Hazel (b. 1923, d. 1924), 54; Douglas Duane (b. 1929), 57; Duncan Alexander (b. 1874, d. 1933), 49; Edith (b. 1885, d. 1959), 49, 55; Edith Blanch (b. 1892,   ), 42; Edith Gwendolyne 'Gwen' (b. 1915), 55; Edna G. (b. 1894), 48; Edward, 56; Edward (b. 1870,   ), 42, 43; Edward (b. 1905), 44; Edward (bt. 1862,   ), 42, 44; Edward (bt. 1871,   ), 41; Edward Gustav, 56; Edward Prince (bt. 1841,   ), 40, 42; Edward Thomas (b. 1868,   ), 45, 50; Edwin (b. 1879), 59; Edwin David 'Bud' (b. 1916), 53; Eleanor Harriet 'Nellie' (b. 1863,   ), 45; Elisabeth (b. 1860, d. 1930), 58, 60; Elise (b. 1890,   ), 44; Eliza (b. 1863, d. 1947), 47, 52; Eliza (b. 1882, d. 1883), 42; Eliza (b. 1903), 44; Elizabeth "Betsy" (b. 1838, d. 1903), 45, 47, 316; Elizabeth (Isabella) 'Lizette' (b. 1820, d.   ), 57; Elizabeth Ann (b. 1876,   ), 48; Elizabeth Helena (b. 1871, d. 1873), 46; Elizabeth Jane (bt. 1864,   ), 42; Elizabeth Mary (b. 1857, d. 1920), 46, 50; Ella (b. 1900), 44; Ellen (b. 1873,   ), 59; Ellen (b. 1879, d. 1899), 42, 44; Ellen Harriet (b. 1884,   ), 59; Ellen Harriet (b. 1886, d. 1967), 51, 56; Ellen Harriet (b. 1887,   ), 60; Ellis Roy (b. 1926), 54; Elsie Irene (b. 1899), 49; Emma Jane (b. 1883, d. 1959), 48; Emory Johnson (b. 1915, d. 1980), 55; Eric Morrison (b. 1913, d. 1913), 52; Erna Mary (b. 1904), 60; Ernest (b. 1918), 53; Esther Jane (b. 1905), 51; Ethel (b. 1917), 52; Ethel Helen (b. 1890, d. 1959), 51; Ethel M. (b. 1900), 50; Eva (b. 1894,   ), 44; Eva Mabel (b. 1907), 44; Eve (b. 1897), 50; Evelina Mary (b. 1895,   ), 44; Evelyn, 53; Fanny (b. 1871,   ), 41; Felix (b. 1893,   ), 49; Flora (b. 1866, d. 1891), 45; Flora Ann (b. 1867,   ), 33, 46; Flora Ann (b. 1868,   ), 47; Flora Ann (b. 1883, d. 1930), 51, 56; Flora Mildred (b. 1893,   ), 60; Florence (b. 1835, d. 1882), 40; Florence Mary (b. 1878, d. 1957), 46; Florence Mary (b. 1880, d. 1917), 48, 53; Frances Emma (b. 1866,   ), 41; Frances Evelyn (b. 1884, d. 1956), 51, 56; Frances Jane (b. 1882, d. 1883), 46; Frances Jane II (b. 1885, d. 1958), 46;

Francis Beddome (b. 1922), 56; Frank Lee (b. 1908, d. 1988), 54, 56; Frederick (b. 1887,   ), 47, 53; Frederick (b. 1888,   ), 42; Frederick George (b. 1877,   ), 41; Frederick Scott (b. 1895,   ), 60; George (, d. 1974), 52; George (b. 1760,   ), 39; George (b. 1838,   ), 40, 41; George (b. 1848, d. 1927), 58; George (b. 1858, d. 1927), 46, 50; George (b. 1895), 49; George (b. 1903), 51; George (b. 1907), 44; George (bt. 1829,   ), 57; George Arthur (b. 1886,   ), 59; George Campbell (b. 1880,   ), 51; George Gray (b. 1897, d. 1897), 47; George II (b. 1799, d. 1844), 39, 40, 253; George III (bt. 1833,   ), 40, 41; George IV (b. 1855,   ), 41, 43; George W. (b. 1892), 50; George Wallace (b. 1911, d. 1959), 55; Gertrude Ethel (b. 1900), 43; Gilbert (b. 1883, d. 1891), 59; Gladys Clement (b. 1895,   ), 44; Glen, 44; Gordon Elmer (b. 1915, d. 1985), 53; Grace Irene (b. 1913, d. 1974), 53; Harriet (b. 1864,   ), 45; Harriet Elizabeth (b. 1887, d. 1959), 49, 55; Hazel (b. 1901), 52; Helen, 56; Helen Charlotte (b. 1880, d. 1960), 46; Hellen (b. 1899), 44; Henriette (b. 1900), 51; Henry (b. 1852,   ), 58, 59; Henry Beddome 'Harry' (b. 1889, d. 1961), 51, 56; Henry Gordon, 56; Herbert (b. 1878,   ), 59; Herbert Anderson (b. 1929), 56; Herbert Chapman (b. 1850, d. 1910), 45, 49; Herbert Chapman (b. 1889, d. 1938), 49; Hilda Esther (b. 1894, d. 1973), 50; Hugh David (b. 1934), 56; Hugh Richard (b. 1891, d. 1962), 49; Hugh Richard (b. 1912, d. 1991), 55; Ida (b. 1884,   ), 49; Ida Martha Henrietta (b. 1894,   ), 43; Isabel (b. 1873, d. 1958), 75; Isabella Mary Ann (b. 1914), 44; James (b. 1794, d. 1878), 45, 77; James (b. 1825, d. 1898), 57, 58, 268; James (b. 1829, d. 1918), 45, 76, 77; James (b. 1851,   ), 58, 59; James (b. 1881,   ), 41; James (b. 1881, d. 1957), 48; James (b. 1898,   ), 54; James Alan (b. 1892,   ), 50; James Brown (b. 1889, d. 1971), 47; James Colin (b. 1857,   ), 46; James Keith (bt. 1833, d. 1863), 40; Jane (b. 1829,   ), 40, 41; Jane (b. 1838,   ), 40, 41; Jane (b. 1852, d. 1943), 78, 123; Jane (b. 1876,   ), 46, 58; Jane (b. 1876,   ), 234, 237; Jane (b. 1887,   ), 43; Jean, 54; Jean (, d. 1982), 52; Jemima (b. 1877,   ), 46; Jessie (b. 1883,   ), 46; Jessie (b. 1884, d. 1884), 47; Jessie Ellen (b. 1885, d. 1961), 48, 53; Jessie Winnie (b. 1889,   ), 42; Joan, 51; John, 56; John (b. 1834, d. 1925), 33, 45, 46; John (b. 1858, d. 1901), 58, 60; John (b. 1865, d. 1866), 47; John (b. 1871, d. 1937), 48; John (b. 1881), 59; John Albert (b. 1888,   ), 60; John Alexander (b. 1899), 42; John Charles (b. 1901), 44; John Colin, 56; John Edward (b. 1881, d. 1882), 51; John Edward (b. 1902), 44; John Jr. (b. 1858, d. 1927), 46, 51; John Kenneth (b. 1914), 56; John Murray (b. 1908, d. 1927), 52; John Rupert Lyall, 56; John Swanston (b. 1839, d. 1841), 40; Joseph (b. 1889,   ), 49; Kathleen (, d. 1991), 52, 56;

67; Andrew (b. 1914), 69; Basile, 67; Clara (b. 1910), 68; David (b. 1877,), 67; Eva Jane (b. 1920), 69; Francois (b. 1860,), 67; Frank J. (b. 1905, d. 1959), 69; Henry (b. 1875,), 68; Henry (b. 1882,), 68; John (b. 1915, d. 1938), 69; Joseph (b. 1874,), 67; Josephine (b. 1908), 69; Louis (b. 1811), 67, 146; Louis (b. 1835, d. 1892), 67; Louis (b. 1880,), 67, 69; Louis (b. 1899), 69; Marie (b. 1846,), 67, 68, 142, 146; Marie Celina (b. 1877,), 68; Marie Jeanne (b. 1879,), 68; Mary (b. 1865,), 67, 69; Mildred F. (b. 1923), 69; Paul (b. 1909), 68; Raphael (b. 1890,), 68; Roger Jerome (b. 1883, d. 1899), 67; Rose F. (b. 1919), 69; St.Ann (b. 1910), 69; Thomas (b. 1844, d. 1884), 67, 68; Thomas (b. 1858, d. 1925), 67, 68; unnamed (b. 1836, d. 1855), 67; Vitaline (b. 1889), 68; William (b. 1914), 69; William J. (b. 1912, d. 1912), 69

Thomas: Adelaide Jane (b. 1896,), 79; Alexander (b. 1869,), 71, 72, 73, 74; Alexander (bt. 1837,), 71; Alexander Charles (bt. 1868, d. 1868), 77; Alexander G. (b. 1911), 74; Alexander 'Sandy' (, d. 1870), 40, 41; Alfred (b. 1849,), 76; Alfred B. (b. 1898,), 73; Alfred Louis (b. 1880,), 77; Alice (b. 1877, d. 1877), 71, 73; Alice (b. 1893,), 78; Alice (b. 1900,), 73; Allan (b. 1905), 75; Ann (b. 1795,), 70; Annabella (b. 1855,), 71, 72; Anne Frances (b. 1895,), 73; Arthur (b. 1906), 74; Arthur Henry (b. 1883, d. 1883), 77; Catherine, 41, 71; Catherine (b. 1810, d. 1834), 75, 76; Catherine (b. 1837,), 76; Catherine (b. 1846, d. 1913), 70, 71; Catherine (b. 1859,), 71, 73; Catherine M. (b. 1875,), 78; Catherine Mary (b. 1879, d. 1966), 71, 72, 73; Charles (b. 1793,), 70; Charles (b. 1814, d. 1904), 70, 73; Charles (b. 1904), 73; Charles (bt. 1837,), 71; Charles Richard (b. 1839, d. 1911), 76, 77, 78, 233, 235; Charlotte (b. 1778, d. 1843), 70; Charlotte (b. 1806, d. 1894), 77, 232, 316; Charlotte Anne (bt. 1876,), 78; Clara (b. 1880,), 78; Colin (b. 1903,), 75; Daniel (b. 1838, d. 1942), 70; Daniel (b. 1853,), 70, 71, 72, 74; Daughter (Mary?) (bt. 1831,), 76; David Henry (b. 1853, d. 1917), 77, 79; Dolly, 78; Edith Mary (b. 1899,), 79; Edward (b. 1801, d. 1802), 70; Edward (b. 1855, d. 1916), 76, 78; Edward Daniel (b. 1881,), 72, 74; Edward F. (b. 1904), 74; Edward John (b. 1863,), 77; Edwin James (b. 1888, d. 1898), 79; Edwin Stewart (b. 1850, d. 1932), 77, 79; Edwin Stuart (b. 1886,), 78; Eleanor (b. 1780,), 70; Eleanor (b. 1838,), 70, 71; Eleanor Harriet (b. 1871,), 78, 79; Eleanor Sophie (bt. 1867,), 76; Eleanore Ann (bt. 1873,), 77; Eleonore (b. 1807,), 71; Elisabeth (b. 1802, d. 1874), 11, 203, 223; Elisabeth (b. 1805, d. 1846), 5, 75, 76; Elise (b. 1845,), 113; Elizabeth, 70; Elizabeth Jane (b. 1887,), 79; Elizabeth Pheobe

(b. 1893,), 78; Ellen (b. 1873,), 73; Ellen Florence (b. 1884, d. 1911), 79; Emily (b. 1904), 75; Eva (b. 1906), 74; Evangeline, 74; Eveline (b. 1904), 74; Florence Alvine (b. 1897,), 79; Florence Louisa (b. 1892, d. 1894), 79; Florence Maud (b. 1886,), 78; Frances, 70; Frances (b. 1795, d. 1843), 75; Frances Jane (b. 1843,), 76, 78; Frances Jane (b. 1882,), 78; Frances Louise (b. 1891,), 77; Frederick George (b. 1889,), 79; George (b. 1852,), 70, 72, 74; George Jr. (b. 1881,), 72; George William (b. 1878,), 78; Gladys (b. 1897,), 78; Harriet Evelyn (b. 1899,), 79; Harriet Maria (b. 1846, d. 1871), 76, 78; Harriet Maria (b. 1877,), 77; Harriet Sophia (b. 1847, d. 1934), 77, 78, 237; Harry James (bt. 1842, d. 1842), 76; Helene (b. 1878), 71, 72, 73, 74; Henry (b. 1805,), 70; Henry (b. 1848,), 71, 73; Henry (b. 1856,), 71; Henry George (b. 1876,), 73, 75; Herbert Charles (b. 1889, d. 1889), 77; Howard (b. 1912), 74; Isabella (b. 1876,), 73, 75; Isabelle (b. 1884,), 77; James (bt. 1852,), 76; James Henry (b. 1872), 71, 72, 73; Jane (b. 1804, d. 1806), 70; Jane (b. 1816, d. 1841), 75, 76; Jane (b. 1845,), 257; Jennie, 78; John (b. 1751, d. 1822), 69, 70; John (b. 1850,), 70; John (b. 1857, d. 1947), 77, 79; John (b. 1867,), 78; John (bt. 1835,), 76; John Edward (bt. 1873,), 78; John Frederick (b. 1904), 79; John George (b. 1866,), 71, 73, 75; John Jr. (b. 1776, b. 1816), 70; Johnny, 74; Joseph (b. 1893), 72; Joseph (b. 1901,), 72; Joseph George (b. 1873, d. 1875), 72; Joseph Lawrence (b. 1913, d. 1985), 299; Josephine (b. 1883, d. 1885), 72; Juliet Jane (b. 1845, d. 1935), 77, 78; Juliet Jane (b. 1884,), 78; Laura (b. 1908), 74; Laurence (b. 1910), 74; Lillie (b. 1892,), 79; Louis (b. 1879, d. 1879), 71, 73; Louisa (b. 1832,), 71, 72; Louisa (b. 1876,), 72; Louison (b. 1874,), 73; Malvina (b. 1920, d. 2004), 200, 201; Margaret, 70; Margaret (b. 1837,), 71, 73; Margaret Jane (b. 1870, d. 1888), 73; Margaret Jane (b. 1885, d. 1896), 77; Marguerite Nancy (b. 1885,), 72, 74; Marie, 288; Marie (b. 1904), 72; Martha Ann (b. 1888,), 79; Mary, 272; Mary (, d. 1863), 32, 232, 233; Mary (b. 1791, d. 1802), 70; Mary (b. 1834, d. 1896), 70, 71, 72, 73, 74, 75; Mary Ann (b. 1800,), 7, 75; Mary Ann (b. 1874, d. 1877), 71, 73; Mary J. (b. 1882,), 78; Mary Josephine (b. 1884,), 72, 74; Mary Margaret (b. 1880,), 78; Mary Maud (b. 1910), 75; Mathilda (b. 1862,), 71, 73, 75; Mathilda (bt. 1837,), 71; Matilda (b. 1907), 74; Nancy (b. 1845, d. 1913), 71, 73; Nancy (b. 1848,), 70, 71, 139; Nancy (b. 1879,), 72, 74; Norman (b. 1901), 75; Peter (b. 1876, d. 1898), 72; Philip (b. 1881,), 72, 74; Phillip (b. 1885,), 71, 73; Phillip (b. 1905), 74; Phoebe (b. 1833, d. 1898), 45, 76, 77; Pierre Richard "Peter" (b. 1875,), 72, 74; Rachel (b.

1910), 74; Richard (b. 1800,), 71; Richard (b. 1858,), 71; Richard Edward (b. 1803, d. 1803), 70; Richard William (b. 1834, d. 1923), 70, 71, 72, 73, 74, 75; Robert Alexander Tache (b. 1882,), 73, 75; Robert Henry (b. 1890,), 79; Sarah (b. 1808,), 75, 76; Sarah (b. 1896), 72, 75; Sarah Elizabeth (b. 1874,), 77; Sarah Elizabeth (bt. 1841, d. 1925), 76; Sidney, 78; Sophia (b. 1805, d. 1858), 75, 76; Sophia (b. 1883, d. 1900), 72; Stanley (b. 1908), 74; Thomas, 70; Thomas (b. 1765, d. 1828), 75; Thomas (b. 1819, d. 1859), 75, 77; Thomas (b. 1875, d. 1900), 72; Thomas (bt. 1834,), 76; Thomas Charles (b. 1849, d. 1849), 77; Thomas James (bt. 1876, d. 1877), 77; Thomas Walter (b. 1897,), 78; Virginie (b. 1893), 72, 74; Walter Charles (b. 1891,), 78; Walter George (b. 1902,), 73; William, 232; William (b. 1806, d. 1875), 45, 75, 76, 235; William (b. 1831, d. 1892), 76, 77; William D. (b. 1865,), 77; William George (b. 1843,), 77, 78; William George (b. 1901,), 79; William Mason (b. 1855, d. 1856), 77; William R. (b. 1882,), 71, 73; William Richard (b. 1880,), 73; William Roy (b. 1894,), 79

Thompson: Cleophas (b. 1891,), 284; Evelyn (b. 1916), 287; John, 135, 137; Louis (b. 1837, d. 1909), 284; Robert, 108

Thomson: Robert Alexander (b. 1875, d. 1945), 311, 313

Thorn: Abraham (b. 1842, d. 1843), 80; Alexander (b. 1884,), 81; Alvina (b. 1884,), 83; Anastasie Nancy (b. 1885,), 83; Anne, 97, 102; Antoine (b. 1884,), 82; Asilda (b. 1884, d. 1900), 83; David (b. 1882, d. 1883), 83; David (b. 1893, d. 1894), 83; David (b. 1897), 83; Ellen (b. 1883, d. 1896), 81; Ernest (b. 1874,), 81; John (b. 1872,), 81; Julie (b. 1857, d. 1875), 80; Lisa A. (b. 1887,), 82; Marie Elise (b. 1881,), 83; Marie Elise (b. 1891,), 83; Marie Esilda (b. 1883, d. 1900), 83; Mary A. (b. 1890,), 82; Nancy (b. 1895,), 83; Paul (b. 1876,), 81; Sarah M. (b. 1895,), 82; William George (b. 1885,), 82; William J. (b. 1899,), 82

Thorne: Angelique (b. 1835,), 80, 81; Bertha (b. 1931), 83; Catherine (b. 1855,), 80, 256, 260; Cecile (b. 1827,), 80; David (b. 1839, d. 1862), 80, 81; David (b. 1859,), 81, 82; David (b. 1882, d. 1898), 81; Elise (b. 1851, d. 1939), 80, 82; Florence (b. 1922), 83; Frances (b. 1890,), 81; Genevieve (b. 1830, d. 1879), 80; George (b. 1859,), 81, 82; George Jr. (b. 1829,), 80; George Sr. (b. 1797, d. 1887), 80, 256, 260; James (b. 1893,), 81, 83; Jeanne (b. 1883, d. 1891), 82; John (b. 1861,), 81; John Francus (b. 1844,), 80, 81; Joseph (b. 1891,), 82; Joseph (b. 1928), 83; Lillian (b. 1920), 83; Maria (b. 1882,), 82; Marie (b. 1837, d. 1862), 80, 81, 148; Marie (b. 1849, d. 1878), 80, 82; Marie (b. 1862, d. 1863),

Louis (b. 1909), 112; Louise (b. 1841, d. 1857), 108; Louise (b. 1897,   ), 112; Louise (b. 1902), 110; Louise (b. 1904), 116; Louise (b. 1908, d. 1948), 114, 120; Louise or Bluehorn (b. 1852, obi. 1944), 24; Madeleine (b. 1822,   ), 38, 106, 107, 261; Marguerite, 163; Marguerite (b. 1796, d. 1879), 105, 106; Marguerite (b. 1825, d. 1902), 106, 108; Marguerite (b. 1828,   ), 106; Marguerite (b. 1857,   ), 108, 112; Marguerite Cecile (bt. 1887,   ), 112; Marie (b. 1831,   ), 106, 108, 113, 304; Marie (b. 1833), 106; Marie (b. 1856,   ), 106; Marie (b. 1859,   ), 108; Marie (b. 1868, d. 1872), 108; Marie (b. 1869,   ), 109, 113; Marie (b. 1871, d. 1888), 110; Marie Anatalie (b. 1876,   ), 111, 116; Marie Cecilia (b. 1877,   ), 110; Marie Edna (b. 1901, d. 1974), 116; Marie Flora (b. 1908), 116; Marie Joseph Andre (b. 1889,   ), 112; Marie Margaret (b. 1896,   ), 115; Marie Marguerite (b. 1871, d. 1880), 107; Marie Rose (b. 1867,   ), 111; Marie Rose (b. 1871, d. 1871), 111; Marie Rose (b. 1885,   ), 113; Marie Rose (b. 1896, d. 1980), 115; Marie Rosine (b. 1876,   ), 110; Marie Veronique (b. 1885,   ), 113; Marie-Anne (bt. 1887,   ), 110; Martin (b. 1905, d. 1936), 110, 115; Martin (b. 1922, d. 1998), 117; Mary (b. 1900,   ), 112; Mary (b. 1915, d. 1921), 118; Mary (b. 1926), 115; Mary Florestine (b. 1904), 118; Mary Louise (b. 1929), 115; Mary Selma (b. 1911), 110; Mathilde (b. 1869,   ), 109, 114; Maxime F. (b. 1900, d. 1969), 116; Medard (b. 1855,   ), 108; Melanie (b. 1876, d. 1876), 111; Michel (b. 1832,   ), 106, 108, 109; Michel (b. 1875,   ), 109; Michel (b. 1904), 114, 119; Moise (b. 1882, d. 1954), 111; Napier (b. 1890,   ), 112; Napoleon "Paul" (b. 1880, d. 1942), 111, 117, 130, 301; Napoleon (b. 1863,   ), 108; Natalie Rose (b. 1877, d. 1880), 111; Norbert (b. 1861,   ), 109, 113, 116; Pascal (b. 1846,   ), 108, 111; Patrice (b. 1866, d. 1880), 106; Patrice (b. 1868, d. 1936), 111, 115, 279, 290; Patrice (b. 1873, d. 1873), 111; Patrice (b. 1902), 116; Patrice (b. 1908, d. 1989), 118; Patrick (b. 1903, d. 1952), 113; Patrick (b. 1907, d. 1985), 117; Peter (b. 1890, d. 1965), 113, 118; Philomene (b. 1872, d. 1893), 109; Raphael (b. 1906, d. 1969), 118; Regina (b. 1905), 117; Remi (b. 1861, d. 1938), 109, 113; Rosalie (b. 1869, d. 1885), 107; Rosalie (b. 1870, d. 1942), 111, 116, 290; Rosalie (b. 1888, d. 1973), 111, 113, 116, 117, 118, 119, 290; Rose (b. 1853, d. 1873), 108, 111; Rose (b. 1871, d. 1958), 107, 110; Rose (b. 1890,   ), 113; Rose (b. 1899), 114, 119; Roselenn (b. 1894), 113; Rosine (b. 1879,   ), 112, 117, 247, 251, 300; Roy Joseph (b. 1923, d. 2002), 115; Sara (b. 1865, d. 1885), 106; Scholastique (b. 1822,   ), 106; Selina (b. 1897), 113; Stan (b. 1905), 114; Stella A. (b. 1897, d. 1964), 115; Suzanne (b. 1873,   ), 110; Tillie Rose (b. 1906, d. 1949), 116; Ursule (b. 1872, d. 1885), 109; Ursule

(b. 1877, d. 1970), 111, 116, 289; Veronique (b. 1890,   ), 112; Victoria B. (b. 1893, d. 1986), 114, 119; Violet (b. 1927), 117; Virginie (b. 1885,   ), 112, 118; Virginie (b. 1886), 113; Vital (b. 1856,   ), 108, 112, 251; William (b. 1864,   ), 109; William (b. 1881, d. 1881), 113; William (b. 1915, d. 2011), 117

Trout: Sally Cree Pa-sa (b. 1780, d. 1874), 242, 272

Trudeau: Rose, 101

Truthwaite: Alexander (b. 1889,   ), 122; Alexander (bt. 1861, d. 1864), 121; Alfred (b. 1883, d. 1930), 122, 123; Alice (b. 1894,   ), 122; Andrew (b. 1849, d. 1936), 121, 122; Andrew T. (b. 1880,   ), 122; Catherine Ann (b. 1877, d. 1943), 122, 123, 234, 237; Catherine R. (b. 1881,   ), 122; Charles Harry (b. 1918, d. 1923), 123; Charles William (b. 1887, d. 1949), 122, 123; Duncan (b. 1887,   ), 123; Edward (b. 1793,   ), 120; Elizabeth (b. 1825, d. 1875), 121; Elizabeth (b. 1885, d. 1886), 123; Elizabeth (b. 1900), 123; Florence M. (b. 1878,   ), 122; Harriet (b. 1831,   ), 121; Harriet Marie (b. 1858, d. 1949), 121, 123; Hector Henry (b. 1897,   ), 123; Helen Marie (b. 1916, d. 2005), 123; Horace (b. 1893,   ), 123; Irene (b. 1915), 123; Isabella (b. 1818, d. 1843), 121, 256; Jacob (b. 1790, d. 1873), 120, 121, 232, 233, 256; Jacob (b. 1855, d. 1940), 121, 122, 123, 237; Jacob (b. 1902), 123; Jane (b. 1816, d. 1843), 121; Jane Mary (b. 1853, d. 1934), 121; Jessie (b. 1892,   ), 122; John Harold (b. 1903,   ), 122; John Thomas (b. 1875, d. 1876), 122; Malcolm Allan (b. 1914), 123; Margaret (b. 1868, d. 1915), 122; Mary (b. 1793,   ), 120, 121; Mary (b. 1895,   ), 123; Mary (bt. 1830,   ), 121; Mathew (b. 1753, d. 1793), 120, 233; Myles McDermot (b. 1900,   ), 122; Nancy "Ann" (b. 1839, d. 1896), 121, 122; Sarah (bt. 1833, d. 1900), 121; Sarah Ann Elizabeth (b. 1851,   ), 121, 122; Sarah Jane (b. 1879,   ), 122; Thomas (b. 1890,   ), 123; Thomas Jr. (b. 1847, d. 1876), 121, 122; Thomas Sr. (b. 1820, d. 1899), 121; Unnamed (b. 1889,   ), 123; Victor Henry (b. 1897,   ), 122

Tucknott: Robert, 301

Turcotte: (--?--), 253; Acilda (b. 1891,   ), 127; Adele (b. 1870,   ), 125; Adelma (b. 1923), 132; Albert (b. 1881,   ), 127; Albert (b. 1903), 127; Albert (b. 1924), 133; Alexina (b. 1878,   ), 127, 131; Alfred (b. 1871,   ), 126; Alfred (b. 1926), 133; Alvina (b. 1929), 133; Alvina Elizabeth (b. 1922), 130; Anastasie (b. 1875), 125; Andrew (b. 1917), 130; Angela (b. 1934), 133; Angelique (b. 1877,   ), 125; Angelique (b. 1878, d. 1952), 125, 130; Antoine (b. 1885), 129, 133; Antoine (b. 1910, d. 1977), 131; Archie (b. 1879,   ), 126; Audrey Vitaline (b. 1932), 130; Benjamin (b. 1924, d. 1997), 132; Caroline (b. 1866,   ), 125; Cecelia (b. 1888), 128; Celina (b. 1883, d. 1949), 126, 130; Celina (b. 1910), 133; Charles

(b. 1886, obi. 1972), 128, 132; Christine (b. 1881,   ), 128; Clara (b. 1861,   ), 125; Clarence Donald (b. 1945), 134; Clarence Walter (b. 1916, d. 1980), 130, 134; Claudine (b. 1929), 134; Collin (b. 1887, d. 1969), 126, 130; Cynthia Alma (b. 1914), 132; Daniel (b. 1873, d. 1951), 117, 125, 129, 301; Daniel Jr. (b. 1892,   ), 129, 133; Delores (b. 1930), 130; Dina Lou (b. 1936), 134; Earl (b. 1920, d. 1924), 132; Edna (b. 1924), 133; Edna Pearl (b. 1921), 130; Effie (b. 1906), 131; Elizabeth 'Betsy' (b. 1812,   ), 253; Elmer Marion (b. 1914), 134; Emily (b. 1896), 128; Emma Louise (b. 1883,   ), 128; Ernest (b. 1912), 131; Eugene (b. 1915), 131; Eva Theresa "Ah-bi-do-th" (b. 1908, obi. 1992), 132; Evelyn (b. 1926, d. 2010), 133; Fred (b. 1912), 130; Gary (b. 1947), 134; Gary (b. 1959, d. 2014), 134; Genevieve (b. 1846, d. 1894), 125, 126, 155, 158, 203; Georgeline R. (b. 1925), 130; Glen (b. 1935), 133; Gloria Bell (b. 1936, d. 1936), 134; Henri (b. 1906), 131; Henrietta (b. 1872,   ), 125, 128; Henry (b. 1929), 130; Horace (b. 1909), 131; Irene (b. 1925), 130; Irma May (b. 1929, obi. 1988), 132; James (b. 1881, d. 1967), 127; James Patrice McKenzie (b. 1864, d. 1874), 125; James Russell (b. 1913), 117, 129, 301; Jane (b. 1894,   ), 127; Jean Baptiste (b. 1837, d. 1902), 125, 126, 300; Jean Baptiste (b. 1860, d. 1873), 125; Joan (b. 1931), 134; John (b. 1882, d. 1960), 128, 132; John A. (b. 1913), 134; John B. (b. 1893,   ), 129, 133, 134; Joseph (b. 1849,   ), 125, 126, 159, 169; Joseph (b. 1872, d. 1955), 126, 131, 158, 169; Joseph (b. 1878,   ), 128; Joseph (b. 1883, d. 1966), 127, 307; Joseph (b. 1902, obi. 1968), 129; Joseph (b. 1904), 129; Joseph (b. 1922), 133; Joseph Ernest (b. 1923), 130; Josephine (b. 1907), 131; Josephine Grace (b. 1922, d. 1929), 130; Juanita (b. 1933), 130; Julie (b. 1851, d. 1927), 125, 126; June Mary (b. 1930), 134; LaRose (b. 1911), 130; Lawrence (b. 1923), 130; Lawrence (b. 1933), 134; Lena Jennie (b. 1888, d. 1965), 128, 131; Leonide (b. 1874,   ), 126, 131; Louis (b. 1912, d. 1936), 130; Louis A. (b. 1915), 130; Louis P. (b. 1928), 130; Lous N. (b. 1918), 134; Lucie Georgina (b. 1886), 127; Lucy Theresa (b. 1890, d. 1981), 128; Madeline (b. 1896, d. 1952), 128; Maggie (b. 1905), 131; Marcel (b. 1904), 131; Marguerite (b. 1853,   ), 125, 126; Marie (b. 1861, d. 1888), 125, 129; Marie (b. 1887), 128; Marie (b. 1887, d. 1956), 128, 133; Marie Alexandrine (b. 1902), 127; Marie Blanche (b. 1906), 131; Marie Cecelia (b. 1916, d. 2009), 130, 134; Marie Claudia (b. 1900, d. 1929), 129, 134; Marie Louise (b. 1883,   ), 129, 133; Marie Mabel Albina (b. 1903), 131; Marie Rose (b. 1878, d. 1963), 128, 131; Martha (b. 1896,   ), 127; Mary (b. 1915), 133; Mary Ann "Ni-ah-do-th" (b. 1911, d. 1964), 132; Mary Bernice (b. 1927), 132; Mary Florestine (b. 1910),

d. 1877), 178, 183, 259; Joseph (b. 1817, d. 1885), 11, 141, 142, 143, 155, 156; Joseph (b. 1824, d. 1873), 155, 186; Joseph (b. 1839,   ), 155, 159; Joseph (b. 1851,   ), 178, 180, 258, 259; Joseph (b. 1852, d. 1927), 156, 162; Joseph (b. 1856, d. 1879), 157, 166, 171, 186, 189; Joseph (b. 1857, d. 1885), 158, 166, 167, 187, 189; Joseph (b. 1864,   ), 143, 156; Joseph (b. 1873,   ), 180; Joseph (b. 1875, d. 1875), 180; Joseph (b. 1879,   ), 161, 171; Joseph (b. 1880,   ), 167, 189; Joseph (b. 1880, d. 1883), 162; Joseph (b. 1883, d. 1885), 163; Joseph (b. 1884, d. 1885), 162; Joseph (b. 1885,   ), 181; Joseph (b. 1891, d. 1952), 162, 174; Joseph (b. 1894, d. 1894), 171; Joseph (b. 1897, d. 1897), 169; Joseph Adelard (b. 1896,   ), 181; Joseph Adelard Celestin (b. 1890, d. 1895), 161; Joseph Aimie (b. 1890,   ), 167, 190; Joseph Albert (b. 1897,   ), 165, 188; Joseph Albert Raymond (b. 1894,   ), 182; Joseph Alexandre (b. 1880, d. 1880), 158; Joseph Alfred (b. 1898), 183; Joseph Amedee (b. 1902), 182; Joseph Edouard William (b. 1905), 169; Joseph Jeremie (b. 1887,   ), 166, 189; Joseph Julien (b. 1904), 170; Joseph Louis (b. 1875,   ), 160, 170; Joseph Louis Frederic David (b. 1893,   ), 168; Joseph Maurice Felix (b. 1910), 169; Joseph Michael (b. 1913, d. 1985), 174; Joseph Norbert (b. 1893, d. 1894), 167, 190; Joseph Olivier (b. 1880,   ), 180; Joseph Patrice Alexander (b. 1900, d. 1901), 169; Joseph Philias (b. 1891,   ), 166, 189; Joseph Roger (b. 1878,   ), 160, 170; Josephine (b. 1855,   ), 156; Josephine (b. 1860, d. 1947), 161, 171; Josephine (b. 1888,   ), 165, 188; Josephine (b. 1891,   ), 182, 184; Josephine (b. 1915), 174; Josephte (b. 1825, d. 1878), 178, 179; Jules Adelard (b. 1900, d. 1901), 170; Julie (b. 1870, d. 1887), 180; Julie (b. 1877, d. 1877), 164; Julien (b. 1878, d. 1936), 160, 170; Julienne (b. 1868, d. 1880), 158; Juliette, 185; Justine (b. 1827, d. 1862), 155; Justine (b. 1870,   ), 179; Justine (b. 1888,   ), 182, 184; Justine (b. 1894,   ), 181, 183; Laura (Dora), 183, 185; Lawrence (b. 1918), 176; Lawrence Edward (b. 1911, d. 1956), 177, 191; Lelie (b. 1879), 181; Leon Salomon (b. 1885,   ), 166, 188; Leona (b. 1913), 183; Leonard J. (b. 1935), 173; Lorene (b. 1929), 175; Louis (b. 1834,   ), 178, 179; Louis (b. 1849, d. 1913), 155, 160, 177, 191; Louis (b. 1863, d. 1936), 179, 183; Louis (b. 1865,   ), 180; Louis (b. 1883, d. 1883), 160; Louis (b. 1895,   ), 182, 184, 185; Louis David (b. 1893, d. 1894), 165, 188; Louis David Avila (b. 1883,   ), 160; Louis Patrick (b. 1917, d. 1986), 174; Louise, 184, 185; Louise (b. 1863, d. 1872), 178; Louise (b. 1879,   ), 162; Louise (b. 1885,   ), 164; Lucille (b. 1947,   ), 184; Madeline (b. 1921), 173; Maggie (b. 1882, d. 1968), 164, 176; Magloire (b. 1889), 164; Majoric (b. 1905), 183, 185; Margaret (b. 1913), 174; Marguerite (b. 1798,   ), 154;

Marguerite (b. 1829,   ), 155, 186; Marguerite (b. 1844,   ), 156, 161; Marguerite (b. 1863, d. 1872), 180; Marguerite (b. 1868,   ), 178; Marguerite (b. 1871, d. 1875), 159; Marguerite (b. 1873,   ), 162; Marguerite (b. 1875,   ), 164; Marguerite (b. 1878,   ), 159, 169; Marguerite (b. 1879,   ), 180; Marguerite Eudore (b. 1898), 167, 190; Maria (b. 1876,   ), 163; Maria (b. 1896, d. 1950), 160, 169; Maria (b. 1905), 182, 184; Marie (b. 1777,   ), 154; Marie (b. 1826,   ), 178, 179; Marie (b. 1858, d. 1862), 157, 187; Marie (b. 1861, d. 1880), 157, 186; Marie (b. 1862, d. 1875), 179; Marie (b. 1867,   ), 179, 182; Marie (b. 1871, d. 1872), 180; Marie (b. 1875, d. 1875), 162; Marie (b. 1877), 159; Marie (b. 1877,   ), 160; Marie (b. 1888, d. 1890), 167, 190; Marie (b. 1890,   ), 163; Marie Adelaide (b. 1884,   ), 167, 189; Marie Adele Delphine (b. 1882,   ), 163; Marie Adele Victoria (b. 1889, d. 1890), 168; Marie Adeline (b. 1876, d. 1886), 162; Marie Adeline (b. 1880,   ), 160, 170; Marie Alvina (b. 1877, d. 1878), 166, 189; Marie Alvina (b. 1882,   ), 160, 170; Marie Amanda "Maude" (b. 1884, d. 1944), 160; Marie Anna (b. 1896, d. 1897), 161; Marie Anna Victoria (b. 1900), 170; Marie Anne, 184; Marie Anne (b. 1868,   ), 180; Marie Anne (b. 1875, d. 1900), 162; Marie Anne Ida (b. 1898,   ), 169; Marie Antonia (b. 1887,   ), 168; Marie Bernadette Eeaerina (b. 1909), 170; Marie Cecelia (b. 1919, d. 2007), 174; Marie Clara "Irene" (b. 1914, d. 1975), 176; Marie Emelie (b. 1877,   ), 165, 176, 188, 191; Marie Emelie (b. 1878, d. 1900), 165, 188; Marie Emma (b. 1899), 183; Marie Ernestine Emelie (b. 1897, d. 1897), 167, 190; Marie Etiennette (b. 1907), 170; Marie Eulalie (b. 1864,   ), 179; Marie Gertrude (b. 1933, obi. 2011), 174; Marie Henriette (b. 1883, obi. 1953), 162, 173; Marie Ida (b. 1903), 169; Marie Isabelle (b. 1876, d. 1961), 160, 169; Marie Isabelle Marguerite (b. 1906), 169; Marie Jane (b. 1862,   ), 158, 187; Marie Jeanne (b. 1871, d. 1872), 158; Marie Louise (b. 1872,   ), 159; Marie Louise (b. 1873,   ), 158, 168, 187, 191; Marie Louise (b. 1895, d. 1896), 167, 190; Marie Louise (b. 1897, d. 1897), 168, 190; Marie Louise (b. 1918), 174; Marie Louise Amanda (b. 1901,   ), 169; Marie Louise Anna (b. 1887,   ), 159; Marie Louise Eva (b. 1892,   ), 161, 171; Marie Lucie Amanda (b. 1891,   ), 159; Marie Melina (bt. 1872,   ), 179; Marie Octavie (b. 1863, d. 1903), 161, 171; Marie Octavie (b. 1876, d. 1880), 158; Marie Octavie (b. 1884, d. 1884), 158; Marie Olivine (b. 1885,   ), 160, 170, 177, 191; Marie Paule (b. 1957), 185; Marie Philomene (b. 1875, d. 1893), 165, 187; Marie Philomene (b. 1902), 183; Marie Regina Eva (b. 1907), 170; Marie Rosalie (b. 1901), 183; Marie Rose (b. 1852, d. 1887), 179,

181; Marie Rose (b. 1863, d. 1900), 158, 168, 210; Marie Rose (b. 1872, d. 1946), 161, 171, 296; Marie Rose (b. 1877,   ), 165, 176, 188, 191; Marie Rose Anna (b. 1879, d. 1881), 160; Marie Therese (b. 1874, d. 1874), 157, 187; Marie Therese (b. 1881,   ), 163; Marie Veronique (b. 1875,   ), 161; Marie Virginie (b. 1879, d. 1904), 166, 171, 177, 189, 191; Mary Catherine (b. 1914, d. 1970), 173; Mary Clara (b. 1901), 164; Mary E. (b. 1911, d. 1997), 175; Mary J. (b. 1913), 171; Mary Jane (b. 1897, d. 1974), 162, 175; Mary Josephine (b. 1905), 183; Mary Louise (b. 1898, d. 1933), 172; Mary May (b. 1920), 175; Mary Petroline (b. 1920, d. 1996), 174; Mathilde (b. 1881, d. 1958), 166, 177, 188, 191; Maurice, 184; Maurice (b. 1895), 182, 184, 185; Melanie (b. 1853, d. 1898), 100, 155, 161; Melanie (b. 1857,   ), 179, 182; Melanie (b. 1858,   ), 158, 166, 187, 189; Melanie (b. 1859, d. 1885), 157, 166, 186, 189; Modeste (b. 1891,   ), 167, 190; Moise (b. 1854, d. 1871), 156; Moise (b. 1881, d. 1882), 164; Moise (b. 1885, d. 1886), 163; Monique (b. 1870), 161; Nancy (b. 1838,   ), 156, 161; Nancy (b. 1861, d. 1899), 158, 168, 202, 208, 209; Nancy Josephine (b. 1884,   ), 159; Napasis (b. 1874, d. 1874), 160; Napoleon (b. 1868,   ), 143, 156; Napoleon Norbert (b. 1895), 165, 188; Noella (b. 1938), 184; Norbert (b. 1868,   ), 158, 167, 168, 187, 190; Norbert (b. 1894), 167, 190; Norman (b. 1857,   ), 157, 164; Octave (b. 1885,   ), 182, 183; Olivier (b. 1861, d. 1879), 178; Patrice (b. 1872, d. 1943), 158, 169; Patrice (b. 1876,   ), 160, 169; Patrice (b. 1877, d. 1878), 166, 189; Patrice (b. 1887, d. 1920), 162, 174; Patrice (b. 1891, d. 1891), 166, 188; Patrice (b. 1913, d. 1990), 175; Peter (b. 1877), 162; Peter (b. 1890, d. 1957), 163, 176; Peter Albert (b. 1916, d. 1994), 176; Phillip (b. 1938), 173; Philomene (b. 1863,   ), 157; Philomene (b. 1864, d. 1865), 156; Philomene (b. 1868, d. 1885), 157, 187; Philomene (b. 1900), 169; Pierre (b. 1787,   ), 154, 155, 186; Pierre (b. 1813,   ), 155, 156; Pierre (b. 1828, d. 1834), 155, 186; Pierre (b. 1829,   ), 178; Pierre (b. 1836,   ), 156, 161; Pierre (b. 1848,   ), 157, 165, 186, 187; Pierre (b. 1874, d. 1877), 179; Pierre (b. 1881,   ), 181, 183, 185; Pierre Arthur (b. 1885,   ), 181; Pierre Louis (b. 1876, d. 1878), 165, 187; Pierre Maxime (b. 1875, d. 1875), 165, 188; Pierre Modeste (b. 1866,   ), 158, 167, 187, 190; Raymond Joseph (b. 1922, d. 1981), 175; Real (b. 1941), 184; Remi (b. 1859, d. 1865), 179; Rene (b. 1936), 184; Rita, 184; Rita Frances (b. 1916, obi. 2002), 174; Robert (b. 1935), 176; Roger (b. 1849, d. 1888), 155, 160; Roger (b. 1938), 185; Rolande (b. 1946), 184; Rosa, 98; Rosa (b. 1898,   ), 181; Rosalie (b. 1840,   ), 156; Rosalie (b. 1859, d. 1901), 158, 167, 187, 190; Rosalie (b. 1882,   ), 160; Rosanna (b. 1888, d. 1889), 168;

Georgianna (b. 1886,), 211; Goodwin (b. 1860,), 204, 212, 213; Henri (b. 1882, d. 1927), 205, 207, 214; Henry (b. 1874,), 204; Henry (b. 1875,), 10, 11, 205, 214; Hermenegilde (b. 1873,), 205, 213; Irene Victoria (b. 1904), 208; Isidore (b. 1880,), 207, 214, 321; Isidore William Remi (b. 1878,), 206; Jacques (b. 1884, d. 1884), 206; James Antoine (b. 1888,), 210; James Leopold (b. 1888,), 206; Jean (b. 1859,), 202; Jean Louis Joachim (b. 1886,), 210; Jeanne, 214; John (b. 1876,), 202, 208; Joseph (, d. 1830), 201; Joseph (b. 1806, d. 1900), 95, 96, 201; Joseph (b. 1832, d. 1885), 201, 202; Joseph (b. 1864, d. 1923), 204, 213; Joseph (b. 1875, d. 1875), 206; Joseph (b. 1876,), 204; Joseph (b. 1878, d. 1879), 204; Joseph (b. 1881, d. 1881), 211; Joseph (b. 1885,), 205, 214, 215; Joseph (b. 1895), 207; Joseph Adelard Alfred (b. 1895,), 206; Joseph Adrian (b. 1895,), 211; Joseph Aime (b. 1882,), 211; Joseph Albert (b. 1873,), 202, 208; Joseph Alexander (b. 1877, d. 1878), 207; Joseph Alexander (b. 1909), 213; Joseph Alexandre (b. 1906, d. 1965), 208; Joseph Alfred (b. 1872,), 203; Joseph Alfred (b. 1872, d. 1873), 204; Joseph Alphonse (b. 1894,), 204; Joseph Arthur (b. 1883,), 206; Joseph Arthur (b. 1888, d. 1893), 209; Joseph Augustin (b. 1891,), 207, 215; Joseph Avila (b. 1882,), 205; Joseph Avila (b. 1898, d. 1899), 213; Joseph Edmond Avila (b. 1912), 214; Joseph Elie Onesime (b. 1897,), 211; Joseph Ernest (b. 1910, obi. 2002), 214; Joseph Georges Alexandre (b. 1885, d. 1937), 206; Joseph Jean (b. 1911), 212; Joseph Jean Alfred (b. 1901,), 210; Joseph Jean Baptiste Georges Homere (b. 1884, d. 1885), 211; Joseph Julien (b. 1891, d. 1959), 209; Joseph Louis (b. 1880, d. 1881), 211; Joseph Michel George (b. 1889, d. 1892), 212; Joseph Napoleon Gregoire (b. 1888,), 211; Joseph Onisime Hermenegilde (b. 1901, d. 1902), 213; Joseph Urbain Albert (b. 1899,), 211; Joseph Victor (b. 1907), 214, 215; Josephine (b. 1884,), 209; Josephte (b. 1870,), 202; Josephte Eugenie (b. 1886, d. 1886), 204; Louis (b. 1837, d. 1902), 168, 201, 203; Louis (b. 1857,), 202; Louis (b. 1859,), 203, 211; Louis (b. 1898,), 210; Louis Albert (b. 1891,), 212; Louis Jean Joseph (b. 1862, d. 1936), 202, 210, 220, 224; Louis Philippe (b. 1893,), 211; Louis Robert (b. 1884,), 202; Lucie Antoinette (b. 1893,), 211; Marguerite (b. 1863, d. 1873), 205; Marguerite (b. 1877,), 205; Marie (b. 1865,), 202, 208; Marie (b. 1869,), 94, 98, 204, 213; Marie (b. 1885,), 207; Marie (b. 1891,), 211; Marie (b. 1903,), 210; Marie Adele (b. 1878, d. 1907), 202, 208; Marie Agnes (b. 1885, d. 1956), 209; Marie Agnes (b. 1905), 214; Marie Alexandrine (b. 1904), 208; Marie Alice Adrienne (b.

1896, d. 1900), 209; Marie Alice Patricia (b. 1899,), 211; Marie Alma (b. 1906), 210; Marie Alvina (b. 1875, d. 1898), 205, 214; Marie Ange Bernadette (b. 1901), 211; Marie Angeline Evangeline (b. 1888,), 207, 214, 215; Marie Anne (b. 1882,), 204, 212; Marie Anne (b. 1894,), 213; Marie Anne (b. 1899, d. 1899), 209; Marie Anne Josephine (b. 1890, d. 1890), 206; Marie Blanche Bertha (b. 1906), 211; Marie Cecile Elise (b. 1910, d. 1910), 214; Marie Delia Clara (b. 1907), 213; Marie Elise (b. 1896), 208; Marie Elise (b. 1908), 212; Marie Elise Zenaide (b. 1893,), 210; Marie Eliza (b. 1868, d. 1885), 203; Marie Elizabeth (b. 1907), 214; Marie Elmyre (b. 1885, d. 1886), 210; Marie Emma (b. 1888,), 204; Marie Ernestine (b. 1885, d. 1885), 209; Marie Ernestine Elise (b. 1908), 212; Marie Eustasie (b. 1873, d. 1909), 204, 212; Marie Eva (b. 1904), 208; Marie Eva (b. 1910), 210; Marie Josephine (b. 1886,), 207; Marie Josephine (b. 1891,), 210; Marie Josephine Elmire (b. 1873, d. 1956), 206, 214; Marie Louise Antoinette (b. 1891,), 211; Marie Louise Eleonore (b. 1893, d. 1893), 212; Marie Mathilde Alexandrine (b. 1875, d. 1886), 207; Marie Oliva Victorina (b. 1903,), 213; Marie Olivine (b. 1900, d. 1900), 210; Marie Olvina Eugenie (b. 1906), 213; Marie Pauline (b. 1874,), 206; Marie Philomene (b. 1871, d. 1871), 203; Marie Rita Patricia (b. 1912), 212; Marie Rosalida (b. 1882, d. 1883), 204; Marie Rosalie (b. 1875, d. 1875), 206; Marie Rose (b. 1874, d. 1875), 206; Marie Rose (b. 1883,), 9, 205; Marie Rose Anna (b. 1869,), 202; Marie Rose Claire (b. 1888, d. 1892), 212; Marie Rose Emma (b. 1876,), 206; Marie Rosina (b. 1882, d. 1906), 207; Marie Victorine (b. 1901, d. 1901), 213; Marie Virginie (b. 1866, d. 1893), 158, 168, 203, 211; Marie Virginie (b. 1870,), 204; Marie Yvonne Emma (b. 1896, d. 1896), 213; Marie-Anna, 205, 214; Mark Alfred (b. 1904), 208; Maxime (b. 1847, d. 1906), 9, 11, 201, 205, 214; Maxime (b. 1872,), 205; Maxime (b. 1905), 208; Melanie (b. 1874,), 204, 212; Michel, 208; Nancy (b. 1883,), 209; Nancy Eugenie (b. 1880, d. 1880), 206; Napoleon (b. 1890,), 207; Norbert (b. 1841, d. 1874), 201, 205; Norbert (b. 1865,), 204; Octave Alfred (b. 1879,), 207; Patrice (b. 1862, d. 1864), 203; Patrice (b. 1876,), 204, 212; Patrice (b. 1876, d. 1898), 203; Patrice Francois (b. 1871, d. 1878), 205; Philibert (b. 1897,), 206; Philomene (b. 1874,), 203, 211; Pierre (b. 1838, d. 1918), 98, 201, 204; Pierre Robert (b. 1881,), 206; Pierre Tobie (b. 1905, d. 1906), 214; Placide (b. 1879,), 205; Remi (b. 1886, d. 1886), 211; Rene Antonio (b. 1916), 203; Roger (b. 1860, d. 1888), 203; Roger (b. 1863,), 202, 207; Rosalie (b. 1867, d. 1918), 204, 213; Rosalie (b. 1878,), 207, 214; Rose (b. 1859, d.

1874), 202; Rose Anne (b. 1892,), 206; Russel, 208; Therese, 214; Toussaint (b. 1849, d. 1930), 93, 96, 201, 206; Toussaint Joseph (b. 1868,), 204; Valentine (b. 1905), 210; Victor Nazaire (b. 1872,), 205; Virginie (b. 1874, d. 1874), 205; Wilfred (b. 1880), 207; William (b. 1854, d. 1865), 201; William (b. 1861, d. 1863), 202; William (b. 1861, d. 1925), 158, 168, 202, 208, 209; William (b. 1877, d. 1936), 204, 212; William (b. 1880,), 204; William (b. 1882,), 209; William Alexandre (b. 1912), 212

Versaille: Albert (b. 1877, d. 1877), 218; Jean Baptiste (b. 1833, d. 1893), 216; Marguerite (b. 1833,), 216; Marie, 258

Versailles: Antoine (b. 1852, d. 1868), 216; David (b. 1845, d. 1906), 216, 217; David (b. 1880, d. 1881), 218; Elise (b. 1868, d. 1887), 217; Euphrosine (b. 1834,), 216, 217; Genevieve (b. 1833, d. 1883), 216, 217; Jean Baptiste (b. 1802,), 216, 265; Joseph Edwin (b. 1864, d. 1890), 217, 218; Joseph Jean Baptiste (b. 1878, d. 1882), 218; Louis (b. 1743,), 215, 265; Louis (b. 1793,), 215; Louis (b. 1890, d. 1890), 218; Louis Marie (b. 1874,), 218; Louise (b. 1802, d. 1857), 216; Marguerite (b. 1872, d. 1889), 218; Marie (b. 1829, d. 1893), 216, 217; Marie (b. 1830,), 216, 217; Marie (b. 1862, d. 1876), 217; Marie Anne (b. 1821,), 216; Marie Anne (b. 1838, d. 1898), 216, 217, 250; Marie Clemence (b. 1870, d. 1888), 218; Pierre (b. 1801, d. 1849), 215, 216, 217; Pierre (b. 1829,), 216; Rosalie (b. 1866, d. 1881), 217; Scholastique (b. 1825,), 216, 217; Susanne (b. 1832,), 86, 216, 217

Vezina: William (b. 1874, d. 1961), 15, 239

Vigar: Maude Eva Mary (b. 1876, d. 1960), 313

Villebrun: Adelaide (b. 1865, d. 1901), 222, 224; Agnes (b. 1900), 224; Albert (b. 1887,), 223; Albert (b. 1900), 224; Alfred (b. 1886, d. 1935), 223; Andre Pierre (b. 1884,), 223; Angeline (b. 1879,), 222; Anonyme (b. 1895, d. 1895), 222; Anonyme dit Plouff (b. 1862, d. 1864), 220; Antoine (b. 1809,), 218, 219; Antoine (b. 1876,), 222, 225; Antoine (b. 1886, d. 1967), 222; Augustine (b. 1899), 224; Brigitte dit Plouf (b. 1805, d. 1888), 94, 95, 218, 219; Caroline (b. 1883, d. 1897), 221; Catherine dit Plouffe (b. 1834,), 219, 222; Christie (b. 1885,), 221; Christine (b. 1866,), 210, 220, 224; Cuthbert Plouffe dit (b. 1857,), 219; Daniel (b. 1849, d. 1921), 219, 221; Earl Romaine (b. 1916, d. 1999), 225; Edward (b. 1897,), 224; Elise (b. 1872,), 220; Elise (b. 1879,), 221; Ellen (b. 1872,), 222; Emma (b. 1874, d. 1891), 109, 220; Eugene (b. 1887,), 223; Flora (b. 1877,), 15, 19, 220, 224; Francis (b. 1897,), 224; Francois (b. 1882,), 220; Francois Jr. (b. 1869,), 221, 224; Francois Sr. (b. 1839,), 219, 221; Frederick (b. 1874,), 221; George (b. 1890,), 222;

Gladman (b. 1868, d. 1896), 234; Josephine Clara (b. 1906), 236; Josephine Clara Stuart (b. 1882, d. 1939), 234; Laura (b. 1870, d. 1947), 233, 234, 236; Laura (b. 1920), 237; Laura Ida Cecelia (b. 1883, d. 1931), 234; Lester James Horden (b. 1899), 236; Lillian (b. 1914), 237; Lillie Annabelle (b. 1882, d. 1883), 235; Louis, 183; Maida May (b. 1884, d. 1900), 235; Mary (b. 1826, d. 1846), 232, 233; Mary (b. 1860, d. 1861), 233; Mary Margaret (b. 1913), 237; Mary Minnie (b. 1867,), 234; Muriel (b. 1921), 237; Myra Maud (b. 1887,), 235; Myrtle (b. 1901), 237; Norah Ann (b. 1889,), 235; Norman (b. 1898), 236; Pheobe Sophie 'Sarah' (b. 1855,), 233; Reginald William (b. 1894, d. 1959), 236; Roderick Lionel (b. 1891,), 235; Samuel L. (b. 1881, d. 1944), 122, 123, 234, 237; Sarah Ann (b. 1885, d. 1887), 235; Sarah Jane (b. 1841, d. 1929), 232, 234, 281; Stanley (b. 1892), 235; Stanley Edgar (b. 1899), 236; Thomas (Archdeacon) (b. 1835, d. 1907), 232, 234, 236; Thomas (b. 1776, d. 1832), 120, 232; Thomas (b. 1810, d. 1851), 232; Thomas (b. 1853, d. 1934), 32, 233, 235; Thomas James (b. 1880,), 235; Unnamed (b. 1909), 236; Vernon (b. 1894,), 236; Walter (b. 1910), 236; Wilfred James (b. 1901, d. 1979), 235; William Charles (bt. 1857,), 233; William John (bt. 1871, d. 1941), 235; William Thomas (b. 1837, d. 1915), 123, 232, 234, 237; William Thomas (b. 1869, d. 1923), 234, 236, 237

Visignault: Alice (b. 1886,), 239; Archibald James (b. 1893, d. 1916), 239; Dinah (b. 1896,), 239; Domithilde (b. 1866,), 239; Edith (b. 1904), 240; Edouard (b. 1877, d. 1878), 239; Elizabeth (b. 1861, d. 1898), 238, 239; Ethel (b. 1907, d. 1913), 240; Jane (b. 1866, d. 1894), 239, 240; Joseph (b. 1864, d. 1932), 238, 239; Joseph (b. 1885, d. 1886), 239; Louis Moise (b. 1868, d. 1945), 239, 240; Mabel (b. 1894,), 239; Marie Louise (b. 1858,), 238; Mary Ann (b. 1891, d. 1893), 239; Moise or Vezina (b. 1830,), 15, 238; Myrtle May (b. 1910, d. 1959), 240; Pierre (b. 1876,), 239; Ruth Lucy (b. 1901), 239; Salomon (b. 1873,), 239; William (b. 1898, d. 1916), 239

Visnaugh: Ellen Harriet (b. 1872, d. 1900), 239

Vivier: Adelaide (b. 1878, d. 1912), 243, 247; Adele (b. 1892, d. 1894), 249; Alexander (b. 1880), 247; Alexander (b. 1898, d. 1952), 250; Alexander W. J. (b. 1883,), 248; Alexandre (b. 1844, d. 1872), 244; Alexandre (b. 1865,), 246, 249; Alexandre (b. 1872,), 246; Alexandre (b. 1898), 246; Alexis (b. 1768, d. 1862), 140, 242, 258; Alexis (b. 1796, d. 1876), 14, 242, 258, 259; Alexis (b. 1825, d. 1924), 242, 244, 245; Alexis (b. 1842,), 242, 246, 258, 259; Alexis (b. 1861,), 245, 248; Alfred (b. 1906, d. 1981), 251; Alma Victoria (b. 1900), 250; Alphonsine

"Rosine" (b. 1869, d. 1955), 66; Ambroise (b. 1856, d. 1929), 302; Ambroise (b. 1870,), 246, 250, 265; Angelique (b. 1855, d. 1870), 244; Annable (b. 1885,), 246; Anonyme (b. 1887,), 249; Bernard (b. 1840, d. 1929), 242, 245, 246, 249; Bernard (b. 1862, d. 1878), 244; Bernard (b. 1870,), 246; Caroline (b. 1845,), 242, 246; Caroline Victoria (b. 1869, d. 1872), 245; Catherine (b. 1849, d. 1929), 130, 171; Catherine (b. 1866, d. 1872), 243; Celestin (b. 1894, d. 1895), 246; Charles (b. 1847,), 117, 242, 246; Charles (b. 1867,), 246; Charles (b. 1894, d. 1966), 250; Christiana (b. 1880), 247; Christianne (b. 1851, d. 1885), 244, 248; Christie (b. 1905), 246; Dolphus Augustin (b. 1853,), 244; Elie (b. 1873, d. 1952), 247, 250; Elise (b. 1868,), 25, 247; Elizabeth (b. 1842), 244; Elizabeth (b. 1919, d. 1920), 302; Ellen Alice (b. 1899, d. 1960), 251; Elzear (b. 1867,), 244, 248; Emelie (b. 1853,), 244, 248; Emile (b. 1860,), 244; Ernest (b. 1923), 302; Ernestine (b. 1912, d. 2000), 117, 251; Esther (b. 1928), 302; Eugene (b. 1914, d. 1988), 251; Flora (b. 1907, d. 1987), 251; Florence Magdelene (b. 1899), 248; Florestine (b. 1873, d. 1898), 247; Francois (b. 1819, d. 1896), 161; Francois (b. 1880, d. 1896), 243; Francois (b. 1902, d. 1934), 251; Guillaume (b. 1863, d. 1865), 245; Guillaume (b. 1870,), 245, 249; Guillaume Jean (b. 1869,), 246, 250; Helene (b. 1879, d. 1897), 247; Iphigenie (b. 1851, d. 1861), 244; Isabelle (b. 1856, d. 1894), 245, 249; Isabelle (b. 1859, d. 1860), 245; Isabelle (b. 1870, d. 1898), 247; Isabelle (b. 1889), 249; Isidore (b. 1857, '), 244; James (b. 1879), 245; James Alexander (b. 1901), 250; Jean (b. 1896), 246; Jean Alexandre (b. 1891), 250; Jean Alfred (b. 1900), 246; Jean Baptiste (b. 1864, d. 1909), 244, 247, 248; Jean Baptiste (b. 1877, d. 1901), 246; Jean Baptiste (b. 1892,), 248; Jean Baptiste (b. 1895,), 248; John Alexander (b. 1883), 249; John Alexandre (b. 1863, d. 1890), 245, 249; Jonas (b. 1855,), 244; Joseph (b. 1813, d. 1890), 242, 243; Joseph (b. 1825,), 13, 14, 242, 245, 249; Joseph (b. 1861,), 245; Joseph (b. 1863,), 243; Joseph (b. 1879, d. 1940), 117, 118, 247, 251, 300; Joseph (b. 1883,), 246; Joseph (b. 1888,), 246; Joseph (b. 1896, d. 1897), 250; Joseph Adelard (b. 1902), 248; Joseph Albert (b. 1905), 248; Joseph Arthur (b. 1896, d. 1896), 248; Joseph Napoleon (b. 1882, d. 1956), 302; Joseph Norman (b. 1898,), 251; Josephte, 67, 68; Josephte (b. 1838,), 68, 242, 245, 264; Josette (b. 1818,), 242, 243; Louis (b. 1878, d. 1878), 246; Louise (b. 1825, d. 1865), 242, 244; Louise (b. 1875,), 247, 251; Madeleine (b. 1811, d. 1875), 242; Madeleine (b. 1878), 248; Madeline (b. 1843, d. 1843), 243; Marguerite (b. 1812, d. 1832), 242, 243; Marguerite (b.

1852, d. 1919), 156, 161, 296, 298; Marguerite (b. 1882,), 249; Marie (b. 1817,), 242, 243; Marie (b. 1832,), 242, 245; Marie (b. 1838,), 110, 128; Marie (b. 1844,), 243, 247; Marie (b. 1846,), 244; Marie (b. 1865,), 244; Marie (b. 1865, d. 1954), 245, 248; Marie (b. 1873, d. 1896), 246, 250; Marie (b. 1881, d. 1890), 247; Marie (b. 1887,), 249; Marie (b. 1894,), 250; Marie Anne (b. 1861,), 242, 247; Marie Bella (b. 1892, d. 1894), 250; Marie Louise (b. 1892, d. 1893), 246; Marie Mabel (b. 1897), 248; Marie Madelaine (b. 1836,), 242, 245; Marie Madeleine (b. 1867, d. 1875), 245; Marie Mathilde (b. 1894,), 248; Marie Melanie (b. 1900,), 248, 252; Marie Rose (b. 1879,), 246, 249; Marie Rose (b. 1892,), 249; Marie Rose (b. 1899), 249; Martin (b. 1909, d. 1974), 251; Mary (b. 1876,), 245; Mary Clara (b. 1909, d. 1912), 302; Mary St.Ann (b. 1905, d. 1977), 251; Maxime (b. 1859, d. 1863), 244; Melanie (b. 1872,), 246; Michel (b. 1820,), 242, 243; Michel (b. 1847,), 25, 244, 247; Modeste (b. 1864,), 243; Modeste (b. 1890,), 246; Napoleon "Johnny" (b. 1926), 302; Nathaline (b. 1872, d. 1894), 246, 250; Norbert (b. 1857, d. 1865), 244; Olivier "Carlouche" (b. 1821), 139, 140, 242, 244; Patrice (b. 1876,), 243; Patrice (b. 1881,), 246; Patrice (bt. 1874,), 245; Philip (b. 1900, d. 1967), 250; Philomene (b. 1891,), 249; Pierre (b. 1878,), 248; Rebecca (b. 1881, d. 1881), 247; Robert (b. 1909), 251; Rosalie (b. 1870,), 246, 250; Rosine (b. 1888,), 248; Rosine (b. 1901, d. 1968), 117, 251, 300; Sara (b. 1884, d. 1893), 247; Scholastique (b. 1848,), 244; Sophie (b. 1853, d. 1855), 244; Sophie (b. 1867, d. 1885), 243; Suzanne (b. 1876, d. 1891), 247; Theresa (b. 1878, d. 1962), 251; Thomas (b. 1864, d. 1894), 245, 249; Victoria (b. 1880), 246; William (b. 1874,), 245; William (b. 1888,), 249; William (b. 1908, d. 1972), 251; William Thomas (b. 1884,), 246

Vizena: Louis (b. 1897, d. 1918), 240; William Hector (b. 1896, d. 1918), 240

Viznaugh: Benjamin (b. 1922, d. 1984), 240; Charlotte Ann (b. 1902), 240; Edna Margaret (b. 1907), 240; John R. (b. 1913, d. 1974), 240; Joseph (b. 1904, d. 1907), 240; Mary Ellen (b. 1892, d. 1961), 240; Norman (b. 1909, d. 1962), 240; Orton Irwin (b. 1907, d. 1956), 240; Peter (b. 1900, d. 1901), 240; Philip (b. 1911, d. 1977), 240; Walter Edward (b. 1894, d. 1901), 240

Vogel: (--?--), 51

Voller: Angus (bt. 1842, d. 1843), 252; Caroline (b. 1851, d. 1917), 252, 253; Catherine (bt. 1839, d. 1840), 252; Charles (chr. 1844, d. 1845), 252; Eliza (b. 1849, d. 1921), 40, 41, 42, 252, 253; Elizabeth (bt. 1837,), 252; James (b. 1800,), 42, 252; Maria (b. 1855, d. 1911), 252, 253; Mary (b. 1832,), 252; Nancy (bt. 1835, d. 1873), 252;

Made in the USA
San Bernardino, CA
09 July 2018